Mastering AutoCAD® Architecture 2010

Mastering AutoCAD® Architecture 2010

autodesk® Press

PAUL F. AUBIN

DELMAR
CENGAGE Learning™

Australia • Brazil • Japan • Korea • Mexico • Singapore • Spain • United Kingdom • United States

DELMAR
CENGAGE Learning

Mastering AutoCAD® Architecture 2010

Paul F. Aubin

Vice President, Career and Professional Editorial: Dave Garza

Director of Learning Solutions: Sandy Clark

Acquisitions Editor: Stacy Masucci

Managing Editor: Larry Main

Senior Product Manager: John Fisher

Senior Editorial Assistant: Dawn Daugherty

Vice President, Career and Professional Marketing: Jennifer McAvey

Marketing Director: Deborah Yarnell

Associate Marketing Manager: Mark Pierro

Production Director: Wendy Troeger

Art Director: David Arsenault

Content Project Manager: Angela Sheehan

Technology Project Manager: Joe Pliss

Production Technology Analyst: Tom Stover

For product information and technology assistance, contact us at
Career & Professional Group Sales Support, 1-800-648-7450

For permission to use material from this text or product,
submit all requests online at **www.cengage.com/permissions.**
Further permissions questions can be e-mailed to
permissionrequest@cengage.com

ISBN-13: 978-0-8400-3158-7

ISBN-10: 0-8400-3158-0

Delmar
5 Maxwell Drive
Clifton Park, NY 12065-2919
USA

Cengage Learning is a leading provider of customized learning solutions with office locations around the globe, including Singapore, the United Kingdom, Australia, Mexico, Brazil, and Japan. Locate your local office at: **international.cengage.com/region**

Cengage Learning products are represented in Canada by Nelson Education, Ltd.

To learn more about Delmar, visit **www.cengage.com/delmar**

Purchase any of our products at your local college store or at our preferred online store **www.ichapters.com**

Notice to the Reader
Publisher does not warrant or guarantee any of the products described herein or perform any independent analysis in connection with any of the product information contained herein. Publisher does not assume, and expressly disclaims, any obligation to obtain and include information other than that provided to it by the manufacturer. The reader is expressly warned to consider and adopt all safety precautions that might be indicated by the activities described herein and to avoid all potential hazards. By following the instructions contained herein, the reader willingly assumes all risks in connection with such instructions. The publisher makes no representations or warranties of any kind, including but not limited to, the warranties of fitness for particular purpose or merchantability, nor are any such representations implied with respect to the material set forth herein, and the publisher takes no responsibility with respect to such material. The publisher shall not be liable for any special, consequential, or exemplary damages resulting, in whole or part, from the readers' use of, or reliance upon, this material.

Printed in the United States of America
1 2 3 4 5 6 7 13 12 11 10 09

CONTENTS

Introduction x

QUICK START GENERAL AUTOCAD ARCHITECTURE OVERVIEW 1

Introduction 1 • Objectives 1 • Create a Small Building 1 • Set Up a Project with Floor Levels 14 • Creating a Presentation 22 • Summary 29

I INTRODUCTION AND METHODOLOGY

CHAPTER 1 THE USER INTERFACE 33

Introduction 33 • Objectives 33 • The Autocad Architecture Workspace 33 • The Autocad Architecture User Interface 37 • Pre-Requisite Skills 69 • Summary 74

CHAPTER 2 CONCEPTUAL UNDERPINNINGS OF AUTOCAD ARCHITECTURE 75

Introduction 75 • Objectives 75 • Parametric Design 76 • The Display System 77 • Object Styles 104 • Anchors 113 • Display Themes 122 • Visual Styles 124 • Content Library 126 • Summary 126

CHAPTER 3 WORK SPACE SETUP 127

Introduction 127 • Objectives 128 • Profiles 128 • Drawing Setup 139 • Template Files 145 • Summary 152

II THE BUILDING MODEL

CHAPTER 4 BEGINNING A FLOOR PLAN LAYOUT 155

Introduction 155 • Objectives 155 • Working with Walls 155 • Working with Doors and Windows 171 • Adding Plumbing Fixtures 191 • Viewers 194 • Creating Wall Plan Modifiers 200 • Finishing Touches 206 • Additional Exercises 208 • Summary 208

CHAPTER 5 SETTING UP THE BUILDING MODEL 209

Introduction 209 • Objectives 209 • Building a Digital Cartoon Set 210 • Setting Up a Commercial Project 211 • Setting Up the Residential Building Model 267 • Congratulations! 267 • Additional Exercises 268 • Summary 268

CHAPTER 6 COLUMN GRIDS AND STRUCTURAL LAYOUT 269

Introduction 269 • Objectives 269 • Structural Members 269 • Column Grids 277 • Column Grid Labels and Dimensions 288 • Structural Framing 295 • Project Structural Category 302 • Creating a Foundation Plan 305 • Additional Structural Content 307 • Additional Exercises 313 • Summary 313

CHAPTER 7 VERTICAL CIRCULATION 315

Introduction 315 • Objectives 315 • Residential Stairs and Railings 315 • Commercial Core Plan 331 • Stair Tower Generation 336 • Custom Stair Creation 345 • Ramps and Elevators 349 • Toilet Rooms 353 • Additional Exercises 354 • Summary 355

CHAPTER 8 THE BUILDING SHELL 356

Introduction 356 • Objectives 356 • Creating the Masonry Shell 356 • Adding and Modifying Curtain Walls 363 • Understanding Curtain Wall Styles 368 • Building a Custom Curtain Wall Style 378 • Direct Manipulation of Curtain Wall Components 403 • Additional Exercises 409 • Summary 410

CHAPTER 9 UNDERSTANDING WALL CLEANUP 411

Introduction 411 • Objectives 411 • What Is Wall Cleanup? 412 • Part 1—Automatic Wall Cleanup 413 • Part 2—Manual Wall Cleanup 427 • Part 3—Wall Component Priorities 432 • Experiment 435 • Additional Exercises 437 • Summary 438

CHAPTER 10 PROGRESSIVE REFINEMENT—PART 1 439

Introduction 439 • Objectives 439 • Wall Styles 439 • Wall Style Display Properties 466 • Demolition 475 • Complete the Second Floor Plan Refinements 481 • Additional Exercises 491 • Summary 492

CHAPTER 11 PROGRESSIVE REFINEMENT—PART 2 493

Introduction 493 • Objectives 493 • Window Styles 493 • Install the CD Files and Load the Current Project 494 • Synchronize Project Standards 502 • Manipulating Window Anchors 503 • Copying Existing Windows 507 • Manipulating Door and Window Display 512 • Creating Custom-Shaped Windows and Doors 523 • Using the Styles in Other Drawings 528 • Adding Window Muntins 530 • Create a Custom Multi-View Block 533 • Additional Exercises 538 • Summary 539

CHAPTER 12 ROOFS AND SLABS 540

Introduction 540 • Objectives 540 • Creating Roofs 540 • Creating Slabs 571 • Building the Commercial Roof Plan File 583 • Additional Exercises 589 • Summary 590

III CONSTRUCTION DOCUMENTS

CHAPTER 13 CREATING REFLECTED CEILING PLANS 593

Introduction 593 • Objectives 593 • Creating Floors and Ceilings Using Spaces 594 • Install the CD Files and Load the Current Project 594 • Generate Spaces from Existing Walls 594 • Working in the Reflected Display Configuration 601 • Working with Ceiling Grid Objects 604 • Adding Anchored Light Fixtures 620 • Other Ceiling Fixtures 629 • Go Further 636 • Restore the Floor Plan 636 • Add an RCP View and Sheet to the Project 637 • Additional Exercises 641 • Summary 641

CHAPTER 14 GENERATING ANNOTATION 642

Introduction 642 • Objectives 642 • Annotation and View Files 643 • Adding Room Tags 646 • Dimensioning AEC Objects 661 • Documentation Content 686 • Additional Exercises 691 • Summary 691

CHAPTER 15 GENERATING SCHEDULES 693

Introduction 693 • Objectives 693 • Overview and Key Features 694 • The Schedule Table Tool Set 694 • Getting Ready to Use Schedule Tables 695 • Adding Schedule Components 695 • Property Set Data 699 • Automatic and Manual Property Sets 714 • Property Set Definitions 720 • Schedule Table Styles 724 • Building a Project-Based Door Schedule (Advanced) 740 • Understanding Display Themes 752 • Additional Schedule Tools 756 • Additional Exercises 757 • Summary 757

CHAPTER 16 GENERATING SECTIONS AND ELEVATIONS 759

Introduction 759 • Objectives 759 • Working with 2D Section/Elevation Objects 759 • 2D Section/Elevation Styles 777 • Subdivisions 787 • 2D Section/Elevation Styles Design Rules 789 • Editing Materials 794 • Editing and Merging Linework 805 • Creating Interior Elevations Using Callouts 811 • Live Sections 813 • Sheet Files 814 • Additional Exercises 814 • Summary 814

CHAPTER 17 GENERATING DETAILS AND KEYNOTES 816

Introduction 816 • Objectives 816 • Details 816 • Keynotes 845 • Challenge Exercise 855 • Additional Exercises 858 • Summary 859

CHAPTER 18 PLOTTING AND PUBLISHING 861

Introduction 861 • Objectives 862 • Sheet Files 862 • Layouts 863 • Page Setup Manager 864 • Viewports 868 • Plot Style Tables 868 • Plotting 873 • Publish a Sheet Set 873 • 3D DWF 877 • eTransmit and Archive 879 • Publish to Web 879 • Publish to PDF 879 • Additional Exercises 879 • Summary 880

IV APPENDICES

APPENDIX A ADDITIONAL EXERCISES 883

Introduction 883 • Install the CD Files and Load the Current Project 883

APPENDIX B WALL CLEANUP CHECKLIST 904

Automatic Wall Cleanup 904 • Other Considerations 904 • Manual Wall Cleanup 905 • Wall Component Priorities 905

APPENDIX C ONLINE RESOURCES 906

Introduction 906 • Web Sites Related to the Content of this Book 906 • Web Sites of Related Interest 907 • Online Resources for ACA Plug-Ins and Training 908

APPENDIX D SPACE AREA CALCULATIONS 910

Introduction 910 • Objectives 910 • Space Geometry 910 • Space Boundaries 912 • BOMA Classifications and Schedules 917 • Summary 922

APPENDIX E SHARING FILES WITH CONSULTANTS 923

Introduction 923 • Objectives 923 • Do They Need a DWG? 923 • Export to AutoCAD 924 • Determining the Required Translation 928 • Sharing ACA Files with Other ACA Users 930 • Understanding Object Enablers 930 • Understanding Proxy Graphics 931 • Sharing ACA Files with Revit Users 932

APPENDIX F WALL CLEANUP SOLUTIONS 934

Index 935

INTRODUCTION

WELCOME

The purpose of this primer is to acquaint the beginning student with the range of graphic tools which are available for conveying architectural ideas. The basic premise behind its formulation is that graphics is an inseparable part of the design process, an important tool which provides the designer with the means not only of presenting a design proposal but also of communicating with himself and others in the design studio.

Frank Ching—Architectural Graphics, *Copyright © 1975 Van Nostrand Reinhold Company, Inc.*

That passage prefaces the book *Architectural Graphics* by Frank Ching. The goal set out by Mr. Ching in this indispensable resource is to convey the intimate relationship between the tools of architectural drafting and the process of architectural design. Over the course of the last three decades, the "graphic tools" available for the conveyance of "architectural ideas" have undergone dramatic change. For most architects, AutoCAD has been at the center of this change. AutoCAD has historically been a "horizontal" product, meaning that it targets a broad base of users—*anyone* needing to produce technical drafting with accuracy. However, as the simple existence of Mr. Ching's reference can attest, generating architectural graphics requires more than simply having a T square (physical or digital). A "vertical" approach in CAD software is needed, one that specifically addresses the uniqueness of architectural graphics and design. AutoCAD Architecture provides such a tool: a computerized tool that can live up to the goal set out by Mr. Ching 30 years ago. The purpose of *Mastering AutoCAD Architecture 2010* is to acquaint the user at all levels with this new breed of graphic tool for the conveyance of architectural ideas.

There are two basic goals to this book: (1) shorten the AutoCAD Architecture learning curve and (2) help you develop a good sound method. All anyone needs for success is a proper understanding of how the program functions and a clear understanding of what the program can and cannot do. This coupled with good procedure may be the magic key to success in *mastering* AutoCAD Architecture.

AUTOCAD AND AUTOCAD ARCHITECTURE: WHAT IS THE DIFFERENCE?

AutoCAD Architecture 2010 (ACA) offers a variety of tools not available in the base AutoCAD drafting package. ACA includes a collection of objects representing the most common architectural components, such as Walls, Doors, Windows, Stairs,

Roofs, Columns, Beams, and much more. All of those objects are able to take advantage of *Display Control* (purpose-built display based on object function and architectural drawing conventions), *Anchors* (physical rule-based linkage between one object and another) and *Styles* (collections of parameters applied to objects as a group) to drive design. AutoCAD does not offer such objects or functionality; instead, it relies on generic geometric components such as lines, arcs, and circles, which need to be assembled by the operator to represent the architectural (or non-architectural) items being designed and organized manually through often complex layer and file schemes.

Success in completing most tasks requires a combination of understanding of one's goals, ample time and planning, and access to the right tools. Although knowledge and planning are critically important, having the proper tool for the job can often determine the overall success or failure of a given undertaking. A handsaw and a power saw are both capable of cutting wood. However, the power saw is generally capable of creating a better cut in less time, provided the operator knows how to use it properly. Used improperly, the results can be dire. The situation is the same in creating architectural documents. While both AutoCAD and AutoCAD Architecture can accomplish the job, ACA is designed specifically for architectural design/drafting and will generally do a better job in less time, provided, of course, the user knows how to use it properly. AutoCAD, while capable of producing architectural documents, is not designed specifically for this task. Having purchased this book, you probably already own ACA or have access to it at work. Read on; and upon completion of this book, you will have the knowledge needed to use ACA properly!

WHAT IS AN INTELLIGENT OBJECT?

An *intelligent* object is an entity within ACA that is designed to behave as the specific "real-world" object after which it is named. The creation of a floor plan in generic AutoCAD involves a process of drafting a series of lines and curves parallel to one another to represent walls, doors, and other elements in the architectural plan. This process is often time-consuming and labor-intensive. When design changes occur, the lines must be edited individually to accommodate the change. Furthermore, a plan created this way is two-dimensional only. When elevations and sections are needed, they must be created from scratch from additional lines and circles, which maintain no relationship to the lines and circles that make up the original plan.

In contrast, AutoCAD Architecture includes *true* architectural objects. These objects are referred to in the software as AEC Objects (AEC stands for Architecture, Engineering, and Construction). Rather than draft lines as in the example above, ACA includes a true Wall object. This object has all of the parameters of an actual wall built directly into it. Therefore, one need only assign the values to these parameters to add or modify the wall within the drawing. In addition, the Wall object can be represented two-dimensionally or three-dimensionally, in plan or in section, using a single drawing element. This means that unlike traditional drafting, which requires the wall to be drawn several times: once for plan, once for section and again for elevation; an ACA Wall need only be drawn once, and then "represented" differently to achieve each type of drawing (plan, section, and elevation). An even greater advantage of the AEC object is that if it is edited, it changes in all views. This is the advantage of its being a single object, and it provides a tremendous productivity boon. With lines, each view remains a separate drawing; therefore, edits need to be repeated for each drawing type—a definite productivity drain.

Objects also adhere to built-in rules that control their behavior under various circumstances. Doors, for example, know they should cut holes in Walls. Spaces (rooms) know to grow and shrink when their controlling edges are reshaped. Columns know to move when the column grid line to which they are attached moves. Stairs remain constrained to restrictions placed on them by building codes. Tags remain attached and continue to report their associated data even across XREFs (separate but linked drawing files). These and many other relationships are programmed into the software. The intelligence of the object extends even further. AEC objects may have graphical and non-graphical data attached to them, which can be linked directly to schedules and reports. All of these features allow us to elevate our ordinary model to a Building Information Model (BIM).

Intelligent objects make the process of creating architectural drawings more efficient and streamlined. Mastery of objects begins with understanding their properties, their styles and their rules. Mastery of AutoCAD Architecture begins with mastery of individual objects but, more importantly, requires mastery of the interrelationship of objects and the procedures and best practices required to take full advantage of them. Through the process of learning ACA, you will learn to construct a Building Information Model—an interconnected series of objects and rules used to generate all of the required architectural documentation and communication, which is greater than the sum of its parts. In general, while both are critical, best practice generally dictates greater emphasis on the "Information" rather than the "Model."

WHO SHOULD READ THIS BOOK?

The primary audience of this book is users new to ACA who have some AutoCAD experience. However, this book is equally suited to existing ACA users. Specifically, this includes anyone who currently uses AutoCAD to produce architectural construction documentation or to design drawings, facilities layouts or interior design studies, and documentation. Architects, interior designers, design-build professionals, facilities planners, and building industry CAD professionals stand to benefit from the information contained within.

You Should Have Some Autocad Background

Although no prior knowledge of ACA is required to read and use this book, this book assumes a basic level of AutoCAD experience. At the very least, you should be familiar with the basics of drafting, layers, blocks, XREFs, object snaps, and plotting.

FEATURES IN THIS EDITION

Mastering AutoCAD Architecture 2010 is a concise manual focused squarely on the rationale and practicality of the ACA process. The book emphasizes the *process* of creating projects in ACA as an interconnected series of objects, rather than a series of independent commands and routines. The goal of each lesson is to help the reader complete their building design projects successfully. Tools are introduced together in a focused process with a strong emphasis on "why" as well as "how." The text and exercises seek to give the reader a clear sense of the value and potential of each tool and procedure. *Mastering AutoCAD Architecture 2010* is a resource designed to shorten your learning curve, raise your comfort level and, most importantly, give you real-life tested practical advice on the usage of the software to create architectural projects.

What You Will Find Inside

Section I of this book is focused on the necessary prerequisite skills and underlying theory behind ACA. The section is intended to acquaint you with the software and put you in the proper mind-set. Section II relies heavily on tutorial-based exercises to present the process of creating a building model in AutoCAD Architecture, relying on the software's built-in Drawing Management functionality. Two projects are developed concurrently throughout the tutorial section: one residential and one commercial. Detailed explanations are included throughout the tutorials to clearly identify why each step is employed. Annotation and other features specific to construction documentation are covered in Section III. Section IV includes several appendices.

What You Won't Find Inside

This book is not a command reference. This book approaches the subject of learning ACA by exposing conceptual aspects of the software and providing extensive tutorial coverage. No attempt is made to give a comprehensive explanation of every command or every method available to execute commands. Instead, explanations cover broad topics of how to perform various tasks in AutoCAD Architecture, with specific examples coming from architectural practice. Dozens of AutoCAD command references are on the market, and any one of them is a good complement to this book. In addition, references are made in this text whenever they are appropriate to ACA's extensive online help and reference materials. The focus of this book is the design development and construction documentation phases of architectural design. The mass modeling and other conceptual design or rendering tools of AutoCAD Architecture are not extensively covered in this book.

STYLE CONVENTIONS

Style Conventions used in this text are as follows:

Text	AutoCAD Architecture
Step-by-Step Tutorials	1. Perform these steps.
Menu picks	**Application menu > Save As > AutoCAD Drawing**
Dialog box and palette input	For the length, type **10'-0"** **[3000]**.
Keyboard input	Type **command** and press ENTER. Type **599** and press ENTER.
File and Directory Names	*C:\MasterACA 2010\Chapter01\Sample File.dwg*

MANAGER NOTE

Especially for CAD Managers—there are many issues of ACA usage that are important for CAD Managers and adherence overall to office standards. Throughout the text are notes to the CAD Manager titled "CAD Manager's Note." If you are the CAD Manager, pay particular attention to these items because they are designed to assist you in performing your CAD Management duties better. If you are not the CAD Manager, these notes can help give you insight into some of the salient CAD Management issues your firm may be facing. If your firm does not have a dedicated CAD Manager, pay close attention to these points because these issues will still be present, only there will not be a single individual dedicated to managing these issues and solving relevant related problems as they arise. If CAD Management is not within your interests or responsibilities, you can safely skip over these notes.

UNITS

This book is written using both Imperial and Metric units. Symbol names, scales, references, and measurements are given first in Imperial units, followed by the Metric equivalent in square brackets [ ]. For example, when there are two versions of the same symbol or file, they will appear in the text as follows:

Aec8_Room_Tag_P [**M_Aec8_Room_Tag_P**], or this "Open the file named *First Floor Imperial.dwg* [*First Floor Metric.dwg*]."

When the scale varies, a note such as this will appear: **1/8"=1'-0" [1:100]**.

If a measurement must be input, the values will appear like this: **10'-0" [3000]**. Please note that in many cases, the closest logical corresponding metric value has been chosen rather than a "direct" mathematical translation. For instance, 10'-0" in Imperial drawings translates to 3048 millimeters; however, a value of 3000 will be used in most cases as a more logical value.

NOTE

Every attempt has been made to make these decisions in an informed manner. However, it is hoped that readers in countries where metric units are the standard will forgive the American author for any poor choices or translations made in this regard.

All project files are included in both Imperial and Metric units on the CD-ROM. See the "Files Included on the CD-ROM" topic below for information on how to install the dataset in your preferred choice of units.

HOW TO USE THIS BOOK

The order of chapters has been carefully considered with the intention of following a logical flow and architectural process. If you are relatively new to ACA, it is recommended that you complete the book from beginning to end. However, if certain chapters do not pertain to the type of work that you or your firm perform, feel free to skip those topics. However, bear in mind that not every procedure will be repeated in every chapter. For example, if you are a designer in an interior design firm, you could skip the Roofs and Slabs chapter. However, for the best experience, you should read the entire book. CAD managers can skip to the CAD Manager Notes to find sections relevant to them. Most importantly, even after you have completed your initial pass of the tutorials in this book, keep *Mastering AutoCAD Architecture 2010* handy, as it will remain a valuable desk resource in the weeks and months to come.

FILES INCLUDED ON THE CD-ROM

Files used in the tutorials throughout this book are included at various stages of completion on the CD-ROM. Therefore, you will be able to load the files for a given chapter and begin working. When you install the files from the CD, the files for *all* chapters are installed automatically. The files will install into a folder on your *C:* drive named *MasterACA 2010*. Files *must* be installed in the *MasterACA 2010* folder on the *C:* drive. The default installation automatically uses this folder, which contains a folder for each chapter. Please note that in some cases, a particular chapter or subfolder will not have any drawing files. This is usually indicated by a text file (TXT) within the folder. For example, the *Chapter03* folder contains no drawing files; instead, it contains a text document in the subfolder *There are no files for Chapter 3.txt.*

NOTE

Please note that the CD does not contain the Autodesk Architectural Desktop software. Please contact your local reseller if you need to purchase a copy.

INSTALLING CD FILES

Locate the *Mastering AutoCAD Architecture 2010* CD-ROM in the back cover of your book. To install the dataset files, do the following:

1. Place the CD in your CD drive.
2. An installer window should appear onscreen after a moment or two.
3. To install the dataset files in Imperial units, click the Imperial Dataset button. To install the dataset files in Metric units, click the Metric Dataset button.

Installation will commence automatically and all files will be installed to a folder named *C:\MasterACA 2010* on your hard drive.

CAUTION

Please do not move the files from this location; if you do, the Tool Catalogs and Project Palettes will not function properly. Moving any of the other files can also cause issues with project files. See the "Repathing Projects" topic below.

If you do not intend to perform the tutorials in certain chapters, you can delete the files for those chapters. Simply delete the entire folder for the chapter(s) that you wish to skip. If you wish to install both the Imperial and Metric datasets, return to the installer and repeat the steps above for the other units. Installation requires approximately 385 MB of disk space per unit type (770 MB if you install both).

Projects

The ACA Drawing Management tools (Projects) are used throughout this text. Please do not open and save files outside the Project Navigator. Although there is no physical difference between a drawing file created inside a project and one created outside a project, procedurally, there are large differences. Please follow the instructions at the start of each chapter regarding how to install files and load the current project files. Furthermore, even though it is theoretically possible to continue working on the files created in Chapter 5 throughout the entire book, at the start of each chapter, you should reload from the installed datasets the files and projects for the chapter on which you are working. Edits may have been made to the files that you will not have if you do not start with the provided CD version.

Completed versions of the exercises for each chapter are provided in the *Complete* folder within each chapter's folder. To view them, use the same procedure outlined at the start of each chapter to load the project within the *Complete* folder instead. You can then compare the version provided with your own.

For an excellent example of an ACA project, load and explore the Sample Project included with the software. From the File menu, choose **Project Browser** and load the **AutoCAD Architecture Sample Project** found in your *My Documents* folder on your hard drive. The first time you load the Sample Project, you will be prompted to repath it. See the "Repathing Projects" topic below.

Project Bulletin Boards and Dataset Updates

When you load a Project in ACA, a bulletin board for that Project will load in the ACA Project Browser window (on the right). Review this page as it loads. If you have a live Internet connection, you will be informed on this page if updates to the Dataset (or the book text as a PDF) are available for download from www.paulaubin.com. If an update is available, you will be able to click the link directly in this page. A live feed (RSS file) is also maintained for this book. For complete instruction on how to load the feed, refer to the "Communication Center" topic in Chapter 1.

Repathing Projects

In some cases when you load a project, you will be prompted to repath the project. This occurs when the project has been moved from its original location. If you move the CD files to a location other than *C:\MasterACA 2010*, a message like the one in Figure P.1 will appear. If you receive this message, click "Repath the project now." This is very important because the project files will not function properly if you ignore this message. It is possible to postpone the decision, but some files may not function properly until you repath.

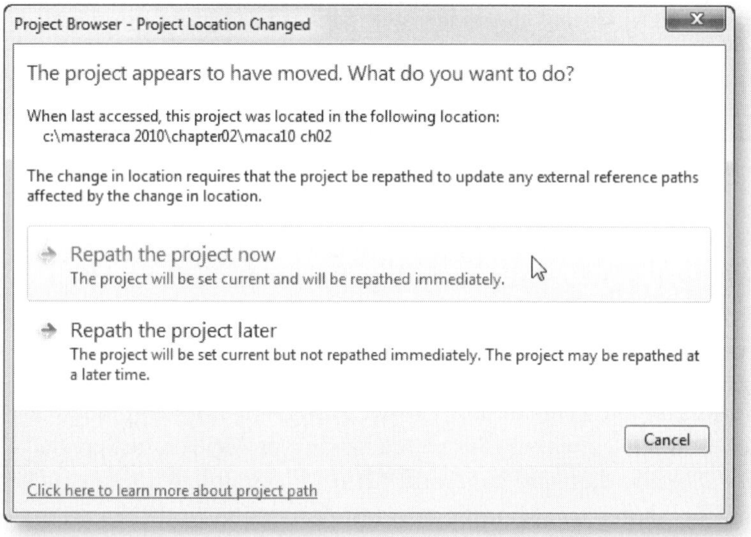

FIGURE P.1 *If a project has been moved, you will be prompted to repath project files. Always repath the project.*

WINDOWS XP AND VISTA COMPLIANT PATHS

AutoCAD Architecture 2010 is Windows logo compliant. Part of achieving this distinction means that the default paths to many resource files are buried deep in the *Program Files* or *Documents and Settings* folder structures. Your CAD Manager may have opted to move these resources out of these locations and to a central location on the server. This book assumes that all files are in the default installed locations. Check with your IT or CAD support personnel for more information on this issue.

If you are using Windows XP and you need to browse the *Documents and Settings* folder to locate ACA resources, the default location (for English language versions) is as follows:

C:\Documents and Settings\All Users\Application Data\Autodesk\ACA 2010\enu

If you use Windows Vista or Windows 7, the path is as follows:

C:\Users\All Users\Autodesk\ACA 2010\enu

It is important to note that the *Application Data* folder is a hidden folder in Windows. Therefore, by default, you will not be able to browse this location. To turn on the display of hidden files, choose **Tools > Folder Options** in Windows Explorer (**Organize > Folder and search options** in Windows 7). On the View tab, choose **Show Hidden Files and Folders** and then click OK. Again, check with your IT or CAD support person before making this change.

Please note: This book was authored on Windows 7. Other than variances in the screen appearance and look of dialog boxes, your experiences working through the exercises of this book should be seamless if you are using Vista or XP.

MISSING OR DAMAGED CD

If you have lost or damaged your CD, please visit the following URL to download the files:

http://www.paulaubin.com/contact.php

Fill out the form, select the "I lost/damaged my CD" option from the type of comment list and then click Submit. You will receive an e-mail explaining how to download the dataset.

SERVICE PACKS

It is important to keep your software current. Be sure to check **www.autodesk.com** on a regular basis for the latest updates and service packs to the AutoCAD Architecture software. Having the latest service packs installed will help ensure that your software runs trouble-free. AutoCAD Architecture 2010 also has the Info Center at the top right corner of the application frame. This tool will alert you when updates and information are available.

WE WANT TO HEAR FROM YOU

We welcome your comments and suggestions regarding *Mastering AutoCAD Architecture 2008*. Please forward your comments and questions to:

The CADD Team
Delmar Learning
Executive Woods
5 Maxwell Drive
Clifton Park, NY 12065-8007
Web site: www.autodeskpress.com

You can also send e-mails directly to the author. Please visit **www.paulaubin.com** and click the Contact link to send an e-mail using the form provided. Paul's services are available to architectural firms using AutoCAD Architecture or Revit Architecture. Please use the contact form to inquire about schedule and pricing.

ABOUT THE AUTHOR

Paul F. Aubin is the author of several books on Revit Architecture and AutoCAD Architecture including *Paul F. Aubin's Mastering Revit Architecture*, *Mastering AutoCAD Architecture* and *Autodesk Architectural Desktop: An Advanced Implementation Guide*. Paul is also the co-author of an all new title: *Mastering AutoCAD MEP 2010*. Paul has a background in the architectural profession spanning nearly 20 years. These experiences include architectural design and production, CAD management, mentoring, and training. Paul is an independent consultant offering training and implementation services to architectural firms using Revit Architecture and AutoCAD Architecture. He is the moderator for *Cadalyst* magazine's online CAD questions forum and has spoken at Autodesk University (Autodesk's annual convention for users) for many years. The combination of his experiences in architectural practice—as a CAD manager and an instructor—give his writing and his classroom instruction a fresh and credible focus. Paul is an associate member of the AIA and is based in Chicago.

Contact Paul directly at: **www.paulaubin.com** (click the Contact link).

Visit Paul's Blog: **paulfaubin.blogspot.com**.

DEDICATION

This book is dedicated to one of my oldest and dearest friends, Ron Bailey.

ACKNOWLEDGMENTS

The author would like to thank several people for their assistance and support throughout the writing of this book. Thanks to Stacy Masucci, John Fisher and all of the Delmar team. It continues to be a pleasure to work with such a dedicated group of professionals.

Sometimes a new release involves big changes. This release was no different. With an all new user interface, nearly every image in the book had to be recaptured and nearly every step re-written. This mammoth task would not have been possible without the assistance of David Koch, RA who assisted me with the re-write of a major portion of this edition. I would like to extend a very heartfelt thank you to David. I could not have completed this edition, and you would not be reading this passage, without David's editorial assistance and meticulous attention to detail.

Thanks to Eric Stenstrom of Wiss, Janney, Elstner Associates, Inc. for technical editing and the folks at Pre-pressPMG, in particular Mary Stone for copyediting and composition.

A special acknowledgment is due the following instructors who reviewed the chapters in detail:

Debra Dorr–Phoenix College, Phoenix, AZ

Joseph Liston–University of Arkansas at Fort Smith, Fort Smith, AR

Jeff Porter–Porter and Chester Institute, Watertown, CT

Margaret Robertson–Lane Community College, Eugene, OR

Edward Rother–Cerritos Community College, Norwalk, CA

Charles West–Dakota County Technical College, Rosemount, MN

Jon McFarland–CAD Instructor, Virginia Marti College of Art and Design, Lakewood, OH

Susan M. Sherod–Engineering Department Chair, Santa Ana College, Santa Ana, CA

There are far too many folks in Autodesk's Building Solutions Division to mention. Thanks to all of them but, in particular, Julian Gonzalez, Jeff Agla, Brook Potter, Chris Yanchar, Jim Awe, Jim Paquette, Kelcy Lemon, Mark Webb, James Smell, Bill Glennie, Dennis McNeal, William (Fitz) Fitzpatrick, Anna Oscarson, Scott Reinemann, Rick Foster, Bryan Otey, Matt Dillon, Tony Michniewicz, Qiong Wu and all of the folks at Autodesk Tech Support.

I am ever grateful for the blessings I have from my lifelong friends, Mark Zifcak and Ron Bailey, and from my family: my parents, Maryann and Del; my brothers, Marc and Tom; and my wonderful children, Marcus, Justin and Sarah Gemma. You are a constant reminder of what is most important in life. Finally, I am most grateful for the constant love and support of my wife, Martha.

QUICK START

General AutoCAD Architecture Overview

INTRODUCTION

This Quick Start provides a simple tutorial designed to give you a quick tour of some of the most common objects and features of AutoCAD Architecture 2010. You should be able to complete the entire exercise in about 45 minutes. At the completion of this tutorial, you will have experienced a firsthand look at what AutoCAD Architecture 2010 (ACA) has to offer.

OBJECTIVES

- Experience an overview of the software.
- Create your first AutoCAD Architecture model.
- Receive a firsthand glimpse at many ACA tools and methods.

CREATE A SMALL BUILDING

Let's get started using ACA right away. For the next several minutes, we will take a whirlwind tour of the ACA tool set. All of the tools covered in the following steps use default AutoCAD Architecture settings. The chapters that follow cover each of these items and settings in detail. This book was authored using Microsoft Windows Vista, although AutoCAD Architecture 2010 works equally well on Windows XP or Windows 7. Both 32bit and 64bit versions are available, see the Preface for further details. Basic AutoCAD knowledge is assumed. Please refer to the Preface for complete details on these and other assumptions.

Lay Out a Simple Building

1. Launch AutoCAD Architecture 2010 from the icon on your desktop or from the *Autodesk > Autodesk AutoCAD Architecture 2010* group in *All Programs* on the Windows Start menu.

TIP

In Windows Vista, you can click the Start button, and then begin typing AutoCAD in the "Start Search field". After a couple of letters, AutoCAD Architecture should appear near the top of the list. Click it to launch to program.

2. From the Application menu (the big "A" button), choose **New > Drawing** (see Figure QS.1).

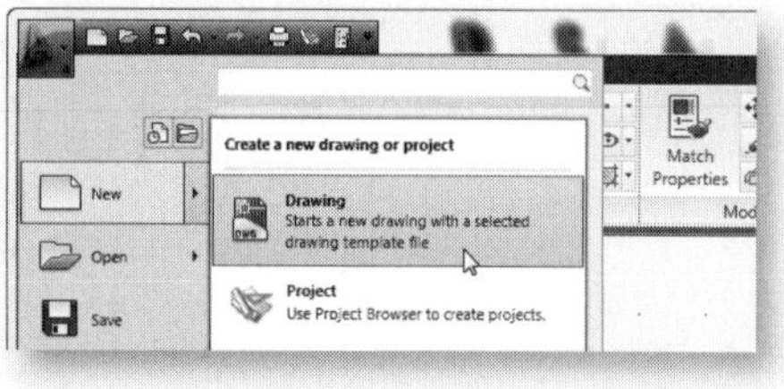

FIGURE QS.1 *Choose an AEC Model template file*

- Choose the *AEC Model (Imperial Stb).dwt* [*AEC Model (Metric Stb).dwt*] template and then click Open.

NOTE

Throughout this book, Imperial units and files will be listed first, followed by Metric units or files in brackets; for example, Imperial [Metric]. See the Preface for complete details on Style Conventions used throughout this book.

For this exercise, be sure to use the **New** command from the Application menu. The New icon on the Quick Access Toolbar calls the AutoCAD QNEW command, which does not prompt for a choice of template file. For more information on QNEW and Template files, refer to Chapter 3.

1. On the Application status bar (at the base of the ACA screen), right-click the Dynamic Input toggle (see Figure QS.2) and choose **Settings**.

   The Drafting Settings dialog should open with the Dynamic Input tab active.

- Place a checkmark in all three options in this dialog to turn them on and then click OK.

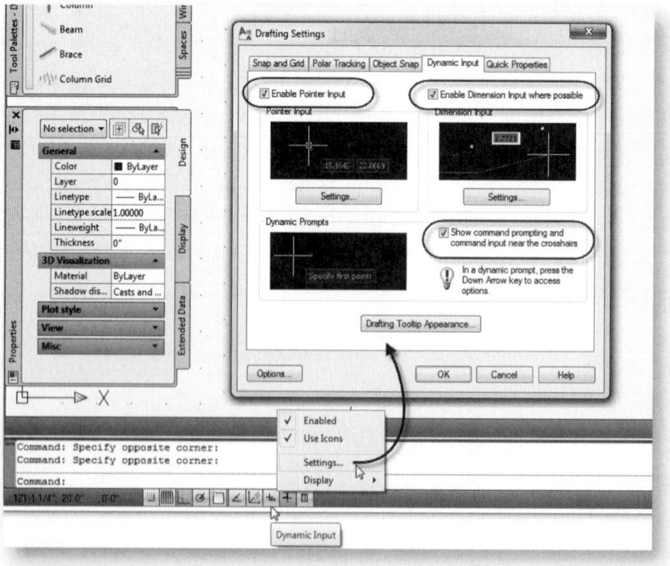

FIGURE QS.2 *Enable all Dynamic Input options*

These settings display prompting and input instructions directly onscreen at the cursor location. Refer to Chapter 1 for more information on these settings. Ribbon tabs run across the top of the screen starting with "Home" right next to the big "A" button. Ribbons contain tools organized in groupings called panels. When referencing a tool, we will refer first to the ribbon tab, then the panel and finally the tool.

2. On the Home tab of the ribbon, on the Draw panel, click the Rectangle icon (see Figure QS.3).

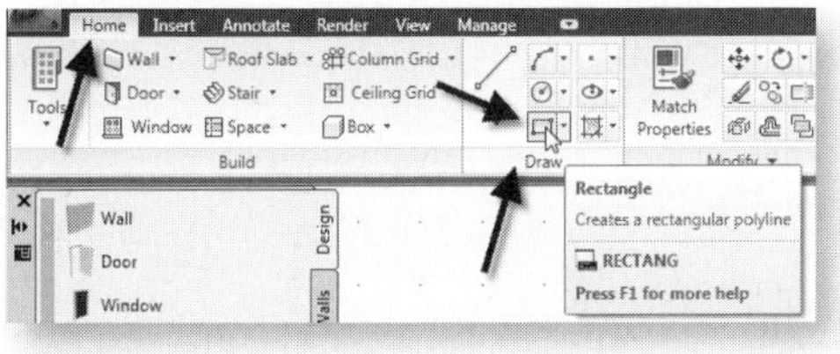

FIGURE QS.3 *Click the Rectangle icon on the Draw panel*

- At the "Specify first corner point" prompt, click a point onscreen.
- At the "Specify other corner point" prompt, press the DOWN ARROW key on your keyboard to access command options of rectangles.
- Arrow down until "Dimensions" is selected and then press ENTER (see Figure QS.4).

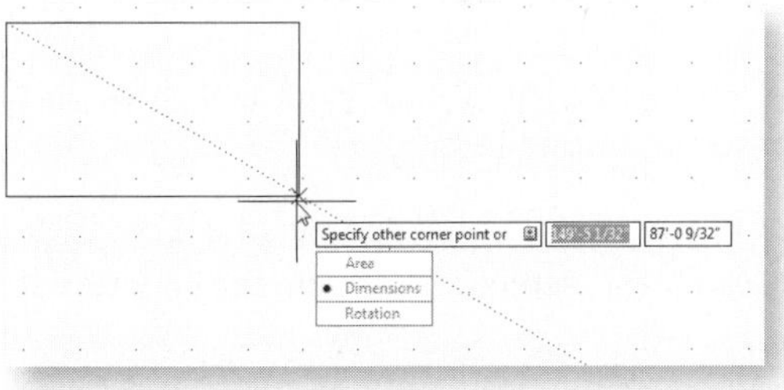

FIGURE QS.4 *Access rectangle command options with the* DOWN ARROW *key*

- At the "Specify length for rectangles" prompt, type **30'** [**9000**] and then press ENTER.
- At the "Specify width for rectangles" prompt, type **20'** [**6000**] and then press ENTER.

  Move your mouse side to side and up and down. Notice that the rectangle is sized based on the dimensions you indicated and that your mouse movements will indicate where the rectangle is placed relative to the first corner point.
- Click your mouse to complete placement (see Figure QS.5).

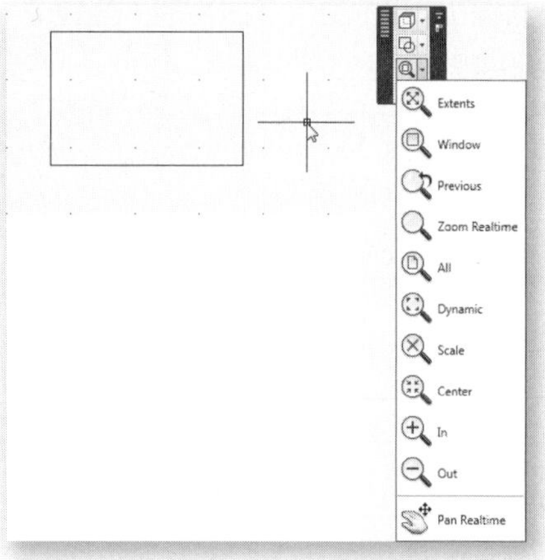

FIGURE QS.5 *Click the mouse to place the rectangle*

3. Zoom in on the rectangle.

If you have a wheel mouse, you can roll the wheel to zoom and drag with the wheel pressed in to pan. You can also use any standard AutoCAD method to zoom. Zoom commands are available on the Zoom flyout located on the View tab on the Navigate panel or on the floating View panel onscreen. Ribbon panels can be "torn off" and left floating onscreen. In the default installation of ACA, the View panel is detached from the ribbon and is floating onscreen. If restored to the ribbon, it reverts back to its location on the right side of the Home tab (see Chapter 1 for more details on the ribbon). To access flyout icons, click the small down arrow next to the icon. Other options will appear. Select the one you wish to use, such as Zoom Window. For more information on Zoom and Pan, refer to the online help.

Most ACA object creation commands are located on Tool Palettes. The Tool Palettes can be floating or docked to the sides of the screen. To open the palettes if they are not already open, press `CTRL + 3`.

4. On the Design tool palette, right-click the Wall tool and choose **Apply Tool Properties to > Linework** (see Figure QS.6).

NOTE

If you do not see the Tool Palettes on your screen, click the *Tools* button on the Build panel of the Home tab.

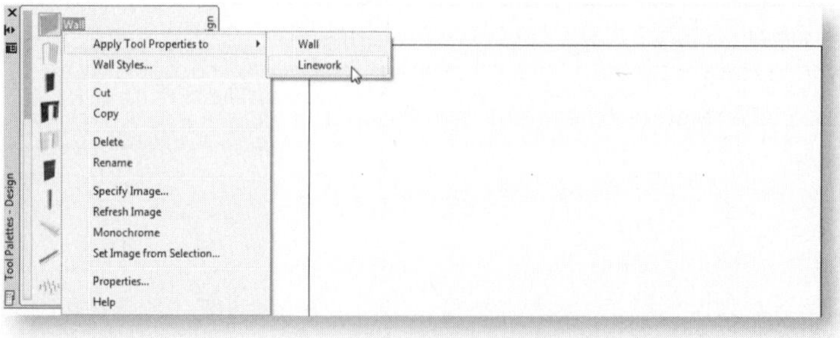

FIGURE QS.6 *Convert Linework to Walls by applying Tool Properties*

- At the "Select lines, arcs, circles, or polylines to convert into walls" prompt, select the rectangle onscreen and then press ENTER.
- At the "Erase layout geometry" prompt, choose **Yes** (see Figure QS.7).

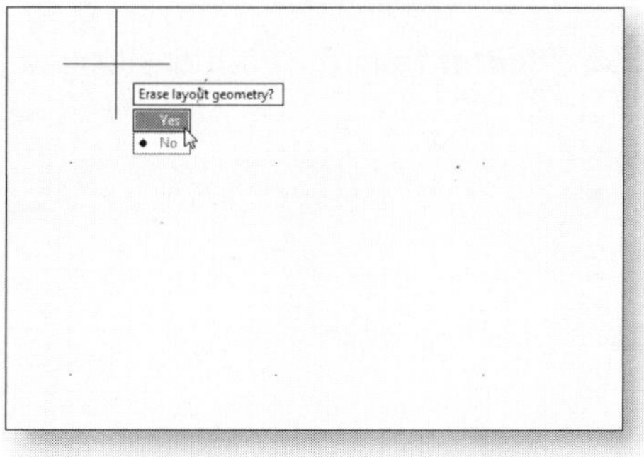

FIGURE QS.7 *Create Walls and erase the layout rectangle*

TIP
If you prefer, you can right-click in the drawing window and choose **Yes** or type **Y** at the command prompt and then press ENTER.

If you have the command line window open (usually docked at the bottom of the screen), it will indicate "4 new wall(s) created." You can also press F2 to make a text window appear that will reveal this message and show a history of past commands. In any case, the rectangle onscreen will be replaced with four Walls that remain selected. More information on Walls can be found in Chapters 4, 9, and 10.

5. With the Walls still selected, on the Properties palette change the Base Height to **8'-0"** [**2400**].

NOTE
If you do not see the Properties palette, you press F1 or right-click onscreen and choose **Properties.**

6. With the Walls still selected, right-click and choose **Insert > Door** (see Figure QS.8).

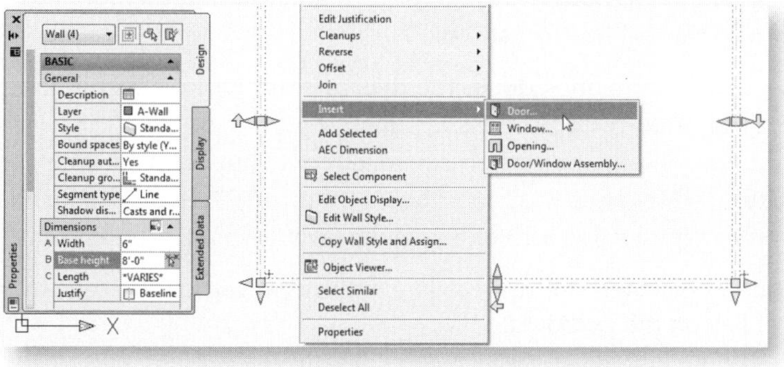

FIGURE QS.8 *Inserting a Door from the Wall's right-click menu*

A Door with some associated "Dynamic Dimensions" will appear, and the Properties palette will appear if it was not already open onscreen. (If only the title bar of the Properties palette appears, move your mouse pointer over it so it will pop open.)

- On the Properties palette, set the Width to **3'-0"** [**910**] and the Height to **7'-0"** [**2110**].
- In the Location grouping, choose **Offset/Center** from the Position along wall list (see Figure QS.9).

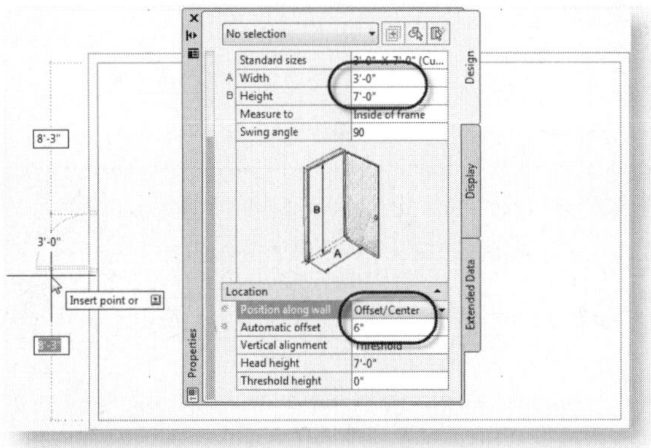

FIGURE QS.9 *Designate Door Parameters on the Properties palette*

- Move the mouse near the center of the left vertical Wall in the drawing.

NOTE Notice that the Dynamic Dimension on either side of the Door shows the same value.

- Move the mouse slightly from side to side. When the Door swings to the outside of the building, click the left button to place the Door.
- Right-click and choose **Enter** (or press ENTER at the keyboard) to end the Add Door routine.

7. Select the bottom horizontal Wall, right-click, and choose **Insert > Window**.

- On the Properties palette, set the Width to **4'-0"** [**1200**] and the Height to **5'-0"** [**1500**]. Leave the Position along wall set to **Unconstrained** this time.
- Click anywhere along the bottom Wall to place a Window and then place two more Windows in the top horizontal Wall.

As the Windows and Doors are being added, the dynamic dimensions surrounding them are "live" and can be used to input precise values. The size of the Window is currently the active dimension and cannot be edited directly, but must be changed in the Properties palette. However, if you press the TAB key, the "active" dimension will cycle, allowing you to type a value into either of the other dynamic dimensions.

8. With the Window command still active, move to the right vertical Wall and then press the TAB key on the keyboard.

   Note that one of the two offset dimensions is now highlighted.

- Type in a value for this highlighted dimension, such as **4'-0"** [**1200**], and press ENTER (see Figure QS.10).

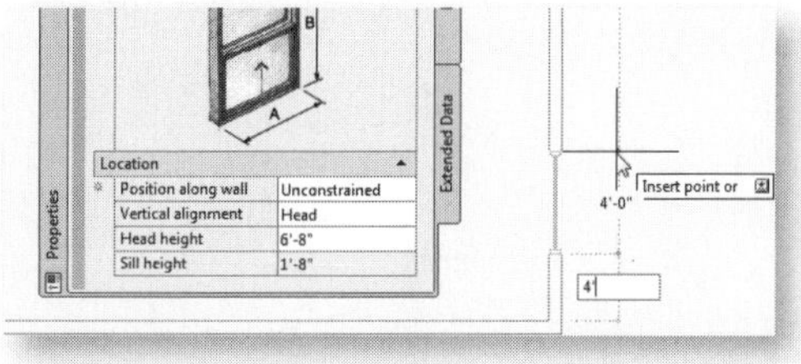

FIGURE QS.10 *Add some Windows using Dynamic Dimension input*

NOTE

Imperial dimensions throughout this text use the "Feet and Inch" format for clarity. However, when typing these values into ACA, neither the inch symbol (") nor the hyphen (-) separating the feet from inches is required. Therefore, 4'-0" can be typed in ACA as either **4'** or **48** to achieve the same result. As you can see, zeros can also be omitted. Hyphens are required only when separating inches from fractions. Therefore 6-½" is typed as **6-1/2.** You can also use decimal equivalents instead of fractions; for example, **6.5**. Metric values in this text are in millimeters and can be typed in directly with no unit designation required. More information on Style Conventions used in this book can be found in the Preface.

The Window appears in the Wall offset from the corner by the exact amount typed in.

- When you have finished adding Windows, right-click and choose **Enter** to end the command (or simply press the ENTER key).

For more information on adding Walls, Doors, and Windows, refer to Chapter 4.

Edit the Model

Objects built with AutoCAD Architecture can be manipulated quickly and easily via the Properties palette or via direct manipulation onscreen. Direct manipulation refers to editing that takes place directly on the object within the drawing window.

1. Move your mouse over any Wall, but don't click yet (see Figure QS.11).

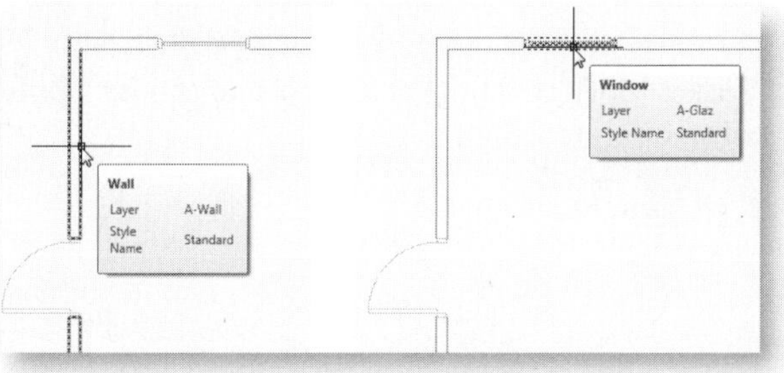

FIGURE QS.11 *Objects under the cursor highlight prior to selection*

Notice that the objects under the cursor will highlight temporarily as the cursor hovers over them. This behavior can be customized and turned on and off in the Options dialog. See Chapter 1 for more information.

2. Click on the top horizontal Wall to select it.

The selection preview will disappear, and a series of grips will appear in various shapes. (Grips are the small geometric shapes placed at strategic editing points when an object is selected.)

3. Hover over one of the grips—do not click it (see Figure QS.12).

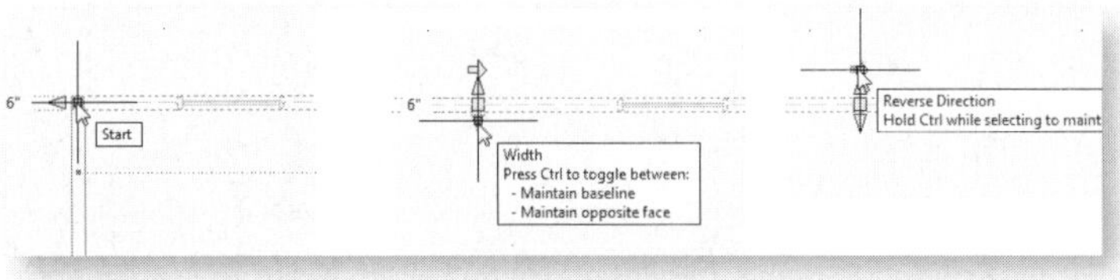

FIGURE QS.12 *Grips provide onscreen tips indicating their function*

A small tip will appear onscreen indicating the function of the highlighted grip and any CTRL key toggle options it may have. When you click a grip, the grip is activated and the tip disappears. At first, don't click the grips; simply move the mouse over each one to see what their functions are.

4. First hover over and then click on one of the triangular-shaped grips at the midpoint of the Wall.

   These grips affect the width of the Wall.

- Make the Wall thicker by dragging away from its center and then clicking (see Figure QS.13).

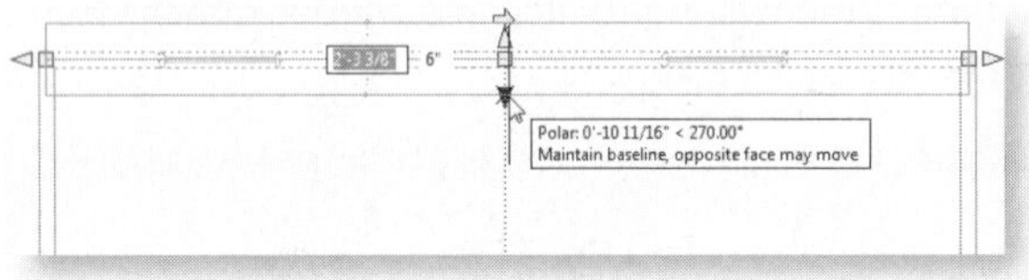

FIGURE QS.13 *Using Grips to edit the thickness of the Wall*

5. With the Wall still selected, right-click and choose **Select Similar**.

   This will select all four Walls, but not the Doors or Windows.

- On the Tool Palettes, click on the Walls tab to show the Walls tool palette.

  This reveals several different types of Walls ready to use in your drawings.

- Right-click on the Brick-4 Brick-4 [Brick-090 Brick-090] tool and choose **Apply Tool Properties to > Wall** (see Figure QS.14).

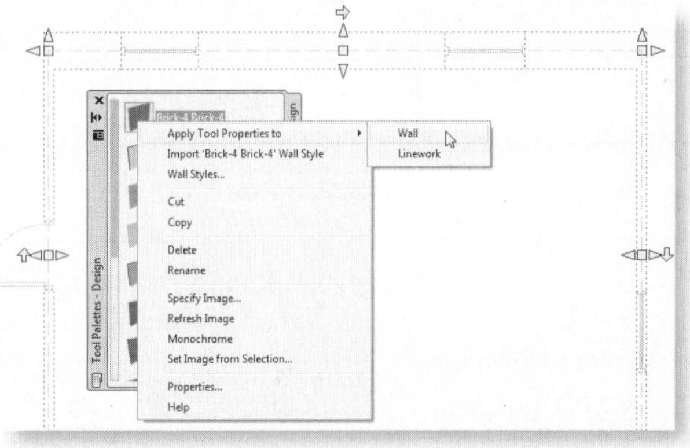

FIGURE QS.14 *Apply a new Wall Style with all four selected Walls*

Hatching will appear within the Walls, and our manually edited Wall will now be the same width as the other Walls. This particular Wall type (called a Wall Style) has a built-in fixed width. For more information on working with and swapping Wall styles, refer to Chapter 10.

- Right-click and choose **Deselect All** (near the bottom of the menu).

6. Select the Door. (Click on it to select).

- Click one of the small arrow-shaped grip points to flip the Door swing. Repeat with the other arrow grip (see Figure QS.15).

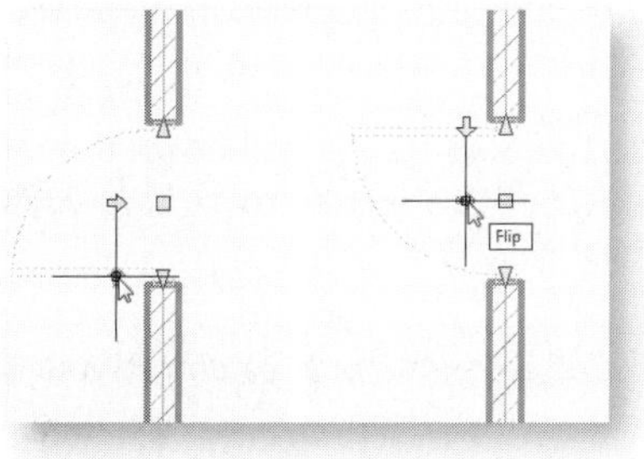

FIGURE QS.15 *Flip the Swing of the Door with Grips*

- Right-click and choose **Deselect All** to complete the change.

7. Right-click in the drawing window and choose **Basic Modify Tools > Move**.

- At the "Select objects" prompt, click on any Window and then press ENTER.
- At the "Specify base point" prompt, click anywhere in the drawing.
- At the "Specify second point" prompt, move the mouse and click a random point (see Figure QS.16).

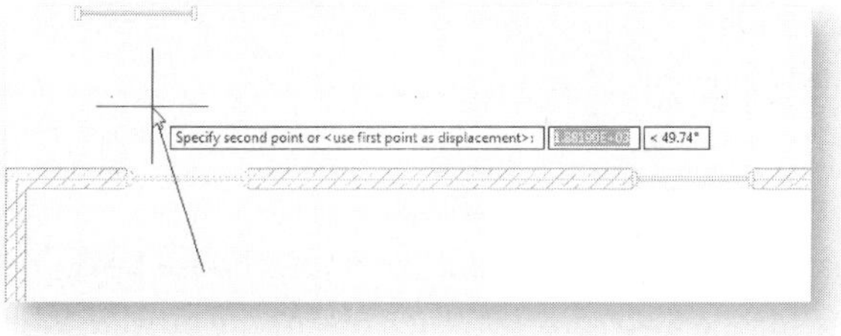

FIGURE QS.16 *Attempt to move the Window out of the Wall*

Notice that the Window did move, but not to the point we picked. Instead, it remained attached to the Wall; therefore, it simply moved along the length of the Wall closest to the point that we clicked. This behavior is determined by an "anchor." Anchors control the relationship of objects to one another, such as keeping the Window attached to a Wall. For more information on anchors, refer to Chapter 2.

8. On the Quick Access Toolbar (QAT) at the top left of the screen, click the Undo icon to return the Window to its original location (See Figure QS.17).

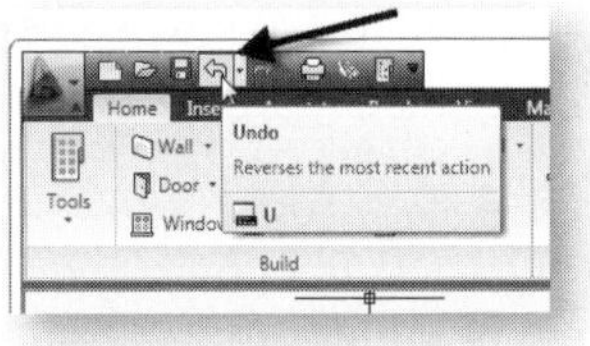

FIGURE QS.17 *Undo the previous operation*

Add a Floor Slab and Roof

We have given our simple building some walls and openings. Let's complete the enclosure with a roof and a floor slab.

9. Click the Design tab of the Tool Palettes; find the Slab tool (scroll down if necessary) and then right-click and choose **Apply Tool Properties to > Linework and Walls.**

TIP

If your Tool Palettes have a scroll bar, you can use it to scroll a palette; or if you move your mouse over an unused portion of the palette, a small hand icon will appear. Click and drag with this icon to scroll.

- At the "Select walls or polylines" prompt, select each of the Walls one at a time and then press ENTER.

TIP

You can click a point outside the model and then surround the entire drawing with a box and click again. Only the Walls will highlight as they are the only object within the selection box eligible to convert to Slabs.

- At the "Erase layout geometry" prompt, choose **No**.

NOTE

If Dynamic Input is OFF (use the Dynamic Input toggle at the base of the screen), right-click and choose **No** or type **N** at the command line prompt and then press ENTER.

- At the "Specify slab justification" prompt, choose **Top**.
- At the "Specify wall justification for edge alignment" prompt, choose **Left**.
- At the "Select the pivot edge for the Slab" prompt, click one of the outside Wall edges (see Figure QS.18).

NOTE

If the outside edge of the Walls do not highlight, press ESC, repeat the steps and try Right for the "Specify wall justification for edge alignment" prompt instead.

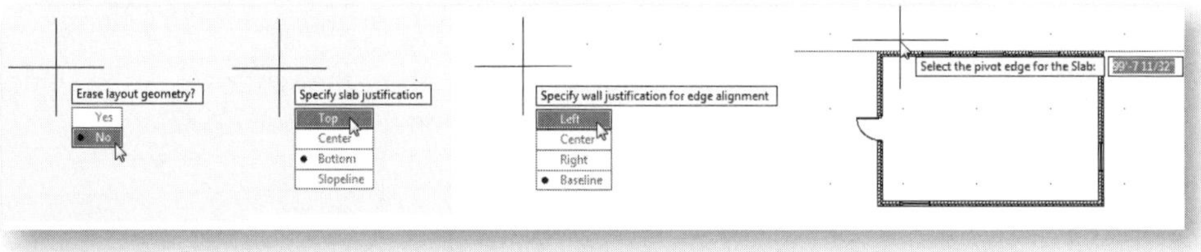

FIGURE QS.18 *Answering the command line prompts of the Apply Slab Properties to Walls command*

10. With the Slab still selected, right-click and choose **Properties**. (If the Slab is no longer selected, click it near the door opening to select it.)
   - On the Properties palette, within the Dimensions grouping, change the Thickness to **1'-0"** [**250**].
   - Scroll down to the Location grouping and type **0** for the Elevation parameter (see Figure QS.19).

   This will make the Slab thicker and move it to the correct location below the bottom edge of the Walls.

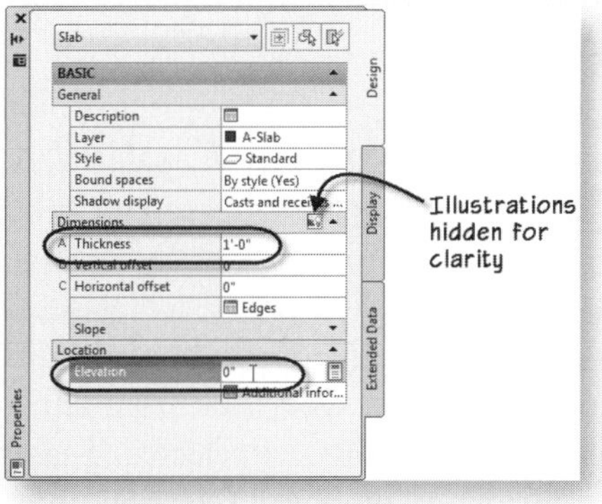

FIGURE QS.19 *Edit the Thickness and Elevation parameters of the slab*

11. On the Design palette, right-click the Roof tool and choose **Apply Tool Properties to > Linework and Walls**.
12. At the "Select Objects" prompt, click to select each of the Walls one at a time and then press ENTER.

NOTE

The window selection method mentioned previously will not work well here. Instead, simply click on each Wall in succession.

13. At the "Erase layout geometry" prompt, right-click and choose **No**.

See Figure QS.20 for the result. For more information on Slabs and Roofs, refer to Chapter 12.

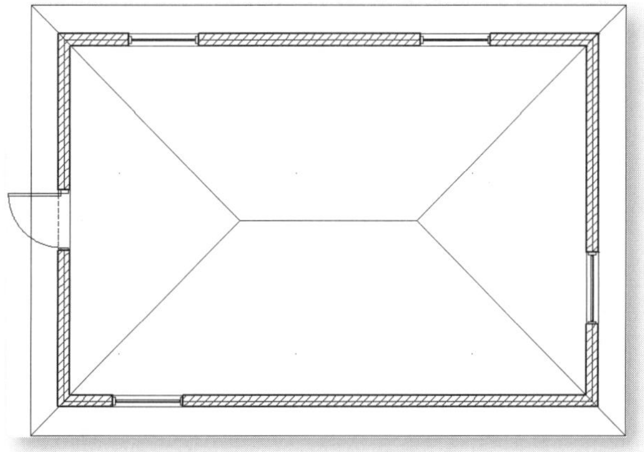

FIGURE QS.20 *Adding a simple Roof based on the existing Walls*

Edit the Model in Elevation

Our top wall contains only one Window. (If you added more, delete the extras for this exercise.) Let's explore how that elevation will look with a few additional windows.

1. Click a point outside and above the model to the right, move the mouse to the outside left of the model just below the upper Wall, and click again (see Figure QS.21).

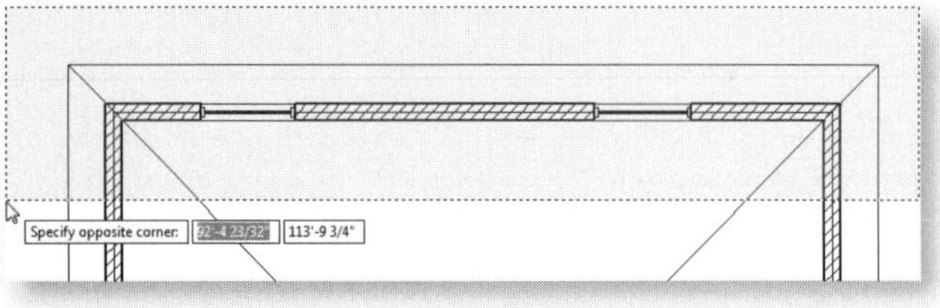

FIGURE QS.21 *Select the upper portion of the model with a crossing window*

This is called a crossing selection window. When you click from right to left, all objects touched by the selection window are selected. When you click from left to right, only those objects completely surrounded by the window are selected. Search for "select objects" in the online help for more information on object selection.

- With the upper Wall, its Window, the Roof, and the Slab selected, right-click and choose **Isolate Objects > Edit in Elevation** (see Figure QS.22).

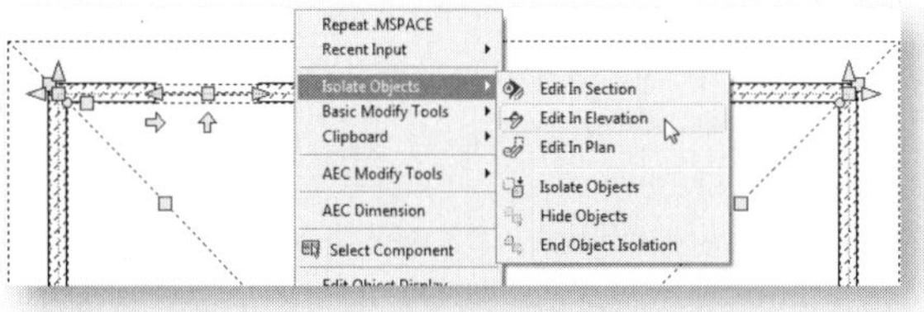

FIGURE QS.22 *Using Edit in Elevation from the right-click menu*

At the "Select linework or face under the cursor" prompt, move the mouse around and note the various edges and surfaces that highlight—do not click yet.

- Highlight the upper edge of the Roof object (a blue line will appear to indicate that the edge is selected) and then click (see Figure QS.23).

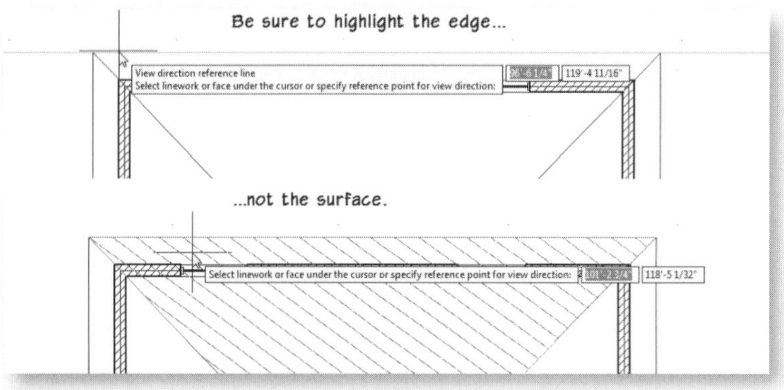

FIGURE QS.23 *Highlight geometry to determine the elevation vantage point*

- At the "Specify elevation extents" prompt, drag down slightly (enough to include the upper Wall) and then click (see Figure QS.24).

The model will change views and zoom to the selected area. All non-selected objects will be hidden temporarily to make editing easier. A small toolbar (labeled "Edit In View") with a single icon will also appear. Use this icon to restore the previous view when editing is complete.

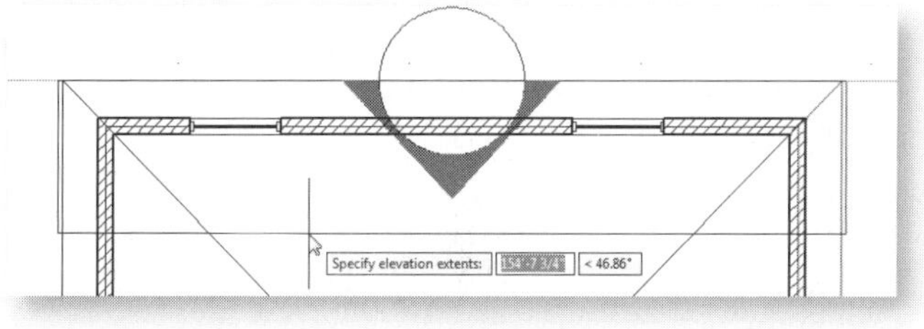

FIGURE QS.24 *Drag to indicate extent of elevation view*

2. Select the Window (now shown in elevation).

   Take note of the grips again.

- Click the square (Location) grip at the bottom edge and drag the Window to a new location on the Wall.

As you can see, all grip editing functions equally well in elevation view as well as in plan view.

- Repeat this process and drag it to the left, placing it a short distance from the left side of the Wall.

3. With the Window still selected, right-click and choose **AEC Modify Tools > Array**.

- At the "Select an edge to array from" prompt, press ENTER.
- Highlight the right vertical edge of the Window and then click (see Figure QS.25).

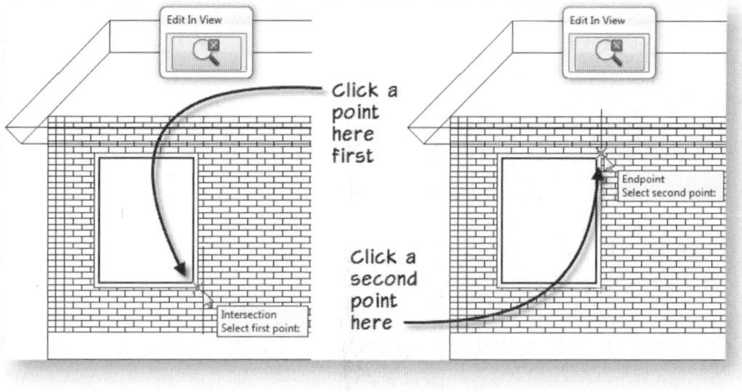

FIGURE QS.25 *Click points to set the start of the array*

- Move the mouse to the right and note the dimension that appears.
- At the "Drag out array elements" prompt, type **8'-0"** [**2400**] and then press ENTER.
- Drag the mouse to the right until two new Windows appear and then click.

There will now be three windows in this elevation. Notice that they cut holes in the Wall just as they did in the plan. It might be nice to space them equally on this wall.

4. Click to select each of the three Windows in this elevation.
5. Right-click and choose **AEC Modify Tools > Space Evenly**.

- At the "Select an axis to space evenly on" prompt, hover over the bottom edge of the Slab to highlight it and then click.
- At the "Select the first point along the axis" prompt, click the outside bottom corner of the Slab.
- At the "Select the second point along the axis" prompt, click the opposite bottom corner of the Slab (see Figure QS.26).

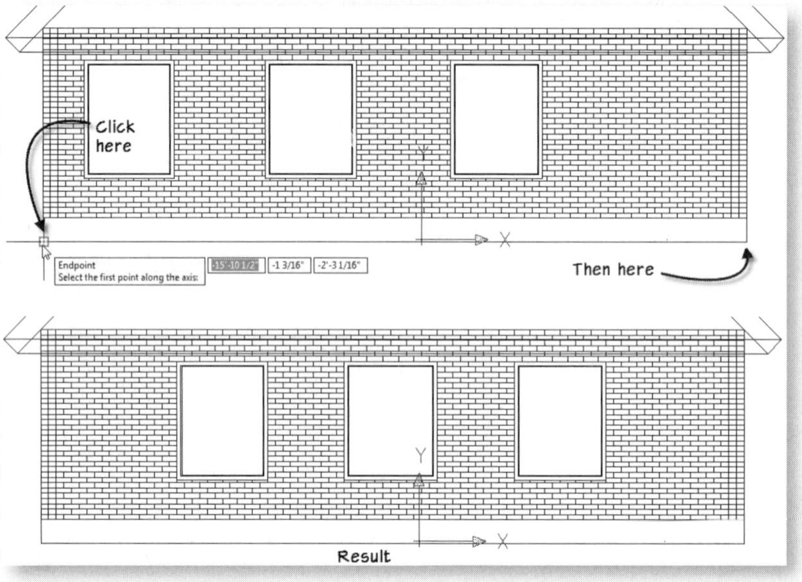

FIGURE QS.26 *Snap from one endpoint to the other to indicate spacing*

6. Click the Exit Edit in View icon to return to the original plan view.

SET UP A PROJECT WITH FLOOR LEVELS

We can quickly take the geometry that we started here and turn it into a multistory building. Let's take a quick look at the Drawing/Project Management System.

7. From the Application menu, choose **New > Project**.

   Verify that the current folder is *My Projects*.

- If it is not, use the drop-down list on the left (below the bank of icons), choose *My Documents*.
- Double-click the *Autodesk* folder and then the *My Projects* folder.
- At the bottom of the window, click the New Project icon (see Figure QS.27).

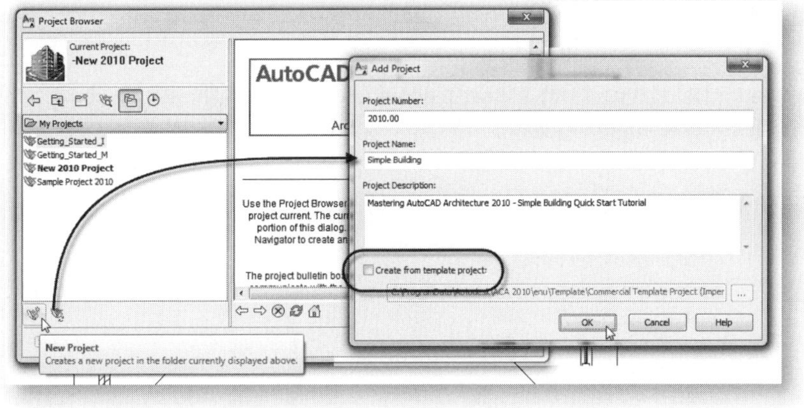

FIGURE QS.27 *Add a new project and give it a name*

- In the Add Project dialog box, type **Simple Building** in the Project Name field.
- If you wish, type a Project number and Description (these are optional) and clear the checkmark from the "Create from template project" checkbox (see Figure QS.27).

8. Click OK to create the project and then click the Close button to dismiss the Project Browser.

The Project Navigator palette should appear onscreen. If it does not, click the **Project Navigator** icon on the QAT or press CTRL + 5.

9. Click the Project tab (if it is not already active). In the Levels grouping, click the small Edit Levels icon (see Figure QS.28).

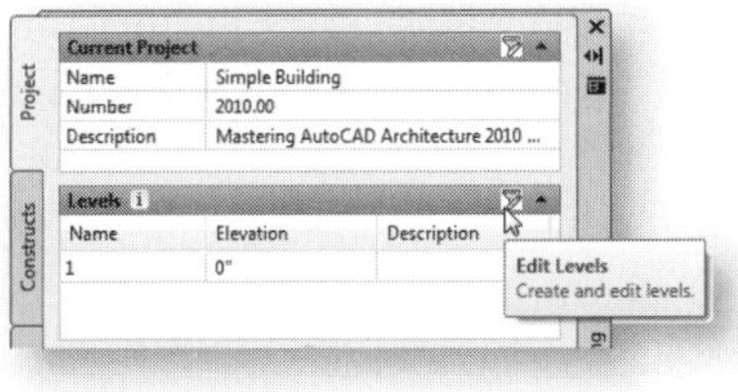

FIGURE QS.28 *Click the Edit Levels icon on the Project tab to change and add floor levels to the project*

- In the Levels dialog box, change the Floor-to-Floor Height for Level 1 to **9'0"** [**3000**].
- Click the Add Level icon (on the right) and then change the Floor-to-Floor Height for Level 2 to **8'-0"** [**2750**].
- Click the Add Level icon again to add a Level 3 and then click OK.

  If an alert dialog box appears asking if you wish to "regenerate all views," click Yes to accept this and dismiss the dialog box.

10. On the Project Navigator palette, click the Constructs tab.

For complete information on Views, regeneration of Levels, Constructs, and the Project Navigator, see Chapter 5.

11. Right-click on the *Constructs* folder and choose **Save Current DWG As Construct**.

- In the Name field, type **First Floor**, place a checkmark in the Level 1 box, and then click OK (see Figure QS.29).

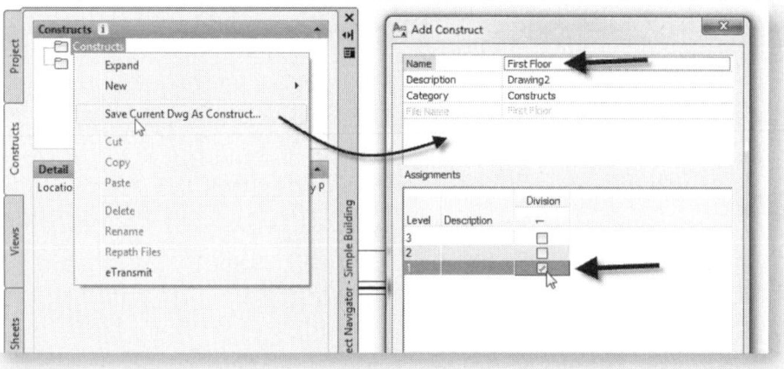

FIGURE QS.29 *Save the current drawing as the First Floor–Level 1 Construct*

12. Click on the Roof object in the drawing, right-click and choose **Properties**.

- In the Dimensions grouping, choose **Plumb** from the Edge cut list.
- In the Dimensions: Lower Slope grouping, change the Plate Height to: **0** (zero) and the Rise to **6"** **[50]**.

13. Click again on the Roof (be sure to click a highlighted edge and not a grip), hold down the mouse, and drag it on top of the Constructs folder of the Project Navigator palette. When the mouse shape changes to an arrow with a small box, release the mouse (see Figure QS.30).

This action will move the Roof from the First Floor file and create a new Construct file from it. If your Roof is changing shape instead of moving, then you selected a Grip (the small colored squares). Press the ESC key, undo any changes to the Roof, and try again. Drag from the highlighted edge, *not* the grip.

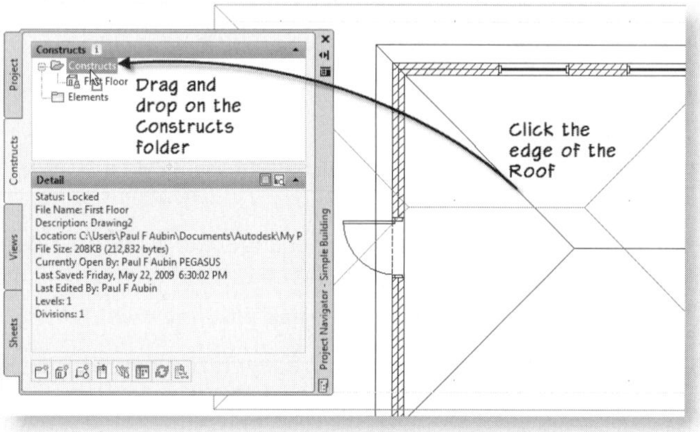

FIGURE QS.30 *Drag the Roof to the Project Navigator palette to create a new Construct*

- In the Add Construct dialog box, name the new Construct **Roof**, check Level 3 for its Assignment, and then click OK.

The First Floor Construct file will still be open onscreen. The Roof will disappear from onscreen. It has moved to the newly created Construct file.

14. On the QAT, click the Save icon (or press CTRL + S).
15. On the Project Navigator palette, right-click on the *First Floor* Construct and choose **Copy Construct to Levels**.

- In the Copy Construct to Levels dialog box, place a checkmark in Level 2 and then click OK (see Figure QS.31).

  We now have an exact copy of the *First Floor* to use for the *Second Floor*.

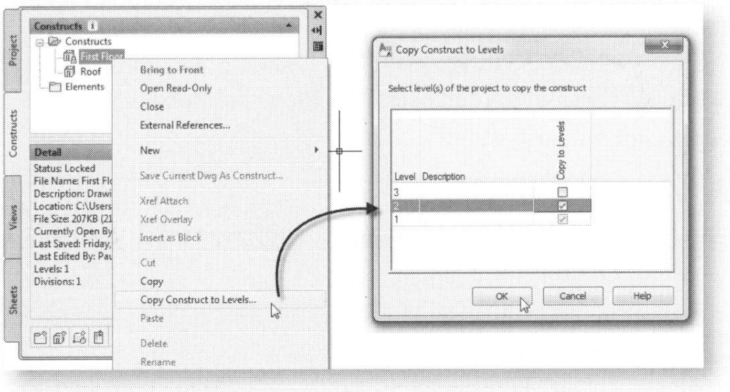

FIGURE QS.31 *Copy the First Floor Construct to the Second Floor Level*

- Right-click on the new Construct—currently named *First Floor(2)*—and choose **Rename**.
- Rename it to **Second Floor**.
- In the "Project Navigator - Re-path Project" dialog that appears, click the Re-path project now option.

NOTE **Re-pathing and Projects will be discussed in detail in Chapter 5.**

16. Right-click on *Second Floor* and choose **Open** (or simply double-click it).

Notice that the geometry on the Second Floor is identical to the First Floor.

17. Select the Door, and then click the small square shaped grip in the center.

- Drag it to the other side of the plan and click when it is near the middle of the vertical Wall on the right side.

  Notice how it stays attached to the Walls as you drag it. Leave this Door here for now; it will open to a patio later in the lesson.

18. On the Tool Palette, click the Windows tab.

- Click on the ***Picture – Arched*** tool.
- On the Properties palette, change the Position along wall setting to: **Offset/Center**.
- Change the Vertical alignment setting to: **Sill** and change the Sill height to **2'-0"** [**600**].
- Click the vertical Wall on the left and place the Window in the middle of the Wall.
- Press ENTER to complete the command.

19. Close the *Second Floor* file.

- Use the small "X" icon in the top right corner of the drawing window, or choose **Close** from the Application menu.
- When prompted; click Yes to save the file.

Create a Model View

Having created the separate parts of our building (Constructs), let's see how they all look together.

1. On the Project Navigator palette, click the Views tab.
2. Right-click on the *Views* folder and choose **New View Dwg > General**.

- For the Name, type **Model** and then click Next.
- On the Context screen, check all three Levels and then click Next.
- On the final screen, click Finish.

3. On Project Navigator, double-click *Model* to open it.

- On the View panel, choose **View, SW Isometric** from the View drop-down button.

  In the default installation, the View panel is torn off and floating onscreen. If yours is not, look for it on the Home tab.

- On the View panel, choose **Visual Styles, Conceptual** from the Visual Styles drop-down button (see Figure QS.32).

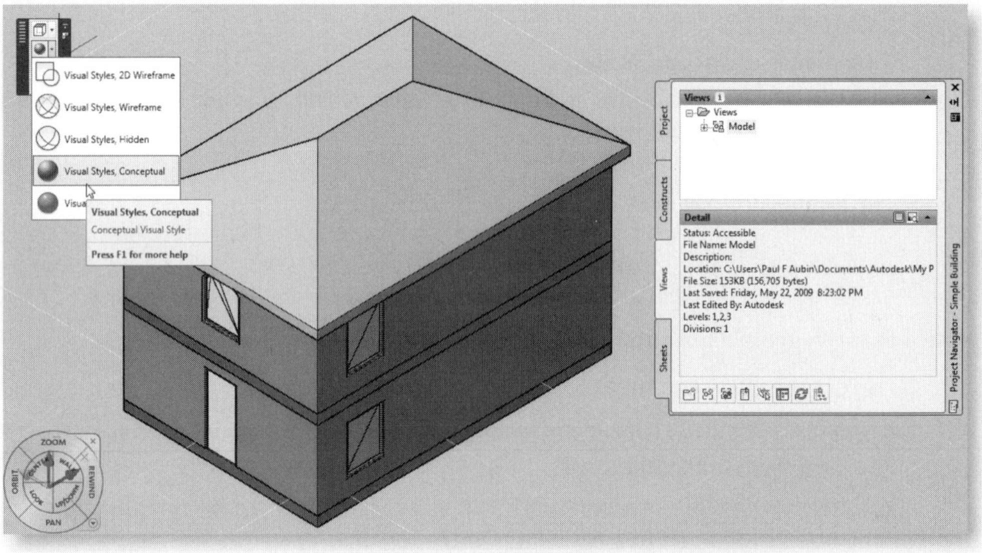

FIGURE QS.32 *View the Model from an Isometric viewpoint in Conceptual shading*

Feel free to try other isometric views and visual styles from the 3D Views and Visual Styles drop-down buttons.

Edit the Model

Viewing the model in 3D gives you the opportunity to see how the design is coming along and consider modifications. It is easy to make changes and then quickly view the results.

1. Click on the second floor in the *Model* file to select it.

Notice how the entire floor plate highlights; the *Model* is comprised of External References (XREFs). A small floating properties palette (called Quick Properties) will appear as you select confirming this. An XREF is a link to the original file that updates when changes to the original are made. Project Navigator automatically creates all XREFs for you when we set up a View. See Chapter 5 for more information.

- Right-click and choose **Open XREF**.

Notice that the *Second Floor* Construct file has opened onscreen. You could have opened it from Project Navigator, but this method can sometimes be faster.

2. Select the vertical Wall on the right.
   If you highlight the Slab instead, press the ESC key and try again.

- Click the square Location grip at the center of the Wall. Begin moving it to the left.
- Type **5'-0"** [**1500**] and then press ENTER (see Figure QS.33).

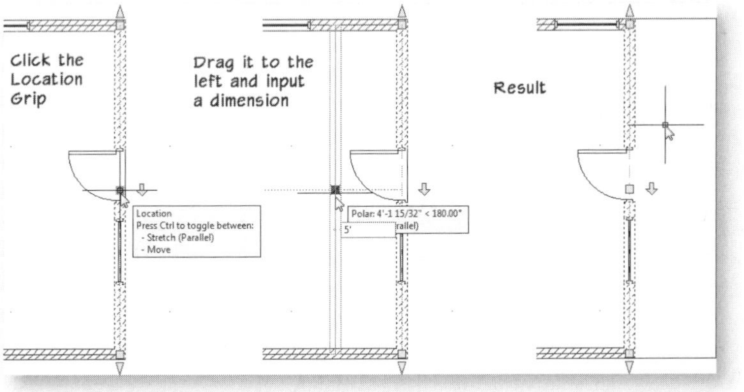

FIGURE QS.33 *Use the Location Grip to move a Wall and simultaneously Stretch its neighbors*

Notice how the two horizontal Walls at the top and bottom are stretched to stay connected to the one we moved. If any of your Windows are now in undesirable locations, you can move them the same way. Select them, then click the square Location grip in the center and move to a new location. You can also use the AEC Modify tools discussed previously to re-center and space Windows if you like.

3. On the Design Tool palette, click the Column tool.

- On the Properties palette, change the Logical length to **8'-0"** [**2750**].
- At the "Insert point" prompt, click a point near the corner of the Slab where the Wall previously was, and then press ENTER to accept the default rotation.
- Repeat at the other corner, and then press ENTER to complete the command.

Add Spaces

On the interior of the building, we can add Space objects that represent the rooms in the plan and that can be used to add room tags and calculate square footage later.

1. On the Project Navigator palette, click the Constructs tab and then double-click the *First Floor* file to open it.
2. On the Walls tab of the Tool Palettes, click the ***Stud 4*** tool.
3. Click a point in between two of the Windows at the top of the plan and then click an opposite point at the bottom of the plan.

TIP

For this exercise, the precise location is not important. Hold down the SHIFT key, and right-click to access the snap menu. Snap Nearest for the first point to Intersection or Perpendicular for the other point.

4. On the Design tool palette, click the ***Door*** tool and then add a Door to the new Wall. Press ENTER to complete the command.
5. On the Design tool palette, click the ***Space*** tool.

- From the "Create type" list, choose **Generate**.
- For the "Ceiling height" type **8'-0"** [**2400**] and for the "Height above ceiling" type **0** (see Figure QS.34).

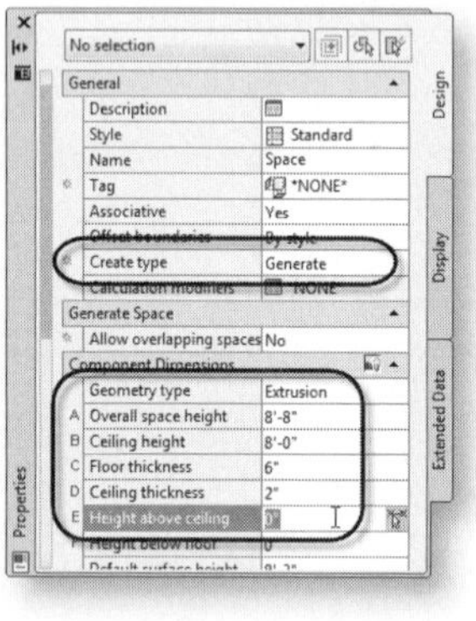

FIGURE QS.34 *Set the parameters of a Space to automatically generate it from bounding Walls*

6. Move the mouse inside the building (see Figure QS.35).

Notice that a red outline appears within the plan surrounding the room. As you move from room to room, the red outline previews the Space that will be created. For this to work, you need to completely enclose a space with Walls or other geometry.

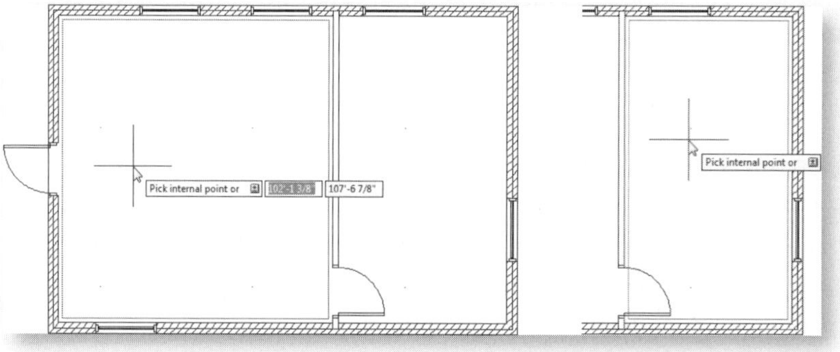

FIGURE QS.35 *Highlight an interior area from which to create a Space*

- Click inside each room to create two Spaces.
- Press ENTER to complete the command.

   Two Space objects represented by cross hatching will appear onscreen.

7. Click the Space on the left. On the Properties palette, click in the Name field and type **Reception**. Press ESC, click the other Space, and change its name to **Office**.

   Try moving the interior Wall. The two neighboring Spaces will update as well!
8. Save and close the *First Floor* file.

The *Second Floor* file should still be open from the edits done previously. Let's add a Space there as well.

9. Repeat the process to add a Space to the *Second Floor*. You can name this Space **Office** as well.
10. Save and close the *Second Floor* file.

Back in the *Model* file (which should still be open onscreen), a small balloon will appear in the lower right corner of the screen (see Figure QS.36).

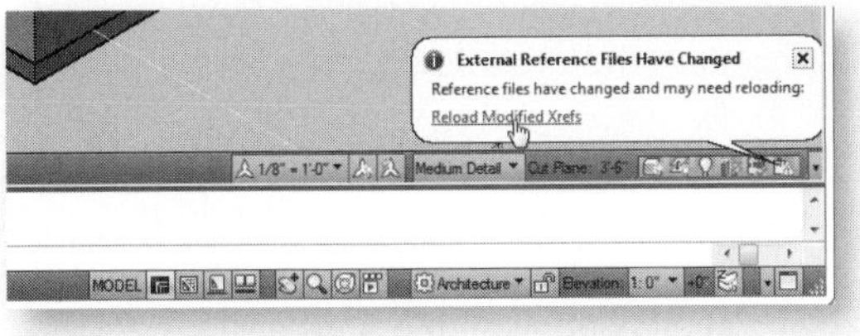

FIGURE QS.36 *After editing the First Floor and the Second Floor, an alert will appear in the Model to reload them*

11. Click the Reload Modified Xrefs link in the External Reference alert balloon.

Notice how the edits made to the *Second Floor* are now visible in the *Model*. The edits to the *First Floor* are here too, they just occur on the inside of the model and therefore do not show in this view.

   Locate the Steering Wheel in the corner of the screen. (It may be concealed behind a palette). The Steering Wheel has many navigation options on it.

12. To Orbit the model, place your mouse over the Orbit area and drag.

   Notice the free-form rotation of the model in 3D (see Figure QS.37).

If you do not like the way it orbits on first attempt, try changing the Center. Move your mouse over the Center portion of the wheel and then drag the icon to a new location onscreen. This will be the center of rotation for subsequent orbits. Try Orbit again. You should get better results.

   Alternative 1: you can simply click and drag on the ViewCube in the corner of the screen.

   Alternative 2: hold down the SHIFT key and simultaneously press and drag with the wheel of your mouse.

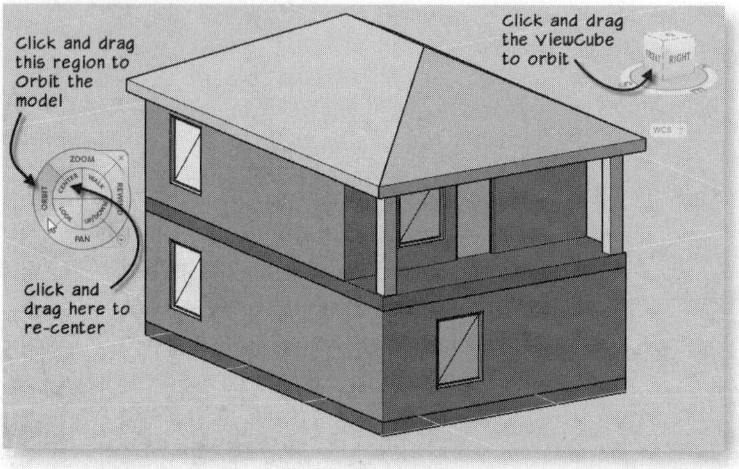

FIGURE QS.37 *Orbit the Model to see the edits in 3D*

13. Using the floating View panel, choose **Visual Styles, 2D Wireframe** and **Views, Top**.
 - Double-click the wheel on your mouse and then roll down two clicks.

These steps are not necessary, but it is best practice to leave a drawing in wireframe and zoomed to extents before saving it.

> **NOTE** If you don't have **a wheel mouse**, use the Zoom Extents option on the View panel.

Notice the different ways in which the objects, particularly the Doors, are displayed in each view. This is the result of ACA display control. (Refer to Chapter 2 for more information.) Consult an AutoCAD Command reference or the online help for more information on zooming, panning, and Visual Styles.

14. Save the *Model* file.

CREATING A PRESENTATION

Let's finish our quick tour of AutoCAD Architecture by generating some plans and elevations and placing them on a sheet for output.

Add the First Floor Plan View

In the preceding section, we built the geometry for the first and second floors. We can use these to create any kind of drawing required for our project. We used both together previously to create a 3D model. Now let's add a few floor plans to our project; one for each floor.

1. Click the Views tab of the Project Navigator.
 - Right-click on the *Views* folder and choose **New View Dwg > General**.
 - In the Name field, type **First Floor Plan** and then click Next.
 - Place a checkmark in the Level 1 box and then click Next.

- At the bottom left corner of the dialog box, place a checkmark in the "Open in drawing editor" checkbox and then click Finish.

  On the Project Navigator palette, *First Floor Plan* will appear on the Views tab and it will open onscreen.

- Use your wheel mouse and zoom in a bit.

2. Right-click the title bar of the Tool Palettes, choose the **Document** group and then click the Tags tab (see the left side of Figure QS.38).

- Click the ***Room Tag – Project Based*** tool.
- At the "Select object to tag" prompt, click the Space on the left and then press ENTER.
- In the dialog that appears, click OK.

  The process repeats.

- Click the other Space, press ENTER and then click OK. Press ENTER again to end the command.

Notice that the names that we typed in the "Add Spaces" topic previously have appeared here automatically. Also note that the rooms have automatically numbered sequentially (see the top right of Figure QS.38).

3. From the Home tab, on the Layers panel, click the Freeze icon.

- At the "Select an object on the layer to be frozen" prompt, click the cross hatching of either Space and then press ENTER (see the lower right portion of Figure QS.38).

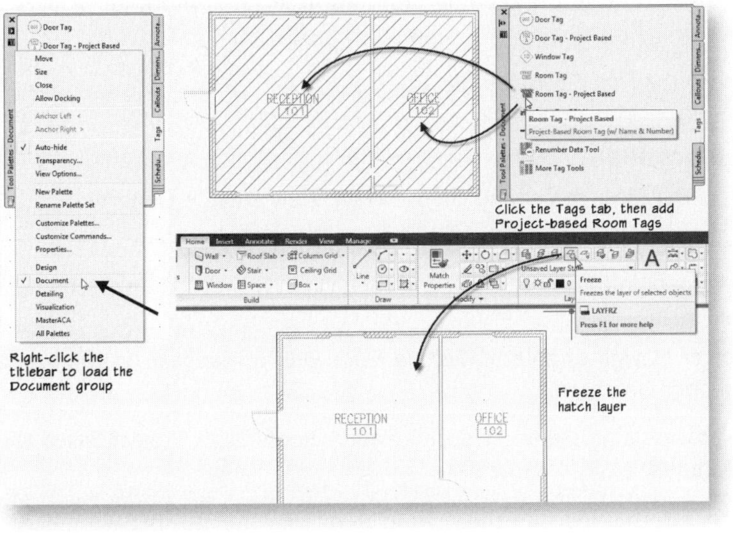

FIGURE QS.38 *Create a first floor plan file, add Room Tags and freeze the Space layer*

The hatching will disappear. In reality, we have just frozen (turned off) its layer. This will make our plans easier to read. The hatching is useful in the Construct (where it is still visible) since you will modify the geometry of the model from the Constructs. But here in a floor plan View, we want things to display more like we wish to print them—thus the reason for freezing the Spaces here.

Change the Scale

Look at the bottom of the drawing window and note that the current drawing scale is 1/8"=1'–0" [1:100]. Since this plan is so small, a scale of 1/4"=1'–0" [1:50] may be more appropriate. You can change the scale of the drawing and the annotation (room tags in this case) will respond accordingly.

1. On the Drawing Status Bar (at the base of the drawing window) click the Scale pop-up and choose **1/4"=1'-0"** [**1:50**] (see Figure QS.39).

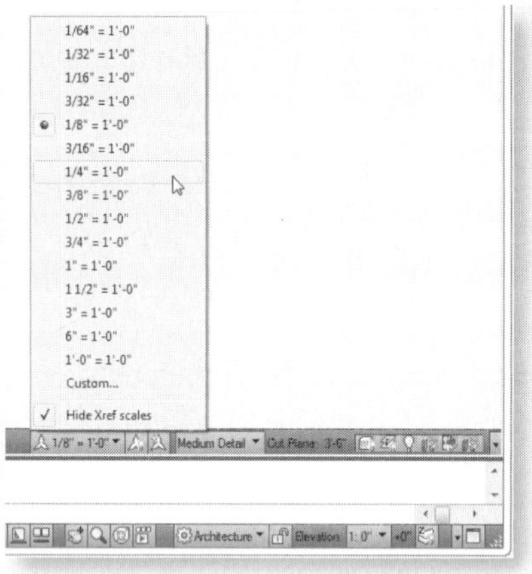

FIGURE QS.39 *Change the drawing scale*

Notice how the tags change size to match the new scale. The annotation scaling feature in AutoCAD is responsible for keeping annotation at an appropriate scale for consistent plotted results. This feature is discussed in more detail in Chapter 14.

2. Save and close the *First Floor Plan* file.

Add the Second Floor Plan View

1. Right-click on the *Views* folder and choose **New View Dwg > General**.

- In the Name field, type **Second Floor Plan** and then click Next.
- Place a checkmark in the Level 2 box and then click Next and then on the next screen click Finish.

  On the Project Navigator palette, *Second Floor Plan* will appear on the Views tab and will open onscreen.

2. Repeat the process discussed previously to add a Room Tag – Project Based and accept all defaults.

Notice that when you tag the Space in the second floor that the number will be 201 automatically using the level for the prefix of the room number. This is a benefit of the "Project based" tag. You would not get this if you used the other Room Tag tool on the same palette.

3. Freeze the Space layer, change the scale and then save and close the file.

Add Callouts and Elevations

The *Model* file should still be open onscreen. Here we will add some elevation callouts and elevations all in one routine. If you closed the *Model* file, reopen it now.

Continue in the *Model* file.

1. On the Tool Palettes, click the Callouts tab and then click the Exterior Elevation Mark A3 tool.

- At the "Specify first corner of elevation region" prompt, click a point below and to the right of the lower right corner of the building.
- At the "Specify opposite corner of elevation region" prompt, click a point above and to the left of the upper left corner of the building (see Figure QS.40).

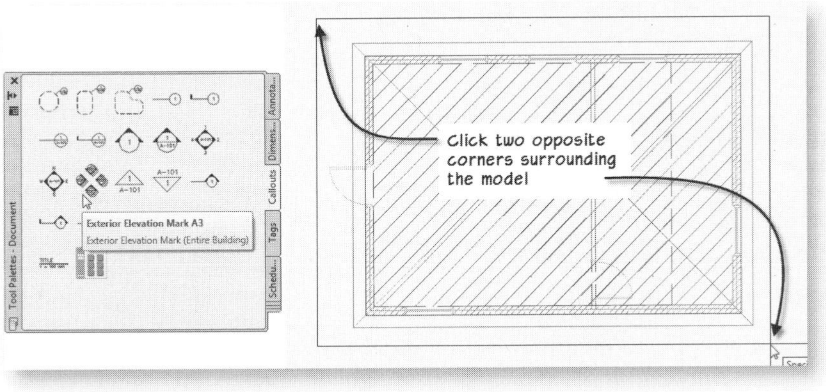

FIGURE QS.40 *Click the Callout tool and then designate a rectangular region in plan*

The "Place Callout" Worksheet will appear.

- At the bottom of the worksheet, choose **1/4" = 1'-0"** [**1:50**] from the Scale list.
- In the "Create in" area, click the Current Drawing icon (see Figure QS.41).

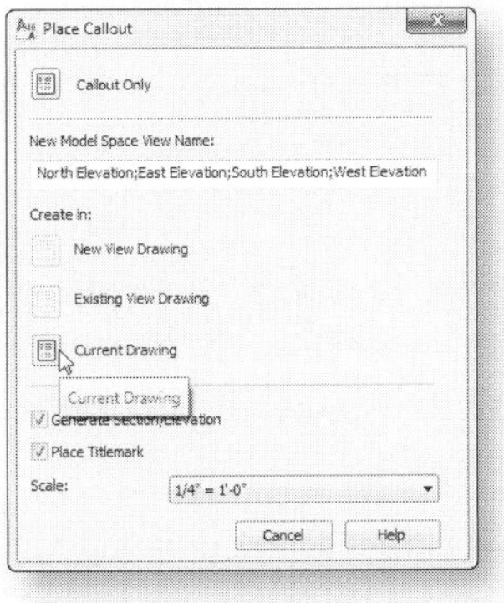

FIGURE QS.41 *Use the Place Callout Worksheet to place Elevations within the Current Drawing*

- At the "Specify insertion point for the 2D elevation result" prompt, click a point to the right of the model.
- At the "Pick a point to specify the spacing and direction of elevations" prompt, move the mouse up slightly and click again.

2. When the operation is complete, zoom out to see the results. (Double-click the wheel of your mouse or use Zoom Extents on the View panel.)

There are now four overall building elevations of the model, complete with callout references. The numbers within these references currently display question marks (?). When we add these elevations to a plotting sheet, these question marks will automatically be replaced with actual numeric references. We will do this in the following sections.

3. Save the file.

Creating Sheets

1. On the Project Navigator palette, click the Sheets tab.
2. Right-click Simple Building at the top of the list, and choose **New** > **Sheet**.

- In the New Sheet dialog, type **A101** in the Number field and **Simple Building** in the Sheet Title field.
- Place a checkmark in the "open in drawing editor" box and then click OK (see Figure QS.42).

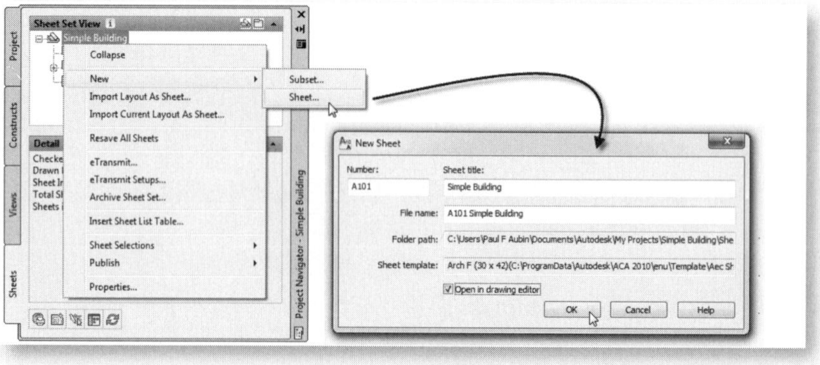

FIGURE QS.42 *On Project Navigator, Sheets tab, create a new Sheet*

The new sheet opens onscreen complete with a title block ready to receive drawings.

3. On the Project Navigator palette, click the Views tab.

- From Project Navigator, drag and drop *First Floor Plan* directly onto the Sheet in the drawing window.
- Zoom with your wheel before placing the drawing.

It is likely that you will need to make some adjustment to the viewports after placement. If you have lots of white space surrounding your plans, just drop them on the Sheet, click the edge of the viewport (which is colored light blue) and using the grips, crop it closer to the drawing.

4. Select the viewport and using the corner grips, crop it closer to the drawing but leave some room on all sides of the plan.

- Drag the cropped viewports to fit on the Sheet better if necessary (see Figure QS.43).

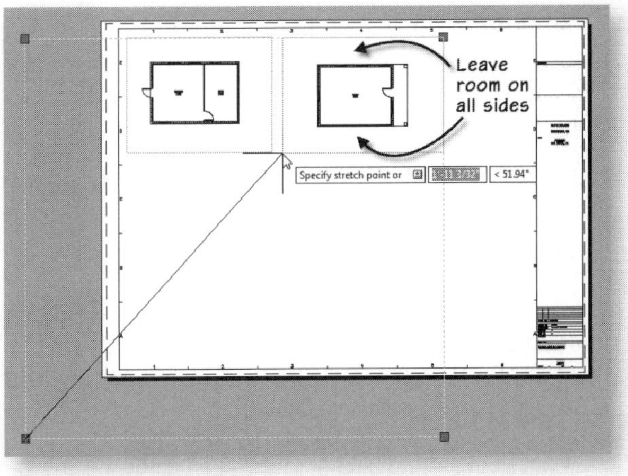

FIGURE QS.43 *Drag the floor plans to the Sheet and grip edit the viewports*

5. Repeat the process to drag the *Second Floor Plan* onto the Sheet and grip edit it as required.

We are leaving room so we can add the elevation callouts to the two floor plans. To add these callouts, we will copy them from the *Model* file and paste them to each plan.

6. On the Project Navigator, double-click to open the *Model* View file.

- Zoom in on the model.
- The callouts are two pieces: the arrow and the round tag. Select both parts of one callout.
- Right-click and choose **Select Similar**.

This should select all four tags and all four arrows.

- Right-click again and choose **Clipboard > Copy**.
- On Project Navigator, double-click to open *First Floor Plan*.
- Right-click again and choose **Clipboard > Paste**. Click a point to place the tags.

TIP

If your symbols do not appear properly as indicated, try toggling the annotation scale to another value and then back again.

7. Repeat the process to copy the same tags to the *Second Floor Plan* View.

- Save and close the *Model, First Floor Plan* and *Second Floor Plan* View files.

8. Back in the Sheet file (which should still be open) click the Reload Modified Xrefs link in the External Reference alert balloon (see Figure QS.44).

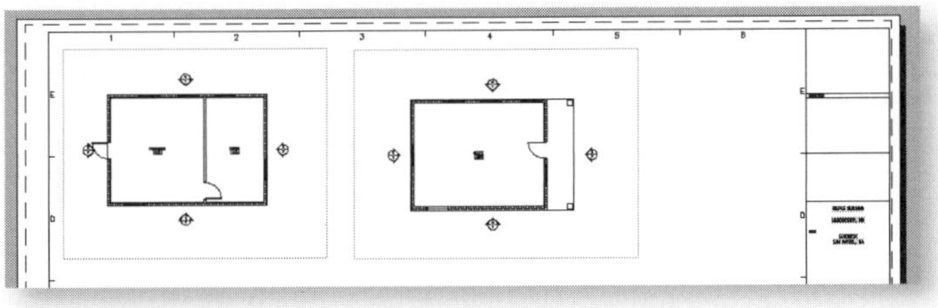

FIGURE QS.44 *After pasting the callouts and reloading the XREFs, they appear in the Sheet*

Notice how the callout symbols appear in both viewports. If the Callouts do not immediately appear, ensure the Annotation Visibility is enabled for all scales. This toggle is located in the lower right next to the scale list pop-up. Let's add the elevations to the Sheet now and see the effect on these callouts.

9. From Project Navigator, drag and drop *Model* directly onto the Sheet in the drawing window.

   A ghosted image of the first elevation will appear ready to be placed at a specific location on the Sheet.

- At the "Specify insertion point" prompt, click a point on the Sheet to place the first Elevation.
- Repeat as prompted for each drawing.

Notice how all of the callouts now display drawing numbers and proper Sheet references. (Zoom in as necessary to see this.) See Figure QS.45 for an example of the final Sheet.

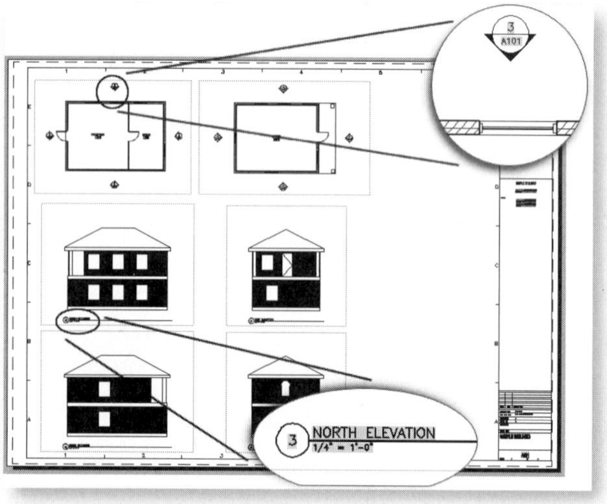

FIGURE QS.45 *Your first complete ACA model presented on a Sheet!*

If you like you can print the sheet.

10. Save and close all project files.

NOTE

Later when you quit ACA, if a prompt appears requesting that you re-path your project, simply accept this and click the Re-path button. Re-pathing and Projects will be discussed in detail in Chapter 5.

SUMMARY

- Getting started with ACA is as simple as clicking a tool on the palettes and locating points in the drawing editor.
- Walls, Doors, Windows and Roofs are added from the Design tool palette. You can edit the parameters using the Properties palette or using grips.
- Objects can be created directly or converted from other objects using a tool's right-click options.
- Projects help you formally establish the overall parameters of an entire building project, such as level management and file organization.
- You can easily make an existing drawing part of the current project.
- Once you have set up a project, it is easy to generate a series of elevations and compose a sheet layout.
- Scale can be adjusted "on the fly" as you compose Sheets, automatically resizing all annotation to the new plot scale.

SECTION

I

Introduction and Methodology

This section introduces the methodology of AutoCAD Architecture 2010. Many concepts will be familiar to the seasoned AutoCAD user; many concepts will be new. If you are a current AutoCAD user, skim through this section looking for concepts unique to ACA, particularly in Chapter 2.

If you do not have AutoCAD experience, please read this entire section. It may also benefit you to complete some basic AutoCAD tutorials prior to reading this section.

Section I is organized as follows:

Chapter 1 The User Interface
Chapter 2 Conceptual Underpinnings of AutoCAD Architecture
Chapter 3 Work Space Setup

CHAPTER 1

The User Interface

INTRODUCTION

This chapter is designed to get you acquainted with the user interface and work environment of AutoCAD Architecture 2010. Collectively, all aspects of the user interface and work environment are referred to as the "workspace." In addition to the workspace, this chapter will also explore any necessary AutoCAD skills required for successful usage of ACA. If you did the Quick Start tutorial prior to this chapter, then you are already familiar with some of the objects and features of ACA. Read on to begin understanding the logic of the workspace and what user interface skills are required to be successful with ACA.

OBJECTIVES

- Understand the AutoCAD Architecture workspace.
- Gain comfort with the user interface.
- Explore the prevalence of the right-click.
- Assess your existing AutoCAD skills.

THE AUTOCAD ARCHITECTURE WORKSPACE

AutoCAD Architecture 2010 is an architectural-*flavored* version of AutoCAD. The workspace of AutoCAD Architecture (ACA) offers a clean and streamlined environment designed to put the tools and features that you need to use most often within easy reach, while allowing for endless customization for those whose needs vary. As such, it shares many similarities with core AutoCAD. However, there are some distinct differences. For instance, ACA has its own collection of highly specialized tool palettes and a different set of ribbon tabs. You'll explore the ACA workspace here and later cover some of the traditional AutoCAD elements. The focus of the AutoCAD items is on those things that are critical to typical ACA usage and success. For more detailed information on the AutoCAD workspace, commands, and features, consult the online help or a book specifically on AutoCAD.

Welcome Screen at Startup

Chapter 1 is not specifically formatted as a tutorial, but you can follow along in AutoCAD Architecture as you read its topics. When you first launch ACA, you may see a Welcome Screen before the program finishes loading. The default installation of ACA presents this dialog to you each time you launch the software, which gives you the opportunity to watch several "Essential Task Movies." You can view these movies to quickly learn what the newest features are and learn some of the core concepts behind ACA (see Figure 1.1).

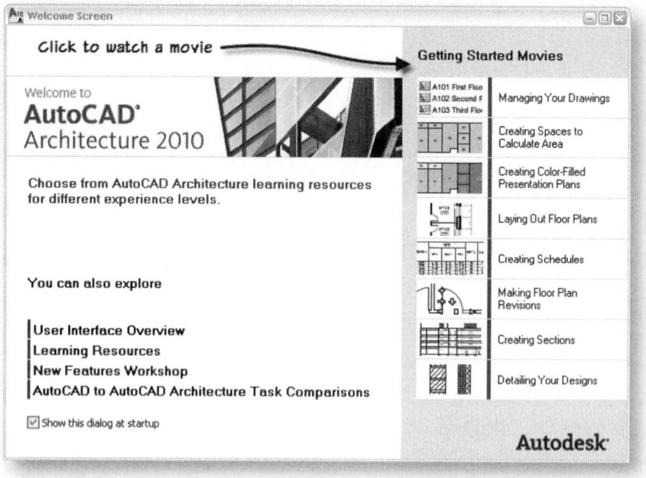

FIGURE 1.1 *The Welcome Screen when launching ACA*

New and seasoned users alike are encouraged to set aside a little time to browse this intuitive and user-friendly way to learn about the core concepts and the latest features of ACA. In addition to the Essential Task Movies, there is also a collection of links to additional movies, slide shows, and documents covering help, support, training, etc. A great deal of effort in recent releases has been devoted to creating learning resources that are easy to use and informative. Take a moment to peruse them. After viewing any of the items on this screen, you can click the Close button in the upper right corner to close the Welcome Screen.

If you deselect the "Show this dialog at startup" option, the Welcome Screen will no longer appear. You will still be able view the Essential Task Movies, New Features Workshop, and other training resources from the Help menu located at the upper right corner of the application frame.

The Drawing Editor

The ACA drawing editor includes many features and controls. Presented here is a simple overview of the most important features (see Figure 1.2). For more information on interface features, choose **Learning Resources** from the Help drop-down menu, located in the InfoCenter and then click the User Interface Overview item.

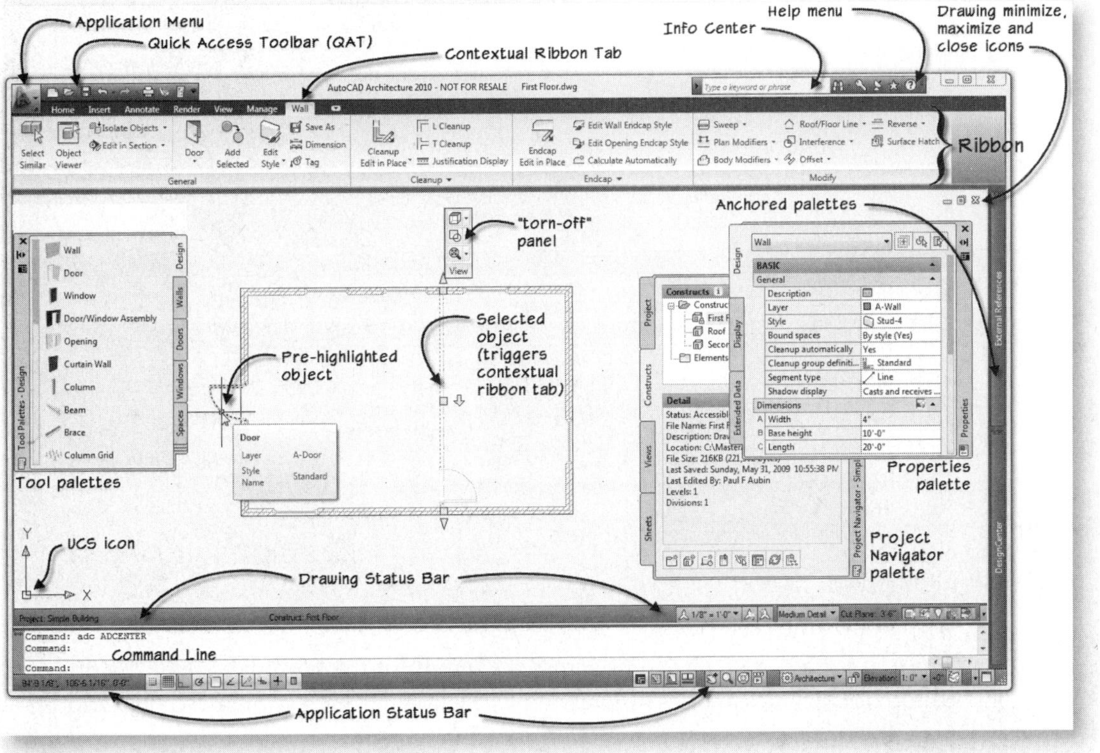

FIGURE 1.2 *Major components of the AutoCAD Architecture drawing editor*

Consistent with most Windows software applications, the ACA screen is framed with the Application Menu, Quick Access Toolbar (QAT), InfoCenter, and ribbon along the top edge; the Windows minimize, maximize, and close icons in the top right corner; and an application status bar along the bottom edge. In addition to these Windows standards, the ACA screen also includes the Command Line, typically docked along the bottom edge of the screen just above the application status bar, and tool palettes. Above the Command Line sits the drawing status bar, which is similar in appearance to the application status bar, but differs in function (see Figure 1.3). The ribbon, command line, and tool palettes are critically important interface elements in ACA and will be elaborated on in topics later. If you are a seasoned AutoCAD user, you are already very familiar with the Command Line. However, as we will see in the topic later, we have a very viable alternative to the Command Line called "Dynamic Input." Other notable elements of the ACA screen include the UCS icon, the Scale and Display Configuration pop-up menus, and the main drawing editor window (see Figures 1.2 and 1.3). Several of these key interface items warrant further discussion and are elaborated on in the topics that follow.

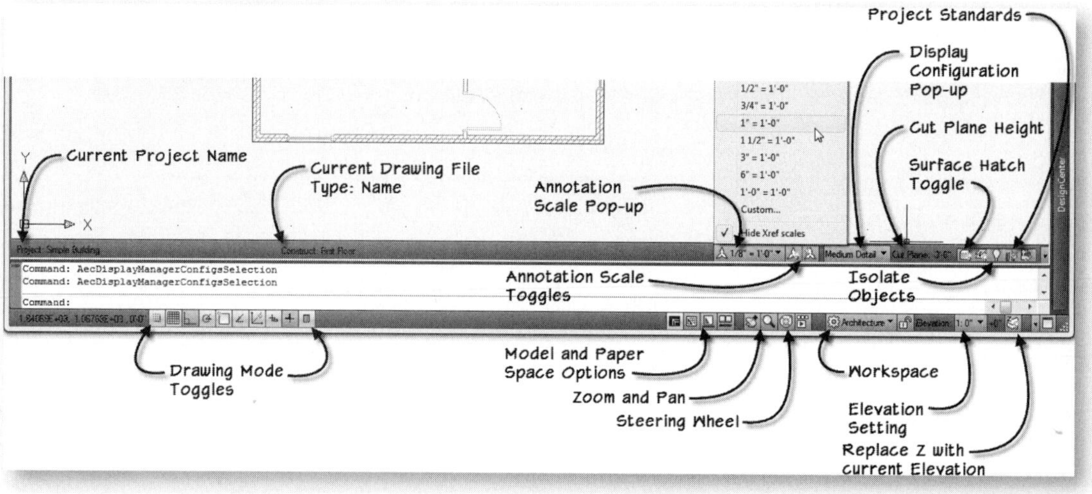

FIGURE 1.3 *The drawing and application status bar areas*

Application Status Bar

The application status bar runs across the length of the bottom edge of the drawing editor and includes a series of Drawing Mode toggles such as Snap Mode, Grid Display, Polar Tracking and Dynamic Input. Each of these modes helps you to control cursor movements and make drawings more accurate. Many of these are covered later and elsewhere in this manual; you can also look them up in the online help.

The next cluster of icons to the right allows you to move between Model and Layouts within the current drawing as well as between all open drawings. Easy access to the `PAN` and `ZOOM` commands and the Steering Wheels is followed by the Workspace Switching menu and the Toolbar/Window position controls, which enable you to lock certain elements of your workspace and prevent them from accidentally being moved or turned off. If you want to maintain the look of your custom user interface (CUI), this tool can be a big help.

With Elevation control, you can quickly set the current Z Elevation in the drawing and then toggle the automatic substitution of this Z value for all clicked points. This can be very handy when working in 2D to keep things "flat" if 3D objects are present in the drawing. It can also be helpful in 3D to avoid inaccurate Z snapping based on view direction. Examples of the use of this tool can be found in Chapter 6.

Drawing Status Bar

The drawing status bar stays attached to the bottom edge of the drawing window and reveals information about the current drawing. As you can see in Figure 1.3, this includes the project name, drawing type and name, if the current drawing belongs to a project in AutoCAD Architecture. (In Figure 1.3, on the left, the current project is "Simple Building" and in the middle, the drawing is a Construct named "First Floor.") The Drawing Management tools in ACA were touched upon briefly in the Quick Start tutorial, and are covered in more detail starting in Chapter 5. On the right side, you will find the Annotation Scaling controls, which will be explored in later chapters. The Current Display Configuration menu allows you to change the currently active Display Configuration within the current drawing window (in Model Space, or viewport in a Paper Space layout). Display Configurations are covered in greater detail in Chapter 2. The Cut Plane height control displays the current height and allows you to change it without opening the Display Manager. Next to this, an icon tray provides quick access to a number of features, including the Surface Hatch toggle, Layer Key Overrides and object Isolation. If the current drawing is part of a project in ACA and drawing standards are enabled, the Drawing Standards icon appears next. Use it to configure standards in an ACA project and synchronize the current drawing to the standards. This feature is first utilized in Chapter 8. If there are external references in the file, the Manage Xrefs icon will appear at the far right of the icon tray. External references (XREFs) are links to other drawing files. Details and techniques on their usage will be covered throughout this book.

InfoCenter

The InfoCenter at the top right corner of the screen provides several means to find or receive information. Some, but not all, of these features require a live Internet connection. The Search feature allows you to do a keyword search on a user-customizable list of resources, including the Help. The Subscription Center provides quick access to subscription benefits and e-Learning lessons for those on Autodesk subscription. The Communication Center displays RSS feeds and, in the Autodesk Channels, notice of available maintenance patches, articles, and tips. You can save links to "favorite" items on the other panels for quick future retrieval in the Favorites panel. You can also open the Help or use the drop-down menu to access specific Help features. Click on the Info Center Settings icon at the upper left corner of any panel to configure them to suit your needs. You can even subscribe to RSS feeds from the various Autodesk websites. In fact an RSS feed has been provided with information about this book. If any updates to the manuscript or dataset are required, the feed will be updated at paulaubin.com and subscribers to the feed will receive the update. If you wish to subscribe to the Mastering AutoCAD Architecture RSS Feed, please perform the following steps:

1. At the top right corner of the screen, click the Communication Center icon (it looks like a satellite dish and is shown in Figure 1.2).
2. In the panel that unfolds, at the top, click the InfoCenter Settings icon.
3. In the InfoCenter dialog that appears, click the RSS Feeds item on the left.
4. At the top, click the Add icon.
5. In the field that appears, type: **http://www.paulaubin.com/rss/paulfaubin_feed.xml** and then click the Add button.
6. In the confirmation dialog that appears click Close and then click OK.

Once you have added the feed, you can use the Communication Center to read it and see if updates have been posted. Simply click an item listed to open the feed and read more.

THE AUTOCAD ARCHITECTURE USER INTERFACE

Now that you have explored some of the common elements of the ACA workspace, it is important to have a look at the most common ways to interface with the product. The Application Menu, Quick Access Toolbar, and ribbon replace the pull-down menus and toolbars as a means of starting commands. Tool palettes allow you to both start commands and import content and styles. Contextual ribbon tabs and right-click context menus provide easy command access when editing existing objects. In addition, you will also frequently interface with objects directly onscreen using dynamic dimensions and grip editing. As you interact with your drawings and models, it will be necessary to move fluidly around your screen and be comfortable viewing the model from all views, zoomed in and out. All of these items will be addressed in this topic.

Application Menu

File access and management tools are grouped under the Application Menu (adorned by the large AutoCAD "A" icon in the upper left). Click on the big "A" to open the Application Menu. At the very top, you will find a command search feature. Type in the name of a command and it will search the Application Menu, static ribbon tabs, any current contextual ribbon tab, and the Quick Access Toolbar and display the results of any matches, including the location. This can be a great help when first learning where things are found in the ribbon.

If this is your first time launching AutoCAD Architecture 2010, the right side of the Application Menu will be empty. But as you open and close files, the list of recent files will begin to populate. ACA remembers the last several files and/or projects you had open and shows them here. You can even click the pushpin icon to permanently "pin" a particular file to the menu, making it easier to load next time (see the left side of Figure 1.4). Right at the top of the Application Menu are two icons to switch the list from Recent Documents to currently Open Documents. These icons are pointed out in the figure. If you switch to Open Documents and you have several project files and/or view windows open, you can use the Application Menu to switch between open windows (see the middle of Figure 1.4). If you hover over an item on either list, you will get a ToolTip that shows the full path of the file, a thumbnail image, and file data.

On the left side of the menu, you will find commands like New, Open, Save and Save As. Sub-menus on many items, denoted by the arrow at the right, give additional, related commands. For example, selecting the Open icon will open the Select File dialog, allowing you to choose a drawing file to open. The sub-menu offers the options to open a project file, a DGN file or an IFC file, in addition to a drawing file (see the right side of Figure 1.4). Hover over each of the icons on the left side and become familiar with the commands available here.

TIP

The Drawing Setup dialog, formerly available on the Format pull-down or Open Drawing menu, can be opened in 2010 through the **Utilities** sub-menu.

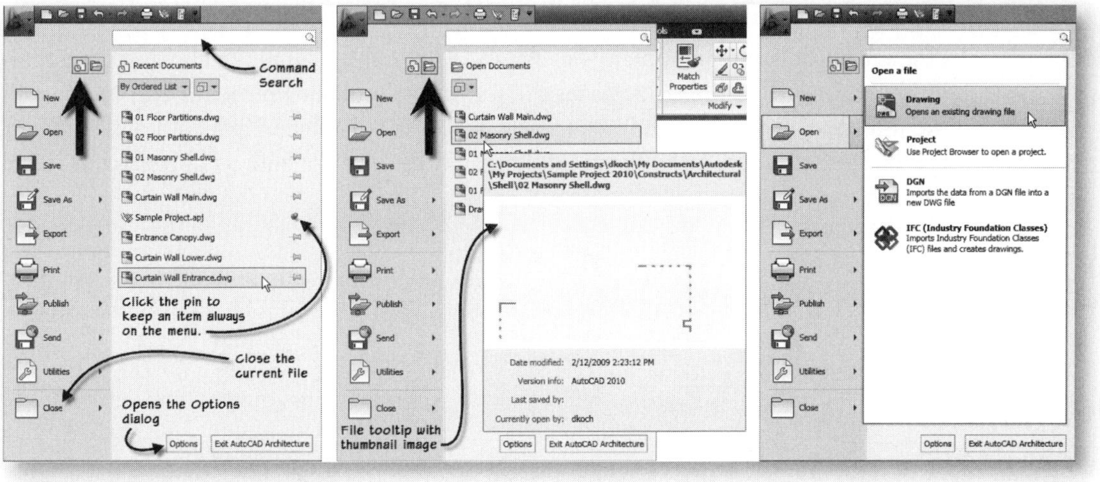

FIGURE 1.4 *The Application Menu*

At the bottom of the Application Menu two buttons appear: Options and Exit AutoCAD Architecture. Exit AutoCAD Architecture is self-explanatory. ACA will prompt you to save your work. Use the Options button to open the Options dialog. This dialog has many program preferences that you can configure. Most of the out-of-the-box settings are suitable for the beginner. There may be some items that you or your CAD Manager will want to adjust. Refer to the online help for more information.

Quick Access Toolbar

The Quick Access Toolbar (QAT) as its name implies is a location for commonly used tools to which you wish to have easy and "quick access." The default QAT includes QNEW, Open, Save, Undo, Redo, Plot, Project Browser and Project Navigator (see the left side of Figure 1.5). You can add buttons to the QAT with the menu on the right end of the QAT itself. The Match Properties command is not part of the default QAT. Simply choose it from the pop-up menu to add it. For other commands, locate them on the ribbon (see the next topic), right-click the tool and choose **Add to Quick Access Toolbar** (see the right side of Figure 1.5). The QAT can be repositioned below the ribbon by choosing **Show Below the Ribbon** from the customize menu at the right end of the QAT, if you are willing to give up the screen space.

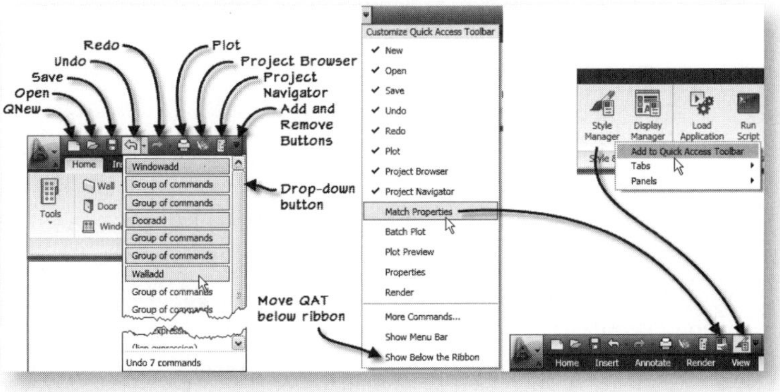

FIGURE 1.5 *The Quick Access Toolbar*

Ribbons

One means of issuing commands in AutoCAD Architecture is by clicking their tools on the ribbon. The ribbon replaces the traditional pull-down menus and toolbars in the interface. A series of six tabs (seven, if you installed the Express Tools) appears just beneath the QAT. Each tab is separated into one or more Panels. Each Panel contains one or more Tools (see Figure 1.6).

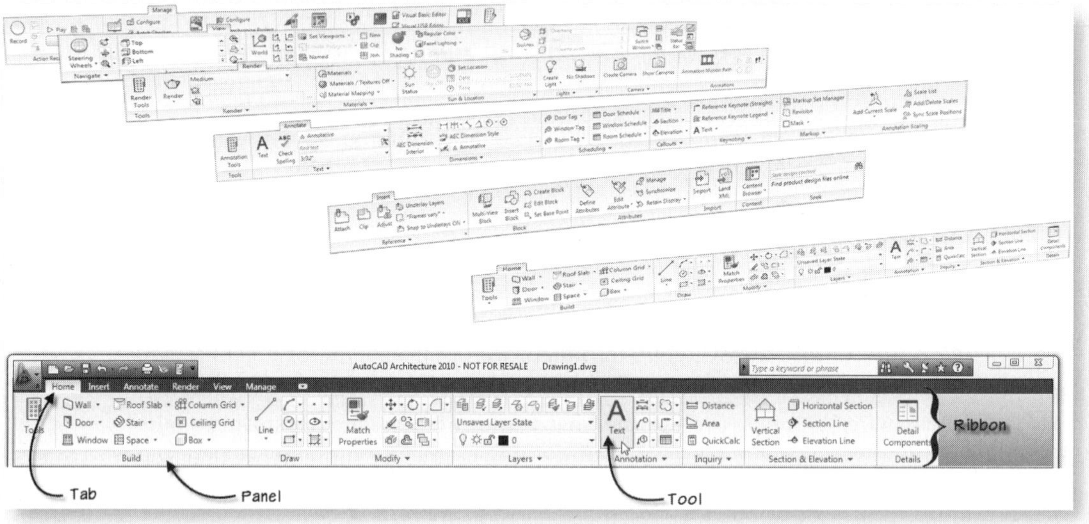

FIGURE 1.6 *A look at the AutoCAD Architecture ribbon tabs*

To navigate the ribbon, click a tab, locate the panel and tool you need and then just click the tool to execute a command. When tutorial instructions are given in this text, you will be directed first to the tab, then the panel and finally the tool. For example, instructions to execute the Wall tool might look something like this:

1. On the Home tab of the ribbon, on the Build panel, click the ***Wall*** tool.

In the context of the exercise, when it is obvious which tab or panel, the description might be shortened to something like:

2. On the Build panel, click the ***Wall*** tool.

Or just:

3. Click the ***Wall*** tool.

Look to "The Static Ribbon Tabs" topic of the online help for a description of each of the six default static ribbon tabs.

Contextual Ribbon Tabs

In addition to the six default "static" ribbon tabs, certain actions you perform in the software will cause other ribbon tabs to appear. These "contextual" ribbon tabs contain tools and commands specific to the item you are creating or editing. For example, if you select a Wall object in the model, a Wall contextual ribbon tab will appear to the right of Manage. If you execute the `MTEXT` tool and begin creating text, a Text Editor tab will appear with the tools and options associated with multi-line text.

When one or more ACA objects of the same type are selected in the drawing editor, a contextual ribbon tab will be displayed.

1. Launch AutoCAD Architecture 2010 if it is not already running.
2. On the Design tool palette, click the Wall tool.

   If the Design tool palette is not visible, refer to the "Understanding Tool Palette Groups" heading below for information on how to make it appear.
3. Click a point anywhere on the left side of the screen within the drawing editor.
4. Move the mouse position to the right side of the screen and click again.
5. Right-click and choose **Enter**.

Notice that "Enter" is the default option at the top of the menu, but that several other options appear as well. Most of the options shown are also available on the Properties palette and the Command Line.

6. Click directly on the newly created Wall object. It will be highlighted, with several grips along its length.

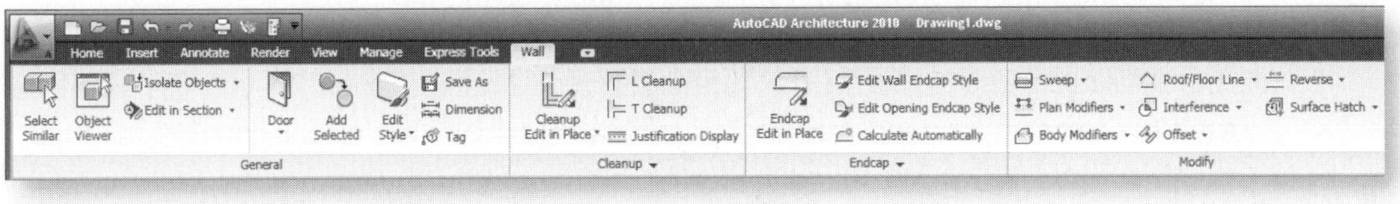

FIGURE 1.7 *Wall contextual ribbon tab*

The Wall contextual ribbon tab appears and becomes current. Notice the green shading of the tab and panel titles. The contextual tabs for all ACA objects will feature this color to distinguish them from the static tabs. Examine the wall-related commands presented on the tab. The static tabs remain available.

7. Right-click and notice that the Wall tab includes most of the wall-related commands previously available through the right-click context menu.
8. Choose **Deselect All** from the menu, and notice that the Wall tab disappears.

When more than one object of different types are selected in the drawing editor, a Multiple Objects contextual ribbon tab, with basic editing commands not specific to any particular object type, will display.

9. On the Home tab of the ribbon, on the Draw Panel, click on the Line flyout and choose the ***Polyline*** tool.
10. Click a point anywhere on the left side of the screen within the drawing editor.
11. Move the mouse position to the right side of the screen and click again.
12. Right-click and choose **Enter** (or press ENTER).
13. Click somewhere in the upper-right corner of the screen (being careful not to click directly on top of any object.)
14. Move the pointer to the lower left corner of the screen and click again. (Both objects should be highlighted. Look up "Crossing Window Selection" in the online help for more information.)
15. Study the contextual tab that appears (see Figure 1.8).

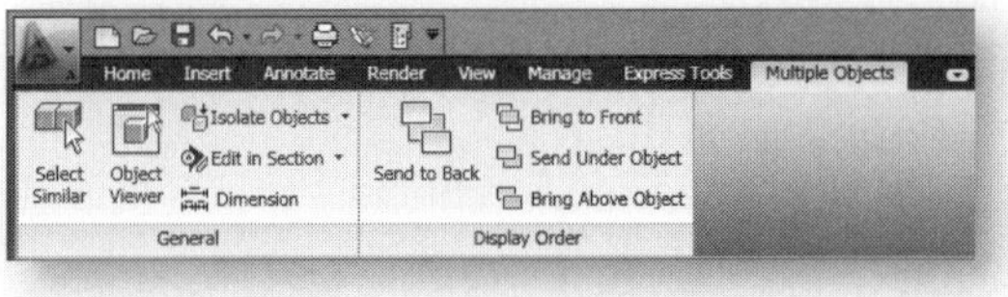

FIGURE 1.8 *Multiple Objects contextual ribbon tab*

16. Notice that the tools available are not object-specific.
17. Right-click and note that the context menu also contains only non-object-specific commands.
18. Choose **Deselect All** from the menu.

If you install any third-party add-on applications, you may also get an Add-Ins tab on your ribbon.

Panels

Ribbons are segregated into panels to help further classify and group the various tools. Panels simply group common tools and make locating the tool you need easier to accomplish. If you use a certain tool frequently, you can right-click on it and add it to the QAT as noted earlier in the "Quick Access Toolbar" topic. If you use all of the tools on a particular panel frequently, you can "tear off" the entire panel. This makes the panel into a floating toolbar on your screen. You can drag such a floating panel anywhere you like, even to a secondary monitor if you have one attached to your system. If you "tear off" any panels, ACA will remember the custom locations of the panels the next time you launch the application (see Figure 1.9). The View Panel is not initially docked to the ribbon when first installed; you can return this panel to the far right side of the Home tab, if you want.

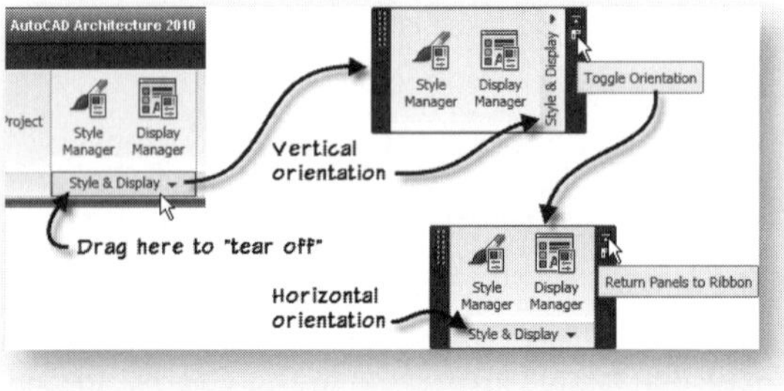

FIGURE 1.9 *Tear off ribbon panels and drag them anywhere you like onscreen*

If you tear off a panel and later wish to restore it, simply move your mouse over the floating panel. This will make gray bars appear on each side. On the left side is a drag bar that you can use to drag the panel around your screen to a new location. On the right side, there are two small icons; the bottom one toggles the orientation of the panel title and the top one restores the panel to its original ribbon tab and location.

NOTE

Feel free to customize your interface by tearing off panels if you wish; however, all instructions in the tutorials that follow assume that panels are in their default locations on the ribbon tabs and refer to them as such.

You can only tear off panels on the permanent default ribbon tabs. Panels on contextual ribbon tabs cannot be torn off and left floating onscreen. However, any of the tools from contextual tabs can be added to the QAT. Refer to the "Quick Access Toolbar" topic for details.

On the panel title bar (bottom edge of the panel), most panels simply show the name of the panel. In some cases, however, a small icon will appear on the right side of the title. This can be one of the two icons. The left side of Figure 1.10 shows a "Dialog Launcher" icon. Clicking an icon such as this will open a dialog. Usually these are settings dialogs that you use to configure several options for a particular type of element.

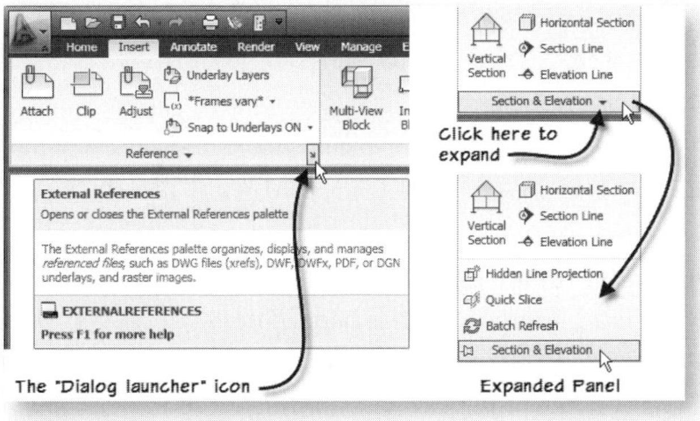

FIGURE 1.10 *Panel with a Dialog Launcher icon on the left and an Expanded Panel on the right*

On the right side of the figure an Expanded Panel is shown. In this case, clicking this icon expands the panel temporarily to reveal additional related tools. Such tools are typically used less frequently than the ones always visible on the panel. Expanded Panels are not ideal, but provide a compromise to what would otherwise be overcrowded ribbon panels in those that use them. Use the push-pin icon to pin the Expanded Panel open if you need to make repeated use of a command in the expanded portion of the panel.

Ribbon View State

The ribbon has three viewing states when docked at the top of the screen. The default state shows the complete ribbon and panels. A portion of the top of the screen is reserved for the ribbon. Click the tabs to switch which tools display, but the same amount of screen space is used regardless of the current tab. This mode makes it easiest to see the tools but uses more precious screen space (see the top of Figure 1.11).

Two alternative states are available that use less screen space. The small icon to the right of the Manage tab is used to toggle to the next state. Click it once to switch to the "Minimize to Panel Titles" state. In this state, ribbon tabs and panel titles are displayed; pass your mouse over a panel title to reveal a pop-up with that panel's tools. Move your mouse (shift focus) away from the panel and it will disappear (see the middle of Figure 1.11).

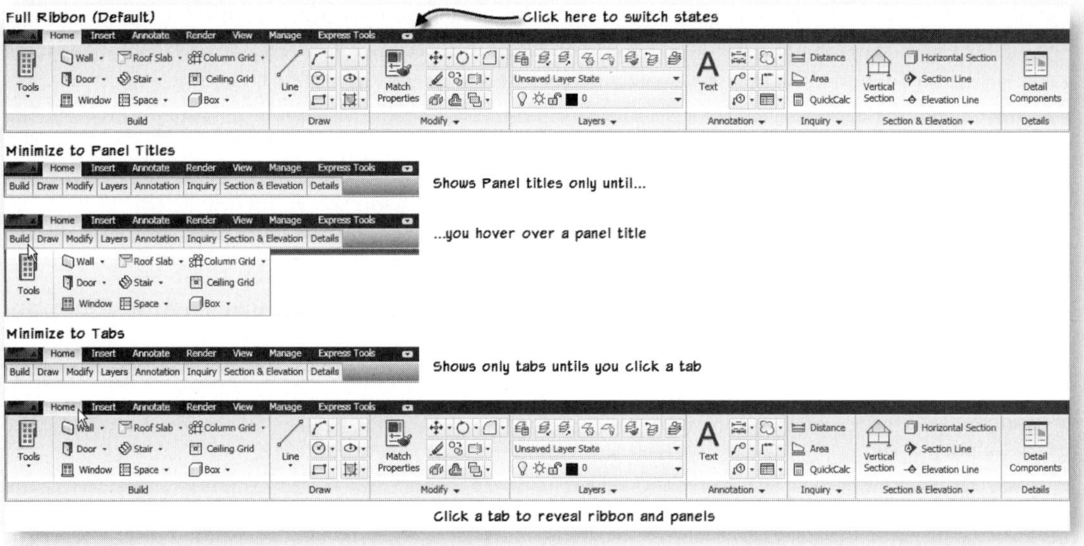

FIGURE 1.11 *Ribbon display states*

The final display state shows only the ribbon tabs (see the bottom of Figure 1.11). Click on a ribbon tab to make the tab pop up. Like the panel titles state, if you shift focus away from a tab, it will disappear. It is easy to experiment with each mode and discover the one that you prefer. Simply click the toggle icon once to switch to panel titles, and click it again to switch to tabs. If you wish to return to the full ribbon, click it again. Each time you click, it toggles to the next state.

Tools

Ribbon panels contain tools. The majority of these tools will use one of three types of buttons: Buttons, Drop-down buttons, and Split buttons. An example of each of these can be found on the Home tab. Examples of a button on the Build panel are the ***Window*** and ***Ceiling Grid*** tools (see the top-left of Figure 1.12). Clicking a button simply invokes that tool.

On the Layers panel, the ***Layer State*** tool is an example of a drop-down button. In this case, if you click the tool, a drop-down list will appear showing the various options for the tool. In the case of the ***Layer State*** tool, we can choose a previously defined named layer state (if any) from a scrolling list box or select from the ***New Layer State***, or ***Manage Layer State*** tools (see the bottom left of Figure 1.12).

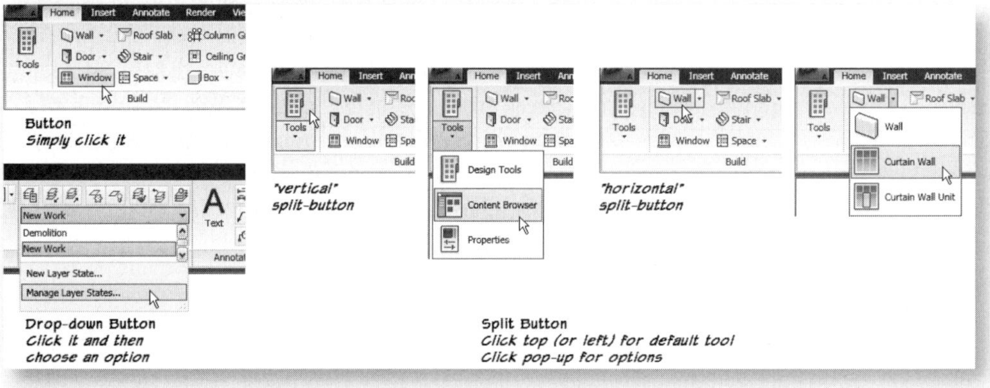

FIGURE 1.12 *Examples of the primary button types on the Home tab*

Split buttons can be either vertical or horizontal. They appear like the other buttons until you pass your mouse over them, at which point it will be clear that that only part of the button highlights under the mouse. The portion of the button with the small pop-up indicator (small triangle) behaves like a drop-down button. The other side behaves like a normal button. On the Home tab in the Build panel, the ***Tools*** and ***Wall*** tools are examples of split buttons (see the right side of Figure 1.12).

Other button types you will find are scrolling list boxes, as seen on the ***Layer State*** drop-down (see the bottom left side of Figure 1.12) or the ***Preset View*** list box located on the View tab in the Appearance panel; text entry boxes, such as the ***Seek*** command, found on the Insert tab in the Seek panel; and slider controls, such as that used for the ***Locked Layer Fading*** control on the Home tab, expanded Layers panel (see Figure 1.13). For the latter, you can either select and drag the bar in the slider control or select the control and key in the desired numeric value.

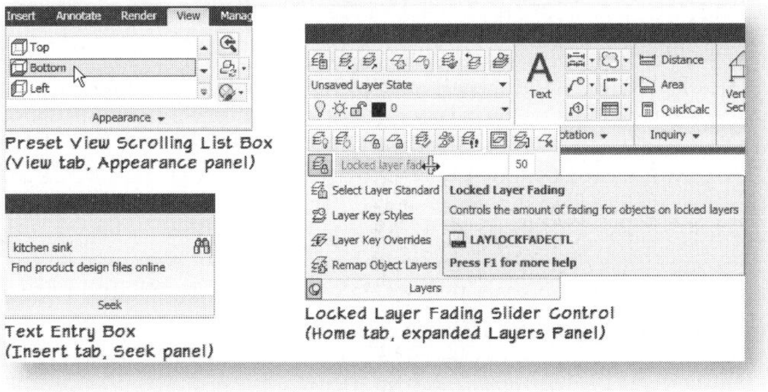

FIGURE 1.13 *Examples of other button types*

Some tools will appear grayed out if the particular command is not available in the current context. For instance, if you select a column grid that was not created from linework, on the Column Grid contextual tab in the Custom Grid panel, the ***Add Grid Lines*** and ***Remove Grid Lines*** tools will be grayed out and inactive. If you select a column grid that was created from linework, all of the tools in the X Axis and Y Axis panels of the Column Grid tab will be inactive.

Right-Click on the Ribbon

1. Move your mouse over any ribbon tab name and then right-click. (If there is empty space to the right of the ribbon, you can right-click there as well.)

   Notice the menu that appears (see Figure 1.14).

NOTE

If you right-click on the ribbon itself instead of the tab name, you will only get the Show Tabs and Show Panels flyouts.

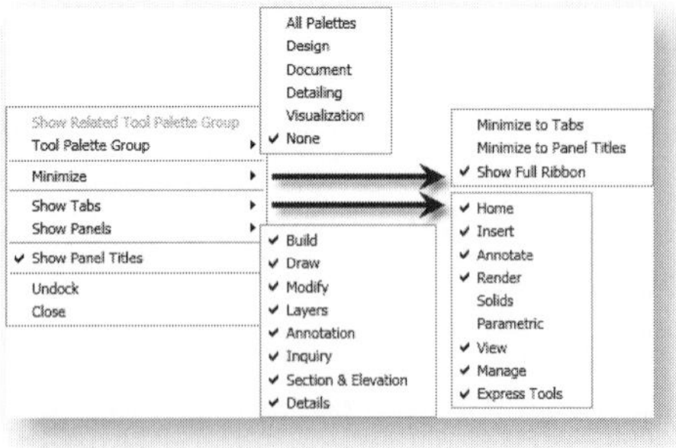

FIGURE 1.14 *Ribbon tab right-click menu*

The first section is related to Tool Palette Groups (see also "Understanding Tool Palette Groups" topic). If a Tool Palette Group is associated with the ribbon tab on which you right-clicked, the first item will be active and choosing it will open the Tool Palettes, if closed, and set the associated Tool Palette Group current. (If you right-clicked to the right of the ribbon tabs, or to the right of the rightmost ribbon panel, the menu will reflect the settings associated with the current ribbon panel.) The Tool Palette Group flyout allows you to associate a Tool Palette Group with a ribbon tab. The check mark indicates the current association. If you do not want an associated Tool Palette Group, choose None.

TIP

You can right-click on an inactive tab name and set the Tool Palette Group associated with that tab current. This will not make that ribbon tab current.

The Minimize sub-menu allows you to directly choose one of the three ribbon view states (see "Ribbon View State" heading).The Show Tabs and Show Panels menu items allow you to hide and display the tabs and panels on the ribbon. Items with a checkmark are displayed. Select them from the menu to toggle off their display. Select again to toggle back on.

The Show Panel Titles menu item toggles the display of the panel titles for the full ribbon display. While you can change this setting when in one of the minimize modes, you will only see the effect when the full ribbon display is restored. You can Undock the ribbon from the top of the screen, turning it into a floating palette, which can then be auto-hidden, docked or anchored to the left or right, like any other palette (see Figure 1.22). Choosing Close will close the ribbon. You can reopen it with the `RIBBON` command at the Command Line.

Customization of the ribbon is beyond the scope of this book; for more information on this topic, refer to the online help.

Tooltip Assistance and ALT-KEY Command Access

When you pause your mouse over tools, a ToolTip usually appears. ToolTips give you the name of a tool, a short description and the name of the command. For certain commands, if you continue to hover an extended tool tip with a more detailed description and possibly a descriptive image will appear. You can find settings to control how much ToolTip assistance you want in the Options dialog on the Display tab, in the Window Elements area in the upper left. (Access the Options dialog from the Application Menu as shown in Figure 1.4 above). If you uncheck **Show ToolTips**, no ToolTip assistance will appear. Figure 1.15 on the top left shows an example of the initial ToolTip you will receive with **Show ToolTips** checked. This will be all you get if you uncheck **Show extended ToolTips**. If you enable ToolTips and extended ToolTips, you can specify the time delay between the display of the initial ToolTip and the expanded ToolTip (Figure 1.15, lower left). To see the expanded ToolTip immediately, set the delay to 0. The **Show shortcut keys in ToolTips** toggle allows you to enable or disable the display of shortcut keys in the ToolTips, for those commands that have a shortcut key assigned.

NOTE

To obtain more information than the ToolTip displays, press F1 to open the Help directly to the page for that command.

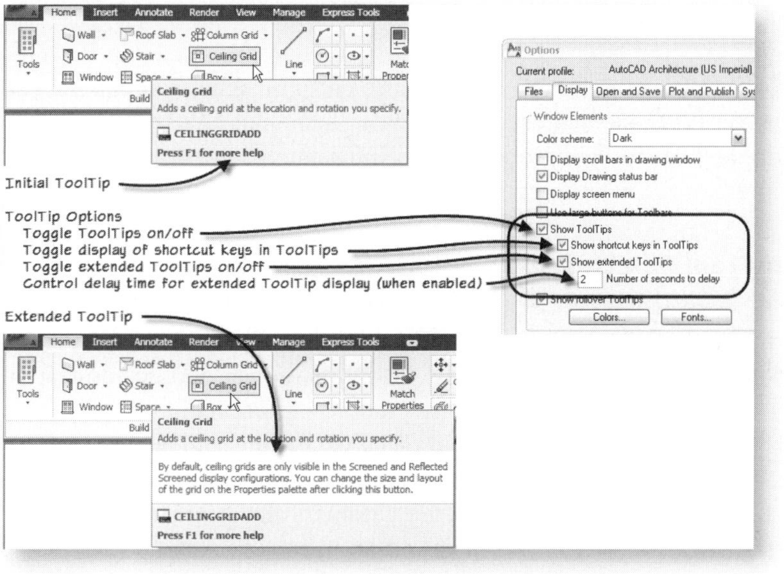

FIGURE 1.15 *Configure ToolTip assistance in the Options dialog*

Another Windows convention supported by AutoCAD Architecture is the ability to invoke ribbon tools with the keyboard using the ALT key and a key letter combination from the desired tool. To try this, press the ALT key. Doing so will place a small label on each tool and tab. Numbers appear on each of the tools on the QAT. Simply press this number to execute that command. Letters appear on each of the Application Menu and ribbon tabs. To invoke a tool on a tab, first press the letter for the tab. This will make a new set of letters appear on all the tools. Next press the key or keys shown on the tool. For example, to access the ***Style Manager*** tool via the ALT key, press the ALT key, then the letters MA and then the letters SM (see Figure 1.16). If a drop-down button is involved, use the arrows on the keyboard to choose the desired tool and then press ENTER to complete the selection.

Please note, even if the tab you want is current, when using the ALT key, you must still press the keystroke for that tab first.

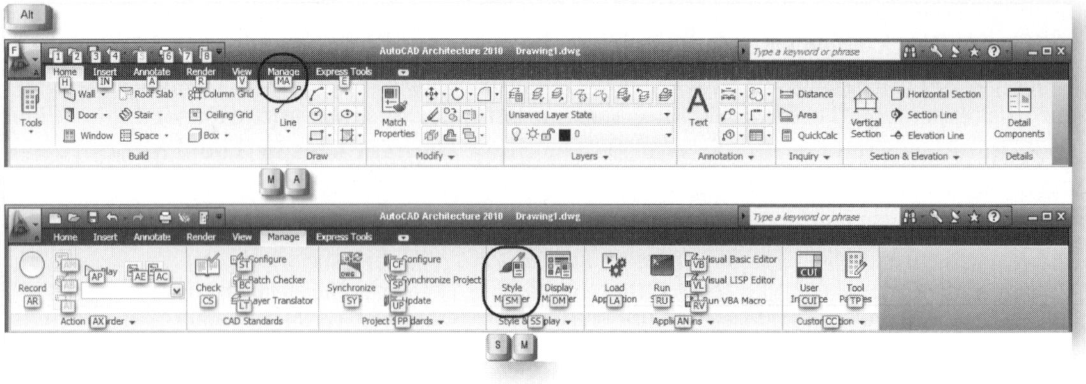

FIGURE 1.16 *Press the ALT key to reveal alternate shortcuts*

As with all AutoCAD-based programs, you can also customize the acad.pgp file and add command aliases for frequently used commands, if you like. Use the ToolTip to identify the command name. For more detailed information on command aliases, consult the "Create Command Aliases" topic in the online help.

Understanding Tool Palettes

Tool Palettes provide instant access to a complete collection of AutoCAD Architecture tools organized in logical groupings. Tool Palettes combine the user-friendly visual icon-based interface of toolbars with the flexibility, power and customization potential of pull-down menus. Simply click on a tool to execute its function (you do not need to drag it). Tools are interactive, and many parameters can be manipulated on the Properties palette while the tool is active. Furthermore, properties can be preassigned to the tools so that default settings are automatically assigned on tool use. Using the Content Browser, you can add tools and complete palettes to your personal workspace at any time—more on the Content Browser below.

The default installation of ACA loads several basic tool palettes populated with a variety of the most commonly used tools. The palettes are organized into Tool Palette Groups (see the "Understanding Tool Palette Groups" topic below). The Design Tool Palette Group contains the most basic architectural object tools. The Design Palette (part of the Design Tool Palette Group) contains a basic tool for each of ACA's architectural object types. The remaining palettes contain tools with more specific parameters. Groups are loaded by right-clicking the title bar. Individual palettes are accessed by clicking their tab on the tool palettes.

NOTE

If you installed and are using a content pack other than US Imperial or US Metric, the specific tool palettes and groups you have might vary slightly from the ones noted and pictured in this text.

Using Tool Palettes is intuitive. The following exploratory steps will help you quickly become acquainted with this critical interface item.

1. Launch AutoCAD Architecture 2010 if it is not already running.
2. On the Quick Access Toolbar (QAT), click the QNEW icon (see Figure 1.17).

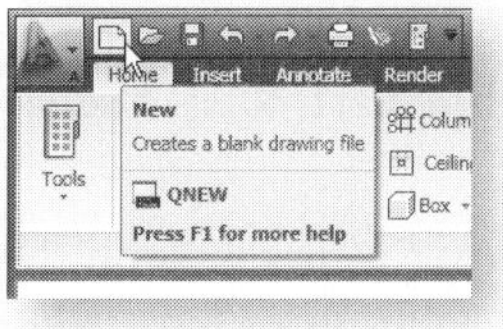

FIGURE 1.17 *Create a new drawing using QNEW*

The QNEW command will automatically create a new drawing file using your default template. If the Select Template dialog appears when you click QNEW, choose the template *AEC Model (Imperial Stb).dwt* [*AEC Model (Metric Stb).dwt*].

MANAGER NOTE CAD

If QNEW fails to load a template automatically, open the Application Menu and click the Options button. Click the Files tab. There, expand the Template Settings item and then the Default Template File Name for QNEW item. Finally, select the entry listed there, click the Browse button, and choose your preferred default template. These steps need only be done once, and will remain in place in the current profile on your machine. For more information on profiles, see Chapter 3.

3. If the Tool Palettes are not loaded, on the Home tab of the ribbon, on the Build panel, click the Tools button (or press CTRL + 3).

Tool Palettes can be left floating onscreen or can be docked or anchored to the left or right side of the drawing editor. Simply drag the palettes by the title bar to the left or right side of the screen. The title bar will dynamically shift from left to right as you move the Tool Palette close to either edge of the screen or it will dock to the edge of the screen (Figure 1.18 shows floating, docked and anchored palettes and Figure 1.19 shows the title bar shifting from the right to left side).

4. Right-click the title bar of Tool Palettes and check the setting of "Allow Docking."

A checkmark next to Allow Docking indicates that the palette will dock (attach) when close to the edge of the screen. No checkmark means that it will stay floating even if moved to the edge of the screen. When Allow Docking is enabled (checked), you will also have the ability to "anchor" the palette. Docked palettes attach to the sides of the screen and reduce the overall width of the drawing area. An anchored palette creates an anchor dock on the left or right side. This small gray strip can contain one or more anchored palettes such as Tool Palettes, Properties or External References. You can even tear off the Command Line from its traditional location at the bottom of the screen and anchor it here. Anchored palettes fly open (such as when Auto-hide is enabled) when you pass the mouse over them (see Figure 1.18).

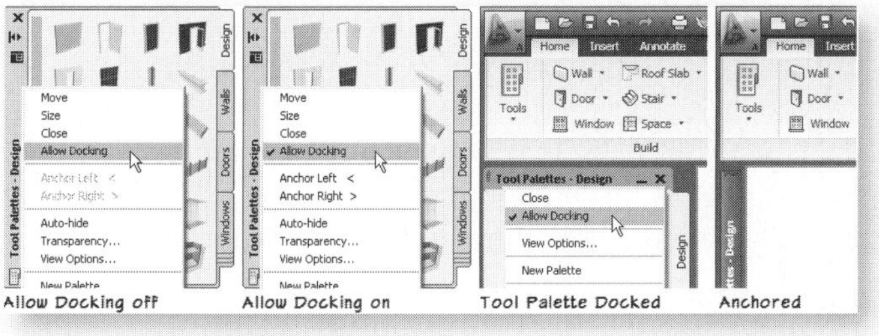

FIGURE 1.18 *The Allow Docking feature toggles docking of the Tool Palettes*

5. Test the behavior with Allow Docking on and then with it off.
6. After enabling Allow Docking, try choosing either **Anchor Left** < or **Anchor Right** >.

If you dock a Tool Palette and wish to return it to floating, you can right-click on the title bar and remove the "Allow Docking" checkmark (shown in the third item from the left in Figure 1.18). You can also click on the title bar and drag the palette into the drawing window or simply double-click on the title bar. The small minus sign icon on the right of the title bar will convert the docked palette to an anchored palette; the "X" icon will close the palette. Right-click the anchored palettes to change the way their labels display.

7. After experimenting, turn off Allow Docking.
8. To see the title bar flip, drag the Tool Palettes first to the left edge of the screen and then to the right.

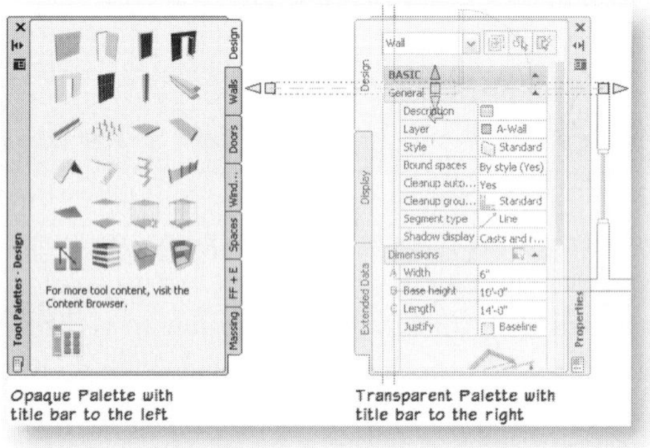

FIGURE 1.19 *Palettes dynamically justify their title bar to the appropriate edge of the screen and can be made transparent*

NOTE

Figure 1.19 shows transparency turned on for the palette on the right. To do this, right-click the title bar (or click the small palette menu icon in the top corner of the palette's title bar—shown in Figure 1.22) and then choose **Transparency**. However, this feature can cause a slowdown in performance on some systems, so make sure you test the feature on your system to gauge performance before using it regularly.

Many of the palettes (Tool Palettes, Properties, etc.) have tabs along the edge (or along the top for DesignCenter). Click these tabs to see other tools and options. For the Tool Palettes, you can customize these tabs and configure their properties; to do so, right-click on a tab (make it current first by clicking on it). When all tabs are not visible, there will be several tabs "bunched up" at the bottom of the Tool Palette; click there to reveal hidden tabs (see Figure 1.20).

Tool Palette tabs can be grouped. A Tool Palette Group includes a small subset of the total available Tool Palettes. The default installation for US Imperial and US Metric includes four groups: Design, Document, Detailing and Visualization. Groups for other content packs may vary.

9. Click on one or more tabs to switch between different palettes.
10. On the Tool Palettes, right-click on a tab.

    Note the menu options.
11. If all tabs are not shown, click on the bunched-up group of tabs at the bottom to see a menu revealing the hidden tabs (see Figure 1.20).

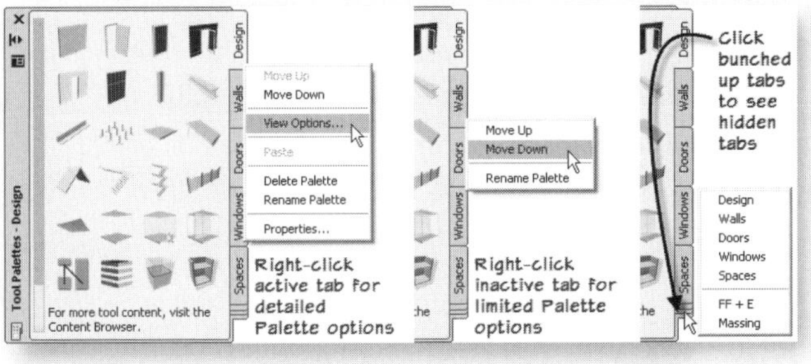

FIGURE 1.20 *Accessing palette options and hidden tabs*

- **Move Up & Move Down**—Shift the location of the selected tab relative to its neighbors.
- **View Options**—Opens a dialog with options for changing the icon size and configuration displayed on the palette(s) (see Figure 1.21).
- **Paste**—Only available after a tool (from this or another palette) has been copied or cut.
- **Delete & Rename Palette**—Allows you to delete or rename the selected palette.
- **Properties**—Allows you to change the Name and Description of the current palette.

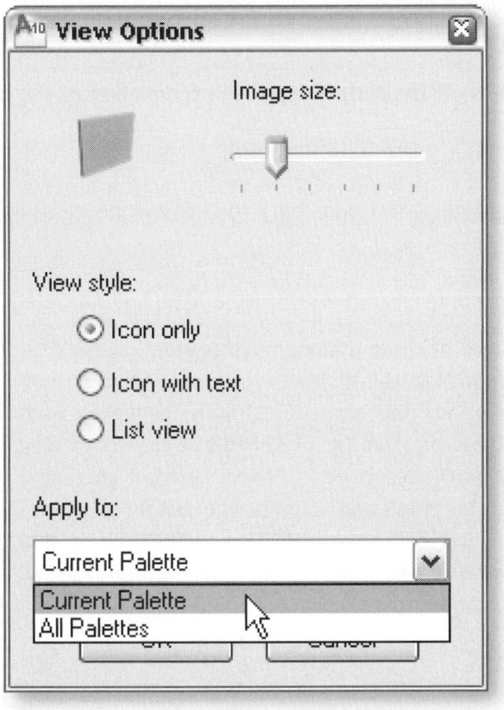

FIGURE 1.21 *View Options changes icon style and size for this palette or all palettes*

Another group of options is available for the entire palette group. In the top corner of the title bar in every palette are three small icons. The first closes the palettes. The second toggles on and off the "Auto-hide" feature of palettes. When this feature is enabled, the palette will automatically collapse to just its title bar whenever the mouse pointer is moved away from the palette. The palette will "pop" back open when the pointer pauses over the title bar again. This same feature can be controlled with the Auto-hide option in the palette Properties menu available by clicking the third icon (in the top corner) or right-clicking on the title bar.

12. On the Tool Palettes, click the small Auto-hide icon (see Figure 1.22).
13. Move your mouse away from the palette.

    Notice that the palette collapses to just the title bar (see Figure 1.22).

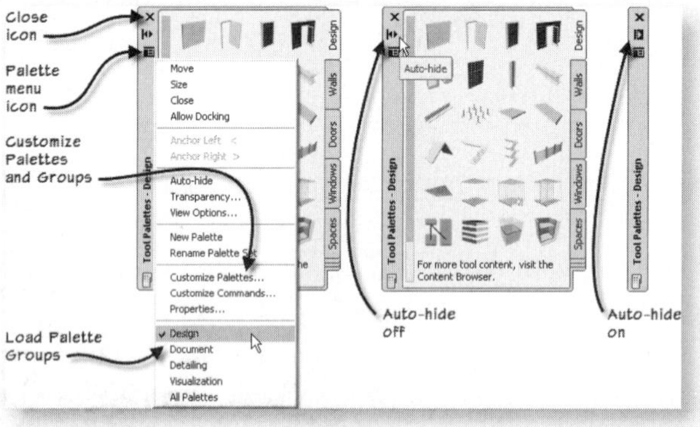

FIGURE 1.22 *Access the Properties menu, load Groups and toggle Auto-hide*

14. Move your mouse back over the collapsed title bar.

    Notice that the palette expands again.
15. Click the Auto-hide icon again to turn it off.

NOTE

For the remainder of this chapter, please turn off the Auto-hide. At the completion of the exercise, you may set it whichever way you prefer.

16. Click the Properties icon (or right-click the title bar) to display the options menu.

    Note the various options.

CAD MANAGER NOTE

Later in Chapters 4 and 6 we will explore some of these options, such as New Palette. Palettes that include any combination of stock and/or user-defined tools can be made. Complete palettes of project-specific tools can be created and subsequently loaded by each member of the project team. Furthermore, these palettes can be linked to a remote catalog location and set to refresh each time AutoCAD Architecture is loaded. This will guarantee that project team members always have the latest tools and settings. The customization potential of tool palettes is nearly limitless. For very detailed information on customizing tool palettes (and many other advanced topics), pick up a copy of *Autodesk Architectural Desktop: An Advanced Implementation Guide*—second edition.

Understanding Tool Palette Groups

As mentioned previously, Tool Palettes can be organized into groups. Right-click the Tool Palettes title bar to access other groups. By default, ACA installs four Tool Palette Groups: Design, Document, Detailing, and Visualization. In addition, when an ACA project is loaded, a Tool Palette Group uniquely named for the project will be added (and potentially made current).

17. Right-click on the Tool Palettes title bar and choose **Document** (to load the Document Tool Palette Group) from the menu (see the left panel of Figure 1.23).

    Notice that all of the Tool Palette tabs change to Documentation functions (see the second item in Figure 1.23).

18. Right-click on the Tool Palettes title bar again and choose **Detailing** (to load the Detailing Tool Palette Group) from the menu (see the third item in Figure 1.23).
19. Right-click on the Tool Palettes title bar again and choose **All Palettes** (to load palettes from all Tool Palette Groups at once).

    Notice that now all of the Tool Palette tabs from all groups appear (not shown in the figure).

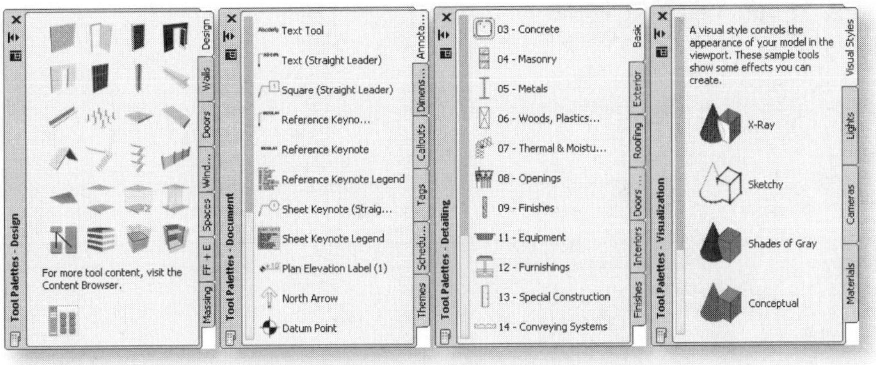

FIGURE 1.23 *Four Tool Palette Groups are included out-of-the-box in US Imperial and Metric*

You can create your own groups if you wish. To do this, right-click the Tool Palettes title bar (or click the palette menu icon shown earlier) and choose **Customize Palettes**. In the Customize dialog, you can create new groups by right-clicking on the right side. Right-click on the left side to create new palettes. Add and remove items from each group by using the drag-and-drop method. The same palette can belong to more than one group. To learn more, create a new palette and then click the "Learn more about customizing AutoCAD Architecture tool palettes" hyperlink on the new empty palette. This will launch the Help window and navigate directly to the Tool Palette topic.

Right-Clicking

In AutoCAD Architecture, you can right-click on almost anything and receive a context-sensitive menu. In fact, we have just seen several examples in the previous topics on the ribbon and tool palettes. These menus are loaded with context-specific functionality.

TIP

As a general rule of thumb, "When in doubt, right-click."

The next several figures highlight some of the more common right-click menus you will encounter in ACA. Do take a moment to experiment with right-clicking in each section of the user interface. You will also discover that the typical Windows right-click menus appear in all text fields and other similar contexts (this is used for Cut, Copy, Paste and Select All). Let's explore the right-click.

Right-Click in Drawing Editor (Default Menu)

1. If AutoCAD Architecture is not running, launch it now.

   Press the ESC key to clear any commands or object selections.

2. Move the mouse to the center of the screen and right-click. Notice the menu that appears (see Figure 1.24).

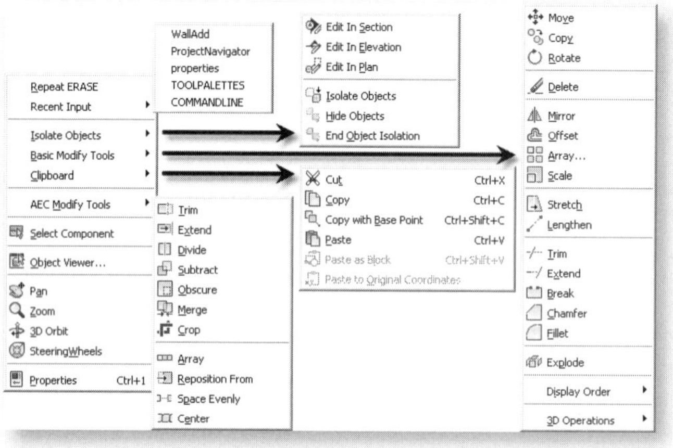

FIGURE 1.24 *The default right-click menu*

The default right-click menu appears when you right-click in the drawing editor with no commands active and no objects selected. It is divided into sections of function. The first item will always show the last command executed and beneath that a flyout list of recent commands. Repeating COMMAND (where COMMAND is the last command run) will give a shortcut to executing the last command. (Figure 1.24 shows the ERASE command.)

TIP

In addition to these two methods of repeating the last command, you can press the ENTER key or the SPACEBAR to repeat the last command. Also, if Dynamic Input is on, you can begin typing the first few letters of a command onscreen or at the Command Line and then press the TAB key until the command you need appears. Press ENTER to execute the command.

The next section includes a flyout menu for the Isolate Objects (used to control visibility of selected objects and access the Edit in View functionality) commands. The Basic Modify commands are next, which include all of the common AutoCAD Modify commands, such as Move, Copy and Rotate. Clipboard functions (Cut, Copy and Paste) occupy the next flyout menu. The AEC Modify Tools flyout menu includes a collection of special ACA editing tools, many of which work on regular AutoCAD entities. The Select Component command allows you to edit the display properties of the components within an AEC object directly on the Properties palette. This will be covered in later chapters. Object Viewer is a separate viewing window for quick study of selected objects. This will be explored in more detail in Chapter 4. Pan, Zoom and 3D Orbit are the standard AutoCAD navigation commands, and finally, Properties will open the Properties palette if it is not open and make it active if it is already open.

MANAGER NOTE

Many Veteran AutoCAD users continue to lament the loss of the right-click to ENTER and repeat the previous command. Although the behavior of the right-click can be reverted to this style, it is recommended that you not do this. In doing so, a great deal of necessary ACA functionality will be lost. Please try the default setting throughout the duration of this book. If after completing the lessons in this manual you are still convinced you will be more productive with the right-click set to ENTER, then at least consider "Time-sensitive right-click" (available on the User Preferences tab of the Options dialog) as an alternative. The Time-sensitive right-click option makes the right-click behave like an ENTER with a "Quick" click of the right button. A "longer click" will display a shortcut menu. This feature will offer a good compromise to many seasoned AutoCAD users. To make this change, choose Options from the Application Menu, click the User Preferences tab, and then the Right-click Customization button.

Please remember that both the ENTER key and the SPACEBAR on the keyboard function as ENTER within the AutoCAD environment. For veteran AutoCAD users, the old "rule of thumb" still applies. Keep your left thumb on the SPACEBAR for a quick ENTER.

Right-Click in the Command Line

When you right-click in the Command Line, a small context menu appears (see Figure 1.25). Choosing Recent Commands shows a menu of the last several commands executed. Use this menu as a shortcut to rerun any of these commands. The Copy History command puts a complete list of all Command Line activity on the clipboard that can then be pasted into any text editing application. You can also access the Options command from this menu. (The Options command is also available on the Application Menu.)

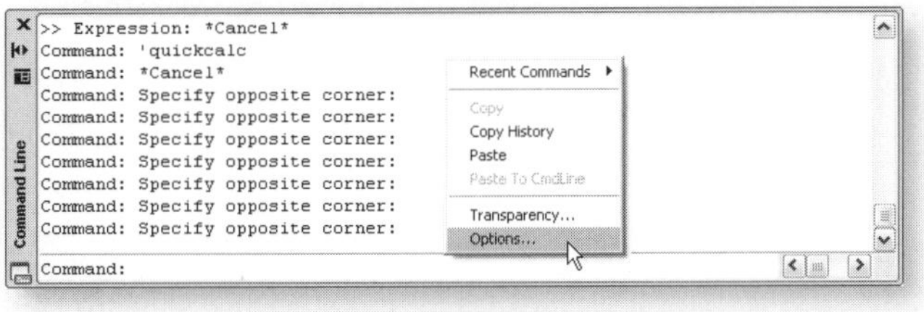

FIGURE 1.25 *Right-click in the Command Line (The image shows the Command Line "torn off" as a palette)*

You can also close the Command Line window. To do this, make the Command Line a floating window. You can float it by dragging the small double gray bar on its edge, and then releasing when the Command Line has "undocked" from the edge of the screen. Once the Command Line is floating, you will see the standard Windows close box (looks like an "X"). Click this box to close the Command Line. When you do this, a warning dialog will appear (see Figure 1.26).

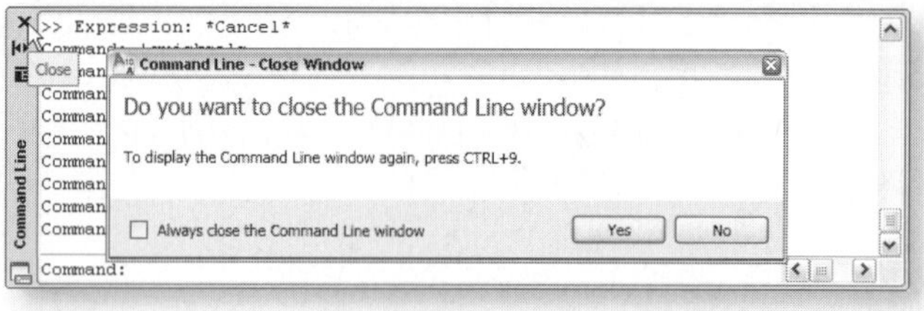

FIGURE 1.26 *You can close (Hide) the Command Line window—use* `CTRL + 9` *to re-display it*

CAUTION

It is highly recommended that you use either the Command Line window or the Dynamic Input dynamic prompts (see the "Dynamic Input" topic below) option. If you disable both of these, it will be very difficult to use the software effectively.

Right-Click While a Command Is Active

Most ACA commands have one or more options. These options can be accessed by typing directly in the Command Line, using Dynamic Input onscreen prompts, or using the right-click menu.

1. On the Home ribbon tab on the Draw Panel, select the Line flyout and choose the ***Polyline*** tool.
2. Click a point anywhere on the lower left side of the screen within the drawing editor.
3. Move the mouse position to the bottom-right side of the screen and click again.
4. Move the mouse to the upper-right corner of the screen and click a third time.
5. With the command still active, right-click (see Figure 1.27).

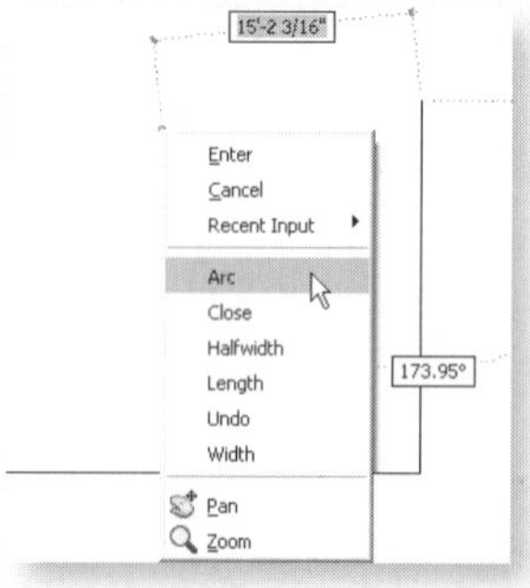

FIGURE 1.27 *Right-click within a command (Polyline in this case) to access its options*

Compare the menu that appears with the options shown in the Command Line. You will see many of the same options are available in both places. (The same options are also listed in the onscreen prompting if you have Dynamic Input enabled—see the "Dynamic Input" topic below.)

6. From the right-click menu, choose **Arc**.
7. Move the mouse to the left of the screen and click again.
8. Right-click and choose **Close**.

Right-Click in the Application Status Bar

The application status bar gives quick access to many of the drafting settings available in AutoCAD Architecture. If you wish to customize the default settings of any of these drafting modes, simply right-click the button and choose **Settings** (see Figure 1.28).

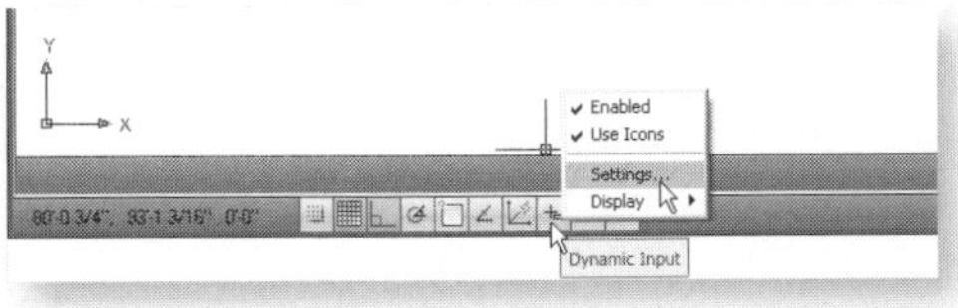

FIGURE 1.28 *Right-clicking the controls on the application status bar to access options*

Choose Use Icons to toggle between icons and the "classic" text modes for displaying these status toggles. Note that ORTHO does not offer the Settings choice. The Model and Layout icons replace the Layout tabs that previously appeared along the bottom edge of the drawing window in earlier versions. By right-clicking, you can restore these tabs instead of the icons shown in the application status bar. We will work in Model Space for most exercises in this book. For the time being, do not click these icons. If you have already clicked the Layout one (named "Work" in the default template with which we started), then you will need to click the Model icon to return to Model Space (see Figure 1.29).

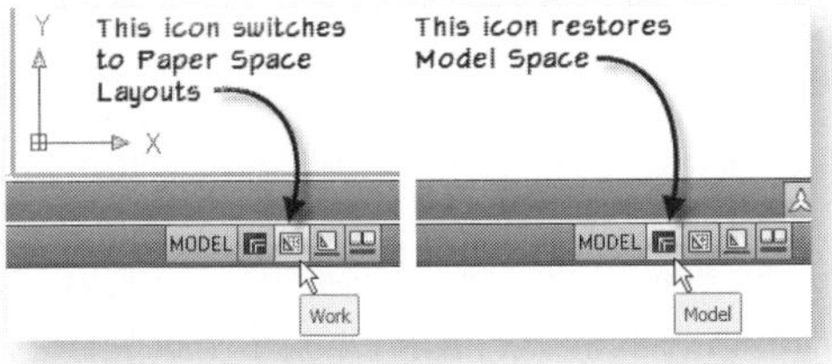

FIGURE 1.29 *Click the Model icon to return to Model Space if necessary*

For more information on Model and Paper Space, refer to the online help.

Dynamic Input

As noted earlier, the Command Line is only way we can interact with and access command options. Dynamic Input—which places command prompts directly onscreen—gives us many cues and prompts to make the interactive process of creating and manipulating objects more fluid and user friendly. Dynamic Input has a simple toggle button in the application status bar alongside the other drafting modes like SNAP, GRID, and POLAR. If you right-click this toggle, you will find many options to customize the Dynamic Input behavior. Let's explore some of those now.

Pointer Input

1. At the bottom of the screen on the application status bar, right-click the Dynamic Input toggle and choose **Settings** (see Figure 1.30).

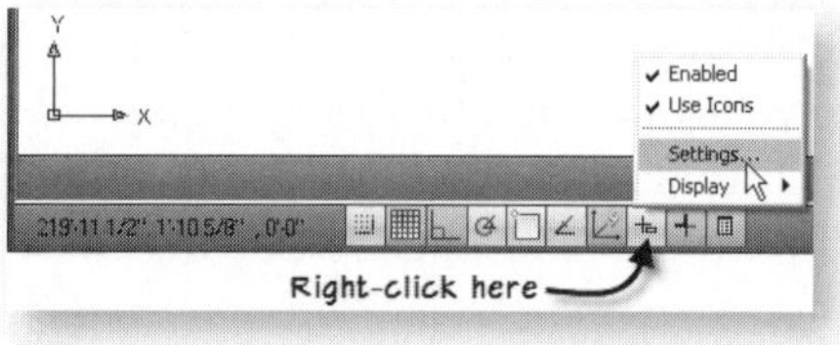

FIGURE 1.30 *Right-click the Dynamic Input icon to access Dynamic Input Settings*

The Drafting Settings dialog will appear with the Dynamic Input tab active.

2. Deselect all checkboxes in this dialog, place a checkmark only in the "Enable Pointer Input" checkbox, and then click OK (see Figure 1.31).

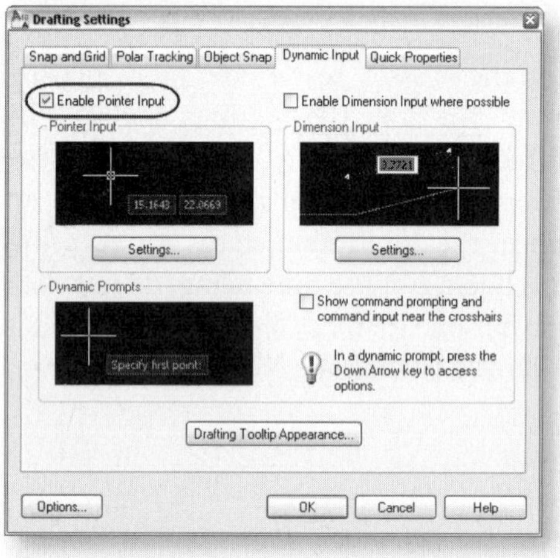

FIGURE 1.31 *Enable only the Pointer Input option*

This option provides text input fields at the cursor where you can type in coordinates as you draw. All objects in AutoCAD/ACA exist in a coordinate grid (referred to as the "World Coordinate System" or "WCS"). Coordinate input can be achieved using two different systems to indicate precise locations in the drawing relative to the WCS—Cartesian and Polar. In the Cartesian system, you input locations using "X" (horizontal) and "Y" (vertical) coordinates. In the Polar system, input is based on a distance (measured in units) and a direction (measured in degrees around the compass). Both systems are valid for input in ACA, and you can switch on the fly simply by varying your input syntax. The syntax for Cartesian input is: **X,Y**—where *X* and *Y* are input as positive or negative numbers in the current unit system (inches, feet, meters, etc.) and the comma is used to separate them. The syntax for Polar is **D<A**—where *D* equals the distance (nearly always a positive number in the units of the drawing) and *A* is the angle along which this distance is measured in degrees, with the "less than" symbol to separate them. Both systems can optionally add a third coordinate for the Z direction when working in 3D. Much of the input needed in ACA and this book will use methods simpler than the traditional coordinate input. View the topic "Use Coordinates and Coordinate Systems" in the online help for more information on coordinate input.

3. On the Design Palette, click the Wall tool and then click a point on the screen.
4. Move the mouse around slowly onscreen and note the two dynamic prompts that appear (see Figure 1.32).

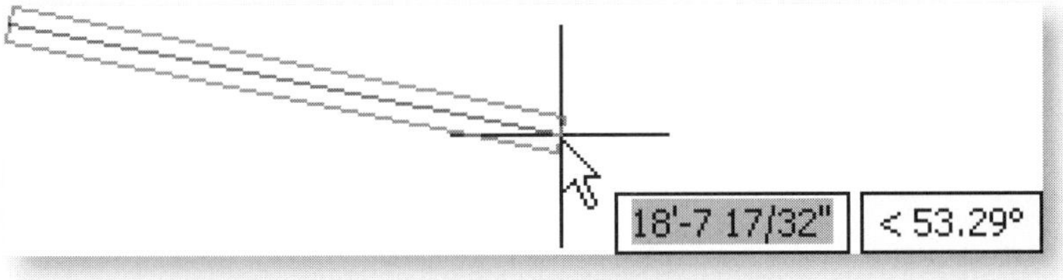

FIGURE 1.32 *Pointer Input gives coordinate prompts at the cursor onscreen*

5. Type a number such as **10'** [**3000**] on your keyboard—do not press ENTER yet.

   Note that the number will automatically appear in the first coordinate field.

By default, ACA uses Polar coordinates as you can see indicated in the second onscreen prompt. However, you can change this default if you like and you can always input values in either system at any time. After you indicate the first value, type a "<" ("less than" sign) to input the Polar angle next, or for Cartesian coordinates, type a comma (,) to interpret the first value as an "X" and then input the "Y" value.

6. On your keyboard, type a comma (**,**)

   Notice that the first value "locks" and the second prompt activates.
7. Move the mouse around a bit.

Notice that the first value of 10' [3000] X is locked in so that the Wall is constrained in width and your mouse movements only affect the vertical position. Do not click yet.

8. Type in a second value such as **10'** [**3000**] again and then press ENTER (see Figure 1.33).

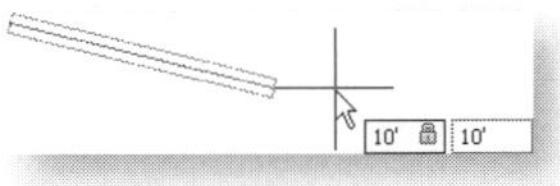

FIGURE 1.33 *Pointer movement is currently constrained to the value in the first (locked) field. Use the mouse or type to set the value of the other*

NOTE

Your screen may look different from the illustrations since the numbers in the illustrations are absolute dimensions. For example, 10' [3000] has a unique location in the WCS. Depending on where you click the first point of the Wall drawn in Figure 1.33, this fixed location could be to the right or the left of your starting point. Otherwise, everything else should function as indicated.

9. Repeat these steps, but instead of locking the first value with a comma, type the less than symbol (<) this time.
10. Move the mouse around onscreen.

Notice that this time the length of the Wall has been locked and you can rotate freely around the first point. Your second value will be interpreted as the rotation angle of the Wall this time. Try it!

11. If you have drawn any Walls, erase them. (Select them, and then press the DELETE key.)

Dimension Input

Let's continue to explore the Dynamic Input settings by enabling the Dimension Input. We will disable Pointer Input and then enable Dimension Input to understand it better.

1. Right click the Dynamic Input toggle and choose **Settings**.
2. Clear the "Enable Pointer Input" checkbox and place a checkmark in the "Enable Dimension Input where possible" checkbox and then click OK (see Figure 1.34).

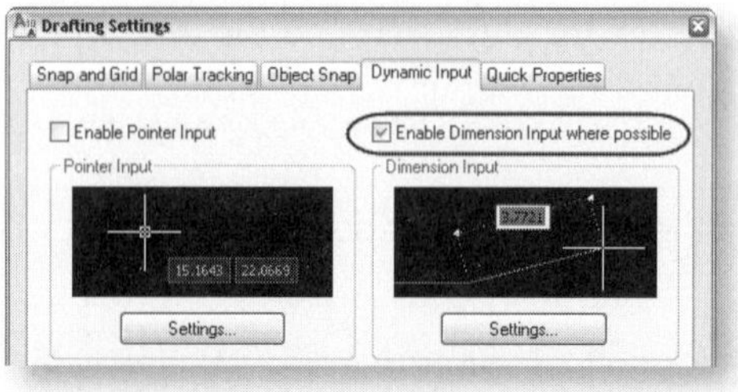

FIGURE 1.34 *Enable only the Dimension Input option*

3. On the Design Palette, click the Wall tool and then click a point on the screen.
4. Move the mouse away from the first point.

Notice the dynamic dimension that appears attached to the length of the Wall and another that indicates the angle of rotation. These dimensions will appear at key points; the content will vary depending on the type of object that you are drawing (see Figure 1.35).

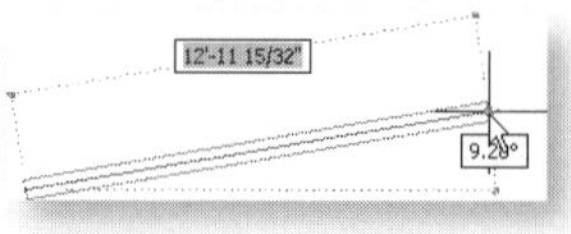

FIGURE 1.35 *With Dimension Input you can type into dynamic dimensions directly onscreen*

5. Try typing in a value such as **10'** [**3000**] again.

Notice that the value will input into the active dimension.

6. With the Wall command still active, press the TAB key once.

You might need to move the mouse slightly after the TAB key. Notice that the angle is now highlighted and ready to receive input. Each time you TAB, the focus cycles to the next dynamic dimension.

7. Press ENTER to complete the Wall command and then erase any Walls drawn.

Dynamic Command Prompting

The third option in the Dynamic Input dialog enables command prompting at the crosshairs. You can use this in place of, or in addition to, the Command Line window. Enable this setting with either or both of the other two settings.

1. Right-click the Dynamic Input toggle once more and choose **Settings**.
2. Place a checkmark in all three boxes this time including the "Show command prompting and command input near the crosshairs" box and then click OK.
3. On the Design Palette, click the Wall tool.

   Notice the command prompt (matching the one shown in the Command Line window) directly at the cursor (see Figure 1.36).

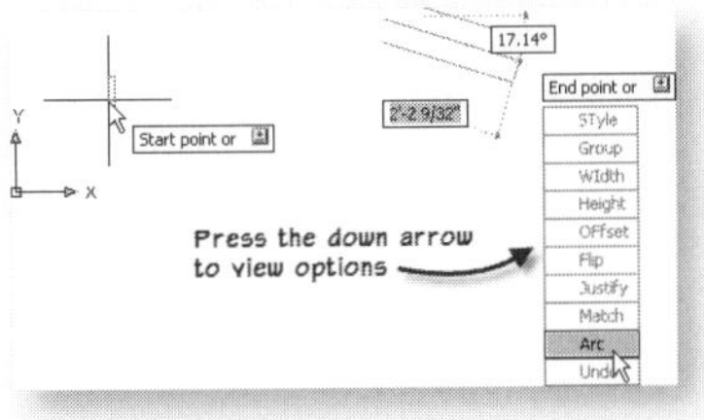

FIGURE 1.36 *With Command Prompting enabled, prompts show directly at the cursor*

4. Click a point to start the Wall.

   Notice the End Point prompt.

5. Click another point.
6. Press the DOWN ARROW on your keyboard.

   A list of command options will appear at the cursor. (This is the same list you would get if you right-clicked at this point.)

7. Press the DOWN ARROW again to begin moving down the list of options. Press ENTER (or click your mouse) to choose the highlighted option.

Continue experimenting as much as you wish. You can return to the Dynamic Input settings at any time and choose different options. For the remainder of this text, it will be assumed that all three Dynamic Input options are active. If you want to learn more about Dynamic Input, return to the settings dialog and then click the Help button at the bottom of the dialog.

Direct Manipulation

Direct manipulation refers to the ability to manipulate object geometry directly in the drawing editor without the need to visit a dialog box or even a palette. To do this, you interact with the various grips of the objects. ACA presents many purpose-specific grip shapes for the various objects. Let's take a look at some of these and basic direct manipulation techniques for them.

1. Using the Wall tool on the Design Palette, create a single horizontal Wall onscreen.
2. Click on the Wall just created to reveal its grips.
3. Hover your cursor over each grip.
   Do not click the grips yet, simply pass the cursor over each one and wait until the tool tip appears (see Figure 1.37).

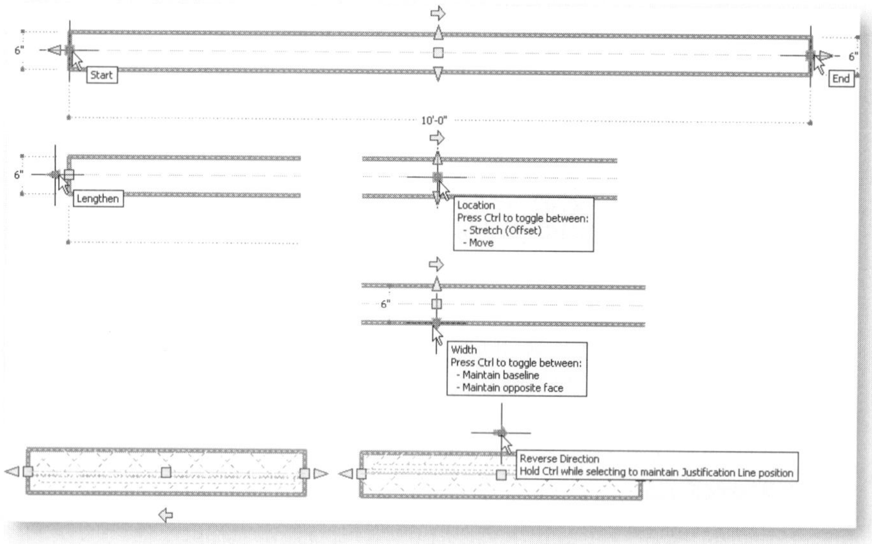

FIGURE 1.37 *Hover over a grip to reveal its function and options*

Notice that each grip shape serves a different function. Hovering over the grip reveals this function in a tool tip. If there are options to this grip (usually invoked by the CTRL key), they will be revealed in the tool tip as well.

4. Click one of the Width grips.
   It is shaped like an isosceles triangle and points away from the width of the Wall.
5. Drag the grip and click to set a new width for the Wall (see Figure 1.38).

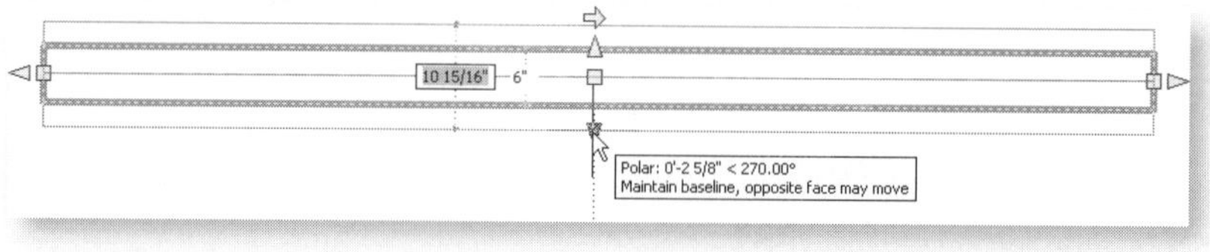

FIGURE 1.38 *Dragging to a new width with the "Width" grip*

6. Try it again; only this time, type a new width into the value field (highlighted onscreen) and then press ENTER to set the width to that value.
7. Try one more time, but press the CTRL key once after you click the triangular grip.

Notice how this method changes the width to distance away from the opposite face of the Wall instead of equally about the center. Pressing CTRL again will cycle back to the baseline option.

8. Try the End and Lengthen grips successively.

Note the difference in behavior between these two grips. With the End (or Start) grip, you have full range of motion and can change the endpoint location as well as the angle of the Wall segment (this is like grip editing an AutoCAD line object). With the Lengthen grip, you can change only the length of the Wall, without affecting its orientation (see Figure 1.39). These are both very powerful tools.

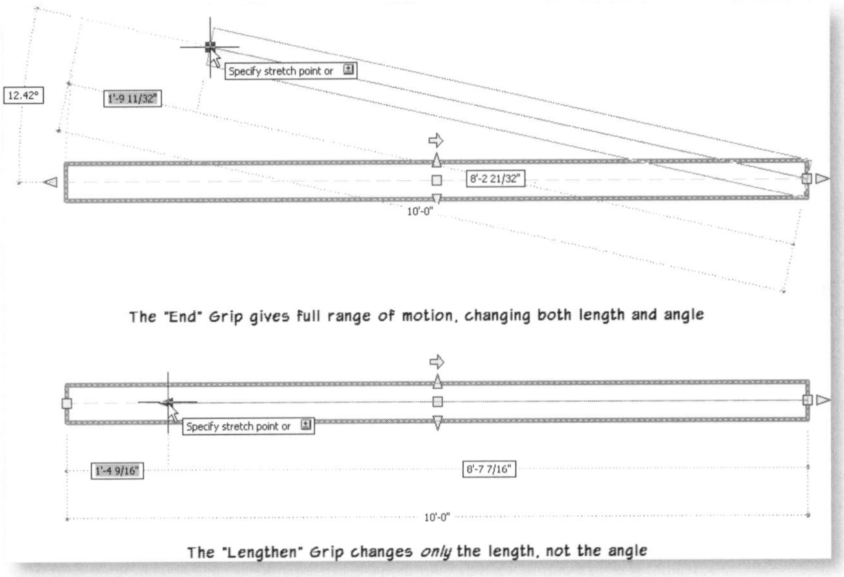

FIGURE 1.39 *Note the difference between the End and Lengthen grips*

This quick overview of grips on Wall objects gives you just some idea of the potential of this very powerful interface item. Look for unique grip shapes on every ACA object. Hover your mouse over them to reveal the tool tip of their function. Doors and Windows offer some exciting possibilities. We will see several more examples throughout this book.

Edge Grips

Profile-based ACA objects (such as Spaces, AEC polygons and In-Place Edit Profiles) have round grips at their corners and long thin grips at the edges.

1. If you did not reload the Design Palette group above, right-click the tool palettes title bar and choose **Design** now.
2. On the Design tool palette, click the Space tool.

TIP

If you are not sure which tool is which, pause your mouse cursor over each one and wait for a ToolTip to appear or right-click the palette tab, choose View Options, and then select an icon with text. Accept all of the defaults and add a Space anywhere in the drawing at a 0° rotation.

3. Click on the Space to reveal its grips.
4. Hover your cursor over each grip.

   Do not click the grips yet; simply pass the cursor over each one and wait until the tool tip appears (see Figure 1.40).

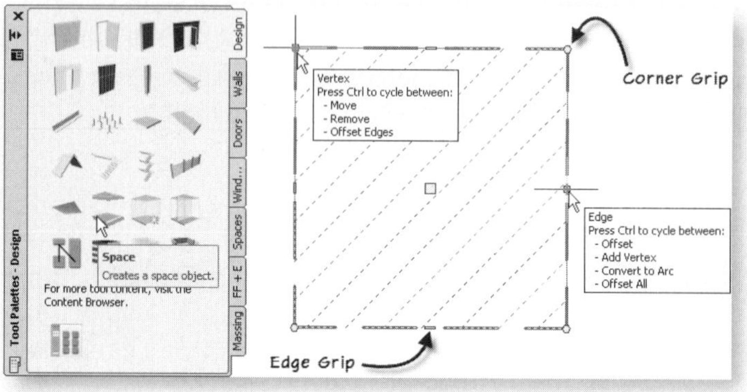

FIGURE 1.40 *Explore the Grip Shape Functions of a Profile-based Object*

5. Click one of the circular-shaped grips and move it. Click again to complete the move.
6. Click on the same circular-shaped grip and then press the CTRL key once.

   Notice that the shape of the Space changes to reflect the removal of this grip. The operation is not complete, however, until you click the mouse again.
7. Click anywhere to complete the removal of the vertex.
8. Undo and then repeat the process by pressing CTRL twice this time.

   This will offset both adjacent edges instead.
9. Click one of the thin rectangular-shaped grips and move it. Click again to complete the move.

   This operation moves the selected edge while stretching the attached edges.
10. Click one of the thin rectangular shaped grips again.
11. Press the CTRL key once.

    Notice that a new vertex is formed.
12. Press the CTRL key again.

    Notice that arc segment is formed.
13. Press the CTRL key once more.

    Notice that all segments will offset around the whole shape.
14. Continue experimenting with any of these functions before continuing.

All of these grip functions work on any ACA object type that uses closed profile shapes. These include Slabs, AEC Polygons and certain Mass Elements. Feel free to draw other objects and experiment.

The Command Line

We have already discussed the Command Line window. This text-based interface, typically docked at the bottom of the AutoCAD Architecture screen, can be set to display one or more text lines at a time; the default configuration displays three lines. The word *Command* will be displayed when the there is no active operation (see Figure 1.41). Most AutoCAD and AutoCAD Architecture commands can be typed into this Command Line area and executed by means of the ENTER key. As we have seen in the previous topic, we can enable onscreen dynamic prompting as an alternative or in addition to the Command Line window prompts. Most common commands can also be executed by choosing them from palettes or ribbon icons. The exact method of command execution is largely a matter of personal preference. As a general rule of thumb, palettes, ribbon icons and onscreen prompting tend to be more user friendly, while the Command Line tends to provide the most options and allow the fullest automation potential as well as a certain familiarity and comfort for experienced AutoCAD users.

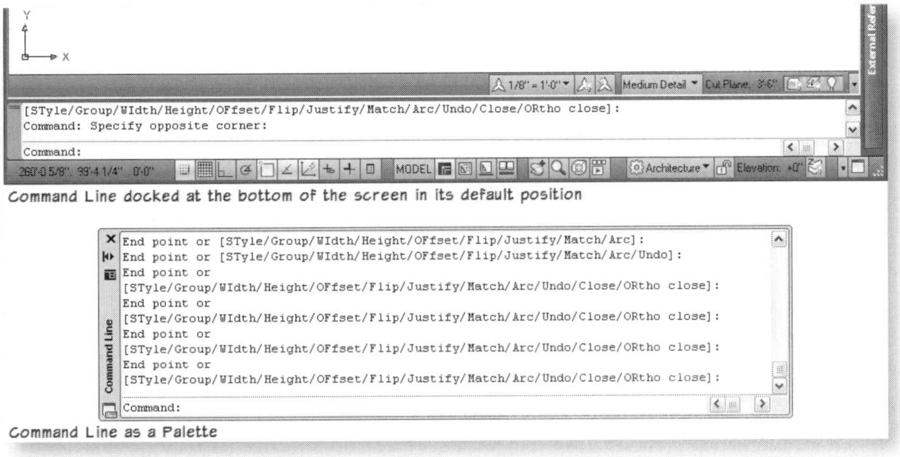

FIGURE 1.41 *The ACA Command Line*

TIP

As any veteran AutoCAD user can attest, there really is only one golden rule to AutoCAD usage: "Always read your Command Line."

Despite the heavy reliance in AutoCAD Architecture on modern interface items such as palettes and direct manipulation, it is still important to understand and pay attention to the Command Line and/or the onscreen prompts. *Remember this rule, and you will be on your way to success with this software package. Disregard this rule and you will surely struggle and be frustrated.* If you need to see more than three Command Lines or want to read back through previously executed commands, press F2 to toggle the AutoCAD text window. The AutoCAD text window is a history window allowing you to scroll back through prior commands.

Even though it is possible to turn off the Command Line and rely solely on the dynamic prompting, many users may find it more comfortable to leave it displayed for those times when Command Line interaction is preferable. However, the Command Line does take up a great deal of screen real estate. One solution to this dilemma is the ability to anchor docked palettes. This was discussed briefly above in the "Understanding Tool Palettes" topic. So a good compromise is to tear off the Command Line from the bottom of the screen, then right-click its title bar and choose **Anchor Right >** or **Anchor Left <**. This will attach it to one or the other side of the screen. When you hover your mouse over the anchor bar at the edge of the screen, the Command Line (and any other anchored palettes) will fly open for use (see Figure 1.42).

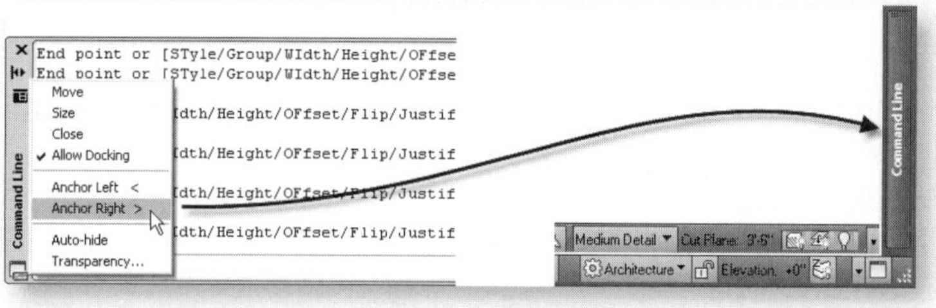

FIGURE 1.42 *Anchoring the Command Line*

Intellimouse

If you have a Windows IntelliMouse, (or any third-party mouse with a middle button wheel and the proper driver,) ACA provides instant zooming and panning using the wheel! If you don't have a wheel mouse, this might be a good time to get one. This modest investment in hardware will pay for itself in time saved and increased productivity by the end of the first day of usage. Using the wheel you have the following benefits:

- **To Zoom**—Roll the wheel.
- **To Pan**—Drag with the wheel held down.
- **To Zoom Extents**—Double-click the wheel. (Do the same type of double-click that you would do with the left button, only on the wheel instead. It takes a little practice at first.)
- **To Orbit in 3D**—Hold down the SHIFT key and simultaneously drag with the wheel held down.

The ZOOMFACTOR command controls the rate of zooming with the wheel. Type ZOOMFACTOR at the Command Line and then press ENTER. Type the percentage you wish to magnify with each rotation of the wheel on your mouse, and then press ENTER again. This setting applies globally, so you only need to do this once. The default setting is 60.

TIP

When typing commands at the Command Line or onscreen dynamic prompts, type the first few letters and then press the TAB key. With each TAB, AutoCAD/ACA will guess the command you want by completing the rest of the command name. Keep tabbing until it shows the command you want and then press ENTER.

If you have tried to use your wheel to zoom and pan and instead you get a menu with Object Snap settings, you will need to adjust the setting for MBUTTONPAN. This command is a toggle setting that turns on and off the wheel zooming and panning feature. At the Command Line type MBUTTONPAN and then press ENTER. Be sure the value is set to 1 and press ENTER again. A setting of "1" turns this feature on, while "0" turns it off. If MBUTTONPAN is set properly and the wheel still does not function properly, you may need to adjust the settings in your Mouse applet in the Windows Control Panel. Usually the wheel works best when the wheel button is set to "Autoscroll." You may also need to update or re-install your mouse driver. Check your mouse manufacturer's website for complete details on mouse driver installation.

View Navigation

With or without a wheel mouse, you make use of the following navigation features in AutoCAD Architecture. For more detail on any of the following items, refer to the "Control the Drawing Views" topic in the online help.

View Panel

The View Panel is torn off as a floating panel by default (see Figure 1.43). If your panel has been returned to its tab, you can find it at the right end of the Home tab. The View Panel consists of three drop-down buttons. The top drop-down button features tools for the standard preset views and for `3D ORBIT`. The middle drop-down button allows you to select from the five out-of-the-box visual styles.

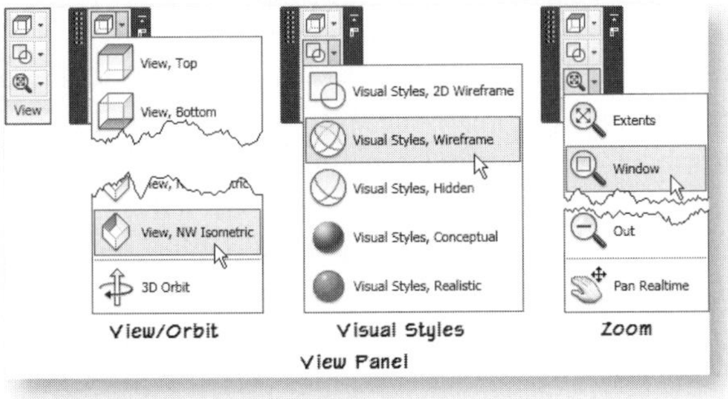

FIGURE 1.43 *The floating View Panel*

The various options for the `ZOOM` command can be found on the bottom drop-down button.

Steering Wheels

The Steering Wheels are a series of "tracking menus" that follow your cursor around and give you quick access to selected groups of navigational commands. The simplest, the 2D Navigation wheel (see Figure 1.44), is only available in Paper Space of a layout, and is the only choice there. In Model Space, you can choose between three different sets of commands, as well as between "full" and "mini" versions of each set. Except in Paper Space, use of the Steering Wheels requires a visual style other than 2D Wireframe. Starting the `NAVSWHEEL` command with the 2D Wireframe visual style current will result in a temporary change in the visual style (noticeable only if you have Grid Display and/or the UCS Icon toggled on) and will return to 2D Wireframe when the command is ended.

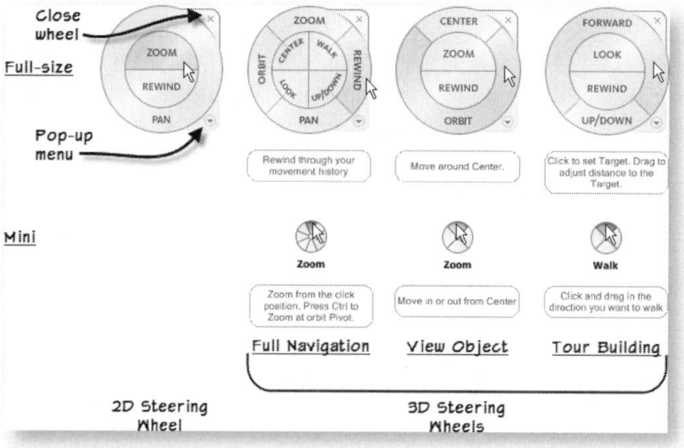

FIGURE 1.44 *The Steering Wheels*

Activate a Steering Wheel by selecting the Steering Wheel icon on the application status bar or, on the View tab of the ribbon, on the Navigate panel, choose the Steering Wheels drop-down button and select one of the Steering Wheels (see Figure 1.45). Right-click or choose the down arrow icon on the full wheels for a pop-up menu of options.

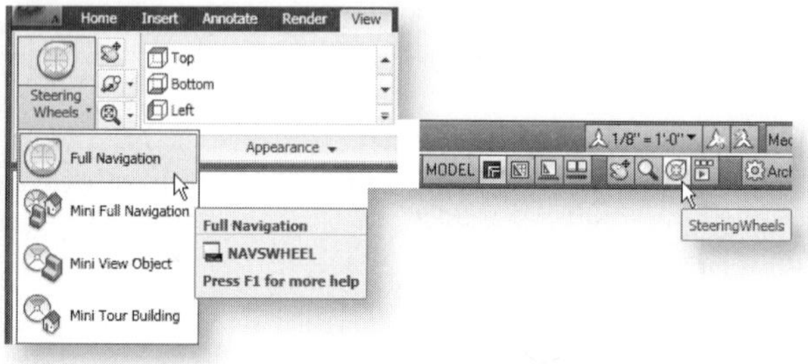

FIGURE 1.45 *Activating a Steering Wheel from the ribbon or the application status bar*

Try out the Steering Wheels in a drawing with some ACA objects. Select the desired option on the wheel and hold down the left mouse button while dragging to use the selected feature. After changing the view several times, try the Rewind feature, which displays a strip of thumbnails of previous views and allows you to return to any one of them (see Figure 1.46).

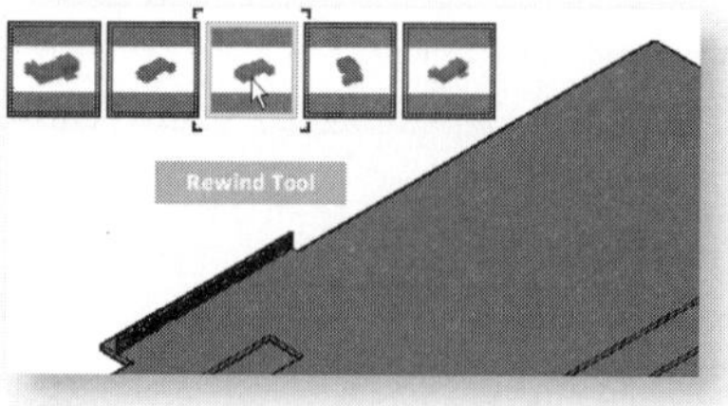

FIGURE 1.46 *Using Rewind to return to a previous view*

The View Cube

Another navigational aid that is only available when the 2D Wireframe visual style is not active is the View Cube. The View Cube allows you to quickly move between any of the preset views as well as rotate when in one of the orthogonal views (front, back, left, right, top or bottom). Unlike the Steering Wheels, the View Cube does not follow the cursor around the screen. The default location is in the upper left corner of the drawing window, but you can specify any of the other three corners by choosing View Cube Settings from the pop-up menu that displays when you hover over the View Cube and select the down arrow icon. This menu also allows you to set a particular view as the "Home" view, then return to it by clicking on the home icon that appears when hovering over the cube. If the View Cube is not enabled in a visual style other than 2D Wireframe, on the View ribbon tab, on the Navigate panel, expand the panel and choose ***View Cube***.

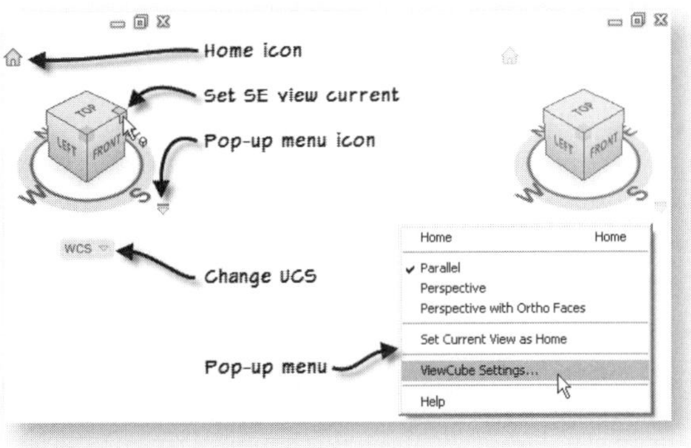

FIGURE 1.47 *The View Cube*

NOTE

The View Cube also appears in the ACA object viewer, the floating viewer available when editing an ACA object style and on the Components tab viewing pane when editing a Wall style.

PRE-REQUISITE SKILLS

The following list of "rules" serves two purposes. For the beginner, it will give you a focused list of topics to research and explore to prepare yourself for the chapters ahead. For the experienced AutoCAD user, treat this list as a self-assessment checklist of pre-requisite AutoCAD skills. Use the list to identify areas where you might need a little brushing up. Please note that this book covers all skills necessary to begin using AutoCAD Architecture effectively and you are not required to purchase or use any other books or lessons. However, there are several core AutoCAD features and topics that are not covered here in the interest of brevity or because they do not have explicit usefulness for architectural design or production. Keep in mind however that all core AutoCAD functionality is present within AutoCAD Architecture. Therefore, any of the dozens of available AutoCAD books, tutorials and videos on the market would provide a nice complement to the lessons covered here.

Autocad Skills—"The Rules"

- **Always read the Command Line (or dynamic prompts)**—This was covered in the previous section, but repetition always aids in retention. Remember: read the Command Line or onscreen prompts (when using Dynamic Input) and you will be on your way to success with ACA. Disregard this rule and you will surely struggle and be frustrated.
- **When in doubt, right-click**—This was also covered earlier, but it is no less important than the others are; therefore it is also repeated here. This is especially critical for ACA commands and functions.
- **Draw accurately and cleanly**—The benefits of a cleanly drafted model, where all corners meet, shapes close, and dimensions make sense, and where double lines and broken lines have been avoided, cannot be overstated. In ACA you will be drafting with Walls instead of lines, but the rule remains the same. Always use tools like Trim, Extend, Offset, Fillet, Chamfer (right-click and select Basic Modify Tools), and Object Snaps. Snap is set to a very small increment and turned on by default in ACA. This is done to help avoid rounding errors and is recommended. Follow these guidelines and the payoff throughout the process will be tremendous.
- **Draw once; use many**—This rule embodies a major purpose of any computer aided design software package. This is certainly true for AutoCAD/ACA. Always look for ways to reuse what you have already created. In ACA this goes beyond the concept of copy and array. In Chapter 2, when we explore the Display System, and Chapter 5 when we look at projects, you will see that "draw once; use many" has numerous applications and interpretations throughout your use of AutoCAD Architecture.

Tools and Entities

Your experience with AutoCAD Architecture will be much more fruitful if you are already familiar with each of the following concepts. While it is beyond the scope of this book to cover each of these topics in detail (as noted earlier), there are dozens of good AutoCAD books and manuals available. The online help system is also a good resource.

- **Object Snaps**—All ACA (or AEC) objects take advantage of the standard AutoCAD Object Snaps. The Node, Center and Insertion Point Object Snaps are used extensively by ACA to mark special reference points within AEC objects. Because the Node and Center Object Snaps are not as frequently used in standard AutoCAD applications, veteran AutoCAD users should train themselves to make use of this powerful ACA feature.
- **Layers**—Layers are like categories that help organize all of the data within a drawing file. AutoCAD has long used layering to keep drawings organized and manageable. ACA objects benefit from "automatic" layering. The specific layer used for an object will depend on the layer Standard used in ACA. For instance, in the United States, the default Layer Standard in ACA is the "AIA (256 Color)" published by the American Institute of Architects. (Actually the Layering Standard installed by default is compliant with recommendations of the most recent version of the AIA Layering as published in the U.S. National CAD Standard.) All layering defaults can be customized to meet your office's layer standard needs. If you use ACA in a country other than the United States, several other Layer Standards are provided. However, it should also be noted that the Display System controls the display properties of ACA objects in a much more thorough way than layering alone can. Please see Chapter 2 for an introduction to the Display System.

- **External References**—An external reference establishes a file link between two or more drawings in a project set. AutoCAD Architecture is designed to take full advantage of the XREF functionality of AutoCAD. (And with the built-in Drawing Management system, it takes it much further.) This allows you to leverage your existing strategies to their fullest advantage (XREFs are used extensively in this book—see Chapter 5 for more information).
- **Layouts (Paper Space)**—Layouts (also called Paper Space) are most often associated with setting up sheets for plotting. ACA takes full advantage of this functionality as well. In addition, the advanced display functionality of AutoCAD Architecture can be combined with the functionality of Paper Space layouts. This allows even more control over output than layouts and viewports alone would allow. With the AutoCAD Sheet Set functionality built right into the ACA Drawing Management system, Layouts take on an even more important role. The topics of Layouts, Page Setup, Sheet Sets and Plotting are discussed in Chapter 18.
- **Template Files**—Template files provide a starting point for any AutoCAD or ACA drawing file. By saving desired settings in a template file, you can ensure that new drawings are begun properly and in conformance to company standards. Out-of-the-box templates are used to begin all drawings in this book.
- **Polylines**—Polylines are used extensively in ACA to help create custom objects. A long list of AutoCAD Architecture objects can have their shapes customized to match the shape of a Polyline. You can even right-click on a Polyline to convert it to certain ACA objects such as Profiles and Mass Elements. When customizing ACA objects, you must use *lightweight* polylines; line and arc segments only, no splines or fit curves.
- **Blocks**—Blocks have been a huge part of AutoCAD productivity for years. A block is a collection of objects that have been grouped together and given a name. They then behave as a single object. Blocks continue to play an important role in customizing ACA objects. Another important issue associated with blocks is that existing libraries of blocks can be incorporated into an ACA work environment fairly seamlessly.

Your existing block libraries can be converted to ACA content (making them "draggable") by adding them to Tool Palettes or by using the AEC Create Content Wizard on the Format menu to put them in the DesignCenter. Blocks, multi-view blocks, mask blocks, entire drawings and custom commands can be converted with this wizard. Refer to the online help or a copy of *Autodesk Architectural Desktop: An Advanced Implementation Guide* for exact steps.

MANAGER NOTE CAD

Important Autocad Tools

This topic includes some important AutoCAD functionality that seasoned AutoCAD users may have overlooked. If you are not familiar with the following tools, you should consult an AutoCAD resource or the online help and become conversant with them.

- **Auto Snap Options**—Parallel and Extension are two Auto Snap features that often go unused by veteran AutoCAD users. Parallel draws a line parallel to an existing line. This can be set as a running snap, but it works best when used as an override. (To use as an override, hold the SHIFT key down and right-click—this calls the OSNAP cursor menu—and then choose **Parallel.**) Extension allows the selection of a point along the extension (trajectory) of an existing line or arc. This provides functionality akin to a *virtual* Extend command.

- **Polar Tracking**—Polar tracking (right-click the POLAR button on the status bar and choose **Settings**) tracks the cursor movement along increments of a set angle, similar to the way ORTHO forces lines to move at multiples of 90°; however, the angle is a user-defined increment such as 45° or 15° (see Figure 1.48). Custom user angles can also be added. Additionally, unlike ORTHO, POLAR does not limit movement to the constraint angles. Instead, it snaps to those angles when the cursor gets close; otherwise it moves freeform. POLAR and ORTHO are not available at the same time. Toggling one on will toggle the other off and vice versa. Access Drafting Settings from the Format menu. The default setting for ACA is an Increment Angle of 30°, with Additional Angles of 45°, 135°, 225° and 315° added. This gives your cursor all of the positions of the traditional 45 and 30/60/90 triangles used in hand drafting.

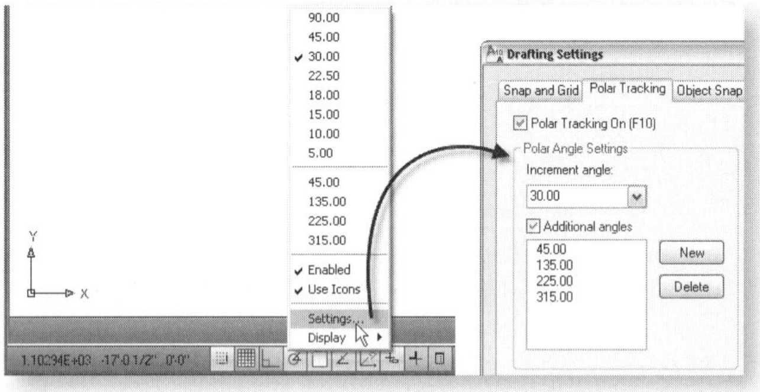

FIGURE 1.48 *Angle choices available in Polar Tracking*

- **Object Snap Tracking**—Uses Object Snap points to set up temporary tracking vectors to align geometry to precise points. Toggle the Object Snap Tracking button on the status bar to turn it on. A temporary alignment path will project from the various Object Snap points in the drawing. To use this feature, both the OTRACK and OSNAP toggles must be on (buttons pushed in on the status bar.) To track, first activate a command, and then hover the mouse over a snap point for a moment. Do *NOT* click the point. As the cursor moves away from the point, a small plus (+) sign will remain indicating that the point has been "acquired" (see Figure 1.49). Moving horizontally or vertically from this acquired point will enable the tracking feature and keep the cursor lined up with the point. Several points can be acquired, and multiple tracking vectors can be used simultaneously to achieve very precise alignments. Check the online help for more information.

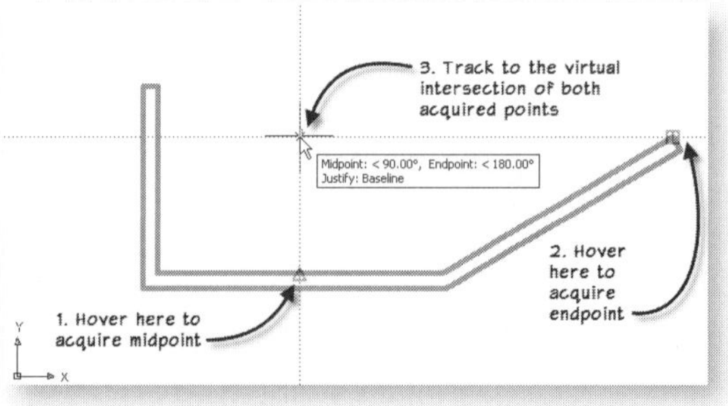

FIGURE 1.49 *Acquiring and tracking from temporary track points*

Autocad Architecture "Rules"

In addition to the summary of basic core AutoCAD skills listed previously, the following list summarizes the overall skills you will want to develop and keep in mind in the coming chapters and as you work on projects with AutoCAD Architecture.

- **Edit at the source**—This is really another way of stating the previous rule of draw once and use many. When building projects in ACA (starting in Chapter 5), you will always seek the source of a particular piece of data in your building information model. When editing the source, you are changing it everywhere! This guarantees coordinated models and helps eliminate errors.
- **Never explode objects**—Never explode an AEC object, hatch or dimension. *Never*! If you explode an AEC object, all its "smarts" are gone. This certainly defeats the entire purpose of using ACA in the first place.
- **Save often**—You only need to lose everything you have done in the last three hours once to realize that Auto-save (in the Options dialog) isn't good enough. Here is a simple test you can do any time while you work to see if it is time to save. Any time you can say to yourself: "boy, I'd hate to draw that again..." it is time to SAVE! Use CTRL + S to save quickly. Creating regular backups is always a good idea as well.
- **Work smarter, not harder**—*Just because you can, doesn't mean you should.* Sure you can make a Wall style that includes 20 components, but is this always a *good* idea? ACA is a wonderful tool, but it can't do *everything* well yet. Learn what it can and can't do well, and learn to discern the often "fine line" between the two. This takes practice, but it is worth the effort. Many examples of this principle will be covered throughout this book.
- **Progressive refinement**—Start with simple, low-detail models and slowly add detail over the course of the project. This process is the basis for all of the tutorials in this book, so you will get plenty of practice.
- **Be consistent**—You will make many small decisions as you work through a project. You will name objects, configure parameters, and establish procedures. There is always more than one way to do things; whatever method you choose, implementing it consistently in similar situations will make it much easier to revisit the issue later. It will also make it much easier to work with other team members on the same project.
- **There are always exceptions to every rule**—Saved the best for last. Rules were made to be broken, were they not? These rules can be ignored or broken, but often at a tremendous loss of productivity (and even loss of data in some cases). However, there are times when breaking a rule will make sense; with practice and experience you will learn when it is appropriate. Like Mother always used to say about falling in love: "When the time comes, you'll just know." Until then, however, it's best to stick to the rules.

SUMMARY

- The AutoCAD Architecture 2010 interface is designed to be streamlined, logical and easy to use.
- Tool Palettes provide ready access to most common AutoCAD Architecture tools and functions.
- Tool Palettes are organized into swappable groups.
- AutoCAD Architecture relies heavily on the functionality of the right-click menu for editing commands.
- When in doubt, right-click.
- The Command Line can be hidden and dynamic onscreen prompting enabled instead.
- A good foundation in basic AutoCAD skills will enhance your learning of AutoCAD Architecture and help you start off on the right foot.
- Several basic concepts like edit at the source, progressive refinement and consistency will provide a solid foundation for all of your efforts with AutoCAD Architecture.

CHAPTER 2

Conceptual Underpinnings of AutoCAD Architecture

INTRODUCTION

AutoCAD Architecture (ACA) is an object-based Computer Aided Design (CAD) software package. It differs from the AutoCAD foundation upon which it is built in a number of ways. The major difference is in its focus on modeling over drafting. The main goal of the software is to facilitate the creation of a virtual building model from which plans, sections, elevations, as well as quantities and other data can be readily extracted. The extracted drawings serve as two-dimensional "reports" of the "live" 3D model data. The advantages of this approach are many. From a 2D production point of view, this means less time drafting and coordinating building data, because plans and sections are both being generated from the same source data. If the data changes, both plan and section receive the change. Schedules and data reports of quantities, component sizes, materials used, and scores of other property data are also within the realm of possibility and fully accessible. To achieve this level of functionality, it is important to understand a bit about what makes ACA tick. That is the goal of this chapter. In particular, the focus will be on three major ACA concepts that are not available in the underlying AutoCAD drafting package. These are: display control, anchors, and object styles. Drawing Management and Property Sets also offer power and flexibility not available within standard AutoCAD; but these topics will be covered extensively in Chapters 5 and 15, respectively.

OBJECTIVES

In this chapter, we will explore the meanings of parametric design, Building Information Modeling and object-oriented CAD. Following the steps of a tutorial on the display system, you will learn how to display a single drawing model in many different ways that serve a variety of architectural drawing and documentation needs. By exploring the Style Manager and anchors, we will begin to gain comfort with some of the critical conceptual underpinnings of the ACA software package. Upon completion of this chapter you will be able to:

- Understand objects and their properties.
- Work with the display system.
- Understand object styles.
- Understand anchors.

PARAMETRIC DESIGN

Objects in ACA are programmed to represent the real-life objects for which they are named. All real-life objects have a series of defining characteristics that determine their shape, size, and behavior. Parametric Design allows us to design while manipulating those real-world parameters directly on the objects.

To get a better sense of what these parameters might be, think of the characteristic to which you would refer if describing the object verbally to a colleague without the benefit of a drawing. Consider, for instance, a door. If discussing a particular door needed in a project with the contractor over the telephone, we would rely on descriptive adjectives and verbal dimensions such as "the door is a particular width, and a particular height, it is solid core and has a hollow metal frame." Once we had settled on the door required and hung up the phone, we would then need to convey graphically in our drawing documents the decisions we had just made regarding that door (and any others like it). In traditional CAD (AutoCAD), this would mean translating dimensions and materials into corresponding lines, arcs, circles and/or blocks that represent the required dimensions and materials in the drawing. In ACA, dimensions and other specifications are simply input into a series of fields and stored with the data for the object. This data remains accessible throughout the life of the object and the drawing via the object's properties. Therefore, the next time we phone the contractor and realize that circumstances on the site have forced us to spec a different door and size, rather than redraw the door and manually adjust the wall in which it sits, as we would in traditional CAD, we now simply re-access the properties for that door and input the new values. Not only does the door itself update because of this change, but the wall in which it is inserted updates as well. Other linked views such as Elevations and Schedules will also receive the change. This is just one example of parametric design. Object parameters are always available for editing; data never needs to be re-created, only manipulated. Some principles of parametric design are as follows:

- **Draw Once**—In traditional CAD, each object needs to be drawn for each required view; therefore the same door or wall may need to be drawn two, three or more times. With ACA, objects need only be drawn once. They are then "represented" in each of the required views of Plan, Section and Elevation.
- **Progressive Refinement**—Complete or final design information is rarely known at the early stages of a design project. Changes occur frequently and often several times. In traditional CAD, it is easy to add new information. However, when major design changes occur, drawings must often undergo time-consuming redrafting. With ACA, designs can be progressively refined over the life of the project. As new data is learned or design changes occur, object parameters may be adjusted appropriately without the need to erase and re-create the drawing. The objects are drawn once, and then modified and refined as required.
- **Style Based versus Object Based**—Most ACA objects make use of styles. A style is a collection of object parameters saved in a named group. When styles are assigned to objects, all properties of the style are transferred to the object in one step. If the style parameters change later, all of the objects using the style will change as well. This is similar to the behavior exhibited by text and dimension styles in traditional AutoCAD. AutoCAD Architecture simply utilizes many more styles, and manages them and their relationships to objects much more completely than the corresponding AutoCAD counterparts. In some cases however, object parameters are assigned directly to the individual objects and *not* controlled by the style. Consider again the Door object as an example.

The Door style would be used to designate the *type* of door, such as a hinged double door. However, double-hinged doors can come in a variety of sizes; the door type double-hinged is a style-based parameter, while the size is an object-based parameter.

- **Live versus Linked**—Some drawing types in ACA are edited directly on the "live" model data. This is the case with floor plans or live sections. The display system (see the next topic) controls what displays on the screen as we are working in ACA. Plans views are live. If changes are made to the objects within the plan, those changes will be seen simultaneously on the live model in all other live views. However, some drawing types, namely 2D sections, 2D elevations, and schedules, are "linked." Rather than being a live view of the model, these separate drawings function as "reports" of the model that maintain a link to the live model data. These views must be periodically refreshed to capture changes made to the model.

THE DISPLAY SYSTEM

Early in our architectural careers, we are taught the traditional rules of architectural drafting. These rules govern such things as what a plan or elevation drawing represents, how to create one, and most importantly, what to include and what not to include in making the drawing "read." Although there are accepted universal rules in place, part of the process involves personal style. Therefore, the rules need to be consistent enough to allow them to convey information reliably, and flexible enough to allow for stylistic variation. Amazingly enough, although CAD software such as AutoCAD has revolutionized the way design drawings are created, prior to ACA, the software offered no specialized tools to assist the architect in achieving the unique graphical look required by architectural documents. Rather, lines were still painstakingly laid out one at a time as they had been in hand drafting, following the internalized prescriptions learned in architecture school. If a plan, section, and elevation were required to convey design intent, three completely separate drawings needed to be created and, more importantly, coordinated. The display system in ACA addresses this situation by incorporating the *rules* of architectural drafting directly into the software. Plans, sections, and elevations can now be generated *directly* from a single building model. This reduces rework and redundancy by requiring one set of objects, with three different modes of display (see Figure 2.1). The tools are flexible and fully customizable, so we can fully benefit from this powerful tool and still introduce the nuances of our own personal style into the process.

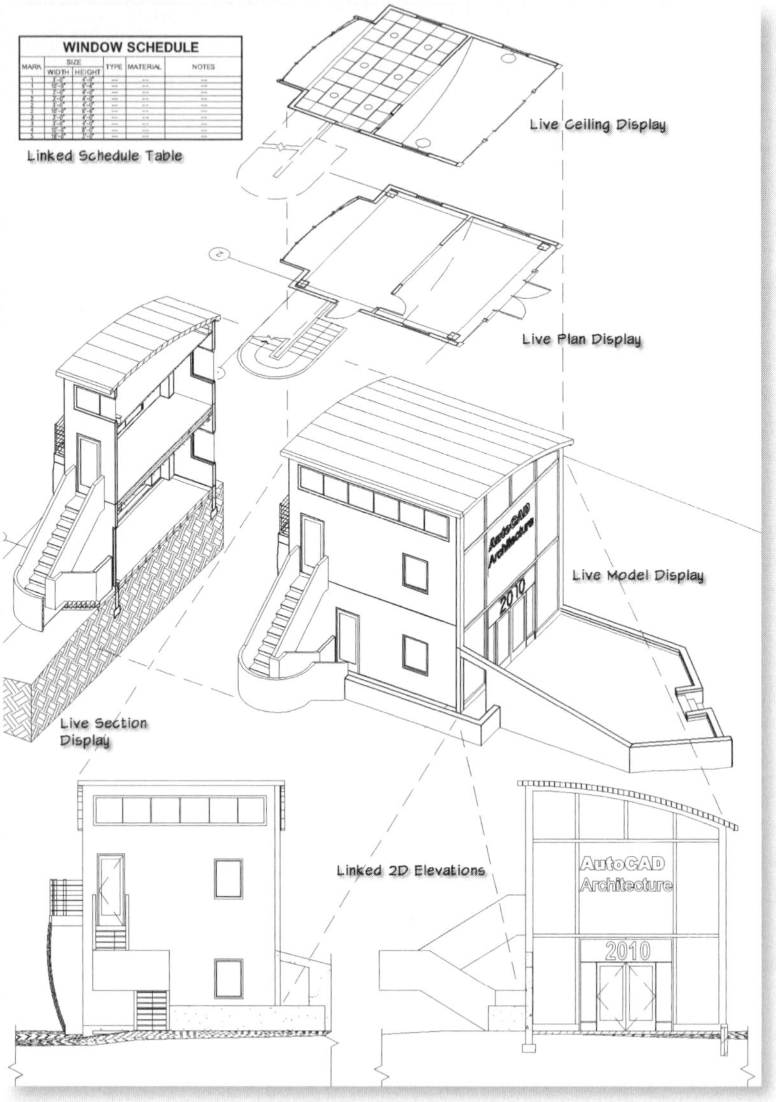

FIGURE 2.1 *Generating plan, section, elevation and schedule views from a single model*

CAD MANAGER NOTE

The best way to quickly understand the display system is to start with the drawing template files (DWT) provided with the software. Much of the display system has already been configured for typical design situations in these templates. For most firms, these templates can be used "as-is" or with minor customization. If you are new to ACA, begin with the out-of-the-box templates and display system configurations and then slowly begin customizing them to suit your firm's particular needs as required. This approach guarantees a complete understanding of the tools as you learn by example using suggested settings. The display system is complex, but it is also extremely powerful. In order to fully master the use of ACA, it is important to become very comfortable with the display system.

The Display System's Relationship to Layers

Objects unique to ACA are referred to as "AEC Objects." They include objects like Walls, Doors, Windows and Schedules. Display control determines how AEC objects are displayed under different viewing conditions and circumstances. (Display control has no effect on AutoCAD entities such as lines, arcs and circles.) Layers are used as a global organizational tool for the management of drawing data, much like a drawing-wide categorization system. All objects (both AutoCAD and AEC) are placed on a Layer when they are created. Display control supplements layers in helping you control what is seen and how it is displayed on the screen and in print. Each AEC object contains a series of components. The display control tools determine the display characteristics of each of these components. In some cases, the display properties of individual AEC object subcomponents are in fact handled by layers, although this is certainly not required (and in many cases not desired either). To summarize, Layers know nothing of Display; however, Display settings can optionally include Layers. Layers work on all entities, AutoCAD and AEC alike, but Display works only with AEC objects. Both can be used to control what is seen onscreen and in print. Layers do this globally in an absolute way—they cannot respond to the condition of the drawing. Display settings can change if the condition of the drawing meets certain criteria. The Display system has been designed specifically with Architectural drawing needs in mind, Layers have not.

Overview and Key Display System Features

The display system offers many features and benefits:

- **AEC objects display differently under various viewing conditions**—Display control settings can dynamically change the display of a building model from plan to elevation to section or 3D model, with a simple change in the viewing direction onscreen.
- **Fully customizable**—Configuration of the display system components and their individual object properties can be customized to suit specialized needs. Customization can be as simple as modifying a setting or two in the configurations provided in the default templates, or as complex as a completely custom-built solution tailored to a project-specific or office-wide need.
- **Understands the nuances of architectural drafting**—Object components such as "Cut Plane" (Walls), "Defining Line" (Sections) and "Muntins" (Windows) allow an architect to configure in a very specific way the precise visual expression a component ought to have in a particular display circumstance. Display modes such as Plan, Reflected, Plan High Detail, and Plan Low Detail allow object components to appear differently and in greater or lesser detail under different scale and presentation conditions.

The Display System Tool Set

The display system tool set consists of a collection of interconnected components. It is important to understand some concepts and terminology related to each of these components before you begin to work with the display system.

- **Object/Sub-Components**—All AEC objects contain one or more subcomponents. These are simply the individual pieces of the object. A door, for example, contains (among others) the following Plan subcomponents: Door Panel, Swing, Stop and Frame. Just like traditional drafted AutoCAD entities (lines, arcs and circles) the entire object (the Door in this case) will be assigned AutoCAD properties such as Layer and LWT, while the individual subcomponents may also receive their own individual properties through their object display settings.
- **Display Properties**—Display properties are the collection of display settings for a particular object. These include Visibility mode (On or Off), Layer, Color,

Linetype, LWT, LTScale, and Plot Style. They also include many object-specific settings like Cut Plane height and Swing Angle. These are applied as "Drawing Default," "Style Override" or "Object Override" level.

- **Drawing Default**—In the hierarchy of display settings, the Drawing Default settings come first and establish the baseline for a particular type of object: all walls, all stairs, etc. within a particular drawing.
- **Style Override**—Style Override affects a subset of drawing objects that belong to the particular style in question only. Establishing the display settings at the object's style level offers many benefits: logical grouping of similar objects, global point of control to make changes, and consistency throughout the drawing and the project. Style-level settings override the Drawing Default settings.
- **Object Override**—Object Override affects only a single object selected in the drawing. Object-level settings override those of both the Drawing Default and, if present, the Style Override. In general, frequent application of object-level overrides should typically be avoided.

- **Display Representation (Display Rep)**—As dictated by the conventional rules of architectural drafting, each type of object has one or more ways in which it may be drawn. Display representations control the behavior of objects under various drawing situations such as Plan, Elevation and Reflected. Representations also control the specific display characteristics of an object's individual subcomponents from a particular viewpoint (see Figure 2.2).
- **Set**—Set describes which objects will display in a particular drawing situation, and in which mode—Display Representation—they will be displayed. A Set closely approximates a particular type of drawing, such as "Floor Plan" or "Building Section" (see Figure 2.2).
- **Display Configuration**—Configuration controls which Display Representation Set will appear on the screen, as determined by a particular viewing direction. Configurations can be "Fixed View" (same set appears regardless of current view direction) and "View Direction Dependent" (loads a different set based upon view direction). See Figure 2.2.

Putting It All Together

Summarizing how all of these components fit together, objects have one or more Display Representations (display modes). These Representations control the On/Off state, Layer, Color, Linetype, LWT, and Plot Style of each of the object's internal subcomponents. These can be assigned in one of three ways: Drawing Default, Style Override, or by Object Override. Most of these settings are available on the Display tab of the Properties palette. Individual objects and their appropriate Representations are grouped together in a Set. Sets are loaded into the viewport based on the conditions outlined in the Display Configuration. Changing the viewport view direction will trigger the display of appropriate Sets based on these conditions. Figure 2.2 shows two examples of these relationships (a door in elevation and in plan) in a flowchart style to illustrate the concept. The far bottom left shows the Views panel. Next to it is the Display Configuration menu on the drawing status bar (first shown in Figure 1.3). These two items together trigger the rest of the items illustrated. The screen captures in the middle of the figure are from the Display Manager, available on the Format menu. The Display tab of the Properties palette is depicted in two scenarios on the right.

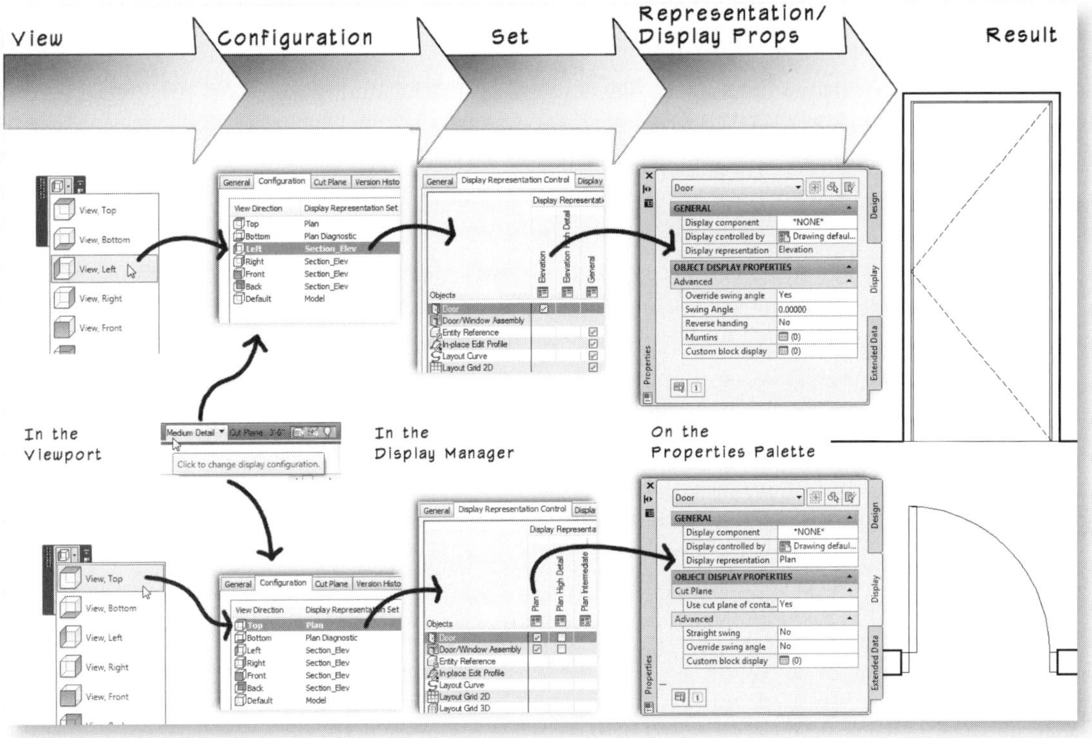

FIGURE 2.2 *The relationship of components in the display system*

The display system is dynamic. Changes made to its settings are immediately evident in the drawing. Many aspects of its configuration can be set up once and used from one drawing to the next, but certain settings will be in a constant state of flux as project needs dictate. The goal of the display system is to provide a unified tool set for controlling the myriad of display needs in architectural drawings. The goal here is two-fold: reduce some of the tedium associated with architectural drafting, and create a single building model that is capable of representing itself in all the ways necessary to display the drawings required in a document set. With the display system, it is no longer necessary to draw the same data two or three times to accommodate plans, sections, elevations and schedules. Features such as those offered by the display system are central to the concept of Building Information Modeling.

Working with the Display System

We begin our exploration of the display system by exploring the settings contained in the default template files. The display system is configured in much the same way in each of the out-of-the-box templates. The Imperial unit dataset used here was created from the *AEC Model (Imperial Stb).dwt* template file. Normally, the metric datasets use the *AEC Model (Metric Stb).dwt* as the starting point. However, in this chapter, since there is no explicit mention of units either Imperial or Metric, a single dataset is provided.

Install the CD Files and Load Sample File

Since the skills covered in this tutorial do not rely on measurement, the dataset used in this chapter is provided in Imperial units only. Both Imperial and Metric datasets have been provided for all subsequent chapters. Please see the "Units" heading in the Preface for additional information.

1. Install the dataset files located on the Mastering AutoCAD Architecture 2010 CD-ROM.

   Refer to "Files Included on the CD-ROM" in the Preface for information on installing the sample files included on the CD.
2. Launch AutoCAD Architecture 2010.
3. On the Quick Access Toolbar (QAT), click the **Project Browser** icon.
4. From the drop-down folder list, choose your *C:* Drive.
5. Browse to the *C:\MasterACA 2010\Chapter02* folder.
6. Double-click MACA10 CH02 to make this project current (you can also right-click on it and choose **Set Project Current**). Then click Close in the Project Browser.

NOTE

The Project Navigator Palette should appear onscreen. If it does not appear, press CTRL + 5**.**

7. On the Project Navigator Palette, click the Views tab and then double-click the *Floor Plan* View file to open it.

Loading a Display Configuration

We are going to load several different Display Configurations. Be sure to Zoom and Pan around the drawing a bit after each change to see the complete effect.

8. On the drawing status bar, on the right side, open the Display Configuration pop-up menu (it currently reads "Medium Detail").

   A menu list of all Display Configurations appears (see Figure 2.3).

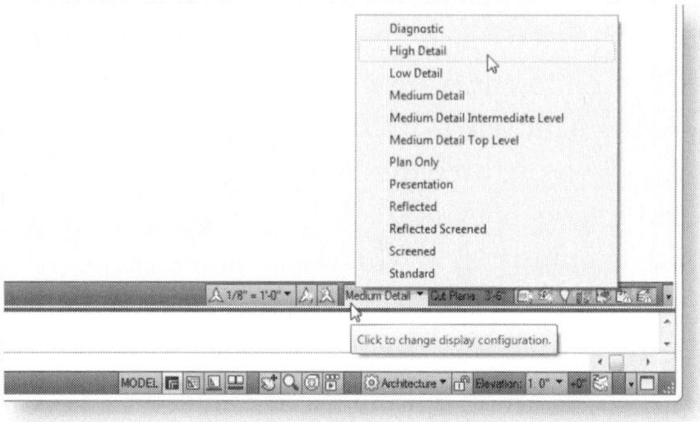

FIGURE 2.3 *The Display Configuration pop-up menu on the Drawing status bar*

9. Choose **High Detail** (see Figure 2.4).

   Zoom and pan around the drawing to see the change. Notice that the hatch patterns in Walls got closer together. The Stair and Railing on the left side of the plan also got more detailed.

NOTE

The images in Figures 2.4 through 2.7 are composites including cropped zoomed-in portions of the entire file to show details.

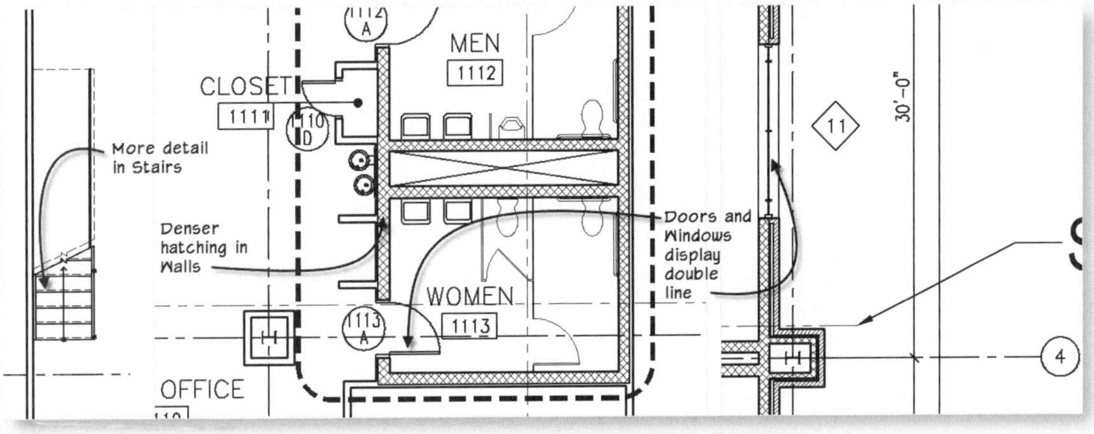

FIGURE 2.4 *Load High Detail from the Display Configurations list*

10. From the Display Configuration pop-up menu on the Drawing status bar, choose **Low Detail** (see Figure 2.5).

    Zoom and pan around the drawing to see the change. Notice that Wall hatching disappeared, Stairs got simpler and the Doors and Windows reduced to single lines.

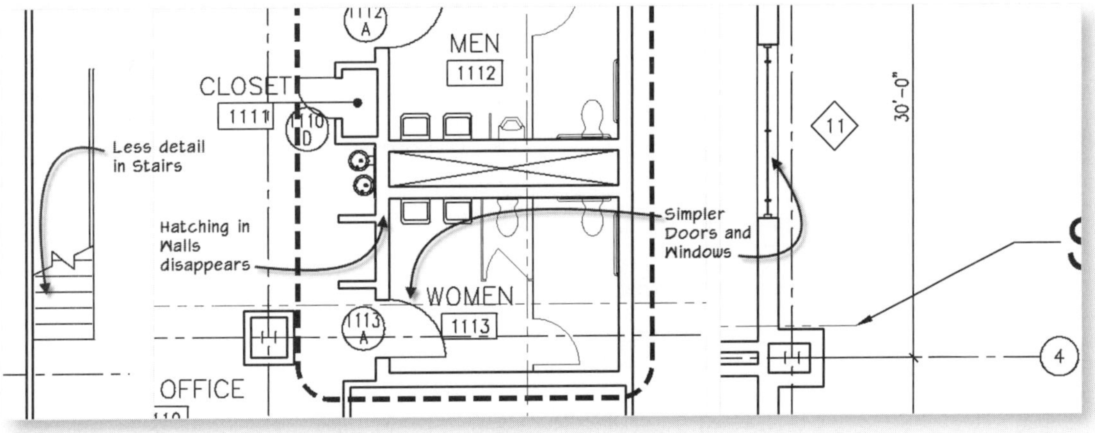

FIGURE 2.5 *Load Low Detail from the Display Configurations list*

11. From the Display Configuration pop-up menu on the drawing status bar, choose **Reflected** (see Figure 2.6).

NOTE

In each case, you may notice the slight delay while the Display Configuration loads and makes the change to the drawing.

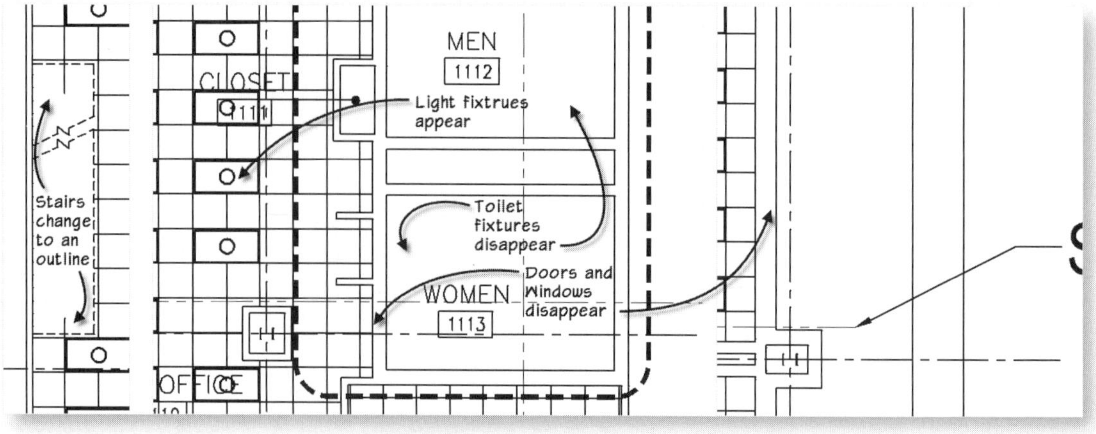

FIGURE 2.6 *Load Reflected from the Display Configurations list*

Notice the change to the drawing: the toilet room fixtures and doors have disappeared and the ceiling grids and lighting have appeared. This configuration is intended for working on reflected ceiling plans; the level of detail is equivalent to the Medium Detail configuration.

12. From the Display Configuration pop-up menu on the drawing status bar, choose **Presentation** (see Figure 2.7).

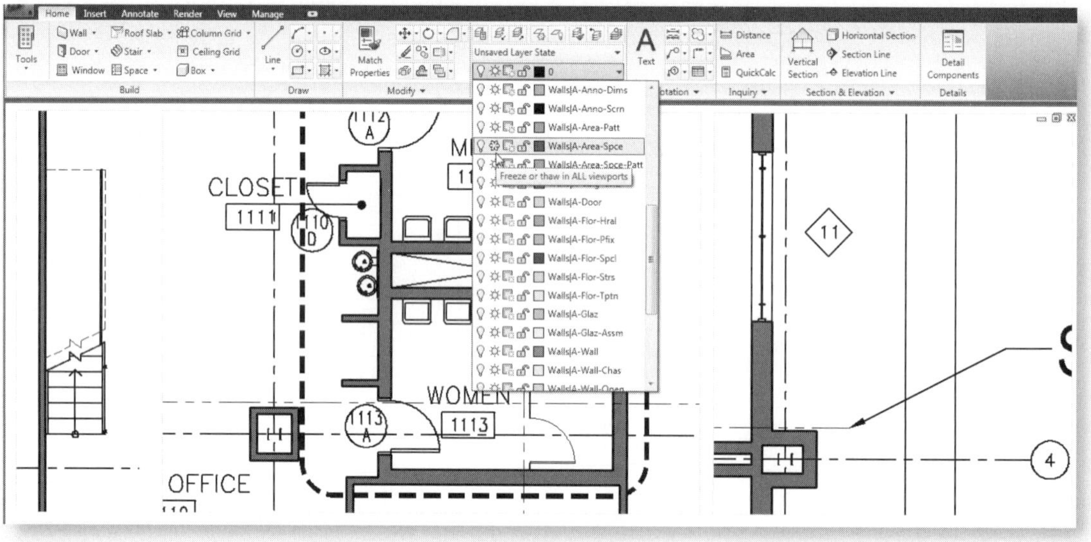

FIGURE 2.7 *Load Presentation from the Display Configurations list*

In this configuration, the Walls are now filled with a solid poché. None of the internal components within the Walls are displayed. If you thaw the Space layer, the Spaces (rooms) would appear in various solid colors as well. If you wish to see this, on the Home tab, on the Layers panel, click the Layer drop-down list and then click the small snow flake icon next to Walls|A-Area-Spce. Please freeze the layer again after experimenting.

As you can see, loading Display Configurations has a broad effect upon the entire drawing. The goal of a Display Configuration is to adjust the display of all AEC objects within the drawing to suit a particular design or presentation situation. Those situations range from floor plans to reflected ceiling plans to presentation plans, at a range of detail levels. Each of the individual configurations provided with ACA by default is designed to serve a particular drawing, modeling or printing task.

MANAGER NOTE

If the solid fill patterns are displaying on top of the other geometry, you may need to adjust the value of Object Sorting Methods. You may do this at the command line (or when Dynamic input is turned on, directly onscreen). To do so, type SORTENTS, press ENTER**, and then type 127 and press** ENTER **again.**

13. Reload the **Medium Detail** Display Configuration.

    Notice the drawing's change back to the default Display Configuration.

By loading these Configurations you can begin to see some of the power of the display system; particularly when it comes to displaying the same information in varying graphical formats or in more or less detail.

14. On the Project Navigator Palette, click the Sheets tab and then double-click to open the *A101 Chapter 2* Sheet.

Sheets and Sheet Sets are used for plotting projects in ACA. While we are currently working in a project, setup and creation will be discussed in more detail in Chapter 5, and Plotting is covered in Chapter 18. Most Sheets have a single Layout using a name similar to the drawing. This project has such a Layout (which is active), but also contains another Layout that we will use for further experimentation. Typically a Layout is used to compose the organization of items within the title block border for printing. The current Layout serves this purpose, and the other one (which is not intended for plotting) was added specifically to showcase the Scale-Dependent qualities of the out-of-the-box Display Configuration.

NOTE

If you prefer the traditional Layout tab display, right-click the Layout or Model icon and choose Display Layout and Model Tabs.

15. At the bottom of the drawing window, on the application status bar, click the Quick View Layouts icon next to the Model and Layout icons.

    A collection of thumbnail previews will appear. Use these to switch between existing Layouts and/or Model Space.

16. Click on the **Scale Dependent** thumbnail to switch to that Layout (see Figure 2.8).

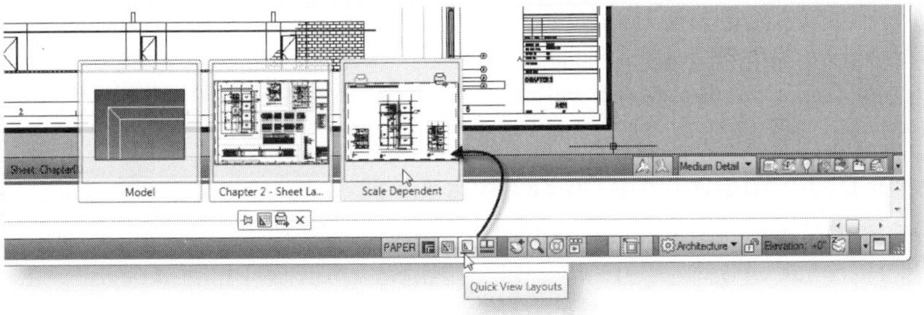

FIGURE 2.8 *Switch to Scale Dependent layout in the Sheet file*

17. Zoom and Pan around the drawing to compare the three viewports to one another (see Figure 2.9).

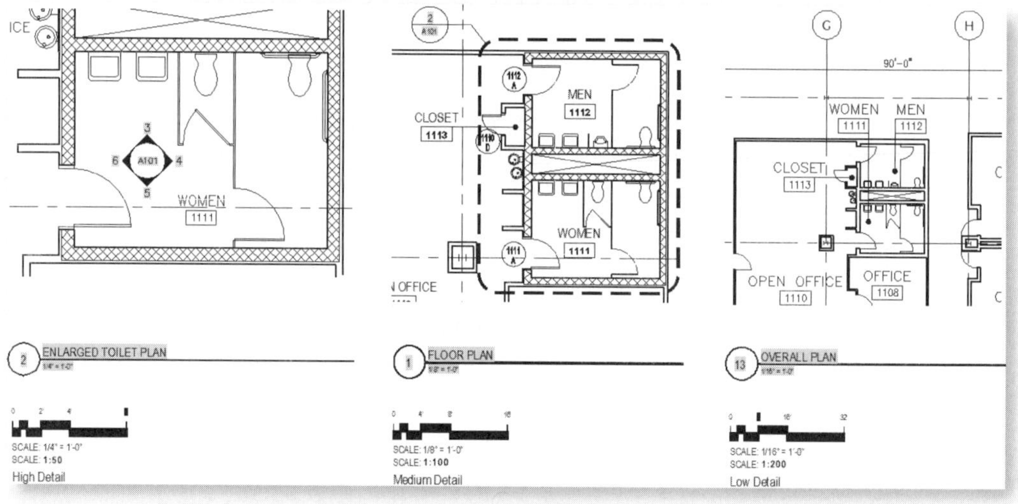

FIGURE 2.9 *Scale Dependent Display Configurations configured at proper scales in a Paper Space Layout*

Changing Display Configurations as we did in Model Space of the *Floor Plan* file is useful and gives a good sense of what the differences in Display Configurations are, but it is not until you view them in a properly configured Paper Space Layout as we have here, with viewports assigned to the appropriate plotting scales and the LWT display turned on (LWT toggle on the application status bar), that you really see how striking the differences are. In addition to the display control differences, changing scales invokes annotation scaling of the tags and dimensions. This keeps the annotation synchronized with the display settings of the AEC objects. We will explore annotation scaling in more detail in future chapters. On the Chapter 2 – Sheet Layout tab, elevations and a schedule are also displayed (use the Quick View Layouts method again to switch back and forth between the two Layouts). Feel free to explore further in this drawing before continuing.

CAD MANAGER NOTE

Introduced in the previous version of ACA, it is also possible to link a Display Configuration to Annotation Scale. To do this, you must run the AECDWGSetup command (Application menu, **Utilities > Drawing Setup**). On the Scale tab, select a scale and then at the bottom choose the Display Configuration that you wish to associate. The effect of such a change will be that ACA will automatically change the Display Configuration when you choose a different scale in the drawing. Unfortunately, this only works one way. In other words, choosing a different scale will automatically change the current Display Configuration; choosing a different Display Configuration will not however change the scale.

View Direction Dependent Configurations

So far we have looked only at the changes that occur in a Plan (Top) view. Display control affects the display of objects in all views. A "View Direction Dependent" configuration is tied into the viewing direction in the drawing or the active viewport. This means that as the view direction is changed, the Display Configuration will automatically adjust what is displayed. View Direction Dependent Configurations contain a default setting and at least one other condition tied to any of the six orthographic views: Top, Bottom, Left, Right, Back and Front. A maximum of six special conditions can be specified; one for each orthographic view. There is always a setting configured for "Default" which will be displayed either when an orthographic view does not have its own override setting, or if a viewing angle other than the six orthographic views (a 3D view) is chosen.

1. On the Project Navigator Palette, click the Views tab and then double-click to open the *Floor Plan* View.

NOTE

If you left the Floor Plan View open previously, then this action will simply make that file active.

2. At the bottom of the drawing window, on the application status bar, click the Layout icon (this is directly to the left of the Quick View Layouts icon and is labeled View Direction Dependent).

   There will be four viewpoints with labels, all of which are currently empty.

3. Double-click in the top right viewport (labeled SE Isometric) to activate it.

   When activated, its border will become bold.

To determine which Display Configuration is currently active onscreen or within a particular viewport, simply glance at the Display Configuration pop-up menu that we used previously.

Note that Medium Detail is currently active.

4. On the View panel, choose **View, SE Isometric** from the View drop-down button (see Figure 2.10).

   In the default installation, the View panel is torn off and floating onscreen. If yours is not, look for it on the Home tab of the ribbon (see Chapter 1 for more details on the ribbon).

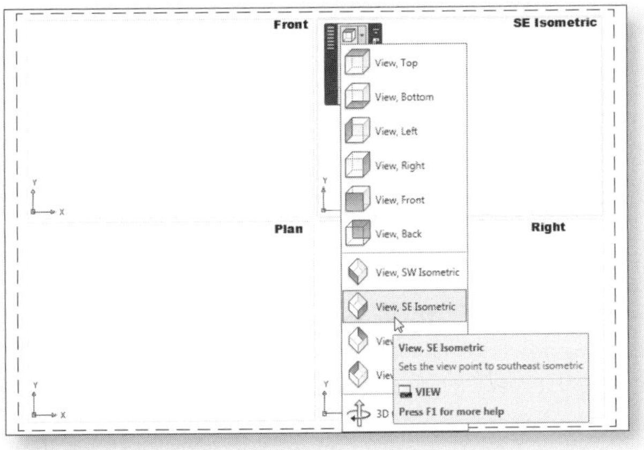

FIGURE 2.10 *Changing viewport view direction using either the View menu or the Views toolbar*

   A three-dimensional model of the drawing will appear.

5. Click in the top left viewport (labeled Front) to activate it.
6. On the View panel, choose **View, Front** from the View drop-down button.
7. Zoom in on the toilet room area (particularly the fixtures and the door swings).

The 2D Plan display graphics have been replaced with graphics appropriate for an elevation.

8. Click in each of the two remaining viewports and set the view direction to match the labels in the corner. (For the Plan viewport, set the view direction to Top.) Zoom in to get a better look at the changes.

The details may be difficult to make out in the elevation and model viewports. To make them easier to see, we can toggle the surface hatching off.

9. Click inside one of the Elevation viewports (Right or Front). At the bottom right corner of the screen on the Drawing Status bar, click the small Toggle Surface Hatch icon next to the Display Configuration pop-up (see Figure 2.11).

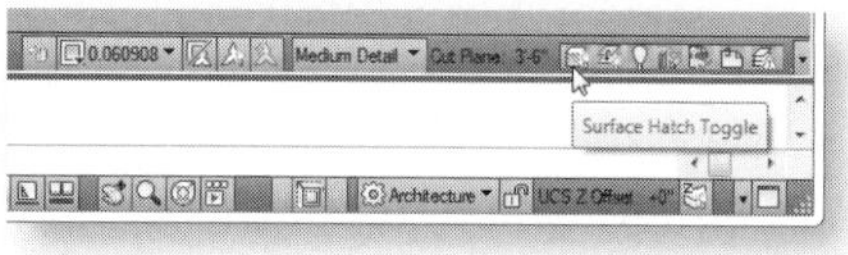

FIGURE 2.11 *Toggle the surface hatching off in the elevation viewports*

Notice that this affects both the Front and the Right viewports. The Display Set loaded by the Medium Detail Configuration is the same for all elevation views, which is why both Front and Right changed; but it is different for Model, which is why SE Isometric did not change. If you wish, you can activate the SE Isometric view and repeat the same process to toggle hatching off there as well.

Even with the hatching disabled, it may still be difficult to see clearly since in wireframe display we are seeing through several walls, which makes discerning certain details difficult. In this file are two Building Section Line objects. They are labeled with text leaders in the drawing. These objects can be used to generate 2D Section/Elevation objects (these are linked 2D drawings derived from the live 3D model) or Live Sections that actually cut away part of the model's display to reveal more clearly the internal objects. Both of these topics are explored in detail in Chapter 16. For now, let's just enable the Live Section display and see the effect on our model.

10. Click inside the SE Isometric view to make it active. Select the Section Line object labeled as Section Line 1, right-click, and choose **Enable Live Section**.

    Do not select the text or leader, but rather the rectangular object to which the leader points.

TIP

If you have trouble selecting the Section Line Object, try Regenerating the Model. Regenerate Model is on the View tab, on the Appearance panel. Click the drop-down button for Regenerate and choose Regenerate Model. Press ENTER **to complete the command.**

11. On the View panel, choose **Visual Styles, 3D Hidden** from the Visual Styles drop-down button (See Figure 2.12).

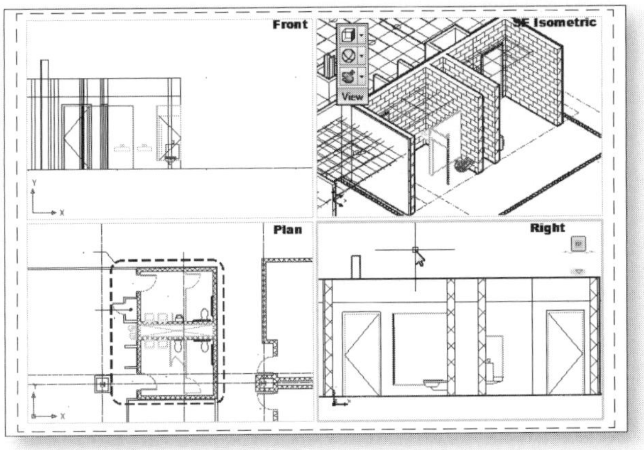

FIGURE 2.12 *Medium Detail Display Configuration from several viewpoints, including an enabled Live Section*

Note the change in the SE Isometric and Right viewports. Although each of these viewports is actually displaying a different Display Set, the Live Section operates at the Display Configuration level. Therefore, all Medium Detail views are affected, including the Front viewport. We do not, however, see any changes to the Top viewport. This is because Live Sections do not display in plan views regardless of the display settings. If you wish to test the behavior witnessed here, try loading High Detail (or any other Display Configuration) in the SE Isometric viewport. Notice that the model will no longer be sectioned. There is also a second Section Line object. Right-click Section Line 1 again, choose **Disable Live Section** to restore the complete model, and then repeat the Enable Live Section steps on the other section line (Section Line 2). If you wish, you can also enable both at the same time. If you wish to see the sectioned portion of the model displayed transparent, right-click the section line after Live Section has been enabled, and choose **Toggle Sectioned Body Display**. This will show the sectioned portion in a transparent gray material.

12. Double-click outside the viewports to toggle back to paper space (or type **PS** and then press ENTER).

    None of the viewport edges should be bold anymore.

As you can see, with a View Direction Dependent configuration, simply changing the viewing direction onscreen will load a different graphical display (Set) of the model.

Fixed View Direction Display Configurations

A Display Configuration need not be view direction dependent. It can be assigned a single fixed configuration. In this case, changing viewing direction has no effect on the Display Configuration. There are two Fixed View Display Configurations provided with the default template files. The "Plan Only" and the "Diagnostic" Display Configurations. As its name implies, the Plan Only configuration shows a two-dimensional plan display from any viewing direction.

13. On the drawing status bar, click the Display Configuration pop-up menu.
14. At the "Select viewports or RETURN for Paper Space viewport" prompt, select all four viewports (click the light blue edges, or use a crossing window selection), and then press ENTER.
15. From the Display Configuration pop-up that appears, choose **Plan Only**.

If all views do not "flatten" to 2D graphics, type REA and then press ENTER. (This regenerates all viewports.)

If you still have the hidden visual style active, choose Visual Styles, 2D Wireframe from the View panel.

Notice that regardless of the active view direction, a simple 2D plan is displayed. In addition, notice that the Live Section display is no longer active.

16. On the drawing status bar, click the Display Configuration pop-up menu.
17. At the "Select viewports or RETURN for Paper Space viewport" prompt, select all four viewports (click the light blue edges, or use a crossing window selection), and then press ENTER.
18. From the Display Configuration pop-up that appears, choose **Diagnostic**.

    Notice that regardless of the active view direction, the model will use the same configuration and as with Plan Only, most (but not all) objects are displayed using 2D Representations.

The Diagnostic Configuration also shows all objects using a single Display Set regardless of view direction. It uses special display modes for several important objects that help you analyze object relationships and troubleshoot problems in the drawing. For instance, Walls are displayed with both the Graph and Sketch Display Representations active, but not the normal Plan or Model Representations. Both of these modes display useful information about the Walls that is not likely to be printed; Graph displays Wall cleanup information (see Chapter 9 for more information), and Sketch shows the Wall's baseline, centerline and direction. All of these terms are explored later in Chapters 4 and 10. When Diagnostic is active, you will also notice that each of the Door and Room Tags has a small curved line attached to another object. These are called "Tag Anchors" and are usually invisible, since we typically don't want them to print. However, they are very useful when you are trying to verify data within Schedule Tags or troubleshoot problems with tag attachments and Schedules. Schedules and Tags are covered in Chapter 15; anchors are discussed later. Another feature of the Diagnostic configuration is the "Decomposed" Display Representation for Spaces. This Representation shows triangulated dimensions useful in creating proof of area reports required by building codes in certain countries. To see this, you need to thaw the Space layer as noted earlier. If you do, be sure to freeze it again before continuing.

It is not important to completely understand the use of the Diagnostic Display Configuration at this time. The point of this exercise is to show the differences between a View Direction Dependent Configuration and a Fixed View Configuration. In the next sequence, we will learn how to set up our own Display Configurations.

19. Click the Model icon on the application status bar to return to model space for the next sequence.

Use the Display Manager

The Display Manager is the primary interface for managing the display system. The Display Manager can be a little overwhelming but fortunately you do not need to visit it often. In this lesson, you will learn the basics of the Display Manager. Our aim in the steps that follow is to give a glimpse at the potential this powerful tool offers. What is important here is attaining a general understanding of the concepts presented. In day-to-day production, you are unlikely to need to visit the Display Manager very often if at all. This heading and the next can safely be considered optional if you wish. More likely you will use the tools and techniques covered later starting in the "Edit Display Properties using the Properties Palette" topic.

1. On the Project Navigator palette, click the Constructs tab and then double-click to open the *Walls* file.

This file looks similar to the *Floor Plan* view file (which references it) but the Space objects are displayed here as solid shading. In the *Floor Plan* file, the A-Area-Spce Layer is frozen rendering Spaces invisible.

2. On the Manage tab, on the Style & Display panel, click the ***Display Manager*** button.
3. Expand (click the plus sign (+) next to) Configurations.

   Study the icons next to the various configurations in the list (see Figure 2.13).

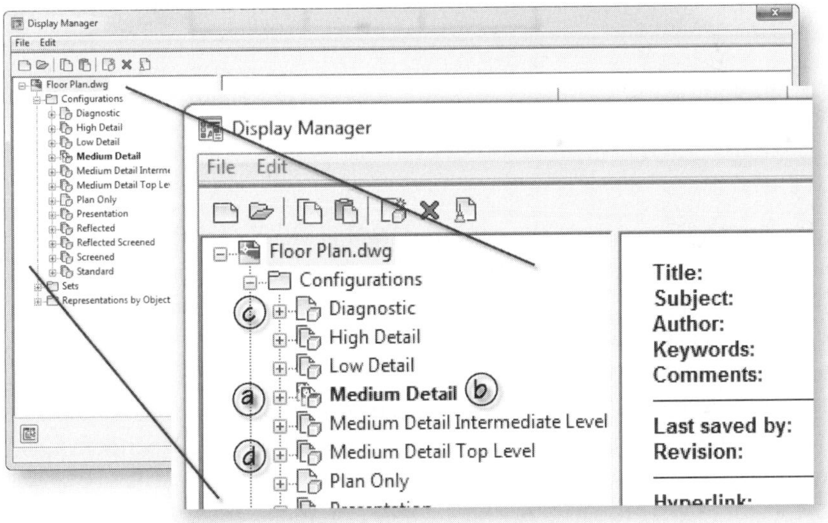

FIGURE 2.13 *Understanding the icons used for configurations*

a. **AutoCAD Drawing Icon superimposed on icon**—Indicates the default display configuration for the drawing (all of the icons have one or more turned corner pages, this one has the AutoCAD icon on the page). The default is used automatically when creating new layouts. To set the default for the drawing, right-click a configuration in the Display Manager and choose **Set as Drawing Default**. In the default templates, Medium Detail is the default.
b. **Bold text**—Indicates that this configuration is active in the current viewport. In Figure 2.13, Medium Detail is current in the active viewport.
c. **A single sheet of paper icon**—Indicates that it is a *Fixed View* Display Configuration. In Figure 2.13, look carefully at the Plan Only and Diagnostic icons. They are both Fixed. (See the "Fixed View Direction Display Configurations" topic.)
d. **A stack of sheets icon**—Indicates that it is a *View Direction Dependent* Display Configuration. In Figure 2.13, all Configurations except Plan Only and Diagnostic are View Direction Dependent. (See the "View Direction Dependent Configurations" topic.)

The Configuration Tab

4. Click on the High Detail Display Configuration in the tree view at left to select it.
5. On the right side of the Display Manager, click the Configuration tab (see Figure 2.14).

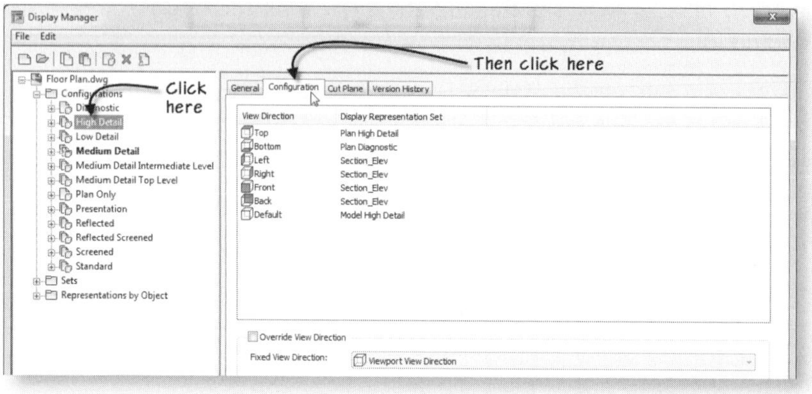

FIGURE 2.14 *A View Direction Dependent Display Configuration has multiple entries*

The Configuration tab lists each of the six orthographic views and also contains an entry for Default under the heading View Direction. Next to each view direction, a Display Representation Set can be loaded. Display Representation Sets are described in detail later. If there is an entry *only* next to the Default, the Display Configuration is fixed. If more than one view direction contains a Set entry, then the configuration is View Direction Dependent (see the "View Direction Dependent Configurations" topic). In this case, we can see that High Detail is a View Direction Dependent Display Configuration, because there is more than one entry.

6. Click on Plan Only in the tree view at the left to select it.

Notice the difference on the Configuration tab. Here, there is only an entry next to the Default view direction. This makes the Plan Only Display Configuration a Fixed Display Configuration (see Figure 2.15). You will also notice a check mark in the Override View Direction checkbox. This allows you to control the behavior of multi-view blocks displayed in this configuration. Multi-view blocks are AEC objects with user-defined graphics. They can be built to display differently from different viewing directions like other AEC objects. See the "Create a Custom Multi-View Block" topic in Chapter 11 for more information on multi-view blocks. When a Configuration is set to "Fixed View Direction" it only displays one of the display blocks in the Multi-View Block—the one normally displayed only in Top view will display all the time in this case.

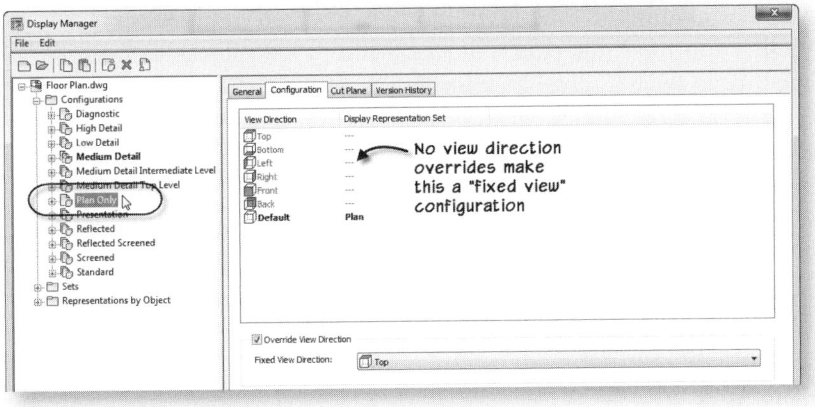

FIGURE 2.15 *A Fixed Display Configuration contains only a Default entry and no others*

There are a few other tabs for Display Configurations: General, Cut Plane and Version History. The General tab contains simply the names and description of the configuration. You can use this tab to edit those values if you wish. Many objects (Walls, Windows, Curtain Walls, etc.) use a cut plane when determining what to draw in plan displays. The Cut Plane tab establishes a single cut plane height that is used by all objects within the drawing. This "Global Cut Plane" is used to help synchronize all of these objects relative to a baseline height in the drawing. If you click the Cut Plane tab, you will see that most of the Configurations use a Cut Plane of 3'-6" [1400] except the two Reflected ones, which use 7'-6" [2300]. We will discuss this feature more in Chapter 8. For now, we will leave the default settings as is. Version History is used in conjunction with the Project Standards feature covered in Chapter 8.

7. Click on the Medium Detail Configuration in the tree view at left to select it and then click the Configuration tab.

In this particular configuration, the Top view direction is configured to use the **Plan** Display Set. (Display Sets determine which AEC objects display and how; see the "Understanding Sets" heading discussed later.) This indicates that whenever the drawing is viewed from the Top, the Plan Display Representation Set will be loaded in the viewport. Next to each of the Left, Right, Front and Back view directions in the Medium Detail Configuration, the **Section_Elev** set is loaded. Plan Diagnostic is used if the drawing is viewed from Bottom. Finally, if none of these conditions is met (the view direction is set to something other than Top, Left, Right, Front, Back or Bottom) the default set will be loaded; in this case, **Model** (see Figure 2.16).

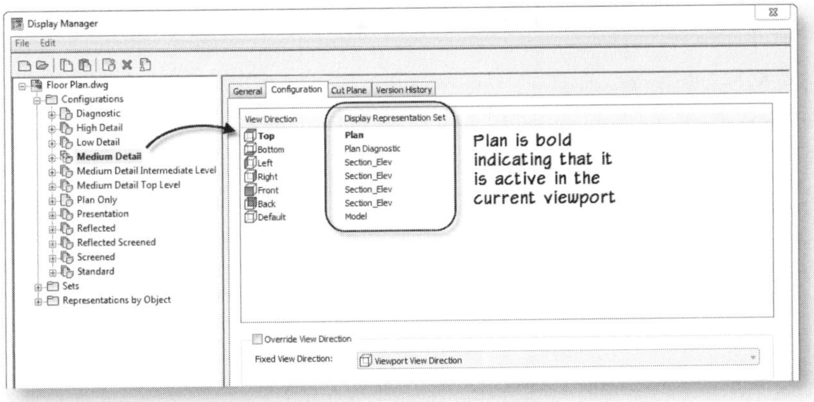

FIGURE 2.16 *Examine each of the assignments in the Medium Detail Configuration*

Note also that this Configuration (and High Detail mentioned earlier) does not override the View Direction for Multi-View Blocks. Multi-View Blocks will display as they are designed to showing a plan block for top, an elevation block for front, back or side views and a 3D model block for 3D views. As you can see from the settings explored here, Display Configurations simply use the viewing direction(s) to decide which Display Sets to show. We saw this behavior interactively in the tutorials discussed previously, but seeing the settings here hopefully helps solidify the concept. Nothing in these settings however tells a Door how to look different than a Wall. What then determines why the objects change their graphics when we switch? Let's have a look at Sets to begin to learn the answer.

Understanding Sets

As defined in the earlier heading, "The Display System Tool Set" determines which objects are displayed onscreen and how (meaning what Display Representation(s) each should use).

1. Continuing in the Display Manager, expand the Sets folder (see Figure 2.17).

   This will reveal all of the Display Representation Sets (or just "Sets") available in this drawing.

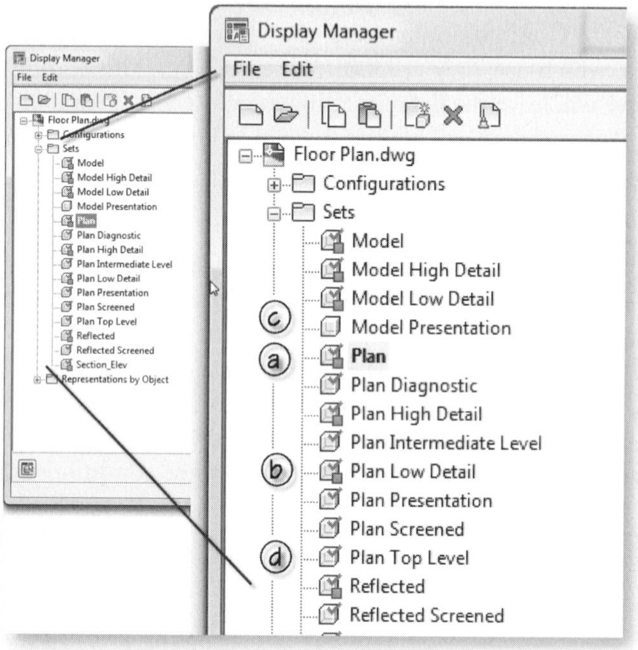

FIGURE 2.17 *Expand the Sets folder*

As noted earlier, the Plan set is the active display set in the drawing. This is evident both on the Configuration tab of the Medium Detail Display Configuration and by the fact that Plan in the Sets list earlier is bold. The Model tab (model space) is currently set to Top view in the drawing.

Notice the icons next to each Set name:

a. **Bold text**—Indicates that this is the current Set. In Figure 2.17, Plan is current.

b. **A green check mark in an icon with green square in the corner**—Indicates that the Set is "in use" by one or more Configurations. In Figure 2.17, several appear this way. The green square indicates that these are default Sets that are auto-created by the software and cannot be purged.

c. **A small box without a check mark and no green square**—Means that the Set is not currently being used by a Configuration and can be purged. In Figure 2.17, Model Presentation is the only Set not in use and purgable.

d. **A red check mark in an icon without shading**—Indicates that the Set is "in use" by one or more Configurations. The lack of green square indicates that these have been duplicated from default Sets. In Figure 2.17, Sets like Plan Top Level, Plan Screened and Plan Diagnostic appear this way.

MANAGER NOTE CAD

Like most named objects in AutoCAD, Configurations and Sets can be purged from a drawing only if they are unused. Highlight the item you wish to delete, and then click the Purge icon at the top of the Display Manager dialog box (it looks like a little broom). Be cautious, as no dialog will appears to confirm deletion. Purged items can be restored with Undo. Please note: the Sets with the small green square in the corner cannot be purged even if they are unused. These are default Sets that are auto-created by the software.

2. Click on the Plan Set in the tree view at left to select it.

Just like the Configuration folder seen earlier, each Set has four tabs. The General tab serves the same purpose as it did for Configurations. You can use it to change Name and Description. (Default Sets, the ones with the small green square, cannot be renamed.) The Version History tab is used in conjunction with the Project Standards feature covered in Chapter 8. There is also a Display Representation Control tab and a Display Options tab. Let's take a look at the Display Representation Control tab.

3. On the right side of the dialog box, click the Display Representation Control tab (see Figure 2.18).

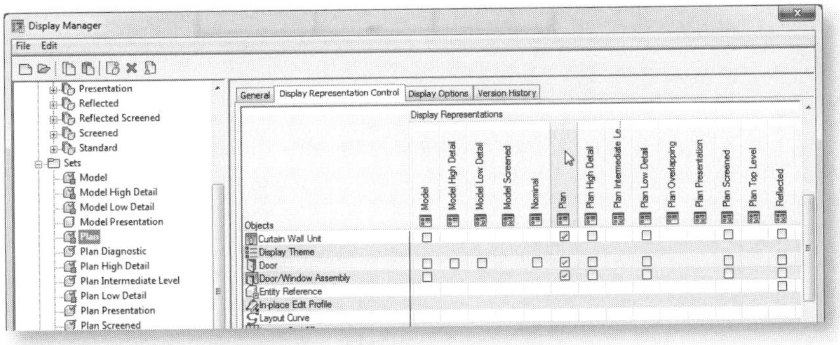

FIGURE 2.18 *Access the display control settings of Sets*

4. Scroll both horizontally and vertically on the right side of the dialog box.

   If necessary, resize the Display Manager window to make the scroll bars appear.

TIP

It is usually a good idea to stretch out the size of this dialog as large as your monitor will allow.

On the left of the Display Representation Control tab is an alphabetical list of all AEC objects. At the top are all of the Display Representations (consolidated from all objects) within the current drawing. Notice that a Set is comprised of a collection of checkboxes. Objects that have one or more of their Display Representations checked in this Set are visible onscreen or in the current viewport. Objects with no boxes checked are invisible.

> **NOTE**
>
> **Not all Display Representations will be available for all object types. If there is no box at all for a particular Display Representation, it means that Representation is not available for that object type.**

For example, perhaps you have decided that Spaces, while very valuable for attaching Room Tags, holding Room Finish data and for their contribution to sections, are not very useful in plans. Using the power of Sets, we can simply turn off Space objects in the current Display Set (Plan) while leaving them displayed in the other Sets such as Model.

5. Locate the Space entry, and click on it.

   This will highlight the complete row in blue.

6. Clear the checkbox in the Plan column (see Figure 2.19).

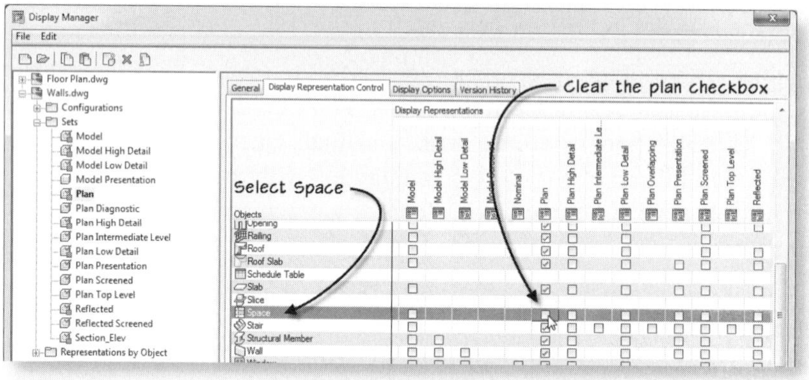

FIGURE 2.19 *Turning off the Spaces in the current view*

7. Click OK to accept changes and return to the drawing.

   There will be a slight delay as the drawing regenerates the current display. Notice that the Spaces (the solid hatching inside of each room) have disappeared (see Figure 2.20).

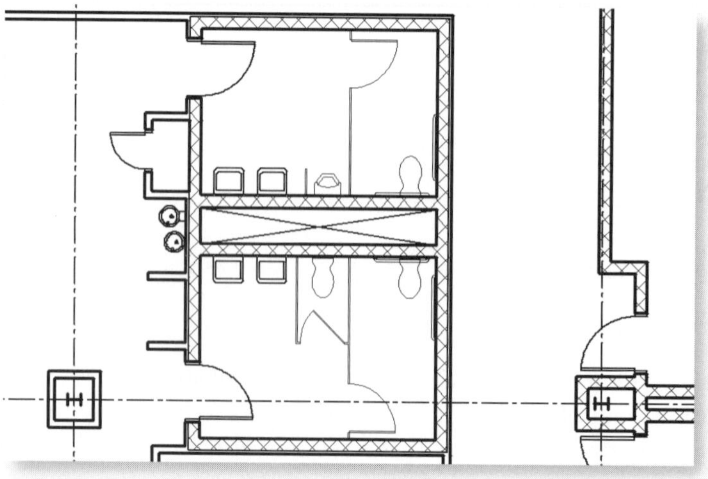

FIGURE 2.20 *The Walls file with Spaces turned off*

It is important to note that this technique is very different from simply freezing the Space object's layer as seen in the *Floor Plan* View file. Had we frozen the layer, Spaces would be invisible in *all* Display Configurations. This might be all right for Display Configurations like Medium and High Detail, but it would not be acceptable for Presentation. See for yourself; try loading other Display Configurations now.

8. Load the **Presentation** Display Configuration using the technique covered earlier in the "Loading a Display Configuration" heading.

   Notice that the Spaces appear here, shaded with solid color fills. Had you frozen the A-Area-Spce Layer like we saw in the *Floor Plan* file previously, they would have been invisible here as well. Try it if you like to see for yourself.

9. Load the **High Detail** Display Configuration.

Notice that the Spaces are still visible in this (and most other) Display Configuration as well. If you load Plan Only, the Spaces will disappear. This is because the Plan Only Configuration and Medium Detail both use the Plan Set.

10. Return to the Display Manager (Manage tab).
11. Expand Sets again and select Plan High Detail (the active set, indicated by bold).

If you made another Configuration active before returning to Display Manager, you do not need to cancel. Expand Configurations, right-click High Detail and choose **Set to Current Viewport**.

12. Highlight Space on the right side again.

    Scroll over and take note of the check mark that appears in the Plan High Detail column.

Although we cleared the Plan Display Representation for Spaces in Medium Detail, there is still a check mark in Plan High Detail for the now active High Detail Display Set. This is why Spaces still display in High Detail.

13. With Space still selected, clear Plan High Detail and instead put a check mark in the Plan Screened column (see Figure 2.21).

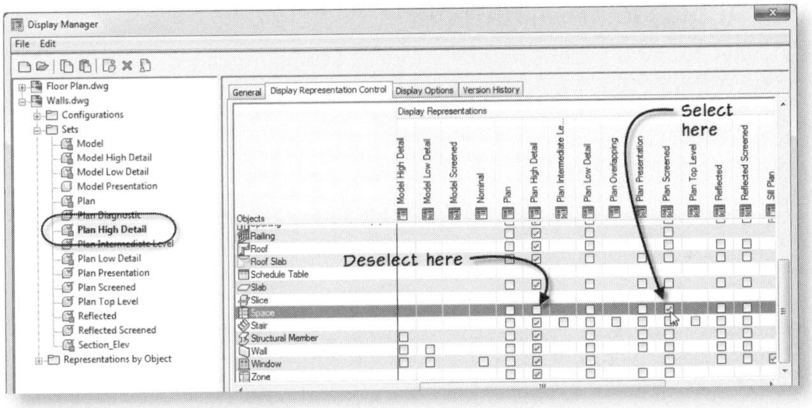

FIGURE 2.21 *Making Spaces display using the Plan Screened Display Representation*

14. Click OK to accept changes and return to the drawing.

Spaces now display using the Plan Screened Display Representation. In model space the hatching lines will appear solid black. To see the halftone effect, from the Application menu, choose **Print > Plot Preview** (see Figure 2.22). When you have finished previewing, press ESC to return to the drawing.

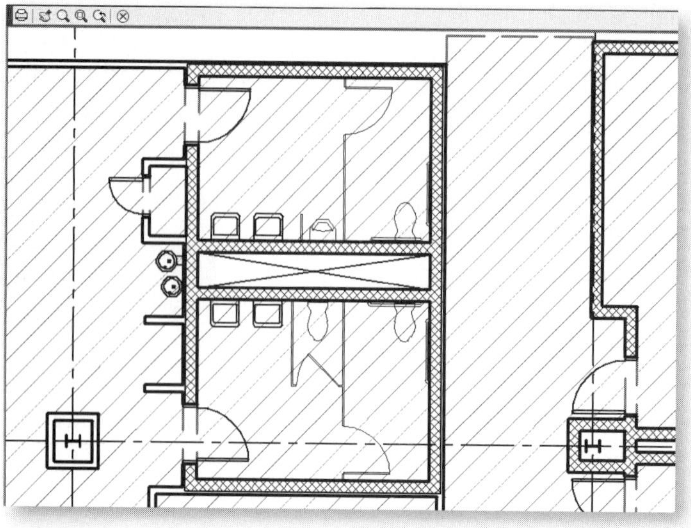

FIGURE 2.22 *Spaces displayed with 50% halftone in a plot preview*

This simple exercise shows the versatility of ACA object display. With the simple selection of a different display mode in the current Set (or none at all), the drawing can take on a dramatically different look. Of the two techniques shown here, changing the display of Spaces to screened is a better option than simply turning them off altogether. If you do turn them off as we did in the first example, you will need to switch to a different Display Configuration such as High Detail or Low Detail whenever you wish to edit Space objects, because when they are turned off, you will not be able to select or edit them in Medium Detail. For this reason, you may wish to return to the Display Manager and turn the Spaces back on in the Plan Set again. Also note that in Medium and High Detail, Spaces use a solid fill pattern by default. This is not governed by the Set. Rather these are style overrides applied to the Spaces themselves. You will see examples of style overrides later.

Understanding Display Representations

Objects in ACA have many different display modes. These are called "Display Representations" (Reps). Each Representation corresponds to a particular drawing type such as Plan or Elevation.

1. Return to the Display Manager.
2. Expand (click the plus sign (+) next to) Representations by Object (see Figure 2.23). This will reveal the complete list of ACA objects.

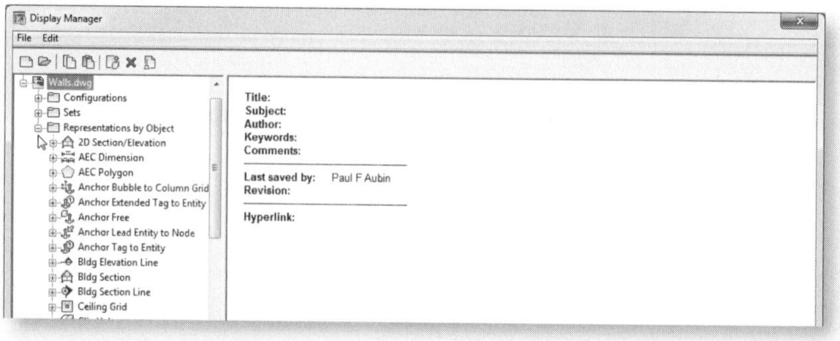

FIGURE 2.23 *Expand the Representations by Object list*

3. From the list of objects in the tree view at left, select Space (see Figure 2.24).

This will reveal a list of all the Display Representations available for this object type in a column on the right side with all of the available Sets listed across the top right. Checkboxes again appear indicating specifically which Space object Representations are utilized in each Set.

An icon appears next to each Display Representation. ACA includes several "built-in" Display Representations. These are part of the core program and can be configured but not renamed or deleted. Additional user-defined Representations can be created to meet needs not addressed by the default Reps. You can create user-defined Representations by duplicating any of the default Reps and renaming the duplicate. User-defined Representations can later be renamed and, provided they are not being used, deleted. A couple of the Reps available for Spaces (and several other object types in this drawing) are in fact user-defined Reps (see Figure 2.24).

- **A "properties" icon**—Indicates that it is one of the default (permanent) representations.
- **A "properties" icon with a portrait icon in the corner**—Indicates that it is a user-defined representation.

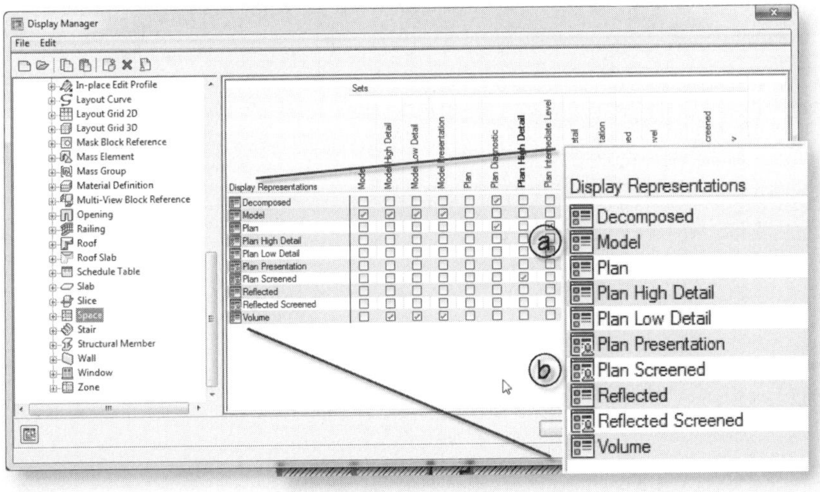

FIGURE 2.24 *Icons differ for default permanent Display Representations and user-created ones*

> MANAGER NOTE
>
> To create a user-defined Display Representation, you must duplicate an existing one that is similar to the one you wish to create. Select the Rep that you wish to duplicate, right-click it and choose **Duplicate**. Give the new Rep a unique name. As with all named objects, choose your name carefully. Once you have created the custom Display Rep, you can configure its parameters and assign it to a Set. Usually, you will also create a custom Set and Configuration along with your new Rep, but this is not required. See the steps that follow for information on building custom Sets and Configurations.

4. Click Cancel to return to the drawing without making changes.

Edit Display Properties Using the Properties Palette

The parameters of a Display Representation control all of the individual subcomponents of each AEC object. For instance, Doors have the door panel, the frame and the swing parameters, among others. The specific subcomponents that an object type contains may vary for each of its Reps. For instance, the Space objects that we have been working with here have a Floor component and a Ceiling component. However, these components are accessible only within the Model Display Representation. In the Plan Representation for Spaces, you will instead see several boundary components; several hatch components and a few others associated with the cut plane. This means that, although the Configurations and Sets determine which objects are visible and invisible onscreen, it is the Display Representations that determine exactly how those objects will be drawn graphically. If we wish to edit the way a particular object or objects in the drawing behaves, we often find it easier to edit the object directly. In this case we would want to work with Space objects.

5. Select the Wall object between the toilet room and the corridor onscreen.
6. Right-click and choose **Properties** (or press `CTRL + 1`) and then click the Display tab.
7. At the bottom left corner of the palette, click the Select Component icon.
8. Click on the hatching inside of one of the Walls (see Figure 2.25).

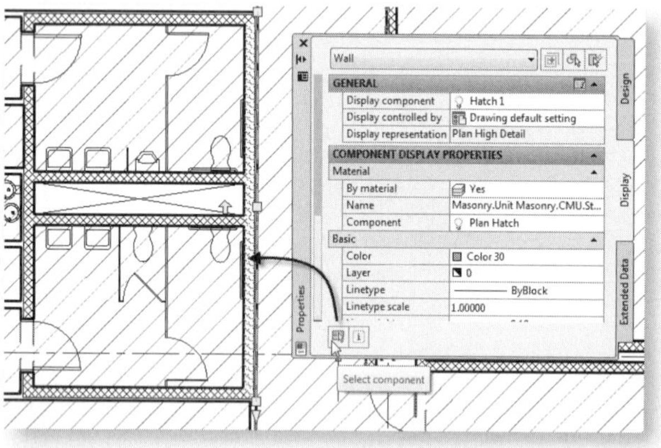

FIGURE 2.25 *Use the Select Component icon to select the Wall hatching*

Notice that the palette will reflect the selection of the hatching by showing that the Hatch 1 component is selected at the top in the Display component list. Beneath this, all of the parameters of the Hatch 1 component such as its visibility, color, material, etc. are listed.

9. Open the Display component list, and then click the lightbulb icon next to Hatch 1.

   A confirmation dialog will appear indicating that you are modifying the drawing default display level—click Yes (See Figure 2.26).

Notice that the hatching in all Walls has disappeared. Notice also that hatching in all Walls has disappeared regardless of their individual styles. This was what the confirmation dialog was indicating. When you edit display properties at the drawing default level, all objects of that kind are affected regardless of style. In this case, it did not matter if the Walls were interior or exterior, corridor walls or toilet room walls; none displays hatching anymore.

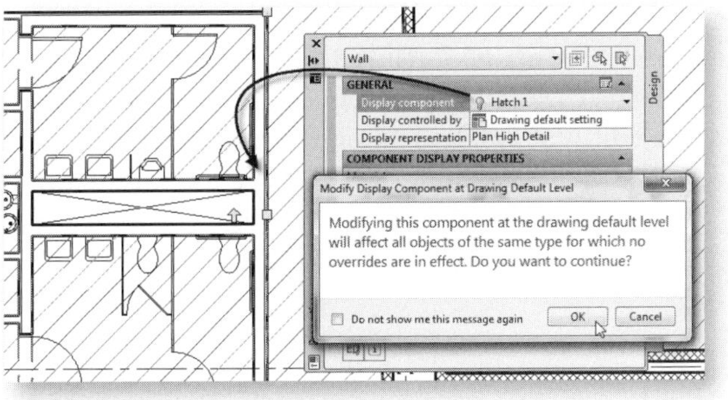

FIGURE 2.26 *Walls no longer display hatching regardless of style*

10. Press ESC to deselect the Wall or right-click and choose **Deselect All.**

Apply a Style Override

Edits to Representations can be applied at three levels: the drawing default, style or object level override. Sets (discussed previously) on the other hand can only be edited in the Display Manager and their effects are global. Let's explore the next level of display manipulation: the style override. Suppose that we wanted to restore the hatching to just the Walls surrounding the toilet rooms.

11. Select the toilet room Wall at the top of the plan.

    If you closed the Properties palette, right-click and choose **Properties** and then click the Display tab.

The word *None* will appear next to the Display component. Beneath this, next to the Display controlled by, it will read Drawing default setting.

12. Click on Drawing default setting and then choose **Wall Style:CMU-8 Furring** from the pop-up list.
13. In the "Add Style Override" dialog, click OK.

This dialog is similar to the one discussed previously and is indicating that we are adding a style override. This means that the change that we are applying will affect only this Wall and others that use the style CMU-8 Furring.

14. From the Display component list, click the lightbulb icon next to **Hatch 1 (CMU)** to turn it back on (see Figure 2.27).
15. Click OK in the confirmation dialog.

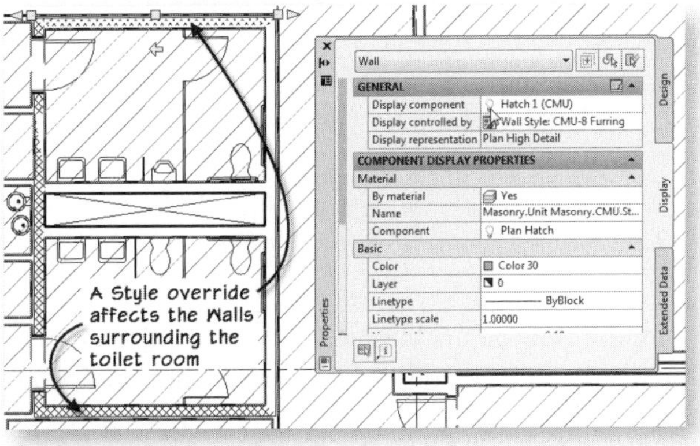

FIGURE 2.27 *Turn the hatching back on for a style affects several Walls*

The hatching will return for the Wall you selected as well as others around the toilet room. This is because they all share the same style. As you will see later in this chapter, a style is a collection of parameters that you apply to an object or objects in your drawing. If you edit the style, the edit will apply to all objects associated with that style. That is, several Walls regained their hatching even though you selected only one to make the edit.

16. Press ESC to deselect the Wall or right-click and choose **Deselect All**.

Apply an Object Override

So far we have seen two of the three levels available to Display Representations. When we turned off the Hatch 1 component at the drawing default level earlier, it applied to all Wall objects in the drawing regardless of their style. Next we applied a Style override to the Walls around the toilet room. However, the Wall adjacent to the corridor did not receive hatching from this change. This is because it uses a different style, even though it appears graphically similar. Let's now apply an Object Override to this Wall to make it match its neighbors. When you apply an object override, it makes that object completely unique: no longer using the parameters of the drawing default nor any attached style overrides.

17. Select the Wall on the right side of the toilet room.

    If you closed the Properties palette, right-click, choose Properties, and then click the Display tab.

18. Click on Drawing default setting and then choose **This object** from the pop-up list.
19. In the confirmation dialog, click OK.

At this point you have seen several of these confirmation dialogs. If you wish, you can select the "Don't show me this message again" checkbox to avoid seeing these messages in the future. However, leaving them enabled can serve as a helpful reminder as to the level at which the display properties are applied. The choice is up to you.

20. Toggle on the lightbulb icon for **Hatch 1 (CMU)** (see Figure 2.28).

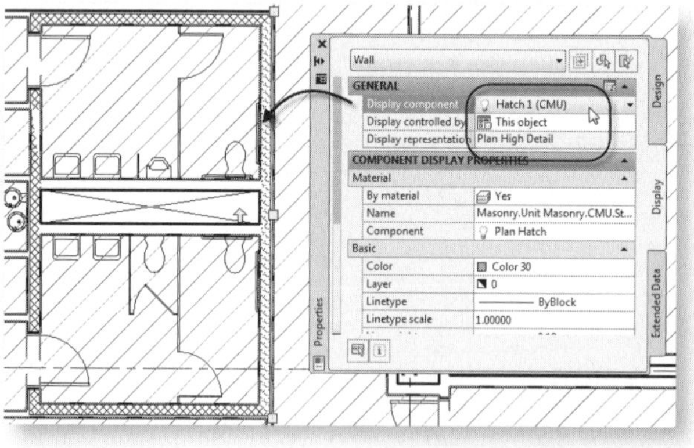

FIGURE 2.28 *Understanding the relationship of Configuration to Representation*

Notice that this time the change applies only to the Wall you selected. At this point, this Wall will no longer respond to display edits made to the style. Furthermore, none of the Walls around the toilet room will respond to edits made to the drawing default of Walls.

21. Repeat the object override process on the small wall on the left side of the men's toilet room at the back of the closet.

At this point, hatching should show in the Walls surrounding the toilet room only. The exterior wall to the far right of the plan will also have some hatching. This is because the style used there has more than one hatch component unlike most of the other Walls in this file. Hatch 1 corresponds to CMU in the Walls we have been modifying. In the exterior Wall Hatch 1 corresponds to the brick. If you wish, you can experiment further to turn off the CMU hatching for the exterior. Think about at what level you should apply the edit: drawing default, style or object. Hint: all exterior Walls on the right side share the same style.

There is one additional point which is very important to note. The three levels of display that we are witnessing here occur for *each* Display Representation. This means that if you change the Display Configuration of the drawing to something other than its current Medium Detail, everything will potentially change. This means that you can use Drawing Default for some Reps, Style Override for others and Object Override for still others — all on the same object and without the need to change layers!

22. From the Drawing status bar, choose **Low Detail** from the Display Configuration pop-up.

    Study the results.

23. Try another configuration such as Medium Detail or Presentation.

Notice that all Walls including the ones we modified now display the same again. This is because in the other configurations, which use different Display Sets (see above), which in turn use alternate Representations for Wall objects have no style or object overrides. If you would like to follow the logic yourself, click one of the Walls, and then look at the Display tab of the Properties palette. In the High Detail configuration, the top Wall has a style override and uses the Plan High Detail Display Representation (see the left side of Figure 2.29). The Presentation configuration has no overrides and uses the Plan Presentation Representation (see the right side of Figure 2.29). Regardless of which configuration you load, if you change the current Display Configuration back to High Detail, your previously applied Style and object overrides will re-display onscreen.

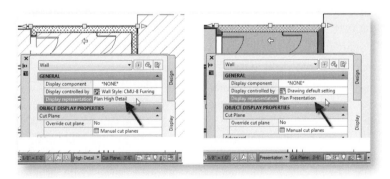

FIGURE 2.29 *Understanding the relationship of Configuration to Representation*

You can experiment further if you wish. Repeat any of these procedures to get a better sense of how all the parts fit together.

24. When you have finished experimenting, please reload the Medium Detail Configuration.

CAD MANAGER NOTE

Much of the configuration of the display system is best left in the realm of office standards. Poll your team and try to determine what Configurations and associated Sets they will require. Try to use the offerings provided out of the box as much as possible. Set up any custom displays required and save them in the office standard templates. (Again, using the default templates as a starting point is an excellent way to begin.) This will greatly enhance overall office productivity. You should seek to create the majority of custom user-defined Display Representations that are required by your team as well. However, individual configuration of the properties of each Display Representation will most likely be tweaked on a regular basis by the users as project needs dictate. Procedures and reasons for doing so are covered throughout the remainder of this book as circumstances dictate. If you decide that you need to customize your templates and include custom Display Configurations and Sets, the topic is covered in more great detail in Chapter 6 of *Autodesk Architectural Desktop: An Advanced Implementation Guide* by Paul F. Aubin and Matt Dillon.

OBJECT STYLES

Virtually all AEC objects use styles to define global object parameters. These can include both physical and display parameters. (We saw examples of style-based display parameters in the previous exercise.) Much like text and dimension styles in core AutoCAD, object styles control all of the formatting and configuration of the object. Using styles is a powerful way to control the behavior of objects and quickly make global changes when the design changes. For instance, at any time during project design, a user could simply go back to a style describing a wall and make a modification, such as changing the size of the concrete block from 6" [150] to 8" [200] or as we saw previously, turn on or off certain components. The change would be reflected throughout the drawing on all wall objects that were associated with that wall style. In most cases, it is best to think of styles as "types" in the same way we commonly distinguish wall types and door types in a construction document set. Each type needed in the CD set would therefore have a corresponding object style.

Working with Styles and Content Browser

Following is an overview of key object style features:

- Editing parameters in the style globally updates all objects within the drawing referencing that style.
- Styles can control physical parameters, display parameters and data property set information used for schedules.
- Styles can be shared between drawings using the tools available in the Style Manager, Tool Catalogs and Tool Palettes.

Collections of similar styles are saved in individual drawing files. These drawings can be part of a particular project or a central library accessible to all people in the office. If you create a style in one drawing and wish to use it in another, you can do so easily by saving the style to a tool catalog. This catalog can be accessed by other users and its tools used in any drawing file, making your style easy to use across multiple project files or throughout the entire office. You can also access a large collection of out-of-the-box tool catalogs provided with ACA. Tool catalogs are accessed from the Content Browser. Content Browser is a Webbrowser–like tool that is designed specifically to browse, store and access ACA Styles and Content items. Before going to Content Browser, it is useful to determine what Styles if any are contained within the current drawing file.

Styles in the Current Drawing

It is easy to determine the name of a particular style that is applied to an existing object within the drawing. To do so, we simply click to select the object in the drawing editor and then view the listing for Style on the Properties palette. You can continue on with the same project loaded from the previous tutorial. If you did not complete the previous tutorial, follow the steps in the "Install the CD Files and Load Sample File" heading discussed previously to install and load the dataset.

1. On the Project Navigator Palette, click the Constructs tab and then double-click to open the *Walls* Construct.

NOTE

If you left the *Walls* Construct open from the previous tutorial, then this action will simply make that file active.

Before continuing, load the Medium Detail Configuration. If you viewed the model in 3D, be sure to return to **View, Top** and **Visual Styles, 2D Wireframe** from the View panel to reset to a simple 2D view.

2. Zoom in on the Toilet Rooms.
3. Select any Wall within the drawing.
4. Right-click and choose **Properties**.
5. On the Properties palette, click the Design tab.

   Toward the top, take note of the Style name.

   You can use the same technique to see what other styles are available within the drawing.
6. With the Wall still selected, click on the Style list on the Properties palette.

   This will activate a pop-up menu for styles.
7. Open the Menu and view the list of styles (see Figure 2.30).

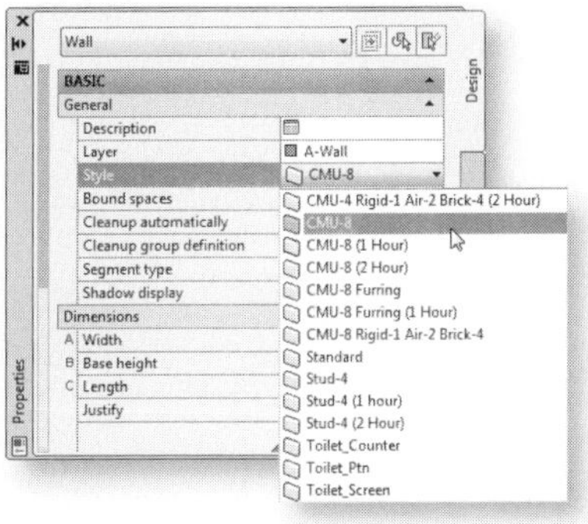

FIGURE 2.30 *View the list of Wall styles contained in the current drawing*

All of the styles on this list are currently available within the current drawing. If you need a style that is not on this list, you will need to create or import it. See the "Working with the Content Browser" heading next for more information on importing styles, and refer to Chapter 10 for more information on creating and editing styles. You can choose a different style from the list to change the style of the selected Wall to a different style that already exists in this drawing.

8. With the Wall still selected, click on the Style list on the Properties palette.
9. From the Style list, choose a different style.

Note the change to the Wall within the drawing.

10. Undo the change by repeating the same steps and then choosing the original name, or press CTRL + Z to undo.

    The same technique could be used for any architectural object in the drawing. Try it on the Doors or Windows if you like. Be sure to undo any changes when you are done experimenting.

Work with the Content Browser

1. On the Home tab, on the Build panel, click the drop-down button on the Tools button.
2. Choose the Content Browser tool (or press CTRL + 4).

The Content Browser window will open. Content Browser is very similar to a Web browser. It is organized in two panes. Navigation is on the left and the content is displayed on the right. Standard Web browser navigation buttons (Back, Forward, Refresh, etc.) are arrayed across the top of the left pane. Action buttons for creating new catalogs and such are placed at the bottom of the left pane. In the Library home (the main page) there are two such buttons: one creates a new catalog and the other modifies the Content Browser view options (see Figure 2.31).

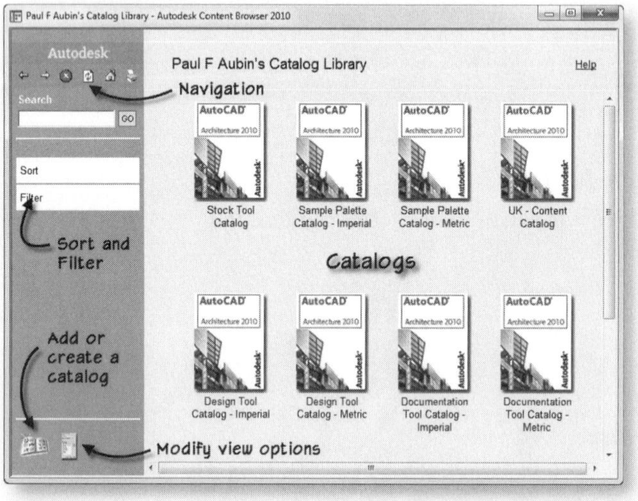

FIGURE 2.31 *The Content Browser main home page (specific catalogs vary depending on installed options)*

AutoCAD Architecture ships with a vast library of premade content. Content items include object styles, symbols and annotation routines. All of these items can be accessed from the Content Browser. The following is a list of each of the catalogs provided with a brief description.

NOTE

The exact list of Catalogs available in your Content Browser varies depending on the options chosen during installation of AutoCAD Architecture 2010. If you performed a Full Install of the US English version, the following Tool Catalogs should be available:

- **Stock Tool Catalog**—Contains all the standard tools that come with ACA. There is a tool for each architectural object type and several other core commands. These tools do not reference any particular unit system.
- **Sample Palette Catalog – Imperial**—Contains four categories corresponding to the four basic tool palette groups installed in the standard out-of-the-box installation. Each of these categories contains a backup copy of the installed palettes belonging to the Imperial units Installation. The palettes contain a mix of stock tools, styles and documentation content.
- **Sample Palette Catalog – Metric**—Contains four categories corresponding to the four basic tool palette groups installed in the standard out-of-the-box installation. Each of these categories contains a backup copy of the installed palettes belonging to the Metric units Installation. The palettes contain a mix of stock tools, styles and documentation content.
- **Design Tool Catalog – Imperial**—Contains tools that refer to all the architectural object styles and AEC design content in Imperial units.
- **Design Tool Catalog – Metric**—Contains tools that refer to all the architectural object styles and AEC design content in metric units.
- **Documentation Tool Catalog – Imperial**—Contains tools that refer to all the documentation object styles, such as schedule tables and area calculation objects, as well as AEC documentation content in Imperial units.
- **Documentation Tool Catalog – Metric**—Contains tools that refer to all the documentation object styles such as schedule tables and area calculation objects, as well as AEC documentation content in metric units.
- **Visualization Catalog**—Contains a large collection of material definitions, lights and cameras for use in rendering.
- **Content and Plug-ins Catalog**—Contains links to Web sites containing styles and other utilities and plug-ins.
- **My Tool Catalog**—This catalog is empty and ready to customize for your own use. Use it to store custom tools or your favorites from the standard tools.

To open a catalog, simply click on it. You can then use the links at the left (or right) to navigate through the categories and palettes to the tools.

Access a Tool Catalog

For most exercises in this book, both Imperial and Metric units and catalogs will be referenced. However, the dataset for Chapter 2 is provided in only Imperial units; therefore this sequence will reference only the Imperial Catalog.

3. With Content Browser open, click on the Design Tool Catalog – Imperial (see Figure 2.32).

NOTE

If you did not install the Imperial catalog, you can browse the Metric one instead.

An introduction page will appear on the right. Read through it and then proceed to the next step.

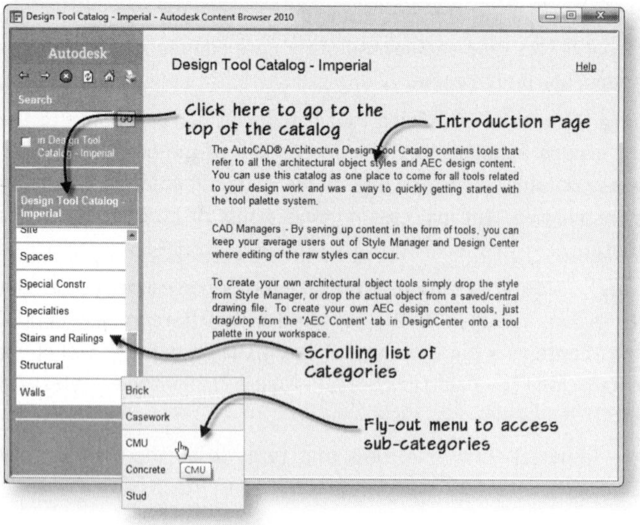

FIGURE 2.32 *Navigating through a Catalog*

4. On the left, scroll the list down to locate the Walls category.
5. Hover your mouse over Walls.

   A submenu will appear.
6. Click on the CMU item in the submenu.

Here you will find several pages of CMU Wall styles ready to drag and drop into your drawings. You can scroll through each page if you wish. We are going to drag and drop one of these CMU Wall style tools into the drawing; it will execute the Wall command and draw a Wall in the selected style.

7. Locate the Wall style named CMU-8 Furring. (It is on the fourth page—use Next and Prev to navigate through the pages.)

Each of the tools located in the Content Browser uses an Autodesk technology called "iDrop." iDrop is a web-based technology that allows content to be dragged into drawings from web pages, complete with all required data, associated parameters and files. In the case of AEC Styles, all style, material and schedule data properties will be included.

8. Place your mouse over the small eyedropper icon; click and hold down the mouse button and then drag the CMU-8 Furring style tool into the drawing window (see Figure 2.33).

   Wait for the eyedropper to appear to "fill up" before dragging.

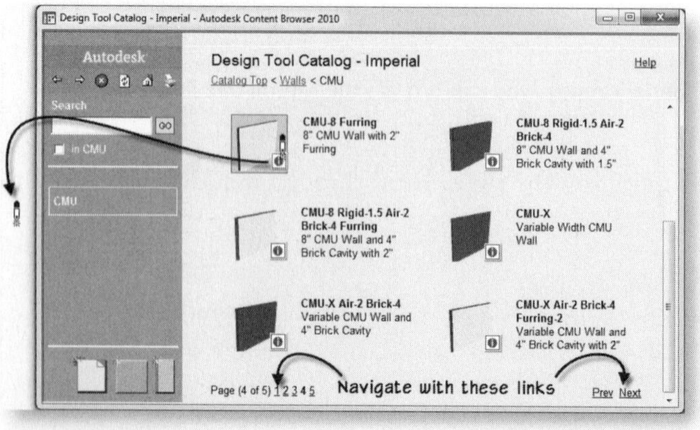

FIGURE 2.33 *Using iDrop to drag and drop styles into the drawing*

The Add Wall command will begin, and all of the parameters on the Properties palette will be set to match the tool just dropped.

9. Following the command prompts, draw a segment or two of Wall with this tool and then press ENTER.

   Notice that this style matches the one used for the Toilet Rooms. You can verify this by selecting a toilet room Wall (not in the plumbing chase) and checking its style on the Properties palette.

Add a Palette

As easy as it is to navigate and drag from the Content Browser, it will be more convenient (and require fewer clicks) to have a palette with the entire collection of styles required for a particular task readily at hand. We can do this by creating a new tool palette.

1. Right-click the title bar of the tool palettes and choose **New Palette** (see Figure 2.34).

   A new tool palette will appear ready to be named.

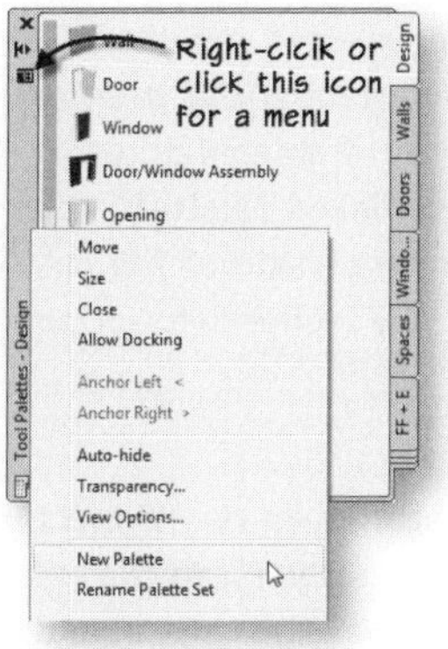

FIGURE 2.34 *Create a new tool palette*

2. Type **Chapter02** for the name and then press ENTER.
3. Bring the Content Browser to the front (press CTRL + 4, or click it on the Windows task bar).

TIP

If you wish, you can right-click the title bar of the Content Browser and choose "Always on Top" to keep it perpetually in front of other windows. This can make drag and drop easier.

4. Click and hold down on the eyedropper icon next to the CMU-8 Furring.

   As before, wait for the eyedropper to appear to "fill up."

5. Drag and drop the tool onto the Chapter02 palette in ACA. When a plus (+) sign appears on the cursor, release it to add the tool to the palette (see Figure 2.35).

NOTE

You can also add and remove tools from any of the out-of-the-box palettes, not just those that you create. In general however, you should consider creating your own palettes for any customization.

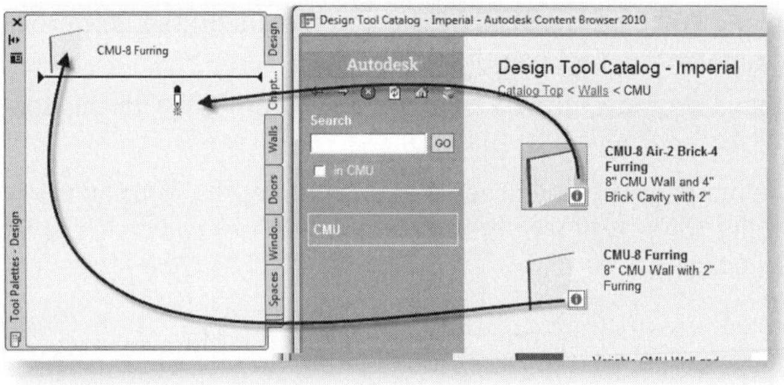

FIGURE 2.35 *Drop a tool on your custom tool palette*

6. On the same page of the Content Browser, locate the CMU-8 Air-2 Brick-4 Furring Wall style, and drag it to the Chapter02 palette as well.

Your custom Chapter02 palette now contains two tools.

CAD MANAGER NOTE

Custom tool palettes offer a great deal of customization potential. Custom palettes are built in the ACA work space as we have done here, and then can optionally be dragged and dropped to a catalog in the Content Browser. In this way, a library of Office Standard tool palettes and tools can be built up and saved to the server. These palettes can then be dragged and dropped by users to their own work spaces. More importantly, the palettes can maintain a back link to the source palette in the Content Browser if so configured. If you do this, when you make changes to the tools contained on these linked palettes, individual users need only click a small "refresh" icon to update their own version of the palettes to the latest version on the server. You can even set the refresh to occur automatically each time ACA is launched.

TIP

The project-based tool palette functionality is part of the project settings. In the "Project Properties" dialog (accessed from the Project tab of the Navigator palette) you can control the type of palette groups you want or turn the feature off. If Project palettes are on, and you create a new palette as we have here, it will *not* remain a permanent part of your workspace. In other words, when you change projects, the palette created here will swap out. If you do not want to use Project Palettes, click the Project tab and click the Edit Project icon at the top right corner of the palette. In the Advanced properties grouping, change the Project Tool Palette Group to None and then click OK.

Apply Tool Properties to Drawing Objects

To run a tool in the drawing, simply click on it. You can also use the tool as a means to import or re-import its associated style. A tool's properties can also be applied directly to objects in the drawing. (You may recall this use of tools from the opening tutorial in the Quick Start.) The two tools that we have here are "Object" tools. An Object tool creates a particular kind of object and requires a certain amount of user interaction, such as changing parameters on the Properties palette or clicking points in the drawing (as with a Wall tool). An important parameter of an Object tool is its style reference. Both of the tools that we built here are Wall tools with the Style setting being the parameter that distinguishes them from one another.

1. Repeat steps 3 through 7 discussed earlier in the "Styles in the Current Drawing" exercise.

   Notice that the CMU-8 Air-2 Brick-4 style is *not* part of the list.

Remember, adding a tool to a palette does not add it to the drawing. Let's apply the tool to a Wall in the drawing now. This will add it to the list of styles in this drawing.

2. Right-click on the CMU-8 Air-2 Brick-4 Furring Tool.

Take note of the menu items that appear. In particular, note the option to: Import "CMU-8 Air-2 Brick-4" Wall Style. Recall the exercise done earlier where we viewed the list of Wall styles that resided in this drawing. When you right-click a tool and the option reads "Import" rather than "Re-import" (as shown later) this indicates that the style is *not* currently available within this drawing (see Figure 2.36). If you were to choose this option, it would import this style into the drawing. It would not however *apply* the style on any particular Wall. To do that, we would choose the first menu option: Apply Tool Properties to. In either case, the style would be imported automatically from the remote library file where it resides to the current drawing.

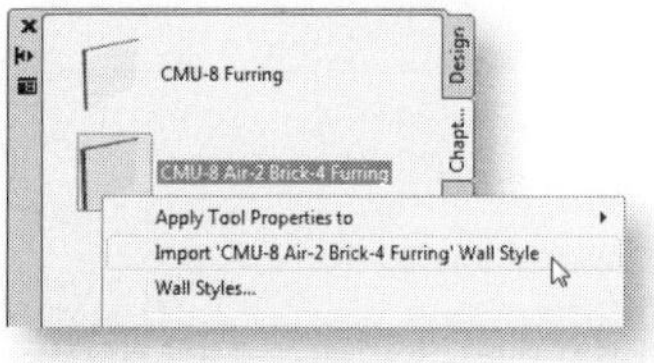

FIGURE 2.36 *Right-click a tool to see options, in particular the Import Style option*

3. Choose **Apply Tool Properties to > Wall.**
4. At the "Select Wall(s)" prompt, click on one or more of the exterior Walls to the right of the plan and then press ENTER.

   Notice the change to the Wall component makeup: the insulation component has been removed. Zoom in as necessary to see.
5. Repeat steps 3 through 7 discussed earlier in the "Styles in the Current Drawing" exercise.

   Notice that the CMU-8 Air-2 Brick-4 style *is* now part of the list.

   Repeat the "Apply to" sequence on other Walls if you like.
6. Zoom in on the toilet rooms in the plan.
7. On the Chapter02 palette, right-click on the CMU-8 Furring Tool (see Figure 2.37).

Take note of the menu items that appear. In particular, note the option to **Re-import 'CMU-8 Furring' Wall Style**. As noted previously, if the style does not currently exist within the drawing, this item will read "Import" and will import that style definition to the current drawing. However, if the style is already present in the drawing, as is the case with the CMU-8 Furring Style, then this option will "re-import" the style from the library file and replace the version of it that exists in the current file. This will "update" the style to the latest design. This tool is very valuable and extremely powerful, but it should be used with caution. Remember that styles are "types." When you re-import the style, all instances of that style in the current drawing will be affected; they will *all* update!

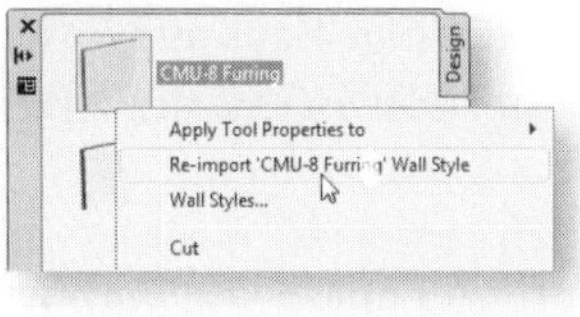

FIGURE 2.37 *Right-click a tool to see options, in particular the Re-Import Style option*

8. Choose **Re-import 'CMU-8 Furring' Wall Style** from the context menu.

Notice the change to *all* of the Toilet Room Walls. The version of the Style that was in this drawing originally had only a single component to represent the furring. The one re-imported from the library has two components: the furring and the drywall (see Figure 2.38). This gives you an example of the potential of the Re-import feature and some of the variety possible with object styles; again, use with caution.

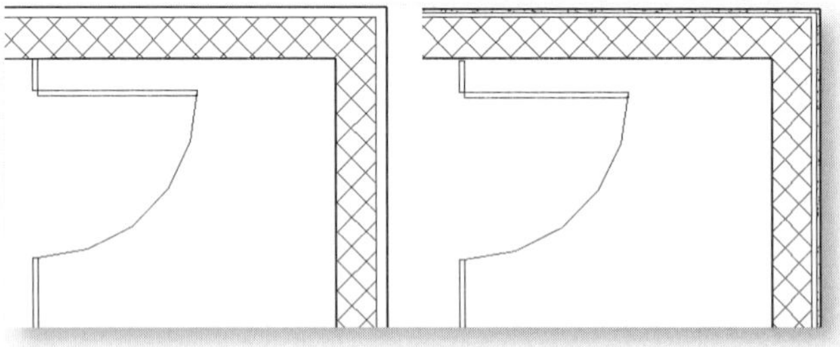

FIGURE 2.38 *Comparing the original style on the left with the re-imported version on the right*

9. Repeat steps 3–8 discussed previously in the "Access a Tool Catalog" heading to draw a segment or two of Wall with the CMU-8 Furring Style from the Content Browser.

Notice that, even though we dragged the Wall tool from the catalog as before, the look of the Style was different in each instance. Earlier it used the simply furring version where now it used the more detailed one. A tool will *not* automatically import its Style from the remote drawing if it already resides in the current drawing. Rather, it will simply use the version resident in the drawing. In this case, the version used in the current drawing originally had less detail, but because the name was the same, importing a more detailed version from the library was as simple as a single right-click.

If this version of the style does not suit you, undo the change. For instance, with the new style you may experience plotting difficulties or Wall Cleanup problems. Wall Cleanup is the automatic interaction between Wall segments that forms "clean" corners and intersections (see Chapter 9 for complete details on troubleshooting Wall Cleanup).

CAD MANAGER NOTE

Another important interface element for working with styles is the Style Manager. You can access the Style Manager on the Manage tab on the Styles & Display panel. Like the Content Browser, it can also be used to retrieve styles saved in remote library files. However, the Style Manager is more than a tool to browse and import styles. You can use it to create new styles and edit existing styles as well. It also provides a convenient way to quickly assess all of the styles contained in the current file. If you have used ACA before, Style Manager will be very familiar to you. We will use the Style Manager to help build and edit styles in later chapters. Feel free to use it if you wish as an alternative to the methods showcased here.

Style Manager also provides access to Project Standards library files if being used in a Project environment. Project Standards provides a way to manage all common Styles (and Display settings) for a project team in one or more library files. These files are typically stored on a network server and made read-only to all team members except the project's team leader or data coordinator. When Project Standards are enabled, library files will appear in a node at the top of the tree listing in Style and Display Manager. Project Standards "synchronize" and "update" functionalities are also integrated throughout the interface of both managers. Project Standards will be explored in greater detail in the chapters that follow.

The potential of object Styles in ACA is nearly limitless and we have only begun to scratch the surface here. Again, the goal of this chapter is to familiarize you with the concepts that are important to working in ACA. As with display control shown earlier, throughout the remaining chapters of this book, styles will play an important part. Here we focused on retrieving and applying styles to objects within our drawing. In Chapters 10 and 11 we will look at editing existing styles and building custom styles. In that discussion, we will also explore the Style Manager that was only mentioned here.

TIP

Think of styles as "types" akin to those types we typically indicate on a construction document set. This will help you in deciding when and how to build and apply styles.

ANCHORS

Anchors are used to build intelligent links between two objects. Anchors enable two objects to be linked together in a logical manner. Usually, this is a physical relationship where one object controls the location and orientation of another. As one object moves or is transformed, the anchored object will move and be transformed in relation to it. The way in which the anchored object moves and is transformed is governed by the rules established within the anchoring parameters. For instance, doors automatically anchor to walls. If the wall moves, the door moves with it. The relationship between the two objects in an anchored relationship is hierarchical. The door is anchored to the wall, not the other way around. Therefore, moving the wall *will* force the door to move, but moving the door *will not* move the wall. However, the door's position as it moves must remain within the confines of the wall (or a neighboring wall). This behavior is controlled by the rules and constraints built into the anchor.

Understanding and fully exploiting the usage of anchors while using ACA is one of the key ingredients to success with the software. Anchors have the following key features:

- Anchors ensure that logical relationships between objects are established and are maintained automatically as edits are made to project files.
- There are many anchor types available, each exhibiting a set of unique parameters. (These include: Wall, Column, Railing and Tag Anchors.)
- Anchoring is often built into other routines in the software; therefore, the anchor is often attached by means of performing a related function (for instance, when a door is inserted in a wall, the anchor is automatically attached).

Types of Anchors

As stated previously, most anchoring occurs automatically as various objects are added to project files. This is true of Doors anchoring to Walls, Railing anchoring to Stairs, Columns anchoring to Grids and Lights anchoring to Ceiling Grids.

However, there are several more generic anchors (which are listed here) which are accessed from the Content Browser in the Stock Tool Catalog in the Parametric Layout & Anchoring category. These anchor commands can be used to establish logical and intelligent relationships between your AEC objects. Brief descriptions of each type are listed here. However, the best way to understand anchors is to use them in real situations. Use the following list as a guide to types of anchors. The tutorial that follows will help to further illustrate the concept of anchors.

- **Curve**—Used to anchor an object along the *length* of another object. A wall anchor used by doors is a type of Curve anchor. (Refer to Chapters 4 and 10 for more information on Walls and Doors.)
- **Leader**—Used to anchor a specific point on an object to a specific point on another object and connect these two points with a *leader* line. A Column Bubble anchor used by column bubbles tools when anchoring to column grids is a type of Leader anchor. (Refer to Chapter 6 for more information on Column Grids and Bubbles.)
- **Node**—Used to anchor an object from its insertion point to a *specific point* (or node) on another object. A column object uses a Node anchor to attach itself to a Column Grid object, as do lighting fixtures to Ceiling Grids. (Refer to Chapter 6 for more information on Column Grids and Chapter 13 for more information on Ceiling Grids.)
- **Cell**—Must be used in conjunction with a 2D or 3D Layout Grid (Layout Grids are defined next). The anchored object will be anchored to the center of a *2D cell* formed by the grid. The anchored object can optionally *reshape* to conform to the shape of the grid cell. Nested objects within Curtain Wall objects use an anchor similar to a Cell anchor. (Refer to Chapter 8 for more information on curtain walls.)
- **Volume**—Must be used in conjunction with a 3D Layout Grid (Layout Grids are defined next). The anchored object will be anchored to the center of a *3D cell* formed by the grid. The anchored object can optionally *reshape* to conform to the shape of the grid cell volume. Nested objects within Curtain Wall objects use an anchor similar to a Volume anchor. (Refer to Chapter 8 for more information on curtain walls.)
- **Object**—Used to anchor one AEC object directly to another AEC object. The original position, rotation and offsets are maintained when using this anchor, thereby making anchoring a simple one-step process.

Layout Tools

When you work with anchors, there are always three objects involved: the object to which you are anchoring, or the "parent," the object being anchored, or the "child," and the anchor itself, which contains the "rules of the relationship." Sometimes the parent object is not an obvious building component (like a Wall, Stair or Curtain Wall), but more of a design relationship itself. Provided with ACA are tools called Layouts whose purpose is to assist in establishing repetitive design relationships such as equal spacing or dimensional repetition. There are three basic types of Layout tools.

- **Curve**—A Layout Curve is a *one-dimensional* Layout tool following the path of a line, polyline, spline, Wall or other linear shape. Even closed shapes like a circle or an ellipse may be used. Anchor points called "nodes" occur along the curve at parametrically defined intervals. Any AEC object can be anchored to these nodes using a Node anchor. Layout Nodes can be spaced equally, repeat a certain distance or be placed at manual intervals.

- **Layout Grid 2D**—The Layout Grid 2D is a *two-dimensional* Layout tool. The X and Y dimensions of the layout form a grid. Anchor points called "nodes" occur at each grid line intersection. Any AEC object can be anchored to these nodes using a Node anchor. AEC objects can also be anchored to the center point of each cell using a Cell anchor, and optionally resize to the cell dimensions. Grid lines can be spaced equally, repeat a certain distance, or be placed manually in both directions. The most common forms of Layout Grids are Column Grids (covered in Chapter 6) and Ceiling Grids (covered in Chapter 13).
- **Layout Grid 3D**—The Layout Grid 3D is a *three-dimensional* Layout tool. The X, Y and Z dimensions of the layout form a volume. Anchor points called "nodes" occur at each 3D grid line intersection. Any AEC object can be anchored to these nodes using a Node anchor. AEC objects can also be anchored to the center point of each 2D cell formed by grid lines running in any two of the three dimensions using a Cell anchor. Finally, the geometric center point of each volume can be anchored to using a Volume anchor, and optionally resize to the cell dimensions. Grid lines can be spaced equally, repeat a certain distance, or be placed manually in all three directions.

Explore Objects with Anchors

Continue working in the same file from the previous exercise. If you closed the file, click the Constructs tab of project Navigator and then double-click the Walls file to reopen it now.

1. Zoom in to the upper right corner of the classroom plan.
2. Click on the Door to the classroom.
3. On the Home tab, on the Modify panel, click the Move tool (see in the left side of Figure 2.39).
4. At the "Specify base point or displacement" prompt, click a point near the center of the Door (see in the middle of Figure 2.39).

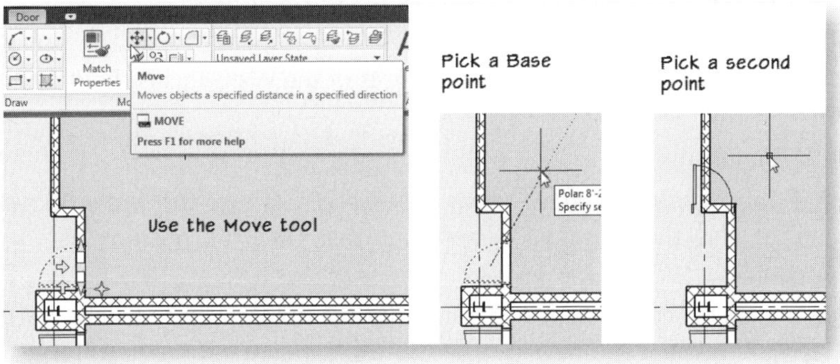

FIGURE 2.39 *Testing a Wall anchor*

5. At the "Specify second point of displacement" prompt, click a random point anywhere within the classroom space (see in the right side of Figure 2.39).

Notice that the Door moves, but stays constrained to a Wall; possibility a different Wall. The most important point is that, even though we picked a point within the classroom space, the Door still remained attached to the closest neighboring Wall.

NOTE

Since we did not use Object Snaps or dimensions to make this move, your Door may have jumped to a different Wall or location.

6. On the QAT, click the Undo icon (or press CTRL + Z) to return the Door to the original location.
7. In the same Classroom, select the Window.

Suppose that you want to shift the position of the Window within the thickness of the Wall. As you saw with the Door, a regular AutoCAD Move command would move the Window, but would not allow you to move it within the Wall's thickness. (Go ahead and try it if you like. Just be sure to undo before continuing.) This is because the Window's anchor controls its position relative to the Wall (including its position within the thickness of the Wall). You can however, move it within the Wall by editing the anchor parameters. The easiest way to do this is by using grips.

8. Hover over the square grip in the middle of the Window and wait for the tool tip to appear (see Figure 2.40).

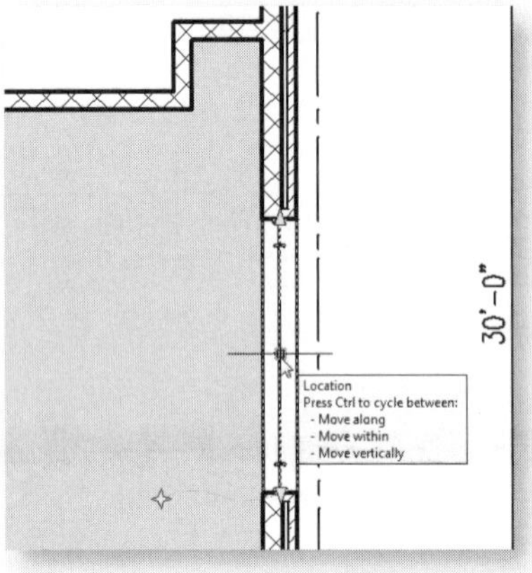

FIGURE 2.40 *Hover over a grip to reveal the various* CTRL *key functions*

Notice that there are three options to cycle through on this grip.

9. Click the Location grip. Move your mouse around.

   Notice that the Window moves along the lengths of the Wall. This is the default option: Move along.

10. Press the CTRL key once.

    Notice that the Window is now moving perpendicular to the Wall (Move within). Notice also the Dynamic Dimensions that track its position as you move your mouse.

11. Move your mouse to the left, type in **3"** and then press ENTER (see Figure 2.41).

NOTE You can simply type **3 and the input will be assumed to be inches.**

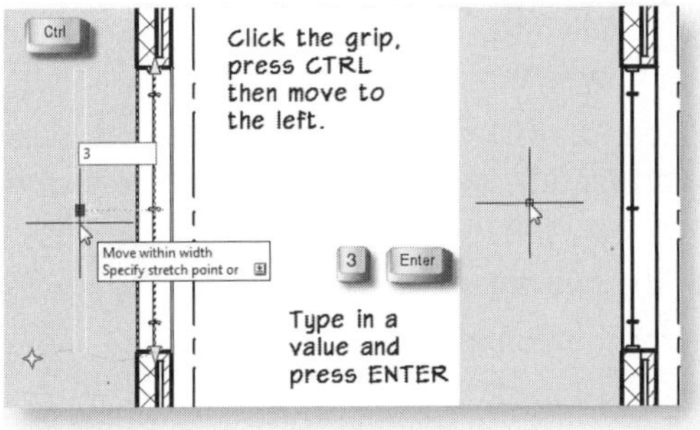

FIGURE 2.41 *Shifting the Window position anchor within the Wall with grips*

12. Right-click and choose **Deselect All** (or press ESC).
13. Zoom in to the lower-left corner of the same classroom, at the column near the Door.
14. Select the column at the lower-left corner of the room.
15. On the Home tab, on the Modify panel, click the Move tool.
16. Click on the Column for the base point.
17. At the "Specify second point of displacement" prompt, click a random point in the hallway nearby (see Figure 2.42).

The MOVE command will appear to have failed. This is because the Column is anchored to the grid and cannot move off the grid line intersection.

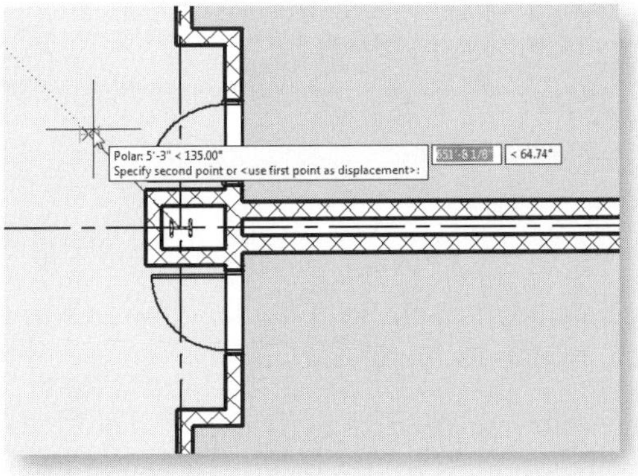

FIGURE 2.42 *Try to move an anchored column*

18. Repeat the MOVE command on the same Column, but this time click the second point much farther away from the original location.

The column will seem to disappear. In fact, what has happened is similar to the door's behavior before. In this case, the column is anchored to the Column Grid object (a type of layout grid, as described earlier). The column has moved to a different node (grid intersection). Most likely, that node was already occupied by another column, and there are now two columns on a single node. This accounts for its apparent disappearance. Be careful of doubling up anchored objects like this.

19. Undo the last MOVE command.

    Anchors control all aspects of an anchored object's position and orientation.

20. Select the column again, on the Home tab, on the Modify panel, click the Rotate tool.

21. Click a base point at the center of the column.
22. At the "Specify rotation angle" prompt, type **90** and then press ENTER.

    Notice that the column has not rotated. To rotate an anchored column, we must manipulate the anchor properties. Fortunately, like the window seen earlier this is easy to do with grips.
23. Select the Column and take note of the two grips.

    The square grip is the location grip for the Column; the diamond-shaped one is the "Roll" (or rotation) grip.
24. Click on the Roll grip.

    Note that the existing Roll for this column is 90°.
25. Begin moving the mouse and note the dynamic dimensions that appear.
26. Type **0** and then press ENTER (see Figure 2.43).

    The Column is now oriented the opposite way.

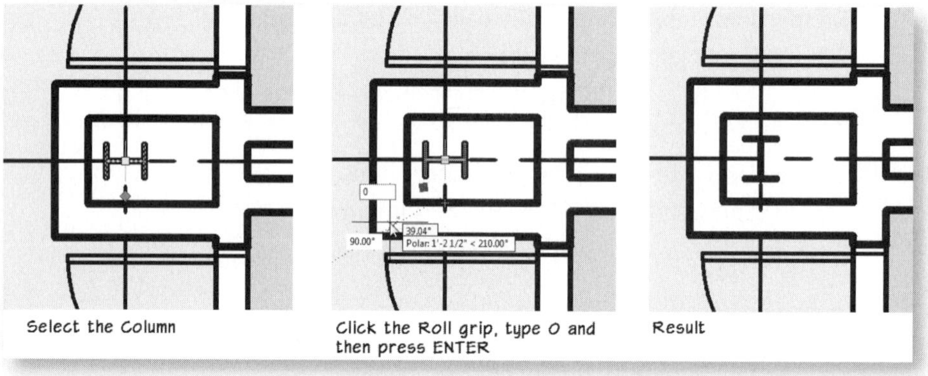

Select the Column
Click the Roll grip, type 0 and then press ENTER
Result

FIGURE 2.43 *Change the orientation of a column with the Roll grip*

Object Anchors

We have explored several anchors that are already present in this file. Now let's use the Object Anchor to establish a new anchor relationship in our file.

In the "Add a Palette" heading discussed earlier, we created a Chapter02 Tool Palette. We will now follow a similar process to add tools to this palette. If you did not complete that exercise, please do so now. You only need the palette for this exercise; it is not necessary to add the Walls tools to it, if you have not done so already.

Make sure that the Chapter02 Tool Palette (created earlier) is active (click on its tab if it is not). If you need to create this palette, right-click the Tool Palettes title bar and choose **New Palette**.

1. Open the Content Browser (press CTRL + 4, or choose it from the Tools drop-down on the Home tab).
2. Click the Home icon at the top left.
3. Click on the *Stock Tool Catalog*, and then from the left navigation bar, choose Parametric Layout & Anchoring Tools.

    A collection of layout and anchor tools will appear on the right (see Figure 2.44).

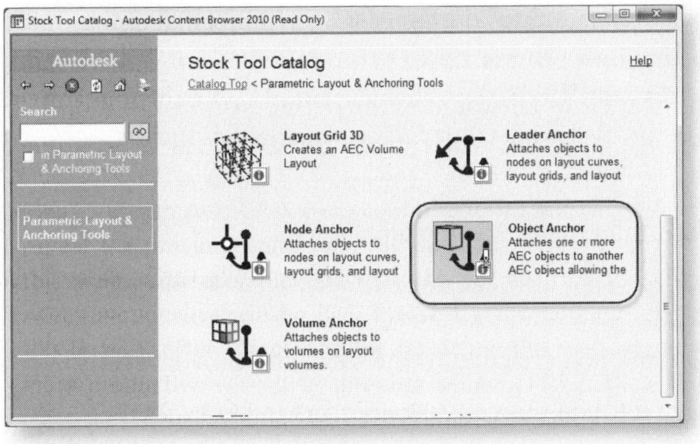

FIGURE 2.44 *Navigate to the Parametric Layout & Anchoring page of the Content Browser*

> **NOTE**
>
> **All of the tools in the Stock Tool Catalog are unit independent, meaning that they work in both Imperial and Metric units.**

4. Click and hold down the eyedropper icon next to the Object Anchor tool (see Figure 2.44).

   Wait for the eyedropper to appear to fill up.
5. Drag and drop the tool onto the Chapter02 palette in ACA. When a plus (+) sign appears on the cursor, release it to add the tool to the palette.

> **NOTE**
>
> **Later we will need two more tools, so let's add them to the palette now, while we are here.**

6. Repeat this process to drag and drop the Layout Curve tool onto the Chapter02 palette. Be sure to drag from the eyedropper icon.
7. Repeat again for the Node Anchor tool.
8. Zoom in on the toilet rooms.
9. On the Chapter02 Tool Palette, click the newly added Object Anchor tool.
10. At the "Select objects to be anchored" prompt, click to select all of the toilet room fixtures adjacent to the horizontal Men's Room plumbing Wall and then press ENTER (see Figure 2.45).

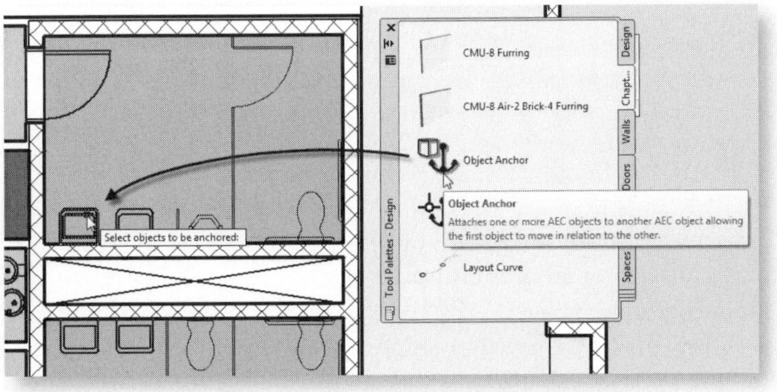

FIGURE 2.45 *Select all of the fixtures on the plumbing Wall of the Men's Room*

11. At the "Select an object to anchor to" prompt, click the horizontal Men's Room plumbing Wall.

The fixtures in the Men's Room are now anchored to the plumbing Wall. If this Wall moves, the fixtures will move with it. If this Wall rotates, the fixtures will also rotate. Let's test this.

12. Click to select the horizontal Men's Room plumbing Wall.
13. Click the square Location grip at the center of the Wall. Move the Wall up a bit and click.

Notice that all of the fixtures remained attached to the Wall and moved with it.

14. Undo the move and try rotating the Wall. (Home tab, Modify panel.)

Notice that all of the fixtures rotated with the Wall. Undo this transformation as well. If you wish, you can also anchor the fixtures in the Women's Room to its plumbing Wall. Notice that in both transformations, the Space object and the "X" within the plumbing Wall cavity were unaffected. To update the Space, right-click and choose **Update Space Geometry**. The "X" which is a chase object, must be updated manually. Do this with the X and Y values on the Properties palette. If later you decide to remove the anchor relationship, click the anchored objects; a small arc will appear connecting the anchored object to the parent object. A small minus (–) sign grip will appear along this arc. Click it to remove the relationship.

Explore Layout Tools

A Layout Curve adds nodes to any linear object such as a line, a polyline or a Wall. AEC objects can then be anchored to those nodes. This provides a valuable architectural design tool.

1. Pan over to the Open Office space in the upper left corner of the plan adjacent to the toilet rooms. (There is a single chair in the upper left corner of the room.)
2. In the upper left corner of the room, draw an arc (use Arc 3 Points on the Draw panel of the Home tab) as shown in Figure 2.46.

   The exact dimensions are not important; simply match the shape shown in the figure. This will be easiest to accomplish if you temporarily disable OSnaps. To do this click the Object Snap icon on the drawing status bar or press `F3`.

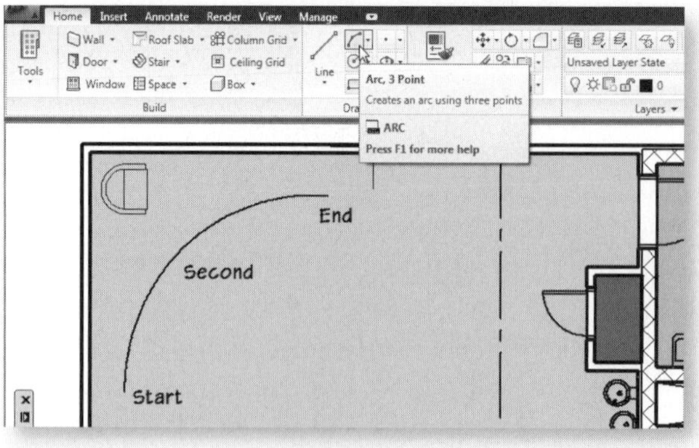

FIGURE 2.46 *Draw an arc in the corner of Open Office*

Earlier at the start of the "Object Anchors" heading, we added several tools to the Chapter02 Tool Palette. We will now use the remainder of those tools to copy and anchor the chair provided here along the arc that we just drew.

3. On the Chapter02 Tool Palette, click the Layout Curve tool.
4. When prompted to "Select a curve," pick the arc just drawn.
5. At the "Select node layout mode" prompt, choose **Space evenly**.

   If you have Dynamic Input disabled, right-click to access this option.
6. Press ENTER at each of the "Start Offset" and "End Offset" prompts to accept the defaults.
7. At the "Number of nodes" prompt, type **6** and then press ENTER to complete the sequence (see Figure 2.47).

   Six small circles will appear along the length of the arc.

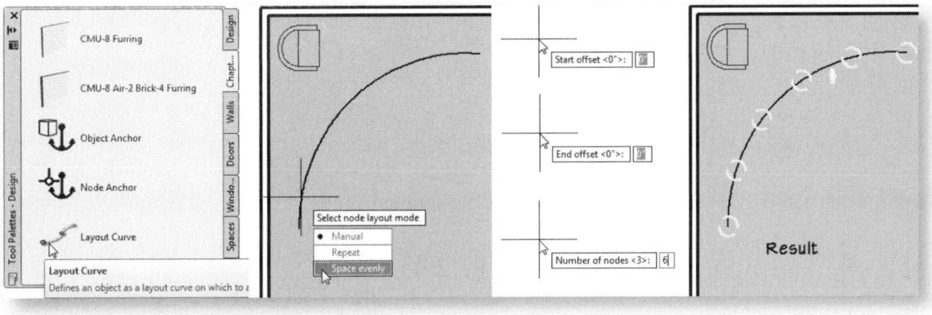

FIGURE 2.47 *Create a Layout Curve along the arc*

We now have a Layout Curve that references the shape of the arc. The Layout Curve and the arc are separate entities, but are linked together. If you change the shape of the arc, the Layout Curve will follow. To change the parameters of the Layout Curve itself, such as the spacing of the nodes, click one of the nodes, right-click and choose **Properties**. Change whatever parameters you wish in the Dimensions grouping of the Properties palette. You can also use the grips. Let's now anchor something to these nodes. We could anchor equipment symbols, plumbing fixtures, lighting fixtures, Walls, Columns, planting symbols or just about anything we wished to have spaced evenly along this arc. In this example, we will anchor chair symbols along the Layout Curve. A chair has already been provided, in this file, in the corner of this room. We will explore browsing, inserting, and creating AEC Content (like this chair) in Chapters 4, 10 and 11.

8. On the Chapter02 Tool Palette, click the Node Anchor tool.
9. At the "Node anchor" prompt, choose **Copy to each node**. (Right-click if Dynamic input is off.)
10. At the "Select object to be copied and anchored" prompt, pick the chair.
11. At the "Select layout tool" prompt, pick one of the six magenta circles (do not pick the arc).

    Notice that, although there are now six chairs anchored to the Curve, they are pointing the wrong way.
12. Press ENTER to complete the Node Anchor command.
13. Delete the original chair.

14. Select all six chairs—Select one chair, and then on the Multi-View Block tab of the ribbon, click the Select Similar button.
15. Right-click and choose **Node Anchor > Set Rotation**.

    Be careful to select only the chairs and not the Layout Curve, the arc or the Space. If you select other objects in addition to chairs, the Node Anchor option will not appear on the right-click menu.
16. At the "Rotation angle about X axis" and "Rotation angle about Y axis" prompts, accept the default of 0 by pressing ENTER.
17. At the "Rotation angle about Z axis" prompt, type **90** and then press ENTER (see Figure 2.48).

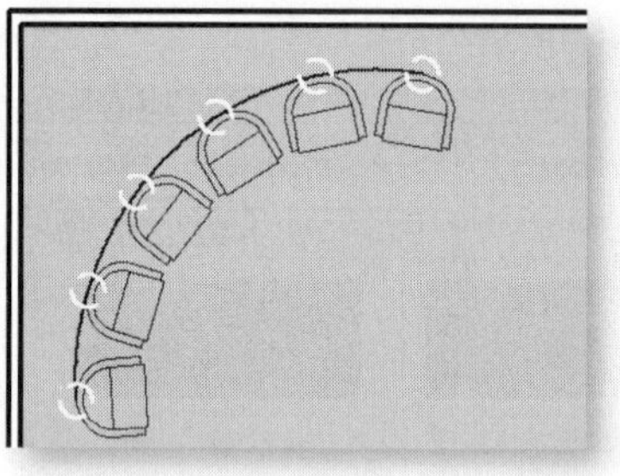

FIGURE 2.48 *Rotating all of the chairs to point into the room*

18. Click on the arc to select it. (Be careful not to select the chairs or the Layout Curve nodes.)
19. Change the shape of the arc using the grips.

    Notice the effect on the Layout Curve and the anchored chairs. Continue to experiment if you wish.

NOTE

Although the Arc must remain in the file since the Layout Curve is attached to it and it governs the shape and location of the Layout tool, you can place the Arc on a non-plotting layer such as A-Anno-Nplt, which is included in the file. In this way, the Arc remains readily available onscreen, but will not plot on final printed drawings.

Anchors ensure that critical design relationships are maintained even as the typical edits and design changes are occurring in the drawing. There are other examples of anchors within this drawing file that you can explore. For instance, try moving the Stair object and note that the Railing goes with it. Switch to the Reflected Display Configuration (see the "Loading a Display Configuration" heading discussed previously) and explore the anchor parameters used to anchor the lighting fixtures to the Ceiling Grid. As you explore, you will get a better sense of the many anchoring possibilities within ACA. In Chapter 7 we will explore Stairs and Railings. In Chapter 13, we will create a ceiling grid layout and further explore these tools.

DISPLAY THEMES

A Display Theme is actually an AEC object that can change the way other AEC objects display. This occurs independently of the current Display Configuration. A Display Theme queries the drawing for certain properties, when the values of these properties meet the conditions outlined within the Display Theme Style, the display of the affected objects is modified. The modified display remains in effect as long as the Display Theme is active. While you can insert as many Display Theme objects into the drawing as you wish, only one can be active at any given time. Previously active Display Themes are automatically disabled when a new one is inserted. You can disable a Display Theme at any time. The topic of Display Themes is introduced here because it related to both the display system and styles: A Display Theme is a Style-based object that affects object Display.

Using Display Themes

The Themes Tool Palette (in the Documentation Tool Palette group) contains a few sample Display Theme Style tools. There are additional examples in the Content Browser in the Documentation catalogs. Use them like any other tool.

1. On the Project Navigator palette, click the Views tab and then double-click the *Floor Plan* View file to open it.

NOTE

If you left the Floor Plan View open from the previous tutorials, then this action will simply make that file active.

2. On the Home tab, on the Layers panel, open the Layer list drop-down and thaw the Walls|A-Area-Spce layer.
3. Right-click the Tool Palettes title bar and choose Document to load the Document tool palette group.
4. Click the Themes tab.
5. Click the Theme by Space Size tool.
6. At the "Upper-left corner of display theme" prompt, click a point next to the plan and then press ENTER at the next prompt (see Figure 2.49).

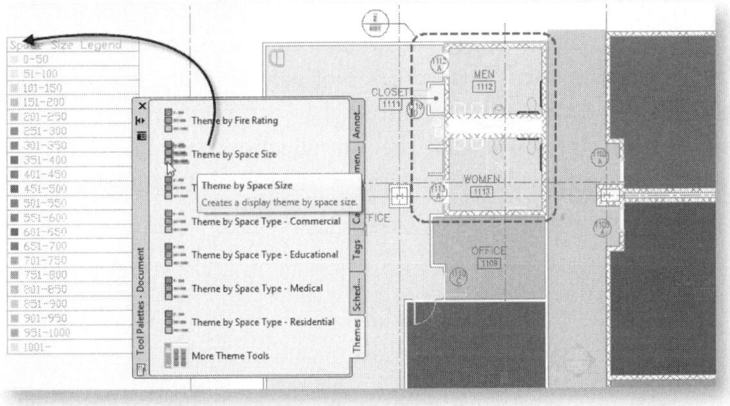

FIGURE 2.49 *Add a Space Size Display Theme*

All of the Space objects in the drawing will be color coded based on their area. The Display Theme object displays a legend defining the range of square footage attributed to each color. This Display Theme will control the color and shading of the Space objects as long as it is active in the file. You can disable or delete it at any time. To disable a Display Theme, right-click it and choose **Disable Display Theme**, delete the Display Theme object (the legend) or add another Display Theme (which will automatically disable the existing one upon insertion).

7. On the Themes tool palette, click the Theme by Fire Rating tool.
8. Click a point to place it in the drawing and then press ENTER to accept the default size.

Notice the changes to the drawing. The spaces return to their previous color display. The existing Display Theme now has a line drawn through it to indicate that it is disabled. The Walls and Doors in the file are now color coded to indicate their respective fire ratings. Since the Spaces use solid hatching by default, it can be a little difficult to read the themed objects. There are a few potential solutions to this. We could modify the Display Theme to change the way that Spaces display, or we could simply turn off the A-Area-Spce layer. For now we will do the later. In future chapters we will explore Themes further and build some custom Display Theme Styles.

9. Freeze the Walls|A-Area-Spce layer again.

There are other Display Theme styles included in the Content Browser; however, they would not yield the desired results in this file as they rely on the names of the Space Style in order to color code the Spaces. If you use the Space Styles found in the Content Browser in the Design Catalog, these additional Display Themes can color code them based on Style name. The potential of Display Themes is nearly limitless.

10. Erase both Display Theme objects (the legends) to disable and remove them from the file.

    You can also right-click and choose Disable instead of deleting them.
11. Close and Save all files to complete the tutorial.

VISUAL STYLES

We have now looked at the display system and display themes. There are other ways to change the appearance of your drawings onscreen and in print. They are Visual Styles and rendering. Rendering is out of the scope of this book. Visual Styles offer an exciting way to apply all kinds of stylistic variations to the onscreen and printed display. You can apply shade, sketchy edges and "Xray" effects. A tool palette with plenty of examples is provided in the Visualization tool palette group. You can use them to explore this feature. To access this palette, right-click the tool palettes title bar and choose **Visualization**. This will load the Visualization tool palette group. Click the Visual Styles tab to see the collection of Visual Styles tools (see Figure 2.50).

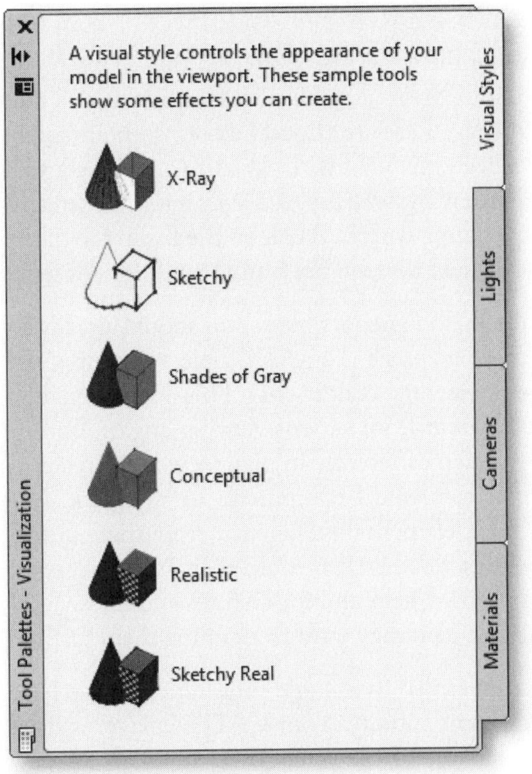

FIGURE 2.50 *The Visual Styles tools in the Visualization tool palette group*

Try each one out in the drawing to see their effects (see Figure 2.51). When you are satisfied with your Visual Styles explorations, choose **Visual Styles, 2D Wireframe** from the View panel to reset the drawing to normal.

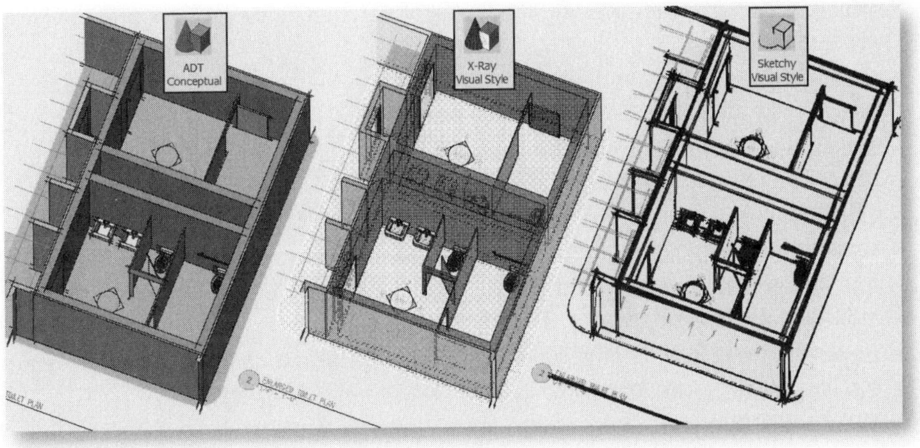

FIGURE 2.51 *Visual Styles add lots of stylistic variation to onscreen display*

If you wish, look up Visual Styles in the help system to learn how to customize and create your own Visual Styles.

CONTENT LIBRARY

Once you have gained an understanding of the concepts covered in this chapter, you will no doubt begin to amass a collection of Styles and Display Configurations that will be useful in future projects. In addition, there are thousands of pre-built styles, blocks, and multi-view blocks that have been included with ACA to get you started. These resources are accessible via the Content Browser, as we have seen. You can also use the Autodesk Seek Web site accessible directly from ACA on the Insert tab of the ribbon. Just input a keyword in the search field to open Seek and search for content.

We have discussed styles, the display system and anchors here. You should already be familiar with AutoCAD blocks. A multi-view block is an AEC object that uses one or more AutoCAD blocks in different viewing conditions. This allows custom objects to be created that need to look different from various viewing angles. For instance, many architectural elements are drawn differently in plan view than in elevation, such as a plumbing fixture, furniture, medical equipment, or millwork. Use custom multi-view blocks to represent these elements intelligently from these different viewing angles. In the display system described earlier, multi-view blocks respond automatically to these different viewing needs. The plumbing fixtures and the chair in this file are examples of Multi-View Blocks. You may want to examine them further.

By default all Styles and Content items are stored in a single root folder on the hard drive. This folder is referred to as the Content Library. Your CAD Manager will set its exact location either on your local machine or on your office network. As new styles and content are accumulated, it is wise to develop a process for adding them to this library. The topics of multi-view blocks and other design content will be covered in more detail in the chapters ahead. We will create a custom multi-view block later in Chapter 11.

SUMMARY

- Usage of ACA is predicated on a process of parametric design and progressive refinement.
- Create objects quickly with whatever information is available, and then continuously modify the objects as the design progresses.
- The display system allows building models to automatically represent a variety of display modes with a click of the mouse.
- Object styles deliver on the promise of progressive refinement by allowing design data to be updated globally as the design evolves.
- Anchors provide complex and robust rule-based relationships between various individual components within the design.
- Object styles, display configurations and custom content can be stored in a central library that grows over time.
- The Content Browser allows you to quickly retrieve tools, styles and content.

CHAPTER

3

Work Space Setup

INTRODUCTION

AutoCAD Architecture is a robust program with many user-customizable options and settings. The available settings cover a wide variety of functions. Items as disparate as the color of the screen's background to the specific template file that ought to be used when creating a new drawing are among the vast collection of configurable settings.

In many cases, these settings are referred to as "system variables." System variables typically change some aspect of the working environment or the behavior of a tool and include a list of two or more specific choices. The simplest system variables are basic *on/off* settings. More complex variables can include a long list of possible settings from which to choose. Some system variables are "global" and need only be set once, and they remain in effect permanently on the computer until changed, regardless of which drawing may be open onscreen. Other system variables are "drawing specific," meaning that their value can change from one drawing to the next. Due to the large quantity of system variables available to AutoCAD, it is useful to have some convenient way to manage them. AutoCAD offers two ways to manage system variables and establish user preferences: *profiles* and *template files.* Profiles provide a means to save global system settings that do not vary per drawing and template files offer a way to start new drawings with all preferred drawing-specific settings.

Depending on the specific installation options chosen, AutoCAD Architecture creates one or more profiles. In the United States, the AutoCAD Architecture (US Imperial) and/or AutoCAD Architecture (US Metric) profile(s) will be created. Several other Content Packs are available during installation including content and profiles tailored for many other regions. Naturally a major difference between the various profiles is the active units settings. There will be other differences in some cases as well. Check the online Help for specifics.

In the US version, ACA will automatically load a template named *AEC Model (Imperial Stb).dwt* [*AEC Model (Metric Stb).dwt*]. The default profile loads the ribbons, palettes, units and system variables for general use. The default template includes the most common drawing settings and Display Control parameters (seen in the previous chapter), and in some cases can also include selected AEC content, such as wall and door styles, layers and so forth. Despite all of these carefully configured defaults, you may find it useful to modify a few of these settings. Such settings and the reasons for editing them will be covered in this chapter. In addition, we will explore the Drawing Setup command, Layer Standards, and default template files.

NOTE

Your company may already have standards for many of the following topics. Please check with your CAD Manager or CAD Support Professional regarding the existence of CAD standards and proper procedures to follow when using them. If you are the CAD Manager for your office, work with office team members to establish the best methods to manage these policies and procedures.

NOTE

Each localized (non-US) version of ACA installs slightly differently. The exact version of ACA that you have installed may vary slightly from that which is indicated here.

OBJECTIVES

The goal of this chapter is to expose you to many of the issues involved in setting up your work space. The following topics will be explored in this chapter:

- Create a profile.
- Assign a profile to a custom ACA desktop icon.
- Explore Drawing Setup.
- Understand layer standards.
- Work with template files.

PROFILES

Profiles are used to manage all of the permanent settings. These settings, once in place, usually do not need to change often or at all. The profile also stores the list of AutoCAD saved Workspaces that are available on launch. A Workspace remembers your entire onscreen interface items including the set of ribbon tabs available at the top of the screen, the currently loaded Status Bar icons, and your tool palette set and its onscreen position. If necessary, more than one Workspace or even more than one profile can be created to facilitate easy swapping of different ribbon sets, palettes, and system variables for different design needs or for several users sharing the same computer. The office CAD Manager or other CAD power user usually handles the creation and management of profiles. If your office has personnel in these roles, check with them before modifying or creating profiles. Profiles are accessed from the Options dialog box. Options can be found on the Application Menu or by right-clicking in the Command Line. As a general rule of thumb, it is a good idea to create a custom profile when you first install ACA if for no other reason than to maintain an easily accessible backup of the default profile.

Create a New Profile

NOTE

The following sequence on creating a Profile is included should you desire to learn how to build or customize ACA Profile(s) or simply to create a backup. However, it is not required that you build your own Profile to use ACA 2010. If you wish, you may skip this topic and simply use the default AutoCAD Architecture Profile in lieu of the "MasterACA" Profile built here with no detriment to the remaining tutorials in this book.

1. Launch AutoCAD Architecture 2010.

   If the Welcome Screen appears (Figure 1.1 in Chapter 1), close it.
2. From the Application Menu, click the **Options** Button.

TIP

You can also right-click in the Command Line area and access the Options command from the context menu.

3. In the "Options" dialog box, click the Profiles tab (use the scroll buttons at the far right to locate it if necessary).

   You will see a list of existing profiles; there might be several. At the top of the dialog box, the currently active profile name is listed.
4. If the active Profile at the top of the dialog is not currently AutoCAD Architecture (US Imperial) or AutoCAD Architecture (US Metric), select one of those and then click the Set Current button. (You can also double-click it.)

   Choose *Imperial* if you are in the United States and/or wish to use Imperial units, otherwise choose *Metric*.
5. Click the Add to List button.

NOTE

The Add to List function actually copies the current profile.

6. In the Add Profile dialog box, type **MasterACA 2010** for the Profile name.
7. For the description type: **Mastering AutoCAD Architecture 2010**.
8. Click Apply and Close.
9. The new entry will appear in the list. Double-click it. (You can also select it and then click the Set Current button.)

   At the top of the dialog box, next to Current Profile, MasterACA 2010 should now appear (see Figure 3.1).

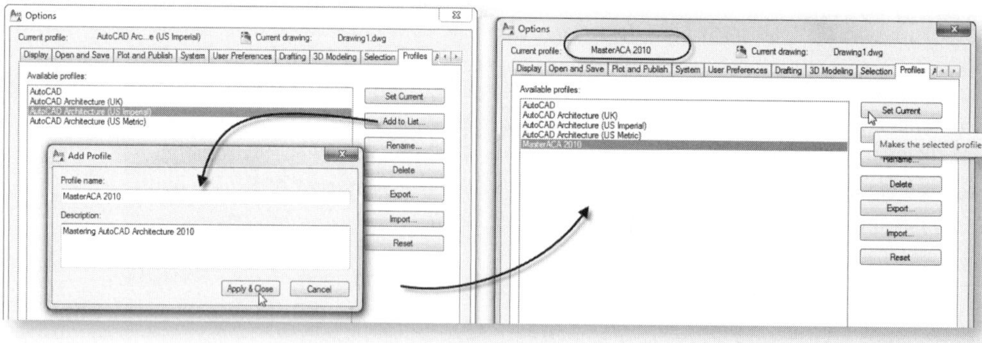

FIGURE 3.1 *Set the new profile MasterACA as the current profile*

Configure the New Profile

10. Click the Files tab located on the far left (use the scroll buttons if necessary).
11. Expand the Template Settings and then the Default Template File Name for QNEW item.
12. Select the item listed there and then on the right side click the Browse button.
13. Browse to the *C:\MasterACA 2010\Template* folder. Select the *AEC Model (Imperial Stb).dwt* [*AEC Model (Metric Stb).dwt*] template file and then click Open (see Figure 3.2).

    Choose the Imperial one if you work in feet and inches. Otherwise select the Metric one.

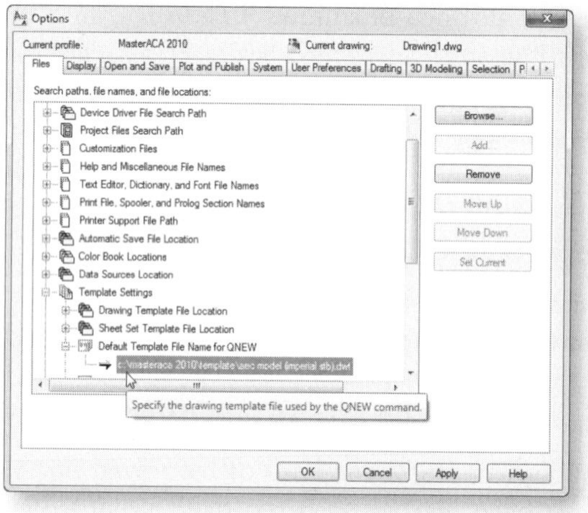

FIGURE 3.2 *Select a template file provided with the book CD as your default*

The "QNEW" command, accessed by clicking the New icon on the Quick Access Toolbar (QAT), will begin a new drawing by automatically loading the template chosen here without a confirmation dialog box. To choose an alternate template or start from scratch, choose **New > Drawing** from the Application Menu.

NOTE

The file that you have just pointed to here is an exact duplicate of the out-of-the-box template file shipped with the software by Autodesk. The reason for pointing to this file instead of whatever may have been selected is to ensure that new files you create while working through the book exercises begin as expected by the tutorials. When you create files for actual production work, use the default profile or one created by your CAD Manager instead. This will ensure that your actual project files are created from your office standard template file rather than the one used here in the book. This example provides one simple advantage to having an alternate profile.

14. Click the Display tab.

Included on this tab are the options for User Interface (UI) Colors and Crosshair size. Many users have their own preferences for UI colors and many prefer the use of a full screen cursor. (The author prefers a white Uniform background under Colors and the default 5% Crosshair size.)

15. Make your preferred choices on the Display tab.

Another item on this tab is the "Show Tooltips" item. This can be turned on and off with the checkbox and determines if tooltips appear when you pause your mouse over an interface item like a ribbon tool, palette tool or dialog box item. In addition, you can select the "Show extended Tool Tips" checkbox to have a more detailed Tool Tip appear if your mouse lingers over the item for the indicated number of seconds. Two seconds is the default. If you do not want the detailed Tool Tips to appear, uncheck this box. If you do not want any Tool Tips, uncheck the "Show Tool Tips" box.

16. Click the Open and Save tab.
17. In the File Safety Precautions area, under Automatic save, change the Minutes between saves value to **20**.

CAUTION

Automatic Save actually functions as an automatic backup. If the file has not been saved by the time entered in the Minutes between saves box, a backup file will be created in the temporary folder on your system (which is listed in the Files tab). It is better to think of the Automatic Save feature as a "Save Reminder" or "Automatic Backup" rather than a save. Should the AutoSave message appear at the Command Line, perform an actual save (Application Menu or press CTRL + S) command immediately to avoid losing work. Also, note that ACA creates an additional backup file with a BAK extension each time you save the file. This file will be saved to the same directory as the DWG file. If a DWG file should become corrupt, rename the BAK to a DWG extension (in Windows Explorer) and open this file. (You will need to turn off the Hide extensions for known types in the Windows Folder Options control panel settings to do this. See Windows help for more information.) You should be able to recover anything up until your last save. No matter what your settings on the Open and Save tab, just remember to save often!

NOTE

The AutoCAD Drawing Recovery Manager makes it much easier to recover files after a system failure. If ACA crashes, the Drawing Recovery Manager will appear the next time you launch the program. The most recent DWG and BAK file will be listed for each drawing that you had open at the time of the crash. You can recover and save these drawings from this interface. The Drawing Recovery Manager will allow you to open BAK files directly without requiring you to rename them in Windows Explorer first. If you do crash, be sure to send the report request that appears. These reports help Autodesk troubleshoot problems in the software and devise fixes for them.

18. In the Demand load XREFs area, verify that "Enabled with copy" is chosen (see Figure 3.3).

    This is the default setting for ACA 2010 and should already be set this way.

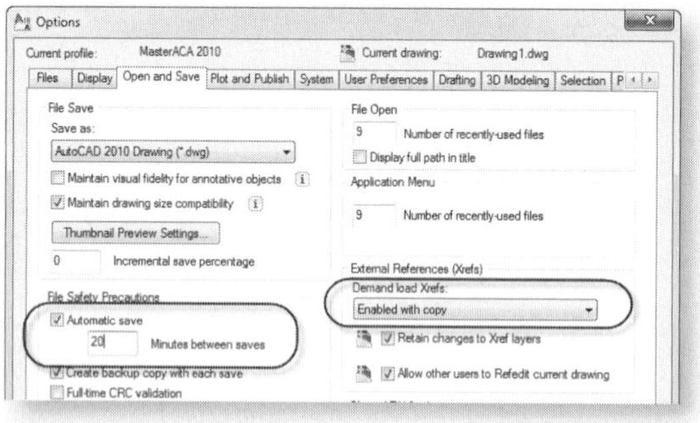

FIGURE 3.3 *Make certain that XREFs use Enabled with copy or Disabled*

CAD MANAGER NOTE

This setting is very important to team environments. If "Disabled" is chosen, the Demand Load feature for XREFs will be turned off and performance may suffer. If the "Enabled" setting is chosen, the user may enjoy better performance, but they will be locking *every* XREF file they load, thereby preventing any one else on the project team from opening those files! "Enabled with Copy" is a good compromise. However, depending on your specific network environment, either "Disabled" or "Enabled with Copy" may be suitable. The only critical thing to remember is that "Enabled" should *never* be chosen when working in a networked environment.

19. Take note of the AutoCAD drawing icon next to some of the items in the Options dialog box (see Figure 3.4).

    This icon indicates a setting saved only in the drawing file. These settings are not saved globally by the profile. Use template files to manage these settings.

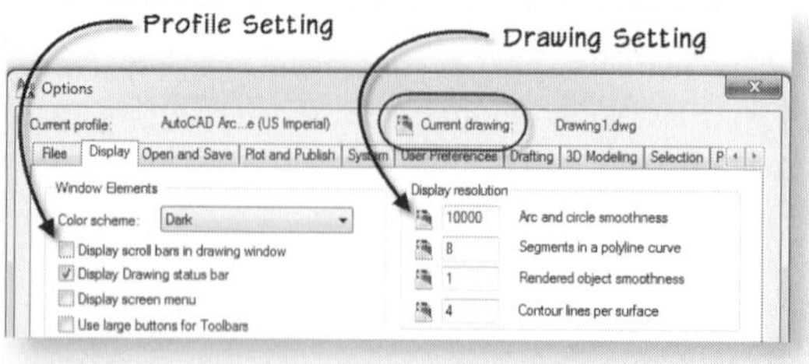

FIGURE 3.4 *Drawing level settings indicated by the colored icon*

Many veteran AutoCAD users have long been accustomed to being able to use the right mouse button as a quick way to press ENTER. However, since ACA makes use of the right mouse button for context menus, many seasoned AutoCAD users have lamented the loss of the simple yet cherished right-click equals ENTER functionality. Fortunately, ACA offers the perfect compromise solution to this dilemma: "Time-sensitive right-click." With this feature enabled, the right-click will behave as it used to in previous versions of AutoCAD by issuing an ENTER. To display the shortcut menu, hold the right-click button down a bit longer. To enable this option, click the Right-click Customization button on the User Preferences tab. If you wish to use this setting, perform the following steps:

20. Click the User Preferences tab.
21. Click the Right-click Customization button.
22. Place a check mark in the Turn on time-sensitive right-click option and then click Apply and Close (see Figure 3.5).

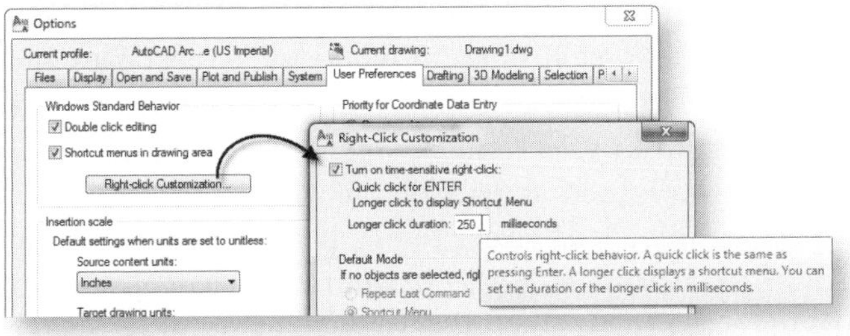

FIGURE 3.5 *Turning on the time-sensitive right-click option*

Remember that using this feature is a matter of personal preference. You are strongly urged to not disable the right-click menu settings. Doing so will make it difficult or impossible to execute many of ACA's core functions. As an alternative to the time-sensitive right-click, remember that you can also press SPACEBAR on the keyboard for ENTER. In this way, you could leave the default right-click behavior as is and rather than right-click to ENTER, simply press the SPACEBAR instead.

That completes our profile settings.

23. Click the Apply button, and then click OK.

Verify and Load Palettes

Many ACA commands may be accessed from Tool Palettes. In this topic, we will be certain that the most common tool palettes are loaded.

24. Verify that the tool palettes are loaded.

    If they are not loaded, from the Home tab of the ribbon, click the **Tools** button or press CTRL + 3.

NOTE

The tool palettes can be left floating, or docked on the edges of the screen. Other settings are available as well. Refer to Chapter 1 for more details.

CAD MANAGER NOTE

ACA installs with a collection of sample Tool Palettes available. The Content Browser provides access to copies of all of these standard tool palettes. It can also be used to set up new or customize existing tool palettes for use by the project team. To open it, choose Content Browser from the Tools drop-down button on the Home tab of the ribbon (or press CTRL + 4). For more information on working with the Content Browser, see the "Working with the Content Browser" heading in Chapter 2.

Create a Tool Palette Group

In Chapter 1, we looked at Tool Palette Groups. Four are provided in the default installation. In the previous chapter we created a custom Tool Palette and looked at the Content Browser. While we are configuring our Workspace, it is a good time to consider additional tool palettes that we might wish to have available in our personal Workspace. While there are endless possibilities, in this example we will focus simply on the tool palettes we already have on hand.

In the last chapter (and in much of the remainder of this book) exercises were performed in the Project Navigator environment. As you saw in the Quick Start and Chapter 2, Project Navigator provides a environment where all project files and resources are readily accessible and linked to one another. Tool Palettes behave slightly differently when working in a project environment. For example, it is possible for Tool Palettes to be configured as part of the project (swapping in and out as the project is loaded or unloaded) rather than a persistent part of your ACA Workspace. If you wish to use such "project palettes" then consult the online help for the "Displaying the Project Tool Palette Group" topic or search for "project palettes."

It is more common and desirable to create tool palettes and groups that will remain available regardless of the project you have currently loaded in Project Navigator. This is the type of tool palette group that we will create now. In order to create such a "persistent" tool palette or group, you must either disable project palettes for your current project or close your current project before proceeding to customize your tool palettes. Even though we did not specifically load a project in this chapter, if you completed Chapter 2, it is likely that the Chapter 2 project is still active in Project Navigator (ACA keeps a project loaded until you load another or close it).

The easiest way to be sure that you are creating persistent tool palettes is to close the current project. You can easily do this on the Project Navigator palette.

25. Make sure the Project Navigator palette is open onscreen. If it is not, click the Project Navigator icon on the QAT.
26. On the Project tab, at the bottom of the palette, click the Close Current Project icon (see Figure 3.6).

Complete the Profile and Save a Workspace

In the "Quick Access Toolbar" and "Ribbon" headings in Chapter 1, several features of the QAT and the Ribbon were discussed including ways to customize them to your preferences. For example, if you wish to relocate the QAT below the ribbon, minimize the ribbon to tabs or panels, add or remove tools from the QAT, or add or remove ribbon tabs and/or panels, you should make those changes now.

34. Make any desired changes to your ribbon tabs, panels and the QAT.

    These will be "remembered" by the MasterACA 2010 Profile.

While you are free to rearrange the ribbon, panels and QAT, it should be noted that the out-of-the-box configuration will be used throughout this book. Therefore, the QAT will be shown above the ribbon tabs, and the ribbon will not be minimized in all figures.

35. Position your palettes (and any floating ribbon panels) the way you like them.

    Remember settings like docking, auto-hide and anchored covered in Chapter 1 (see Figure 3.10).

Review the controls available for palettes in the "Understanding Tool Palettes" topic in Chapter 1 Open any hidden palettes you anticipate using frequently and either anchor them to side of your workspace or turn on auto-hide. Good candidates to have open and anchored are the Layer Manager, External References palette, the DesignCenter and the QuickCalc palettes. Once you have all palettes and ribbons organized the way you like them, proceed to the next step.

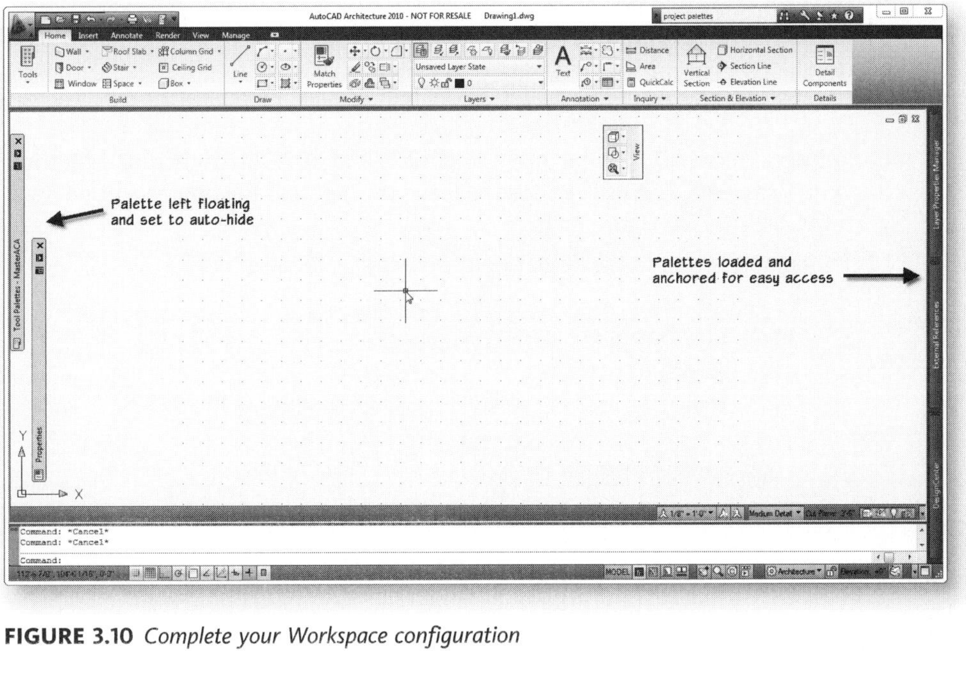

FIGURE 3.10 *Complete your Workspace configuration*

Create a Desktop Shortcut

To make your new Profile easy to access, you can create a custom shortcut on the desktop.

36. From the Application Menu, choose **Exit**. (You can also press CTRL + Q. If asked to save a drawing, click No.)
37. On the Windows desktop, locate the AutoCAD Architecture 2010 icon.
38. Right-click it and choose **Copy**.
39. Right-click next to it and click **Paste**.
40. Right-click the new copy and choose **Rename**. Type **MasterACA** and then press ENTER (see Figure 3.11).

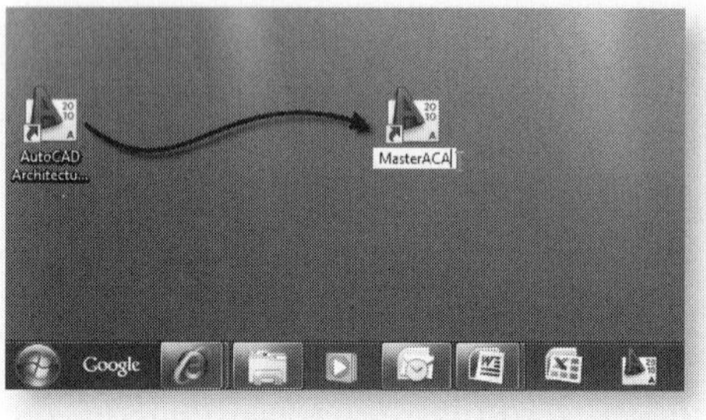

FIGURE 3.11 *Copy, paste and rename the new icon*

41. Right-click the newly named MasterACA icon and choose **Properties**.
42. Click the Shortcut tab.

    In the Target field locate the following string:

    `/p "AutoCAD Architecture (US Imperial)" [/p "AutoCAD Architecture (US Metric)"]`

43. Replace "AutoCAD Architecture – Imperial" ["AutoCAD Architecture – Metric"] with **"MasterACA 2010"**. Be sure to leave the "/p" and the quotes around MasterACA 2010 (see Figure 3.12).

    The complete text in the Target field will read as follows:

    ```
    " "C:\Program Files\AutoCAD Architecture 2010\acad.exe" /ld
    "C:\Program Files\AutoCAD Architecture 2010\AecBase.dbx"
    /p "MasterACA 2010"
    ```

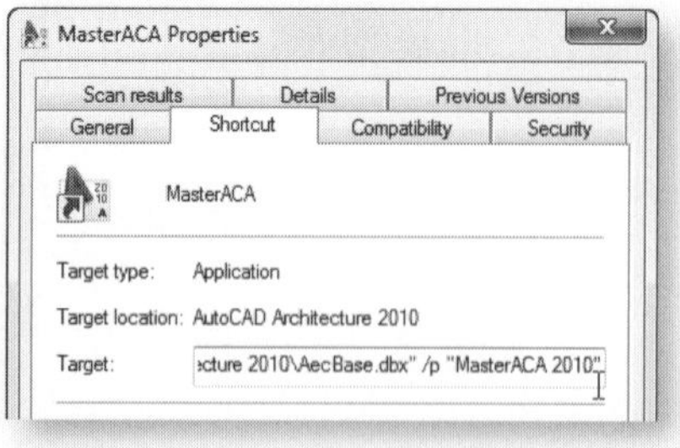

FIGURE 3.12 *Replace the default profile call with MasterACA 2010*

The first part of the Target field tells the Windows shortcut which application to load, in this case "*acad.exe*" (or AutoCAD). Following that, "/ld" instructs the shortcut to load the ACA functions immediately upon launch. Without this switch, we would be loading just standard AutoCAD. The "/p" switch in the Target box tells ACA to launch into the profile listed after /p, in our case "MasterACA 2010."

NOTE

The use of quotes in the text strings of the Target box is required if spaces occur in any of the paths or names. In the default strings, both "Program Files" and "AutoCAD Architecture" include spaces, and therefore require the use of quotes around the entire string. In our case, "MasterACA 2010" also has a space. Be sure to include the quotes.

44. Click OK to close the MasterACA Properties dialog box.

Test the New Icon

45. Double-click the new icon to test it.
46. If the Welcome Screen appears, close it.
47. Verify that the MasterACA profile is active by returning to the Options dialog box.

    Visually inspect the screen to see if all of your QAT, ribbon, panel and palette setup remained from the previous exit.

TIP

If any error messages appeared, go back through the steps discussed earlier to troubleshoot the problem or contact your CAD or IT support person. One of the advantages of making the duplicate profile is it leaves the default one intact to return to as a backup should something go wrong.

DRAWING SETUP

Once you have a profile in place to manage all of the global settings, you can turn your attention to the drawing-specific settings. These include items such as units, layers, and scale. The Drawing Setup command is used to configure these settings within the current drawing. All settings in the Drawing Setup dialog box are saved within the drawing. (There is also an option to save the settings as the default for future drawings.)

Understanding the Relationship of Units and Scale

In this sequence, we will explore the interaction of the Units and Scale settings by switching between Imperial and Metric units. The steps in this sequence apply to users of both Imperial and Metric units.

1. From the Application Menu, choose **Utilities > Drawing Setup**.
2. Click the Units tab (see the left side of Figure 3.13).

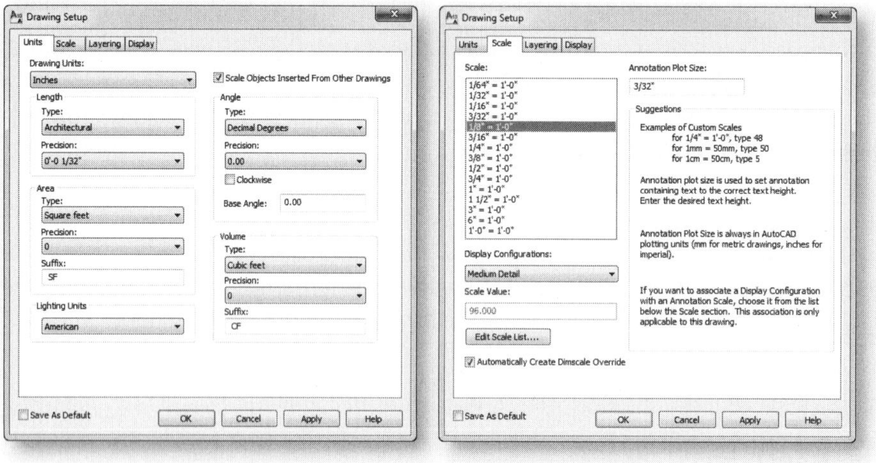

FIGURE 3.13 *The Units and Scale tabs of the Drawing Setup dialog*

3. In the top left corner under Drawing Units, choose **Inches**.

The settings available in the other four sections, Linear, Angular, Area, and Volume, will adjust as required to be consistent with the base Drawing Unit (in this case Inches). For example, in the Area grouping, the Type list shows three choices, all listed in Imperial units of measure. When you choose an item from the list, the suffix field will update appropriately.

4. Experiment with the settings in all fields.
5. At the top of the Drawing Setup window, click the Scale tab (see the right side of Figure 3.13).

Drawing Scale lists all of the most common architectural scales. Annotation objects, such as targets, tags, symbols, text, dimensions and schedule tables, automatically scale to the value assigned here. In order to choose the right drawing scale, it is necessary to know at which scale the final drawing will plot. When you choose a scale such as 1/4" = 1'-0" the field below Custom Scales changes to 48.000 to reflect the new choice. Notice also that the Display Configuration may change as you switch scales. This is an optional feature that automatically changes the drawing Display Configuration when you change the drawing scale (refer to Chapter 2 for more detail on Display Configurations).

If the scale you wish to use is not listed, you can enter it as a custom scale. Determine it by dividing the drawing unit by the scaled unit. For example, to work at 1"=10', divide 10' (120") by 1" to arrive at the scale factor of 120.

NOTE

If the scale that you want is not already on the list, you can click the Edit Scale List button to add to or edit the list.

The Annotation Plot Size value (on the right in Figure 3.13) controls the plotted height of text contained within symbols inserted in the drawing. The value represents the height of the text portion of the symbol in the *final* printed output. The most typical text height sizes are 1/8" [3] and 3/32" [2.5]. The graphic portion of the symbol will scale proportionally to whatever factor is necessary to achieve the correct Annotation Plot Size for text. Both this value and the scale factor from the list at the left are multiplied together to arrive at the final automatic scale factor for all ACA annotation routines. Annotation is explored in more detail in Chapter 14.

6. Return to the Units tab.
7. In the Drawing Units section, choose **Millimeters**.

   Notice the change in the Length section. The unit Type has changed to Decimal.

In the Area grouping, if you open the Type list again you will notice that all of the available choices now reflect metric settings. Like we saw previously, if you choose a value from the list such as **Square Millimeters** the suffix will change accordingly.

8. Experiment again with the settings in all fields.
9. Click the Scale tab again.

   The choices under Drawing Scale now represent the most common metric architectural scales.

This time, choose a metric scale in the Drawing Scale list, such as **1:100**. This will result in a value of 100 in the Custom Scales field to reflect the new choice. As before, if the scale you wish to use is not listed, click Other, and type in a scale factor in the Custom Scale field or click the Edit Scale List to add to the preset list.

Notice that the Length unit Type is Decimal, *not* Architectural.

NOTE

Architectural and Engineering unit formats are available only when the base unit is inches. Both feet and inches can be entered when you work in Architectural or Engineering as long as you distinguish feet from inches at the Command Line and in text input boxes with an apostrophe (') following the number. To enter inches, typing only the number is required. Hyphens are not required to separate feet from inches. Hyphens are used to separate fractions from whole numbers. For more complete information on valid input of Imperial units in the ACA, refer to Table 3.1 and the online help.

TABLE 3.1 *Acceptable Imperial Unit Input Formats*

Value Required	Type This	Or This
Four feet	4'	48
Four inches	4	4"
Four feet four inches	4'4	52
Four feet four and one half inches	4'4-1/2	4'4.5 or 52.5

NOTE

Typing the inch (") mark is acceptable as well; however, it is not required. Dimensions throughout this text use the Feet and Inch format for clarity. However, feel free to enter dimension values in whatever formats you prefer. Eliminating the inch mark reduces keystrokes and is recommended despite the inclusion of it in this text.

Understanding Layer Standards

Layers provide an important organization and management tool to AutoCAD and AutoCAD Architecture alike. Part of the core functionality of AutoCAD, layers provide a means to centrally control object color, visibility, linetype, lineweight, and plotting properties. Because a typical architectural drawing can contain dozens or even hundreds of layers, several tools have been devised over the years to make layer management easier and more useful. Layers and layering strategy have kept many a CAD Manager busy and have been the topic of many books, including the popular *CAD Layer Guidelines, Second Edition* published by The American Institute of Architects and its successor, the *US National CAD Standard* (now in its fourth edition). For reasons such as these, CAD Managers and users alike will be pleased to learn that layering of AEC objects is handled automatically by the software. (Please note that drafted entities such as lines, arcs and polylines are *not* auto-layered.)

Layer Usage in AutoCAD Architecture

Layers are an important part of any ACA drawing. There are many popular notions regarding the definition and usage of layers. The most common description of layers is the "sheets of acetate" analogy. This description of layers and layering uses the metaphor of several sheets of acetate, each with a different piece of drawing information, stacked on top of one another. When taken together as a composite, they represent a complete drawing. This metaphor, though illustrative, is not complete. While effectively conveying a good mental picture of a collection layers, it fails to convey any information as to why we might use layers in the first place. It also implies properties that are not characteristic of layers such as "stacking" or the implication that one layer could "cover" the information on another. This is not possible with layers. A more evocative way to comprehend the potential of layers is to think of them as categories. Layering is simply a drawing-wide categorization system. When we think of layers this way, it is easy to understand their full potential. It is also easy to decide when a new layer is appropriate and what it ought to be named.

Thinking of layers this way is appropriate in generic AutoCAD, but it is especially helpful when we attempt to reconcile their role together with Display Control in ACA. As detailed in the previous chapter, Display Control offers a completely different way to control visibility, color, and lineweight of objects. Determining when to use the display system and when to use layering can sometimes be tricky. However, if we treat layering as a global drawing-wide categorization system, the distinction becomes much clearer. Display Control addresses very specific object-level display needs, while layers are much more general and pervasive. As such, it is appropriate to approach layering in ACA in "broad brush" fashion. In the default configuration, all walls are placed on a Wall layer regardless of type or style, likewise with doors, and all other objects. Each major ACA object class has a unique default layer assignment. Internal object subcomponents of ACA objects typically rely less on layers and more on Display Control parameters. For example, the control of individual object components like the swings of doors, the row lines of a schedule table, or the color of 3D components is often better handled with Display Control parameters instead. However, it is just as common to use both display settings and layers to achieve desired display results.

The strategy will become clear in the chapters that follow. The first step is to understand how automatic layering works. Objects are automatically placed on a layer as they are created. The current Layer Standard (rules for layer naming based on an established office or industry standard naming convention) and Layer Key Style (a list of potential layers that ACA can create as required on-the-fly) determine the exact layer they use. Layering assigned to internal object components is typically a parameter of the object style. Tools on tool palettes can also contain Layer Key information that supersedes the defaults of the particular object class.

MANAGER NOTE CAD

You can customize the Layer Standard and Layer Key Styles to comply with your existing office standard layering scheme. This is done by assigning a Layer Standard/Key file in the "Drawing Setup" dialog. Once assigned, you can save it as the default. You can be sure that your latest settings are available to all users by also checking the Always import Layer Key Style when first used in drawing option. Within the file you designate are both a Layer Standard and one or more Layer Key Styles. Layer Key Styles are used to assign AEC objects to their required layers. If a layer does not exist at the time the object is created, the Layer Key for that object will generate the layer on-the-fly. All AEC objects and any object or group of objects inserted from the AEC Content tab of the DesignCenter as well as objects created from tool palette tools can use Layer Keys.

Set the Layer Standard

ACA automatically places all new architectural objects on a predetermined layer. Layer standard files which facilitate this feature can be loaded in the "Drawing Setup" window.

1. From the Application Menu, choose **Utilities > Drawing Setup**.
2. Click the Layering tab.

   Take note of the file listed in the Layer Standards/Key File to Auto-Import box.
3. If the Layer Standards/Key File to Auto-Import field is blank or incorrect, click the small browse (...) button to the extreme right of the window, and locate the correct file. *AECLayerStd.dwg* is the default (see number 1 in Figure 3.14).

   Your particular office's standards might be set to Auto-Import a file other than *AECLayerStd.dwg*. If this is the case, then leave the setting as is. Check with your CAD Manager or CAD support personnel for more information.

MANAGER NOTE CAD

AutoCAD Architecture 2010 uses Windows compliant file locations for all resources (this is true for all versions of Windows from Windows XP to the present). This means that the path to the *AECLayerStd.dwg* drawing file in XP defaults to: *C:\Documents and Settings\All Users\Application Data\Autodesk\ACA 2010\enu\Layers* and in Vista and Windows 7 it is: *C:\Users\All Users\Autodesk\ACA 2010\enu\Layers*. This path may vary with locale. If you have installed a non-English version of ACA, or non-US version, this path might vary slightly. It is also important to note that the *Application Data* folder is a hidden folder by default in Windows. Therefore, you will need to set your Folder Options in Windows Explorer to show hidden folders. Bear in mind that this path and any other support file search path can be changed to any location that you find suitable, including locations on a network server. In fact, it will often be much easier to administer resources for several users if certain common files like the layer file are stored on the server. The option to move most content and support files to alternate locations on your system or a network server are available during software installation. For complete recommendations on installation options and layer standards, refer to chapters 1 and 5 in *Autodesk Architectural Desktop: An Advanced Implementation Guide* by Paul F. Aubin and Matt Dillon. This resource was last updated for the 2007 version of the software, but most of its recommendation remain relevant to ACA 2010.

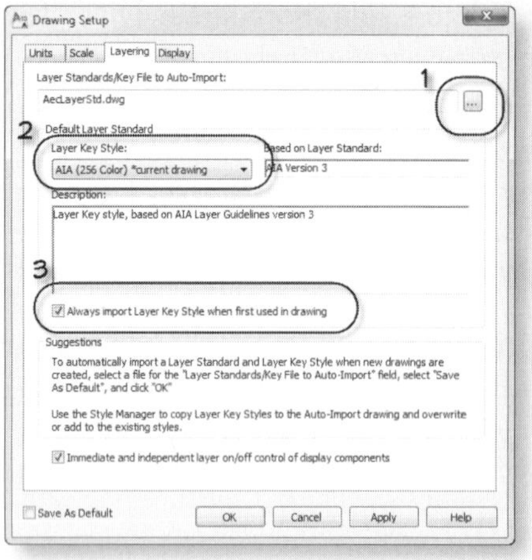

FIGURE 3.14 *The browse button used to load a Layer Standards file and Layer Standards included in the AECLayerStd file*

The *AECLayerStd.dwg* file includes many built-in industry standard layering schemes such as the one published by The American Institute of Architects (AIA)—which is a part of the US National CAD Standard (NCS) and several other layering schemes. From the Layer Key Style list, you can choose the layer key style appropriate to your firm's office standards (see number 2 in Figure 3.14). If your firm uses a standard not included in this file, your CAD Manager can advise you regarding the proper file to load here. If you are a sole practitioner or otherwise do not have a CAD Manager or an established office standard, it is recommended that you adopt one of the standards in this file, such as AIA (256 Color) as your layering standard. This Layer Key Style is fully compliant with the NCS. Adopting an industry standard provides immediate benefit to you and your firm:

- Sharing drawings with other firms is easier because the layering systems are more likely to be compatible.
- Orientation is easier when new employees are hired.
- The developers of AutoCAD Architecture have already done the work of configuring the standard and including it in the software.
- Changes to the standard will be implemented automatically by Autodesk in future releases of the software without your staff being burdened with the task.
- The structure is logical and extensible.

One additional setting on the Layers tab bears mention. The "Always import Layer Key Style when first used in drawing" checkbox instructs ACA to check the default Layer Standards/Key file each time a drawing is opened to see if there is a more recent version of the Layer Key Style. If so, it will update the current drawing to the latest version of the Layer Key Style. This setting is very useful for maintaining CAD Standards across the office.

4. Place a check mark in the Always import Layer Key Style when first used in drawing box (see number 3 in Figure 3.14).
5. Click Apply and then OK to dismiss the Drawing Setup dialog box.

Once they have been established, the majority of settings in the Drawing Setup dialog box do not need to change. Typically, as project needs dictate, the Scale setting might be changed as the project progresses. However, it is important to note that changing the values in the Units, Scale and Layering tabs may impact objects already contained in the drawing. For instance, if you change the Units setting, a dialog box will appear when you apply the change. This dialog box will give you the option to rescale all objects in the drawing to the new Unit. It will be your choice, which you should consider carefully depending on what you are trying to achieve. Regardless, all objects created from that point on would use your new settings. Re-layering of objects is NOT automatic. (A command to remap layers is, however, provided on the Layers panel. On the Home tab, click the Layers panel to expand it. Click the Remap Object Layers button). The final tab of the "Drawing Setup" dialog is the Display tab. This tab gives access to the System Default Display Control settings. This is an alternative to the Display Manager discussed in the previous chapter.

TEMPLATE FILES

AutoCAD has long used template files as a means to quickly apply setup information, enforce company standards and project-specific settings, and save time. AutoCAD Architecture takes full advantage of the same benefits. In much the same way as other popular Windows software packages, ACA uses template files at the time of file creation to establish a whole host of user settings and overall configuration. (Please note that template files apply only at the time of drawing creation.) A template file is an AutoCAD drawing file preconfigured for a particular type of task. Template files have a DWT extension and are available from the Application Menu. Choose the **New > Drawing** command or click the New icon on the QAT. In addition to the time saved when drawings are created from templates, templates help to ensure file consistency by giving all drawings the same basic starting point. ACA 2010 ships with several premade template files. These templates are ready to be used "as is." However, because office standards and project-specific needs vary, feel free to modify the default templates as necessary. The exact composition of the template used to create a drawing is not as important as ensuring that a template is used to create all new drawings. Table 3.2 shows the AEC template files included in the box with ACA 2010. Previously in the "Configure the New Profile" heading, we pointed our custom profile's QNEW setting to a copy of the *AEC Model (Imperial Stb).dwt* [*AEC Model (Metric Stb).dwt*] template file in the *C:\MasterACA 2010\Template* folder. The templates in this folder are exact copies of the out-of-the-box versions that ship with AutoCAD Architecture.

TABLE 3.2 *Out-of-the-Box Template Files*

Template File Name	Drawing Units	Plot Style Type
AEC Model (Imperial Ctb).dwt	Inches	Color
AEC Model (Imperial Stb).dwt	Inches	Named
AEC Model (Metric Ctb).dwt	Millimeters	Color
AEC Model (Metric Stb).dwt	Millimeters	Named
AEC Sheet (Imperial Ctb).dwt	Inches	Color
AEC Sheet (Imperial Stb).dwt	Inches	Named
AEC Sheet (Metric Ctb).dwt	Millimeters	Color
AEC Sheet (Metric Stb).dwt	Millimeters	Named

Notes on Table 3.2:

AEC Model—Template files are used for creating "Model" files. A model file is a file containing actual full-scale building data. This template is used to create files in which all of the day-to-day work is performed. The Constructs we will create later in this book use this template.

AEC Sheet—Template files are used for creating "Sheet" files. A sheet file is used *exclusively* for printing drawings.

In addition to the DWT templates listed here, the *Template* folder also contains Project templates and Sheet Set templates. (Refer to Chapter 5 for more information.)

NOTE

Please refer to the "Elements, Constructs, Views and Sheets" heading in Chapter 5 for complete information on Model and Sheet files.

CAUTION

Please avoid creating drawings without a template. This is because a scratch drawing requires an enormous amount of user configuration before serious ACA work can begin.

CAD MANAGER NOTE

ACA saves virtually all data and configuration within the drawing file. This includes system variables, blocks, object styles, and display configurations. Therefore, template files provide an excellent tool for promoting and maintaining office standards. ACA 2010 ships with several sample template files to help you get started. These include Model and Sheet templates for both Imperial and Metric units. Refer to Table 3.2 for more information. Certainly, you will find one of these pairs of templates suitable for your firm's needs. When you establish and configure office standards, it is highly recommended that these default templates be used as a starting point. Modify them to suit individual project or office-wide needs. Styles, blocks, and other resources can also be stored in separate drawing files stored on the network or hard drive. The resources can be accessed with custom tool palette tools. This keeps the template file size smaller by including only those items needed in all drawings, yet it provides a central repository for additional office standard items. This method also provides additional ongoing flexibility because new items can be easily added to the office standard library. It also makes it easier to update existing drawings when standard styles are modified.

In addition, ACA has the ability to establish Project Standards. Project Standards allow you to establish one or more drawing or template files as the source for all project styles and display configurations, and then use them to keep all other drawings synchronized with the standard. Use of this feature requires that the drawing management system be used to manage projects. ACA projects are covered throughout this book starting in Chapter 5. Project Standards are covered beginning in Chapter 8.

Understanding What Is Included in a Template

The best way to demonstrate the importance of using template files is to compare drawings created with and without template files. A drawing begun with the Start from Scratch option has little in the way of architectural settings. (To start from scratch, from the Application Menu, choose **New > Drawing** and then click the small arrow on the Open button to reveal a small menu. Then choose either **Open with no Template – Imperial**, or **Open with no Template – Metric**. See Figure 3.15.) Of the three major tools covered in the previous chapter, the display system, object styles, and anchors, display configurations and object styles make excellent additions to a template file. The "scratch" drawing will have no useful settings for any of these critical items.

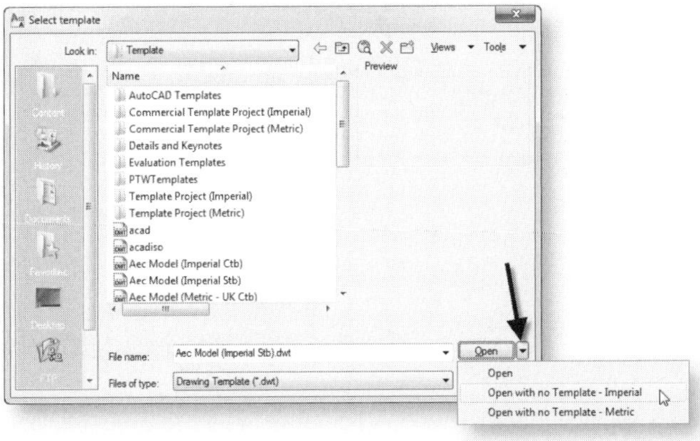

FIGURE 3.15 *Accessing the No Template (Start from scratch) option*

MANAGER NOTE

For actual production work, using template files is the only viable option; however, using Start from Scratch can be an excellent way to troubleshoot styles or a corrupted file or to import a file from another CAD package or outside vendors.

A drawing created without a template will have the following characteristics (see Figure 3.16):

- Scratch drawings include two Layout tabs; neither has its Page Setup configured for plotting architectural drawings.
- Layer 0 is the only layer typically present in a scratch drawing.
- There are no ACA styles in a scratch drawing. (Figure 3.17 shows the Style Manager with all object classes empty.) Access the Style Manager from the Format menu.
- The Display System is not initialized in a scratch drawing. If you run an ACA command, a collection of the most basic Display Configurations and Display Control settings will be auto-created. But you will have few of the benefits of the Display System showcased in the previous chapter.
- Scratch drawings start in model space zoomed in to a size roughly equal to a sheet of notepaper (US Letter Size or A4 Size).

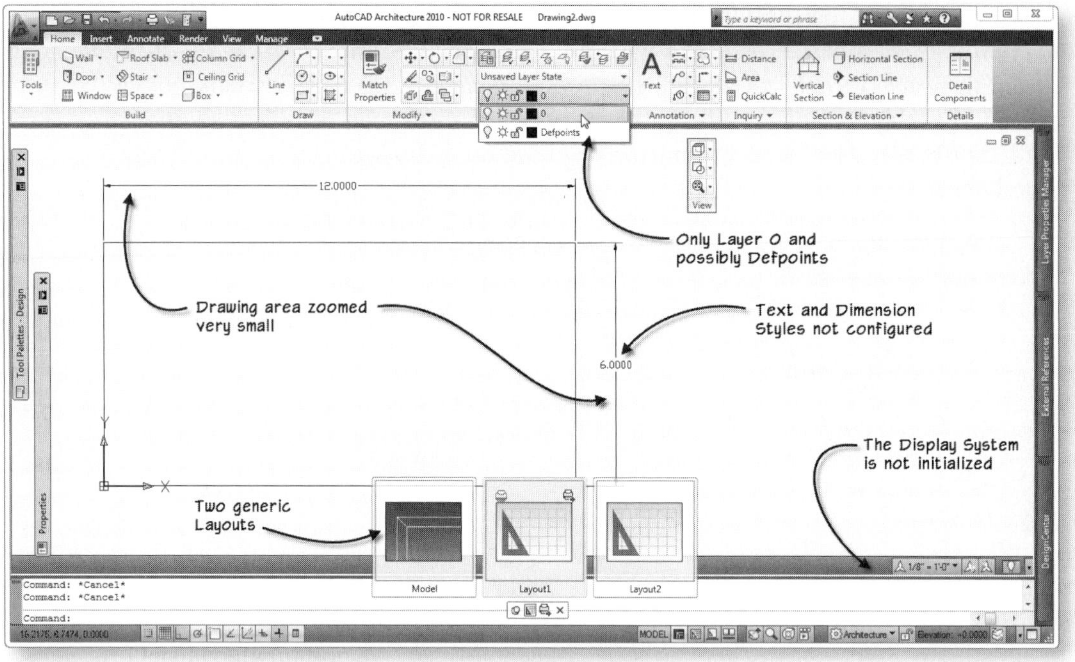

FIGURE 3.16 *Scratch drawings contain no useful ACA settings*

As noted previously, and as you can see in Figure 3.17, no ACA styles appear in a scratch drawing. Open Style Manager from the Manage tab to see this.

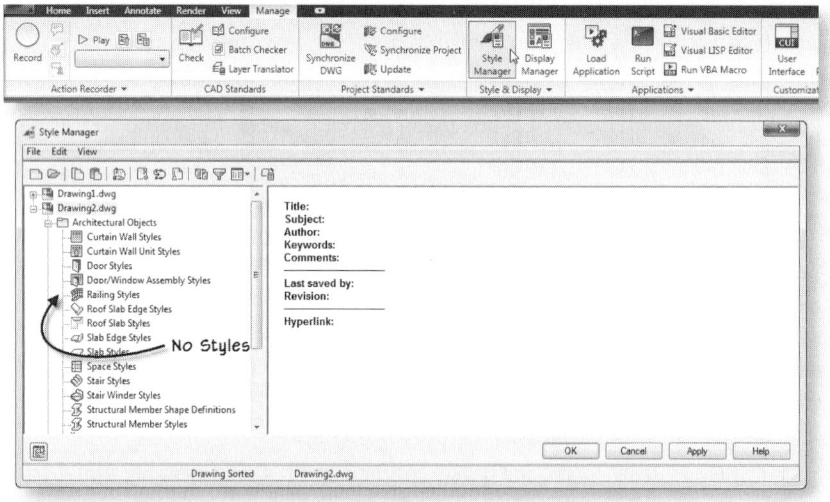

FIGURE 3.17 *The Style Manager showing no styles in a scratch drawing*

By contrast, a drawing created with one of the out-of-the-box template files will have the following characteristics (see Figure 3.18):

- Template drawings typically include purpose-built Layouts. These are preconfigured for purposes like Working or Plotting at a particular Sheet size. The Model template includes a single "Work" Layout that includes a 2D and 3D viewport. The Sheet templates include several Layouts—one for each common sheet size. When you create a Sheet from these templates, only the sheet size you need is copied to the newly created sheet file (see Chapter 5 for more information on Sheets).

- Templates contain several premade layers. However, it is usually desirable to keep the number of layers in a template file to a minimum including only those layers that cannot be auto-created using the Layer Key system discussed previously.
- Perhaps the greatest benefit of using an AEC template is the preconfigured Display Configurations and Display Control settings. Nearly all of the advantages of the Display System discussed in the previous chapter are lost if you do not begin your drawings with a well-conceived template file. This is the most compelling reason to use the out-of-the-box template files as the seed for any of your in-house customization.
- Template drawings start in model space zoomed out to a size appropriate for building models.

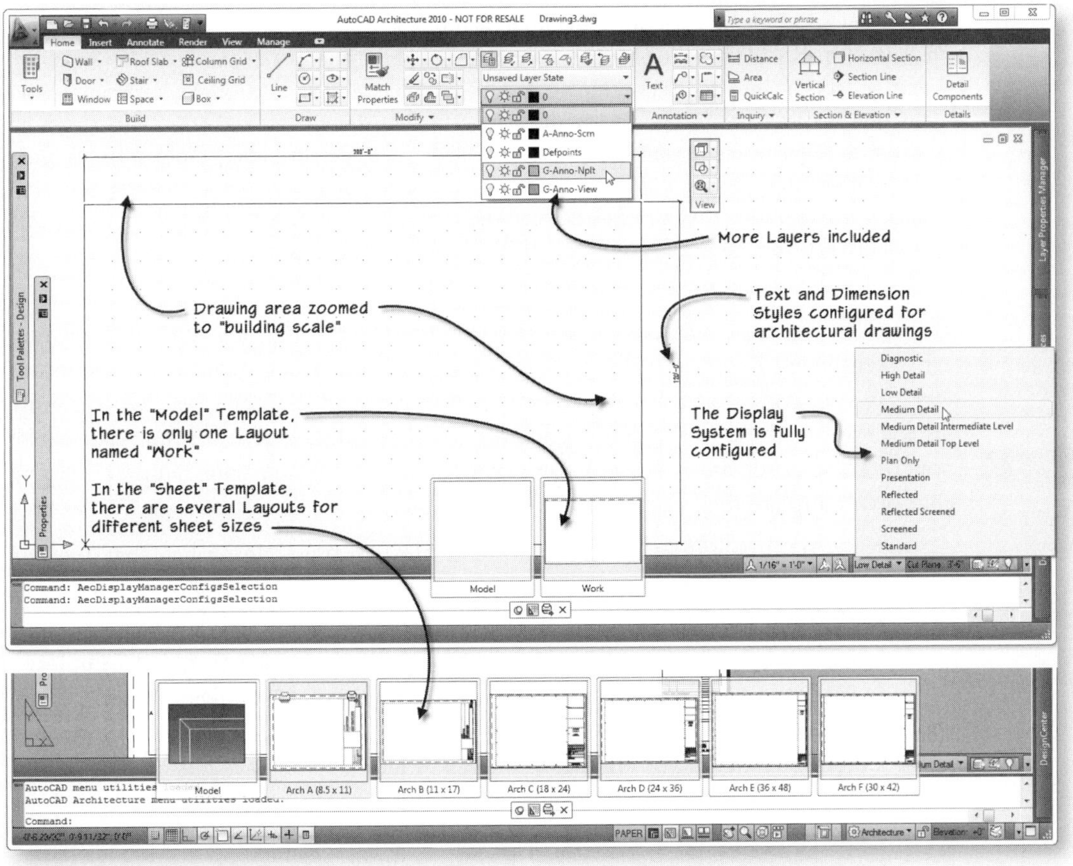

FIGURE 3.18 *Templates use purpose-built settings useful for architectural modeling and printing tasks*

- Templates often contain some ACA Styles—these "Standard" styles are often auto-created by the software. Figure 3.19 shows the Style Manager with several classes populated with styles. A plus sign (+) next to a class indicates that styles are present.

NOTE

Because of a Tool Palette's ability to automatically import a remote Style, the inclusion of Styles in a Template is not a critical factor.

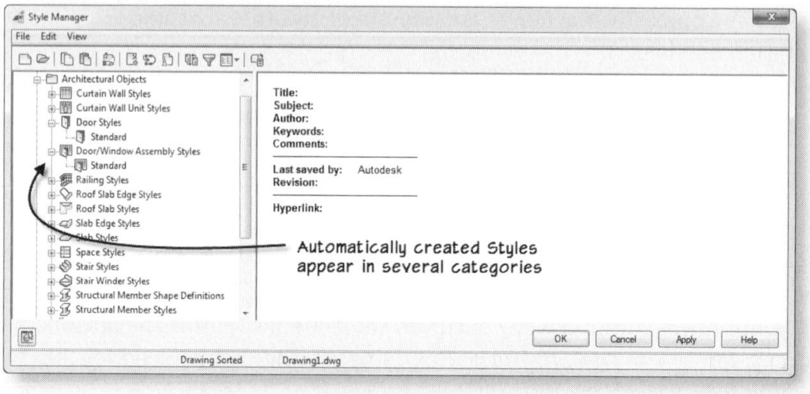

FIGURE 3.19 *A Template is often pre-populated with Styles in one or more categories*

CAD MANAGER NOTE

The templates shipping with AutoCAD Architecture are ready to use straight out-of-the-box. If you wish to build your own office standard template, the out-of-the-box offerings are excellent starting points for developing your own template file(s). It is highly recommended that you become comfortable with the out-of-the-box templates and then if necessary, customize them to meet your firm's specific needs. Consider including those settings and display items that people will use most frequently. Once you have a standard template in place, it is imperative that all users be required to use it, or a project-based derivative of it, for all project work. (See Chapter 5 for more information on Projects.)

Hopefully, you are beginning to see the benefits to starting new drawings with an AEC template. There is really no compelling reason to begin drawings any other way. As you work through the exercises in the coming chapters, you will certainly discover areas where the default templates could be enhanced and improved. Make note of these observations as you go. When you are ready, try your hand at creating your own template file. The basic steps are simple:

1. Create a new drawing using the template that most closely matches the one you wish to create.
2. Edit any settings as you see fit.
3. From the Application Menu, choose **Save As > AutoCAD Drawing Template.**
4. From the Files of type list, make sure that AutoCAD Drawing Template File (*.dwt) is chosen (see Figure 3.20).
5. Type a name for your new template and then click the Save button.

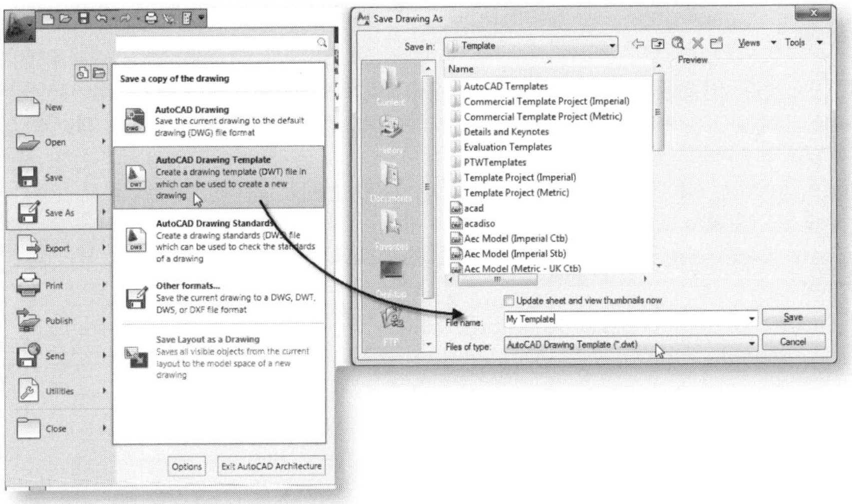

FIGURE 3.20 *Saving a new template file*

> **NOTE**
>
> Choosing AutoCAD Drawing Template File (*.dwt) as the file type automatically switches to the correct folder for saving templates. This location is configured on the Files tab of the Options dialog (see the "Configure the New Profile" heading). Check with your CAD Manager before saving templates to be sure of the correct location.

Templates will also be used in ACA by the Drawing Management system. This very important and powerful tool set will be covered extensively throughout this book starting in Chapter 5 (see Figure 3.21).

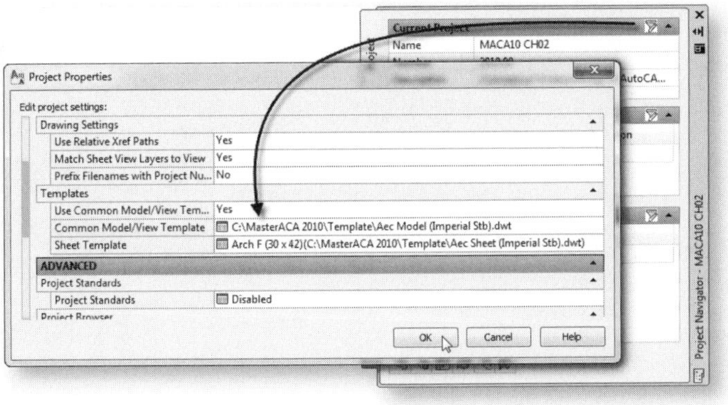

FIGURE 3.21 *ACA Projects automatically use Template files to create all drawings*

Whether or not you choose to use this powerful ACA drawing and XREF management system, template files are *the* way to start new AutoCAD Architecture drawings.

SUMMARY

- A profile helps manage the system level settings in ACA.
- Adding a profile switch (/p) to the ACA icon on the desktop loads the profile automatically when you launch ACA.
- Choose Drawing Units before all other settings in the Drawing Setup dialog box; this will set other choices to appropriate matching values.
- To create a "persistent" Tool Palette or Group, close the Current Project before proceeding.
- The Layer Standard chosen determines which layers will be auto-created by objects in the drawing.
- Using the Start from Scratch option to create new drawings is not recommended for typical usage.
- The AEC templates come preloaded with a variety of useful sample content and settings.
- Adopt templates as your office/project standards to manage standards, quality control and support issues when managing ACA drawings.

SECTION

II

The Building Model

In this section, we will explore in detail the creation of the Building Model. We will work on two projects from start to finish throughout the course of this book: one residential (beginning in Chapter 4) and the other commercial (beginning in Chapter 5). In Chapter 5, we begin using the Drawing Management system in ACA to create and link several drawing files, each with its own unique focus, but used together to create the complete composite building model of each project. In Chapters 6 through 12, we undertake a thorough exploration of the major AutoCAD Architecture AEC object types such as Walls, Doors, Curtain Walls, Column Grids, Stairs, Roofs and Fixtures, each with its own special focus on how the parts fit into the complete building model. A great deal of emphasis is placed on the actual process of using such tools throughout and how they fit into the drawing management system.

Section II is organized as follows:

Chapter 4 Beginning a Floor Plan Layout

Chapter 5 Setting Up the Building Model

Chapter 6 Column Grids and Structural Layout

Chapter 7 Vertical Circulation

Chapter 8 The Building Shell

Chapter 9 Mastering Wall Cleanup

Chapter 10 Progressive Refinement—Part 1

Chapter 11 Progressive Refinement—Part 2

Chapter 12 Roofs and Slabs

CHAPTER

4

Beginning a Floor Plan Layout

INTRODUCTION

Any discussion about using AutoCAD Architecture to create floor plan layouts needs to begin with walls. After all, walls are the major component of any building. In this chapter, we'll make our first thorough examination of an AEC object—the Wall object. We will look at other objects as well, but Walls will be the primary focus. The last several chapters were intended to get you comfortable with the theoretical underpinnings of ACA. Now that you are in the correct mindset, get ready to roll up your sleeves—it is time to produce some drawings!

OBJECTIVES

Two projects will be completed in this book—one commercial and one residential. Throughout the course of the following hands-on tutorials, we will lay out the existing conditions floor plan for our residential project. In this chapter, we will explore the various techniques for adding and modifying walls, doors, and windows. In addition, we will add plumbing fixtures and other elements to make the floor plan more complete.

- Understand Wall objects.
- Add and modify Walls.
- Explore Wall properties.
- Add and modify Doors and Windows.
- Add plumbing fixtures.
- Work with Wall Modifiers and associated tools.

WORKING WITH WALLS

Basic object creation in ACA involves frequent interaction with the Tool and Properties palettes as well as a heavy use of the ribbon and right-click menus. An overview of the ribbon and various right-click menus can be seen in Chapter 1. Although many of the command options do appear at the Command Line, remember that it is often quicker and more direct to interact with the Properties palette or the ribbon and right-click menus. If you have Dynamic Input enabled (see Chapter 1), you will also receive heads-up prompts directly onscreen at your cursor location. Working with walls is very similar to drawing simple lines. You add Walls point by point just as you do lines, and like a line, each Wall segment remains a separate entity distinct from its neighbors. However, unlike lines, Walls know that they are Walls and behave accordingly. Walls will "cleanup" with intersecting Walls. Walls have height and width parameters, can have custom shapes and profiles, and can receive Doors and Windows by automatically creating openings and anchors for them. Finally, like lines, Walls can also be copied, trimmed, filleted, extended, offset and arrayed. Don't worry if you do not have experience with AutoCAD, many of these commands will be used with Walls in this chapter; however, if you wish, you can consult an AutoCAD reference or the online help for further information on these and other basic AutoCAD commands.

Install the CD Files

1. If you have not already done so, install the dataset files located on the Mastering AutoCAD Architecture 2010 CD-ROM.

   Refer to "Files Included on the CD-ROM" in the Preface for information on installing the sample files included on the CD.
2. Launch AutoCAD Architecture 2010 from the desktop icon created in Chapter 3.

If you did not create a custom icon, you might want to review "Create a New Profile" and "Create a Desktop Shortcut" in Chapter 3. Creating the custom desktop icon is not essential; however, it makes loading a custom profile easier.

3. Create a new file using the *AEC Model (Imperial Stb).dwt* [*AEC Model (Metric Stb).dwt*] template.

   Depending on your system's settings, this can normally be done by simply clicking the QNEW icon on the Quick Access Toolbar (QAT).

Getting Started with Walls

AutoCAD Architecture has two "New" commands: the "NEW" command on the Application Menu and "QNEW" on the QAT. QNEW automatically uses a default template file, whereas NEW presents you with a dialog box of templates from which to choose (see Figure 4.1). To set a default template, see the "Configure the New Profile" heading in Chapter 3. It is highly recommended that you always begin ACA files from an ACA Template file. Review the "Template Files" heading in Chapter 3 for more information.

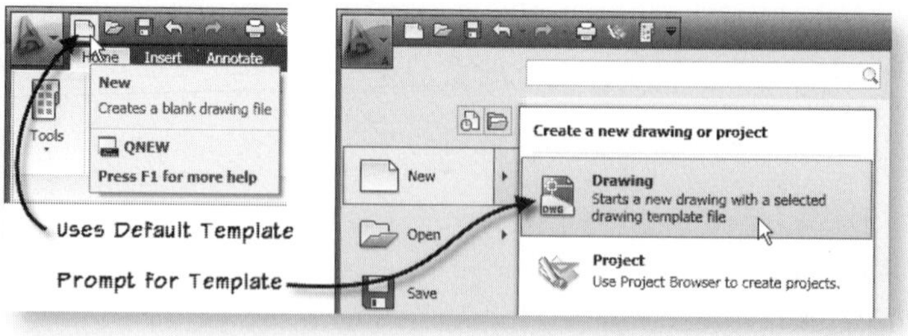

FIGURE 4.1 *The QNEW setting on the Files tab of the Options dialog box*

4. On the Design palette, click the Wall tool (see Figure 4.2).

NOTE

If the Tool Palettes are not open onscreen, on the Home ribbon tab on the Build panel, choose the Home tab, Build panel, Tools flyout, *Tools* tool (top half of split button), or press `CTRL + 3`. If the Design Tool Palettes Group is not visible, right-click the Tool Palettes title bar and choose Design. See the "Tool Palette Groups" heading in Chapter 1 for more information.

The Properties palette will appear when the Wall tool is clicked. If it was already open on your screen, then the parameters listed within it will now be for the new Wall that you are creating. If you have your Properties palette open but set to Auto-hide, then you will have to hover your mouse over the title bar to make it pop open to view or edit the Wall creation parameters (see the "Understanding Tool Palettes" heading in Chapter 1 for more information on Auto-hide).

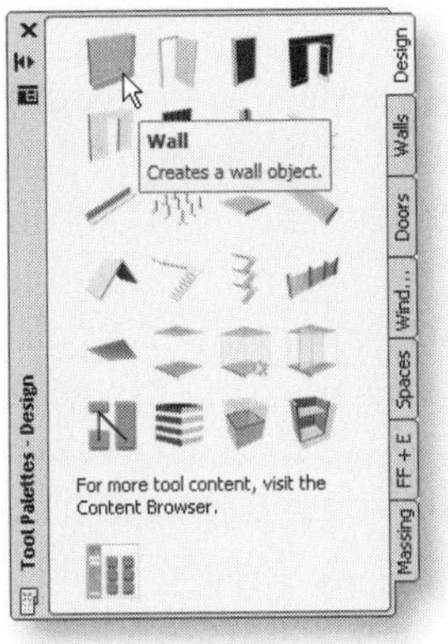

FIGURE 4.2 *The Wall tool on the Design palette*

5. On the Properties palette, change the Width to **8"** [**188**], change the Base Height to **9'** [**2750**], and change the Justify to **Center**.

The following list explains the major fields and controls in the Properties palette while you are adding a Wall (see Figure 4.3).

General Properties:

- **Description**—Click to give this particular Wall a detailed Description.
- **Style**—Contains a list of all Wall styles within the current drawing file. Think of Wall styles as "wall types." (Refer to the previous chapter and Chapter 10 for more information.)
- **Cleanup automatically**—A Yes or No value that determines whether or not this Wall will automatically clean up with other Walls. This is Yes by default, and should rarely be changed (refer to Chapter 9 for more information).
- **Cleanup group definition**—Used to limit cleanup of Walls to other Walls within the same Group. (This topic is covered in Chapter 9.)
- **Segment type**—Walls can be added with Line or Arc segments. Adding Straight segments is like adding lines. Adding Arc segments is like drawing 3 point arcs.

Dimensions Properties:

- **Width**—The thickness of the Wall. This is also referred to as the "Base Width."
- **Base height**—The Floor to Ceiling height of the wall.
- **Justify**—One of four possible points within the thickness of the Wall from which the Width is referenced. The Wall's grip points will occur at its justification. Center places the grips at the middle of the Wall width. Left and Right justification correspond to the left and right edges of the Wall width when looking from the Wall's start point toward its end. (Refer to Figure 9.1 in Chapter 9.) Baseline justification occurs at the zero point of a Wall's width as determined by its style. (Refer to Chapter 10 for information on editing and creating Wall styles.)
- **Offset**—Can be used to place the Wall at a specified distance parallel to the points actually picked in the drawing.
- **Roof line offset from base height**—The top edge of Walls can be projected above the Base height in elevation and 3D.
- **Floor line offset from baseline**—The bottom edge of Walls can be projected below the Base height in elevation and 3D.

All of these parameters are shown in the illustration included on the Properties palette.

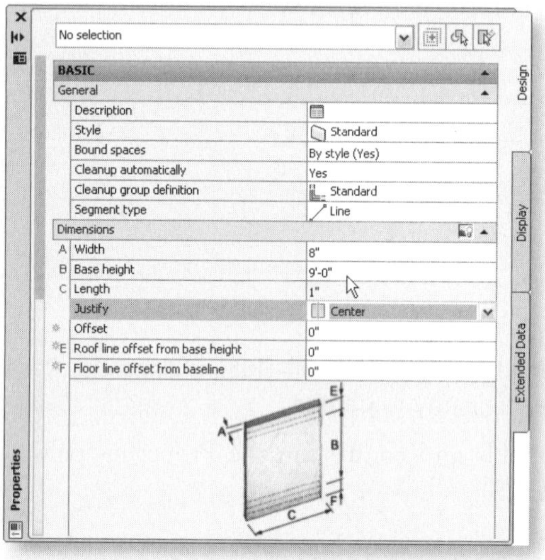

FIGURE 4.3 *The Properties palette for adding Walls*

6. At the "Start point" Command Line prompt, click a point toward the lower left corner of the screen to start the first Wall (see Figure 4.4).

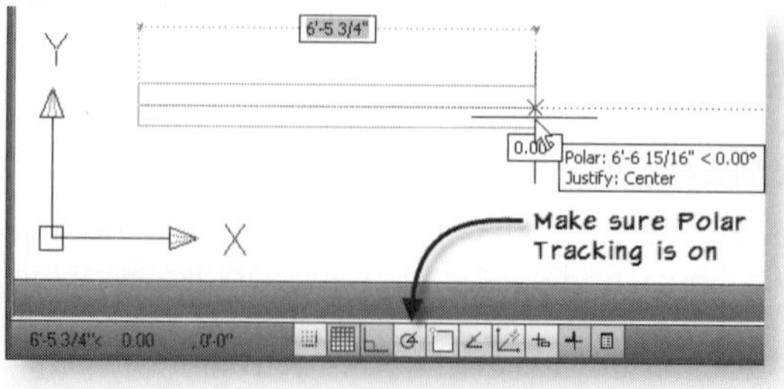

FIGURE 4.4 *Click start and end points to draw Wall segments*

7. Verify that Polar Tracking is active.

   The Polar Tracking button at the bottom of the screen (on the Application status bar) should appear with a light blue-green background. If it is gray, click it to enable it.

8. Move the cursor directly to the right.

   Use the Polar Tracking as a guide to be sure you are drawing the wall perfectly horizontal.

9. Type **30'** [**9000**] and then press ENTER (see Figure 4.5).

TIP

Look up Direct Distance Entry and Use Dynamic Input in the online help for information on this technique.

10. Move the cursor straight up (90°).

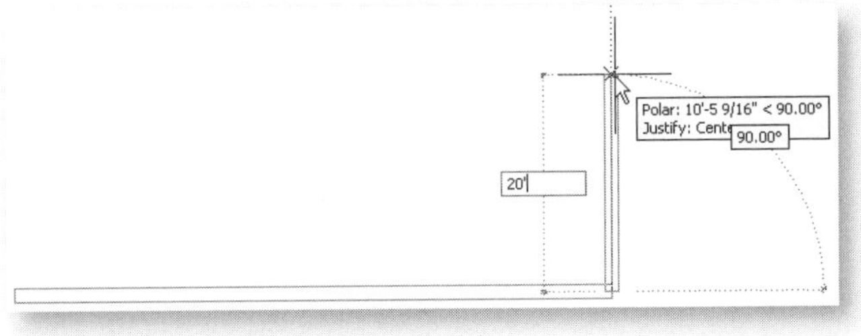

FIGURE 4.5 *Using Direct Distance Entry with Polar Tracking*

11. Type **20'** [**6000**] and then press ENTER.

    Notice that the corner where the two Walls join has formed a clean intersection.

12. Move the cursor to the left (180°), type **15'** [**4500**], and then press ENTER.

Use Polyline Close

13. With the command still active, press the down arrow to reveal command options. (You can also right-click in the drawing window to see a menu). With either method, choose **Close** from the context menu (see Figure 4.6).

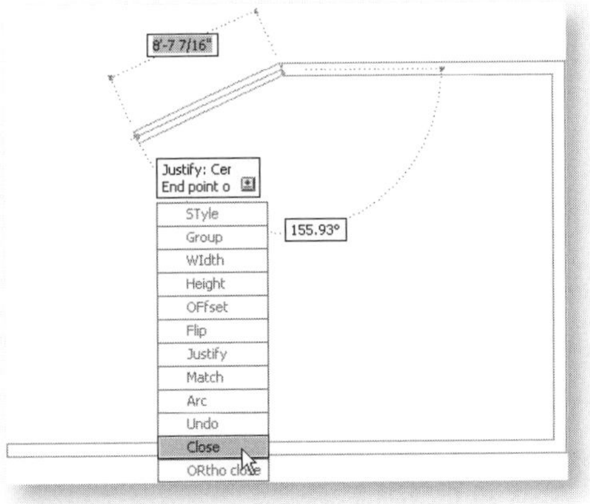

FIGURE 4.6 *Use the Polyline Close option*

Choosing the Close option will add a single Wall segment joining the current wall to the first Wall drawn in this sequence, and then complete the add Wall command.

Add a Curved Wall Segment

Let's add a curved Wall segment this time.

14. On the Design palette, click the Wall tool.
15. On the Properties palette, choose **Arc** for the Segment type.
16. Click a point anywhere outside the existing room drawn in the last sequence.
17. At the "Mid point" prompt, click anywhere within the room.

    Move the mouse slowly before clicking in the next step to get a sense for the behavior of the curve.
18. At the "End point" prompt, click anywhere outside the room again (on the opposite side).
19. Right-click and choose ENTER to end the command (see Figure 4.7).

    Notice that the curved Wall segment also cleans up nicely with the others.

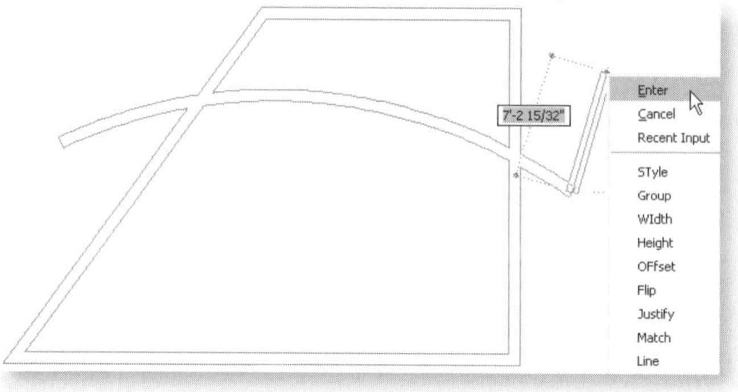

FIGURE 4.7 *Adding a curved wall*

20. Close the file without saving the changes (**Application Menu > Close**).

Create an Existing Conditions Plan

Now that we have practiced adding a few Walls and seen some of the properties available while doing so, let's begin creating an actual model. We will start with the first floor existing conditions plan for our residential project.

1. Create a new file using the *AEC Model (Imperial Stb).dwt* [*AEC Model (Metric Stb).dwt*] template.

   Remember, depending on your settings, you should be able to use the QNEW icon to do this.

   This file will later become our first floor existing conditions for the residential project.
2. At the Command Line, type **z** (for zoom) and then press ENTER.
3. Type **−120,−360** [**−3000,−9000**] and then press ENTER.
4. Type **480,120** [**12000,3000**] and then press ENTER.

Any time that the command prompt requests a point (location, corner, etc.), you are able to either use your mouse to click a point or type in a coordinate entry. Should you choose keyboard input, there are two types of coordinate entries available: absolute and relative. Absolute coordinate entry is so called since it references the absolute 0,0,0 point of the drawing—called the "origin." Relative coordinate entry, by contrast, is measured from (that is, relative to) the current point. In this case we have used absolute entry to zoom in to a region of the drawing starting from down and to the left of the origin, to up and to the right. Under normal circumstances, it is rare that you would zoom this way, but for purposes of the tutorial, it is effective since we will begin drawing at 0,0 and it is desirable to see the layout we are drawing at a comfortable zoom level. For more information on coordinate entry, consult the "Use Coordinates and Coordinate Systems" topic in the online help.

Use Ortho Close

The Ortho Wall menu option is a close command that will complete the Wall Add sequence by adding two wall segments. The first will follow the angle indicated by the next mouse click. The other will be placed perpendicular to the first wall segment drawn in this sequence. Let's try it out.

5. On the Design palette, click the Wall tool.
6. Set the Width to **12"** [**300**], the Height to **9'** [**2750**], and the Justify to **Right** (see Figure 4.8).

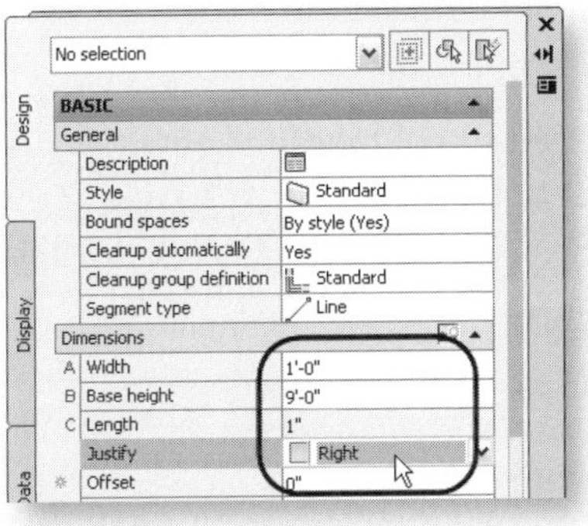

FIGURE 4.8 *Change the settings on the Design palette*

7. At the "Start point" Command Line prompt, type **0,0** and press ENTER.
8. With Polar Tracking active (click on the Application status bar or press F10), move the cursor down (270°), type **24'** [**7300**], and press ENTER.
9. Using Polar Tracking, move the cursor to the right (0°), type **33'** [**10000**], and then press ENTER.
10. Press the down arrow to access the Wall command options or right-click in the drawing window and choose **Ortho close**.

If we point straight up with the mouse in this case, we get a rectangular shape.

The Command Line should prompt "Point on wall in direction of close:"

11. To make a rectangular space, use Polar Tracking to click 90° straight up (see Figure 4.9).

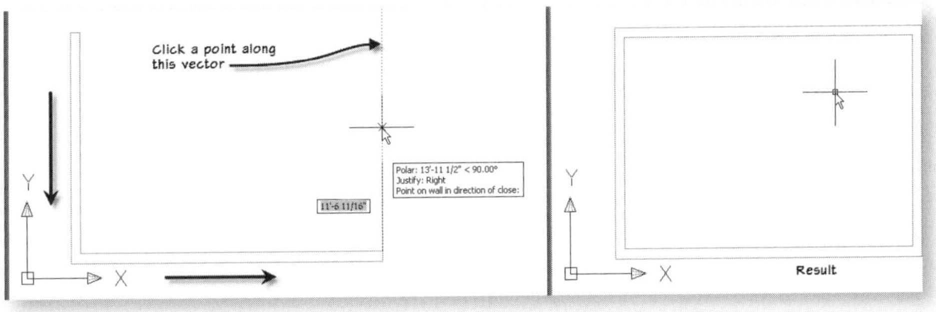

FIGURE 4.9 *Using the Ortho close option*

This option is very commonly used to create rectangular spaces. However, plenty of other shapes are possible depending on the angle you indicate with the mouse (see Figure 4.10).

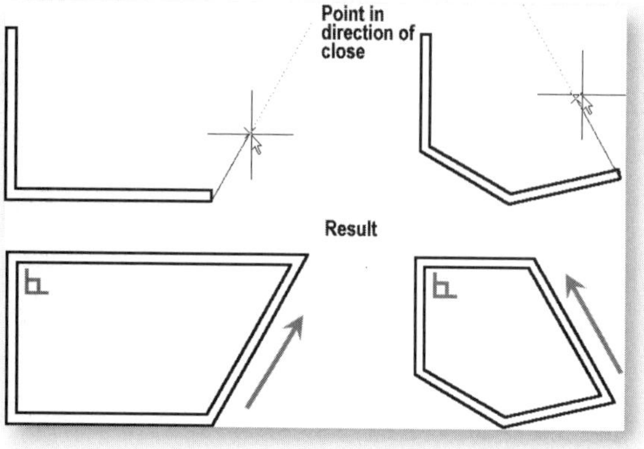

FIGURE 4.10 *Using the Ortho close option*

If you experimented and drew any additional Walls, please erase them now before continuing. We need only the four Walls making the 24' [7300] × 33' [10000] rectangular shape.

Offset Walls

Most standard AutoCAD editing commands work normally on Walls. We will use offset, trim, extend and fillet to continue to add the interior walls of the floor plan layout for the residential project. All of these commands are available on the Home ribbon tab on the Modify panel, or you may use the right-click menu via the Basic Modify Tools submenu. Type the appropriate Command Line version, command alias or other valid AutoCAD method for the command. (Refer to the online help for more information on Command Line versions of the commands.)

12. On the Home ribbon tab on the Modify panel, choose the ***Offset*** tool (third row, second from left).

TIP

You can also use command aliases for many commands as well if you wish. The alias for offset is O (followed by enter). If Dynamic Input is turned on, typing will appear directly at the cursor onscreen, otherwise, it will appear at the Command Line.

13. At the "Specify offset distance" prompt, type **12'-11.5"** [**3950**] and then press ENTER.
14. At the "Select object to offset" prompt, click on the lower horizontal Wall.
15. At the "Specify point on side to offset" prompt, click a point anywhere within the building (see Figure 4.11).

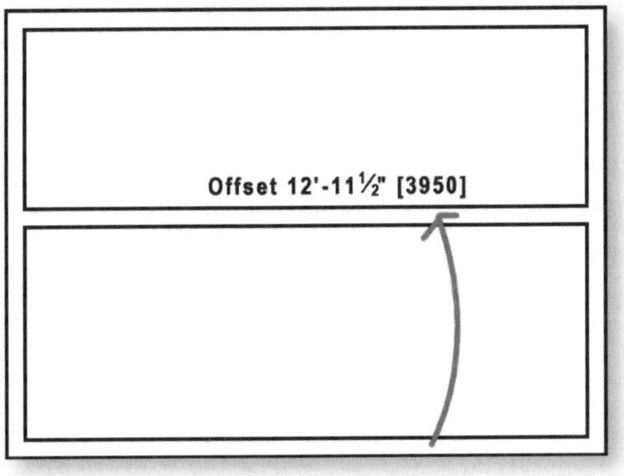

FIGURE 4.11 *Offsetting a new wall*

16. Press ENTER to end the offset command.
17. Press ENTER again to repeat the offset command.

TIP

Remember that except for text editing commands, the SPACEBAR functions like an ENTER key at the Command Line. This would also be a good time to use the "thumb on SPACEBAR" technique to repeat the previous command.

18. Type **12'-8.5"** [**3874**] for the offset distance this time.
19. Click the leftmost vertical wall, and offset it inside as well (see Figure 4.12).

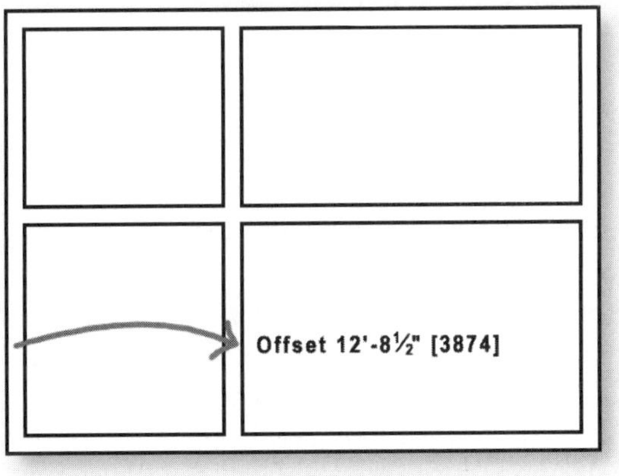

FIGURE 4.12 *Two new Walls offset inside*

20. Press ENTER to end the offset command.
21. From the Application Menu, choose **Save As**.
22. Save the file to the *C:\MasterACA 2010\Chapter04* folder, using the name *First Floor Existing.dwg*.

One of the features that makes AutoCAD Architecture such a powerful tool is the ability to change an object's parameters at any time, as design needs change. Throughout this book, we will refer to this as "progressive refinement."

Modify Walls on the Properties Palette

Let's take a look at modifying some of the Walls as we continue with the layout of the first floor existing conditions for the residential project.

23. Select the two internal Walls created in the "Offset Walls" heading earlier.
24. Right-click, and choose **Properties**.
25. On the Properties palette, set the Width to **5"** [**125**] and the Justify to **Center** (see Figure 4.13).

    Notice the change to the drawing, particularly the way the walls shift when changing justification.

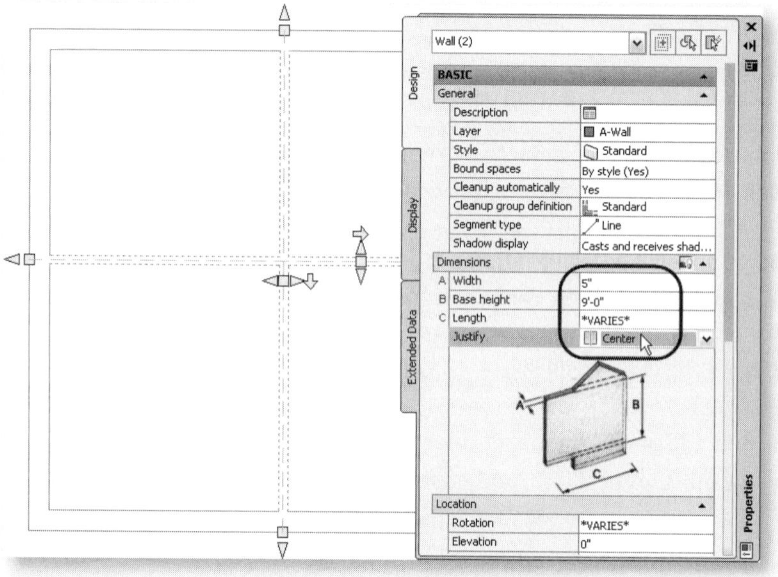

FIGURE 4.13 *Manipulate Wall properties in the Properties palette*

26. Right-click and choose **Deselect All** (near the bottom off the menu) or press the ESC key.

Justification is an important consideration when working with walls. Again, the Properties palette allows you to receive immediate feedback on the change while the object selection is still active. Therefore, if you decide you are not happy with the change, you can simply try another on the fly. When calculating offset distances, you must take the wall's width and justification into account. Offsets performed with the AutoCAD Offset command are measured between the justification lines of the walls (or center to center), and the Trim and Extend commands use the justification line as the Cutting/Boundary edge. We will look at alternative techniques that do not behave this way on the Wall's contextual ribbon tab or right-click menu later.

Layout the Remaining Walls

Now that we have the interior walls at the correct width and justification, we will continue adding walls using the same technique.

27. Using the offset command, offset the interior horizontal Wall up **4'-3"** [**1295**] and the interior vertical Wall to the left **2'-11"** [**889**] and **6'-11"** [**2108**] to the right (see Figure 4.14).

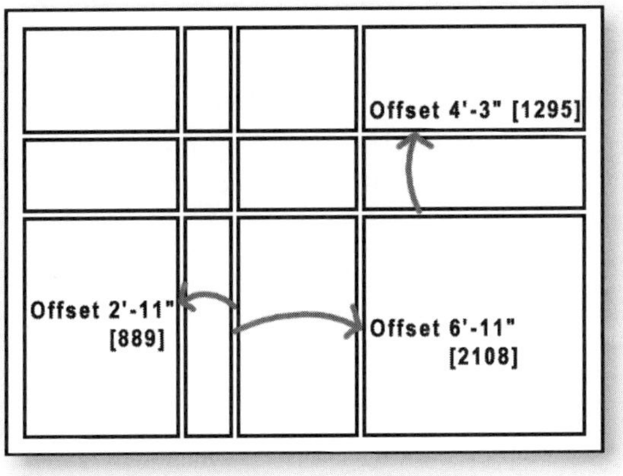

FIGURE 4.14 *Offset three more Walls*

At this point we have several Wall segments crossing one another. Before we add any more Walls, it is best to clean up what we have. We will use the AutoCAD Trim command to eliminate the unwanted portions of the Walls. If you are familiar with the AutoCAD Trim command, it works the same way with Walls as it does with other AutoCAD geometry. If you are not familiar with this command, pay close attention to the command prompts as you execute it.

The first prompt reads: "Select cutting edges." At this prompt you can select one or more objects that will be used as trim points for other objects (pressing ENTER at this prompt will select *all* objects in the drawing as edges). All of the interior Walls will be used as cutting edges in this step. You can do each one in a separate Trim command or do them all together. It is up to you.

28. On the Home ribbon tab on the Modify panel select the drop-down arrow to the right of the Trim/Extend button (second row, first tool from the right) and choose the ***Trim*** tool (or type **TR** and then press ENTER).
29. At the "Select cutting edges" prompt, select all of the interior walls as Cutting Edges.
30. Press ENTER to complete the selection of cutting edges.

This is an important step. Before you can move on to the "Select object to trim" prompt, you must press ENTER at the "Select objects" prompt to stop selecting cutting edges. For more information on Trim, consult the online help.

31. At the "Select object to trim" prompt, and using Figure 4.15 as a guide, Trim all of the unneeded Wall segments.

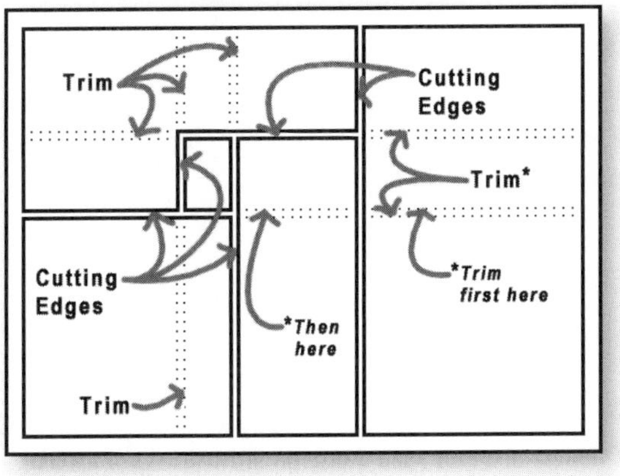

FIGURE 4.15 *Trim away unnecessary Wall segments*

The layout is coming along. We need to offset two more Walls to frame out a powder room at the top of the plan. We could use the AutoCAD offset command as we did earlier; however, as we have pointed out, the distances must be calculated carefully since AutoCAD Offset does not give an option for the reference point. On the Wall contextual ribbon tab, there is such an option. Using the **Offset > Copy** function, we can offset Walls from face to face rather than center to center.

32. Select the rightmost interior vertical Wall (labeled "Wall A" in Figure 4.16), and on the Wall ribbon tab on the Modify panel click the Offset drop-down button and choose the ***Copy*** tool.

    Move the mouse left and right and notice the red line that shifts from side to side on the Wall.

33. Click to set the red line on the left edge of the Wall (see panel 1 in Figure 4.16). This is the offset edge.

    Begin moving the cursor further to the left and note the dynamic dimension.

34. Type **4'-4"** [**1323**] and then press ENTER (see panel 2 in Figure 4.16). Like the AutoCAD Offset command, this offset function will repeat. Press ENTER again to complete the command.

35. Using **Offset > Copy** again, offset "Wall B" up **1'-8"** [**510**] (see panel 3 in Figure 4.16).

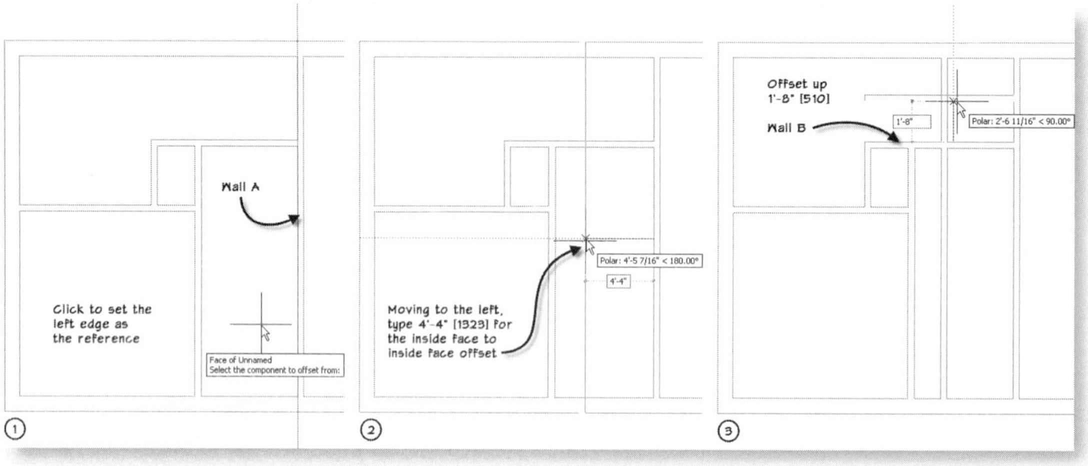

FIGURE 4.16 *Offset Walls for the powder room*

36. On the Home ribbon tab on the Modify panel, select the drop-down arrow to the right of the Fillet/Chamfer button (first row, first tool from the right) and choose the ***Fillet*** tool (or type **F** and then press ENTER).

37. Using Figure 4.17 as a guide, remove the unneeded wall segments. Be sure to click on the part of the Wall that you wish to keep.

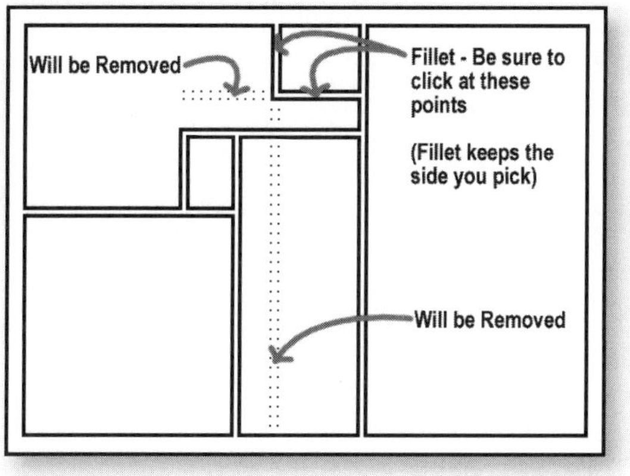

FIGURE 4.17 *Fillet away unnecessary Wall segments*

38. **Offset > Copy** two more walls to frame out the stairway in the center of the plan. Offset from the left wall of the hallway to the right **3'-1"** [**942**], and up **5"** [**129**] from the horizontal wall on the left of the plan (see Figure 4.18).

    If you would rather use the AutoCAD Offset command, add 5" [125] to each dimension to account for the thickness of the Wall. (Please note that the look of your dimensions might vary slightly from those in the figure.)

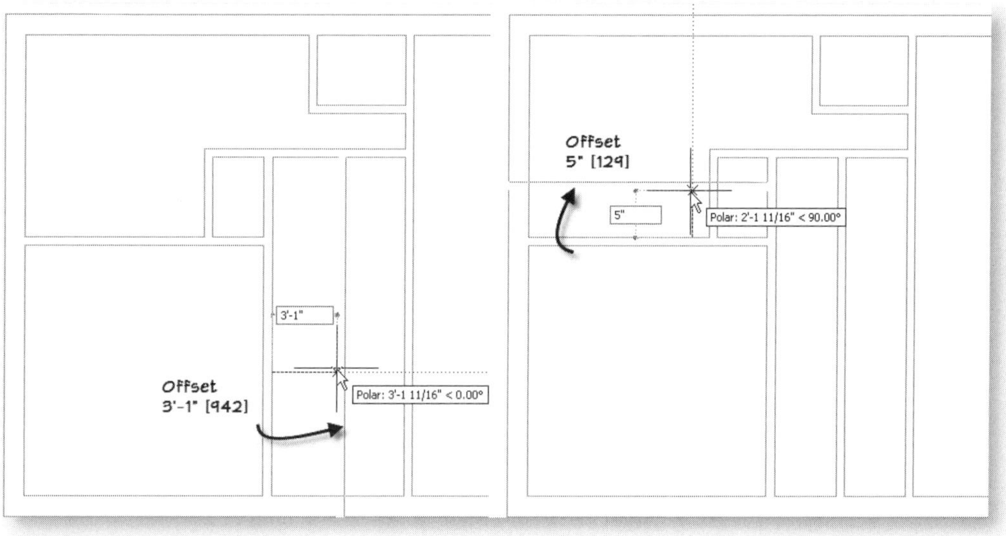

FIGURE 4.18 *Offset Walls for the stairway*

39. Using the EXTEND command (on the Home ribbon tab on the Modify panel, same split button drop-down as the TRIM command) and Figure 4.19 as a guide, extend the required wall segments.

    If you are new to the EXTEND command, its prompts are nearly identical to the TRIM command. Follow the Command Line closely as you work.

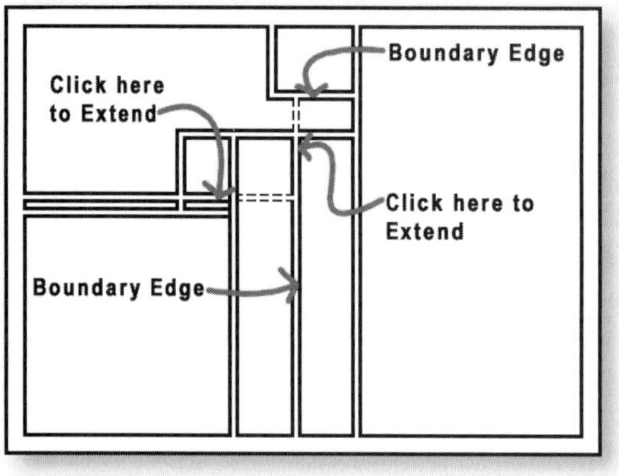

FIGURE 4.19 *Extend Wall segments*

40. Using the TRIM command, and Figure 4.20 as a guide, trim the unneeded Wall segments.

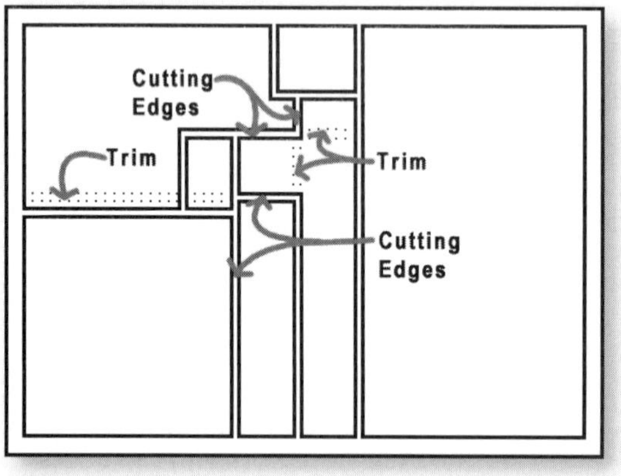

FIGURE 4.20 *Trim away unnecessary Wall segments*

41. Select the vertical Wall bounding the right side of the stairway in the center of the plan.
42. Click the triangular shaped grip at the bottom end of the wall to make it "hot."
43. Drag the triangular grip up (See Figure 4.21).

    The triangular or "Lengthen" grip will keep movement constrained to the existing angle of the Wall without the need for Polar Tracking or Ortho Mode. To test it, try moving the mouse side to side and note that the wall angle does not change.

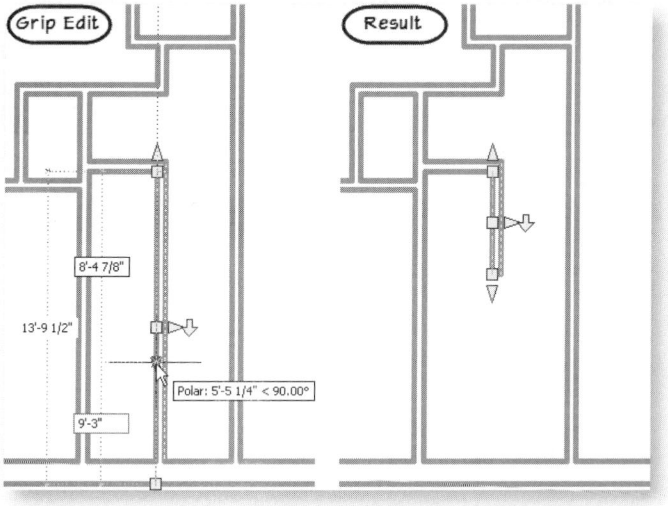

FIGURE 4.21 *Grip stretching the Wall bounding the stairway*

Three dynamic dimensions will appear: one overall, one representing the new length of the Wall, and the other representing the amount added or subtracted to the Wall's original length (the delta). One of the three will be highlighted. If the one highlighted is not the delta portion, press the TAB key. Repeat until the correct one is highlighted.

44. With the delta dynamic dimension active, type **9'-3"** [**2820**] and then press ENTER.
45. Deselect the Wall and save the file.

To verify the dimensions of your plan, use the ***Distance*** tool on the Home ribbon tab on the Inquiry panel or type DI at the command prompt.

Create and Assign a Wall Style

We have completed the layout of existing walls on the first floor of the house. Assigning Wall styles to the walls will help us distinguish them as existing construction as the project progresses. Wall styles can be thought of as "wall types" and usually indicate the construction of the Wall and a variety of other parameters. Styles were covered in general in the previous chapter and Wall styles will be covered in detail in Chapter 10. For now, let's simply create and assign a new Wall Style to our Walls and place them on an existing construction layer.

Continue in the *First Floor Existing.dwg* file.

46. Select all of the Walls in this drawing. (The easiest way to do this is to use a window selection or to press CTRL + A.)
47. On the Wall contextual ribbon tab on the General panel, choose the ***Save As*** tool (in the upper right corner of the panel).
48. In the Wall Style Properties dialog that appears, click the General tab if it is not already chosen, and type **Existing** for the name.
49. In the Description field, type **MasterACA Existing House** and then click OK.

You will not see any change on the screen. This very simple change merely created a new Style named "Existing" and assigned it to all of the selected Walls. If you wish to verify this, click to select any Wall and check the Style setting on the Properties palette.

Create a Layer

In addition to the Style, Layers are typically used to distinguish existing construction from new. In this sequence, we will create a Layer for existing walls. AutoCAD Architecture includes Layer Standards to simplify the creation of Layers and help to standardize naming.

50. On the Home ribbon tab on the Layers panel, click the ***Layer Properties*** tool (top row, first button from left).
51. On the toolbar across the top, click the New Layer from Standard icon (see Figure 4.22).
52. In the New Layer from Standard dialog, click the small browse (...) icon next to the Status field (scroll down if you don't see it).

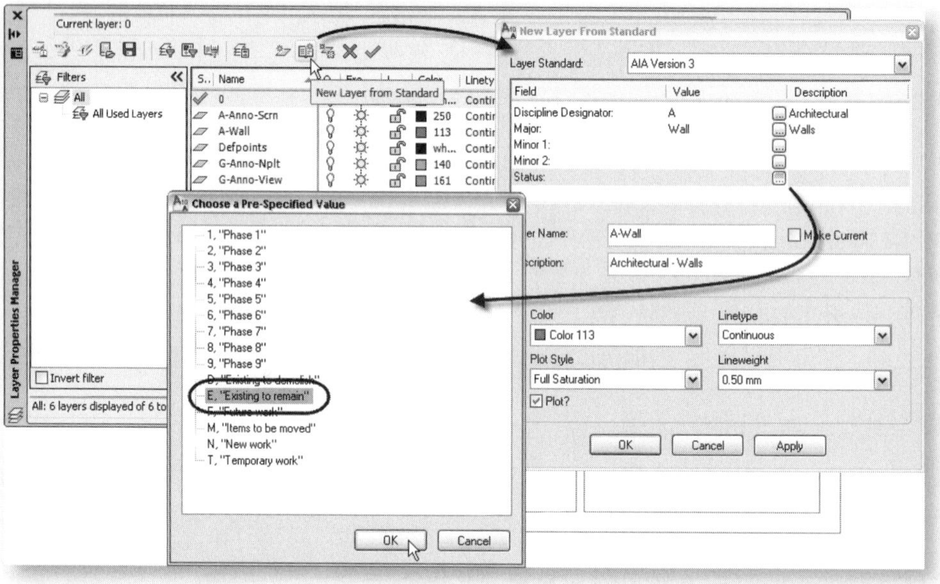

FIGURE 4.22 *Create a new layer based on a Layer Standard*

53. In the Choose a Pre-Specified Value dialog, choose **E, "Existing to remain" [X, "Existing"]** and then click OK.
54. Back in the New Layer from Standard dialog, from the color list, choose Select color, choose color **#64**, and then click OK.
55. Change the Plot Style to **Full Saturation** and the Lineweight to **0.35 mm** and then if you wish, close the Layer Properties Manager palette.

You will now have an existing conditions wall Layer named: A-Wall-E [A-Wall-GX]. Next we will assign all of our Walls to this Layer.

CAD MANAGER NOTE

This book makes use of two out of the box Layering systems, AIA (256 Color) for Imperial files and BS1192 Descriptive (256 Color) for Metric files. Your firm may use a different Layering scheme and Standard. You can discuss this with your CAD Manager and/or CAD Support Personnel to identify what issues and standards are in place at your firm. Feel free to use whatever Layering system is in place at your firm in place of the ones suggested in this text.

Apply a Layer to Walls

56. Select all of the Walls within the drawing. (Use the same procedure as before.)
57. On the Properties palette, choose **A-Wall-E** [**A-Wall-GX**] from the Layer list.
    Notice that all of the Walls change color.
58. Right-click in the drawing and choose **Deselect All** to complete the operation.
59. Save the file.

MANAGER NOTE CAD

The process outlined here is a simplification of that which would typically be required were you to wish to incorporate such a layer into your ongoing standards. It is effective for changing the Walls in the current drawing to the desired layer; however, the layer that we created exists only in this file. Furthermore, when adding additional Walls, those Walls will not automatically use this layer. To achieve a more automated solution, you must open the default Layer Standards/Layer Key file (*AEC Layer Standard.dwg* by default briefly covered in Chapter 3) and add a new Layer Key for Existing (and Demolition Walls). You can then create custom Tools on your Tool Palettes that automatically create the required layers based upon these layer keys. Refer to Chapter 10 for more information on building Demolition Wall Styles, Tools and Layer settings. For complete details on configuring layer standards for your office, consider purchasing a copy of *Autodesk Architectural Desktop: An Advanced Implementation Guide* by Paul F. Aubin and Matt Dillon and refer to Chapter 5 therein.

WORKING WITH DOORS AND WINDOWS

Doors and Windows automatically interact with Walls when inserted to create the opening and anchor themselves to the Wall in a parametric way. (As discussed in Chapter 2, anchors establish the rules that physically link two AEC objects together.) Doors and Windows have a dedicated Elevation Display Representation that makes controlling display of Doors and Windows in sections and elevations more manageable. Doors and Windows offer a variety of routes to customization, resulting in virtually no Door or Window condition that cannot be rendered with accuracy and relative ease in ACA. Let's continue work on our floor plan layout by adding the required doors and windows. We will cover the basics here. For more detailed information on Door and Window usage and customization, refer to Chapter 11.

Add Doors

For this exercise, turn off your Object Snaps (click the Object Snap toggle on the Application status bar or press F3). Object Snaps can actually hinder the proper placement of Doors and Windows by causing them to "jump" to the wrong Wall. Use the Location settings on the Properties palette when adding Doors and Windows. These provide greater precision than Object Snap and less possibility for error.

1. Continuing in the *First Floor Existing.dwg* file, at the bottom of the screen, click the Object Snap icon to turn it gray (see Figure 4.23).
   If it is already gray, do nothing.

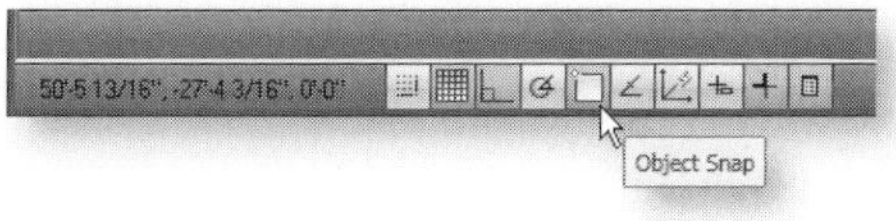

FIGURE 4.23 *Turn off the Object Snaps while adding Doors and Windows*

2. On the Design palette, click the Door tool (see Figure 4.24).

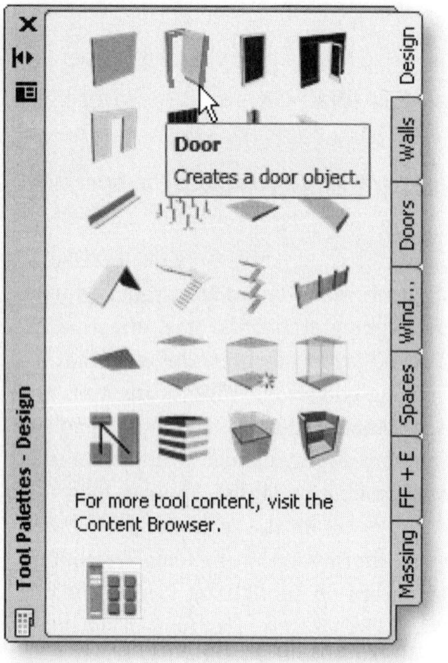

FIGURE 4.24 *Choose the Door tool to add Doors*

On the Properties palette, open the Style list (in the Basic Properties area under the General grouping).

Notice that there is only the Standard style currently available in this drawing. Most of the time, you will wish to use a style other than Standard for Doors and Windows. To do this, you use a tool from a different palette. Tools have the ability to reference a specific style (external to the current drawing), which will be automatically imported as the tool is executed.

Click the Doors tab to make the Doors tool palette active.

3. Click the Hinged – Single tool.
4. On the Properties palette, choose **3'-0"** × **6'-8"** [**900** × **2200**] from the Standard sizes list.
5. In the Location grouping, choose **Unconstrained** from the Position list (see Figure 4.25).

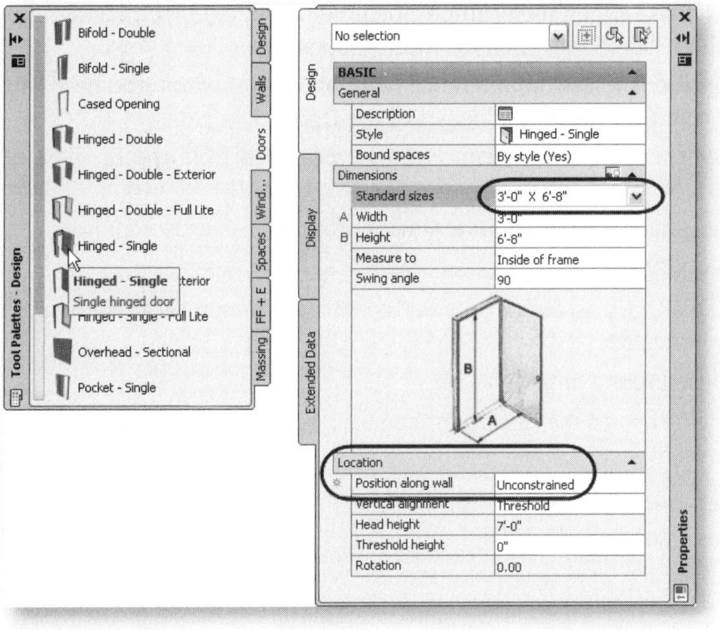

FIGURE 4.25 *Setting Door parameters on the Properties palette*

The following list explains the major fields and controls in the Properties palette while adding Doors.

General Properties:

- **Description**—Click to give this particular Door a detailed Description.
- **Style**—Contains a list of all Door styles within the current file. Think of Door styles as door types. (Refer to Chapter 11 for more information.)

Dimension Properties:

- **Standard Sizes**—List of standard sizes built into the Door style. Choose from this list or type in a Width and Height manually. (Please note that not all Styles have Standard Sizes.)
- **Width**—Width of the door opening. Refer to the Note below the Width and Height fields to see if this door measures to the inside or outside of the frame.
- **Height**—Height of the Door opening. Refer to the Note below the Width and Height fields to see if this door measures to the inside or outside of the frame.
- **Measure to**—Determines whether the Door size relates to the Door Leaf or the Frame size.

NOTE

To change whether the dimensions measure to inside or outside of the frame, choose an option from the Measure to list.

- **Swing Angle**—Use to set the number of degrees open that the Door swing should be drawn.

Location Properties:

- **Position along Wall**—When set to Offset/Center, ACA automatically sets the position of the Door relative to Wall intersections and midpoints.

- **Automatic Offset**—When the Position along Wall is set to Offset/Center, this value determines the offset from Wall intersections.
- **Vertical Alignment**—Sets the reference point and offset within the height of the Wall to which to measure the height of the Door.
- **Head height**—Location of the Door Head as measured from the Baseline of the Wall.
- **Threshold height**—Location of the Door Threshold as measured from the Baseline (floor line) of the Wall.

6. At the "Select wall, grid assembly or Enter" command prompt, click the topmost horizontal exterior Wall.
7. Move the mouse around onscreen a bit.

   Move to the left, then to the right, and then back again.

Notice how the door you are placing keeps up with the mouse movements, but at all times remains attached to a wall. Notice also the dynamic dimensions showing the Door size and location relative to the Wall (see Figure 4.26).

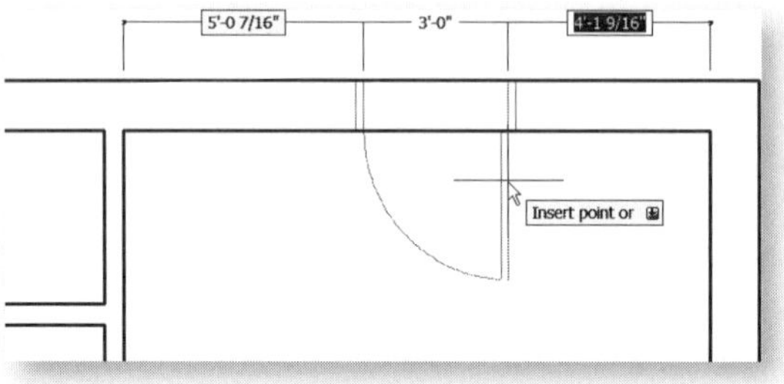

FIGURE 4.26 *Dynamic Dimensions interactively show Door location and size*

8. Move the mouse back to the top right side of the plan.
9. Position the Door roughly (don't try to be precise at this step) in the center of the top exterior Wall and then click the mouse (see Figure 4.27).

Notice that the Door appears in the drawing and cuts a hole in the Wall.

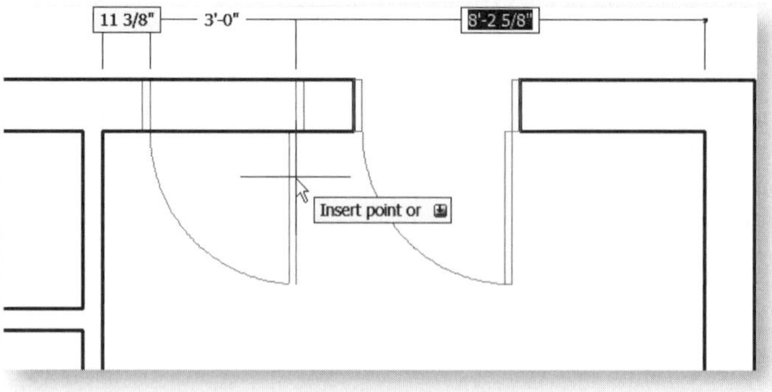

FIGURE 4.27 *The new Door cuts a hole in the Wall*

As you add doors, you can change settings on the fly by simply clicking back into the Properties palette, changing the desired setting(s) and then returning to the main drawing window.

10. On the Properties palette, change the Standard Size to **2'-6" × 6'-8"** [**760 × 2200**].

    Move the cursor to the upper left corner of the plan and position it so that the Door is being added to the topmost horizontal exterior Wall.

Dynamic Dimensions may also receive keyboard input. Use the TAB key to cycle through each editable dimension, and then type the desired value.

   Press the TAB key. Repeat until the dimension indicating the offset to the left of the Door is highlighted.

11. Type **2'-4"** [**762**] and then press ENTER (see Figure 4.28).

A door will appear offset 2'-4" [762] from the top left exterior Wall intersection.

12. Press ENTER again to complete the command.

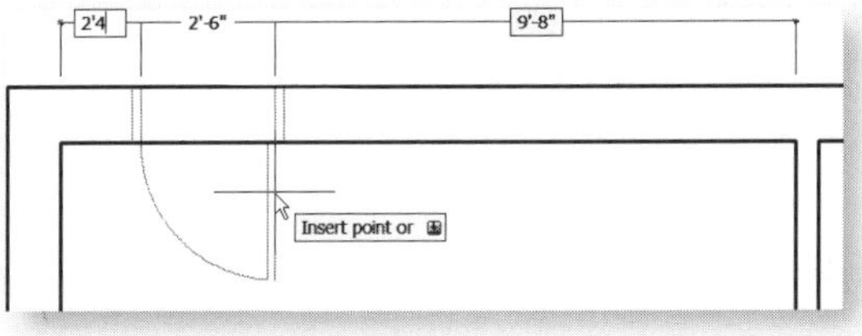

FIGURE 4.28 *Using Dynamic Dimensions for accurate placement*

13. On the Doors palette, click the Bifold – Single tool.
14. On the Properties palette, from the Standard Sizes list, choose **2'-2" × 6'-8"** [**660 × 2200**].
15. In the drawing window, click the right vertical Wall of the closet in the middle of the plan (see Figure 4.29).

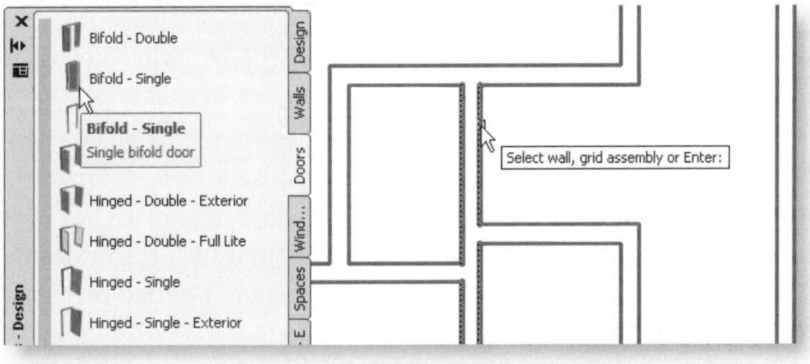

FIGURE 4.29 *Add a Bifold Door to the closet*

16. On the Properties palette, beneath the Location grouping, change the Position along Wall to **Offset/Center**. In the Automatic Offset field, type **4"** [**100**] in the text box (see Figure 4.30).

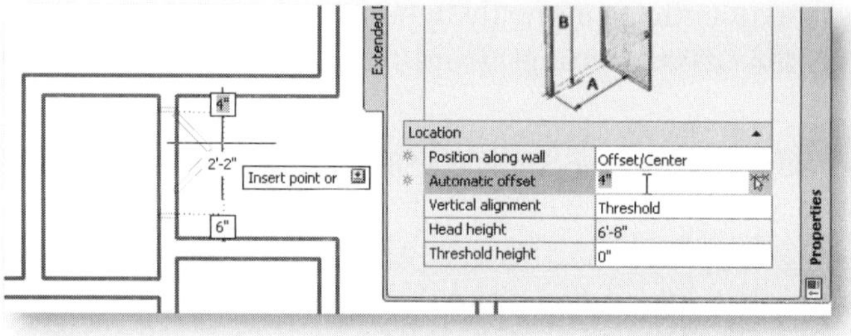

FIGURE 4.30 *Configure the Automatic Offset/Center feature*

17. Move the mouse around near the closet again. (If the cursor is unresponsive, click once in the drawing to shift focus away from the Properties palette.)

    Do NOT click the mouse to place the door yet. If you did so accidentally, right-click and choose Undo.

18. Make your mouse movements slower and more deliberate.

Notice the behavior with Automatic Offset/Center active. The door automatically snaps to a set distance (4'' [100] in this case) from a nearby corner or jumps to the center of the room. (In this case, both dynamic dimensions will show 5'' [128] when it is centered.)

Notice also that slower and more deliberate movement allows you to control the direction of the swing of the door more precisely as it is being placed (see Figure 4.31).

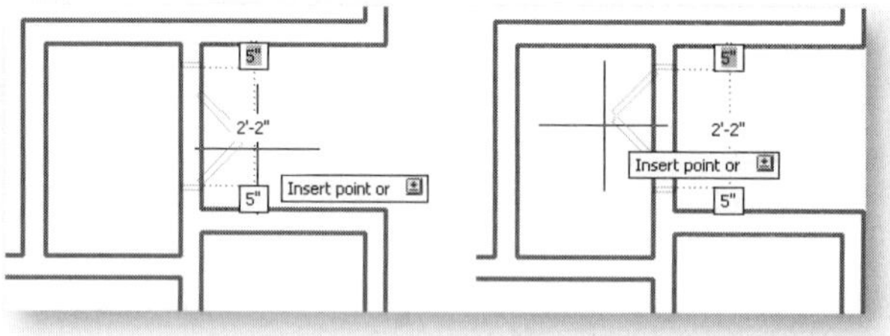

FIGURE 4.31 *Controlling the position and swing direction with the Automatic Offset/Center feature*

19. When you are happy with the placement of the door and its swing position, click the mouse to place the door.
20. Right-click and choose **Enter** to end the command (or press ENTER).

Change Door Swing with Direct Manipulation

Sometimes you will make a mistake when adding a Door or Window, or later decide you wish to change it. Resist the urge to press ESC and/or Undo. To manipulate or relocate a Door (or Window), simply use its grips.

21. Click on the hinged Door at the top right (the first Door placed in the previous steps earlier).

Notice there are several grips: two triangular shaped, one square and two arrows. Each of these grip shapes performs a different function. The arrow grips are "trigger" grips. A trigger grip will perform a designated function with a single click and then return to the previous condition with a second click. In this case, the arrow triggers are used to change the Door swing direction.

22. Hover over either one of the two arrow trigger grips.

    It will turn light red and a "Flip" tool tip will appear to indicate its function (see Figure 4.32).

23. Click either one of the two arrow trigger grips to flip the Door swing.

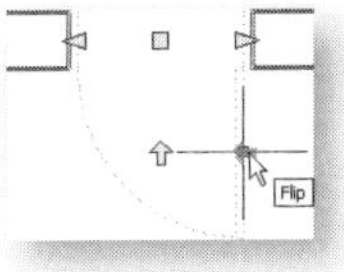

FIGURE 4.32 *Using trigger grips to perform an object-specific function*

Change Door Size with Direct Manipulation

The two triangular grips allow you to interactively resize the Door object. If the Door Style contains a list of "Standard sizes" (see the definition given previously), then movement of these grips will snap to these Standard sizes. If there are no standard sizes saved in the Style, then resizing will be unconstrained. Door styles are covered in more detail in Chapter 11.

24. Hover over one of the two triangular grips and pause for a moment.

    A tool tip will appear indicating the grip's function as well as a Dynamic Dimension indicating its current size (see Figure 4.33).

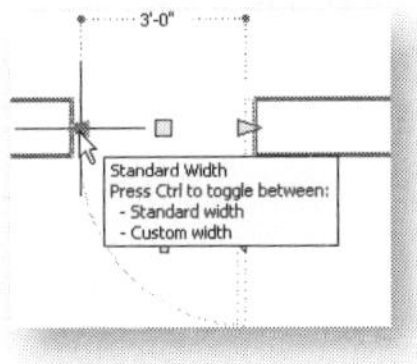

FIGURE 4.33 *Hover over a grip to reveal its function in a tool tip*

25. Click on one of the triangle grips and begin dragging it (see Figure 4.34).

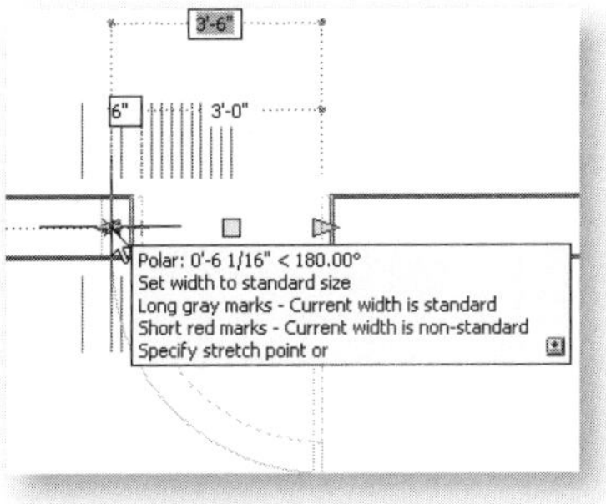

FIGURE 4.34 *Snap marks (gray or red) indicating standard sizes appear while grip editing*

Click on one of the gray marks to snap to a standard size.

NOTE

In some cases, some of the tick marks may appear red and a bit shorter than the gray ones. This indicates that the size has a standard width, but that the height is not standard. This cannot be seen with the Door style that we have used here, but if you use another style, you may encounter this behavior.

TIP

If you wish to use a non-standard size, press the CTRL key and then drag to the new size. You may also type a value into the Dynamic Dimensions to set the new non-standard size accurately.

Move a Door Precisely with Object Snap Tracking

The square grip in the middle of the Door is a "location" grip. With this grip, you can change the location of the Door relative to the length, thickness or height of the Wall. (Use CTRL to cycle between modes.)

26. Right-click on the Object Snap toggle at the bottom of the screen and choose Settings (see Figure 4.35).

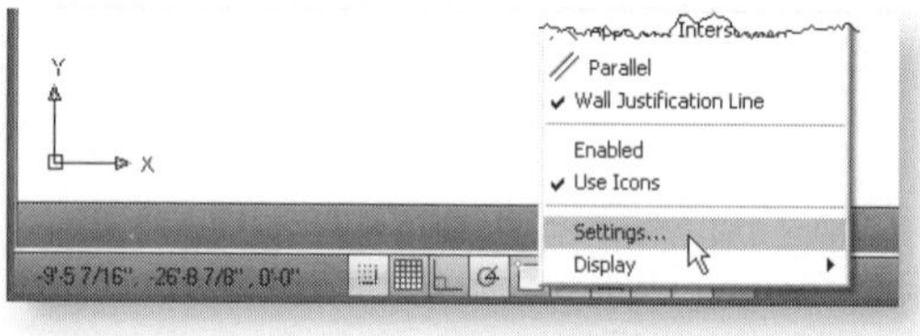

FIGURE 4.35 *Access the settings of Object Snap*

27. In the Drafting Settings dialog box, on the Object Snap tab, place a check mark in Object Snap On (F3), Object Snap Tracking On (F11) and Midpoint (see Figure 4.36).

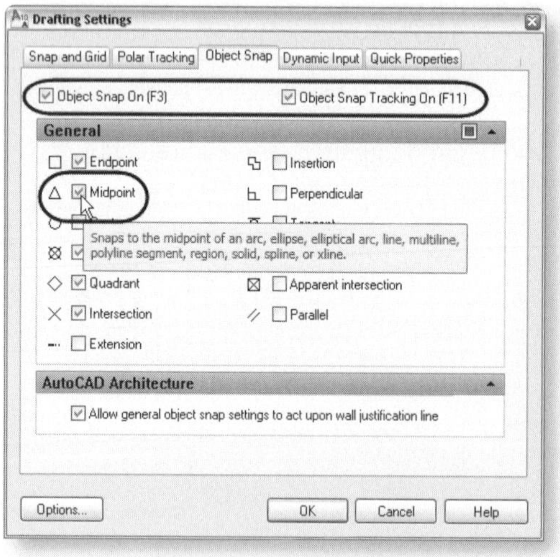

FIGURE 4.36 *Configure the Drafting Settings*

It is not necessary to deselect any of the other Object Snap modes that may be turned on in this dialog box; simply make certain that Midpoint is among those selected. For future reference, make note of the keyboard shortcuts F3 and F11 listed next to Object Snap and Object Snap Tracking. You can use these to quickly turn on and off these features.

28. Click OK to dismiss the Drafting Settings dialog box.

    Continue to work with the Door at the top right corner of the plan.

29. Select the square grip point in the middle of the Door to make it hot (the grip turns dark red when "hot").
30. Move the mouse to the bottom horizontal wall of the room and hover over the Midpoint. Do NOT click yet.

    A small tick mark should appear on the edge of the Wall at the midpoint. The midpoint is indicated by a triangle symbol.

31. Move the mouse all the way back straight up to the original Wall (see Figure 4.37).

    A light dotted tracking vector will trace your movement and keep you lined up with the Midpoint at the bottom. If you move too far to the left or right, it will vanish, so keep it lined up.

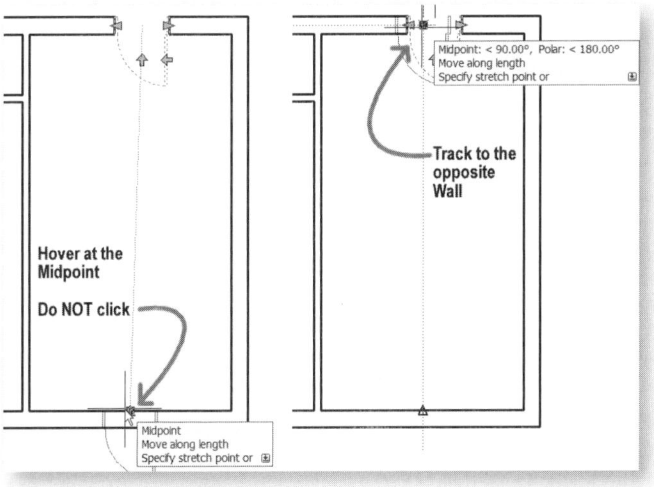

FIGURE 4.37 *Using Object Snap Tracking for precise alignment*

32. When your mouse is over the original Wall, click the mouse to set the new position.

TIP
Polar Tracking (F10) can make this process even easier, by giving additional tracking vectors in the opposite direction.

33. Right-click and choose **Deselect All**, or simply press the ESC key to deselect the Door.

NOTE
You can also hold down the SHIFT key, right-click and choose Mid Between 2 Points and locate the middle of the Wall by snapping to each corner of the room instead.

Add the Remaining Doors

Using Figure 4.38 as a guide and the techniques covered earlier, place the remaining doors in the plan.

HINT

You can select a Door, then on the Door contextual ribbon tab on the General panel choose the ***Add Selected*** tool as a way of quickly adding Doors with similar parameters.

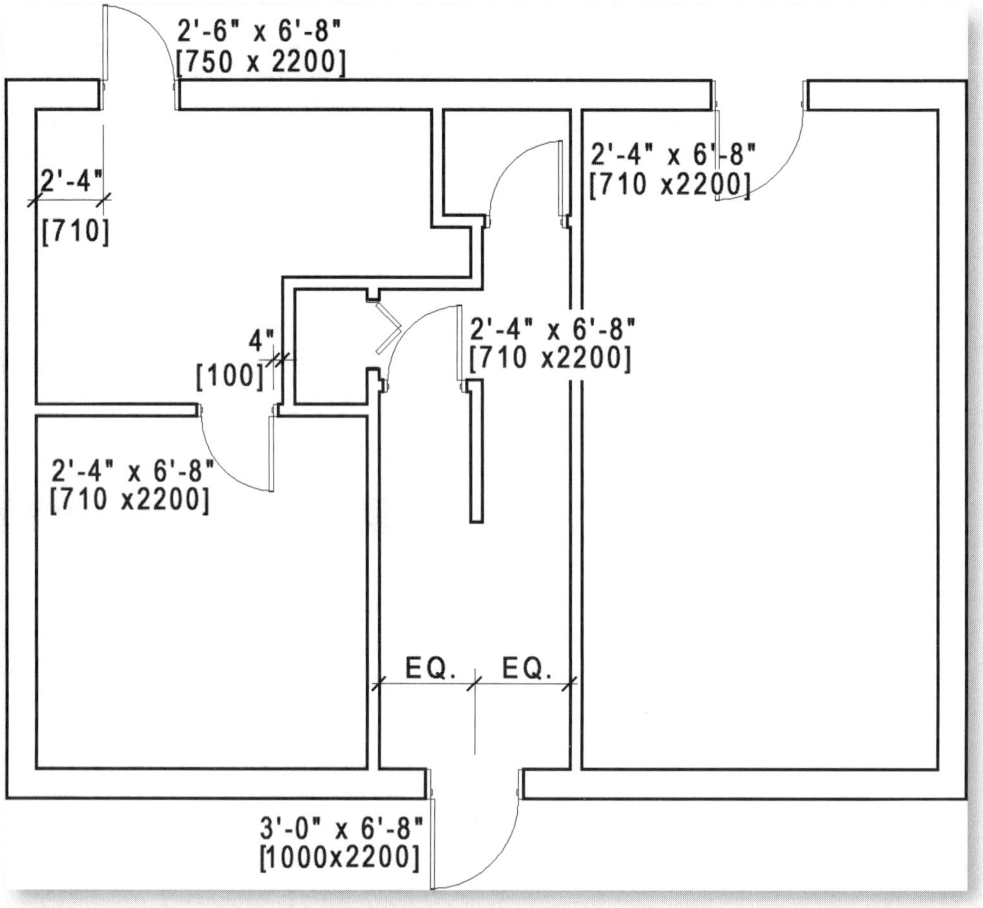

FIGURE 4.38 *Place the remaining Doors in the plan*

34. Save the File.

You may want to create an A-Door-E and an A-Glaz-E layer for the Doors and Windows, respectively. Follow the procedures used for the Walls if you choose to do so.

Add Windows

Working with Windows is nearly identical to working with Doors. Many of the parameters are the same and placement and manipulation of Windows works the same as with Doors.

35. On the Windows palette, click the Double Hung tool.

Refer to "Add Doors" before for a description of each of the settings on the Properties palette that are active while adding Windows, except that with Windows, "Swing Angle" becomes "Opening Percent" and "Threshold Height" becomes "Sill Height."

36. For the Width type **3'-0"** [**900**] and for the Height type **4'-8"** [**1400**].

    The Standard Size will indicate that this is a Custom Size.

37. In the Location grouping, choose **Offset/Center** from the Position along Wall list.

    Set the Automatic Offset value to **2'-6"** [**750**] (see Figure 4.39).

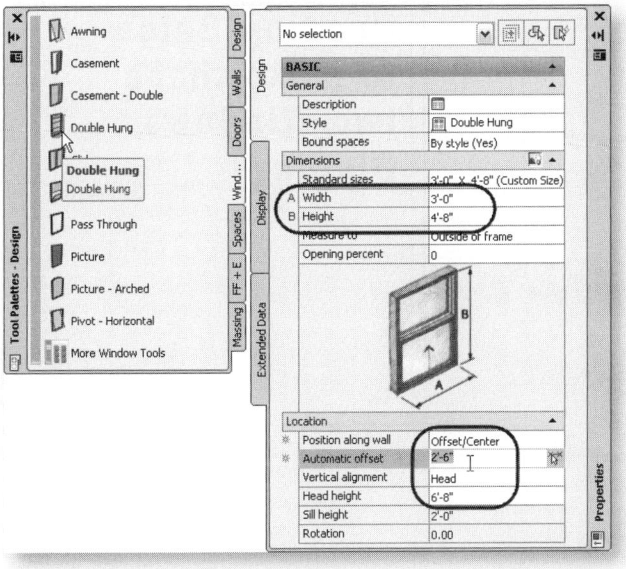

FIGURE 4.39 *Set parameters on the Properties palette for adding Windows*

Just as we were able to do for Doors, when adding Windows we can set the position of the Window vertically within the Wall. We will not see the effect of this setting in plan view, but you will see it later when you generate an elevation from your plan or view the model in 3D. The Vertical Alignment setting includes two options in a list used to toggle the reference point from Sill to Head and a text box for each to set the offset from these points relative to the Wall's Baseline. For this exercise, verify that the Head is chosen for Vertical Alignment and that 6'-8" [2200] appears for the offset. Using Head Height as the Vertical Alignment point measures the window height *down* from the position set for the Head, in this case 6'-8" [2200]. Using Sill would measure the window height *up* from the position set for the Sill.

38. At the "Select wall, grid assembly or Enter" command prompt, click on the exterior wall at the bottom of the screen.

39. Position the Window in the center of the horizontal Wall in the bottom left room.

40. Using Figure 4.40 as a guide, place the remaining double-hung Windows. Add them all at the same height initially and then change to the height on the Properties palette for the two Windows at the top of the drawing. When you do this, they will seem to disappear. Please see the "Adjust Cut Plane" heading later to correct this.

41. Right-click and choose ENTER when finished.

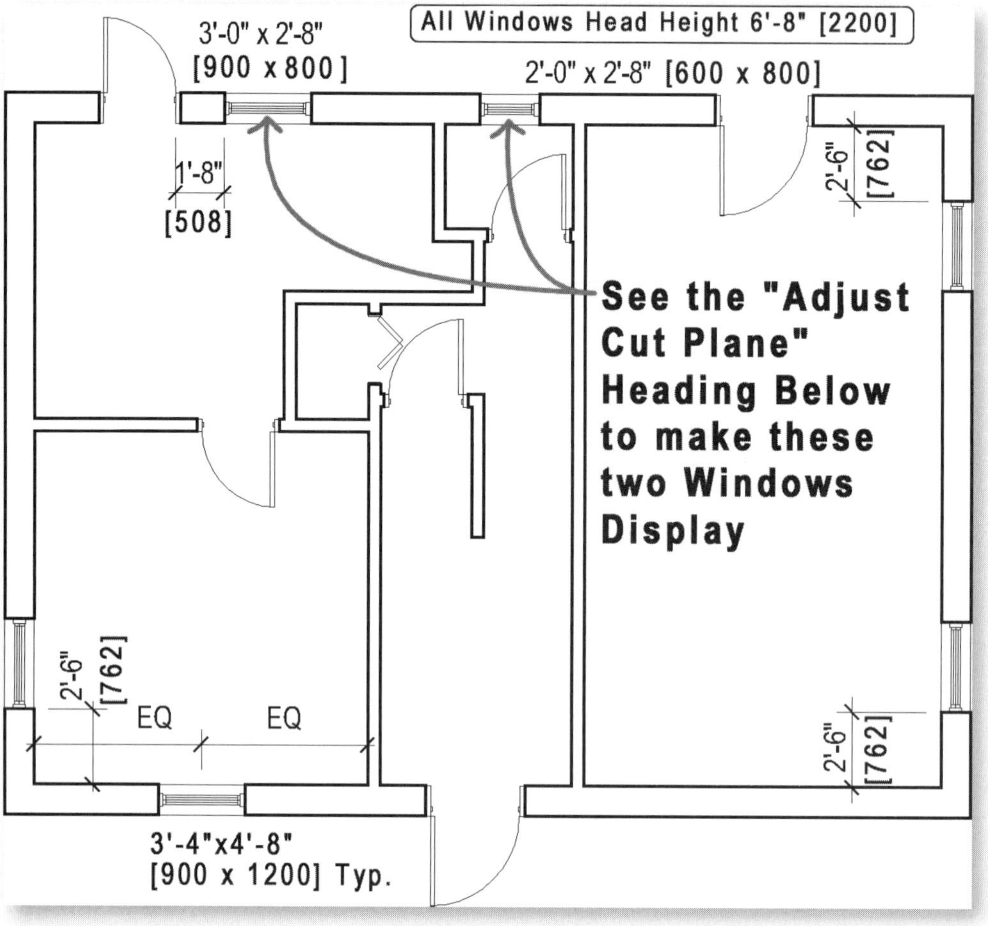

FIGURE 4.40 *Double-hung Window placement*

Adjust Cut Plane

When you add the two Windows at the top and then adjust their height, they seem to disappear. Do not repeat the steps again or undo them. Although the two windows do not appear, they are in fact still there. The problem here is a matter of the way in which the display parameters are configured in the default templates. The display parameter in question is the Cut Plane. Just as taught in traditional architectural drafting, the Cut Plane is an imaginary plane parallel to the ground plane that cuts through the entire floor plate. This plane determines the way in which each AEC object will be drawn in a Plan Display Configuration. (If you are unfamiliar with Display Configurations, please review Chapter 2.) In this particular instance, the default Cut Plane height of 3'-6" [1400] is not high enough to cut through these two Windows at their new height; therefore, they are excluded from the Plan display. However, if you were to view the drawing as an elevation or in 3D display, they would appear. To fix this problem, we will simply override the Cut Plane height for the Wall in which the two problem Windows reside. This is *not* the only way to correct this situation, but for now it is effective and simple to achieve.

42. Select the top horizontal Wall, and on the Properties palette, click the Display tab.
43. From the Display controlled by list, choose **This object**.

    An Add Object Override dialog will appear unless you have previously disabled the warnings. If the warning box does appear, click OK.
44. Beneath the Object Display Properties grouping in the Cut Plane category, set the Override cut plane property to Yes.
45. Set the Cut Plane Height property value to **4'-6"** [**1400**] (see Figure 4.41).

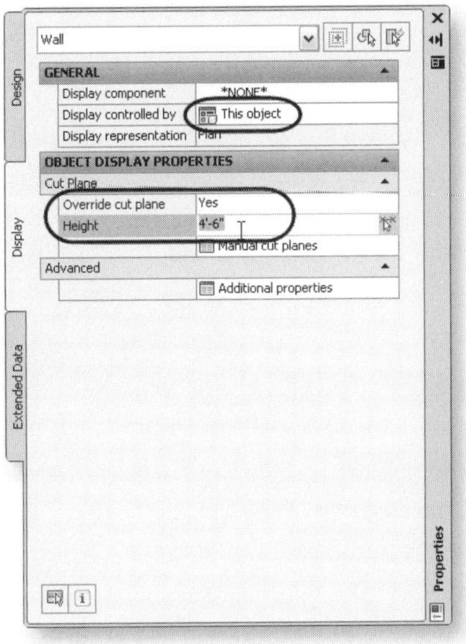

FIGURE 4.41 *Use the Display tab on the Properties palette to edit the Cut Plane of the Wall*

The Windows at the rear of the house should now be displayed. If you inadvertently added some extra ones, please delete them now. For a more detailed discussion of this topic, see the "Explore Display Representations" heading in Chapter 10.

46. Save the file.

> **TIP**
>
> All other techniques covered previously for Doors work the same for Windows—Automatic Offset/Center, Grip Edits, Standard Sizes, etc.
>
> Try repeating the grip editing steps described earlier on some of the Windows. All of the earlier techniques for Doors work the same way for Windows.

Add Openings

An Opening is a parametrically defined "hole" in a Wall. Openings do not use styles, but do use a Shape definition. All parameters of an Opening object apply directly to the Opening object. So far, when adding Doors and Windows, we have used tools on the various tool palettes. However, Doors, Windows, Openings, and Door/Window assemblies can be inserted directly into a Wall from the Wall object's contextual ribbon tab. We did not use this technique for Doors and Windows because we wanted their respective tools to automatically import the required Styles. Since Openings do not use Styles, we will practice this alternative technique now by placing a few Openings.

47. Select the left vertical Wall of the hallway.
48. On the Wall contextual ribbon tab on the General panel select the bottom half of the Door split button, and choose the ***Opening*** tool from the drop-down.

49. On the Properties palette, set the Shape to Rectangular, the Width to **2'-6"** [**762**], the Height to **6'-8"** [**2200**] and the Automatic Offset/Center to **6"** [**150**].

NOTE

You must type these values, as Openings do not have a Standard Sizes list.

50. Place openings in the locations shown in Figure 4.42.

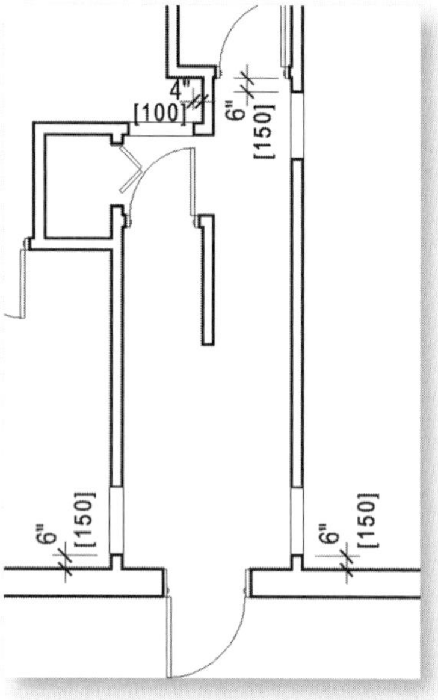

FIGURE 4.42 *Opening locations*

An Opening is unique in the sense that it is a "negative" object. No other object in ACA is used exclusively to represent a hole within another. In order to access the parameters of the Opening object however, it must be selectable; this is why some lines appear in the hole rather than nothing at all. The easiest way to manage this situation is with the Opening object's layer or its display properties. Opening objects are placed on the layer like all other AEC objects; "A-Wall-Open" if using the AIA layer scheme. Simply access the Layer Properties dialog box and set this layer to No Plot (click the little printer icon off). This will leave the layer visible onscreen but render it invisible when printed. The other way to manage Openings is to turn them off in the current Display Set (see Chapter 2 for more information on Display Sets).

CAD MANAGER NOTE

You can make this change the default in the Layer Key Style file (if using the Layer technique) and template files (for the Display option) for the office. This will save the users from making this change manually within each drawing. Other choices would include leaving the Opening objects displayed for plotting, and change the linetype, lineweight or other display parameters to match your office graphic standards.

Load Custom Tool Palette

There is one additional opening object type that we can add to Walls: a Door/Window Assembly object. These objects behave very much like Doors, Windows and Openings in the way you add and manipulate them, but have the potential for more complex Styles and designs. Using a Door/Window Assembly, you can define opening styles containing one or more integral Doors and Windows as well as any variety of Frame and Mullion conditions. Door/Window Assembly objects are nearly identical in concept and function to Curtain Wall objects. You can learn more about Curtain Wall and Door/Window Assembly design and composition in Chapter 8. For now, we will focus on how to import and use a premade Style. A content file containing a custom Door/Window Assembly Style and a custom tool palette is included with the other Chapter 4 files from the Mastering AutoCAD Architecture 2010 CD-ROM. In this sequence, we will load the Mastering AutoCAD Architecture Tool Palette and use its tools to import a custom Door/Window Assembly Style for the picture window at the front of the existing house.

NOTE

The process portrayed here specifically showcases the importing of a Door/Window Assembly style, but can be used to import any type of ACA style.

Recall in the "Create a Tool Palette Group" topic from Chapter 3, that we need to close the active ACA Project before adding a palette.

51. From the QAT, choose **Project Browser**. Right-click the active project and choose **Close Current Project.** Click OK to close the Project Browser.
52. On the Insert ribbon tab on the Content panel, click the top half of the ***Content Browser*** split button (or press CTRL + 4).

The Content Browser window will open. (Refer to the "Content Browser" topic in Chapter 2 for more information).

53. In the bottom-left corner of the Content Browser, click the Add Catalog icon.
54. In the Add Catalog dialog box, choose **Add an existing catalog or website** from the bottom and then click the Browse button.
55. Navigate to the *C:\MasterACA 2010\Catalog* folder, choose the *MasterACA 2010.atc* file, click Open and then click OK (see Figure 4.43).

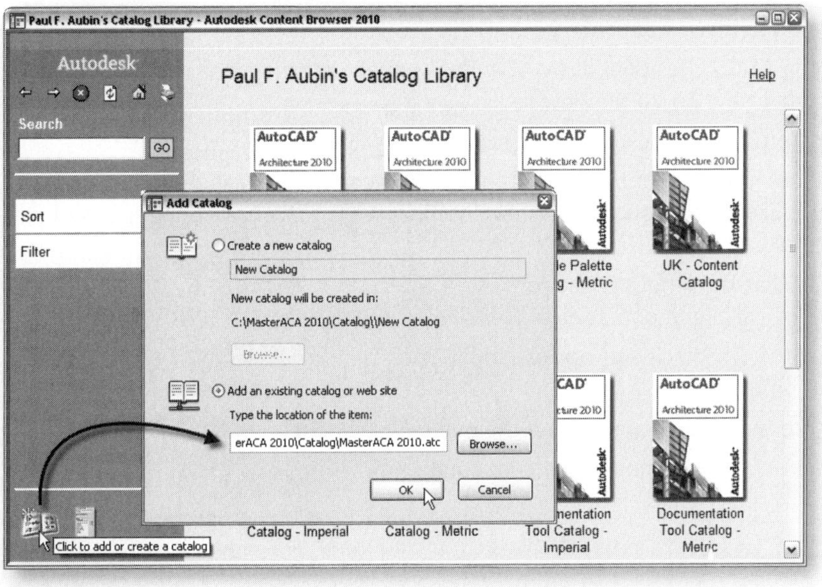

FIGURE 4.43 *Add the Mastering ACA 2010 Catalog to your library*

Idrop a Tool Palette

56. Right-click the Tool Palettes title bar and choose **MasterACA** to load the tool palette group created in Chapter 3.
57. Click on the newly loaded catalog (click on the image to open it).

    Contained within the MasterACA 2010 Tool Catalog are four tool palettes named *MACA Residential*, *MACA Residential - Metric*, *MACA Commercial* and *MACA Commercial - Metric*.
58. Click and hold down the mouse on the small eyedropper icon for the *MACA Residential* [*MACA Residential - Metric*] tool palette and drag it into the ACA drawing window.

    A new *MACA Residential* [*MACA Residential - Metric*] tab will appear on your Tool Palettes.

You will see three tools contained in this palette, two Wall tools and one Door/Window Assembly tool. We will use the Door/Window Assembly tool next.

TIP

You can create a Tool Palette Group and move the new tool palette to this group to consolidate the number of tabs on your Tool Palettes. The process was covered in Chapter 3. If you did not complete Chapter 3, right-click the Tool Palettes title bar and choose Customize. Create a new group and then drag the MasterACA palette to it. For more information, see the "Tool Palette Groups" heading in Chapter 1, the "Create a Tool Palette Group" heading in Chapter 3 and the online help.

CAD MANAGER NOTE

You might want to have a single central location on your system or on a network server (where all users have access) to store all catalogs and content files. This will make it easy to access and maintain the company library of content and styles. Establish a procedure for submitting new content to the library as the team creates it. It is also wise to develop a standard for locating project-specific content that may or may not become part of the firm-wide library. These project resources can then be made available to project team members via a project-specific tool palette. See the "Setting up Standard Tools in a Project" and the "Project Standards" topics in the online help for more information.

Add a Door/Window Assembly

59. On the MACA Residential [MACA Residential - Metric] tool palette, click the Existing Living Room Window tool.
60. When prompted, click the lower horizontal Wall.

    The Tool has many of the settings already preconfigured including the Style reference like other tools that we have used, as well as the basic dimensions of the assembly.
61. Verify that the length is set to **8'-0"** [**2400**], the Height to **6'-0"** [**1800**] and the Vertical alignment is set to Head with a Head height of **6'-8"** [**2200**].
62. Using the Offset/Center option, add a Door/Window Assembly centered in the room on the right.

    Be sure that the sill appears on the outside (see panel B in Figure 4.44).
63. Press ENTER to complete the command.

TIP

If you add the Assembly with the sill to the inside (see panel A in Figure 4.44), do not erase it and start over. Instead, select the Door/Window Assembly (you must click the sill to select it, do not click the nested Windows within it), right-click and choose **Wall Anchor > Flip Y**. This will reverse the direction of the Assembly relative to the Wall.

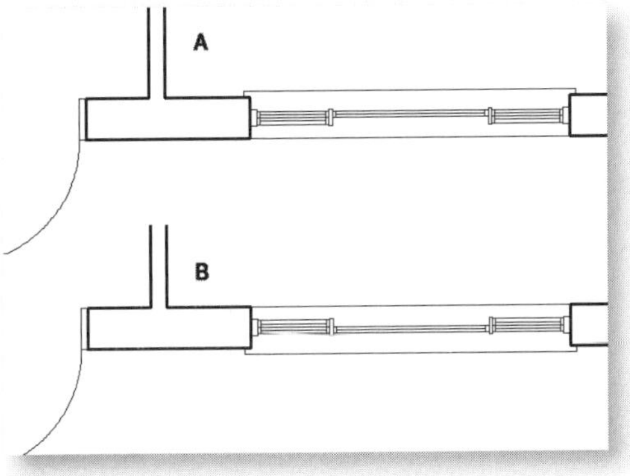

FIGURE 4.44 *Place a Door/Window Assembly with the sill on the outside*

Modifying Door Size and Style

Modifying Doors and Windows is easy. We can use the direct manipulation techniques already covered previously, or we can also use the Properties palette. The following steps will show you the technique to follow when using the Properties palette.

1. Select the Single Hinged door in the top-right corner of the plan (the first one we added), right-click and choose **Properties.**

This will open the Properties palette if it is not open already. On the Design tab of the Properties palette, you can change many of the basic parameters of the Door: Layer, Size, Style and Anchor point.

2. Change the Width to **6'-0"** [**1800**] and then press ENTER.

   Repeat the steps in "Move a Door Precisely with Object Snap Tracking" to re-center the door in the space. (You should be able to track to the center of the Door/Window Assembly this time.)

This Door is now a bit large to remain a Single Hinged Door. However, if you keep the Door selected and look at the available styles in the Style list on the Properties palette, no double Door style is currently available. We will need to import a double Door style into this drawing. We could use the Content Browser as before; however, it is always a good idea to first check what is available on your tool palettes. The tools on tool palettes often have built-in styles that can be applied to existing drawing objects.

3. Right-click the Tool Palettes title bar and choose **Design**, and then click the Doors tab.
4. Locate the Hinged – Double tool and right-click its icon.
5. Choose **Apply Tool Properties to > Door**.

The selected Door will change to match the properties of the tool, including the application of the Hinged – Double style. Here we used a Door tool, but you can perform this process with most tool palette tools on most types of AEC objects.

If you have already deselected the Door that we enlarged previously when you right-click the tool, you will be prompted to "Select Door(s)." Select the Door in the top-right corner of the plan that we enlarged and press ENTER.

NOTE

You can use this technique to convert nearly any object type into any other. For instance, a Door or Opening can be converted to a Window. A Window can be converted to a Door/Window Assembly. When we begin exploring other object types in later chapters, we will also see further examples of conversions that we can perform.

Adjust Door Swing Angle

If you wish to use 45° Door Swings for existing Doors, perform the following steps.

6. On the Properties palette, click the Quick Select icon (the small icon with the green rectangle, cursor arrow and lightning bolt). (See the left side of Figure 4.45.)

Quick Select allows you to select objects within the drawing that have one or more properties in common.

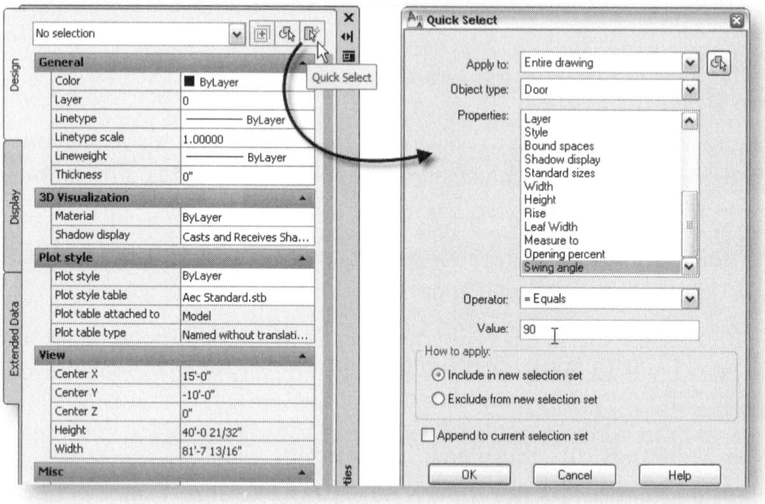

FIGURE 4.45 *Use the Quick Select command to select objects with similar properties*

7. From the Apply to list, choose **Entire Drawing**.
8. From the Object type list, choose **Door**.
9. From the Properties list, choose **Swing angle**.
10. Leave Operator set to = **Equals** and type **90** for the Value (see the right side of Figure 4.44).

NOTE

In Palettes and dialog boxes such as these, the degree (°) symbol is not necessary, 90 will be correctly interpreted as 90°.

11. Click OK to apply the selection criteria to the drawing.

All of the hinged (both single and double) Doors should be selected. We could have right-clicked one of the doors here and chosen Select Similar, but since we had both Single and Double hinged door types, only the ones of the same type as the one right-clicked would have been selected. To select both types with Select Similar, you would have to first select one of each type. In most cases, Select Similar is much quicker and easier. However, in this case we can see that Quick Select is also very useful and offers more control.

12. On the Properties palette, type **45** for the Swing angle.

    The doors you selected now have 45° swings.

13. Right-click and choose **Deselect All** or simply press the ESC key.

NOTE

The Bi-fold Door remains unchanged. This is because the parameter for this type of Door is actually "Open percent" rather than Swing angle.

14. Select the Bi-fold Door (in the closet at the center of the Plan).
15. On the Properties palette, change the Open percent to **75** and then press ENTER.
16. Save the file.

All of the techniques described previously would also work for Windows. (Windows would typically not have a "Swing Angle" but rather an "Opening percent".) Most would apply to Door/Window Assemblies and Openings as well. The overall process using both the Properties palette and the "Apply Tool Properties to" object techniques will work with all AEC objects. Try out a few variations on your own if you wish.

Adjust Door Threshold Display

In this sequence, we will look at adding thresholds to the exterior Doors.

17. Select the exterior double Door (top right corner).
18. On the Doors palette, right-click the Door tool labeled Hinged – Double – Exterior and choose **Apply Tool Properties to > Door**.
19. Right-click and choose **Deselect All**.

    Notice that the Door now shows a Threshold on the exterior.

20. Repeat the same process on the two remaining exterior Doors. Use the Hinged – Single – Exterior this time.

This process worked fine for the Door at the top, but the Door in the center of the bottom exterior Wall (which happens to be the house's front door) has the threshold on the wrong side. Changing the swing (with the grips as explained previously) would flip both the swing and the threshold. But if we want to keep the Door swinging out, and have the threshold to the outside as well, we must edit the Display Properties of the Door.

TIP

Be certain to select only one object when using the Edit Object Display command. If you select more than one object before you right-click, only the General Properties tab will be available.

21. Select only the Door in the bottom exterior Wall and on the Properties palette, click the Display tab.
22. From the Display representation list, choose **Threshold Plan**.
23. From the Display controlled by list, choose **This object**.

    An Add Object Override dialog will appear unless you have previously disabled the warnings. If the box does appear, click OK.

For most objects, the Display Representation list would show only one Representation. For Doors however, there are actually two choices—Plan and Threshold Plan. When we explored Sets in Chapter 2, we learned that a Set determines whether an object displays at all and if so which Display Representation(s) it will show. Also recall that a Representation is a specific set of graphics used to convey a particular type of drawing such as Plan or Elevation. In this case since we see two items in the list—"Plan" which shows the panel, swing and frame and so forth and "Threshold Plan" which shows the threshold lines. (For more information on the display system and Display Representations, refer to Chapter 2.)

Remember that there are three levels of display properties. Most objects use drawing default or style overrides. However, this will be the second example of an object override used in this drawing. (We applied an object override previously for the Wall when we adjusted the Cut Plane.)

- **Drawing Default**—Applies to all objects of a particular type (in this case all Doors) regardless of style.
- **Style**—Applies to all objects of the same style (in this case all Hinged - Double Doors). All Drawing Default settings are ignored at this level. Objects of other styles are not affected.
- **Object**—Applies only to the selected object (in this case the main entrance Door of the existing house). All Drawing Default and Style based settings are ignored at this level. No other objects in the drawing are affected in any way.

These three property sources apply hierarchically. When you apply a style-level override, for instance, the Drawing Default settings are copied to the style. You can then edit those settings at the style level, which would then apply to all Doors of that style.

TIP

As a general rule of thumb, apply Display Properties first at the Drawing Default level, then at the Style level, and finally, only if necessary, at the Object level. Try to avoid object level overrides if you can.

24. Returning attention to the Properties palette, select the Display component property (at the top of the General area), click on the down arrow icon at the right to display the drop-down list.

The drop-down list includes all of the Display Components assigned to the selected display representation, in this case Threshold Plan. Visibility is controlled by the light bulb icons, which are toggled directly on the list. Additional parameters (display by material, color, linetype, etc.) for each component can be edited by selecting a specific component. For now we will focus only on Threshold A and B. Threshold A is the threshold for the swing side of the door, Threshold B is on the opposite side.

25. Click the light bulb next to Threshold A to turn it on.
26. Click the light bulb next to Threshold B to turn it off (see Figure 4.46).

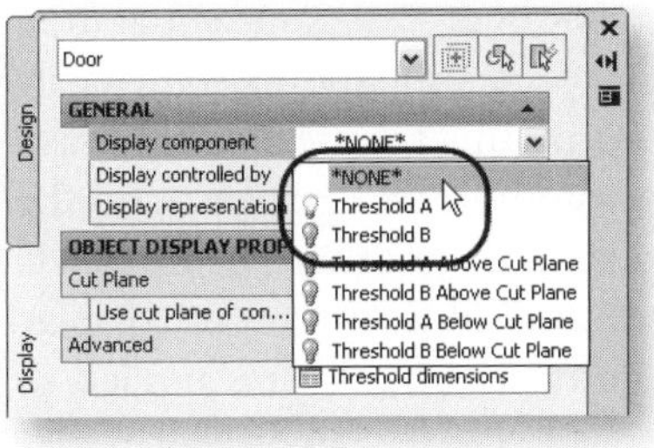

FIGURE 4.46 *Changing which threshold displays for the selected Door in the Threshold Plan*

27. Select *NONE* to close the drop-down list without choosing a component.

    Notice the change to the thresholds in the drawing.

28. Select the Threshold dimensions worksheet icon (under the Object Display Properties group, Advanced category) to control the size and offset of the threshold.

    Values A and B apply to Threshold A, while C and D apply to Threshold B.

29. Set A- Extension to **2"** [**50**] and B- Depth to **4"** [**100**] (see Figure 4.47).

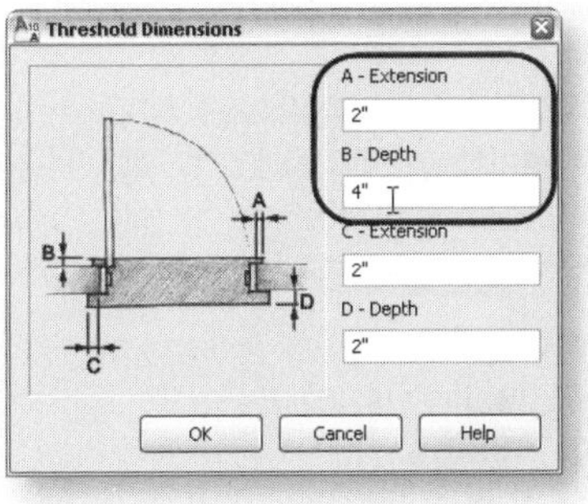

FIGURE 4.47 *Configure Threshold settings*

30. Click OK to return to the drawing.

    Notice the change. Repeat these steps for the other Hinged – Single – Exterior door on the left side of the top exterior Wall.

31. Save the file.

Object Display Properties are very powerful tools for all AEC object types. They can also be very complex. Having guidelines and procedures firmly established in your office for their proper use will yield enormous benefit. For instance, Door styles with various typical size thresholds can be included in the office library, and made into tools on all users' tool palettes, thereby preventing the need (as in this example) to attach Object level overrides.

MANAGER NOTE CAD

ADDING PLUMBING FIXTURES

A vast library of drawing components has been provided with AutoCAD Architecture. Items such as furniture, toilets, trees, parking lot layouts, equipment, electrical fixture symbols, targets, tags, and much more have been included. Most of these items are created from an AEC object called a Multi-View Block. A Multi-View Block (MVB) is similar to an AutoCAD block; however, as implied by its name, it has the addition of display control intelligence (or "multiple viewing") built in. This allows completely separate AutoCAD blocks within the same MVB to be displayed under different viewing conditions. Items that have not been programmed as true parametric objects such as toilets, furniture, and many others mentioned previously can be created as MVBs. The two major benefits in doing this are the ability to take advantage of ACA display control (Chapter 2) with custom-drawn graphics and the ability to anchor design items such as furniture and fixtures to other AEC objects (also Chapter 2). AutoCAD entities such as lines, arcs, and circles cannot use display control or anchors. In addition, property data and keynotes can also be applied to MVBs.

Add Plumbing Content from the Content Browser

MVB content provided with ACA can be accessed through the Content Browser and tool palettes. (In Chapter 13, we will also use the AutoCAD DesignCenter to access AEC Content.) If you use the same content frequently, you can add it to a custom tool on a tool palette as we did in the "Add a Palette" heading in Chapter 2.

1. On the Insert ribbon tab on the Content panel, click the top half of the ***Content Browser*** split button (or press CTRL + 4).
2. Click the Design Tool Catalog - Imperial [Design Tool Catalog - Metric] to access its contents (see Figure 4.48).

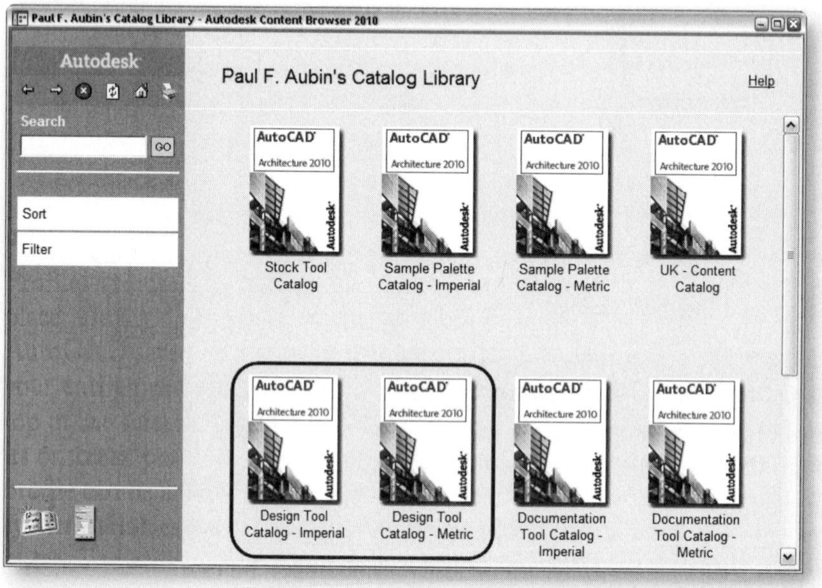

FIGURE 4.48 *Access the ACA Design Tool Catalogs*

This will reveal a text page describing the contents of this catalog.

As we have seen, the Content Browser has several catalogs. (See "Work with the Content Browser" in Chapter 2 for a complete list with descriptions.) *The Design Tool Catalog - Imperial* and the *Design Tool Catalog - Metric* both contain a mixture of Style definitions and AEC Content. We will browse within these catalogs to locate the plumbing fixtures that we need.

3. On the left side on the Navigation pane, scroll to and choose the desired category.

   If you are using Imperial units, hover over *Mechanical* and then choose *Plumbing Fixtures*. A collection of categories will appear on the right; click the Toilet category (see the left pane of Figure 4.49).

   If you are using Metric units, hover over *Bathroom* and then choose *Toilet* (see the right panel of Figure 4.49).

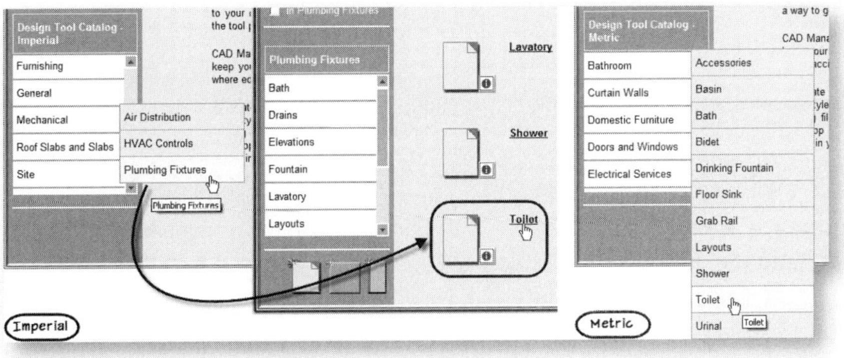

FIGURE 4.49 *In the Content Browser, browse to the Toilet Fixtures location*

   A collection of toilet symbols will appear.

4. Click and hold down over the eyedropper for the toilet named Tank 1 [3D Toilet – Standard] (wait for it to fill up) and then drag it to the drawing window and release (see Figure 4.50).
5. Click a point to place the toilet in the drawing.

   The exact position is not important, because we will move it precisely in the next step.

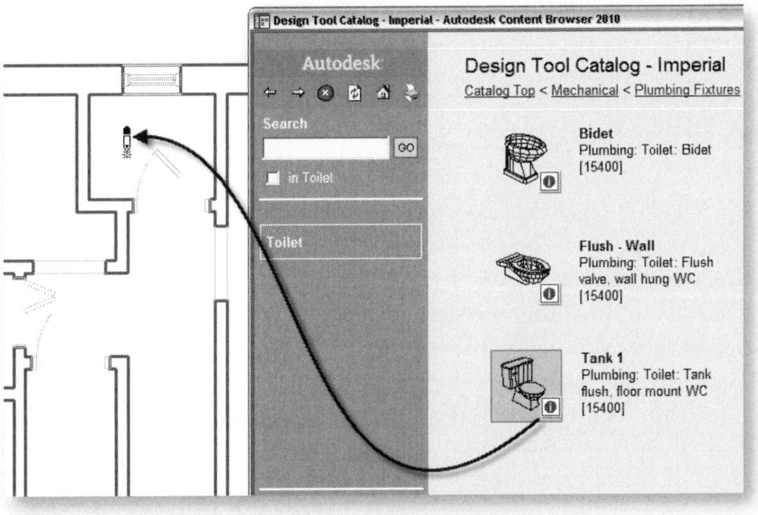

FIGURE 4.50 *Drag the eyedropper icon into the drawing to insert the symbol*

6. Press ENTER to complete the insertion.

Notice that although the icon in the Content Browser was in 3D, once dragged into the current drawing, the symbol came in "flat – 2D." This is typical behavior for a Multi-View Block.

The MVB contains one or more view blocks used to portray the object under different viewing conditions. In the Content Browser, you will often see a 3D icon used; however, it is automatically adjusted to show a simple 2D symbol when viewed from top (Plan) view; appropriate to a floor plan in this case. As a matter of convention, 3D icons typically convey symbols that are multi-view, while a 2D icon typically indicates a 2D–only symbol.

7. On the left side of the Content Browser, click the Back icon. (Content Browser should still be open on your Windows Task Bar; simply click it to make it active again.)

NOTE

You can also use any common Web browser technique to go back as well.

8. Click the Lavatory [Basin] link.
9. Locate the symbol called Wall 1 [Oval] and drag it (also using the eyedropper icon) into the drawing and release.

NOTE

In the Imperial catalog, Wall 1 is onscreen 3, so you will need click Next a few times to locate it.

10. Pick your insertion point and then press ENTER to complete the insertion.
11. Move (and Rotate if necessary) the toilet and the Lavatory [Basin] to a proper location in the small half bath at the top of the plan, as shown in Figure 4.51.

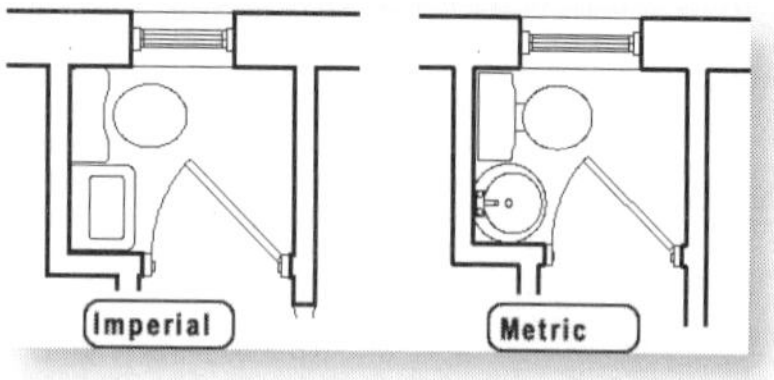

FIGURE 4.51 *Adding fixtures to the half bath*

VIEWERS

Being able to visualize a design change quickly from many angles and under a variety of display settings is critical to the design process. Throughout ACA a series of viewers provide this functionality. We will consider the Object Viewer here. With the Object Viewer, you can quickly study any selection of objects from all angles, in 2D or 3D, in a separate floating window. In addition, the viewers provide full access to display configurations. Access the Object Viewer from the contextual ribbon tabs.

Use the Object Viewer

1. Using a crossing selection window, select all of the objects in and around the small powder room (see Figure 4.52).

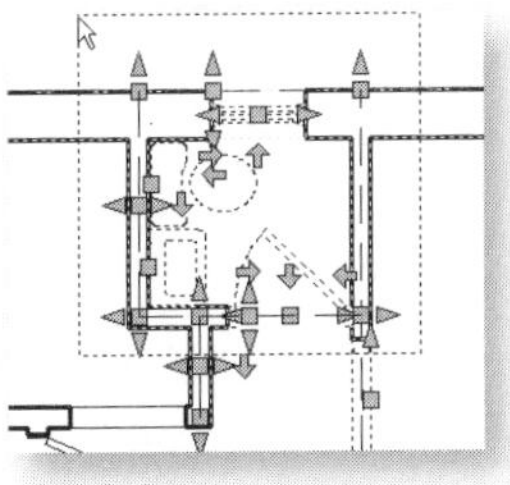

FIGURE 4.52 *Select the powder room and surrounding walls*

TIP
To make a crossing selection, click below and to the right of the room, move the cursor up and to the left, click again outside and above the room. More information on object selection can be found in the AutoCAD online help.

2. On the Multiple Objects contextual ribbon tab on the General panel, choose the ***Object Viewer*** tool.

Only the current selection will appear within the Object Viewer, making it easy to isolate portions of the model for quick study. At the top of the object viewer is a collection of icons and menus.

3. From the Display Configuration list, choose **Medium Detail**. From the Visual Styles list, choose **3D Wireframe**.
4. On the ViewCube, click on the "N" at the top of the cube, or, from the View Control list (located at the top right), choose **Back** (see Figure 4.53).

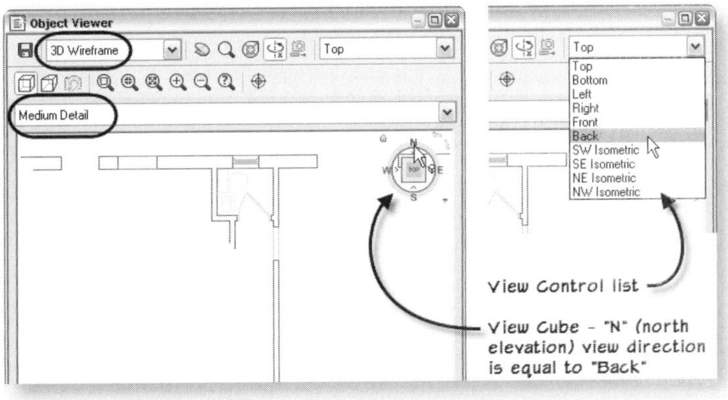

FIGURE 4.53 *Change the viewing angle to Back and display configuration to Medium Detail*

5. If you have a wheel mouse, roll the wheel up a click or two to zoom in on the image. If you don't have a wheel mouse, choose one of the Zoom icons and zoom in on the bathroom.

TIP
When you use your mouse wheel in the Viewer and choose a view direction in the View Control list, be sure to click in the Viewer window first before rolling the wheel or the focus will remain on the View Direction menu and change the view direction rather than zoom.

Notice the height of the window sill. Also notice the diagonal swings for the doors and the direction arrows for the double-hung windows. These are features rendered by the display system (see the "View Direction Dependent Configurations" heading in Chapter 2 for more information).

6. Choose the Constrained 3D Orbit icon.
7. Drag within the viewer to orbit the model dynamically into 3D view.

Drag slowly and watch the toilet and sink as you drag. They will appear as 2D elevation symbols until you release the mouse. This experiment showcases the qualities of the Multi-View Blocks. With "Back" view active, a 2D elevation view block is displayed. When you orbit to a 3D isometric view, the MVB dynamically swaps out the 2D symbols with 3D models (see the left side of Figure 4.54).

Experiment with starting the dragging from different positions in the viewer window. Each orbits differently. If the Orbit shifts the image off screen, switch to Pan (If you have a wheel mouse, simply drag with your wheel held down) to bring it back into view, and then return to Constrained 3D Orbit. If you don't have a wheel mouse, hold down the SHIFT key and drag in the Object Viewer; this will temporarily pan. Hold down the CTRL key and drag to zoom temporarily. For more information, search for "Object Viewer" and "3D Orbit" in the online help.

8. From the Visual Style drop-down list, choose **Conceptual** (see the right side of Figure 4.54).

Notice that the lavatory [basin] is sitting on the floor. Many of these symbols have an insertion point that places them this way. The practical application of such an insertion point is that it allows this content item to be mounted at different heights. We will explore how in the next topic.

9. Close the Object Viewer to return to the main drawing window.

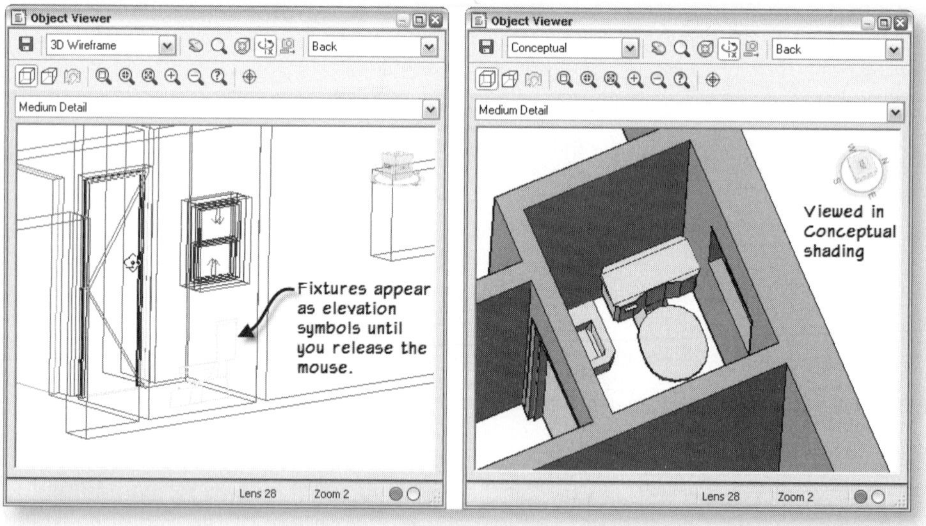

FIGURE 4.54 *Orbiting and shading the model in 3D within the Object Viewer*

If you prefer, you can do most of this viewing directly in the drawing window. To orbit with your wheel mouse, hold down the SHIFT key and drag simultaneously with the wheel. If you make a selection first, ACA will orbit just the selection until you let go of the wheel. You can also use the orbit icon on the Navigation toolbar. As you have seen in previous chapters, you can then change the Display Configuration and/or the Visual Style. Be sure to return to the 2D Wireframe Visual Style and the

Top view direction in Medium Detail before continuing. This is one advantage of the Object Viewer over such live viewing—when you close the Object Viewer, the main drawing window remains as you left it.

Using Edit in View

As useful as the Object Viewer is to quickly study an isolated selection of drawing objects, it does not allow any edits to be made. As its name implies, objects may only be "viewed" in the Object Viewer. If you wish to study an isolated selection of objects and edit them in place, use the Edit in View commands.

1. Press ESC to clear the previous object selection, if necessary. Click beneath the door to the half-bath and then move the mouse up and to the left crossing through the left vertical wall and the topmost horizontal wall (see left panel of Figure 4.55).
2. Click again to complete selection.
3. On the Multiple Objects contextual ribbon tab on the General panel, select the drop-down list arrow at the right side of the "Edit In View" split button (middle button on right side of panel) and then choose the Edit in Section tool (see right panel of Figure 4.55).

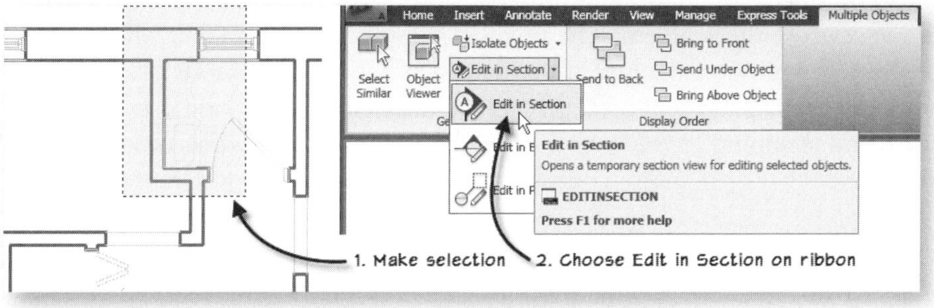

FIGURE 4.55 *Choose Edit in Section from the Isolate Objects menu*

4. At the "Specify first point of section line or Enter to change UCS" prompt, click beneath the door, move the mouse straight up (using Polar Tracking or Ortho Mode) and click again outside the window and then press ENTER.
5. At the "Specify section extents" prompt, move the mouse to the left past the left vertical wall and then click (see left panel of Figure 4.56).

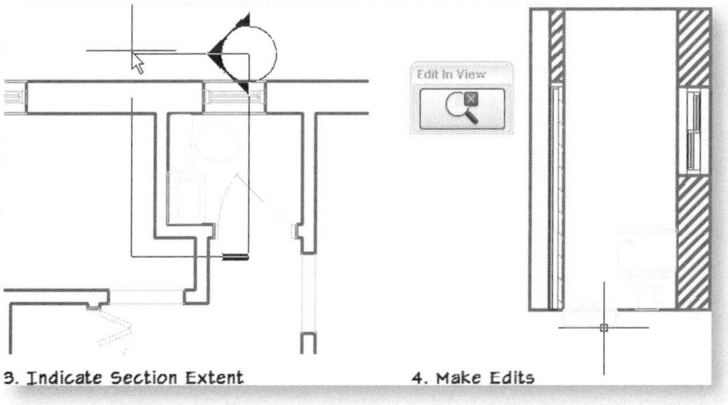

FIGURE 4.56 *Following Edit in Section prompts, designate the portion of the model to edit*

The drawing will enter the Edit In View mode. The selected objects will be isolated and the drawing will automatically zoom to the selected region (see right panel of Figure 4.56). When you execute one of the Edit In View commands, the objects you select are isolated. Isolating objects allows you to temporarily hide the unselected objects in the drawing thereby isolating the selected objects and making them easier to view and edit. When objects are isolated, you can continue editing the visible objects normally. In this case, we can now see that the sink is not mounted at the proper height and we can edit it directly in this view.

The simplest solution is to move it in this view. This method which seems obvious and is quick and easy, can cause undesirable results (that are not obvious) in the plan view. As we have said already, a Multi-View Block is an AEC object that contains one or more AutoCAD Blocks within it. It is basically a "smart" container object that will only display one of its view blocks in any given viewing angle.

6. Click the sink MVB, on the Properties palette set the Elevation parameter to **3'-0"** [**900**].
7. Use the Object Viewer (or the commands on the **View > 3D Views** menu) and view the half bath from all directions.

So far, everything appears fine; however, if you use the Object Viewer starting from a Top view and slowly rotate the view into 3D (or use the Plan Only Display Configuration), you can see the problem. The sink will show as 2D in plan, but will appear to "float" above the plane of the rest of the floor plan (see Figure 4.57). This situation can prove undesirable as the project progresses. Problems can include issues with object snaps and snapping to the wrong Z height, and problems when you export the drawing to a 2D background for consultants. We can use Insertion Offsets to correct this problem.

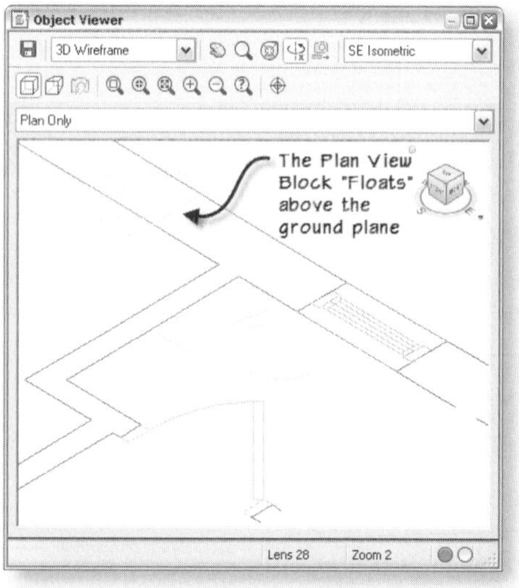

FIGURE 4.57 *Use the Plan Only Configuration to see the 2D symbol "float"*

8. On the Edit In View toolbar, click the Exit Edit In View icon.

Notice that once you exit the Edit In View mode, all of the hidden objects return to view and the drawing's viewpoint before the Edit In View is restored.

Adjust the Lavatory [Basin] Height with Offsets

In the previous sequence, we moved the entire symbol. In this sequence, we will see that we can also offset some (or all) of its internal view blocks. Display Control allows AEC objects to have both a 2D (flat) Plan display component and a 3D Model component. If we move the Multi-View Block up in 3D, we move all of its views, including its Plan view. This would mean that the 2D symbol used to represent the Plan would be floating above the Plan even though the correct fixture mounting height would be displayed on the Properties palette. To get the best of both situations, we will offset the Plan view block so that it returns to 0 while allowing the 3D and elevation views to continue to display at the correct height. This method takes a bit more effort, but is more accurate.

9. Select only the lavatory [basin] symbol, right-click and choose **Properties**.
10. Click the Insertion offsets icon in the Advanced area of the Properties palette.

This worksheet lists each of the view blocks contained within the MVB. The names of the view blocks are the same except for the suffix at the end. The one that ends in "_P" is for Plan, "_M" for Model, "_F" for Front and so on. Using this interface, we can shift any of the view blocks in any direction: X, Y or Z.

11. In the Z offset column, type **-3'-0"** [**-900**] for in the plan "_P" block (the "_P" block is indicated in Figure 4.58 by a small dot).
12. Click OK to dismiss the worksheet.

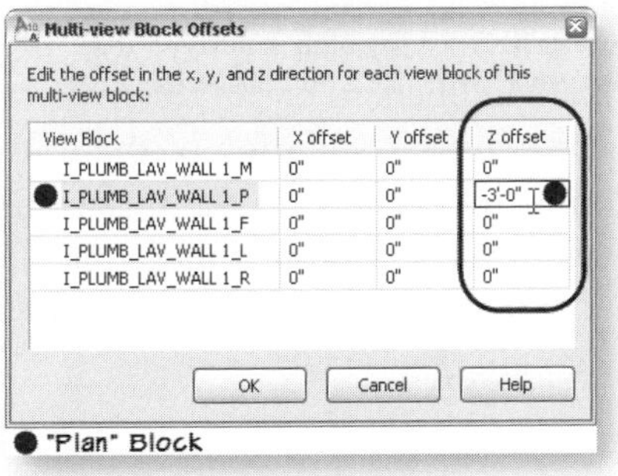

FIGURE 4.58 *Using Insertion offsets to move the plan block along the Z axis back to zero*

13. Reselect the same objects as before, and return to the Object Viewer to view the change in both 3D and the Plan Only Configuration.

Notice that this time, when you use the Object Viewer and orbit from a Top view to a 3D view that the sink remains "flat" and on the floor. Even though a bit more effort to achieve, this is the recommended approach to dealing with mounting heights of Multi-View Block symbols.

CAD MANAGER NOTE

Please note that the insertion offsets are applied at the object level. You cannot make these changes at the style level for the Multi-View Block. However, if you always wish to insert a particular symbol with the same offsets, there are two options. In the first, open the content item within the library and edit the actual view blocks contained within. You can move the graphics up relative to their respective insertion points. In this way, even though the insertion point remains at Z=0, the block itself would appear at the correct height. The problem with this approach is that your newly edited MVB will work only at one height. If you have no intention of inserting the item at a different height, then this approach is acceptable. However, in the example of the Lavatory [Basin] showcased here, some design scenarios might require mounting it at a height other than 3'-0" [900] (for ADA compliance for example). In that case, if you use this technique, you would need to make, potentially, several copies of the same piece of Content, one for each height. In the second approach, leave the MVB Definition unchanged (with all of its view blocks inserted at Z=0), and instead, create a custom tool (on a tool palette) referencing this Content item, and adjust the Insertion Offsets of this tool. The process to create such a tool is a bit more advanced, but the advantage is greater flexibility with a single piece of Content. For more information, search for "Creating a Multi-View Block Tool" in the online help. Whichever approach you choose, you should document your choice clearly so that team members will know how to use the content items you provide properly.

You can create your own Multi-View Blocks to meet specialized needs. Refer to Chapter 11 for a complete tutorial on the process.

CREATING WALL PLAN MODIFIERS

The first floor existing conditions plan is nearly finished. We still need to add the fireplace in the living room. We will use wall Plan Modifiers to create this type of condition. A wall Plan Modifier is a variation in the surface condition of the wall. Wall Plan Modifiers can represent any protrusion or indentation in the surface of the wall, such as pilasters, piers, column enclosures, or niches. While this is not the only way to achieve a fireplace (we could also use Mass Elements or Body Modifiers for example), it will prove effective in this existing conditions layout.

Configure Osnap Settings

Let's make sure that the Osnap settings are appropriate to our next task.

1. At the bottom of the screen, right-click on the Object Snap button and choose **Settings**.
2. In the Drafting Settings dialog box, click on the dark gray square at the right side of the General area header.
3. Put a check mark in Endpoint and Midpoint.
4. Put a check mark in Object Snap On (F3) and Object Snap Tracking On (F11), if they are not already on, and then click OK.

Add a Wall Modifier

5. Select the right exterior vertical Wall.
6. On the Wall contextual ribbon tab on the Modify panel, select the Plan Modifiers drop-down button and choose the ***Add*** tool.

7. At the "Select start point" Command Line prompt, place the cursor over the lower right outside corner of the building and hover for a second or two.

NOTE

Important: Do Not click yet.

A small tick mark will appear at the corner.

8. Using Polar Tracking or Ortho Mode, slowly move the cursor up 90° (see Figure 4.59).

   This will activate Object Snap Tracking.

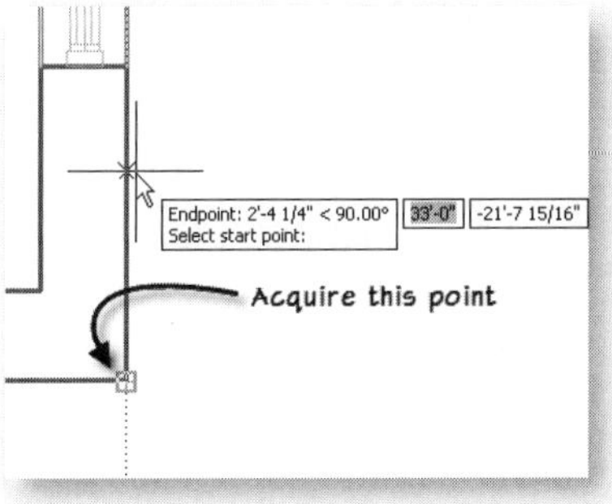

FIGURE 4.59 *Tracking the first point of the wall modifier*

Note the small tick mark at the corner point. This is referred to as an "acquired" point. By thus acquiring a point, we are able to reference it with a dimension at the Command Line. For more information on Object Snap Tracking, refer to the online help.

9. Type **7'-9"** [**2370**] at the Command Line and press ENTER.

   This sets the first point of the Wall Modifier.

10. At the "Select end point" Command Line prompt, continue tracking up at 90°, type **6'-2"** [**1880**] and then press ENTER.

NOTE

It will appear as though nothing has happened with the second dimension; however, if the Command Line prompts "Select the side to draw the modifier:" then everything is working correctly. Always remember to read the command prompts! Review the "Prerequisite AutoCAD Skills" heading in Chapter 1 if you have not done so already. If you have Dynamic Input enabled (the Dynamic Input toggle on the status bar is blue-green) then the prompts will appear onscreen as well.

11. At the "Select the side to draw the modifier" prompt, move the cursor outside the plan (to the right) and click anywhere.

    This indicates whether the modifier is a "protrusion" or an "indentation" of the Wall's surface.

12. At the "Enter wall modifier depth" prompt, type **10"** [**250**] and press ENTER.

    The Add Wall Modifier dialog box will appear.

The following options are available in the Add Wall Modifier dialog box:

- **Modifier Style**—Choose from an existing list of styles. Modifier styles determine the shape of the modifier in plan. The default Standard Style is rectangular in shape; custom shapes can be described by drawing polylines (see below).
- **Wall Component**—Assigns the modifier to a specific component of the Wall. Wall components are determined by the Wall style. The Walls in this file have only a single component called "unnamed." (Refer to Chapter 10 for more information on multi-component Wall styles.)
- **Offset Opposite Face**—Shapes the opposite side of the Wall component to the same shape as the side with the modifier. This is useful for showing Gyp. Board wrapping around a column as shown in Figure 4.66.
- **Start and End Elevation Offsets**—Use these to make a modifier that is not the full height of the Wall. Useful for niches and buttress type protrusions. We will make use of this below to shape the Hearth and Mantel.

13. Accept all the defaults by clicking OK (see Figure 4.60).

This creates a modifier representing the exterior shape of the chimney.

FIGURE 4.60 *The completed wall modifier for the protrusion of the chimney on the exterior*

Import Objects with the Clipboard

14. Open the file named *Fireplace.dwg* [*Fireplace-Metric.dwg*].

This file is among the files installed with the Chapter 4 sample files. You will find it in the *C:\MasterACA 2010\Chapter04* folder.

15. Select both polylines onscreen, and then on the Home ribbon tab expand the Modify panel and choose the ***Cut*** tool (second row in the expanded area, first button on left).
16. Hold down the CTRL key and press the TAB key to switch back to the *First Floor Existing* file.

TIP **Use this CTRL + TAB technique to quickly cycle between open drawing files.**

17. On the Home ribbon tab expand the Modify panel, select the down arrow of the Paste split button, and choose the ***Paste to Original Coordinates*** tool from the drop-down list.

MANAGER NOTE CAD

If you have shunned the use of clipboard commands in AutoCAD due to past functionality, please note that the clipboard commands no longer add anonymous blocks by default to the drawing when pasting (unless you deliberately choose Paste as Block). Therefore, please do not hesitate to use this excellent functionality, particularly the "Paste to Original Coordinates" feature showcased here. By contrast, you will typically want to avoid "Paste as Block."

Convert Polylines to Wall Modifiers

18. Again select the right exterior vertical Wall, on the Wall contextual ribbon tab on the Modify panel select the Plan Modifiers drop-down button and then choose the ***Convert Polyline to Wall Modifiers*** tool.
19. Click on the hearth Polyline shape (see Figure 4.61).

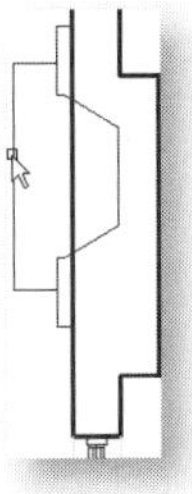

FIGURE 4.61 *Creating a hearth from a polyline*

20. At the "Erase layout geometry" Command Line prompt, select **Yes** from the Dynamic Input list (or right-click and choose **Yes** or type **Y** and press ENTER).
21. In the New Wall Modifier Style Name box, type **Hearth** and then click OK.
22. In the Add Wall Modifier dialog box, verify that the Start Elevation Offset is set to **0''** and choose **Wall Baseline** in the "from" list.
23. Set the End Elevation Offset to **2''** [**50**] and choose **Wall Baseline** in the "from" list (see Figure 4.62).

The Wall Baseline is equivalent to the floor line. Therefore we are making this modifier 2'' [50] thick and setting it at the floor.

24. Click OK.

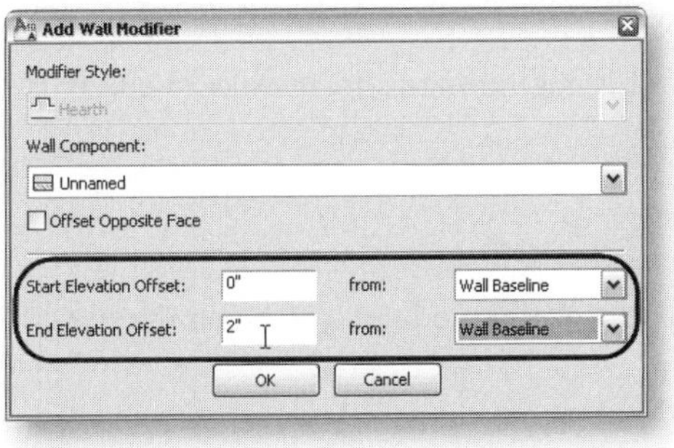

FIGURE 4.62 *Setting the vertical limits of the Wall Modifier 2'' [50] from the floor*

One obvious effect of this new modifier in plan view is the change in color of the hearth component. We will study the total effect in the Object Viewer after the next sequence.

25. Select the same Wall once more, on the Wall contextual ribbon tab on the Modify panel select the Plan Modifiers drop-down button and then choose the ***Convert Polyline to Wall Modifiers*** tool again.
26. Click the firebox Polyline shape this time.
27. Again, select **Yes** from the Dynamic Input list (or right-click and choose **Yes**) at the "erase the layout geometry" prompt.
28. Type **Firebox** for the New Wall Modifier Style Name and then click OK.
29. In the Add Wall Modifier dialog box, change the Start Elevation Offset to **2"** [**50**] and choose **Wall Baseline** in the "from" list.

    This will start the firebox just above the hearth.
30. Set the End Elevation Offset to **3'-9"** [**1140**] and choose **Wall Baseline** in the "from" list.
31. Click OK (see Figure 4.63).

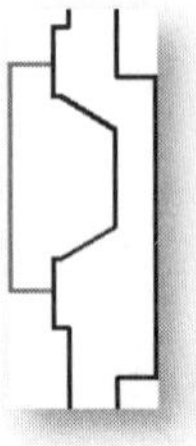

FIGURE 4.63 *The results of adding both polyline Modifiers*

Edit in Place for Plan Modifiers

It is perhaps now obvious that the chimney is not centered on the firebox and hearth. Although it is possible that this could be the true configuration, in this case, this represents an error in our original numbers used to create the first Plan Modifier. This is easy to rectify with the Edit in Place feature.

1. Select the same Wall again, on the Wall contextual ribbon tab on the Modify panel select the Plan Modifiers drop-down button and then choose the ***Edit Profile In Place*** tool.

NOTE

If a message stating: "The Wall has a modifier that is not drawn to size. In order to edit it, it must be converted" appears, simply click Yes.

Several grips will appear around the Wall modifier.

2. Click the cyan triangle grip in the center of the modifier and begin dragging it up (see Figure 4.64).

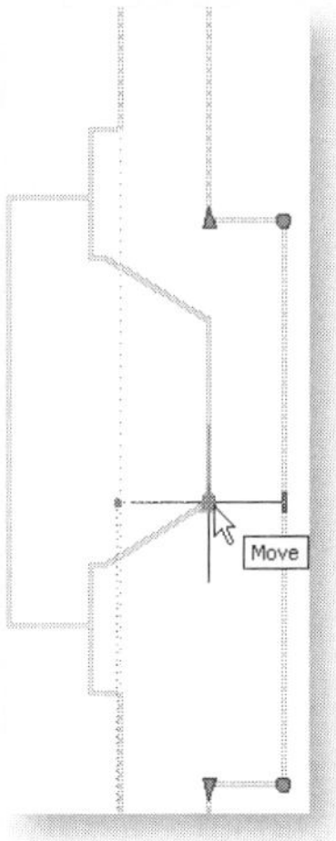

FIGURE 4.64 *Move a Wall modifier while in edit in place*

3. Snap it to the Midpoint of the firebox (or the hearth; either one will suffice).

> **NOTE**
>
> **The triangular grips will always move in an angle constrained to the original. This is why you can snap to either Midpoint.**

The other grips around the modifier can be used to reshape the chimney vertex by vertex if you like. Notice that they are magenta while the one that we just edited was cyan. When you edit shapes in place like this, cyan indicates an edit unique to the selected object while magenta indicates that the edit will be applied to the style. In this case the style would be the rectangular shaped Plan Modifier style. If you edited its shape and then added another Modifier using this same Modifier Style somewhere else, it would match the same shape.

4. Click the rectangular grip at the midpoint of the right edge of the chimney modifier.
5. Drag it to the right **5"** [**130**]. (If you have Dynamic Input on, you may want to toggle it off prior to entering the offset. Use Ortho Mode or Polar Tracking to keep the offset perpendicular to the Wall face.)
6. On the Edit In Place: Wall Plan Modifier ribbon contextual tab on the Edits panel, click the Finish icon (see Figure 4.65).

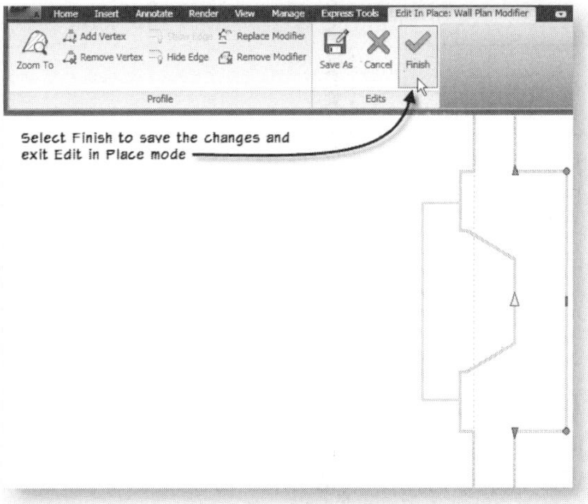

FIGURE 4.65 *Exit the Edit in Place mode and save all changes*

7. Select this Wall and bring it into the Object Viewer (see above).
   Have a look at it in 3D.

The fireplace could use a mantel and possibly some more articulation on the chimney. However, because there will be no new work done in the living room of this project and therefore no sections or elevations of the fireplace, that extra level of detail is unnecessary for this tutorial. What we have created works well for the plan. If you wish to try it anyway for the practice, feel free. Use the add wall modifier command as in the first sequence, with a 3'-9" [1140] Start Offset, and perhaps a 4'-0" [1220] End Offset, both measured from the Wall Baseline, to make the mantel. Experiment with other modifiers by drawing more polylines to make it fancier.

Another point to note as we move further into ACA functionality: the process that was used here to create a fireplace is one of several possible approaches. Since there is no dedicated parametric ACA fireplace object, you can model the fireplace with whatever technique you see fit. Other options include modeling it with Mass Element objects, creating a Multi-View Block or using Wall Body Modifiers. Many of these objects will be covered in the chapters that follow. If you wish to apply materials to the fireplace created here (like bricks), then you would need to build it differently. In this example, the fireplace is integral to the Wall. Therefore, without some modification, we could not assign a brick material to it without applying that material to the entire Wall. Again, since this is the existing part of the house, the approach used here is fine since it is not necessary to show materials on the existing construction. Materials will be covered in more detail in several upcoming chapters.

8. Save the file.

CAD MANAGER NOTE

To best take advantage of wall Plan Modifiers, create a "graphics standards" section in your office CAD manual. Show a few project examples of the best graphic conditions in which to take advantage of wall Plan Modifiers. Figure 4.66 provides an example.

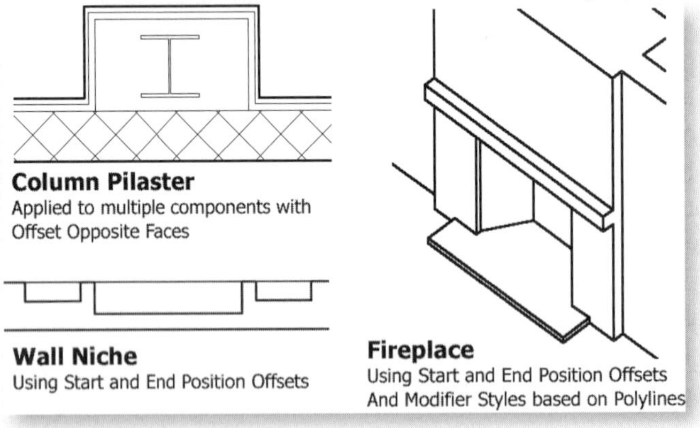

FIGURE 4.66 *Examples of Wall modifiers*

FINISHING TOUCHES

The last item needed in our first floor existing conditions file is the stairs. (Stairs are covered in detail in Chapter 7.) For now, we will copy and paste some pre-built stairs in the file to finish it. Later, when we have explored Stairs in depth, we will revisit the Stairs in this file and build them over again from scratch.

Import Stairs

1. Open the file called First *Floor Stairs.dwg* [*First Floor Stairs - Metric.dwg*].

This file is among the files installed with the Chapter 4 sample files. You will find it in the *C:\MasterACA 2010\Chapter04* folder.

2. Press CTRL + A to select all objects.
3. On the Home ribbon tab, expand the Modify panel and choose the ***Cut*** tool.
4. Close the file without saving.
5. In the *First Floor Existing* file, on the Home ribbon tab, expand the Modify panel, select the down arrow of the Paste split button, and choose the ***Paste to Original Coordinates*** tool.

This will add the Stairs to the floor plan. Congratulations, the first floor existing conditions file is finished (see Figure 4.67).

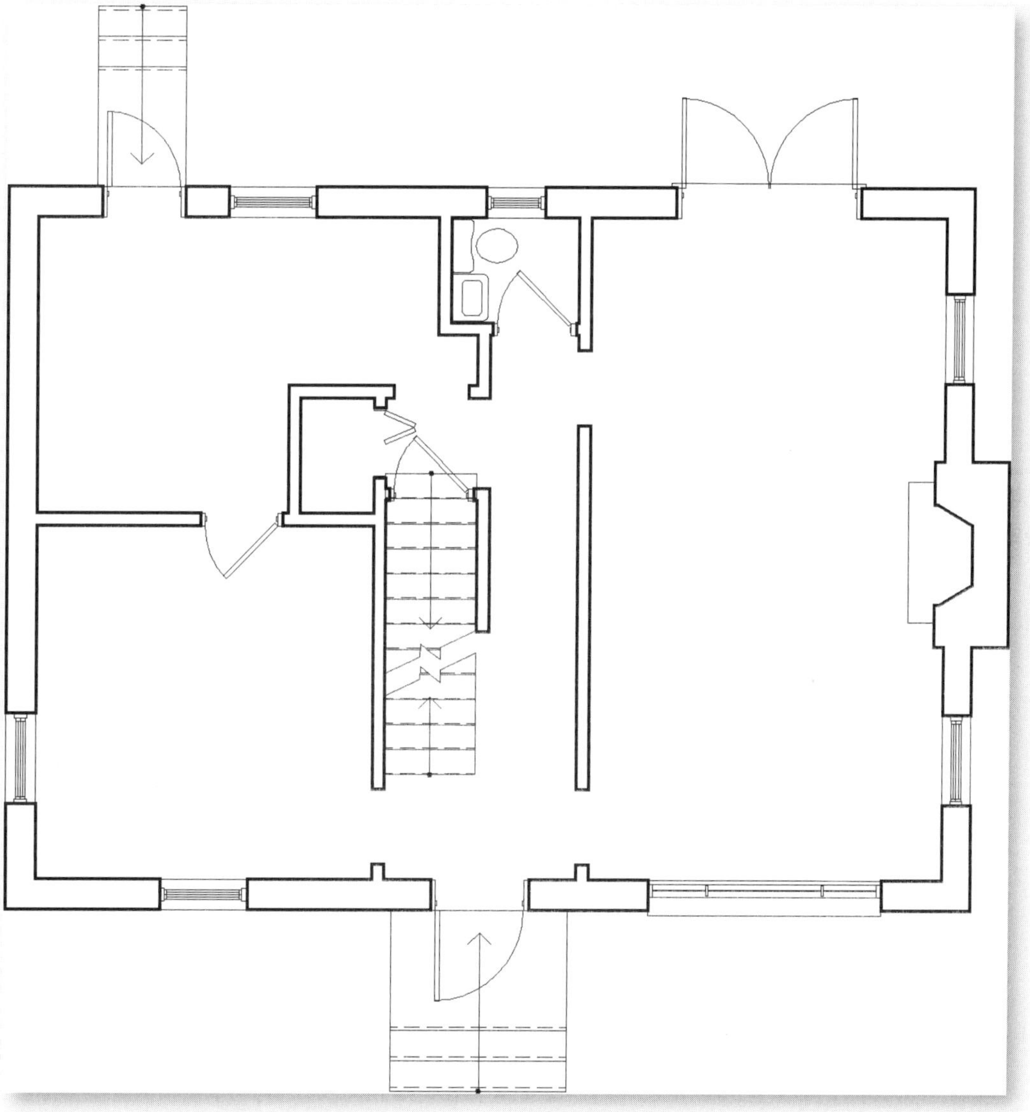

FIGURE 4.67 *The final first floor existing conditions*

6. Save and Close the file.

ADDITIONAL EXERCISES

Additional exercises have been provided in Appendix A. In Appendix A, you will find exercises for the Basement and Second Floors of the Existing Conditions as well as an exercise for completing a commercial Floor Plan. It is recommended that you complete these exercises for practice with techniques covered in this chapter before continuing to the next chapter. However, if you prefer, each of the drawings has been provided in completed form in the files from the CD. You will find them in the *C:\MasterACA 2010\Chapter04\Complete* folder.

SUMMARY

- When adding objects in ACA, remember that the Properties palette remains open and interactive as you work.
- Walls can be added one segment at a time (or converted from sketch lines as shown in the Quick Start).
- Doors, Windows, Openings and Door/Window Assemblies automatically "cut" a hole in, and remain attached to, the receiving Wall.
- Add Walls, Doors and Windows quickly, and modify their properties to add detail later.
- Use normal AutoCAD commands to erase, move, copy, trim, extend, fillet or offset Walls.
- Wall, Door and Window styles give access to a variety of Wall, Door and Window types.
- Ortho close and Close offer convenient ways to close Wall geometry while drawing.
- Direct manipulation of objects via their grips makes shifting Door and Window placement and orientation simple.
- Through the Content Browser, you can access the vast ACA content library.
- Multi-View Blocks are like AutoCAD blocks with display control added for different views in elevations or 3D.
- Use Object Viewer to quickly study design changes of selected objects in 2D or 3D.
- Wall Plan Modifiers offer a simple way to articulate the surface of Walls.

CHAPTER

5

Setting Up the Building Model

INTRODUCTION

AutoCAD Architecture can be used successfully in all types of architectural projects and within all phases. This is due in part to the versatility of the architectural tools provided and in part to ACA being built on the AutoCAD foundation. This book focuses mainly on the design development and construction documentation phases. The tutorial exercises in this book will explore two building types concurrently, starting at different points in the project cycle, to give you some sense of the variety of ways you can approach the design process. Don't be limited by the techniques covered here. The aim of the tutorials is to point you in the right direction. Exploration and playtime are highly encouraged.

Programmatic and preliminary design information might be received by the project team in a variety of forms, such as hand-drawn sketches, SketchUp Files, AutoCAD files, or other CAD files. ACA supports the import of DWG, DXF, and now even IFC files. You can also attach image files in popular formats as underlays and trace over them.

Getting started is sometimes the most difficult part. Regardless of the source of preliminary design data, gather all project data together in ACA early in the project cycle and consider developing a digital "cartoon set." A cartoon set will allow you to quickly assess the quantity and composition of each of the drawings and files required in the final document package. Remember, like everything else in ACA, the cartoon set will evolve and become more refined as the project progresses. The goal is to simply build a rough road map and gain a jump start on production. This chapter will demonstrate how to set up a project in ACA using the drawing management (Project Navigator) feature and create a digital cartoon set.

OBJECTIVES

In this chapter, we will explore the Drawing Management features of AutoCAD Architecture to create several files that will provide the basis for the projects explored throughout the rest of the book. One of the projects will be a commercial office building, while the other is a residential addition to a single family home (detailed lesson provided on the CD-ROM). The main goal of this chapter is to help you understand the procedure used to set up a project using the Drawing Management tools in ACA. The techniques covered here can be used on all types and sizes of projects. The following list summarizes the goals of this chapter:

- Set up preliminary files for ongoing tutorial projects.
- Build comfort with Drawing Management.
- Set up all preliminary Model and Sheet files.
- Set up callouts, elevations, and sections.
- Work with Sheets and Sheet Sets.
- Print a digital cartoon set.

BUILDING A DIGITAL CARTOON SET

When the time comes in a project cycle to begin thinking about how many sheets of drawings will be required and what those sheets will contain, it is time to build a digital cartoon set. Just like the traditional paper-based cartoon set, the digital version will help you make good decisions about project documentation requirements and the impact on budget and personnel considerations. One extra advantage of the digital cartoon set is that it is the actual set of CAD files for the project and will evolve as the project develops. This means that the layout of a cartoon set is actually the layout of the real building model and the eventual document set! Don't be concerned with the finality that this seems to imply. The documents remain completely flexible and editable, making this approach consistent with the goal of progressive refinement as defined in Chapter 2.

CAUTION

Please do not skip this step when setting up your own projects. Establishing the digital cartoon set (or the Building Information Model structure) at the beginning of a project is critical to maximizing the potential of the ACA tools and methods and will go a long way toward ensuring success.

In this chapter, we will set up the project structure for two different types of projects. Both project structures involve a heavy dose of external references (XREFs). However, using the Drawing Management system in ACA, the use of XREFs is made easy and nearly transparent. If you are uncomfortable with XREFs, do not shy away from this task—complete the exercises in this chapter anyway. You will find that most of the work associated with the attachment and maintenance of the required XREFs is handled automatically and intelligently by the software. File naming strategies and organization used herein are based on accepted industry standard practices. Although practices vary from company to company (and region to region), the recommendations made by the *United States National CAD Standard* (NCS) are the most prolific (in the US). Therefore, these guidelines will be suggested and utilized throughout this chapter and the rest of the book. More specific information can be found in that publication. Every attempt has been made to follow NCS recommendations wherever possible and appropriate. We will see however, that certain modifications to NCS naming recommendations are necessary to accommodate the specific needs of building information modeling when working with the ACA drawing management system. It is hoped that the intent is still discernable if not directly applied.

While NCS naming is utilized throughout the tutorials in this book, specific best practice guidelines and recommendations will also be made as appropriate (for example, see the "File Naming Guidelines" sidebar later in this chapter). Therefore, if your firm has specific naming guidelines in place that differ from the US National CAD Standard, feel free to utilize your firm's naming scheme for files created in this text instead. The exact file name that you choose should not negatively impact the intent or function of the file assuming that the naming scheme used is logical and understandable and that naming guidelines mentioned herein have been considered.

SETTING UP A COMMERCIAL PROJECT

The first project is a 30,000 SF [2,800 SM] commercial office building. The project is mostly core and shell with some build-out occurring on one of the tenant floors. The project will run through construction documents and will include plans, sections, and elevations. The tutorials that follow walk through the setup of the commercial project in several stages: setting up the project, creating Model files (Constructs and Elements), configuring plans, elevations, and sections (Views), and then generating sheet files and printing the cartoon set (Sheets). The completed files for the project are installed with the files from the CD in the *C:\MasterACA 2010\Chapter05\Complete* folder on your hard drive. There you find the completed ACA project files and a DWF (Design Web Format) file of the complete set of printed sheets as they appear at the end of the chapter.

Install the Cd Files and Launch Project Browser

In this first exercise, we use the Project Browser, a tool used to navigate through and manage all of your AutoCAD Architecture projects, to set up a new project.

1. If you have not already done so, install the dataset files located on the Mastering AutoCAD Architecture 2010 CD-ROM.

   Refer to "Files Included on the CD-ROM" in the Preface for information on installing the sample files included on the CD.

2. Launch AutoCAD Architecture 2010 from the desktop icon created in Chapter 3.

If you did not create a custom icon, you might want to review "Create a New Profile" and "Create a Desktop Shortcut" in Chapter 3. Creating the custom desktop icon is not essential; however, it makes loading the custom profile easier.

3. On the Quick Access Toolbar (QAT), click the Project Browser icon (see Figure 5.1).

By default, when you install AutoCAD Architecture, a folder named *Autodesk* that contains a subfolder named *My Projects* will be created in the current user's *My Documents* folder. When you open the Project Browser for the first time, it will be set to this location. However, if you completed Chapter 1 or 2, it will remember the location of the last project that you had loaded there instead.

It is not necessary that you create projects in the *My Documents* location and in fact, in a team environment it is preferable to work from a network server location instead. Files installed from the Mastering AutoCAD Architecture 2010 CD-ROM are installed in the *C:\MasterACA 2010* folder (see the "Files included on the CD-ROM" section of the Preface for more information). Even though you will typically work from a server location on your real projects, for the tutorials in this book, it is highly recommended that you work in this location.

The Project Browser is a file browser mechanism that allows you to locate project files (APJ files) anywhere on your computer (local or network). Using the Project Browser, you can locate projects and make them current, and move, copy, and create projects.

Figure 5.1 illustrates the various icons and controls within this window and includes brief descriptions of each in the caption following the figure.

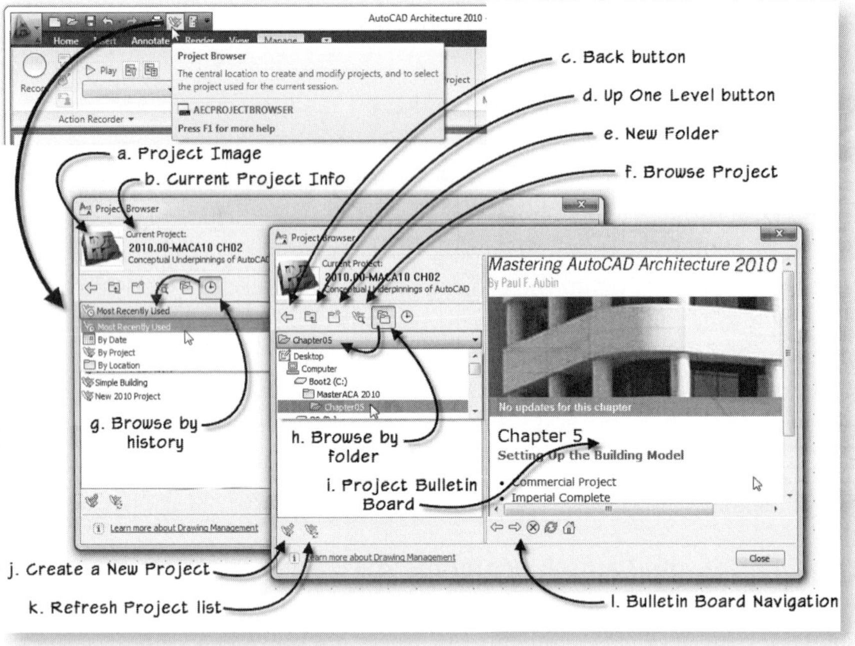

FIGURE 5.1 *The Project Browser window*

a. **Project Image**—A custom-defined BMP image can be assigned to the project and displayed here. For example, load the client's logo here.
b. **Current Project Info**—The Name, Number and Description of the current project will display here.
c. **Back**—Click to go back to the previous folder.
d. **Up One Level**—Click to go to the parent folder.
e. **Create a New Folder**—Create a new folder in the current location.
f. **Browse Project**—Click to open a standard Browse Window to locate and load project files (projects have an APJ extension).
g. **Project History**—Click to browse for projects that were previously active (see image inset for additional history view options). While in the History view, you can right-click and remove items from the history list as well as reset the list.
h. **Project Folder**—Click to browse for projects within the folder tree. This option gives access to My Computer, My Documents, Network location such as mapped drives and any additional locations that you add to the AEC Project Location Search Path (see Figure 5.2).
i. **Project Bulletin Board**—The user-defined Project Bulletin Board Web Page, a fully customizable project-specific HTML Web page. ACA starts with a simple generic page; you can load your own custom one in the Project properties.
j. **New Project**—Creates a new project within the current folder.
k. **Refresh Project**—Refreshes the current folder.
l. **Project Bulletin Board Navigation Tools**—Typical browser functions for the bulletin board page.

MANAGER CAD NOTE

You can add to the default search path locations used by the Project Browser in the Options dialog box. From the Application Menu choose Options, and then click the AEC Project Defaults tab. There you can add paths to the AEC Project Location Search Path. You can also edit the default Project Templates, Project Bulletin Boards, and Project Images on this screen. It is recommended that at the time of installation, you reset these paths for users to a location on the server where project templates and files are typically stored.

Create a New Project

4. In the Project Browser, be sure that the Project Folder icon (see item in Figure 5.1) is active and then choose *Computer* (*My Computer* in XP) from the list.
5. Double-click the *C:* Drive, then the *MasterACA 2010* folder, and finally the *Chapter05* folder.
6. With the *Chapter05* folder showing in the drop-down list, click the New Project icon (see item **j** in Figure 5.1) at the bottom of the Project Browser window.

NOTE

Be sure to browse to the folder first, then click the New Project icon. Review items c through h in Figure 5.1 for the tools used to navigate within Project Browser.

The Add Project worksheet will appear.

7. In the Project Number field, type **2010.1**.
8. In the Project Name field, type **MACA Commercial**.
9. Click in the Project Description field, and in the small dialog box that appears, type **Mastering AutoCAD Architecture 2010 Commercial Project**.
10. Make sure the "Create from template project" checkbox is selected and then click the small browse button (...) (see Figure 5.2).

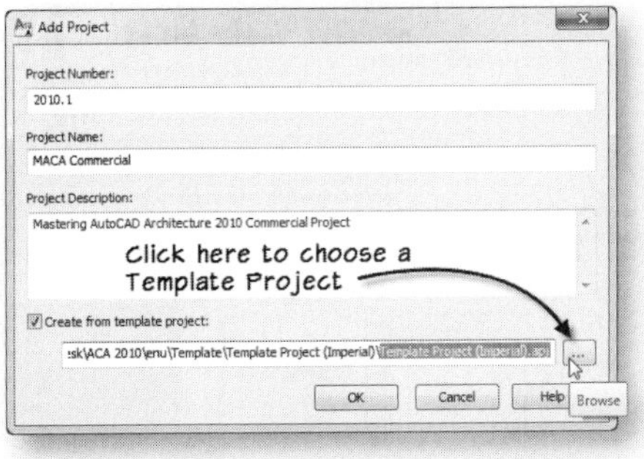

FIGURE 5.2 *Input the name, number and description of the new project*

11. In the dialog that appears, in the shortcut bar at the left, click the *Content* folder icon.

    This will take you to the default content location located at: *C:\ProgramData\Autodesk\ACA 2010\enu*.

    (*C:\Documents and Settings\All Users\Application Data\Autodesk\ACA 2010\enu* in Windows XP).
12. Double-click the *Template* folder.

A template project is much like a drawing template (DWT): it provides a preconfigured starting point for a new project that can potentially include settings, drawing template file references, tool palettes and even premade drawing files. Two template projects have been included with AutoCAD Architecture for both imperial and metric units: *Template Project (Imperial).apj* [*Template Project (Metric).apj*] and *Commercial Template Project (Imperial).apj* [*Commercial Template Project (Metric).apj*]. The *Template Project* is a very basic template project that includes no premade drawing files, but does include some basic project settings. The *Commercial Template Project* provides a better example of the potential of template projects. It includes pre-configured levels and a collection of premade Constructs, Views and Sheets (these are drawing files—see later) and other settings as well. In this chapter, our primary focus is learning the Drawing Management system. With this goal in mind, the following tutorials will use the simpler template project instead. In this way, you will learn how to build an ACA project completely from scratch. You are however, highly encouraged to create a project from the *Commercial Template Project* as well. In fact, at the end of this chapter, you are directed to an additional exercise in Appendix A for this purpose. You can also find a detailed description of the Commercial Template Project in the help file. Type: "Appendix 1: Template Projects" in the Info Center search field at the top-right corner of the screen to locate this topic in the online help.

13. Double-click the *Template Project (Imperial)* [*Template Project (Metric)*] folder, then select the *Template Project (Imperial).apj* [*Template Project (Metric).apj*] file and click Open (see Figure 5.3).

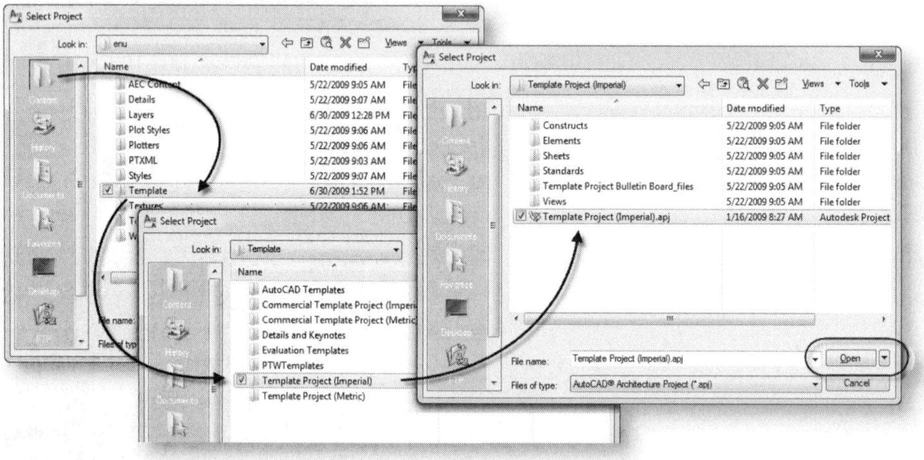

FIGURE 5.3 *Create the Project from a template project*

This will return you to the "Add Project" worksheet.

14. In the Add Project worksheet, click the OK button to create the project.

The new **MACA Commercial** Project will appear in the Project Browser (highlighted in bold to indicate that it is current), and the Bulletin Board and Project Image will update as well.

MANAGER NOTE CAD

The project template that we used to create the project included a bulletin board. You can replace the default one with something more specific to the project. Any HTM or HTML file can be used as a project Bulletin Board. You can use virtually any word processor, text editor, or HTML editor to create or edit project Bulletin Board files. A project Bulletin Board can be used by a Project Coordinator or CAD Manager to keep project team members informed on project news, or as a way to provide links to project standards, project tool palettes, or even a DWF of the project. (A good example of this is seen in the ACA Sample Project included with the software—the ACA Sample Project is located in the *My Documents\Autodesk\My Projects* folder). The Project Web page displays in its own integrated Web Browser window within the Project Browser, complete with its own Back, Forward, Home, and Refresh icons (see item **i** and item **l** in Figure 5.1). In this way, the project Bulletin Board can actually reference a home page to an entire intranet project Web site. If you prefer not to use the Bulletin Board feature in projects, simply leave the reference to the default Bulletin Board page unchanged.

The Project Image file is a logo for the project. Any image file can be used for this image, but it must be saved in BMP format. Use Photoshop, Windows Paint or any other image editor to save the image file. If your project has its own logo, you can load it here. Otherwise, you can use your company logo, the client's logo, or this can be left set to the default ACA image. If you prefer not to use the Project Image feature, simply leave the reference to the default Image.

15. Right-click on the MACA Commercial project in Project Browser and choose **Project Properties** (see Figure 5.4).

Some firms like to include the job number as a prefix to drawing file names. This can be accomplished automatically with the "Prefix Filenames with Project Number" option. To set this option, simply choose **Yes** from the drop-down next to this feature in the "Project Properties" dialog to enable it. For simplicity in this book, the Project Number Prefix has not been used. However, feel free to use this feature if you wish. You can also choose different default template files for each of the various files managed by the ACA Drawing Management system, such as Constructs, Elements, Views, Sheets, and Sheet Sets. (Each of these file types is explained later.)

You can optionally map each of the required root folders of the project to different physical locations. For example, you could map the *Constructs* folder to a folder named *Models* and even place it on another server.

There are also three options to how paths can be stored:

- **UNC paths:** *\\servername\share\Project folder\Constructs\File Name.dwg*
- **Mapped drives:** *P:\My Client\Project folder\Constructs\File Name.dwg*
- **Relative paths:** *..\Constructs\File Name.dwg*

Relative paths are turned on by default. If you set "Use Relative Paths" to "No," ACA will use either UNC or mapped drives depending on how you browse to the project within the Project Browser. If you locate the project via Windows Network Places, you will get UNC. If you browse via a drive letter, you will get mapped drives.

Also found in the Modify Project worksheet is the "Match Sheet View Layers to View" setting. This setting covered later in the "Create Views" heading allows the View file layer settings to control the layers in the Sheet file viewports. View and Sheet files are covered in detail later in this chapter.

16. For “Use Relative Xref Paths,” choose **Yes**.
17. For “Match Sheet View Layers to View,” choose **Yes**.
18. And for “Prefix Filenames with Project Number,” choose **No** (see Figure 5.4).

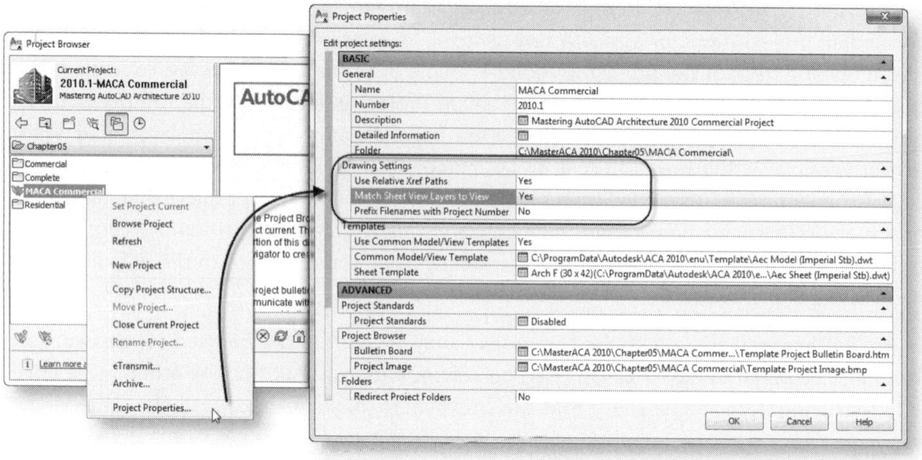

FIGURE 5.4 *The Project Browser—editing properties of the newly created project*

When you create a new project, a Tool Palette Group (refer to Chapter 1) can optionally be associated with the project. If you have Tool Palettes within this group, they will automatically load in project team members’ workspaces. We will not use Project-based Tool Palette Groups in this book. Therefore, let’s verify that they are turned off.

19. In the “Project Properties” dialog, beneath the Advanced grouping, scroll down and locate the Tool Palettes item. For “Project Tool Palette Group” ensure that **None** is selected and then click OK.

Some additional tools can be found on the right-click menu within the Project Browser; right-click on the project name to access this menu (shown on the left of Figure 5.4). Use these tools to set the current project, refresh, copy, and browse project files. You can also close the current project and rename and move inactive (not current) projects. You will not find an option to delete projects in the Project Browser. To delete a project, first make another project current, then exit ACA, navigate to the project location in Windows Explorer, and delete the folder containing the project files. Please exercise caution when doing this, however, as this will completely and *permanently* remove the project and *all* of its drawing files.

TIP

If you wish to have the Project Browser appear automatically each time you open ACA, choose Options from the Application Menu, and click the AEC Project Defaults tab. There, place a check mark in the Show Project Browser at startup box and then click OK. With this active, the Project Browser will launch each time you start ACA.

20. Click Close to close the Project Browser and return to ACA.

    The Project Navigator palette will appear onscreen.

You can also load your project directly from Windows Explorer before even launching ACA. Simply browse to the directory where the ACA project is found and double-click on the APJ file located directly in the project’s folder. AutoCAD

Architecture will launch a new session and make selected project current. If ACA is already running, launching a project through Windows Explorer will open a second session.

Project Navigator Terminology

Projects in AutoCAD Architecture consist of a collection of drawing files and project information files saved together in a common location. Taken together, this collection of graphical and non-graphical data is used to assemble a complete Building Information Model (BIM). The graphical drawing data associated with the project fall into four types of ACA drawing (DWG) files: *Constructs*, *Elements*, *Views*, and *Sheets*; each defined later. The non-graphical project information files include a single Autodesk Project Information file (APJ) that contains the basic framework of a project (all of the data we entered and looked at so far is stored in the APJ file), a Sheet Set file (DST) that determines the organization and configuration of the list of printed Sheets within the project, and several individual project data (XML) files (one per drawing) describing how each individual drawing fits into the overall project structure.

When you create a project, you enter the basic descriptive information (as we did previously), such as Name, Description and Project Number. The next task is to determine how the building will be subdivided into Levels and Divisions. Levels are the floor Levels and divide the building horizontally. You can also subdivide the building laterally into Divisions. Although you can edit Levels and Divisions at any time, it is typical to establish the Levels and Divisions that will describe the basic framework of our Project at the onset. These tasks are performed in the Project Navigator.

TIP

If Project Navigator did not appear automatically onscreen when you created the project, click the **Project Navigator** icon on the QAT (or press ctrl + 5).

Levels and Divisions (Project Framework)

- **Level**—A horizontal separation of building model data. A Level is typically an actual floor level in a building. Levels can be established for actual building stories, and also for mezzanines, basements, and other partial levels. You also use Levels to establish Grade level, Roofs and Datum levels (see Figure 5.5).
- **Division**—A vertical separation of the building model data. Divisions are typically used to articulate a physical separation such as a Wing, an Annex, or an Addition to a building. Divisions can be used to subdivide large floor plates into pieces that are more manageable in size (See Figure 5.5).

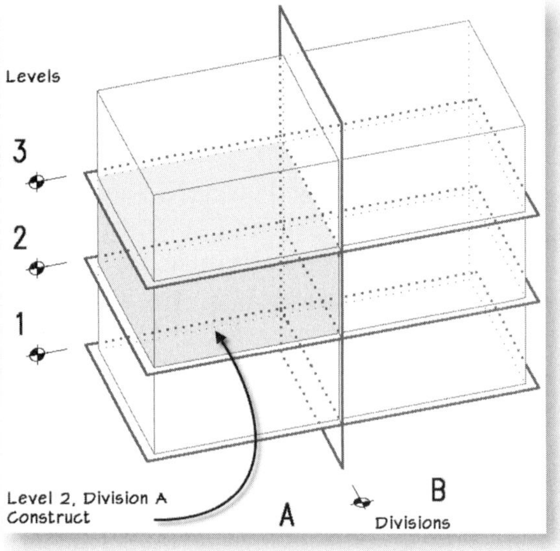

FIGURE 5.5 *Divide your building into Levels and Divisions to create your project structure*

NOTE See next topic for a definition of Construct.

Model and Sheet Files

Standard industry practice and the US National CAD Standard (NCS) recommend the creation and maintenance of two types of file: Model files and Sheet files. We will set up both Model and Sheet files in this book. This practice is widely used in the industry and offers many benefits.

- **Model File**—A file containing actual building data drawn at full size (1 to 1 scale.) This is a file in which all of the *day-to-day* work is typically performed. In the ACA Drawing Management system, Constructs, Elements, and Views can all be considered Models in the traditional sense; see definitions later.
- **Sheet File**—A file that is used *exclusively* for printing drawings. No data is saved in this file. It typically contains only a title block and external references to the project's various Model files.

Model files are referenced to Sheet files for printing (or when appropriate, other Model files). Most daily work is performed in Model files. In contrast, Sheet files exist solely for printing final documentation sets for distribution. One or more Model files are "gathered" by the Sheet file, composed on a title block sheet, scaled properly with the proper Display Configuration (see Chapter 2) active, layers and objects visible, and then printed. The Sheet is saved in this state so that documents can be printed again any time, at a moment's notice. To perform physical edits and design changes, return to Model files and perform the changes there. Those changes will appear in the Sheet file the next time the XREFs in that Sheet are reloaded, which happens automatically when the Sheet is opened.

CAUTION The Sheet file's "ready-to-print" status is maintained only if all project team members agree to work only in Model files and not in the Sheet files.

Elements, Constructs, Views, and Sheets (Project Drawing Files)

AutoCAD Architecture formalizes the creation of project files based on the Model/Sheet concept in the Drawing Management system and accompanying procedures. To fully realize the goals of the Model/Sheet file concept, ACA provides the project navigation system that we have begun to see in the preceding passages (as well as in tutorials in the previous chapters). This system incorporates the industry-standard use of Model and Sheet files and introduces an additional layer of granularity (Elements, Constructs, and Views) to help formalize the process. This is necessary simply because Model/Sheet file recommendations as published in the *NCS* and its predecessor the *AIA CAD Layer Guidelines* are not written specifically for ACA or even for AutoCAD. Rather they are general CAD guidelines applicable to any software package. Therefore, when we apply these recommendations to the specific toolset offered by ACA, we find that the Element, Construct, View, and Sheet framework greatly enhances our ability to fully achieve the Model/Sheet file intent and push the functionality and usefulness much further than envisioned in the previously referenced publications.

NOTE

Some of the recommendations made in the UDS Module 01 (part of NCS) refer to the earlier "AIA CAD Layer Guidelines - Second Edition" document. The overall intent of these documents has been summarized here. However, for the complete explanation of these recommendations and all supporting materials, you are encouraged to purchase and refer to the previously referenced documents directly.

ACA Model Files

- **Element**—A discrete piece of a design *without* explicit physical location within the building. Often an Element represents components that are repeated more than once in the design (typicals). Elements are also ideal for storage of project resources that you wish to have readily accessible. Elements are drawing files that are XREFed to other files (Constructs, Views, Sheets, or even other Elements) as project needs dictate.
- **Construct**—A discrete piece of a design *with* explicit physical location within the building. More specifically, it is a unique piece of the building occurring within a particular zone (Division) on a specific floor (Level) of the building. Constructs typically contain only items representing "real" building components, and typically do not contain any annotation, notes, or dimensions. Constructs are not specific to any particular type of drawing. They are not "Plans" or "Sections" but rather Models that can be used to generate plans, sections, or any other type of drawing. A Construct is distinguished from an Element by its unique identifiable physical location within the building. Constructs are drawing files that are XREFed to other files (other Constructs, Views, and Sheets) as project needs dictate.
- **View**—A slice of the building model configured to match a standard architectural drawing type. A View gathers all of the Constructs (and their nested Elements) required to correctly represent a specific portion (or *slice*) of the building. Views are akin to a particular type of drawing such as a "plan" or "section" and will contain those project annotations like notes, dimensions, and tags appropriate to the drawing type and scale in question. Views are drawing files containing XREFs of Constructs that are in-turn XREFed into Sheets as project needs dictate.

For example, imagine a three-story commercial building. You might create Elements to represent a typical restroom layout (see an example of this in the out-of-the-box Commercial Template Project), with core configuration or even furniture grouping configurations. You would have at least one Construct for each floor, although there could be, and often are, several. For instance, in many cases it is advantageous to separate the interior from exterior construction. In this case, you would have a "First Floor Interior" Construct and a "First Floor Exterior" Construct. Nested within the interior Construct would be Elements for stairs and toilet rooms. A similar structure would be established for each of the other floors. If some unique element occurred on one or more of the upper floors, such as a Curtain Wall that spans from second to third floors on three sides of the building, it would be built in its own "Spanning" Construct. This Construct would then be referenced to both (or all) the floors to which it applies. When you were ready to begin creating construction documents to communicate your design, you would start creating drawing-specific Views. A View allows you to create a unique snapshot of a portion of the building. For instance, if you wished to work on the Third Floor East Wing in plan, you would create and work in a View that would gather and correctly represent all of the Constructs (and their nested Elements) that are required by that *physical* portion of the building. Another similar View could be made of the same physical slice of the building but configured for a reflected ceiling plan, and yet another for furniture or finishes. Views are not limited to just plans. Views can be made to accommodate the creation of Sections, Elevation, Schedules, Details, and even full 3D Models. Be careful, however, to distinguish the "working" nature of Views from the "output" or plotting nature of Sheets. In other words, we still perform edits in Views, but Sheets are for plotting only.

ACA Sheet Files

- **Sheet**—A "just for printing" view of the building model. While Elements, Constructs, and Views can all be considered *Models* as defined by NCS/AIA, the ACA Sheet exactly emulates the purpose and intent of the NCS/AIA recommended Sheet file as noted previously. A Sheet file will gather all required building model components (Views with their annotations and all nested Constructs and Elements) and compose them on a title block sheet, at a particular scale ready to print.

There are those who argue that annotation and dimensions ought to be placed in the Sheets. Some go further to promote that these items be placed in the Layout (Paper Space) on top of viewport images of the project files. While both these approaches are certainly possible, the ACA Drawing Management toolset instead supports the approach championed by this text as indicated in the definition of "Sheet" earlier. It is the position of this text that Sheets should be set up once and maintained from then on as "for plotting only" files. The goal is to provide a set of files (one for each physical paper sheet in a document set) that is always ready to be opened and printed with no advance notice or *tweaking* required.

When project team members are allowed (or encouraged) to *work* in Sheet files, it is possible or even likely that they will leave the drawings in a state that is less than ideal for "ready printing." For instance, one might close the drawing with model space active, or change the LtScale, or accidentally forget to freeze or thaw the correct layers. These are just some examples of the types of small mundane settings that if set incorrectly at the time of plotting can result in re-printing a drawing. Not only is this frustrating to the person making the plots, but it needlessly wastes time, paper, and money. It is therefore *strongly* recommended that Sheets be used for plotting only, and all daily work be done in Elements, Constructs, and Views. To help you achieve this goal, the "Match Sheet View Layers to View" feature when turned on (as we did previously) will synchronize all changes in the View files to the corresponding Sheet viewports automatically. This feature powerfully supports the workflow intended by the ACA system and the process that will be recommended and followed throughout the tutorials in this book. More details on this feature can be found later in the "Create Views" heading.

Establish the Project Framework

Now that we have defined the Drawing Management terms that we will be using throughout the rest of this chapter (and the entire book), we are ready to add some structure to our commercial project.

Set up Project Levels

1. If the Project Navigator palette is not showing onscreen, choose click the Project Navigator icon on the QAT (or press ctrl + 5).

There are four tabs on this palette. The first one, labeled Project, should already be active. On the Project tab is listed the Current Project information, Divisions, and Levels. If you wish to edit any of these, click the small Edit icon (a small pencil icon as seen in Figure 5.6) next to the appropriate item.

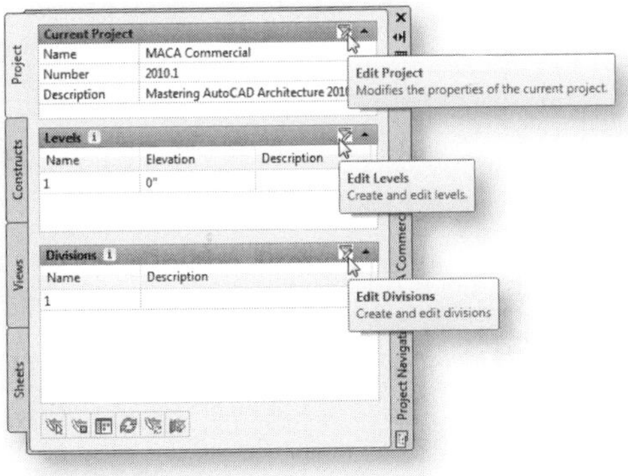

FIGURE 5.6 *The Project tab of the Project Navigator and the accompanying Edit icons*

This project will have four stories, site conditions, and a roof. We will establish a Level for each of these.

2. In the Levels area, click the Edit Levels icon (see Figure 5.6).

   The default Level is named "1." We need to make a few edits to its ID, Floor Elevation, and the Floor to Floor Height.

3. Click in the Floor Elevation column, and edit the value to **3'-0"** [**900**].
4. Change the Floor to Floor Height to **12'-0"** [**3650**].
5. Change the ID to **G** and edit the Description to read **First Floor** (see Figure 5.7).

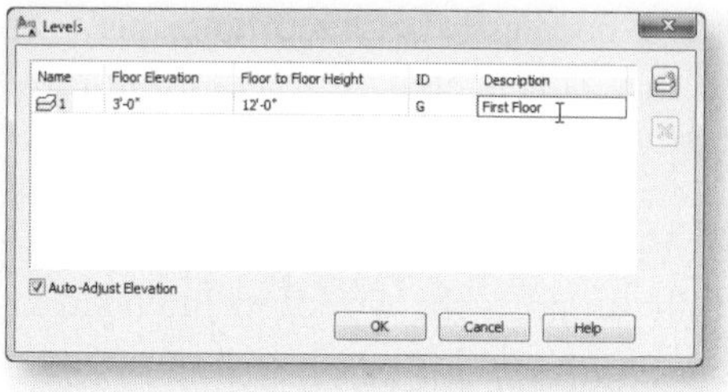

FIGURE 5.7 *Edit the parameters of the First Floor Level*

6. At the top-right corner, click the Add Level icon.

Notice that the new Level has automatically been named "2" and the Floor Elevation begins at 15'-0" [4550]. This is due to the Auto-Adjust Elevation setting, which is on by default (see the bottom-left corner of Figure 5.7).

7. Edit the Description to read **Second Floor**.
8. Click the Add Level icon twice more and edit the Descriptions for **Third Floor** and **Fourth Floor** (see Figure 5.8).

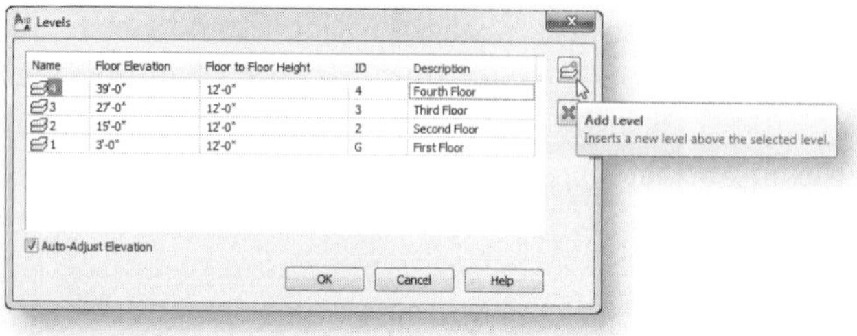

FIGURE 5.8 *Add and edit each of the four Floors*

As stated earlier, we will also require a Level for the Site and another for the Roof.

9. Be sure that Level 4 is still selected, and then click Add Level again.
10. Click in the ID column and change the value to **R**.
11. Change the Floor to Floor Height to 3'-0" [900] (the parapet height) and type **Roof** for the Description (see Figure 5.9).

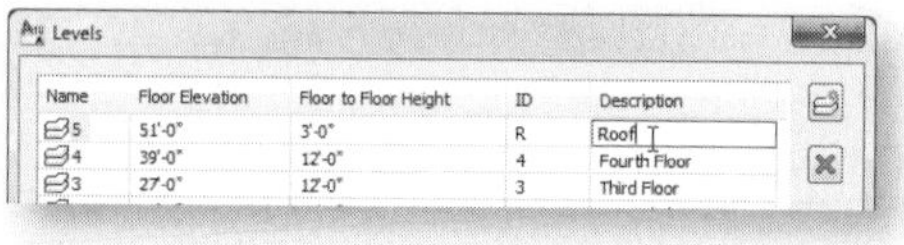

FIGURE 5.9 *Add the Roof Level*

12. In the Name column, select 1, right-click, and choose **Add Level Below** (see Figure 5.10).

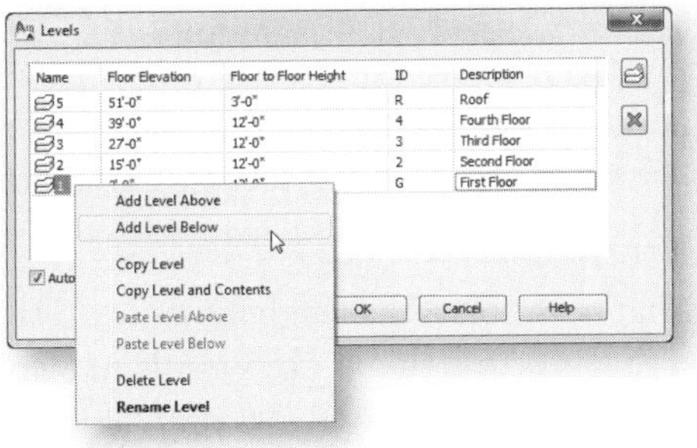

FIGURE 5.10 *Add a Level below the current level*

A Level is added below the current level; it is named "6." This name and the Floor Elevation of this Level require adjustment.

13. Click in the Name column (on the number "6"), pause a moment, and then click again.

    This should activate the rename mode for Level 6. You can also right-click and choose **Rename Level**.

14. Change the Name to **0**.
15. Click in the Floor Elevation column and edit the value to **0**.

    This will distort all of the other Floor Elevation values. Don't worry, with Auto-Adjust on, it is easy to fix.

16. Change the Floor to Floor Height to **3'-0"** [**900**].
17. Change the ID to **S** (for "Street") and the Description to **Street Level** (see Figure 5.11).

FIGURE 5.11 *Completing the edits to the Project Level Structure*

18. Click OK to accept the values and dismiss the Levels worksheet.
19. A prompt will appear asking you to "Update all Project Views." Click the Yes button (see Figure 5.12).

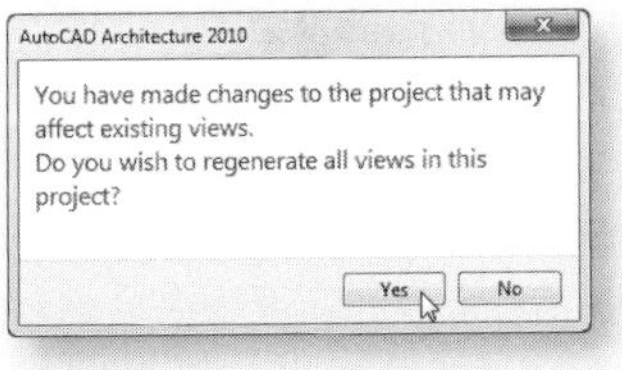

FIGURE 5.12 *Completing the edits to the Project Level Structure*

Answering "Yes" to this prompt will update all drawings that reference the Project Levels to incorporate the new values just entered. There are not yet any drawings in this project that would require such updating, but you should typically answer "Yes" to this prompt regardless. This will ensure the integrity of your project files and their relationships to one another.

This project has a small and simple footprint that requires only a single Division. (All projects must have at least one Division.) By default, this single Division is named simply "1." We can, if we wish, change that name, but for this project we will leave it set to the default (see Figure 5.13).

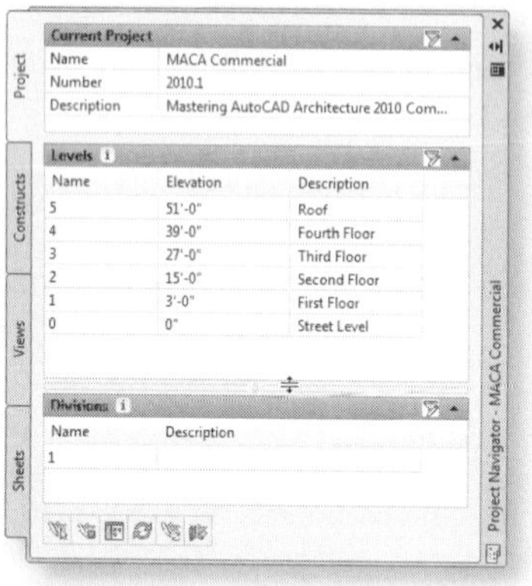

FIGURE 5.13 *The Project Navigator complete with Divisions and Levels*

At this point, we have completed the general project parameters and established that the building will be divided into six Levels (including the Street and Roof Levels) and a single Architectural Division. Keep in mind that we can revise this structure later if necessary and adjust the Level and Division structure as changing project needs dictate. Naturally we would want to try to avoid drastic changes to the Level and Division structure wherever possible. The important point of note here is that this structure *can* be adjusted later if required.

The next step is to build the files called Constructs and Elements that will populate this building framework. These will be comprised of drawing files that represent various portions of the building information model as defined later in the next topic.

Create Constructs

Now that we have created the project database, the first files that you need to create in your new project are the Constructs. These files will make up the pieces of the building model, and therefore are required before you can do any meaningful work on Views and Sheets. It is not necessary that you create every Construct that your project will eventually have at the early cartoon set phase, but you typically will create each of the major building components at this stage. For instance, in this sequence, we will create a Construct for each level of the building as well as the site.

Open an Existing Site Conditions File and Create a Construct

The first Construct that we will create is the Site. We will build a Site Terrain Model utilizing some existing data. For this tutorial, we will assume that we received a sketch of the site plan as a drawing file. This drawing is in rough form, with only basic outlines of roads and alleys that define the site and some simple contours, but it is enough to help us get started. We will first save this file within the project structure as the project's site Construct.

1. Click the Open icon on the QAT (or choose **Open** from the Application Menu).
2. Navigate to the *C:\MasterACA 2010\Chapter05\Commercial* folder and locate the file named *Site.dwg* [*Site-Metric.dwg*].

   Even though the site data is preliminary, it gives us the most important information required at this point in the project: the extent of the building footprint.

As stated previously, the Building Model is composed of a collection of Constructs (and as appropriate, their nested Elements). To incorporate the provided Site data contained in this file into our project structure, we will create a Construct from it and assign it to the Street level defined earlier.

3. On the Project Navigator palette, click the Constructs tab.

Notice that there are two folders shown on this tab: *Constructs* and *Elements*. (Later, we can add additional sub-folders to these as project needs dictate.)

MANAGER NOTE

Creating a well-planned Folder (Category) structure for your projects can prove extremely beneficial. Category sub-folders can be added to each of the root folders: *Constructs*, *Elements*, and *Views*. While you can also add folders to *Sheets*, the Sheets typically use Sheet Set Subsets for organization. These folders can be added within the Project Navigator or in Windows using standard folder creation methods. Once you have established a suitable folder structure, you can even re-use it in future projects by the **Copy Project Structure** command (available as a right-click option in the Project Browser), which will copy all of the sub-folders in the project to a new Project name and location that you specify. This will help you maintain consistency in project setup. Please note that **Copy Project Structure** does not copy any of the files. To create a project from another including all of its folders, Constructs, Views and Sheets, use the project as a project template when creating new projects.

4. Right-click on the *Constructs* folder and choose **Save Current Dwg As Construct**.

   The Add Construct dialog box will appear.
5. Type **Site** in the Name field.
6. Click in the Description field and type **Site Information**.
7. In the Assignments area, place a check mark next to Street Level (see Figure 5.14).

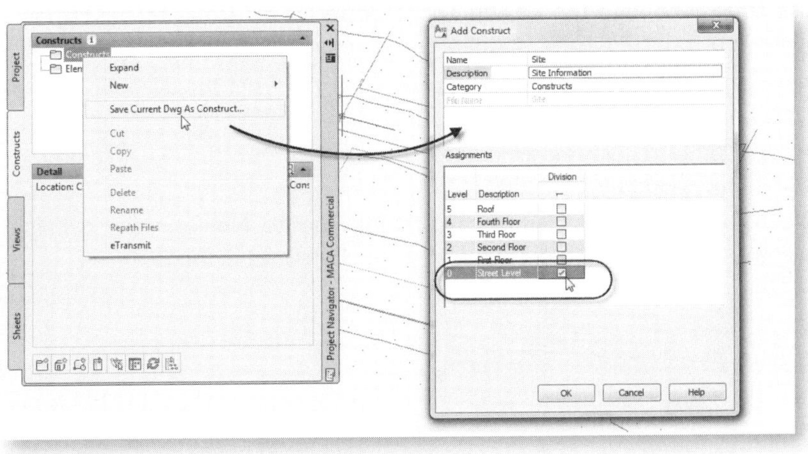

FIGURE 5.14 *Name the new Construct and assign it to the Street Level*

The Assignments area of the Add Construct dialog box is very powerful. It is here that you tell ACA and the Project Management system which portion of the building this particular Construct represents. Since the Project Management system is aware of all the Levels and Divisions within a project, ACA will be able to correctly XREF and locate this Site Construct drawing relative to all other drawings in the project.

8. Click OK to accept all values and create the new Construct.

Notice that there is now a new Construct in the Project Navigator (Constructs tab) named Site (see Figure 5.15).

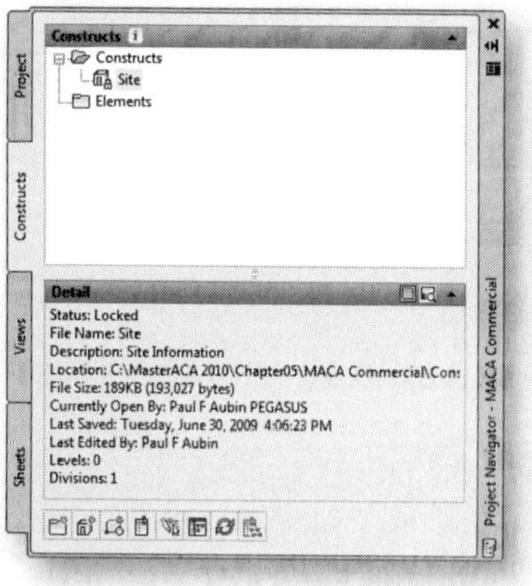

FIGURE 5.15 *The new Site Construct appears on the Project Navigator palette in the Constructs folder*

Build a Terrain Model from the Site Data

The *Site* Construct should still be open. If it is not, double-click it on the Constructs tab of the Project Navigator. Looking carefully at the geometry in the file, you will notice that there are polyline contours that have been set at their respective heights in the Z direction. To see this, click on one of the polylines, right-click and choose **Properties** and on the Properties palette, check the value of the Elevation field. Note that each polyline you do this to has a different elevation. We will use these elevated polylines to generate a terrain Mass Element.

9. Select one of the gray polyline contours, right-click and choose **Select Similar**.
10. With the gray polylines selected, on the Massing tool palette, click the Drape tool.

    If the Massing palette is not available, right-click the tool palettes title bar and choose **Design** to load the Design Tool Palette Group (refer to the "Understanding Tool Palettes" topic in Chapter 1 for more information).
11. At the "Erase selected contours" prompt, choose **Yes** from the dynamic prompt (or type **y** and then press ENTER).
12. At the "Generate regular mesh" prompt, choose **No** from the dynamic prompt (or type **n** and then press ENTER).
13. At the "Generate rectangular mesh" prompt, choose **No** from the dynamic prompt (or type **n** and then press ENTER) (see Figure 5.16).

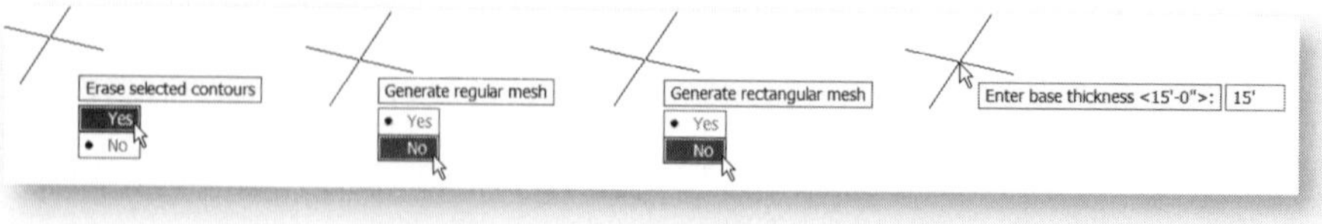

FIGURE 5.16 *Establish the rectangular bounds of the Drape object*

14. At the "Enter base thickness" prompt, type **15'-0"** [**4500**] and then press ENTER.

    Upon completion of the Drape, you will have a 3D Mass Element terrain model.

We erased the contour lines in the first prompt because they were only needed to generate the terrain model. When creating your own terrain models, if you wish to keep the contours to display in a site plan, you can instead choose **Yes**. In this example, we actually have a second set of contours on a frozen layer for that purpose which we will thaw in the exercise later. The "regular" mesh prompt determines whether a uniform number of mesh segments is created in the X and Y directions. If you choose **Yes** for this prompt, you are then prompted to indicate how many mesh segments you wish in each direction. By choosing **No** here, the Drape instead generated a varying number of mesh segments determined by the shape of the contours. This type of mesh will give more segments only where they are needed. The "rectangular" mesh prompt determines the shape of the plan footprint of the mesh. It can be either rectangular in shape (in which case you indicate the extent of the rectangle onscreen) or irregularly shaped based on the extent of the selected contours. This is the option we used by choosing **No** for a rectangular mesh. If you like, you can undo the command and try it again with different answers to the prompts.

Next we will restore a hidden 3D Mass Element shaped like the roads. We will use this Mass Element to cut the shape of the roads away from the Drape. We would not have been able to achieve the same thing with the linework that we erased earlier.

15. On the Drawing Status Bar click the red lightbulb icon and choose **End Object Isolation** from the popup menu (see Figure 5.17).

TIP

If the lightbulb icon does not appear red, right-click in the drawing and choose **Isolate Objects** > **End Object Isolation** instead. This will achieve the same result.

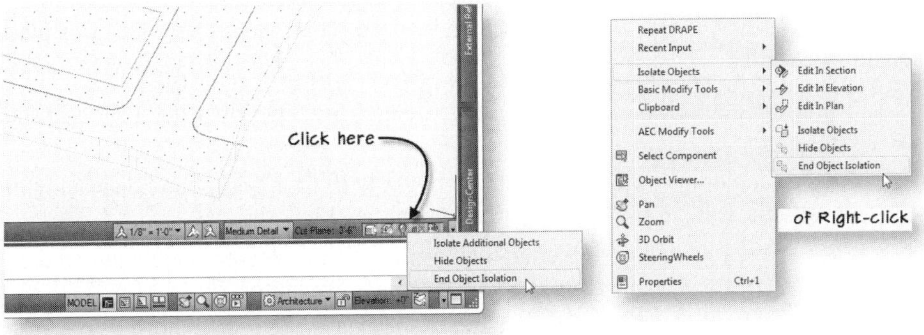

FIGURE 5.17 *End Object Isolation to reveal a hidden Mass Element*

In the original Site file that contained the contours, there was also a hidden Mass Element object. The Isolate Objects tool (small lightbulb on the Drawing Status Bar) allows you to hide and isolate selected objects in a file. If objects in the file are hidden, then the small lightbulb appears red. As mentioned in the tip earlier, sometimes the icon fails to appear in red. Use the right-click menu instead in this case.

16. Select the Drape (green colored Mass Element) that you just created.
17. On the Mass Element tab of the ribbon, click the Boolean tool and choose **Subtract**.

18. When prompted, select the gray Mass Element representing the roads (the one that was hidden) and then press ENTER.
19. At the "Erase layout geometry" prompt, choose **Yes**.

    The result is subtle, but the shape of the roads is now carved out of the terrain Mass Element. To get a better look, select the terrain, right-click and choose **Object Viewer** and then orbit the model around a bit. Try the Visual Styles icons in the viewer as you orbit.
20. Place your mouse over the Layer Properties Manager palette docked on the side of your screen.
21. When the palette flies open, click the snowflake icon on the A-Site-Clin Layer to thaw it.

NOTE

If you did not dock the Layer Properties Manager to the side of the screen back in Chapter 3, you can do so now, or use the Layer drop-down list on the Home tab, on the Layers panel to achieve the same result.

This reveals some more accurately depicted contour lines than the ones we erased previously. They are set at 1'-0" [300] intervals, rather than the 6" [150] ones used to generate the terrain and convey the curb cuts on the roads. Although these contours could have been used to generate the terrain, the Drape tool uses a smoothing algorithm that would have smoothed all the sharp edges at the curb lines. This is why we did the two-step technique shown here.

22. Save the file. (Don't close it yet).

Begin the First Floor Construct

Each floor of our project will consist of one or more Constructs. In fact, there will often be several Constructs per floor. The next several steps continue from the previous exercise (building the site) and will walk through the process of beginning a Construct for the first floor. This will in turn be used when we create first floor plan View and Sheet files.

1. Select the light blue rectangle in the middle of the *Site* Construct. (Click on the edge.)

   The rectangle in the center should highlight with four grip points displaying at its corners. It is on the Layer: G-Anno-Nplt.
2. Click and hold down on the edge (not a grip) of the selected rectangle and drag it on top of the *Constructs* folder of the Project Navigator.
3. Press and hold down the ctrl key, and then release the mouse button to create the Construct (see Figure 5.18).

NOTE

Holding down the ctrl key while dragging makes a copy of the rectangle and leaves the original rectangle in the Site file. Had we simply dragged, it would have moved the rectangle (deleting it from the original file).

If you have the auto-hide feature turned on for Project Navigator, drag the rectangle over the title bar of the Project Navigator until it pops open and then continue to drag the item to the Constructs folder.

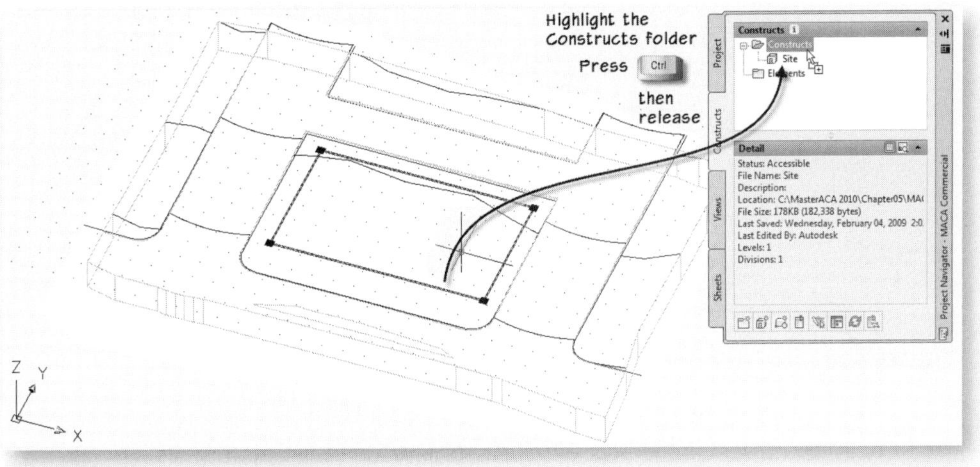

FIGURE 5.18 *Drag drawing geometry to the Project Navigator to create a Construct*

4. In the Add Construct worksheet, type **01 Shell and Core** for the Name.
5. In the Description field, type **First Floor Core and Exterior Shell**.
6. In the Assignments area, place a check mark in the First Floor Level checkbox and then click OK to finish (see Figure 5.19).

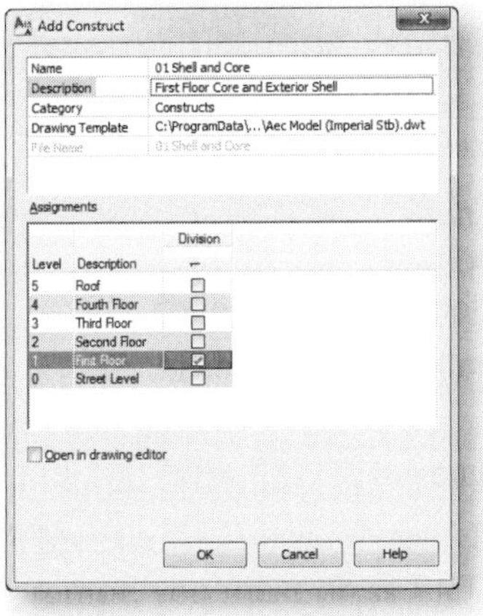

FIGURE 5.19 *Name the Construct and assign it to a Level 1*

7. Save and close the *Site* Construct file. (Application Menu, or use the close (X) icon in the upper right corner of the drawing.)
8. On the Project Navigator, double-click *01 Core and Shell* (or right-click the *01 Core and Shell* Construct, and then choose **Open**).
9. Zoom in on the rectangle.
10. On the Design tool palette, right-click the Wall tool and choose **Apply Tool Properties to > Linework** (see Figure 5.20).

NOTE

If the Tool Palettes are not open, on the home tab, click the Tools button (or press ctrl + 3).

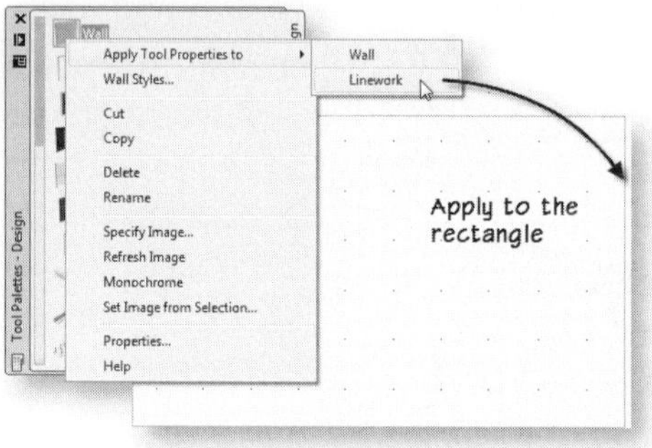

FIGURE 5.20 *Access the Wall tool's right-click options*

11. At the "Select lines, arcs, circles, or polylines to convert into walls" prompt, click on the edge of the rectangle.
12. Press ENTER to accept the selection.
13. At the "Erase layout geometry" prompt, choose **Yes** (or type **y** and press ENTER).

We are erasing the rectangle, because we needed it only to provide the overall shape of our building footprint. The rectangle has now been replaced with four Walls. They are still highlighted, and the Properties palette has appeared (or has become active if it was already onscreen) with the properties of the selected Walls showing.

The Walls will remain selected.

14. On the Properties palette, change the Width to **1'-0"** [**300**] and the Height to **12'-0"** [**3600**] (see Figure 5.21).

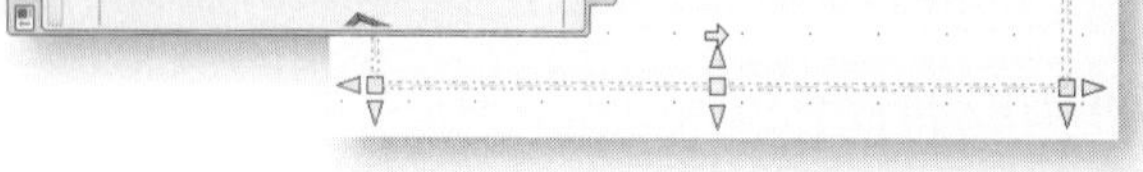

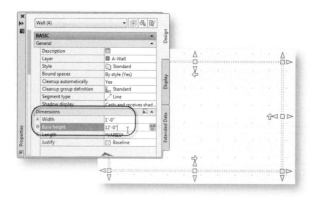

FIGURE 5.21 *Change the dimensions of the selected Walls*

The Walls generated in this file are temporary *stand-ins* for the real Walls that we will add later. For purposes of the cartoon set, it is necessary to have some objects in each file as *placeholders* and to provide the rough size and shape of the building. Think of them as a sketch similar to what you might create by hand in the traditional paper-based cartoon set.

Preparing for Project Standards

In the coming chapters, we will progressively add refinements to the simple sketch models that we are building here. With the Project Standards feature, we will be able to establish a master library file for our Wall styles (types) and other styles and then synchronize changes across the entire project. In this way, you can quickly make an edit to a style in one file and then apply it to the entire project. At this stage of the project, we do not want to concern ourselves with developing the specifics of a Wall style. However, we can simply name the style being utilized here so that later when we do get more specific, it will be a simple task to update these stand-in Walls with the latest version.

15. Make sure the four Walls are still selected, if you deselected, please reselect them now.
16. On the Wall tab of the ribbon, on the General panel, click the Save As button.
17. In the "Wall Style Properties – Standard (2)" dialog, choose the General tab.
18. In the Name field, type: **Exterior Shell**.
19. In the Description field, type: **Mastering AutoCAD Architecture Commercial Project Exterior Building Shell Wall** and then click OK.
20. Save and Close the file.

Create the Upper Floor Constructs

Once you have built one floor, you can easily copy its Construct to create additional floors via the Project Navigator where we are able to copy a Construct to other levels.

1. On the Project Navigator, right-click on the Construct *01 Core and Shell.*
2. From the context menu, choose **Copy Construct to Levels** (see the left side of Figure 5.22).

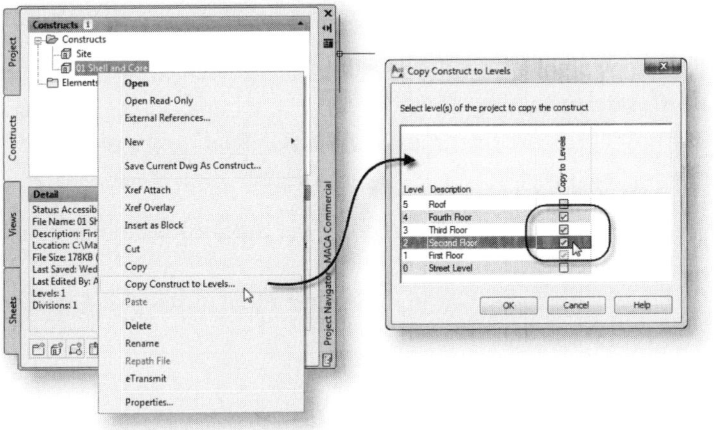

FIGURE 5.22 *Copy Construct to Levels command*

3. In the Copy Construct to Levels dialog box, place a check mark in the Second, Third, and Fourth Floor boxes, and then click OK (see the right side of Figure 5.22).

   The first floor Construct has been duplicated to each of the other floors. However, notice that the names read "*01 Core and Shell (2)*" and so on.

CAD MANAGER NOTE

This method is useful to maintain drawing consistency when starting a project. It ensures that every project file uses the same template files and maintains a consistent global origin for XREFs. Also, when setting up a project in anticipation of using project standards as noted earlier, this method in copying the first floor "Exterior Shell" Walls also will make it easy to synchronize our styles later.

4. Right-click on *01 Core and Shell (2)* and choose **Rename**.
5. Type **02 Core and Shell** and then press ENTER.

The "Project Navigator – Repath Project" dialog will appear. When you rename a file, it can affect the integrity of the XREFs in the project. Repathing is highly encouraged as it maintains proper naming and pathing. However, you can postpone the repath until you are done renaming all the files. ACA will queue up all the changes and apply them when you are ready.

6. In the "Project Navigator – Repath Project" dialog, click Repath project later (see Figure 5.23).

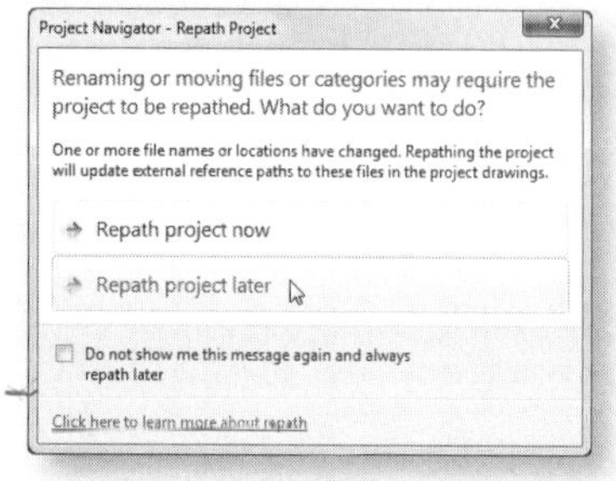

FIGURE 5.23 *Postpone the repathing until all files are renamed*

7. Repeat the process for the third making it **03 Core and Shell**, and again postpone the repath.
8. Repeat once more for the fourth as **04 Core and Shell**. This time choose Repath project now.

Once you choose to repath, it clears the queue and fixes any XREF paths required.

9. Right-click on *02 Core and Shell* and choose **Properties**.

   Notice that the check mark for the level is correctly at the Second Floor but that the description incorrectly refers to the first floor.
10. Click in the Description field, change it to **Second Floor Core and Exterior Shell**, and then click OK (see Figure 5.24).

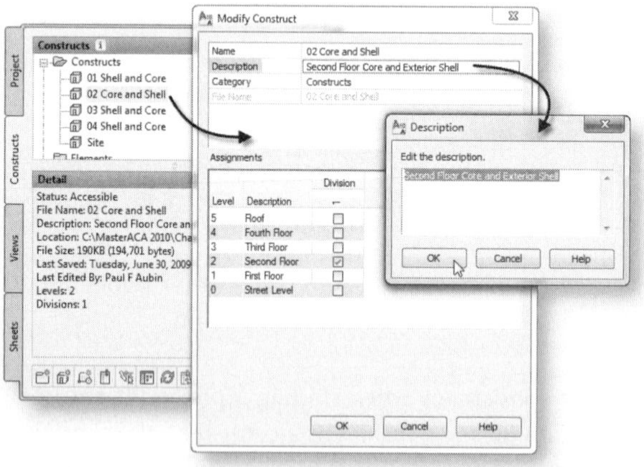

FIGURE 5.24 *Editing the Descriptions of the copied Constructs*

11. Repeat these steps for the Third and Fourth floors as well.
12. To display the Constructs in the correct numerical order, click the Refresh icon (second from the right at the bottom of the palette).

Create a Spanning Construct

In Chapter 8, we will build a Curtain Wall Element that spans the Second through Fourth floors of the front façade of the building. Building components that occupy more than one level in an ACA Model are referred to in Project Navigator as "spanning" Constructs. Spanning Constructs will automatically be added to Views that reference them for each floor in which they span. In this case, we will build a spanning Construct for a future front façade condition that has yet to be designed at this stage of the project. However, as is often the case in the early stages of a project, the designers usually have some notion of the types of design elements that they hope to incorporate. Remembering our aim in this chapter, to build a mock-up set to be fleshed out as the project progresses, we will not allow ourselves to get carried away with the particulars of this design element; rather we will simply add a Construct for now with a simple Wall as a placeholder for the future Curtain Wall design. This approach is consistent with the rest of the steps taken here so far and the notion of progressive refinement promoted throughout this book.

1. In Project Navigator, on the Constructs tab, select the *Constructs* folder and at the bottom of the palette, click the Add Construct icon.
2. For the Name type **Front Façade**.
3. For the Description type **Front Façade Spanning Curtain Wall**.
4. In the Assignments area, check the Second, Third and Fourth floors.
5. Take note of the message that appears at the bottom of the Add Construct worksheet indicating that by selecting *more than* one Level, we have made this a "spanning" Construct (see Figure 5.25).

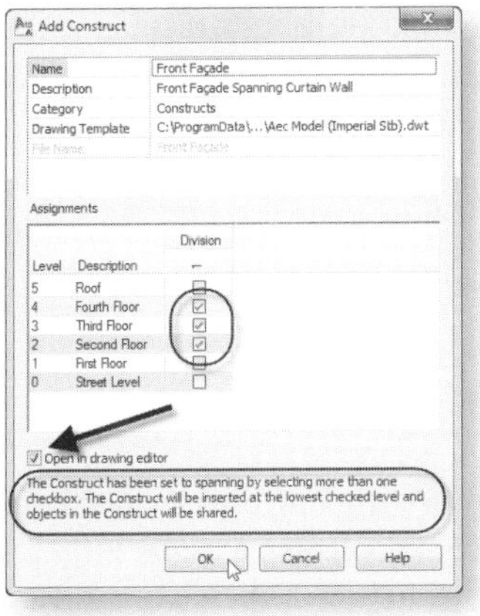

FIGURE 5.25 *Assigning the Construct to multiple levels makes it a "spanning" Construct*

6. At the bottom of the "Add Construct" dialog, place a checkmark in the "Open in drawing editor" checkbox and then click OK.

This checkbox opens the drawing immediately after creating it. If you forget to check this, you will need to double-click the file to open it.

7. On the Insert tab, on the Block panel, click the Insert Block tool.

8. Click the Browse button, and in the *C:\MasterACA 2010\Chapter05\Commercial* folder, locate the file named *Base Curve.dwg* [*Base Curve-Metric.dwg*] and then click Open.
9. In the Insert dialog box, in the Insertion point area, deselect the Specify On-screen checkbox and leave the values for X, Y and Z set to **0**.
10. Place a check mark in the Explode checkbox and then click OK.

The *BaseCurve.dwg* file contains a single arc segment. This segment is a sketch of the curved Curtain Wall footprint that we will build in Chapter 8. We will now convert this arc to a Wall to serve as a temporary stand-in for this future Curtain Wall.

11. On the Design tool palette, right-click the Wall tool and choose **Apply Tool Properties to > Linework**.
12. At the "Select lines, arcs, circles, or polylines to convert into walls" prompt, select the arc segment and then press ENTER.
13. At the "Erase layout geometry" prompt, choose **Yes**.
14. On the Properties palette with the Wall still selected, change the height to **36'-0"** [**10,950**].

NOTE

The metric value is shown here with a comma separating the thousands. This is done for clarity. Please type the value without the comma in ACA.

15. On the View tab, on the Appearance panel, scroll through the list of preset views and choose SE Isometric.
16. Save and Close the file.

We now have four *Core and Shell* Constructs, a single spanning *Façade* Construct, and a *Site* Construct. We will create additional Constructs for this project as needs dictate in later chapters. But for now, we have all of the Constructs we will require for our cartoon set.

The next step in project setup will bring all of these floor plate Constructs together with the site to form a single composite model of the whole building in its current (albeit very schematic) form. This composite model will be our first *View* file as defined earlier in the "Elements, Constructs, Views, and Sheets (Project Drawing Files)" topic under the "Project Navigator Terminology" heading. There can be many reasons to create such a composite model early on. The most common reason is simply to use a check to verify that all of the pieces (Constructs) are fitting together properly as expected.

Enable View Layer Synchronization

Project Navigator has the ability to synchronize the layer settings of Sheet viewports with the corresponding View files so that the Sheet viewport's layer settings are updated from the layer settings within the XREFed View drawing. The layer settings include the layer states (on/off, thawed/frozen) and the layer properties (layer, color, linetype, plotstyle) of all geometry within to the View file as well of all layers contained in external references attached to the View drawing. The synchronization option can be activated at any time; however, the update within the Sheet viewport will not take effect until the external references are reloaded or the drawing file is reopened. We enabled this feature earlier, "Create a New Project" topic, but let's verify that it is set correctly now.

1. On the Project Navigator Palette, click the Project tab, and then click on the Edit Project icon in the upper-right corner (this icon is shown in Figure 5.6).
2. For Match Sheet View Layers to View, verify that it is set to **Yes**.
3. Click OK to close the Project Properties worksheet.

With this setting, veiwports on Sheets you create in the project will be using the layer settings of the associated view drawing. Existing sheet views will be synchronized the next time they are opened or their external references are reloaded.

NOTE

Verify that VISRETAIN is set to 1 both in the View files and in the Sheet drawing files in order for the synchronization to be successful.

Build a Composite Model View

A composite model View will help us visualize what we have so far. The tools in Project Navigator make creating a View easy. By simply designating which portions of the building we wish to include in the View, we can have the system gather all of the required XREFs for us and assemble them at the correct relative locations and heights.

4. In Project Navigator, click on the Views tab to activate it.

   There are currently no files on this tab.
5. At the base of the palette, click the Add View icon (second from the left).
6. In the "Add View" dialog that appears, choose Add a General View.
7. For the Name, type **A-CM00** and for the Description, type **Composite Building Model** (see Figure 5.26).

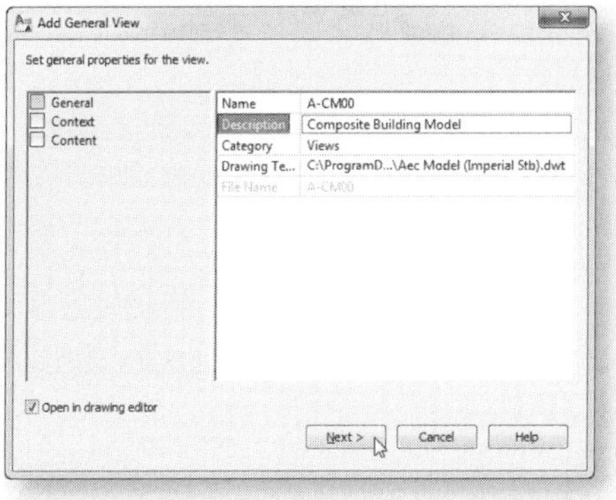

FIGURE 5.26 *The first page of the Add View wizard*

File naming conventions vary widely from one firm to the next. While it is possible to adapt existing file naming conventions to Project Navigator files when migrating to ACA, it is often necessary to make some adjustments. In this book, we will use simple descriptive names for Constructs (as you saw earlier) and both descriptive names and US National CAD Standard (NCS) names for Views. See the "File Naming Guidelines" sidebar later for recommendations on Project file naming. Feel free to use your firm's file naming strategies rather than those recommended in this text. Changing the names of the files will not alter the tutorials in any way. In this case, for our Composite Model, "A" stands for "Architectural," "CM" for "Composite Model," and "00" is simply a placeholder for enumeration. For a floor plan this would be a floor number designation and for sections and elevations it is typically a simple sequential number.

8. Click Next to move to the Context page.
9. Right-click anywhere in the Levels area and choose **Select All** (see Figure 5.27).

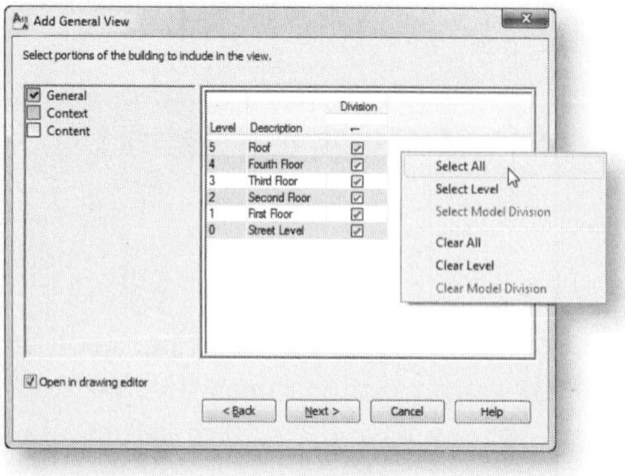

FIGURE 5.27 *Include all of the Levels (and Divisions) in the View*

10. Click Next to move to the Content page.
11. On the Content page, verify that all Constructs are selected, that the "Open in drawing editor" checkbox is selected and then click Finish (see Figure 5.28).

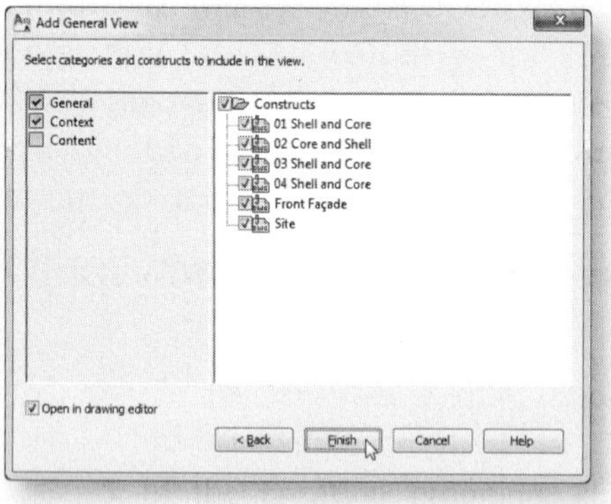

FIGURE 5.28 *Complete the Add View wizard by verifying that all Constructs are included*

12. On the View tab, on the Appearance panel, scroll through the list of preset views and choose SE Isometric.
13. Next to the view list, click the drop-down button on the Visual Styles tool and choose the Conceptual tool (See Figure 5.29).

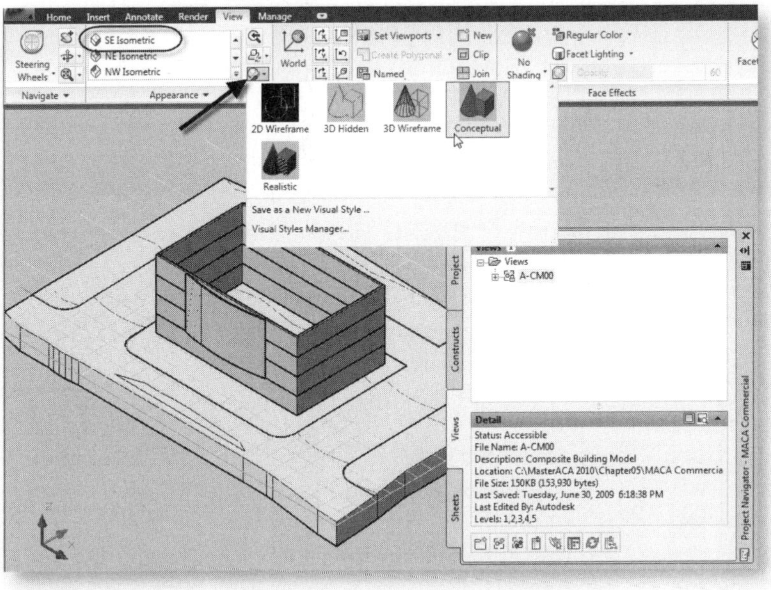

FIGURE 5.29 *The composite model viewed from the South East*

Note that all of the Construct files have been XREFed into this View file and inserted at their correct locations and heights respectively relative to the Levels settings on the Project tab of the Project Navigator. This is one of the major benefits of the Project Management system in ACA. Once the basic parameters have been established, all of the Level and height information as well as which files are required to assemble a particular View are handled automatically by the system.

Naturally we still have quite a bit of work to do. For instance, there is no roof, but at this early stage of design, this model begins to give a good idea as to how this proposed project will sit on the site and a sense of the overall proportion of the building.

14. Save and Close the file.

Visual Styles provide a wonderful way to visualize your designs in different graphical presentations such as hidden line or the Conceptual style shown here. However, if you do not have a suitable video card, performance can suffer when viewing a drawing in Visual Styles other than 2D Wireframe. To see if your video card is recommended by Autodesk for use in AutoCAD Architecture, visit www.autodesk.com.

TIP

If you experience slowness when working with Visual Styles, return to 2D Wireframe when finished viewing and before closing the file. This will enable the program to load quicker the next time you open the file.

FILE NAMING GUIDELINES

- In general, try to name all files as descriptively as possible. Whether this is with names that include the actual contents of the file, like: "Architectural First Floor Plan," or with well-established abbreviations like: "A-FP01," the name should evoke the file's contents in some way.
- **Naming Element files**: Use names that describe the contents such as "Typical Toilet Room" or "Temporary Building Outline." Elements don't belong to specific levels and should not include Level or Division descriptors in the names.

(*Continued*)

- **Naming Construct files**: Use names that describe the contents of the file such as "01 Partitions" or "First Floor New" or "North Stair Tower." Do *not* name Constructs with names evocative of specific drawing types. For example, Constructs should *not* be named as "Plans," "Sections," or "Elevations." Constructs are hybrid models and are used to generate all of these types of drawings. Name them for what they contain. Drawing "type" names should be used for View files instead.
- **Naming View files**: Views *are* created with a particular type of drawing in mind. Views can be named descriptively with a name that evokes the type of drawing that they will spawn, such as "First Floor Plan," "Exterior Building Elevations," "Third Floor Interior Elevations," or "Door and Frame Details." Views can also be named using existing naming conventions or industry-standard naming conventions such as the U.S. National CAD Standard. For instance, using NCS names, you might end up with View names like "A-FP01 (for Architectural Floor Plan First Floor)," "A-EL01" (for Architectural Elevations number one) and "A-SP00 (for Architectural Site Plan)." NCS style names are used for Views in this book.
- **Naming Sheet files:** Sheets are typically named after their Sheet number in many architectural firms. The AutoCAD Sheet Set functionality is incorporated directly into Project Navigator. The default behavior of Sheet Sets is for the file name to combine both the Sheet number and the Sheet title in the drawing file name. This is done automatically and is tedious to override. For example, Sheet "A-101" titled "Floor Plans" is automatically named "A-101 Floor Plans" by Project Navigator (and its integral Sheet Set). Since the Sheet Set will automatically manage all Sheet files, it is recommended that you simply adopt this default behavior.

Create Floor Plan Views

The next task we have is to create a series of Floor Plan View files. Like the Composite Model, these will also be "General" Views; however, they will each include only one level of the project rather than all levels as in the composite model. Remember, when creating a View, that the software will automatically gather all of the correct Construct files required to make the View at a particular Level and Division combination. The View file thus created will be ready to receive notes, dimensions, and other annotation appropriate to floor plans (or whatever specific type of drawing is intended). Later we can then compose one or more of these Views (including their drawing specific annotations) onto a Sheet for printing.

Create a Site Plan View

We will start at the bottom of the model and work our way up beginning with a Site Plan View.

1. At the base of the palette, click the Add View icon (second from the left).
2. In the "Add View" dialog that appears, choose Add a General View.
3. Name the file **A-SP00**, give it a Description of **Building Site Plan**, and then click Next.
4. On the Context page, place a check mark in the "Street Level" box and then click Next.
5. On the Content page, verify that only the *Site* Construct is included and then click Finish.

   The new View file has been created and opens onscreen.
6. Zoom as required to see the complete Site Plan file.

Try switching to 3D as we did previously and note that this time only the Site Construct is included. Return to plan view (**Top**) before closing and saving the file.

7. When you are satisfied that the file has been created correctly, save and close the file.

Create the First Floor Plan View

The process for the first floor is nearly identical. However, we will take the floor plans a bit further.

8. On the Project Navigator palette, on the Views tab, click the New View icon and then choose to add a General view.
9. Name the file **A-FP01**, give it a Description of **Architectural First Floor Plan**, and then click Next.
10. On the Context page, place a check mark in the First Floor box and then click Next.
11. On the Content page, verify that only the *01 Shell and Core* Construct is included and then click Finish.

    The new First Floor Plan View file has been created and opens onscreen.

Notice that only the four Walls that make up the First Floor Construct have been XREFed into this file. Neither the front façade, which begins on the Second Floor, nor the Site Plan has appeared here. This is correct based on the levels that we specified for this View.

Add a First Floor Plan Model Space View

Because View files are created with specific architectural drawing types in mind, like plans in this case, we can go further than simply gathering the correct Constructs as we have here. Let's make some decisions about how we would like this particular View to appear on a Sheet for plotting. For instance, we can designate the portion of the model that we wish to appear within the viewport of our Sheet Layout even before creating the Sheet. We can assign a display configuration, a title, and plotting scale ahead of time as well. To aid us in this process, we will insert a guideline from another file that represents the correct size and scale that we need for the First Floor Plan viewport. This step is optional in your own projects, but it is being shown here because even though this adds an extra step, it will be much easier to later compose your Sheets if you make this extra bit of pre-planning effort up front.

12. On the Insert tab, on the Block panel, click the Insert Block button.

NOTE

To save time in this tutorial, the 2D Layout Grid is provided in a separate file for quick retrieval. See the CAD Manager Note later for how this object was created.

13. Click the Browse button, and in the *C:\MasterACA 2010\Chapter05\Commercial* folder, locate the file named *Live Area Guide.dwg* [*Live Area Guide-Metric.dwg*] and then click Open.
14. In the Insert dialog box, in the Insertion point area, be sure that the Specify Onscreen checkbox is not checked and leave the values for X, Y and Z set to **0**.
15. Place a check mark in the Explode checkbox and then click OK.

The *Live Area Guide.dwg* file contains an AEC Layout Grid 2D (available from the Stock Tool Catalog in Content Browser—ctrl + 4). It will appear as a dashed purple rectangle surrounding the plan (see the left side of Figure 5.30). We will use this rectangular gridline to create a Model Space View that we will use for the creation of our Sheet viewport later. AEC Layout Grid 2D objects automatically appear on a non-plotting layer by default.

CAD MANAGER NOTE

The best way to plan these items is to know on what size title block the Sheets will be composed. For this project, we will be using the default Sheet size 42″ × 30″ [1189 × 841] and the default title block provided out-of-the-box. In order to plan how our floor plan will fit on the final Sheet, we must know the "Live Area" of the title block. The Live Area is the portion of the title block minus all borders, margins and title strips available to place drawings. This title block has a Live Area measuring 36″ × 28 ¾″ [1040 × 780]. We can create a rectangular boundary using this Live Area dimension within our View file. This will give a visual reference for how much of our View file's geometry can fit on the title block at a given scale. In order for this guide to be valid, we must insert it into the View at a scale equal to that which we intend to plot. A simple rectangle would do for this purpose, but consider using an ACA Layout Grid 2D (available in the Stock Tool Catalog in Content Browser—ctrl + 4). Using such a grid makes it easy to compose Sheet layouts where multiple viewports are involved. This is because it has parameters for the number of cells in both the X and Y directions. To do this, you set both X and Y directions to "Space Evenly" and then input the number of bays you desire. In this case, both were set to 1 bay. But for an elevation View, you might do 2 or 4 vertically (in Y) and 1 in X, while a detail sheet might be 5 high by 6 wide for example.

16. On the Project Navigator palette, select the Views tab, right-click the *A-FP01* file, and choose **New Model Space View** (see the right side of Figure 5.30).

NOTE

A Model Space View is simply the AutoCAD Named View that is essentially a "saved zoom." You could achieve almost the same result by going to the View tab of the ribbon, on the Viewports panel and clicking the Named tool.

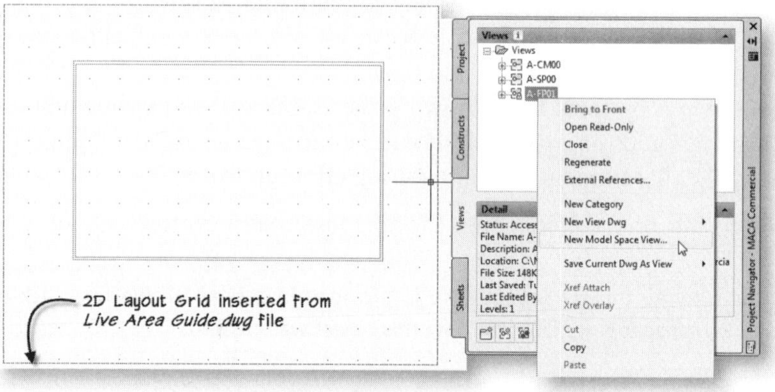

FIGURE 5.30 *Create a New Model Space View in the A-FP01 file*

17. In the Name field, type **First Floor Plan**.
18. Verify that the Scale is set to **1/8″ = 1′-0″** [**1:100**].

    It is not necessary to type a Description for this exercise.
19. Click the Define View Window icon on the right (see Figure 5.31).

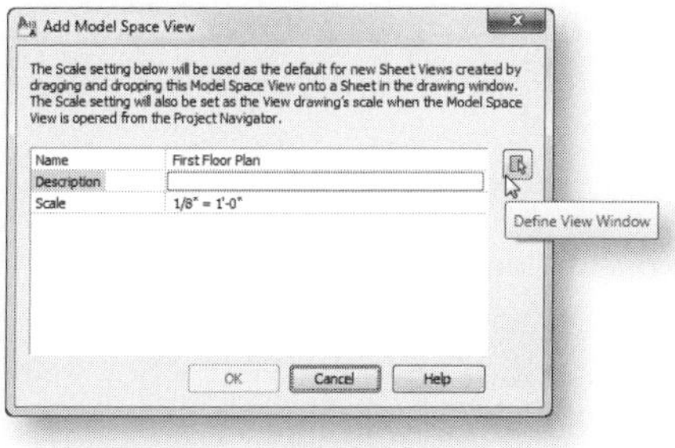

FIGURE 5.31 *Name the View and then designate its boundaries*

20. At the "Specify first corner" prompt, snap to the lower-left corner of the dashed purple rectangle (the one just inserted).
21. At the "Specify opposite corner" prompt, snap to the upper right corner of the dashed purple rectangle (the one just inserted), and then click OK to dismiss the Add Model Space view worksheet.

In Project Navigator, indented beneath *A-FP01*, an icon labeled "First Floor Plan" should appear. AutoCAD Named Views (Model Space Views) appear in Project Navigator on both the Views and Sheets tabs. You can select these in Project Navigator to view detailed information or a preview at the bottom of the palette just as you can the actual drawing files. You can toggle between the Detail and Preview views with the icons on the preview pane (see bottom right corner of Figure 5.32). To open a file and zoom right to the Model Space View, double-click the Model Space View in Project Navigator.

22. In Project Navigator, double-click First Floor Plan beneath *A-FP01* (see Figure 5.32).

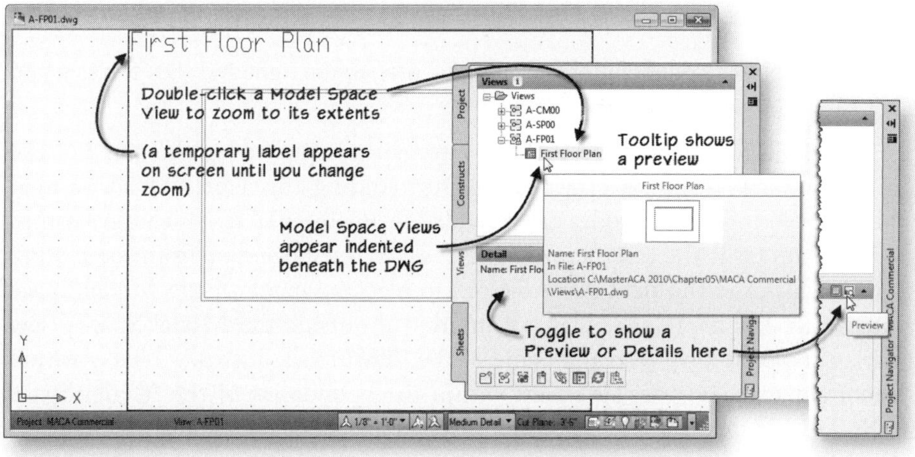

FIGURE 5.32 *Name the View and then designate its boundaries—double-click to zoom to it*

A temporary label will appear onscreen with the Model Space View name (First Floor Plan in this case). This will vanish the next time you zoom or pan.

Add a Titlemark

In addition to providing a convenient way to zoom to a particular portion of a View file directly from Project Navigator and giving us a way to preassign the extents of a

Sheet Viewport (as we will see later), the name of the Model Space View is referenced automatically into drawing Titlemarks.

23. Right-click the title bar of the Tool Palettes and choose **Document** to load the Documentation tools group.
24. Click the Callouts tab, and then click the first Titlemark tool (the one with both title and drawing number bubble).

    Move the mouse around onscreen. You will notice that the First Floor Plan Model Space View shows a temporary label and border and that whenever you move your mouse within it, the border highlights in red—this indicates that it will be associated to the Model Space View name.
25. At the "Specify location of symbol" prompt, click a point within the highlighted border and beneath the plan (see Figure 5.33).

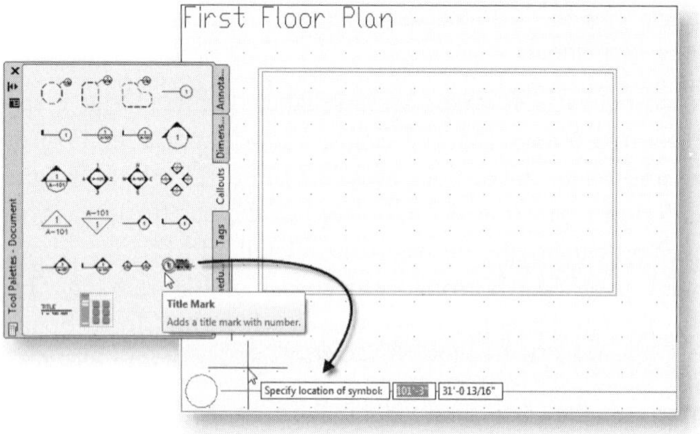

FIGURE 5.33 *Add a Titlemark beneath the Plan, within the First Floor Plan Model Space View boundary*

26. At the "Specify endpoint of line" prompt, drag to the right and click to designate the length of the title bar.

Notice that the label of the Title Bar has automatically picked up the name of the Model Space View. There is gray shading surrounding this label. This indicated that this is a field code. Field codes can be added to any piece of text including within Block Attributes (as is the case here) and then set to reference data from some other location. In this case, the field is configured to read the name of the Model Space View in which it is contained. Had we inserted it outside the Model Space View boundaries, it would have read the name of the drawing file instead. This is why it was important to insert the Titlemark within the boundaries of the Model Space View. Notice that the Scale has also been inserted as a field code and correctly reads the values that we assigned earlier.

Finally, there is a third field code within this Titlemark: the number within the round bubble. Currently it is displaying a question mark (?). This is because it is tied to the actual drawing number for this plan from the Sheet. Since we have not yet built the Sheet, the field cannot yet display the correct number. Later when we build our Sheets, this question mark will automatically be replaced with the correct designation (see Figure 5.34).

FIGURE 5.34 *The Titlemark contains field codes that reference the drawing name and scale*

27. When you are satisfied that the file has been created correctly, save and close the file.

Create the Second Floor Plan View

To create the remaining floor plans, we could repeat all of the steps done earlier. In this example, we will copy them from the First Floor Plan View and then edit them.

28. On the Project Navigator palette, choose the Views tab, right-click on *A-FP01*, and then choose **Copy**.
29. Right-click again and choose **Paste**.

    The new file will be named *A-FP01 (2)*.
30. Right-click *A-FP01 (2)*, and choose **Rename**. Change the name to **A-FP02** and press ENTER to accept the new name.

    A repath message like the one we saw earlier will appear again.
31. Click Repath project later.
32. Right-click on the newly renamed *A-FP02* and choose **Properties**.
33. On the General page on the left, change the Description to **Architectural Second Floor Plan**.
34. Click on the Context page on the left, and then clear the check mark next to Level 1 and place a check mark in Level 2 (see Figure 5.35).

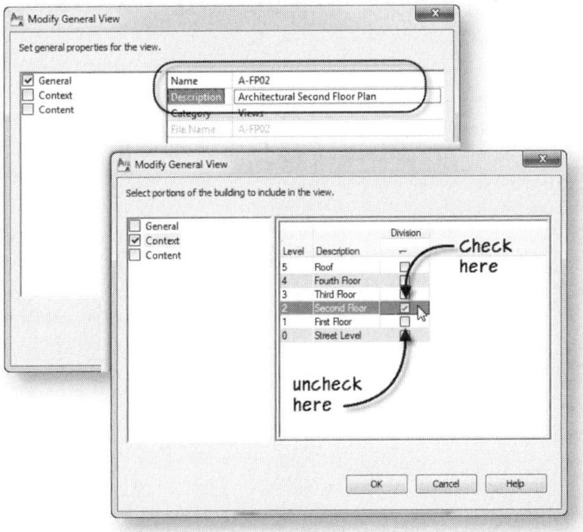

FIGURE 5.35 *Changing the Properties to reference Level 2*

35. On the left, click the Content page.

    Notice that the Constructs included are now *02 Shell and Core* and *Front Façade*. This is because the context has now changed to the second floor.
36. Click OK to dismiss the Modify View dialog box.
37. Double-click on *A-FP02* to open it.

Post Linking Field Codes

Notice that the title bar under the plan still reads "First Floor Plan." The reason for that is because the field codes within the Titlemark still reference the First Floor Plan Model Space View from the *A-FP01* View file.

38. On the Project Navigator palette, right-click the Model Space View indented beneath the *A-FP02* file (currently named "First Floor Plan") and choose **Properties**.
39. Change the name to **Second Floor Plan** and then click OK.

    You can test it by double-clicking on the newly named Model Space View. It should zoom to the rectangle in *A-FP02*.

The Model Space View name is now changed. Let's redirect the link of the fields now from the original copy of the file (*A-FP01*) to *A-FP02*.

40. Using a crossing window selection, select all pieces of the Titlemark.

TIP

To make a crossing selection, click to the right of the Titlemark and then move the mouse to the left until it is near the other side of and surrounding the bubble and click again. The crossing selection will appear in color—green by default.

There should be three objects selected. You can verify this on the Properties palette at the top: "All (3)" should appear in the selection list.

41. Click and hold down on any of the highlighted items and drag to the Project Navigator. (Do not click on any grips; drag from the highlighted edge.)
42. Drop the selection directly on top of the Model Space View indented beneath *A-FP02* (the one we just renamed to "Second Floor Plan," see Figure 5.36).

This procedure is called "post linking" and is used to link up the values in existing field codes with particular nodes within the Project Navigator. The Titlemark should now correctly reference the new name (Second Floor Plan) assigned to the Model Space View in *A-FP02*.

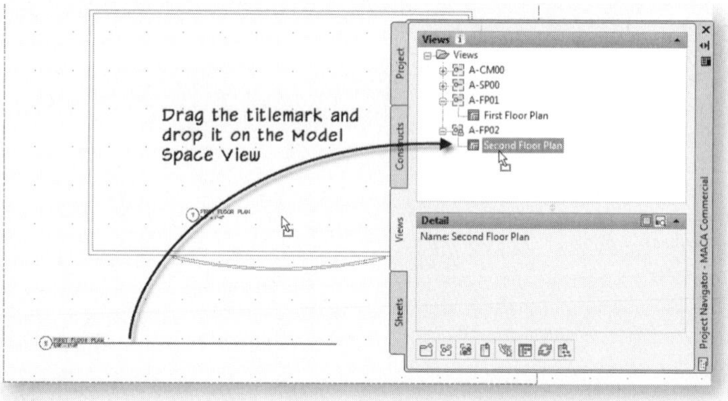

FIGURE 5.36 *Drag and drop the Titlemark to the Second Floor file to "post link" the field codes*

43. When you are satisfied that the file has been created correctly, save and close the file.

Create the Third and Fourth Floor Plan Views

The process for creating the upper floors is the same. Simply repeat the procedure.

44. Repeat the steps in the "Create the Second Floor Plan View" and "Post Linking Field Codes" topics to create the Architectural Third and Fourth Floor Plans.

    If you prefer, you can repeat the steps in "Create the First Floor Plan View," "First Floor Plan Model Space View" and "Add a Titlemark" instead.

45. Name them **A-FP03** and **A-FP04** respectively.

> **TIP**
>
> **Be sure to open the new file before renaming its Model Space View and post linking. There can be problems with applying the new name if you do not open the file first.**

46. Save and close all the Floor Plan View files.

We have copied and renamed several files. To make all changes permanent and avoid broken XREFs later, we must instruct Project Navigator to repath all XREF files. We have been postponing it in the prompts; we can now use the Repath Xref icon to perform the repath.

47. At the bottom of the Project Navigator palette, click the Repath Xref icon and then click Repath in the dialog box that appears (see Figure 5.37).

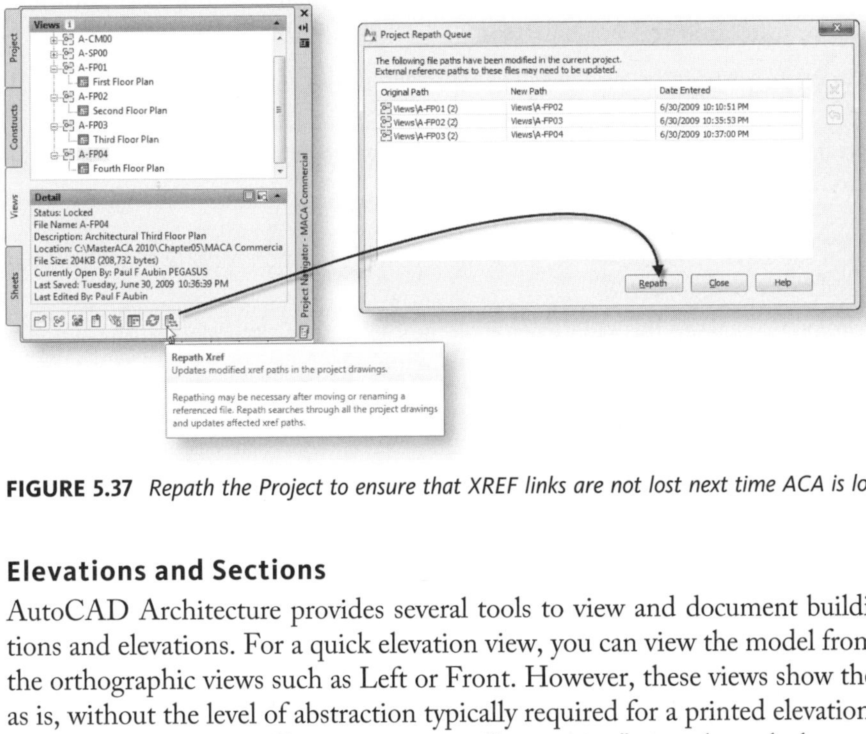

FIGURE 5.37 *Repath the Project to ensure that XREF links are not lost next time ACA is loaded*

Elevations and Sections

AutoCAD Architecture provides several tools to view and document building sections and elevations. For a quick elevation view, you can view the model from one of the orthographic views such as Left or Front. However, these views show the model as is, without the level of abstraction typically required for a printed elevation or section. With a bit more effort, you can cut a "live section" view through the model that crops away the portion behind the Section line and reveals the sectioned portion in a live view. Depending on how these are cut and configured, live sections can even be printed under certain circumstances.

For most design development and construction document needs, the ACA 2D Section/Elevation object gives us the required level of control by creating a separate two-dimensional drawing that remains linked to the original building information model and can be updated when the original changes. This linked drawing functions like a graphic report of the data within a building model. To get just the right section or elevation requires a bit of careful configuration. (In Chapter 16, we will explore the 2D Section/Elevation object in detail.)

In this exercise, we carry on from the previous exercise and generate simple elevations that will serve as placeholders in our cartoon set, in the same way that the basic walls we added earlier serve as stand-ins for our plans.

Create the Building Elevation View

We can generate sections and elevations from any ACA model. For instance, for quickly assessing design edits and changes, Live Sections can be enabled in any Construct or View file. These are used typically for this purpose and rarely for printed documentation. However, Live Sections can be printed if desired and can make very interesting presentation drawings. In these cases, they ought to be generated in separate View files and then dragged to Sheets.

2D Section/Elevation objects can also be created in any ACA file, but often should be created in separate Elevation/Section Views. The benefit of this approach is that each Section/Elevation View can be uniquely configured for its specific purpose, and it enables flexibility in work flow by enabling different team members to work simultaneously on different parts of the project. Following this rationale, we will start by creating a new Section/Elevation View file for our building elevations. We will use the Callout routines on the Tool Palettes to assist us with this task.

1. In Project Navigator, on the Views tab, double-click *A-FP01* to open it.

NOTE

If you left the First Floor Plan View open earlier, then this action will simply make that file active.

2. On the Callouts tool palette, click the Exterior Elevation Mark A3 tool (see the right side of Figure 5.38).

   If you do not see this palette or tool, right-click the Tool Palettes title bar and choose **Document**, and then click the Callouts tab.

You may be wondering, if we intend to create a separate Section/Elevation View file, why we have begun the process in the First Floor Plan file. The callout routine will add four elevation callouts, one on each side of the building, and then generate four corresponding elevations. The callouts will be placed in the current file (in this case *A-FP01*), and when prompted, we will generate the elevations in a new Section/Elevation View file. Therefore, always begin the callout routines in the file where you want the callouts placed. ACA will prompt you for the location of the generated section(s) or elevation(s).

3. At the "Specify first corner of elevation region" prompt, click a point below and to the left of the building.
4. At the "Specify opposite corner of elevation region" prompt, click a point above and to the right the building (see Figure 5.38).

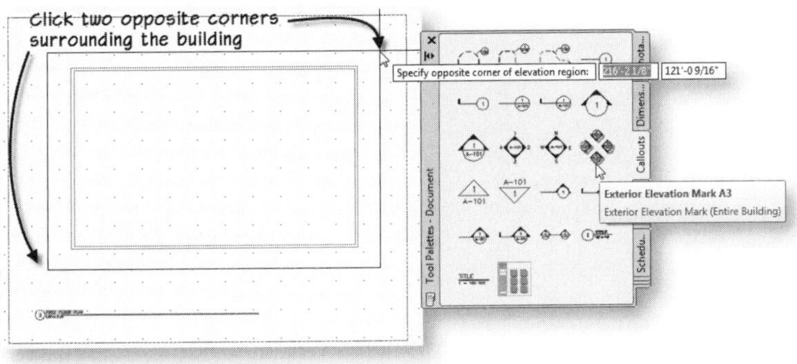

FIGURE 5.38 *Designate the extent of the building elevation region*

The Place Callout worksheet will appear.

5. In the Place Callout worksheet, verify that a check mark does appear in the Generate Section/Elevation and the Place Titlemark checkboxes (at the bottom).
6. For Scale, verify that **1/8" = 1'-0"** [**1:100**] is chosen from the list.

These are the default settings for the exterior elevation callout routine. The Generate Section/Elevation checkbox instructs ACA to create a 2D Section/Elevation object from each of the four sides of the rectangular region designated in the previous steps. The Place Titlemark setting is used to add a Titlemark beneath each 2D Section/Elevation like the ones we added manually to the plans earlier.

7. In the New Model Space View Name field, change the text to read **North Building Elevation;East Building Elevation;South Building Elevation; West Building Elevation**.

TIP

You can add multiple names like we have here as long as you separate each name with a semicolon (;). Do not include a space between names.

When the 2D Section/Elevation object is created, a Model Space View (like the ones we created previously for our Plans) will be created around each one. These Model Space View names must be unique within the project, so plan carefully. You can use any names that you find suitable. Remember, these are the names of the Model Space Views being created, which in turn will become the names automatically referenced by the Titlemarks. The Scale setting is applied to this Model Space View and is also used to scale annotation applied to the 2D Section/Elevation object such as the automatically created Titlemark.

8. Verify that your settings match Figure 5.39.

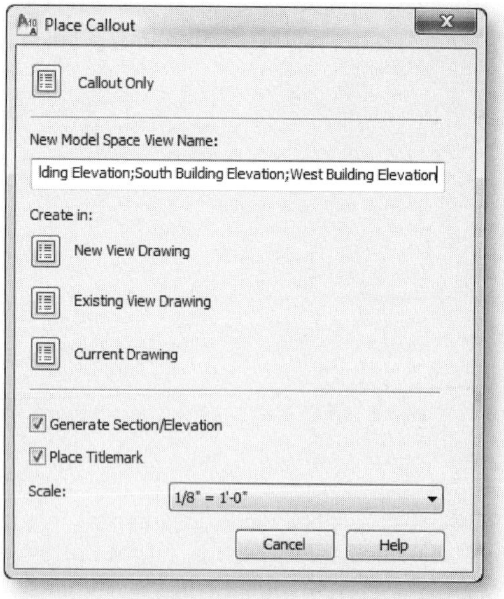

FIGURE 5.39 *The Place Callout worksheet*

There are four behaviors in this dialog box. If you choose Callout Only at the top, you will simply get the section/elevation Callouts, and nothing else will be generated. This is useful if the section or elevation already exists somewhere and you simply wish to have a callout reference it; such as on an upper floor. The other three icons allow different options for the destination of the generated section or elevation. The choices are a new View drawing, and existing View drawing or the current drawing. In this case, we are creating the elevations and a new View drawing in the same operation.

9. In the middle of the Place Callout worksheet, in the "Create in" area, click the New View Drawing icon.

TIP

Make sure the other settings are configured correctly before clicking one of the destination icons as this will move on to the next step which dismisses the "Place Callout" dialog.

The Add Section/Elevation View wizard will appear. This is the same wizard that we have worked through already to create the composite model and plan View files.

10. For the name, type **A-EL01**, type **Architectural Building Elevations** for the Description, and then click Next (see item 1 in Figure 5.40).
11. Verify that all levels are selected and then click Next (see item 2 in Figure 5.40).

A Section/Elevation View differs from a General View only slightly. Basically, the Section/Elevation View assumes that you wish to create your section or elevation from all levels and has them all preselected, while the General View, as we have seen, does not start with any items selected. Also if you look carefully on the Content screen, you will note that the XREFs for a Section/Elevation View use Overlay, unlike those of the General View, which use Attach.

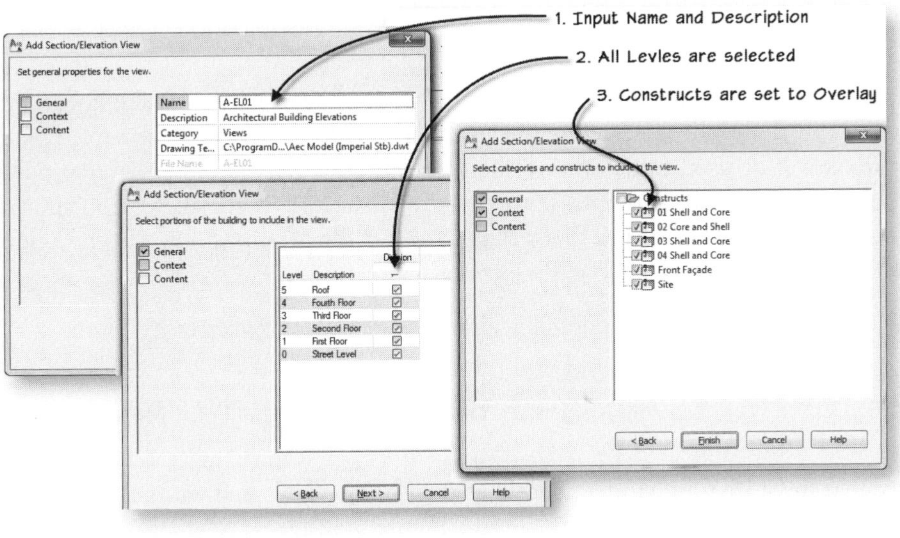

FIGURE 5.40 *The Add Section/Elevation View wizard*

12. Verify that all Constructs are selected and then click Finish (see item 3 in Figure 5.40).

CAUTION

Do not press the ENTER **or** ESC **keys. You are not done with the Callout routine yet!**

Look at the Command Line and notice the message that has appeared. It will read:

```
** You are being prompted for a point in a different view
drawing **
```

You will also see a prompt at your cursor if Dynamic Input is on. (Refer to Chapter 1 for more information on Dynamic Input.) When you create elevations to an existing or new View file, you still must indicate where you would like the elevations to be created in the other file. This prompt serves to inform you of that. Since the Section/Elevation View file being created will XREF the same Constructs that appear in the current file, it is usually best to pick a point off to the side of the plan.

13. At the "Specify insertion point for the 2D elevation result" prompt, click a point in the drawing to the right of the floor plan beyond the purple rectangle (see Figure 5.41).

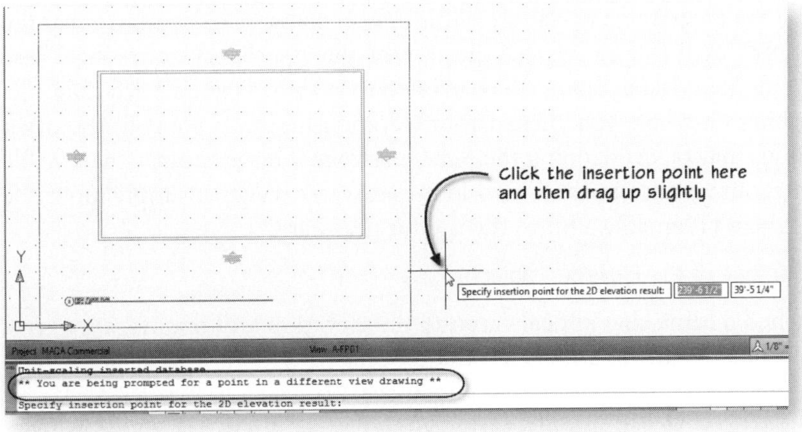

FIGURE 5.41 *Click two points to the side of the drawing to indicate the insertion point and direction to generate elevations*

14. At the "Pick a point to specify the spacing and direction of elevations" prompt, move the mouse up slightly and then click again.

The first point is the insertion point of the elevations and will become the lower-left corner of the elevation object. The distance and direction between the second and first points will be used to determine the direction in which to draw the elevations and how far apart to space them. At this point, the routine is complete. You should have four Callouts in your First Floor Plan–*A-FP01* file. There should also be a new View file named *A-EL01* on your Project Navigator.

If any of your Callouts are overlapping other geometry, feel free to move them.

15. Save the *A-FP01* file.
16. On the Project Navigator palette, click to expand the small plus (+) sign next to *A-EL01*.

Notice that there are four Model Space Views with the names that we assigned earlier already configured within this View file (see Figure 5.42).

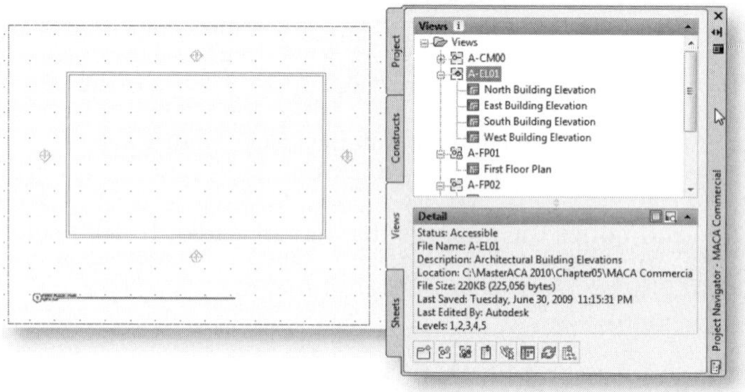

FIGURE 5.42 *The First Floor Plan now contains Callouts, and the new A-EL01 View appears in Project Navigator complete with four Model Space Views*

17. On the Project Navigator palette, double-click *A-EL01* to open it and then Zoom Extents.

Examine the Elevation objects in this file. Notice that there are four of them, spaced one on top of the other as we indicated previously. If you zoom and pan around a bit, you will also notice that the building appears to "float" above the ground in each of the elevations. Don't worry; we will address this in later chapters. Also notice that the Titlemark beneath each one references the title of the associated elevation. These titles come from the Model Space View names that were created with this file. Finally, depending on where you clicked your elevation insertion point in the other file, the elevations may be overlapping the *Site* Construct. This is because the *Site* file is included here, but was not in the First Floor Plan View. We can simply move the elevations and their Titlemarks a bit to the right if necessary.

18. Click on one of the Elevation objects.

Notice the dashed outline that appears around the elevation and the magenta grips on each edge. This is the boundary of the associated Model Space View. The magenta grips allow you to resize the Model Space View (see Figure 5.43). If you move the 2D Section/Elevation object, the Model Space View will move as well. This is very handy, as we will see. You will also notice that the Bldg Elevation

Line associated with this elevation also highlights in red when the associated elevation is selected. The Bldg Elevation line is an object that determines what portion of the plan is to be included in the section or elevation. We will look more at this object in Chapter 16.

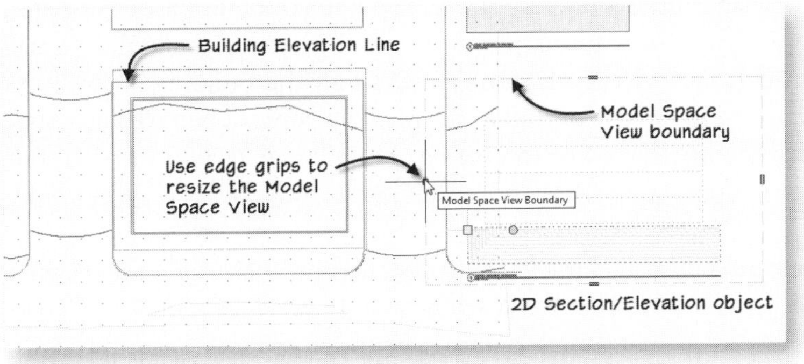

FIGURE 5.43 *The Model Space View associated with each elevation moves with the elevation and can be grip edited*

19. Select all four elevations and all four Titlemarks.

TIP

Be sure to select all three pieces of each Titlemark. Use a window selection to select everything easily. Make a window selection by clicking above and just to the left of the top elevation, and then clicking again below and to the right of the bottom one. Your window must surround all of the items to select them. The Window selection will shade in color—blue by default. It will not select items not completely surrounded like the Site Construct in this case.

All four elevations and their associated Model Space View boundaries and Titlemarks should all be highlighted—16 objects total.

20. Move all selected items to the right until they no longer overlap any of the XREFs.

These elevations are very simplistic; however, they are more than adequate for us to use in planning an elevation Sheet file. This is our main goal at this time: to set up the required Model and Sheet files and to print a cartoon set. As the design evolves in the upcoming chapters, these elevations remain linked to the model, and we will update them periodically.

21. Save and Close the *A-EL01* file.

MANAGER NOTE CAD

At the start of this tutorial, we encouraged you to explore the Commercial Template Project. The Commercial Template Project already includes four building elevations and two building sections complete with callouts on all floor Plan Views. All you have to do when using that project as a seed for your own projects, is draw geometry in the Constructs, open the pre-built elevation or section Views, and then refresh the provided elevation and/or section objects. They will automatically update to reflect the newly added geometry as will the ones you have created manually here. The only difference is that the Commercial Template Project saves you a little work in the setup phase.

Create a Section View

We can create sections using a nearly identical process. On the Callouts tool palette are several variations of Callout symbols, each with slightly different behaviors tailored to their intended functions. There are two types of section that we can create in ACA: the 2D Section/Elevation object (like the ones created in the previous sequence) is typically used for Design Development and Construction Documentation purposes, and the Live Section is more of a design and presentation tool. We will begin by creating a 2D Section/Elevation object through the building following a process nearly identical to the steps covered in the previous topic. Then we will create a Live Section from the same Bldg Section Line. This will give us two ways to consider how the design is shaping up throughout the course of the design.

> **NOTE**
>
> **Please note that both types of section use the same Bldg Section or Elevation Line object. Therefore, any Section or Elevation Line object can be used to generate both 2D and Live Sections and Elevations.**

22. In Project Navigator, on the Views tab, double-click *A-FP01* to open it.

> **NOTE**
>
> **If you left the First Floor Plan View open earlier, then this action will simply make that file active.**

We are going to run a section line vertically through the middle of the plan.

23. On the Callouts tool palette, click the Section Mark A2T tool.

    If you do not see this palette or tool, right-click the Tool Palettes title bar and choose **Document**, and then click the Callouts tab.

24. At the "Specify first point of section line" prompt, click a point on the Construction Line near the top of the plan just beneath the Elevation Callout (see the top of Figure 5.44).

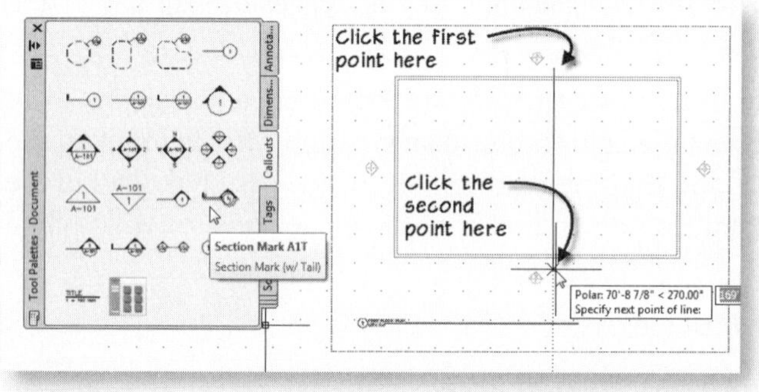

FIGURE 5.44 *Draw a Construction Line through the middle of the plan*

25. At the "Specify next point of line" prompt, move the mouse down to just beneath the lower horizontal Wall and slightly above the elevation callout and click (see the bottom of Figure 5.44).
26. At the subsequent "Specify next point of line" prompt, press `ENTER` to complete the operation.
27. At the "Specify section extents" prompt, move the mouse to the left side of the section line and then click outside the building Walls.

Use the interactive dashed section line boundary as a guide to click in the right spot (see Figure 5.45).

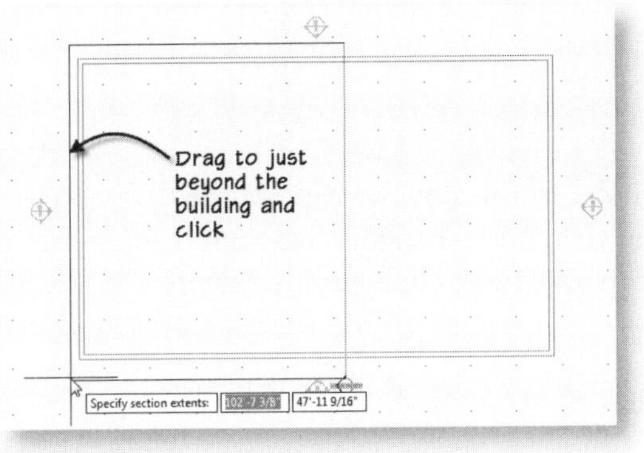
Drag to just beyond the building and click
Specify section extents:
47'-11 9/16"

FIGURE 5.45 *Drag the dashed section line boundary to enclose the left of the building*

28. In the Place Callout worksheet, type **Transverse Building Section** for the Model Space View name and accept all other defaults.
29. In the "Create in" area, click the New View Drawing icon.
30. For the name, type **A-SC01** and **Architectural Building Sections** for the Description, and then click Next.
31. On the Context page, verify that all levels are selected and then click Next.
32. On the Content page, verify that all Constructs are selected and then click Finish.

CAUTION

Do not press ENTER or the ESC key. You are not done with the Callout routine yet!

33. Pan over to the left side of the plan a distance about equal to the plan itself.

Remember to pay close attention to the Command Line here. Refer to the "Create the Building Elevation View" topic and Figure 5.41 for the Command Line warning during this routine. We are placing the section on the opposite side of the plan this time. However, the insertion point of the section is still the lower-left corner; this is why we need to pan to the left to allow enough room for the section in the new View drawing. If you click too close to the plan, it is not a big concern. You can always move the generated section later, as we saw with the elevations earlier.

34. At the "Specify insertion point for the 2D elevation result" prompt, click a point in the drawing to the far left of the floor plan.
35. Save the *A-FP01* floor plan file.

The routine is now complete, and there should be a new *A-SC01* View drawing on the Project Navigator and a new section Callout in the current plan file. Notice that the section line is continuous for the full height of the plan. In some cases, it is desirable to break this line in the middle to make it easier for the plan drawing to read. You can do this now, using the AutoCAD Break command or wait until later when the plan is more fleshed out. Either way, breaking this polyline in the plan file, will have no impact on the actual section object in the *A-SC01* file.

36. On the Project Navigator palette, double-click *A-SC01* to open it.
37. Zoom Extents.

If the section overlaps the XREFs at all, use the process previously in the "Create the Building Elevation View" topic to move the section, its Model Space View, and Titlemark over to the left until it no longer overlaps.

38. Save the file.

Enable a Live Section

Working in the same file, *A-SC01*, we can enable a Live Section from the Bldg Section Line created by the Callout routine. In this way, we can use the Live Section to assist in making design decisions, and then once changes have been made, refresh the 2D Section/Elevation object to incorporate those changes into the printed Sheets that we will set up later.

39. On the Project Navigator palette, double-click *A-SC01* to open it.

NOTE **If you left the Section View open earlier, then this action will simply make that file active.**

40. Change the active Display Configuration to **High Detail**.

The active Display Configuration can be chosen from a list at the bottom right corner of the screen on the Drawing status bar. (See the "Loading a Display Configuration" topic in Chapter 2 for more information.) Live Sections apply to the active Display Configuration. Since the one we are enabling here will be used as a design tool, it is useful to enable it in the High Detail Display mode. The change will not be evident at this stage, but later in the project as the model becomes more detailed, the choice of High Detail will become more apparent.

41. Select the Section line object in the middle of the plan.
42. On the Building Section Line tab, on the Live Section panel, click the Enable Live Section button.
43. On the View tab, on the Appearance panel, scroll through the list of preset views and choose SE Isometric (see Figure 5.46).

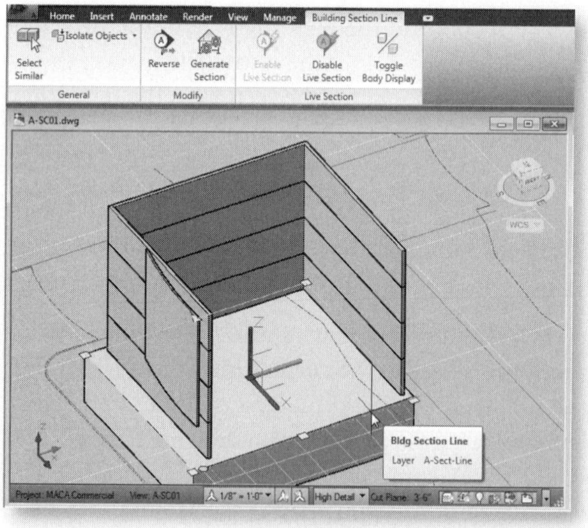

FIGURE 5.46 *A view of the Model with a live section enabled*

Notice that the entire model has been sectioned transversely through the middle. Hatching appears at the section line. Also notice that the 2D Section/Elevation object has disappeared. There is no cause for alarm. Recall the lessons of Chapter 2 in the "Working with the Display System" topic. There we explored the way ACA objects change their display behavior under different viewing conditions. Here, because we are viewing the model in 3D, the 2D Section/Elevation object has simply been turned off. If you return to Top view, it will re-appear.

To make the model easier to see, zoom in a bit, choose **Hidden** or **Conceptual** from the Visual Styles tool on the View tab of the ribbon. Drag the ViewCube to orbit the model to a better angle if you wish.

TIP

Drag the ViewCube or hold down the shift key and drag with the mouse wheel pushed in to orbit.

44. Save and Close the file.

We will look more at this Live Section in later chapters.

Add Elevation and Section Callouts to Upper Floor Plans

When we drag the elevations to a Sheet below, the field codes embedded within the Callouts in the First Floor Plan file will update to reference the correct elevation number and Sheet number. We would also like to see Callouts referenced to the same information appearing on the upper floors of the project. We could repeat the same Callout routine in the Second and other upper floors and simply choose the "Callout Only" option this time. (The Callout Only option creates only the Callout symbols and does not create a 2D Section/Elevation object or a View file.) The only problem with that approach is that we would then need to use the technique covered earlier in the "Post Linking Field Codes" topic to properly reference the fields in the Callouts to the correct elevations. We would have to drag and drop each callout (four in total) and then repeat for each floor plan. It is much easier to simply copy and paste the required Callouts from the First Floor Plan to the other floors. Recall the behavior earlier before we post-linked the Titlemark copied from the first floor to properly reference the second floor. At first, it simply continued to link to the original reference. In this case, this is exactly the behavior that we want. Therefore, post linking will be unnecessary!

45. On the Project Navigator palette, click the Views tab and then double-click *A-FP01* to open it.

NOTE

If you left the First Floor Plan open earlier, then this action will simply make that file active.

46. Select all four elevation Callouts, the section Callout, and both ends of section line.

NOTE

Each Callout is comprised of two separate objects. Be sure to select both in each case, or eight objects total. Likewise, the section callout and line is four separate objects total. You should have 12 objects total in your selection set.

47. On the Home tab, click on the Modify panel title (see the left side of Figure 5.47). The panel will expand to reveal several additional tools.

48. Click the Copy to Clipboard tool (see the middle of Figure 5.47).

TIP

The shortcut for Copy to Clipboard is ctrl + c.

TIP

You can select one elevation callout, one section callout and the section line and then right-click and choose Select Similar to select the rest.

49. On the Project Navigator palette, double-click *A-FP02* to open it.
50. Expand the Modify panel again, click the drop-down button on the Paste tool and choose Paste to Original Coordinates (see the right side of Figure 5.47).

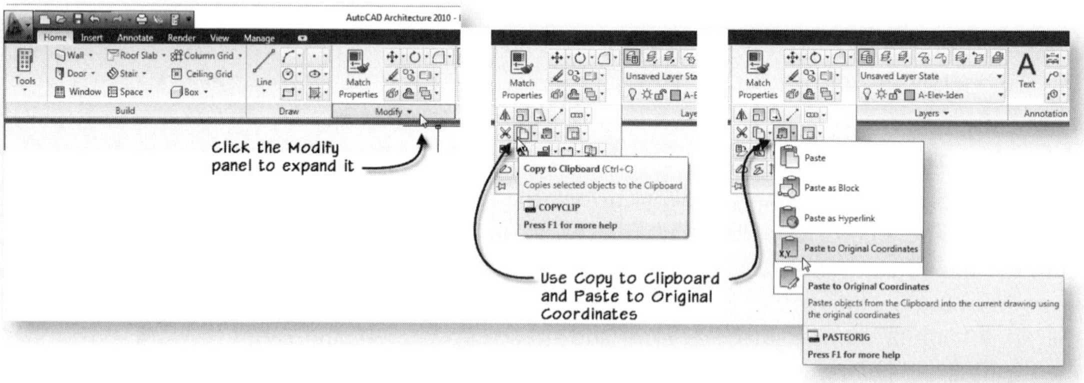

FIGURE 5.47 *Copy and Paste to Original Coordinates*

51. Repeat the Paste to Original Coordinates in both *A-FP03* and *A-FP04*.

Paste to Original Coordinates places the copied objects in exactly the same location relative to the original file. You can use ctrl + v as an alternative, but it will not paste to the same location. Rather, you will be prompted for the new location. If you choose to do this instead, simply type **0,0** and then press ENTER when prompted to place the copies in the same location.

52. Save and Close all Floor Plan files.

Sheet Files and the Cartoon Set

In this exercise, we will create Sheet files for each of the floor plans as well as an elevation and section Sheet file. Finally, we will print the cartoon set. The AutoCAD Sheet Set functionality is fully incorporated into Project Navigator. When you click the Sheets tab, you will see a hierarchical series of items that look similar to a folder tree. These are the Sheet Set and its nested Subsets. Sheet Sets are used to organize drawing files and their Layout tabs for plotting. Coupled with all of the other functions of Project Navigator, Sheets Sets provide the final component of the ACA Drawing Management system.

When you create a new project, a Sheet Set will automatically be created. A Sheet Set Template is used to create all of the initial Subsets. If you click on the Sheets tab of Project Navigator, you will see that the default Sheet Set template creates a General and an Architectural Subset. The Architectural Subset contains several additional Subsets that further help to organize a large document set.

MANAGER NOTE CAD

The entire collection of Subsets is completely customizable. If your firm uses Sheet categories different from those included here, they can easily be modified to suit your firm's needs. To do this, open a project and then modify the Sheet Set by adding, modifying or deleting Subsets. Right-click each Subset and choose its Properties, such as template file to use. Once you are satisfied with the Subset organization, copy the DST file from Windows Explorer to your ACA templates folder. From the Application Menu, choose Options and click the AEC Project Defaults tab to set this DST as the default for new projects that are created without template projects. If you are planning to implement the project template feature (used at the start of this chapter to create the Commercial Project) then you will want to load that template project (using Project Browser) and then modify its Sheet Set instead. This will give all future projects created from that template project a standard and consistent Sheet Set with office standard Subsets and Sheet templates.

Create the Site Plan Sheet File

Let's begin with the Site Plan. Let's create this new Sheet within the Architectural – General Subset.

1. On the Project Navigator palette, click the Sheets tab (see Figure 5.48).

   Be sure that the Sheet Set view is active. If it isn't, click the Sheet Set icon at the top-right corner of the Sheets tab. If Sheet Set View is active, but only MACA Commercial shows in the list, click the plus (+) sign icon to expand.

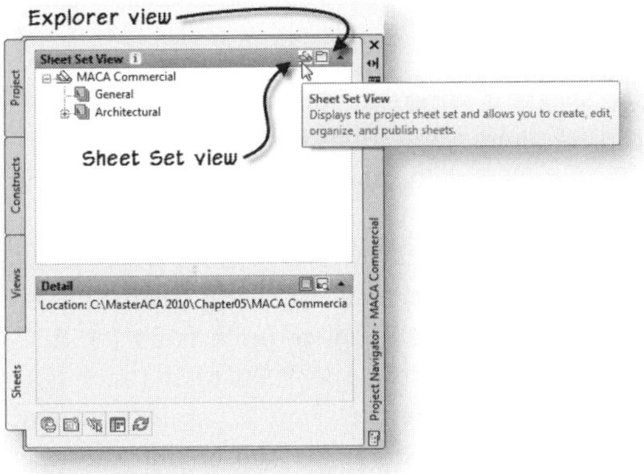

FIGURE 5.48 *Be sure the Sheet Set view is active*

2. Expand the *Architectural* Subset.
3. Select the *General* Subset beneath the *Architectural* Subset.
4. At the base of the palette, click the Add Sheet icon.
5. For the Number, type **A-100** and for the Sheet Title, type **Site Plan**. Click OK to dismiss the New Sheet dialog box (see Figure 5.49).

   Notice that the File Name is created automatically by concatenating these two fields. You are able to edit the File name field manually before clicking OK.

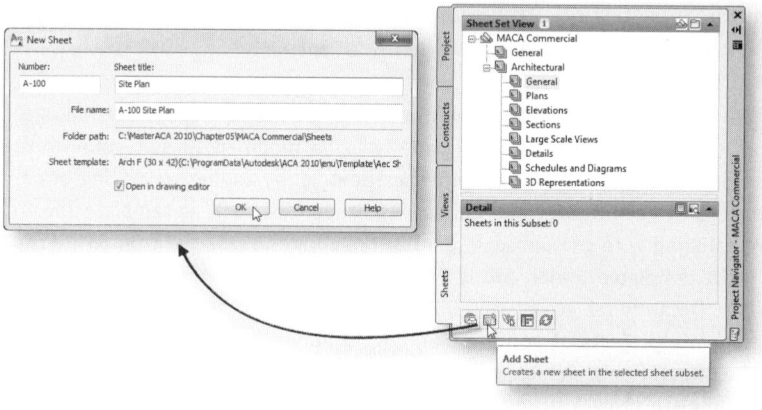

FIGURE 5.49 *Create a new Sheet for the Site Plan*

TIP

When you rename a Sheet file, you can choose whether the associated drawing file renames as well. When you do this, you will have the option to use the Name only or the Name and Number in the new file name. To see these options, select a Sheet, right-click and choose **Rename and Renumber**.

Like other files types in Project Navigator, there is also a checkbox here to open the drawing in the editor after creation. This is on by default and so the new sheet should open automatically.

6. Zoom in on the titleblock and examine the fields. Notice that many of them have filled in automatically with project data field codes.

CAD MANAGER NOTE

You will notice that the template used for Sheets is different from the one used by the other file types. When you first set up a project, there are settings for this. You can assign the template used directly to the Sheet Set, or each individual Subset can have its own template—this can be very useful in multi-discipline firms. We are using the defaults here (based on the template project which we used to create MACA Commercial), which loads the *AEC Sheet (Imperial Stb).dwt* [*AEC Sheet (Metric Stb).dwt*] template file to create Sheets. You can change these settings for projects begun without template projects on the AEC Project Defaults tab of the Options dialog box or within the Sheet Set of the template project that you use to create a project. To do this, make the template project current using Project Browser and then right-click on the Sheet Set at the top of the tree (the top node of the Sheet Set will have the same name as the project) and choose **Properties.**

7. On the Project Navigator palette, click the Views tab.
8. Drag and drop the *A-SP00* View from the Project Navigator palette directly onto the Sheet Layout (see Figure 5.50).

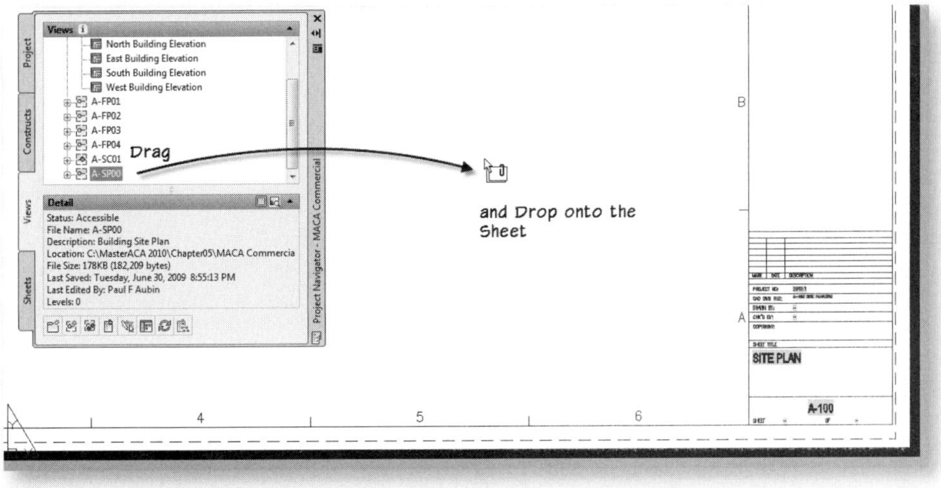

FIGURE 5.50 *Drag the Site Plan from the Project Navigator onto the drawing sheet*

The image of the file will appear onscreen with the lower-left corner attached to the cursor.

9. Move the Viewport to position the Site Plan to an optimal position onscreen.

   You may need to fine tune the position or size of the viewport after placement. You can move it around and resize it with the grips.

Dragging the View onto the Sheet in this way has created a single Viewport scaled at 1/8" = 1'-0" [1:100]. (We can verify the scale by selecting the Viewport object. A small Quick Properties panel will appear showing the layer and scale of the Viewport.) Notice that the viewport is also locked. This prevents the viewport scale from being changed accidentally when someone has the viewport active and then zooms. Notice also that the viewport is automatically placed on a non-plotting layer.

10. Save and close the Site Plan Sheet.

Create the Remaining Floor Plan Sheet Files

Let's now create another Sheet and add the remaining floor plans to it.

11. In Project Navigator, click the Sheets tab.
12. Select the *Plans* Subset beneath the *Architectural* Subset.
13. Click the Add Sheet icon.
14. For the Number, type **A-101** and for the Sheet Title, type **Floor Plans**. Click OK to dismiss the New Sheet dialog box and open the sheet.

    In the numbering scheme used here, "1" stands for Plans (Horizontal Views), and 01 is the floor. Previously, "1" was also used for the Site Plan, because it is a horizontal view, but "00" was used to denote the Street level.

15. On the Views tab, expand the plus sign (+) next to *A-FP01* and then drag and drop the "First Floor Plan" Model Space View onto the Sheet (see Figure 5.50).
16. Snap the lower-left corner of the viewport to the midpoint of the left vertical border of the Sheet (immediately adjacent to the letter C on the border—see the inset in Figure 5.51).

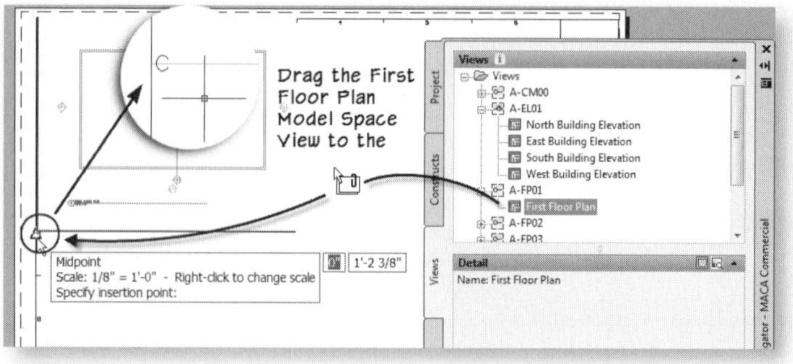

FIGURE 5.51 *Drag the First Floor Plan Model Space View onto the Sheet to create a viewport from the pre-defined boundary*

Notice that the bubble next to the Titlemark for the First Floor Plan has filled in automatically with the number 1. This is because this is the first drawing on this Sheet. When we drag in the Second Floor Plan next, it will become number 2, and so on. The elevation Callouts have not yet updated. This will happen after we drag the elevations to their own Sheet.

17. Expand the plus (+) sign next to *A-FP02* and then Drag and drop the Second Floor Plan Model Space View onto the Sheet.
18. Snap the lower-left corner of the viewport to the lower right corner of the First Floor Plan viewport.

Again note that the Titlemark updates immediately to reflect this change.

19. Repeat this process to drop the Third and Fourth Floor Plan Model Space Views onto the Sheet (see Figure 5.52).

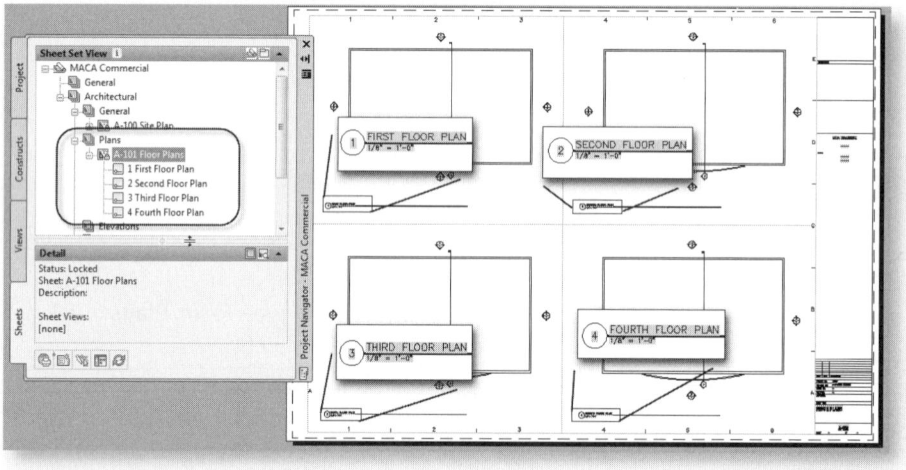

FIGURE 5.52 *The Floor Plans Sheet with all of the Plans added*

Take a look at the Sheet Set in Project Navigator. Notice that once we have dragged several plans onto the *A-101 Floor Plans* Sheet, there are now four Views indented beneath the Sheet name (see Figure 5.52). These are more AutoCAD Named Views. (We have been calling them Model Space Views till now; however, that name is not applicable in Paper Space Layouts.) These Named Views represent the area of the

Sheet that is associated to a particular number. Try double-clicking on one of these Views. It will simply zoom to that location on the Sheet.

20. Save and close the *A-101 Floor Plans* Sheet.

Create the Elevation Sheet File

We create the Elevation Sheet in the same fashion.

21. On the Sheets tab of the Project Navigator, create a new Sheet in the *Architectural – Elevations* Subset numbered **A-201** and with the Sheet Title set to **Building Elevations**.

    "2" is the code for elevations, and "01" makes it the first elevation sheet.

22. On the Views tab of the Project Navigator, drag and drop *A-EL01* onto the Sheet.

NOTE

Drag the entire View file this time—not the individual Model Space Views. ACA will successively insert each Model Space View and number them accordingly.

23. As each Model Space View is inserted, place it on the Sheet until all four elevations are placed.

    Make any necessary adjustments to the position and size of the viewports. You can use the grips to stretch the viewports if needed.

Examine all the elevation numbers. Notice that similar to the plan views, they have been automatically numbered in the sequence in which they were added to the Sheet (see Figure 5.53).

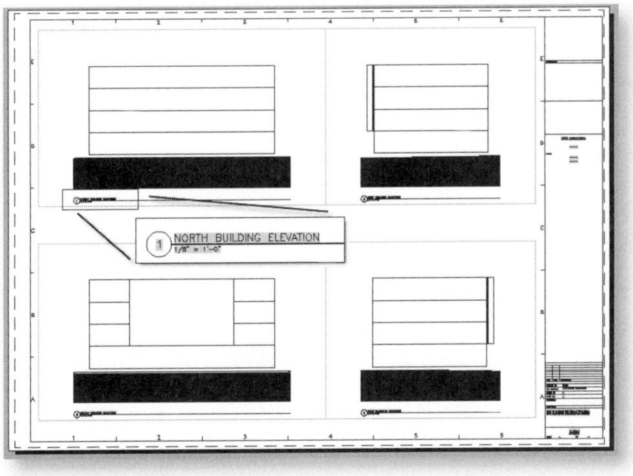

FIGURE 5.53 *Complete the setup of the Elevation Sheet*

24. Save and Close the file.

Create the Section Sheet File

Although we generated both a 2D Section/Elevation object and a Live Section earlier, here we will place only the 2D Section/Elevation object on the Sheet.

25. On the Sheets tab of the Project Navigator, create a new Sheet in the *Architectural – Sections* Subset numbered **A-301** and with the Sheet Title set to **Building Sections**.

    "3" is the code for sections (Vertical Views), and "01" makes it the first section sheet.

26. On the Views tab of the Project Navigator, drag and drop *A-SC01* onto the Sheet—do not click to place it yet.
27. Before placing the viewport, right-click.

Notice that a menu of standard scales appears. Suppose that at the time you created the View file, you chose a scale, or perhaps forgot to set a scale that you now realize is incorrect in relation to the Sheet. Using this menu, you can set a different scale for this viewport on the fly.

28. From the list of scales, choose **1/4" = 1'-0"** [**1:50**], and then place the viewport on the Sheet (see Figure 5.54).

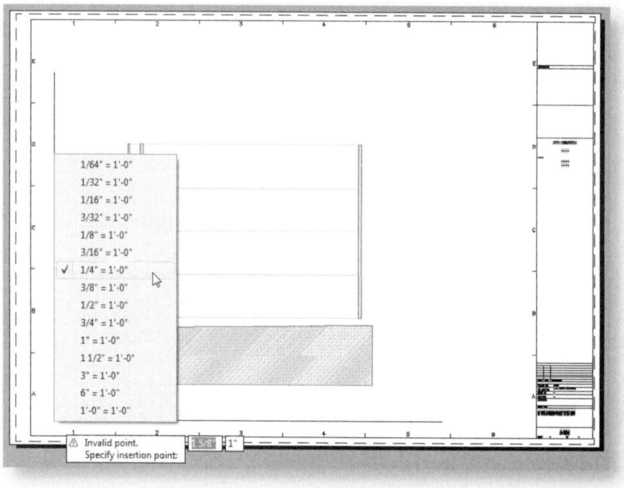

FIGURE 5.54 *Right-click while placing a viewport to change the scale*

Making an edit such as this on the fly can be handy, but you will need to make adjustments to the View file anyhow. Let's take a look at that now.

29. Save and Close the file.
30. On the Project Navigator palette, click the Views tab and then double-click Transverse Building Section beneath *A-SC01* to open it.

Notice that this action opens the *A-SC01* file and then automatically restores the Transverse Building Section Model Space View. A temporary label will appear with this name onscreen until you change the zoom or pan. If you saved the file in a visual style, it will look as though the view is empty. Restore the 2D Wireframe visual style to correct this.

31. On the Project Navigator palette, right-click on Transverse Building Section beneath *A-SC01* and choose **Properties**.
32. In the Modify Model Space View worksheet, change the scale to **1/4"=1'-0"** [**1:50**] and then click OK.
33. Select all parts of the titlemark callout.

34. On the Annotate tab, on the Annotation Scaling panel, click the Add Current Scale button.

The titlemark should adjust in scale and become smaller. It is now correctly displaying for 1/4"=1'-0" [1:50] scale. This usually happens automatically, but when you change the scale of the view via the viewport in the Sheet file, it does not occur.

35. Save and Close the file.
36. On the Sheets tab of the Project Navigator palette, double-click *A-301 Building Sections* to open it.

    Notice that the Titlemark is now displaying and is the correct size. If you left this file open, a balloon should appear alerting you that the XREF file has changed. Simply click the link in this balloon to reload the *A-SC01* XREF file.
37. Save and close the *A-301 Building Sections* file.
38. On the Sheets tab of the Project Navigator palette, double-click *A-101 Floor Plans* to open it.

Zoom and pan round the file and notice that now that we have created the elevations and sections Sheets, all of the Callouts now correctly display the associated elevation or section to which they reference on all four floors. If you left the file open before, then you will need to force the fields to update with the new information manually. On the View tab, on the Appearance panel, locate the Regenerate tool (next to the views list). Click the drop-down button on the Regenerate tool and choose Regenerate Drawing and Viewports. You do *not* need to reload the XREFs for this update to occur.

39. Save and Close the file.

Create a Cover Sheet

Let's create one more Sheet before printing our cartoon set. A Cover Sheet template has been provided with the Chapter 5 dataset files. We will use it now to give our set a Cover Sheet.

1. On the Sheets tab of the Project Navigator, right-click the *General* Subset and choose **Properties**.

   Be sure to choose the *General* category above *Architectural* and not the one indented beneath *Architectural*.
2. Place a check mark in the Prompt for Template checkbox and then click OK (see Figure 5.55).

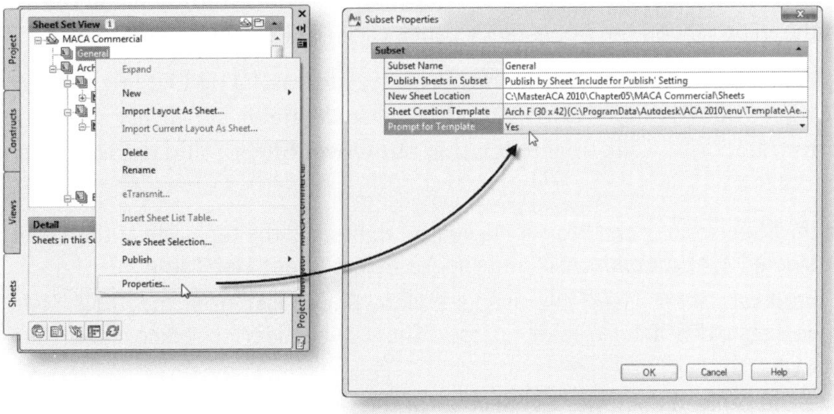

FIGURE 5.55 *Enable the "Prompt for Template" option for the General Subset*

Each Subset of a Sheet Set can reference its own template file. This is very useful for multi-discipline firms where, for instance, the MEP Consultant uses a different titleblock than the Architects do. In this case we are specifying that we wish to be prompted for a template. You will not typically want this setting in most Subsets; however, it seems appropriate here in the General category, which will have a Cover, perhaps a Legend, and other types of Sheets that can use slightly different templates.

3. Select the *General* Subset and then click the Add Sheet icon.

Notice that a dialog box appears to prompt you to select a template file for this Sheet.

4. Click the Browse (...) icon next to the Drawing template file name field.

The default template folder on your system will be displayed. This could be in the *Documents and Settings* folder of your system, on your office server, or any other location. The template we want to use here has been provided in the same location as the other dataset files.

5. In the Select Drawing dialog box, on the left side, click the Desktop icon, double-click *My Computer*, and then browse to the *C:\MasterACA 2010\Chapter05* folder.
6. Choose *Cover Sheet.dwt* [*Cover Sheet-Metric.dwt*] and then click Open.

In the bottom half of the dialog box, any Layouts saved in the template will appear. Choose a Layout here, and it will be used to create the new Sheet.

7. Choose Cover Sheet (30x42) [Cover Sheet (841 x 1189)] and then click OK to continue to the New Sheet dialog box.
8. For the Number, type **G-100** and for the Sheet Title type **Cover Sheet** and then click OK (see Figure 5.56).

   "G" indicates "General," where "A" indicates "Architectural" on all of the other Sheets. "100" is used here for consistency with the naming of the other Sheets and simply indicates that it is the first Sheet.

It is a pretty simple Cover Sheet. Naturally, you can customize this template or use your own in real projects. Notice that several of the fields have empty values. These are retrieved from the project database. At this time, we have not yet entered those values. We can edit these values now, and the Cover Sheet will update.

9. In Project Navigator, click the Project tab, and then click the Edit Project icon at the top (shown in Figure 5.6).
10. In the Basic > General grouping, click the worksheet icon next to Detailed Information.
11. Edit any fields that you wish, and then click OK twice to return to the drawing.
12. On the View tab, on the Appearance panel, click the Regenerate tool.

The first field below the Project title is the "Project Address." The Date field is actually the "Project Start Date." "Owner" and "Architect" fields are clearly noted in their respective categories. One final touch that our Cover Sheet could use is a Sheet Index.

13. On the Sheets tab of the Project Navigator, right-click the top node of the Sheet Set labeled *MACA Commercial* and choose **Insert Sheet List Table**.
14. In the Insert Sheet List Table dialog, choose **Sheet List** from the Table Style Name list, place a checkmark in the "Show subheader" checkbox and then click OK.
15. Place the Table in the lower right corner of the Cover Sheet in the space labeled for it (see Figure 5.56).

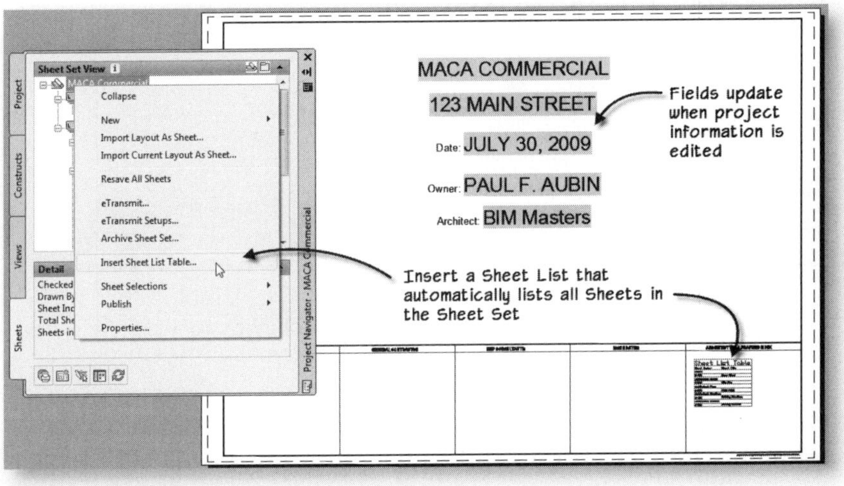

FIGURE 5.56 *Create a Cover Sheet from a different template, update its fields, and insert a Sheet List*

CAD MANAGER NOTE

Traditionally, a title block is an AutoCAD Block with attributes within it. In ACA, the title block graphics (borders and lines) are still an AutoCAD Block, but instead of attributes, field codes are used within Mtext objects to input the values in the title block. You can open the out-of-the-box Sheet template files to see examples of this. You can find the default template files (DWT) located in the *C:\ProgramData\Autodesk\ACA 2010\enu\Template* folder (*C:\Documents and Settings\All Users\Application Data\Autodesk\ACD-A 2008\enu\Template* folder in Windows XP). The name of the default file is: *AEC Sheet (Imperial Stb).dwt* [*AEC Sheet (Metric Stb).dwt*]. This template file contains multiple Layouts—one for each standard sheet size. When you create a new Sheet in the Sheet Set, only the Layout needed for the sheet size assigned to the current subset is actually added to the new Sheet file. You can see that in the Sheet created here. Each contains only a single Layout named after the file name.

16. Save and Close the file.

Publish the Cartoon Set

Now that all of the preliminary files have been created, we can publish our Cartoon Set.

17. On Project Navigator, click the Sheets tab.
18. At the top of the Sheet Set list, right-click the *MACA Commercial* node and choose **Publish > Publish to DWFx**.
19. In the Select DWF File dialog box, accept the default name (*MACA Commercial.dwfx*), browse to the *C:\MasterACA 2010\Chapter05\Commercial* folder, and then click Select.

Sit back and watch it process the entire Sheet Set. You can access this same command from each node of the Sheet Set. Therefore, you can Publish the entire drawing set as we have done here, or you can publish smaller Subsets. You can even create custom Sheet Selections and publish only those. We will explore this technique in Chapter 18. When the DWFx is complete, a balloon will appear in the status bar (see left side of Figure 5.57). Click on it to see a report.

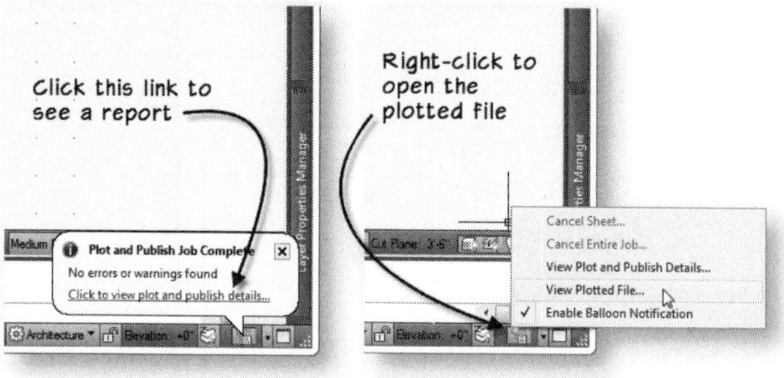

FIGURE 5.57 *A notification appears when a Plot and Publish job is complete, right-click for options*

The Publish routine can create hard-copy plotted Sheets using the settings saved in the Page Setup of each file, or it can also create a multi-page DWF or DWFx (Design Web Format) file. This single file will contain several pages, one for each Sheet, and can be distributed electronically. This is what we have created here. To view and print DWF files, use the free Autodesk Design Review software available from Autodesk.com and installed automatically with AutoCAD Architecture. If you plot a DWFx and your recipient is using Windows Vista or later, they can open and view the file directly in Windows Explorer without any additional software. If the recipients wish to mark up the DWF file, they can do so in Design Review. Markups generated in Design Review can be loaded back into ACA for reference while picking up changes. Let's view the DWF file now.

20. On the Application status bar, at the right side, right-click the small Plot and Publish icon and choose **View Plotted File** (see right side of Figure 5.57).
21. Explore the file in Design Review (see Figure 5.58).

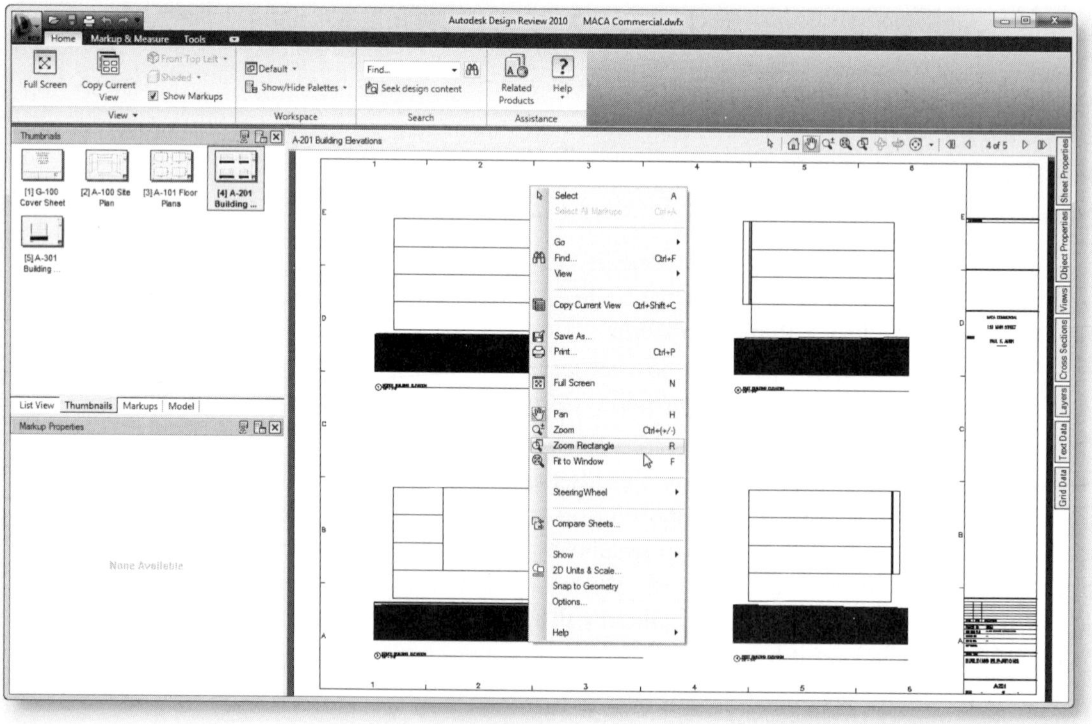

FIGURE 5.58 *Viewing multi-sheet DWF files in Design Review*

All Sheets of the set will appear in a panel on the left as icons, or in a list. Click the icon to view a particular Sheet. All Callouts from the original files will contain hyperlinks in the DWF file. Simply hold down the ctrl key and click a link to jump directly to the referenced Sheet in the DWF. You can make markups directly on top of the DWF file, save them, and then load them back into ACA. Right-click for additional options and navigation controls.

22. Close Design Review when you are finished viewing the DWF file.

If you prefer paper plots, and you are already familiar with AutoCAD plotting, choose the Plotters named in page setups option instead, and proceed to generate "real paper" plots. (For more information on plotting in ACA, refer to Chapter 18 of this book or consult the online help.)

23. Save and Close all Commercial Project files.

MANAGER NOTE CAD

Although your office standards may vary considerably from the file naming and XREF structure presented here, the more important issue is the strategy of using consistent file naming and XREF structures from one project to the next. It is also critical to set up the project files as early in the project life cycle as possible. Building the set early allows for easier setup and maintenance and allows the project team members to follow an established standard.

If you are also planning to utilize the Project Standards features of AutoCAD Architecture, then you will also want to configure project standards files, and potentially Project Content Browser libraries and Project Tool Catalogs as well. All of these items can be included in your own custom Project Template that can then be used to create future projects. Examples of some of these items can be found throughout future chapters such as Chapters 8, 10 and 11.

SETTING UP THE RESIDENTIAL BUILDING MODEL

The second project in this book is an 800 SF [75 SM] residential addition. Since the focus of this chapter was on the commercial project, also included as a special bonus on the CD-ROM is a PDF mini-chapter with a detailed tutorial for the setup of the residential project files. Download and view this PDF mini-chapter onscreen or print it out to perform the tutorials for setting up the residential project.

CONGRATULATIONS!

You have set up your first ACA Projects and completed your first AutoCAD Architecture cartoon set. The files are now ready to receive project design data. At any time, you can open the Sheet files to assess your progress, compare with your schedule and budget projections, and re-plot as necessary. The completed set of files has been provided with the files from the CD. You will find them in a folder named *Chapter05\Complete*. Launch the Project Browser, and load the completed versions to compare them to the ones created here if you wish. (Both commercial and residential projects are provided.)

NOTE

When you wish to view the completed versions of the Projects from the CD, be sure to use Project Browser to make the project current. If you are prompted to "Repath" the project, always answer yes to this query. This will ensure that all required XREF paths are properly configured for your machine.

ADDITIONAL EXERCISES

Additional exercises have been provided in Appendix A. In Appendix A you will find an exercise for adding a Furniture Element file to the Project dataset and then using it to build a Furniture Plan. You will also find an exercise to create a project using the out-of-the-box Commercial Template project instead of the template project used in this chapter. It is not necessary that you complete these exercises to begin the next chapter. They are provided merely for your information and practice.

SUMMARY

- Thorough project setup can help give a good sense of project drawing requirements early in the project cycle.
- Using the Project Browser and Project Navigator tools makes setting up a project quick and easy.
- ACA Drawing Management tools make use of XREFs to relate files to one another.
- XREF Overlay is used when you want the XREF to go only one level deep.
- XREF Attach creates nested references, which create a hierarchical reference structure.
- Model files are full-scale drawings used to generate actual project data on a daily basis.
- Constructs and Elements are Model files representing individual pieces of a complete building model.
- Constructs have a unique physical location (an address) within the Building Model; Elements do not.
- Views are used to gather a collection of Constructs (and any nested Elements that they may contain) for a specific viewing purpose.
- Views make an excellent location for adding annotation.
- Several provided Callout routines make the process of creating sections and elevations with linked annotation as simple as following a wizard.
- Sheet files are used for setting up "ready to plot" sheets for printing document sets.
- Sheet Sets can be quickly plotted to Multi-Sheet DWF files that can be opened, viewed, plotted and redlines in Design Review.

CHAPTER 6

Column Grids and Structural Layout

INTRODUCTION

In this chapter, we will explore the layout of structural components for the commercial project begun in the last chapter. As we have seen, the design is a four-story structure of modest footprint. We will begin with the layout of the column bay grid. We will add framing members and explore how to incorporate these items into appropriate files within our project structure and revisit the Residential Project to create a foundation plan.

OBJECTIVES

We will begin adding a Column Grid and Columns to a file that will be used as a typical layout on all floors. This grid layout will be added to each level of the project including bubbles and dimensions. We will then add Beams and Joists to complete the framing. The main tools covered in this chapter include the following:

- Explore the Structural Member Catalog.
- Explore the Structural Member Wizard.
- Work with the Column Grid tools.
- Annotate a Column Grid with bubbles and dimensions.
- Create Structural Beams and Braces using automated layout routines.
- Create a Foundation Wall with integral footings.

STRUCTURAL MEMBERS

A structural member is an AEC object that is used to represent Columns, Beams or Braces. Each structural member belongs to a style, which in turn must reference one or more "Structural Member Shapes." The shape is simply the cross section of the structural member at a given point along its length. A structural member must contain at least one shape, but may have several. A shape is extruded along the path of the structural member. (A Structural Member may optionally have more than one shape along its path.) Structural Member shapes are retrieved from an extensive catalog of industry-standard structural shapes. This catalog includes typical sizes of concrete, timber and steel. A simple wizard can also be used to create shapes. Custom shapes can also be defined, thus, the potential of structural members is virtually limitless. In order to be used in a design, shapes located in the catalog (or custom-defined shapes) must be referenced in styles in the current drawing. In this tutorial, we will import a few steel shapes from the catalog and wizard and define them as styles for our commercial project.

Install the CD Files and Load the Current Project

If you have already installed all of the files from the CD, simply skip down to step 3 below to make the project active. If you need to install the CD files, start at step 1.

1. If you have not already done so, install the dataset files located on the Mastering AutoCAD Architecture 2010 CD-ROM.

   Refer to "Files Included on the CD-ROM" in the Preface for information on installing the sample files included on the CD.
2. Launch AutoCAD Architecture 2010 from the desktop icon created in Chapter 3.

If you did not create a custom icon, you might want to review "Create a New Profile" and "Create a Desktop Shortcut" in Chapter 3. Creating the custom desktop icon is not essential; however, it makes loading the custom profile easier.

3. From the Quick Access Toolbar (QAT), choose the ***Project Browser*** icon.
4. Click to open the folder list and choose your *C:* drive.
5. Double-click on the *MasterACA 2010* folder, then the *Chapter06* folder.

   One or two commercial Projects will be listed: *06 Commercial* and/or *06 Commercial Metric.*
6. Double-click *06 Commercial* if you wish to work in Imperial units. Double-click *06 Commercial Metric* if you wish to work in Metric units (you can also right-click on it and choose **Set Current Project**). Then click Close in the Project Browser.

NOTE

Important: If a message appears asking you to repath the project, click the "Repath the project now" option. Refer to the "Repathing Projects" topic in the Preface for more information.

If you want to learn more about ACA Projects, refer to Chapter 5.

Create a New Element File in the Project

The same Column Grid layout will occur on all four floors of the project. We could build the grid layout, and then copy it to each of our existing floor plates, but an easier approach will be to take advantage of Project Elements, as described in Chapter 5. By making the Column Grid an Element, we can use it in each floor level Construct, while maintaining a link to the original Element file. If the Column Grid layout needs to change, we simply edit the Element file, and it will update in all of the Constructs. Naturally this approach would be less effective on buildings where the column layout varies from floor to floor. However, anytime that you have a repetitive portion of your building design—such as a typical Stair, Toilet Room or Column Grid as in this case—you can use Element files in Project Navigator to manage them. Refer back to the "Elements, Constructs, Views and Sheets (Project Drawing Files)" heading in Chapter 5 for more information.

7. On the Project Navigator, click the Constructs tab. (If the Project Navigator did not open automatically when you closed Project Browser, press `CTRL + 5` to open it now.)
8. Right-click on the *Elements* folder and choose **New > Element**.
9. Type **Column Grid** for the Name and **Typical Column Grid** for the Description and then click OK (see Figure 6.1).

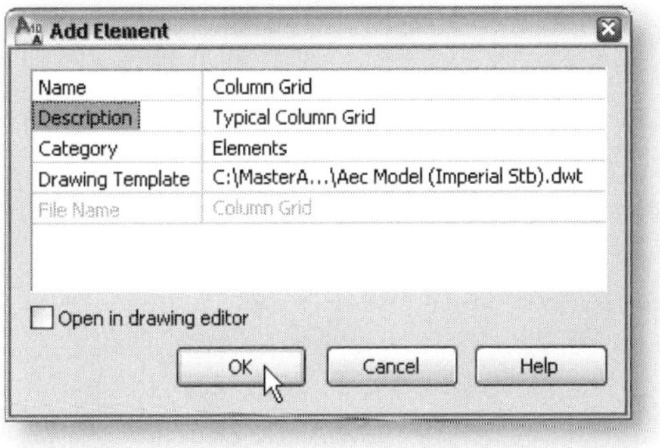

FIGURE 6.1 *Create a new Column Grid Element file*

10. Double-click on the *Column Grid* Element file to open it.

TIP

You can also select the "Open in drawing editor" checkbox before clicking OK to create and open the drawing in one step.

Access the Structural Member Catalog

Let's now import some Structural Member Shapes to use in our Grid layout.

11. On the Manage ribbon tab on the Style & Display panel, expand the panel and choose the ***Structural Member Catalog*** tool (see Figure 6.2).

Disclaimer:

The shapes used in this book are chosen only for illustration purposes and are not presented as a design solution or to be construed as a recommendation of structural integrity. No structural analysis of any kind has been performed on the designs in this book.

Navigate the Structural Member Catalog in the same way as you would Windows Explorer. On the left are two main categories: *Metric* and *Imperial*.

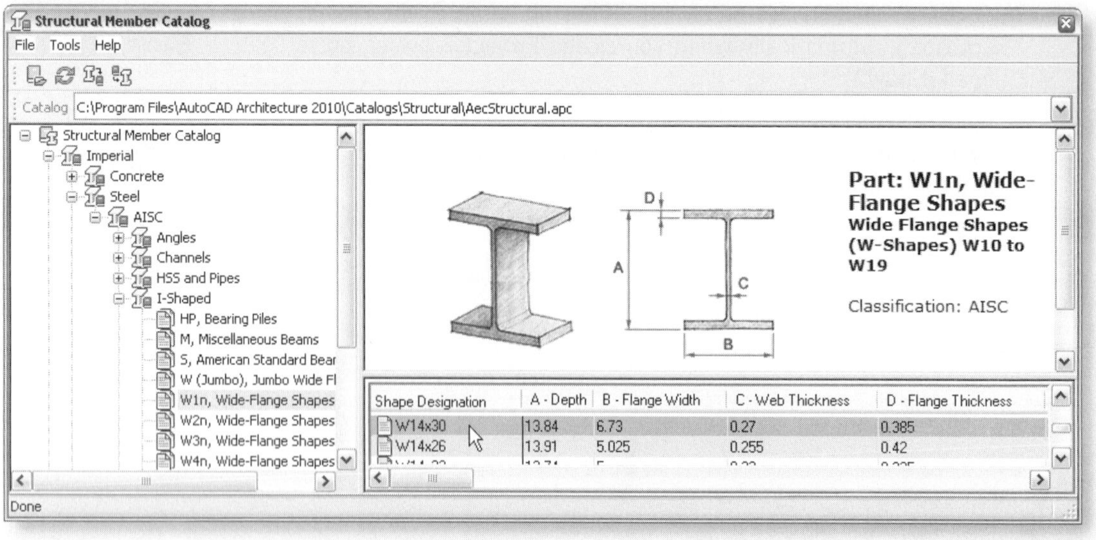

FIGURE 6.2 *The Structural Member Catalog*

12. Click the Plus (+) sign next to each category to expand the tree.

    Both *Imperial* and *Metric* are divided into three sections based on material: *Concrete*, *Steel* and *Timber*. However, the divisions within each material vary regionally (see Figure 6.2).

13. Expand the *Steel* entry, then the *AISC* entry and finally *I-Shaped* [for Metric, expand one level deeper to *Wide Flanges*].

> **NOTE**
>
> **Nearly every imaginable industry standard shape is included in this hierarchy. However, as new shapes become available, the catalog's XML format makes it very easy to update.**

14. Select the *W1n, Wide-Flange Shapes* [*W3nn, Wide Flanges*] category.

15. Scroll through the list, locate the W12x87 [W310x97] shape and select it (see Figure 6.3).

    Scroll horizontally and notice the complete list of properties associated with each shape.

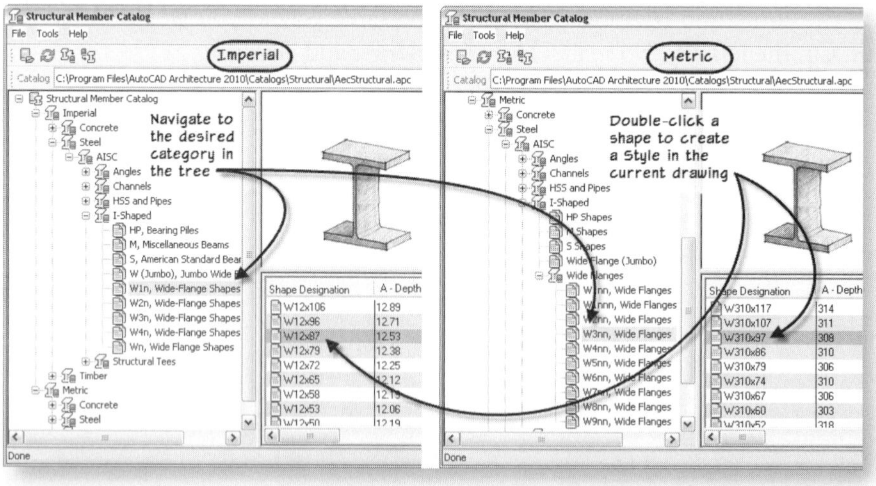

FIGURE 6.3 *Create a new Structural Member style by double-clicking the shape in the catalog*

16. Double-click W12x87 [W310x97].

    The Structural Member Style dialog box will appear. Double-clicking a shape name imports the shape into the current drawing and creates a style that references it.

There are three types of structural members available in ACA: Columns, Beams and Braces. The shapes available in the Structural Member Catalog are used for all three forms of Structural Members. When you double-click a shape, ACA will suggest that the name of the shape being imported be used as the name for the style being created. Nothing in particular about the shape names themselves indicates your intent to use them as columns, beams or braces in your project. Therefore, you might want to add a descriptive suffix when creating Structural Member styles, like "Main Columns," or "First Floor Beams." This is optional, and if you prefer, you can simply accept the name that is offered instead.

17. Type **W12x87 (Main Columns)** [**W310x97 (Main Columns)**] and then click OK (see Figure 6.4).

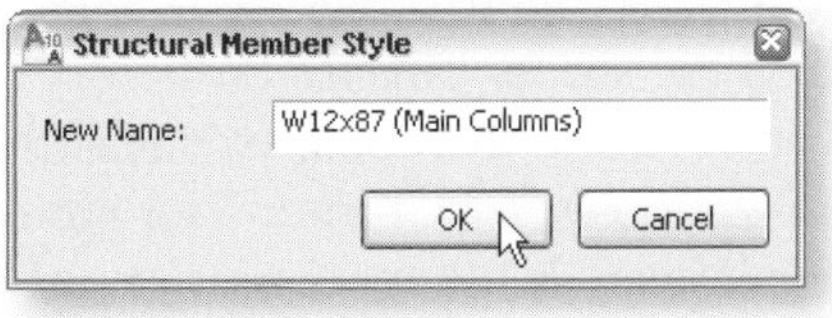

FIGURE 6.4 *Name the new Structural Member style with a descriptive suffix*

18. Continue browsing the Structural Member Catalog if you wish. When finished, close the Structural Member Catalog.

Use the Structural Member Style Wizard

If you wish, you can bypass the Structural Member Catalog when creating Structural Member styles. This is useful if you have not yet consulted your structural engineer and you wish to create a shape based on overall size. To do this, we use the Structural Member Style Wizard. Later, when accurate sizes have been calculated by your structural engineer, you can swap those styles in to replace the ones created with the Wizard.

19. On the Manage ribbon tab on the Style & Display panel, expand the panel and choose the ***Structural Member Wizard*** tool.
20. From the list under the *Steel* category, choose **Wide Flange (I)** and then click Next.
21. For both the Sectional Depth and Sectional Width, type **8"** [**210**] and then click Next.
22. For the Style Name, type **Front Skin Columns** and then click Finish (see Figure 6.5).

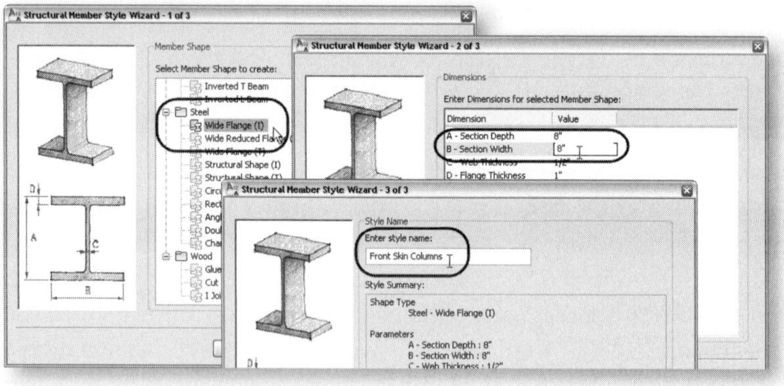

FIGURE 6.5 *The Structural Member Style Wizard*

23. Save the file.

Viewing Structural Member Shapes in Style Manager

Structural Members, as we have mentioned, contain one or more Structural Member Shapes as cross sections. You can view and edit these shapes directly in the Style Manager. Each Structural Member Shape can contain up to three shapes: one each for High, Medium and Low Detail Display Configurations (see Chapter 2 for more information on Display Reps and Display Configurations). It is not necessary to utilize all three Display Reps, but doing so gives Structural Members based on the Shapes a great deal of flexibility. To understand this better, let's take a look at the Style Manager and preview the Shapes that we just added to the drawing.

24. On the Manage ribbon tab on the Style & Display panel, choose the ***Style Manager*** tool.
25. On the left side under ColumnGrid.dwg, expand the Architectural Objects and Structural Member Shape Definitions and click on the W12x87 [W310x97] Shape.

Note that here we are looking at the Structural Member Shape Definitions, not the Structural Member Styles that reference the Shapes. Therefore, the name listed here is simply the Shape name, not the longer name (including "Main Columns") that we assigned to the Structural Member Style above.

26. On the right side of the Style Manager, click the Design Rules tab.
27. Click through each level of detail and note that the corresponding Shape will highlight in green (see Figure 6.6).

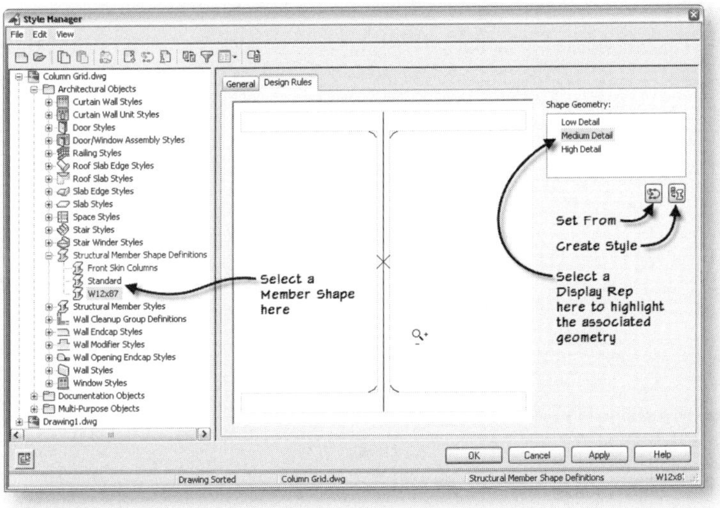

FIGURE 6.6 *Viewing Structural Member Shape Definitions in the Style Manager*

There are two icons beneath the Display Reps. The one on the right (Create Style) allows you to create a Structural Member Style from the Shape that you are viewing. The icon on the left (Set From) will return you to the drawing editor and allow you to select linework from which to create the selected Shape. If you wish to create your own Shape, you can start with the polylines embedded in an existing Definition or draw new ones from scratch. To start with the existing ones, you would exit the Style Manager and on the Manage ribbon tab on the Style & Display panel, expand the panel and choose the ***Member Shape*** tool. This will open the Insert Member Shapes dialog, which has a viewing pane similar to that in Style Manager and which allows you to select one or more of the rings embedded in the Shape to insert into the drawing. Once there, you can edit them and then return to the Style Manager to reassign them to the Shape Definition with the "Set From" icon. Feel free to try this on your own later. Remaining in Style Manager, let's take a look the Structural Member Style that references the Shape that we have been viewing here.

28. On the left side in the tree view, expand Structural Member Styles and then select W12x87 (Main Columns) [W310x97 (Main Columns)].
29. On the right side, on the General tab, type **Main Structural Columns All Bays** in the Description field.
30. Click the Design Rules tab.

Any shapes referenced by the Structural Member Style are listed here. This is where the Structural Member Shapes that we just explored are assigned to the Structural Member Style. A basic Structural Member Style will have only one Shape. However, it is possible to design a very complex and intricate Member style incorporating several Shapes at various cross sections along the length of the Structural Member. (The Add and Copy buttons at the bottom right of the dialog would be used to accomplish this.) Member styles can be tapered, and a variety of parameters such as rotations, mirroring and offsets can be built into the style. To access these advanced functions, click the Show Details button (see the bottom of Figure 6.7). We will skip over the remaining tabs at this time.

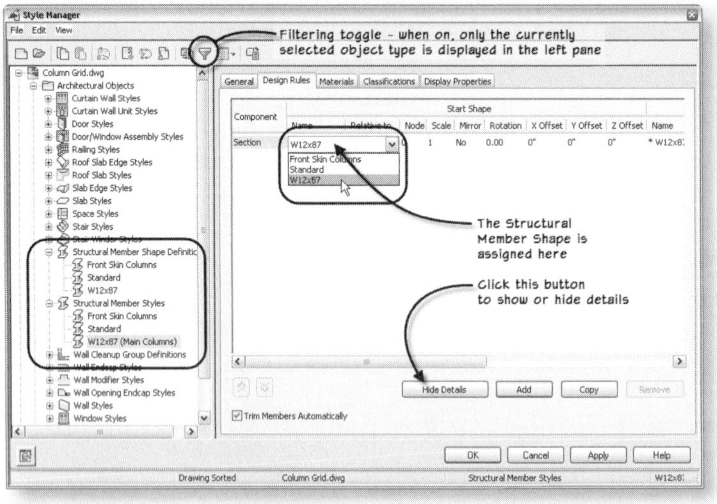

FIGURE 6.7 *Understanding how Structural Member Shapes are assigned to Structural Member Styles*

31. Click OK to dismiss the Style Manager and return to the drawing.

Work with Structural Members

Now that we have seen how to create Structural Styles and how their components fit together, let's use them in the drawing.

1. On the Design tool palette, click the Column tool.

   If you do not see this palette or tool, right-click the Tool Palettes title bar and choose **Design** (to load the Design Tool Palette Group) and then click the Design tab.

2. On the Properties palette, choose W12x87 (Main Columns) [W310x97 (Main Columns)] from the Style drop-down list.

3. At the "Insert point" prompt, click a point anywhere onscreen and then press ENTER to complete the command. Press ENTER again to complete the routine.

   Zoom in as required to see the Column.

Structural members, like most AEC objects, have three levels of detail: Low Detail, Medium Detail and High Detail. In the Style Manager, it was a bit difficult to see each of the Shapes clearly. Let's have a look at the Structural Member in the drawing now in each Display Configuration to see this more clearly. The scale of the drawing will typically determine which level of detail is appropriate (see Figure 6.8).

- **Low Detail**—Single-line diagram, good for small-scale drawings.
- **Medium Detail**—Basic double-line display with square corners; good for 1/8" = 1'-0" [1:100] and 1/4" = 1'-0" [1:50] scales.
- **High Detail**—Shows a high level of detail including filleted corners; good for large-scale details, 1/2" = 1'-0" [1:25] and larger.

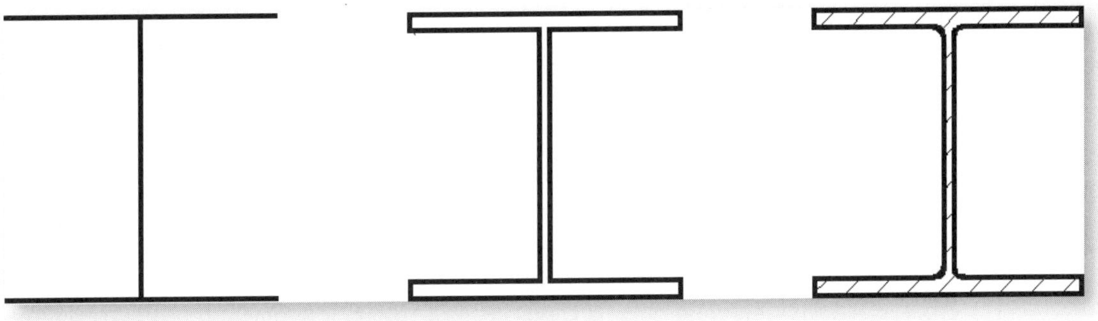

FIGURE 6.8 *Three levels of display detail*

If you are not zoomed in on the Column, zoom in on it now.

4. Change the current Display Configuration to **Low Detail**.

   Note the change to the structural member; a simple line sketch.

5. Change the current Display Configuration to **High Detail**.

Again note the change to the display of the structural member; In High Detail, the fillets and hatching are shown. Hatching is a parameter of the Structural Member Style, not the Shape. Therefore, we did not see hatching in the Style Manager preview above.

6. Change the current Display Configuration back to **Medium Detail**.
7. Erase the Column onscreen before proceeding to the next sequence.
8. Save the file.

COLUMN GRIDS

An overview of layout tools and Anchors appears in the "Anchors" topic of Chapter 2. A Column Grid object is a type of 2D Layout Grid. There are two shapes, rectangular and radial. Grid spacing, orientation and location are controlled parametrically. Spacing can be set to equal spacing, repeat spacing or manual spacing. A Node Anchor point exists at each grid intersection. Column objects can be anchored to these points. Anchored column line labels generate automatically, and AEC dimensions contribute to form a complete assembly of components. It is also possible to create a manual grid from linework. We will explore these features in detail by building the Column Grid layout for our commercial building.

Add a Column Grid with Anchored Columns

1. Zoom back out a bit; on the Design palette, click the Column Grid tool.
2. On the Properties palette, choose **Rectangular** for the Shape.

The overall size of the Column Grid is set in the Width and Depth fields. This should correspond to the size of the overall building footprint. In buildings with a non-rectilinear footprint, you can use more than one grid and set the Width and Depth to the size of the section of the building for which you're designing the grid.

3. In the Dimensions grouping, set the X - Width to **80'-0"** [**24,000**] and set the Y - Depth to **60'-0"** [**18,000**].

There are two ways to set the initial bay spacing within the grid. The total Width or Depth dimension can be divided by a certain quantity of bays. To do this, choose **Space Evenly** from the Layout type list. A fixed bay dimension can also be used. To do this, choose **Repeat** for the Layout type instead. In this example, we will do one of each to compare and contrast.

4. Be sure the X Axis Layout type is set to **Repeat**, and set the X - Baysize to **20'-0"** [**6000**].
5. For the Y Axis Layout type choose **Space evenly**, and set the Number of bays at **3**.
6. In the Column grouping, choose W12x87 (Main Columns) [W310x97 (Main Columns)] from the Style drop-down list.
7. Set the Logical Length to **11'-5"** [**3475**] (see Figure 6.9).

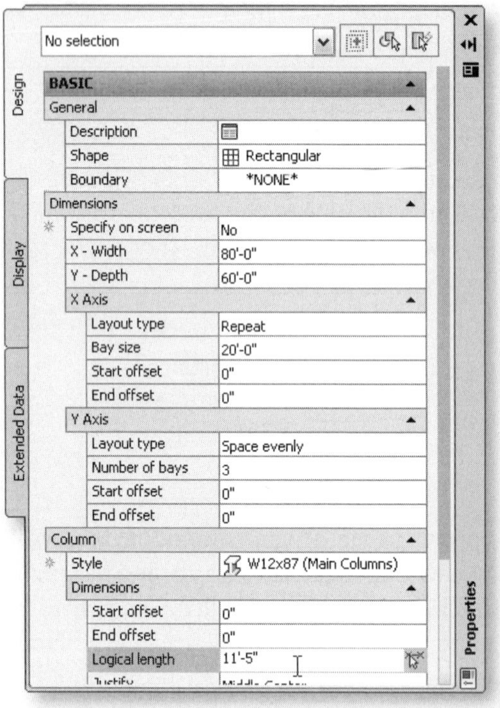

FIGURE 6.9 *Set Structural Grid and Column parameters*

8. At the "Insertion point" Command Line prompt, click a point anywhere onscreen to place the grid.

   Slowly move the mouse and notice that the grid's insertion point is its lower-left corner and that you are able to rotate the grid relative to this point.

9. Press ENTER to accept the default rotation of **0°**. Press ENTER again to complete the routine.

   Zoom out as necessary and notice the appearance of the Grid with a Column at each intersection (see Figure 6.10).

FIGURE 6.10 *A Column Grid with anchored columns*

Move Column Grids and Columns

If you try to move the Column Grid Object, you will notice that all columns move with it. This is the effect of the anchor used to link the Columns to the Grid. Likewise, if you try to move a single column a small amount (say 3'-0" [900] in any direction), it would seem that the column did not move at all. If instead you try to move the column nearly a full bay or more, it would seem to have disappeared. In fact, what has happened is that it has moved to a different Node. The reasons behind the behavior of the column are explained in the rules of the Node Anchor relationship which states that the middle center point at the base of the column must be attached to a grid intersection—it does not matter which one. Therefore, if you move too far, you force it to "jump" to the next Node. If you did such a move and then made a window selection around the Node you moved toward, you would find that there would now actually be two Columns located there. If you tried any of these experiments, undo the changes before proceeding.

TIP

You can undo a series of Zoom and Pan commands with a single Undo. To enable this feature, choose **Options** from the Application Menu and then click the User Preferences tab. Place a check mark in the "Combine zoom and pan commands" checkbox and then click OK.

Identify Anchors

It is not always obvious when objects are anchored to one another. Over time, with practice and experience it does become more obvious, but initially it can be a little confusing. The next few steps are an exercise designed to help you identify when objects are anchored. There are a few simple techniques.

10. Select any Column and right-click (see Figure 6.11).

    Notice the Node Anchor item on the right-click menu. The presence of this sub-menu indicates that the object is anchored. (The type of Anchor varies, such as Wall Anchor, Cell Anchor, Leader Anchor or Node Anchor, as is the case here.) Review the different options on the Node Anchor menu. Make sure to undo any changes after you are done.

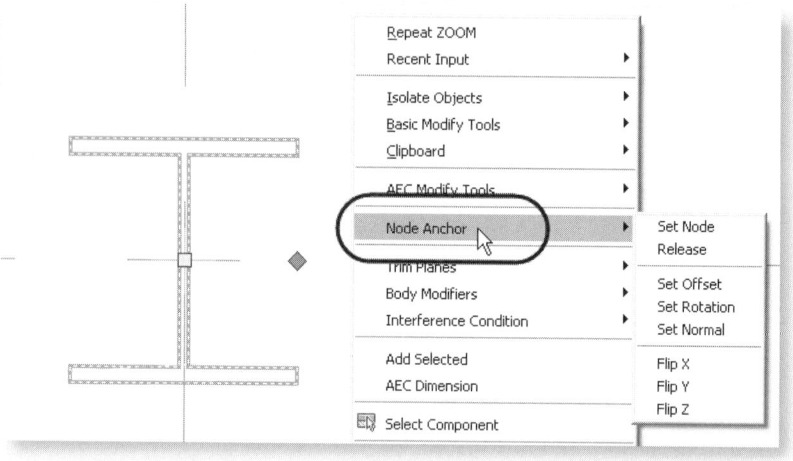

FIGURE 6.11 *An "Anchor" sub-menu indicates the presence of an anchor*

11. Choose **Properties** from the right-click menu.

    In the Location grouping, notice that there is a "Location on node" grouping and that an Anchor worksheet icon is present beneath it. An Anchor worksheet icon will always be present in the Properties palette for any object with an anchor. Clicking this icon (See Figure 6.12) will open a worksheet with some of the same parameters as in Figure 6.11.

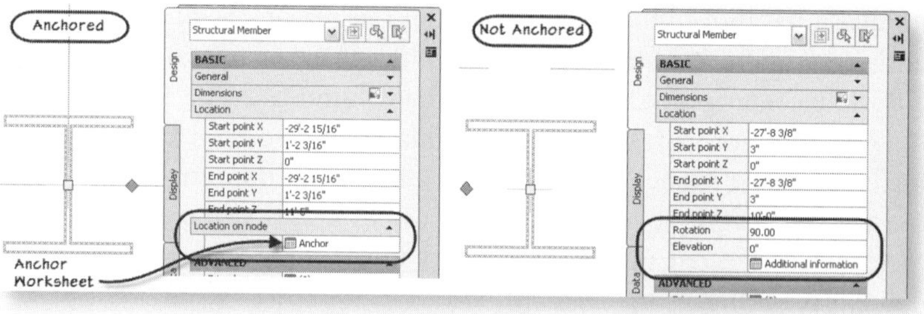

FIGURE 6.12 *Identifying the presence of an anchor on the Properties palette*

Move the Grid to the Correct Coordinates

When we added the Column Grid object, we placed it randomly. Because this object is not anchored to another, it can move and rotate freely and all of the anchored columns will automatically follow. Notice the absence of an Anchor option under the right-click menu of the Grid. In order for this Column Grid to be useful in our

Commercial Project, we need to locate it correctly relative to the rest of the building. To do this, we will XREF one of the floors.

1. Open the Project Navigator palette if it is not already open (Quick Access Toolbar, or CTRL + 5).
2. On the Constructs tab, drag the *01 Shell and Core* file (in the Constructs folder) and drop it anywhere onscreen (see Figure 6.13).

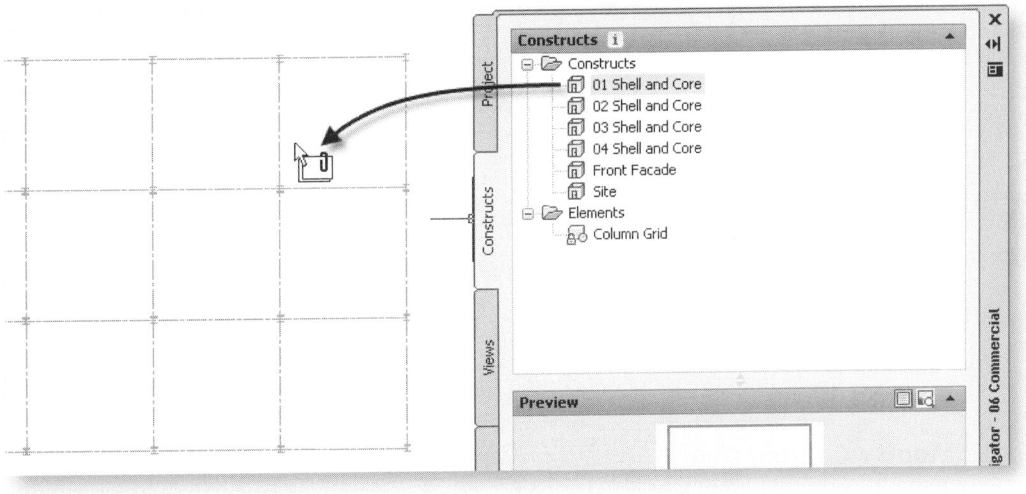

FIGURE 6.13 *XREF the First Floor Shell for reference when placing the grid*

This gives us the First Floor Walls to use for reference so that we can place the Grid in the correct location. You can use this technique anytime you want to use another floor's geometry for reference. To save you a bit of trouble, however, the exact coordinates are provided in the next few steps.

3. Select the Column Grid (just the Grid, not any Columns) and then right-click and choose **Properties**.
4. In the Location grouping, click the Additional Information worksheet icon.
5. In the Insertion Point X field, type **105'-5"** [**32,130**], in the Y field, type **53'-0"** [**16,154**], and then click OK (see Figure 6.14).

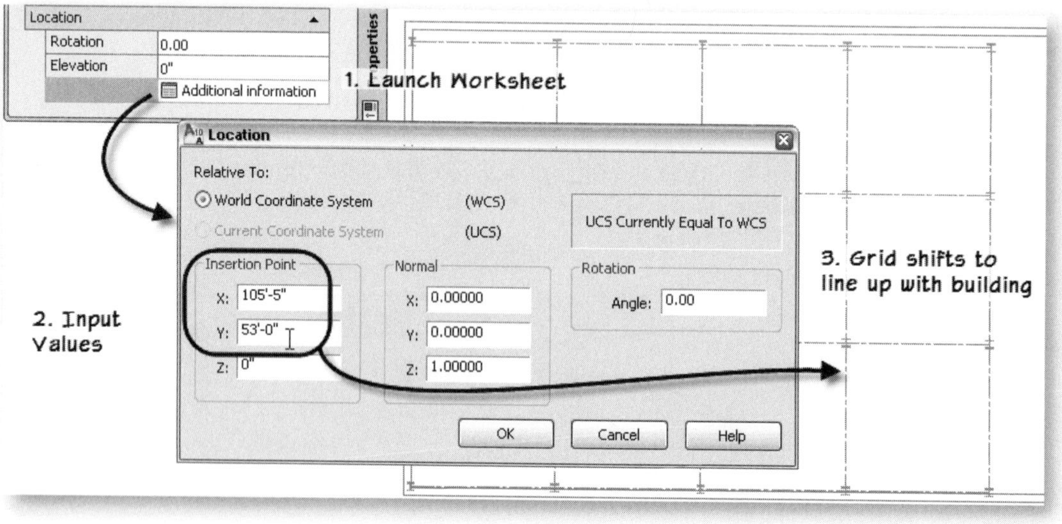

FIGURE 6.14 *Open Location worksheet and input coordinates of building footprint*

Notice the grid and its anchored Columns shift to its new location.

Modify Column Grids

The parameters established for the grid upon creation continue to control its dimensions as modifications are made.

6. Select the Column Grid object.

   Notice the four grip points, one at each corner of the grid.
7. Click the upper-right grip point to make it hot.
8. Slowly drag the grip up and to the right. Do NOT click yet.
9. Move about half a bay in each direction.

   Notice that the bays in the X direction do not appear to be affected; however, in the Y direction, the spacing is changing dynamically as the mouse moves.
10. Continue moving the mouse slowly up and to the right.

    Notice that at approximately one bay width to the right, a new bay begins to appear.

The behavior in both the Y and the X directions is simply based on the original parameters set at the time of creation. We built this grid to use a fixed bay size of 20'-0" [6000] in the X direction and to evenly space the entire Depth (Y direction) by 3 bays.

11. Click the mouse anywhere to finalize the change and add one bay to the right.

    Notice that new Columns were *not* added in the X direction.

When you add a Column Grid, you are able to simultaneously add Columns, but these are separate and distinct objects. To add Columns to the new bay, we would need to add them manually. This can be accomplished with the Column tool on the Design tool palette or simply by copying one of the existing Columns. When copying an object with anchors, the copy will *also* be anchored. Try it out.

12. Select all four Columns (just the Columns, not the grid) at the extreme right of the grid.

13. On the Home ribbon tab on the Modify panel, choose the ***Copy*** tool (on the second row, middle button; not the ***Copy to Clipboard*** tool on the expanded Modify panel).

CAUTION

If you use the Copy to Clipboard tool on an anchored object, it will also copy the parent object when pasted, thereby anchoring the newly copied objects to this newly copied parent object. This is not what we want in this case.

14. Click a "Base point" near the original Columns and a "Second point of Displacement" near the new bay.
15. Be sure to press ENTER to complete the Copy command.

Because of the anchor, we do not need to use Object Snaps on this operation. The rules built into the anchor have higher priority to ACA than Object Snaps. As a rule, however, using Object Snaps is always a good idea; particularly when Anchors are not involved. Many objects do not use anchors, and for them, Object Snaps are often the only way to guarantee accuracy.

You should now have a five-bay-wide by three-bay-high Column grid with Columns anchored to all points.

16. Save the file.

Manipulate Column Line Spacing

It is rare that a building has a perfectly regular Column grid bay spacing. The automatic spacing we used in the beginning of this exercise is a good way to get started, but the grid will likely need to be manipulated manually to achieve the proper spacing of bays in your design.

1. Continuing in the *Column Grid* file, select the Column Grid, right-click and choose **Properties**.

   In the Dimensions grouping, notice that the X Width and the Y Depth parameters have both changed because of the grip editing in the last sequence.

2. In both the X-Axis and the Y-Axis groupings change the Layout type to **Manual**.

   Notice the appearance of grips at each of the grid lines in the X and Y directions. Notice also that all parameters on the Properties palette have been replaced with a worksheet icon.

3. Near the bottom-left corner of the grid, select the second grip point from the left to make it hot (see Figure 6.15).

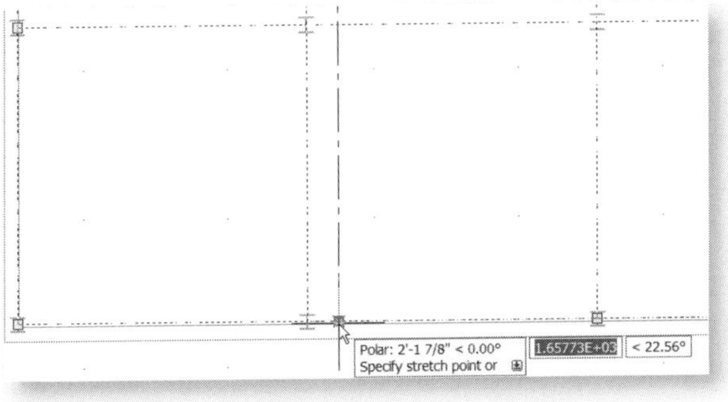

FIGURE 6.15 *Select the grip point of a single grid line*

4. Make sure that either POLAR or ORTHO is on and Dynamic Input is off, move the mouse directly to the right, type **2'-7"** [**860**], and then press ENTER.

   Notice that only the selected grid line has shifted and that each of the anchored Columns along its length has shifted with it.

This method is effective for simple modifications where immediate feedback is needed. However, if several bays need to shift, it is easier to perform the change in the Column Grid Properties worksheet.

5. On the Properties palette, in the Dimensions > X-Axis grouping, click the worksheet icon next to Bays.

   Notice that each Column Line in the X direction is listed with two sets of dimensions.

- **Distance to Line**—is measured from the origin (lower-left corner) of the grid.
- **Spacing**—is measured from the previous grid line.

6. Type **14'-4"** [**4400**] in the Spacing Column for Column Line Number 2 and press ENTER.

   Notice that the difference between the new value and the old value has been applied to the next Column Line (Number 3) and that each Column Line in the X direction is listed with two sets of dimensions.

TIP

For this reason, you should always begin at the top of the list and work your way down.

7. Work your way down the list and set the following values: Column Line 3 = **28'-0"** [**8500**], Column Line 4 = **14'-4"** [**4400**], Column Line 5 = **22'-7"** [**6860**] (see Figure 6.16).

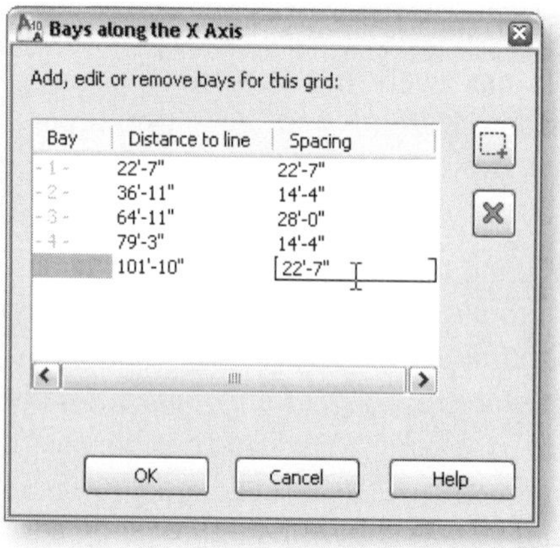

FIGURE 6.16 *Change the values of the grid lines in the X Axis*

   Notice that as you change the Spacing values, the Distance to Line values also change.

8. Click OK to close the Bays along the X-Axis worksheet.
9. Click the worksheet icon next to Bays in the Dimensions > Y-Axis grouping.
10. Set the Spacing for each grid line as follows: Column Line 1 = **20'-0"** [**6100**], Column Line 2 = **21'-9"** [**6600**], Column Line 3 = **20'-0"** [**6100**].
11. Click OK to close Bays along the Y-Axis worksheet.

12. Right-click in the drawing and choose **Deselect All**.
13. Save the file.

Rotate an Anchored Column

Column orientation can be adjusted to suit design needs. When objects are anchored to the grid as these Columns are, the standard AutoCAD Rotate command will not do the trick. We must change the parameters governing the anchor of the Columns we wish to rotate. Fortunately this is easy to do with grips.

If you previously turned off Dynamic Input, please turn it back on now.

14. Select one of the Columns on the left edge of the grid.
15. Click the diamond-shaped grip and move the mouse.

    Notice the dynamic angular dimensions that appears.
16. Type **90°** and then press ENTER.

NOTE

The degree symbol (°) is used here for clarity. You need only type "90" into the dynamic dimension to rotate. ACA is already expecting input in degrees for this value.

You can use this method to rotate all of the Columns on the left and right edges one at a time, or it is possible to perform the rotation on all of them at once. The method to do so, however, is not quite as intuitive.

17. Select all of the Columns on both the extreme left bay and the extreme right bay. (Do NOT select any Columns in the middle.)
18. On the Properties palette, click the Anchor worksheet in the Location on node grouping.
19. In the Orientation area, change the Rotation Y to **90°** and then click OK.

TIP

If you prefer, you can perform this rotation on all selected Columns via the right-click menu instead. With them selected, right-click and choose Node Anchor > Set Rotation, and then input 90° for each of the X, Y and Z rotations.

Why Rotate "Y"?

A Structural Member can be a Column, a Beam or a Brace. Each of these items has a different default orientation. If all of the rotation values were set to **0°**, we would essentially have a Beam. Therefore, although not very intuitive, in this case rotating the Y value was appropriate to achieve the desired effect. Had we been rotating any other anchored object in the plan (such as a piece of furniture, a light fixture, etc.) we would have actually been rotating around the Z axis instead.

Remove Unnecessary Columns

The front of the building (at the bottom of the screen) will receive a curtain wall in an upcoming chapter. A secondary Column Grid will be placed here with a different type of Column. Therefore, we will remove the unnecessary Columns at the bottom row of the grid.

20. Select the two middle Columns along the bottom row.
21. On the Home ribbon tab on the Modify panel, choose the ***Erase*** tool (on the second row, left button, or just press DELETE).
22. Save the file.

Convert Linework to a Column Grid

Along the front of the building will be a gently curved curtain wall. To provide support for this object, we will create a second Column Grid object. Sometimes it is easier to simply draw the grid we want with lines and then convert those lines into a Column Grid.

1. Click on the Manage XREFs quick pick icon located in the lower-right of the Drawing status bar (looks like a small binder clip—or type XR and then press ENTER).
2. Select the *01 Shell and Core* XREF, right-click and choose **Detach** from the menu. Close the External References palette, or allow it to auto-hide.

   This will make it easier to see the grid as we work.
3. From the second grid intersection of the bottom-left corner of the grid, draw a Line **6'** [**1800**] long straight down (270°).

TIP

Zoom in as required to snap accurately to the Endpoint of the Column Grid, and not to the points on the Column (or use a Node object snap on the Column Grid near the second grid intersection). This is where a wheel mouse comes in very handy for zooming.

4. Repeat for the next three grid intersections moving to the right or just copy this line three times (see Figure 6.17).

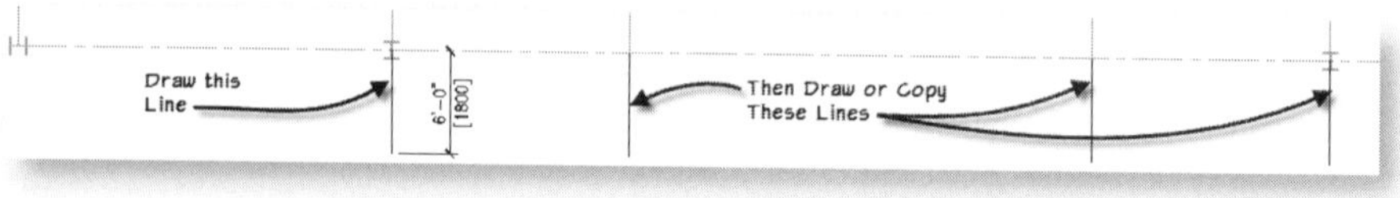

FIGURE 6.17 *Draw the vertical grid lines for the second Column Grid*

5. Offset the two inner lines **9'-0"** [**2700**] toward the middle (see Figure 6.18).

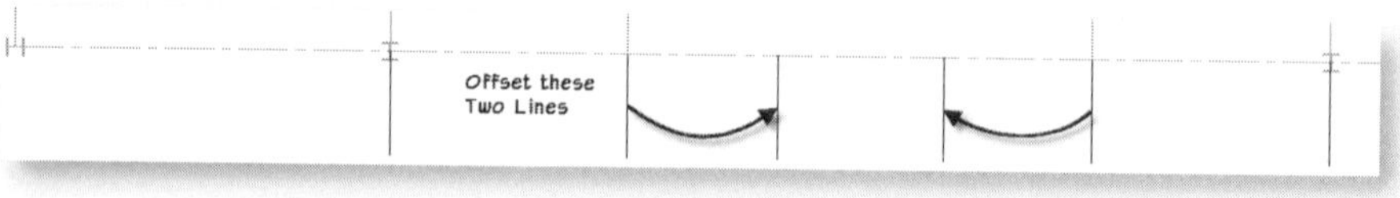

FIGURE 6.18 *Offset two additional vertical lines*

6. Draw a line from the bottom endpoint of the line at the far left to the bottom endpoint of the line at the far right.
7. Offset this line up **8"** [**200**].
8. Move both horizontal lines up **2'-0"** [**610**] (see Figure 6.19).

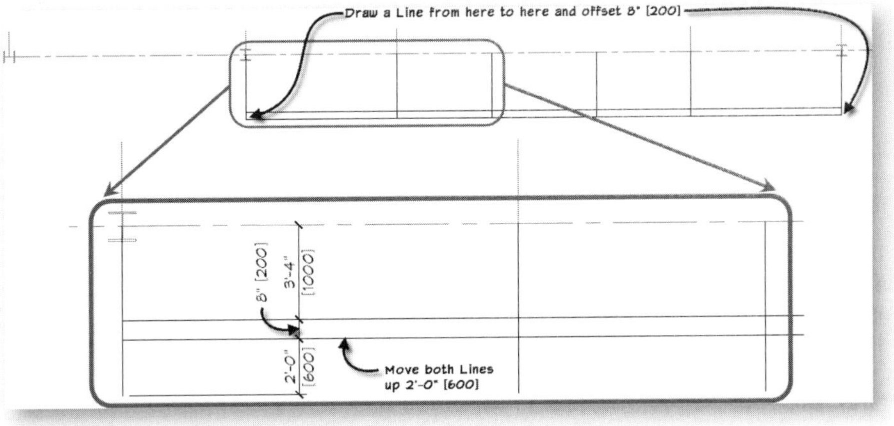

FIGURE 6.19 *Complete the grid lines with two horizontal lines*

9. On the right side, extend each of the horizontal lines about **12'-0"** [**3600**] using the grips.
10. On the Design palette, right-click the Column Grid tool and choose **Apply Tool Properties to > Linework**.
11. Select the eight lines just drawn and then press ENTER.
12. At the "Erase selected linework?" prompt, choose **Yes**.

You should now have a small custom Column Grid in place of the lines.

Add Columns to the New Grid

13. On the Design tool palette, click the Column tool and on the Properties palette, change the Style to **Front Skin Columns** and the Logical Length to **11'-5" [3475]**.

    The prompt will read: "Insert Point."
14. On the Application status bar turn off the Osnaps by clicking the Object Snap toggle (or press F3 on the keyboard).

Columns will automatically Anchor to a Grid if you click on one. As you move the mouse around onscreen, if you hover over a Grid, you will see this behavior and options will appear at the cursor. This is why we will temporarily turn off the Osnaps.

15. Move the mouse over the new Grid that we just created and pause for a moment—do not click yet (see Figure 6.20).

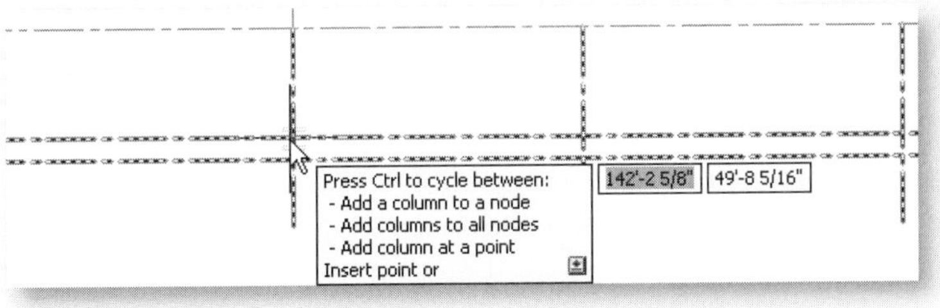

FIGURE 6.20 *Hover over a Grid to see automatic Node Anchor options*

- **Add a column to a node**—This is the default option and will add a single column to a single node on which you click.
- **Add a column to all nodes**—Press CTRL once to toggle to this option. A column will be attached to all nodes with a single click.
- **Add column at a point**—This simply adds a freestanding, non-anchored column.

If you wish to try the "all nodes" option, feel free to do so. Just Undo before proceeding to the next step.

16. At the "Insert point" prompt, click on each of the intersections indicated as "Add New Columns" in Figure 6.21 and then press ENTER.

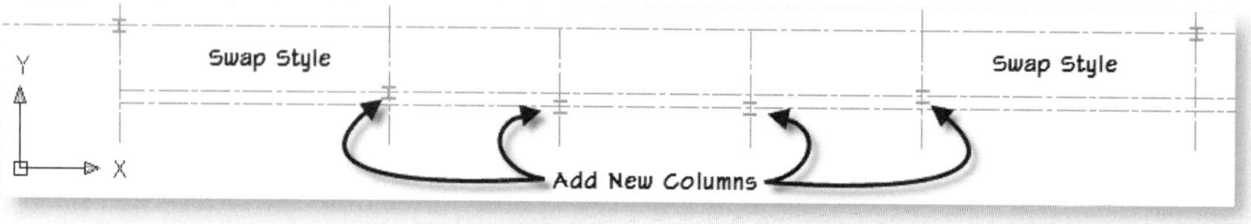

FIGURE 6.21 *Add Front Skin Columns to new Column Grid by picking the nodes*

17. Select the two Columns (on the original grid) indicated as "Swap Style" in Figure 6.21 and change the Style on the Properties palette to **Front Skin Columns**.
18. Right-click and choose **Deselect All**, and then Save the file.

Add and Delete Grid Lines

Column Grids (both parametric and manual) can be further manipulated. While in the Column Grid Bays worksheet, in either the X or Y direction, click in the blank space below to add a new grid line. Select a grid line by clicking in the Number column. Delete a grid line by selecting it by number and pressing DELETE. Grid lines can also be added and deleted in the drawing using the Column Grid contextual ribbon tab. To do this, select the grid, and then on the Column Grid ribbon tab on the X-Axis panel choose the ***Add Grid Line*** or ***Remove Grid Line*** tool or on the Y-Axis panel choose the ***Add Grid Line*** tool, etc. To add grid lines to a manual grid, draw the line in the place where you want it, then select the manual grid and on the Column Grid contextual ribbon tab on the Custom Grid panel, choose the ***Add Grid Lines*** tool. Choose ***Remove Grid Lines*** from the same panel to delete a line. Notice that the Column Grid ribbon panel knows what type of grid(s) have been selected, and disables the commands that do not apply. If you select both a parametric and a manual Column Grid, all three panels (X Axis, Y Axis and Custom Grid) will be disabled. Feel free to experiment with some of these techniques before continuing. Either Undo to return the file to the point saved here, or save the file before you begin experimenting and then simply close the file without saving when you are done and then reopen it to continue.

COLUMN GRID LABELS AND DIMENSIONS

Once you have a Column Grid, grid labeling and dimensioning can be accomplished easily. Grid labels are Multi-View Blocks with Leader Anchors to attach them to the Grid. The dimensioning routine provided quickly adds AEC

Dimensions in two strings. These dimensions stay linked to the Grid and update as the Grid changes.

Set Drawing Scale

1. From the Application Menu, choose **Utilities > Drawing Setup**.
2. Click the Scale tab. In the Annotation Plot Size box, type **5/32"** [**4**].

   This value works with the Drawing Scale to determine the final scale factor used for scaling annotation symbols. The value typed here represents the final plotted height of the text portion of annotation symbols. The default is **3/32"** [**3.5**] but for Column Bubbles you will typically want a larger value.

CAUTION

The Scale list, which could be used to set the drawing scale in the 2008 and prior releases, can now only be used to review the scales defined for the current drawing and to associate a Display Configuration with a particular scale. Set the drawing scale from list on the Drawing status bar.

3. Click OK and choose the "Update to match my changes" option that appears.
4. On the Drawing status bar, use the Scale list to set the drawing scale to **1/8" = 1'-0"** [**1:100**].

   ACA annotation objects and symbols will automatically scale relative to this setting.
5. Click OK.

Typically, Scale and Annotation Plot Size settings are configured properly in each ACA View file in Project Navigator (see Chapter 14 for more information). Regardless, it is a good habit to check this setting before adding annotation to the drawing. Changing this setting after annotation is placed will also cause existing annotation to be resized (a REGEN may be needed to see the effect). If necessary, existing ACA Annotation objects can be scaled after insertion on the Properties palette.

MANAGER NOTE CAD

In general, if you refer back to the "Elements, Constructs, Views and Sheets (Project Drawing Files)" heading in Chapter 5, you will note that you are intended to build your model geometry in Constructs and that annotation should be added to Views. However, Column Grids present a bit of a limitation with regard to the annotation in this approach. The limitation is a function of the Anchors that are used with Grids. Technically, the Columns which are part of the model should be in Constructs (or Elements as we are doing here) and the Grid which is actually technically annotation should be in the View file. The same would be true of the bubbles and the dimensions. However, Anchors unfortunately do not function across XREFs. Therefore, in order to keep all of the parts anchored, the Columns, Grid, Bubbles and Dimensions are all typically kept together in the Construct or Element file. Theoretically you could choose not to Anchor these objects and thereby place them in the proper file. However, this is a situation where "breaking the rule" is considered to have more benefit overall than following it. Therefore, it is recommended that you keep all of these components together in the Construct or Element file as we are doing here in your own projects.

Add Column Grid Labels

6. Select the main grid, and on the Column Grid contextual ribbon tab on the Label panel, choose the ***Label*** tool.

7. In the Column Grid Labeling dialog box, on the X - Labeling tab, put a check mark in the "Automatically Calculate Values for Labels" checkbox.

This will automatically calculate the values of the labels based on the first value you enter.

8. In the Automatic Labeling Rules area, choose **Ascending**, place a check mark in the Never Use Characters checkbox, and type **I,O** in the text field. (Be sure to type this uppercase.)

This will allow you to type certain characters that you wish to have the software skip when calculating the automatic numbering values (in this case, capital "I" because it looks very similar to "1" and capital "O" because it looks very similar to "0").

9. In the Bubble Parameters area, place a check mark in both "Top" and "Bottom" checkboxes and set the Extension to **12'-0"** [**4000**].

These settings will add bubbles to both the top and bottom of the plan and will place them 12'-0" [4000] away from the edge of the grid. Choose this value based on the size of your project and the scale at which it will print.

10. Make sure "Generate New Bubbles On Exit" is checked.

    This will replace any labels already in the drawing and add new ones.

    This is valuable if you renumber the column lines during design.

11. On the left side of the dialog box, type **H** (uppercase) in the first Number box and then press ENTER.

    Notice how the remaining values fill in automatically based on the parameters we set, including skipping the letter "I."

12. Click the Y - Labeling tab.
13. Set everything the same as on the X - Labeling tab, except type **1** for the first value this time (see Figure 6.22).

TIP

It is not necessary to choose "Never Use Characters" on the Y Labeling because we are labeling with numerals here rather than letters.

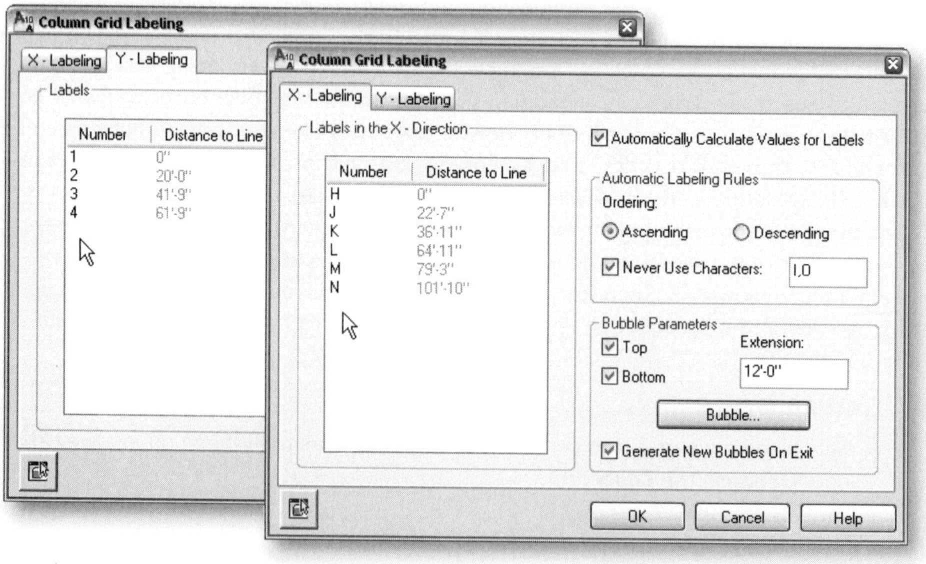

FIGURE 6.22 *Configure the Column Grid Labels*

14. Click OK to add the labels.

TIP

If you make a mistake while labeling, just select the *Label* tool again, adjust the settings and click OK. The column bubbles will be adjusted to the proper settings, provided you place a check mark in the "Generate New Bubbles on Exit" checkbox.

Create Grid Line Extensions and Load the Commercial Palette

In many cases, the labels are desired on only one side of the plan. This is easy enough to accomplish by simply not checking one of the choices of Top, Bottom, Left or Right as the bubbles are being added. However, it is also often desirable to have the column grid lines extend past the end of the grid. There is no Grid parameter to do this, which is why we added bubbles to both sides. The following steps illustrate a workaround that will resolve this situation and convert the bubble on one side to grid extensions.

In order to understand the logic, it is necessary to understand exactly what the column bubbles are in ACA. As covered in Chapter 4, a Multi-View Block (MVB) is an AEC object containing one or more AutoCAD blocks. The Grid bubbles use an MVB called "StandardGridBubble." This MVB is anchored to the Column Grid using a Column Grid Anchor. The Column Grid Anchor behaves similarly to the Node Anchor, except that a visible leader attaches it to the Grid Node. (See the discussion on Anchors in Chapter 2 and in the headings above.) If you click on one of the bubbles, you will note that the leader is highlighted with the bubble. If you delete one of the bubbles, you will note that the leader is deleted as well—the two are connected and cannot be separated. What we need to do is make one set of bubbles in each direction where the actual bubble is *invisible.* We can make the bubble invisible without losing the leader. When we do this, it will "appear" as though the grid lines extend past the limit of the grid.

We will open Content Browser to access a custom Multi-View Block tool that we will use to swap out the bubble on one side to create extensions. The Mastering AutoCAD Architecture 2010 catalog should already be loaded in your Content Browser library. This was done in the "Load Custom Tool Palette" topic in Chapter 4. If you did not complete Chapter 4, please refer to that topic for instructions on how to load the catalog.

15. Right-click the Tool Palettes title bar and choose **MasterACA** to load the Tool Palette Group created in Chapter 3.

This group should contain the Chapter 02 and the MACA Residential palettes. We will now add the MACA Commercial palette.

16. On the Home tab, click Tools drop-down button and choose Content Browser.
17. Click on the *Mastering AutoCAD Architecture 2010* catalog (loaded in Chapter 4) top open it.
18. Click and hold down the mouse on the small eyedropper icon for the *MACA Commercial* [*MACA Commercial - Metric*] tool palette and drag it into the ACA drawing window (see Figure 6.23).

    A new *MACA Commercial* [*MACA Commercial - Metric*] tab will appear on your Tool Palettes.

Several tools will appear on the palette. For this exercise, we only need the Grid Bubble Extension tool. The others will be used in later chapters.

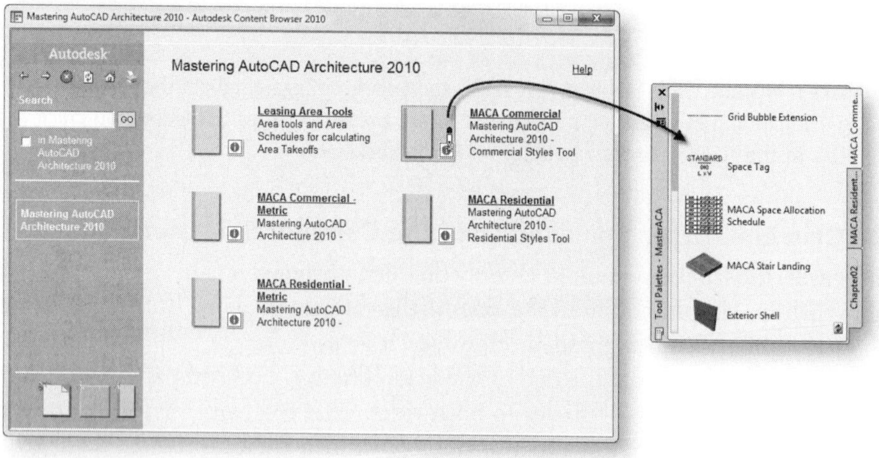

FIGURE 6.23 *iDrop the MACA Commercial tool palette and add it to the MasterACA tool palette group*

19. Carefully select all of the bubbles at the bottom and right sides of the plan.
20. Right-click on the Grid Bubble Extension tool on the MACA Commercial [MACA Commercial – Metric] tool palette and choose **Apply Tool Properties to Multi-View Block Reference**.

    Notice the change to the drawing. It now appears as though there are grid line extensions.

If you wish to see what makes this Multi-View Block display this way, select one of the Column Grid Extensions and on the Multi-View Block contextual ribbon tab on the General panel, choose the ***Edit Style*** tool (top half of the split button). Then click the View Blocks tab and notice if you click the General or Model Display Representation on the left, all the View Direction checkboxes are cleared on the right. Even though a View Block named BubbleDef is loaded, by having no boxes checked, it is effectively *invisible*. Therefore, all we see in the drawing is the extension line that is the Column Bubble Anchor (a type of Leader Anchor).

If you prefer, you can create this Multi-View Block yourself rather than use the provided tool. To do this, select all of the Bubbles on the bottom and the right, and on the Multi-View Block contextual ribbon tab on the General panel, choose the ***Save As*** tool. On the General tab, rename it to: **Grid Bubble Extension** and on the View Blocks tab, deselect all checkboxes in both the General and Model Display Reps. Click OK to see the results.

CAD MANAGER NOTE

This method might seem a bit complicated, and it might be tempting to add labels to only two sides and create the extension by drawing a line manually. This practice is NOT recommended. The line workaround is not properly anchored to the grid. AutoCAD objects such as lines cannot use anchors. The workaround suggested above, although not perfect, keeps the Grid intact and can be modified globally by editing the Multi-View Block to modify the bubbles back to the original or to a new graphic standard. In addition, if Column Grid lines move, the extensions created in the technique above will move as well since they are anchored. Give it a try.

Add Labels and Extensions to the Second Grid

The second Grid is a manual Grid created from linework. Manual Grids do not use the automatic labeling routine. Instead we will use the Column Bubble tool on the Annotation tool palette.

21. Right-click on the title bar of the Tool Palettes, load the **Document** group and then click the Annotation tool palette. On the Annotation tool palette, click the Column Bubble tool.
22. At the "Select node to label" prompt, click the vertical line just to the right of Column Line K.
23. In the Create Grid Bubble dialog box, type **K.3** for the Label, and set the Extension to **8'-0"** [**2400**] (see Figure 6.24). Click OK.

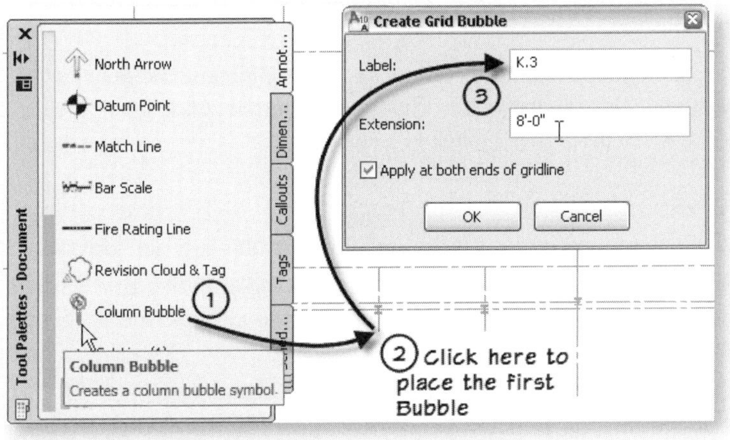

FIGURE 6.24 *Add a manual Grid Bubble*

The prompt will repeat.

24. At the "Select node to label" prompt, click the vertical line just to the left of Column Line L (and the right of the one you just labeled).
25. In the Create Grid Bubble dialog box, type **K.7** for the Label this time, leave the Extension set as is.
26. Repeat the process again for the two horizontal grid lines. Add the bubbles only to the left this time by clearing the "Apply at both ends of gridline" checkbox.

    Use **0** and **0.1** for the Labels and **12'-0"** [**4000**] for the Extension.
27. Click OK to complete the routine.
28. Adjust the Bubbles with Grips.
29. Select the two bubbles (K.3 and K.7) at the top.
30. On the Properties palette, change the Definition to **GridBubbleExtension**. (Or repeat the steps above to apply the Grid Bubble Extension tool properties.)
31. Click on bubble 0 at the left.
32. Click the grip point in the middle of the leader to make it hot.
33. Move the mouse straight down (using Polar Tracking or Ortho Mode), type **6'-0"** [**1800**] and press ENTER (see Figure 6.25).

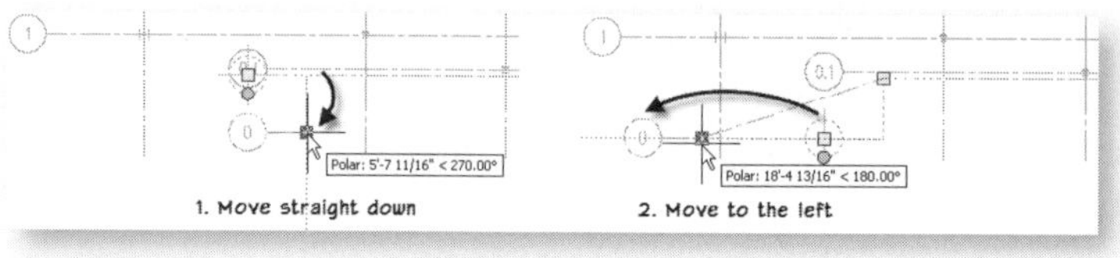

FIGURE 6.25 *Grip editing bubble extensions*

34. Click the same grip point again and move it directly to the left **22'-7"** [**6860**]. This will make it line up with the bubbles from the other grid.
35. Repeat with Grid line 0.1 moving it down only **2'-0"** [**600**] this time. Move it to the left by the same amount.

TIP

If you have trouble grip editing the Grid lines, temporarily turn off the Dynamic Input toggle on the Application status bar.

Grid bubble values can be modified manually without regenerating all of the bubbles by right-clicking the bubble you wish to change and choosing Properties. Click the Attribute worksheet icon in the Advanced properties grouping.

Add AEC Dimensions

36. On the Dimensions tool palette, click the AEC Dimension - Exterior tool.

    If you do not see this palette or tool, right-click the Tool Palettes title bar and choose **Document** (to load the Document Tool Palette Group), and then click the Dimensions tab.
37. Select the top horizontal edge of the main Column Grid and then press ENTER.
38. Click a point above the grid to place the Dimensions.

TIP

Tweak dimension placement by using the small triangular-shaped grip.

39. Repeat the Dimensions steps on the left side of the grid.
40. Select one of the dimensions and on the AEC Dimension contextual ribbon tab on the General panel choose the ***Save As*** tool.
41. In the dialog that appears, name the new style **Column Grid**.
42. Click the Chains tab and change the Number of Chains to 2.
43. Click the Display Properties tab, select Plan and then click the Properties icon on the right.
44. In the Display Properties dialog, on the Other tab, place a check mark in the Use Fixed Length Extension Lines checkbox and then click OK twice.
45. Select the other AEC Dimension object and on the Properties palette, change it to the new Column Grid style (see Figure 6.26).

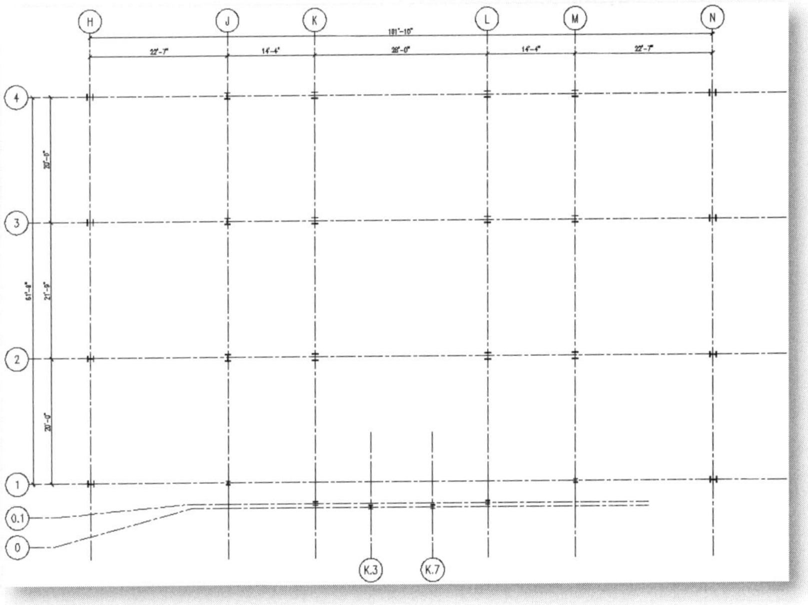

FIGURE 6.26 *The complete Column Grid*

46. Save the file.

NOTE

Both the parametric Column Grid and the manual (converted from linework) grid were showcased here. Both techniques are suitable for creating Column Grids for use in real projects. The choice of which technique to use is largely a matter of personal preference. Parametric grids work well for repetitive spacing while manual grids work well for irregular spacing and orientation. Sometimes using a little of both is appropriate (as we have done here).

STRUCTURAL FRAMING

So far we have limited our exploration of Structural Members to Columns only. Beams and Braces are also part of the AutoCAD Architecture structural toolset. Let's explore these now.

Add Beams

Let's start by revisiting the Structural Member Catalog and importing some more shapes.

1. Following the steps above in the "Access the Structural Member Catalog" heading, create two new Structural Member Styles: W18x40 [W460x52] and L6x6x3_8 [L152x152x9.5].

   Name them **W18x40 (Beams)** [**W460x52 (Beams)**] and **L6x6x3_8 (Braces)** [**L152x152x9.5 (Braces)**]

We'll use the "W" shape for the Beam in this exercise. Later we will use the "L" shape for the Braces.

2. Close the Structural Member catalog when finished.
3. On the floating View ribbon panel (if you have it docked, it is on the Home ribbon tab), choose the ***View, SE Isometric*** tool.
4. Right-click on the title bar of the Tool Palettes, load the **Design** group and then click the Design tool palette. On the Design tool palette, click the Beam tool.
5. On the Properties palette, choose W18x40 (Beams) [W460x52 (Beams)] for the Style.
6. In the Dimensions Grouping, choose **Edge** for Layout Type.

The Edge option will place beams along grid lines between two columns. The Fill option will array the Structural Members within one or more bays.

7. Slowly move your cursor around onscreen hovering over the Column Grid—do not click yet.

A tool tip similar to the one we saw above for the columns will appear indicating the various CTRL key options for placing beams. Notice also that this tip changes as you move off of the Grid object. Furthermore, notice that when the Grid highlights, the Beam will automatically match the length of the nearest Grid bay (see Figure 6.27).

TIP

Turn off Object snaps to facilitate the automatic placement of Structural Members. The easiest way to toggle them off is to press the F3 key or click the Object Snap toggle (to make it gray) on the Application status bar.

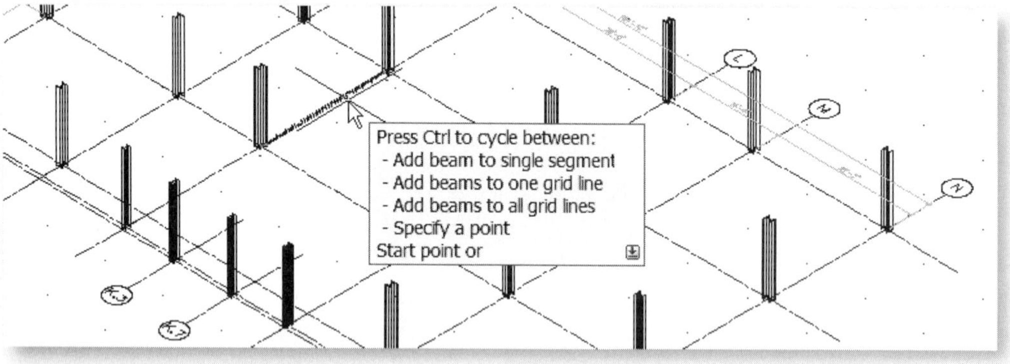

FIGURE 6.27 *Beams have many CTRL key options and automatically match the size of Grid cells*

8. Click the mouse to create a Beam. Press ENTER to end the command.

The only trouble with the Beam that we just placed is that it is attached to the same height as the Grid. We have a tool that can be used to override this behavior.

9. At the bottom of the screen, on the Application status bar, click the number next to the word Elevation (see item 1 in Figure 6.28).
10. In the Elevation Offset worksheet that appears, click the Pick point icon (see item 2 in Figure 6.28).
11. Using your Object Snaps (toggle them back on with F3 if they are still turned off from above) snap a point to the top of one of the columns and then click OK when the Elevation Offset worksheet returns (see item 3 in Figure 6.28).
12. Next to the Elevation value on the Application status bar, click the small Replace Z toggle icon—it will stay pushed in to indicate that it is active (see item 4 in Figure 6.28).

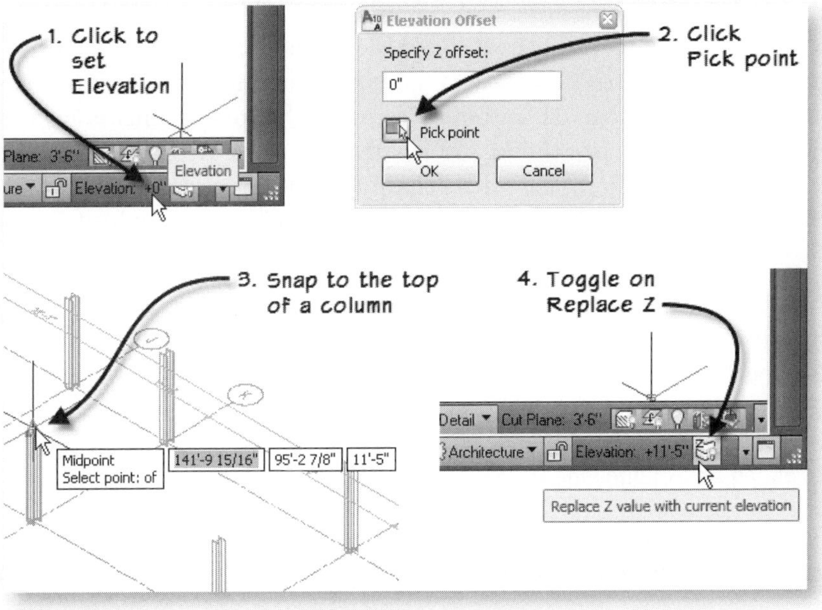

FIGURE 6.28 *Set the Z Elevation snap*

This procedure has now moved the Z Elevation up to the top of the columns. If we repeat the Beam placement from above, the Beams will now appear at the top of the columns. If you still have a stray Beam down at Z = 0, delete it now.

13. On the Design tool palette, click the Beam tool.
14. On the Properties palette, choose W18x40 (Beams) [W460x52 (Beams)] for the Style.
15. From the "Trim automatically" list, choose **Yes**.
16. From the "Layout type" list, choose **Edge**.

    Verify that "Justify" is set to Top Center.
17. Hover over one of the outer edges of the Column Grid—do not click yet.
18. Press the CTRL key once (see middle of Figure 6.29).

    Note that beams will be added to all bays along a single edge.
19. Press the CTRL key again (see right side of Figure 6.29).

    Notice that now Beams will be added to all edges.

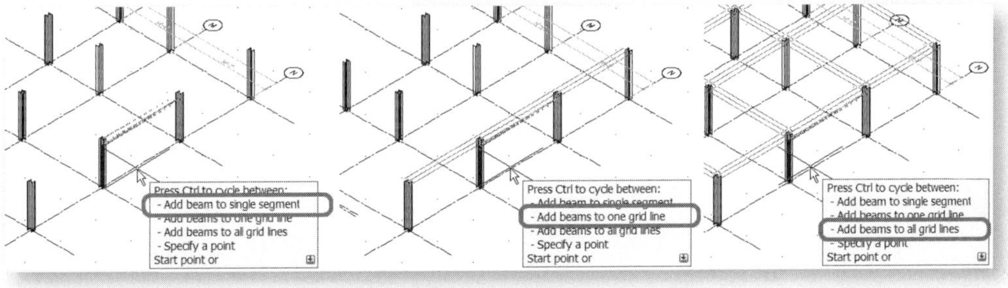

FIGURE 6.29 *Cycling through the Beam placement options*

20. Click the mouse to place the Beams. Press ENTER to end the command.

At this point we have the makings of a nice framing model. However, if you take a look at the front of our building where we added the small manual Grid, the beams don't quite match the columns. This is easy to fix. It is important to realize, however, that all of our Structural Members are currently "connected" to one another in logical ways. Try selecting any Beam or column and lengthening or shortening it with the grips. Notice that when you do so, the other "connected" beams and columns adjust as well. While this behavior looks similar to anchoring, it is not a result of using Anchors. This is special behavior by which Structural Members relate to one another. Undo any grip edit that you made.

21. Delete the Beam on Column Line 1 between lines K and L.
22. Using the lengthen grip (pause over each grip to find lengthen), begin to lengthen the Beam on Column Line K.
23. Press the CTRL key once to toggle off the connected behavior and then snap to the Column on Column Line 0.1.

TIP

Hold down the SHIFT key, right-click and then choose Node Osnap. The Node snap will allow you to easily snap to the middle center of the column.

24. Repeat this process for the Beam on Column Line L.
25. On the Design tool palette, click the Beam tool.

    Verify that all of the previous settings are still configured: "Style" is W18x40 (Beams) [W460x52 (Beams)], "Trim automatically" is **Yes**, "Layout type" is **Edge** and "Justify" is **Top Center**.
26. Move the mouse near the Column at Column Line K0.1. When the Column highlights, click the mouse (no Osnap is necessary).
27. Highlight the free-standing Column at Column Line K0 and click.

    A Beam will appear between these two columns trimmed neatly to fit between them (see Figure 6.30).

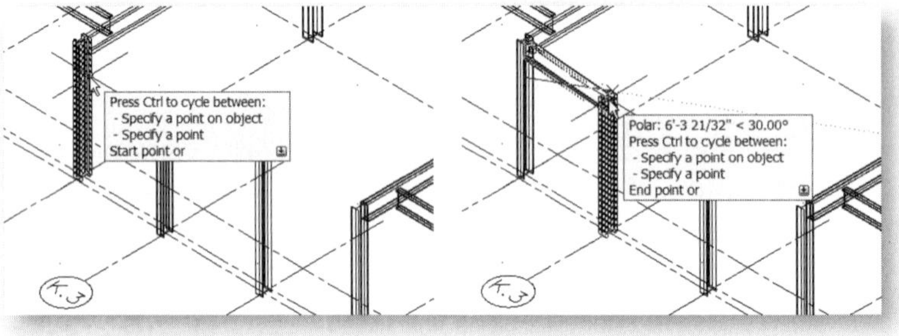

FIGURE 6.30 *Create a Beam that automatically connects to neighboring Columns*

28. Repeat the process to add two more Beams (see Figure 6.31).

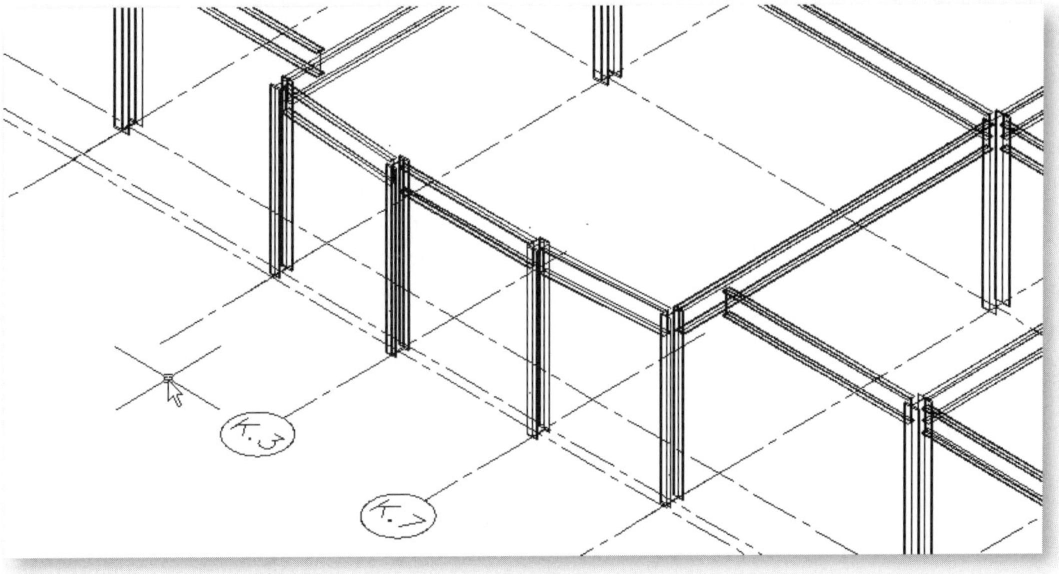

FIGURE 6.31 *Add three Beams to complete the front façade bay*

29. Save the file.

Add Braces

We can add braces using similar methods. Let's add a few Braces where the building core will be. We will add our first brace along Column Line 3 between lines L and M.

30. Zoom into the area near Column Lines K through L and 3 and 4.
31. On the Design tool palette, click the Brace tool.
32. On the Properties palette, choose L6x6x3_8 (Braces) [L152x152x9.5 (Braces)] for the Style.
33. From the "Trim automatically" list, choose **Yes**.
34. From the "Specify rise onscreen" list, choose **No**.
35. For the "Method" choose **Distance** and for both "Distance along first member" and "Distance along second member" type **6'-0"** [**1800**].

TIP

If Replace Z is still toggled on, click on the icon on the Application status bar to turn it off so that your braces do not end up with both ends at the top of the columns.

36. At the "Start point (Pick Beam or Column)" prompt, hover over the Column at grid intersection L3 and then click.
37. At the "End point (Pick Beam or Column)" prompt, hover over the horizontal Beam at grid line 3 and then click.
38. Repeat the same process to add an additional Brace between the same Beam and Column M3.

If you are having difficulty getting the Braces to link up to the Columns and Beams properly, try using the Edit in Section command on the Isolate objects right-click menu to get a better view and indicate the relationship with more precision. The Edit in View commands allow you to isolate a small selection of objects and zoom directly to them in either Plan, Elevation or Section. In this case, we can add the Braces using Edit in Section.

Select just the Columns and Beams on and between Column Lines L3 and M3. On the Structural Member contextual ribbon tab on the General panel, select the drop-down arrow at the right of the Edit in View split button and then choose the Edit in Section tool. Following the prompts, click two points in front of the Column object and parallel to Column Line 3 and then press ENTER. (This is sometimes easier to do if you go to a Top view first.) When prompted, drag the temporary section line back large enough to surround the Columns and then press ENTER again. You will be automatically zoomed to a section view of the selected objects and all other objects will temporarily disappear. Add your Braces following the steps here, and then click the Exit Edit in View icon when finished. This will return you to the drawing, restore the previous view and all the hidden objects will return.

Place one more Brace.

39. Click near the base of Column K3 and near the top of Column K4 (see Figure 6.32).

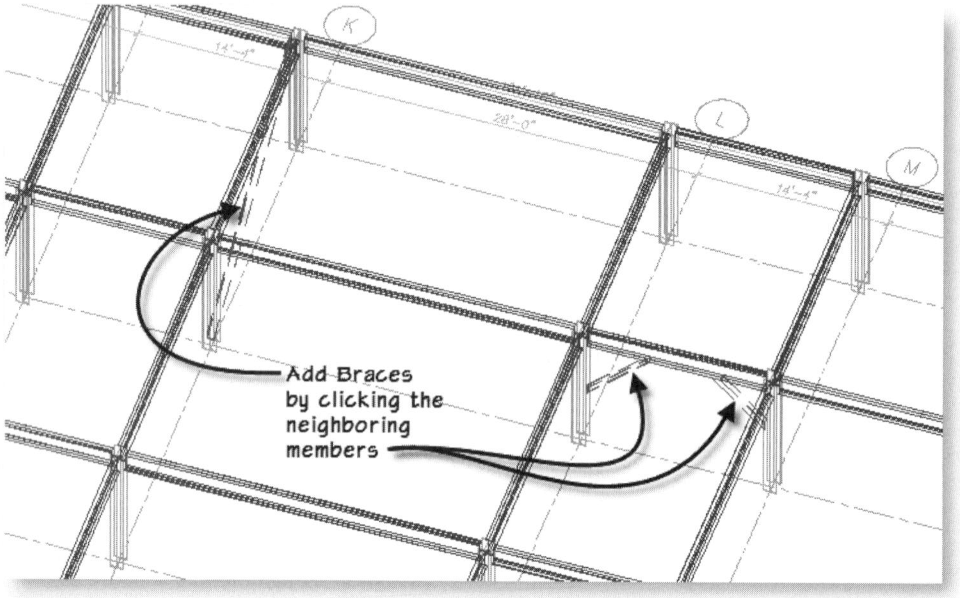
K
L
M
28'-0"
Add Braces
by clicking the
neighboring
members

FIGURE 6.32 *Add Braces between the existing Columns and Beams*

There are several methods of placement for Braces. Feel free to experiment with others if you like. Most of the methods require that a Brace be placed between two perpendicular members such a Column and Beam. However, as you can see from our last example, you can achieve results between parallel members like two Columns as well.

Add Joists

To complete our structural layout of the commercial project, let's add some joists. For this task, we could return to the Structural Catalog or Wizard to create a new joist Beam Style. However, there are some premade steel bar joists provided in the library with the software. These are accessed via the Content Browser. Recall in Chapter 4 that we utilized the Content Browser and even loaded a custom catalog. In this exercise, we will simply access one of the out-of-the-box catalogs. Please note that the bar joists are provided only in the Imperial catalog.

40. On the Insert ribbon tab on the Content panel, select the down arrow on the bottom half of the Content split button and choose the ***Content Browser*** tool (or press CTRL + 4).
41. Click on the *Design Tool Catalog – Imperial* catalog to open it.
42. On the left side, choose the *Structural > Bar Joist* category.
43. Click and hold down the mouse on the small eyedropper icon next to the Steel Joist 16 tool.

    Wait for the eyedropper to "fill up" and then drag it and drop it into the ACA drawing window (see Figure 6.33).

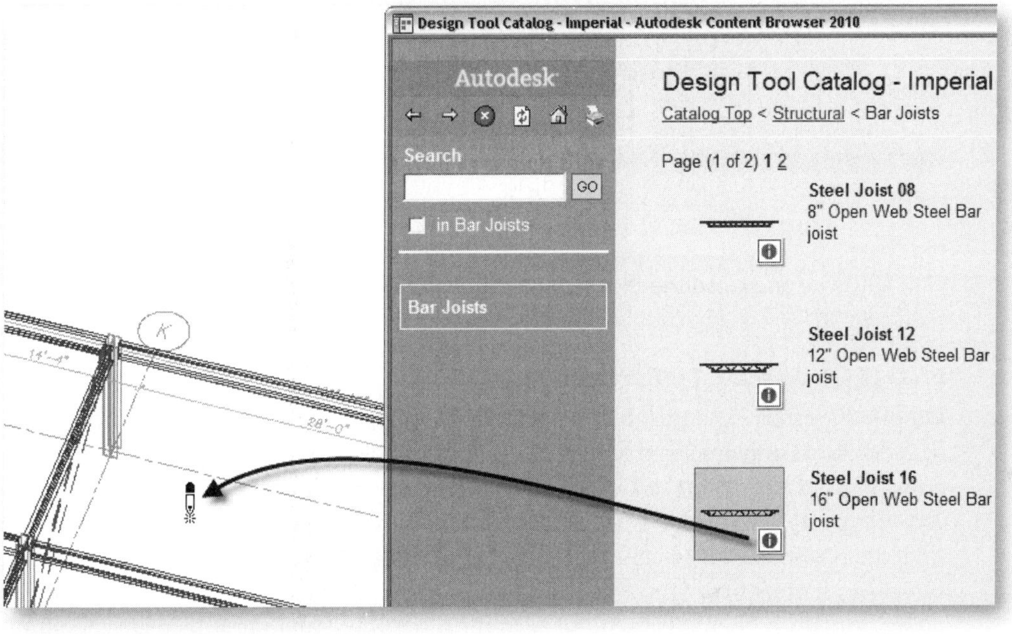

FIGURE 6.33 *The complete Column Grid*

The Structural Beam command will execute and the Steel Joist 16 Style will automatically import and become active in the Properties palette.

44. On the Properties palette, change the "Layout type" to **Fill** and the "Justify" to **Baseline**.
45. In the Layout grouping, set "Array" to Yes, "Layout method" to Repeat and set the "Bay size" to **2'-0"** [**600**].
46. Verify that the Replace Z icon is toggled on and that Object Snap is toggled off. Hover the mouse over a grid line—do not click yet.

Notice that the entire Grid cell will be filled with members. Try moving the mouse to hover over both horizontal and vertical Grid edges. Notice that the orientation of the joists flips to match the highlighted edge.

47. Press the `CTRL` key once.

    Notice that now all cells are highlighted with joists.

48. Orient the joists parallel to the lettered grid lines and then click the mouse to create joists in all bays (see Figure 6.34).

Use the `EXTEND` command and choose the beams between the Columns on Column Lines 0 and 0.1 to extend the joists in the structural bay between Column Lines K, L, 1 and 2 to those beam. You may also want to erase any joists that fall on or very near to the W18x40 beams, such as those along Column Line M.

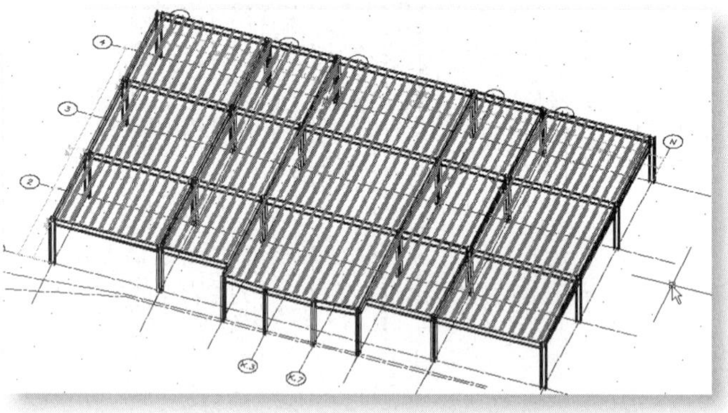

FIGURE 6.34 *The complete structural framing system*

49. Save and close the file.

PROJECT STRUCTURAL CATEGORY

Despite the effort expended in Chapter 5 to get the project set up, you will often identify additional drawings and Sheets that are required as the project progresses. This in no way invalidates the goals of Chapter 5. Rather it exposes a situation that occurs very frequently in *real* projects. In this case, we could simply take the Element file (that we previously had open) and attach it to each of the *Shell and Core* Constructs. However, if your firm is multidisciplinary, or if you would like greater flexibility in project structure, then it is useful to keep the disciplines separate and create a Column Grid Construct for each floor.

Add a Structural Category

1. On the Project Navigator (Quick Access Toolbar or press `CTRL + 5`) click the Constructs tab.
2. Right-click on the *Constructs* folder and choose **New > Category**. Name the new Category **Structural**.

   A Category will appear as a folder in the Project Navigator.

3. Repeat this process and make a new Category in *Constructs* named **Architectural**.
4. Repeat this process again in the *Elements* folder, creating the same two Categories, **Architectural** and **Structural**.

5. In the *Elements* folder, drag the *Column Grid* Element file onto the *Elements\Structural* folder to move it to that folder.

Like we saw back in Chapter 5, you will receive a warning message asking if you want to repath the project now or later. While you can certainly repath after each file is moved, you may want to defer repathing until directed to do so below.

6. In the *Constructs* folder, drag and drop each of the existing Constructs onto the *Architectural* folder.

Unfortunately, this must be done one Construct at a time.

Create Structural Grid Construct Files

Now that we have extended our project folder structure to accommodate a Structural discipline, let's build a Column Grid Construct for each floor of the building.

7. Right-click on the *Structural* folder and choose **New > Construct**.
8. For the Name type **01 Grid**, and for the Description type **First Floor Structural Grid**.
9. In the Assignments area, place a check mark next to First Floor and then click OK (see Figure 6.35).

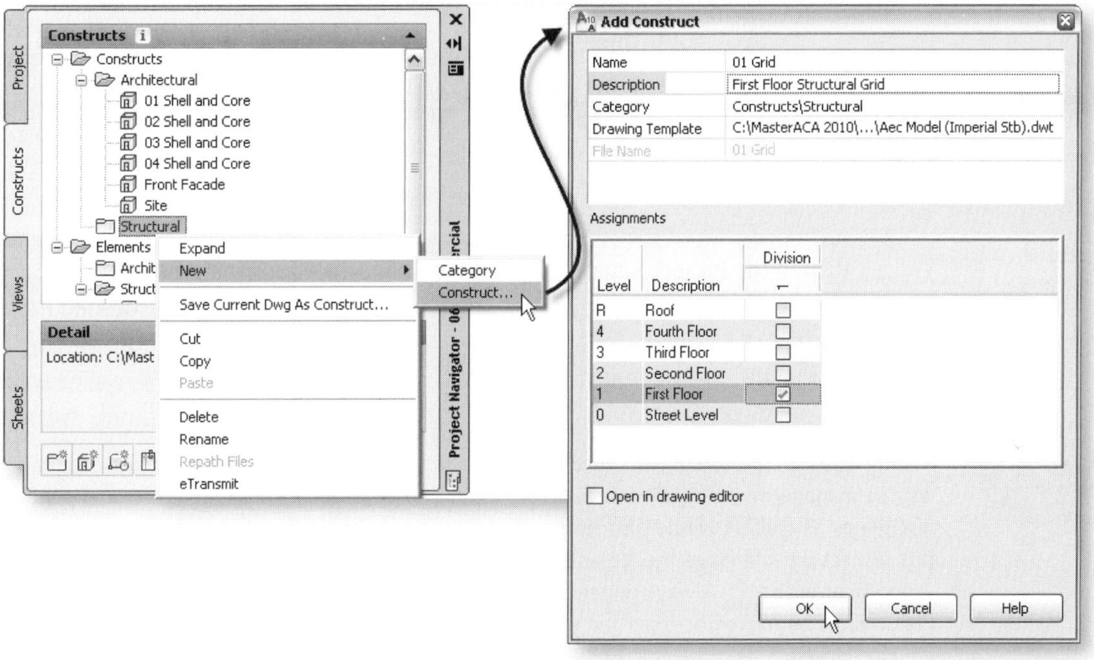

FIGURE 6.35 *Create a First Floor Column Grid Construct within the Structural Category*

10. Repeat these steps to create **02 Grid**, **03 Grid**, and **04 Grid**. Edit the Descriptions and Level assignments accordingly.
11. In the *Elements\Structural* folder, right-click the *Column Grid* Element file and choose **Attach Element to Constructs**.
12. Place a check mark in the checkbox next to the *Structural* folder and then click OK (see Figure 6.36).

    This will XREF Attach the *Column Grid* Element to each of the Grid Constructs.

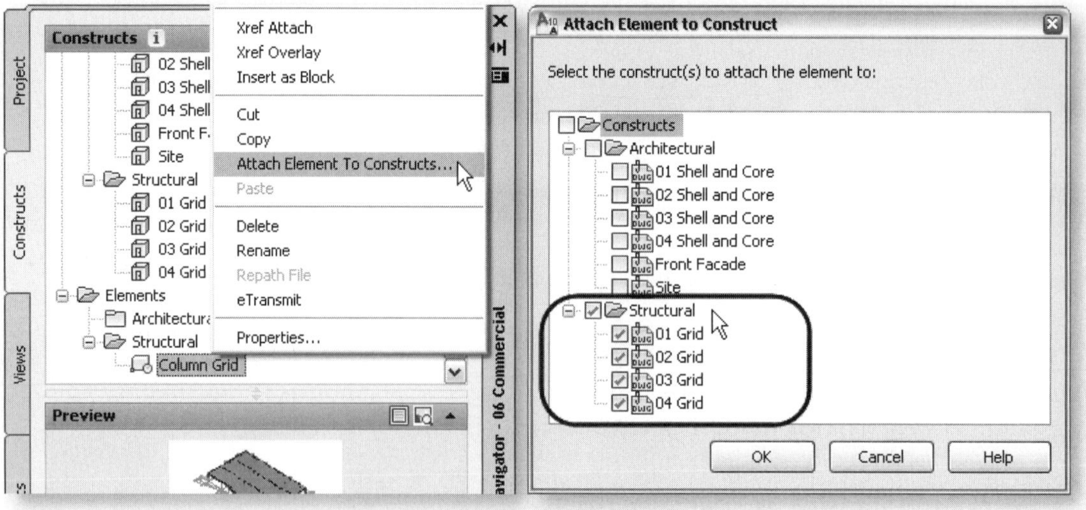

FIGURE 6.36 *Attach the Column Grid Element to each of the Grid Constructs*

13. On the Constructs tab, in the *Constructs\Structural* folder, double-click *01 Grid* to open it.

    Note that the Grid has been XREFed to this file. Feel free to open others as well.

Since moving Constructs to different categories literally moves the drawing files to a different folder, the XREF paths will fail if you do not repath the project. Also, when you rename files you can experience broken XREF links. For these reasons, we must repath all of the XREFs in the project. Refer to the "Create the Upper Floor Constructs" heading in Chapter 5 for more information on these issues.

14. At the bottom of the Project Navigator palette, click the Repath Xref icon, and then in the Project Repath Queue dialog box, click the Repath button.
15. That completes the setup of the Structural Column Grid and all associated Project files.
16. Save and Close all project files.

CAD MANAGER NOTE

Adding subfolders (Categories) to the Constructs and Elements folders is a very common way to manage multidiscipline firms. You could add additional folders for MEP and other disciplines as well. It would also be fairly common to add subfolders to the Views tab. In this project we will leave the Views tab uncategorized for simplicity. However, feel free to experiment with this. Always remember to repath after moving and/or renaming files. Also, files cannot be moved or repathed while they are open for editing, so be sure that all files are closed first.

Update Project Views

The Constructs that we have created here will need to be added to the Project Views (refer to Chapter 5 for complete details on Views). In particular, we would typically wish to see Column Grids in the Floor Plan Views and in the overall Composite Model and Section Model. It would not be useful to have the Column Grids appear in the Composite Elevation Model.

17. On the Project Navigator, click the Views tab.
18. Right-click on *A-CM00* and choose **Properties**.

19. Click on the Content page. Check all Grid files and then click OK.
20. Repeat the same steps on *A-SC01*, and all of the Plan Views.

    Naturally in each Plan View, only one Structural Grid file will be selected for that particular level.

CAUTION

Be sure to check the Content page after each change or the updates may not Regenerate properly.

21. Right-click on the *A-EL01* View and choose **Properties**.
22. Click on the Content page, place a check mark in the Structural folder and then remove it.

    This action will deselect the entire Category and all future files from this View. It is not necessary to load Structural Grids for the exterior Building Elevations.
23. Right-click on the Views folder and choose **Regenerate**.

This will update all of the View files with the changes that we just made. Go ahead and open any of the Views to verify the addition of the Column Grid to each of them.

If you wish, open the *A-SC01* View file, select the Section object and on the 2D Section/Elevation contextual ribbon tab on the Modify panel choose the ***Regenerate*** tool. In the Selection Set area of the Generate Section/Elevation dialog, click the Select Additional Objects button, select the Grid files with a crossing window and click OK to see all the framing added to the section. Publish an updated DWF of the entire set on the Sheets tab as well if you wish.

24. Save and Close all commercial project files before continuing.

CREATING A FOUNDATION PLAN

In addition to Columns and Grids, the structural tools in ACA include Beams, Braces, Slabs and certain Wall styles. In this exercise, we will look at a concrete Wall style with integral footing. We will do this in the context of the Residential Project. However, any of the techniques we will cover would work equally well in the Commercial or any other Project.

Load the Residential Project

Be sure that all drawings from the Commercial Project are saved and closed.

1. On the QAT, choose **Project Browser**.
2. Navigate to the *C:\MasterACA 2010\Chapter06* folder and make the *06 Residential* [*06 Residential Metric*] project current.

   If the Repath dialog appears, simply click the Repath icon to continue. There may still remain some queued XREF path changes in the Commercial Project. This operation will ensure that none of them are missed before you change the current project. *Always* click the Repath button when asked! It is possible you could get this alert twice here, once for closing the commercial project and then again for opening the residential project. Always click Repath.
3. On the Constructs tab, double-click the *Basement New* file to open it.
4. On the Walls palette, right-click the Concrete-8 Concrete-16x8-footing [Concrete-200 Concrete-400x200-footing] tool and choose **Apply Tool Properties to > Wall**.

If you do not see this palette or tool, right-click the Tool Palettes title bar and choose **Design** (to load the Design Tool Palette Group), and then click the Design tab.

5. At the "Select Wall(s)" prompt, select all three Walls in this drawing and then press ENTER.

   Notice the change in the Walls and the appearance of the footing line below. The Walls, however, still need some adjustment.

6. On the Project Navigator palette, drag and drop the *Basement Existing* Construct into the drawing.

NOTE

When you drag one Construct into another Construct, the file will be XREFed as an Overlay. Overlaid XREFs apply only to the current drawing and do not carry forward if the current drawing is XREFed to another.

Adding the Overlaid XREF of the Existing Basement Conditions reveals that the foundation Walls on the addition do not properly align with the existing construction.

7. With the same three Walls still selected, right-click and choose **Properties**.
8. On the Properties palette, change the Justify to **Baseline**.

   Notice that the face of the concrete Wall is now aligned with the existing construction (rather than the face of the footing as before), but the wrong face is aligned.

9. With the Walls still selected, on the Wall contextual ribbon on the Modify panel select the Reverse drop-down button and choose the ***Wall Reverse Baseline*** tool (see Figure 6.37).

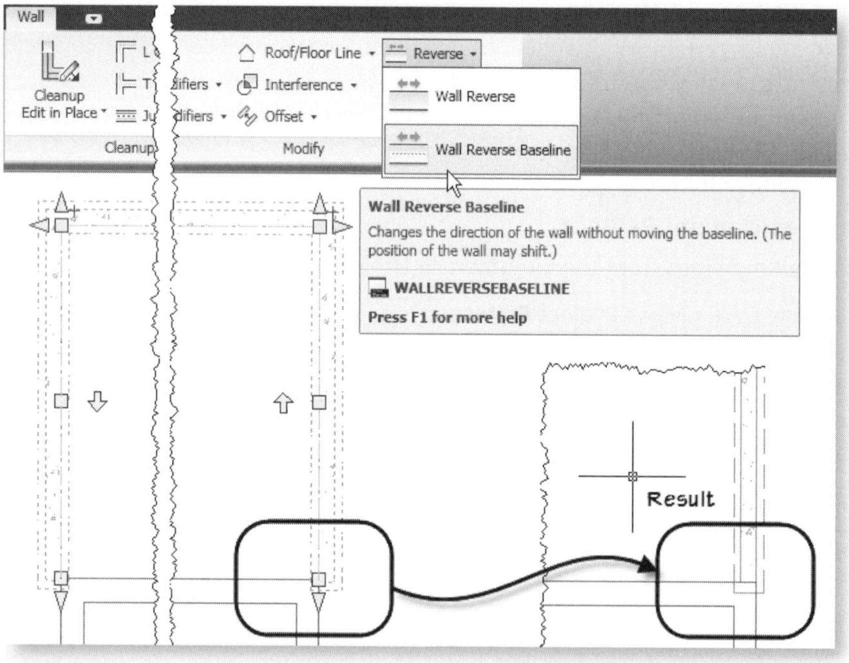

FIGURE 6.37 *Use the ribbon to reverse the direction of the Walls*

10. Select all three Walls again and on the Properties palette, change the Base Height to **8'-9"** [**2600**].
11. Right-click and choose **Deselect All**.

    There will be a small galley and new basement stair on the left side of the new addition.
12. Offset the left vertical Wall into the plan (toward the right).

    For the Offset Distance type **5'-0"** [**1500**].
13. Using both of the vertical Walls at the left as cutting edges, trim off the piece of horizontal Wall between them (see Figure 6.38).

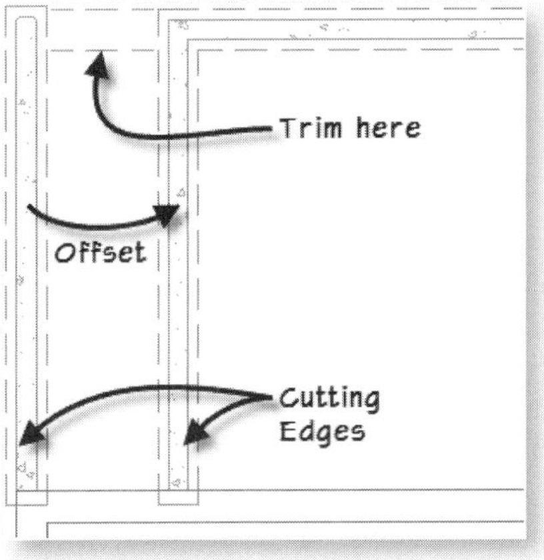

FIGURE 6.38 *Adding a Basement access gangway*

A few more things need attention in this file. For instance, the foundation Wall appears to encroach on the existing Wall [and does not touch in the Metric file]. This is easily remedied with Wall Endcaps. However, we will save those edits for later chapters.

14. Save and Close the file.

ADDITIONAL STRUCTURAL CONTENT

In addition to the Wall tool that we accessed here, there are also many Wall Styles in the Content Browser that can be used for footings of various kinds. Some are concrete Wall Styles with integral footings like the one showcased here, others are styles of just the footing that you add separately from any Walls. One of the advantages of using Wall Styles for footings is that like other Walls, you get automatic cleanup (see Chapter 9) and the ability to control how they display below the cut plane (see Chapter 10).

Structural Styles in the Content Browser

To view the many styles provided, return to the Content Browser (as covered above) and browse to the *Design Tool Catalog – Imperial* [*Design Tool Catalog – Metric*] and then the *Walls > Concrete* category. There you find several concrete footing and wall with footing styles ready to iDrop into your projects (see Figure 6.39). Some of these styles are Wall Styles while others are Mass Elements. Try them out in a sample drawing or your own projects.

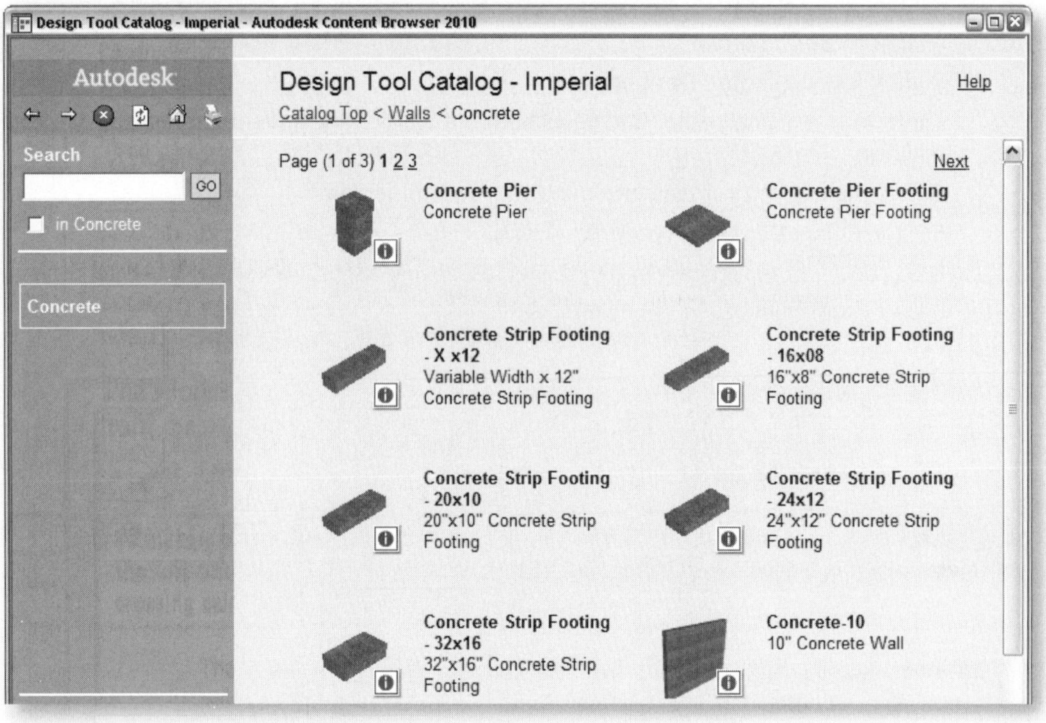

FIGURE 6.39 *Concrete Footing Styles in the Content Browser library*

Structural Members—Custom Block Customization

You can apply Boolean operations to custom display blocks within Structural Members. You can also apply Booleans directly to the members themselves. An out-of-the-box example of a structural member that incorporates the Boolean block feature is the castellated beam, styles for which are found in the Content Browser. Since we have finished with the Commercial project structural layout, we can simply open the Content Browser and take a quick look at the styles provided. We can also explore how these structural members are created.

1. Start a new drawing using the *AEC Model (Imperial.stb)* [*AEC Model (Metric.stb)*] template.
2. Open the Content Browser (as covered above) and browse to the *Design Tool Catalog – Imperial* [*Design Tool Catalog – Metric*] and then the *Structural > Members* [*Structural Members*] category (Figure 6.40).

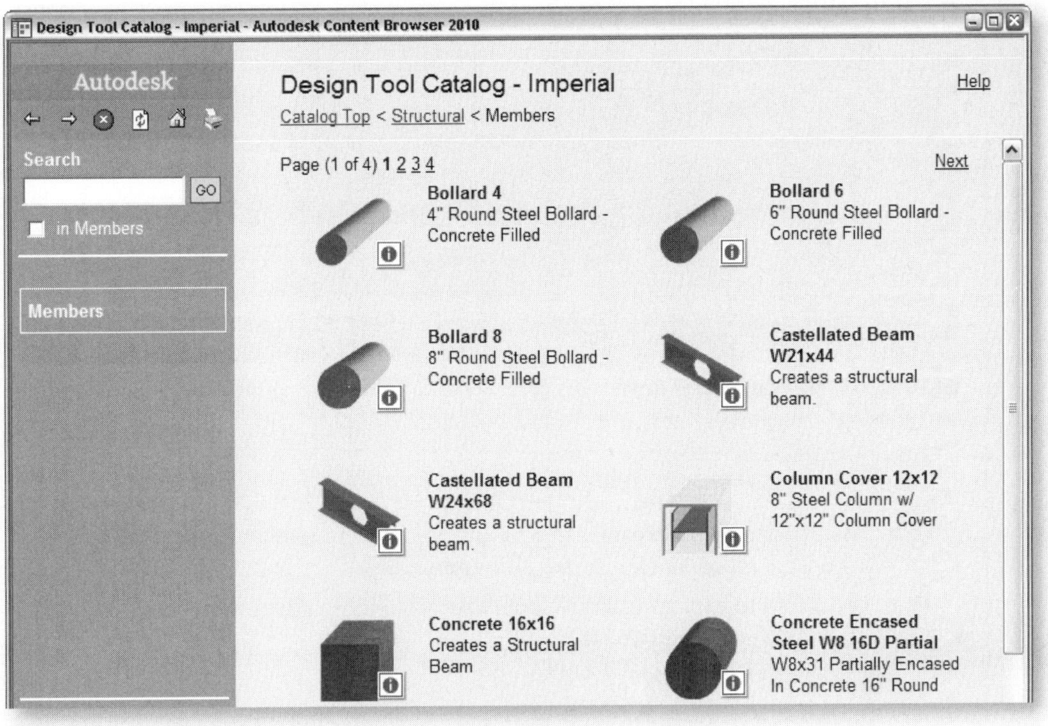

FIGURE 6.40 *The Content Browser library showing Castellated Beam Structural Member styles*

3. Using the iDrop icon, drag the Castellated Beam W21x44 [Castellated Beam W530x66] tool into the drawing and draw a Beam.
4. Draw a **20'-0"** [**6000**] length of Beam.
5. From the floating View panel, expand the View drop-down button by selecting the down arrow at the right side of the top split button and choose the ***View, SE Isometric*** tool.

   Reminder: If you docked the floating View panel, you can find it at the right end of the Home ribbon panel.
6. From the floating View panel, expand the Visual Styles drop-down button and choose the **Visual Styles, Conceptual** tool.

If you like, you can also add the other style: Castellated Beam W24x68 [Castellated Beam W610x82] from the Content Browser as well. Castellated Beam W21x44 [Castellated Beam W530x66] repeats a round hole, while Castellated Beam W24x68 [Castellated Beam W610x82] repeats a hexagonal one (Figure 6.41).

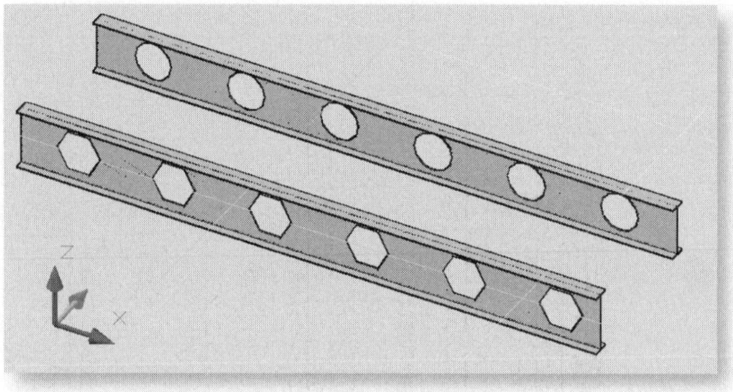

FIGURE 6.41 *The Castellated Beam styles have a repeating "hole" along their length*

To understand how these styles were created, simply reverse engineer them.

7. Select one of the Beams, and on the Structural Member contextual ribbon on the General panel choose the ***Edit Style*** tool.

   Feel free to explore each tab, but what gives these styles their holes is found on the Display Properties tab.

8. Click on the Display Properties tab.

Notice that there is a Style Override applied to both model and elevation Display Representations. All of them are configured the same way, but let's edit the Model Rep.

9. Click on the Other tab, select round duct [hexagon duct] and then click the Edit button.

In the Custom Block window, notice the name "round duct [hexagon duct]" next to the Select Block button. This block has been added as a display component of the Structural Member. (In Chapter 11, we will see a similar example adding a custom display block to a Door Style.) On the right side, the "Repeat Block Display" checkbox is selected, making this block repeat along the length of the Beam. The dimensions here are used to indicate the offset from either end of the Beam and how far apart the repeated blocks should be spaced. On the left side, within the Boolean area, Subtractive has been chosen for the Operation. This makes the blocks mass cut away from the Member rather than add to it. This is how we end up with holes (see Figure 6.42).

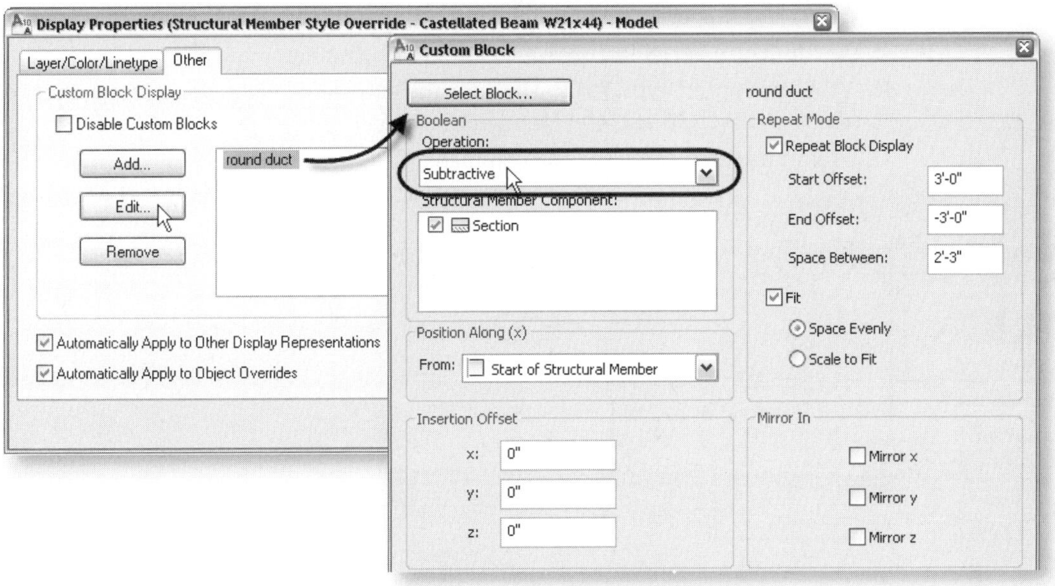

FIGURE 6.42 *The Block Round Duct is set to a Subtractive operation along the length of the Member style*

10. Click OK twice to return to the drawing.

If you wish to see the block, choose Block from the Insert menu, select round duct [hexagonal duct] from the list and then place it anywhere in the drawing. You will need to zoom in close to see it because it is very small. This block was created by drawing a circle, then right-clicking it and choosing **Convert To > Mass Element**.

11. Close the temporary file. It is not necessary to save it.

Structural Members—Body Modifier Customization

Body modifiers can be added directly to Structural Members. To demonstrate this feature let's work with a trellis for the Residential project.

12. On the Project Navigator palette, double-click to open the file named *Trellis* in the *Elements* folder.
13. From the floating View panel, expand the View drop-down button and choose the ***View, NW Isometric*** tool.

This file has some Structural Members placed in a trellis configuration. They are positioned relative to the back entrance of the new addition. If you like, drag the *First Floor New* Construct from Project Navigator and drop it in this file. While there are no Doors or Windows in this Construct yet, it will at least give you an idea what the context for the trellis is. In later chapters we will add the Door, a porch and other elements to the *First Floor New* Construct. For now we will simply use this file to learn about the new Boolean features of Structural Members.

The Structural Members used in this file were created from the Catalog as shown at the start of this chapter. You can create similar ones by browsing the Lumber category and choosing an appropriate size. A 2 × 6 [50 mm × 150 mm] was used here. Take notice of the polyline placed at the end of one of the Structural Members. We will extrude this into a Mass Element and then attach it as a Body Modifier to the Structural Members.

14. Select the shape, right-click and choose **Convert To > Mass Element**.
15. At the “Erase Selected Linework” prompt, choose Yes.
16. When prompted, type **1 1/2"** [**150**] for the extrusion height (this corresponds to the width of the Structural Member).
17. Press ENTER to complete the command (see Figure 6.43).

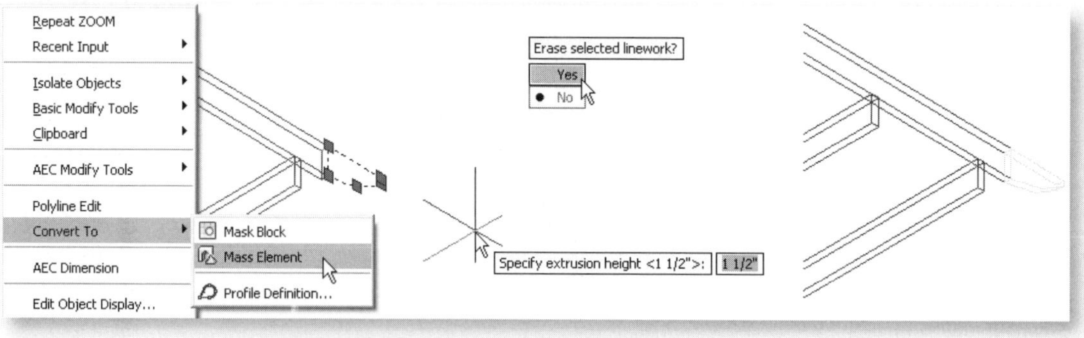

FIGURE 6.43 *Convert the Polyline to a Mass Element*

When the polyline is converted to a Mass Element, the curve becomes segmented. You can make the segmentation more closely match the original curve with the AEC-FACETDEV command.

18. Type AECFACETDEV and then press ENTER.
19. The default value of this setting is 1/2" [12.70]. A smaller value will make the curve smoother.
20. Type **.05** [**1**] and then press ENTER.
21. Select the Structural Member adjacent to the new Mass Element, on the Structural Member contextual ribbon tab on the Modify panel select the Body Modifier drop-down button and choose the ***Add*** tool.
22. At the “Select objects to apply as body modifiers” prompt, select the Mass Element and then press ENTER.
23. In the “Add Body Modifier” worksheet, choose **Section** for the “Structural Member Component,” **Additive** for “Operation,” and place a check mark in the “Erase Selected Object(s)” checkbox (see the left side of Figure 6.44).

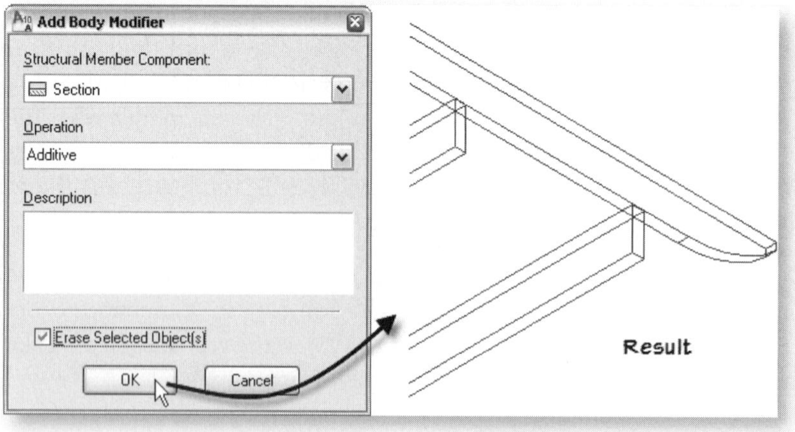

FIGURE 6.44 *Convert the Mass Element to a Body Modifier*

24. Click OK to view the results (see the right side of Figure 6.44).

Now that we have completed the modification to the Structural Member, we can array it to complete the trellis. You can use either the AutoCAD ARRAY command or the Array option on the AEC Modify Tools right-click menu.

25. Array the Beam using a spacing of **1'-4"** [**400**] (see Figure 6.45).

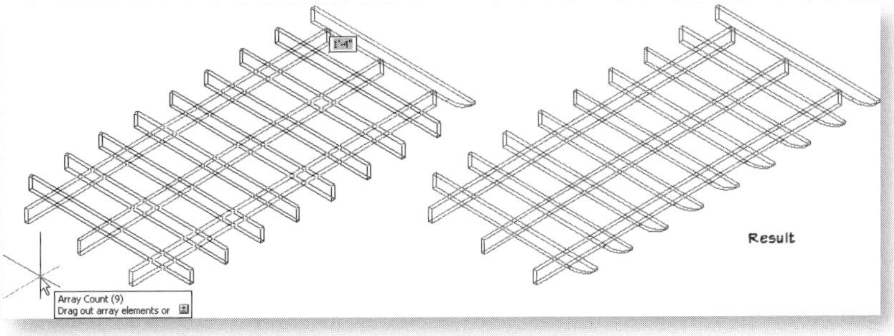

FIGURE 6.45 *Array the Beam to complete the Trellis*

26. Save and Close the file.

ADDITIONAL EXERCISES

Additional exercises have been provided in Appendix A. In Appendix A you will find an exercise for updating the Basement Existing Construct of the Residential Project to include the Beams and Columns. It is not necessary that you complete this exercise to begin the next chapter, it is provided to enhance your learning experience. Completed projects for each of the exercises have been provided in the *Chapter06/Complete* folder.

SUMMARY

- Use either the Structural Member Style Wizard or the Structural Member Catalog to import shapes into your file and generate Structural Member styles.
- Column Grids can be inserted with Columns already anchored to each intersection.
- Anchors provide powerful parametric relationships between the Columns and the Column Grid.
- A parametric Column Grid object can have grid spacing set to a fixed bay size, or equally divide the total grid size by a fixed number of bays.
- Grid spacing of parametric grids can be manually adjusted to meet any design or existing conditions requirement.
- You can draw a grid exactly the way you want it using lines and then convert those lines to a Column Grid object.
- Automatic grid labeling and dimensioning are fast and flexible tools for annotating a Column Grid.
- Grid Extensions can be achieved with a custom Multi-View Block used in place of the standard bubble.
- Beams, Braces and Joists can be added to your parametric Column Grid using many powerful automated placement routines.

- Categories can be added to the Project folders to organize the project files by discipline.
- Wall Styles with integral footings can be used to create foundation plans.
- Many footing styles both integral to Walls and independent can be found in the Content Browser library.
- Structural Members can utilize Boolean operations within display Blocks assigned to their Display Representations.
- Body Modifiers can be applied to Structural Members to customize them individually.

CHAPTER

7

Vertical Circulation

INTRODUCTION

In this chapter, we will look at Stairs and Railings. The core plan of the commercial building will include Stairs, elevators and toilet room layouts. The exterior entrance plaza leading up to the commercial building calls for Stairs, a ramp and Railings. The lobby will include a feature Stair. The Residential Project contains existing Stairs on the interior and an existing exterior Stair at the front entrance.

OBJECTIVES

- Add and modify Stairs.
- Add and modify Railings.
- Add and modify ramps.
- Add a Custom Stair.
- Lay out elevators and restrooms.
- Working with Stair Tower Generate.
- Stairs and Railings.

RESIDENTIAL STAIRS AND RAILINGS

When we work with Stairs, most parameters are configured in the style (refer to Chapter 2 for an overview of Object styles in ACA). Style-based settings include riser and tread relationships, stringer settings, landing rules and display settings. Width and height parameters and clearances belong directly to the Stair object (and are therefore not part of the style). Stairs do not automatically include Railings; however, rules can be assigned to the Stair objects that control the placement of Railings. Railings are then added as a separate object, anchored to the Stair (refer to Chapter 2 for an overview of Anchors). Multi-View Blocks are used to generate elevators, and ramps are created from specially configured Stair styles included with the out-of-the-box ACA content library.

Adding and modifying Stairs is much like adding and modifying any other ACA object. Choose the appropriate tool from the tool palettes and set the initial parameters in the Properties palette, then you place the object into the drawing. Finally, you progressively refine the Stair over time as project needs dictate. To begin our exploration of Stairs, we will revisit our first floor existing conditions plan for the Residential Project. In this file, we will build the existing Stairs in the main house.

Install the CD Files and Load the Current Project

If you have already installed all of the files from the CD, simply skip down to step 3 below to make the project active. If you need to install the CD files, start at step 1.

1. If you have not already done so, install the dataset files located on the Mastering AutoCAD Architecture 2010 CD-ROM.

   Refer to "Files Included on the CD-ROM" in the Preface for information on installing the sample files included on the CD.
2. Launch AutoCAD Architecture 2010 from the desktop icon created in Chapter 3.

If you did not create a custom icon, you might want to review "Create a New Profile" and "Create a Desktop Shortcut" in Chapter 3. Creating the custom desktop icon is not essential; however, it makes loading the custom profile easier.

3. From the Quick Access Toolbar (QAT), choose the ***Project Browser*** icon.
4. Click to open the folder list and choose your *C:* drive.
5. Double-click on the *MasterACA 2010* folder, then the *Chapter07* folder.

   One of two residential Projects will be listed: *07 Residential* and/or *07 Residential Metric.*
6. Double-click *07 Residential* if you wish to work in Imperial units. Double-click *07 Residential Metric* if you wish to work in Metric units. (You can also right-click on it and choose **Set Project Current**.) Then click Close in the Project Browser.

NOTE

Important: If a message appears asking you to repath the project, click the "Repath the project now" option. Refer to the "Repathing Projects" topic in the Preface for more information.

Add a Stair to the Residential Plan

7. On the Project Navigator, double-click *First Floor Existing* in the *Constructs* folder.

This is the first floor existing conditions file from Chapter 4. At the end of that lesson, we inserted some pre-built Stair objects into our Residential First Floor Existing Conditions file. The interior Stair in the main hallway has been removed here so that we can learn the techniques needed to build it ourselves. To assist us in establishing a good starting point, let's add a construction line.

8. On the Home ribbon tab on the Draw panel, select the down arrow on the bottom half of the Line split button and click the ***Construction Line*** tool.

   Make sure the Dynamic Input is enabled (the Dynamic Input toggle on the Application status bar is blue-green).
9. Following the prompts, highlight the inside edge of the bottom horizontal Wall and then click.
10. Type in **3'-6"** [**1075**] for the dynamic dimension and then press ENTER (see Figure 7.1).

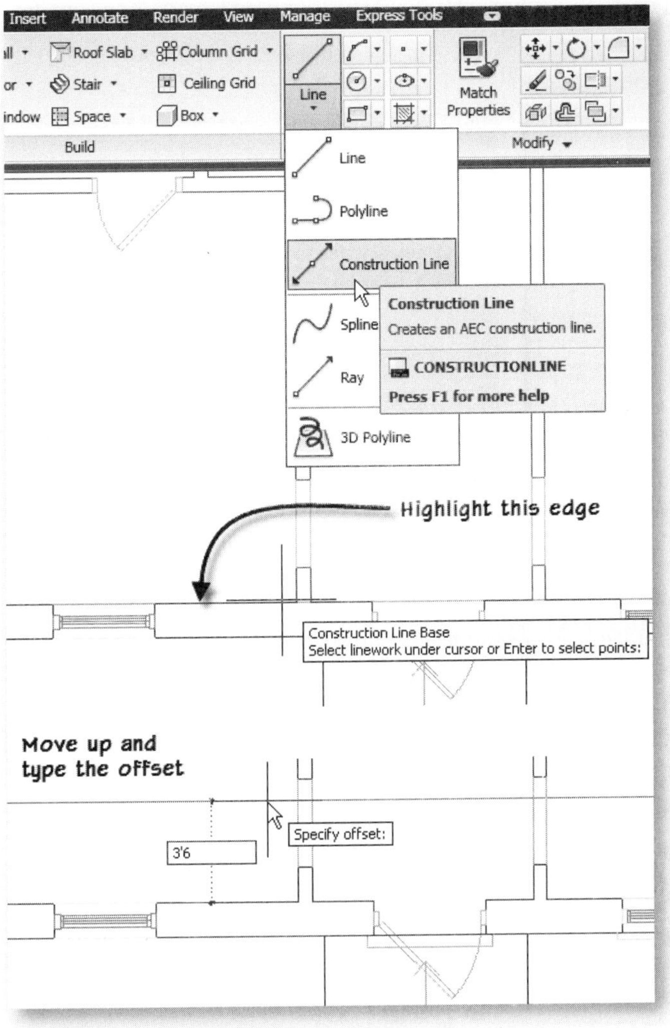

FIGURE 7.1 *Create a Construction Line to aid placement*

11. Press ESC to end the command.

To draw the Stair, we will start with a predefined Stair style and modify it to suit our needs. We can find a suitable style in the Content Browser. We have visited the Content Browser in a few exercises in previous chapters, so you should now be getting comfortable with it.

12. Open the Content Browser (on the Insert ribbon tab on the Content panel, click on the ***Content Browser*** tool (select the down arrow on the bottom half if the ***Content Browser*** tool is not displayed in the top half) or press CTRL + 4).
13. Click on *Design Tool Catalog - Imperial* [*Design Tool Catalog - Metric*]
14. Navigate to the Stairs and Railings category and then the Stairs category.
15. Using the eyedropper icon, drag the Wood-Saddle tool into the drawing window.

    The Add Stair command will begin and on the Properties palette, Wood-Saddle will be set as the Stair Style.
16. On the Properties palette, choose **Straight** for the Shape and choose **Left** for Justify.
17. Set the Width to **3'-1"** [**942**], the Height to **9'-0"** [**2750**] and the Tread to **11"** [**280**] (see Figure 7.2).

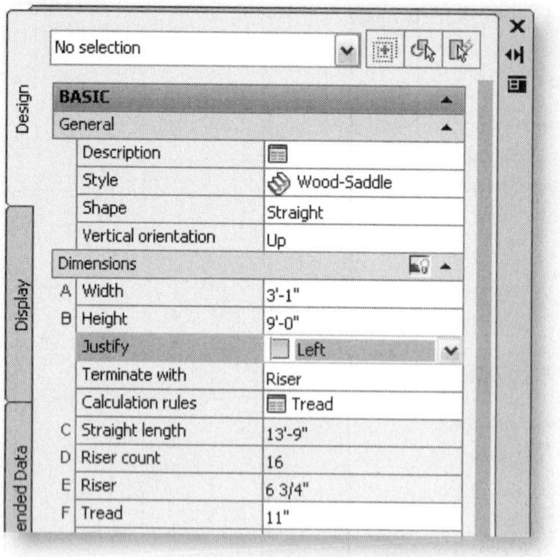

FIGURE 7.2 *Set the parameters for adding a Stair*

18. At the "Flight Start Point" prompt, snap to the intersection of the Wall on the left side of the entrance hallway and the construction line drawn above.
19. From that point, move the mouse straight up (90° using Polar Tracking or Ortho Mode), click the mouse to place the Stair. Press ENTER to complete the command (see Figure 7.3).

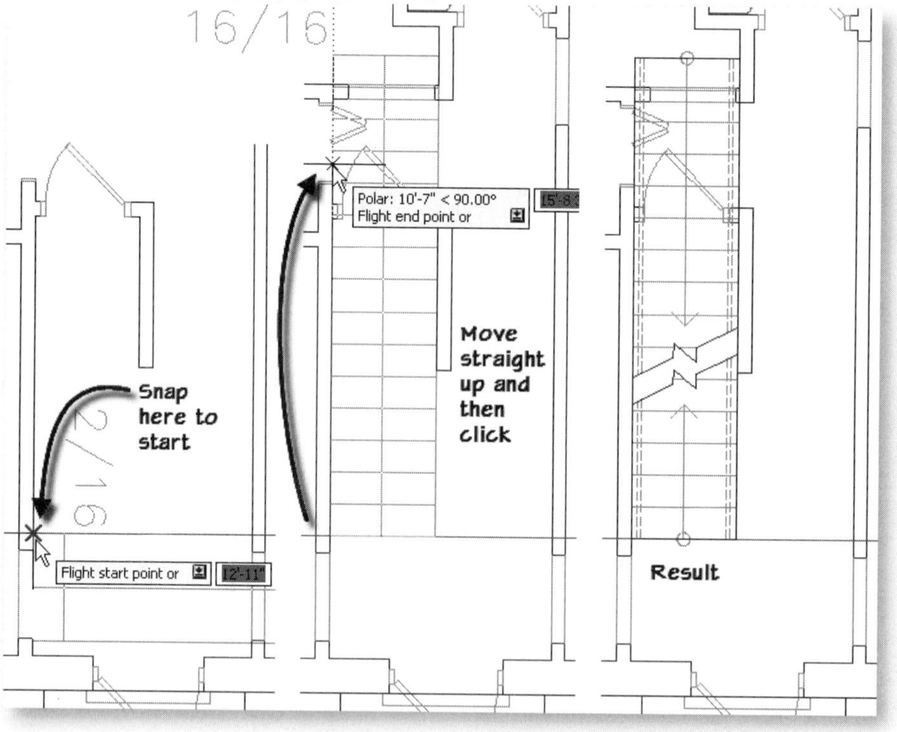

FIGURE 7.3 *Click two points to place the Stair—The Stair is too long*

Notice the overall box defining the footprint of the Stair as it is being placed. There is also feedback on the number of risers placed (in this case 16 out of 16). This is based on the riser-to-tread relationship and the 9'-0" [2750] height we assigned. In this case, the box is too long. By default, the Stair is placing too many risers for the space available. Furthermore, there are rules that govern the relationship of treads to risers in the Stair style. To correct this, we will first edit the Stair style, and then the Stair properties.

Work with Stair Styles

In this sequence, we will edit the parameters of the Stair style and make some minor modifications to it to help it conform to the needs of the existing structure. This will involve removing the constraints enforced by Design Rules. Since the stairs existing in this house were built before current code requirements were in place, an "Existing Stair" style needs to be created allowing more freedom.

20. Select the Stair that you just placed and on the Stair contextual ribbon tab on the General panel choose the ***Save As*** tool.
21. In the Stair Styles dialog, on the General tab, change the name to **Existing Stairs**.
22. Change the Description to: **Existing Conditions Stair – Residential Project**.
23. Click the Floating Viewer icon in the lower-left corner of the dialog box and set it to **SE Isometric** view and **Conceptual** (see Figure 7.4).

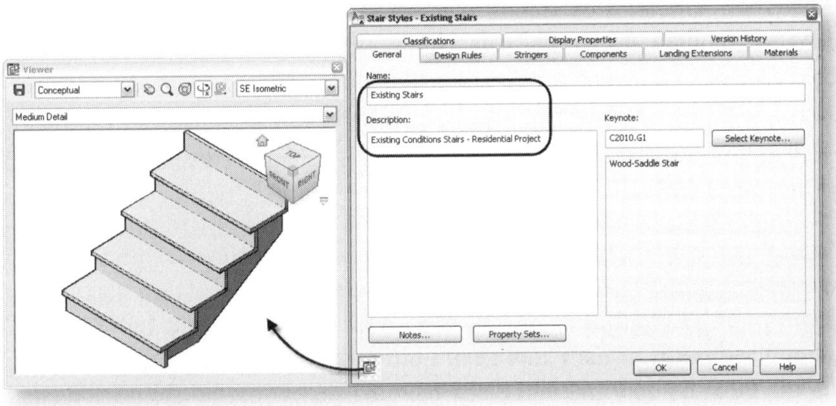

FIGURE 7.4 *Rename the Stair style and open the floating viewer in the style editor*

24. Click the Design Rules tab.

    Notice the parameters.

Here you can enter a range of values for minimum and maximum tread and riser. You can also enter building code values for your jurisdiction in a rule-based calculator. Values assigned to these rules will constrain the parameters of the Stair as it is being created. This is an existing Stair, so we will draw what is actually there rather than what the building code states *should* be there. Therefore, we will set the limits very broadly so that we can enter actual values without restriction.

25. In the Maximum Slope fields, type **12"** [**300**] for Riser Height and **8"** [**200**] for Tread Depth.

    The Optimum Slope and Minimum Slope values can remain as they are for this Stair.
26. Clear the Use Rule Based Calculator checkbox (see Figure 7.5).

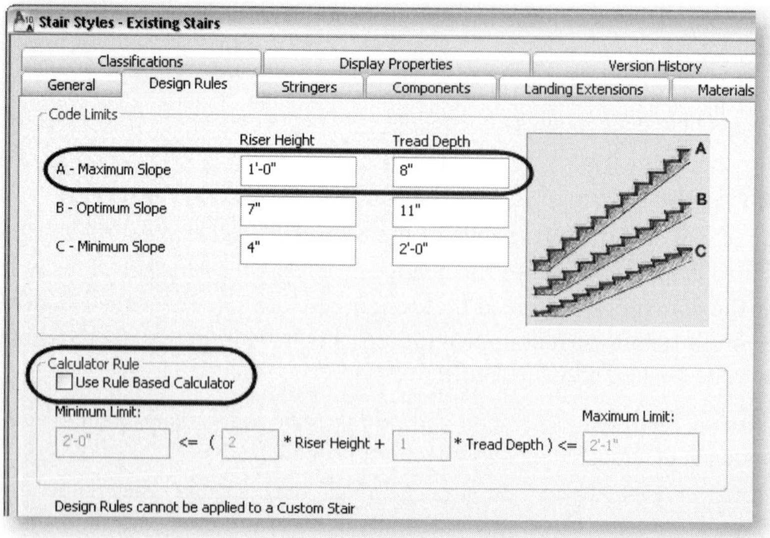

FIGURE 7.5 *Enter broad code limits to accommodate existing conditions*

These settings will give us the freedom we need to create the existing Stair. (We hope we never run across a 12" [300] riser with 8" [200] tread, but you never know.)

27. Click the Stringers tab.

ACA Stairs can have four different types of stringer. The choices are Saddled, Housed, Slab and Ramp. A Saddled stringer is notched in the shape of the treads and risers and supports the treads from underneath. The Housed stringer occurs at the edges of the Stair with the treads spanning in between. A typical wooden Stair would use Saddled, while a steel pan Stair would be Housed. Slab creates a solid mass of material across the full width of the Stair underneath the treads and risers. Solid Slab is used primarily for poured concrete Stairs. In ACA, there is no dedicated Ramp object. To create a ramp, you use a Stair style with Ramp stringers (see the tutorial later in this chapter). Take a quick look at the other settings and match them up with the letters in the diagram at the left of the dialog box. We do not need to change anything here for our existing Stair.

28. Click the Components tab.

This tab contains the tread and riser settings. Match up the settings with the letters in the diagram. Deselect tread or riser if you do not wish to display either of these components. For instance, by deselecting the Riser checkbox, you can create an open riser Stair. Check Sloping Riser for steel pan Stairs; leave it unchecked for our Wood Stairs.

29. Place a check mark in the Allow Each Stair to Vary checkbox (see Figure 7.6).

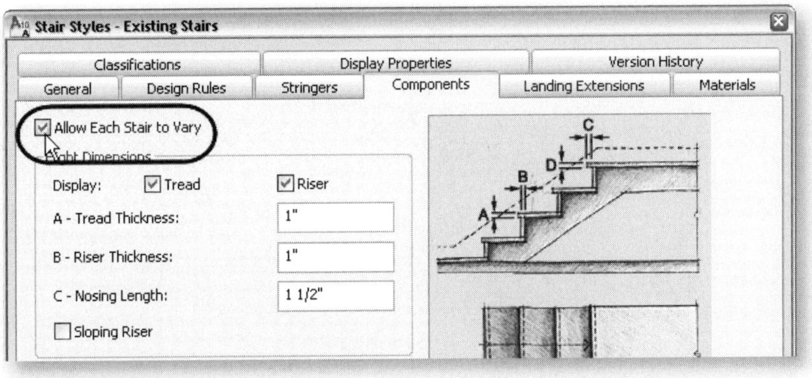

FIGURE 7.6 *The Components tab controls the Tread and Riser dimensions*

This is another helpful setting for an existing Stair. Each Stair you create will take its original parameters from the style. However, when you allow each Stair to vary, all style-based parameters can be edited on each individual Stair object without affecting the others. This setting is recommended only if your project has few Stairs that share the same constraints. The alternative is to simply make a style for each unique situation. This setting is being used here because this is an existing Stair.

30. Click the Landing Extensions tab.

    Study the settings. For this Stair, we will not set any extensions, but when we return to the commercial core plan, we will look further at this feature. Don't worry about the other tabs yet. We will edit those parameters later.

31. Click OK to accept the changes and return to the drawing.

Modify Stair Properties

32. Select the Stair, right-click and choose **Properties**.
33. In the Dimensions grouping, click the Calculation rules worksheet icon, labeled Tread (see Figure 7.7).

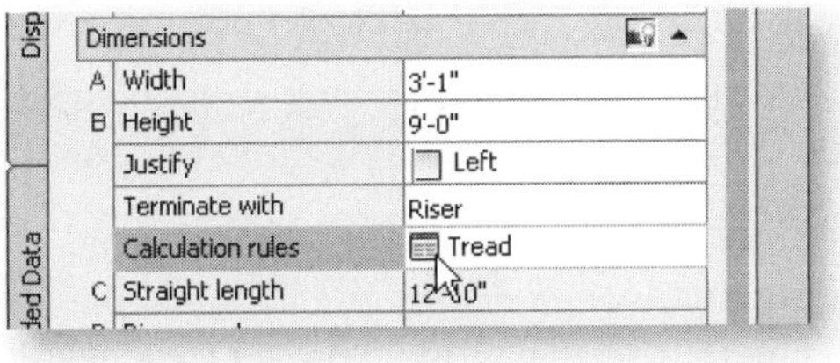

FIGURE 7.7 *Access Calculation rules worksheet*

34. Change D - Tread to **10"** [**250**].
35. Click the Automatic (lightning bolt) icon next to Riser Count (see Figure 7.8).

    This will make the Riser Count field editable.

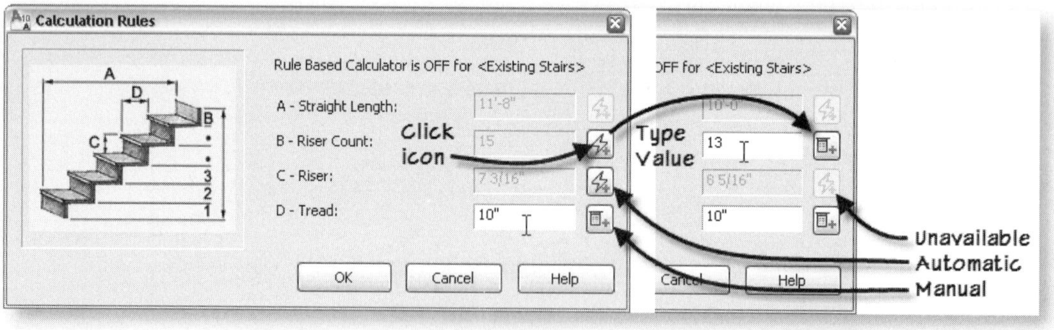

FIGURE 7.8 *Unlock and edit the Riser Count field*

36. Type **13** in the B - Riser Count field and then click OK.

    Notice the dynamic reduction in Stair length. This is due to the now shallower treads and taller risers.

37. Save the file.

Modify Stair Display

The default display characteristics for the current Stair style in plan are to represent the Stair as two flights; one up and the other down. This is helpful in many plans, but it does not work well in all plans. If the Stairs on each floor are different heights or shifted slightly from one another, this graphic representation will not be accurate. Also, this representation is incorrect if there is really only one Stair. At the early *stages* of a project, it might be acceptable to leave the Stair representation as is, but it will likely need to be changed as the design enters a more refined state. Editing the Display Properties of the Stair object will allow us to produce whatever graphic display our specific design scenario requires. In this residential plan, the floor-to-floor height of the first to second floor is 9'-0" [2750]; however, it is only 8'-9" [2675] from basement to first floor. To resolve this situation, we will edit the display of the Stair we created in the last step to show only the Stairs going up. Then we will copy this Stair and modify it to show only the basement Stairs going down.

NO TIME FOR THE BOOK, SEE THE MOVIE

AutoCAD Architecture includes three sets of display components for Stairs in plan. These components allow better control over the accuracy of Stair plan display. A file named *Understanding Stair Display* has been included in the *Elements* folder of the residential project. This file begins with two Stair objects: one running up and the other running down. The display properties of the Stair have been color-coded to help illustrate the three ranges available: Up, Down and Above Cut Plane. If you wish, you can open the file and explore its settings. Space limitations in the text did not permit the inclusion of a tutorial on these components, but a movie file (which can be opened and played with Windows Media Player) named *Stair Plan Display.wmv* has been included with the files from the CD-ROM (in the *Chapter07* folder). The movie illustrates the details of the settings in the Understanding Stair Display file. The modified file (as it appears at the end of the video) has been included in the *07 Residential Complete* project's *Elements* folder. In the next several steps, we will make some edits to the display of our Stair in the current file. Before proceeding, take a few moments and play the video file and then optionally open and explore the accompanying drawing file.

38. Select the Stair, right-click and choose **Edit Object Display**.
39. Click the Display Properties tab.

Ordinarily, we would prefer to edit display properties at the Style level. You can see that this particular Stair already has style overrides applied to several Display Representations. If you watched the video file noted above, this is how the edits were made. However, in this situation, we need to change the cut height of the stair differently for the first floor and for the basement. Therefore, we will find it easier to edit at the Object level.

40. In the Display Representation column, highlight Plan (it should be bold).
41. In the Object Override column, click the checkbox next to Plan.

Since we are unable to rely on the Display Configuration Cut Plane setting for this Stair, we will need to leave the override applied (on the Other tab—see the video file). This means that we will need to manually adjust which components are visible on the Layer/Color/Linetype tab.

42. On the Layer/Color/Linetype tab, click the lightbulb icon next to Stringer Up.

This will turn off the dashed stringer lines and make the plan a bit less cluttered.

43. Turn off each of the Above Cut Plane components (see Figure 7.9).

    The lightbulbs will turn dim, indicating that the display of these components is off.

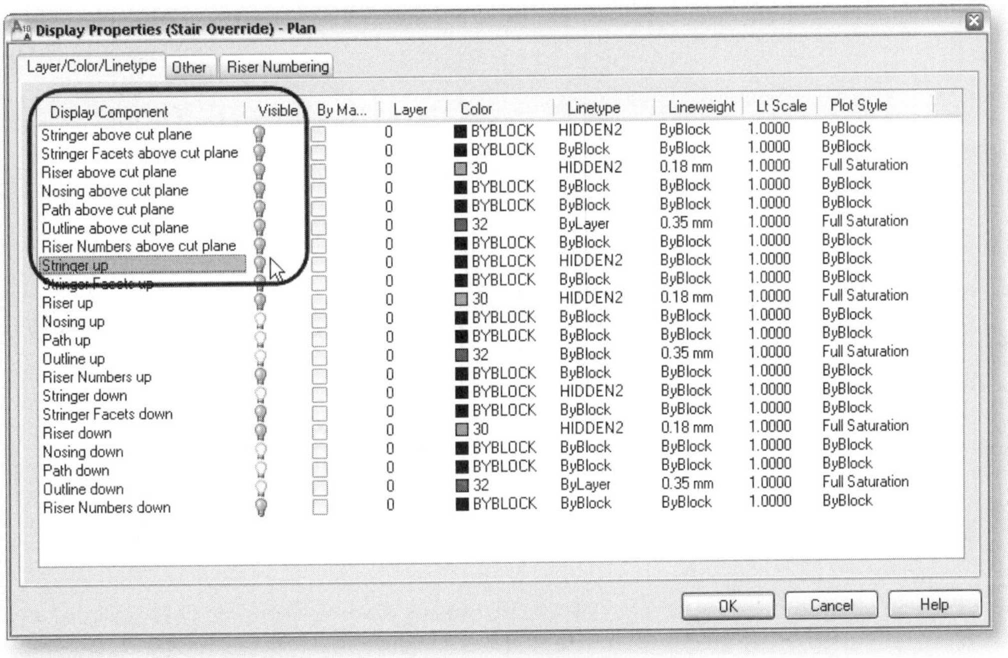

FIGURE 7.9 *Turn off the Stringers and all "down" components*

44. Click the Other tab and change the Height in the Cut Plane area to **6'-0"** [**1800**].

    This will move the diagonal break line and show more of the Stair in plan.

In the video, this override was removed to make Stairs use the Cut Plane setting assigned to the current Display Configuration (Medium Detail in this case).

By leaving the override applied, you can move the Cut Plane of this Stair without affecting the cut height of any other objects.

45. Click OK twice to return to the drawing.

    Notice that the above cut plane flight has disappeared, and the stringers going up have disappeared as well. In addition, the Cut Plane moved, showing us more of the Stair in plan.

Create the Basement Stair

Starting with the current Stair, we can create another that will go from the first floor down to the basement.

46. Select the Stair, and on the Stair contextual ribbon tab on the General panel choose the ***Add Selected*** tool.
47. On the Properties palette, change the Vertical Orientation to **Down**.
48. Change the Height to **8'-9"** [**2675**] and the Justify to **Right**.

After a Stair is created, the justification is no longer relevant. It is used simply to assist you in placement of the Stair as it is being drawn.

49. Click the point at the basement doorway (shown in Figure 7.10) as the Start Point of the Stair.

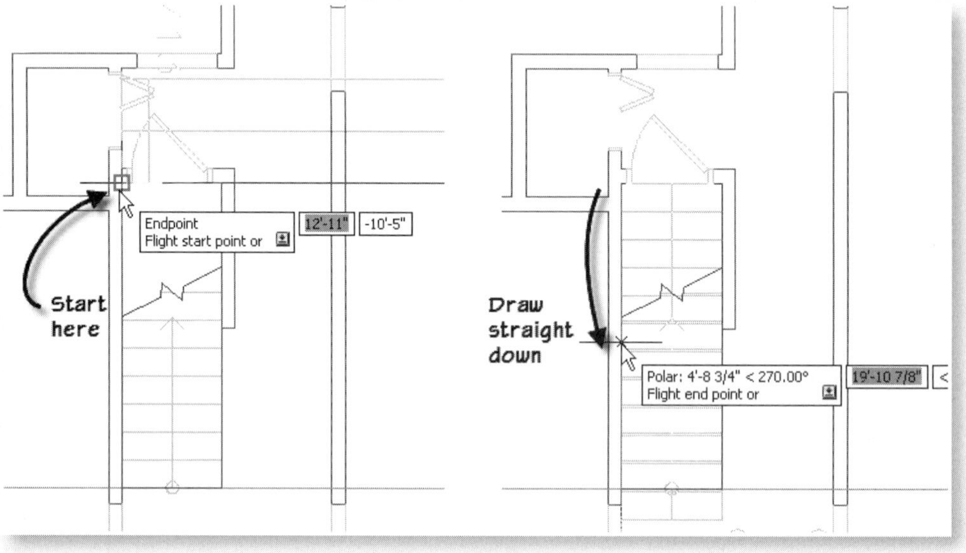

FIGURE 7.10 *Pick the Endpoint at the Basement Door as a start point—draw straight down*

50. Pull the mouse straight down 270° (using Polar Tracking or Ortho Mode) and then click. Press ENTER to end the command.

    A new Stair, very similar to the first, will appear in nearly the same spot as the first (see Figure 7.11).

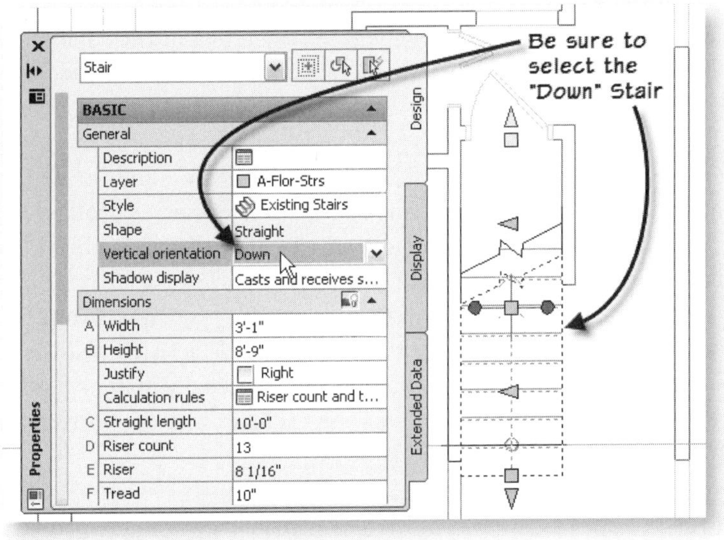

FIGURE 7.11 *Select the newly created overlapping Stair*

51. Select the newly created Stair, right-click and choose **Edit Object Display**.

TIP

To be certain that you selected the correct one, check the Vertical orientation on the Properties palette; the newly created Stair should have a "Down" orientation. If the one you selected is "Up," deselect it and try again.

52. Return to the Display Properties tab.

    The Stair object level override is already attached because it was copied from the original Stair when we used the Add Selected command.

53. Click the Edit Display Properties button in the top-right corner of the dialog box (or double-click Plan).
54. On the Layer/Color/Linetype tab, click the lightbulb icons next to Nosing Above Cut Plane, Path Above Cut Plane and Outline Above Cut Plane to turn them on.
55. Click the lightbulb icon next to each of the Up components to turn them off (see Figure 7.12).

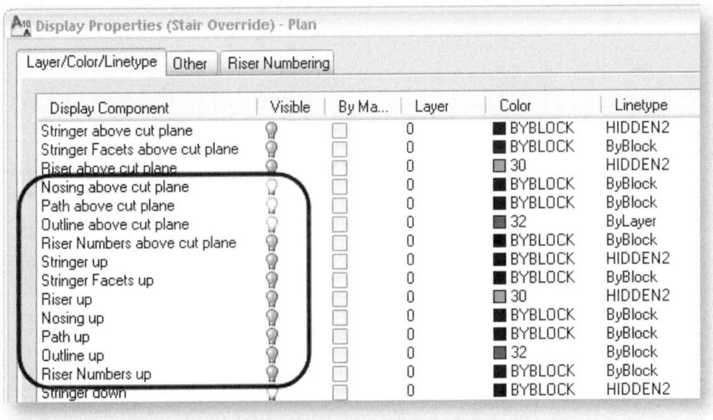

FIGURE 7.12 *Turn on several "above cut plane" components—turn off all "up" components*

56. On the Other tab, change the Elevation in the Cut Plane area to **6'-6"** [**1600**] and then click OK twice to return to the drawing.

Notice that the Stairs now display correctly. The change in Vertical orientation is not yet evident because we are viewing the plan. (We will see the effect of this change in the "Adjust Wall Roof Line" sequence below.) If you like, switch to an isometric display and have a look. Be sure to return to Top View before continuing to the next exercise. In this example, we had to use the Above Cut Plane components to represent the visual portion of the Stair. This again has to do with the behavior of the Override Display Configuration Cut Plane setting. When this option is enabled (as it is in both of these Stairs), the Display Configuration Cut Plane (seen in the video file above) is ignored and the Cut Plane is measured independently for each Stair object. Therefore, in this case, the 6'-6" [1600] value we used is measured from the bottom of the basement Stair. So, even though the entire Stair is actually below the Display Configuration Cut Plane of the first floor, the Stair is actually being cut relative to its own bottom, which occurs at the basement floor. This is why the portion we want to see is actually "above" the cut plane in this case.

Project a Stair Edge

The edge of the Stairs can be customized to conform to neighboring objects or polylines. In this sequence, we will widen the Stair as it passes the short Wall in the middle of the hallway.

57. Draw a polyline (Home ribbon tab on the Draw panel on the drop-down of the bottom half of the Line split button) from the outside corner of the half wall in the center of the plan straight down past the end of the Stair (see Figure 7.13).

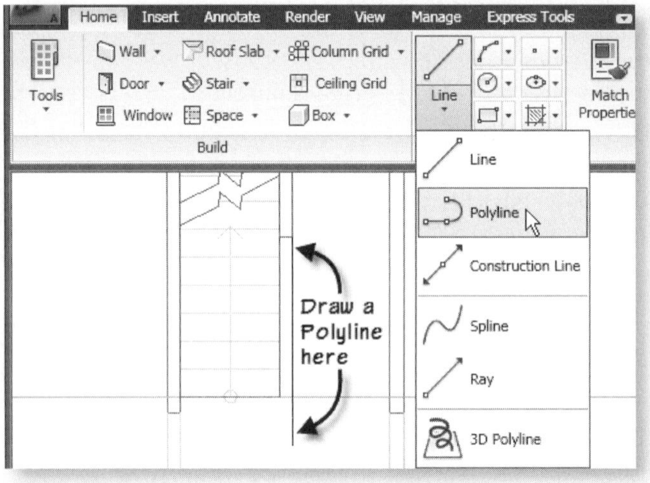

FIGURE 7.13 *Draw a polyline as an edge for the Stair edge projection*

58. Select the first floor Stair, and on the Stair contextual ribbon tab on the Modify panel, select the Customize Edge pull-down button and choose the ***Project*** tool.
59. At the "Select an edge of a stair" prompt, select the right edge of the Stair.
60. At the "Select a polyline or connected AEC objects to project to" prompt, select the polyline just drawn and press ENTER.

    The edge of the Stair projects to the line defined by the polyline.
61. Erase the polyline (see Figure 7.14).

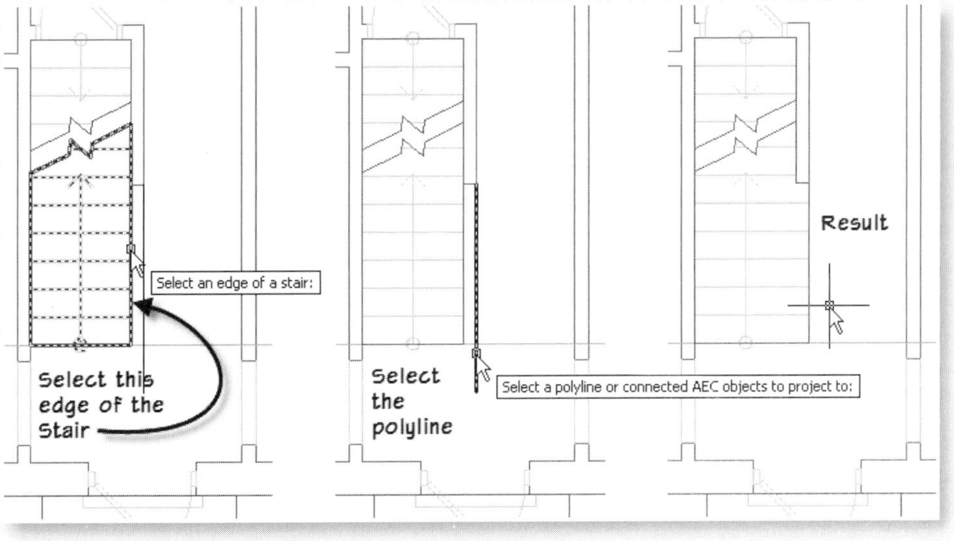

FIGURE 7.14 *Project an edge of the Stair to make it flush to the Wall line*

Adjust Wall Roof Line

Although our Stairs look fine in plan, a 3D View would reveal that the Wall at the Basement Door is too tall and intersects the Stair.

62. Using a crossing window, select both Stairs and the surrounding walls and doors of the hallway.
63. On the Multiple Objects contextual ribbon tab on the General panel, choose **Object Viewer**.
64. Use the Orbit (click and drag in the viewing pane) to dynamically change the view to 3D (or use the View Cube or choose a preset view from the View Control list like **SE Isometric**).

We can now see the effect of the Down orientation of the basement Stair. However, if you look at the top of the first floor Stair, it is passing right through the wall. If you will use this drawing only for plans, you could ignore this situation. However, it will be noticeable in 3D or Sections. Let's see the steps to fix it in 3D View.

65. Close the Object Viewer.
66. Click on the small horizontal wall with the door leading to the basement (the one that passes though the Stair); select just the Wall.
67. On the Wall contextual ribbon tab on the Modify panel, select the Roof/Floor Line drop-down button and choose the ***Modify Roof Line*** tool (see the left side of Figure 7.15).

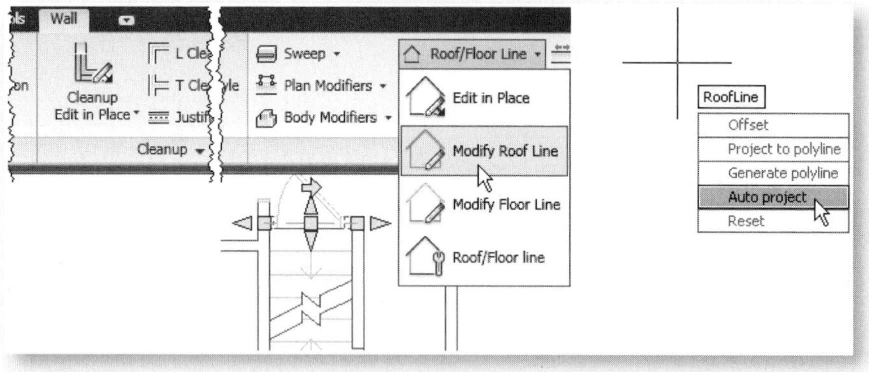

FIGURE 7.15 *Choose Roof Line to edit the top of the Wall*

68. If you have Dynamic Input turned on, choose **Auto project** from the list of options, otherwise, right-click and choose it from the list of options (see the right side of Figure 7.15).
69. At the "Select objects" prompt, click the first floor Stair (not the one going to the basement) and then press ENTER.

    The Command Line in response should read something like "[1] Wall cut line(s) converted." Please note that if you have turned off the Command Line, this prompt will not appear dynamically, but you can press F2 to see it in the text window.
70. Press ENTER again to end the command.
71. Select the Stairs, walls and doors of the hallway again, and on the General tab, return to Object Viewer to view the results (see Figure 7.16).

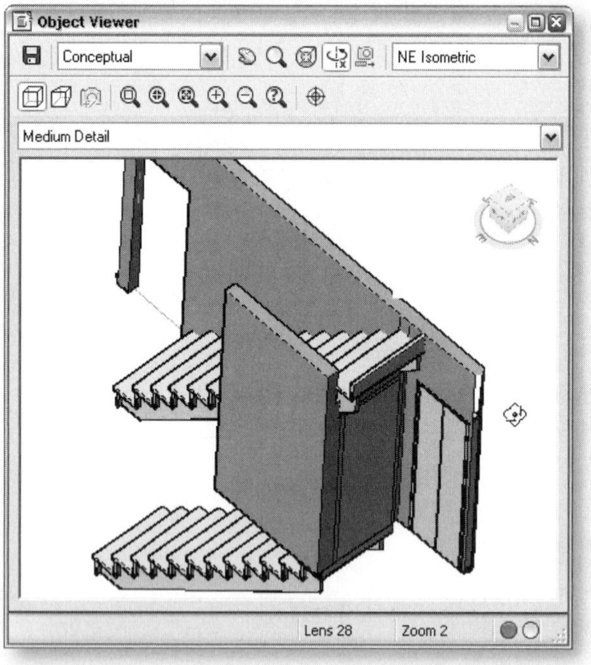

FIGURE 7.16 *The top of the wall now stops below the Stair*

72. Save the file.

Add a Railing

Railings can be added to Stairs or drawn as free-standing guardrails. We will look at both types in this chapter. In this sequence, we will add a Railing to the existing Stair.

1. Open the Content Browser (CTRL + 4).
2. In the *Design Tool Catalog - Imperial* [*Design Tool Catalog - Metric*], browse to the *Railings* category. Click Next to go to the second page of Railings.
3. Drag the eyedropper icon for Guardrail - Wood Balusters 01 and drop it into the drawing.
4. On the Properties palette, choose **Stair** from the Attached to list, and from the Automatic placement list choose **No** (see Figure 7.17).

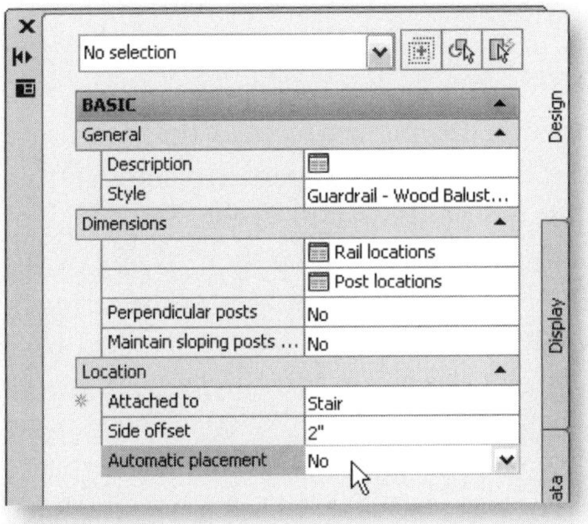

FIGURE 7.17 *Set the parameters to attach the Railing to the Stair*

When you turn off automatic placement, you will indicate the extent of the Railing with two clicks of the mouse. When you turn on automatic placement, the Railing will automatically extend to the full length of the Stair. In this case, we only need the Railing at the lower portion of the Stair.

5. At the "Select a stair" prompt, click the right side of the first floor Stair.
6. At the "Railing start point" prompt, click near the bottom of the Stair.
7. At the "Railing end point" prompt, click the endpoint of the Wall where the Stair jogs (see Figure 7.18).

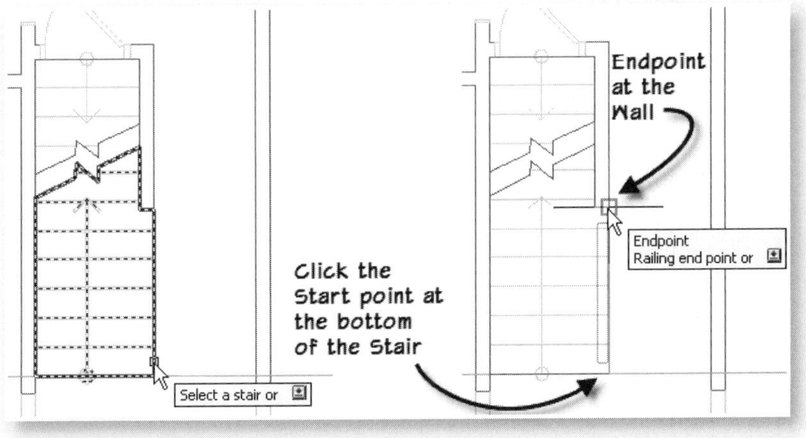

FIGURE 7.18 *Manually click the start and end points of the Railing*

8. Right-click and choose **Enter** (or press ENTER) to end the routine.

There is a slight gap between the end of the Railing and the wall. We can adjust this with grips.

9. Click on the Railing.

There are two triangular-shaped grips at each end: The one that is directly over the end of the Railing (End Offset) will lengthen the Railing, and the one that is offset from the end of the Railing (Fixed Post Position – it may be beyond the Railing end or within the Railing, depending upon your relative zoom at the time you select the Railing) will move the post. If you are unsure which is which, just hover the mouse over each one for a tool tip.

10. Click the Fixed Post Position grip at the top of the Railing and drag it slightly up till it snaps to the Wall.

Adding a Body Modifier to a Stair

Sometimes you want to add some details or embellishment to a Stair that can prove difficult with the parameters available in the Style or the Properties palette. To do this, we can add a Body Modifier to Stairs just like you can with Walls. You first create a 3D object that you wish to use as a modifier, then you apply it to one of the components of the object. In the case of the Stair, you can apply it to the stringer, tread or riser components. To save a bit of effort, a couple of Mass Elements have been included in this file. They are currently invisible using the Isolate Objects feature that we already saw when preparing the terrain model in Chapter 5. We will employ a similar process here.

11. On the Drawing status bar, click the red lightbulb icon and choose **End Object Isolation** from the pop-up menu (see Figure 5.17 in Chapter 5).

    Two Mass Elements will appear at the base of the Stair. We will use these to add a bullnose treatment to the bottom tread.

NOTE

To create Mass Elements like the ones here, simply draw a closed polyline, select it, right-click and choose Convert to Mass Element. Follow the prompts.

12. Select the first floor Stair, and on the Stair contextual ribbon tab on the Modify panel select the Body Modifier pull-down button and choose the ***Add*** tool.
13. At the "Select objects to apply as body modifiers" prompt, select the smaller (inner) Mass Element shape and then press ENTER (see the left side of Figure 7.19).

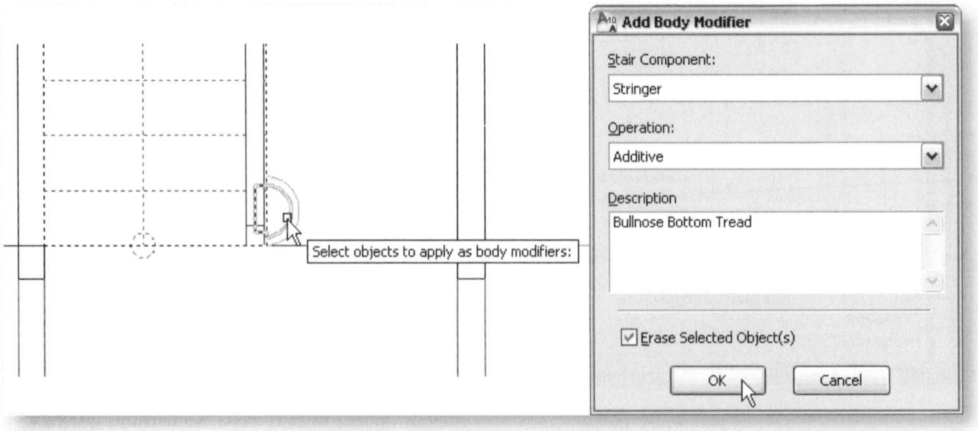

FIGURE 7.19 *Add a Mass Element as a Body Modifier*

14. In the "Add Body Modifier" worksheet that appears, choose **Stringer** for the Stair Component, leave the Operation set to **Additive**, add a description and select the "Erase Selected Object(s)" checkbox (see the right side of Figure 7.19).
15. Click OK to complete the operation.

    Since we told it to erase the object, the Mass Element disappears. Let's apply the other one and then look at the final result in the Object Viewer.
16. Repeat the entire process. Select the other Mass Element and apply it to the Tread component this time.

Using the grips again, you can fine tune the placement of the post at the end. Also, if you like, you can edit the Railing style and reduce the setting for "A - Extension of ALL Posts from Top Railing" on the Post Locations tab. This will reduce the height of the posts so that the railing passes through them instead.

17. Select the Stairs, walls and doors of the hallway again, right-click and return to Object Viewer to view the results (see Figure 7.20).

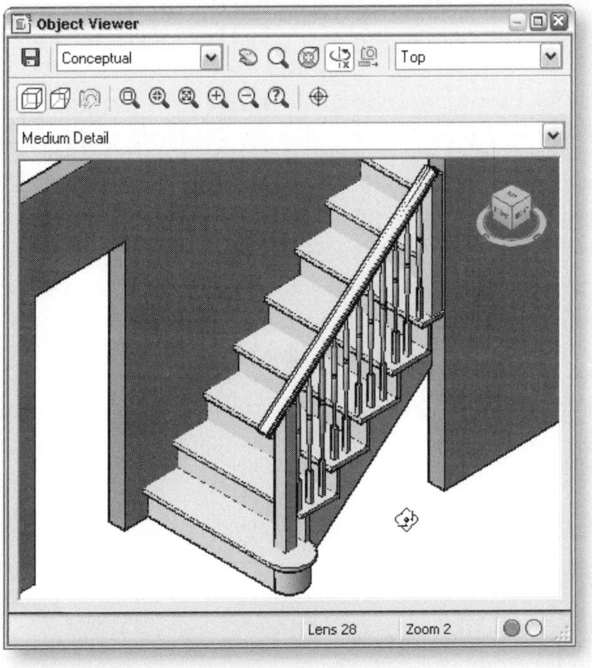

FIGURE 7.20 *The residential Stair complete with custom post locations and bullnose first tread*

18. Save and Close the file.

COMMERCIAL CORE PLAN

The Commercial Project files for Chapter 7 include a new Element file named *Core*. This file, included in files installed from the Mastering AutoCAD Architecture 2010 CD-ROM, already includes the core walls. This will allow us to focus exclusively on the vertical circulation elements.

Load the Commercial Project

Be sure that all drawings from the Residential Project are saved and closed

1. On the Quick Access Toolbar, choose **Project Browser**.
2. Navigate to the *C:\MasterACA 2010\Chapter07* folder and make the *07 Commercial* [*07 Commercial Metric*] project current.

3. On the Constructs tab, double-click the *Core* file in the *Elements\Architectural* folder to open it.

   As stated above, you will find core Walls already laid out in this file.

Add a New Stair to the Commercial Plan Core

The Column Grid created in the last chapter is already XREFed to this file as an overlay. With Overlay as the reference type, the Column Grid will not be included as a nested XREF whenever the Core file is attached to other drawing files.

4. Open the Content Browser (CTRL + 4).
5. In the *Design Tool Catalog - Imperial* [*Design Tool Catalog - Metric*] catalog, navigate to the *Stairs and Railings* category and then the *Stairs* category.
6. Using the eyedropper icon, drag the "Steel" tool into the drawing window.

   The Add Stair command will begin and on the Properties palette, "Steel" will be set as the Stair Style.
7. On the Properties palette, choose **U-shaped** for the Shape.
8. Set the Width to **3'-8"** [**1100**], the Height to **12'-0"** [**3650**] and the Tread to **11"** [**280**].
9. Choose **1/2 Landing** for the Turn type, choose **Clockwise** for the Horizontal Orientation, choose **Outside** for Justify and choose **Riser** for Terminate with.

Shapes include U-shaped, Multi-landing, Spiral and Straight. The Width is measured from stringer to stringer across the flight of stairs. The Height is measured floor to floor. Justification assists with placement of the Stair as it is being added, but it has little impact after placement. Horizontal Orientation determines which leg of the U-Shaped Stair is the starting leg. Terminate with determines what type of component, riser, tread or landing, will be placed at the end of the Stair.

The Stair tower is the upper-left space in the *Core* file. Make sure that OSNAP is on in the Application status bar at the bottom of the screen. This will aid in placement of the Stair.

10. Snap the first point at the corner of the inside wall intersection (see the left side of Figure 7.21).
11. Move the pointer straight up and snap to the opposite corner of the stair tower space (see the middle of Figure 7.21).
12. Press ENTER to complete the routine.
13. Move the Stair horizontally to the left **5' 8"** [**1800**] (see the right side of Figure 7.21).

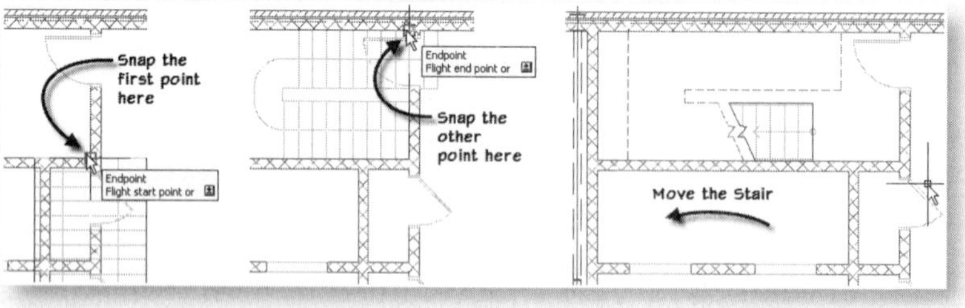

FIGURE 7.21 *Place the Stair by snapping to points on the Wall, then moving it to the correct location*

Note that the two flights are not even.

14. Select the Stair, right-click and choose **Properties**.
15. On the Properties palette, beneath the Advanced > Constraints grouping, choose **Lower flight** from the "Uneven tread on" list (see Figure 7.22).

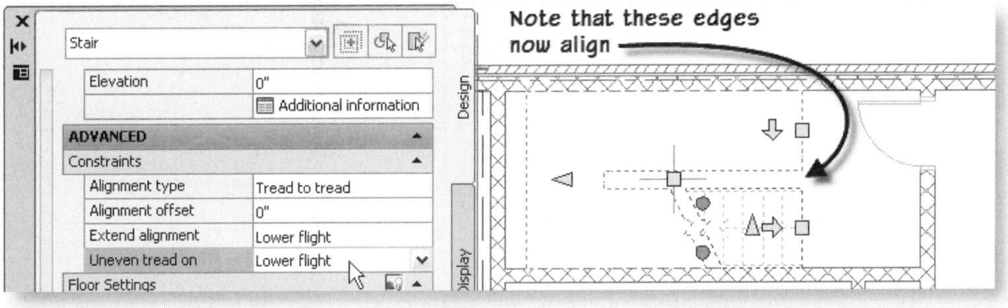

FIGURE 7.22 *Change the way the uneven tread is applied*

Extend the Landing

Like most ACA objects, we can use grips to fine tune the shape of the Stair after it is placed. In this case we will enlarge the landing.

16. Click on the Stair to activate the grips.

    As we have seen in previous exercises, if you pause your mouse over a grip, a grip tip will appear indicating the function of that grip point and shape.

17. Locate the "Edit Edges" Trigger Grip (it is a small gray circle) for the outer edge and click it (see Figure 7.23).

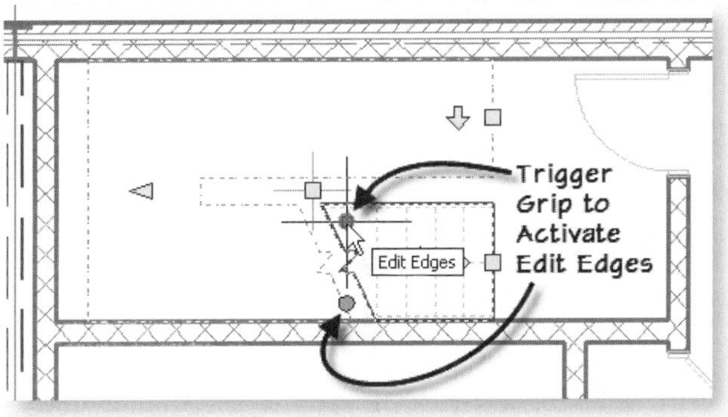

FIGURE 7.23 *Activate the Edit Edge Grips with the small gray Trigger Grip*

Several more Grips will now appear around the outer edge of the Stair. Hover over each one to see their function.

18. On the left side of the Stair, in the middle of the landing are two grips, one square shaped, the other triangular. Click the triangular-shaped grip.

    This grip shape manipulates the width of the landing.

19. Drag this grip point and snap it perpendicular to the core Wall to the left of the Stair (see Figure 7.24).

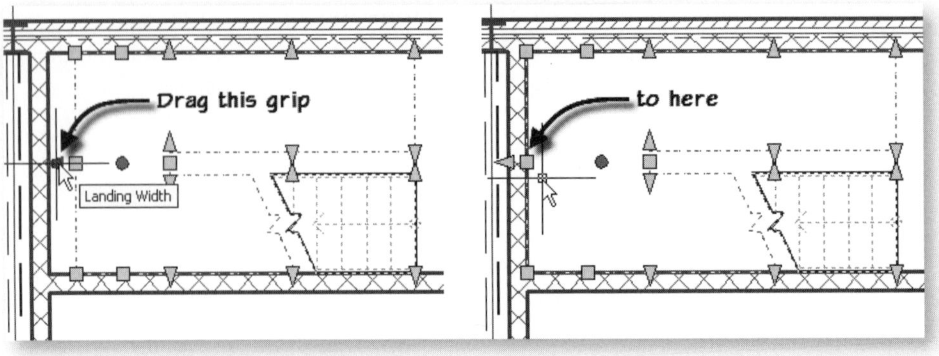

FIGURE 7.24 *Grip editing the Stair shape*

20. Experiment with additional grip edits. Undo when finished.

TIP

Grip editing offers an excellent way to get the shape of the Stair exactly the way you want it. Using the `CTRL` key while grip editing a Midpoint will extend just that edge without moving the ones connected to it. Try it out on one of the horizontal edges of the landing. Undo when finished experimenting.

Copy and Assign the Stair Style

Now let's make some modifications to the Stair Style for the Commercial Building Core.

21. Select the Stair, and on the Stair contextual ribbon tab on the General tab, choose the ***Object Viewer*** tool.

    In Object Viewer, view the Stair in 3D. You will notice that this particular Stair style has open risers. Let's change this to a Steel Pan configuration.

22. Select the Stair, and on the Stair contextual ribbon tab, on the General panel, click the ***Save As*** tool.
23. On the General tab, change the name to MACA Steel Pan, and type **Mastering AutoCAD Architecture Commercial Project Steel Pan Stair** for the Description.

Unlike the Residential Project, the Commercial Project is all new construction. Therefore, we will leave the Rule-based calculator on for the Commercial Stair. View the settings on the Design Rules tab if you wish. If you change anything, be sure to Undo the change before you proceed.

24. Click the Stringers tab and change the A - Width for both Stringers to **2"** [**50**].
25. Change the E - Waist (for the Landing) for both Stringers to **8"** [**200**].

    This will drop Stringers surrounding the Landing platform down relative to the landing.

26. Click the Components tab.

    We need to make some adjustments here to transform this open riser Stair into a Steel Pan configuration.

27. In the Flight Dimensions area, place a check mark in the Riser checkbox.
28. Change the A - Tread Thickness to **2"** [**50**], the B - Riser Thickness to **½"** [**12**] and place a check mark in the Sloping Riser checkbox.
29. In the Landing Dimensions area, set the D - Landing Thickness to **2"** [**50**] (see Figure 7.25).

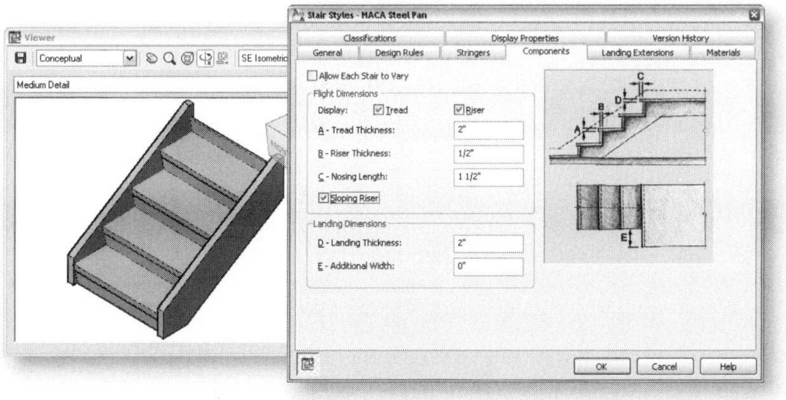

FIGURE 7.25 *Set the parameters for a Steel Pan Stair on the Components tab*

We do not need to change any of the other settings on the other tabs at this time.

30. Click OK to see the results.

    Use the Object Viewer to see the effect of all the changes in 3D.

Add Railings

As mentioned earlier, Railing objects do not appear automatically when a Stair is placed. They are separate objects. However, they can be anchored to Stairs. In this way, the Railing will respond to changes made to the Stair. Railing rules applied to the Stair object help control the exact placement of the Railing relative to the Stair as well as any extensions required by building codes. As with the Stair (and any other object type), we can use the Content Browser to locate an appropriate style.

31. Open the Content Browser (CTRL + 4).
32. In the *Design Tool Catalog - Imperial* [*Design Tool Catalog - Metric*], navigate to the Stairs and Railings category and then to the Railings category.
33. Using the eyedropper icon, drag the Guardrail - Pipe + Rod Balusters tool into the drawing window.

    The Add Railing command will begin and on the Properties palette, Guardrail - Pipe + Rod Balusters will be set as the Railing Style.

34. From the Attached to list, choose **Stair**. Set the Side Offset to **1"** [**25**], and choose **Yes** for Automatic placement.
35. At the "Select a Stair" Command Line prompt, click the inside edge of the Stair and then press ENTER to complete the routine.

    Notice that the Railings follow the inside edge of the Stair. If you zoom in a bit, you will also notice that they are displaying posts in plan. Let's simplify the Plan display.

36. Select the Railing, and on the Railing contextual ribbon tab on the General panel, choose the ***Edit Style*** tool.
37. On the Display Properties tab, place a check mark in the Style Override checkbox next to Plan.
38. On the Layer\Color\Linetype tab, turn off (click the lightbulb) all of the Post components (there are several) and then click OK twice to return to the drawing.

    The railing posts no longer display in Plan.

39. Return to the Content Browser and click Next twice to go to last page of Railing Styles.
40. Drag the eyedropper of the Handrail - Round + Return (Escutcheon) Style into the drawing.
41. On the Properties palette, change the Side offset to **-1 1/2"** [**-50**] and then choose **Stair Flight** from the Attached To list.
42. At the "Select a Stair" prompt, click the bottom edge of the Stair, and then click to the top edge when the prompt repeats. Press ENTER to complete the routine.
43. Using a crossing window, select the Stair and the Railings that were added, and on the Multiple Objects contextual ribbon tab on the General panel, choose the Object Viewer, and set to **SW Isometric** to view the results of the added Railings (see the left side of Figure 7.26).

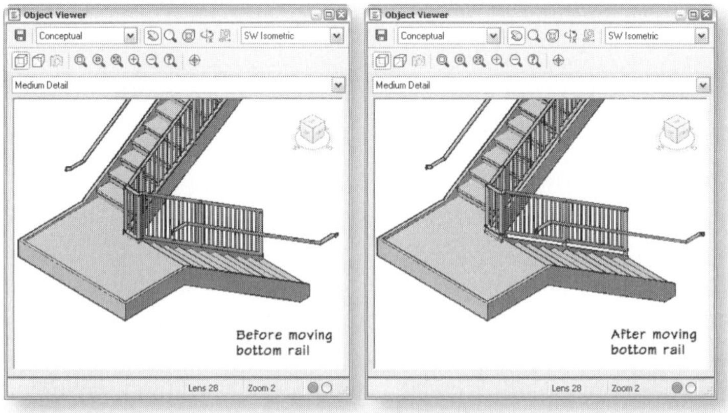

FIGURE 7.26 *The completed Commercial Stair with Railings*

Notice that the bottom rail of the inner railing nearly sits directly on top of the Stair Stringer. We can adjust this in the Railing Style.

44. Close the Object Viewer, select the inner Railing and on the Railing contextual ribbon tab on the General panel, choose the ***Save As*** tool.
45. On the General tab, change the name to MACA Guardrail - Pipe + Rod Balusters, and type **Mastering AutoCAD Architecture Commercial Project Guardrail - Pipe + Rod Balusters** for the Description.
46. On the Rail Locations tab, change both C - Horizontal Height and C - Sloping Height to **6"** [**150**].

    Feel free to explore the other tabs in this dialog and experiment with additional changes.
47. Click OK to close the dialog and accept the changes. Select the Stair and Railings again, and return to Object Viewer to see the results (see the right side of Figure 7.26).
48. Save the file.

STAIR TOWER GENERATION

In this topic, we will explore the Stair Tower Generate routine. Using this tool, we can create a single "spanning" Stair Tower for use in all floors of the project. (As we saw in Chapter 5, in Project Navigator the term "Spanning" refers to a Construct that occupies more than one Level or Division.) The routine *must* be used within the context of the ACA Drawing Management system. If you do not have a Project active in Project Browser, the routine will fail. The routine will automatically copy a Stair, and optionally any Railings and Slabs associated with it, to one or more levels of the project. Stair heights will automatically be adjusted to match the level floor-to-floor heights.

Since we are going to use this routine to create our Stair Tower, it might be useful to create a Slab for the landing between the Stair and the Door to the Stair Tower. Slab objects are AEC objects used to represent floor slabs, or nearly any horizontal surface. They can be simple flat slabs, sloped or embellished with custom edge conditions. Slabs will be explored in more detail in Chapter 12. For now, a tool with an associated pre-built custom Slab Style has been included on the MACA Commercial tool palette. (This palette was added in the "Create Grid Line Extensions and Load the Commercial Palette" topic of Chapter 6).

Use Isolate Objects

Let's begin by hiding the Railings so we can work with the Stair more easily.

1. On the Drawing status bar, click the Isolate objects icon, and then choose **Hide Objects**.

   It appears as a small lightbulb icon in the bottom-right corner of the screen (shown in Figure 1.3 in Chapter 1).

2. At the "Select objects" prompt, select all three Railing objects (zoom in as required) and then press ENTER.

> **NOTE**
>
> The Isolate Object icon will turn red, indicating that Object Isolation Mode is active. In other words, there are currently some invisible objects in the drawing. To display all objects, simply click the Isolate Objects icon again and choose **End Object Isolation**.

Add a Landing Slab

3. Right-click on the Tool Palettes title bar and load the MasterACA Tool Palette Group.
4. On the MACA Commercial tool palette, click the MACA Stair Landing tool.

If you did not complete Chapter 6, please visit the "Create Grid Line Extensions and Load the Commercial Palette" topic to learn how to load the tool palette.

5. At the "Specify start point" prompt, snap to the inside-right corner of the Stair tower (the same point indicated as "Snap the first point here" in Figure 7.21 above).
6. At the "Specify next point" prompt, snap to the inside-upper corner of the room (directly above the first point and the Door).
7. Continue adding points as shown in Figure 7.27, right-click and choose **Close** to finish the Slab, and then press ENTER to end the command.

   Points 3 and 4 are the top Endpoints of the Stringer, and Points 5 and 6 are the bottom Endpoints of the Stringer. Endpoint snaps will appear at these locations onscreen.

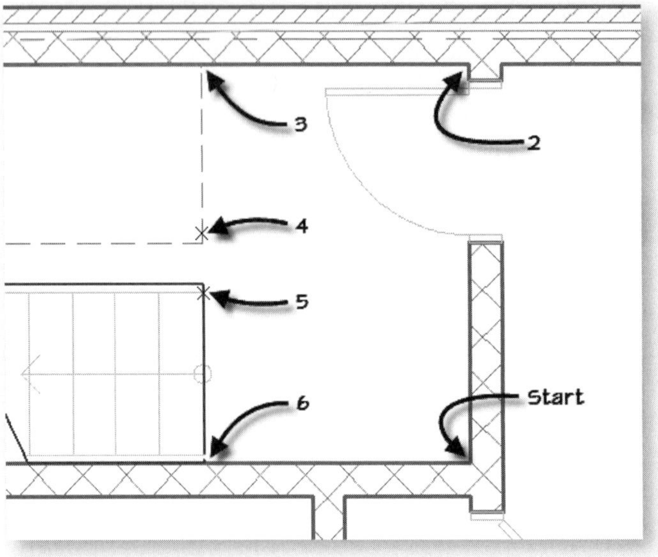

FIGURE 7.27 *Snap to the Stringer Endpoints to complete the Slab*

Edit the Landing Slab

The Slab extents appear to extend beyond the points selected. This is due to the Slab Edge condition, which has been designed to emulate the Stringer of the Stair. We of course need to make a few adjustments.

8. Click on the Slab and note the Grips, which are on or along the lines defined by the points that were selected. On the Properties palette, click the Display tab. Select the Display controlled by property, click on the down arrow to display the list and choose **Slab Style**. If a dialog appears, click on OK to accept the addition of a style override.
9. Select the Display component property and then click on the down arrow to display the list. Click on the dim light bulb icon next to **Fascia** to turn on this component. If a dialog appears, select OK to accept the change to all objects using this style.

A second line, connecting the selected points as well as the rectangular Edge Grips appears. Continue with the following adjustments.

10. With the Slab still selected, Click the top Edge Grip (rectangular shape on the top horizontal edge) and move it down **2"** [**50**].
11. Click on the bottom Edge Grip (rectangular shape on the bottom horizontal edge) and move it up **2"** [**50**].
12. With the Slab selected, on the Slab contextual ribbon tab on the Edge panel, choose the ***Edit*** tool.
13. At the "Select edges of one slab" prompt, click the vertical edge to the right (at the Door) and the two vertical edges to the left that abut to the Stair flights.

    The three edges should highlight. Press ENTER to complete edge selection. In the Edit Edges dialog, Edge 1, 3 and 5 should be listed.
14. In the Edit Slab Edges dialog, change the Edge Style of all three edges to **None** and then click OK (see Figure 7.28).

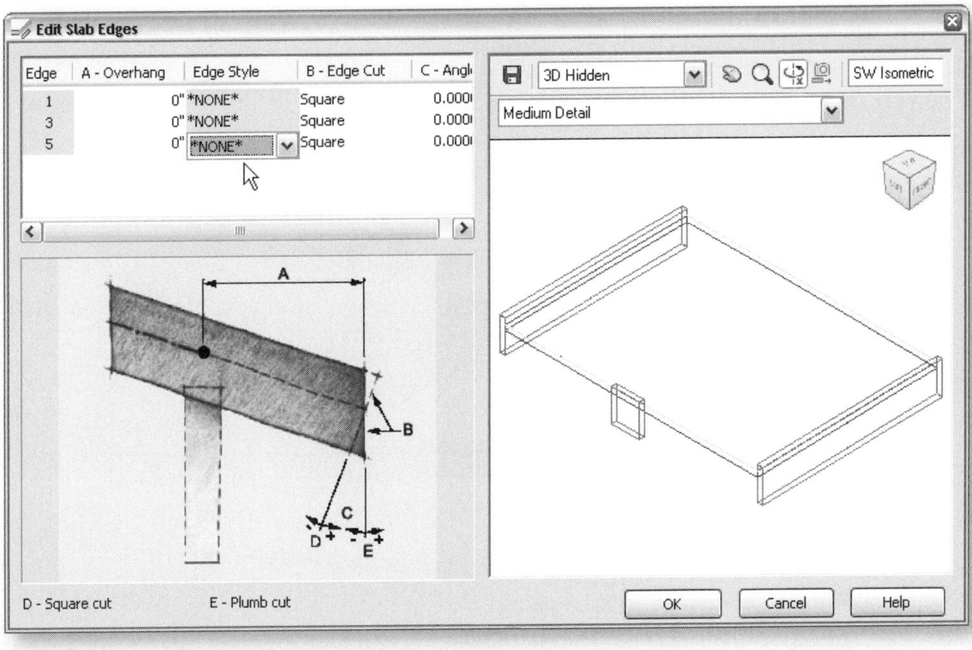

FIGURE 7.28 *Edit the Slab Edges to remove the Edge Style*

15. Click on the Slab and click the Edge Grip between the two Stair flights (small vertical segment).
16. Drag the Grip to the right with Polar Tracking or Ortho Mode type **2"** [**50**] and then press ENTER.

If you snapped points 4 and/or 5 to the stringer corner away from the treads, use the Edge Grip on the top and/or bottom of the small vertical segment to move point 4 up **2"** [**50**] and/or point 5 **2"** [**50**] down, so that the emulated stringer is wide enough to receive the stringers of the Stair.

17. Right-click and choose **Deselect All**.
18. On the Drawing status bar, click the Isolate Objects icon and then choose **End Object Isolation**.

Anchor a Railing to the Slab

The last item we need to create for the Stair core before using the Stair Tower routine is a small piece of Railing between the two Stair flights. We can anchor this Railing to the Slab.

19. Select the inner Railing (zoom in as necessary), and on the Railing contextual ribbon tab on the General panel, choose the ***Add Selected*** tool.
20. On the Properties palette (Design tab), from the "Attached to" list, choose **None**.
21. Following the prompts, snap from Midpoint to Midpoint as indicated on the left side of Figure 7.29.

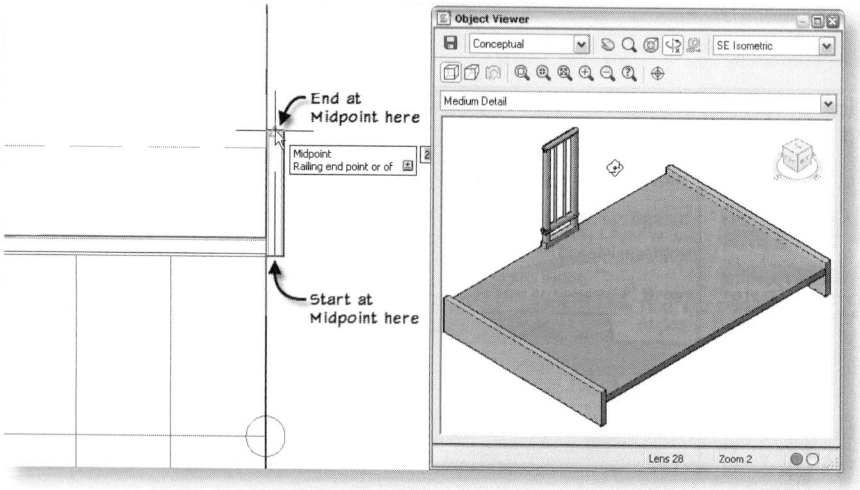

FIGURE 7.29 *Draw a Railing manually*

Remain zoomed in on the Railing.

22. Select the new Railing, and on the Railing contextual ribbon tab on the Anchor panel choose the ***Set to Objects*** tool.
23. At the "Select AEC Objects" prompt, select the Slab and press ENTER. Press ENTER twice more to accept the other defaults.
24. Select both the Slab and the new Railing, and on the Multiple Objects contextual ribbon tab on the General panel, choose **Object Viewer** to examine the results (see the right side of Figure 7.29).
25. Close the Object Viewer and Save the file.

Edit the Slab Display

One last finishing touch for our Slab: let's get rid of that line in plan at the Door.

26. Select the Slab, and on the Slab contextual ribbon tab on the General panel, choose the ***Edit Style*** tool.
27. On the Display Properties tab, double-click on Plan to edit it.
28. On the Layer/Color/Linetype tab, turn off (dim the lightbulb) the Below Cut Plane Outline component and then click OK twice.
29. Select the Slab, right-click and choose **Properties**.
30. On the Properties palette, scroll down to the Location grouping and change the Elevation to **12'-0"** [**3600**].

We don't need a landing at the bottom level so we have moved it to the top of the Stair run. By turning off the Below Cut Plane Body Shrink Wrap component, we won't get a line around the Slab. However, this is only evident at the edges we set to None, so we still get lines at the stringer locations.

Move Stair and Railings to the Spanning Stair Tower Construct

Now that we have all of the pieces of our Stair—the Stair itself, the Railings and the Landing Slab—we are ready to generate a Stair Tower. To do this, we must work in a Spanning Construct (see the "Create a Spanning Construct" heading in Chapter 5 for more information). A Construct named Stair Tower has been included in the Chapter 7 dataset. We will open this file (which is currently empty), move the Stair, Railings and Slab to it and then we will generate the Stair Tower.

NOTE

This file was provided simply to save a few steps. The file itself is empty, but it has already been added to all of the floor plan Views in the project.

1. On the Project Navigator palette, click the Constructs tab, and expand the *Architectural* folder.
2. Right-click the *Stair Tower* Construct and choose **Properties**.

In the Assignments area, notice that all levels (except Street Level) are selected and at the bottom notice the message indicating that the Construct is "Spanning" (this message is illustrated in Figure 5.25 in Chapter 5).

3. Click OK to return to the drawing.
4. In the *Core* file, select the Stair, all four Railings and the Landing Slab.
5. Drag them onto the Project Navigator palette, and release them on the *Stair Tower* Construct (in the *Architectural* folder).

   The Stair, Railings and Landing Slab will disappear from the *Core* file.

   If you prefer, you can select the Home ribbon tab, expand the Modify panel and choose the ***Cut*** tool and then open the *Stair Tower* file, select the drop-down button on the Paste tool and choose ***Paste to Original Coordinates***.
6. Save and Close the *Core* Element file.

Generate the Stair Tower

The Stair Tower Generate routine copies a selected Stair to one or more levels in the project. It will automatically adjust the height of the copied Stairs to match the levels in your project.

7. Double-click the *Stair Tower* Construct to open it.
8. Zoom in on the Stair.
9. On the Design tool palette, click the Stair Tower Generate tool.

   If you do not see this palette or tool, right-click the Tool Palettes title bar and choose **Design** (to load the Design Tool Palettes Group) and then click the Design tab.
10. At the "Select a stair" prompt, click the Stair. (Do NOT press ENTER.)
11. At the "Select railings and slabs" prompt, select the Railings and Slab and then press ENTER.
12. In the Select Levels dialog, verify that all available levels are selected, and then place check marks in both the "Include Anchored Railings" and the "Keep Landing Location when Adjusting U-Shaped Stair" checkboxes (see Figure 7.30).

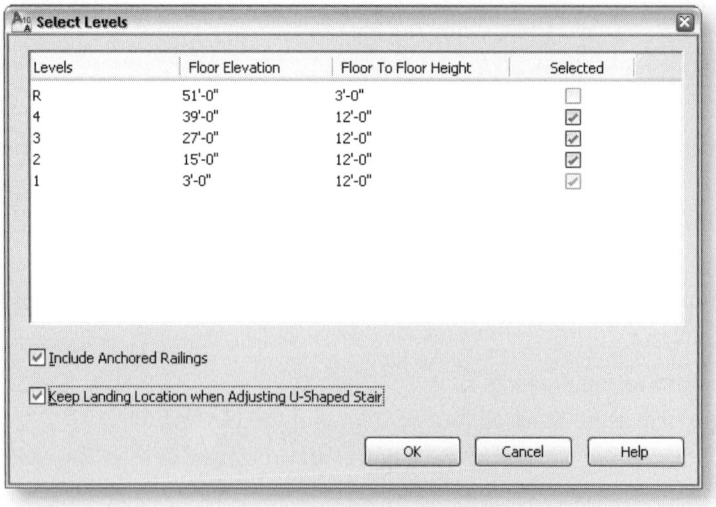

FIGURE 7.30 *Select Levels and Options for Stair Tower Generate*

The "Include Anchored Railings" option will copy the Railings to each level with the Stairs. The "Keep Landing Location when Adjusting U-Shaped Stair" will stack all copied Stairs relative to the landing position regardless of the height of the level. With this option turned off, the start of the Stair flight will be maintained on each floor and if the floor heights vary, the landings will not be aligned in the plan.

13. Click OK to complete the operation.
14. From the floating View panel (if you returned this to the ribbon, select the Home ribbon tab), click on the down arrow icon at the right side of the View split button and choose the ***View, Front*** tool (see Figure 7.31).

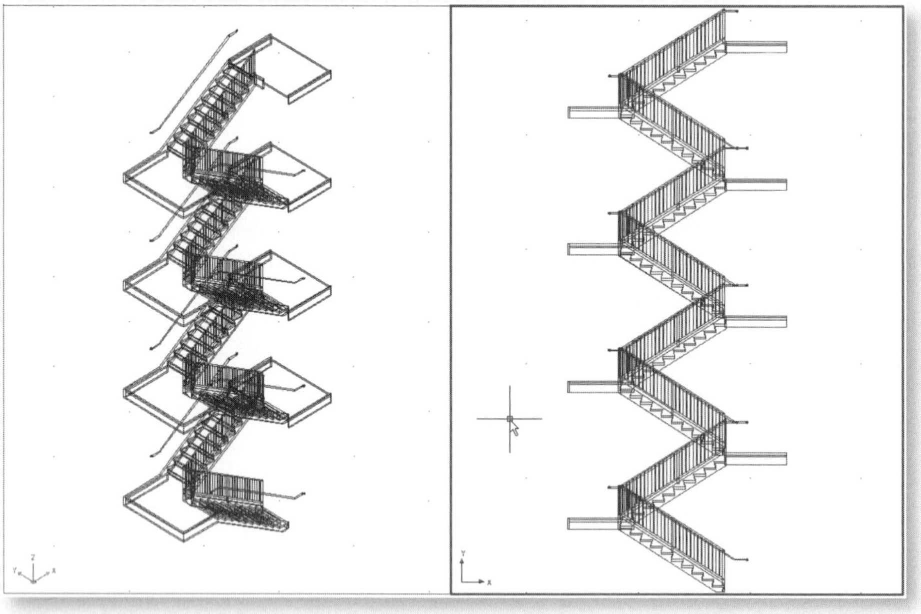

FIGURE 7.31 *Study the results of the Stair Tower Generate routine*

15. Save and Close the file.

Attach Core to Constructs

Before we open the Plan View files and view the Stair display, let's add the *Core* Element from above to each of the *Shell and Core* Constructs. This will give our Stair Tower its enclosure on each floor.

16. On the Project Navigator palette, on the Constructs tab, right-click the *Core* Element in the *Elements\Architectural* folder and choose **Attach Element to Constructs.**
17. In the Attach Element to Construct dialog, select all of the *Shell and Core* Constructs and then click OK (see Figure 7.32).

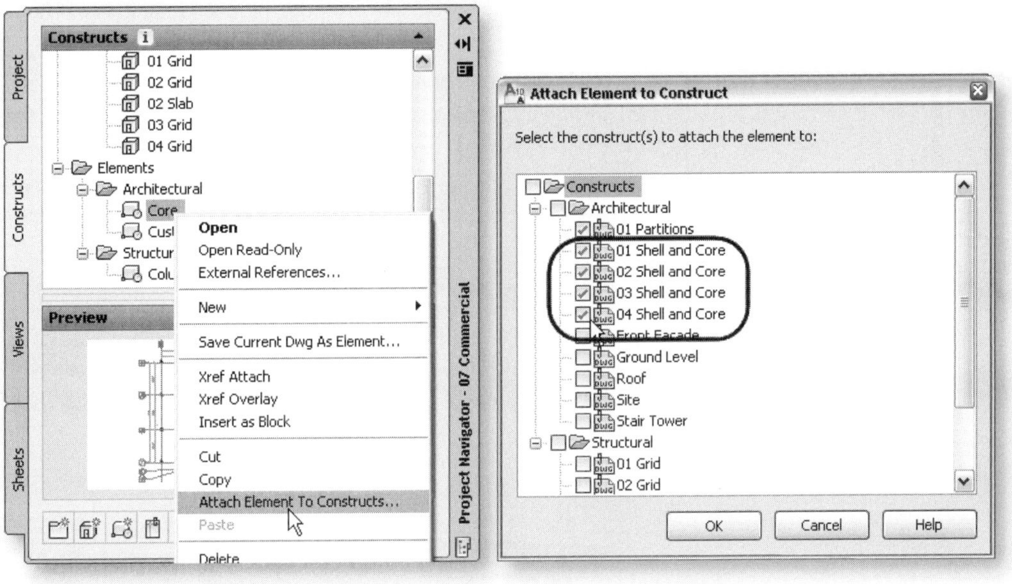

FIGURE 7.32 *Attach Element to all Shell and Core Constructs*

Viewing Spanning Stairs on Various Levels

The out-of-the-box template files (DWT) have been configured to show Stairs properly on various floor levels. On the lowest level, only the up direction will show. On intermediate levels, both up and down will show and on the top level only the down direction will show.

18. On Project Navigator, click the Views tab and then double-click *A-FP01* to open it.

    Zoom in on the Stairs and note that only the up direction is currently showing.
19. On Project Navigator, click the Views tab and then double-click *A-FP02* to open it.

    Zoom in on the Stairs and note that both up and down are currently showing.

It can be difficult to notice, but the way that the Stairs currently display, you can see some overlapping geometry. The default out-of-the-box drawing template file (DWT) used to create these files includes three versions of the Medium Detail Display Configuration: Medium Detail, Medium Detail Intermediate Level and Medium Detail Top Level. The only difference in these three is the way they display Stairs. Since *A-FP02* is an intermediate level, we should use the appropriate Configuration to display it.

20. From the Display Configuration pop-up menu, choose **Medium Detail Intermediate Level**.

Again, the change will be subtle, but some of the overlapping geometry will disappear.

21. Close *A-FP02*.
22. Repeat the process in *A-FP03* and *A-FP04*.

A simple Roof Plan Construct and View have been added to the project so we can see that the Stairs there only display the down direction. We will build a proper Roof file in Chapter 12. For now, let's open the simple version of *A-FP05* provided here.

23. On Project Navigator, click the Views tab and then double-click *A-FP05* to open it.

    Zoom in on the Stairs and note that only the down is currently showing. However, the Stair is still being cut diagonally. It might be better to display the entire Stair going down.
24. From the Display Configuration pop-up menu, choose **Medium Detail Top Level** (see Figure 7.33).

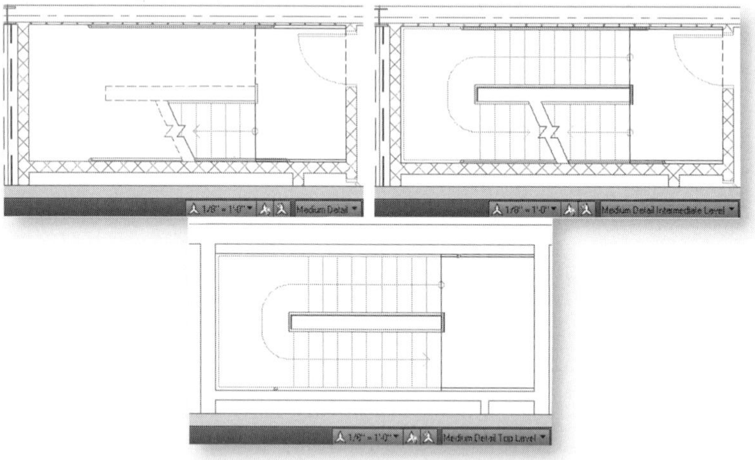

FIGURE 7.33 *Displaying the Stair using the built-in Display Configurations*

25. Save and Close any open View files.

Override Xref Display

In the First Floor Plan, even though the Stairs correctly display up only, we may wish to see more of the Stairs than is currently displayed. It is also often desirable to have the cut occur after the landing. This can be accomplished with an XREF Display Override.

26. On Project Navigator, open the *Stair Tower* Construct.
27. On the Manage ribbon tab on the Style & Display panel, choose the ***Display Manager*** tool.
28. Expand *Configurations*, select Medium Detail and then on the right side, click the Cut Plane tab.

29. Change the Cut Height to **8'-6"** [**2250**] and then click OK.

    The change will be immediately visible in the *Stair Tower* Construct, but to see it in the first floor View file, we need to apply an XREF Override.

30. Save and Close the *Stair Tower* Construct.
31. On the Project Navigator, open the *A-FP01* View file.
32. Click on the Stair in *A-FP01*, right-click and choose **Edit Object Display**.

    Since this is an XREF, you will get a slightly different dialog.

33. Click the XREF Display tab, and place a check mark in the "Override the display configuration set in the host drawing" checkbox.

This reveals the list of Display Configurations available in the XREF file, in this case *Stair Tower* Construct. Even though the names are the same, we have just changed the way that Medium Detail in the XREF looks compared to the version of it in the host file.

34. From the list of Display Configurations, choose Medium Detail and then click OK (see Figure 7.34).

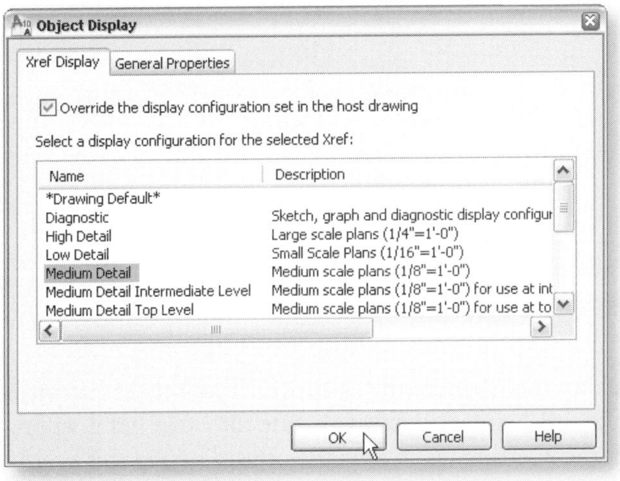

FIGURE 7.34 *Apply a Display Override to an XREF*

Note the change to the Stairs in the First Floor Plan. Feel free to reopen the *Stair Tower* file and repeat the process for Medium Detail Intermediate Level and then apply overrides to the other floor plan Views as well.

35. Save and Close all Plan View files.

CUSTOM STAIR CREATION

In this next sequence, we will create a custom feature Stair for the Commercial Project lobby using the Stair's "from Linework" command. Using this routine, you can sketch out a plan of both the Stairs stringers and risers or you can draw a series of treads. In either case, you can then convert this Linework to a custom Stair object. To assist us in this task, some files have been added to the project.

Attach an Element File

1. On the Constructs tab, double-click to open *01 Partitions.*

There is a large lobby space near the bottom of the plan. We will add our feature Stair to this space. The blue dashed lines are from a Slab object set at the height of the second floor. Linework for the Stair has already been drawn and provided in the *Elements* folder.

On the Project Navigator, expand the *Elements\Architectural* folder.

2. Drag the *Custom Stair* file and drop it anywhere in the *01 Partitions* drawing window (see Figure 7.35).

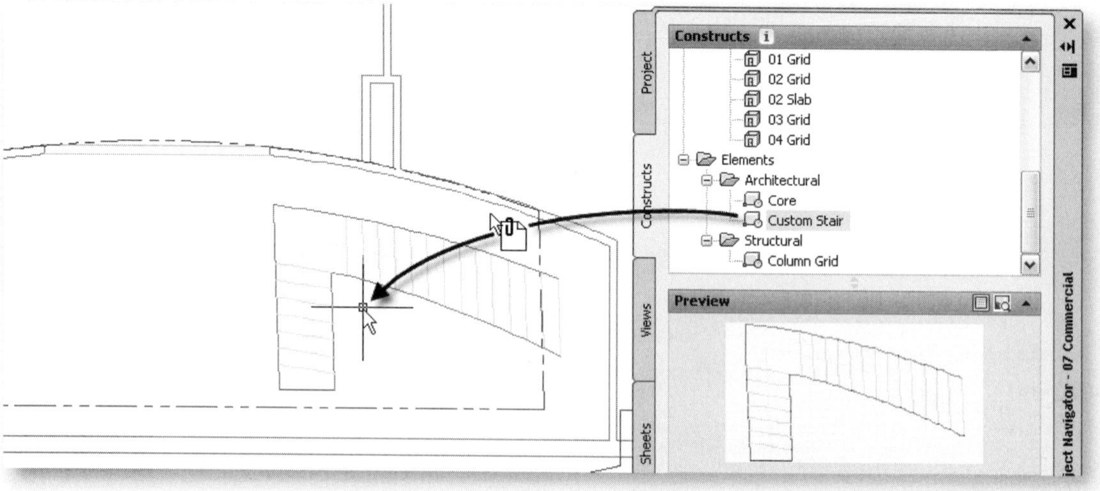

FIGURE 7.35 *Attach the Custom Stair Element as an XREF to 01 Partitions*

The drag-and-drop action attaches the Element file as an XREF to the *01 Partitions* file. We will open the Custom Stair Element directly to create the Stair, but dragging the XREF in is consistent with the way that we created the other Stairs in this project above. In order to create a custom Stair from Linework, you need to have either several closed polylines that represent the actual treads, or a series of open polylines like we have here. At a minimum, you need a polyline for each edge of the Stair and then one for every riser. All risers must touch the edges.

Create a Stair from Linework

3. Select the sketch we just dragged in, and then, on the External Reference contextual ribbon tab on the Edit panel, choose the ***Open Reference*** tool.
4. Make the MACA Commercial tool palette active.

If you don't see this palette, right-click the tool palettes title bar and choose **Master-ACA** to load the Mastering AutoCAD Architecture Tool Palette Group and access this palette.

5. Open the Content Browser (click the icon on the Navigation toolbar or press CTRL + 4).
6. Click on *Design Tool Catalog - Imperial* [*Design Tool Catalog - Metric*].
7. Navigate to the Stairs and Railings category and then the Stairs category.
8. Using the eyedropper icon, drag the Cantilever tool and drop it on your MACA Commercial palette.

This will add the tool to your palette. For this exercise, having the Command Line visible is helpful. If you have hidden it, on the View ribbon tab, on the Windows panel, click the ***Command Line*** button or press CTRL + 9 to display it.

9. Right-click the new Cantilever tool and choose **Apply Tool Properties to > Linework**.
10. Follow the command prompts and select the appropriate geometry:

    For left and right sides, select the magenta polylines and then press ENTER.

    For the Stair path, use the yellow polyline and then press ENTER.

    Press ENTER to accept the default and use the left and right sides and the path for the stringers.

    The first tread at the current level is the blue polyline.

    The remaining treads are the green polylines (see Figure 7.36).

NOTE

It is not necessary to color-code your own sketches. The colors are simply used to facilitate easy selection in this tutorial.

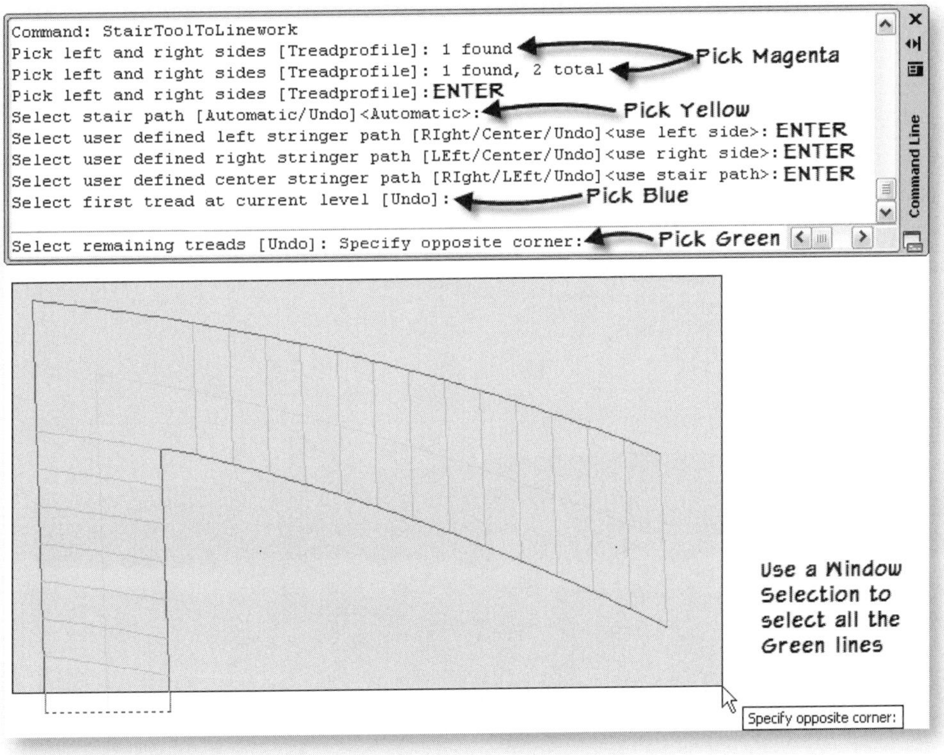

FIGURE 7.36 *Follow the prompts to select the appropriate linework*

11. Select all of the green tread polylines and press ENTER.

The "Convert to Stair" worksheet will appear. Make sure that the style reads Cantilever. If it does not, cancel the command and try again. Accept all the remaining defaults. If you want to erase the sketched Linework, place a check mark in the "Erase Layout Geometry" checkbox.

12. In the "Convert to Stair" worksheet, verify the settings and then click OK (see Figure 7.37).

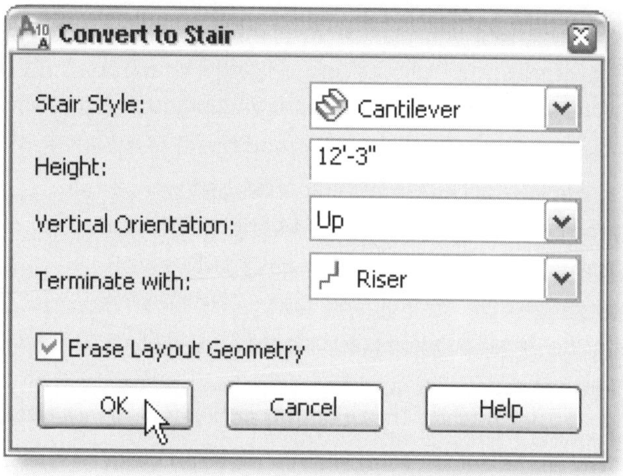

FIGURE 7.37 *Verify the settings to create the Stair*

13. Using the Object Viewer, study the new Stair in 3D.
14. Return to the Content Browser and drag in a suitable Railing and apply it to both sides of the Stair.
15. Save and Close the *Custom Stair* Element file.
16. Back in *01 Partitions*, reload the *Custom Stair* XREF.
17. View the model in 3D or in the Object Viewer (see Figure 7.38).

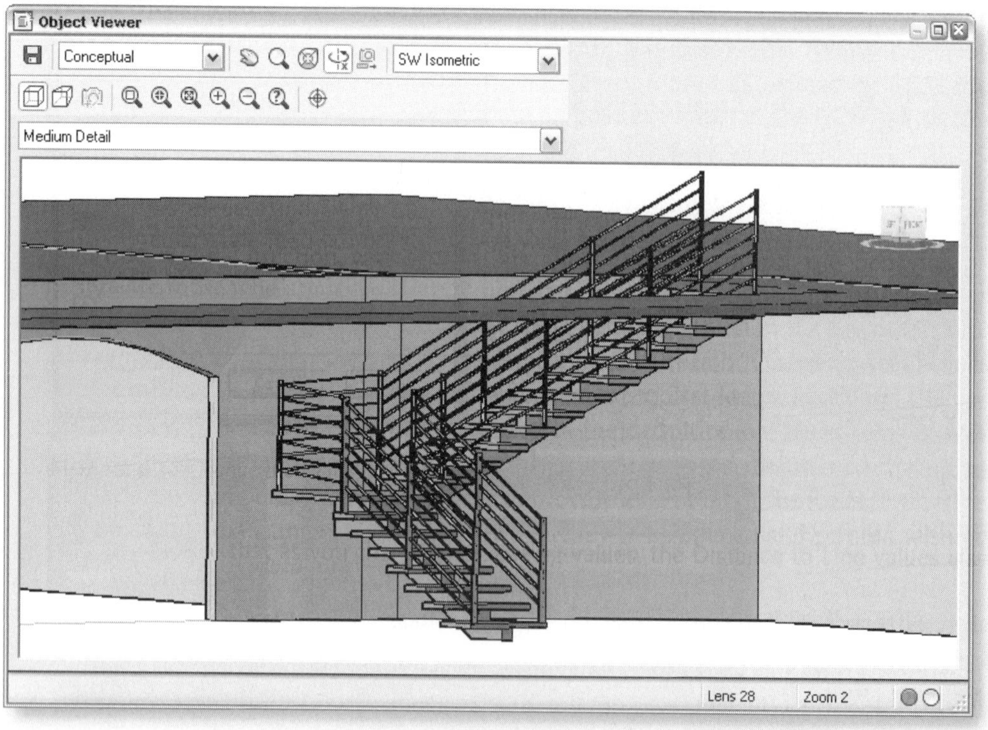

FIGURE 7.38 *The completed custom Stair reloaded back into the first floor partitions file*

18. Save and Close the *01 Partitions* Construct.

RAMPS AND ELEVATORS

In this section, we will add some ramps and elevators. Ramps and elevators are handled quite differently from one another. To create a ramp in ACA, use a Stair style defined for ramps. There are a few examples provided in the Content Browser. Elevators are created from Multi-View Blocks. There are a few sample Elevator Multi-View Blocks in the Content Browser as well.

Add a Ramp

A ramp is made by configuring a Stair style to "look like" a ramp. This is accomplished by two tricks: First, the ramp is actually a very wide stringer. Second, on the Components tab, both Tread and Riser are removed. In this way, a wide stringer is drawn without any Treads or Risers. This gives us a ramp. In all other ways, it has the same behavior and parameters as any other Stair.

1. On the Project Navigator, double-click the file named *Ground Level* in the *Constructs\Architectural* folder.

This file has been added to the project structure for Chapter 7.

2. Open the Content Browser again, and return to the Stairs category.
3. Drag (using the eyedropper icon) the Ramp - Concrete Curb tool into the drawing.

NOTE

Don't worry if it looks like a Stair while attached to your cursor. It won't when we are finished.

4. On the Properties palette, change the Shape to **Multi-landing** and set the Turn type to **1/2 Landing**.
5. Set the Width to **3'-0"** [**900**], the Height to **2'-8"** [**810**], Justify to **Right** and Terminate with to **Tread**.

Three sets of polylines have been included in this file. We will use the magenta one to draw the ramp.

6. At the "Flight start point" prompt, snap to the endpoint of the magenta polyline. (Snap to the lower one along the angled leg of the polyline.)
7. At the "Flight end point" prompt, snap to the next endpoint along the angled magenta polyline (see Figure 7.39).

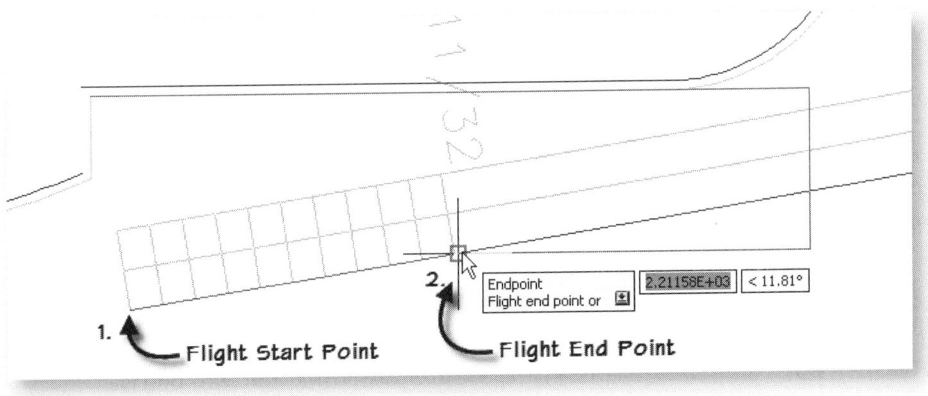

FIGURE 7.39 *Begin drawing the ramp by tracing points on the magenta polyline*

8. With either Polar Tracking or Ortho Mode on, move directly to the right (0°), type **3'-0"** [**900**] and then press ENTER.

The prompt changes back to "Flight start point." When you have a multi-landing Stair, you draw a flight of Stairs (or section of ramp in this case), then indicate some space for a landing, and then draw the next flight. The distance between the last "Flight end point" (or the top of the last flight) and the next "Flight start point" is the size of the landing.

9. The next point ("Flight end point") is the bottom-right corner endpoint of the magenta polyline.
10. Click the top-right corner endpoint of the magenta polyline next—this is the end of the landing and the start of the next run of ramp (see Figure 7.40).

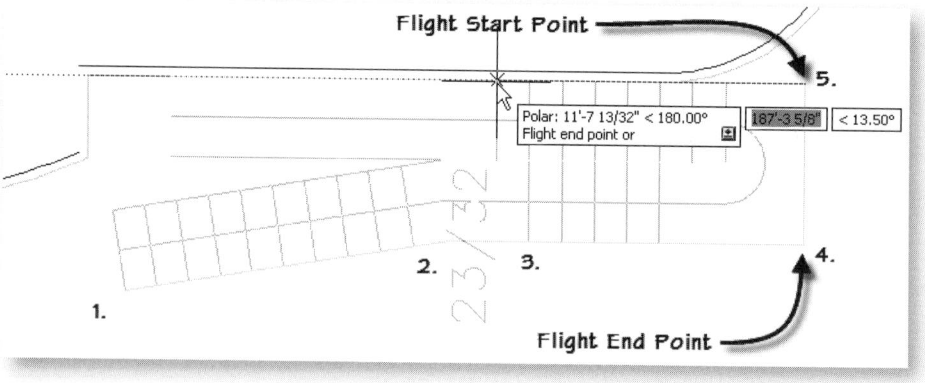

FIGURE 7.40 *Continue alternating between ramp and landing*

11. With either Polar Tracking or Ortho Mode on, move directly to the left (180°), type **12'-0"** [**3650**] and then press ENTER.
12. With either Polar Tracking or Ortho Mode on, continue moving directly to the left (180°), type **3'-0"** [**900**] and then press ENTER.
13. Snap to the final endpoint (top left) of the magenta polyline to complete the ramp (see Figure 7.41).

NOTE

Important: If you still have lots of leftover ramp, or if the ramp completely disappears, check your Properties palette, and be sure that the Calculation Rules are set to Height. To do this click the worksheet icon next to Calculation Rules and lock all settings by clicking the icons to change them to lightning bolts.

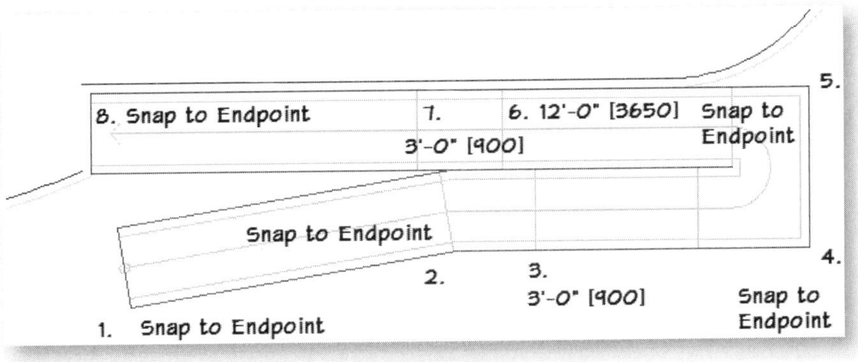

FIGURE 7.41 *Completed ramp with each point labeled*

14. Using the steps above in the "Add Railings" topic, add a Railing to the ramp.
15. Select the new ramp and Railing, and on the Multiple Objects contextual ribbon tab on the General panel, choose the ***Object Viewer*** tool (see Figure 7.42).

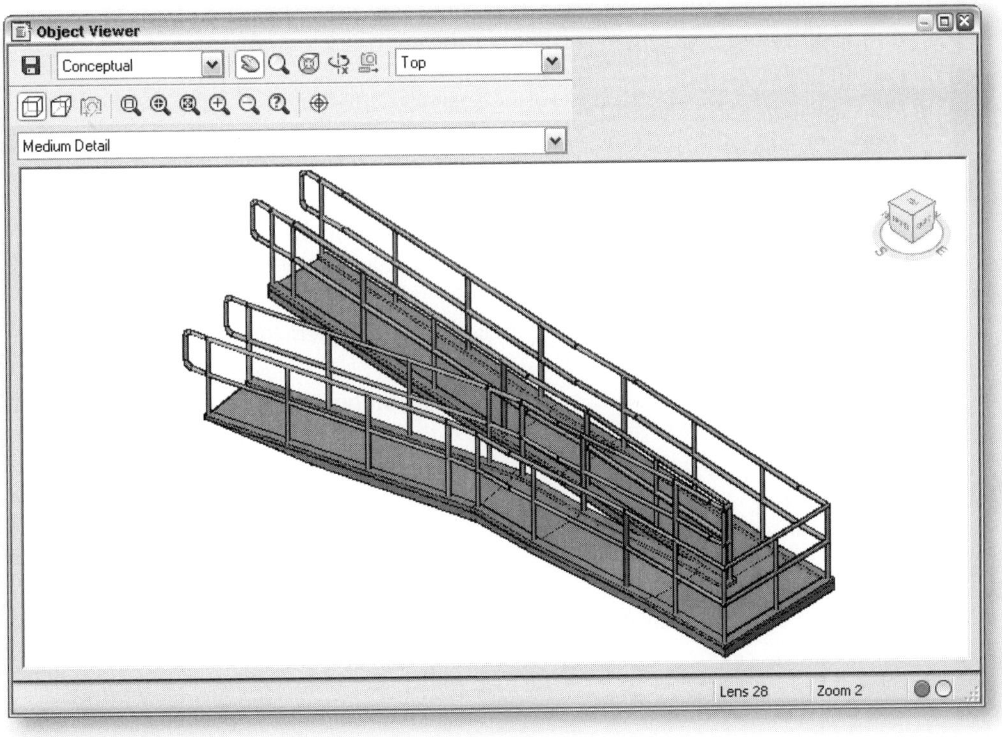

FIGURE 7.42 *The ramp and Railing in the Object Viewer*

16. Mirror the ramp and Railings to the other side.

Complete Entrance Terrace

17. On the Design tool palette, right-click the Slab tool and choose **Apply Tool Properties to > Linework and Walls**.
18. At the "Select walls or polylines" prompt, click on the green polyline and then press ENTER.

19. At the "Erase layout geometry" Command Line prompt, right-click and choose **Yes** (or type **Y** and press ENTER).
20. At the "Specify slab justification" prompt, press ENTER to accept the default. At the "Select the pivot edge for the Slab" prompt, move the cursor near the top edge of the polyline (a red line will appear when you get close) and click to select it.
21. With the Slab still selected, change the Thickness on the Properties palette to **2'-8"** **[810]** and the Elevation (scroll down) to **2'-8"** **[810]**.
22. With the Slab still selected, on the Slab contextual ribbon tab, on the General panel, click the ***Save As*** tool.
23. On the General tab, change the name to MACA Entrance Terrace. For the Description, type **Mastering AutoCAD Architecture 2010 Commercial Project Entrance Terrace**.
24. Click the Materials tab and change the Unnamed component material to Concrete.Cast-in-Place.Flat.Grey and then click OK.
25. On the Design tool palette, right-click the Railing tool and choose **Apply Tool Properties to > Polyline**.
26. Follow the prompts to convert the three blue polylines to Railings and delete the polylines. On the Properties palette, choose the same Railing Style that you used for the Ramp.

    Feel free to experiment further in this file. Use the technique above to anchor the three railings to the terrace Slab.
27. Save and Close the file.

Add Elevators

28. On the Project Navigator palette, right-click the *Elements\Architectural* folder and choose New Element. Name the new Element file *Elevators*. Double-click *Elevators* to open it.
29. On the Project Navigator, right-click the *Core* Element file and choose XREF Overlay. Zoom in on the Core.
30. Open the Content Browser (CTRL + 4) and in the Design Tool Catalog - Imperial, navigate to the *Conveying* category and then the *Elevators* category.

NOTE

The Metric Catalog does not contain Elevator symbols. However, the Imperial ones will automatically scale when inserted.

There are three Elevator Multi-View Blocks from which to choose.

31. Drag the eyedropper icon of the Elevator named Square into the drawing file.

    It does not matter where you drop it; we will move and rotate it in the next step.
32. Rotate the elevator 270° and then move it into position in the space below the Stair tower.
33. Copy the elevator next to the first to create the second one (see Figure 7.43).

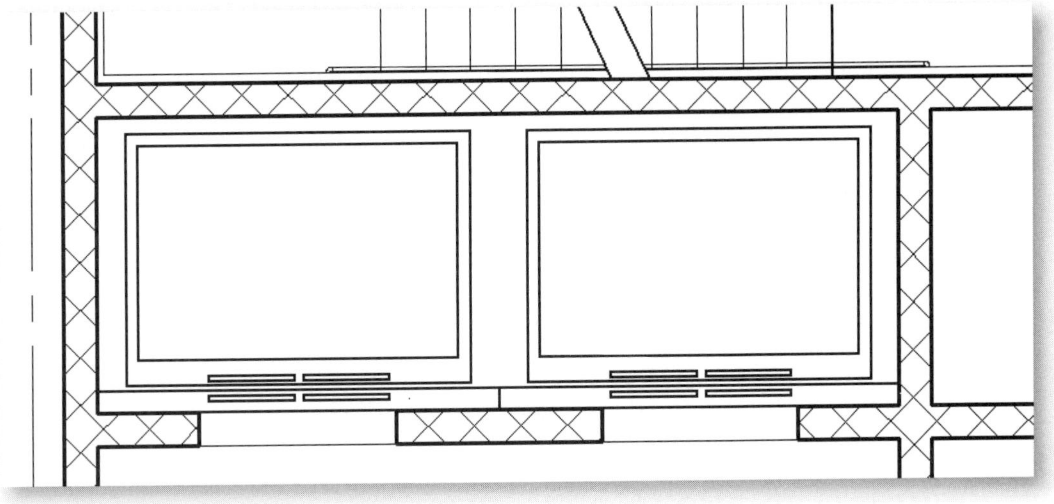

FIGURE 7.43 *Elevators XREFed to the Core file*

34. Select both elevators, right-click and choose **Object Viewer**.
35. View from all sides, and close the Viewer when finished.
36. Save and Close the file.

NOTE

These Elevators are Multi-View Blocks. You can edit them to suit your needs. If you receive blocks from an Elevator manufacturer, you can build your own, or customize this Multi-View Block from those files. See Chapter 11 for more information on creating and editing Multi-View Blocks.

We could have simply added the Elevator Multi-View Blocks directly to the *Core* file rather than create a new and separate *Elevators* file. However, by taking this extra step, we can later add the Elevators just once to the composite model from which we will cut our sections. This way, we will only see one set of elevator cabs in the section cut rather than one on every floor. If you are primarily concerned with plans, you can skip the step of creating the *Elevators* file above and add the elevators directly to the *Core* Element file.

TOILET ROOMS

The last item needed in our core plan is the restrooms. There are premade fixture layouts in the Content Browser, as well as a collection of individual fixtures.

Add Toilet Layouts

1. On the Project Navigator palette, double-click the *Elements\Architectural\Core* Element File to open it.
2. Open the Content Browser (CTRL + 4).
3. In the *Design Tool Catalog - Imperial* [*Design Tool Catalog - Metric*] catalog, navigate to the *Mechanical > Plumbing Fixtures > Layouts* [*Bathroom > Layouts*] category.

4. Drag the eyedropper for the Rest Room (Women) [Toilet (Women)] layout into the drawing.
5. The Insert Block dialog box will appear; accept all defaults and click OK. (However, if Explode is checked, uncheck it.)

This object is actually an AutoCAD block containing several AEC objects. Leave it as a block to position it in the room. Explode it to manipulate the actual pieces of the layout. Be sure to explode it only once! If you explode a second time, you will destroy the nested ACA Multi-View Blocks within.

6. Use the single grip point at its insertion to position it in one of the rooms at the right.
7. Move, rotate and mirror as necessary.
8. Once it is positioned correctly, explode the block.

CAUTION

Be sure to explode the block only once. If you explode it again, you will destroy its nested ACA objects. If you accidentally do it twice, please Undo.

9. Delete one stall, and move the counter and lavatories to fit the room.
10. Repeat the steps above for the Rest Room (Men) [Toilet (Men)] layout (see Figure 7.44).

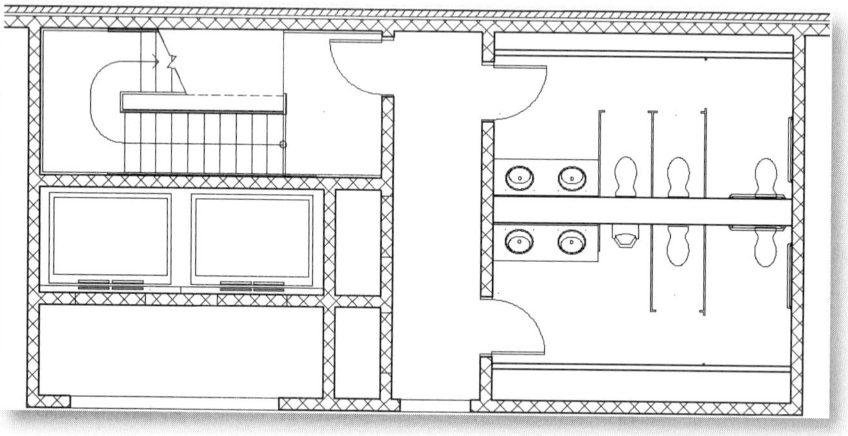

FIGURE 7.44 *The final core plan layout*

11. Save and Close all project files.

ADDITIONAL EXERCISES

Space limitations prevent a discussion of all of the powerful features of Stairs. You are encouraged to search for additional stair topics, such as Interference Conditions, in the online help. Additional exercises have been provided in Appendix A. In Appendix A you will find an exercise for adding a new Stair to the *Basement New* construction file of the Residential project. There is also an exercise to complete the front entry plaza for the Commercial project. It is not necessary that you complete this exercise to begin the next chapter; it is provided to enhance your learning experience. Completed projects for each of the exercises have been provided in the *Chapter07/ Complete* folder.

SUMMARY

- Stairs and Railings offer flexible configuration with style-based parameters and optional object-based variations.
- A single Stair object can be configured to represent one or two flights in the Display Properties.
- Stair shapes can be manipulated with grips.
- Slabs can be used with Stairs to create Landings.
- Stair Tower Generate can be used with ACA Project Navigator to create Spanning Stair Constructs.
- Custom Display Properties can be configured to show Stairs correctly on the bottom, middle and upper levels.
- Display Overrides can be attached to XREF files to force them to display in a different Display Configuration than the host drawing.
- Railings can be anchored to Stairs or drawn free-form as guardrails.
- Custom Stairs can be created from a series of sketched polylines used to represent the stringers, treads and risers.
- Ramps are created from Stair styles.
- Premade elevators and toilet layouts are included in the Content Browser.

CHAPTER

8

The Building Shell

INTRODUCTION

In this chapter, we will enclose our Commercial Project with a building skin. The skin will be comprised of masonry enclosure on three sides, with a Curtain Wall on the front of the building. The Curtain Wall is a "spanning" element beginning on the second floor and spanning the third and fourth floors. The correct display graphics of the spanning Curtain Wall on each floor is a built-in benefit of Project Navigator.

OBJECTIVES

In order to complete the shell of the Commercial Project, we will edit the Wall style applied to the Shell files created in Chapter 5 and use the Project Standards feature to synchronize the change to all floors. We will also build a custom Curtain Wall for the front façade. We will take a comprehensive look at ACA's Curtain Wall object to build this front façade—this will be the major focus of the chapter. The main tools covered in this chapter include the following:

- Use Project Standards to synchronize styles.
- Convert Walls to Curtain Walls.
- Build a Curtain Wall.
- Create a Custom Curtain Wall style.
- Convert an Elevation Sketch to a Curtain Wall.
- Work with Curtain Wall In-Place Edit.

CREATING THE MASONRY SHELL

In this exercise, we will refine the *Shell and Core* Construct files (created in Chapter 5) with an appropriate Wall style from the Content Library and then synchronize the change across the project.

Install the Cd Files and Load the Current Project

If you have already installed all of the files from the CD, simply skip down to step 3 below to make the project active. If you need to install the CD files, start at step 1.

1. If you have not already done so, install the dataset files located on the Mastering AutoCAD Architecture 2010 CD-ROM.

   Refer to "Files Included on the CD-ROM" in the Preface for information on installing the sample files included on the CD.

2. Launch AutoCAD Architecture 2010 from the desktop icon created in Chapter 3.

If you did not create a custom icon, you might want to review "Create a New Profile" and "Create a Desktop Shortcut" in Chapter 3. Creating the custom desktop icon is not essential; however, it makes loading the custom profile easier.

3. On the QAT, click the Project Browser icon.
4. Click to open the folder list and choose your *C:* drive.
5. Double-click on the *MasterACA 2010* folder, and then the *Chapter08* folder.

   One or two commercial Projects will be listed: *08 Commercial* and/or *08 Commercial Metric.*

6. Double-click *08 Commercial* if you wish to work in Imperial units. Double-click *08 Commercial Metric* if you wish to work in Metric units. (You can also right-click on it and choose **Set Current Project.**) Then click Close in the Project Browser.

NOTE

Important: If a message appears asking you to repath the project, click the "Repath the project now" option. Refer to the "Repathing Projects" topic in the Preface for more information.

Copy Walls Between Files

In Chapter 5 we built four Shell files containing four Walls in the basic shape of the building's footprint. This was useful for the early stage of the project. It is now time to begin adding some more detail to these files and refine the Wall layout.

1. On the Project Navigator palette, in the *Constructs\Architectural* folder, double-click the *Ground Level* Construct to open it.

   The Walls in this file more accurately portray the desired Wall layout for the upper floors. We will copy and paste a couple of them to assist with the upper floors.

2. Select the two short vertical Walls on either side of the entry terrace (see Figure 8.1).

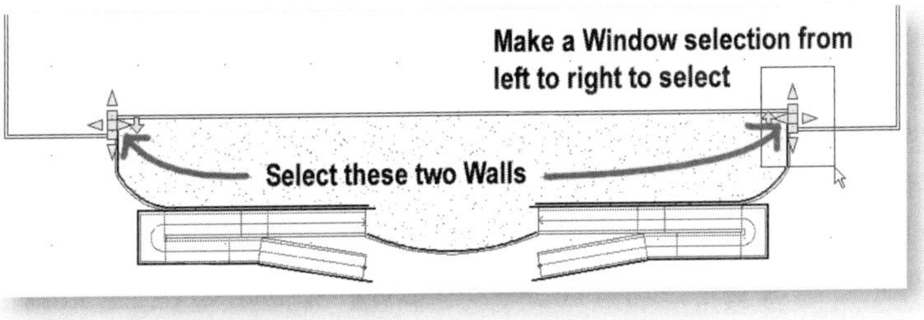

FIGURE 8.1 *Select the two short vertical Walls*

3. On the Home tab, expand the Modify panel and then click the Copy to Clipboard tool (or press CTRL + C).
4. Close the *Ground Level* Construct (it is not necessary to save) and then on the Project Navigator palette, double-click the *01 Shell and Core* Construct to open it.
5. On the Home tab, expand the Modify panel and then click the drop-down button on the Paste button and choose the Paste to Original Coordinates tool.
6. On the Modify panel, click the drop-down button on the AEC Trim tool and choose Trim (or type **TR** at the Command Line and then press ENTER).
7. At the "Select cutting edges – Select Objects" prompt, select both of the small Walls just pasted and then press ENTER.

TIP

Remember, to receive onscreen prompts, turn on Dynamic Input by activating the toggle icon on the Application Status bar. Refer to Chapter 1 for more information.

8. At the "Select object to trim" prompt, click in the middle of the bottom horizontal Wall and then press ENTER to complete the command (see Figure 8.2).

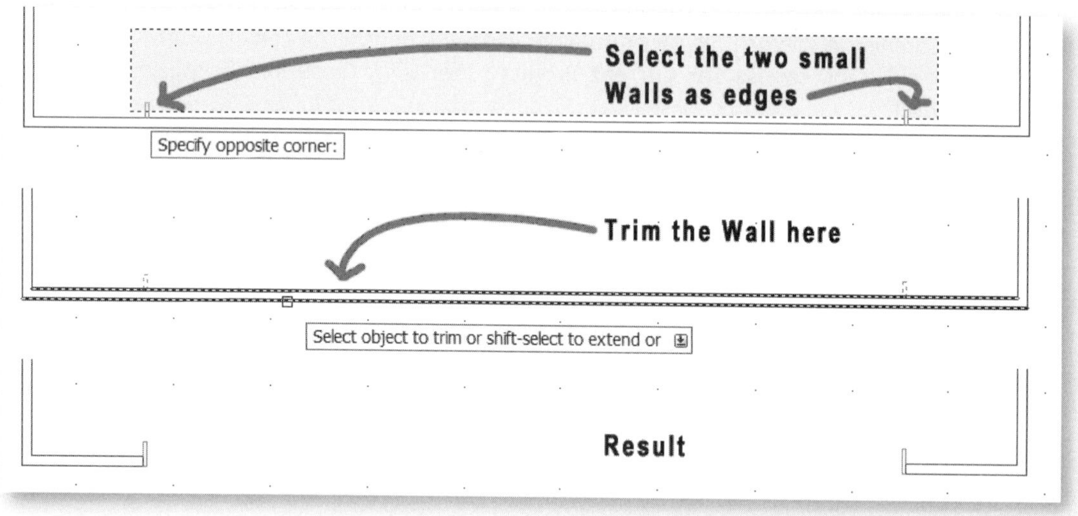

FIGURE 8.2 *Trim the middle segment of the Wall away using the two pasted Walls as edges*

The two small Walls need some slight adjustment.

9. Hover your mouse over one of the small Walls and note the tool tip.
10. Move the mouse over one of the shell Walls and note the tool tip (see the left side of Figure 8.3).

Notice that the shell Walls use the style: Exterior Shell (as assigned to them back in Chapter 5) and the two pasted short Walls use the Standard style. We can use Match Properties to correct this.

11. On the Home tab, on the Modify panel, click the Match Properties button.
12. At the "Select source objects" prompt, select one of the shell Walls.
13. At the "Select destination object(s)" prompt, select both short pasted Walls and then press ENTER (see the right side of Figure 8.3).

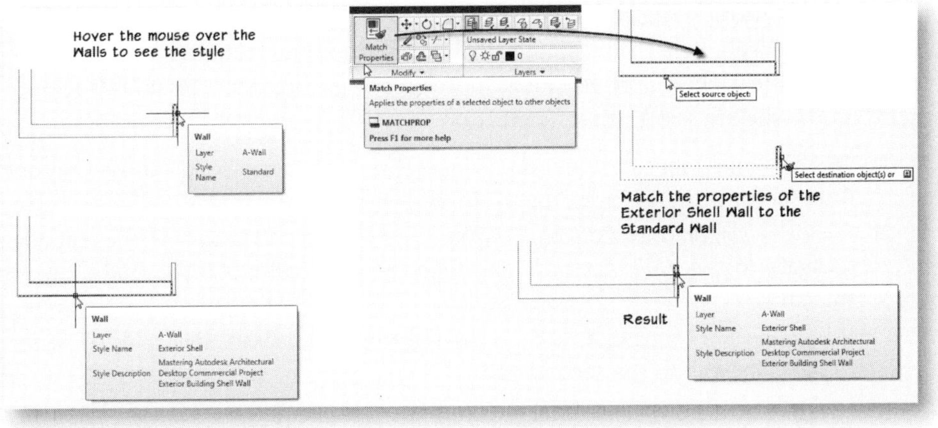

FIGURE 8.3 *Use the iDrop icon to drag the tool from Content Browser to the drawing window*

This approach applies the style and any AutoCAD properties such as layer. However, as you can see, it did not change the width or justification. We can edit those on the Properties palette.

14. Select both of the small pasted Walls.
15. On the Properties palette, set the Width to: **1'-0"**, the Base height to: **12'-0"** and the Justify to **Baseline**.
16. Right-click and choose **Deselect All**.
17. Save the file.

Working With Project Standards

Recall that in Chapter 5 when we set up the project and created these basic shell Walls, we saved a new style and named it "Exterior Shell." This was done in the "Preparing for Project Standards" topic. Let's now use the Project Standards feature to edit the style definition for the Exterior Shell Wall and then synchronize the new version of the style to the other project drawings. To use Project Standards, we must designate one or more drawing files to be "Standards Drawings." For this we will use a file named: *Commercial Styles.dwg* [*Commercial Styles - Metric.dwg*]. In that file, we will edit the Wall style and apply a "Version ID" to it. Next we enable Project Standards, and then instruct our project files to synchronize with the Standards Drawing. When you synchronize, ACA will compare Style names and Version IDs looking for matches and Styles that are out-of-date. Let's begin in the standards drawing and create a newer version of our Wall style.

18. On the QAT, click the Open icon.
19. Navigate to the *C:\MasterACA 2010\Chapter08\MACA Commercial\Standards\Content* [*C:\MasterACA 2010\Chapter08\MACA Commercial Metric\Standards\Content*] folder and open the *Commercial Styles.dwg* [*Commercial Styles - Metric.dwg*] drawing file.

NOTE

This file must be opened manually; it is not accessible from Project Navigator.

This file is the "Style Library" for the project. We will create a Wall Style in this file for the exterior shell of our building. To do this, we will start with one of the out-of-the-box Wall styles provided in the default Content Browser library. We'll bring it into our Style Library file and then rename it to "Exterior Shell." Alternatively we could build the Wall style from scratch. We will learn about building Wall styles in Chapter 10, so the process here will focus more on using the Project Standards feature rather than the specifics of Wall style creation.

20. On the Home tab, click the drop-down on the Tools button and choose Content Browser (or press CTRL + 4).
21. Click the *Design Tool Catalog - Imperial* [*Design Tool Catalog - Metric*] catalog, navigate to the *Walls* category and then the *CMU* category. (Navigation is on the left.)

    In the *Imperial* Catalog, browse to the fourth page of CMU Styles, in the *Metric* Catalog, browse to the second page.
22. Locate the CMU-8 Air-2 Brick-4 [CMU-190 Air-050 Brick-090] tool, click and hold down the mouse on the small eye-dropper icon and then drag the tool into the drawing window in ACA.

    Release the mouse button anywhere in the ACA drawing window to begin drawing a Wall with the tool.
23. Draw a small horizontal segment of Wall in the file next to the other objects onscreen and then press ENTER to complete the command.
24. Select this Wall onscreen, on the Wall tab of the ribbon, click the Edit Style button.
25. On the General tab, rename the style to: **Exterior Shell** add: **Mastering AutoCAD Architecture Commercial Project Exterior Building Shell Wall** to the Description and then click OK (see Figure 8.4).

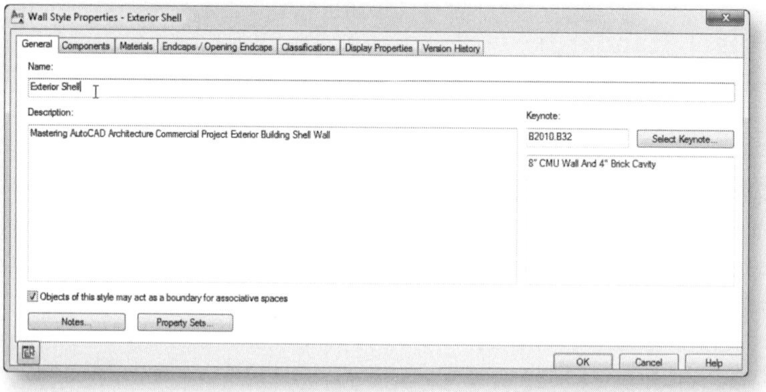

FIGURE 8.4 *Rename the imported Wall style to match the one used in the project*

By renaming the style to match the name we used to set up the project in Chapter 5, we will make it possible to synchronize the change to the rest of the project using the Project Standards feature. Adding the description is optional, but usually a good idea. If you wish, you can explore the other tabs in the Wall Style Properties dialog; however, these will be covered in detail in Chapter 10.

26. Save the *Commercial Styles.dwg* [*Commercial Styles - Metric.dwg*] drawing file.

CAD MANAGER NOTE

You will notice the text object beneath each of the objects already in the Commercial Styles file. When you create a Style Library, consider adding a piece of text beneath each object and then insert a field within the text. The field should reference "Objects" from the Field Category and then click the "Select Object" icon to pick the object onscreen. Finally, choose "Style" from the Property list to have the field automatically read the Style name of the selected object. This makes it easy to see the names of the items within your library at a quick glance. Feel free to add such a note to the new Wall Style in this file.

Set up Project Standards

We now have a style that requires synchronization. However, before we can synchronize, we must configure the Project Standards.

27. On the Project Navigator palette, click the Project tab.
28. Click the Configure Project Standards icon at the bottom of the palette (see item 1 in Figure 8.5).

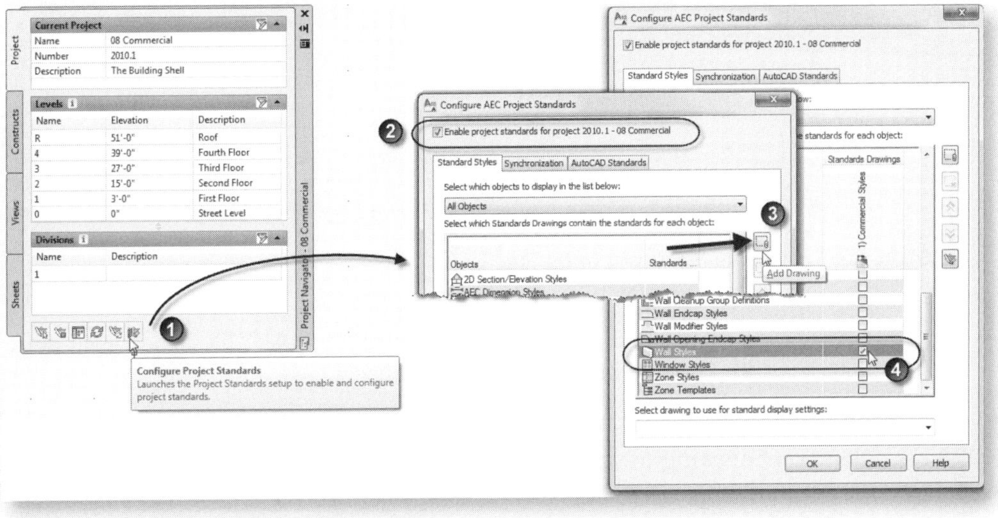

FIGURE 8.5 *Configure Project Standards*

29. At the top of the Configure AEC Project Standards dialog, place a check mark in the "Enable project standards for project 2010.1 - 08 Commercial" checkbox (see item 2 in Figure 8.5).
30. On the right side of the dialog, click the Add Drawing icon (see item 3 in Figure 8.5).
31. Navigate to the *C:\MasterACA 2010\Chapter08\MACA Commercial\Standards\Content* [*C:\MasterACA 2010\Chapter08\MACA Commercial Metric\Standards\Content*] folder and open the *Commercial Styles.dwg* [*Commercial Styles - Metric.dwg*] drawing file.
32. In the Objects list, scroll down and place a check mark next to Wall Styles (see item 4 in Figure 8.5).
33. Click the Synchronization tab, verify that "Manual" is selected.

A detailed explanation of each of the synchronization options is provided. While there are potential advantages to the Automatic and Semi-automatic options, Manual is the best method for the purposes of learning the tool.

34. Click OK to complete the configuration.

    A Version Comment dialog will appear.

35. In the Version Comment dialog, type: **Initial Standards Configuration** and then click OK.
36. Save and close the file.

Project Standards compares Style names and Version IDs. In order to assist you in deciding which version is most current, comments are requested (and highly encouraged) when you configure standards.

37. On the Project Navigator palette, on the Project tab, click the Synchronize Project icon (see Figure 8.6).

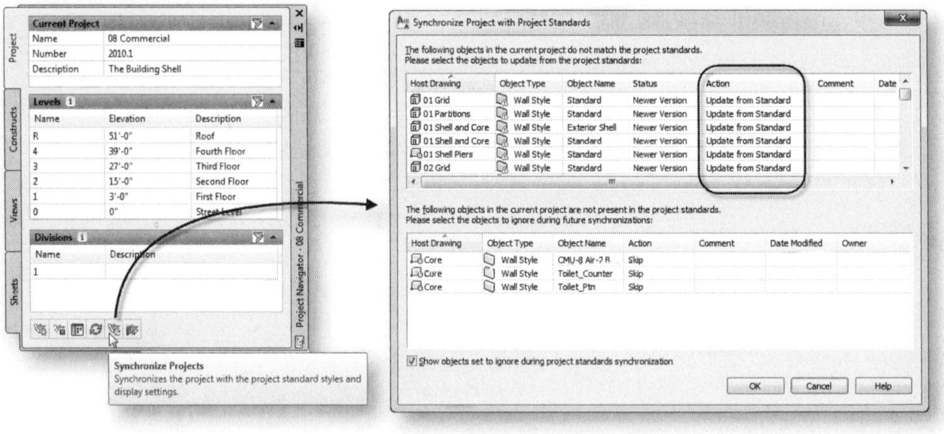

FIGURE 8.6 *Synchronize the Project to the Standards*

After the progress bar completes the scan of all project files, the Synchronize Project with Project Standards dialog will appear.

38. Scroll through the list at the top.

Notice that every drawing in the project and each of their Wall styles is listed. All of these possible variations are being compared against the versions of the style in the *Commercial Styles* standards drawing. Where differences are found, the version in *Commercial Styles* will overwrite the version in the host file(s).

39. Verify that **Update from Standard** is chosen in the Action column for all entries and then click OK.

    If you still have the *01 Shell and Core* file open, the Wall should change to new version of the style now displaying brick and block.

40. On the Project Navigator palette, double-click to open each of the other *Shell and Core* Constructs (*02 Shell and Core*, *03 Shell and Core* and *04 Shell and Core*).

    Notice the more detailed brick and block wall in place of the previous simple two-line wall in each of these files as well.

41. In the *01 Shell and Core* Construct file, copy the two small vertical Walls to the clipboard.
42. Paste them into each of the other three *Shell and Core* Constructs and repeat the trim steps from above.

MANAGER NOTE CAD

This has been a very brief introduction to the powerful Project Standards feature. A complete set of tools is available on the Manage tab on the Project Standards panel. You can use the basic process followed here to configure additional Style types to synchronize. It is also possible to load more than one Standards Drawing and organize them hierarchically for synchronization. Using the Project Standards, you are also able to synchronize Display Configurations, Sets and Representations. We can also update Standards files with the styles and display settings from project drawings. We will see additional examples later in this book. Also, please refer to the online help for more detailed descriptions of all the various Standards functions.

43. When you are finished, Save and Close all of the *Shell and Core* Constructs.

The strategy just employed would be referred to as "Progressive Refinement." This concept has been mentioned in previous chapters. In ACA, your goal is often to start by simply populating your drawings with very basic geometry and then throughout the course of the project, you slowly and progressively refine the detail and data contained within those files. The parametric nature of AEC objects makes this approach not only practical, but very desirable.

ADDING AND MODIFYING CURTAIN WALLS

The Curtain Wall object is similar to the Wall object in use and function. Add Curtain Walls to the drawing in the same way that you add Walls or even convert existing Walls to Curtain Wall objects. What makes the Curtain Wall object special is its ability to represent complex grid patterns and designs within its mass. A series of interwoven horizontal and vertical members defines cells, which are filled by other nested grids or infill objects such as Door/Window Assemblies or panels. A common use for the Curtain Wall object will be to represent the exterior skin of a building. Whether the design is expressed with steel and glass skin, or heavy masonry piers and infill panels, the Curtain Wall object offers tremendous flexibility and design potential. In fact, Curtain Walls can be used to model all sorts of objects that would not necessarily be thought of as a Curtain Wall. Casework, Seating configurations and Wrought Iron fences are just a few examples of objects that have been modeled with the Curtain Wall object.

To begin our exploration of Curtain Wall objects, we will open the first floor Shell file, modified earlier in this chapter, and begin adding Curtain Wall objects to the front entry Wall.

Add a Curtain Wall

1. On the Project Navigator, in the *Constructs\Architectural* folder, double-click the *01 Shell and Core* file to open it.

Some column pier enclosures at the front entrance of the building have been provided in a separate file. For convenience, this file has been saved to the *Elements* folder. The *Elements* folder is a handy location to store temporary project files, such as this one, until they are given a permanent location in the project structure. Let's insert these piers from the *Elements* file to assist us with building the Curtain Wall along the first floor front façade.

2. In the *Elements* folder of the Project Navigator, right-click the *01 Shell Piers* and choose **Insert as Block** (see Figure 8.7).

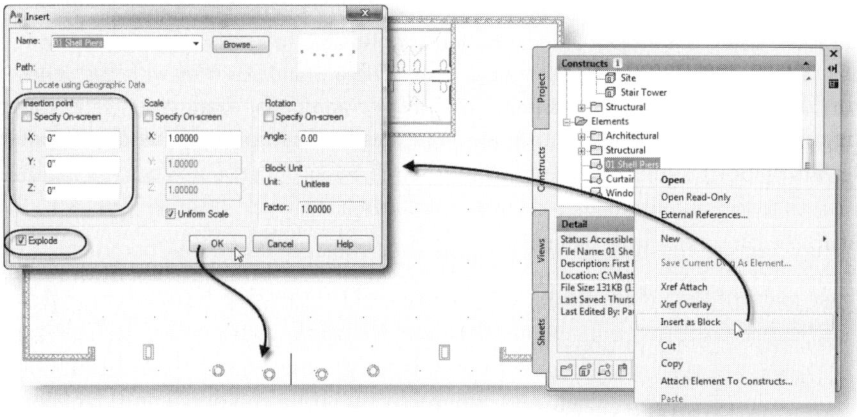

FIGURE 8.7 *Insert the First Floor Shell Piers into the 01 Shell and Core Construct*

3. In the Insert dialog, clear the "Specify onscreen" check mark for Insertion Point, place a check mark in the "Explode" checkbox and then click OK.

   Several column pier enclosures will appear in the void at the bottom of the plan.

4. On the Home tab, on the Build panel, click the drop-down button on the Wall tool and choose Curtain Wall.
5. On the Properties palette, set the Base Height to **12'-0"** [**3650**].

We will draw the Curtain Wall across the space at the bottom of the plan, just above where we trimmed away the Wall at the start of the chapter.

6. Using tracking, set the first point of the Curtain Wall **6"** [**150**] below the end of the short vertical masonry Wall on the left (see Figure 8.8).

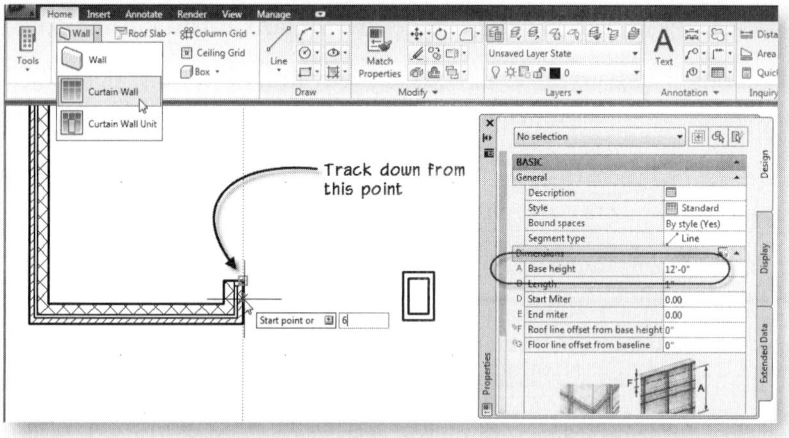

FIGURE 8.8 *Start point of Curtain Wall at the small vertical Wall on the left*

7. Using tracking again (or Perpendicular), set the endpoint **6"** [**150**] below the end of the masonry Wall on the other side (see Figure 8.9).

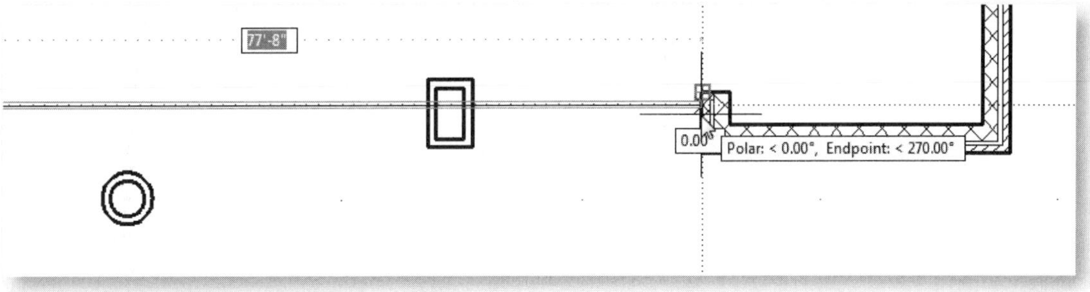

FIGURE 8.9 *End point of the Curtain Wall at the small vertical Wall on the right*

8. Press ENTER to complete the command.

Trim the Curtain Wall

Like Walls, Curtain Walls can be offset, trimmed and extended.

9. Zoom in to the left end of the Curtain Wall just added.
10. Trim the piece of the Curtain Wall that passes through the column enclosure, using the two Walls as cutting edges (see Figure 8.10).

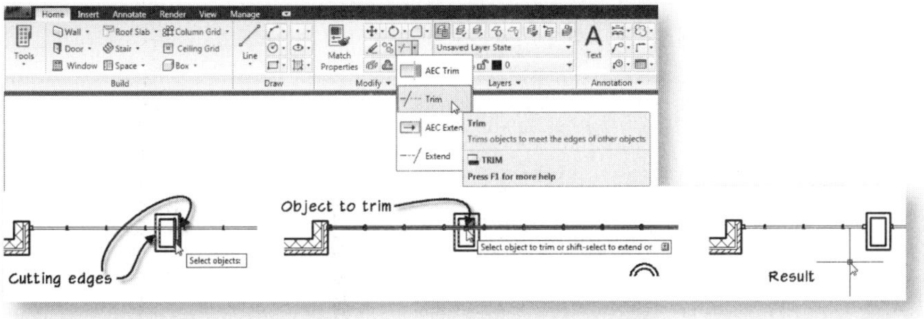

FIGURE 8.10 *Trim the Curtain Wall*

11. Repeat the same steps on the other side.

NOTE

The Trim action in this case yielded the precise result we needed because the position of the justification of the Walls is Left (outside edge relative to the column enclosure). Trim and Extend use the justification line of the Wall or Curtain Wall as the cutting or boundary edge. Keep this is mind as you work, and plan ahead accordingly.

Merge Cells

Examine the Curtain Wall onscreen. The small rectangles are "frames" and "mullions" and the spaces in between are "cells." The cells of a Curtain Wall style are "filled" parametrically, in this case with a simple infill panel expressed here as two parallel lines in plan. There are times, however, when the parametrically defined infill isn't appropriate for a particular cell, such as the front entry bay of the building. Rather than redesign the entire Curtain Wall style, we can apply an override to a particular cell.

12. Select one of the Curtain Walls and then on the Curtain Wall tab of the ribbon, click the Select Similar button.
13. With all three Curtain Walls thus selected, on the Curtain Wall tab, click the Save As button.
14. On the General tab, name the Style **MACA Front Entry**. For the Description, type **Mastering AutoCAD Architecture 2010 Commercial Project Front Entrance**.
15. Click OK to dismiss the Curtain Wall Style Properties dialog.

REMEMBER

It is important to create a new style this way so that you are not inadvertently editing the Standard style.

16. Zoom in to the middle of the Curtain Wall (between the round columns).
17. Right-click and choose Deselect All and then select just the Curtain Wall object in the middle.
18. On the Curtain Wall tab, on the Modify panel, click the Infill drop-down button and then choose Merge.

Between each pair of round columns are three cells. We will use the Infill > Merge command to merge these three cells into one for each pair of columns (three total).

19. At the "Select cell A" prompt, click one of the cells between a pair of round columns (see "First Merge" in Figure 8.11).

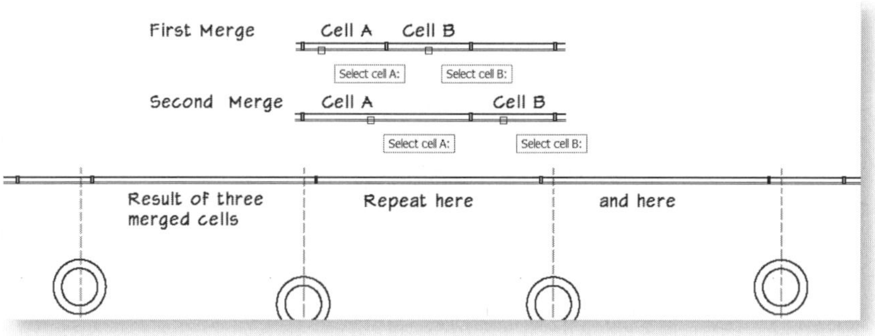

FIGURE 8.11 *Select a cell to merge cells*

20. At the "Select cell B" prompt, click the cell adjacent to the one selected for Cell A.

    Notice how the two cells have fused into one larger cell.
21. Repeat the process to merge the double cell with the third cell adjacent to it (see "Second Merge" in Figure 8.11).
22. Repeat the entire process (to make three large cells total) for each of the additional pairs of round columns.

TIP

This is an excellent time to use the "Rule of thumb" to repeat the last command. Just press the SPACEBAR to repeat the Infill > Merge command.

Add the Front Entry Infill Override

When all merges are complete, the Curtain Wall should look like the lower portion of Figure 8.11. We will now add a revolving door entry to each of these large cells.

23. Open the Content Browser (CTRL + 4).
24. In the *Design Tool Catalog - Imperial* [*Design Tool Catalog - Metric*] catalog, navigate to the *Doors and Windows* > *Door and Window Assemblies* category.
25. Browse to the sixth (6) page of the *Door and Window Assemblies* category.
26. Using the eyedropper icon, drag the Revolving 6-0×6-8 Ctr + Sidelights + Transom [Revolving 1800×2050 + Sidelights + Transom] (page 6 Imperial, page 5 Metric) tool into the drawing window.
27. At the "Select wall, grid assembly or RETURN" prompt, click the Curtain Wall.
28. At the "Select grid assembly cell to add door/window assembly" prompt, click one of the large merged cells.
29. In the Add Infill worksheet, choose the "Add as Cell Override" radio button.

    "New Infill" will be the only available option in the Infill section.
30. Type **Front Entry Infill** for the name.
31. In the Override Frame Removal area, place a check mark in the Left, Right and Bottom boxes and then click OK (see the left side of Figure 8.12).

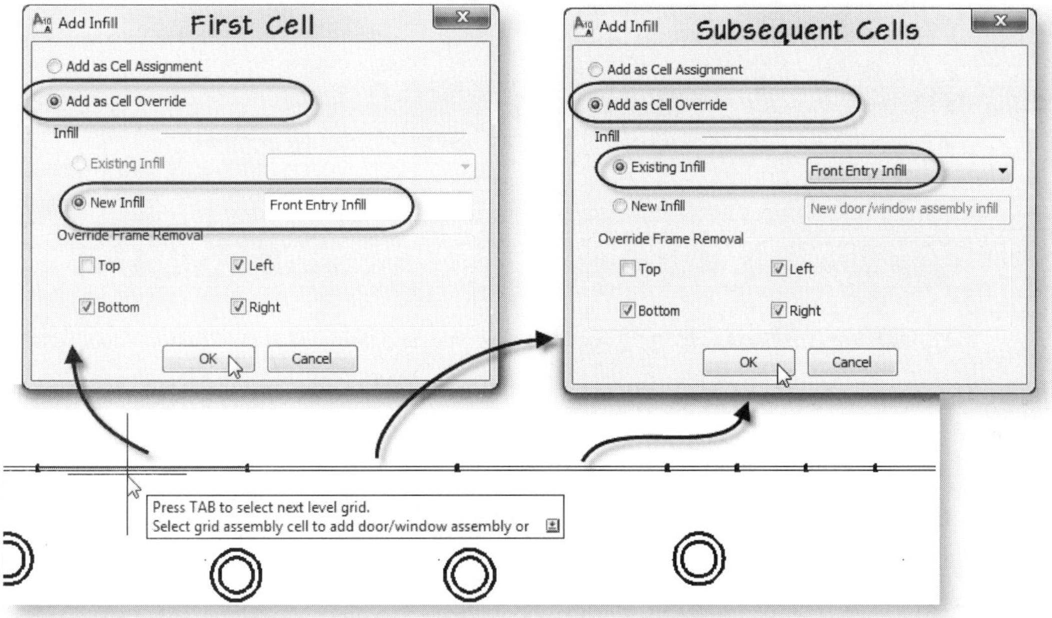

FIGURE 8.12 *Override the Cell Assignment of each of the three large merged cells*

The "Select grid assembly cell to add door/window assembly" prompt will repeat.

32. Select the next large merged cell and, this time, choose "Existing Infill," but all other settings should match the first (see the left side of Figure 8.12).
33. Repeat again for the third cell. Press ENTER to finish.
34. From the View tab, choose SE Isometric (or choose SE Isometric from the View drop-down button on the View panel).
35. Select one of the Curtain Wall objects. (Be careful not to select the Front Entry Infills.)

36. On the Curtain Wall ribbon tab, click the Edit Style button.
37. On the Materials tab, for the Default Infill component choose **Doors & Windows.Glazing.Glass.Clear.**
38. For both the Default Frame and Default Mullion components choose **Doors & Windows.Metal Doors & Frames.Aluminum Frame.Anodized.Dark Bronze. Satin.**

Since our MACA Front Entry Curtain Wall style was saved from Standard above, it did not have any materials assigned to it. This is why we have to assign them now. The Material Definitions we used were imported automatically as part of the Door/ Window Assembly tool used above. This saved our having to import them first.

39. Click OK when finished to return to the drawing and then click the Realistic Visual Styles on the View tab, on the Appearance panel (see Figure 8.13).

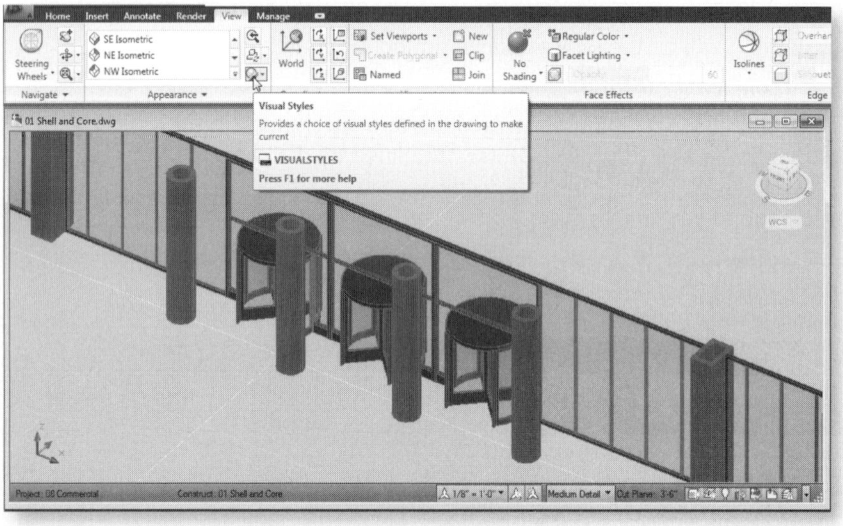

FIGURE 8.13 *The Front Entry Infill inserted as overrides and displayed in the Realistic Visual Style*

40. Save the *01 Shell and Core* file, but leave it open for the next sequence.

UNDERSTANDING CURTAIN WALL STYLES

After that quick primer on the Curtain Wall object, it is time to get more advanced. The true power and utility of the Curtain Wall object comes in its endless customization potential. It is perhaps the most complex and powerful object offered by AutoCAD Architecture. For this reason, developing good procedures is critical to success. In this lesson, we will walk through the process of designing and building a custom Curtain Wall style. The process involves detailed planning and good procedure. To begin, we will open a sample file and add some Curtain Wall objects using the Convert from Walls feature. This technique allows you to place Walls in your design in the early stages as "stand ins" for the Curtain Walls you will add later. This way, you are not hindered with the specifics of a complex Curtain Wall design before the project warrants it. The Curtain Wall style, like those of many AEC objects, can start very simply and then be slowly refined and embellished with detail as the design evolves.

Understanding Curtain Wall Terminology

The basic structure of a Curtain Wall is actually quite simple. One or more grid structures are nested together to form a complex design. Each grid can be horizontal or vertical, spaced evenly or repetitively, and might have other grids nested within it. In order to work successfully with Curtain Walls, you must first understand some basic terminology (see Figure 8.14 and Figure 8.15).

- **Grid**—Establishes the quantity and orientation of the *cells* in a particular design. A grid references a *division* to determine its orientation and spacing. A division is NOT a grid, but rather the rules used to create one. Each grid is a distinct item, but several grids can reference the same division.
- **Cell**—The space formed by the intersecting *grids*. This space can be filled with the contents of an Infill or another Nested Grid.

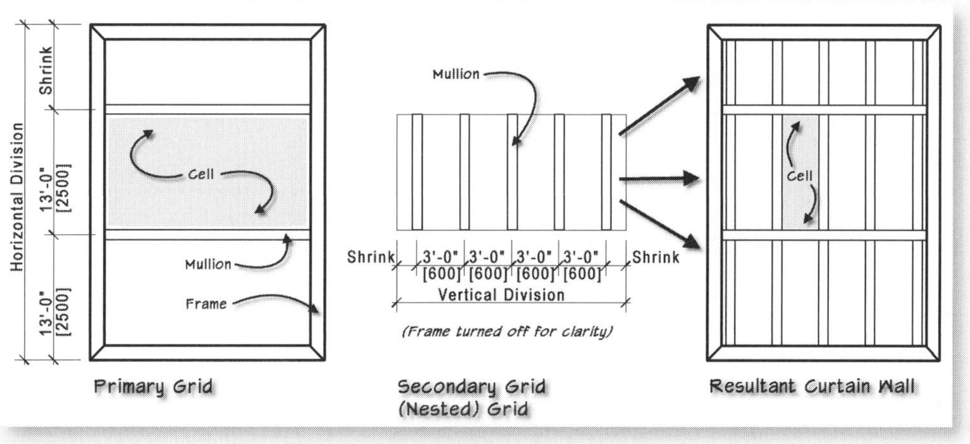

FIGURE 8.14 *Understanding the relationship of grids, divisions and cells*

In order to create the two basic structural components (grid and cell), a Curtain Wall design makes use of four "Element Definitions": Divisions, Infills, Frames and Mullions. Each of these is defined as follows:

- **Division**—Sets the spacing and orientation of the Curtain Wall bays. Orientation can be either horizontal or vertical. Spacing can be configured to repeat (use a specified bay dimension), space evenly (divide the total equally into a specified number of bays) or space manually (specify each mullion explicitly). A horizontal division can also be set to reference the baseline and base height of the Curtain Wall object. A vertical division can be configured to use a polyline for the spacing. In this configuration, each vertex of the polyline will become a mullion division in the grid.
- **Infill**—Determines what each grid cell contains. Each cell of each grid is filled with either an Infill definition or a Nested Grid. Infills can use a simple panel (solid slab of material) or they can reference a Door, Window, Curtain Wall Unit, Window Assembly or AEC Polygon style as the infill.
- **Frame**—The outer edge of each grid and nested grid. The Frame can be the same on all four sides, or each one can be different. Frames can also be turned off on internal nested grids if not required by the design. Each Frame component is defined by its width and depth and can also optionally use a custom profile shape.
- **Mullion**—Has the same parameters as frames, but is used for the internal grid divisions to separate each cell from one another. Mullions can also use a custom profile shape.

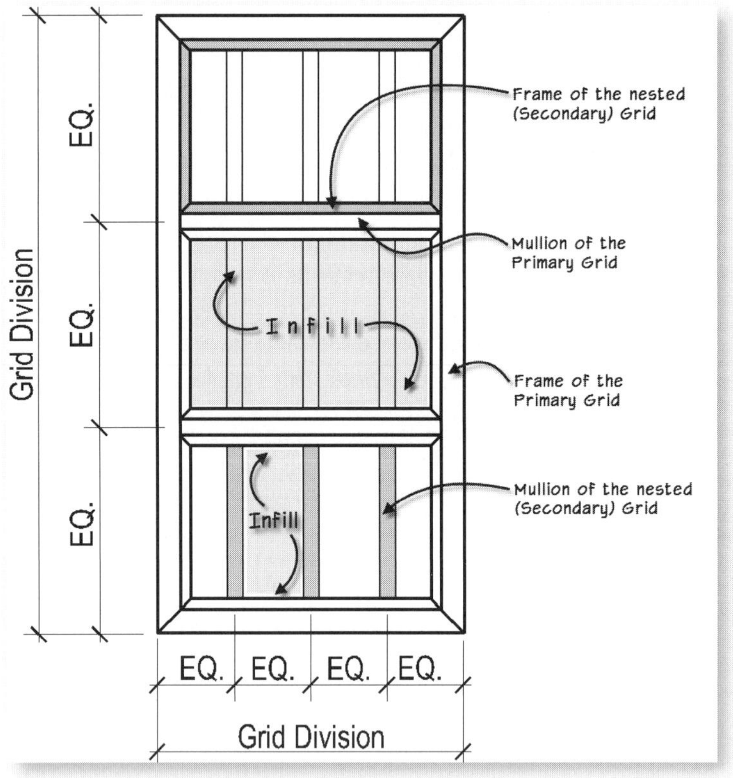

FIGURE 8.15 *Curtain Wall Element Definitions*

Putting It All Together

In summary, a *grid* is a collection of one or more cells defined by a division. A *division* defines the spacing of each grid of the Curtain Wall. A division establishes the number of cells in a single direction. To define a basic rectangular grid pattern requires two grids, one horizontal and one vertical. The *frame* is the outermost edge of a grid on all sides. Each nested grid can have its own frame definition. The edge between each cell is a *mullion*. The *cell* is the space defined by frames and mullions. Each cell can contain another nested grid, or an infill. An *infill* can be comprised of solid material or it can reference one of several object style types.

Exploring Existing Curtain Wall Styles

To further understand some of these elements and their relationships, let's dissect some existing Curtain Wall styles in order to understand the hierarchy and function of elements. We will explore the Curtain Wall interface in the *01 Shell and Core* file by examining the composition of the Style used here. This Style was copied from the Standard style, so with the exception of the Infill we added above, it is identical in composition.

Explore the Interface

1. Select the main segment of the Curtain Wall, and on the Curtain Wall tab of the ribbon, click the Edit Style button.
2. Click the Design Rules tab (see item 1 in Figure 8.16).

3. Click the Viewer icon at the lower-left corner and position the windows onscreen to be next to one another, enlarging them as much as your screen will allow (see item 2 in Figure 8.16).
4. In the Viewer, change the View Direction to **SE Isometric** (see item 3 in Figure 8.16).

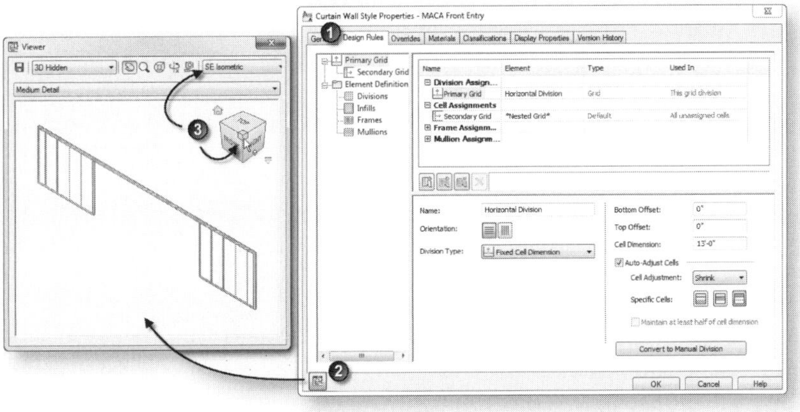

FIGURE 8.16 *Position windows to maximize screen real estate*

The Design Rules tab of the Curtain Wall Style Properties dialog box can be challenging to master. However, once you get the hang of it, you will see that it is organized quite logically (see Figure 8.17). The left side of the dialog box is a tree view divided into two sections. At the top of the tree, one or more grids are organized hierarchically. The main grid is listed at the top (in this case, it is called "Primary Grid"). If there are additional nested grids, there will be a minus (–) sign in front of main grid, and they will be listed indented below. Click on the minus sign to collapse the grid tree. In this case "Secondary Grid" is the name of the only nested grid. Also in the tree view is the Element Definitions node (depicted by a folder icon). Here you gain quick access to the definitions for each of the four Curtain Wall Element types: Divisions, Infills, Frames and Mullions (see definitions). The right side of the dialog box is divided into two areas. The top-right section lists (or previews) whatever item is selected at the left tree view. At the bottom right, detailed parameters will be available for the item selected at the top right (where appropriate).

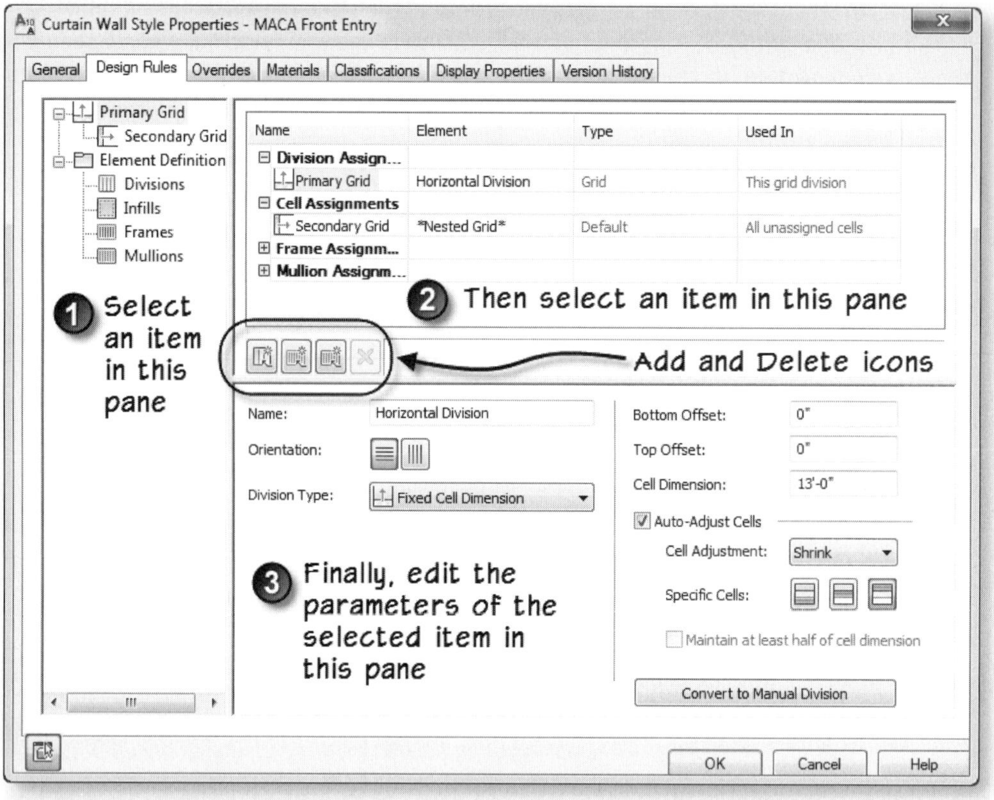

FIGURE 8.17 *Understanding the Curtain Wall Style Properties dialog box interface*

The basic flow of movement through the dialog box is as follows:

- Choose an item on the left tree view, either a Grid (at the top) or an Element Definition (at the bottom) (see item 1 in Figure 8.17).
- On the right at the top, select an item to edit. (Depending on the selection at left, there could be several choices. See item 2 in Figure 8.17.)
- Edit the parameters at the bottom half of the window (see item 3 in Figure 8.17).

All changes occur immediately. Buttons to add and delete elements are located in a strip across the middle of the right pane (circled in Figure 8.17). Hover your mouse and pause over each icon to see a tool tip indicating its function.

Explore the Element Definitions

5. On the left-hand tree view, under Element Definitions, choose **Divisions**.

   On the right side at the top, two divisions will appear: Horizontal Division and Vertical Division.

6. Choose **Horizontal Division** and review its settings in the bottom half of the window (see Figure 8.18).

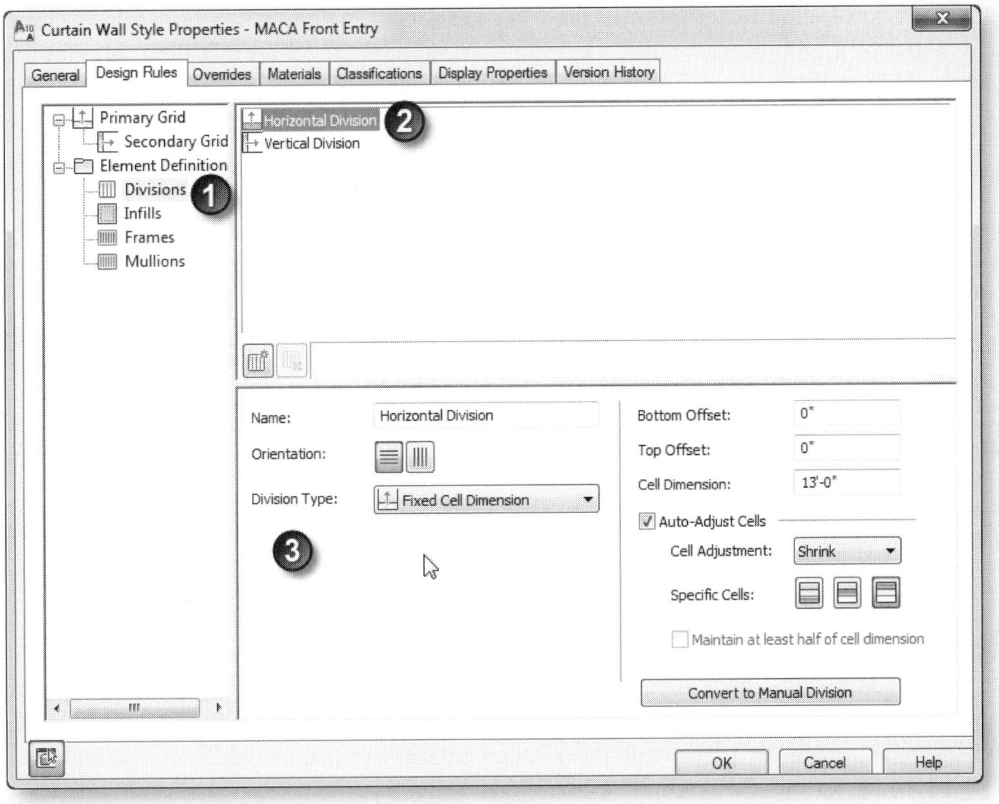

FIGURE 8.18 *Study the parameters of the Horizontal Division*

Next to Orientation, the Horizontal button is depressed, thus the name Horizontal Division. Below that is a list of Division Types. This particular division uses the Fixed Cell Dimension type. To the right of these settings, the Cell Dimension is 13'-0" [2500] with zero unit offsets. Finally, if the grid does not work out to be an exact multiple of 13' [2500], it will reduce (Shrink) the size of the Top cell. In summary, this division will repeat a 13' [2500] bay until it runs out of space; the final bay at the Top will be allowed to be smaller than 13' [2500].

7. Choose **Vertical Division** and review its settings (see Figure 8.19).

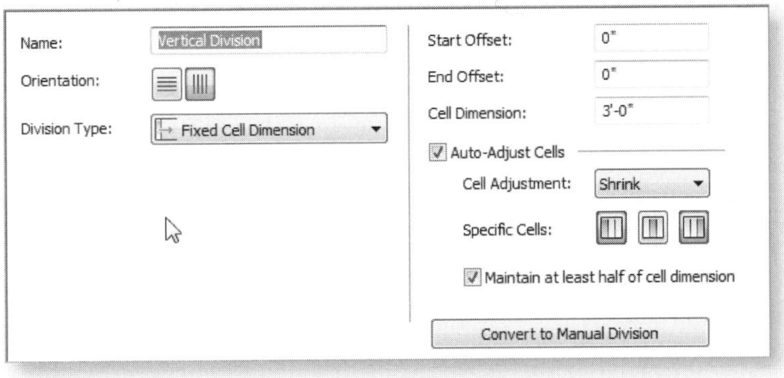

FIGURE 8.19 *Study the parameters of the Vertical Division*

Next to Orientation, this time the Vertical button is depressed. This one is also a Fixed Cell Dimension, with a Cell Dimension of 3'-0" [600] this time. Should the grid not multiply evenly by 3' [600], both the Start and the End will equally shrink to accommodate the variance. However, we also have a setting to instruct the Curtain Wall style to maintain at least half the Cell dimension size when dividing the difference between two or more Cells. In summary, this Division will repeat 3' [600] as many times as possible and split the leftover between both ends as long as it can do so while maintaining half the Cell size.

8. On the left-hand tree view, under Element Definitions, select Infills.

There is only a single Infill Definition named Default Infill. This Infill is a two-inch [10 millimeter] thick Simple Panel. A Simple Panel is drawn graphically as a solid slab of material (two parallel lines in plan). Infill panels can be aligned to left, right or center.

9. Select Frames next.

There is only one Frame Definition, called Default Frame. It is 3" [50] square. Frames may have offsets and use profiles for their shapes (see below).

10. Select Mullions.

There is also one Mullion Definition, Default Mullion, 1"×3" [30×30]. Mullions may have offsets and use profiles for their shapes (see below). Now that we have explored the elements, let's look at how they are put together.

Explore the Grid Structure

11. On the left-hand tree view, at the top, select the Primary Grid item.

    On the right side, the parameters of the Primary Grid will appear.

12. On the right, click the minus (–) sign next to each entry (see Figure 8.20).

    This will help you to focus on just the component you are working on at any given moment.

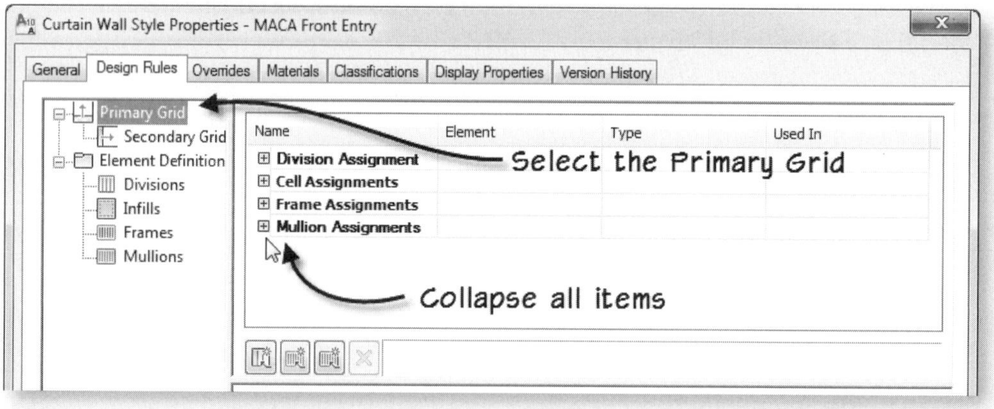

FIGURE 8.20 *Collapse all components*

13. Expand *only* the Division Assignment (click the plus (+) sign).

Reading in the Element column, the Division Assignment for the Primary Grid is Horizontal Division. As shown above, the Horizontal Division establishes a 13' [2500] horizontal spacing. We also saw that the spacing begins at the bottom, divides the total height by 13' [2500] cells and leaves any uneven space at the Top. Each of the Cells resulting from this Grid will have an Assignment as well. To see what component is loaded into each Cell, expand the Cell Assignments item.

14. Expand the Cell Assignments.

    Here the Element is a Nested Grid. (This means that these Cells will be subdivided further. This is illustrated diagrammatically in Figure 8.14 and Figure 8.15 above.)

15. Open the list of choices by clicking on *Nested Grid* (see Figure 8.21).

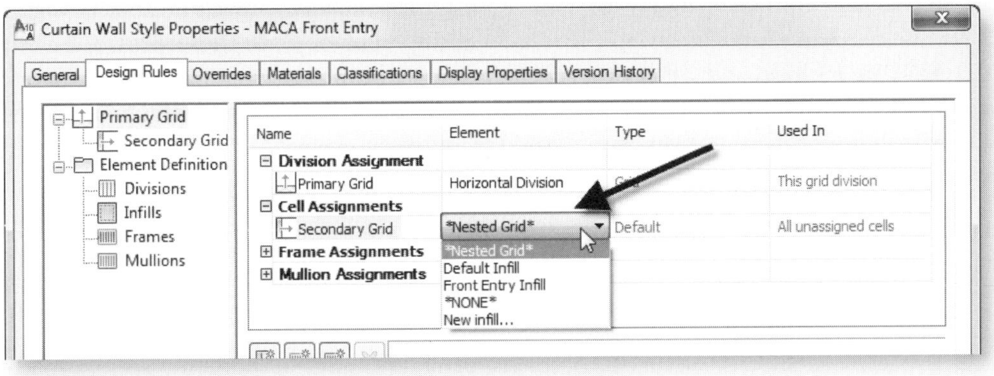

FIGURE 8.21 *Infill elements available in the current style*

Two choices will always be available, ***Nested Grid*** and ***NONE***. The asterisks indicate that these are hard coded into the software. In addition, **Default Infill** and **New infill** are available. **Default Infill** is the simple two-inch [50 millimeter] thick panel we looked at above in the Infill Definitions item. Choosing **New infill** allows a new component to be created on the fly. Additional infills will appear on this list as they are defined (see later in this exercise). In this case, each of the 13' [2500] horizontal Cells created by the Horizontal Division are "filled" with another Grid called Secondary Grid.

16. Expand Frame Assignments.

There is only one Frame Assignment as well; it uses the Default Frame Definition looked at above, and it is applied on all four sides of the Primary Grid as seen in the Used In column.

17. Expand Mullion Assignments.

There is also only one Mullion Assignment. It occurs between any two cells (of the Primary Grid in this case) and is expressed with the 1"×3" [30×30] Default Mullion explored above.

18. On the left-hand tree view, at the top, select the Secondary Grid item.

This is the Nested Grid referenced by the Cell Assignment of the Primary Grid. It has similar parameters to the Primary Grid, with a few notable differences. First, its Division Assignment uses the Vertical Division. This creates the 3' [600] mullion spacing as seen above. The Cell Assignment for the Secondary Grid is the **Default Infill**. This means that the grid does *not* subdivide any further and each 3' [600] Cell is simply filled with the Simple Panel designated by the Default Infill definition. The last item to note is the Frame Assignment. The Default Frame *is* assigned here as well; however, in the Used In column it specifies "None." Therefore, the Frame, although assigned, is not *expressed* at this level of the design. The Mullion Assignment is however the same as the Primary Grid, forming a flush appearance between Primary and Secondary Grid Mullions in the final design (see Figure 8.14 above).

19. Click Cancel to return to the drawing.

Out-Of-The-Box Curtain Wall Styles

Until now, we have used the Content Browser to access the styles and content provided out of the box with ACA. There is another tool that we can use to access styles, in this case Curtain Wall styles. You can use the following procedure to access and work with any kind of style, Curtain Wall or other objects, those provided with ACA in the box, and others that your firm may have in library files on a network server. This is simply an alternative method. This method is also useful when styles exist, but tools have not yet been created from them.

The Curtain Wall should still be selected. If it is not, please select it again.

20. On the Curtain Wall tab of the ribbon, on the General panel, click the drop-down button on the Edit Style tool and choose Curtain Wall Styles.

    The Style Manager dialog box will appear. The Style Manager is used to create and edit ACA Styles.

21. Across the top of the Style Manager dialog box is a row of icons. Click the Open Drawing icon.
22. On the left side of the dialog box that appears is a series of icons. Click the Content icon on this toolbar.

    This shortcut opens a folder with several more folders (see Figure 8.22).

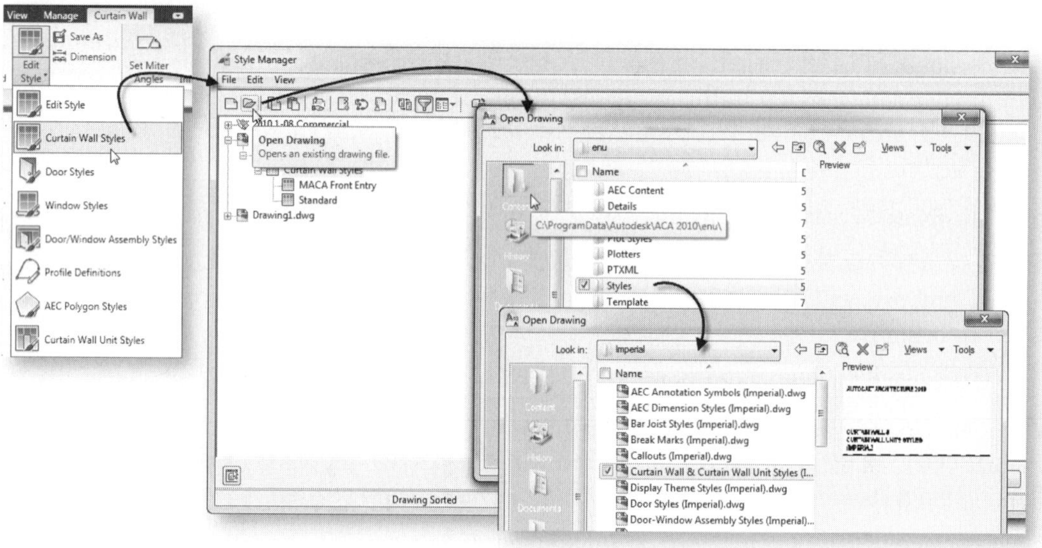

FIGURE 8.22 *Use the Content icon to access the Out-of-the-Box Style Library*

23. Double-click the *Styles* folder, and then if you wish to use Imperial Styles, double-click the *Imperial* folder [if you wish to use Metric, double-click the *Metric* folder instead] (not shown in the figure).
24. Finally, double-click the *Curtain Wall & Curtain Wall Unit Styles (Imperial).dwg* [*Curtain Wall & Curtain Wall Unit Styles (Metric).dwg*].

This will return you to the Style Manager with the *Curtain Wall & Curtain Wall Unit Styles (Imperial).dwg* [*Curtain Wall & Curtain Wall Unit Styles (Metric).dwg*] file loaded on the left in the tree view. You can expand this drawing to reveal the *Architectural Objects* category.

25. Expand the *Architectural Objects* category and then the *Curtain Wall Styles* item.
26. At the top of the Style Manager, click the "Inline Edit Toggle" icon.

    This will enable the interactive viewer directly in the Style Manager.

ACA offers the ability to edit a style inline within the Style Manager. The toggle icon used here toggles between a viewer and the inline edit behavior. If you double-click a style in the list, it also toggles to the Edit inline mode. Notice also that if Project Standards are enabled (as we did above) any Standards Drawing(s) in use in your project will be listed at the top of the Style Manager tree. You can expand the Standards Drawing node(s) and view and edit the styles like any other branch in the tree. Right-click to get additional Standards options.

27. Select any Curtain Wall Style on the left to preview it in an interactive Viewer on the right. Be sure not to double-click (see Figure 8.23).

TIP

The interactive viewer and the ability to edit inline are the primary features that set the Style Manager apart from the Content Browser. If you wish to preview and edit styles interactively, use Style Manager.

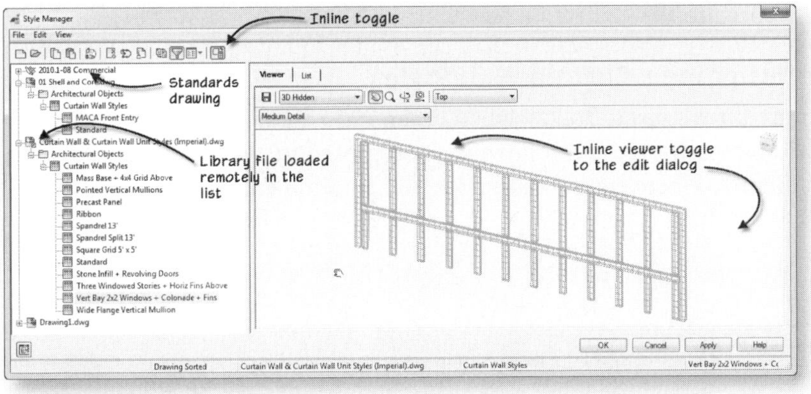

FIGURE 8.23 *Select styles on the left to preview or edit them on the right*

NOTE

One limitation of the Viewer within the Style Manager is that it does not preview any nested components. Some of the Curtain Wall styles reference other AEC styles for Infills. This was mentioned above. Those nested styles will not preview in the Viewer. You would need to add a Curtain Wall of that style to the drawing to properly see those infills.

28. In the tree, drag the ***Mass Base + 4×4 Grid Above*** Style from the *Curtain Wall & Curtain Wall Unit Styles (Imperial).dwg* [*Curtain Wall & Curtain Wall Unit Styles (Metric).dwg*] file and drop it on top of the *01 Shell and Core.dwg* file. (You can also right-click and copy and paste instead.)

    This action will import the style into your current drawing.
29. Stay in Style Manager; beneath the *01 Shell and Core.dwg* file, double-click on the style that you just imported in the list.

    This will toggle the Inline Edit in the right pane.

30. Repeat the procedure that we performed above in the "Explore the Element Definitions" topic.

    You will notice several differences from the Standard Style explored previously.

31. Continue this process on as many styles as you wish. Click OK to close the Style Manager when you are finished.

NOTE

If a dialog box asking you to save the Content file appears when you click OK, choose No. This is asking you if you wish to save the library file, not the drawing you have onscreen. You should not save any changes to the Library file at this time.

The exercise just completed will help you to get familiar with strategies and techniques to planning and building a Curtain Wall style. In the next exercise, we will build a custom Curtain Wall Style from scratch.

BUILDING A CUSTOM CURTAIN WALL STYLE

The Standard Curtain Wall style defines a single Frame, Mullion and Infill component, each called Default. For example, the mullion defined in the Standard Curtain Wall style is called Default Mullion. You can name the elements anything you wish. There are two predefined Division elements: one for the default horizontal Grid, the other for the default vertical Grid. Each of the default elements can be renamed and redefined, and additional elements can be created. When creating your own style, careful naming of each component is critical to successful implementation of your design, as it helps to avoid confusion and keep you organized. Outlined below is the recommended procedure for creating a new Curtain Wall style.

Process for Designing a Curtain Wall Style

Outlined next are three steps to follow when designing a custom Curtain Wall style. Curtain Walls can be complex, but following good procedure when you lay them out can mean the difference between successful implementation and frustration.

FIGURE 8.24 *Make a sketch of the design first*

Step 1—Plan

Make a sketch of your design ideas on paper first (see Figure 8.24). A simple sketch is all you need in order to help you determine the basic grid structure and orientation. This sketch will also reveal how many Division, Frame, Mullion and Infill elements you will need. The purpose of the sketch is to establish the proper organization and structure of the Curtain Wall design. The dialog box interface of the Curtain Wall object is complex, and having a clear "road map" before beginning will help keep you on track.

Don't worry about making the sketch too perfect or refined, because it will likely change as the design develops.

Step 2—Create the Element Definitions (Build a Kit of Parts)

Referring to the Curtain Wall terminology covered above, you can begin to understand the primary goal of the sketch. The purpose of the sketch is to help you determine what Element Definitions (Divisions, Frames, Infills and Mullions) will be required by your design. Once you have your rough sketch, create all of the elements you will need in your design. You can create additional elements on the fly later, but it will be easier to choose from a ready-made kit of parts as you work. First, refer to your sketch, and determine how many Divisions you will need; each level of your grid structure will be defined by a Division (see Figure 8.25).

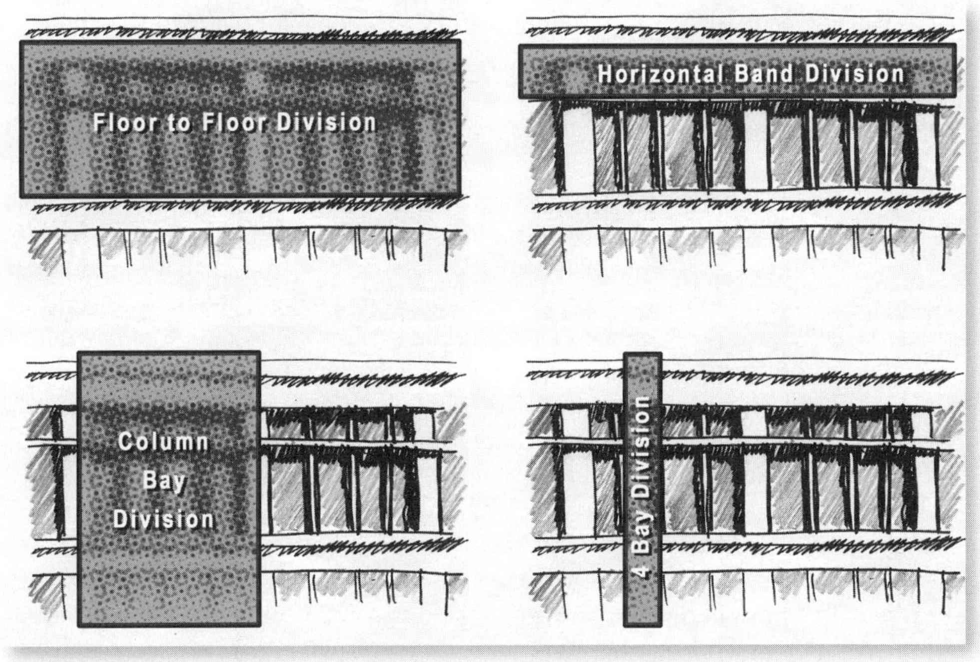

FIGURE 8.25 *Determine the required Divisions*

Next determine what will go inside each Cell (a Nested Grid or Infill). Finally, consider how each Grid level will be "edged" with Frames and Mullions (see Figure 8.26).

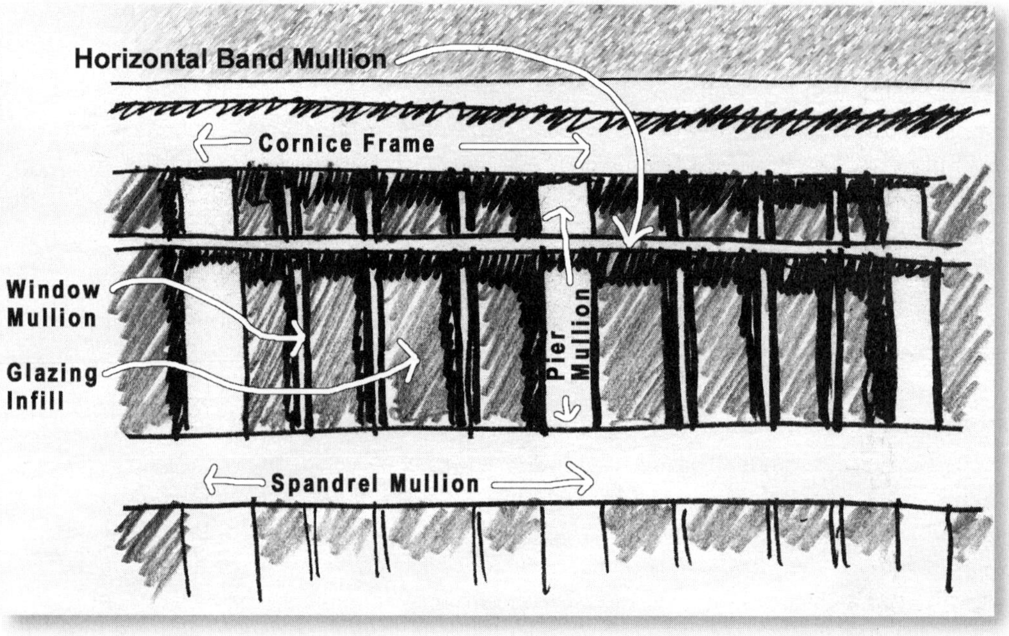

FIGURE 8.26 *Determining the required Element Definitions*

Following the recommendation of Step 1, a rough design has been sketched out in Figure 8.24. Figure 8.25 reveals that four divisions will be required in the Curtain Wall style. Finally, according to the sketch in Figure 8.26, several frames and mullions will also be needed. Table 8.1 summarizes the required Element Definitions.

Step 3—Build the Grid Structure

Once you have your kit of parts built, it is short work to put all of the pieces together in a grid structure that will yield the results you desire. You can add as many grids as necessary to achieve the desired effect. However, as a general rule, if your design requires more than five nested grid levels, you might want to consider creating Infills that reference Curtain Wall Unit styles or Door/Window Assembly styles (see the note below). If you add these types of components to your design, the possibilities are limitless, and the grid structure of the design remains manageable. The most important consideration when establishing the grid structure is careful planning of the hierarchy. Using descriptive naming throughout will aid tremendously in this endeavor. This tip cannot be stressed enough: although it is tempting to accept the default names while creating elements, it is highly recommended that you take the time to consider your naming scheme carefully and pick names that make sense for the design. More important still, pick names that will still make sense two or three months after the design is complete. You never know when you will need to revisit a design scheme and when that happens, good naming will pay back tenfold. For all of these reasons, you should also avoid the default names (such as "Primary Grid," "Horizontal Division" and "Default Mullion"). These are simply not descriptive enough in most cases. The strategy can be summarized as follows:

- Limit your design to three to five nested grids.
- Create Infill Definitions that refer to Curtain Wall Units or Door/Window Assemblies in complex designs.
- Have variations of styles, both Curtain Wall and Infill, for quick swapping and "what if" scenarios.
- Plan your grid hierarchy carefully!
- Use clear, descriptive and simple naming!
- Avoid complex naming schemes with cryptic abbreviations or acronyms.

TABLE 8.1 *MACA Front Façade Curtain Wall Style Element Definitions List*

Element Name	Type	Dimensions	Other
Divisions			
Floor to Floor Division	Fixed Cell Dimension	12'-0" [3650]	Shrink Top
Column Bay Division	Fixed Cell Dimension	10'-0" [3000]	Shrink Left & Right Don't Maintain half Cell
Horizontal Band Division	Manual	3'-8" [1100] from Top	
4 Bay Division	Space Evenly	4 equal	
Infills			
Glazing Infill	Simple Panel	1" [25] thick	
Frames			
Vertical End Frame	Basic (No profile)	6" [150] wide × 8" [200] deep	
Cornice Frame	Basic (No profile)	24" [600] wide × 12" [300] deep	
Mullions			
Pier Mullion	Basic (No profile)	12" [300] wide × 12" [300] deep	
Spandrel Mullion	Basic (No profile)	24" [600] wide × 12" [300] deep	
Horizontal Band Mullion	Basic (No profile)	4" [100] wide × 18" [450] deep	
Window Mullion	Basic (No profile)	4" [100] wide × 6" [150] deep	

Curtain Wall Units and Door/Window Assemblies

Curtain Wall Units and Door/Window Assemblies are very similar to Curtain Walls in form and function, with a few minor differences. Curtain Wall Units are meant specifically to be smaller components of a larger Curtain Wall design. Use them as nested infill elements rather than building endless nested Grids and Divisions directly within the Curtain Wall Style. They are intended to be nested within Curtain Wall cells, and because they are style based, they offer a powerful way to consider alternate schemes and contingencies while designing. A Door/Window Assembly can be used in similar fashion as an infill in a Curtain Wall, and it can be inserted in a Wall just like a door or window. In this way, Window Assemblies are ideal for doors with sidelights, complex grouping of windows, transoms and storefronts. Refer to the exercise under the "Add the Front Entry Infill Override" heading above, and to the "Add Window Assembly" topic in Chapter 4 for some specific examples. Although we will not specifically build Curtain Wall Units and Door/Window Assemblies in this lesson, the interface to these items is nearly identical to that of the Curtain Wall and all of the same techniques apply.

Creating a Custom Curtain Wall Style

We now have a strategy to follow when contemplating a Curtain Wall. Let's put it into practice and get started building a custom Curtain Style Wall for the Mastering AutoCAD Architecture Commercial Project.

Convert the Walls to Curtain Walls

1. On the Constructs tab of the Project Navigator in the *Constructs\Architectural* folder, double-click the *Front Façade* Construct file to open it.

You may recall from Chapter 5 that we built a file for the front façade of the building and placed a stand-in Wall in that file as a temporary place holder. Some additional Wall segments are included in this file to help complete the Curtain Wall shape. The first step will be to convert these Walls to Curtain Walls, and then we will adjust the basic height parameters. Once we have a Curtain Wall in place, we can begin developing our custom Curtain Wall design.

2. On the Design tool palette, right-click the Curtain Wall tool and choose **Apply Tool Properties to > Walls**.

   If you do not see this palette or tool, right-click the Tool Palettes title bar and choose **Design** (to load the Design Tool Palette Group) and then click the Design tab.
3. At the "Select Walls" prompt, select all of the Walls onscreen (five total) and then press ENTER.
4. At the "Curtain Wall baseline alignment" prompt, choose **Center** (if you don't have Dynamic Input toggled on, right-click and choose **Center**).
5. At the "Erase layout geometry" prompt, choose **Yes** (or type **y** and then press ENTER).

   We now have Curtain Wall objects in place of the Wall objects. Let's configure the basic height parameters.
6. With the Curtain Walls still selected, right-click and choose **Properties**.
7. Set the Base height to **35'-0"** [**10,650**].
8. With the Curtain Walls still selected, right-click in the drawing and choose **Roof Line/Floor Line > Modify Floor Line**.
9. At the "Floorline" prompt, choose **Offset** (if you don't have Dynamic Input toggled on, right-click and choose **Offset**).
10. At the "Enter offset" prompt, type **-12"** [**-300**] and then press ENTER twice (see Figure 8.27).

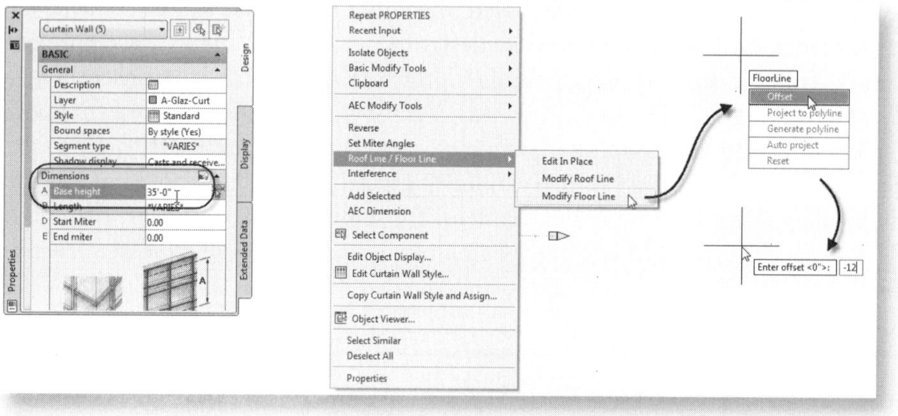

FIGURE 8.27 *Setting the height parameters and Floor Line offsets*

With the Floor Line projected down slightly, the Curtain Wall will cover the floor slab of the second floor in the building model. Likewise the Base Height that we assigned will allow enough room for a Roof Slab above.

11. On the View tab of the ribbon, on the Appearance panel, choose **SE Isometric**.

Create a New Curtain Wall Style

12. Select all of the Curtain Walls onscreen (five total), on the Curtain Wall tab, click the Save As button.
13. On the General tab, name the New Style **MACA Front Façade**.

On the General tab, it is usually a good idea to put a description. Typical descriptions include a reference to the project, a detailed description of components in the design or reference to the manufacturer if it is prefabricated.

14. In the Description field, type **Mastering AutoCAD Architecture 2010 Commercial Project Front Façade Curtain Wall**.

As you make edits, it will be handy to see some visual feedback. For this reason, it is always useful to have the floating viewer open as you work.

15. If the Viewer is not already open, click the Floating Viewer icon at the bottom-left corner of the dialog box to open the Viewer window, and choose **SE Isometric** from the View Control list.

Notice that even though the viewer appears to be showing us the correct style, its image does not look like the Curtain Wall we have in the drawing. This occurs in the floating viewer when you select multiple objects before editing Styles as we did here. It is easily remedied.

16. Click OK to accept the changes and dismiss the Curtain Wall Style Properties dialog.
17. Deselect all objects, and then select just the curved front Curtain Wall. On the Curtain Wall tab of the ribbon, click the Edit Style button.

Notice that the viewer now displays only the curved front Curtain Wall segment. This will be much more useful as we progress.

Create Divisions

As we work through the Design Rules, they will at first be very familiar to those explored above. This is because the Curtain Walls here were created from the generic Curtain Wall tool on the Design tool palette. This tool uses the Standard style, making the "MACA Front Façade" style a copy of Standard. We have not yet configured its Design Rules to make it vary from Standard.

18. Click the Design Rules tab.
19. Under Element Definitions (on the left in the tree), click Divisions.
20. Choose **Horizontal Division** at the top right.
21. In the bottom-right area, in the Name field, rename it to **Floor to Floor Division**.
22. Change the Cell Dimension to **12'-0"** [**3650**].

Leave the Orientation set to **Horizontal** and the Division Type set to **Fixed Cell Dimension**. Leave the Auto-Adjust Cells section configured as is. This will reduce the Top cell if the Curtain Wall's height does not multiply cleanly. Experiment with the alternative setting of Grow and the other choices under Specific Cells. Check the results in the Viewer as you experiment, and change it back to **Shrink** and **Top** when you are done.

23. In the top-right pane of the dialog box, choose "Vertical Division" and rename it **Column Bay Division**.
24. Change the Cell Dimension to **10'-0"** [**3000**] and leave the remaining settings as they are.

Notice the effect of the settings in the Viewer. With the current settings, the curved Curtain Wall ends up divided into six bays. The two at the end are a bit smaller. For this design, we would actually prefer a center bay with an equal number of bays on either side of it. To do this, we need to experiment with the "Maintain at least half of cell dimension" setting. When this is turned on, cells smaller than a half Cell are not permitted, so rather, all Cells will be shifted. If this setting is not checked, then the two Cells at the ends can be any size, thereby not requiring a shift in Cells. Experiment with the Maintain at least half of cell dimension setting as well as some of the other Auto-Adjust Cells settings.

25. When finished experimenting, be sure that Auto-Adjust Cells is set to **Shrink Left** and **Right** (these buttons pushed in), and that Maintain at least half of cell dimension is *not* checked (see Figure 8.28).

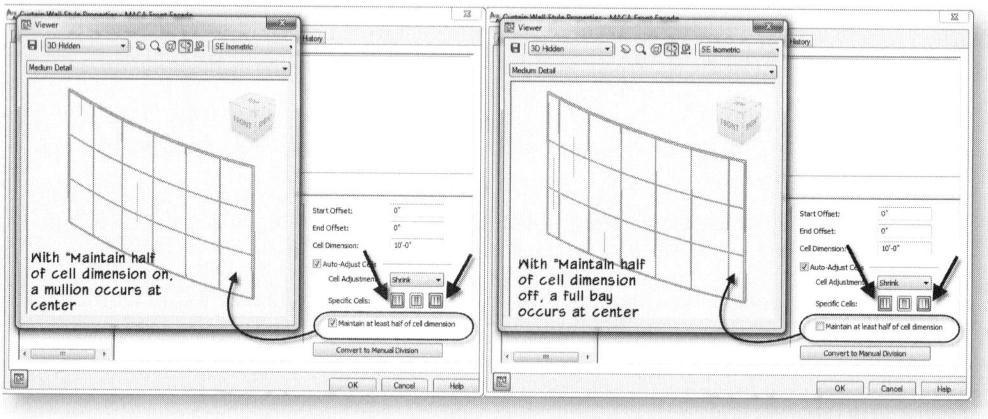

FIGURE 8.28 *Comparing the effect of the Maintain at least half of cell dimension setting*

These changes occur immediately because the two Divisions are already assigned to items in the grid structure. Review the steps in "Explore the Element Definitions" above for more information.

In the middle of the window, there are a couple of icons similar to those circled in Figure 8.17 above. These icons will change function when you select a different node on the tree at the left. Pause your mouse over each icon to see a tool tip indicating its function. In this case, only the New icon is available. There is also a Delete icon, but you cannot delete items that are being used in the grid design. This is why the Delete icon is currently grayed out.

26. Click the New icon.
27. Name the New Division **Horizontal Band Division**.
28. Click the Horizontal icon next to Orientation.

29. Expand the Division Type list and choose **Manual** for the type.
30. To the right of the window, click the Add Gridline icon. (If you don't see this icon, try stretching the window a little)
31. Change the Offset of Gridline 1 to **3'-8"** [**1100**], and the From point to **Grid Top** (see Figure 8.29).

    We will use this to form a single horizontal band across the top of each main horizontal cell (you can look back to our design sketches above in Figure 8.25).

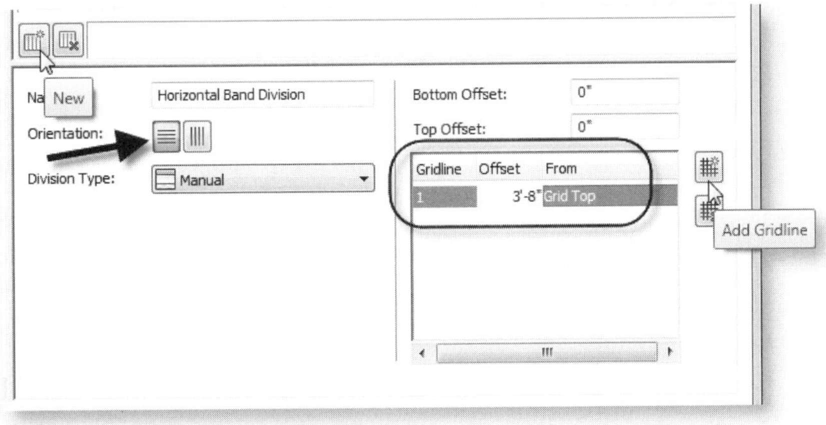

FIGURE 8.29 *Add a manual grid line*

> There will not be any feedback on this change in the viewer. This is a new Division and until it is added to the Curtain Wall design, the effect will not be apparent.
>
> **NOTE**

32. Click the New icon again.
33. Name it **4 Bay Division** and change the Orientation to **Vertical**.
34. Choose **Fixed Number of Cells** from the Division Type list and set the Number of Cells field to **4**.

> You will now notice that the Remove icon is available when the 4 Bay Division and the Horizontal Band Division are selected. This is because they are not yet used in the design and therefore can be deleted.
>
> **NOTE**

Create Infills, Frames and Mullions

35. On the left in the tree, select Infills under the Element Definitions heading.
36. Select the Default Infill and rename it to **Glazing Infill**.
37. Change the Panel Thickness to **1"** [**25**].
38. On the left in the tree, select **Frames** under the Element Definitions heading.
39. Select the Default Frame and rename it **Vertical End Frame**.
40. Set the Width to **6"** [**150**], and the Depth to **8"** [**200**].

> Since this item is already used in the design, the change will be immediately apparent.
>
> **NOTE**

41. Click the New icon (in the middle).
42. Name the new Frame **Cornice Frame** and make its Width **24"** [**600**] and its Depth **12"** [**300**].
43. Following the same procedure, refer to Table 8.1 and create the Mullions.
44. Create all new Mullion Definitions. Do *not* rename and reuse Default Mullion this time.

TIP

You may want to click OK here, save the drawing and then return to the Curtain Wall Style to continue. It is a good habit to save after you have completed a procedure, and unfortunately, you cannot save while in a dialog.

Build the Grid Structure

1. Select the Primary Grid node at the top of the tree. Pause for a second and then click again.

   This will allow the item to be renamed. This is the same technique used to rename items in Windows Explorer.
2. Type **Level 1 Grid** and then press ENTER.

On the right, note that the Level 1 Grid is already referencing the Floor to Floor Division, because we simply renamed the existing division in the steps above. This is a good time to pause and make certain that you understand this behavior. It is important to grasp this interrelationship between the parts. Here again, good naming will help you keep the hierarchy and relationships straight.

3. In the top-right pane, expand Frame Assignments, click in the Used In field and then click the small browse (...) button within the field.
4. In the Frame Location Assignment dialog box, deselect Top and Bottom and then click OK (see Figure 8.30).

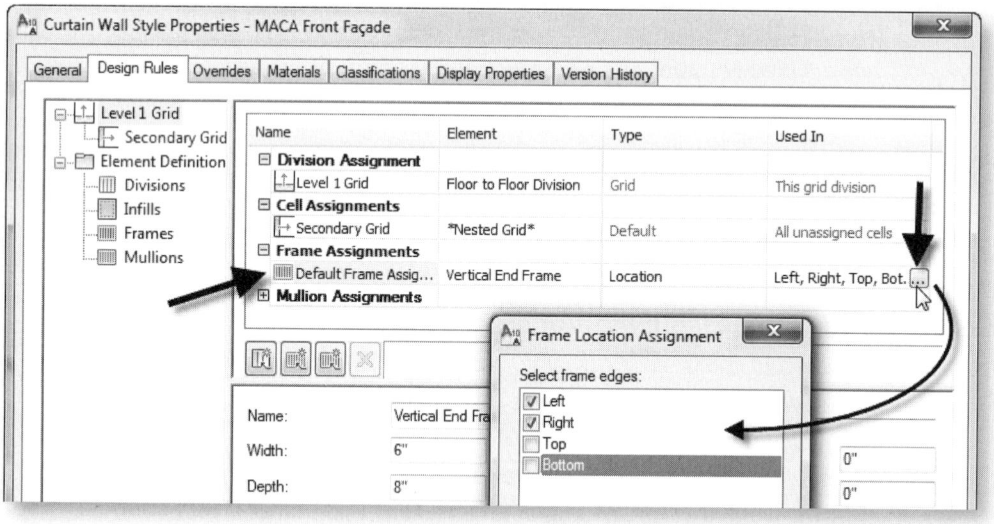

FIGURE 8.30 *Frame Location Assignment Location button*

The Element currently referenced by the Default Frame Assignment is the Vertical End Frame. We only need the Vertical End Frame to show at the left and right edges of the Curtain Wall.

Notice that the frame has disappeared in the top and bottom edges in the Viewer window.

5. In the middle of the dialog box, click the New Frame Assignment icon (second from the left).

   A new entry labeled "New Frame Assignment" will appear in the Frame Assignments grouping in the top pane (see Figure 8.31).

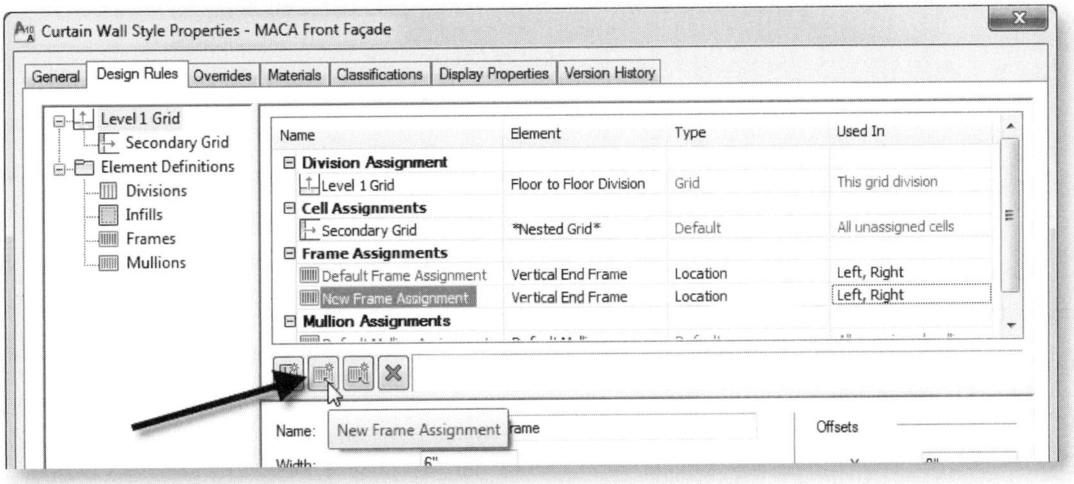

FIGURE 8.31 *Renaming the Frame Assignment*

Element assignments and element definitions are not the same thing. An element assignment, such as the frame assignment we are discussing here, is part of the actual grid structure of the Curtain Wall design. Element definitions are members of our "kit of parts," which are available for *use* in element assignments. Another way to look at it: an element assignment uses an element definition, not the other way around. Please note that unlike all of the other components we have seen in this dialog box so far, the Default Assignments cannot be renamed.

For example, a wall is often framed with a top and bottom plate, and studs at 16" on center. 16" OC would be a Division assignment, as would be the specification of a top and bottom plate. The inclusion of both together as a specification for wall construction would be a Grid in the Curtain Wall. Furthermore, you could use 2×4s or 2×6s to do the actual framing. A 2×4 is an element definition, as is a 2×6, whereas their use for all of the members spaced at 16" OC is the element assignment.

6. Click in the Element column (currently reading "Vertical End Frame").

   A small menu will appear.

7. Choose **Cornice Frame**.

Notice that the list includes the Frame elements we took the time to define in the previous sequence. It is much easier to simply choose from a premade list of elements than to create them as you build the grid hierarchy.

8. Click in the Used In field, click the browse (...) button and place a check mark in Top and Bottom; clear Left and Right this time.

   Notice the change in the Viewer. A much heavier frame now occurs at the top and bottom edges (see Figure 8.32).

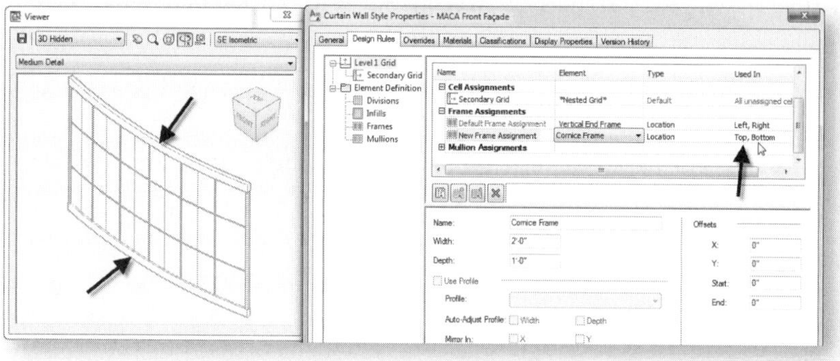

FIGURE 8.32 *Create a Frame Assignment for the Top and Bottom edges*

9. Beneath the Mullion Assignments grouping, next to Default Mullion Assignment, choose **Spandrel Mullion** from the Element list.

   Notice the change in the Viewer. Again, having predefined the list makes the process of assigning them much simpler.

That completes the first grid in the structure. Now we can begin nesting other grids within the cells of this main grid to build a more complex design.

10. On the left in the tree, click and rename Secondary Grid as we did above for Primary Grid. Call it **Level 2 Grid**.

Here we are going to make changes that are slightly more dramatic than those for the Level 1 Grid.

11. In the Division Assignment area for Level 2 Grid, choose **Horizontal Band Division** from the Element list.

    Notice the change in the Viewer. The design has become entirely horizontal. This will prove temporary as we continue (see Figure 8.33).

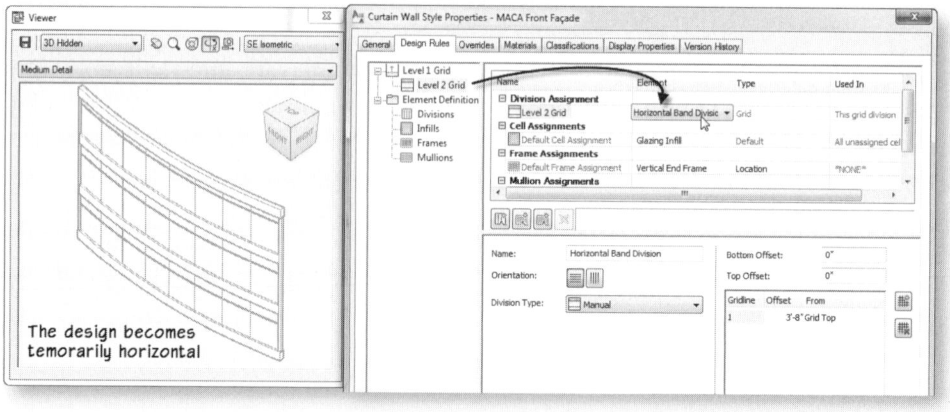

FIGURE 8.33 *Adding the Horizontal Band Mullion grid*

12. Skip down to Mullion Assignments and choose **Horizontal Band Mullion** from the Element list for the Default Mullion Assignment.

    Notice the change in the Viewer. The Level 2 Grid Mullion is now a bit deeper.

13. Move up a bit to Cell Assignments, open the list in the Element column, and choose ***Nested Grid*** (see Figure 8.34).

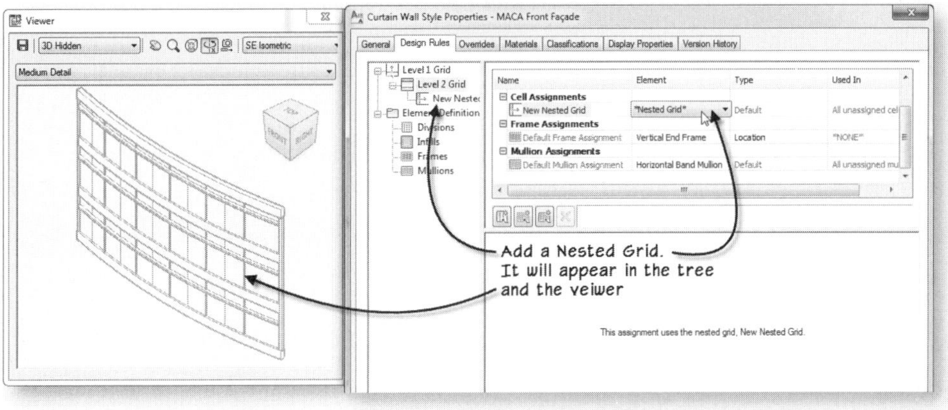

FIGURE 8.34 *Add a new Nested Grid as the Level 2 Grid Cell Assignment*

Notice the appearance of a new node in the tree called "New Nested Grid" and the appearance of a new grid in the Viewer.

14. Select New Nested Grid in the tree on the left, and rename it **Level 3 Grid**.
15. With Level 3 Grid still highlighted in the tree on the left, in the Division Assignment area, ensure that **Column Bay Division** is selected from the Element list (it should automatically default to this choice).
16. In the Mullion Assignments area, choose **Pier Mullion** from the list.
17. In the Cell Assignments area, choose ***Nested Grid*** once more.
18. In the tree on the left, rename the New Nested Grid to **Level 4 Grid**.
19. Change the Division Assignment to **4 Bay Division** and the Mullion Assignment to **Window Mullion**.

We don't need to change the Cell Assignment this time, because we do not need any more Grids and it is already referencing the Glazing Infill by default. As with the other nested grids above, the Frame Assignment is irrelevant because it is not assigned to any edges (in the Used in column).

Take a good look at the design in the Viewer (see Figure 8.35). Click the Visual Styles button to see the details even better. The design is coming very close to the intention of the sketch, but it could use some improvements. For instance, the entire thing is currently a dull gray with no material articulation. To make this design read better, we need to assign some materials.

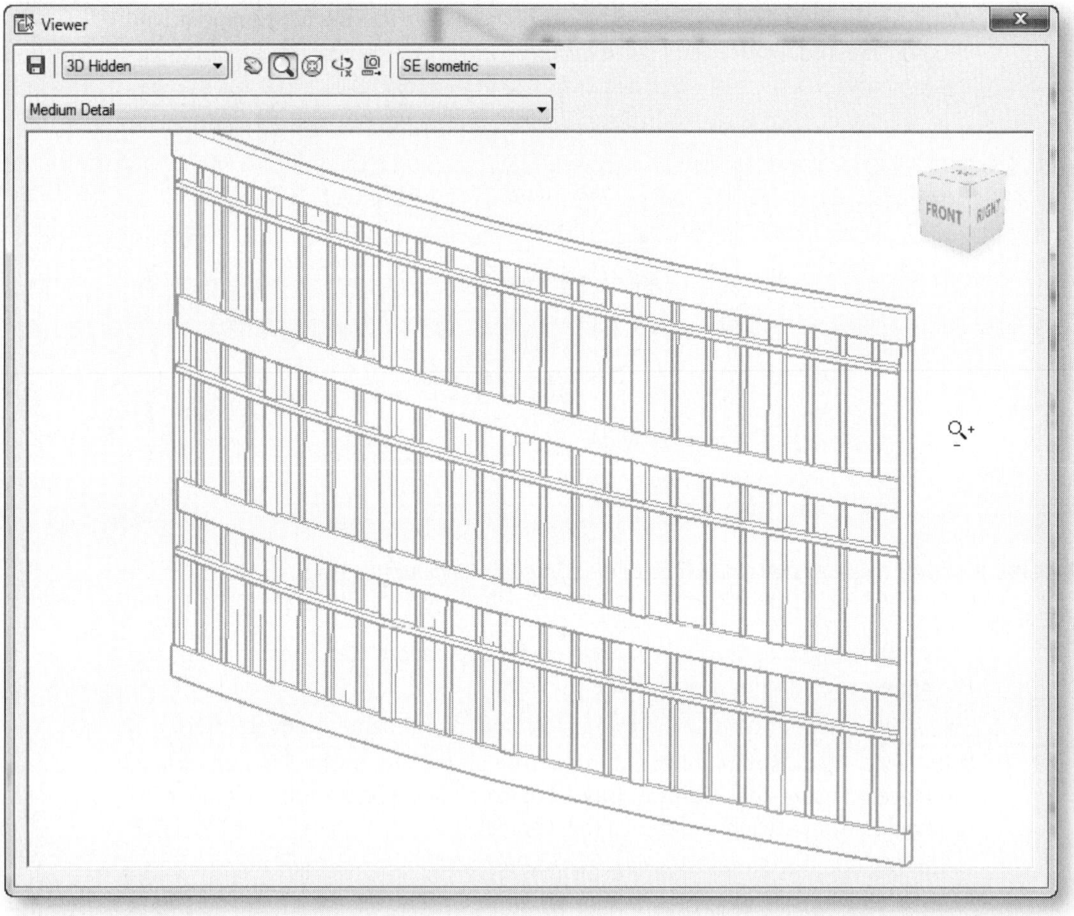

FIGURE 8.35 *Completed Grid Assignments*

Assign Materials

Material Definitions offer a powerful way to articulate the plan, surface, section and 3D parameters of any component in any ACA style. Materials define linework properties such as layer, color and linetype. They also designate hatching and rendering material parameters for all components in all Display Configurations.

1. In the Curtain Wall Style Properties dialog box, click the Materials tab.

There are two columns on this tab. On the left are listed all the Components of the Curtain Wall design that we just added (each Element Definition is listed). The right column shows which Material has been assigned to that component. Currently all components are assigned to the Standard material. The Standard material simply uses the Layer color in plan and usually yields a dull gray in 3D. Let's assign materials to each of our components.

2. Click on Standard in the Material Definition column next to Glazing Infill.

   This will reveal a drop-down list. Notice that the only choice is Standard and clear glass. This will limit our ability to enhance the Materials of this design.

3. Choose **Doors & Windows.Glazing.Glass.Clear**.

There are a few ways to import Material Definitions into a drawing. You can use the Style Manager and the technique covered in the "Out-of-the-Box Curtain Wall Styles" heading above to load a drawing with Materials and drag and drop or copy and paste them into the current drawing. However, in many cases, you can also import the desired Materials simply by using a Style that references them. In other words, since Materials are not stand-alone objects, they are always assigned to other Styles. Therefore, if you know a Style that already uses the Material you want, simply use that Style and the Material will automatically be imported with the Style. For instance, if you wanted a basic Brick Material, you could simply use one of the Wall tools on the Walls palette to import it. Try it out if you like. Click on any Wall tool on the Walls palette and then return to the Materials tab of the Curtain Wall Style. You will now have the Material(s) from that Wall in addition to Standard and clear glass.

4. Click OK to dismiss the style properties dialog.
5. On the View tab, on the Appearance panel, click the Visual Styles tool and then choose Realistic.

   The Glazing Infills should now be transparent.
6. On the Manage tab, on the Style & Display panel, click the Style Manager button.

   The *Curtain Wall & Curtain Wall Unit Styles (Imperial).dwg* [*Curtain Wall & Curtain Wall Unit Styles (Metric).dwg*] file should still appear in the list from when we loaded it earlier.
7. Beneath the *Curtain Wall & Curtain Wall Unit Styles* file expand the *Architectural Objects* category and then select the *Curtain Wall Styles* item.

   This will reveal all the Curtain Wall style in that file in a list on the right side.
8. In the tree, drag the ***Mass Base + 4X4 Grid Above*** Style from this file and drop it on top of the *01 Shell and Core.dwg* file. (You can also right-click and copy and paste instead.)

   This action will import the style into your current drawing. More importantly, all of the nested Material Definitions used in that style will also be imported.

No need to exit Style Manager. We can continue editing our style directly from here.

9. Beneath the *Front Façade* file expand the *Architectural Objects* category and then select the *Curtain Wall Styles* item.

   You see MACA Front Façade, Mass Base + 4×4 Grid Above and Standard in the pane at the right.
10. Double-click MACA Front Façade to edit it.
11. On the Materials tab, hold down the CTRL key and select Vertical End Frame, Horizontal Band Mullion and Window Mullion.

    This will select all three.

    Click on the Material assignment next to any of the highlighted items and then choose: **Doors & Windows.Metal Doors & Frames.Aluminum Frame. Anodized.Dark Bronze.Satin**
12. Click in the white space below to apply the change (see Figure 8.36).

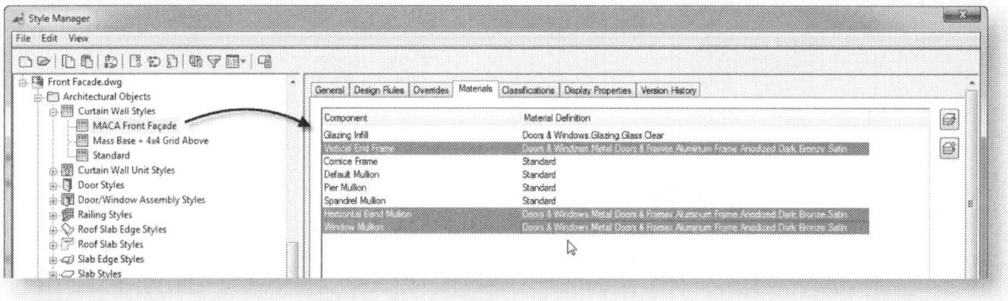

FIGURE 8.36 *Assign Materials to the Curtain Wall components in Style Manager*

13. Select each of the remaining components excluding the Default Mullion.
14. Assign the **Masonry.Stone.Marble.Square.Stacked.Polished.White-Brown-Black** Material and then click OK to view the results (see Figure 8.37).

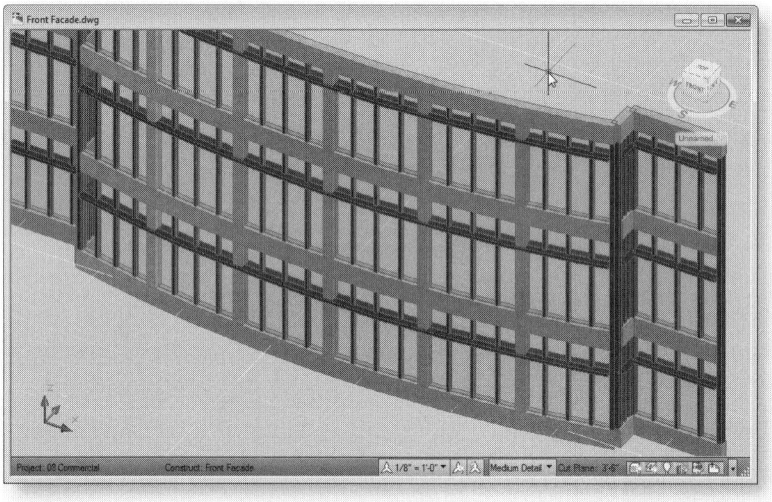

FIGURE 8.37 *Materials Assigned and Realistic Visual Style turned on*

15. Save the file. (Do not close the file.)

TIP	There is no rule of ACA that is more important than remembering to Save often!

Check Dimensions

At an early stage of design, the Curtain Wall style we have built would be sufficient. However, closer examination would reveal some issues that need to be resolved, particularly the way the Frame and Mullion Elements are placed relative to the Curtain Wall dimensions and Grid Divisions. For convenience, let's explore these issues in another file.

16. In the *Elements* folder (on the Constructs tab) of the Project Navigator, double-click the file named *Curtain Wall Offsets* to open it.

This is a version of our design as it appears so far. Note the two dimensions on the left side of the screen. 35'-0" [10,650] is the height parameter and 1'-0" [300] is the projection of the bottom edge. These were applied to the Curtain Wall at the beginning sequence. These two values total: 36'-0" [10,950], or exactly three vertical bays according to the 12'-0" [10,650] dimension used in the Level 1 Grid. The important issue to note is the difference in the way that frames and mullions are applied relative to these overall dimensions. The frame falls *completely* within the limits of the Curtain Wall on all sides. However, mullions are always *centered* relative to the cell divisions by default. The problem this presents is fairly obvious—the space within the bays at the ends will not be equal to those in the middle. To resolve this situation, we will explore the Offset parameters of the Frame and Mullion Elements.

17. Select the Curtain Wall and then on the Curtain Wall tab, click the Edit Style button.
18. On the Design Rules tab, choose Frames from the Element Definitions listing in the tree, and then select the "Cornice Frame" on the right.

    Make sure the Viewer window is open and set the View to Front.

On the bottom right of the dialog box are four fields in the Offsets area. The X and Y offsets adjust the position of the frame component relative to the Curtain Wall. The Start and End offsets adjust the length of the Frame material (see Figure 8.38).

- **A positive X**—Moves the frame *out* away from the Curtain Wall center.
- **A negative X**—Moves the frame *in* toward the Curtain Wall center.
- **A positive Y**—Shifts the frame in plan view above the baseline (relative to a Curtain Wall drawn from left to right). When viewed in elevation as we have here, again with the start point on the left and the endpoint on the right, a positive Y will move the component away from us.
- **A negative Y**—Shifts the frame in plan view below the baseline (relative to a Curtain Wall drawn from left to right). When viewed in elevation as we have here, again with the start point on the left and the endpoint on the right, a negative Y will move the component toward us.
- **Positive Start or End offsets**—Shorten the length of the frame component.
- **Negative Start or End offsets**—Extend the length of the frame component.

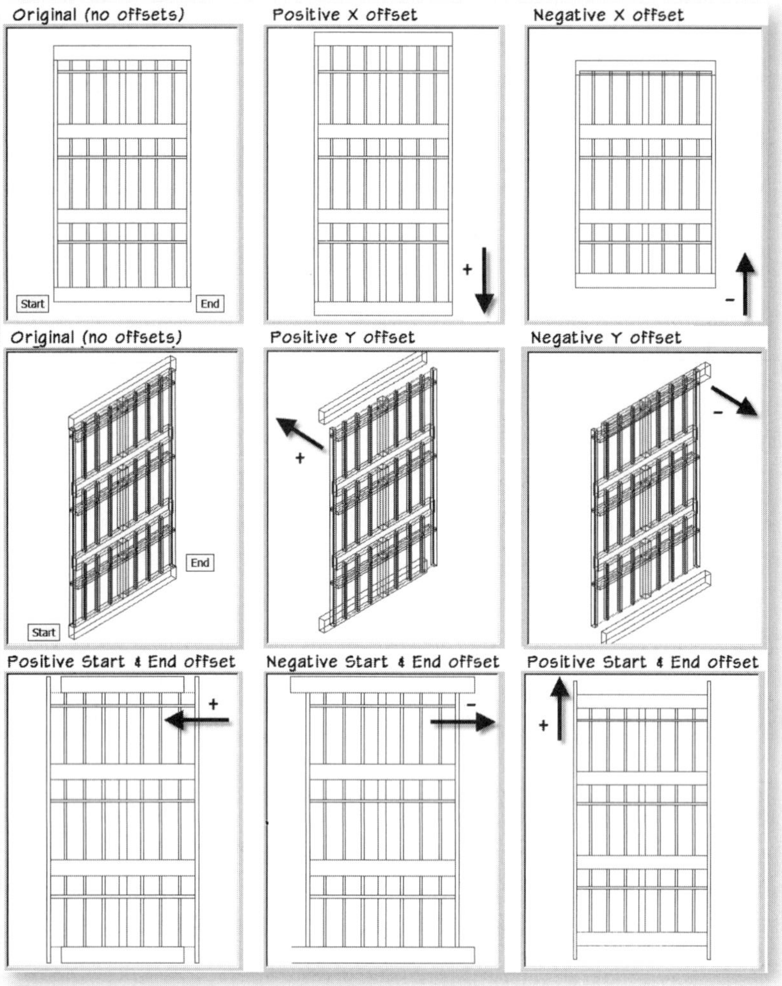

FIGURE 8.38 *The various effects of offsetting Frames and Mullions*

19. Type **2'-0"** [**600**] in the X Offset box and then press ENTER.

    Note the change in the Viewer. The top Cornice frame will move up and the bottom one will move down.

20. Change the X Offset to **-2'-0"** [**-600**].

    The Cornice frames will move in the opposite direction.

21. Change the Viewer to an isometric view and then experiment with the Y Offsets.

    Note that the movements of the Cornice frames are now relative to the depth of the Curtain Wall.

22. Type **2'-0"** [**600**] in the Start Offset box and then press ENTER.

    Note the gap on the left side of the Cornice frame. The Cornice frame length has been shortened by 2'-0" [600].

23. Continue to experiment with the various offsets and compare the results to Figure 8.38.
24. Return all Offsets to **0** (zero) before continuing.
25. Beneath Element Definitions, select the Cornice Frame component again.
26. Type **1'-0"** [**300**] in the X Offset field and then click OK.

    Notice the shift of the Frame component on both the top and bottom (relative to the dimensions).

A check of the dimensions will now yield evenly spaced horizontal bays. We will perform a similar technique on the mullion spacing.

27. Return to the Design Rules tab of the Curtain Wall Style Properties dialog box.
28. Under Element Definitions, select Divisions.

Divisions can also have offsets just like Frames and Mullions.

29. Select the 4 Bay Division, type **4"** [**100**] in both the Start and End Offsets, and click OK to see the change.

The Start and End Offsets will move the points used to divide the cell closer to the center (reduce the width of the cell). Notice that the distance between the face of the mullions and the face of the frames is now the same as the distance between the face of the mullions in relation to each other (see Figure 8.39). You can check this spacing using either the AutoCAD Distance (type **DI**) command or by grip editing the existing dimensions to the new points.

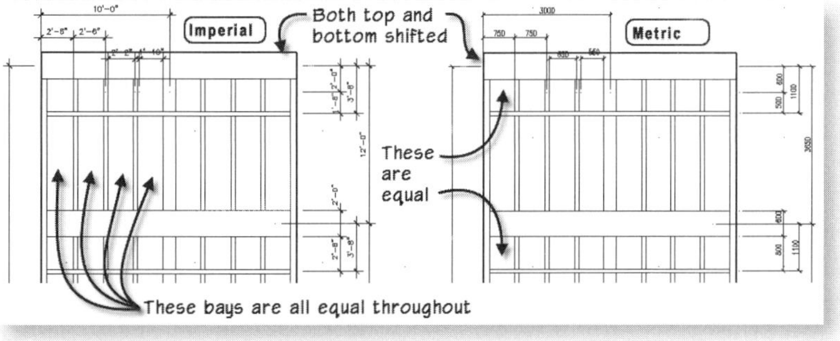

FIGURE 8.39 *Equalizing spacing between components with Division and Frame Offsets*

30. Save the *Curtain Wall Offsets* file.

Update Project Standards

We are now ready to apply the changes to this Style to the version in the *Front Façade* Construct. There are actually several ways to do this in AutoCAD Architecture. We could use the Style Manager to manually copy the new version and overwrite the one in the Front Façade file; we could create a Tool on our MACA Commercial palette and use it to "Re-import" the Style into the Front Façade file or we could use Project Standards. (We could also do all three or any combination of them if we wished—see the CAD Manager Note below.) All methods would achieve the same initial result, but over the life of the project, the Project Standards approach is the most useful. To do this, we need to return to Style Manager and copy this updated version of our style to the standards file (established at the start of this chapter). Then we need to edit the settings for project standards and synchronize.

1. Open Style Manager.
2. Beneath the *Curtain Wall Offsets* file expand the *Architectural Objects* category and then select the *Curtain Wall Styles* item.
3. At the top of the file list, expand the *2010.1-08 Commercial* item.

   This will reveal the project standards file: *Commercial Styles.dwg*.
4. From the right side, drag the ***MACA Front Façade*** Style from this file and drop it on top of the *Commercial Styles.dwg* file. (You can also right-click and copy and paste instead.)

5. Beneath the *Commercial Styles* file expand the *Architectural Objects* category and then select the *Curtain Wall Styles* item.
6. On the right side, double-click the MACA Front Façade style to edit it.
7. Click the Version History tab and then click the Version button.
8. For the comment, type: **Adjusted Offsets** and then click OK.
9. Click OK to close the Style Manager.
10. When prompted to save the standards file, click Yes.

We have just copied the modified version (with adjusted offsets) of MACA Front Façade to the project standards file and to ensure that it is understood as the latest edit, we applied a new Version to it. Now we need to adjust the settings of project standards which are currently configured to synchronize only Walls to include Curtain Walls as well.

11. On the Project Navigator, click the Project tab and then click the Configure Project Standards icon.
12. Click on the Standard Styles tab.
13. Place a check mark next to Curtain Wall Styles beneath the Standards Drawings column and then click OK.
14. When prompted to apply a Version, type **Modified synchronization options** for the comment and then click OK (see Figure 8.40).

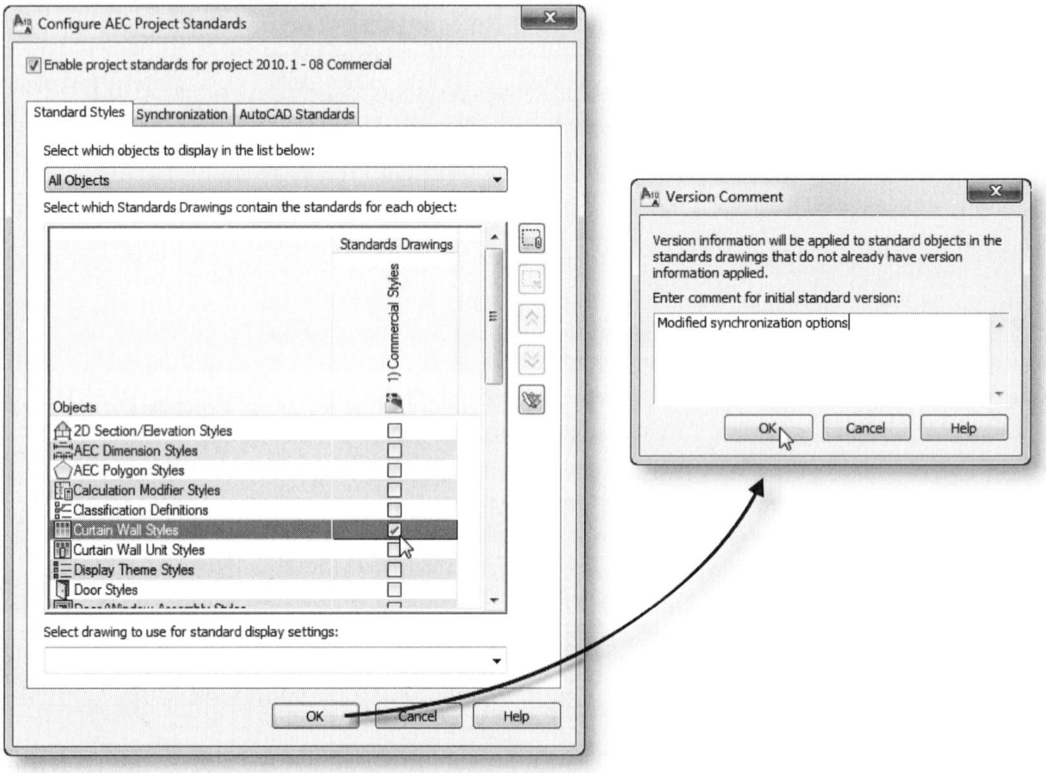

FIGURE 8.40 *Assign the Curtain Wall Offsets as a Standards Drawing for Curtain Wall Styles*

Notice the message in the "Version Comment" dialog. It says that Version information will be applied to those styles that do not already have Version information. Since we already applied a Version to the MACA Front Façade style, this Version comment will be applied to other Curtain Wall styles in the file such as Standard.

15. Save and close the *Curtain Wall Offsets* file.

Synchronize a Single Drawing

Now let's synchronize the *Front Façade* file to the updated Standards Drawing.

16. On the Project Navigator, from the *Constructs\Architectural* folder, double-click *Front Façade.*

    If you left *Front Façade* open above, this action will make it the current drawing.

17. At the bottom-right corner of the drawing, right-click the AEC Project Standards quick pick and choose **Synchronize Drawing** (see Figure 8.41).

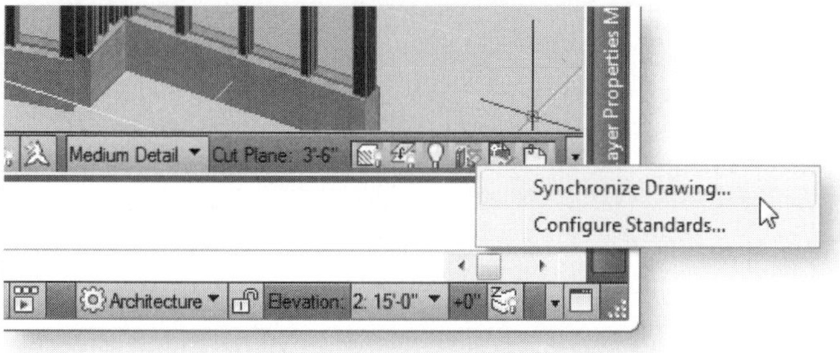

FIGURE 8.41 *Synchronize the Front Façade Construct*

18. Be sure that the Action reads "Update from Standard" and then click OK.

You should see the Curtain Wall adjust to reflect the new offset settings.

CAUTION

Remember, once you designate a drawing as Standards Drawing, it controls the composition of that Style from then on. If you should make a change to the Style in any other project drawing, it can be overwritten the next time you synchronize the standards. This is a very powerful tool in ACA. However, make certain that you really want to overwrite the existing style before you synchronize. Once it has been overwritten, the original style is gone. It is always a good idea to save often and perform regular backups. Changes made in project drawings can be "pushed" to the Standards Drawing where appropriate. The process is called "Updating." Refer to the "Updating Project Standards Drawings" topic in the online Help for more information.

MANAGER NOTE

As noted above, there are other ways to update the Style. We could make a custom tool from our Curtain Wall style on our Project Tools palette. Even if you use Standards to synchronize the Styles, it is often useful to create tools for the most common project styles as well. We have seen examples of this already. Objects from the drawing can be dragged to Tool Palettes to create tools. You can also drag styles from the Style Manager to create tools. When you create a new tool, it will write the full path to the host drawing file as the Style source location. An icon is also generated automatically for the new tool. It is best to work in Standards Drawings when you make tools. This way, the tool's style reference will point to the master version of the Style and there will be no ambiguity as to which version is most current. To try this out, open one of the Standards Drawings, make the MACA Commercial palette active and then drag an object (or Style from Style Manager) to the palette. After the tool is created, right-click the new tool and choose **Properties**, and then look at the Style Location field. It will reference the Standards Drawing name and path.

Please note, that it is very important to save the file before you drag to create the tool. This is the only way that the file reference in the Style Location field will be correct. The style must exist in the saved version of the file before a tool that references it can be properly made.

If you are unhappy with the icon image that was automatically created, you can scroll to the bottom of the Tool Properties worksheet and adjust the image in the Viewer to your liking. When you have finished, right-click the icon image at the top of the worksheet and choose **Refresh image**. Specify image allows you to choose an image file from your hard drive (these should be small, 64-pixels square). Finally, if you close the Tool Properties worksheet, you can right-click on the tool and choose **Set Image from Selection**, and then have an icon generated from an object selection in the drawing (see Figure 8.42).

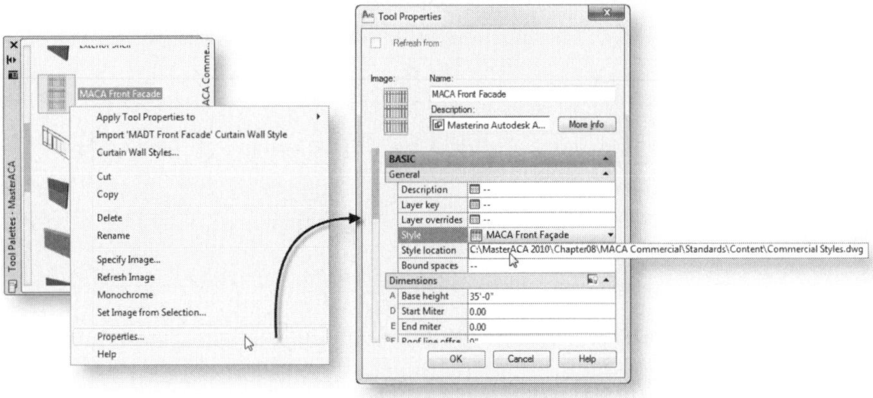

FIGURE 8.42 *Create a Project Tool for the Curtain Wall and customize the image*

Once you have built a tool of this sort, it can be applied to objects in other drawings in the project by simply right-clicking the tool and choosing "Apply to." You can also "Re-import" style to manually update a drawing without performing a Standards Synchronization.

Finally, if you create tools in your workspace, they must still be made available to other team members on a project. This can be done via the Content Browser. Copy and paste the tool to a common catalog in Content Browser to which all team members have access.

Refining the Maca Front Façade Curtain Wall Design

Editing the offsets to help equalize the frame and mullion spacing was helpful, but there are a few additional refinements that we can make to the design to make it more visually appealing.

Due to the "Shrink" rule of the Grid Division, the cells on the ends are smaller than the ones in the middle. Subdividing them into four cells, like the other full-sized bays, does not work well in this circumstance. In addition, the corner conditions need some refinement as well. We will redefine the style so that the Level 4 Grid (4 Bay Division in this case) does not apply to the first and last cells. Then we will apply overrides to the corners to get nicer transitions and cleanup. Finally, because the two segments parallel to the front of the building do *not* need the Start and End cell override that the others do, we will make a copy of the original Curtain Wall style to apply to them.

Address the End Bays

1. Make sure that *Front Façade* is the current drawing.

   If it isn't, choose Front Façade from the Window menu, press CTRL + TAB to cycle it into view, or simply double-click it on the Project Navigator palette again.

2. Select the two straight horizontal Curtain Wall segments on the right and left (the ones that will intersect the masonry Walls).
3. On the Curtain Wall tab of the ribbon, click the Save As button.
4. In the Curtain Wall Style Properties dialog box, click the General tab and type **MACA Front Façade 3 Bay** for the name and then click OK.

We now have two styles that will work independently of one another. This will enable us to edit them separately and create slight variations to the design between the main Curtain Wall and the two smaller pieces that frame it.

5. Deselect All and then select the curved Curtain Wall segment.
6. On the Curtain Wall tab of the ribbon, click the Edit Style button.
7. On the Design Rules tab, click the Level 3 Grid node in the tree.
8. Click the New Cell Assignment icon.

   Verify that in the Element column, Glazing Infill appears and that "Used In" displays Start, End (see Figure 8.43).

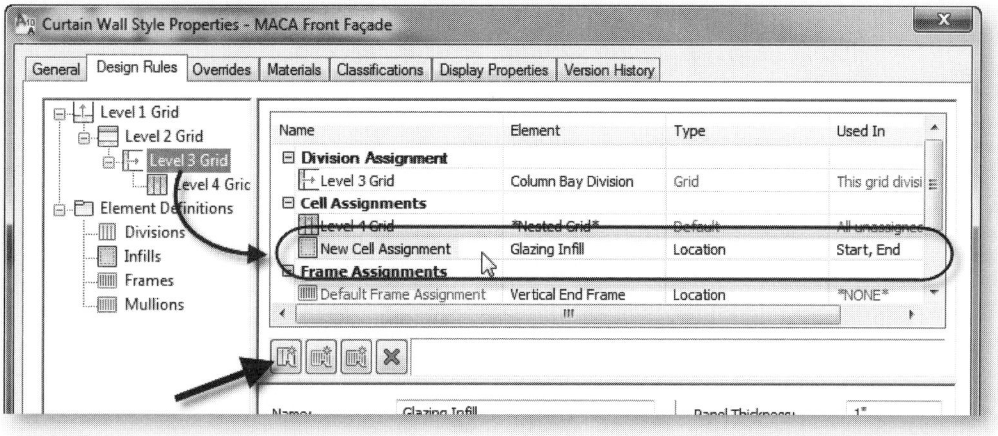

FIGURE 8.43 *Add a new Cell Assignment for the end bays*

9. Click OK to accept the changes and close the dialog box.

Notice the change to the drawing from the adjustment of the Level 3 Grid. The Curved Curtain Wall and the small perpendicular segments now look better. Since we first copied and applied a new style to the two horizontal segments that will join up with the masonry Walls, they are unaffected. However, these might look better with only three bays instead of four.

Edit Divisions in Place

10. On the View tab, from the Appearance panel, choose **Front**.

    If you have been working in shaded mode, you might want to choose **2D Wireframe** for the next operation. This will make it easier to see while you work.
11. Select the straight horizontal Curtain Wall segment on the left.
12. On the Curtain Wall tab of the ribbon, click the Design Rules drop-down button and choose Transfer to Object.
13. Click the small round gray (Edit Grid) grip at the bottom of the Curtain Wall (see item 1 in Figure 8.44).

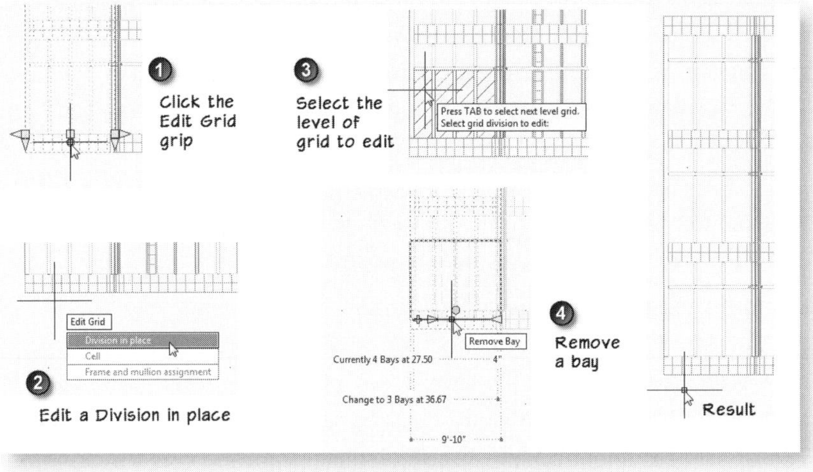

FIGURE 8.44 *Edit Grid of the Curtain Wall and edit the Division in Place*

14. At the "Edit Grid" prompt, choose **Division in Place** (see item 2 in Figure 8.44).

    Move the cursor over the Curtain Wall and notice the way the grid cells highlight.
15. Press the TAB key as required to highlight one of the 4-Bay Divisions as shown in item 3 in Figure 8.44 and then click to select it.

    A series of grips will appear.
16. Hover over each grip to see a tool tip indicating its function.
17. Click the minus sign (–) grip to remove one bay (see item 4 in Figure 8.44).

    Notice that this applies to the entire Curtain Wall not just the selected bay.
18. On the Edit In-Place: Grid Division tab, click the Finish button.
19. Select the same Curtain Wall; on the Curtain Wall tab, click the Design Rules button and then choose Save to Style.
20. In the Save Changes worksheet, click OK.

This action will apply the edit made to the first Curtain Wall to the one on the other side as well. Let's return to an isometric view and study the changes.

21. On the View tab, choose **SE isometric**.

The design is starting to shape up nicely. However, corners still don't cleanup very nicely. Let's resolve that next.

Override Corner Conditions

22. On the View tab, choose **Top**.

    If you have been working in shaded mode, you might want to choose **2D Wireframe** for the next operation. This will make it easier to see while you work.

TIP In general, when viewing Top, you should always choose 2D Wireframe.

23. Zoom in on the right side of the plan where the three segments of Curtain Wall come together.
24. Select the horizontal Curtain Wall segment, on the Curtain Wall tab, click the Edit Style button.

25. On the Design Rules tab, in the tree, beneath Element Definitions, select the Frames item.
26. Click the New Frame icon.
27. Name the new Frame **Corner Frame**.
28. Set both the Width and Depth to **8"** [**200**], and the X Offset to **4"** [**100**].
29. Click the Materials tab and set the material for Corner Frame to **Doors & Windows.Metal Doors & Frames.Aluminum Frame.Anodized.Dark Bronze. Satin** and then click OK to return to the drawing.

 Now let's apply this new Element to the corners that need it.

30. With the horizontal Curtain Wall segment still selected, on the Curtain Wall tab, click the Frame/Mullion drop-down button and then choose Override Assignment.
31. At the "Select an edge" prompt, click the Frame to the left (see Figure 8.45).

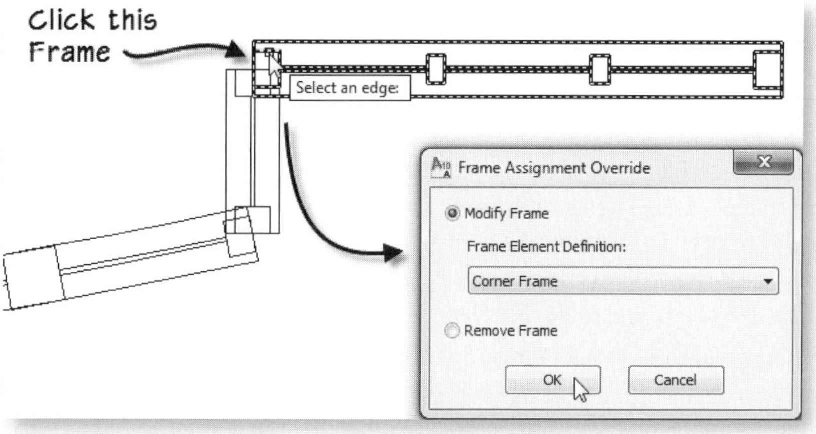

FIGURE 8.45 *Select the Frame edge to override*

32. In the "Frame Assignment Override" dialog box that appears, choose **Corner Frame** from the Frame Element Definitions list and then click OK.
33. Repeat the entire process on the small perpendicular Curtain Wall segment (see Figure 8.46).

NOTE

you need to create the element definition again, since the small perpendicular Curtain Wall uses a different style.

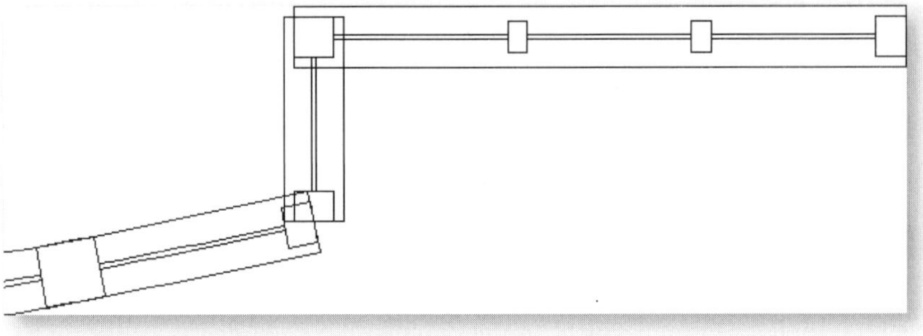

FIGURE 8.46 *Result of the Square Corner Override applied to both segments*

It was necessary to repeat all of the steps including the definition of the square Frame component, since these two segments are now two different styles. You will need to repeat the Override steps again on the other side of the plan as well. However, in this case, since the Corner Frame is already defined for both styles, you can simply repeat the Override Frame steps. If you wish, you can delete the two segments on the left side and mirror them over instead.

34. Select the small perpendicular Curtain Wall segment or the curved one, and on the ribbon choose Edit Style.
35. On the Design Rules tab, select Level 1 Grid.
36. In the Frame Assignments area, next to the Default Frame Assignment item, click in the Used In box, then click the (...) button.
37. Deselect the Right and Left checkboxes, and then click OK.

    The Used In will now display *NONE*.
38. Click OK again to view the change (see Figure 8.47).

    The Frame edges of the Curtain Wall will disappear. However, the square edge of the small perpendicular Curtain Wall retained its override.

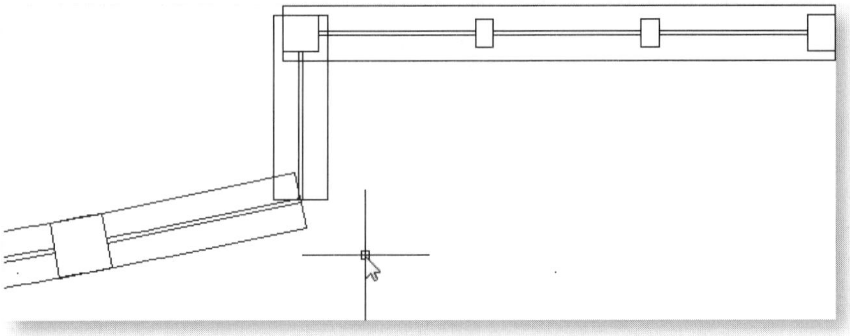

FIGURE 8.47 *The result of removing the Frame Assignment*

Apply a Miter to the Corners

39. Select the curved Curtain Wall segment and the small perpendicular segment.
40. On the ribbon, click the Set Miter Angles button (see Figure 8.48).

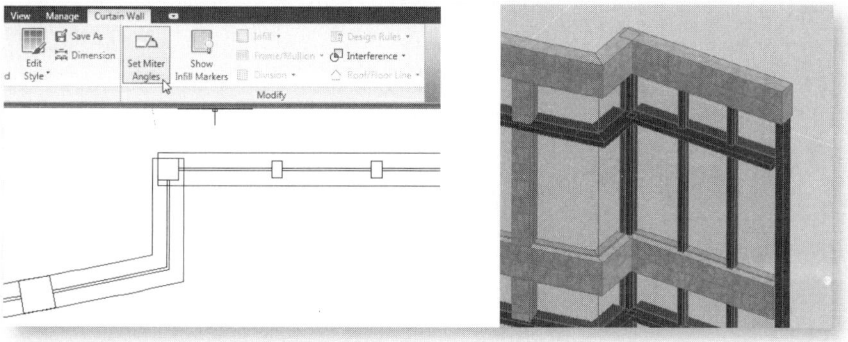

FIGURE 8.48 *Miter the corners*

41. Repeat the Miter on the other side and on the intersection between the horizontal and perpendicular straight Curtain Wall segments.

NOTE

If the angles calculated by the Set Miter Angles command are not correct, you can manually adjust them in the Properties palette.

42. On the View tab, choose **SE Isometric**, zoom in on the corner, turn on Realistic Visual Style and study the result.
43. Save the file.

DIRECT MANIPULATION OF CURTAIN WALL COMPONENTS

In many respects, the preceding tutorial could be considered "the hard way" of designing and building Curtain Walls, Curtain Wall Units and Door/Window Assemblies. The overall goal of the exercise was to convey a complete understanding of Curtain Wall terminology and procedure. The result of what we created was a fully parametric Curtain Wall design. However, there are easier ways to build Curtain Walls. Perhaps the simplest method is to convert linework to a Curtain Wall, Curtain Wall Units or Door/Window Assembly object. In addition, we have several in place edit and direct manipulation functions as well. Let's look at a few here.

Customize a Mullion Profile

The shape of all of our Frames and Mullions are rectangular at this point. But they can be any shape we like. For the next sequence, we do a bit of experimentation. Be sure that the *Front Façade* file is open onscreen.

1. On the View tab, choose **SE Isometric** (or choose the SE Isometric icon on the Views toolbar).
2. Zoom in close on one of the square Pier Mullions in the center bay of the Curtain Wall.
3. Select the Curtain Wall, on the ribbon, click Frame/Mullion > Add Profile.
4. At the "Select a frame or mullion of the grid assembly to add a profile" prompt, click on one of the Pier Mullions in the center.

TIP

If you have trouble selecting one of the Pier Mullions, change to Top view first and then try again.

5. In the Add Mullion Profile dialog box, be sure that Profile Definition is set to **Start from scratch**.
6. Type **Pier Mullion Profile 1** for the name, and make sure that "To Shared Mullion Element Definition" is chosen (see Figure 8.49).

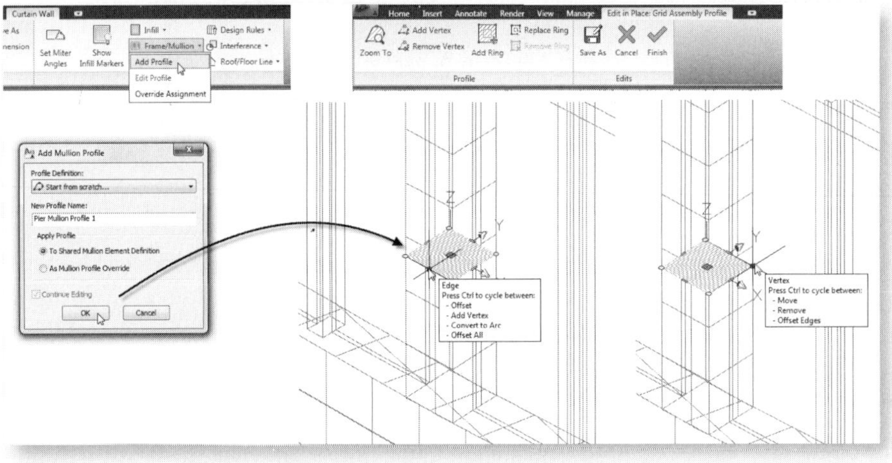

FIGURE 8.49 *Enter Edit in Place for a new Mullion profile*

An Edit in Place profile will appear with grips at each corner, one at each midpoint and one at the center. You can edit the shape of the profile with these grips, or you can use the contextual ribbon tab (or right-click) for more options. Like most ACA grips, each shape has a different function. Hover your mouse over a shape to see a tip indicating its function and any CTRL key options. For instance, with the thin rectangular grips, you can add vertices and convert the edge to an arc. On the small circular grips, you can move or remove vertices. You can also add and remove vertices from a right-click menu, as well as add, remove and replace rings. A ring is a shape that you draw with a closed polyline first, and then incorporate into the Edit In Place profile. Feel free to experiment with these grips before proceeding. You can stretch and reshape the profile any way you wish. The Curtain Wall will respond interactively. When you are finished experimenting, be sure to undo the edits until you return the Edit In Place profile to its original square shape. For our purposes here, we will make a very simple edit.

7. Click the small rectangular grip on the edge facing out and then press CTRL once to add a vertex.
8. Drag the new point using POLAR or ORTHO perpendicular to the Curtain Wall **2"** [**50**] and then press ENTER (see Figure 8.50).

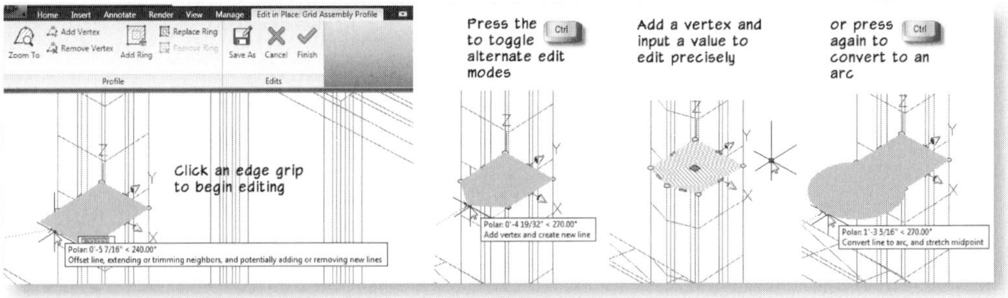

FIGURE 8.50 *Edit the shape of the Edit in Place profile*

9. On the Edit in Place: Grid Assembly Profile tab, click the Finish button.

   Note the change to all of the Pier Mullions in the design.
10. Zoom in on the middle bay of the top row of the Curtain Wall.
11. Select the Curtain Wall, on the ribbon, click Frame/Mullion > Add Profile.
12. When prompted to "Select a frame or mullion of the grid assembly to add a profile," click the third Pier Mullion from the left (in the top row).
13. In the Add Mullion Profile dialog box, be sure that Profile Definition is set to **Start from scratch** again.
14. Type **Pier Mullion Profile 2** for the name, and choose "As Mullion Profile Override" from the Apply Profile group this time.

    By choosing this option, the edit will be applied to only the selected Mullion.
15. Repeat the Add Vertex steps exactly as before. (Or press CTRL twice and add an arc segment this time.)
16. Click the same grip again, and drag it back in the opposite direction **2"** [**50**] this time and then click the Finish button on the Edit In-Place contextual ribbon tab.

    Where the first profile produced a pointed Mullion profile, this edit produces a concave shape.
17. Select the Curtain Wall, on the ribbon, click Frame/Mullion > Add Profile once again.
18. This time, select the third Pier Mullion from the right.
19. Instead of "Start from Scratch," this time choose **Pier Mullion Profile 2** from the Profile Definition list and be sure that **As Mullion Profile Override** is chosen from the Apply Profile group again.

    You may repeat these steps to add the Pier Mullion Profile 2 to as many of the top row Mullions as you wish.
20. Save the file.

    If you like, open the *A-CM00* Composite Model file on the Views tab of the Project Navigator to see your Curtain Wall in the context of the entire building.

Update Project Standards

Recall that we mentioned above that if we were to synchronize the project right now with the Standards, we would lose most of the changes that we have just made. This is because the Standards Drawing still contains the old Version of the Style. While it is typical that the workflow will be for changes to be made in the Standards Drawing and then synchronized to the project files, it is possible to take changes made in the project file and push them back to the Standards file. This is called "Updating" the Standards Drawing.

We will use this process to update the MACA Front Façade style and to copy the new MACA Front Façade 3 Bay style to the Standards Drawing.

1. On the Manage tab, click the Style Manager button.
2. Expand the *Architectural Objects* category and then highlight the *Curtain Walls* category.

Notice the small orange badge on the style icon. This indicates that the style is newer than the standards version.

3. Right-click the MACA Front Façade style and choose **Version Style**.
4. In the "Version Objects" dialog, type: **Modified End Bays and Added Corner Frame** for the Version Comment and then click OK.

5. Repeat this process for the MACA Front Façade 3 Bay style using the comment: **Created 3 Bay Variation**.
6. Right-click the Curtain Wall Styles node on the left and choose **Update Standards from Drawing**.
7. Verify that the action next to MACA Front Façade is **Update Project Standards** and that the action next to MACA Front Façade 3 Bay is **Add to Project Standards** and then click OK (see Figure 8.51).

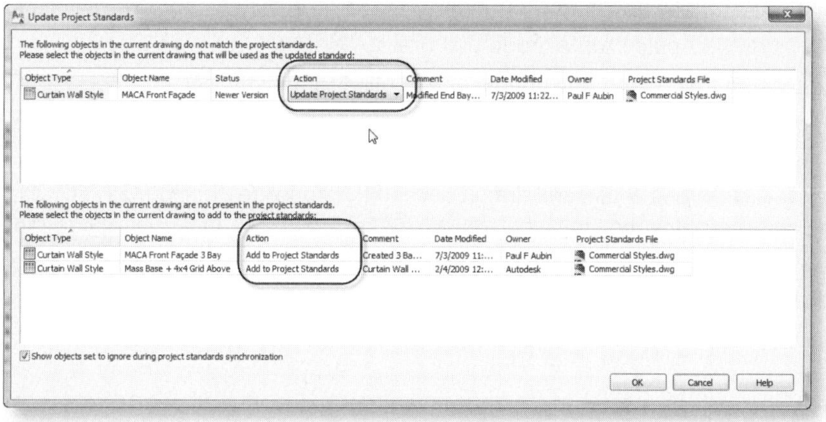

FIGURE 8.51 *Update Project Standards from the current Drawing*

8. Click OK to close the Style Manager. In any "Save Changes" dialogs that appear, click Yes.

If you wish, you can open the *Commercial Styles.dwg* file, open the Style Manager and edit the Curtain Wall styles. Click the Version History tab to see that the new Version with the "Modified End Bays and Added Corner Frame" comment is the current Version.

That completes our work on the Front Façade file. Feel free to continue your personal experimentation further if you wish. Otherwise, you can close the file.

Convert Linework to a Door/Window Assembly

9. On the Project Navigator palette, click the Constructs tab.
10. In the *Elements* folder, double-click *Window Assembly Sketch* to open it.

    This file was added to the dataset for this chapter.
11. On the Design tool palette, right-click the Door/Window Assembly tool and choose **Apply Tool Properties to > Elevation Sketch**.
12. At the "Select elevation linework" prompt, select all of the lines in the drawing and then press ENTER.
13. At the "Select baseline or RETURN for default" prompt, press ENTER.
14. At the "Erase layout geometry" prompt, choose **Yes**. (If you do not have the Dynamic Input toggle turned on, right-click and choose **Yes**.)

    A new Door/Window Assembly will be made from the linework. Let's add a Door to the main Cell.
15. On the Doors tool palette, click the Hinged - Double - Full Lite tool.
16. At the "Select grid assembly cell to add door" prompt, click the middle bay of the Door/Window Assembly object.

17. In the Add Infill worksheet, choose the "Add as Cell Override" option.
18. Type **Door Infill** for the New Infill name and then place a check mark in the Bottom box for Frame Removal (see Figure 8.52).

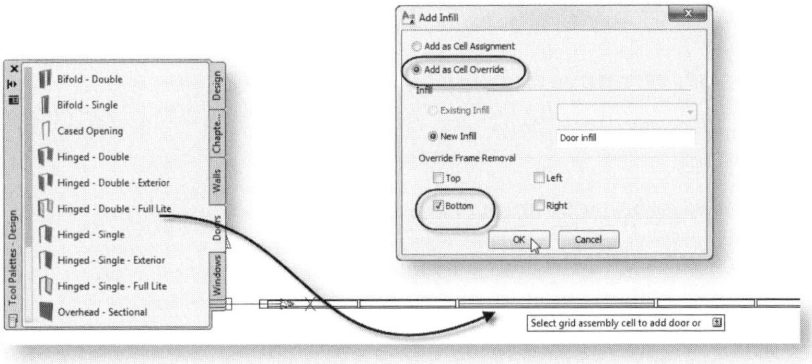

FIGURE 8.52 *Select a Cell to receive a Door Infill override*

19. Click OK to see the results and then press ENTER to complete the command.
20. Switch to SW Isometric view.
21. Select the Door/Window Assembly and on the Door/Window Assembly tab of the ribbon, click the Design Rules button and choose Save to Style.
22. Click the New icon, type **MACA Retail Store Front** for the name and then click OK.
23. Place a check mark in the "Transfer Infill Overrides to Style" checkbox and then click OK (see Figure 8.53).

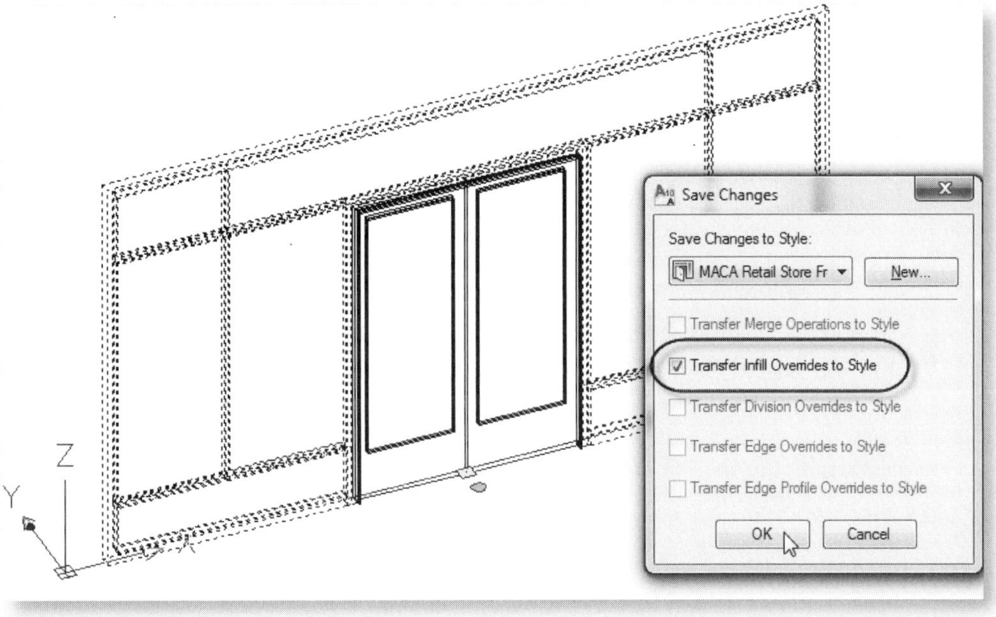

FIGURE 8.53 *Saving the custom Door/Window Assembly to a new Style*

24. With the object still selected, click the Edit Style button on the ribbon.

25. On the Materials tab, apply the Doors & Windows.Glazing.Glass.Clear Material to the Default Infill component.
26. Click OK and then Save the file.

For more detailed instruction on using the Material tool, refer to the "Assign Materials using a Material Tool" heading.

Create a Custom Door/Window Assembly Tool

27. Right-click the tool palettes title bar and choose **MasterACA** to load the book Tool Palette Group.

This tool is already on the MACA Commercial palette. However for the education value, let's go through the process of creating it.

28. Right-click the tool palettes title bar and choose New Palette.
29. Name the new palette **Chapter08**.
30. Select the Door/Window Assembly and the nested Door, press CTRL + C.
31. From the Application menu, choose **Open > Drawing**. Browse to the Standards\Content folder for the current project and open the *Commercial Styles* [*Commercial Styles Metric*] drawing file.
32. Press CTRL + V and then click a point onscreen to locate the pasted object.
33. Save the *Commercial Styles* [*Commercial Styles Metric*] drawing file.
34. Select the Door/Window Assembly object and (being careful not to select a grip) drag it and drop it on the Chapter08 palette.

    You will receive a warning about saving the drawing. This is important because the tool will not work if the drawing is not saved.
35. Click OK to dismiss the warning.
36. Right-click the new tool and choose **Set Image from Selection** and then when prompted, select both the Door/Window Assembly and the nested Door and then press ENTER.
37. Save and Close the *Commercial Styles* [*Commercial Styles Metric*] drawing file.

Add the Door/Window Assembly to the 01 Partitions Construct

38. On the Project Navigator, double-click *01 Partitions* (in the *Constructs\Architectural* folder) to open it.

    This file was added to the dataset for this chapter. It contains a few Walls defining a lobby and an XREF Overlay of the *01 Shell and Core* file for reference. Notice how your changes to the *01 Shell and Core* file appear here.
39. On the Chapter08 tool palette, click the MACA Retail Store Front tool.
40. Add one to each of the two vertical Walls in this file and then press ENTER when finished (see Figure 8.54).

TIP

for best results, use the Offset/Center positioning feature on the Properties palette.

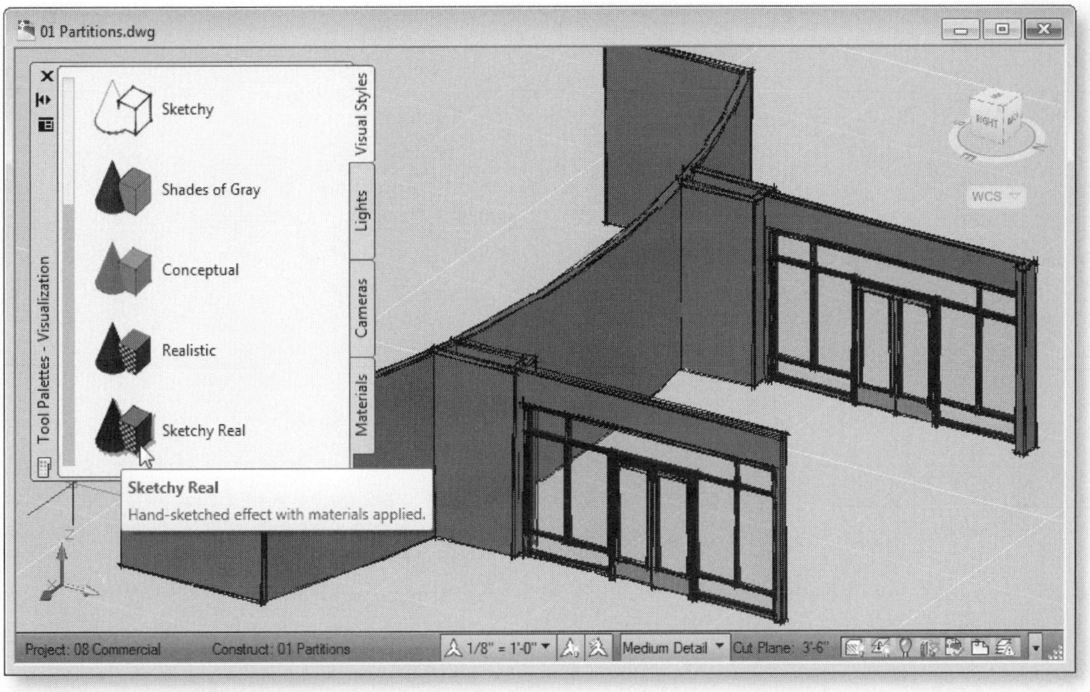

FIGURE 8.54 *Adding the Door/Window Assemblies to the 01 Partitions file (XREF hidden for clarity)*

41. Save and Close both the *Window Assembly Sketch* and the *01 Partitions* files.
42. Save and Close all project files.

Here are a couple of additional tools to explore:

- **Roof Line/Floor Line**—Includes options such as Project, which will match the top edge (Roof Line) or bottom edge (Floor Line) to the shape of an open polyline. Change to an elevation view; draw a polyline above or below the Curtain Wall in the shape that you want it to project. Select a Curtain Wall and click the Roof Line/Floor Line drop-down button to access Modify Roof Line, Modify Floor Line or Edit in place. Choose the Project option, and when prompted, select the polyline. The ribbon tools only work with a single object selected. To edit the Roof Line or Floor Line of multiple objects at once, right-click instead.
- **Reference Shape**—Allows the baseline in plan of the Curtain Wall to follow another shape. Draw a polyline, spline or ellipse in the plan in the drawing. On the Design palette, right-click the Curtain Wall tool and choose **Apply Tool Properties to > Referenced Base Curve**. Follow the prompts. The Curtain Wall will remain linked to the shape as it changes.

ADDITIONAL EXERCISES

Additional exercises have been provided in Appendix A. In Appendix A you will find an exercise for building a screen porch in the Residential Project using a Curtain Wall (see Figure 8.55). In it you will review topics covered here, and explore the Edit in Place functionality further. It is not necessary that you complete this exercise to begin the next chapter, it is provided to enhance your learning experience. Completed projects for each of the exercises have been provided in the *Chapter08/Complete* folder.

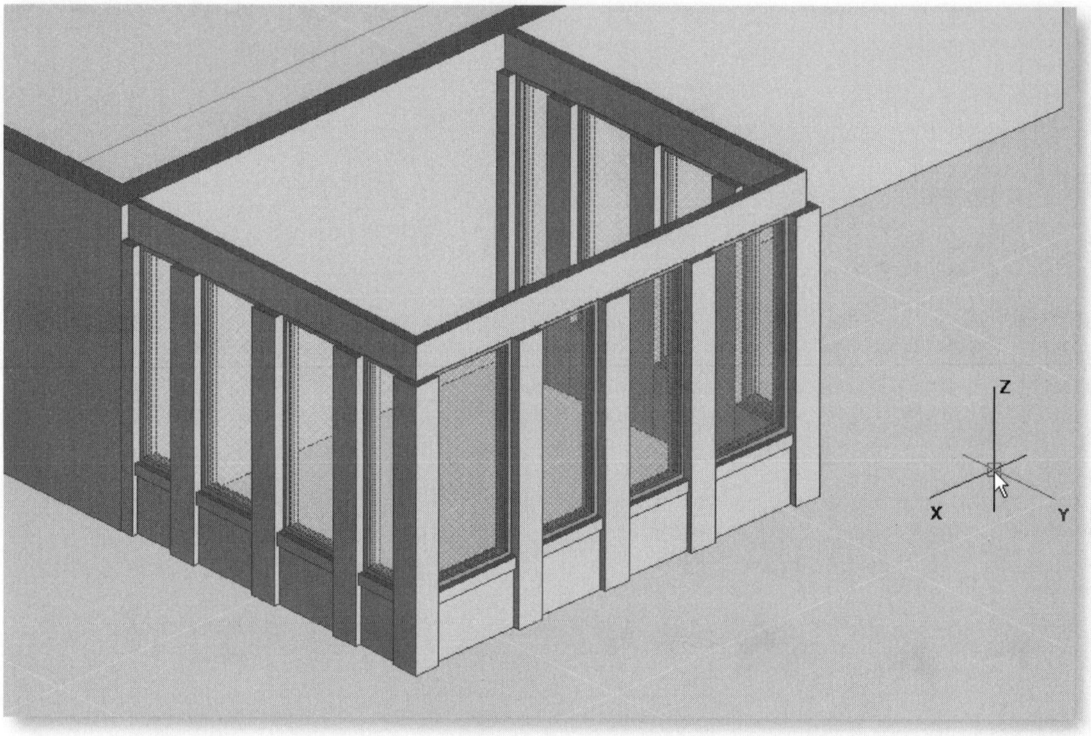

FIGURE 8.55 *Add a Sun Porch to the rear of the Residential Project*

SUMMARY

- Project Standards offer a way to keep all Styles (and Display settings) in a project synchronized with one or more master Standards Drawing files.
- Create Project Tools that point to the styles in your Project Standards files for additional functionality and convenience.
- The Curtain Wall object is a powerful and flexible tool for designing a building skin.
- Proper planning and good naming are critical to successful Curtain Wall designs.
- Sketch out your design intent first.
- Try to determine and build as many of the components as you will need ahead of time—Kit of Parts.
- Assemble the style from your Kit of Parts.
- Establish proper offsets on the Frame and Mullion elements to ensure proper cell spacing.
- The Edit in Place mode allows for flexible "what if" scenarios that can be saved back to the original style or to a new style.

CHAPTER

9

Understanding Wall Cleanup

INTRODUCTION

Wall cleanup determines the interaction between Wall objects and controls all aspects of their successful intersection. Previous editions of this book presented the topic of wall cleanup as one of the most critical skills to success in AutoCAD Architecture. While the importance of properly cleaned up Wall intersections remains critically important, the extent to which you as the user of the software must tinker with Walls to tease meaningful cleanup solutions from them is greatly diminished. ACA has seen so much significant improvement in its automated cleanup behavior in the past few releases that the retirement of this chapter altogether was seriously considered. However, since nearly all of the lessons contained herein remain valid and continue to provide valuable insight into how the software performs Wall cleanup functions, the chapter remains. No one can dispute that walls are the major component of any floor plan or building model. You will find that in the large majority of circumstances, ACA will give you cleanup conditions you expect automatically. In those cases where it does not, or where you wish to make manual adjustments, this chapter will give you the tools you need to make necessary adjustments.

OBJECTIVES

In this chapter, we will take a break from our dual projects and instead explore the concepts of wall cleanup in several small files prepared specifically to focus on individual aspects of the topic. As we work through the lessons, we will be building a list of rules and guidelines to follow when performing and troubleshooting wall cleanup. These rules and guidelines are summarized in Appendix B—Wall Cleanup Checklist. Keep it handy for ongoing reference. The objectives of this chapter are:

- Understand the internal "rules" of automatic wall cleanup.
- Learn to manipulate wall cleanup parameters.
- Understand the Justification Display Representation.
- Learn when to use "manual" wall cleanup (Wall Merge) and Edit in Place.
- Understand Wall component cleanup priorities.

WHAT IS WALL CLEANUP?

Let's begin with some terminology associated with wall cleanup.

- **Wall cleanup**—The interaction between two or more Wall segments that causes them to respond to one another and form "correct" and/or "clean" corners and intersections.
- **Baseline**—The zero point of a Wall object's width as defined by its style. The parallel edges of a Wall are measured from this point. The Baseline and its significance in Wall Styles are explored in detail in the next chapter.
- **Justification line**—The point within the Width of the Wall that is used for reference as the Wall is drawn. This is the line where the Wall's grips will appear in the drawing. The justification can be Right, Left, Center or Baseline. Right and Left are relative to the direction of the Wall as determined when looking toward the end point from the start point (see Figure 9.1). You can easily see which end is the start and which is the end by hovering the cursor over the grips. The justification line is also used to calculate cleanup (see Figure 9.2).

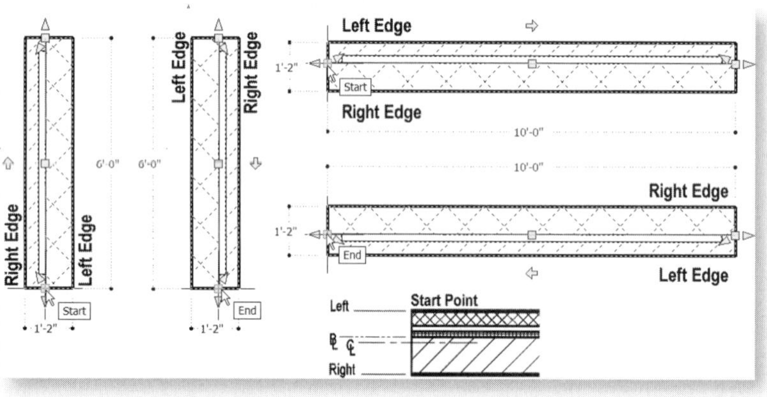

FIGURE 9.1 *Wall justification and its relationship to Wall orientation*

- **Cleanup Circle**—A tolerance applied at each end of a Wall segment and each intersection between Walls to force wall cleanup to occur. Also referred to as "cleanup radius" (see Figure 9.2).

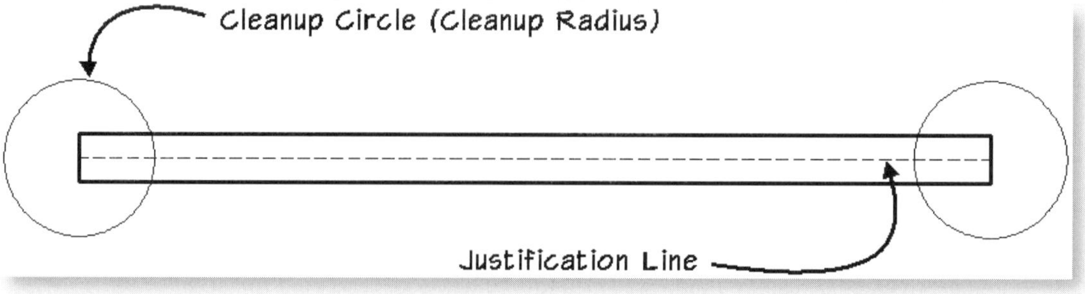

FIGURE 9.2 *Graph line and cleanup circles*

- **Solution Tip Icon**—A small triangular marker with an exclamation point within it indicating display calculation errors in the drawing. These usually appear when wall cleanup cannot be calculated properly. Hover your mouse over the icon for a tooltip with potential solutions (see Figure 9.3).

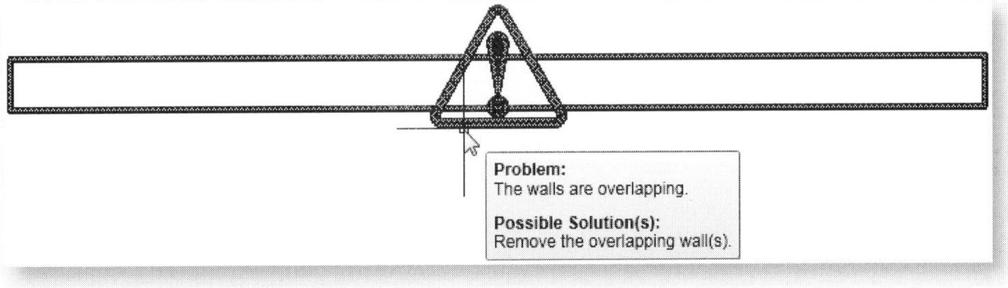

FIGURE 9.3 *Solution Tip Icons—Hover over them for potential solutions*

PART 1—AUTOMATIC WALL CLEANUP

Whenever walls intersect one another in ACA, an automatic cleanup is typically performed. When automatic cleanup is successful, it requires no user interaction—It simply works! The first topic in this chapter will help you understand how the software performs automatic cleanup. We will first understand exactly what factors determine if automatic cleanup will occur, and then what to do about it if it is not successful.

Install the Cd Files and Open a Sample File

If you have already installed all of the files from the CD, skip step 1. If you need to install the CD files, start at step 1.

1. Install the files for Chapter 9 located on the *Mastering AutoCAD Architecture 2008* CD-ROM.

   Refer to "Files Included on the CD-ROM" in the Preface for information on installing the sample files included on the CD.
2. Launch AutoCAD Architecture 2010 from the desktop icon created in Chapter 3.

If you did not create a custom icon, you might want to review "Create a New Profile" and "Create a Desktop Shortcut" in Chapter 3. Creating the custom desktop icon is not essential, however, it makes loading the custom profile easier.

3. On the QAT, click the Open icon and then browse to the *C:\MasterACA 2010\Chapter09* folder.
4. Open the file named *Wall Cleanup1.dwg* [*Wall Cleanup1-Metric.dwg*].

Rule 1—Use Wall Justification Display

Wall cleanup is calculated automatically by the software using the justification line of the Wall and an optional cleanup circle occurring at either end of the Wall. Using these components, the software constructs a "graph" of all Walls and then applies all of the other Wall parameters like width, endcap conditions and openings to draw the actual plan display onscreen and in print. The position of justification lines within the width of the Wall and the radius of cleanup circles (where present) are configured individually for each Wall object. Wall justification lines can be displayed onscreen to assist in understanding and achieving proper wall cleanup. Displaying them gives you insight into issues affecting the cleanup of each Wall intersection. To display Wall justification lines, use the following steps:

Toggle the Wall Justification Display

Several Walls appear onscreen in the *Wall Cleanup1.dwg* [*Wall Cleanup1-Metric.dwg*] file.

5. Select any Wall onscreen.
6. On the Wall tab of the ribbon, on the Cleanup panel, click the Justification Display tool (see Figure 9.4).

TIP You can also right-click and choose **Cleanups > Toggle Wall Graph Display.**

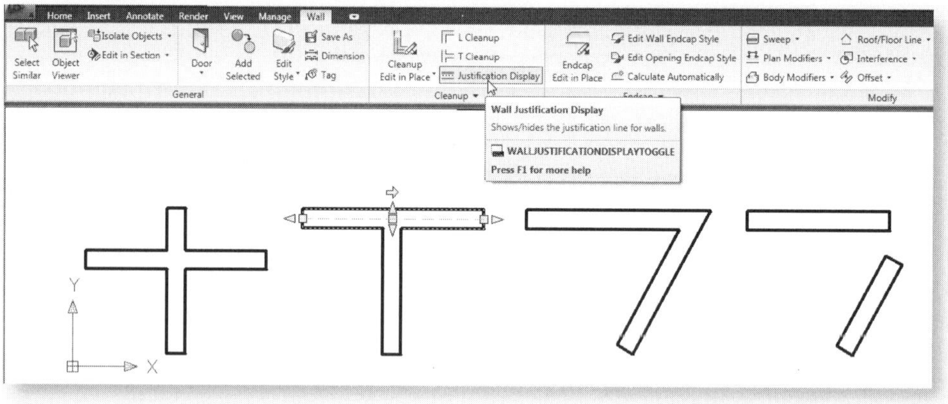

FIGURE 9.4 *Toggle Wall Justification Display on the ribbon*

When the Wall Justification Display is toggled on, it reveals the justification lines and radii for all Walls in the drawing (this is why you can select any Wall from which to execute the command). Each of these components (justification "Edge" and cleanup circle "Radius") is usually color-coded (this is done in the display settings for the Graph Display Representation) to help them stand out. (If your drawing contains Walls within XREFs, you may need to Regen the drawing before the justification lines will display for the XREFs.) Examine each condition in this file. Notice that two intersecting radii (the right-most condition) do *not* cause cleanup (see Figure 9.5). Cleanup will occur if any of the following conditions occurs:

- The justification line of one Wall intersects the justification line of another Wall.
- The justification line of one Wall intersects the cleanup radius of another Wall.
- The cleanup radius of one Wall intersects the justification line of another Wall.

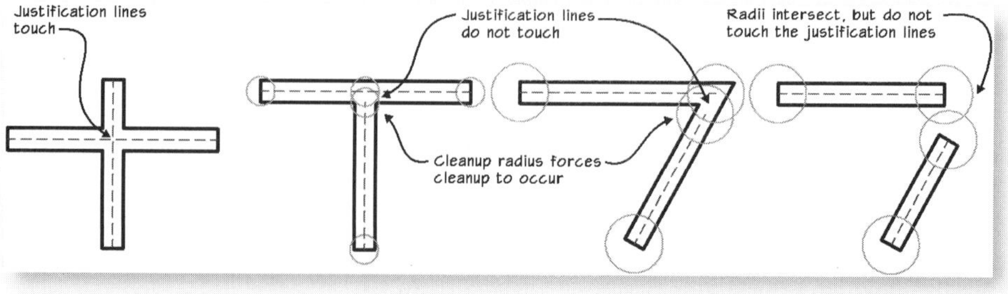

FIGURE 9.5 *Walls with Justification Display on*

TIP

Toggle Wall Justification Display on whenever you are working with Walls. Toggle it off before printing.

MANAGER NOTE CAD

The justification lines and cleanup circles are color-coded by default in the *AEC Model (Imperial Stb).dwt* [*AEC Model (Metric Stb).dwt*] template files. This is very helpful when using Graph Display mode (which is toggled on when you enable Justification Display). Choose unique colors and/or linetypes that are not being used anywhere else in your company's standards. To change the Graph Display settings, edit the Drawing Default property source of the "Graph" Display Representation of Walls in your template file(s). In addition, assign these components to a non-plotting layer such as A-Anno-Nplt. By default, the "Edge" component (justification lines) is blue, and the "Radius" (cleanup circle) is cyan. A third component: the "Wall Cleanup Override" component is color 254. (Cleanup overrides will be discussed below.) All three are on the A-Anno-Nplt layer by default. Chapter 2 discussed Display Representations.

Justification Display is your best diagnostic tool to assess Wall cleanup issues. Toggling Justification Display on is akin to the doctor's taking an X-Ray to assess whether you have broken a bone. Just as it would be very difficult to assess many medical conditions without the benefit of an X-Ray, it is nearly impossible to correctly assess a Wall cleanup situation without using the Justification Display.

Rule 2—Start with a Cleanup Radius of 0 (Zero)

As you can see in the *Wall Cleanup1.dwg* [*Wall Cleanup1-Metric.dwg*] file, a cleanup radius can make two Walls cleanup even if they do not actually intersect. The larger the Cleanup radius, the farther away from a true intersection the Walls can actually be. In some cases, this is desirable to achieve a particular cleanup effect, but in general, large Cleanup radii should be avoided, and any cleanup radii should be as small as possible. Also, notice from the image at the left in Figure 9.5 that the cleanup radius can be set to a value of 0 (zero, no radius). As a rule, all cleanup radii should initially be set to 0 and only increased when proper cleanup requires it. With the radius set to 0, you are forced to close your geometry. The benefits of good, cleanly drafted floor plans and models go far beyond simple wall cleanup, as any veteran AutoCAD user can attest (more on this in Rule 3).

Verify the Drawing Default Cleanup Radius

When you draw Walls with the Wall tool on the Design Tool Palette (or any tool that does not have its own Cleanup radius value), you can designate a cleanup radius value on the Properties palette. ACA will remember the last value set for cleanup radius. This setting becomes the drawing default. This is true even after you have quit and restarted ACA.

1. On the Design Tool Palette, click the Wall tool.
2. On the Properties palette, scroll down to the Cleanups grouping in the Advanced category.
3. Verify the value of Cleanup radius and set to **0"** [**0**] if necessary and then press ENTER (see Figure 9.6).

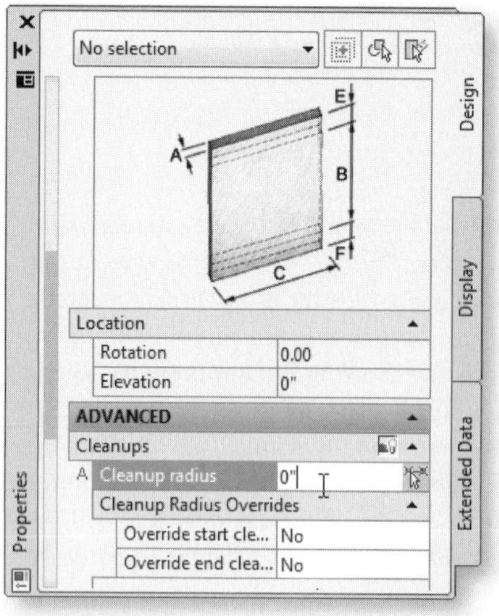

FIGURE 9.6 *The Wall Cleanup radius setting on the Properties palette*

Ultimately, regardless of whether the value is preset in the Properties palette or preset in a Wall tool, the Cleanup radius can always be changed directly on the Wall object (see Rule 4). Having the default in place, however, helps to avoid any inadvertent errors. A zero cleanup radius is the default setting in AutoCAD Architecture out-of-the-box. This default should be maintained.

4. Draw a short Wall and then press ENTER to end the command.

CAD MANAGER NOTE

The default Wall Cleanup radius set to 0 (zero) is another good value to have set in the office template files. This is easy to do if you are using the default out-of-the-box templates as your standard, since it is already set this way.

Rule 3—Practice Good, Clean Drafting

This is perhaps the most important rule of all. A striking majority of all cleanup problems can be avoided by simply practicing good, clean drafting technique. All AutoCAD editing commands can be performed on Walls. Commands such as Move, Copy, Array, Rotate, Break, Fillet, Chamfer, Trim and Extend are among the many commands useful for editing Walls (many of these were utilized in the tutorials in Chapter 4). There are several wall-specific command options as well. Always use Object Snaps! Always type in dimensions when they are known. Use Offset, Trim and Extend and the 'L' and 'T' Cleanup tools often. They offer an excellent means of performing layout tasks quickly while nearly always facilitating proper cleanup. Review the tutorials in Chapter 4 for proof of this statement. In that chapter, we laid out an entire floor plan without discussing the rules of wall cleanup. This was possible because the first three rules of wall cleanup, as covered here, were anticipated and built into the exercise. We will look at a few good drafting techniques in particular in the next section.

Avoid "Doubles"

5. Select any Wall in the drawing, on the Home tab, on the Modify panel, click the Copy tool.
6. For the base point, type **0,0** and then press ENTER.
7. For the second point, type **0,0** and then press ENTER again.

   Notice the triangular solution tip icon appearing on the Wall.

Avoid deliberately or inadvertently creating double Walls. The problem is that the Wall is trying to cleanup with itself. As you can see, it is not having an easy time of it. Hover your mouse over the solution tip and it will suggest removing the overlapping wall.

8. Erase the duplicate Wall.

TIP

Click the solution tip icon to easily select the duplicate Wall. If you have several duplicates, try using a crossing selection to select all of them (note the quantity on the properties palette) and then hold down the SHIFT key and deselect just the one on top. Then erase the remaining selected duplicates.

9. Close the file. You do not need to save it.

Use Extend and Trim

1. In the C:*MasterACA 2010\Chapter09* folder, open the file named *Wall Cleanup2.dwg* [*Wall Cleanup2-Metric.dwg*].

   Notice that the Wall justification lines are already displayed in this file. There are also text labels to help you work through this tutorial.

2. On the Home tab, on the Modify panel, click the drop-down button on the AEC Trim tool (next to Copy) and choose Extend.

NOTE

If you prefer, you can execute the command by typing it in the Command Line or using the right-click menu.

3. On the upper-left side of the drawing (labeled Extend), click the left-most horizontal Wall (at the top) as the "boundary edge" and then press ENTER.
4. At the "Select object to extend" prompt, click near the top of the left-most vertical Wall (at the top) and then press ENTER (see Figure 9.7).

   Notice that the Wall has actually extended from its centerline to the centerline of the boundary Wall.

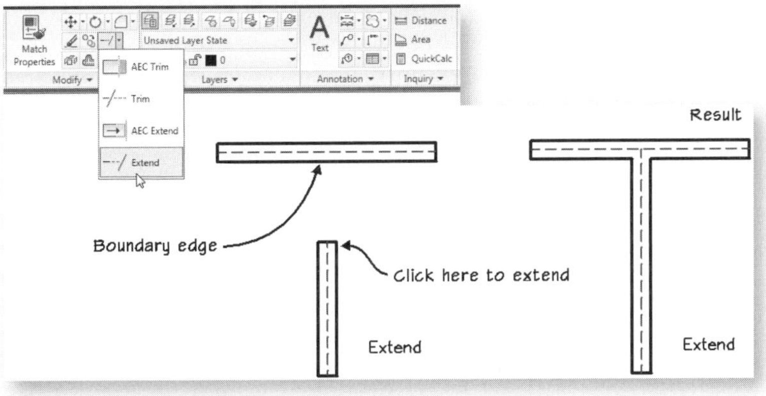

FIGURE 9.7 *The justification line of the Wall is used with Extend*

5. From the same drop-down button, choose Trim.
6. On the upper-middle section of the drawing (labeled Trim), click the middle horizontal Wall (at the top) as the "cutting edge" and then press ENTER.

7. At the "Select object to trim" prompt, click near the top of the middle vertical Wall, and then press ENTER (see Figure 9.8).

Notice that the Wall has actually trimmed from its centerline to the bottom edge (the justification) of the cutting Wall.

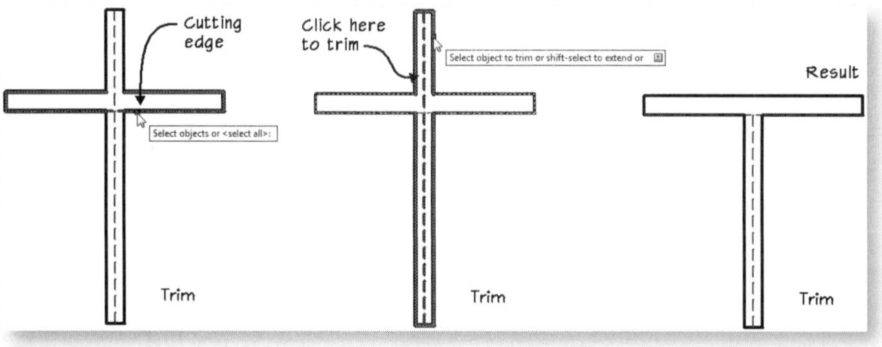

FIGURE 9.8 *The justification line of the Wall is used with Trim*

8. In the next set of Walls in the top-right corner of the drawing (labeled Fillet/Chamfer); try performing a Fillet and Chamfer. Undo after each operation.

   Change the Fillet Radius and the Chamfer Distances and try them again.

AutoCAD editing commands such as Trim, Extend, Fillet, Chamfer and Offset reference the justification line of Wall segments. It is important to consider this fact when using these functions with Walls and other similar AEC objects, such as Curtain Walls (recall the trim we performed on the Curtain Wall object back in Chapter 8). With practice, you begin to anticipate this behavior and incorporate it into your process as you work.

L and T Cleanups

In addition to the standard AutoCAD commands, there are two very useful tools unique to Walls. L Cleanup is similar to Fillet, and T Cleanup is like Extend or Trim. Although the results are similar to these well-known AutoCAD counterparts, the usage varies a bit.

9. On the bottom-left side of the drawing ('L' Cleanup), select the horizontal and the left-most vertical Walls.
10. On the Wall tab of the ribbon, on the Cleanup panel, click the L Cleanup tool.
11. Repeat on the same horizontal Wall and the other vertical Wall that intersects it (see Figure 9.9).

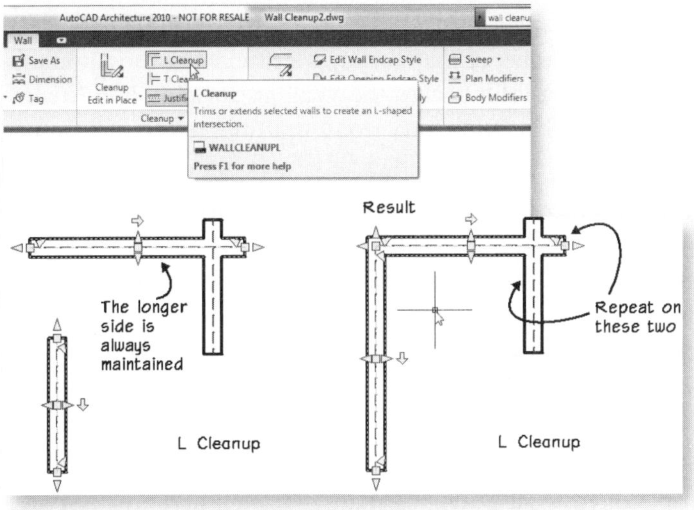

FIGURE 9.9 *Using the 'L' Cleanup routine*

In both cases, the two Walls overlap forming a long and short side. In the L Cleanup routine, unclick the standard AutoCAD Fillet command (where you click the side you want to keep); the longer side is always maintained.

The T Cleanup routine works in a similar fashion, but requires you to select the Wall that you wish to trim or extend first, run the T Cleanup command and then select the bounding Wall when prompted.

12. In the bottom-middle section of the drawing (T Cleanup), select the vertical Wall.
13. On the Wall tab of the ribbon, on the Cleanup panel, click the T Cleanup tool.
14. At the "Select boundary Wall" prompt, click the upper horizontal Wall.
15. Undo the edit, sue the grips and shorten the vertical Wall.
16. Repeat the process.

Like the L Cleanup, the longer side of the Wall will be maintained. In the first attempt, the part above the boundary Wall should be trimmed away to form the "T." After you undo and shorten the Wall, the lower portion should be removed forming an "upside-down T" this time (see Figure 9.10).

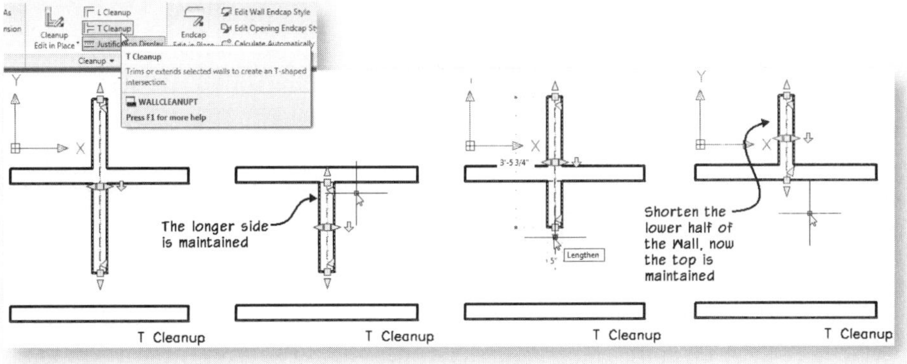

FIGURE 9.10 *The longer side is always maintained in both L and T Cleanup*

17. Repeat for the lower Wall.

Explore Autosnap

When grip-editing Walls, there is a special snap setting that facilitates the automatic intersection of Wall baselines. It basically makes the Wall justification line "sticky" as if it had magnetic attraction. This helps force good drafting and ensure proper cleanup.

18. In the bottom-right section of the drawing (labeled Grip Edit), click on the right-most vertical Wall (at the top) to highlight it.
19. Select the top grip point (either the square or the triangular one) and begin stretching the Wall up.
20. Use the Midpoint Object Snap to snap to the bottom face of the horizontal Wall.

    Notice that the grip point jumps to the top edge (the justification line) of the horizontal Wall.

With the Autosnap Grip Edited Wall Baselines setting enabled, if a grip edit falls within the drawing's designated Autosnap radius setting, the grip point will automatically snap to the justification line of the Wall. This behavior can be toggled on or off. As a general rule, keep this setting turned on, with a modest Autosnap radius (the default is 6'' [75]). Turn the setting off in situations where you deliberately need to grip edit within the allowable tolerance.

21. Click the right-most vertical Wall to highlight it again.
22. On the Wall tab, click the Add Selected button.

TIP

Add Selected is a great way to add a Wall (or any other object) with the same parameters as an existing one.

23. Set the start point to the left of this Wall.
24. Move straight up and snap Perpendicular to the same horizontal Wall as in the last sequence.

    Notice that the behavior is the same as with the grip editing; the Wall has automatically "snapped" to the justification line of the horizontal Wall (see Figure 9.11).

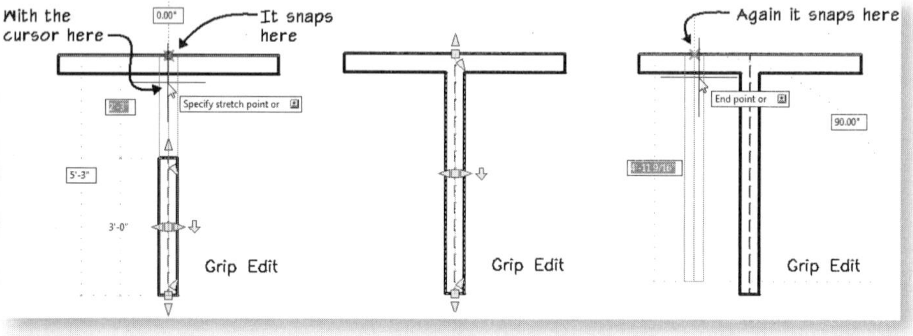

FIGURE 9.11 *Using Autosnap on existing and new Walls*

25. Press ENTER to end the command.

The Autosnap New Wall Baselines feature uses the same Autosnap radius as the grip editing Autosnap feature. Both features are configured in the Options dialog box, on the AEC Object Settings tab. Both features can be turned on or off independently and the snap strength can be adjusted as well.

26. From the Application Menu, choose **Options** (you can also right-click in the Command Line and choose **Options**).
27. Click on the AEC Object Settings tab (see Figure 9.12).

The Autosnap options are in the Wall Settings area. Clear the checkbox next to Autosnap Grip Edited Wall Baselines to turn it off. Clear the checkbox next to Autosnap New Wall Baselines to turn it off. Place a check mark in either box to turn them on.

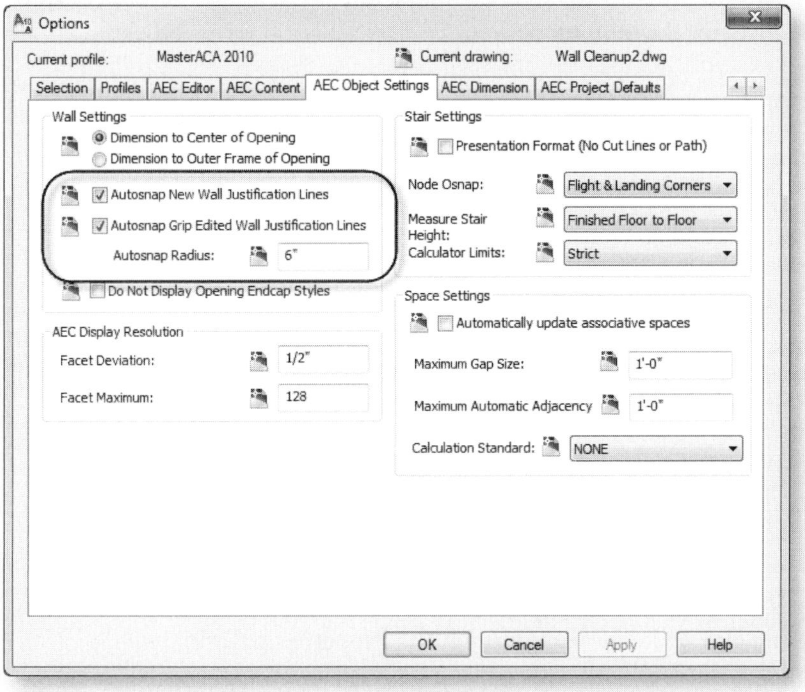

FIGURE 9.12 *Autosnap features on the AEC Object Settings tab of Options*

When either of these Autosnap features is active, the Autosnap Radius field controls the tolerance level. Enter a larger value if you want the effect to be stronger; enter a smaller value if you want the effect to be weaker.

28. Click Cancel to close the dialog without making changes.

Both of these settings (and all of the others on this tab) are saved in the current drawing as indicated by the drawing icon (refer to Chapter 3 for more information).

Rule 4—Tweak the Cleanup Radius

Sometimes, despite graph line position and good drafting techniques, cleanup might still prove troublesome. In many cases, tweaking the cleanup radius can solve the problem. It is usually easier to solve problems by increasing the radius than by decreasing; therefore start with low initial values, and slowly increase until the optimal setting is reached. When it becomes necessary to increase the initial value, the best way to do this is to edit the radius of a selected Wall segment on the Properties palette or on each end of the Wall using the grips.

Explore Common Cleanup Radius Situations

1. In the *C:\MasterACA 2010\Chapter09* folder, open the file named *Wall Cleanup3.dwg* [*Wall Cleanup3-Metric.dwg*].

A common example of a troublesome situation occurs when two Walls of varying thickness touch end to end. Their justifications will be parallel and may not fall in the same line. Consider the conditions on the left of Figure 9.13. These are good examples of when it is appropriate to increase the cleanup radius.

Adjusting the radius helps both conditions achieve cleanup. This is the only way to solve the condition on the bottom (labeled as 2 in the figure). An alternative for the first condition is to simply perform an L Cleanup. This will join the necessary justification lines and achieve the cleanup desired.

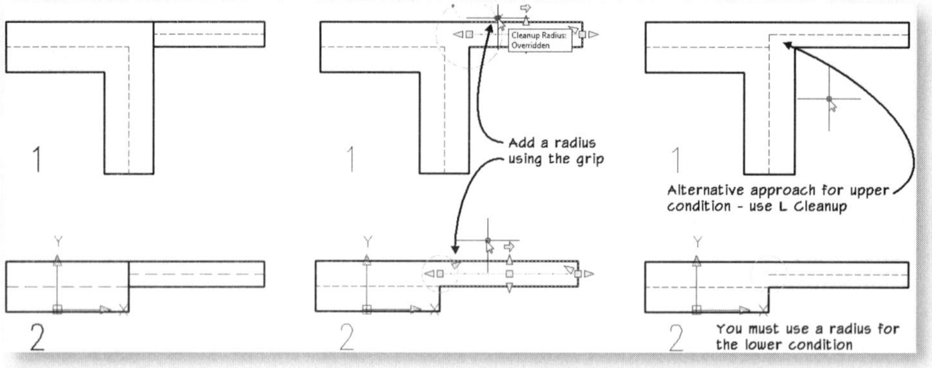

FIGURE 9.13 *Cleanup radii offer an alternative to make parallel Walls cleanup*

The grips are usually the easiest way to adjust the cleanup radius when necessary. However, you can also make the same edit on the Properties palette.

2. In condition 1, select the thinner Wall at the right, right-click and choose **Properties**.
3. Scroll down to the Advanced category, and locate the Cleanups grouping.

When editing the cleanup radius with the grips, stretch it just enough to touch the justification line of the other Wall. When using the Properties palette, use the following guidelines to determine how large a radius to use:

- If the justification is Center or Baseline, choose a value between 1/2 and 3/4 times the width of the largest segment in the intersection.
- If the justification is Left or Right, choose a value between 1/2 and 1 times the width of the largest segment in the intersection.

In this case, the Walls in situation 1 are 12" [300] and 6" [150] in thickness. The 12" [300] Wall therefore is larger; the value ought to be between 6" [150] (1/2 × 12" = 6" [1/2 × 300 = 150]) and 9" [225] (3/4 × 12" = 9" [3/4 × 300 = 225]). However, this is not an exact science. The goal is simply to get the cleanup circle of the Wall large enough to touch the justification line of the neighboring Wall.

4. In the Cleanup radius field type a value in the middle of the calculated range like **7"** [**175**] and then press ENTER (see the left side of Figure 9.14).

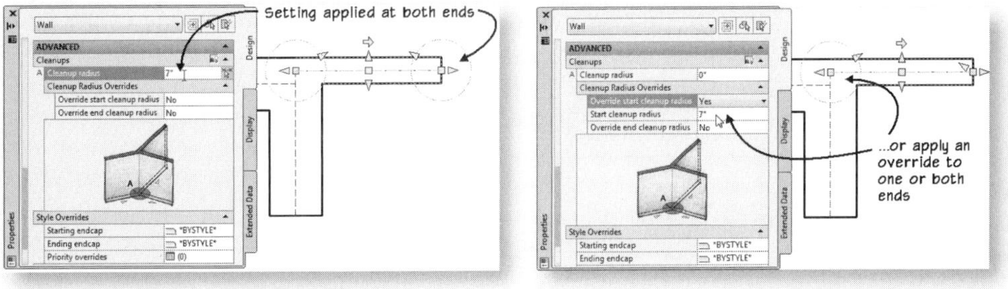

FIGURE 9.14 *Edit the value of the Cleanup radius*

If you want to see the results of the intersection without the graph lines, toggle the Justification Display off temporarily. (Select any Wall, then click the Justification Display tool.) Be sure to toggle it back on to complete the rest of the exercise.

When you use the grip to edit the radius instead, it applies an override to just the selected end of the Wall. The same can be done on the Properties palette (as shown on the right side of Figure 9.14). However, the grip is usually easier.

Situation 2 is nearly identical to the first. There are just two Walls of varying thickness, but again, the graph lines are parallel and will never touch. This situation will give us the opportunity to look at an alternative (and easier) way to set Cleanup radius for a particular Wall.

5. In situation 2, select the thinner Wall at the right.

   Notice that there are two triangular-shaped grips (one at each end of the Wall) that are at a slight angle to the Wall's centerline. These are the Cleanup radius grips (see Figure 9.15).

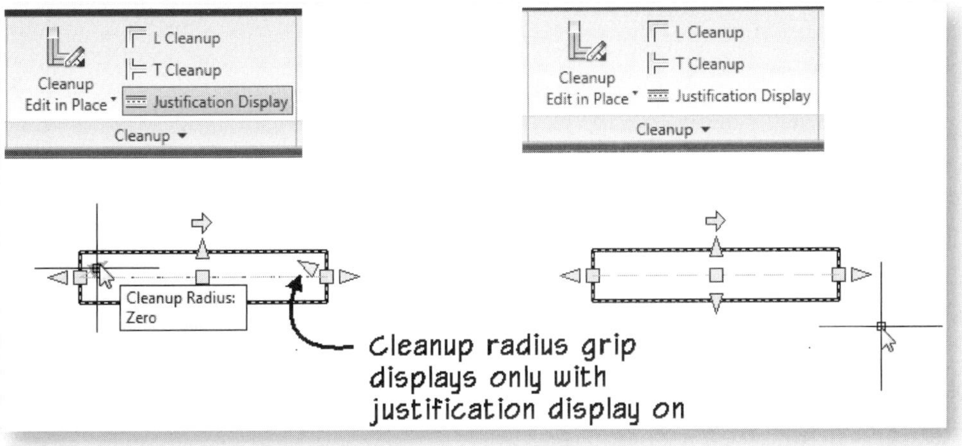

FIGURE 9.15 *Cleanup radius grips show only when the justification lines are displayed*

6. Click the Cleanup radius grip (on the left end of the Wall) and drag it outward.

Notice the Radius enlarges interactively. There is also a dynamic dimension into which a value may be typed if you wish, or you can simply click the mouse to set the size of the radius just large enough to touch the neighboring justification line. In most cases, this is much easier than performing the calculations detailed above.

7. Drag the grip until the Cleanup Circle just crosses the graph line of the thick Wall, and then click to set the radius (see Figure 9.16).

   If you prefer, using the formula in the bullet points above, you could type **6"** [**150**] and then press `ENTER`.

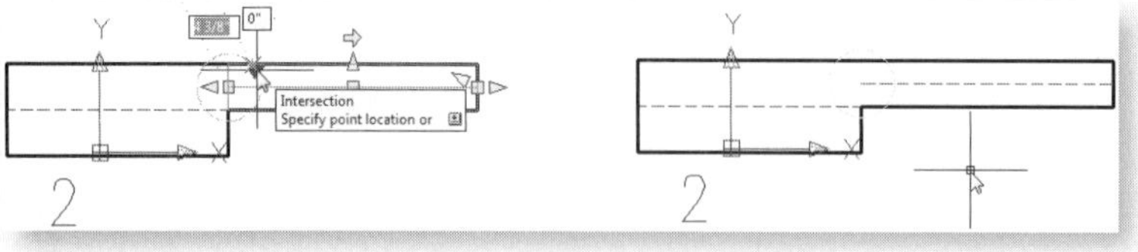

FIGURE 9.16 *Assigning the Cleanup radius using grips*

8. Deselect the Wall segment.

NOTE

The first technique covered here works on selections of multiple Walls. The grip edit method must be done on one Wall at a time. However, in most cases, the grip edit technique is much quicker.

Examine Situation 3

This is a tricky situation and represents what happens when the Cleanup radii are too large. The "one-half to three-quarters" rule should not be used if the radius ends up being larger than the length of the Wall segment itself. If this happens, the start of the Wall attempts to cleanup with the end of the Wall and defects occur. Change all of the radii back to 0" [0] and these Walls should cleanup properly. This will certainly be true in this case. However, if you encounter a similar situation in your own files and they don't cleanup after taking these measures, set the value as close as possible to the allowable Cleanup radius range without exceeding the length of any of the Wall segments involved. If none of these techniques works, refer to the "Part 2—Manual Wall Cleanup" section below.

In general, when troubleshooting cleanup, run through the list of "rules" in the order presented here. Turning on Justification Display is the first step and usually helps you assess the problem. Looking at the condition in situation 3, revealed that a zero cleanup radius was the best solution. Next, following good clean drafting is the "golden rule" of cleanup as we saw in situation 1. Only situation 2 required our adjusting the cleanup radius as dictated by rule 4. Most cleanup situations can be solved this way. There are however plenty of situations that require a bit more effort. Read on for further tips and techniques.

Other Automatic Cleanup Tips

In addition to the rules listed in the steps above, keep the following additional considerations and guidelines in mind:

Wall Justification

- The choice of justification will have an impact on cleanup. Typically you will want to use Center justification for most interior partitions. Baseline is often used for structural bearing Walls and exterior Walls. Left and Right can in some cases solve problems that would otherwise require radii with Center or Baseline, such as situation 2 in the previous topic.

- Left and Right justification will work well for exterior Walls or interior conditions where alignment with some existing feature (existing construction or building setback line, for instance) is needed.
- Use Baseline justification for multi-component exterior Walls where drafting based on the line of demarcation between structural and non-structural components is desirable.

In the *C:\MasterACA 2010\Chapter09* folder, open the file named *Wall Cleanup4.dwg* [*Wall Cleanup4-Metric.dwg*]. There you will find several combinations of Wall justifications and graph line positions (see Figure 9.17). Experiment with additional variations in this file. Use a combination of the techniques covered above in your explorations.

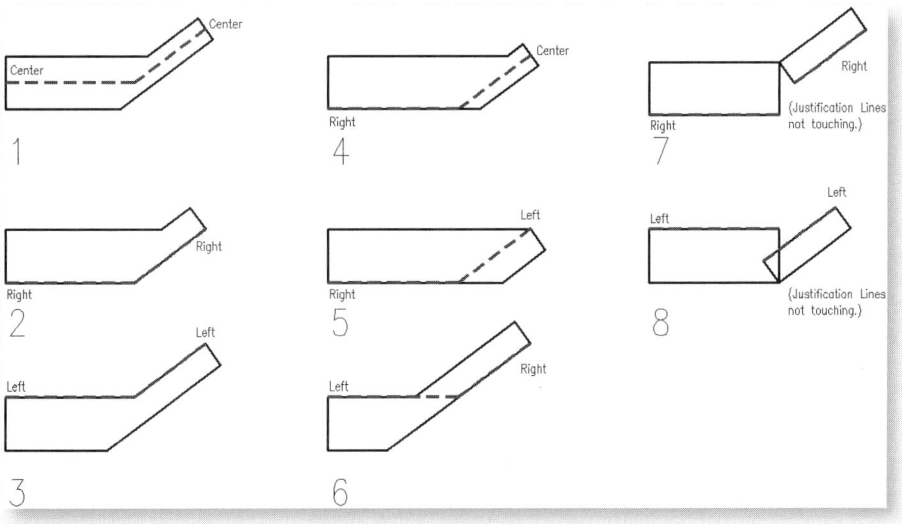

FIGURE 9.17 *Justification can have an impact on wall cleanup*

You can also experiment with situations 1 and 2 in *Wall Cleanup3.dwg*. For example, in condition 2 select one of the Walls, right-click and choose **Edit Justification**. Hold down the CTRL key and click the top diamond grip to set the justification to left. Repeat on the other horizontal Wall (see Figure 9.18).

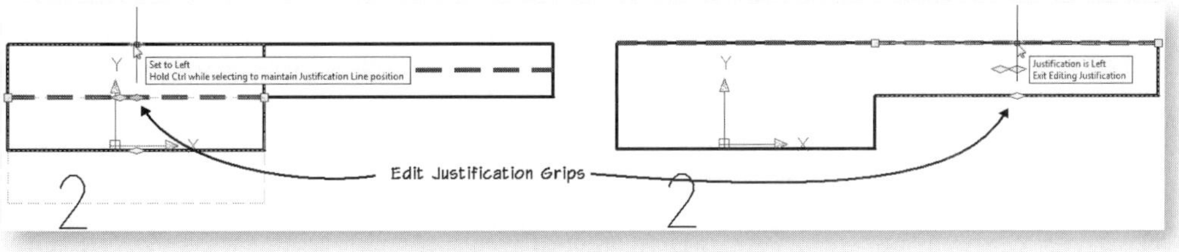

FIGURE 9.18 *Editing Justification can eliminate the need to increase the Radius*

This can be a good alternative to using a cleanup radius in some situations. However, moving the justification line using this procedure will often have a "chain reaction" effect whereby other Walls attached to the Walls you edit will require adjustments after making the justification change. Editing justification and using cleanup radii are both valid approaches. Use whichever you prefer in any given situation.

Cleanup Groups

- A Cleanup Group limits cleanup to Walls sharing the same group. Walls will not cleanup outside their group. This is often used to prevent one type of Wall, such as new construction, from cleaning up with another type, such as demolition. The next chapter covers some examples of this in more detail. Another common use is to isolate Wall styles used to create countertops from the Walls to which they are attached. Examples of such Wall styles can be found in the Content Browser library. Change the Cleanup Group of a selection of Walls on the Properties palette or preassign it to a Wall tool.
- In order for cleanup to occur between an XREF and its Host, the "Allow Wall Cleanup between host and XREF drawings" setting in the Cleanup Group must be enabled. Wall Cleanup Group Definitions are accessed from the Style Manager, as described below.

XREF Cleanup is controlled with Wall Cleanup Groups. To configure a Cleanup Group for XREF cleanup, choose **Style Manager** on the Manage tab. Expand the *Architectural Objects* folder, and then the Wall Cleanup Groups category. Create a new or edit an existing Wall Cleanup Group. Edit the new Group and on the Design Rules tab of the Wall Cleanup Group Definition Properties dialog box, place a check mark in the "Allow Wall Cleanup between host and XREF drawings" box (see Figure 9.19). Be sure to do this in at least the XREF file. You can do it in both the XREF and host drawing if you wish, but it is not required in the host drawing.

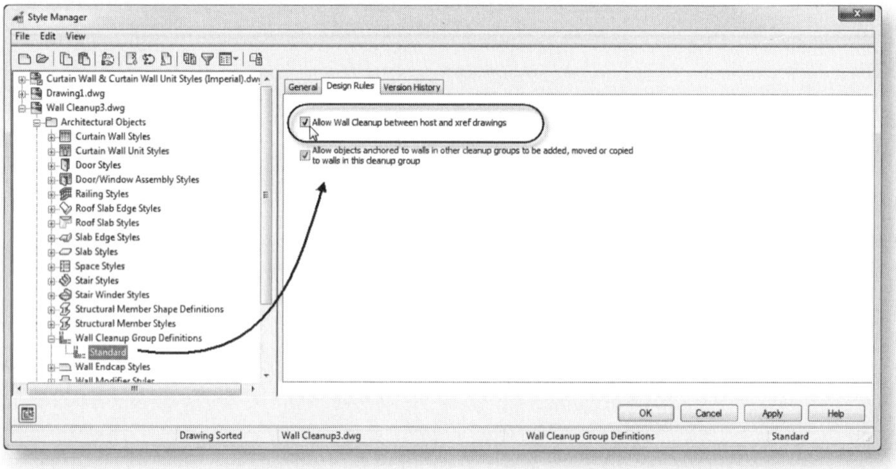

FIGURE 9.19 *Turn on XREF Cleanup in the Wall Cleanup Group Definition Properties dialog box*

CAD MANAGER NOTE

This setting is enabled in the out-of-the-box drawing template files (DWT). It is recommended that you keep this setting in your office template files. It is more likely that this will be the best default setting for typical project files. Users can always turn it off for special cases.

Sloped Walls

- Do not rotate Walls in 3D to make canted Walls. Use a Wall Sweep instead. See Chapter 12 for more information on Sweeps.

Component Priorities

- Complex Wall styles use Component Priorities to determine how their individual subcomponents cleanup; refer to the "Wall Component Priorities" topic below.

Wall Merge and Edit in Place

- If all attempts at automatic cleanup do not achieve the desired result, you can manually modify the cleanup using Wall Merge or Edit in Place. This is the subject of the next topic.

PART 2—MANUAL WALL CLEANUP

So, you followed all of the rules and guidelines listed here in an attempt to get some stubborn Walls to cleanup to no avail. Frustration is the natural reaction, and in some cases people are tempted to give up. Fortunately, if the automatic cleanup tools and procedures fail to generate the desired cleanup condition, we have the ability to manually force the cleanup condition we need. There are a couple ways to do this. The first is "legacy" Wall Merge Tool; the other is the more "modern" Edit in Place. In this lesson, you will learn how to perform manual wall cleanup in situations where automatic cleanup fails to achieve the desired effect. Please bear in mind that we should try all of the techniques covered in the last lesson before resorting to manual methods. This is because using manual cleanup requires that you maintain the edit manually from then on. Resorting to manual editing can therefore exact more effort than otherwise required.

Review the "Rules" to Trigger Automatic Cleanup

1. In the *C:\MasterACA 2010\Chapter09* folder, open the file named *Wall Cleanup5.dwg* [*Wall Cleanup5-Metric.dwg*].

This file contains Wall situations that will not cleanup properly using the automatic cleanup techniques covered earlier. The various recommendations are at odds with one another due to the complexity of the intersection (see Figure 9.20). On the left is the file as it appears when you open it, and on the right is the desired result. Remembering that the rules outlined in the last lesson are meant to be applied in order, let's see if we can achieve the required results.

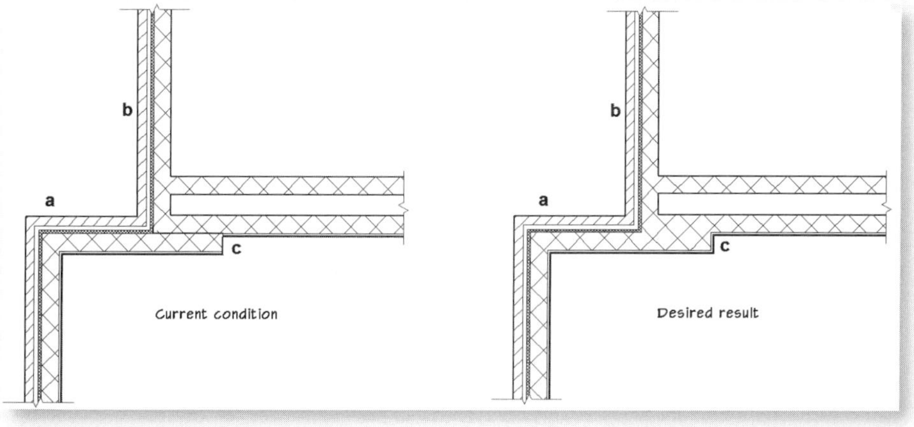

FIGURE 9.20 *Improper wall cleanup*

2. Beginning with Rule 1: Select any Wall onscreen and then on the Wall tab, click the Justification Display button (see Figure 9.21).

This situation was extracted from a larger floor plan. The three Walls on the left are exterior Walls and the two parallel ones on the right enclose a cavity for cross-bracing. The three exterior Walls use Baseline Justification as you can see and the two interior ones use Center. The lower portion (labeled "c" in the figure) is actually another small Wall segment. However, as you can see on the left side of Figure 9.20, this Wall does not cleanup properly with the others. Further, as you can see in Figure 9.21, there is no drywall on the exposed end of this short Wall.

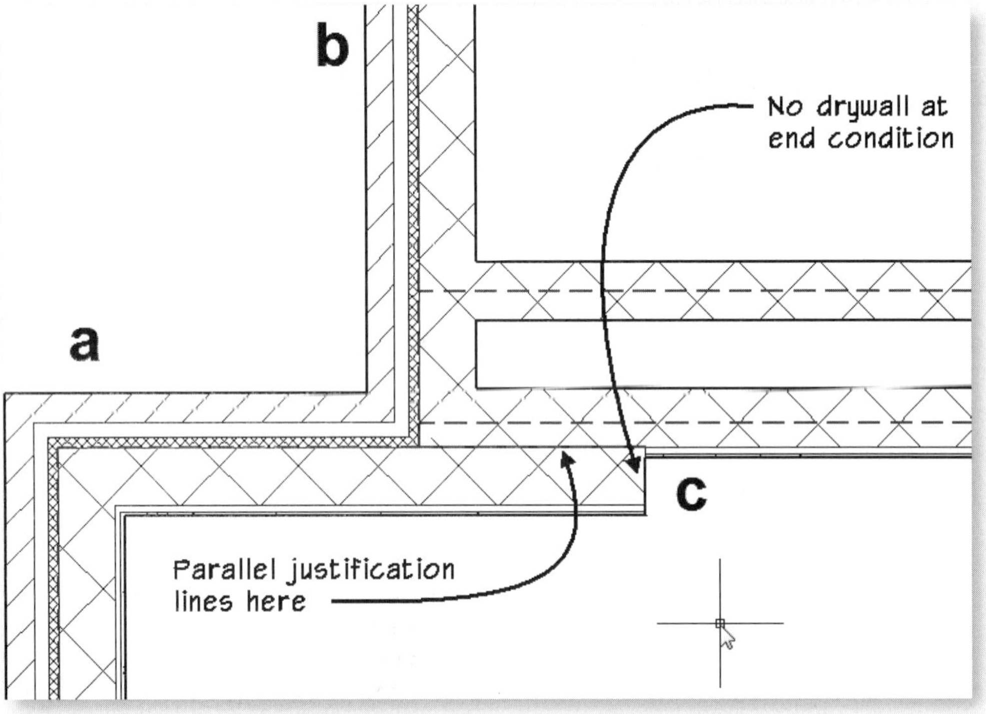

FIGURE 9.21 *Toggle Graph Display on*

With the Justification Display toggled on, you can see that that rule 2 is already satisfied as there are no cleanup radii applied. Further, all Walls touch in clean intersections satisfying rule 3. This leaves only rule 4. However, as already noted, the two Walls that are not cleaning up are parallel and adding a radius would actually make matters worse.

3. Select the small horizontal Wall (Wall "c") and use the grip to increase the cleanup radius (see Figure 9.22).

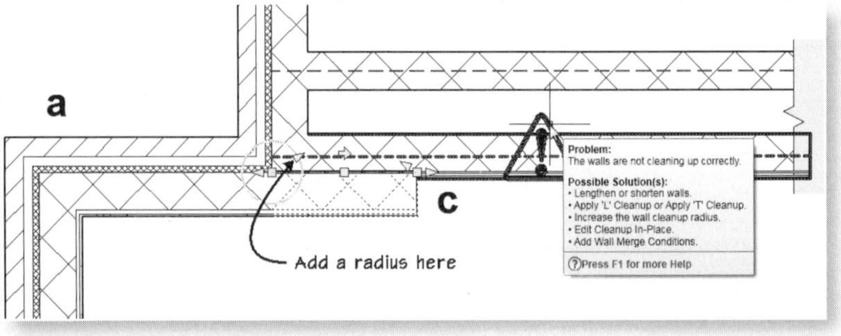

FIGURE 9.22 *Rules 1 through 4 do not help in this case*

4. Place your mouse over the solution tip icon for possible solutions.

   Notice that two of the options include Wall Merge and Edit in Place.

We can solve this situation using either a Wall Merge or Edit in Place. To use Wall Merge, we also would need to add an Endcap to the Wall that requires a drywall return. Endcaps are covered in several places in Chapter 10 starting with the "Endcaps" topic. Therefore, we will quickly look at the Wall Merge option and then undo it to focus on Edit in Place.

Apply a Wall Merge

5. Undo to remove the cleanup radius.
6. Select Wall "c."
7. On the Wall tab, click the Cleanup panel title to expand it.

   This reveals more tools.
8. Click the Add Wall Merge Condition tool (see the left side of Figure 9.23).
9. At the "Select Walls to merge with" prompt, select the horizontal Wall above "c."

   The Wall will be highlighted as it is selected, the command prompt will acknowledge with "1 found" and the "Select Walls to merge with" prompt will be repeated.
10. Press ENTER to complete command.
11. To get a better look at the result, toggle off Justification Display (see the right side of Figure 9.23).

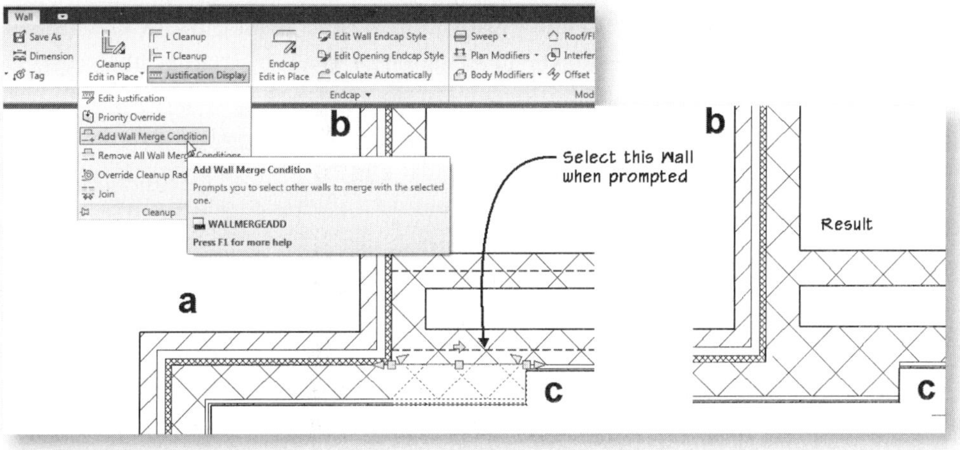

FIGURE 9.23 *Wall Merge helps, but without an Endcap, the solution is not complete*

When Wall Merge works, it is quick and easy to apply. If you want to skip ahead to Chapter 10 and learn about creating custom Endcaps, you can finish this condition by building and applying a custom Endcap to the right side of Wall "c."

Use Cleanup Edit in Place

There are many cases, however, when Wall Merge will not yield acceptable results. In those cases when you need more control, use Edit in Place. With Edit in Place, you can draw the condition exactly the way you need. For the next exercise, it will actually be easier to delete Wall "c" and build a custom cleanup solution using Edit in Place.

12. Delete Wall "c" (see Figure 9.24).

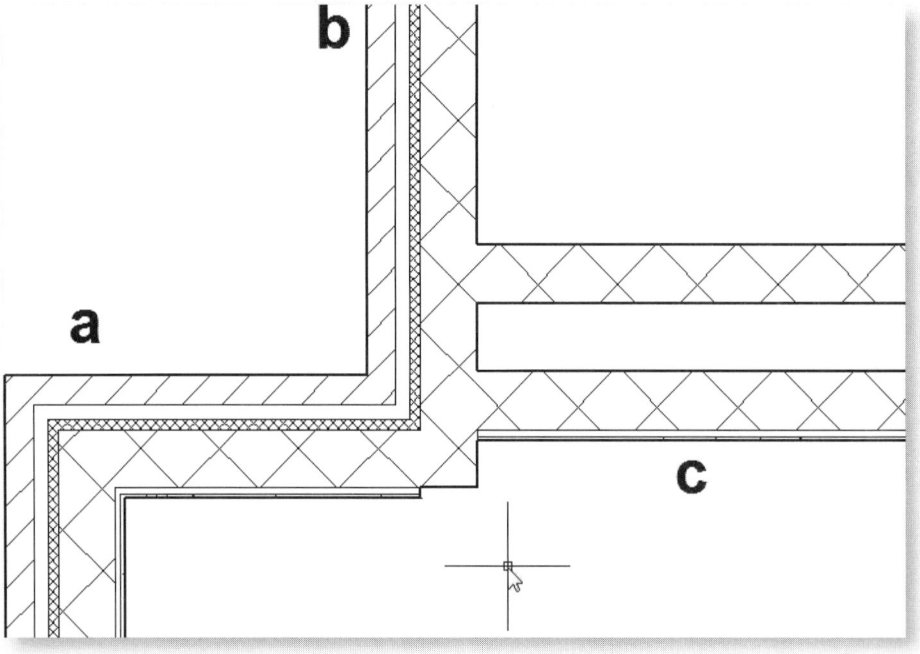

FIGURE 9.24 *After deleting Wall "c," the drywall terminates in an odd way*

Notice the odd way that the drywall terminates after deleting the Wall. This is because Wall "a" includes furring and Wall "b" does not. The furring ends where it does because Wall "b" uses Baseline justification. If you would like to experiment with this, you can temporarily edit the justification of Wall "b" (right-click menu) to the right side. If you do this, be sure to undo to return it to Baseline before continuing.

In this sequence, we will use simple rectangles and the Edit in Place functionality to change the way this corner (or "Wall Joint") cleans up. To save time, the required polylines have been provided in the file on a frozen layer.

13. Thaw the layer named: A-Wall-Temp.

With the Cleanup Edit in Place tool we can "show" ACA the exact cleanup condition we require. The disadvantage is that we must maintain this intersection manually from this point on. For this reason, use such manual edits sparingly and only after you have exhausted the other possibilities. Remember to follow the rules before resorting to a Merge or Edit in Place!

14. Select the long horizontal Wall at "c."
15. On the ribbon, click the Cleanup Edit in Place button.

A collection of boundary lines in green will appear; one for each component of the Wall. You can select any one of these boundaries and edit its shape in a variety of ways. Make sure that none of the boundaries are selected before continuing. If any are selected, press ESC to clear the selection.

16. Place your mouse over the edge of the CMU component and click to select it (see Figure 9.25).

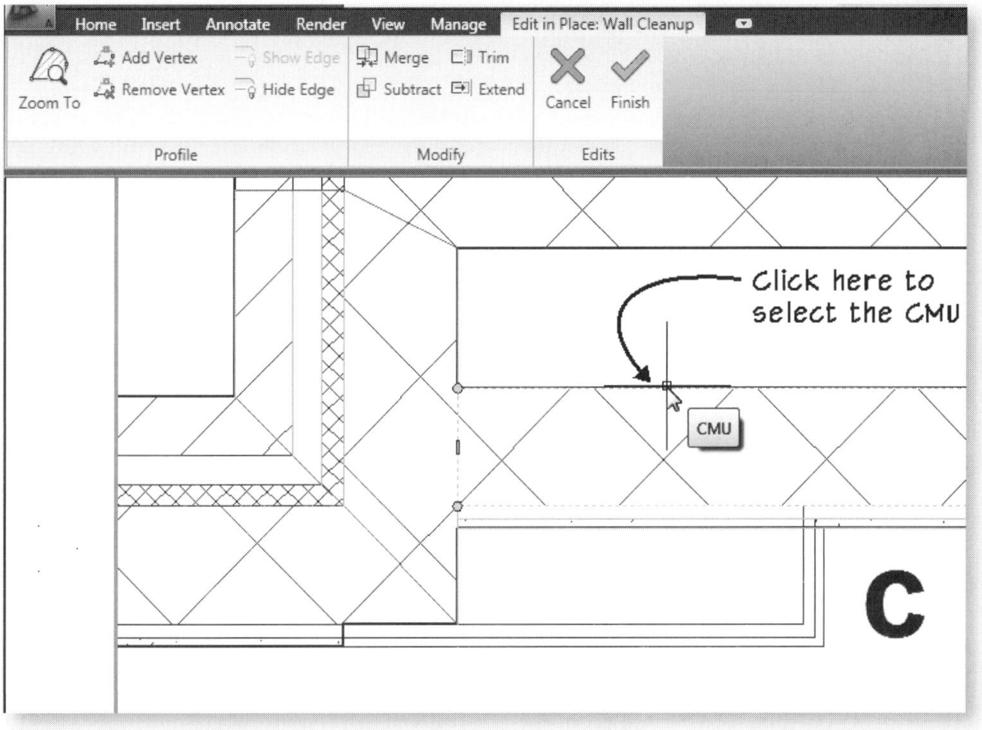

FIGURE 9.25 *Each component has a selectable boundary*

Feel free to experiment with the grips to edit. Pause your mouse over each grip for a tip of its function and available CTRL key options. Grip edits in this mode can be a little unpredictable, so take some time to get comfortable with them. Remember, you are editing a Wall cleanup joint. So the edits you make have to be reasonable when applied to the condition. Undo any changes before continuing. You can also click the Cancel button to discard your changes and then repeat the command to start again.

Rather than use the grips, we will use the Merge tool with the provided polylines to reshape the cleanup joint. A polyline has been provided for each Wall component in the joint.

17. With the CMU green boundary selected, on the Edit in Place Wall Cleanup tab, on the Modify panel, click the Merge button.

NOTE **please do not confuse this with Wall Merge used above. They share the same terminology, but are very different commands.**

18. At the "Select object(s) to merge" prompt, select the rectangle onscreen and then press ENTER (see Figure 9.26).
19. At the "Erase selected linework" prompt, choose Yes.

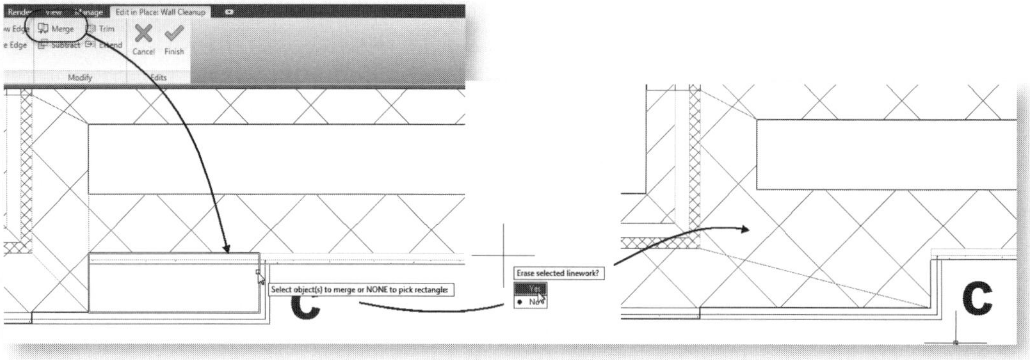

FIGURE 9.26 *Merge the provided rectangle into the CMU component*

There are two additional "L" shaped polylines; one for the Stud and the other for the GWB component.

20. Select the Stud component next and then repeat the process to merge in the inner "L" shaped polyline.
21. Repeat once more on the GWB component with the final polyline.
22. Finally, select the Stud again, on the ribbon click the Hide Edge tool and then click the small vertical edge on the left.
23. Repeat for the GWB component (see the left side of Figure 9.27).

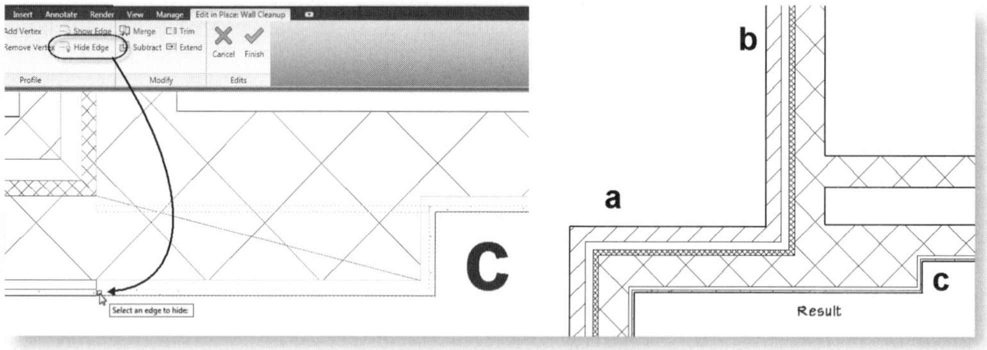

FIGURE 9.27 *Merge the other components and hide the shared edges*

24. On the ribbon, click the Finish button.
25. You will need to repeat the Hide Edge process on the Stud and GWB of the neighboring Wall on the left.

    The result should look like the right side of Figure 9.27.
26. Save and close the file.

As you can see, Edit in Place can be a few more steps, but you do gain the ability to edit the joint in virtually any way required to achieve the desired result.

PART 3—WALL COMPONENT PRIORITIES

Up to this point in this book, we have worked mostly with the Standard Wall style. The Standard Wall style is a simple two-line Wall (that contains a single component), centered relative to its width. Walls, however, can include several subcomponents as defined by their style. The previous exercise used several "multi-component" Walls.

Many such Walls are included on the Walls tool palette and in the Content Browser library (in Chapter 10, you will learn to create your own multi-component Wall styles). These multi-component Walls have an additional factor to consider when calculating cleanup. The Walls must determine how each component within the Wall will cleanup with each of the components of the neighboring Wall. The parameter used to control this behavior is the component's "priority." In this lesson you will learn how cleanup priorities assigned to Wall components interact and influence overall wall cleanup behavior.

Explore Wall Component Priorities

1. In the *C:\MasterACA 2010\Chapter09* folder, open the file named *Wall Cleanup6.dwg* [*Wall Cleanup6-Metric.dwg*].

Study the intersection between the two Walls. Each Wall is of a different Wall style. The horizontal Wall at the top uses the Style CMU-12 Air-2 Brick-4 Furring [CMU-300 Air-050 Brick-090 Furring], while the Wall at the bottom uses the Style CMU-8 Furring Both Sides [CMU-190 Furring Both Sides]. Notice that all the internal component materials are cleaning up properly with the corresponding materials in the other Wall. This is due to the component priorities assigned to each component within their respective Wall styles.

NOTE

A complete discussion on editing and building Wall styles follows in the next chapter.

2. Select the horizontal Wall (brick veneer), on the Wall tab, click the Edit Style button.
3. Click the Components tab.

Study the list of components. Notice that there are five components in this Wall style, and that each component has a number in the Priority column. The numbers are as follows: Brick = 810, Air Gap = 700, CMU = 300, Stud = 500 and GWB = 1200 (see Figure 9.28).

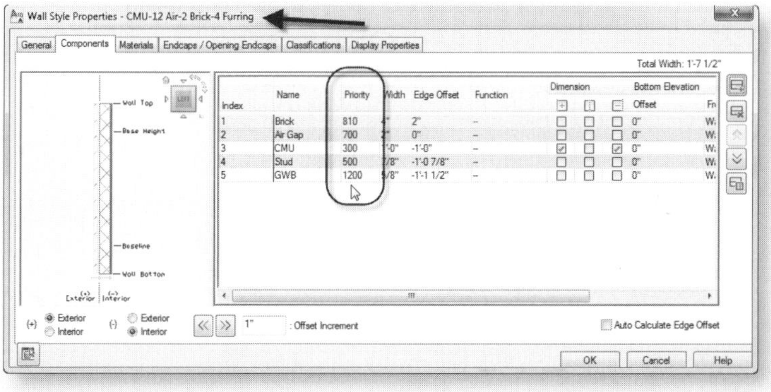

FIGURE 9.28 *Component Priorities of the CMU-12 Air-2 Brick-4 Furring [CMU-300 Air-050 Brick-090 Furring] style*

4. Click Cancel to dismiss the dialog box.
5. Deselect the Wall, select the vertical Wall (Gyp Bd. Both sides) and then on the ribbon, click the Edit Style button.
6. Click the Components tab (see Figure 9.29).

Notice that this style also has five components, many of them the same as the previous style. Note that the Priority numbers for the like components match. This is why the two styles cleanup properly with one another.

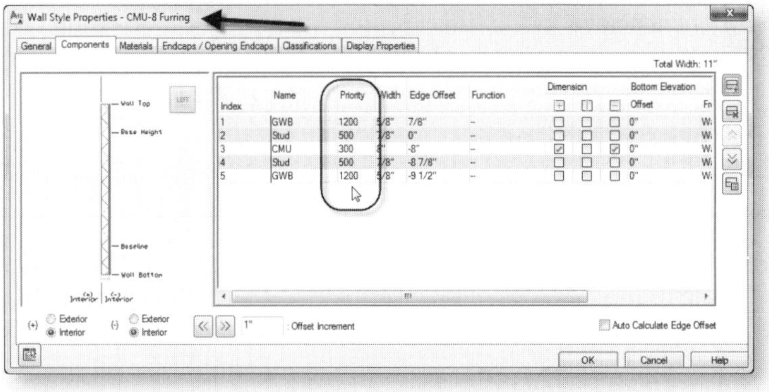

FIGURE 9.29 *Component Priorities of the CMU-8 Furring Both Sides [CMU-190 Furring Both Sides] style*

7. Click Cancel.

Change Component Priorities

Let's perform an experiment:

8. Edit the style of the horizontal (brick veneer) Wall.

To see the full effect of priorities, let's mess these Walls up a bit.

9. On Components tab, select Index 1 (Brick), change the Priority to **10** (see Figure 9.30) and then click OK.

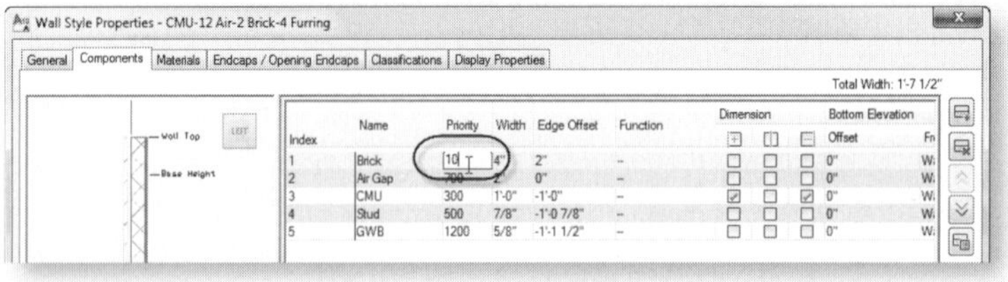

FIGURE 9.30 *Change the Brick component Priority to 10*

No obvious changes yet—perform the next step.

10. Select the vertical Wall (Gyp Bd. Both sides), and edit its style.
11. Select Index 3 (CMU), change the Priority to **10** and then click OK.

Notice how the CMU of the vertical Wall now passes through the CMU of the horizontal and attempts to cleanup with the Brick beyond (see Figure 9.31).

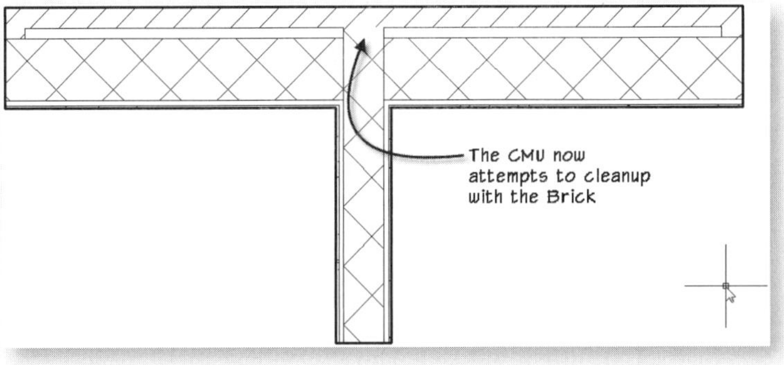

FIGURE 9.31 *Brick and CMU are now attempting to cleanup*

Let's keep going.

12. Edit the vertical Wall (Gyp Bd. Both sides) style again.
13. Select Index 2 (Stud) and change the Priority to **20**.
14. Select Index 4 (Stud), change the Priority to **20** and then click OK.
15. Edit the horizontal Wall (brick veneer) style.
16. Select Index 2 (Air Gap), change the Priority to **20** and then click OK (see Figure 9.32).

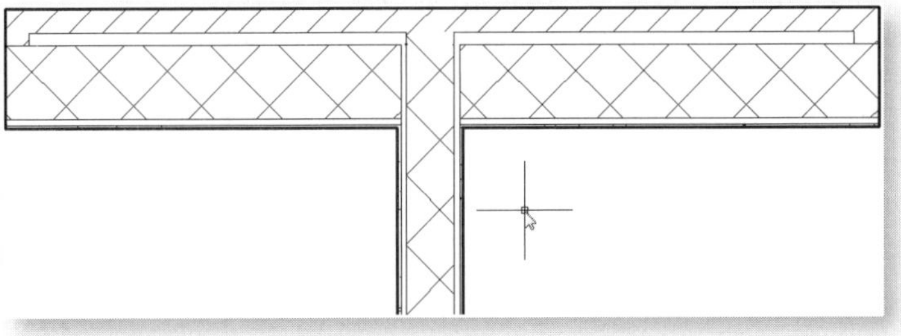

FIGURE 9.32 *Interesting, but it is not exactly a construction-worthy detail*

EXPERIMENT

Do a few more experiments; see how badly you can mess it up. Then try to fix it.

Understanding Wall Component Priorities

Having completed the previous tutorial, you can probably begin to draw some conclusions about the behavior of component priorities. Priorities determine which materials will cleanup with one another and which will be interrupted. Priorities function like this:

- Components with the *same* priority number will cleanup.
- Lower-numbered components will interrupt (pass through) higher-numbered components.
- Wall priorities will take precedence over drawing order. (The order in which Walls were drawn has no bearing.)
- Component priorities work with all of the other rules and cleanup behaviors. Priority should be considered in addition to the other considerations not instead of them.

Establishing a consistent and logical material and priority list is critical to successful cleanup and having a useable library of Wall styles. All sample Wall styles provided with ACA use the same list of priorities. The default list is based on the order of construction. Materials installed first, like poured concrete, get low numbers, while items installed last like stucco and toilet partitions get high numbers. Numbers in the chart deliberately do not start at one (1). The reason for this is that number 1 is the highest Priority. To allow for flexibility and future expansion, numbers start in the hundreds. For all practical purposes, there is no lower limit. Table 9.1 includes a complete list of all the priorities used in the sample content provided with ACA. You are not required to use this list, but it is *highly* recommended that you do. Check with your CAD Manager for the actual list used at your firm. If you are your own CAD Manager, use this list! It works, it is done already and some 200 or so Wall Styles that ship with the product are configured with these values.

NOTE

The first two items, "Existing to Remain" and "Demolition," are not part of the default ACA offerings. They are included in the chart here as recommended additions to the default list, and they have been incorporated into files used in the tutorials of this book.

TABLE 9.1 *Wall Component Cleanup Priorities*

Component Name	Priority Number
Existing to Remain (Mastering ACA Recommendation)	50
Demolition (Mastering ACA Recommendation)	100
Concrete	200
Concrete (Footing)	200
CMU	300
Air Gap (CMU/CMU)	305
CMU Veneer	350
Precast Panel	400
Rigid Insulation (Brick)	404
Stud	500
Air Gap (Stud/Stud)	505
Insulation (CMU/Brick, Stud/Brick)	600
Air Gap	700
Brick	800
Air Gap (Brick/Brick)	805
Brick Veneer	810
Siding	900
Metal Panel	1000

TABLE 9.1 *(Continued)*

Component Name	Priority Number
Stucco	1100
Glass	1200
GWB	1200
GWB (X) - First Layer	1200
GWB (X) - Second Layer	1210
GWB (X) - Third Layer	1220
GWB (X) - Fourth Layer	1230
Bulkhead	1800
Casework - Upper	2000
Casework - Base	2010
Casework - Counter	2020
Casework - Backsplash	2030
Toilet Partition	3000

MANAGER NOTE CAD

It is recommended that you adopt the preceding chart as your office standard. Consistency in assigning wall cleanup priorities is perhaps as important as an office standard Layer scheme. Having consistency will make it easy to add Wall styles created on specific projects to the office library without having to rework them first. A consistent list will also save hours wasted in needless cleanup troubleshooting related to incompatible priority lists. Note that plenty of space has been left between each material. (They jump in increments of 100.) It is recommended that you follow this guideline and maintain an adequate increment between numbers if you develop your own list. This will give you flexibility and room for future expansion in between materials without needing to redefine your entire collection of office standard styles each time the priority list changes. Following this method, a new material component can be slipped in wherever it fits best.

ADDITIONAL EXERCISES

Additional cleanup exercises have been provided in Appendix A. In Appendix A you will find the Third Floor Partitions (*03 Partitions*) file of the Commercial Project. Load the project (using Project Browser on the File menu) and open the *03 Partitions* Construct. Follow the guidelines outlined in this chapter as you move around the plan. Fix all of the cleanup problems you encounter. It is not necessary that you complete this exercise to begin the next chapter; it is provided to enhance your learning experience. However, it is highly recommended that you do complete this exercise for practice with techniques covered in this chapter before continuing to the next chapter. Completed projects for each of the exercises have been provided in the *Chapter09/Complete* folder. The solution to the wall cleanup exercise is provided in Appendix E.

SUMMARY

- Intersecting Wall justification lines or Wall justification lines intersecting Wall Cleanup radii cause Walls to automatically cleanup.
- Rule 1: Toggle the Justification Display of Walls on while working with cleanup.
- Rule 2: Start with the Cleanup radius set to 0 for all Walls.
- Rule 3: Practice good clean drafting using normal AutoCAD editing commands such as Offset, Trim, Extend and Object Snaps.
- Rule 4: When necessary, tweak the Cleanup radius to between 1/2x and 1x the Wall width. (Use the cleanup radius grip.)
- Justification, Cleanup Groups and XREFs all affect cleanup success or failure.
- Use Wall Merge or Edit in Place when automatic wall cleanup fails to produce desired results.
- Two Walls with matching component priority numbers will cleanup; lower priority numbers interrupt components with higher priority numbers.
- It is recommended that you adopt the out-of-the-box priority list for your firm's standard.

CHAPTER 10

Progressive Refinement—Part 1

INTRODUCTION

As a design scheme progresses, it is often desirable to begin including more detail in the articulation of Walls, Doors and Windows. We may want to begin indicating construction materials of Walls with poché and other articulation. We have stressed throughout the book that ACA is designed to allow us to add objects with little detail early in the design cycle and progressively refine our design as more information becomes known. The key to being able to achieve this is working with the various object styles. In this chapter—part 1 in our exploration of progressive refinement—we will focus on Wall styles, Wall Endcaps and Opening Endcaps.

OBJECTIVES

In this chapter, we will refine the first and second floor plans of the residential project. First, we will assign styles to all of the Walls. Then we will look at the steps involved in editing an existing and creating a new Wall style. We will explore the following topics:

- Understand Wall styles.
- Import Wall styles.
- Edit Wall styles.
- Understand Wall and Opening Endcaps.
- Create custom tools.
- Build a Custom Wall style.

WALL STYLES

A Wall style is analogous to a Wall type in the Construction Document set. One Wall style might represent a stud Wall, while another represents a 2-hour fire rated masonry Wall. As you develop your floor plan, think in terms of having a Wall style for every Wall type you will have in your Wall type legend. Wall styles control the component makeup of a Wall type, and they control the display characteristics of the Walls as well. Wall styles control virtually every aspect of Wall configuration.

In this lesson, you will learn how to import Wall styles from other drawing files and use them in an existing floor plan and we will build some custom Wall styles from scratch.

Install the CD Files and Load the Current Project

If you have already installed all of the files from the CD, simply skip down to step 3 below to make the project active. If you need to install the CD files, start at step 1.

1. If you have not already done so, install the dataset files located on the Mastering AutoCAD Architecture 2010 CD-ROM.

   Refer to "Files Included on the CD-ROM" in the Preface for information on installing the sample files included on the CD.
2. Launch AutoCAD Architecture 2010 from the desktop icon created in Chapter 3.

If you did not create a custom icon, you might want to review "Create a New Profile" and "Create a Desktop Shortcut" in Chapter 3. Creating the custom desktop icon is not essential; however, it makes loading the custom profile easier.

3. From the Quick Access Toolbar (QAT), choose the Project Browser icon.
4. Click to open the folder list and choose your *C:* drive.
5. Double-click on the *MasterACA 2010* folder, then the *Chapter10* folder.

   One or two residential Projects will be listed: *10 Residential* and/or *10 Residential Metric*.
6. Double-click *10 Residential* if you wish to work in Imperial units. Double-click *10 Residential Metric* if you wish to work in Metric units. (You can also right-click on it and choose **Set Current Project**.) Then click Close in the Project Browser.

NOTE

Important: If a message appears asking you to repath the project, click the "Repath the project now" option. Refer to the "Repathing Projects" topic in the Preface for more information.

Wall Style Basics

AutoCAD Architecture ships with a vast library of premade styles. Before we embark on the process of creating our own styles, let's explore some of the out-of-the-box offerings. There are two ways to access this content. We could use the Content Browser to access the style that we need, draw a Wall with it, and then copy and edit the Style. The other method is to use the Style Manager to access a remote Style library drawing and then either copy or edit it. Both methods are valid and have already been covered in previous chapters. As a general rule of thumb, we have been using Content Browser to access and *use* styles, reserving Style Manager for creation and editing. We will continue that practice in this chapter and work mostly with Style Manager for the following tutorials.

Import Styles from a Content File

The default templates shipped with ACA 2010 contain very few embedded styles. Therefore, we must typically open a remote content file to import styles for use in the current drawing.

7. On the Project Navigator palette, click the Constructs tab.
8. In the *Constructs* folder, double-click the *First Floor New* file to open it.

The plan has been refined a bit since we last opened it. The new construction has been laid out with the Standard Wall style. Doors and windows have been added, as has a screen porch on the back of the house (top of the plan). (The screen porch is built using Curtain Walls and was the subject of an additional exercise for Chapter 8. Details on its construction can be found in Appendix A.) Throughout this chapter, we will work with this file and refine it. By now, you should also be getting comfortable with the Project Navigator and the process of working in ACA projects. When the *First Floor New* file opens, the Existing Conditions file is not showing. However, as you work on new construction, it will be helpful to have the existing conditions visible as you work. To do this is an easy drag-and-drop process from Project Navigator.

9. On the Project Navigator, drag the *First Floor Existing* file and drop it into the drawing area workspace.

   You will note that it appears in the correct location at the bottom of the plan.

It is important to note that when you drag a Construct into another Construct (as we have here); the XREF is overlaid, *not* attached. This is very important. If the file were attached, you would receive "circular reference" errors later when you tried to work with your project's Views and Sheets. If you wish to verify that the *First Floor Existing* file is in fact overlaid, click the Manage Xrefs quick pick in the Drawing status bar to open the XREF Manager and have a look.

10. Select any Wall onscreen.
11. On the Wall tab, click the Edit Style drop-down button and choose **Wall Styles** (see Figure 10.1).

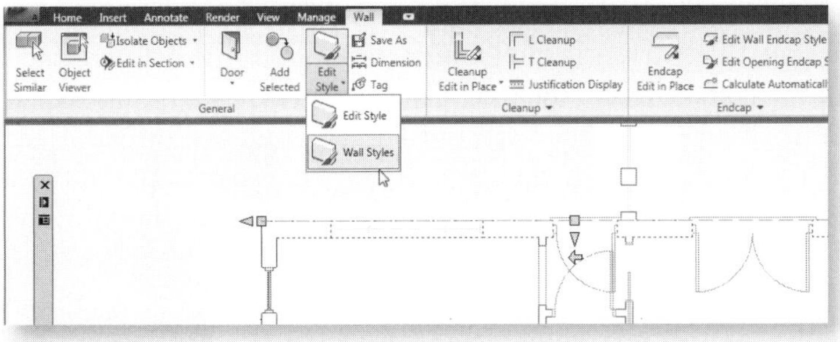

FIGURE 10.1 *Access Wall Styles from the ribbon*

12. On the row of icons appearing across the top of the Style Manager, click the Open Drawing icon (see Figure 10.2).

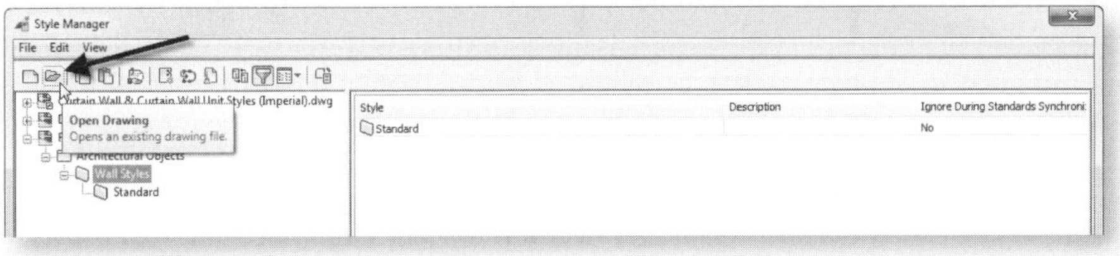

FIGURE 10.2 *Click the Open Drawing icon in the Style Manager*

13. In the "Open Drawing" dialog box, click the Content icon in the icon bar at the left and then double-click the *Styles* folder (see Figure 10.3).

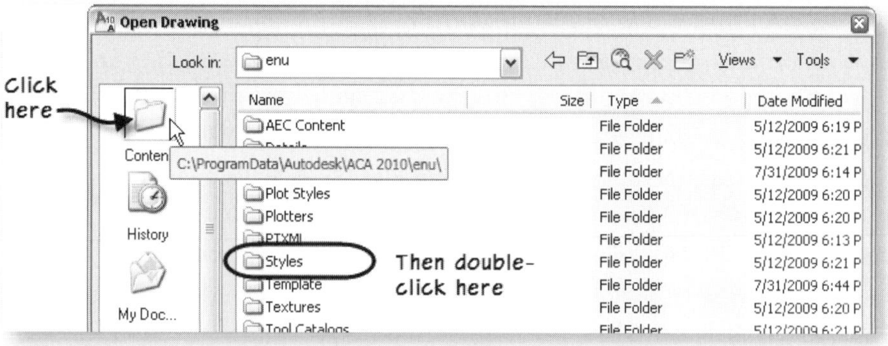

FIGURE 10.3 *Use the Content shortcut on the Outlook bar to access the Content folder on your system*

Style content is saved in ACA drawing files. These can be referred to as library files. The default ACA Style Content folder is located at *C:\ProgramData\Autodesk\ACA 2010\enu\Styles*. If you work with a non-English version of ACA, this path might be slightly different. Also, your firm may have located this folder elsewhere on your company's network. Check with your CAD manager in this case for the correct location. The Content icon on the icon bar is a shortcut to this location, which makes it much easier to navigate there. Even if the location varies from the one indicated here, the *Content* link should take you to the modified location instead. In the default content folder, several Wall style (and other style type) library files are provided. Each file contains styles of a particular construction type. Be sure to explore each of these files at some point to get a good sense of what has been provided with the software. Don't spend time building custom styles until you are familiar with what has been provided.

CAD MANAGER NOTE

Please note that the *ProgramData* folder is hidden by default in Windows Vista or Windows 7. You can turn on all hidden files in Windows Explorer. Click the Organize drop-down button and choose **Folder and Search options** and then click the View tab. Some CAD Managers may be uncomfortable at the prospect of users' turning on hidden files on their systems. This is required if the users want to view the files in Windows Explorer or browse to this folder manually; however, it is *not* required to access the files from ACA when using the Content shortcut provided on the icon bar. Another way to avoid the issue is to relocate the *Styles* folder to a Server location. If you do this, you will need to edit the tools in the Content Browser to point to the new location as well. It is much easier to do this when you install the software. Options to do so are offered at the time of installation when you use the deployment wizard. If you installed ACA with the defaults, you will need to uninstall it and then reinstall and use the options in the installation wizard to locate Content on the server.

14. Double-click the *Imperial* [*Metric*] folder, select the file named *Wall Styles – Stud (Imperial).dwg* [*Wall Styles – Stud (Metric).dwg*] and then click Open.

This will return you to the Style Manager, and this content file will now be listed among any other files you have open in ACA. Your tree view in Style Manager should look something like Figure 10.4.

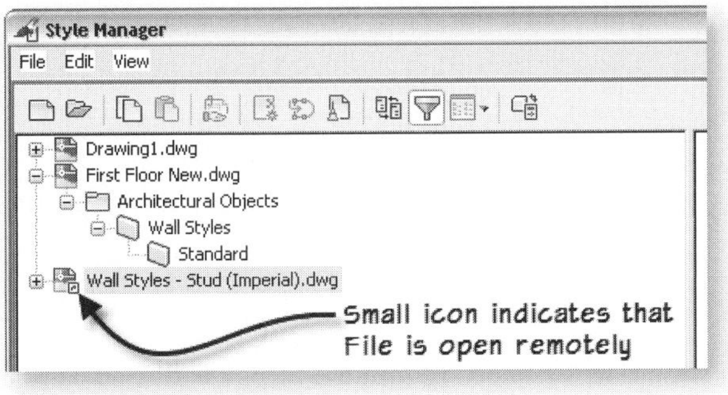

FIGURE 10.4 *The library file appears in the tree view of Style Manager with a small icon indicating that it is open remotely*

NOTE

The special icon (similar to a Windows Shortcut icon) indicates that the file is open remotely in the Style Manager, and not directly in ACA.

15. Expand the *Wall Styles – Stud (Imperial).dwg* [*Wall Styles – Stud (Metric).dwg*] file and the *Architectural Objects* folder and then the list of Wall styles.
16. On the Style Manager toolbar, click the Inline Edit Toggle icon (farthest to the right).

    This toggles the style edit worksheets for the inline preview window.
17. Click on each entry, one at a time, in the list in the tree.

As you click on a Style name in the tree, a preview will appear to the right. The preview window is interactive like the others in ACA. Feel free to use Zoom or Orbit or to change shading.

18. Locate the style named Stud-5.5 Air-1 Brick-4 [Stud-140 Air-025 Brick-090].
19. Right-click it and choose **Copy** (see Figure 10.5).

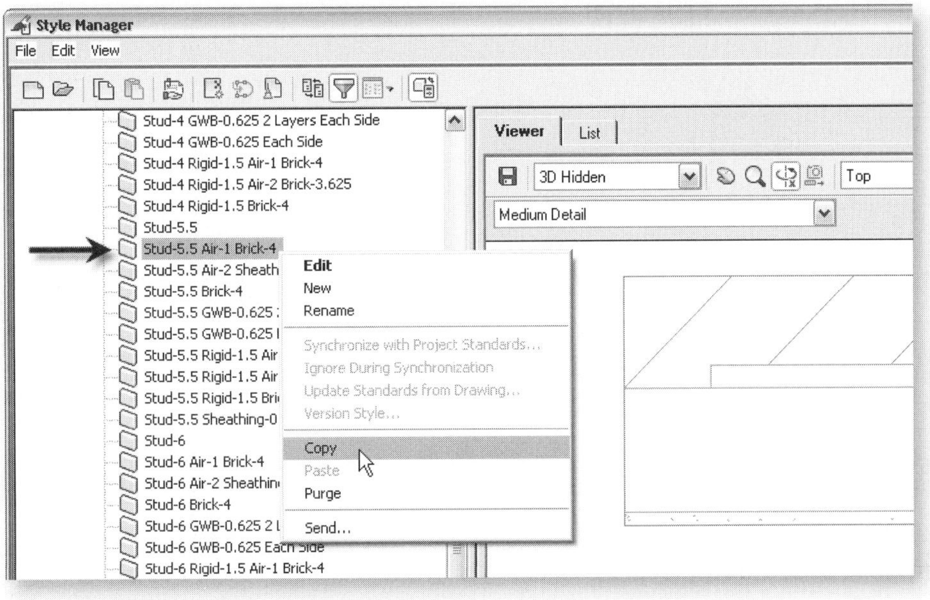

FIGURE 10.5 *Copy a style from the remote file*

20. Scroll the list back to the top, right-click on *First Floor New.dwg* and choose **Paste**.

You have now imported the style into the current drawing file. When you copy a style in Style Manager, you can right-click on the file name, the *Architectural Objects* folder, or the *Wall Styles* category to paste. Regardless of the specific node you select, ACA will paste it to the proper category. When you copy, if you right-click the file name, the folder or category, you will be copying all styles from that drawing, folder or category. If you want just one, be sure to right-click directly on the style you want.

TIP

Multiple styles can be copied at the same time by selecting with the SHIFT and CTRL keys on the right side of the Style Manager. Select the heading *Wall Styles* at left to see the list appear at right. Multiples cannot be selected at the left.

21. Click OK to close the Style Manager.

    If prompted to save the content file, answer No.

CAD MANAGER NOTE

When Content files are accessed remotely as we have done here, ACA will often prompt you to save the remote file even if all you did was copy something from it. In general, you will not want users to have the ability to save the library content files, particularly if you moved them to the server. To prevent this, simply make the *Styles* folder read only in Windows for typical users. If the folder is read only, users will still be able to remotely open files and copy styles as we have done here, but they will not be able to edit the styles directly in those remote files. The message to save the file will also cease to appear, since the file can no longer be saved.

Swap Styles

22. Click to select the three exterior Walls of the addition (right, left and top, not the screen porch).
23. If the Properties palette is not open onscreen, right-click and choose **Properties**.
24. From the Style list, choose Stud-5.5 Air-1 Brick-4 [Stud-140 Air-025 Brick-090].

    Notice the change to the drawing and notice that the brick is on the wrong side (see Figure 10.6).

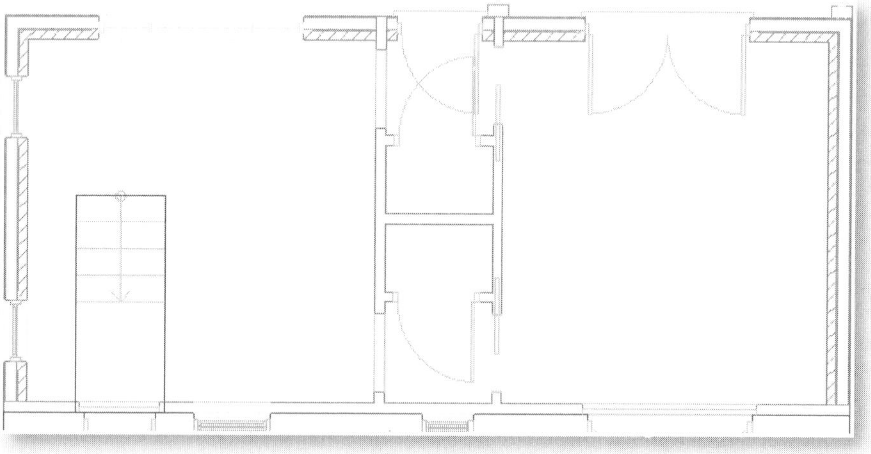

FIGURE 10.6 *The new style applied to the Walls*

25. With the same three Walls selected, on the Wall contextual ribbon tab on the Modify panel, click the Reverse drop-down button and choose the ***Wall Reverse Baseline*** tool.

NOTE

You could also use the Reverse Direction (arrow-shaped) grip to reverse each Wall directly one at a time.

That solved the problem of the brick, but now the justification line (in this case, Right) of the Walls is on the inside of the plan and the Walls are sticking out. (The justification line is the edge with the grips.) Right justification was chosen when these Walls were added so that they would remain flush with the existing house. Now that we have reversed the Walls, we need to switch the justification to Left to maintain the flush relationship and shift the Walls back where they belong. We can do this for all three Walls at once on the Properties palette. We can also change the justification of the Walls directly with grips, one at a time, using a tool on the Wall contextual ribbon tab. Let's look at both techniques.

26. Deselect the Walls and select only the vertical Wall on the right.
27. On the Wall contextual ribbon tab, click the Cleanup panel title bar to expand the panel and then choose the ***Edit Justification*** tool.

    Four diamond-shaped grips will appear in the middle of the Wall. Each one corresponds to a different Wall justification. The gray one is the current justification (in this case, Right).
28. Hover your mouse over each grip point to see the grip tip indicating its function.

Notice that the grip tips indicate that holding down the CTRL key will maintain the baseline. This means that the Wall footprint will not move when the justification is repositioned. If you do not hold the CTRL key, then the Wall will shift. You can see this indicated before you click by the small gray ghost line that appears when you hover over the grip. In this case, we need the Wall to shift back to its original position before we reversed it, so we will *not* use the CTRL key.

29. Click the Left justification grip (see Figure 10.7).

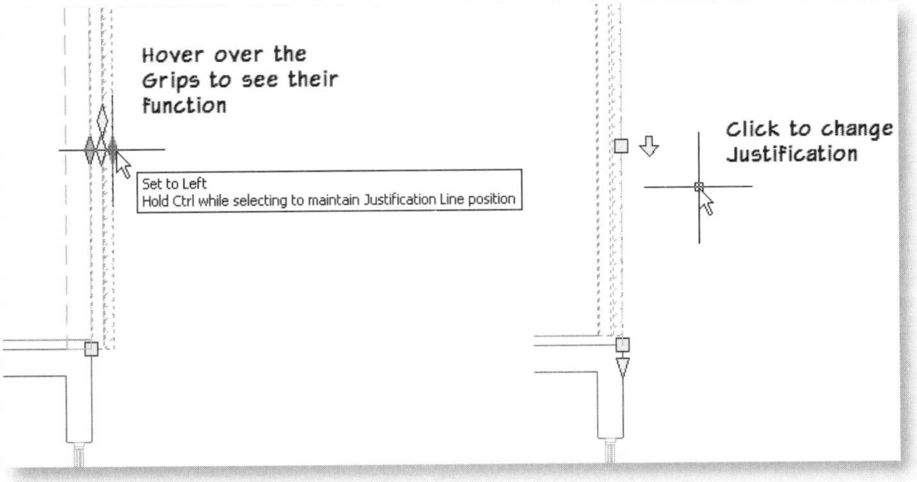

FIGURE 10.7 *Left justify positions the Walls correctly*

The Wall is now oriented, positioned and justified correctly.

30. Deselect the first Wall and then select the other two Walls, right-click and choose **Properties**.
31. On the Properties palette, in the Dimensions grouping, change the Justify to **Left**.

TIP

In some situations, when you perform these types of edits, the Walls will no longer clean up. The L Cleanup routine covered in the previous chapter can easily fix this.

Be careful of the sequence and exact technique you use to perform such edits. As you can see from the previous exercise, when we reversed the Walls, their respective justifications caused them all to "flip" to the outside. Changing the justification in this case from right to left fixed the problem by flipping them back. An alternative approach would be to use the Wall Reverse ribbon tool instead of Wall Reverse Baseline ribbon tool. Wall Reverse would have flipped the brick *without* shifting the Walls. This would initially have appeared to be correct; but upon closer investigation, you would have discovered that the justification line would then be the inside edge rather than the outside edge. Therefore, we would still have had to shift the justification lines to Left and potentially use the L Cleanup tool when finished. When you use the justification grips shown above, you can hold down the CTRL key as you click a grip to maintain the Wall's position without a shift occurring, as we saw here. If you like, undo back to the point where we reversed the Walls and try it the other way. Either approach is valid as long as the end result—having the brick and the justification flush to the edge of the existing house—is achieved.

Despite the fact that the exterior Walls are now displaying properly and in the correct orientation, the cleanup between them and the interior Walls is incorrect. It appears as though the interior Walls penetrate through the brick veneer on the exterior. This clearly needs to be addressed. This is actually an example of a simple cleanup problem like those we explored in Chapter 9. The issue is that the interior Walls use the Standard Wall style, which uses a Cleanup Priority of 1 and therefore does not interact nicely with other Wall Styles. The priorities of the components in the exterior Wall style that we just applied are all much higher than 1 (refer to Chapter 9 for detailed information on Wall Component Priorities). However, this situation is easily resolved when we apply a Wall style other than Standard to the interior Walls as well.

TIP

As a general rule of thumb, you should build your plan entirely from the Standard Wall style or not use it at all.

32. Deselect all Walls.
33. Select one of the interior Walls, and, on the Wall contextual ribbon tab on the General panel, click the ***Select Similar*** button (see Figure 10.8).

Select Similar is quick and powerful. With a click, you can select all objects in the drawing that match (Style and Layer) the one selected.

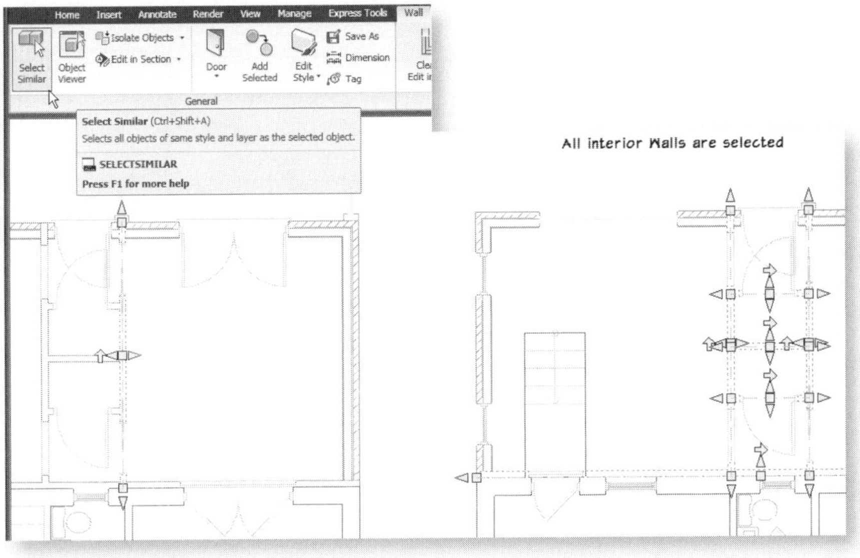

FIGURE 10.8 *Use Select Similar to select objects of the same type and layer*

All of the interior Walls in the new addition will be highlighted. This is because they were all similar to the one you originally selected.

34. Right-click the Tool Palettes title bar, choose Design (to load the Design Tool Palette Group) and then click the Walls tab.

    If your Tool Palettes are not displayed, on the Home tab, click the Tools button.

35. On the Walls tool palette, right-click the Stud-4 GWB-0.625 Each Side [Stud-102 GWB-018 Each Side] tool and choose **Apply Tool Properties to > Wall**.

All of the selected Walls now use the style that was built into the tool.

36. Zoom in to the top middle of the plan where the interior Walls meet the exterior.

Study the Walls on all sides of the closet, including the way they join and clean up with the exterior. Note that the stud Walls are made from a stud component with a layer of gypsum wallboard (GWB) on each side (represented here by the extra set of internal Wall lines). The masonry Wall is composed of a stud structure with a brick veneer. The stud component of the interior walls and the stud backup of the masonry walls now clean up properly with each other. Recall the Wall Component Priority lesson in Chapter 9 and note the way the interior Walls behave before and after, as shown in Figure 10.9. Toggle on the Wall Justification display as a check. All of these features are built into the respective Wall styles of each Wall object. Toggle off the Justification display when you are satisfied.

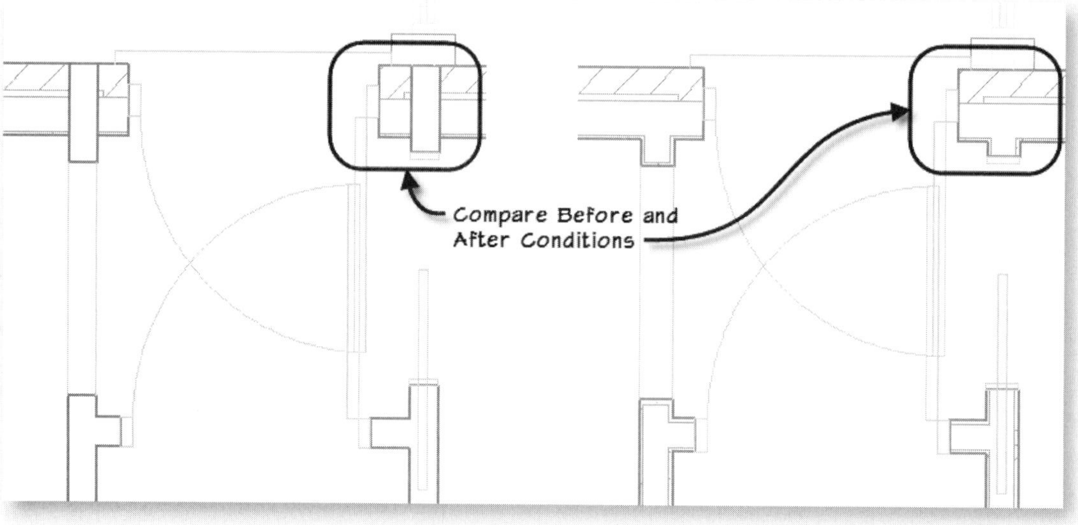

FIGURE 10.9 *Wall cleanup in standard versus stud Wall*

Building and Editing Wall Styles

It has been stated already that there are hundreds of pre-built Wall styles provided with the software. They are stored in library files like the one we accessed in the steps above. When you begin contemplating the creation of your own custom Wall styles, you should first thoroughly explore the ones that ship with the product. Even if the "out-of-the-box" offerings do not meet your needs, it will usually be much easier to start with one of the existing styles and edit it, rather than build one completely from scratch. Reverse engineering existing styles also provides an excellent means to learn about Wall style composition.

Explore the Wall Style Properties

1. Select the exterior masonry Wall (the one at the top of the screen) and, on the Wall contextual ribbon tab on the General panel, click the ***Edit Style*** button.

The Wall Style Properties box has seven tabs: General, with name and description fields, and six others, most of which will be covered in the upcoming exercises (see Figure 10.10). On the General tab, there are also some other buttons: Notes, Property Sets and the Keynote assignment area. (Notes simply calls a dialog box with a single, large text field. You can enter any information here you wish: notes to the drafter, information on the style etc.) Property Sets are covered in Chapter 15, "Generating Schedules." Keynotes provide a means to assign construction notes to the Style from a central database. These notes can then be referenced with field codes on the printed sheets and even pass through to elevations, sections and details (see Chapter 17 for more information).

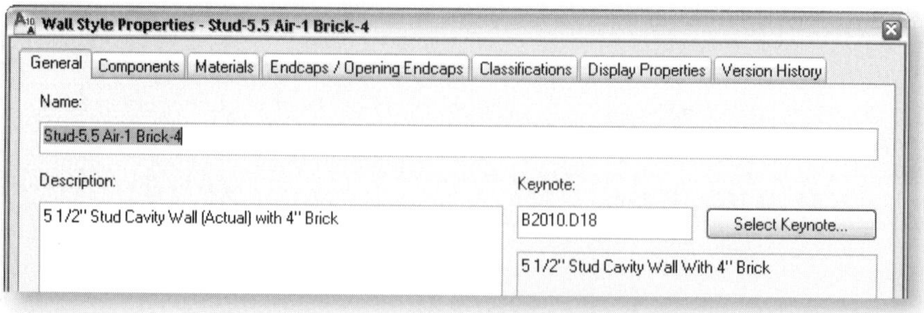

FIGURE 10.10 *The tabs of the Wall Style Properties dialog box*

2. Click the Components tab.

Components in the Wall Style represent the major elements of the Wall Style's construction. A Wall style contains a minimum of one component and can contain several. The Components tab is used to define each component's width, height and position within the Wall, both horizontally and vertically. At the left is an interactive Viewer that defaults to a vertical end (Left) view of the Wall style. You can use Zoom and Pan in this Viewer as well as access a standard right-click menu as needed. The View Cube and your wheel mouse will work in this Viewer as well. The main center section contains an interactive list of all the Wall components. On the right is a bank of icons to add, remove and shuffle components within the list (see Figure 10.11).

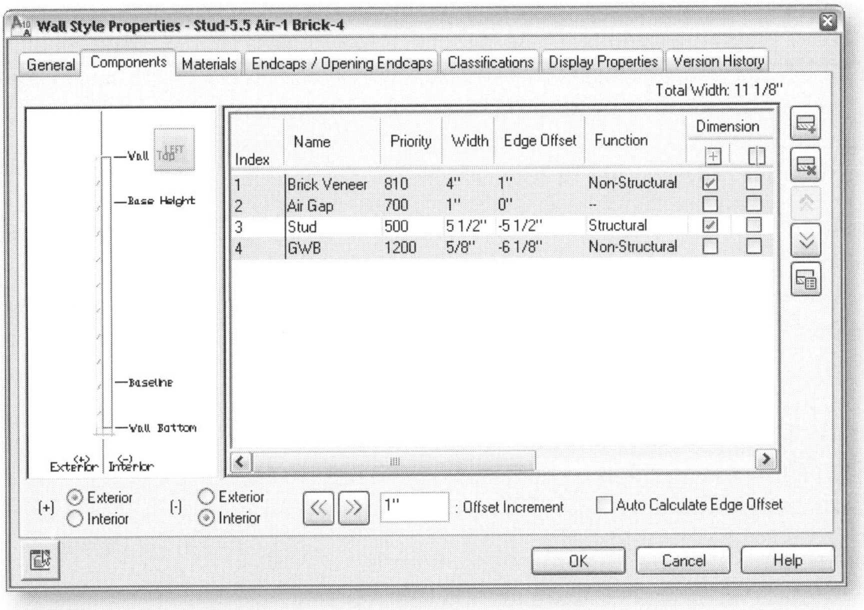

FIGURE 10.11 *The Wall Style Components tab*

To edit the properties of a particular component, select it in the list. Set the horizontal dimensions in the left columns; configure the vertical dimensions in the columns at the far right. Let's define the relevant terminology on the Components tab.

- **Index**—A number assigned by ACA starting at 1. Indexes are always in numeric order; however, you can use the icons at the right of the dialog box to reorganize (and thereby re-index) any of your components.
- **Name**—User-defined designation; usually refers to the material that the component represents. Naming schemes should be standardized throughout the office. A complete list of common components (with their associated priorities) appears in Table 9.1 in Chapter 9.
- **Priority**—Numeric value used to determine how the component will clean up with components of other Walls. Refer to Chapter 9 for complete information on priorities.

Geometrically, each component is basically a long thin box. In plan, this is some portion of the total width of the Wall. The Edge Offset and the Width parameters define the two lines that are used to draw a component relative to the Wall Baseline.

- **Baseline**—The "zero point" of the Wall's width (in plan) and height (in elevation). Its location relative to the Wall section (and plan) is indicated by the long red vertical line in the Viewer. A Baseline text label indicates its location relative to elevation (see Figure 10.12 below).
- **Edge Offset**—Locates first edge of the component, it is measured from the Baseline. This can be a positive or negative value.
- **Width**—The *true* width of the component, measured from the Edge Offset, *not* the Baseline. This can be positive or negative.

TIP

When trying to understand or build a Wall style, remember that the Edge Offset is measured from the Baseline, while the Width is measured from the Edge Offset.

Positive and negative are used to indicate direction in the Wall style. Small plus (+) and minus (−) signs are shown at the top of the Viewer for reference. When a Wall is drawn from left to right in plan, the positive direction is up and the negative is down. Another way to think of it is to imagine standing at the start point of the Wall and looking toward the endpoint. In this orientation, positive offsets would be to your left, while negative offsets would be to your right.

You can also designate whether each side of the Wall style represents an interior or exterior edge. Look at the bottom left corner of Figure 10.11 above. A series of four radio buttons appears in this location—an exterior and an interior option next to the (+) side of the Wall and the same two choices on the (−) side. You simply choose the appropriate radio button to indicate whether that side of the Wall is exterior or interior. In this case, you can see that the Wall style we have onscreen has its positive side (with the brick) as exterior and its negative side (with the drywall) as the interior side. Each of the out-of-the-box Wall styles will already have these designations pre-configured logically.

We also have the Function and Dimension columns.

- **Function**—Indicates whether the component is structural or non-structural. The list is fixed. There are three choices: Structural, Non-Structural and Not assigned (--). All out-of-the-box Wall styles will have these values preselected for most components. In this case, the Stud component of the current Wall style is the only Structural component. The Function of a component is utilized by AEC Dimensions. In order to use this feature, your AEC Dimension style must be set to dimension Wall Components using "Structural ByStyle." AEC Dimensions (and the Function value of Wall styles) are explored in Chapter 14.
- **Dimension**—The choices here include the left, center and right edges of the component. By selecting one or more of these boxes, you indicate to AEC Dimension objects which points you prefer to dimension. In order to use this feature, your AEC Dimension style must be set to dimension Wall Components using "ByStyle." AEC Dimensions and the Dimension settings of Wall styles are explored in Chapter 14.

Let's continue to look at the geometric values of the components.

- **Top and Bottom Elevation Offset**—Establishes the default top and bottom heights of a component in elevation relative to one of four possible points along the Wall height. Typically, components have no offset (zero) from both Wall Bottom and Wall Top. This makes them "full height" components. Change these values for components that occur in elevation; for example, horizontal bands; footings; and even countertops, moldings or soffits. Vertical components can be referenced from the following four points within the height of the Wall (see Figure 10.12).

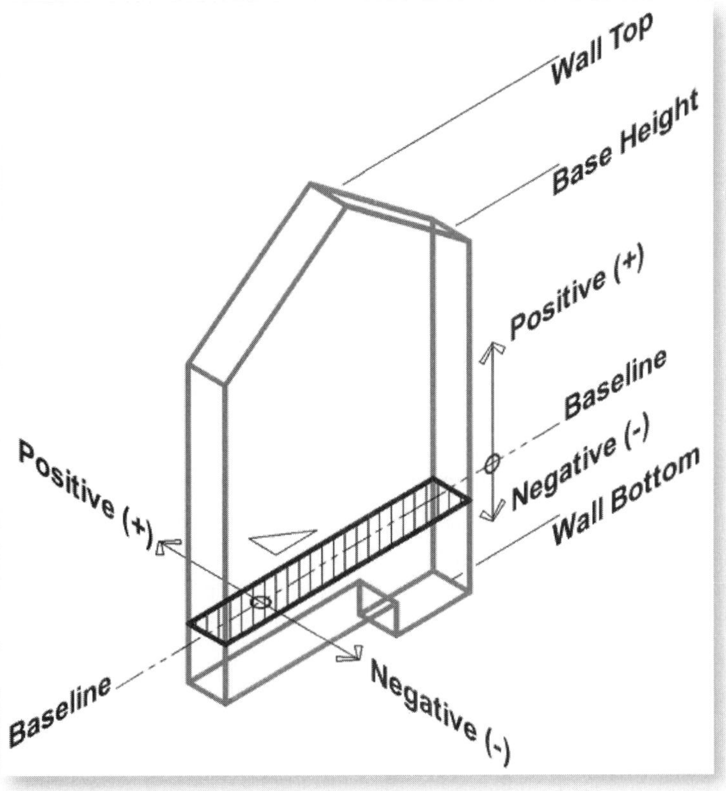

FIGURE 10.12 *Key datum points within a Wall object*

- **Wall Bottom**—In elevation or 3D, the absolute lowest point on the Wall's height when measured normal to the ground plane. Wall Bottom defaults to Baseline (typically at Z = 0). Use the Floor Line command (on the Wall contextual ribbon tab) or the Roof/floor Line worksheet on the properties palette to change it on an individual Wall object. (Recall the use of Floor Line and Roof Line Offsets in the Curtain Wall style in Chapter 8 and the Wall at the residential Stair in Chapter 7.) Floor Line offsets can also be specified in the properties of a Wall tool or on the properties palette at the time of Wall creation.
- **Baseline**—The datum line of the Wall in elevation or 3D. This point corresponds to the Wall's Z location (on the properties palette) and is typically Z = 0. This point corresponds to the finish floor line in most cases.
- **Base Height**—The basic height parameter of the Wall on the properties palette as seen in elevation or 3D. In most cases, it is best to think of this point as the finish ceiling line of the Wall.
- **Wall Top**—In elevation or 3D, the absolute highest point on the Wall's height when measured normal to the ground plane. Wall Top defaults to Base Height. Use the Roof Line command (on the Wall contextual ribbon tab) or the Roof/floor Line worksheet on the properties palette to change it on an individual Wall object. Roof Line offsets can also be specified in the properties of a Wall tool or on the properties palette at the time of Wall creation.

NOTE

The Wall Bottom in some cases may be above the Baseline. The Wall Top in some cases may be below the Base Height although neither of these scenarios is common. Typically, Wall Bottom will be equal or lower than Baseline while Wall Top will typically be equal or higher than Base Height.

Change the Air Gap Width

Now that we have an understanding of the basic terminology used in Wall styles, let's explore the specific settings of the Wall style that we are currently editing (see Figures 10.11 and 10.13).

Look closely at the settings for the Air Gap and the Stud. The Air Gap begins at zero and is 1 [25] wide. The Stud is offset negative 5 1/2" [140] from zero, with a width of 5 1/2" [140] (see Figure 10.13). This puts the left edge of the Stud component directly at zero. This means that this Wall style is built with a Baseline at the edge between the Stud and the Air Gap. This is the edge of the structural material (in this case, the Stud). Placing the Baseline at the edge of structure is a common approach seen in nearly all out-of-the-box styles. This enables you to draw this Wall with Baseline justification, trace along the slab edge or a beam and have the Wall properly positioned as you work. It also allows you the freedom to adjust the width of the structure, or the veneer, at a later stage in the design process without needing to move the Walls. It is not required that the Baseline be positioned this way; it is done for the convenience of the user. Also remember that regardless of Baseline position within the Wall Style, you can always choose to draw with Left, Right or Center justification instead.

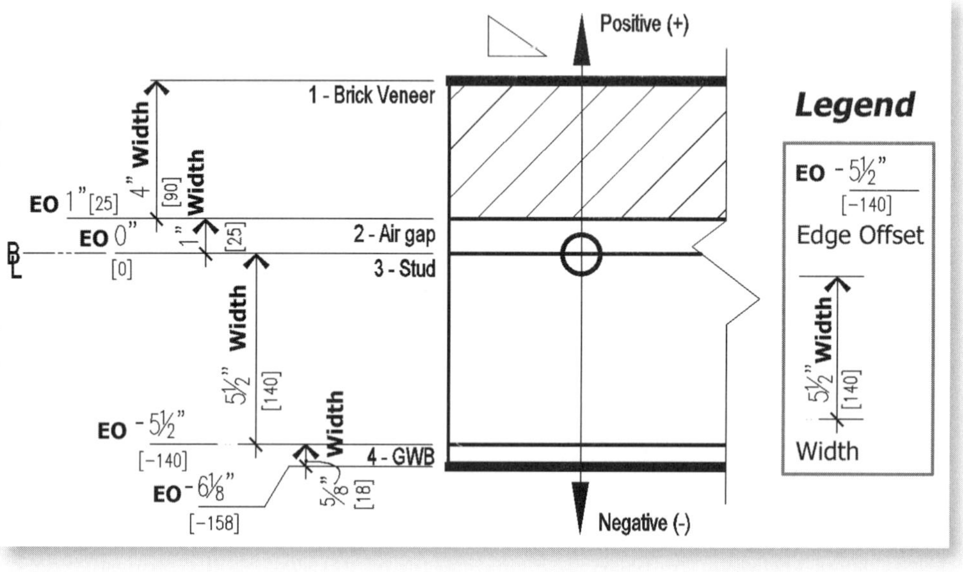

FIGURE 10.13 *Note each component's Edge Offset and Width and their relationship to the Baseline*

Let's assume we wanted to change the width of one of the components. For instance, suppose we wanted to have a 2" [50] Air Gap.

3. Select the Air Gap component (Index number 2).

   Notice it is highlighted in green in the Viewer.

4. Click in the Width column, change the value to **2"** [**50**] and then press ENTER (see Figure 10.14).

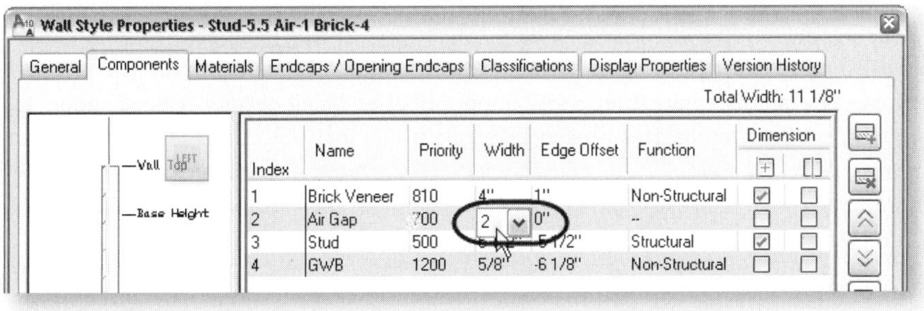

FIGURE 10.14 *Change the Width of the component*

Now that we have made the width of the Air Gap larger, the Brick no longer has the correct Edge Offset. (At an Edge Offset of 1" [25], it overlaps the Air Gap, which is not recommended.)

5. Click on the Brick Veneer component (Index 1).
6. At the bottom left corner of the dialog box, verify that the Offset Increment is **1"** [**25**] and then click the Increment Wall Component Offset icon (see Figure 10.15).

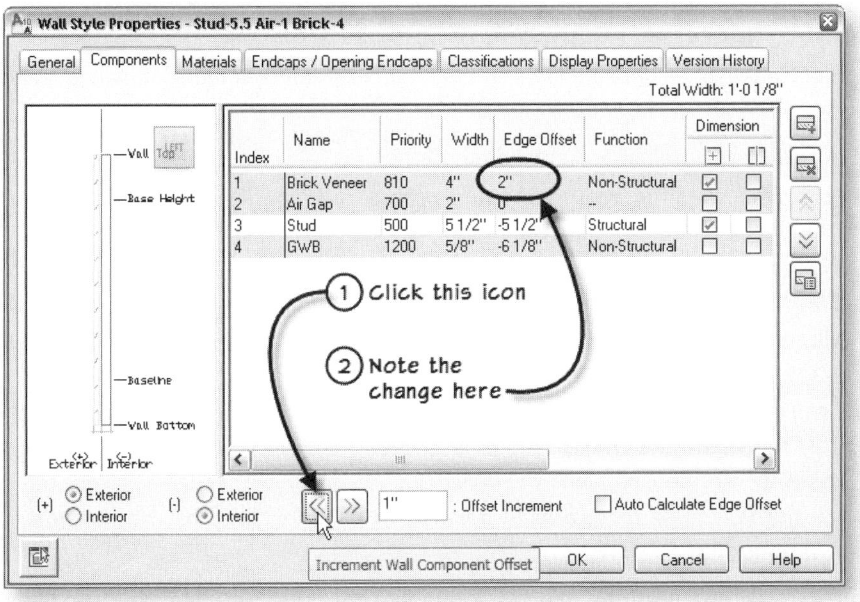

FIGURE 10.15 *The Brick Veneer is still flush, but the Endcaps need work*

Notice the change to the Edge Offset for the Brick component. It is now 2" [50]. (If it went to zero, you clicked the Decrement icon. If so, click the Increment icon twice to fix it.)

With this tool, you can interactively adjust the position of components within a Wall style without the need to calculate the values. Adjust the offset Increment as appropriate before clicking the Increment and Decrement icons.

7. On the General tab, rename the Style to Stud 5.5 Air-2 Brick-4 [Stud-140 Air-050 Brick-090] and then click OK to return to the drawing and view the change.

NOTE

We are keeping the component-based naming convention in this example. If you choose, you could use a more descriptive name such as "Exterior Wall" like we did in the commercial project. The exact naming convention is less important than being certain that you apply it consistently across the project. This is especially true if you intend to use Project Standards to synchronize styles, as we did in the commercial project. Another popular naming convention is to incorporate an abbreviation for your firm's name in the renamed style such as PFA Stud 5.5 Air-2 Brick-4.

Note that the exterior Walls have become wider. However, the exterior edge has remained flush with the exterior of the existing building just as we required. This is because the justification of the Walls is Left. Had we used Baseline instead, the brick veneer would have shifted 1" [25] all the way around the building and we would have been forced to move the Walls to compensate. This is an example of how understanding the interaction of the various Style parameters (component dimensions) and Object-based parameters (justification in this case) provides insights valuable to forming good strategy. This is also why we so carefully considered these options above when applying the Wall style and shifting the justification.

8. Save the file.

Guidelines to Successful Component Composition

There are a few issues to consider when setting up the components of a new Wall style.

- Will you use Nominal or Actual dimensions?
- How much detail is appropriate and necessary (quantity and composition of components, hatching choices, etc.)?
- Where should you position the Baseline (relative to the edge of the structural component or elsewhere)?
- Will the Wall style use a fixed (hard-coded) Width or a variable (user-specified on the properties palette) Width?
- If you use a variable Width, will the variable (Base Width on the properties palette) represent the overall width of the entire Wall or a single component within the Wall, such as just the CMU?
- Will the Wall style require fixed heights for some or all of its components in elevations and 3D?

The answers to these questions depend somewhat on your personal philosophy or project needs. For example, should a brick component be 3 5/8" or 4"? Compelling arguments can be made to support either approach. Will you design the Wall style to draw lines representing each layer of drywall, or will you simply represent the major structural components or overall wall width? Be sure to consider the scale at which the drawings will be printed when deciding on an appropriate level of detail and quantity of components. Keep in mind that the default template includes three levels of detail: Low, Medium and High (see Chapter 2). You will need to consider these points at each level of detail that you plan to use. On most default out-of-the-box ACA Wall styles, the Baseline is at the face of the structural component. This is typically a good location, but it is not critical. Once you have determined your own personal leanings concerning these criteria, the following three guidelines will help guarantee the successful creation of your new Wall style.

a. Regardless of nominal or actual, make sure that your math works. Solution tip icons are a virtual certainty if any of your Edge Offsets and Widths do not add up properly.

b. Leave no gaps within the thickness of your Wall. If your Wall is 12" [300] in total Width, make sure that your entire component Widths total exactly 12" [300] and that each component is touching one another without overlap. Air Gaps (in construction, such as between brick and CMU) should be defined as Air Gap components with Display Properties turned off. Otherwise, you will experience display, cleanup and area/volume calculation problems.

c. In any decision, be consistent! This is the golden rule. No matter what you decide, actual or nominal, do it consistently. If you like to use negative Edge Offsets and positive Widths, do it consistently. If you change the component priority for brick in a new Wall style, assign it consistently. Making good decisions that support the way your firm works is half the battle. Following those decisions with consistency will make your job and those who work with you much easier.

MANAGER NOTE CAD

The key to solid and consistent building models and drawings involves a combination of technical and drafting standards. Do not simply address file naming, layer naming, XREF/block creation and plotting methodologies. Your firm may already have a drafting standard, perhaps created in the days prior to CAD. Management needs to be aware of the opportunities and options the CAD software offers, because production time will be affected. A project methodologies guideline and CAD/Drafting Guideline are essential in order to take advantage of many ACA features. It is not necessary, as the CAD Manager, to create every possible Wall style anyone in the firm could ever need. Rather, if good guidelines based on time-tested drafting standards and object modeling best practices are put in place (incorporating the suggestions noted here), it will become much easier for all members of the team to be involved in the process of populating and using the library.

Endcaps

While components are the major aspect of a Wall Style, there are several other settings and characteristics of a Wall Style to consider; for example, how they terminate at the ends.

1. Zoom in on left side of the plan, where the masonry Wall meets the existing house.

Notice that the ends of the Walls at both the connection to the existing house and penetration of the windows show a special condition for the brick, yet appear a bit disjointed because of the change to the Air Gap component. Let's explore Endcaps to learn how to solve this problem.

Where the Edge Offset and Width define the two parallel lines that represent the component, an "Endcap" terminates the component on both its ends and at each opening (penetrations such as windows and doors). An Endcap is simply the condition at the end of a Wall. Specifically, it is the termination of each component within the Wall. The simplest form of Endcap is a straight line. The default Endcap named Standard is simply a straight line. Graphically, this will terminate the Wall as if it were cut straight across all components. However, Endcaps can be virtually any shape; look at Figure 10.16 for some examples of Endcap conditions. Shown are four Wall styles contained in the out-of-the-box Content files. The name of the style is at the top; beneath each style is a sketch of the polylines used to create the Endcap. Next is the description of the Endcap condition and finally an image of the resultant Wall condition.

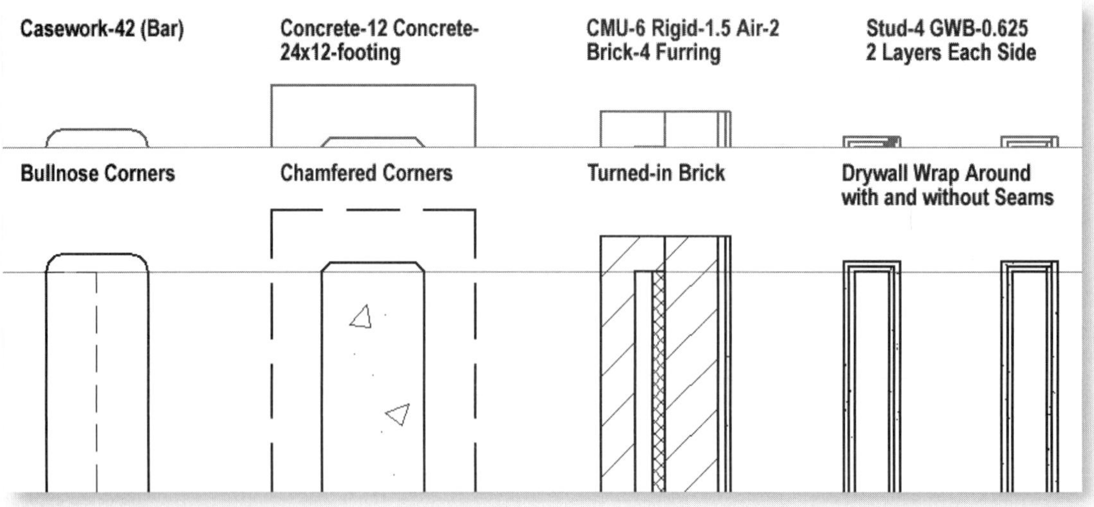

FIGURE 10.16 *A selection of sample Endcap conditions*

Assign a Different Endcap

Let's start by assigning a different Endcap.

2. Select the vertical masonry Wall at the left, and, on the Wall contextual ribbon tab, on the General tab, click the ***Edit Style*** button.
3. Click the Endcaps/Opening Endcaps tab (see Figure 10.17).

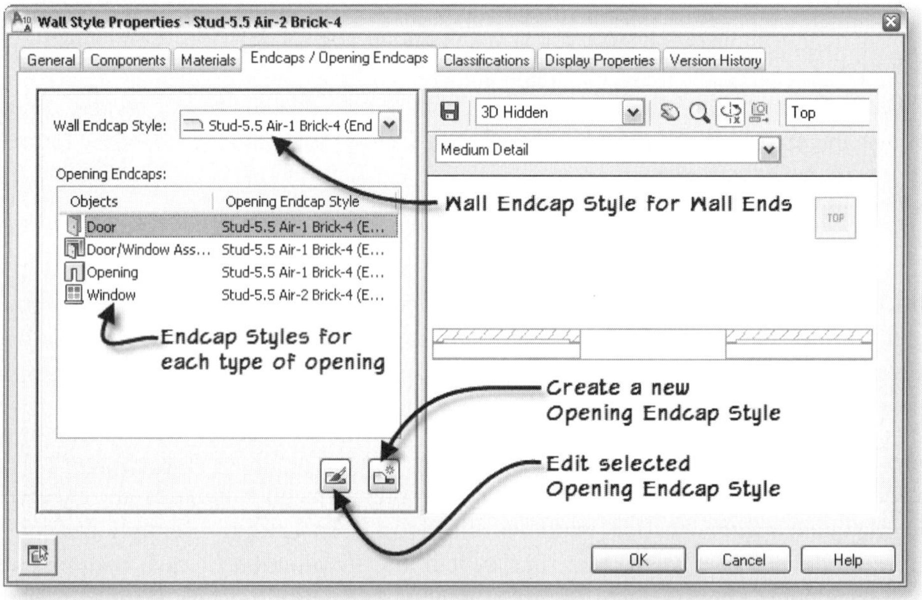

FIGURE 10.17 *Endcaps can be assigned to the Wall ends and each type of Opening*

There are three areas on this tab. In the top left corner, you can assign from a list the Endcap to use for the Wall's ends. Beneath this are the Opening Endcaps assignments; a different Opening Endcap style may be assigned for each type of Wall Opening. The third area of this tab is the familiar Viewer. If the Wall style is complex and requires a more articulated termination, a custom Endcap can be devised.

To create an Endcap, simply draw the way that each material should end with a polyline. You can also use the in-place edit functionality to create a custom Endcap without first drawing polylines. We will build a new Endcap for this style below; but before we do that, let's assign a different Wall Endcap style from the predefined list. Currently, the Wall uses an Endcap named Stud-5.5 Air-1 Brick-4 (End 1) [Stud-140 Air-025 Brick-090 (End 1)]. This Endcap turns the brick veneer in to close the Air Gap. However, because it is rare to have a Wall of this type in a freestanding situation, the brick needs to turn in only at the openings and not at the ends. Therefore, let's assign the Standard Endcap (which, as mentioned above, is a simple straight line) to the Wall Endcap Style condition.

4. From the Wall Endcap Style list, choose **Standard** (see Figure 10.18).

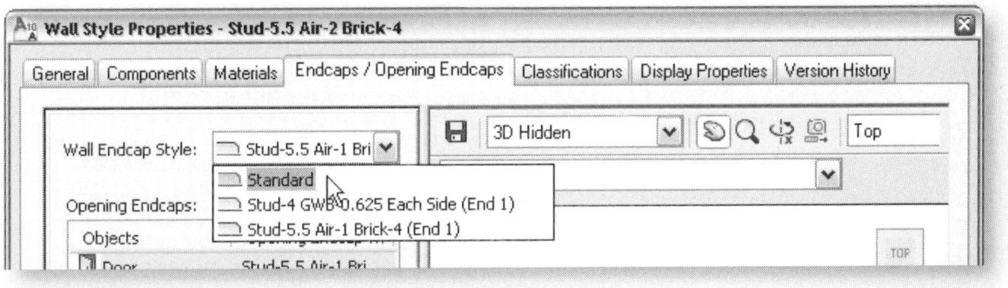

FIGURE 10.18 *Choose Standard from the list*

5. Click OK to return to the drawing and view the change (see Figure 10.19).

   Notice the condition where the new walls meet the existing walls. The brick now simply terminates into the existing wall rather than turning in. Notice also that this change occurs on both sides of the addition. This is because the change was made in the Wall Style.

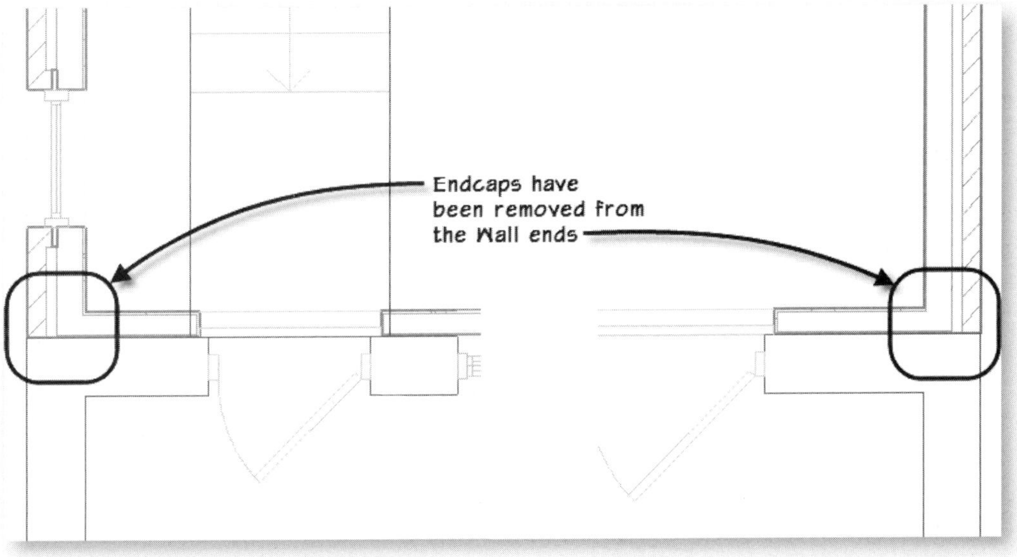

FIGURE 10.19 *Standard Endcap applied to the ends*

Edit an Endcap in Place

We have solved the condition where the new and existing come together nicely. However, if you observe the condition at the Windows and other Wall penetrations, you will note that the problem caused by increasing the Air Gap is still evident. To fix this, let's edit the existing Endcap style.

6. Select the vertical masonry Wall at the left, and, on the Wall contextual ribbon tab on the Endcap panel, click the ***Endcap Edit in Place*** tool.
7. At the "Select a point near Endcap" prompt, click near one of the Window frames (see the left side of Figure 10.20).

   This will activate the Edit in Place mode. The end of the Wall will shade, and grip-editable shapes will appear at the end of each component. The In-Place Edit ribbon will also appear.
8. Click on the hatching inside the turned in Brick shape.

   Grips will appear on this shape (see the right side of Figure 10.20).

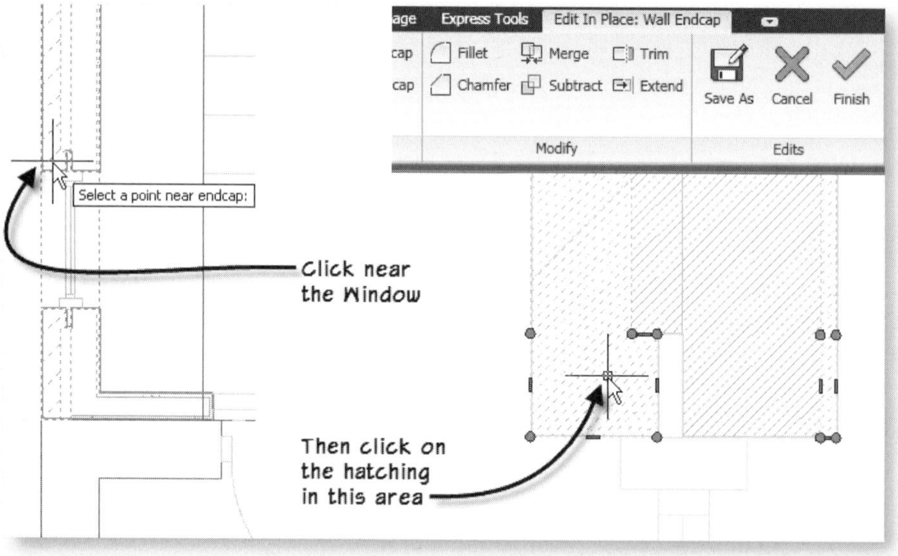

FIGURE 10.20 *Click the hatching in the Brick component to reveal its In-Place Edit Grips*

You can use any of the grip points to edit the shape of the Endcap. Corner grips (round shape) edit just that vertex. The midpoint edge grips (long thin rectangle) move the entire edge parallel to itself.

9. Click the edge grip on the vertical edge of the selected profile.
10. Snap this point to the perpendicular edge across the Air Gap (see Figure 10.21).

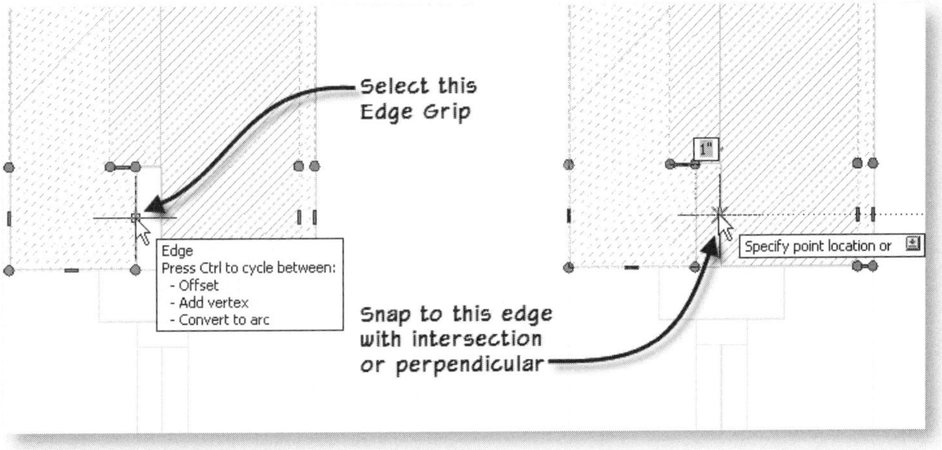

FIGURE 10.21 *Draw polylines for a custom Endcap*

11. On the Edit In Place: Wall Endcap contextual ribbon tab, on the Edits panel, click the ***Save As*** tool and select the profile we just edited at the prompt.
12. In the "Opening Endcap Style" dialog, leave the two "save as" checkboxes near the top of the dialog checked.
13. Change the name of the new opening Endcap style to: **Stud-5.5 Air-2 Brick-4 (End 1)(2-Sided)** [**Stud-140 Air-025 Brick-090 (End 1)(2-Sided)**].
14. Change the name of the new wall Endcap style to: **Stud-5.5 Air-2 Brick-4 (End 1)** [**Stud-140 Air-025 Brick-090 (End 1)**].
15. Leave the balance of the dialog settings as is and click OK (see Figure 10.22).

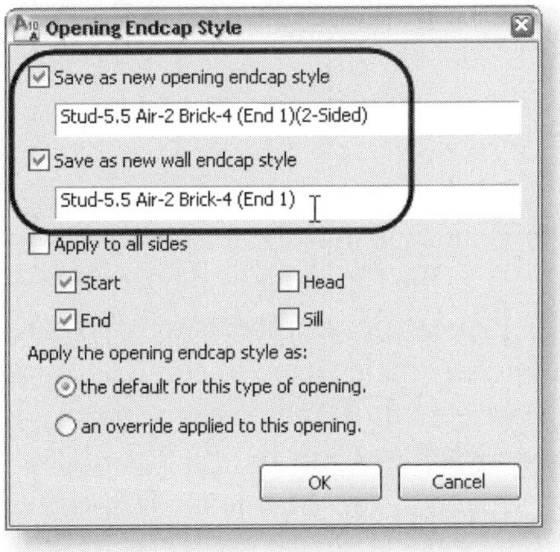

FIGURE 10.22 *Rename the Wall Opening Endcap and Wall Endcap Styles*

16. Zoom in to one of the windows in the plan.

Notice the change to the Endcap. Because we created and assigned a new one at a Window, the change was immediate and applied to all Window locations. However, even though we have successfully redefined this Endcap at Windows, we still need to add the new Opening Endcap Style to the other opening types.

17. Select the Wall again and, on the Wall contextual ribbon tab on the General panel, click the Edit Style button.

18. On the left side Endcaps/Opening Endcaps tab (see Figure 10.17 above), select the Door entry.
19. From the pop-up list in the Opening Endcap Style column choose Stud-5.5 Air-2 Brick-4 (End 1)(2-Sided) [Stud-140 Air-025 Brick-090 (End 1)(2-Sided)].
20. Repeat for Door/Window Assembly and Opening (see Figure 10.23).

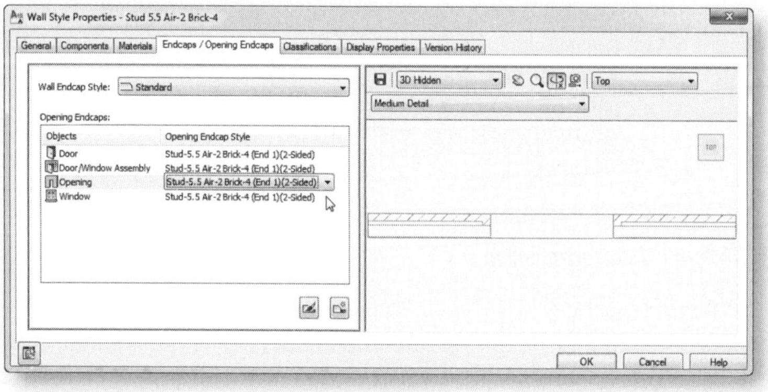

FIGURE 10.23 *Assign Opening Endcap Styles*

21. Click OK and examine the Endcap conditions at the Doors and Door/Window Assembly in the top exterior Wall.

An Opening Endcap Style is used at Doors, Windows, Openings and Door/Window Assemblies. It is a style that can apply one or more Wall Endcap Styles to each of the four sides of an opening: Sill, Head and both Jambs. This is why we had to rename two different styles. One was the Opening Endcap Style; the other was the nested Wall Endcap Style within it.

22. Save the file.

Endcaps with Invisible Segments

When an Endcap is built, all components in the Wall style must be terminated individually. However, take a close look at the Endcap at the Opening at the left side of the small foyer at the top middle of the plan. The gypsum board appears to wrap continuously around the opening. It appears as though a single shape in the Endcap is being used to terminate two gypsum board components. In fact, what is occurring is that the shapes used in the Endcap contain some invisible edges. In other words, because each layer of gypsum *must* be terminated separately, an edge is made invisible where the two Endcap pieces "touch." To see this more clearly, let's edit the Endcap in-place.

23. Select the Wall on the left side of the small foyer at the top middle of the plan.
24. On the Wall contextual ribbon tab, on the Endcap panel, click the ***Endcap Edit in Place*** tool.
25. At the "Select a point near Endcap" prompt, click near one of the Opening (without a Door).

    This will activate the Edit in Place mode. The end of the Wall will shade, and grip-editable shapes will appear at the end of each component. The In-Place Edit ribbon will also appear.
26. Zoom in closely on the Endcap shapes.

Move your mouse over the shaded shapes of the Endcap. Each of the GWB components have an Endcap shape. The one on the left wraps across the Stud component eliminating the need for this component to have its own shape. The GWB component on the right has a smaller and simpler shape (basically a square). Notice that there is a vertical red line between these two shapes. As you pre-highlight each shape, you will notice that they each have a red edge. These red edges are "invisible" or hidden edges. Notice also that there is a Show Edge button and a Hide Edge button on the Edit In Place: Wall Endcap contextual ribbon tab. Use these tools to hide and show edges. Feel free to experiment with them if you like. Just undo any changes when you finish exploring (see Figure 10.24).

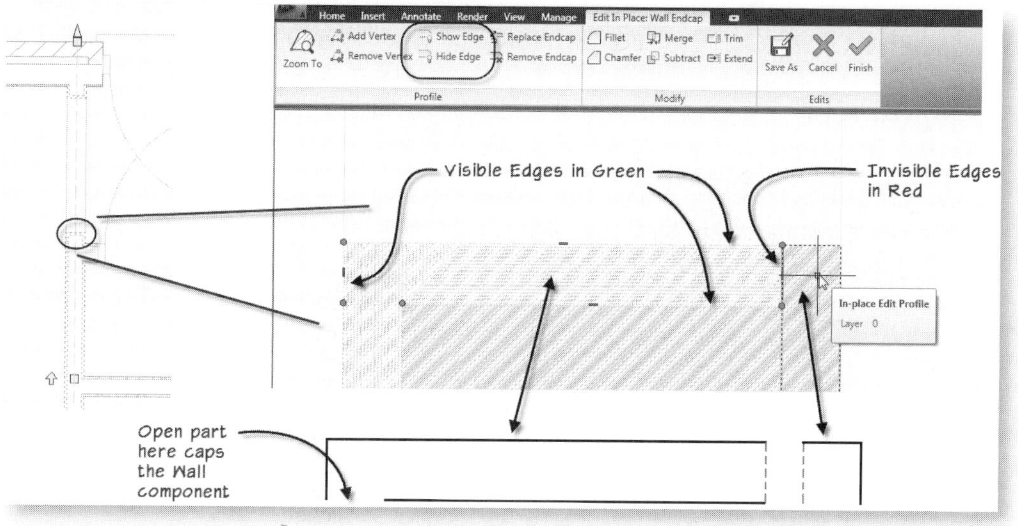

FIGURE 10.24 *Segments with non-zero Width render invisible in the final Endcap*

The lower illustration in the figure shows the shapes independently to help clarify them. The open portion is where the shape connects to the Wall component and the two hidden edges overlap to give the illusion of a wrap-around component.

27. On the ribbon, click the Cancel button to exit without making changes.

Customize a Wall Style

Along the Wall between the existing house and the addition, a new Stud Wall is needed to abut the Masonry Wall of the existing house. Currently, this Wall uses the same Stud Wall style as the other interior Walls. However, it is not likely that a layer of drywall would be installed between the existing brick and the new stud. Therefore, it would be good for us to create a new Wall style that has drywall on only one side. This will also require a custom Endcap for the Openings that penetrate this new Wall.

28. Select the horizontal Wall between the existing house and the addition and, on the Wall contextual ribbon tab, on the General tab, click the ***Save As*** button.

    The "Wall Style Properties" dialog will appear ready to receive edits for the new style.

29. On the General tab, change the name to Stud-4 GWB-0.625 One Side [Stud-102 GWB-018 One Side]. Edit the description as appropriate.

30. Click the Components tab.
31. Select component number 3 – GWB and then click the Remove Component icon (see Figure 10.25).

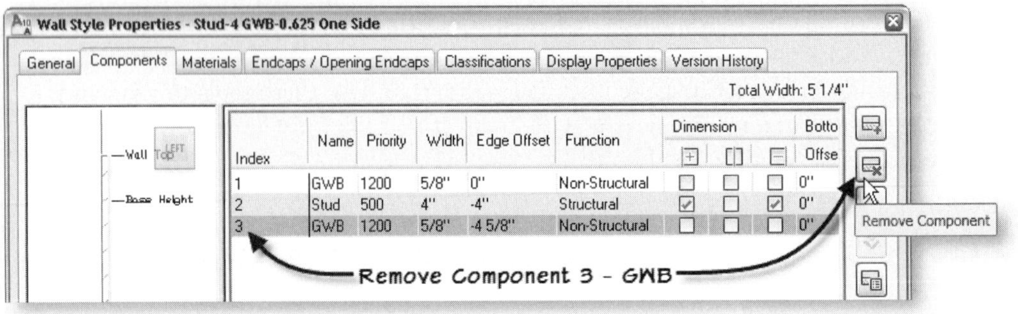

FIGURE 10.25 *Remove one layer of GWB – Component Index number 3*

In some cases, making such an edit would require you to change the dimensions of the components remaining in the style. Refer back to the "Guidelines to Successful Component Composition" listed above. Be certain that all criteria are met before you leave the components tab. In this case, the removal of the second GWB component simply makes the Wall narrower. This is fine in this case since this is what would really occur.

32. Click the Endcaps / Opening Endcaps tab.
33. Change all Endcap entries to **Standard** (see Figure 10.26).

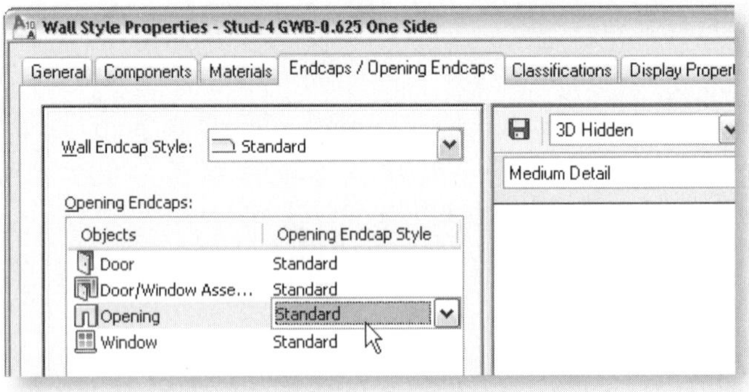

FIGURE 10.26 *Change all Endcap entries to Standard for the new Wall style*

34. Click OK to return to the drawing.

Notice that the Wall got a bit narrower, moving the remaining layer of drywall closer to the existing house. If you click the Wall you can see why. The justification of this Wall is Right. This keeps that bottom face of the Wall touching the existing house no matter what we do to the component composition. This is another good example of choosing your justification carefully (see Figure 10.27).

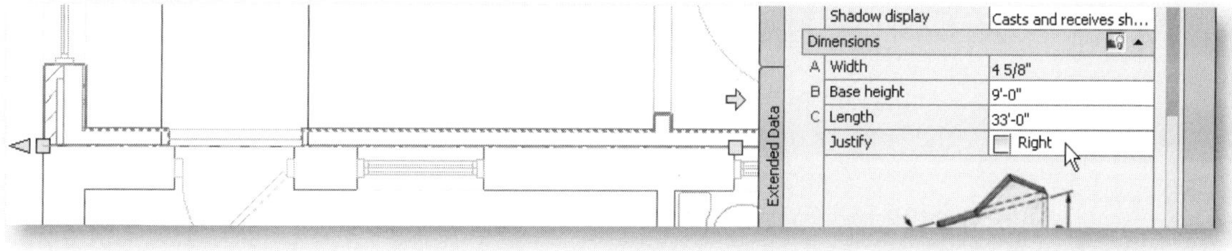

FIGURE 10.27 *The Style is already positioned properly due to careful choice of justification*

Create a Custom Endcap

So far, this process has taken care of removing the unnecessary layer of drywall. However, we now need to build a custom Endcap style for the Openings that penetrate this Wall.

35. Zoom in on the Door between the kitchen and the new addition.
36. Select the horizontal Wall between the existing house and the addition.
37. On the Wall contextual ribbon tab, on the Endcap panel, click the ***Endcap Edit in Place*** tool.
38. At the "Select a point near Endcap" prompt, click near the left side of the Door.
39. Draw a rectangle 5/8" [18] wide by 4" [102] tall in the space next to the Door opening (see item 1 in Figure 10.28).

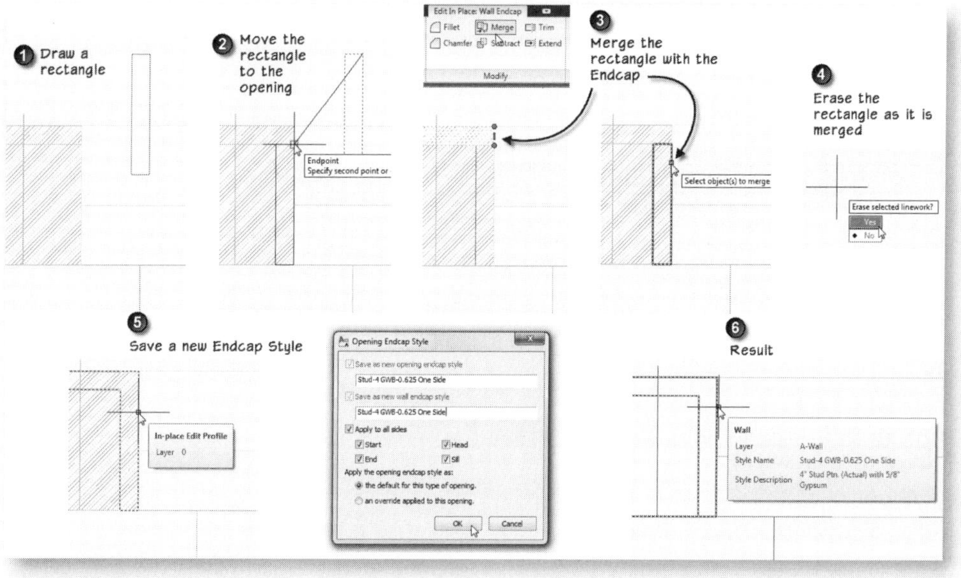

FIGURE 10.28 *Create a new Wall off to the side*

You can draw the rectangle using the tool on the Home tab and relative coordinates.

40. Move the rectangle and snap it to the point between the Stud and GWB components (see item 2 in Figure 10.28).
41. Click near the end of the GWB component on the green Endcap edge.
42. On the Edit In Place: Wall Endcap ribbon tab, on the Modify panel, click the Merge button and then select the rectangle when prompted (see item 3 in Figure 10.28).

43. Press enter to complete the selection. At the "Erase selected linework" prompt, answer Yes (see item 4 in Figure 10.28).
44. On the Edit In Place: Wall Endcap contextual ribbon tab, on the Edits panel, click the ***Save As*** tool and select the profile we just edited at the prompt.
45. In the "Opening Endcap Style" dialog, type **Stud-4 GWB-0.625 One Side [Stud-102 GWB-018 One Side]** in place of Standard (2) in both fields.
46. Accept the remaining defaults and then click OK (see item 5 in Figure 10.28).

The result will be the drywall wrapping over the stud to finish the opening as shown in item 6 in Figure 10.28.

Understand Opening Endcap Styles

So far, we have focused on simple Wall Endcap styles. Openings do not use Wall Endcap styles directly; they actually use an Opening Endcap style, which then references one or more Wall Endcap styles. This is done because you can build an Opening Endcap Style that has a different Wall Endcap at its Sill, its Head and each Jamb.

1. Select the Wall and on the ribbon, click the ***Edit Style*** button.
2. Click the Endcaps / Opening Endcaps tab.

Notice that Endcap assigned to Openings is now the one we just created.

3. At the bottom of the dialog box, click the "Edit the selected Opening Endcap Style" icon (see Figure 10.29).

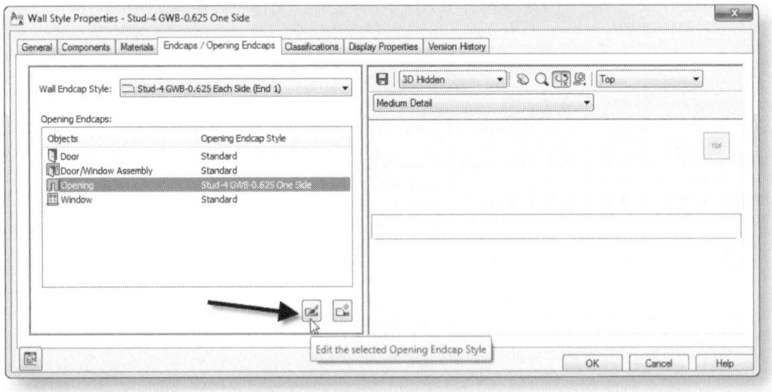

FIGURE 10.29 *Edit the selected Opening Endcap Style*

4. Click the Design Rules tab.

Notice that there are four Positions available. Each can have its own Endcap style assignment. In this case, the Endcap we build above have automatically assigned the same style to each of the four Positions. If you had a different condition for one of them, you could edit it here (see Figure 10.30).

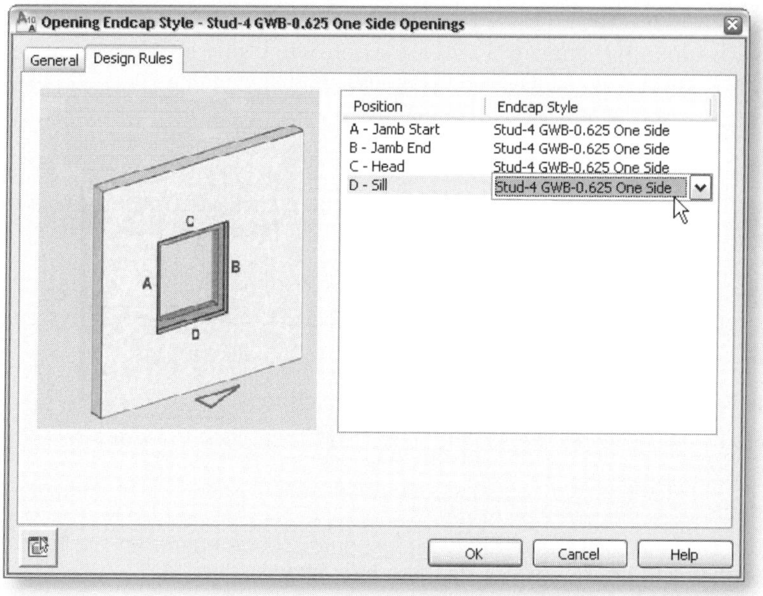

FIGURE 10.30 *Each of four Positions can optionally receive a different Endcap setting*

5. Click OK to return to the Wall Style Properties dialog box.
6. Confirm the Opening Endcap for all Opening Objects is Stud-4 GWB-0.625 One Side [Stud-102 GWB-018 One Side] and then click OK.
7. Zoom out and pan around the drawing to see the result.

Some extra lines show at the door between the existing house and the new addition. This is because there are actually two Walls here: the existing Wall in the *First Floor Existing* Construct XREF and the new Wall in the current file. Opening objects have been added to the new Wall at each of the Door and Window locations between the existing and new house. The two outer lines are this ACA Opening object, and are on their own layer: A-Wall-Open [A-Opening-G]. You can make this layer non-plotting in the Layer Properties Manager by clicking the small Plot\NoPlot icon next to this layer. The third line in the center is the threshold from the existing Door (see Figure 10.31).

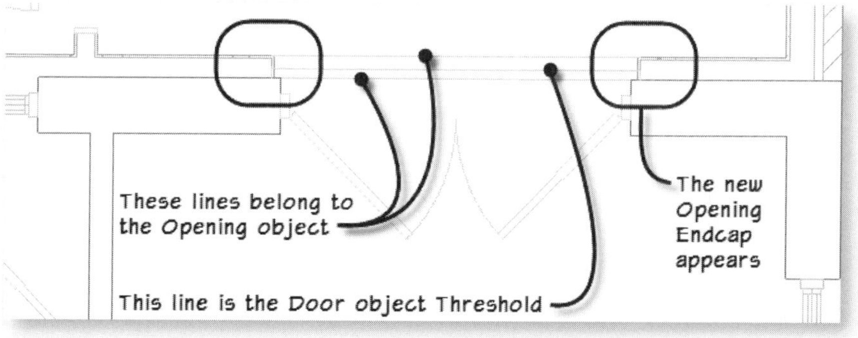

FIGURE 10.31 *The result of the new Wall style and its Custom Endcap*

8. Save the file.

Add a Brick Sill

The possibilities with Opening Endcap Styles are extensive. Using an Endcap Style, we can create Sills for our Windows that penetrate the masonry Walls. To save time, some of the work has been done for you and provided in a file in the *Elements* folder of Project Navigator.

9. On Project Navigator, on the Constructs tab, double-click the *Opening Endcaps* file in the *Elements* folder.

In this file is a segment of the Wall style used in our exterior Wall. A Wall Endcap Style that incorporates a Brick Sill shape has already been defined (using the steps above) and applied as an override to the end of one of the Wall segments.

10. Select the Wall on the right with the Endcap applied to it.
11. On the Home tab, expand the Modify Panel and then click the ***Copy to Clipboard*** tool.
12. Close the file. (It is not necessary to save.)
13. Back in the *First Floor New.dwg* file (which should still be open), on the Home tab, expand the Modify Panel, and click the ***Paste*** tool.
14. Press ESC to cancel the command without placing the pasted Wall.

    This was done as a quick way of importing the Endcap style to the current drawing. You could have used other methods like the Style Manager for example.
15. Select any exterior masonry Wall, on the Wall tab, on the General tab, click the ***Edit Style*** button and then click the Endcaps/Opening Endcaps tab.
16. Click the Add a new Opening Endcap Style icon and on the General tab, name this new style **Stud 5.5 Air-2 Brick-4 Openings** [**Stud-140 Air-050 Brick-090 Openings**].
17. On the Design Rules tab, change Jamb Start, Jamb End and Head to Stud-5.5 Air-2 Brick-4 (End 1) [Stud-140 Air-050 Brick-090 (End 1)].
18. Change Sill to Stud-5.5 Air-2 Brick-4 Sill [Stud-140 Air-050 Brick-090 Sill] and then click OK.
19. Back in the "Wall Style Properties" dialog, assign this new style to Windows and then click OK.

NOTE

Do not add this style to the other Opening types, only Windows.

You will not see the effect of this change in Plan. Furthermore, even if you were to switch to 3D, this change would not yet be readily apparent. This is because by default, this sort of Endcap will show only in High Detail. We need to make a slight modification to the Display Properties of this Wall style to see it in Medium Detail. Wall style display properties are covered next. In the "View Opening Endcaps in 3D" heading below, we will look at our new Opening Endcap Style in 3D.

WALL STYLE DISPLAY PROPERTIES

Chapter 2 stated that the display system determines how AEC objects are displayed under different viewing conditions and circumstances. In the context of Wall styles, the display properties that will concern us are the individual components of the Wall in plan, section, elevation and 3D Model. Within the Display Properties of a Wall, Layer, Color, Lineweight, Hatching, Cut Plane and level of detail are among the myriad of settings available.

Explore Display Properties

1. Select any masonry Wall.
2. Click the Display tab of the Properties palette.

You may recall that in Chapter 2, we learned that the display system contained Configurations, Sets and Representations. In Chapter 2, we explored the display system as a global set of controls that affected the display of the entire drawing and, as such, focused mostly on Configurations and Sets. In this exercise, we will approach display from the other end of the spectrum and consider very specific display characteristics at the object level (of Walls in particular). Therefore, we will be focused entirely on Display Representations in this sequence. Looking at the Display tab, you can see that the active Display representation will vary automatically if you change viewing angle in the drawing (see Figure 10.32).

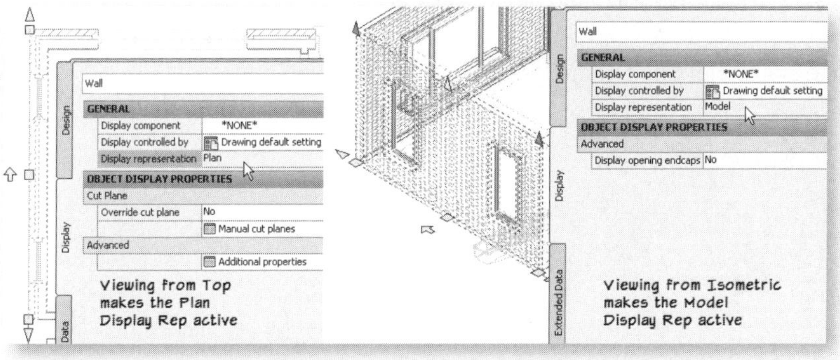

FIGURE 10.32 *The Display representation varies with viewing direction*

There can be several representations for a particular object. When using the Display tab of the Properties palette to edit them, you will see only the active one(s). In general, the various Representations serve the purpose of representing the object in a fashion appropriate to their names. For instance, "Plan High Detail," "Plan" and "Plan Low Detail" are used to represent the object with 2D Plan graphics in three levels of detail. Three similar Representations for 3D Models—"Model High Detail," "Model" and "Model Low Detail"—present 3D model geometry, while "Reflected" gives a reflected ceiling plan display. To see these reps on the Properties palette, change the active Display Configuration using the display configuration pop-up menu on the Drawing Status Bar (see Chapter 2) and then select the wall again.

In the Display controlled by setting, a pop-up list shows the following three possible values:

- **Drawing default setting**—Affects all objects of a particular object class globally that are not overridden at the style or object level. In this case, all Walls regardless of style.
- **Style**—Affects all objects of a particular object class that belong to the same style. In this case, all Walls of the type Stud-5.5 Air-2 Brick-4 [Stud-140 Air-050 Brick-090]. No other Walls would be affected.
- **This object**—Affects *only* the selected object. No other objects are affected regardless of object class or style.

If you still have a wall selected, you can see that the display representation uses the drawing default display properties. This makes managing those properties simple since virtually anything we do while editing this Wall simultaneously affects all other Walls in the drawing.

3. Change the view direction to an isometric view; with a wall selected, click the Display tab of the Properties palette and note the active Display Representation (see right side of Figure 10.32).
4. Open the Display component list.

Note the list of components (see the right side of Figure 10.33).

5. Change the view direction to a plan view and repeat the process.

Note the list of components (see the left side of Figure 10.33).

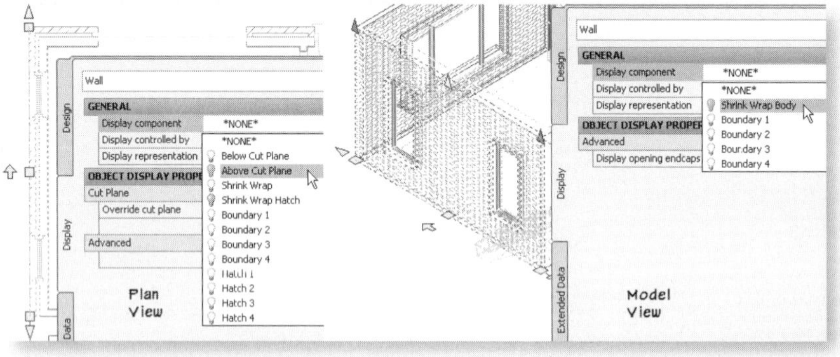

FIGURE 10.33 *Display components vary with the active viewpoint and display representation*

While some of the components were common to both lists, you will notice that the lists do vary. Each display representation has its own list of components, which, in turn, have their own settings. All plan display reps for Walls have the first four components, which are related to the Cut Plane of the Wall. The Cut Plane is a user-definable distance above the floor line from which the floor plan graphics are derived. (We manipulated the Cut Plane of one Wall in the residential project back in Chapter 4.) Each 2D plan representation has its own Cut Plane parameters.

- **Below Cut Plane**—Any edges visible below the Cut Plane height will be rendered to this component.
- **Above Cut Plane**—Any edges visible above the Cut Plane height will be rendered to this component (see Figure 10.34).
- **Shrink Wrap**—A continuous outline drawn around the outermost edge of all of the Walls after cleanup has occurred and derived at the height of the Cut Plane.
- **Shrink Wrap Hatch**—An infill within the shape of the shrink wrap using any standard AutoCAD hatch pattern.

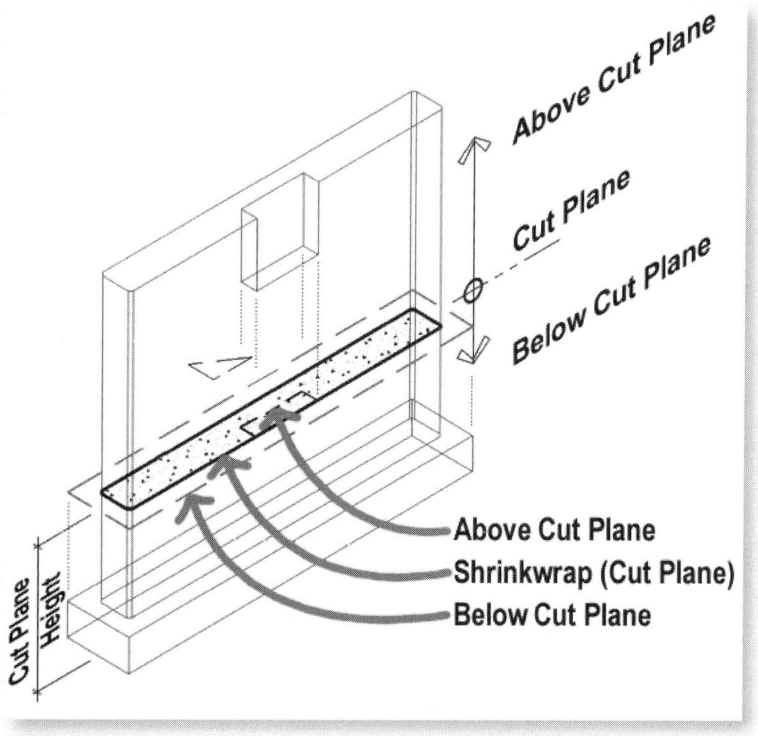

FIGURE 10.34 *How Above and Below Cut Plane components are determined*

> **NOTE**
>
> Keep in mind that even though the content of these components is determined from the 3D Wall body, the resulting Plan graphics are drawn two dimensionally on the X,Y plane at Z = 0.

In addition to the components defined here, notice that there are several "Boundary" components and several corresponding "Hatch" components as well.

6. Select any Boundary or Hatch component (see Figure 10.35).

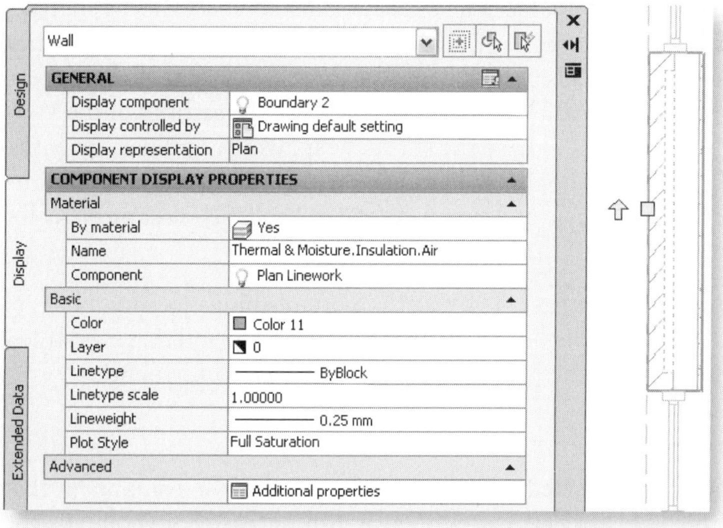

FIGURE 10.35 *Select a component to edit on the Properties palette*

The "lit" lightbulb next to the component name indicates that the component is turned on in the drawing. To change the visibility of a component, open the Display component list and click on the lightbulb icon next to the component name, changing the icon from "lit" to "off" or "off" to "lit". In the "Component Display Properties" grouping, the first section is for Material. In this particular Wall style, the brick is showing as hatched in plan, but the stud shows no hatching. Notice that regardless of the specific boundary or hatch component you have selected, the "By material" setting reads Yes. This means that the component's respective hatching (or lack of it) comes from the Material assigned to that component, not the Wall style itself. Assigning display settings By Material allows the display settings to remain at the drawing default level while still allowing us to differentiate Boundary and Hatch 1 in one Wall Style from any other Style without applying a Style Override to each style. In other words, the By Material setting allows the overall Drawing Default Wall properties to govern all Styles, while also allowing each Style to display its own unique hatching and display parameters.

It is important to understand what is occurring here. Each component can have its own Layer, Color, Linetype, Lineweight and Plot Style settings. Or we can defer all of these settings to the Material Definition. A Material Definition is an ACA style that represents a real-life material such as brick or wood or concrete. By controlling an object's display properties with Materials, we get a more realistic set of plans and models and the management of the display parameters is much simpler. It is simpler because we need to configure the parameters of brick only once in the brick Material definition, rather than having to duplicate those settings in each Wall style that uses brick. Materials are covered in more detail in later chapters.

7. Select the Shrink Wrap component.

Notice that the settings of this component are a little different from those of the Hatch or Boundary components. Specifically, it is not by material, it is assigned to Layer 0, and the other properties are assigned "ByBlock." Every object in AutoCAD is assigned to a Layer, Color, Linetype, Lineweight and Plot Style. Walls are no exception. The layer of Walls in this drawing is A-Wall [A-Wall-G] (the default for ACA). By assigning a component to Layer 0, it is like not assigning it to a layer at all. This means that it defers to the layer of the Wall itself (in this case A-Wall [A-Wall-G]). Likewise, the ByBlock property is a special AutoCAD property that allows the components within the object to likewise defer to the Color, Linetype, Lineweight or Plot style of the object itself. Think of ByBlock as "By Object." Using this property allows individual Walls to hold overrides for these properties if required. If no override is assigned to a specific Wall, then they will use the settings of the Wall layer. The net result in this case is to have the shrink wrap, which outlines the entire Wall (and all adjoining Walls), to appear bolder than the components within (assuming the Lineweight and/or Plot Style of Layer A-Wall [A-Wall-G] is set properly for this to occur).

This may all be a bit confusing at first. The most important things to remember are that the Wall layer is controlling the properties of the shrink wrap and that everything else at the cut plane comes from the Materials assigned to each component.

Using Select Component

In the explorations so far, we selected a Wall and then selected the component that we wanted to edit from the list. In many cases, it will be easier to point to the component directly onscreen. To do this, we will use the Select Component command. You can find this on the right-click menu, or there is an icon for it at the bottom left corner of the Display tab on the Properties palette.

8. On the Display tab of the Properties palette, click the Select Component icon.
9. Click on the brick hatching in one of the exterior Walls (see Figure 10.36).

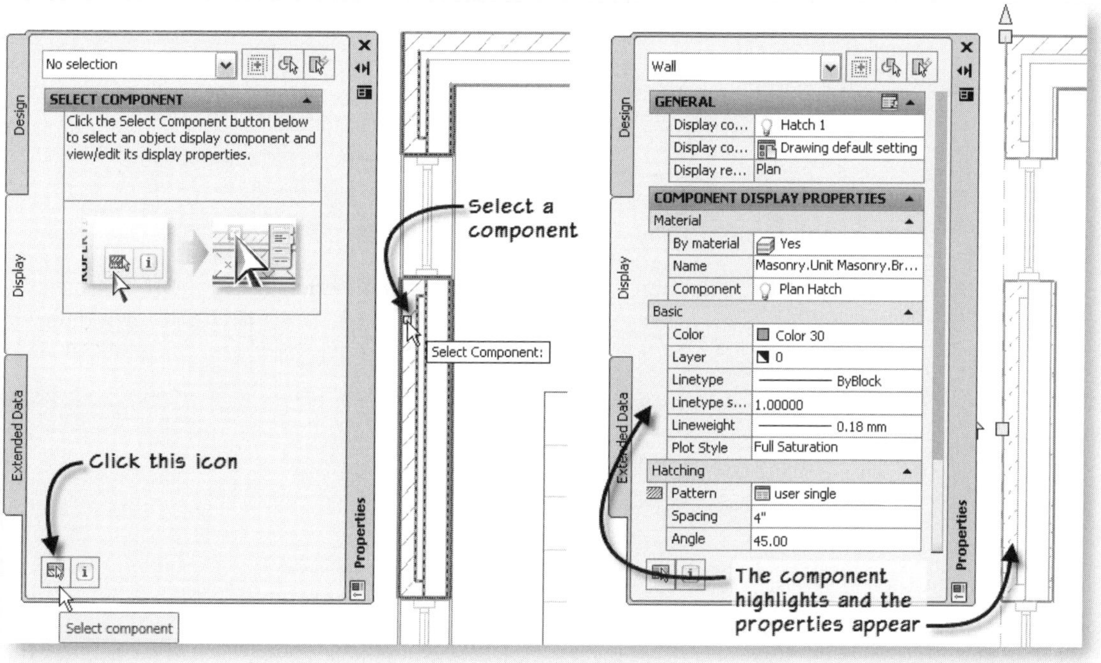

FIGURE 10.36 *Using the Select Component tool to edit display properties*

The advantage of this tool is that you do not need to know the name of the component that you wish to edit. By simply clicking on it, you will be taken directly to the appropriate properties. Note also that when you edit a hatch component that is set to by material (as we have here), the properties that you will edit are those of the Material definition. Therefore, if you were to edit the spacing of the hatching, for example, all brick in the drawing would change, not just the selected Wall.

Apply an Object-Level Display Override

The Cut Plane for all objects is an imaginary plane that sits at a fixed height above Z = 0. All objects are cut at this height to determine their outlines and which graphics to draw in 2D plans. The height of the Cut Plane is 3'-6" [1400] by default. This value is configured on the current Display Configuration (see "Use the Display Manager" topic in Chapter 2 for more details) and applies to all AEC objects. (This is sometimes referred to as "Global Cut Plane.") You may recall that we made an adjustment to the Cut Plane of one of the walls in the existing house back in Chapter 4. Let's review that process now to make a similar adjustment to the abutting Wall on the new construction.

As we saw above, there is a new stud-bearing Wall sistered to the existing masonry Wall for support of the new addition. Since this gives us a double Wall at this location, Openings have been added to the stud Wall where the existing Doors occur.

The same has been done for the Window above the kitchen sink on the left side of the existing plan. However, although it appears as though both Windows are covered over, only the Window in the existing bathroom should be covered over. The reason the Opening is not displaying is that it is inserted above the Display Configuration Cut Plane (3'-6" [1400] by default). To see this, view the Wall in the Object Viewer in 3D. We need to raise the Cut Plane height of this Wall.

10. Select the horizontal stud Wall separating the addition from the existing house.
11. On the Display tab of the Properties palette, for Display controlled by, choose **This object**.

    If a warning dialog appears, click OK.
12. Set the Override cut plane property to Yes (see Figure 10.37).

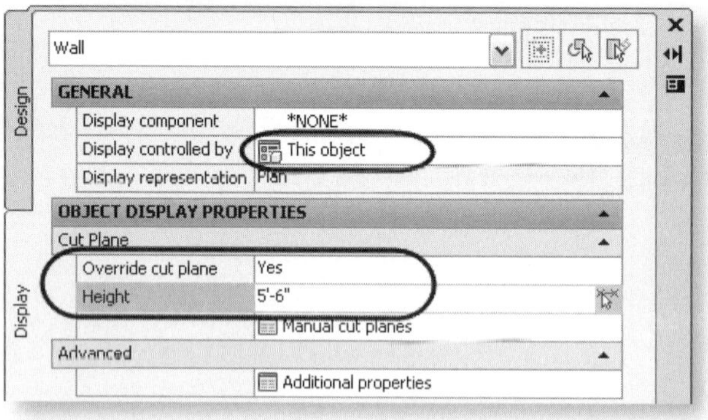

FIGURE 10.37 *Override the Cut Plane for a single Wall*

13. In the Height property that appears, change the value to **5'-6"** [**1650**] (see Figure 10.38).

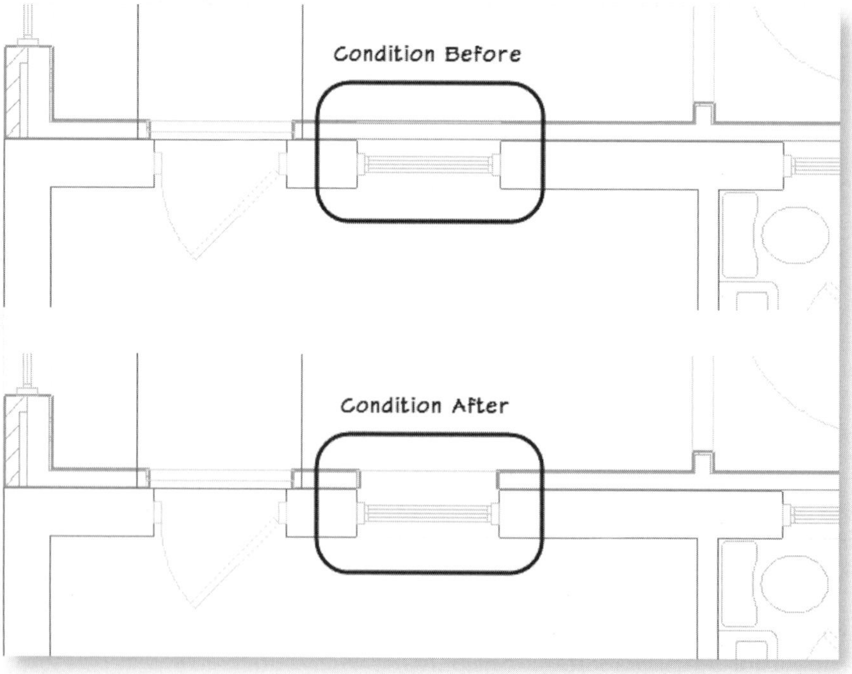

FIGURE 10.38 *The Opening at the kitchen Window now displays in plan*

Notice that the custom Endcap Style that we applied above is now visible at this opening. You may need to zoom in to see it.

View Opening Endcaps in 3D

Recall that we added Sills to the Windows in the masonry Wall, yet we have not seen them. Displaying Endcaps in 3D is within the province of Display Properties.

14. On the floating View panel, click the down arrow icon at the right side of the View split button and choose the ***View, NW Isometric*** tool.

    As an alternative, on the View tab, on the Appearance panel, choose **NW Isometric** from the View list.

    Notice that all of the Walls of the addition are displaying materials.

15. Zoom in on one of the Windows.

    Notice that the Sills are not displaying (see Figure 10.39).

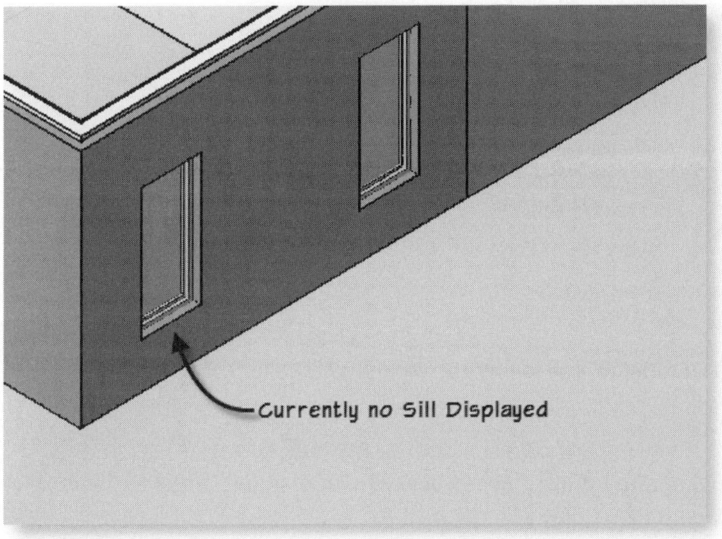

FIGURE 10.39 *When the Windows are viewed in 3D, the Sills do not yet display (shown in Conceptual Visual Style)*

16. On the Drawing Status Bar, click the Display Configuration pop-up menu and choose **High Detail**.

You should immediately see a change in the brick hatching. (Use a Visual Style such as 3D Hidden to see the hatching clearly—the figure, however, is displayed in Conceptual to show the window sills.) It will now be denser and show the mortar as well as the bricks. However, the sill still may not display. If this is the case, the model must be regenerated to force a display update. To do this, use the tool on the View ribbon tab.

17. On the View ribbon tab on the Appearance panel, click the down arrow icon at the right side of the Regenerate split button and select the ***Regenerate Model*** tool and then press ENTER.

The brick sills should display when regeneration is complete. Keep this "Regenerate Model" tool in mind. It is very helpful when you want to force the Display System to recalculate all (or selected) objects in the drawing. This often corrects most display abnormalities. Switching to High Detail has enabled the display of the custom Endcaps, but now everything is more detailed. We can instead modify the Medium Detail display to show Opening Endcaps in 3D if we wish.

18. On the Drawing status bar, click the Display Configuration pop-up menu and choose **Medium Detail**.
19. Select the masonry Wall and click the Display tab of the Properties palette.
20. In the Object Display Properties grouping, set the Display Opening Endcaps property to **Yes** (see Figure 10.40).

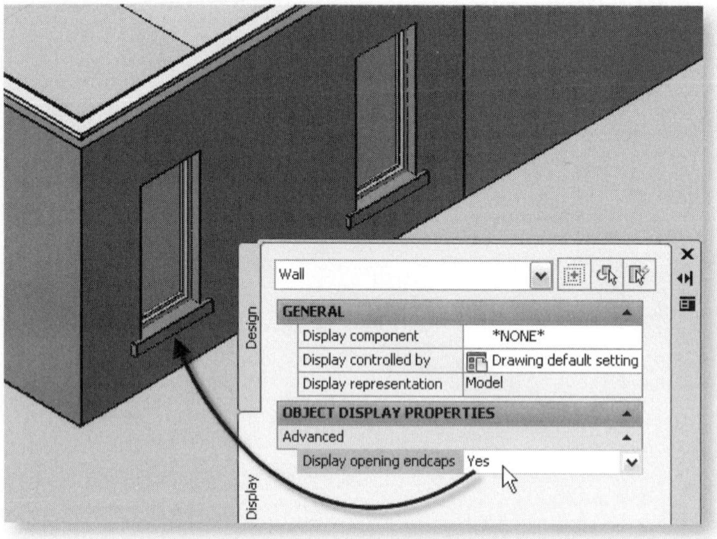

FIGURE 10.40 *With Display Opening Endcaps turned on, Endcaps display in 3D (shown in Conceptual Visual Style)*

Again, use Regenerate Model if necessary to force Medium Detail to display the new settings.

Note that the large picture window on the adjacent wall already shows a sill before this change. This is because the object used for the picture window is actually a Door/Window Assembly object. Door/Window Assembly objects are nearly identical to Curtain Wall objects; and as such, you can define custom frame components for one or more sides of the style. (Curtain Wall Styles were covered in detail in Chapter 8.) In this case, a custom Frame component of the Door/Window Assembly forms the "sill" for this style.

21. On the floating View panel, click the ***View, Top*** tool (or, on the View ribbon tab on the Appearance panel, choose **Top** from the View list).

    If you turned on a Visual Style like Conceptual, go back to 2D wireframe.

NOTE

The Display Opening Endcaps setting is a 3D Model setting only. It will not appear in the Plan view. To make sills appear in Plan, use the Sill Plan Display Rep. More information on the Sill Plan Display Rep is found in the next chapter.

22. Save the file.

DEMOLITION

There are just a few more changes left to be made to the first floor plan. We need to show the items that must be demolished. The simplest way to achieve this is to move the "demo" items to another layer.

Demolish Existing Items

1. Select the *First Floor Existing* XREF, and, on the External Reference contextual ribbon tab, on the Edit panel, click the ***Edit Reference In-Place*** tool.
2. In the "Reference Edit" dialog box, click OK.

   The *First Floor New* file will be gray, and the Edit Reference panel will be added to the current ribbon tab while you are in the XREF Edit mode.
3. Open the Layer Manager and create a new Layer named **A-Demo**.

NOTE

If you followed the recommendations in Chapter 3, your Layer Properties Manager is docked as an anchored palette on the side of your screen. Otherwise, you can click the Layer Properties button on the Home tab.

4. Choose a dashed linetype, a gray color, a .25 mm lineweight and the 50 Percent plot style; then click OK.
5. Select the Door and Window in the kitchen (on the left), the Window in the bathroom and the Stair along the Wall between the new work and the existing.
6. From the Layer list on the Properties palette, choose **A-Demo** (see Figure 10.41).

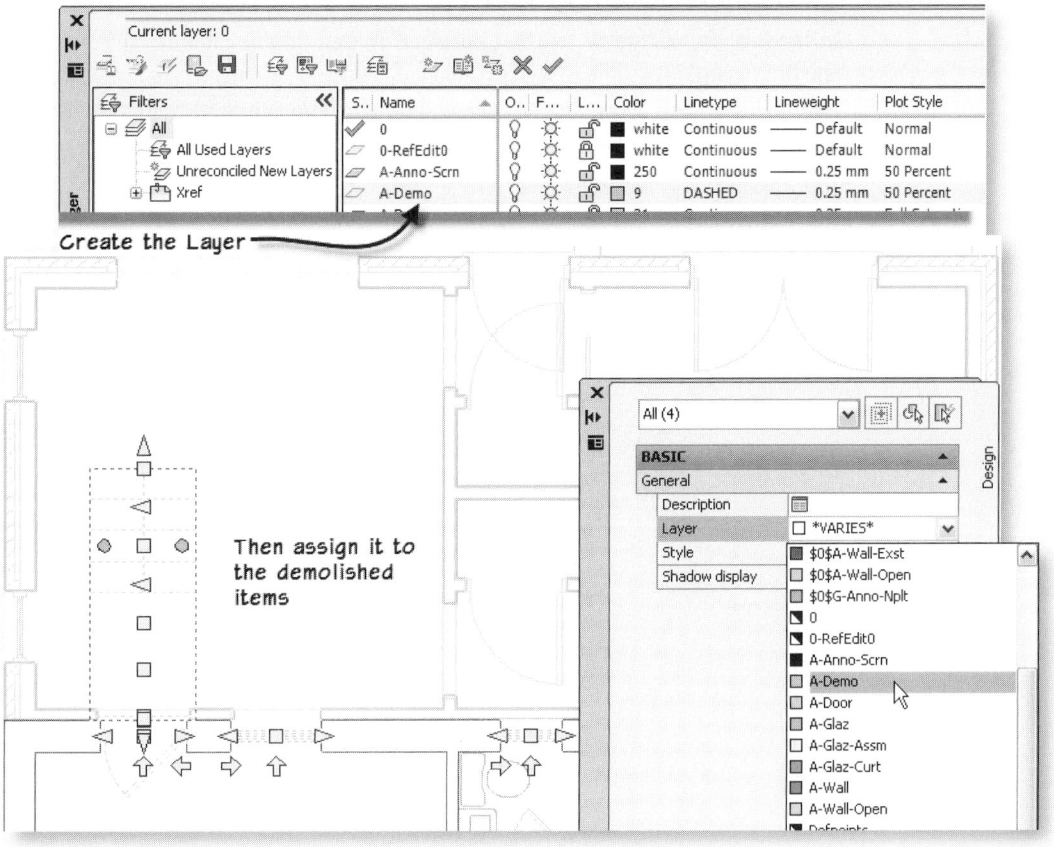

FIGURE 10.41 *Select the items and move them to the A-Demo layer*

7. Right-click and choose **Deselect All**.
8. On the Edit Reference panel, click the ***Save Changes*** tool.
9. Click OK in the confirmation dialog that appears.
10. Save the *First Floor New.dwg* file.

CAD MANAGER NOTE

The layer we have created here is not in strict compliance with U.S. National CAD Standard (NCS) recommendations. If you prefer, you could create A-Door-D, A-Glaz-D and A-Flor-Strs-D layers instead. Each layer can use the same settings. This would make things more compliant with the NCS. You can also use a different layer scheme if your company standard is not the NCS. The exact name of the layer and its settings do not change the overall process.

Demolition Wall Style

These items are now properly showing as demolition. The second floor plan requires a little more demolition. On this plan, we need to remove some of the Walls. We could use the same technique we just covered, but it can also be worthwhile to use a Wall style and tool palette tool specifically for demolition. In Chapter 4 you recall that we created the MACA Residential tool palette. That tool palette contains the Existing Conditions Wall style and the Door/Window Assembly tool that we used in that chapter. It also has a Demolition Wall style on it that we will use now. If you did not load this tool palette, please review the "Load Custom Tool Palette" topic in Chapter 4 before continuing.

Review the Demo Wall Tool Properties

1. On the Project Navigator, in the *Constructs* folder, double-click the *Second Floor New* file to open it.
2. Drag and drop the *Second Floor Existing* file from the Project Navigator into the *Second Floor New* drawing window to overlay the XREF.
3. Right-click on the tool palettes title bar and choose **MasterACA** to load our custom tool palette group.

   Again, please review the "Load Custom Tool Palette" topic in Chapter 4 if you don't have this tool palette group.
4. On the MACA Residential palette, right-click the Demo Wall tool and choose **Properties** (see Figure 10.42).

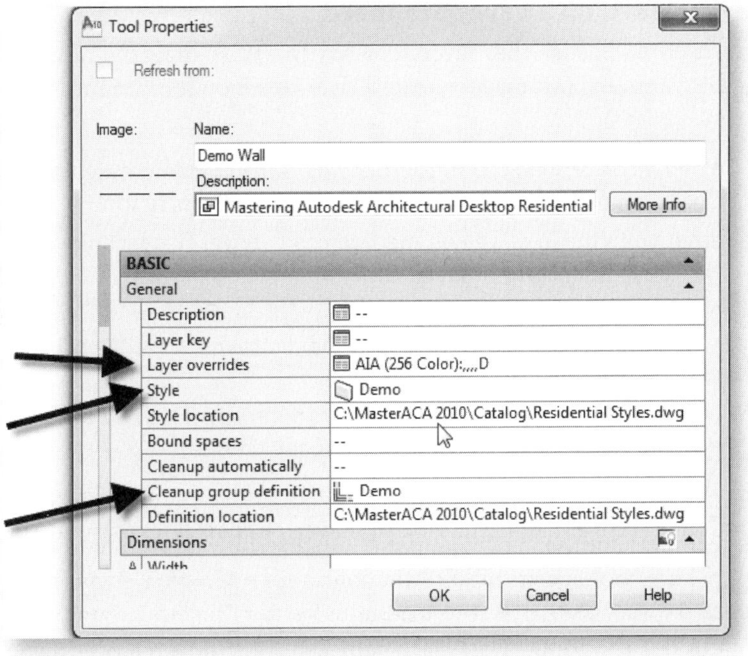

FIGURE 10.42 *The Properties of the Demo Wall tool*

All of the salient features of this tool are evident in the first few fields. In the Basic parameters grouping, we find a Layer override, the Style and the Cleanup group definition. The Wall style is actually quite simple—so simple, in fact, that this tool could just as easily reference the Standard Wall style to similar effect. If you were to edit the Demo Wall style, you would find a simple single component Wall style with variable width. The only difference between its parameters and those of the Standard Wall style is the Cleanup Priority of 100 as recommended in Chapter 9. Also evident in the "Tool Properties" is the use of a "Demo" Cleanup group definition. You may recall the mention of Cleanup Groups in Chapter 9. The function of a Cleanup Group is very simple. Walls will clean up only with other Walls in the same Cleanup Group. If they belong to different groups, they will not clean up. Therefore, using a Demo Cleanup Group allows this Wall style to be used freely and without concern that it will attempt to cleanup with existing or new construction.

Perhaps the most significant setting of this tool is the Layer override. This setting references the rules set by the current Layer Standard to automatically place Walls drawn with this tool on a Wall Demolition layer.

5. Click Cancel when you have finished viewing the settings.

Now that we have seen the way this tool behaves, there is one small issue that we must address. This tool overrides the normal Wall Layer name by adding a suffix to it to indicate that it is Demo. However, it does this using the same parameters that are assigned to the existing Wall Layer. Typically, we would want different settings for a demolition Wall Layer. Therefore, we will create the Wall Demo Layer first and then use the tool. If the Wall Demo Layer already exists in the drawing, the tool will use the existing one rather than create one based on the Wall Layer.

Create a New Layer Based on a Layer Standard

Layer Standards are used to ensure that layers created in ACA drawings use the proper layer naming conventions. It is easy to create a layer based on the current Layer Standard.

6. Select the *Second Floor Existing* file in the drawing, on the External Reference contextual ribbon tab, on the Edit panel, click the ***Open Reference*** tool.

   This is an alternative to the in-place edit method used above. This technique actually opens the file in a separate window. Either approach is perfectly valid. It is a matter of personal preference.

7. On the Layer Properties Manager, at the top of the dialog, click the "New Layer from Standard" icon (see the top of Figure 10.43).
8. In the "New Layer from Standard" dialog, choose AIA Version 3 [BS1192 Descriptive] from the Layer Standard list (if it was not already chosen).

The layer name defaults to A-Wall. We will start with this, add a Status field to the end of the name and change the parameters of the layer to display as desired for demolition.

9. Click the small browse icon (...) next to the Status field.
10. From the Status list, choose **D**, "Existing to demolish" [**R**, "To be removed"] and then click OK.
11. In the bottom of the dialog, assign Color to **9**, Plot Style to **50 Percent**, Linetype to **Hidden2** and Lineweight to **.25mm** (see Figure 10.43).

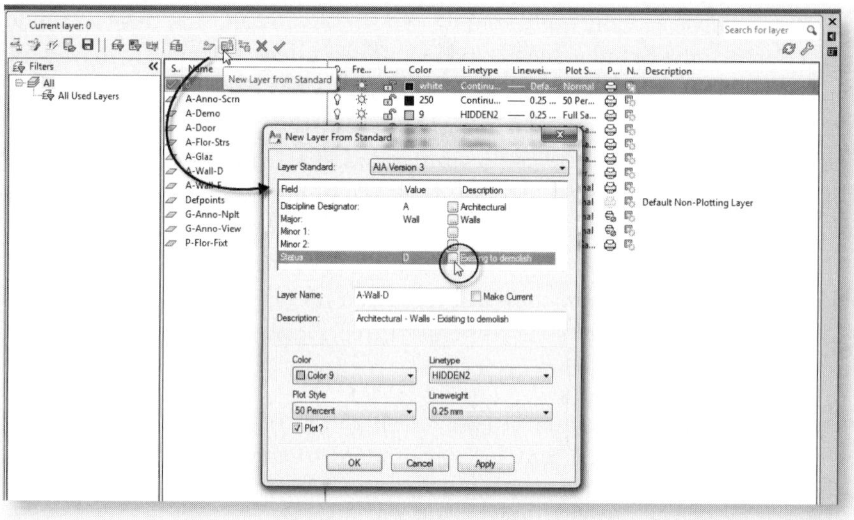

FIGURE 10.43 *Create a new layer based upon a Layer Standard*

12. Click OK to accept the new layer and return to the drawing.

MANAGER NOTE CAD

To implement the Demo Wall tool properly, you should edit the Layer Key style for your firm. A Layer Key style is a collection of instructions on which layers should be auto-created by AutoCAD Architecture and how they should be configured. The reason that we had to build this layer is because it is not included in this default Layer Key style. The default Layer Key style is imported into a drawing automatically from a static location on your user's hard drive or a network server. In most cases you will want to move it to the server so that there is only one file to keep up to date. (See the "Layer Standards" topic in Chapter 3 for more information.) Regardless of the location of the default Layer Key style, if you edit it to include a Layer Key for the custom tools that you create, you can reference those Layer Keys and/or Overrides in the tool Properties. This would prevent you from having to include the Layers in your template or project files. For instance, in this case, if a WallDemo Layer Key had been established in the default Layer Key style, it would have been unnecessary to include the A-Wall-D Layer in the current file. For complete recommendations on layer standards, refer to Chapter 5 in *Autodesk Architectural Desktop: An Advanced Implementation Guide* by Paul F. Aubin and Matt Dillon.

Test the Demolition Wall Tool

Now that we have our Wall Demo Layer defined, we are ready to test the Demo Wall tool.

13. On the MACA Residential tool palette, click the Demo Wall tool.
14. Click a random point outside the building to the left.
15. Click another point on the right side of the building.

    Allow the Wall to pass diagonally through the building and cross through several of the other Walls.
16. Add another segment or two in any direction (see Figure 10.44).

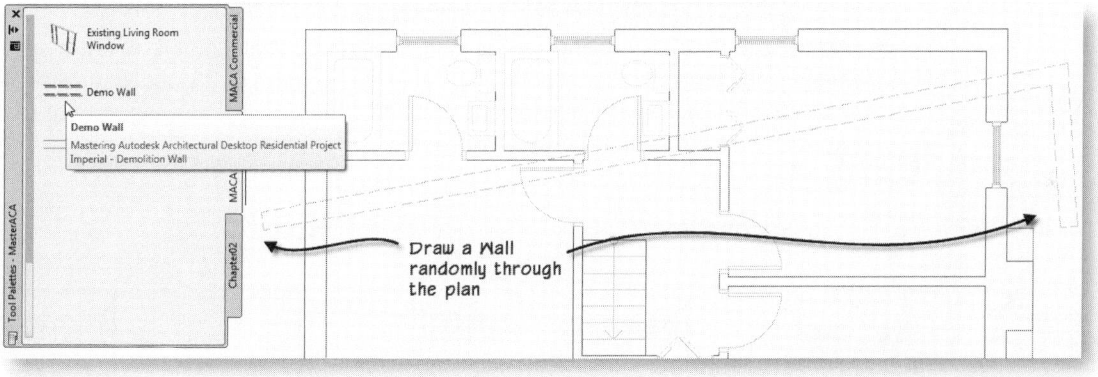

FIGURE 10.44 *Draw a few random Demo Walls*

17. Press ENTER to end the Add Wall command.

View the result. Notice that the segments of Demo Wall have properly cleaned up with one another but have completely ignored the other Walls. The Demolition Cleanup Group defined with the Demo Wall style governs this behavior. Also notice that the Demo Walls are properly displaying on the Demolition layer with a gray dashed linetype.

18. Erase the Demo Walls just drawn.

Demolish Existing Walls by Applying Tool Properties

19. Turn on the Justification Display as covered in Chapter 9 (select any Wall, and on the ribbon, click the Justification Display button).

    The Graph lines will make the next several steps easier.

20. On the Home tab, expand the Modify panel and click the Break tool (or type **BR** and press ENTER at the Command Line).
21. Select the existing horizontal Wall at the bathrooms at the top of the plan where the new and existing construction meet.
22. Right-click in the drawing and choose **First point** (or type **F** and press ENTER at the Command Line).
23. At the "Specify first break point" prompt, snap to the point where the closet Wall and outside Wall meet (see Figure 10.45).

NOTE Notice how easy it is to pick the desired point by snapping to the Graph line endpoint.

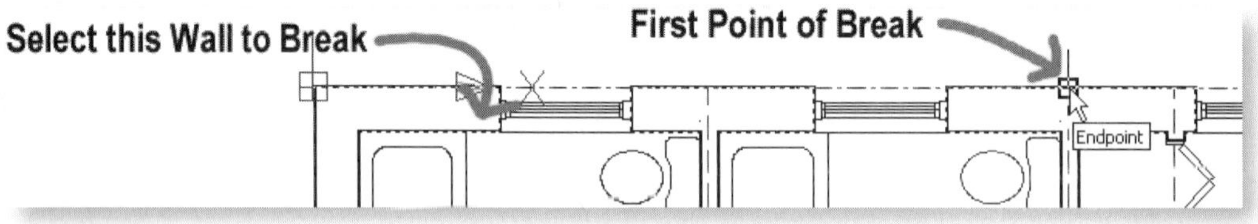

FIGURE 10.45 *Select the Wall to Break and use the "Specify the first point" option*

24. Click the same point again for the second point.

    The Wall segment has now been broken into two segments.

25. Repeat the Break command on the same horizontal Wall and break out a segment of the horizontal bathroom Wall equal to the width of the abutting vertical Wall (see Figure 10.46). Choose your first and second points at endpoints of the vertical Wall separating the two bathrooms.

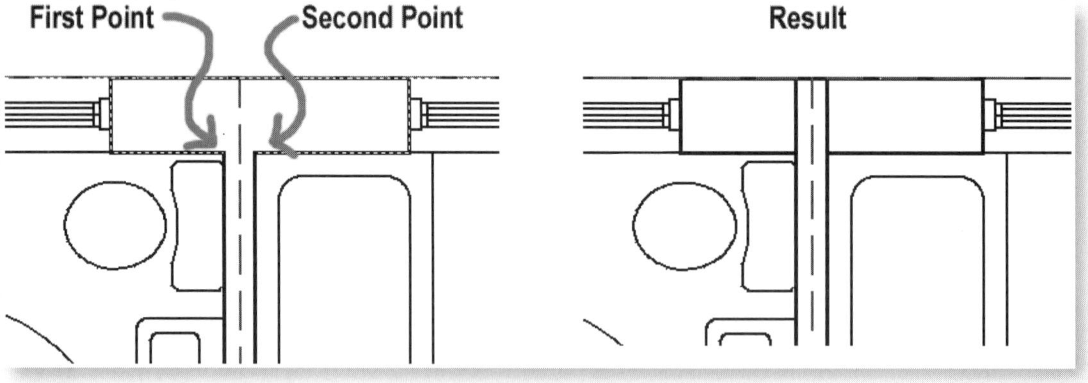

FIGURE 10.46 *Use Break to remove a small segment of Wall*

26. Select the two horizontal exterior bathroom Walls.
27. On the MACA Residential tool palette, right-click the Demo Wall tool and choose **Apply Tool Properties to > Wall**.

    Notice that the Demo Walls now overlap the existing ones.
28. Use the Wall Lengthen grips (the triangular ones) to adjust the Demo Walls as shown in Figure 10.47.
29. Follow the steps above to change the layer of the two Windows and the bathtub on the left to the A-Demo layer.
30. Toggle the Wall Justification Display off.

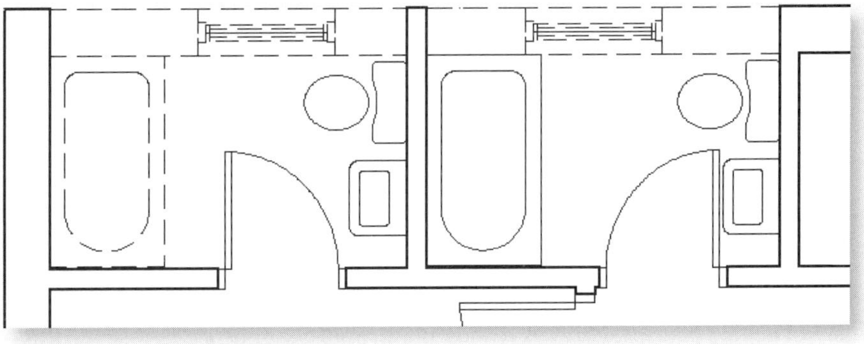

FIGURE 10.47 *Fine-tune how the Existing and Demo Walls meet*

31. Save and close the file.

    When you close the file, you will return to the *Second Floor New* file, which was left open in the background. A message should appear in the bottom right corner of the screen alerting you that the XREF has changed.
32. Click on this message to reload the *Second Floor Existing* XREF (see Figure 10.48).

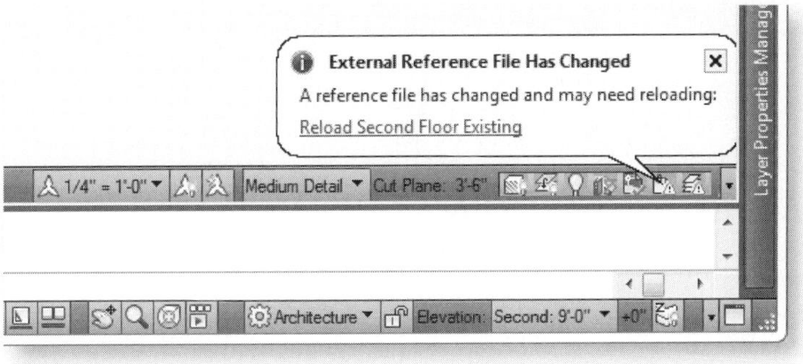

FIGURE 10.48 *An alert pops up to let you know an XREF has changed*

COMPLETE THE SECOND FLOOR PLAN REFINEMENTS

The second floor plan looks much like the first did at the start of this chapter. All of the Walls currently use the Standard style. Rather than repeat all of the steps that we performed on the first floor, we can save time by reusing the styles that we developed there. To do this, we will make tools from the styles that we used on the first floor. This will help us maintain consistency throughout the project and streamline workflow. We will also need to create a new Wall style for the second floor patio condition that does not occur on the first floor.

Create Custom Tools

The styles from which we will create our tools currently reside in the *First Floor New* Construct file. You can create tools directly from this file if you like, but if you are working in a team of more than one person, then it is best not to have tools reference their styles directly from project drawing files, but rather a separate dedicated "library" file instead. Even if you are the only one on the project, maintaining separate library files can still be considered "best practice."

Look back to above and the entry next to the Style setting. The styles referenced in that tool point to a drawing located in the *C:\MasterACA 2010\Catalog* folder and called *Residential Styles.dwg*. This is the "library" file provided for this project. A library file is just a drawing file that contains styles and content. It can be stored in any location that is convenient to the project team. The location is typically on a network server. In this example, we will simply add the Wall styles from the first floor to this same library file and then create tools from them. This will make the styles easy to use in other project drawings.

1. On the Project Navigator, on the Constructs tab, double-click the *First Floor New* Construct to open it.

   If you left *First Floor New* open above, this action will simply switch to this file.

There are several ways to copy styles from one file to another. The two most common are using the Style Manager or Copy and Paste. Let's use the Copy and Paste method.

2. Select one of the exterior brick Walls, one interior stud partition (with GWB on both sides) and the single stud wall with GWB on only one side (between the new and existing construction).
3. With all three Walls selected, on the Home tab, expand the Modify panel and then click the Copy to Clipboard tool (or press CTRL + C) (see Figure 10.49).

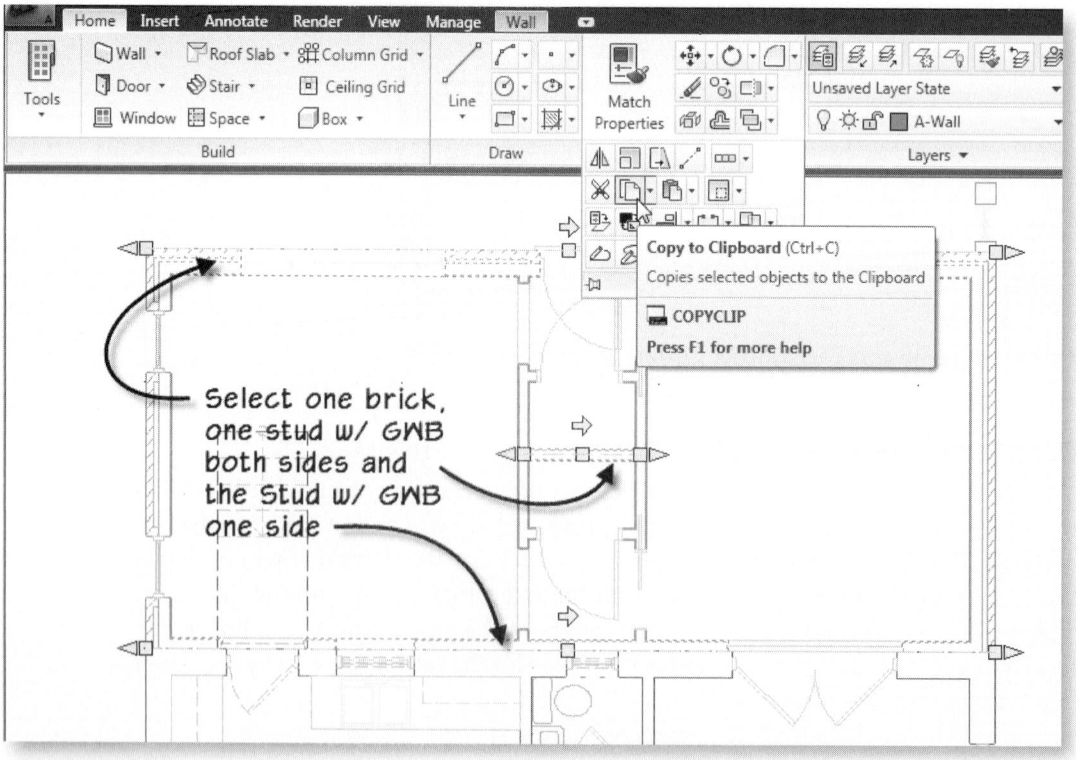

FIGURE 10.49 *Copy one of each type of Wall from the First Floor New file*

4. On the QAT, click the Open icon.
5. Browse to the *C:\MasterACA 2010\Catalog* folder.
6. Select *Residential Styles.dwg* [*Residential Styles - Metric.dwg*] and then click Open.

This file contains one of each of the objects that are currently included on the MACA Residential palette. We need to copy the additional styles from the *First Floor New* file over to this file before making tools from them.

7. Right-click and choose **Clipboard > Paste** and click a point anywhere onscreen to paste the Walls.

   Zoom as necessary to place them in a convenient spot. The exact location is not important.

If you wish, you can adjust the lengths of the Walls to more closely match those of the Walls already in the file. You can also add text labels to them like the other objects. These steps are not required, but they do make for a cleaner library file. The labels in this file use field codes. To add a field, add a piece of text; and while editing it, right-click and choose **Insert Field** (or press CTRL + F). Choose Objects for the category and click the Select Object icon. Select the Wall and then in the Field dialog, choose the property you want to report, such as the Style name.

8. Save the *Residential Styles* [*Residential Styles – Metric*] file.

TIP

Always remember to save before creating tools.

Make sure the MACA Residential palette is active and turn off auto-hide.

9. Click on the first pasted Wall and drag it to the Project Tools palette (see Figure 10.50).

   Be sure to not click a grip when you drag.

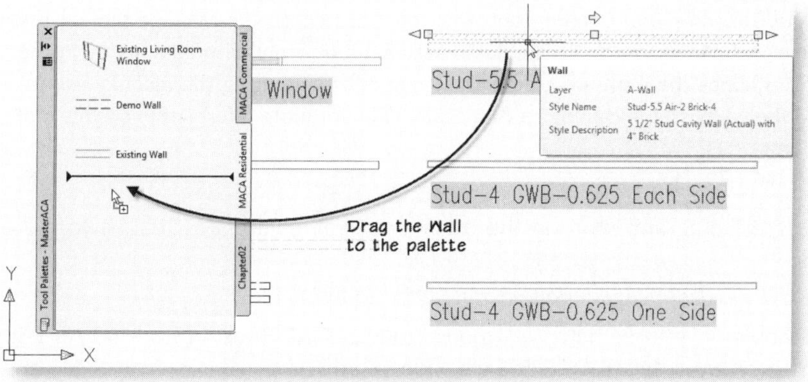

FIGURE 10.50 *Drag a Wall to the palette to make a tool*

A new Wall tool should appear. Previous chapters have noted that we can make tools in two ways: we can drag a style from Style Manager and drop it on a palette, or we can drag an object from the drawing and drop it on a palette. In both cases, the result is nearly the same. They vary slightly in the defaults that will be written to the new tool.

10. Right-click on the new tool and choose **Properties** (see Figure 10.51).

Notice that the Wall Style and Style location correctly reference the current file and Wall Style. Scroll down a bit and notice that both the Base height and the Justify parameters have been set automatically to match the Wall that was dragged. This will be useful later when we apply the tool properties to the Walls in the *Second Floor New* file.

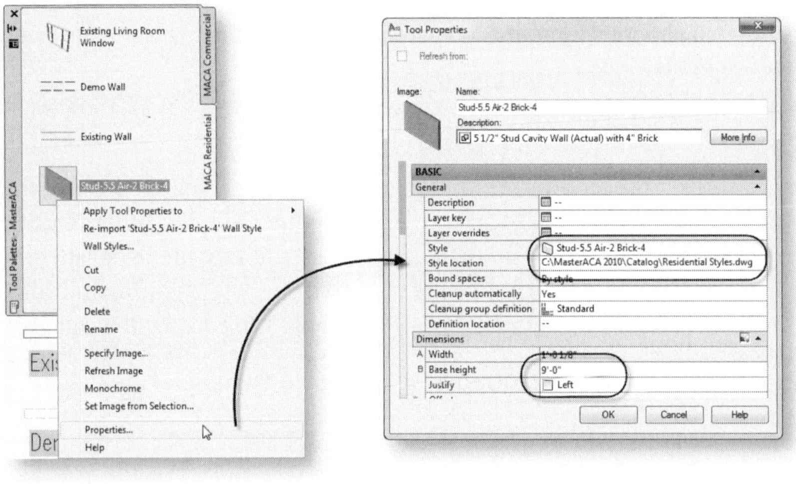

FIGURE 10.51 *Properties of a tool dragged from an object match the properties of the original object*

11. Click OK to dismiss the Tool Properties worksheet.

CAD MANAGER NOTE

You can edit several tools' common properties at the same time. To do this, hold down the CTRL key, select two or more tools of the same type (such as two or more Wall tools), right-click and choose Properties. You can then edit common parameters as appropriate, such as Width, Base height or Justify. This makes creating several tools with custom properties quick and easy. Furthermore, if you wish to create several tools from the styles in a file, you can use the Generate Tool Catalog tool. This tool, located on the Manage tab, on the Customization panel allows you to create tools automatically from all of the styles in the drawing or folder. Once the tools are created, you can edit them using the techniques outlined here and then publish the catalog to your team. Look for more information on this tool in the online help.

12. Repeat the drag and drop on the other two Wall objects to create two more tools.
13. Save the *Residential Styles* [*Residential Styles – Metric*] file.

    You should have three new Wall tools: Stud-5.5 Air-2 Brick-4 [Stud-140 Air-050 Brick-090], Stud-4 GWB-0.625 Each Side [Stud-102 GWB-018 Each Side] and Stud-4 GWB-0.625 One Side [Stud-102 GWB-018 One Side].

We now have our tools that correctly reference styles in the *Residential Styles* [*Residential Styles – Metric*] file. If you are a single-person firm or have a single-person project team, you do not need to do anything else. You can use the tools as configured directly from the MACA Residential palette. However, if you wish to share the same collection of tools with several members of a project team, proceed to the next topic to learn how to create a linked-shared tool palette.

Set Up a Shared Tool Palette

Now that we have tools created, we want to make them accessible to all project team members. To do this, we access or create a catalog in Content Browser and then copy our palette or tools there. You should start with just a single catalog for all office-wide custom tools. However, depending on how many custom tools and palettes you anticipate creating, you may wish to have more than one catalog. For example, you could have a catalog for commercial projects and another for medical jobs. You create a catalog following a procedure similar to the steps covered in the "Load Custom Tool Palette" topic in Chapter 4. In the "Add Catalog" dialog, instead of choosing the "Add an existing catalog or web site" option (shown in Figure 4.43 in Chapter 4), choose the "Create a new catalog" option. Be sure to browse to a server location and give it a good name.

A new catalog will appear with a generic blue cover icon. Remember where you saved it, as you will need to share this information with your team later. Right-click the new catalog and edit its properties. To add a custom image, create a TIF, TIFF, PNG, JPG or BMP image about 90 pixels by 120 pixels. Right-click the image in the "Catalog Properties" dialog and choose Specify Image to designate your custom image. At the bottom of the dialog, check the "Link items when added to workspace" checkbox if you want the palette(s) in the ACA workspace to be refreshable. This means that users of the palettes are essentially "subscribing" to the palettes and if they change on the server, the users simply click the refresh icon on the corner of the palette to download the latest changes (see Figure 10.52).

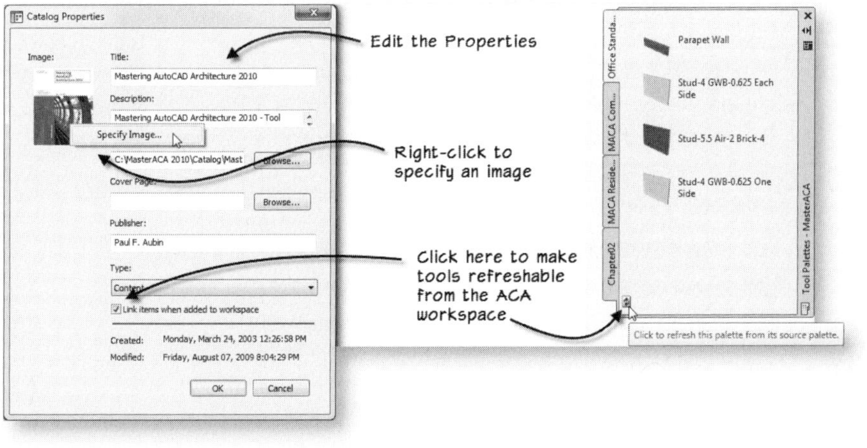

FIGURE 10.52 *Create a catalog in Content Browser and a linked palette in ACA*

After you have finished creating your catalog on the server, you can either drag and drop or copy and paste palettes and tools to it. While it is possible to add freestanding tools, adding full palettes is more efficient when there are many tools. After you have tested everything to make sure it is functioning properly, simply inform your team where the catalog is located on the server. They can follow the steps in Chapter 4 to add the catalog to their Content Browser Library. Then drag and drop the palettes to their ACA workspace. If you set the catalog to be linked, they can click the refresh icon when you make changes to update their copies.

Apply Tool Properties to Another File

Our tools and their palettes are now ready to be used.

14. If the *Second Floor New* file is not open, double-click it on the Project Navigator to open it now.
15. Using the technique covered above in the "Demolish Existing Walls by Applying Tool Properties" topic, break the two Walls (top horizontal and left vertical) as indicated by the "Break here" notes onscreen.

TIP **Remember to toggle the Justification Display to make it easier to break at the correct point.**

Erase the two "Break here" notes when finished.

16. On the MACA Residential tool palette, right-click the Stud-5.5 Air-2 Brick-4 [Stud-140 Air-025 Brick-090] tool and choose **Apply Tool Properties to > Wall**.
17. At the "Select Wall(s)" prompt, click the three exterior Walls shaded dark in Figure 10.53 and then press ENTER.

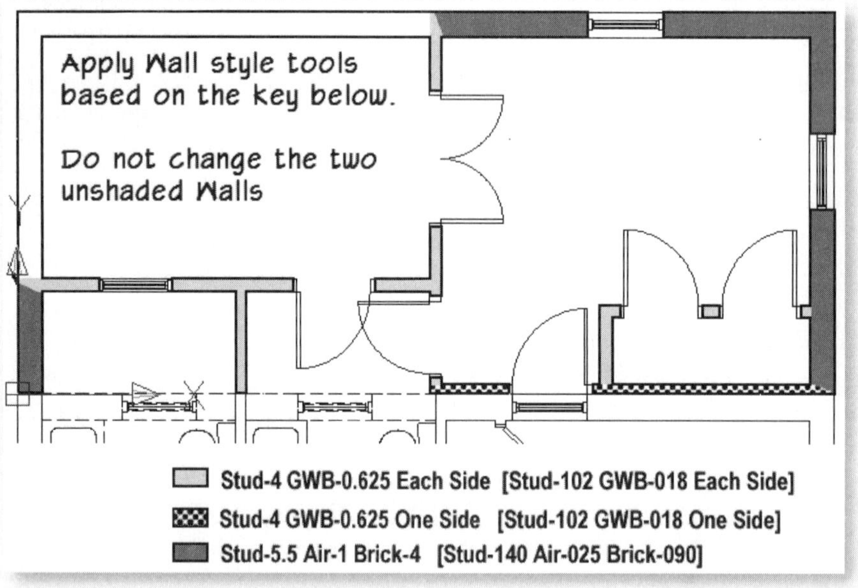

FIGURE 10.53 *Apply the new Wall tools to the existing Walls*

18. Following the key in Figure 10.53, repeat these steps for the remaining Walls.

    Do not change the two unshaded Walls at the top left of the plan.

Override an Endcap

19. Zoom in on and select the new section of Wall between the two bathrooms.
20. On the Wall tab, expand the Endcap panel and click the Override Endcap Style button.
21. At the "Select a Point" prompt, click a point at the end of the Wall where the new and old Walls meet.
22. In the "Select an Endcap Style" dialog box, choose Standard and then click OK.

Notice the change. This technique quickly removes the unnecessary layer of drywall between new and existing construction.

23. Adjust the justification of any of the Walls as required.

Building a Custom Wall Style from Scratch

To complete the second floor and this chapter, we will build a complete Wall style from scratch. It is rare that you will need to build a Wall style from scratch; in most cases, you can modify an existing one more quickly (as we did above). Nonetheless, it is beneficial to chronicle the steps needed to build your own style. In this exercise, we will build a parapet Wall style for the patio on the second floor. We will then apply it to the two remaining Standard Walls (at the top and left of the plan).

Create a New Style

To be consistent with our approach, let's build the new Wall Style for the patio parapet in the Style Library file for the project. This will make it easy to create a tool for it following the same procedure outlined above. It will also keep all of our project's styles in a nice, tidy location. Remember the "rules" above: Be consistent!

1. From the Application Menu, choose *Residential Styles.dwg* [*Residential Styles - Metric.dwg*] from the Open Drawings list.

   If you closed the file above, on the QAT, click the Open icon, browse to the *C:\MasterACA 2010\Catalog* folder, select *Residential Styles.dwg* [*Residential Styles - Metric.dwg*] and then click Open.
2. Select any Wall onscreen. On the Wall tab, click the Edit Style drop-down button and then choose **Wall Styles**.
3. On the right side of the Style Manager, right-click and choose **New**. (There is also a New Style icon on the Style Manager toolbar.)
4. Type **Parapet Wall** for the Name of the new style.
5. Click on the Parapet Wall style to edit it.
6. On the right side, choose the General tab, type **Mastering AutoCAD Architecture Residential Project Patio Parapet Wall** for the Description.

Use the Wall Style Components Browser

7. Click the Components tab.

This Wall style will have three components: two wythes of brick and a stone cap. We could define each of these components from scratch, but it will be easier to use the Wall Style Browser to locate existing components that have already been defined and copy them to our new style. We can then modify them as required for the current design.

8. On the right side of the Component tab, click the Wall Style Browser icon (the one at the bottom).

The "Wall Style Components Browser" is organized much like the Style Manager. It has a tree view at the left and a list view and viewer at the right. By expanding the Wall styles listed at the left, you can drag and drop components from existing styles to use in the one you are creating. Currently, the left tree view is showing the styles that reside in the current drawing. We need to create two brick components. One of the existing Wall styles has brick in it, so let's start by copying this component to our new style.

9. In the tree of the Wall Style Components Browser, select Stud-5.5 Air-2 Brick-4 [Stud-140 Air-050 Brick-090].

   This will list all of its components on the right (see Figure 10.54).

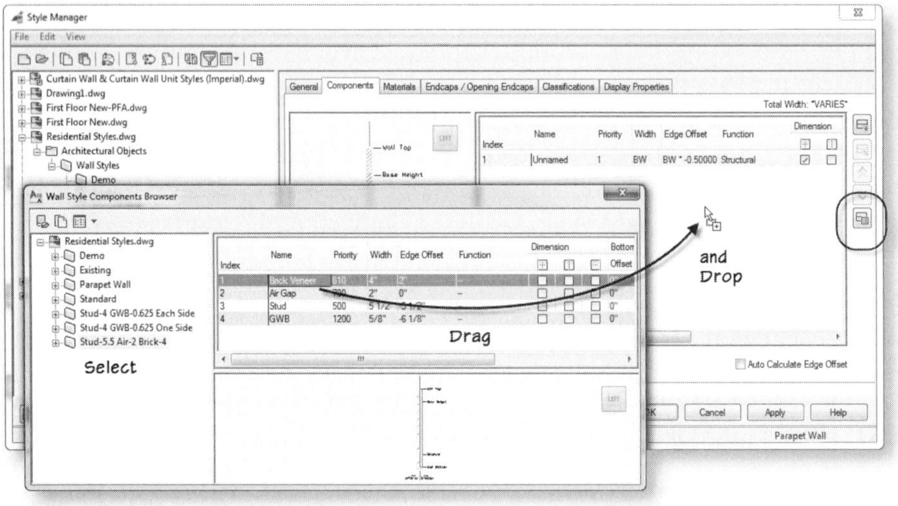

FIGURE 10.54 *Browsing Wall style components*

10. Drag Brick Veneer from the "Wall Style Components Browser" and drop it in the Wall Style Editor (anywhere on the Components list).
11. At the top of the Wall Style Components Browser, click the Open Drawing icon.

    The dialog box should default to the last location that you were browsing, which should be the *Catalog* folder.
12. Click the Content icon in the icon bar at left and navigate to your *Styles* folder and then to either *Imperial* or *Metric* depending on your preference.
13. Open the *Wall Styles – Brick (Imperial).dwg* [*Wall Styles – Brick (Metric).dwg*] file.
14. In the tree of the Wall Style Components Browser, select Brick-4 Brick-4 [Brick-090 Brick 090].
15. Drag the Brick Veneer (Structural) component from the Wall Style Components Browser and drop it in the Wall Style Editor anywhere on the Components list.
16. Repeat the process and open the *Wall Styles - Concrete (Imperial)*.dwg [*Wall Styles - Concrete (Metric).dwg*] file.
17. In the tree of the Wall Style Components Browser, select Concrete-10 [Concrete-250].
18. Drag the Concrete component from the Wall Style Components Browser and drop it in the Wall Style Editor anywhere on the Components list.

    Those are all of the "raw" components that we will need.
19. Close the Wall Style Components Browser.
20. Click the Materials tab.

Notice that all of the Materials are already assigned to each component. When you use the Wall Style Components Browser to create your components you gain many benefits:

- The basic sizes and parameters are already set.
- The names are always consistent.

- The Cleanup Priorities are properly configured.
- All Material Definitions are already assigned.

21. Click back to the Components tab.

    Now we need to make some adjustments to the dimensions because all of these components are on top of one another.

22. Select the Unnamed component and then click the Remove Component icon at the right.

The Unnamed component is the default component added to all Wall Styles when created from scratch. It cannot be deleted if it is the only component in the style, which is why we add the new components first and then delete it here. We can adjust the order of the components in any way that suits us.

23. Using the Up and Down arrow buttons on the right, organize the components so that the Brick Veneer component comes first (index 1), Brick Veneer (Structural) is next (index 2) and Concrete is last (index 3).

Earlier this chapter outlined several points to consider when building a Wall style. One that we must decide on before we can continue is where we wish our new Wall Style's Baseline to be. Remember that the Baseline is the "zero point" of the Wall. For this Wall style, it will be most useful to have the Baseline at the face of the brick. This way, we can easily flush the brick from this Wall with the adjacent Walls.

24. Change the values of each component as shown in Table 10.1 and Figure 10.55.

TABLE 10.1 *Parapet Wall Style Component Parameters*

		Bottom Elevation		**Top Elevation**	
	Edge Offset	**Offset**	**From**	**Offset**	**From**
1-Brick Veneer	-4" [-90]	0	Wall Bottom	2'-6" [850]	Baseline
2-Brick Veneer (Structural)	-8" [-180]	0	Wall Bottom	2'-6" [850]	Baseline
3-Concrete	-9" [-215]	2'-6" [850]	Baseline	3'-0" [1000]	Baseline

TIP

You should maximize the width of the Style Manager as wide as your screen will allow so it is easy to work with. You can type the values for the Edge Offsets directly into the fields or use the Offset Increment icons beneath the viewer. The Top and Bottom Elevation offsets must be typed into the fields.

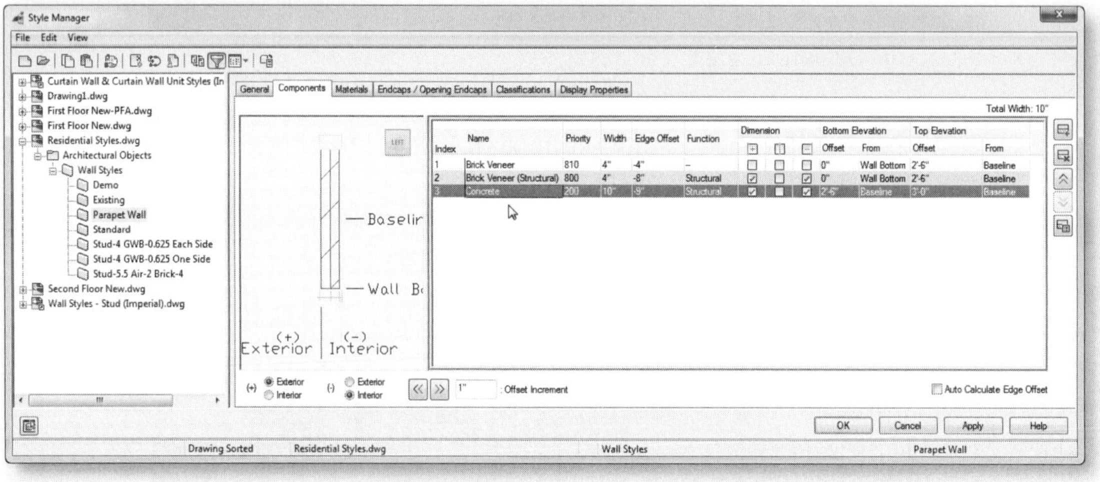

FIGURE 10.55 *Reorganize the components in the list and configure the dimensions*

This Wall style will butt into the other surrounding Walls and will not have any penetrations; therefore, we do not need to configure anything on the Endcaps/Opening Endcaps tab. We also will not configure anything on Classifications or Display Properties.

25. Click OK to complete the Wall Style edit and close the Style Manager.

NOTE

While it is possible to drag the style directly from the Style Manager to a palette to make a tool, we must save the drawing first before the tool can be created properly. Unfortunately, we cannot save the drawing while Style Manager is open.

26. Select any Wall onscreen (and its text label if it has one) and make a copy of it to any available location onscreen. (The exact location is unimportant.)
27. Select the new Wall and on the Properties palette, change the Style to Parapet Wall and change the Justify to **Baseline**.

The new Wall should appear as two lines in plan. This is because all of the components that we defined occur below the cut plane. Therefore, we are simply looking down on the topmost component (the Concrete cap) only. If you added a text field referencing the style name, it will update when you save.

28. Save the file.
29. Drag the Parapet Wall from the drawing onto the MACA Residential tool palette as before.
30. Close and save the *Residential Styles.dwg* [*Residential Styles - Metric.dwg*] file.

Apply the New Style to the Model

All that remains is to apply the new Wall Style to the model. It might be nice to do this in a view other than plan. NW Isometric view on the View tab will give you the best vantage point.

31. Using the same technique as before, apply the new Parapet Wall tool's Properties to the two patio Walls.

    You will need to do some grip-editing and other fine-tuning to resolve the intersections where the Parapet meets the house (see Figure 10.56). The specifics are left to you as an exercise. You may want to consider some items that were already covered:

- Grip editing the Parapet Wall ends
- Endcap overrides for the exterior masonry Walls of the addition
- Wall Cleanup rules
- Wall Cleanup issues if any

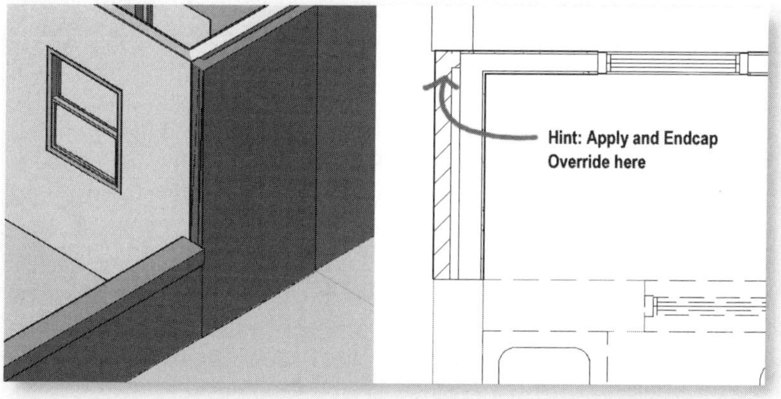

FIGURE 10.56 *The completed patio parapet Wall*

ADDITIONAL EXERCISES

Additional exercises have been provided in Appendix A. In Appendix A, you will find suggestions for adding Casework and Equipment to the Residential and Commercial Projects. Special Wall styles are defined to behave as countertops (look in the *Wall Styles - Casework (Imperial).dwg* [*Wall Styles - Casework (Metric).dwg*] file), with and without cabinets (see Figure 10.57). A collection of pre-built cabinet Multi-View Blocks (MVBs) are available in the Content Browser. Equipment, Appliances and Furniture are also available as MVBs in the Content Browser. It is not necessary that you complete this exercise to begin the next chapter. It is provided to enhance your learning experience. Completed projects for each of the exercises have been provided in the *Chapter10/Complete* folder.

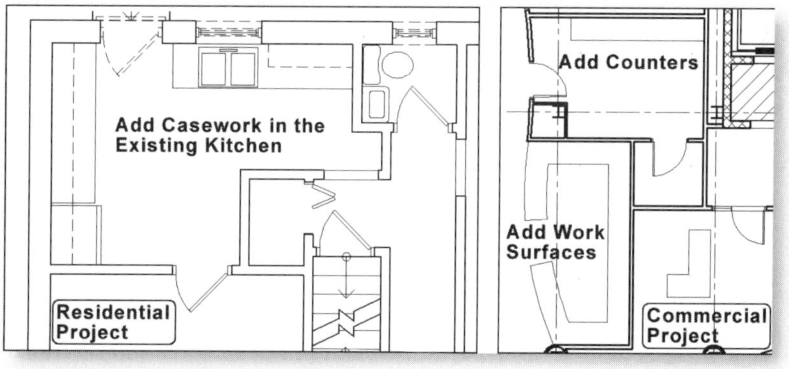

FIGURE 10.57 *Add Casework to both projects*

SUMMARY

- Wall styles control default size and shape, internal component makeup and graphical display settings of Walls.
- Default settings such as Wall width, justification and cleanup behavior can be preset in Wall tools.
- A Wall style can contain several internal components, each comprised of a boundary (two parallel edges) and a hatch infill.
- The termination of each component of a Wall is controlled by Endcap styles at both ends of the Walls and at all Wall penetrations.
- Cleanup Groups limit Wall cleanup to other Walls belonging to the same group.
- Display Properties can be assigned at the style level to control how a specific Wall style is displayed graphically onscreen and in print.
- Most Wall styles use the Drawing Default Display Properties and reference the By Material setting for lineweights and hatching.
- You can build tool palette tools that reference specific styles in your project and then use those tools to apply the parameters throughout any drawing in the project.
- Building custom Wall Styles is easy when you use the Wall Style Component Browser to start with premade components.

CHAPTER 11

Progressive Refinement—Part 2

INTRODUCTION

As a design scheme progresses, it is often desirable to begin including more details in the articulation of Walls, Doors and Windows. We have stressed throughout the book that ACA is designed to allow us to add objects with little detail early in the design cycle and progressively refine our design as more information becomes known. In the previous chapter, we took an exhaustive look at Wall styles and Wall Endcaps. In this chapter, we will focus on Door and Window styles. In addition, we will fine-tune the placement of Doors and Windows along the Walls they are anchored to and within the thickness of the Walls. We will also take a look at Multi-View Block content.

OBJECTIVES

In this chapter, we will refine the masonry shell of the Commercial Project and continue to work on first and second floors of the Residential Project. Now that styles have been applied to all of the Walls, we will shift our focus to fenestration. In the commercial shell file, we will adjust the placement of the Windows within the walls and look at the Sill Plan Display Representation. Returning to the Residential Project and some ancillary sample files, we will explore the features of the Door and Window styles. The chapter will conclude by finishing the residential floor plans with the creation of a custom Multi-View Block for the second floor bathroom.

- Understand Door and Window styles.
- Manipulate Door and Window Anchors.
- Customize Door and Window display.
- Build a Multi-View Block.

WINDOW STYLES

The simple Door and Window placement provided by the Add Door and Add Window commands is easy to achieve and perfectly acceptable for early design phases. However, as the design scheme becomes more refined, so too must the graphics used to represent the building fenestration. In this chapter, we will begin with a return to the

Commercial Project. The shell wall on three sides of the building includes punched Window openings. We will add sills to these Windows on their exterior and reposition them within the thickness of the Wall.

INSTALL THE CD FILES AND LOAD THE CURRENT PROJECT

If you have already installed all of the files from the CD, simply skip down to step 3 below to make the project active. If you need to install the CD files, start at step 1.

1. If you have not already done so, install the dataset files located on the Mastering AutoCAD Architecture 2010 CD-ROM.

   Refer to "Files Included on the CD-ROM" in the Preface for information on installing the sample files included on the CD.
2. Launch AutoCAD Architecture 2010 from the desktop icon created in Chapter 3.

If you did not create a custom icon, you might want to review "Create a New Profile" and "Create a Desktop Shortcut" in Chapter 3. Creating the custom desktop icon is not essential; however, it makes loading the custom profile easier.

3. On the Quick Access Toolbar (QAT), choose **Project Browser**.
4. Click to open the folder list and choose your *C:* drive.
5. Double-click on the *MasterACA 2010* folder, then the *Chapter11* folder.

   One or two commercial projects will be listed: *11 Commercial* and/or *11 Commercial Metric*.
6. Double-click *11 Commercial* if you wish to work in Imperial units. Double-click *11 Commercial Metric* if you wish to work in Metric units. (You can also right-click on it and choose **Set Current Project**.) Then click Close in the Project Browser.

NOTE

Important: If a message appears asking you to repath the project, click the "Repath the project now" option. Refer to the "Repathing Projects" topic in the Preface for more information.

Copy and Assign a New Window Style

Let's get started right away and build a new Window style for the commercial project masonry shell.

NOTE

Nearly every technique that we explore here is interchangeable for Windows or Doors. Feel free to experiment with either or both.

7. On the Project Navigator, in the *Constructs\Architectural* folder (Constructs tab), double-click to Open the *01 Shell and Core* file.

Some of the required Windows have been added to this file. The process to add Windows was covered in Chapter 4. We will start with these Windows and create a new style, then adjust their Anchor parameters and their Sills. Later we will copy several of them to complete the layout.

8. Select one of the Windows, and, on the Window contextual ribbon tab on the General panel, choose the ***Select Similar*** tool.

All of the Windows will highlight. (Please note that the front façade Curtain Wall will not highlight.)

9. With all of the Windows selected, on the Window contextual ribbon tab on the General tab, choose the ***Save As*** tool.
10. On the General tab, type **Shell Window** for the name.

11. In the Description field, type **Mastering AutoCAD Architecture Commercial Project - Window with fixed glazing and Sills** (see Figure 11.1).

TIP

It is a good habit to put a description for new styles. This will help you and others recognize the intention of the style at a future date.

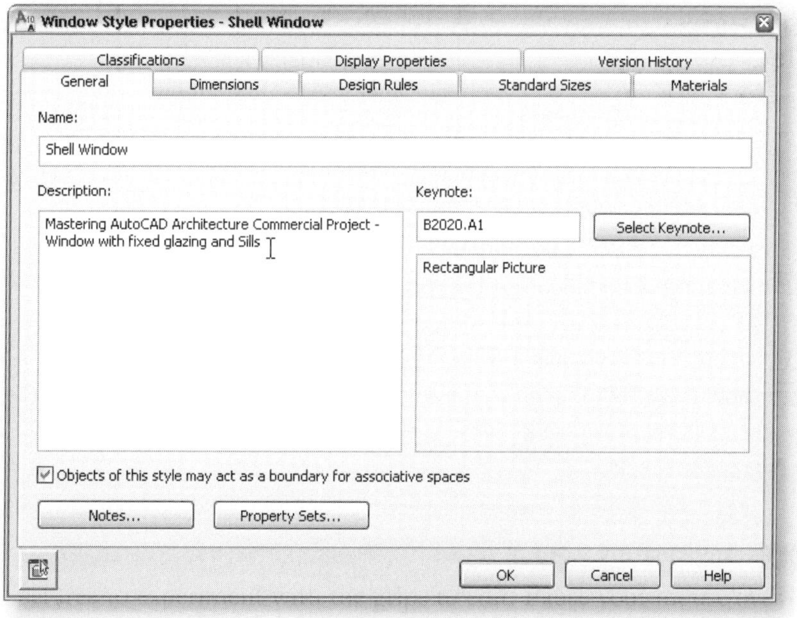

FIGURE 11.1 *Create and Edit the new style*

In addition to the Name and Description, notice that we also have Property Sets, Notes and a Keynote assignment area. Property Sets are covered in Chapter 15, "Generating Schedules." Notes simply calls up a dialog box with a single large text field. You can enter any information here you wish: notes to the drafter, information on the style, etc. Keynotes provide a means to assign construction notes to the Style from a central database. These notes can then be referenced with field codes on the printed sheets and even pass through to elevations, sections and details.

Edit the New Style

12. Click the Dimensions tab.

The settings on this tab allow you to configure the basic sizes of each of the major Window components. Use the diagram at the left of the dialog box to help you understand what each setting controls.

13. In the Frame area, set the Width to **3"** [**75**] and the Depth to **5"** [**125**].
14. In the Sash area, set the Width to **3"** [**75**] and the Depth to **4"** [**100**] (see Figure 11.2).

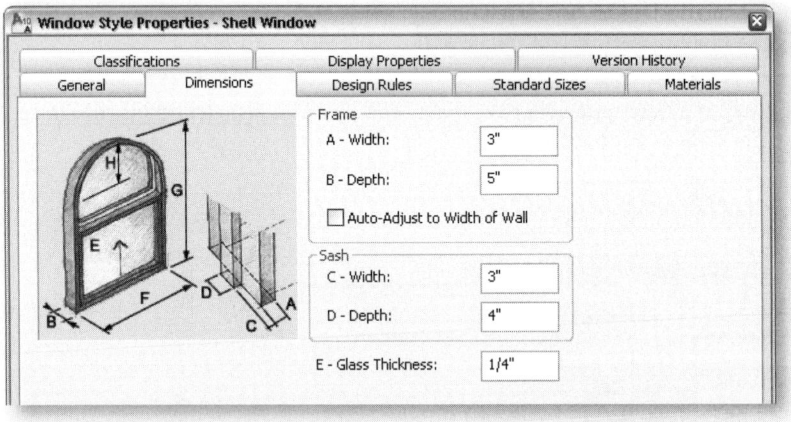

FIGURE 11.2 *Experiment with the settings on the Dimensions tab*

15. Click the Floating Viewer icon in the lower left corner of the dialog box (see Figure 11.3).
16. From the list of Views, choose **Top** (see Figure 11.3).

    This will show the effect in plan of the settings we just changed. The size of the Frame and Sash are now exaggerated.

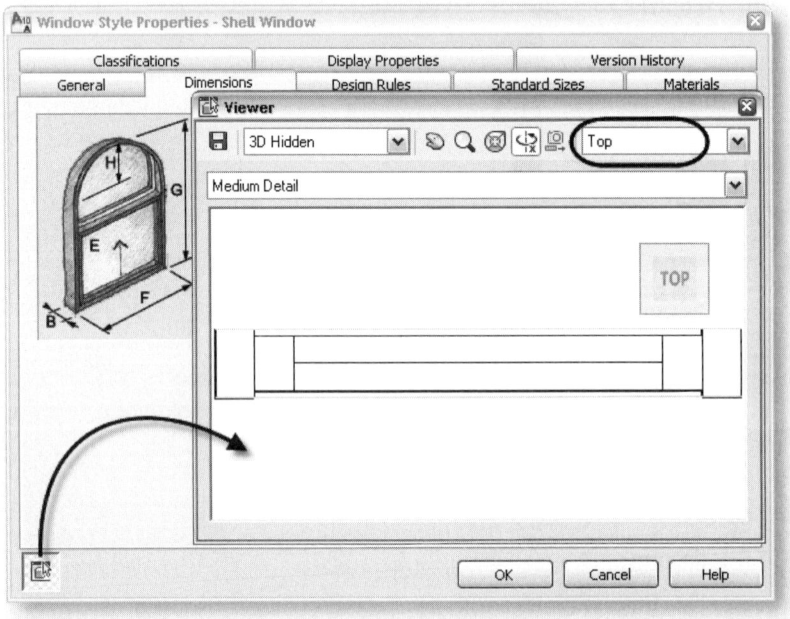

FIGURE 11.3 *Open the Floating Viewer*

Leave the Viewer open but position it next to the main dialog box on your screen so that it will remain visible.

17. Click the title bar of the Window Style Properties dialog box.

    This will shift focus away from the Floating Viewer and back to the Window Style Properties dialog box while leaving the Viewer open.
18. Change the Width of the Frame to **2"** [**50**] and leave the Depth of the Frame set to **5"** [**125**].

Note the change in the Viewer. The Frame is now a more reasonable size.

For the Window style that we are designing, we are looking for a very simple look graphically. For instance, showing the Sash component for this style is not desired. Removing it can be achieved in a number of ways. It seems that the logical place to remove the display of Sashes would be in the Display Properties. Let's have a look.

19. Click the Display Properties tab.

In the last chapter, we manipulated the display of Walls with the Properties palette. The same types of modifications made there can also be made using the Display Properties tab of the style dialog box. Notice that there is a list of display representations and that two of them are bold: Plan and Sill Plan. This indicates that Plan and Sill Plan are currently active for Windows in this drawing. If you recall the lessons of Chapter 2, we saw this possibility when discussing sets. Notice also that the drawing default setting controls all display representations for Windows. In the previous chapter, we used the Properties palette to apply style and object overrides to Walls. You can apply a style override in this dialog using the checkbox in the right column. If you do not check the box, you are editing the currently applied level which, in this case, is drawing default.

20. Select Plan from the list.
21. Click the Edit Display Properties icon at the top right corner.
22. On the Layer/Color/Linetype tab, click the small lightbulb icon next to the Sash component to turn it off; it should go "dim" (see Figure 11.4).

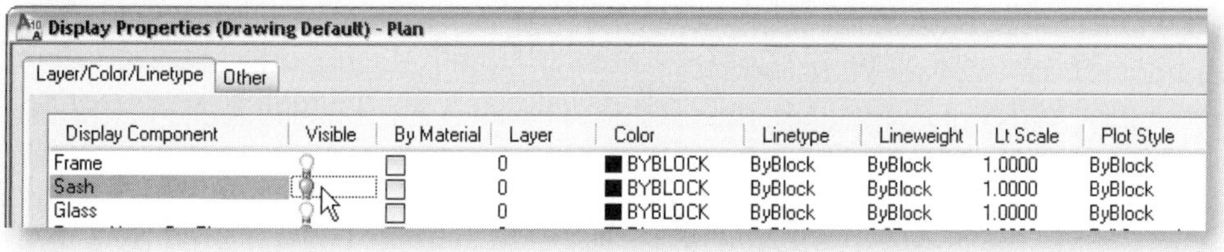

FIGURE 11.4 *Turn off the Sash component in the Display Properties*

23. Click OK once to return to the Display Properties tab.

Notice the result in the Viewer. The Sash is no longer displayed, but there is now a gap between the Frame and the Glazing. If you don't want to display sashes in plan, this is obviously not the best technique to achieve your goal.

24. Click the Edit Display Properties icon again.
25. Click the small lightbulb icon next to the Sash component to turn it back on.
26. Return to the Dimensions tab.
27. Set the Width of the Sash to **0"** [**0**] (see Figure 11.5).

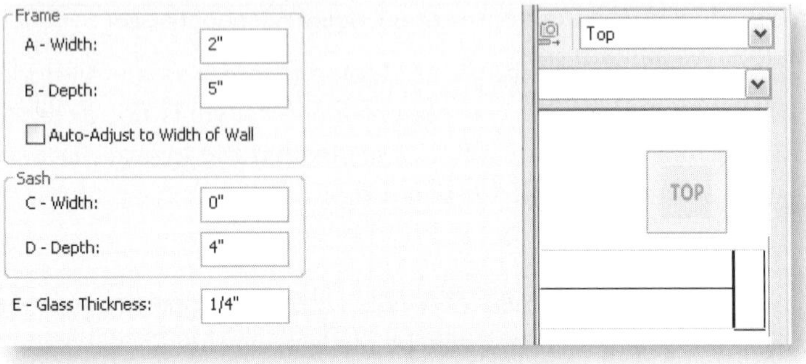

FIGURE 11.5 *Adjusting the Sash Dimensions to Zero*

28. Click OK to return to the drawing and see the result.

This will remove the sash more effectively. As you can see, this is different from turning off the Sash component in the Display Properties tab. There is no gap between components this time. There is one more way that our goal could be achieved. We could use the Nominal Display Representation for Windows in the current Display Configuration. (To do this, you would need to edit the current display set in the Display Manager as covered in Chapter 2.) However, this technique would affect all Windows in the drawing, which may not be desirable either. Zeroing out the Sash is the best compromise approach for our purposes here.

Add Sill Extensions

In the previous chapter, we saw that we could use Opening Endcaps to add Sills in the 3D and Elevation views of the Model. However, you may recall that those Sills did not appear in plan. To make the sills appear in plan, we need to edit the display properties. This time we will use the technique covered in the previous chapter, which is a bit more user friendly.

29. Select one of the Windows, right-click and choose **Properties**; then click the Display tab.

Sill components belong to a special Display Representation called Sill Plan (Threshold Plan for Doors). So we will make sure that we are editing the Sill Plan. We want to adjust the way the sills are displayed on the current style only; therefore, we will apply the override for Window Style.

30. Choose **Sill Plan** from the Display representation list.
31. From the Display controlled by list, choose **Window Style:Shell Window**.

NOTE

Be sure that you choose Sill Plan before applying the override; otherwise, the override will apply to Plan instead.

If a warning dialog appears, click OK (see Figure 11.6).

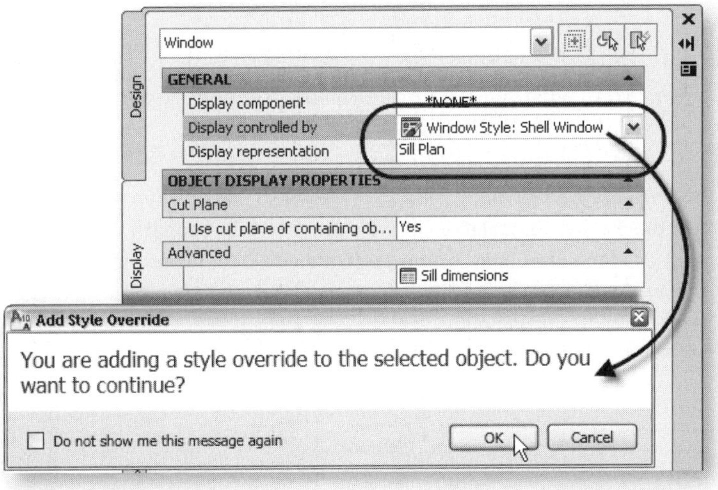

FIGURE 11.6 *Attach a style override to the Sill Plan Display Representation*

All such warnings include a "Do not show me this message again" checkbox. If you selected it previously, the warning will not appear. The message reminds you that applying a style override applies any changes to all objects sharing this style. In this case, this is precisely what we want.

If you open the Display components list, you will notice that two components are visible: Sill A and Sill B. (Also, some other above and below components are currently off.) Sill A occurs on the "swing" side of the window or door (the side with the arrow-shaped "Flip" grips), and Sill B occurs on the opposite side. Our Window is fixed and, therefore, does not have a swing at all. In this case, we will treat Sill A as the *outside* and Sill B as the *inside*. We are going to leave Sill B flush to the inside face of the Wall and project Sill A outward.

32. Click the Sill dimensions worksheet icon.

There are four dimensions here. A - Extension and B - Depth apply to Sill A, while C - Extension and D - Depth apply to Sill B.

33. In the Sill Dimensions area, change A - Extension to **2"** [**50**] and change B - Depth to **4"** [**100**] (see Figure 11.7).

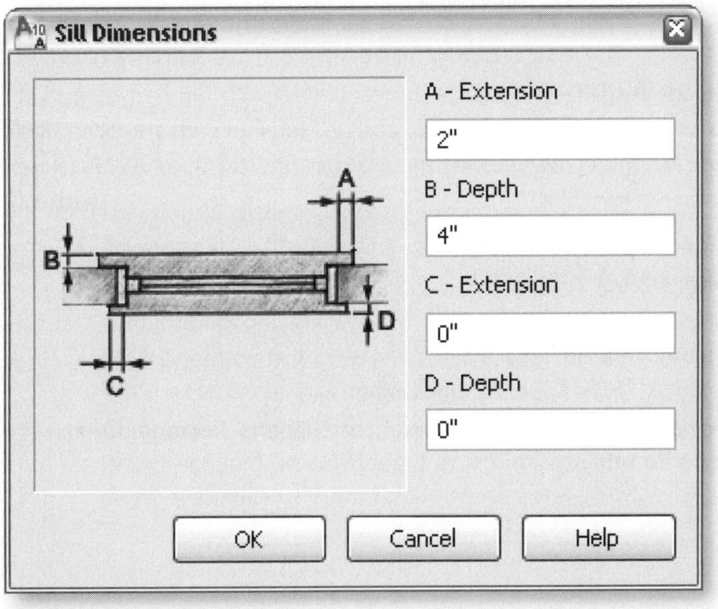

FIGURE 11.7 *Edit the dimensions of the sills*

34. Click OK to return to the drawing.

Notice the addition of sills on the Windows (see Figure 11.8). Some of them, however, are oriented the wrong way, with the sill on the inside. We will correct this later in the chapter.

TIP

The extra lines at the openings are part of the Walls. To make these lines disappear like the figure, select the Wall, on the Properties palette click the Display tab, beneath Advanced, click the Additional Properties worksheet icon. In the "Wall – Additional Properties" dialog, check the "Hide Lines Below Openings Above Cut Plane" checkbox and then click OK. Do this in your template file to make it permanent.

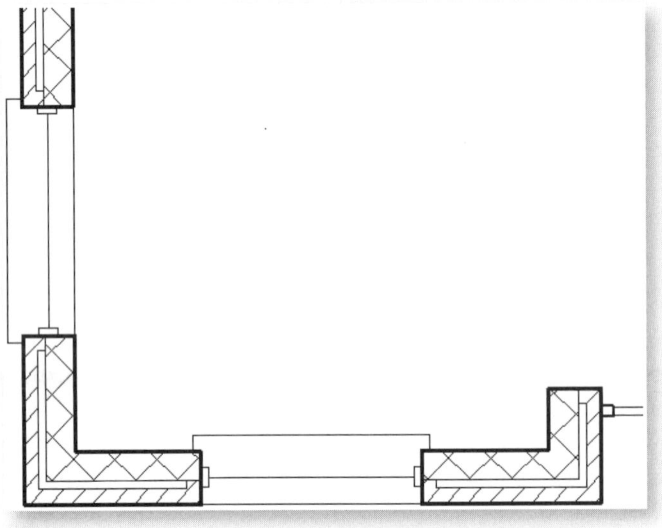

FIGURE 11.8 *The Sills now extend past the Window Frames*

NOTE

Sill Plan display is available for Door\Window Assemblies and Openings as well. All parameters are configured the same way as shown here. A similar Display Representation exists for Doors called Threshold Plan. It is configured and behaves the same way as Sill Plan except that the components are named Threshold A and Threshold B.

Complete the Custom Window Style

There are a few other tabs in the Window style dialog box. Let's take a quick look at them.

35. Select one of the Windows, and, on the Window contextual ribbon tab on the General panel, choose the ***Edit Style*** tool.
36. Click the Design Rules tab.

    On this tab, the basic shape and type of Window are configured.
37. Change the Viewer to an isometric view and experiment with the various Predefined Window Shapes and Window Types.
38. When you are finished experimenting, reset the Shape to **Rectangular** and the Window Type to **Picture**.
39. Click the Standard Sizes tab.

Standard Sizes appear in a list on the Properties palette when Windows of this type are being added to the drawing. You are also able to snap to Standard Sizes while grip-editing the size of a Door or Window that uses them. For this reason, Standard Sizes can be very useful. We will be using this Window in two situations, so let's add two Standard Sizes.

40. Click the Add button and in the Add Standard Size dialog box, type **Shell Windows** for the Description, **5'-0"** [**1500**] for Width, and **6'-0"** [**1800**] for Height; then click OK (see the left side of Figure 11.9).
41. Select the Standard Size: **3'-0"** [**900**] Wide by **5'-0"** [**1500**] High by clicking in the Description column. Click the Edit button, input **Core Windows** for the Description and click OK (see the right side of Figure 11.9).

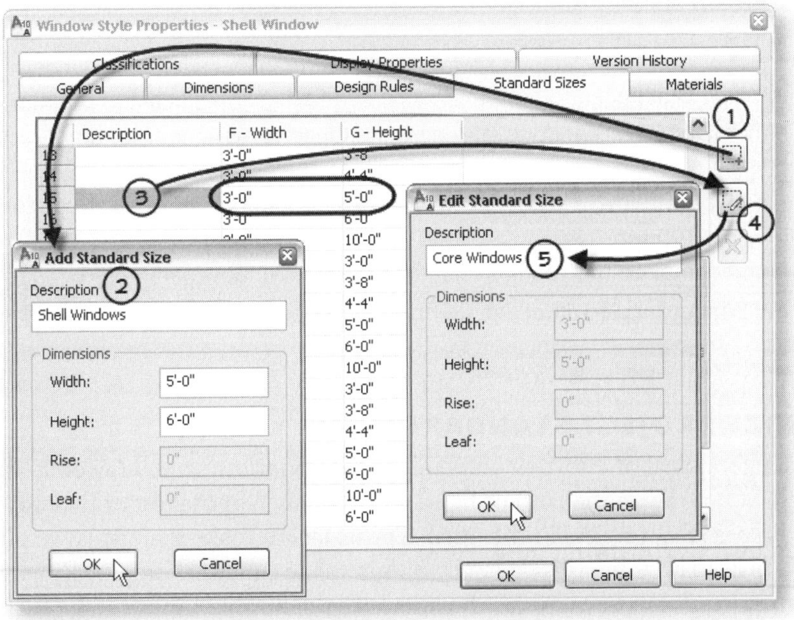

FIGURE 11.9 *Add some Standard Sizes to the Window style*

TIP

If you wish to have only the two standard sizes that we are adding and remove all of the others, you can select the entire list by clicking on the small cell in the first column next to the description at the top left corner. With all cells highlighted, click the Remove button. Then add the two sizes indicated above.

42. Click the Materials tab.

We have seen plenty of examples of Materials so far. Material Definitions control all hatching and textures applied to various AEC objects. They control the lineweights in plans, sections and elevations and determine special parameters such as transparency for glass. This drawing already contains a few basic Material Definitions. We will simply verify the settings. More information about accessing, creating and editing Materials can be found in Chapter 16.

43. Change the Material for Muntins (currently Standard) to Doors & Windows.Metal Doors & Frames.Aluminum Windows.Painted.White (see Figure 11.10).

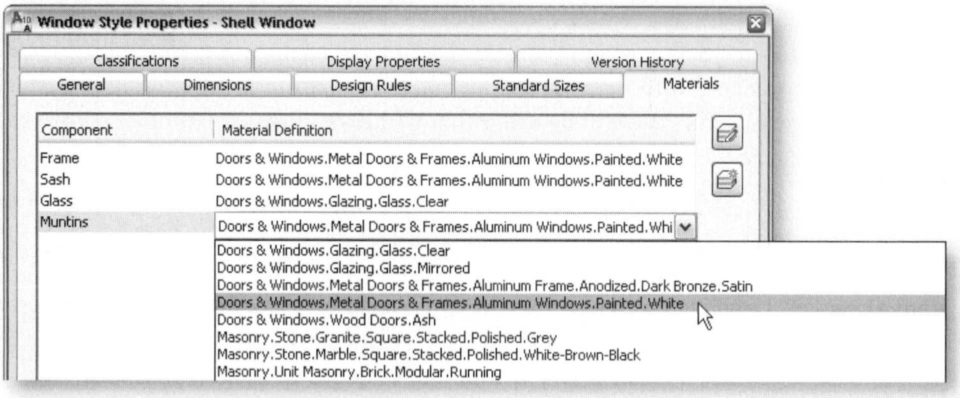

FIGURE 11.10 *Assign Material Definitions to the Window components*

44. Verify that Doors & Windows.Metal Doors & Frames.Aluminum Windows. Painted.White is assigned to both the Frame and Sash components.
45. Verify that Doors & Windows.Glazing.Glass.Clear is assigned to the Glass component.
46. In the Viewer window, choose **SE Isometric** and choose Realistic from the Visual Styles drop-down list.
47. Click OK to complete the configuration of the Shell Window parameters.

    The new Window Style will be applied to all Windows. Zoom in and study the results.

SYNCHRONIZE PROJECT STANDARDS

We have spent a good deal of effort on configuring this Window style. However, all of these changes occur only in the current file. To use the style in the rest of the project, we need to repeat this process in the other Constructs to make the display in all files consistent. Instead of doing this manually, this is an ideal place to employ Project Standards. We explored the use of Project Standards to synchronize object styles back in Chapter 8.

Some of the Windows have already been placed in the upper floors. The name "Shell Windows" has been applied to these Windows, but none of the style edits made so far have been applied. Let's synchronize the project so that all of the files will be updated to match the Shell Window.

1. On the Constructs tab of the Project Navigator, double-click 02 Shell and Core in the Constructs\Architectural folder.
2. Zoom in on one of the Windows.

Notice that this Window looks the same as the Window in the first floor before we made any modifications. It would be quite inefficient to make those modifications again. We can use Project Standards to update the current drawing to the latest version of this style. The style that we configured above has already been copied to the *Commercial Styles* [*Commercial Styles – Metric*] file to save you a few steps. This file has also been configured to synchronize Window Styles for the project. Refer to the "Set up Project Standards" heading in Chapter 8. for more information on these configurations.

3. At the bottom right corner of the drawing on the Drawing status bar, click the AEC Project Standards quick pick and then choose **Synchronize Drawing**.

4. For now, verify that the only item that has the action of "Update from Standard" is the Shell Window style and then click OK (see Figure 11.11).

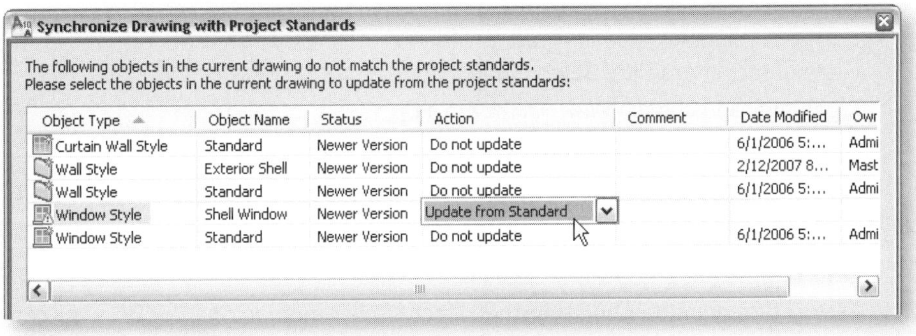

FIGURE 11.11 *Update only the Shell Window Style for now*

AutoCAD Architecture will process all drawing files in the entire project and synchronize them. If you have any drawings open onscreen, they might indicate that XREFs need to be reloaded. The Window should now match the one that we configured above.

MANAGER NOTE

Only the basic "user level" procedures of the Project Standards features are being showcased in this text. If you wish to use Project Standards in your firm, you will want to read the online documentation for complete details on all of its features. For instance, you can generate log files of synchronizations, perform standards audits and check AutoCAD Standards via the AEC Project Standards functions. A project can use a combination of project-based standards files (as showcased here) and office wide standards files at the same time. For instance, you might choose to have all Display Setting synchronization come from the office standard drawing template (DWT) file that contains all of the accepted Display Settings, while the Style might come from both office standard and project-based files. With most procedures, careful consideration of the options available and consistent implementation of chosen options are paramount to achieving desired results.

MANIPULATING WINDOW ANCHORS

Let's return to the first floor and continue working on our Windows. We now have sills applied to our punched Windows, but many of the Windows are pointing in different directions. We can flip the Windows manually with grips, which works well for a small selection of Windows; but when many Windows are involved, a more efficient approach is needed. Among the many parameters controlled by anchors is their orientation relative to their parent Wall. We can access Anchor parameters through the Properties palette on the Anchor worksheet or on the right-click menu.

Change the Orientation of All Windows

To flip the orientation of a single Window is easy. You simply click the arrow-shaped grip.

1. Return to *01 Shell and Core* and then select any two Windows.
2. Click the arrow-shaped grip pointing perpendicular to one of the selected Windows.

   Each time you click, the Sill will flip from inside to outside and back again.

This method is quick and easy; but notice that even though more than one Window is selected, only the one whose grip you clicked actually flips. Therefore, although quick and easy, this technique works best for a single Window or a small selection of Windows; it could get tedious for a large selection such as we have here.

3. With the Windows still selected, on the Window contextual ribbon tab on the General tab, choose the ***Select Similar*** tool.
4. Right-click and choose **Wall Anchor > Flip Y**.

Notice that this action *did* flip all of the Windows. However, they all flipped opposite relative to their existing positions; so we are no better off than we were before. To flip only those Windows that point to the inside and make them point to the outside, we must use the Anchor worksheet.

1. Reselect the windows by using the Select Similar method. On the Window contextual ribbon tab on the Anchor tab, click the ***Settings*** tool (see Figure 11.12).

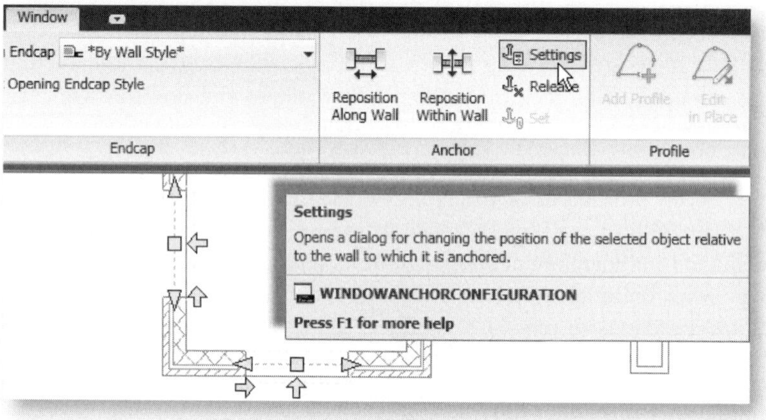

FIGURE 11.12 *Access Anchor worksheet from the Window Contextual Ribbon Tab*

The direction of the Windows is controlled by the three checkboxes at the bottom right corner of the dialog box, labeled "Flip X," "Flip Y" and "Flip Z." The check marks in Flip X and Flip Y are currently grayed over because some of the Windows are flipped and others are not. The X direction is parallel to the parent wall; the Y direction is perpendicular to it. Therefore, changing the Y setting will flip the Windows either in or out of the building. Unlike the right-click technique, this worksheet will orient all of the Windows in the same way relative to the Wall. The trick is figuring out which way they will flip, in or out. (In other words, we are not yet certain if we need the check mark in the Flip Y box or need it cleared.)

2. Clear the check mark in the Flip Y box (see Figure 11.13).

The initial orientation of each Window is determined at the time of insertion by the mouse movements. There is no *simple* way to know whether the Windows must be flipped, but there is a 50 percent chance we will guess right.

3. Click OK to complete the change.

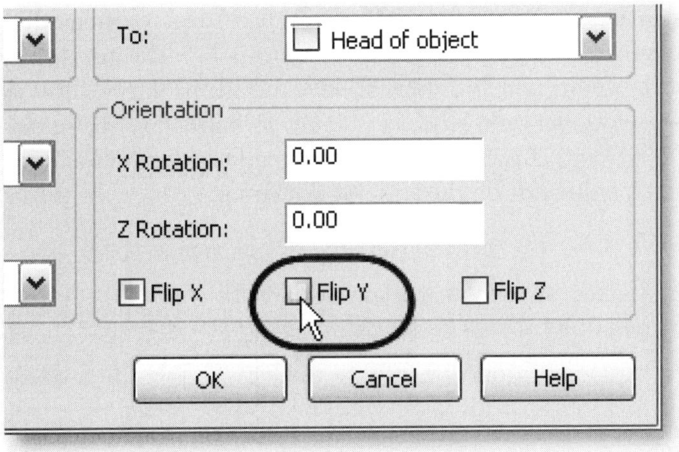

FIGURE 11.13 *Clear the check mark in the Flip Y box*

Notice that all of the Windows have flipped to the same direction relative to their parent Walls. In this case, we got lucky and the odds were with us. However, had chance gone the other way, we would have repeated the steps and placed a check mark in the Flip Y box or right-clicked and chosen **Wall Anchor > Flip Y**, which would have given the desired results since all of the Windows are now pointing the same way. Give it a try if you like.

Adjust the Window Position

An anchor controls the Window's position within the wall as well as its orientation. (We began to explore this in Chapter 2.) By manipulating the properties of the anchor, you can shift the position of the Windows. Every AEC object has its own X, Y and Z directions (see Figure 11.14). Typically, object direction is determined as follows:

- The Width of the object corresponds to X.
- The Depth of the object corresponds to Y.
- The Height of the object corresponds to Z.

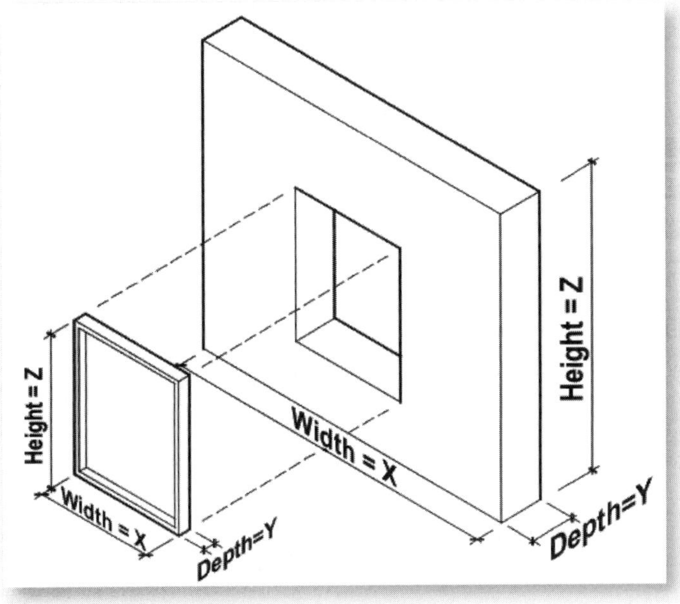

FIGURE 11.14 *Typical Orientation of AEC objects*

Feel free to experiment with the settings in the Anchor worksheet and see their effect on the Windows relative to these orientations. However, there is a much simpler way to manipulate the position of Doors and Windows relative to their parent Walls. We can use the Location grip in conjunction with the CTRL key for individual manipulations (see the "Explore Objects with Anchors" heading in Chapter 2 for an example), or we can use the reposition commands on the right-click menu.

Make sure that all of the Windows are selected using the Select Similar technique.

4. With all Windows selected, on the Window contextual ribbon tab on the Anchor panel, choose the ***Reposition Within Wall*** tool.

A red line will appear that can be positioned relative to the faces or the center of the Window object. It is best to zoom in with your wheel on a single Window as you perform the next few steps.

5. At the "Select position on the opening" prompt, click the inside face of the Window (see Number 1 in Figure 11.15).
6. At the "Select a reference point" prompt, click the adjacent corner on the inside face of the Wall (see Number 2 in Figure 11.15).

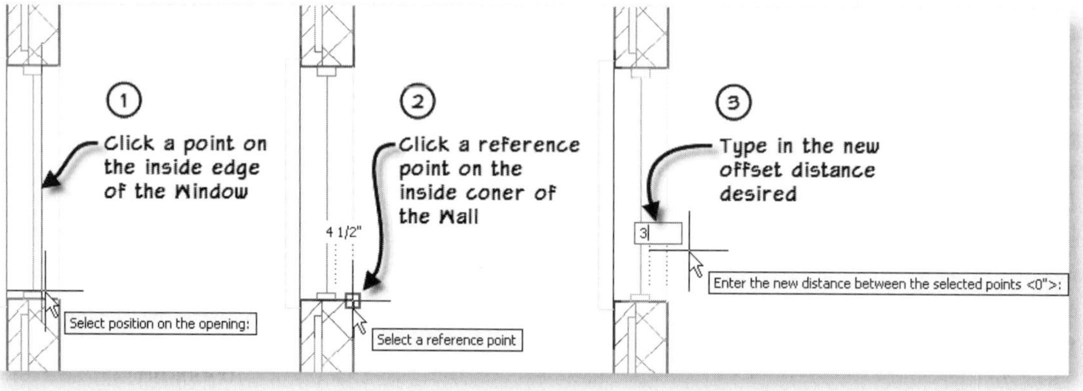

FIGURE 11.15 *Select the position on the Window and the Wall and indicate the new offset*

7. At the "Enter the new distance between the selected points" prompt, type **3"** [**65**] and then press ENTER (see Number 3 in Figure 11.15).

The change is subtle, but all of the Windows have shifted the same relative amount and now are a bit closer to the inside edge of the Wall. You can repeat the process and try other offsets and reference points if you wish. Once you have clicked your two reference points (one on the Window, the other on the Wall), a smaller number will move the Window closer to the point on the Wall and a larger number will move it away from the point on the Wall. If you like, you can select the Window and, on the Window contextual ribbon tab on the General panel, choose the ***Edit Style*** tool, and edit the dimensions of the Frame on the Dimensions tab to further manipulate the overall relationship of the Window to the Wall.

8. Save the file.

COPYING EXISTING WINDOWS

We now have several Windows with a nicely configured Window Style, which are carefully positioned relative to the width of the Walls and have sills pointing to the outside. However, our left and right vertical Walls could use a few more Windows. Naturally, if we copy one of the Windows inserted here, the new copy will use the same Style. Also, as we saw in Chapter 2, when you copy an anchored object, all of the Anchor parameters (such as position within the Wall, Sill height and orientation to the outside) will also be copied. We will use two ACA routines here: Edit in View and the Array AEC Modify Tool.

Using Edit in Elevation

We can perform the copying of Windows in any view and use any ACA or AutoCAD tool. In this sequence, we showcase a few items in our ACA arsenal—starting with Edit in Elevation.

1. Select the right and left vertical exterior masonry Walls and the two Windows within them.
2. On the Multiple Objects contextual ribbon tab on the General panel, select the down-arrow icon at the right side of the Edit in... split button and choose the ***Edit in Elevation*** tool.
3. At the "Select linework or face under the cursor or specify reference point for view direction" prompt, move the mouse close to the outside edge of the right vertical Wall. When the blue construction line appears, click the mouse (see Figure 11.16).

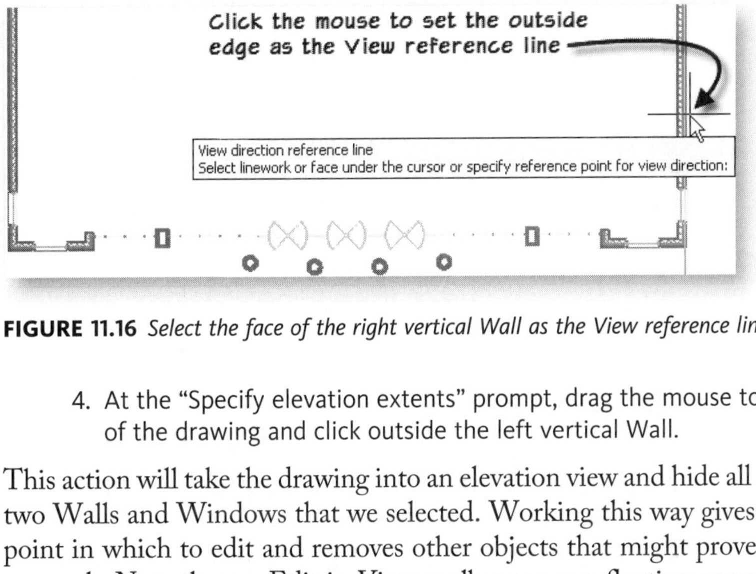

FIGURE 11.16 *Select the face of the right vertical Wall as the View reference line*

4. At the "Specify elevation extents" prompt, drag the mouse to the opposite side of the drawing and click outside the left vertical Wall.

This action will take the drawing into an elevation view and hide all objects except the two Walls and Windows that we selected. Working this way gives us a nice vantage point in which to edit and removes other objects that might prove distracting while we work. Note that an Edit in View toolbar appears floating onscreen. This toolbar has a single icon that is used to return to the previous viewpoint and restore all hidden objects once we are finished editing.

Using AEC Modify Array

We made certain to include vertical Walls and their Windows in the elevation's isolated selection so that we could array them together in the next step. Even though from the current vantage point it appears as though there is only one Window, you can still select them both and array them together.

5. Click above and to the left of the Windows onscreen; then moving down and to the right, surround the Windows and click again.

The Properties palette should read Window (2) at the top. If it says "All (#)" instead, right-click and choose **Deselect All** and try again.

6. With the two Windows selected, on the Home ribbon tab expand the Modify panel, select the down-arrow icon at the right side of the Array split button (rightmost icon on the first row of the expansion) and choose the ***AEC Array*** tool (see Number 1 in Figure 11.17).
7. At the "Select an edge to array from or Enter to pick two points" prompt, hover over the left side of the Window and when the blue construction line appears on the outside of the frame, click the mouse to set the reference edge (see Number 2 in Figure 11.17).

   If you can't get the vertical edge to highlight, press ENTER and then object-snap to the bottom left and upper left corners of the Window.

Whatever edge you select, the array will move parallel to it. So be certain to highlight a vertical edge. At this point, if you move the mouse left or right, you will see the array indicated interactively. Since we are all the way to the left of our Wall, we need to move our arrayed objects to the right. A default distance between objects will appear in the dynamic dimension. Make sure the Dynamic Input icon on the Application status bar is toggled on, or you will not get the necessary feedback for this part of the command.

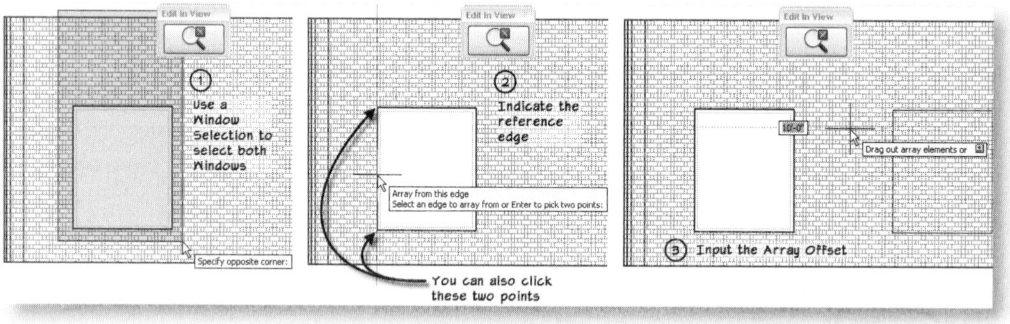

FIGURE 11.17 *Use the Array AEC Modify Tool to copy Windows along the Wall*

8. In the dynamic dimension that appears onscreen, type **10'-0"** [**3000**] and then press ENTER (see Number 3 in Figure 11.17).
9. At the "Drag out array elements" prompt, drag the mouse to the right all the way to the other end of the Wall. When six Windows are indicated in the Array Count, click the mouse to complete the routine.

You should now have six Windows along the Wall in elevation. (There are actually 12 total, with 6 directly in front of the other 6.) Notice that despite working in elevation, the Windows behave exactly as they would in plan and cut holes in the parent Wall.

10. Click the Exit Edit in View icon on the Edit in View toolbar to exit the Edit in Elevation mode and return to the previous plan view.

Notice that all of the Windows have their sills correctly pointing outside the building.

Add the New Windows to the Upper Floors

Now that we have all of our Windows in the first floor, we need to copy them to the upper floors. Initially, we will use the same Window layout on all floors. Later, if the design warrants, we can move Windows around on each floor as required. Our first instinct would likely be to copy and paste to original coordinates the Windows from the first floor to the other floors. While this would work, the only difficulty would be that when you copy and paste Anchored objects, they include their parent object. Therefore, we would end up with a duplicate Wall in the other files. While it would be easy enough to erase the duplicate Wall, let's explore an alternative approach. After performing the following steps to copy the Windows to the second floor, you can decide if you would like to adopt this process or use the copy and paste method instead.

11. Repeat the steps in the "Using Edit in Elevation" heading above to return to Edit in Elevation.

    Select the same two Walls, but also be sure to select all 12 attached Windows this time.

12. On the Project Navigator palette, click the Constructs tab and then drag the *02 Shell and Core* file from the *Constructs\Architectural* folder and drop it anywhere in the drawing window.

    This will XREF the *02 Shell and Core* file into the current file and stack it at the correct vertical height based on the settings in the Constructs and the Project's levels.

13. Double-click the *02 Shell and Core* XREF.

    This will activate a "RefEdit" session, allowing us to edit the XREF in place.

14. In the Reference Edit dialog, be sure that *02 Shell and Core* (and not *Core*) is selected and then click OK (see Figure 11.18).

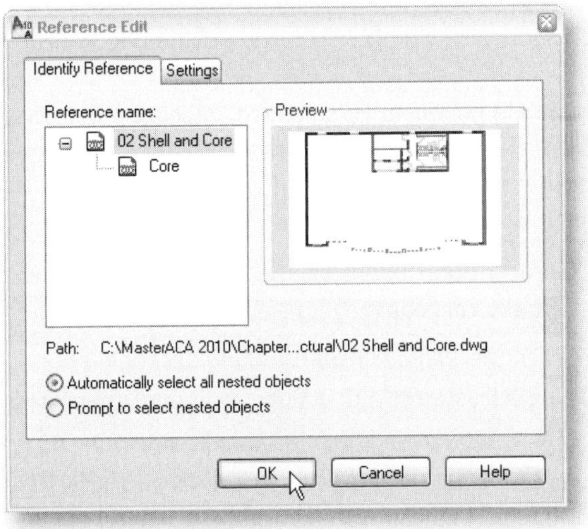

FIGURE 11.18 *Use RefEdit to edit the 02 Shell and Core file*

An Edit Reference panel will be added to the right side of your current ribbon tab, and the first floor will screen back a bit. (Depending upon the tab that was active and the width of your screen, the Edit Reference panel may be in a minimized state – click on the title panel to expand it to access its tools.) When you activate a RefEdit session, you are actually editing the geometry in the XREF file. Any changes you make will apply to that file when you save the session. The XREF file is locked for editing while you are in RefEdit. Therefore, no one else on the project team can open the file and edit it while you are in RefEdit. It is as though you had opened the file directly except that you can see the XREF file in context of the host file (the first floor in this case). A "Working Selection Set" is automatically applied to the reference file at the start of RefEdit. This selection set includes all objects in the XREF file and excludes all objects in the host file. However, you can modify this selection set if necessary, which is what we need to do here. By adding the Windows to the working set, we can easily copy them to the second floor.

15. Click above the second floor and drag slightly down and to the left (crossing window) below the top edge of the horizontal Walls.

    The Properties palette should confirm the selection by showing Wall (2) at the top.
16. Press the DELETE key to erase the two Walls.
17. On the Edit Reference panel, click the ***Add to Working Set*** tool (see Figure 11.19).

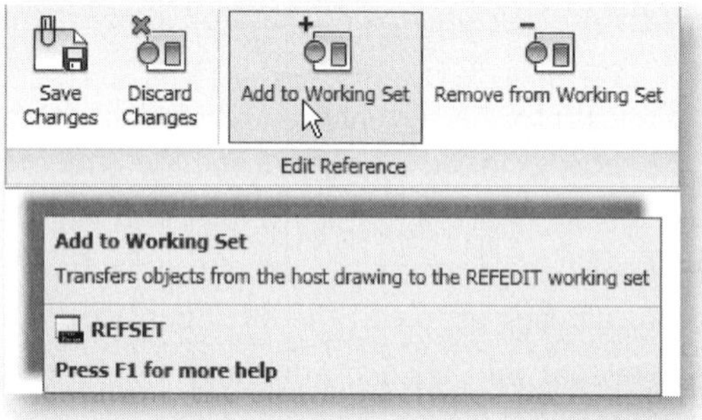

FIGURE 11.19 *Temporarily add the Windows to the RefEdit selection set*

18. Using a crossing window selection, select all 12 Windows and the two Walls on the first floor and then press ENTER.

    The 12 Windows and 2 Walls should no longer be screened, indicating that they are now part of the working set. If you have the Command Line active, you should see this message: 14 Added to working set.
19. Select all 12 Windows and the 2 Walls and copy them up **12'-0"** [**3650**].

You can use the ***Copy*** tool on the Home ribbon panel on the Modify panel or the ***AEC Array*** tool on the same panel to make this copy.

20. On the Edit Reference panel, click the ***Remove from Working Set*** tool.
21. Select all 12 Windows and the 2 Walls on the first floor again and then press ENTER.

It is necessary to remove these objects from the working set before closing the RefEdit session, or they will remain part of the second floor file and be removed permanently from the first floor.

22. On the Edit Reference panel, click the ***Save Changes*** tool (see Figure 11.20).

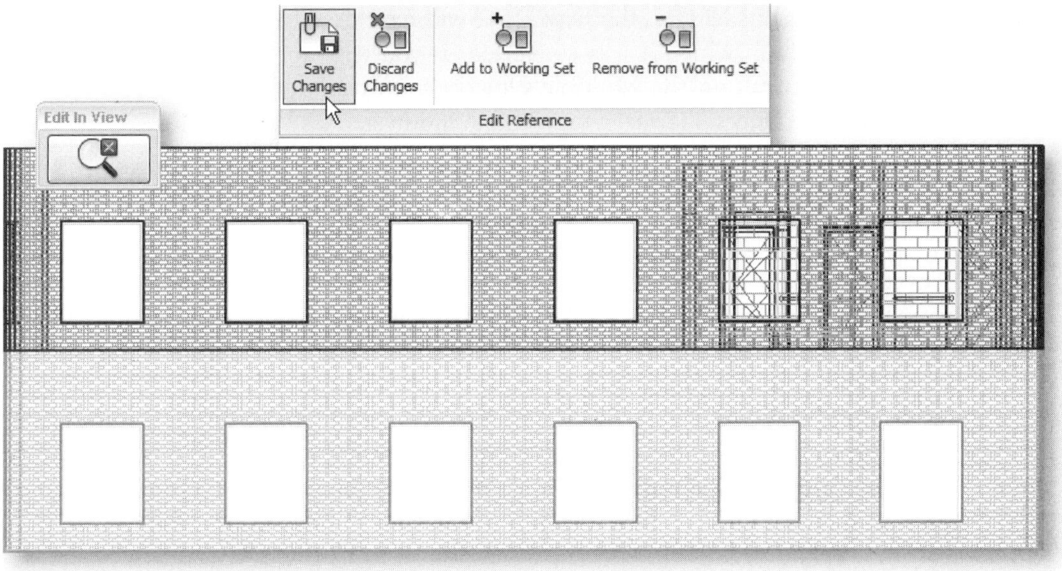

FIGURE 11.20 *Return the Windows to the first floor file by removing them from the Working Set and then Save the edits back to the Reference*

23. In the confirmation dialog, click OK.
24. On the Drawing status bar, click the Manage Xrefs quick pick, right-click the *02 Shell and Core* file and then choose **Detach**. If you wish to close the External Reference palette, click the "X" on the title bar of the palette.
25. On the Edit in View toolbar, click the Exit Edit in View icon.
26. Save the file.
27. On the Project Navigator palette, double-click the *02 Shell and Core* file to open it.

    Notice that all of the Windows have been added to this file in the correct locations. Close the file when you are satisfied.
28. Using the RefEdit procedure again, repeat the process to copy the Windows to the third and fourth floors. Use offsets of **24'-0"** [**7300**] and **36'-0"** [**10950**] this time.

As indicated previously, if you prefer, you can copy the Windows to the clipboard, open the third floor, and use **Paste to Original Coordinates**. Remember that if you choose this option, you will want to delete the duplicated Walls *before* pasting, and to use the Paste to Original Coordinates icon on the Home ribbon, Modify panel.

Convert a Window to a Door

A few small modifications remain for the first floor shell file. There is a Window in the Core area where there ought to be an egress door. We can easily convert this Window to a Door.

29. If you closed *01 Shell and Core*, reopen it now from Project Navigator.
30. On the tool palettes, right-click the title bar and choose **Design** to load the Design tool palette group if it is not already loaded.
31. On the Doors tool palette, right-click the Hinged - Single – Exterior tool and choose **Apply Tool Properties to > Door/Window Assembly, Opening, Window.**
32. At the "Select door/window assemblies, openings, and/or windows to convert" prompt, click the Window in the Core at the end of the small corridor and then press ENTER.

When you use this feature, the new Door will have exactly the same dimensions as the Window from which it was converted. If you wish to see this, select the Wall and Window, and, on the Multiple Objects contextual ribbon tab on the General panel, choose **Object Viewer** to view the Window and its Wall in 3D.

33. Select the new Door and on the Properties palette, change the Height to **7'-0"** [**2200**], change the Vertical alignment to **Threshold** and change the Threshold height to **0"** [**0**].

At the start of the chapter, we noted that most settings and procedures for Windows worked the same way as for Doors and other openings. Notice that this Door has a threshold line on the side opposite the swing. We need this door to swing out and want the threshold on the outside as well. This "Threshold Plan" Display Representation works the same way as the Sill Plan for Windows above. We could simply flip the Door with the grip. However, then the swing would point in, which would likely not meet fire codes. Instead, let's change the side of the threshold.

Make sure the Door swings out. If it does not, click the "Flip" grip.

34. Select the Door, right-click and choose **Properties**; then click the Display tab.
35. For Display representation, choose **Threshold Plan**.
36. Select the Display component property and click the down arrow to the right of the current value (***NONE***).
37. On the drop-down menu, turn on Threshold A and turn off Threshold B by clicking on the light bulb icon at the left of each component, and then reselect the ***NONE*** component. If you get a warning message about style overrides, click OK.
38. On the Display tab, click the Threshold dimensions worksheet icon and change both A - Extension and B - Depth to **2"** [**50**].
39. Click OK to return to the drawing.

Let's make one more edit to complete the first floor. In Chapter 6, we added a custom tool palette, MACA Commercial [MACA Commercial Metric], to the MasterACA tool palette group. That palette has a tool referencing a custom Wall Style for the lower exterior Walls of our project. Let's apply that tool's properties to the shell Wall of just the first floor. This will give our building a rusticated base on the lowest level.

40. On the tool palettes, right-click the title bar and choose **MasterACA** to load the MasterACA tool palette group.
41. Select one of the exterior Walls, and, on the Multiple Objects contextual ribbon tab on the General panel, choose the ***Select Similar*** tool.
42. On the MACA Commercial [MACA Commercial Metric] tool palette, right-click the Exterior Shell Lower Level tool and choose **Apply Tool Properties to > Wall**.
43. Save and close the file.

MANIPULATING DOOR AND WINDOW DISPLAY

There is much more to Door and Window display properties than simply turning components on and off and manipulating Sill and Threshold dimensions. To customize the graphics of Doors and Windows, you can manipulate the display properties of Door and Window styles. You can change the Layer, Color, Linetype, Lineweight and Plot Style properties of any component; and you can add custom components. Adding custom components to Doors and Windows is, however, a little different than it was for Walls in the previous chapter. Custom components are added to Doors and Windows using AutoCAD blocks and are applied at the display level. Let's have a look at the potential contained in the display parameters for Doors and Windows.

Enable a Live Plot Preview

1. On the Project Navigator, in the *Elements\Architectural* folder, double-click the file named *Core* to open it.

   We last had this file open in Chapter 7. No additions have been made to this file since then; however, the redundant Wall along the back of the building has been removed.

2. At the bottom of the drawing window, on the Application status bar, click the layout toggle icon.

This will toggle to the Layout named "Work." This Layout is intended to provide a convenient way to view your model as you work in 2D (on the right) and 3D (on the left). This can be very useful indeed. The trickiest part of using it is paying attention to which space—Model Space or Paper (Layout) Space—you are in. For the task that we are about to complete, we want to preview the model the way it will be plotted. The only way this can be done in Model Space is by using the Plot Preview command. However, in a Layout such as this, we can turn on the "Display Plot Styles" and the "Display Lineweights" options and preview the model in a kind of *live* plot preview. Elements and Constructs use a Model template and are not intended for plotting. Therefore, we must make a few changes to the Work Layout settings to view the model as it will plot. The critical aspects of a plot preview are white paper with black linework, lineweights displayed and the proper scale.

NOTE

You should understand that we are not intending to print from the Element or Construct. Rather, we are looking for a convenient way to preview how it will look when plotted.

With the Work Layout active, you should see a white background (the ACA default). If you do not, it is possible that your settings on the Display tab in the Options dialog box (**Application Menu > Options**) have been modified from the defaults (see Chapter 3). Although it is not critical that you use a white background in Paper Space Layouts, it is recommended. To see all of the linework in black, we need to display the Plot Styles.

3. On the Application Menu, choose **Print > Page Setup**.
4. Only one item will be in the list: *Work*. With it selected, click the Modify button.
5. In the Page Setup – Work dialog, in the top right corner, place a check mark in the Display plot styles checkbox, click OK and then click Close (see Figure 11.21).

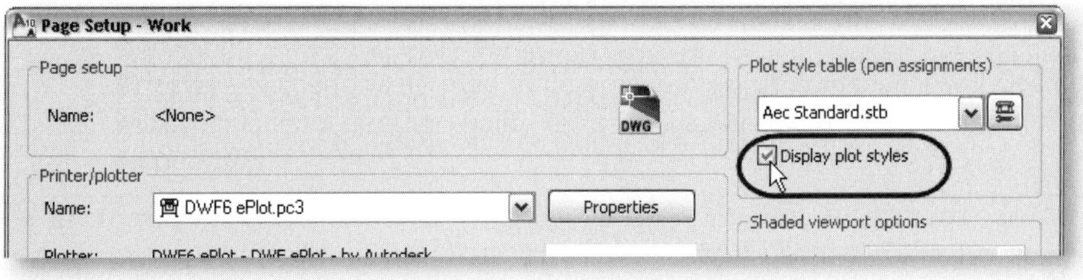

FIGURE 11.21 *Turn on Display Plot Styles in the Paper Space Layout*

The drawing should now be displayed with all black linework. (If you have a black background, the linework will display all white instead.) If your lines are still displaying in color rather than black and white, either the default *Plot Style Table - AIA Standard.stb* is missing or the layers in this file are assigned to the "Normal" Plot Style, which prints as it is seen onscreen. Check with your System Administrator or CAD Support person for assistance.

NOTE

Neither the proper display of Plot Style nor the absence of a white background in your Work Layout will hamper you from completing the Door Display exercise below; however, it is much easier to see the results accurately when everything is displayed in black and white.

Let us now address Scale and Lineweight.

6. Make sure that you are working in floating model space and that the right-hand viewport (the one displaying in plan) is active.

   You can tell this by the shape of the UCS icon (L-shaped vs. triangular). Also, the Plan viewport edge will be bold when floating Model Space is active and not bold when Paper Space is active (see Figure 11.22).

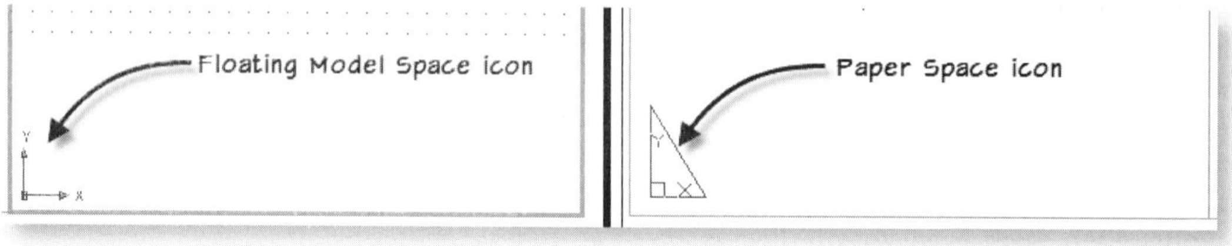

FIGURE 11.22 *The UCS icon and the Model/Paper toggle indicate whether model or paper space is active*

If the plan viewport is not active, double-click inside it to activate it. (Its edge will become bold.)

7. On the Drawing status bar, on the right side, click the Viewport Scale pop-up menu and choose **1/4" = 1'-0"** [**1:50**].

   Pan the view as necessary. Do *not* zoom or roll your mouse wheel! This will change the scale.
8. On the Application status bar, click the Show/Hide Lineweight button (make the background a blueish green color) to turn on Lineweight display (see Figure 11.23).
9. Finally, on the Drawing status bar, click the Lock/Unlock Viewport icon, immediately to the left of the Viewport Scale pop-up menu to change the icon to a closed, bluish gray lock (see Figure 11.23).

TIP

As an alternative, you can lock a viewport using the right-click menu or the Properties palette. With Paper Space active and the viewport selected, right-click and choose **Display Locked** > **Yes** or on the Design tab of the Properties palette, set the Display locked property to **Yes**.

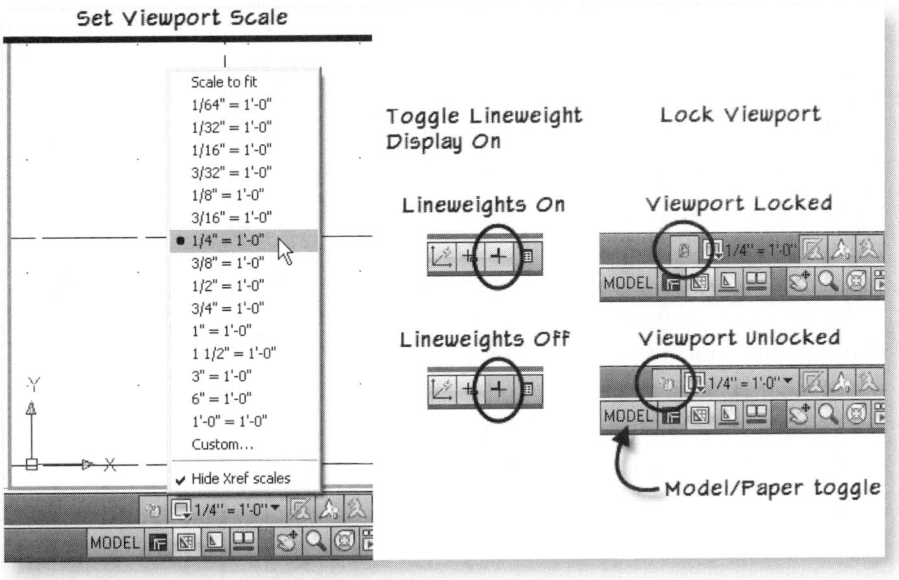

FIGURE 11.23 *Click the Show/Hide Lineweight button to toggle Lineweight display*

You should now have a display that is nearly identical to the way the drawing will appear when plotted. With the viewport display locked, you can freely zoom and pan in both Paper Space and Floating Model Space. Try it out.

Work with Door Display Properties

Like all AEC objects, a Door has several components in each Display Representation. Each Display Representation has components appropriate to that Representation. In many cases, the same component will show in one or more Display Representations (such as Door Panel and Frame); in other cases, they will show in some and not others (such as Glass and Swing). Each component has its own layer, color, linetype, lineweight and plot style. Each can be turned on or off. Additional subcomponents in the form of custom display blocks can also be added; we'll cover those in the next exercise. Figure 11.24 shows the basic components of a Door object in the Model, Plan and Elevation Display Representations.

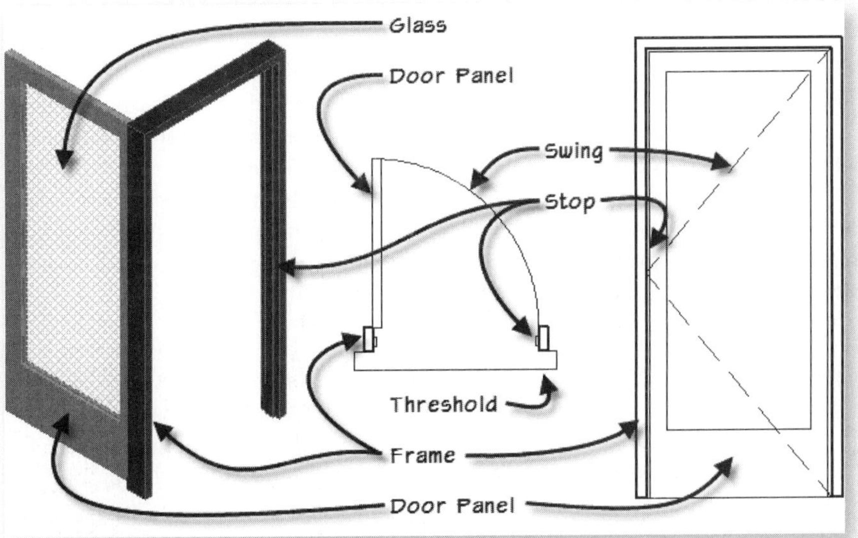

FIGURE 11.24 *Basic components of the Door object in three Display Representations*

Now that the drawing is giving us the proper visual feedback (as configured in the previous "Enable a Live Plot Preview" heading), we can begin fine-tuning the adjustments to the Door object display. For instance, it might be desirable to have the door swing display in a lighter lineweight than the rest of the door in plan.

10. Zoom in on one of the Doors in the women's restroom (top right of the plan).

    Notice that with the viewport display locked, as we did above, the scale is preserved even when zooming in on the viewport.

11. Right-click in the drawing area and choose **Select Component** from the pop-up menu.
12. Select the door swing of the Door to the women's restroom (top right) and on the Properties palette, click the Display tab.

    The properties of the Door's Swing will display.

13. From the Lineweight list, choose **0.18mm** (see Figure 11.25).

    If a warning dialog appears, click OK.

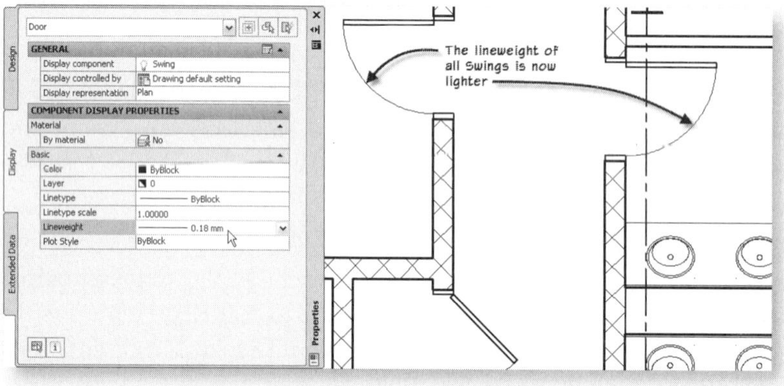

FIGURE 11.25 *Change the Lineweight of the Swing component*

NOTE

Due to variances in video card displays, you may need to zoom in or out a bit for the difference between the swing and panel Lineweight to become apparent onscreen.

CAD MANAGER NOTE

Traditionally, many firms would have achieved the same result by assigning different layers to each component. You may need to coordinate your choices with your specific plotting standards and/or service bureau. The approach showcased here takes better advantage of the benefits of the AutoCAD Architecture Display System. Although the multilayer approach is possible within the Display Properties of AEC objects, it is not necessary. Also note that the change we made affects *only* the Plan Display Representation; other Representations remain unaffected—including other plan displays such as High or Low Detail. Layers do not offer this level of control.

Using lineweight display will give you a good idea of the final look before committing to a plot. If you zoom around the plan, you will see that this is a global change that affects all Doors. This is because the Door Plan Representation edits that we made were part of the *Drawing Default*. (Drawing Default affects all objects (Doors in this case) that do not have a Style or Object override.) However, the toilet stalls appear to be unaffected. This results from their having been inserted on a different layer than the Doors. The toilet stall layer uses the same lineweight settings that we assigned to the Swing component, so the entire stall door (including the Swing) is lighter.

NOTE

All of the techniques apply to editing the Display Properties of Windows. Try the previous steps on some Window objects if you would like to see for yourself. For instance, you could add variance between the lineweight of the Frame and the glass.

14. Return to model space by clicking the Model icon on the Application status bar.
15. Turn off the Show/Hide Lineweight toggle.
16. Save the file.

MANAGER NOTE CAD

Note that we just made a Display System change only in a single drawing file. If you wanted this change to apply to all Doors in all files, you could use Project Standards to synchronize the project. First, edit the Project Standards to include Display synchronization; then open Style Manager or Display Manager, right-click the Core file and choose **Update Standards from Drawing.** This will update the Standards Drawing with the changes that were made here. Then you can Synchronize the project to update all of the other files.

Adding Custom Display Blocks in Plan

The default graphics used to display AEC objects are suitable for most situations. Occasionally, however, the default graphical display of a particular object or a subcomponent within an object fails to convey the information required by the particular architectural drawing. Even with the flexibility of available object parameters, it is often necessary to add custom components to Doors and Windows to make them look precisely as required by the project's needs. Any AutoCAD block can be added to the Door or Window style in any of its Display Representations as a custom display component. This allows you to build complex Doors such as revolving and overhead doors. You can also use this functionality to add hardware and custom frames or to create bay windows.

View a Door with Custom Blocks

As you recall, in Chapter 8 we built a Curtain Wall storefront for the first floor and added some revolving Doors for entries. These revolving Doors use custom display blocks in lieu of the default graphics for the Revolving Door type.

1. On the Project Navigator palette, in the *Constructs\Architectural* folder, open the *01 Shell and Core* file.
2. On the Doors palette, click the Revolving - Simple tool.
3. In the drawing, press ENTER to dismiss the "Select wall" prompt and add a freestanding Door.
4. Click a point in front of the building as an insertion point and press ENTER twice to accept the default rotation and to dismiss the command (see Figure 11.26).

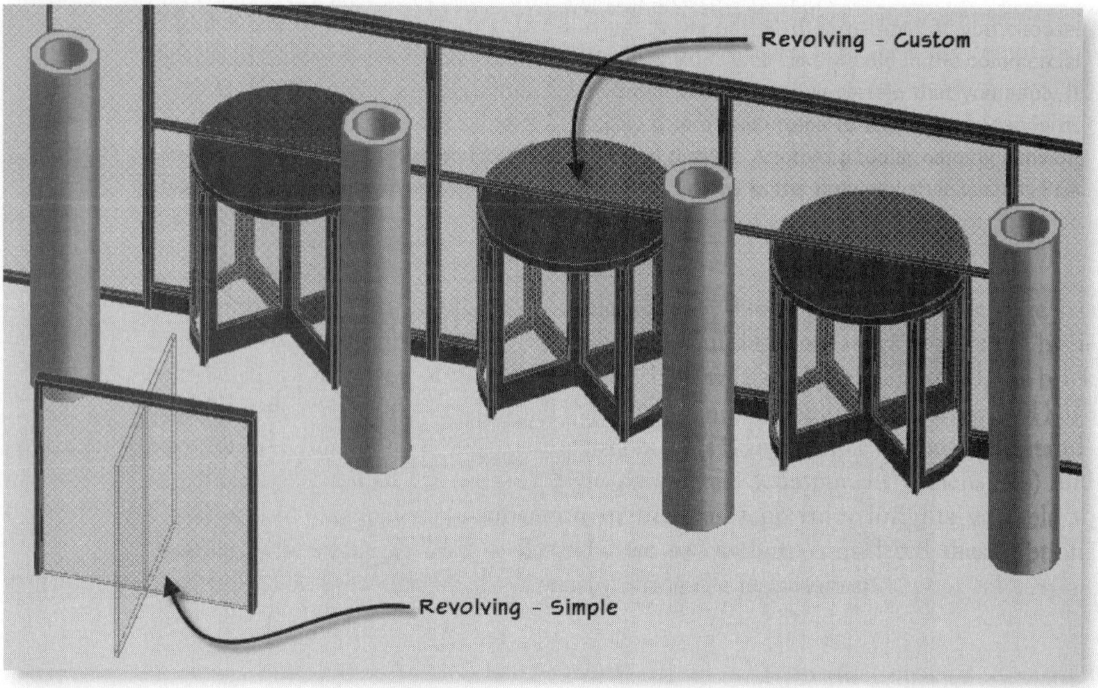

FIGURE 11.26 *Insert a freestanding Revolving - Simple Door next to the others to compare*

Naturally, you will see a big difference between the two Revolving Door styles. If you select either Revolving Door and choose the ***Edit Style*** tool from the Door contextual ribbon tab on the General panel, you will find many similarities between both styles. You will note only minor differences on the Dimensions, Design Rules and Materials tabs. However, none of these differences is enough to account for the presence of the enclosure surround in the Revolving - Custom Style or the absence of it in the Revolving - Simple. These differences occur in the Display Properties of the styles.

5. Click the Revolving - Simple Door, which you just inserted, and on the Properties palette, click the Display tab.

The active display representation is Plan. Note that it uses the drawing default settings. These settings are more than adequate for most Doors, but they do not suffice for a Revolving Door.

6. Press the ESC key and then repeat the steps on the Revolving - Custom.

This time Door Style Override occurs on the Plan representation instead of drawing default.

7. On the floating View panel , click on the down arrow icon on the View split button and choose the ***View, SE Isometric*** tool. (If your View panel is docked, you can find it on the Home ribbon tab.)
8. Select the Revolving - Custom Door again and then, on the Door contextual ribbon tab on the General tab, click the ***Edit Style*** tool.
9. Click the Display Properties tab if it is not already current. Verify the Model Display Representation is selected and click the Edit Display Properties button in the upper right.

Notice that in addition to the typical components that we are accustomed to seeing for a Door on the Layer\Color\Linetype tab, there are two additional components: Aec_Door_Rev3D and Aec_Door_Rev3D_Glass. These are AutoCAD blocks that have been added to this Display Representation on the Other tab.

10. Click the Other tab.

You will see both of these blocks listed under Custom Block Display. We will go through detailed steps to add a custom display block in the next sequence and therefore will forego the specifics of the currently selected door. However, if you wish, select one of them and click the Edit button to view its parameters. This is a great way to learn how to use this feature. Please feel free to repeat the exploration on other Display Representations as well. For instance, you will find that in this particular Door style, there are different blocks used for Plans than for Model.

11. Click Cancel to dismiss all dialog boxes when you are finished exploring.
12. Close the *01 Shell and Core* file without saving it.

Add a Custom Display Block

In the next sequence, we will add a hollow metal frame to a Door style in our *Core* file. If you closed the *Core* file, please reopen it now.

1. In the *Core* file, change the current Display Configuration to **High Detail** (Drawing status bar, see Chapter 2).
2. Select the Door to the stairwell and on the Display tab of the Properties palette, choose **Door Style: Hinged – Single** from the Display controlled by list.

   If a warning dialog appears, click OK.

The hollow metal frame block we will add will replace the default Frame and Stop. Therefore, we need to turn off the default Frame. The Stop should already be turned off.

3. From the Display component list, click on the lightbulb icon to the left of **Frame** to toggle it off (dark bulb icon).
4. Still on the Display component list, choose ***None***.

   If a warning dialog appears, click OK.
5. Click the Custom block display worksheet icon.

Here we can add custom display blocks. A block named 5HMFrame [150HMFrame] has already been drawn and included in this file. The base point has been located on the left middle point of the frame. Two scaling points have been included on the Defpoints layer to force the block to scale properly when attached to the Door (see Figure 11.27).

NOTE

If you are unfamiliar with creating AutoCAD Blocks, consult a resource on creating Blocks in AutoCAD, such as the online help.

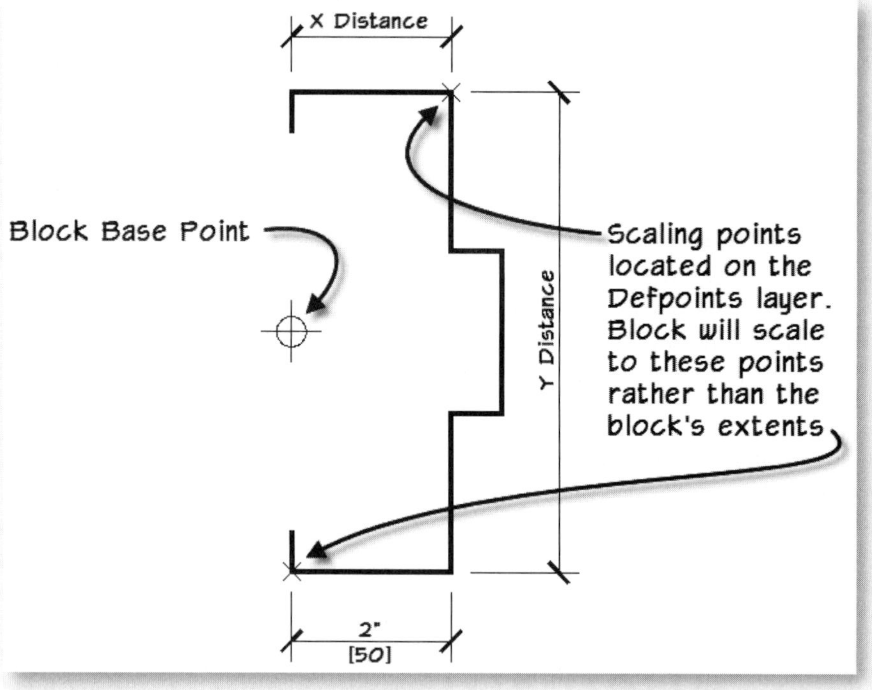

FIGURE 11.27 *Adding custom scaling points to a block*

A custom display block can be drawn at the specific size that you choose, or it can be scaled dynamically when added to the Door style. If you choose scaling, by default, a custom display block will scale to the extents of the component that it is replacing. For instance, if the Door Frame is 2" × 5" [50 × 250], the custom block will scale to fit within a 2" × 5" [50 × 250] rectangle. However, if you add two scaling points to the block, the scaling will be calculated in such a way as to fit the X Distance between the scaling points to the Width of the component (2" [50] in the current example) and fit the Y Distance to the Depth (5" [250] in the current example). A scaling point is simply an AutoCAD point entity that is placed on the Defpoints layer and included inside the block. If ACA finds point entities on Defpoints within a custom display block, it will treat them like scaling points. If you wish to see these point objects, insert the block in the drawing, edit it in place and then list the various components. Be sure to cancel or undo any edits you make while exploring.

6. In the Custom Block Display dialog, click the Add button (see Figure 11.28).

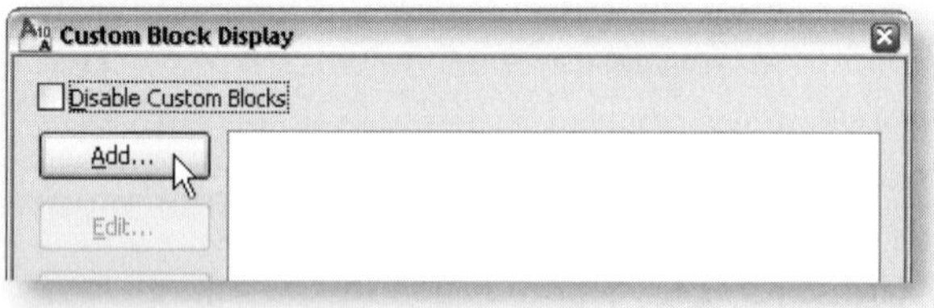

FIGURE 11.28 *Click Add to add a custom display block*

On the right side of the dialog box is an embedded Viewer window.

7. Click the Zoom button to activate the zoom mode and drag down slightly within the viewer to zoom the image out a bit (or you can use your wheel mouse).

   This will make the changes easier to see.
8. Click the Select Block button at the top left corner of the dialog box.
9. Choose 5HMFrame [150HMFrame] from the list and click OK.
10. Put a check mark in the Depth checkbox in the Scale To Fit area.

    This will match the 5HMFrame block depth (the "Y Distance" shown in Figure 11.27) to the frame depth set in the Door style.
11. In the Insertion Point area, change the Y Insertion Point to **Center** (see Figure 11.29).

    Notice the frame block shift in the Viewer.

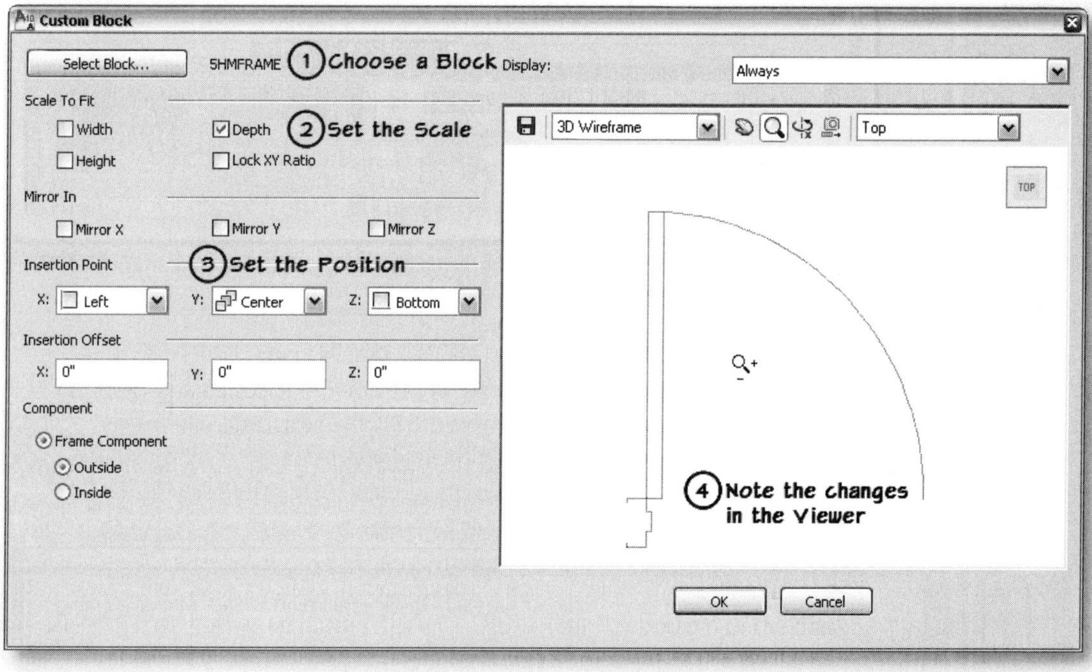

FIGURE 11.29 *Choose and configure the block*

This completes the setup for the frame on the left, but we need to repeat the steps for the frame on the right.

12. Click OK.

    Notice that 5HMFrame has been added to the list field at the right.
13. Click the Add button again.
14. Click Select Block; choose the same block, 5HMFrame [150HMFrame] and then click OK.
15. Adjust the zoom in the Viewer as before.
16. In the Scale to Fit area, again check Depth.
17. In the Mirror In area, put a check mark in Mirror X.

    This flips the block for use on the other side.

TIP

If the Viewer does not update, click OK, select the second 5HMFrame [150HMFrame] in the list, and then click Edit. This will return you to the same dialog box with the Viewer updated.

18. In the Insertion Point area, choose **Right** for X and **Center** for Y.

In the Viewer, notice that the frame is shifted a bit. This is because the insertion point of the block (see Figure 11.27) is on the left side of the block and we have shifted the block to the right (see Figure 11.30). Adding an offset equal to the width of the block will correct the problem.

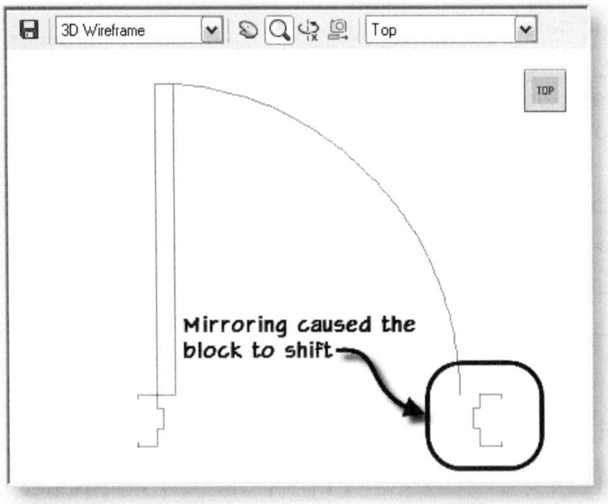

FIGURE 11.30 *The block is shifted*

19. In the Insertion Offset area, type **-2"** [**-50**] for the X offset and press ENTER (see Figure 11.31).

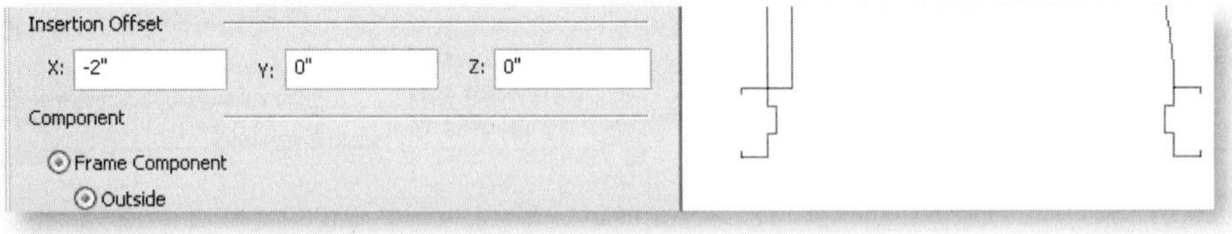

FIGURE 11.31 *Add an offset in the X direction to compensate*

This will correct the offset of the block.

20. Click OK to return to the drawing.
21. With the stair door still selected, on the Door contextual ribbon tab on the General panel, select the ***Edit Style*** tool. On the Display Properties tab, verify the Plan High Detail Display Representation is highlighted and select the Edit Display Properties button at the upper right. Click the Layer/Color/Linetype tab.

    Notice that the two custom blocks have been added as custom components. You could now change their layer and other properties if required. In this case, the default settings are fine.
22. Click OK to return to the drawing and notice the change to all of the Doors (see Figure 11.32).

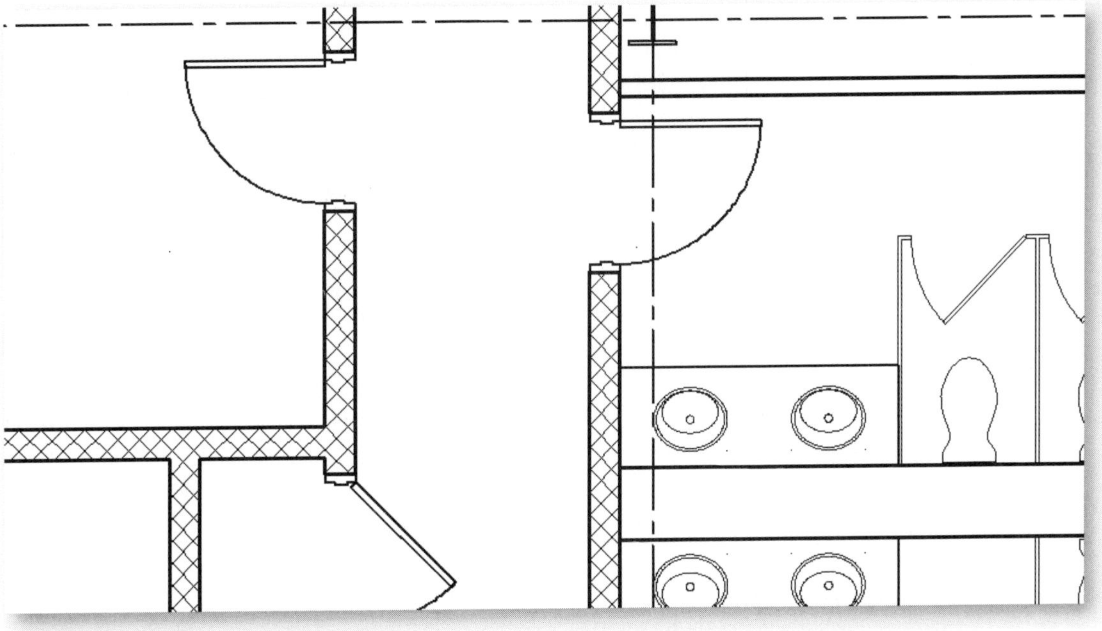

FIGURE 11.32 *All Doors now have a hollow metal frame in the High Detail Display Configuration*

23. Change the current Display Configuration back to **Medium Detail**.

Notice how all of the Door Frames revert back to the simple rectangle. This is another example of the power of the Display System. By adding the Custom Display Block only to the High Detail Display Configuration, we can easily swap between simple and high detail frames.

24. Save and close all Commercial Project files.

CREATING CUSTOM-SHAPED WINDOWS AND DOORS

Several predefined shapes are available for Window and Door styles. However, as the need arises, custom shapes can be defined. Any Profile Definition (a type of ACA Style used to form the shape of several object types) in the drawing can be used to customize the elevation shape of a Window or Door style. Profile definitions appear in a list of Custom Shapes on the Design Rules tab of the Door and Window Style Properties dialog boxes. A profile is simply one or more closed polylines that have been named and saved as profiles. Using the powerful edit-in-place functionality, customizing the shape of Doors and Windows is simple. We will begin our exploration in a separate file and then import the styles we create back to the project files.

Load the Residential Project

We will continue our exploration of Doors and Windows with a return to the Residential Project. Be sure that all files from the Commercial Project have been closed and saved.

1. From the Quick Access Toolbar, choose the **Project Browser** icon.
2. Click to open the folder list and choose your *C:* drive.
3. Double-click on the *MasterACA 2010* folder, then on the *Chapter11* folder.

   One or two residential Projects are listed: *11 Residential* and/or *11 Residential Metric.*

4. Double-click *11 Residential* if you wish to work in Imperial units. Double-click *11 Residential* Metric if you wish to work in Metric units. (You can also right-click on it and choose **Set Current Project**.) Then click Close in the Project Browser.

NOTE

Important: If a message appears asking you to repath the project, click the "Repath the project now" option. Refer to the "Repathing Projects" topic in the Preface for more information.

Modify the Window Shape

Two small files have been added to the Residential Project since the previous chapter. They are both within the *Elements* folder. Elements are typically used for project components that repeat in one or more Constructs. The *Core* and *Column Grid* files in the Commercial Project are good examples of this. However, you can also use Elements as a convenient place to store project resources that are not specifically tied to the building model in the way Constructs are. We have seen a few examples of this in the previous chapters. For more information on Projects and Project terminology, see Chapter 5.

5. On the Project Navigator, in the *Elements* folder, double-click the *Door and Window* file to open it.

The simplest way to customize the shape of a Window or Door is to use the edit-in-place functionality. Let's add a new profile to the Windows in this file using edit in place.

NOTE

Profiles are not just for Windows and Doors. Many AEC objects (Slab Edges, Roof Edges, Railings, Curtain Walls, etc.) can have their shape customized by referencing Profiles. Similar techniques will apply to those objects. Examples are provided in Chapters 8 and 12.

6. Select one of the Windows onscreen, and, on the Window contextual ribbon tab on the Profile panel, choose the ***Add Profile*** tool.
7. In the Add Window Profile dialog box, be sure that Start from Scratch is chosen for the Profile Definition, type **Window – Chamfered Corners** for the name, and then click OK (see Figure 11.33).

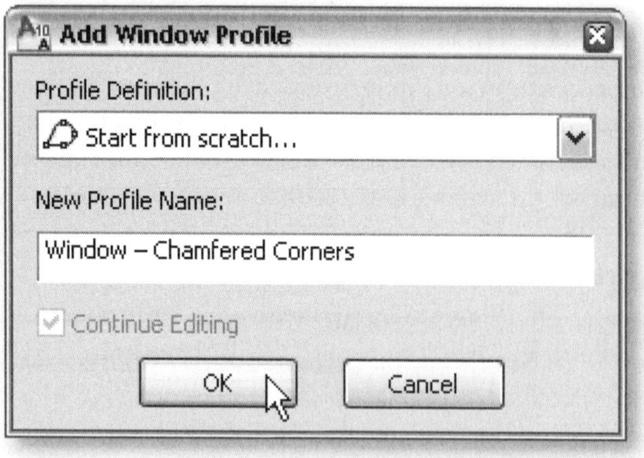

FIGURE 11.33 *Start a new Window Profile from Scratch*

The In-Place Edit profile will appear, as will the Edit In Place: Window contextual ribbon tab. Try some random grip editing to get the hang of the In-Place Edit mode. Undo when done experimenting.

8. Select the thin rectangular grip at the top edge of the Window and then press CTRL once to toggle to Add Vertex mode.

   There are several edit modes once a grip is activated. A tip will appear onscreen to indicate them. Use the CTRL key to cycle through the choices.

9. Move the mouse directly to the right with either Polar Tracking or Ortho Mode on and then type **8"** [**200**] (see Figure 11.34).

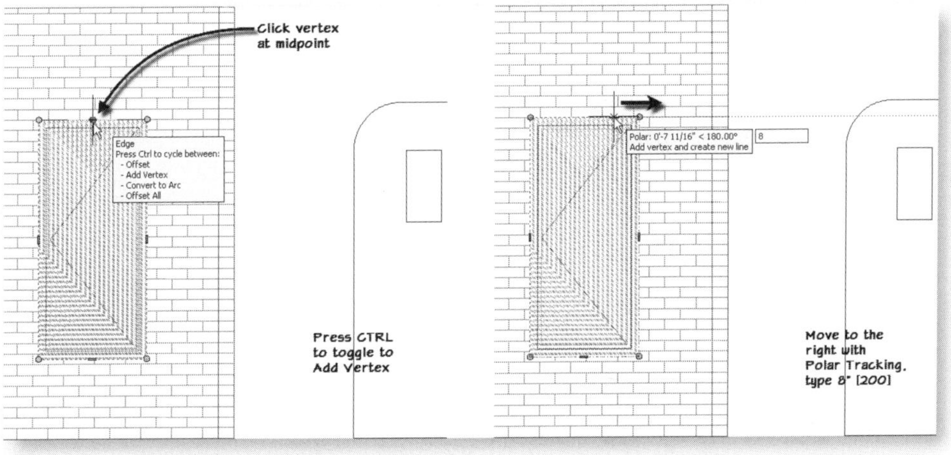

FIGURE 11.34 *Use the CTRL key to toggle to Add Vertex mode*

You should now have two segments across the top.

10. Repeat the process on the longer segment on the left at the top. Drag the new vertex to the left **5"** [**125**] (see Figure 11.35).

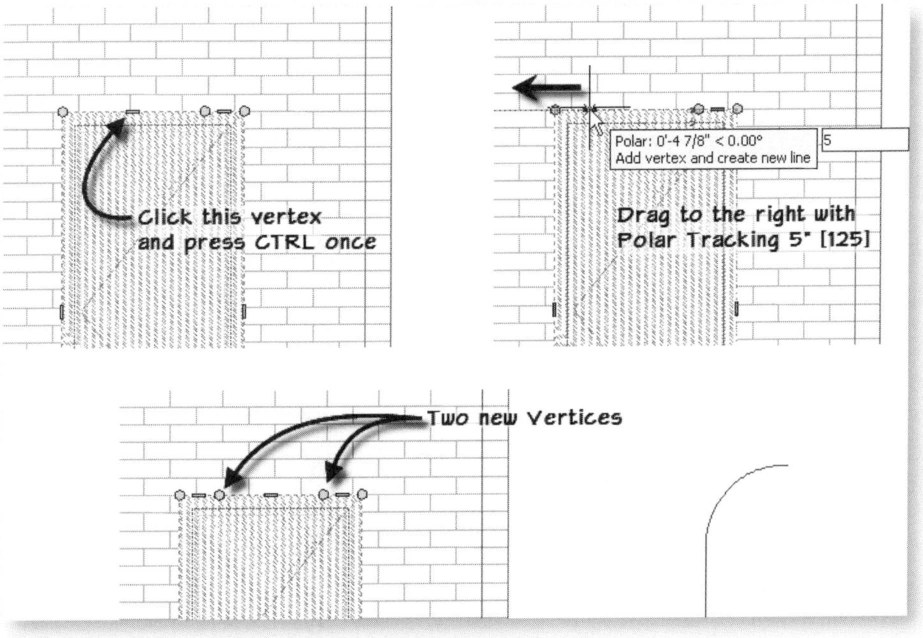

FIGURE 11.35 *Add another vertex to the opposite side*

11. Click the top right corner grip (small circle) to make it hot and move it straight down (with Ortho Mode or Polar Tracking).
12. Type **8"** [**200**] and press ENTER.
13. Repeat on the other side (see Figure 11.36).

TIP

Sometimes edits like this are easier to make with Dynamic Input toggled off temporarily.

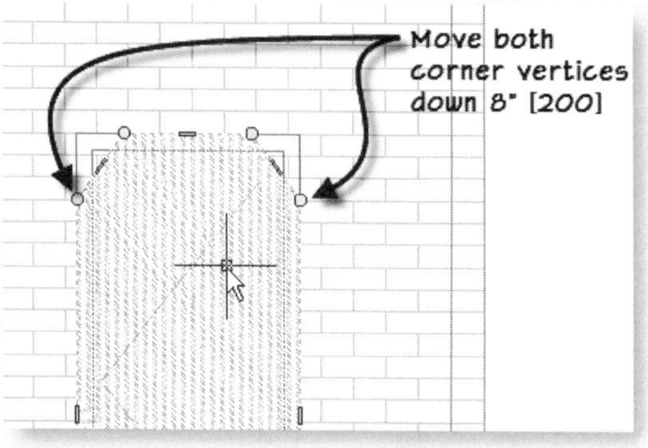

FIGURE 11.36 *Grip-edit the corners of the shape*

14. On the Edit In Place: Window contextual ribbon tab on the Edits panel, click the ***Finish*** tool.

    Note the results. The shape has been applied to both Windows. This was a Style-level edit.
15. Select either Window, and, on the Window contextual ribbon tab on the General panel. Choose the ***Edit Style*** tool.
16. Click the Design Rules tab.

Notice that Use Profile is now chosen for the Shape of this Window style and that Window - Chamfered Corners is chosen for the Profile.

17. Click Cancel to dismiss the dialog box.

Create a Custom-Shaped Door

Creating profiles for Doors is slightly different than for Windows. If you will be changing only the outer shape of the Door's elevation, use the same process covered in the previous exercise. If you wish your Door to have vision panels or lites, you can add another shape to the Profile. Also note that you can draw polylines for the shapes of both inner and outer rings while in the In-Place Edit routine.

18. Off to the side of the drawing are two polylines. Move them directly on top of the Door.

    You can snap the bottom midpoint of the large outer polyline to the bottom midpoint of the Door Panel.
19. Select the Door, and, on the Door contextual ribbon tab on the Profile panel, choose the ***Add Profile*** tool.
20. In the Add Door Profile dialog box, be sure that Start from Scratch is chosen for the Profile Definition and Type **Door Round Corners – Small Vision Panel** for the name; then click OK.

21. On the Edit In Place contextual ribbon tab on the Profile panel, choose the ***Replace Ring*** tool.
22. At the "Select a closed polyline, spline, ellipse or circle" prompt, click the outer polyline shape (the one with the rounded corners).
23. At the "Erase layout geometry" prompt, select **Yes** from the Dynamic Input menu or right-click and choose **Yes** (see Figure 11.37).

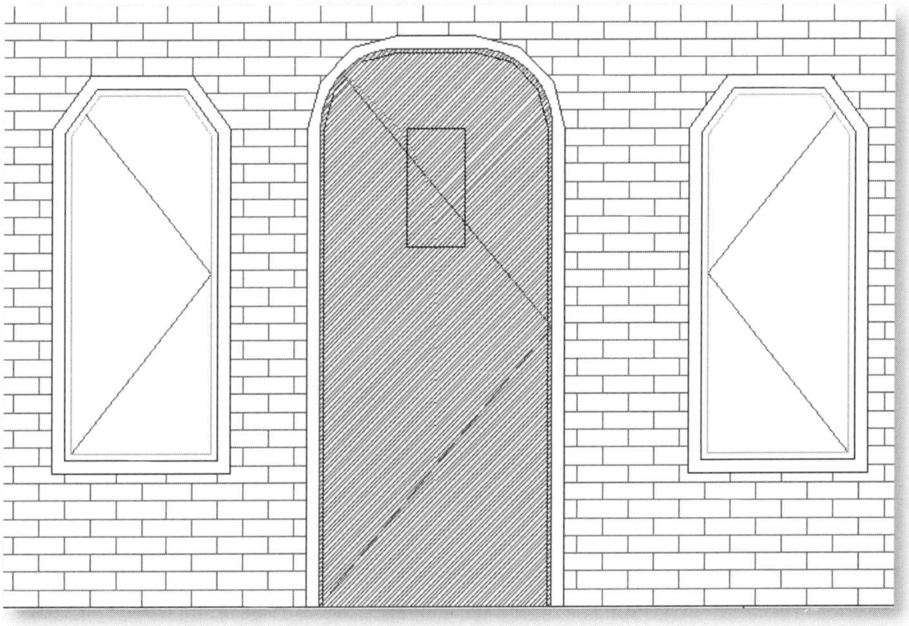

FIGURE 11.37 *Click the outer polyline to replace the ring*

24. Select the In-Place Edit profile (click the blue hatching), and, on the Edit In Place contextual ribbon tab on the Profile panel, choose the **Add Ring** tool.
25. When prompted, select the inner rectangle and answer **Yes** to erase it.
26. On the Edit In Place: Door contextual ribbon tab on the Edits panel, click the ***Finish*** tool and view the results (see Figure 11.38).

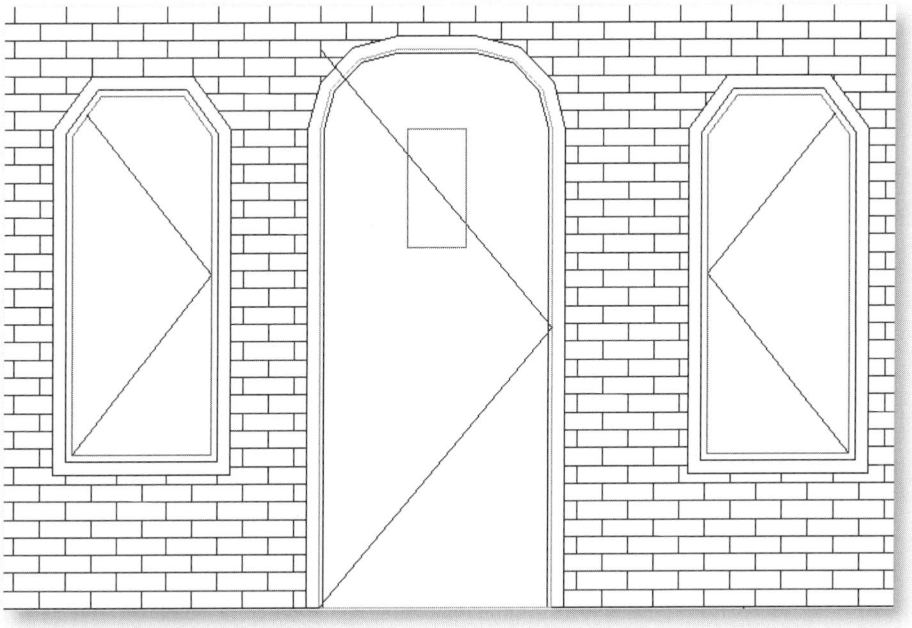

FIGURE 11.38 *Add the inner ring as a void*

As before, if you were to edit the Door style, you would find that this new profile has been added as a custom shape on the Design Rules. Select the Door, and, on the Door contextual ribbon tab on the General panel, bring it into the Object Viewer, and have a look at it in 3D. Notice that the lite correctly renders as a void in the Door. However, the glass is not transparent. Let's make that correction.

27. Close the Object Viewer, and, with the Door still selected, on the Door contextual ribbon tab on the General panel, choose the ***Edit Style*** tool.
28. Click the Materials tab and assign Doors & Windows.Glazing.Glass.Clear to the Glass component.
29. Assign Doors & Windows.Metal Doors & Frames.Aluminum Frame.Anodized.Dark Bronze.Satin to the Muntins component and then click OK.

    You may notice that the curves on the Door appear faceted after the edit is complete. There is a setting that controls this.
30. Type AECFACETDEV and then press ENTER.
31. At the "Set new Facet Deviation" prompt, type **.001** and then press ENTER.

The smaller the number, the smoother the curves will render; but performance can suffer. If your drawings become too slow at the **.001** setting, try **.01** instead.

32. Save the file.

USING THE STYLES IN OTHER DRAWINGS

Once you have built a custom style in one drawing, you will often wish to use it in other drawings in the project or even on future projects. To apply these styles to the Doors and Windows in the project files, we will add them to our MACA Residential [MACA Residential – Metric] tool palette, added to the MasterACA tool palette group in Chapter 4.

Create the Tools

1. On the tool palettes, click the MACA Residential [MACA Residential – Metric] tab to make it active.

   If this tab is not available, right-click the tool palettes title bar and choose **MasterACA** to make that tool palette group active.

If you did not do the tutorials in Chapter 4, please review the "Create a Tool Palette Group" topic of Chapter 3 before proceeding.

Be sure that the file has been saved.

2. Select the Door and drag and drop it onto the Project Tools palette.

   A New Addition Rear Entry tool will appear on the palette.
3. Select one of the Windows and drag and drop it onto the Project Tools palette (see Figure 11.39).

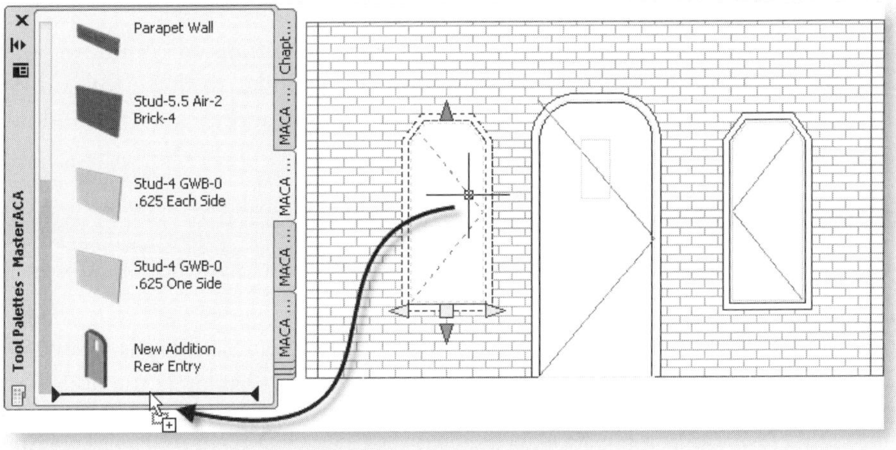

FIGURE 11.39 *Add new Door and Window tools to the Project Tools palette by dragging from the drawing*

4. Save the *Door and Window* file.

Apply Custom Styles to Residential Plan

Now let's apply the tool properties to some objects in the project.

5. From the Project Navigator, open the *First Floor New* file.
6. Select the two Windows on the left exterior wall of the addition.
7. Right-click the New Addition Single Casement tool and choose **Apply Tool Properties to > Window**.
8. Repeat the process for the New Addition Rear Entry tool on the rear exterior Door in the addition.

There will be little evidence of the change in plan. Try using the Object Viewer or one of the preset 3D Views in the drawing window to see the styles applied to the model. You can also hold down the SHIFT key and drag with the wheel to orbit the model interactively (see Figure 11.40).

FIGURE 11.40 *Applying the custom styles to the model*

9. Save the *First Floor New* file.

ADDING WINDOW MUNTINS

Window muntins can be added to the Display Representations of Windows and Doors parametrically. The interface and procedure are similar to those for adding custom display blocks. In the following steps, we will add muntins to a Window; however, the procedure is identical for Doors.

Access Window Muntin Display Props

10. Switch to the *Door and Window.dwg* file. If you have closed the file, reopen it from the *Elements* folder.

The first thing we need to determine is in which Display Representations we would like the muntins to be displayed. Unique to Muntin Block Display is the ability to link the Muntins Blocks from all Display Representations so that editing one of them edits them all. For this exercise, we will add muntins to the Model, Model High Detail and Elevation Display Representations. We will leave them out of Model Low Detail.

11. Select one of the Windows and on the Display tab of the Properties palette, choose **Window Style: New Addition Single Casement** from the Display controlled by list.
12. Click the Muntins worksheet icon.

Verify that "Automatically Apply to Other Display Representations and Object Overrides" is checked (see Figure 11.41).

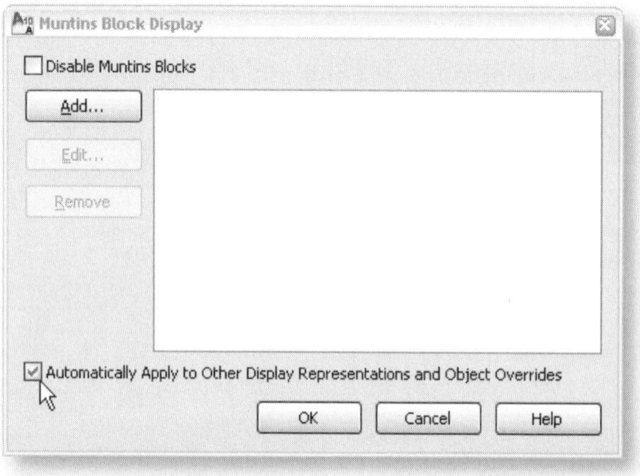

FIGURE 11.41 *Overrides are applied to two Model Display Representations, and Elevation is active*

13. In the Muntins Block Display dialog, click the Add button and then click OK twice.

All we have done here is add the Muntin Block, but we will wait to configure it until after we have added one to each Display Representation. This way when we edit it in one Display Representation, the edit will apply to the others as well. This synchronized editing cannot occur if the Muntins Block does not exist in a particular Representation.

14. From the floating View panel, click on the down arrow icon at the right side of the View split button and choose the ***View, SE Isometric*** tool.
15. Reselect the same Window.

16. Repeating the same process, add a style override to the Model representation, add a Muntins Block and then click OK.

    At this point, you should have added an override to both the Model and Elevation reps.

17. On the Drawing status bar, choose **High Detail** from the Display Configuration pop-up.
18. Reselect the same Window, repeat the process to add a style override and Muntins block once more, but don't close the dialog.

This time we will configure the Muntins Block, so don't dismiss the dialog box. Because we had the "Automatically Apply to Other Display Representations and Object Overrides" box checked in the Model and Elevation Representations, any edits we make here in Model High Detail will automatically apply to those Representations. In the Window Pane area at the top left of the dialog box, you can designate which window pane should receive muntins. Choices include Top, All, or a specific pane designated by index number.

19. Choose the "Other" radio button and then choose the "All" radio button.

NOTE

If you need muntins in the Top and one other pane, you must add two Muntins Blocks. This is not an issue for this Window Style since it has only one pane.

In the Lights area, you can set the number of lights you wish in each direction.

20. For Lights High, use **3** and for Lights Wide, use **2** (see Figure 11.42).

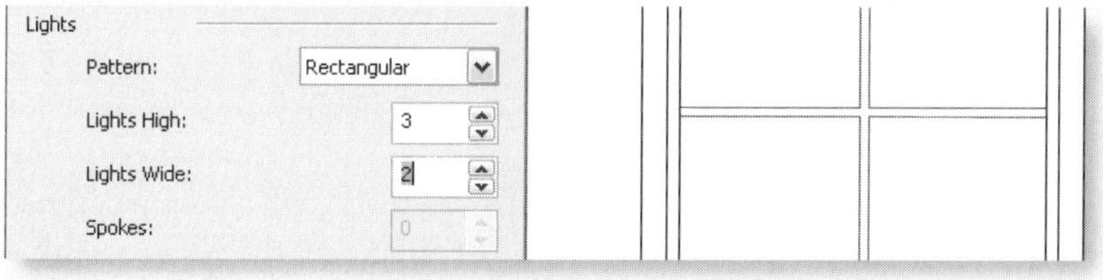

FIGURE 11.42 *Add a Muntins Block and configure the settings*

21. Take note of the check marks in the Clean Up Joints and the Convert to Body checkboxes (see Figure 11.43).

    Notice that all intersections between horizontal and vertical muntins clean up when Clean Up Joints is turned on. If you uncheck Clean Up Joints, the vertical and horizontal mullion lines will cross each other, rather than clean up. Experiment with this if you like, but restore the check before continuing.

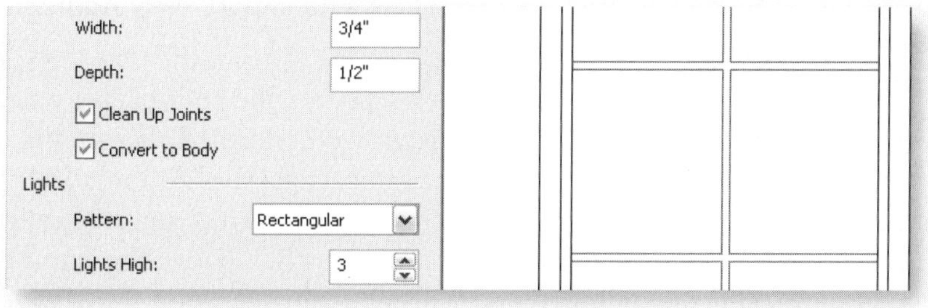

FIGURE 11.43 *Use Clean Up Joints to resolve intersections*

22. From the Pattern list, experiment with each of the four choices and then settle on one that you like.
23. Click OK twice to return to the drawing and view the effect of the changes (see Figure 11.44).

FIGURE 11.44 *Pick a pattern type to complete the muntins*

24. Save and close the *Door and Window.dwg* file.

Re-Import Styles

You may recall from the last chapter that when you drag a style to a tool palette, it records the path to the file where the style is saved. In this case, the two tools that we just made point back to the *Door and Window.dwg* file. Since we just made additional edits to the Window style in the *Door and Window.dwg* file, our *First Floor New* file is no longer up to date. This situation allows us to see another benefit of the tool palette system.

25. Return to the *First Floor New* file. If you closed it, reopen it from Project Navigator.
26. On the floating View panel, click on the down arrow icon at the right side of the View split button and choose the ***View, SW Isometric*** tool.
27. Zoom in on the two Windows in the addition.
28. On the MACA Residential [MACA Residential – Metric] tool palette, right-click the New Addition Single Casement tool and choose **Re-import 'New Addition Single Casement' Window Style**.

The two Windows should inherit the change from the source file and display with muntins. As you can see in Figure 11.45, even though we performed the muntins edits with the Model High Detail Display Representation active, the "Automatically Apply to Other Display Representations and Object Overrides" feature automatically applied those edits to the Model Display Representation as well. Change the current Display Configuration to High Detail, and you will see them there too. However, since we did not apply them to the Model Low Detail Representation, the muntins will disappear if you load Low Detail. Give it a try. At any future time, we can return to the *Door and Window.dwg* file, make edits, save them and the use the Re-import feature to apply those changes across the project.

FIGURE 11.45 *The results of re-importing the style with muntins*

Again, we are merely showcasing an alternative method to the Project Standards approach. Tools can be used to keep styles in synch as shown here. However, the tool system cannot update the styles without manual intervention. To update a style with a tool, you must open the file that needs updating and then perform the steps listed here. This is fine for small projects with few custom styles that need only infrequent updates. If you have more styles, frequent updates or large project teams, the Project Standards are a more efficient and powerful tool. Furthermore, while not covered in this text, Project Standards can be set to semi-automatic or automatic updates in which the update process can become partially or completely automated, respectively. Consult the online help for more details.

29. Save and close the *First Floor New* file.

CREATE A CUSTOM MULTI-VIEW BLOCK

Plumbing fixtures were added in the previous chapters. As we saw in those exercises, plumbing fixtures are Multi-View Block (MVB) objects. ACA ships with a vast library of pre-built Multi-View Blocks. However, in some circumstances, the symbol required for a specific item will not be available in the default library. In that case, you can build your own Multi-View Block content. We will look at the steps to build a custom Multi-View Block for the new whirlpool bathtub on the second floor of the residential project. To make a Multi-View Block, you must create an AutoCAD block for each unique view your Multi-View Block will require. Be certain that all of the insertion points line up in the same spot and create elevation views "upright" in the correct plane. Plan and elevation views are typically drawn two-dimensionally (see Figure 11.46) and often contain a flat surface behind the linework. (An AEC Polygon object can be used for this.) This surface will conceal objects behind the Multi-View Block when it is used to generate 2D Section/Elevation objects. (See Chapter 16 for more on 2D Section/Elevation objects.) In this exercise, the required AutoCAD blocks have already been provided in a file. The blocks were adjusted from files provided by a plumbing fixture manufacturer. Each manufacturer builds its CAD files differently, so the amount of rework you need to do and your results in using them will vary. Therefore, we will focus on the steps to create the Multi-View Block once the blocks are available and complete.

NOTE

Several manufacturers provide AutoCAD Blocks and/or ACA Styles and Content. Some of the providers are listed in the Content Browser. On the Insert ribbon tab on the Content panel, choose the *Content Browser* tool (not the one on Project Navigator) and look for the *AutoCAD Architecture and VIZ Render Plugins* catalog.

1. On the Project Navigator, in the *Elements* folder, double-click to open the file named *Whirlpool Tub.dwg.*
2. On the tool palettes, click the MACA Residential [MACA Residential - Metric] tab to make it active.

   Four blocks are inserted in this drawing. The red nodes indicate the insertion points. Notice that the same relative corner is used consistently.

NOTE

If you do not see nodes in your file, type DDPTYPE **at the Command Line and then choose an appropriate style.**

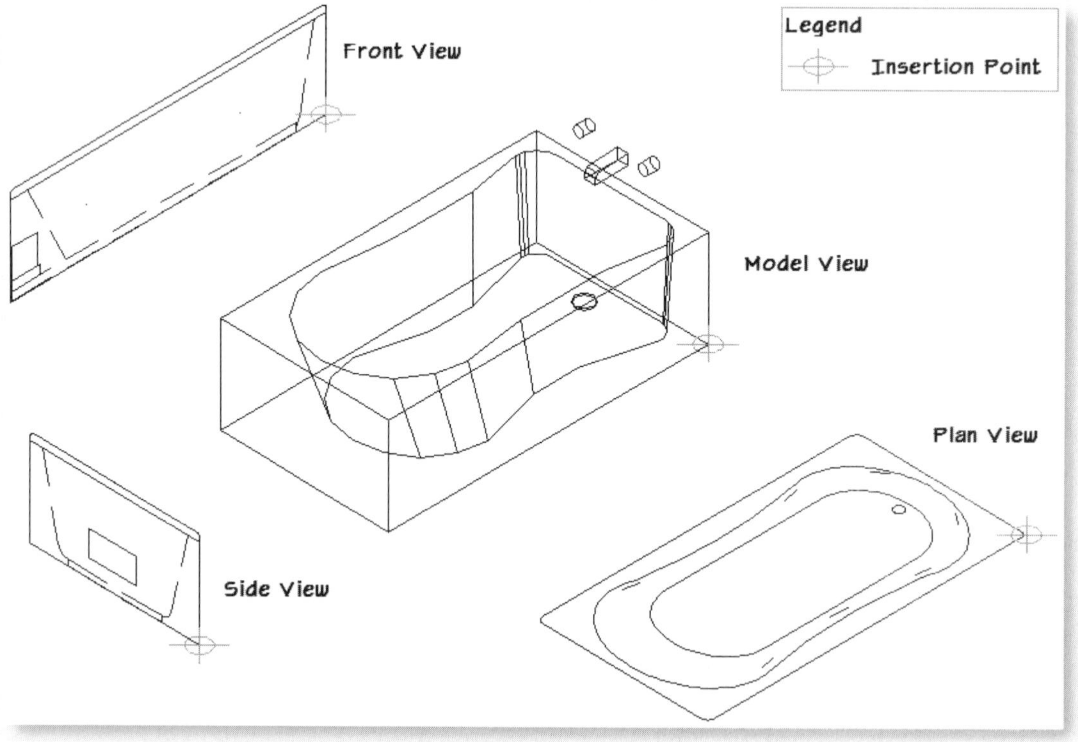

FIGURE 11.46 *Create the AutoCAD blocks with proper alignment and insertion points*

3. On the Manage ribbon tab on the Style & Display panel, choose the ***Style Manager*** tool.
4. Expand *Multi-Purpose Objects* and then select **Multi-View Block Definitions**.
5. On the right side, right-click and choose **New** and call it **Whirlpool Tub**.
6. Right-click on the Whirlpool Tub style and choose **Edit**.
7. On the General tab, change the Description to **Mastering AutoCAD Architecture 2010 - Whirlpool Tub – Residential Project** and then click the View Blocks tab.

In the View Blocks tab, a column on the left lists the Display Representations of the Multi-View Block object type, a column in the middle lists any blocks that are loaded, and a column on the right lists the seven possible View Directions. Building a Multi-View Block is actually quite simple. Choose a Display Representation, load a block and then check which View Directions should trigger the display of that block. In our case, we have a plan, front, side and 3D model View Block. The General Display Representation is used to set up all orthographic drawings (plans, sections and elevations). The Model Display Representation is exclusively for 3D. Plan High Detail and Plan Low Detail are for scale-dependent symbols (symbols that change size and/or level of detail in response to drawing scale). Finally, the Reflected Display Representation is used for reflected ceiling plans. In this case, only Blocks need to be added to the General and Model Representations.

8. Click the Add button.
9. In the list of blocks, choose Whirlpool_Tub_P and then click OK.

The "_P" suffix indicates that this is the "Plan" block. Notice that all of the check marks under View direction are checked by default.

10. Leave Top and Bottom checked and clear the rest.
11. Click Add again, choose Whirlpool_Tub_F and then click OK.
12. Leave Front and Back checked and clear the rest.
13. Click Add again, choose Whirlpool_Tub_S and then click OK.
14. Leave Left and Right checked and clear the rest (see Figure 11.47).

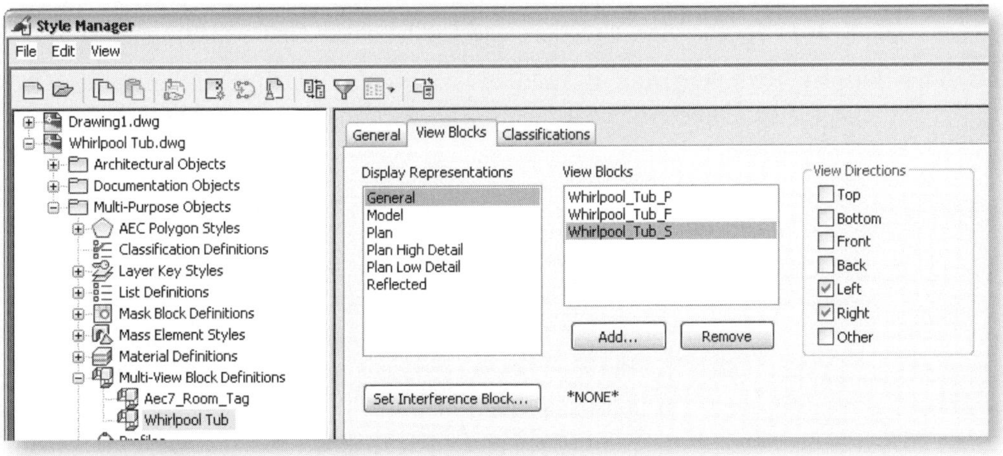

FIGURE 11.47 *Add the Plan and the Side View Blocks*

15. Click Add again, choose Whirlpool_Tub_M and then click OK.
16. Leave Other checked and clear the rest (see Figure 11.48).

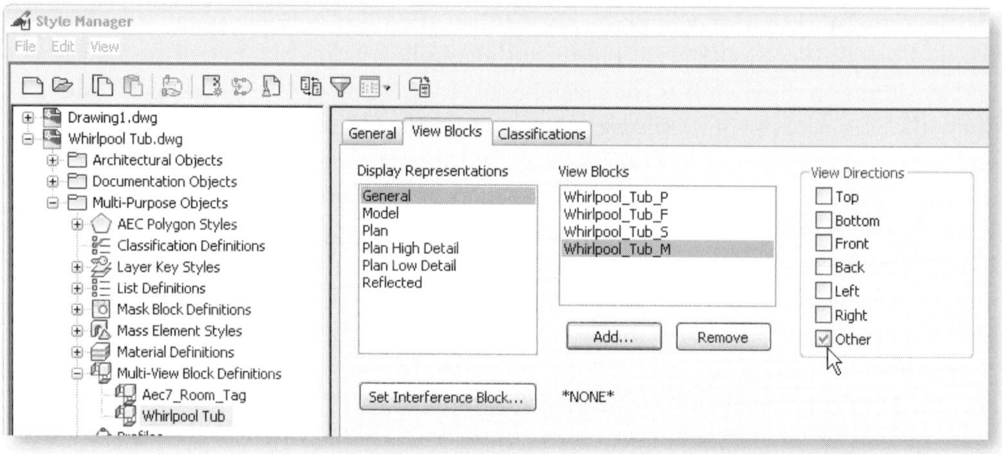

FIGURE 11.48 *View Blocks for the General Display Representation*

NOTE

Even though the General Display Representation is typically used for plans and elevations, occasionally you will view the Multi-View Block in elevation, but from an oblique angle (that is, not 90°). These oblique views will trigger the display of the block loaded in the "Other" view Direction. Loading the 3D model block (_M) will ensure that the Multi-View Block displays something.

17. On the left, click the Model Display Representation.
18. Click Add, choose Whirlpool_Tub_M and then click OK.
19. Leave all of the View directions checked here (see Figure 11.49).

This Display Representation is used exclusively for 3D applications; therefore, regardless of View Direction, we want the 3D block to be displayed here.

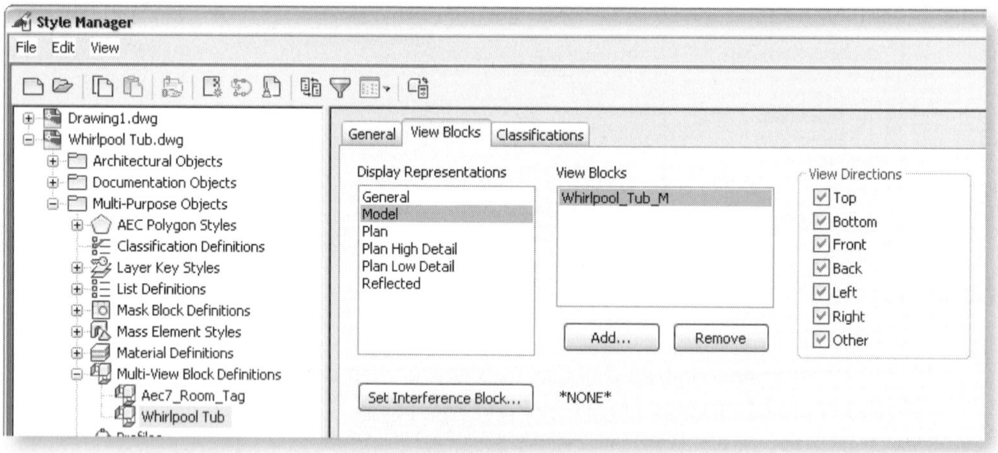

FIGURE 11.49 *The completed View Block configuration*

20. Drag the new Whirlpool Tub Multi-View Block Definition from the Style Manager and drop it on the MACA Residential [MACA Residential – Metric] tool palette.

NOTE

If the MACA Residential [MACA Residential – Metric] tool palette is not in front, click OK to exit the Style Manager and click the MACA Residential [MACA Residential – Metric] tab on the tool palettes to make it active. Then return to Style Manager and the Multi-View Block Definitions category and perform the drag and drop.

A warning will appear indicating that the tool will fail unless you save the file.

21. Click OK twice to dismiss the warning message and the Style Manager.
22. Save and close the *Whirlpool Tub.dwg* file.

NOTE

Important: Don't forget to Save the Whirlpool Tub file, or the tool will not work!

23. On the MACA Residential [MACA Residential – Metric] tool palette, right-click the new Whirlpool Tub tool and choose **Properties**.

    As before, this tool maintains a link to the definition in the *Whirlpool Tub.dwg* file.
24. Click on the Layer Key worksheet icon and choose PFIXT from the list.
25. Beneath Location, choose **Yes** from the Specify Rotation Onscreen list.

    If you are satisfied with the default icon generated for this tool, click OK to dismiss the Properties dialog box. Otherwise, use the following steps:

- Scroll to the bottom of the worksheet and right-click in the Viewer.
- Choose **Preset Views** > **NW Isometric** (or use the ViewCube).
- Right-click again and choose **Visual Styles** > **Conceptual**.
- At the top of the worksheet, right-click directly on the existing icon (directly below the label "image") and choose **Refresh image** (see Figure 11.50).

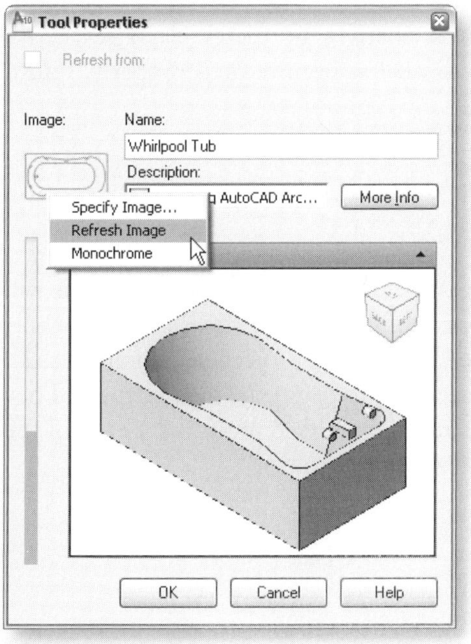

FIGURE 11.50 *Refresh a tool image*

26. Click OK to dismiss the Tool Properties worksheet and complete the tool configuration.
27. In Project Navigator, in the *Constructs* folder, open the *Second Floor New* file.
28. Click the new Whirlpool Tub tool and add the tub to the upper corner of the bathroom on the left (see Figure 11.51).

    Notice that the tub is added on the correct layer and that it prompts you for rotation after you place it. This is the result of the settings that we added in the Tool Properties worksheet.

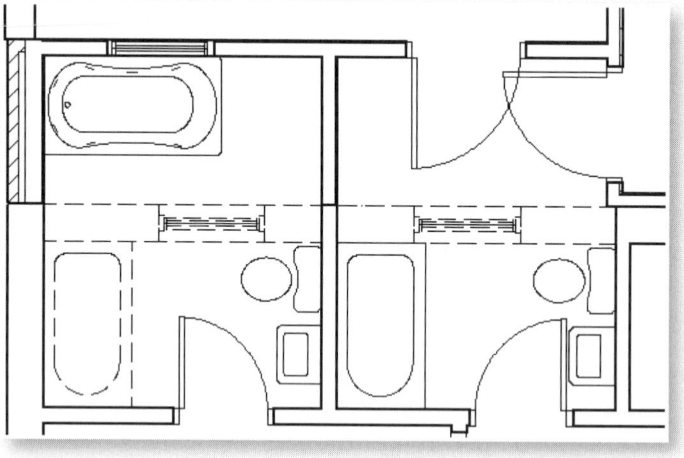

FIGURE 11.51 *Adding the new tub to the plan*

29. Using the tools on the floating Views panel, change the drawing from **Top** to **Left** to **Front** and then to any Isometric View.

Notice the way the new Multi-View Block changes to match each respective viewpoint. When you are satisfied that the MVB has been created properly, return to Top view.

30. Save and close all project files.

ADDITIONAL EXERCISES

Additional exercises have been provided in Appendix A. In Appendix A, you will find suggestions for adding a bay window to the dining room of the Residential Project and Column enclosures to the shell of the Commercial Project (see Figure 11.52). It is not necessary that you complete these exercises to begin the next chapter. They are provided to enhance your learning experience. Completed projects for each of the exercises have been provided in the *Chapter11/Complete* folder.

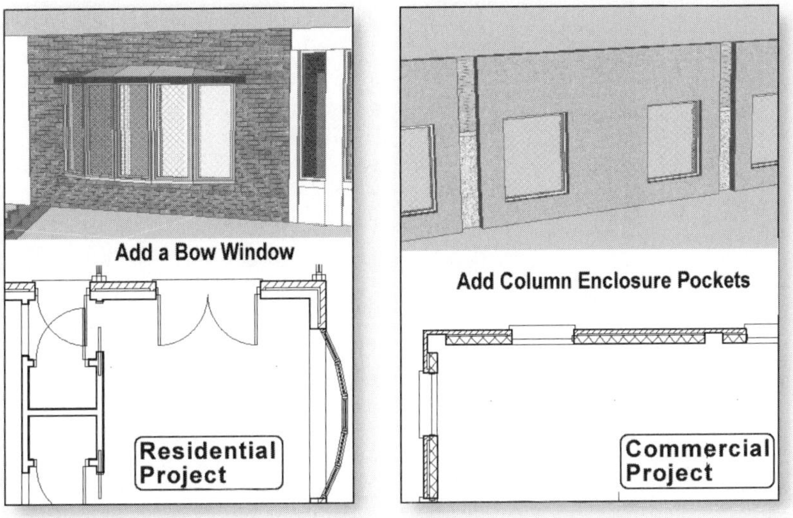

FIGURE 11.52 *Appendix A additions to the projects*

SUMMARY

- Door and Window positions are controlled by their anchor settings.
- Basic type and shape settings occur on the Dimensions and Design Rules tabs of the Door Style and Window Style dialog boxes.
- Door and Window positions can be manipulated in place with grips and contextual ribbon tab functionality or in worksheets from the Properties palette.
- The Edit in View tools provide a powerful way to isolate and edit a selected portion of the model in a convenient plan, section or elevation view.
- Profiles can be used to customize the shape of Doors and Windows.
- Profiles can include lites (rings set as voids) in Door styles.
- Each default component of the Door and Window can have its own Layer, Color, Linetype and Lineweight.
- AutoCAD blocks can be used to customize component display in any view.
- To establish custom scaling points within the custom block, you should include two scaling points on the Defpoints layer within the AutoCAD block definition to establish scaling.
- Window muntins can be added parametrically without the need for a separate display block.
- A Multi-View Block is composed of one or more AutoCAD blocks designed to represent the object from different viewing angles.
- A Multi-View Block tool can be made with presets for layer and rotation.

CHAPTER 12

Roofs and Slabs

INTRODUCTION

In this chapter, we will add the various horizontal surfaces of the building—specifically, Roofs and Slabs. AutoCAD Architecture offers two types of Roof objects: the standard (one-piece) Roof and the Roof Slab. With a variety of parameters including Rise, Run and Edge conditions, these tools allow us to model complete roof structures and assemblies. Horizontal planes and slabs can be built with the Slab object. Slabs have many parameters in common with Roof Slabs—they can be flat or pitched, and they can vary in thickness and include holes. Slabs are beneficial for 3D modeling of complex horizontal planes and for generating sections. Floors and ceilings can be modeled using Slab or Space objects depending on your project needs. In this chapter, we will explore creating Floors using Slabs. In the next chapter, we will create Space objects.

OBJECTIVES

- Build Roofs.
- Learn to create and modify Roof Slab objects.
- Build a Dormer.
- Learn to create floor Slabs.
- Work with Slab interference conditions.

CREATING ROOFS

There are two types of Roof objects in AutoCAD Architecture: the standard Roof and the Roof Slab. The standard Roof object will be referred to here as the one-piece Roof. This is because it is comprised of a single monolithic piece of material that includes all of the sloping faces. A Roof Slab is an individual sloping roof surface. The advantage of the one-piece Roof is that all joints miter automatically since it is a single continuous object. The advantage of the Roof Slab over the one-piece Roof is that each edge of the Slab can be manipulated separately, and Roof Slab Styles now include multiple components similar to Walls. As a general rule, it is useful to begin your roof design with the one-piece Roof and take it as far as its somewhat limited parameters will allow. This is easier because you do not need to be concerned with the mitering of edges and the intersection of roof planes. However, once the design progresses, you will likely need to convert it to Roof Slabs to gain more control and to articulate the design properly. This basic prescription will be followed for the Residential Project in the sequence that follows.

Install the CD Files and Load the Current Project

1. If you have not already done so, install the dataset files located on the Mastering AutoCAD Architecture 2010 CD-ROM.

   Refer to "Files Included on the CD-ROM" in the Preface for information on installing the sample files included on the CD.
2. Launch AutoCAD Architecture 2010 from the desktop icon created in Chapter 3.

If you did not create a custom icon, you might want to review "Create a New Profile" and "Create a Desktop Shortcut" in Chapter 3. Creating the custom desktop icon is not essential; however, it makes loading the custom profile easier.

3. From the Quick Access Toolbar (QAT), choose the ***Project Browser*** tool.
4. Click to open the folder list and choose your *C:* drive.
5. Double-click on the *MasterACA 2007* folder, then the *Chapter12* folder.

   One or two residential Projects will be listed: *12 Residential* and/or *12 Residential Metric*.
6. Double-click *12 Residential* if you wish to work in Imperial units. Double-click *12 Residential Metric* if you wish to work in Metric units. (You can also right-click on it and choose **Set Current Project**.) Then click Close in the Project Browser.

NOTE

Important: If a message appears asking you to repath the project, click the "Repath the project now" option. Refer to the "Repathing Projects" topic in the Preface for more information.

Working with the One-Piece Roof

Roofs can be added manually by placing them point by point or by converting existing geometry into a Roof. In many circumstances, it is easier to convert existing geometry to a Roof. To do so, you draw a polyline outline of the roof perimeter, then convert it to a Roof. In this exercise, we will explore both techniques. First, using the Add Roof Command, we will manually trace the footprint of the existing floor plan in the residential building. Later we will convert some existing polylines for the roof over the new addition. As you work, you will indicate to ACA at each point whether you wish to create a sloped surface or a gable end.

Create a New Construct

1. On the Project Navigator, right-click the *Constructs* folder and choose **New > Construct**.
2. Name the new Construct **Roof New** with a Description of **Roof - New Construction**.
3. In the Assignments area, place check marks in both the "Roof - New" and "Roof - Existing" checkboxes and then click OK.

The roof of the existing house already exists in rough form in the *Roof Existing* file. However, since the roof will undergo major reconstruction and the entire roof will be reshingled in this project, we will recreate the entire Roof structure in this file. Later, if you wish to see Views of the project as they existed before the new work, you will reference only the *Roof Existing* file. If you wish to see the house after new construction, you will reference the *Roof New* file. (See Chapter 5 for more information on Views.)

4. A new file named *Roof New* will appear. Double-click to open it.

TIP

As an alternative, check the "Open in drawing editor" checkbox to create and open it in one step.

5. From the Project Navigator, drag and drop the *Second Floor Existing* file into the drawing.
6. Repeat this process for the *Second Floor New* file as well. Zoom in on the XREFs.

We will construct the Roof of the Residential Project in this file. We have XREFed the second floor files into this drawing to assist us in placing the various portions of the Roof.

Add Roof

As was already stated, we will begin with the one-piece Roof and lay out the existing portion of the Roof. We will add this Roof point by point so that you can see the manual process. It is also possible to convert a polyline of the roof outline or the Walls of the Second Floor Existing file directly into a Roof. An example of this technique can be found in the "Quick Start" tutorial at the beginning of the book.

7. On the Design tool palette, click the Roof tool.

   If you do not see this palette or tool, right-click the tool palettes title bar and choose **Design** (to load the Design Tool Palette Group) and then click the Design tab.
8. On the Properties palette, in the Dimensions grouping, set the Thickness to **10''** [**250**] and the Edge cut to **Plumb**.

In the Next edge grouping, the Shape list includes two choices: Single Slope and Double Slope. Single Slope creates a hip or gable roof; Double Slope creates a Mansard or Gambrel roof.

9. Choose **Single Slope** for the Shape.
10. Set the Overhang to **6''** [**150**].
11. Set the Plate Height to **0''** [**0**] and the Rise to **6''** [**50**] (see Figure 12.1).

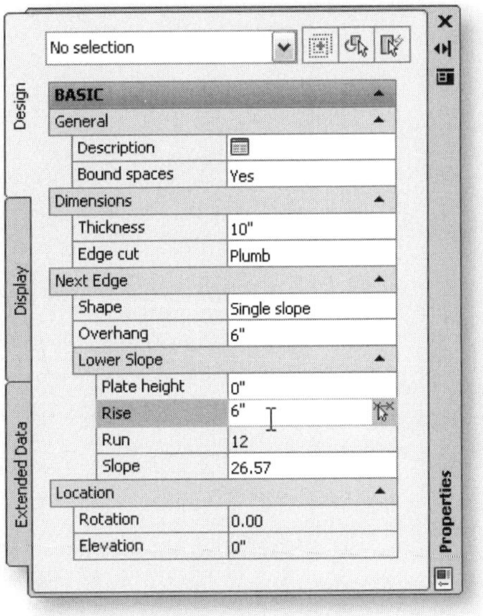

FIGURE 12.1 *Set the parameters for the first edge of the Roof on the Properties palette*

The Run is always 12 [100], but we can assign the Rise to achieve the required roof pitch. The Overhang is how far the roof projects past the perimeter walls. And we are using a zero Plate Height because the *Roof* file will be referenced in at the correct height in other Views by the Drawing Management system.

12. Use an Endpoint Object Snap and set the first point of the Roof at the outside lower right corner of the existing house (see Figure 12.2).

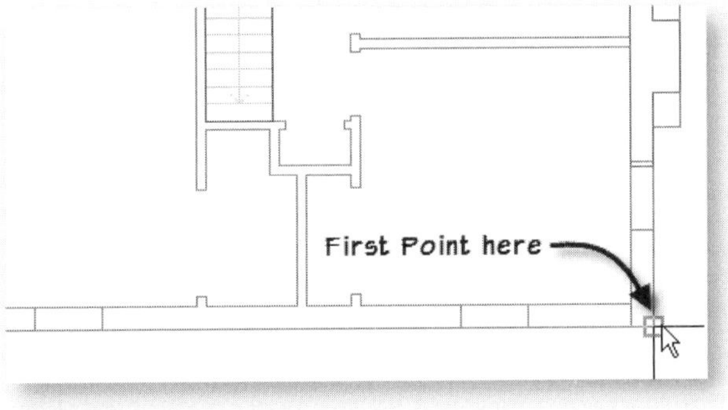

FIGURE 12.2 *Start at the lower right corner*

13. Snap the next point to the outside lower left corner.
14. Right-click in the drawing and choose **Gable**; then at the "Is Gable" prompt, choose **Yes** to the dynamic prompt (if active) or right-click again and choose **Yes** (see Figure 12.3).

    This will make the next edge of the Roof a gable. To use this correctly, remember to turn it off once the edge is drawn.

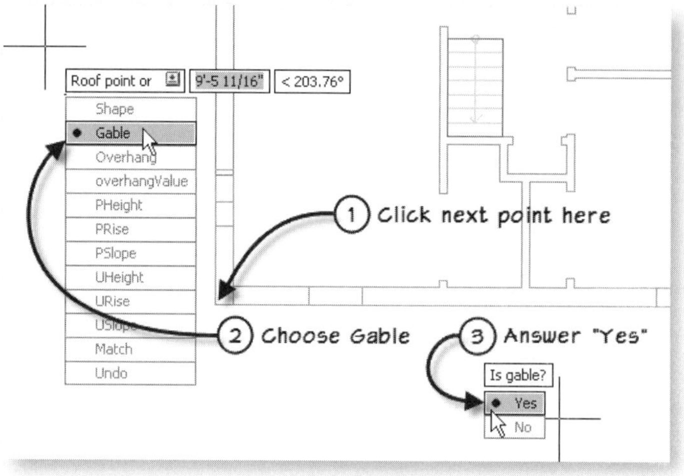

FIGURE 12.3 *Make the next edge a gable*

15. Click back to the drawing and set the next point at the intersection between existing and new construction on the left.
16. Right-click and choose **Gable** again; at the prompt, choose **No** (see Figure 12.4).

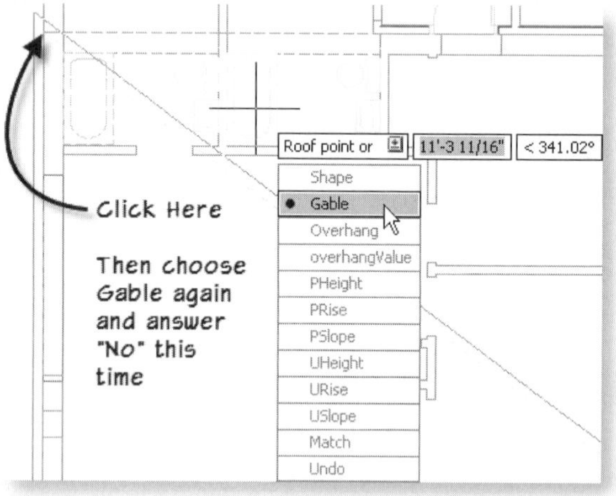

FIGURE 12.4 *Deselect Gable for the next edge*

17. Set the last point at the right between the existing and new construction (see Figure 12.5).

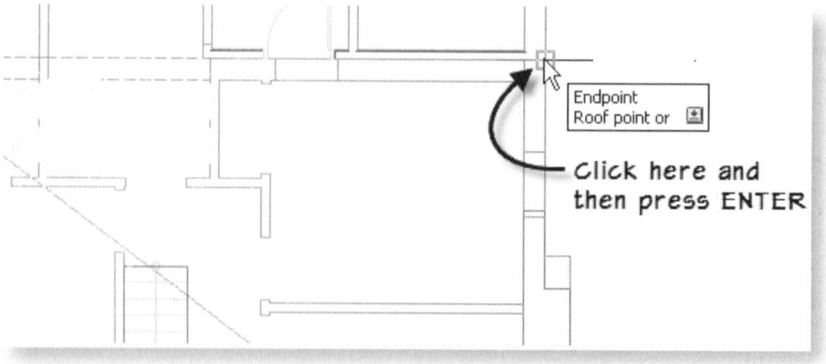

FIGURE 12.5 *Place the last point and then press enter*

18. Press ENTER to end the command.

    Notice that the left side has drawn a gable end, but the right has a hip. This can be fixed easily with grips.

19. Click on the Roof and highlight the grip at the ridge where the three hipped sides meet (see Figure 12.6).

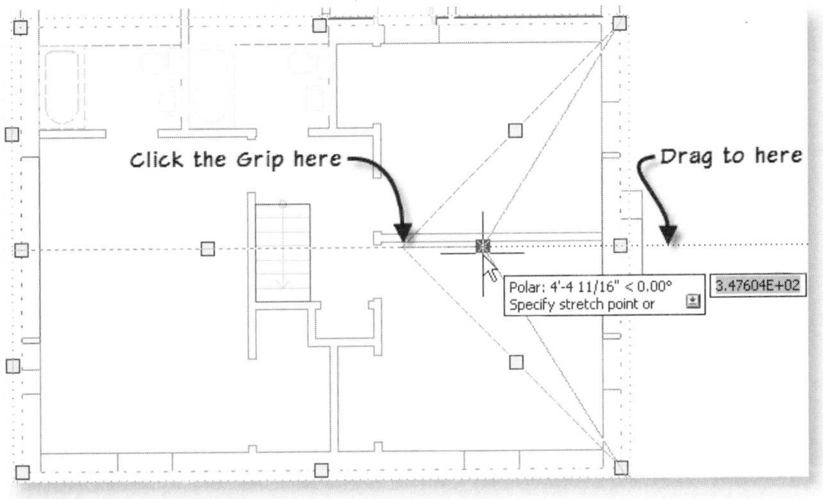

FIGURE 12.6 *Grip-edit the right face to transform it to a gable*

20. Drag the grip all the way to the right, past the edge of the Roof, and click with your mouse to complete the Roof in-place edit.

    The right is now a gable end as well. With the newly drawn Roof still selected, on the Roof contextual ribbon tab on the General panel, choose the ***Object Viewer*** tool. Have a look at it from all sides. Close the Viewer when you are finished.

Convert to Roof

For the new construction, the Roof is a bit more complex. Therefore, we will convert some polylines into Roofs.

21. On the Project Navigator, in the *Elements* folder, right-click the file named *Roof Outlines* and choose **Insert as Block**.

22. In the Insert dialog box, clear the check mark in the "Specify on Screen" checkbox for Insertion Point (accept the default 0,0,0 insertion point), place a check mark in the "Explode" checkbox and then click OK.

    Notice the two magenta rectangles that appear. By checking Explode, we have inserted the contents of the file as individual objects rather than objects grouped together as a block.

Any closed polyline can be converted to a Roof. We will convert these two closed polylines to Roofs.

23. On the Design tool palette, right-click the Roof tool and choose **Apply Tool Properties to > Linework and Walls**.

24. At the "Choose walls or polylines to create roof profile" prompt, click *one* of the rectangles and then press ENTER.

NOTE

Important: Don't select both polylines at the same time, or you will get a single Roof from their combined shape (see the right side of Figure 12.7).

25. At the "Erase the layout geometry" prompt, choose **Yes** (or type **Y** and press ENTER).
26. Right-click and choose **Deselect All**.
27. Repeat the steps on the other polyline.
28. Select both Roofs and on the Properties palette, verify that the parameters match those of the previous Roof. If not, change any settings (Plate Height, Rise, Overhang and Edge Cut) as required to match the previous Roof (see Figure 12.1 above).

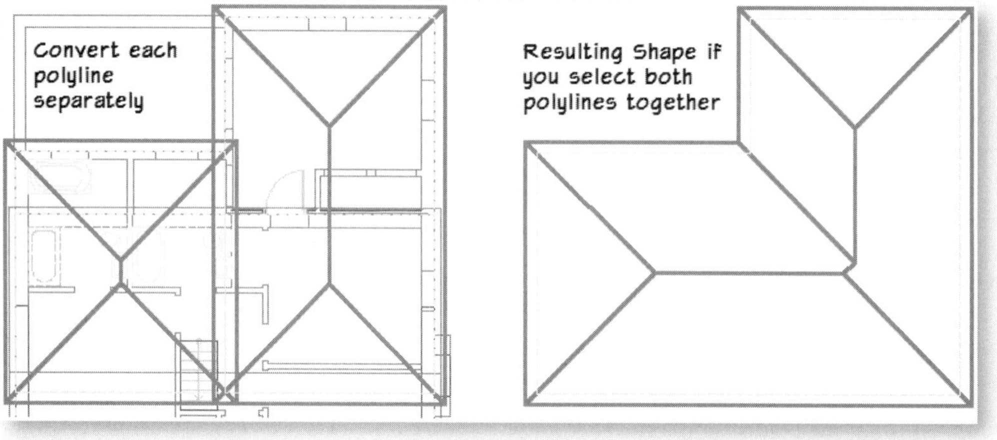

FIGURE 12.7 *Convert two polylines to Roofs*

The default shapes of the converted Roofs will be hip Roofs. By using the grip editing technique covered above, we can transform them into gable Roofs.

29. Use grips to edit the hip roof ends into gable roof ends (see Figure 12.8).

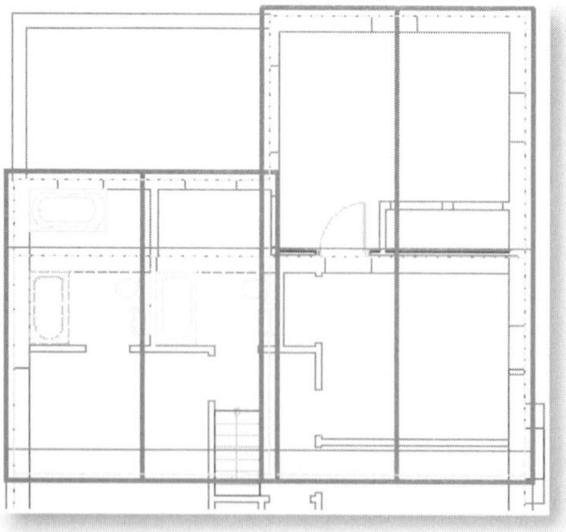

FIGURE 12.8 *Grip-edit the ends to form gables*

30. On the floating View panel (if you have docked the View panel, find it on the Home ribbon tab), select the down arrow icon at the right side of the View split button and click the ***View, Back*** tool.

    Take a look at the Roofs' overall relationship to each other (see Figure 12.9).

This will give you a better sense of what we have so far.

FIGURE 12.9 *Viewing the Roofs from the back*

31. Select all three Roof objects, hold down the SHIFT key, and then drag with the wheel of your mouse.

    The action with your wheel is press, hold and drag—exactly like you do when panning; however, holding the SHIFT key down orbits the model in 3D instead!

NOTE

If your wheel does not behave this way, check the settings of your mouse driver in the Mouse Control Panel on your system.

32. Orbit the Roofs around in 3D and study them from all sides.

Notice that when objects are selected, only those objects display while orbiting. However, when you release the mouse, the remainder of the model reappears. If you wish to see only the Roofs, you can unload the XREFs; but an easier approach is to use the Isolate Objects command.

33. With the three Roofs still selected, on the Roof contextual ribbon tab on the General panel, choose the ***Isolate Objects*** tool.

    If you prefer, you can choose the same command from the lightbulb icon on the Drawing status bar.

34. On the View ribbon tab on the Appearance panel, select the Visual Styles button in the lower right corner and click the ***Conceptual*** tool (see Figure 12.10).

    If you prefer, you can choose the ***Visual Styles, Conceptual*** tool from the floating View panel, by selecting the down arrow icon at the right side of the Visual Styles split button (middle button).

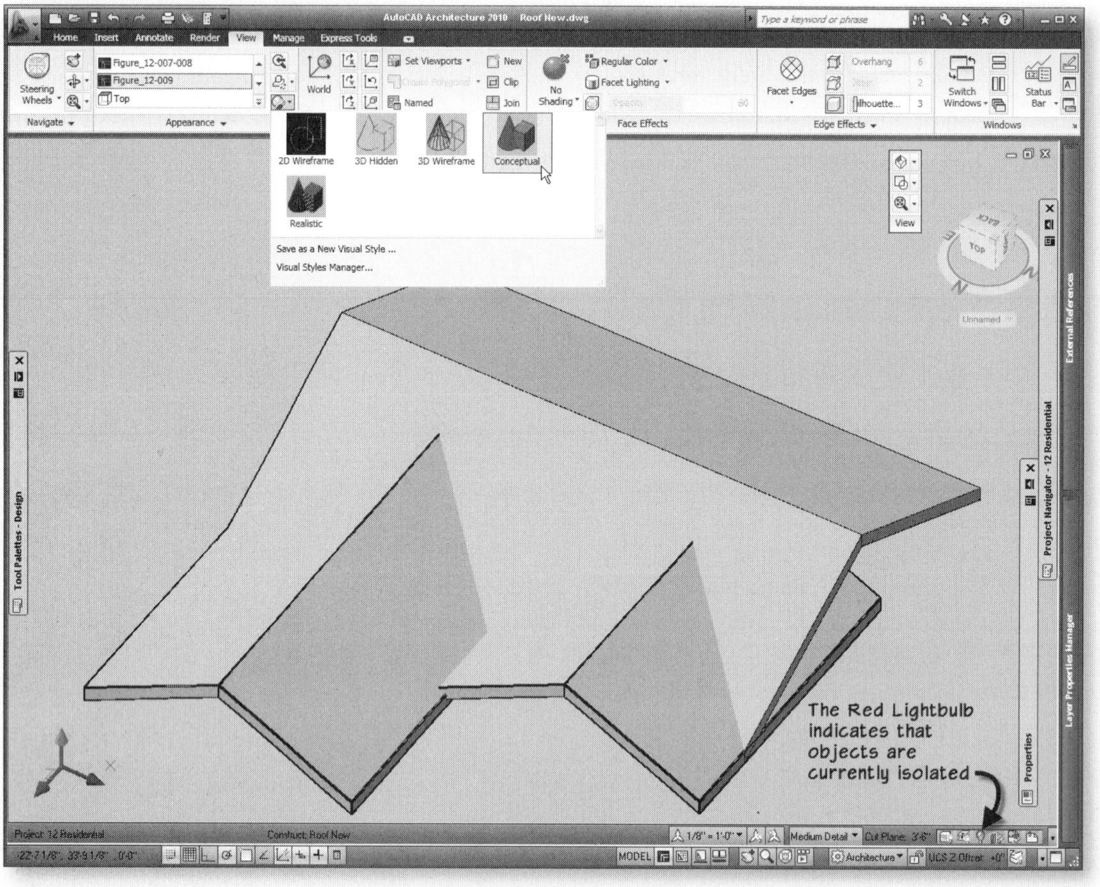

FIGURE 12.10 *Bring the Roof into the Object Viewer*

Try other Visual Styles if you wish. Continue to orbit and study the Roof from different angles until you are satisfied. The one-piece Roof is a relatively simple object. It is not Style-based and has few parameters. However, do not be fooled into thinking that the one-piece Roof is too simple to be valuable. It is precisely this simplicity that makes it valuable. Because it is a single continuous object, you can easily modify critical parameters such as the Roof pitch and quickly change the faces from hips to gables. As you make these changes, all faces automatically join and miter correctly because the Roof is a single continuous object. This feature is very valuable in the early stages of design where changes are frequent. Use the one-piece Roof in early design phases to rough out the roof configuration. Do not convert to Roof Slabs until project needs it. To make complex Roof designs, simply create multiple one-piece Roof objects as we have done here. At the schematic design and early design development phases, do not be concerned with how the Roofs interact with each other. You will notice that the two smaller Roofs here intersect with the larger Roof. Before moving on to Roof Slabs, let's take a look at a few one-piece Roof properties.

35. Select any Roof and modify some of its parameters on the Properties palette.
36. Click the Edges/Faces worksheet icon in the Dimensions grouping.

Individual edges can be edited in this dialog box. For instance, to make a saltbox style Roof, change the Plate Height of just one Edge. The Overhang parameter can be edited one edge at a time as well. Some of the values are calculated by the software as a result of other parameters. For instance, you will not be able to edit the Eave value, Segments or Radius. The Eave is a result of the pitch. When you change the Rise, Run or Angle in the Modify dialog box or in the lower portion of this tab, the Eave adjusts accordingly. Segments and Radius are available only when you convert a polyline with curved segments to a Roof. Even though it converts the arc segment of the polyline into several straight segments, this parameter remains available for edit so that you can increase or decrease the quantity of segments used to describe the curve. The only problem with editing edges this way is that there is no easy way to tell which edge is which. For this reason, the Modify Edges command can be a better choice, as explained below.

37. Finish your experiments and click OK to close the worksheet.
38. Undo any changes made in the Properties palette or the Edges/Faces worksheet.
39. On the floating Views panel, choose the ***View, Top*** tool.
40. On the View ribbon tab on the Appearance panel, select the Visual Styles button in the lower right corner and click the ***2D Wireframe*** tool (or choose the ***Visual Styles, 2D Wireframe*** tool from the floating View panel).
41. On the Drawing status bar, click the small red lightbulb icon and choose **End Object Isolation** from the pop-up menu that appears (or right-click in the drawing window and choose **Isolate Objects > End Object Isolation**).

Visual Styles offer a wonderful way to view and study your model as it progresses. If you have a certified video card (visit www.autodesk.com for a complete list), you can consider working while Visual Styles are active. If you do not have a proper video card (or even in some cases if you do), working in 2D Wireframe is more practical, particularly when working in plan view.

Modify Roof Edges

42. Select any Roof, and, on the Roof contextual ribbon tab on the Modify panel, choose the ***Edit Edges*** tool.
43. Click a single Edge of the Roof that you wish to edit and then press ENTER.

Notice that there is now a single entry in the Edit Edges dialog box, making it impossible to edit the wrong edge (see Figure 12.11).

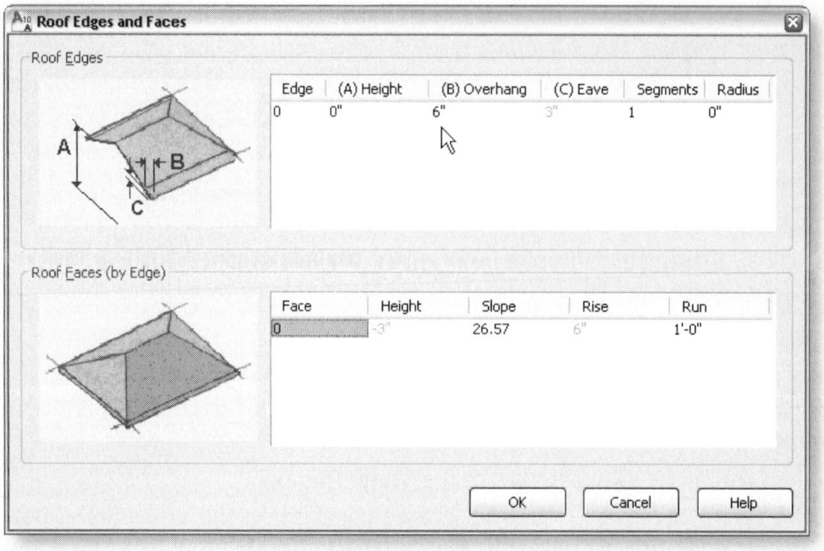

FIGURE 12.11 *Only a single edge is available to edit*

44. Make any changes and experiment on other edges if you wish; then click OK.
45. Undo the changes and save the file when you are finished.

Working with Roof Slabs

As you probably noticed, the parameters of the one-piece Roof are limited. Building a Roof that achieves the complexity of the typical architectural project often requires several Roofs. However, separate one-piece Roofs do not interact with one another. Furthermore, the one-piece Roof gives very little control over eave, soffit and fascia conditions. For those situations, we have the Roof Slab. Roof Slabs offer all of this additional functionality, and their styles can contain multiple components similar to Walls.

Convert to Roof Slabs

Our design has progressed to the point where the one-piece Roofs no longer suit our needs. We will convert them to Roof Slabs.

1. Select all three of the Roofs, and, on the Roof contextual ribbon tab on the Modify panel, choose the ***Convert*** tool.

   A small Convert to Roof Slabs worksheet will appear.
2. Place a check mark in the "Erase layout geometry" checkbox and then click OK.

Although it is possible to keep the original one-piece Roofs after conversion, this would only be advisable if you intended to spin off more than one scheme from the original Roof, or if the client is still actively making changes. If planning to do so, you can choose to keep the layout geometry after conversion. You can then freeze the Roof layer. Roof Slabs use a separate layer by default.

A flurry of grips will appear, as well as some additional linework (see Figure 12.12).

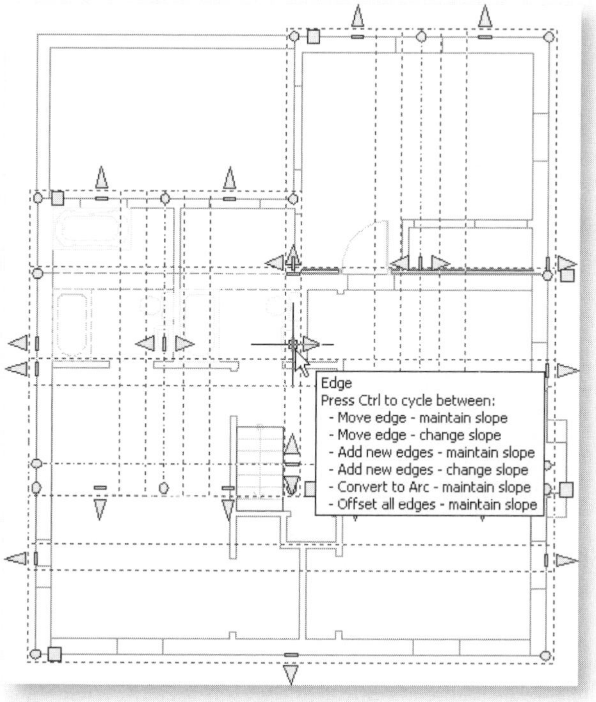

FIGURE 12.12 *The one-piece Roofs converted to several separate Roof Slabs*

As usual, the grips have a variety of shapes and functions. Hover your mouse over each grip to see a tool tip of its function. If you click any grips and make any edits, be sure to undo before continuing.

All of this additional linework makes it a bit difficult to see what is going on. Perhaps it is time that we turned off the display of the XREFs.

3. At the bottom right corner of the drawing, on the Drawing status bar, right-click the Manage XREFs quick pick and choose **External References** (see Figure 12.13).

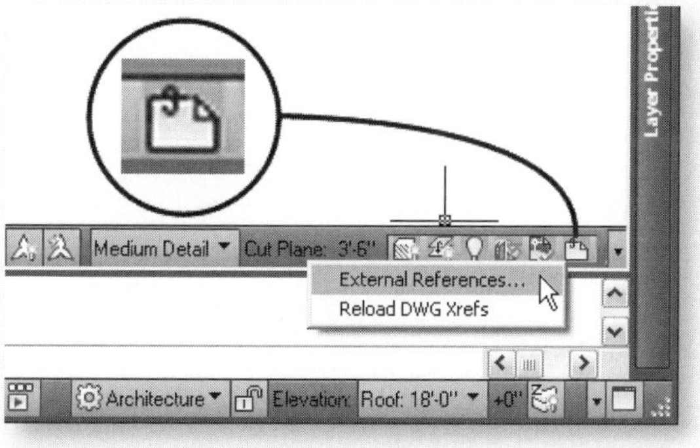

FIGURE 12.13 *Use the XREF Quick Pick to open the External References palette*

4. Select both the *Second Floor New* and the *Second Floor Existing* XREFs, right-click and choose **Unload**.

The second floor plan will disappear. Now that we have the entire Roof in rough form, the XREF is no longer needed. However, just in case, we chose Unload so that we can quickly retrieve it should design needs require it again.

If you wish, you can set the External References palette to Auto-Hide, Dock, Anchor or close. Refer to Chapter 1 for explanations of the various options.

If you select one of the newly created Roof Slabs and look at its properties on the Properties palette, you will notice that the thickness is no longer 10" [250] as we indicated for the Roof object above. This is because the Roof object set to a Plumb Edge Cut measures the thickness vertically rather than the true thickness of the roof surface as the Roof Slab does. So let's make a few minor adjustments to the Roof Slabs we just created.

5. Select all of the Roof Slabs.
6. On the Properties Palette, set the Thickness to **10"** [**250**] and the Elevation to **0**.
7. On the View ribbon tab on the Appearance panel, select the Visual Styles button and click the ***Conceptual*** tool (or choose the ***Visual Styles, Conceptual*** tool from the floating View panel).

Notice that the top half of the Roof seems to disappear. Like other AEC objects, Roof Slabs are affected by the Cut Plane assigned to the drawing. In this case, the default 3'-6" [1400] Cut Height cuts through the Roof Slabs and shows only the lower portion. In some cases, this may be the appropriate display condition (such as in an attic plan); but in this case, it will be easier to edit the Roof Slabs if we can see the entire object. There are a few ways that we can achieve this. For now, we will use the Display Manager and move the Cut Height above the highest point on the Roofs. We can also edit the Display Properties of the Roof Slab objects and turn on the display of the Above Cut Plane Body Shrinkwrap or even apply a Cut Plane override to the Slabs themselves. Feel free to experiment with these options on your own if you wish.

8. On the Manage ribbon tab on the Style & Display panel, choose the ***Display Manager*** tool.
9. Expand the *Configurations* folder; select Medium Detail; and then on the right side, click the Cut Plane tab.
10. In the Cut Height field, type **10'-0"** [**3000**] and then click OK (see Figure 12.14).

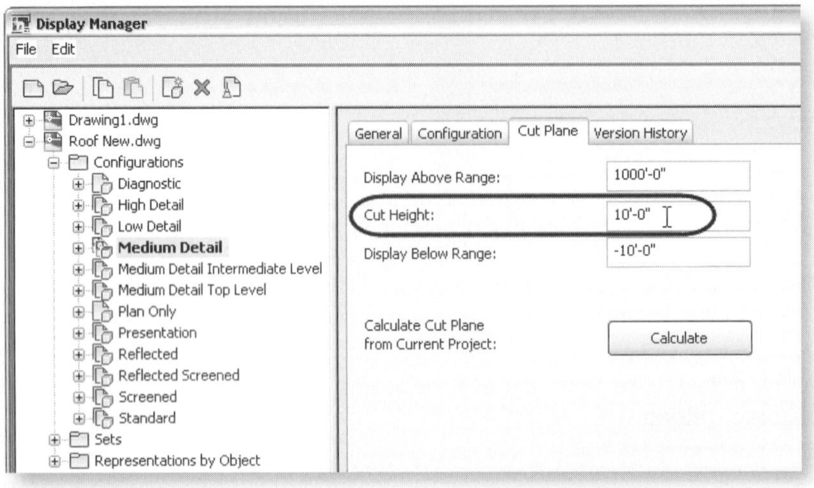

FIGURE 12.14 *Change the Cut Height to better show the Roof*

11. On the View ribbon tab on the Appearance panel, select the Visual Styles button and click the ***2D Wireframe*** tool (or choose the ***Visual Styles, 2D Wireframe*** tool from the floating View panel).

NOTE

As an alternative, you can use the Cut Plane control on the Drawing status bar and use the "Global Cut Plane" worksheet to reset the value. Making the change that way affects the current Display Configuration.

Trim the Roof Slab

At the moment, the two Roofs for the new addition pass through the existing Roof. In this sequence, we will look at ways to trim the Roof Slabs to the intersection point instead. In order to do this, we need to rough out the shape we need on the roof of the existing house first and then miter all the Roof Slabs together. We will draw a simple polyline to assist us in this task.

12. On the Application status bar (at the bottom of the screen as shown in Figure 1.2 in Chapter 1), right-click the Polar Tracking button and choose **Settings**.
13. Verify that there is a check mark in the "Polar Tracking On" checkbox.
14. Verify also that the Increment angle is set to 30° and the additional angles are set as shown in the left side of Figure 12.15.
15. Click the Object Snap tab.
16. Be sure that "Object Snap On," "Object Snap Tracking On," "Endpoint" and "Midpoint" are all checked, turn off any other snaps and then click OK (see the right side of Figure 12.15).

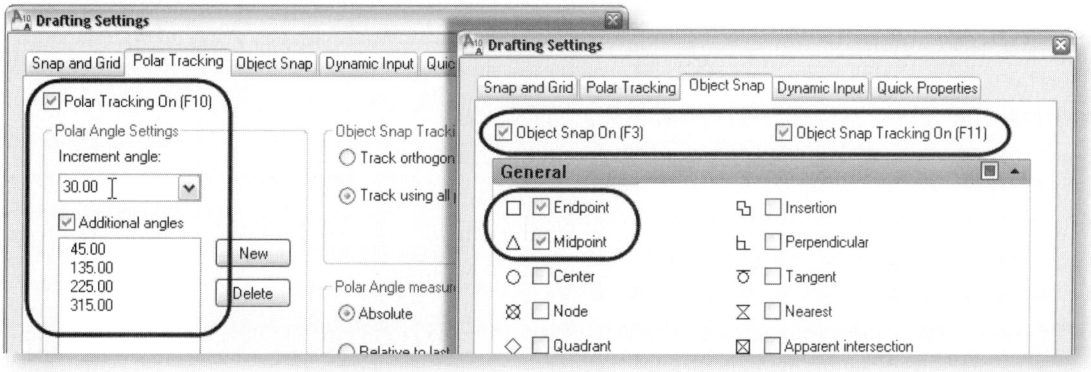

FIGURE 12.15 *Set up Polar Tracking and Object Snap settings*

17. On the Drawing status bar, disable the Allow/Disallow Dynamic UCS icon. (Make sure that the icon background is gray, not bluish green.)

Dynamic UCS is a feature that allows the cursor to automatically align to the coordinate system of any surface in 3D. Since we are working on sloping roof surfaces, this feature would potentially align the cursor to the plane of the roof as we are trying to draw the polyline. In this case, this is not what is needed.

One more setting that we want to adjust before we begin the polyline is to turn on the Baseline component of the Roof Slab objects. This will assist us in snapping to the proper points. We will use the ability to modify the display property settings for a selected object in the current display representation directly from the Properties Palette.

18. Select any Roof Slab and on the Properties Palette, click the Display tab.
19. On the Display component list, click on the light bulb icon to the left of **Baseline** to make the baseline component visible (see Figure 12.16).
20. If a warning dialog appears noting that the change will apply to all objects of the same type with no override, select OK; otherwise, select the *NONE* component to collapse the component list.

A blue dashed line will appear around each Roof Slab object (see the right side of Figure 12.16).

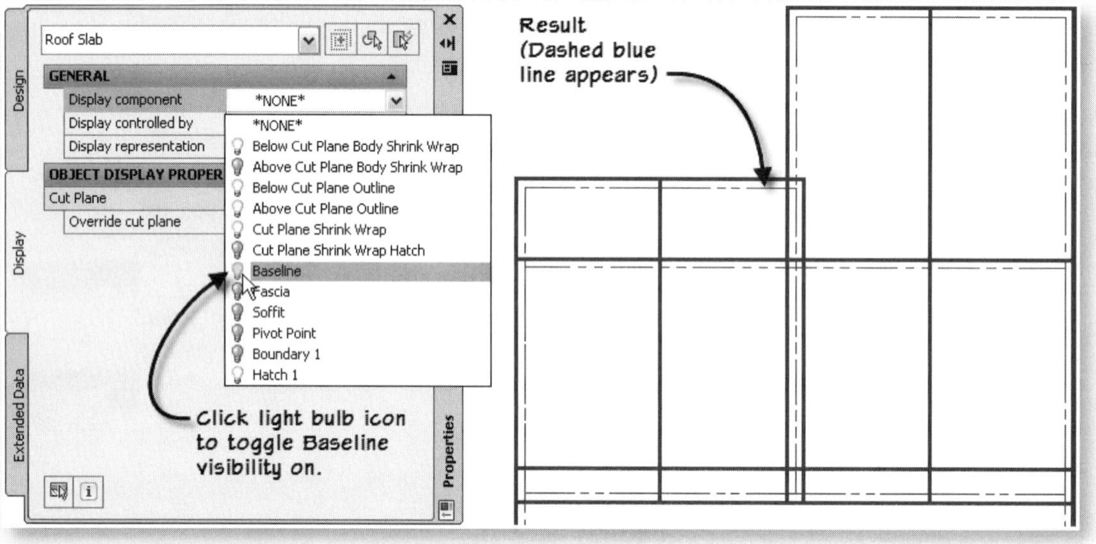

FIGURE 12.16 *Turn on the Baseline component of the Roof Slab objects*

The Baseline component represents the outside edge of the Walls beneath the roof. It is the edge of the Roof Slab minus the overhang.

TIP

When you trim and miter Roof Slabs, try to do so relative to the Baseline rather than the overhang for more predictable results.

21. On the Home ribbon tab on the Draw panel, select the down arrow icon on the Line split button (bottom half) and click the ***Polyline*** tool (or type **PL** at the Command Line and press ENTER).
22. At the "Start point" prompt, click the Endpoint at the left of the plan where the two Roof Slab Baselines meet (see Figure 12.17).

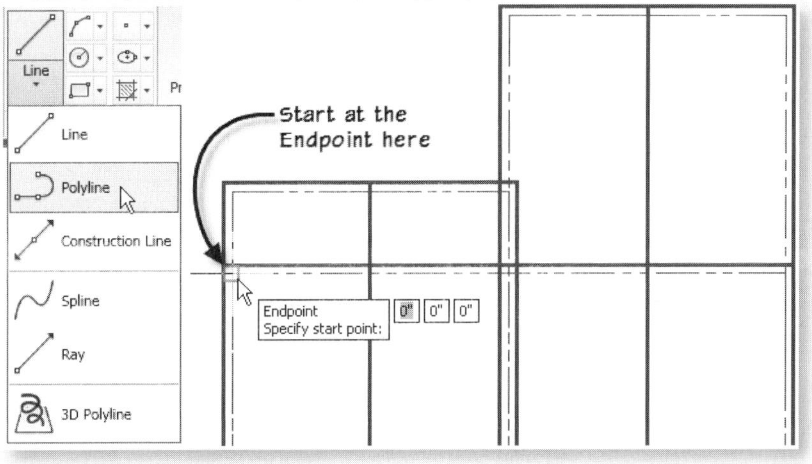

FIGURE 12.17 *Start the polyline where the Roof Slabs meet*

23. Using tracking, acquire the ridge point and track it down to the 45° valley (see Figure 12.18).

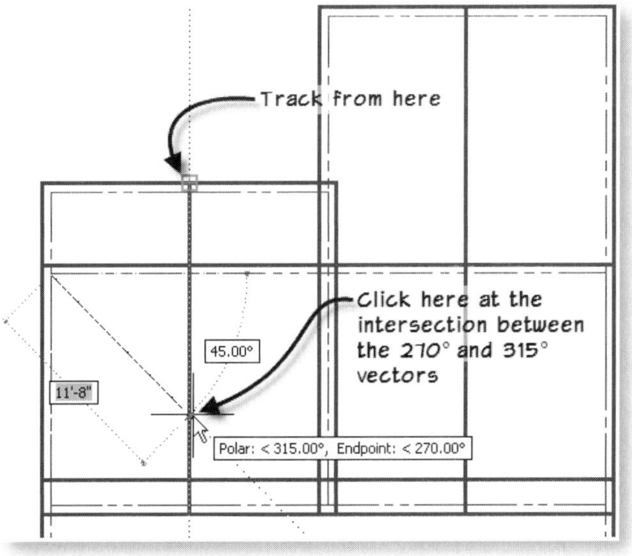

FIGURE 12.18 *Set the next point using tracking*

24. Complete the polyline using Figure 12.19 as a guide.

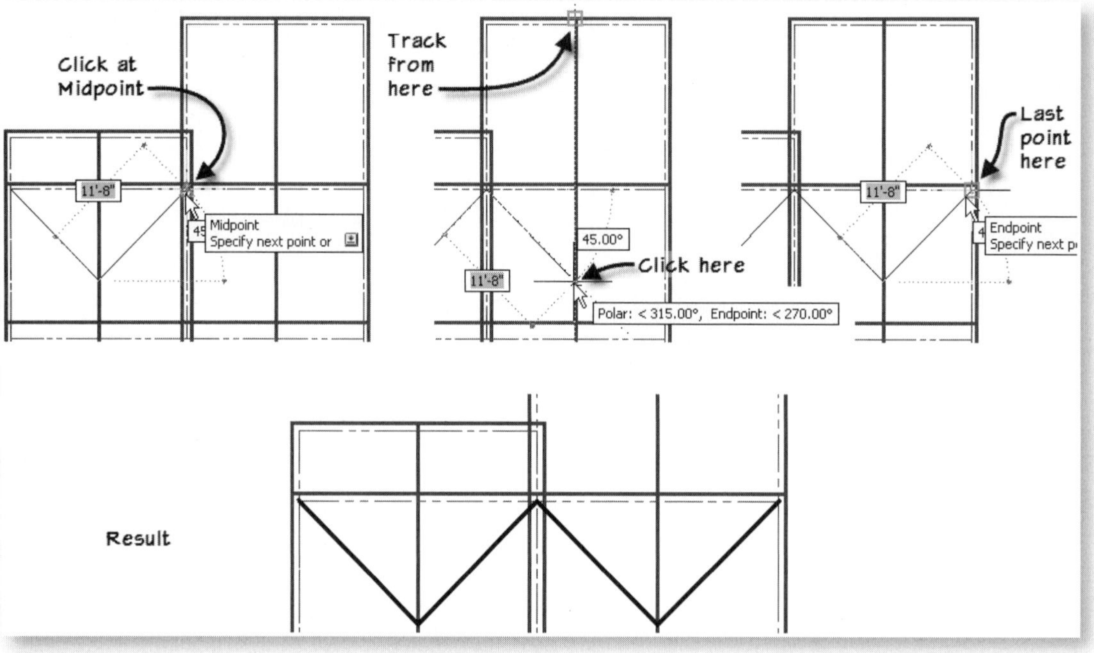

FIGURE 12.19 *Follow the valleys of the Roof to complete the polyline (Top). The final polyline appears at the bottom (polyline enhanced in the figure for clarity)*

If you have any trouble creating the polyline, you can right-click the file named *Roof Trim Polyline* in the *Elements* folder of Project Navigator and choose **Insert as Block**. Use the same settings as above. This will add the required polyline to your file.

25. On the floating View panel, click the ***View, NW Isometric*** tool.
26. Select the Roof Slab shown in Figure 12.20, and, on the Roof Slab contextual ribbon tab on the Modify panel, choose the ***Trim*** tool.

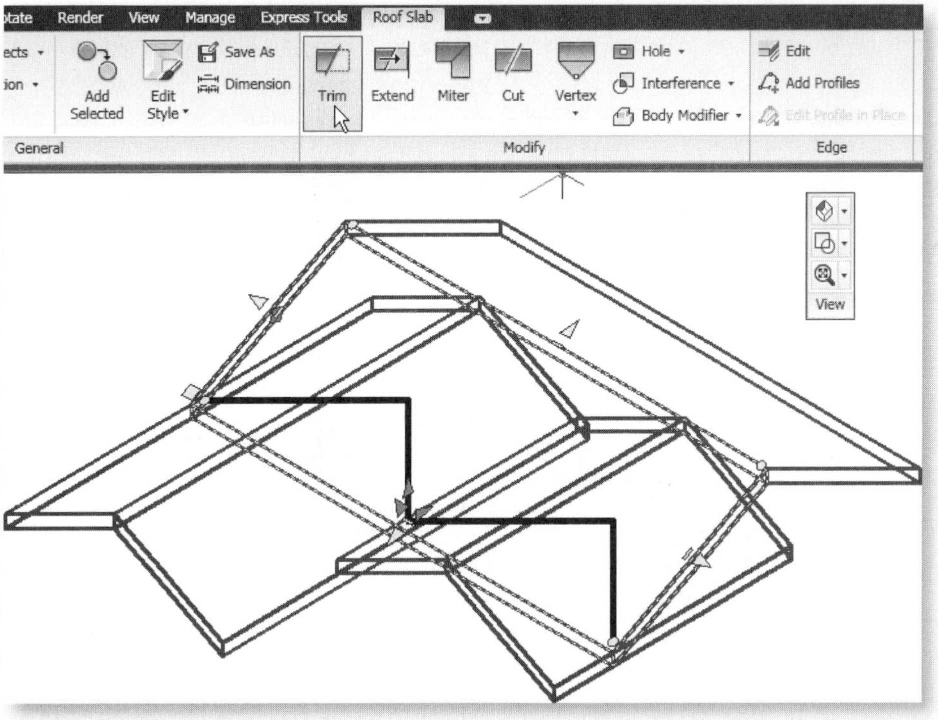

FIGURE 12.20 *Select the Slab to trim*

27. At the "Select trimming object" prompt, click the polyline.
28. At the "Specify side to be trimmed" prompt, click down and to the left of the Roof (see Figure 12.21).

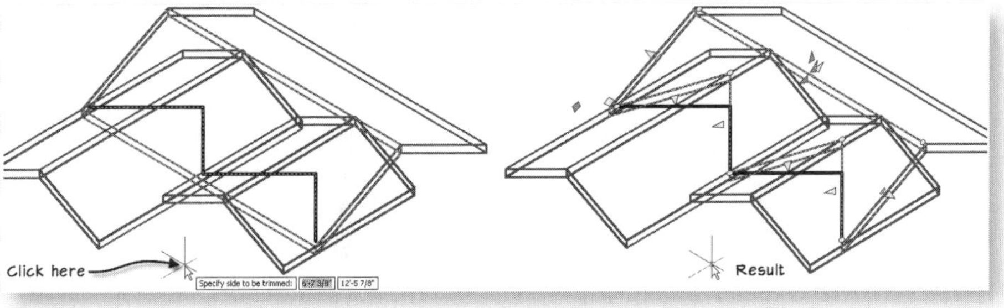

FIGURE 12.21 *Exaggerate your pick when designating the side to trim*

TIP

Because we are working in a 3D view, click far enough away from the object so that ACA trims the correct side. If the wrong side is trimmed, Undo and try again, clicking farther away this time.

Notice that the Roof Slab has been trimmed to the shape defined by the polyline as projected along its sloped faces.

NOTE

Occasionally, you will need to Undo and start a particular sequence over. AEC objects do not always automatically regenerate properly. To force an AEC object to update, use the Regenerate Model tool on the View ribbon tab on the Appearance panel, by selecting the down arrow icon on the Regenerate split button (or type objrelupdate at the Command Line and press ENTER **twice).**

29. Erase the polyline.

Miter the Roof Slabs

Now that the edge has been cut to the shape of the polyline, we can miter the intersecting Slabs with the trimmed one.

30. Select the Roof Slab we just trimmed, and, on the Roof Slab contextual ribbon tab on the Modify panel, choose the ***Miter*** tool.
31. At the "Miter by" prompt, choose **Edges**.
32. At the "Select edge on first slab" prompt, click the edge along the trim line closest to you (see Figure 12.22).

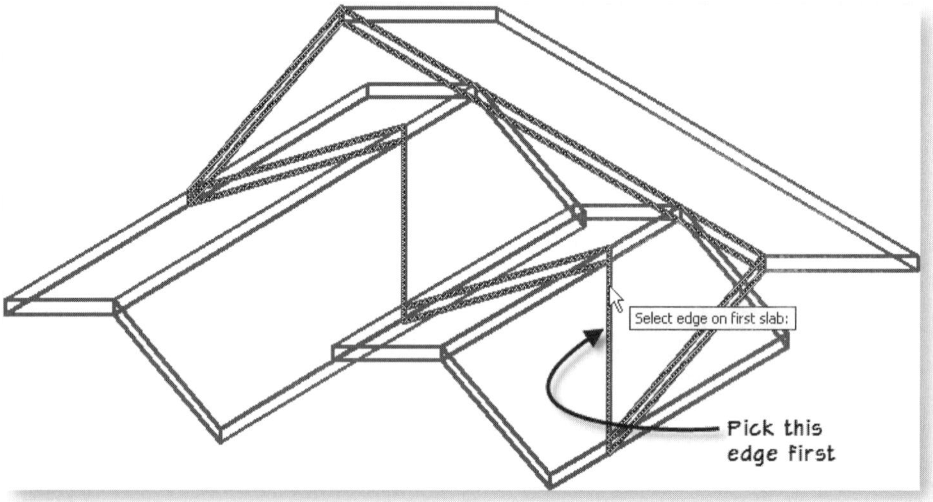

FIGURE 12.22 *Select the first edge of the miter*

33. At the "Select edge on second slab" prompt, click the concealed edge of the intersecting Slab (see Figure 12.23).

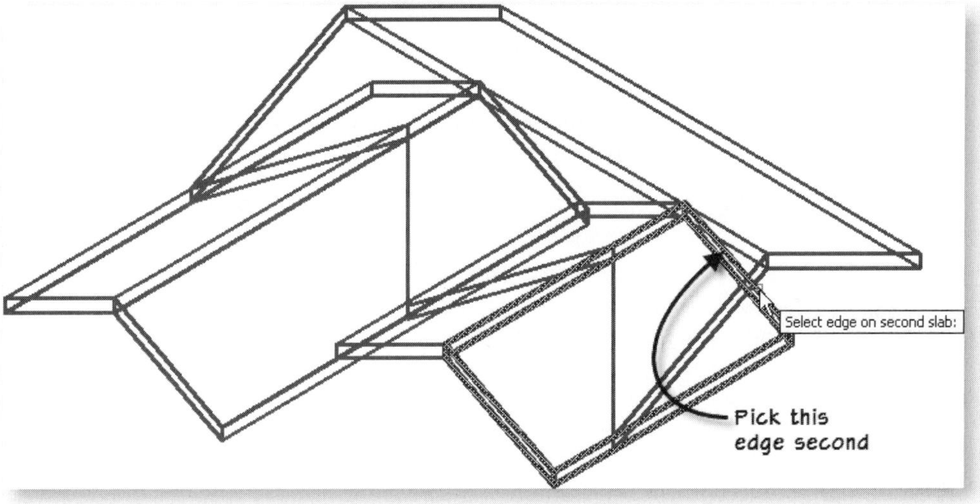

FIGURE 12.23 *Select the second edge of the miter*

34. Repeat the same steps for the remaining three miters—you can press the SPACEBAR to quickly repeat the command (see Figure 12.24).

Be sure to use the Edges option and not the Intersection option. The Edges option gives you the control to select each edge you wish to miter. The Intersection option searches for the intersection without your input. For simple miters, Intersection will work well; but for complex situations such as the ones here, use the Edges option.

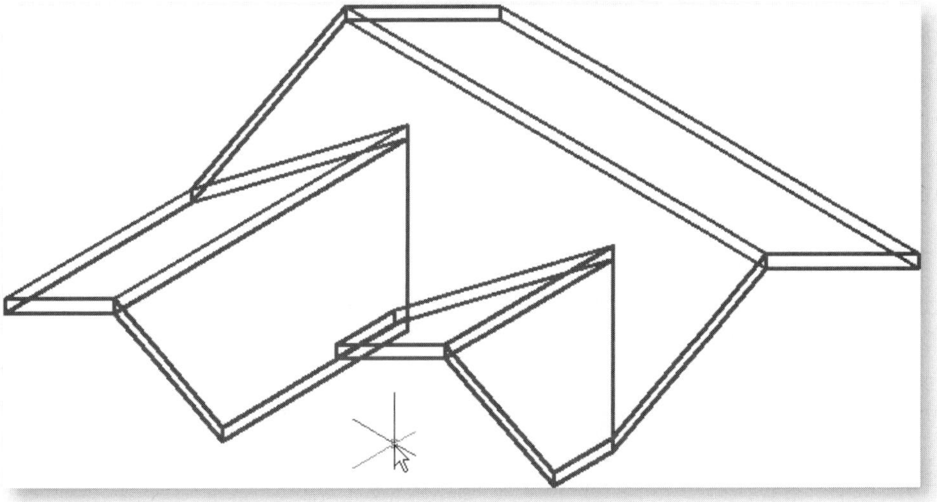

FIGURE 12.24 *The completed mitered Roof Slabs*

35. Save the file.

Working with Roof Slab Styles

In addition to being able to trim and miter edges as in the previous sequence, we can apply articulated conditions at the edges of the Roof Slabs. These are called Roof Slab Edge styles. Furthermore, we can use styles that have multiple components representing the various materials used in their construction. The fastest way to get started with both of these tasks is to use some premade styles included with ACA. Several sample styles have been included on the Roof Slabs catalog, which is available in the Content Browser under the Design Tool catalog. We can also use either of the two methods covered so far in this book, Content Browser or Style Manager, to import other styles that are not included on this palette.

36. Open the Content Browser (available on the Insert ribbon tab on the Content panel) and then browse the Design Tool Catalog.
37. From the Roof Slabs and Slabs menu on the left, choose **Roof Slabs**.
38. Add the 04 - 1×8 Fascia [100 - 25×150 Fascia] tool and the 04 - 1×8 Fascia + Soffit [100 - 25×200 Fascia + Soffit] tool to the MACA Residential tool palette (see Figure 12.25).

    Be sure to drag them using the eyedropper icon or right-click and choose **Copy**, then **Paste**.

A Roof Slab style controls the parameters of the Roof Slab. A Roof Slab Edge style controls the shape of the individual edges. The tools on this tool palette allow us to import either or both quickly. In this exercise, we will use styles from two different tools.

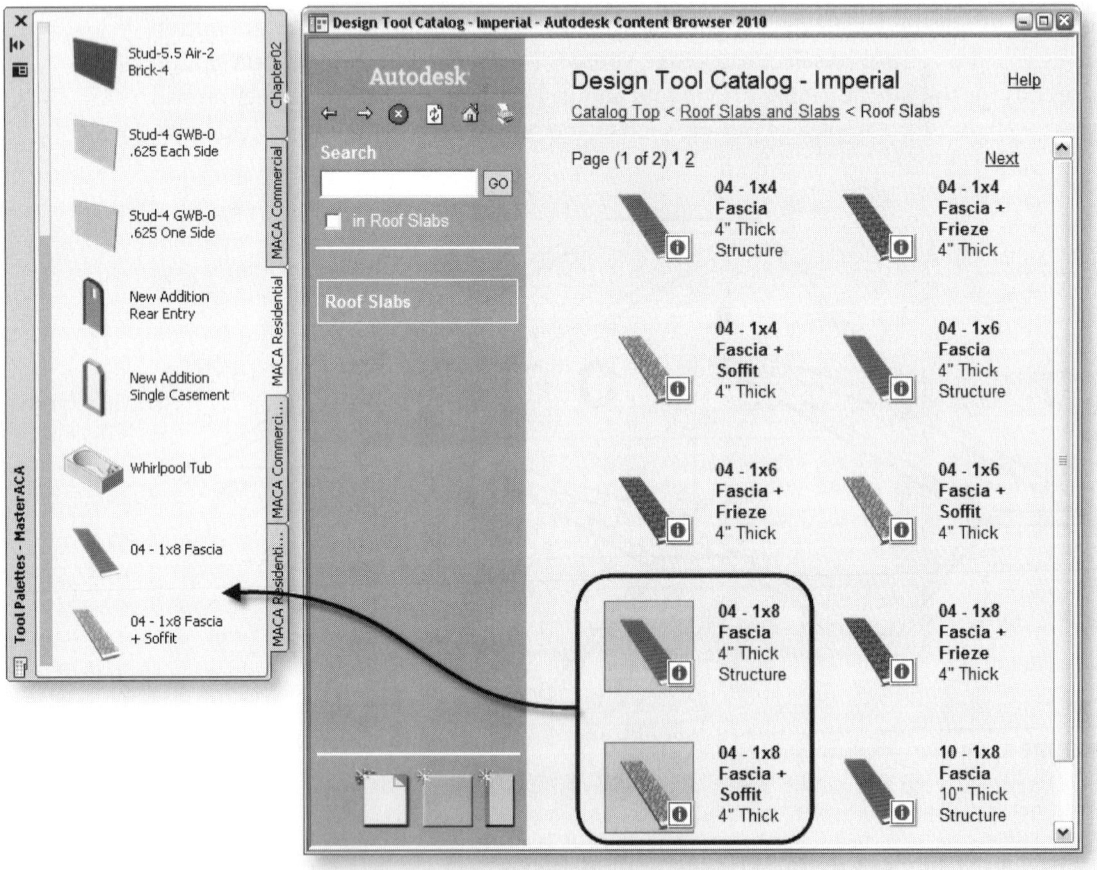

FIGURE 12.25 *Add Roof Slab styles to your MACA Residential palette*

Now let's apply some of the tools to Roof Slabs in the model.

39. Select the four Roof Slabs that make up the roof of the new addition (see Figure 12.26). Do not select the existing house Roof.

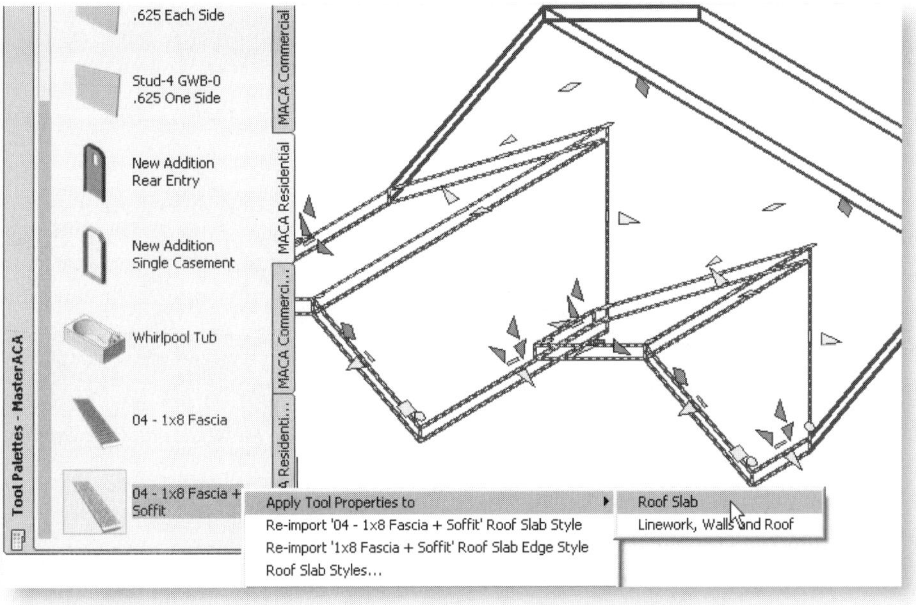

FIGURE 12.26 *Select the Roof Slabs of the new addition and apply a tool's properties*

40. Right-click the 04 - 1×8 Fascia + Soffit [100 - 25×150 Fascia + Soffit] tool and choose **Apply Tool Properties to > Roof Slab**.

Several things have occurred with this step (see Figure 12.27). The most obvious is the appearance of Materials on the Roof Slab surfaces. If you zoom in a bit, you will also notice that the horizontal edges of the Roof Slabs have edge profiles (Roof Edge styles) applied to them and that the Roof Slabs have shifted vertically. Even less obvious is a change in the Roof's thickness. Some of these effects were desired. Let's address some of those that weren't.

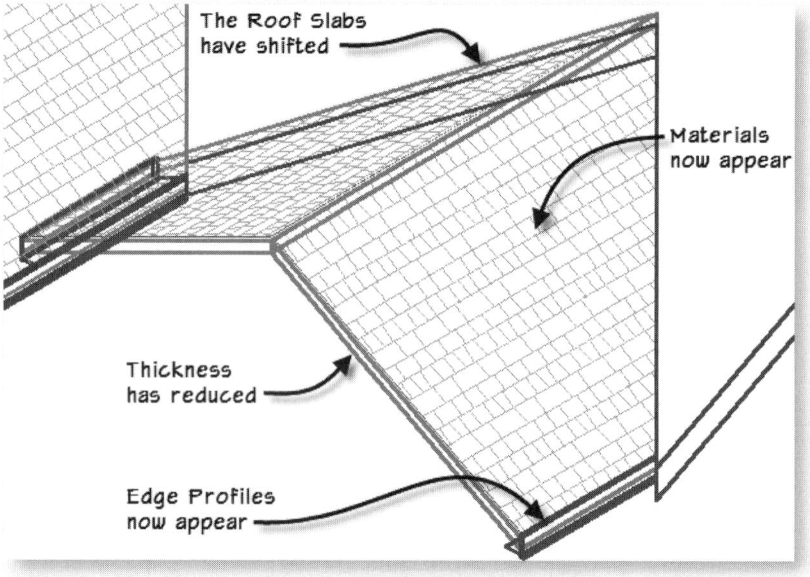

FIGURE 12.27 *The Roof Slabs have shifted vertically, and they now have Materials and Edge Profiles*

41. With any of the four Roof Slabs selected, on the Roof Slab contextual ribbon tab on the General panel, choose the ***Edit Style*** tool.
42. On the General tab, rename the Style to **MACA New Construction**.
43. Click the Components tab.

This tab lists three components: Shingles, Sheathing and Joist. Each has a "Thickness Offset" and a "Thickness" parameter. The joist in this particular style is a bit small. Let's increase its thickness.

44. Select the Joist component and change the Thickness to **7 ¼"** [**185**].
45. Change the "Thickness Offset" of the Sheathing component to **7 ¼"** [**185**] and the Shingles component to **8"** [**200**] (see Figure 12.28).

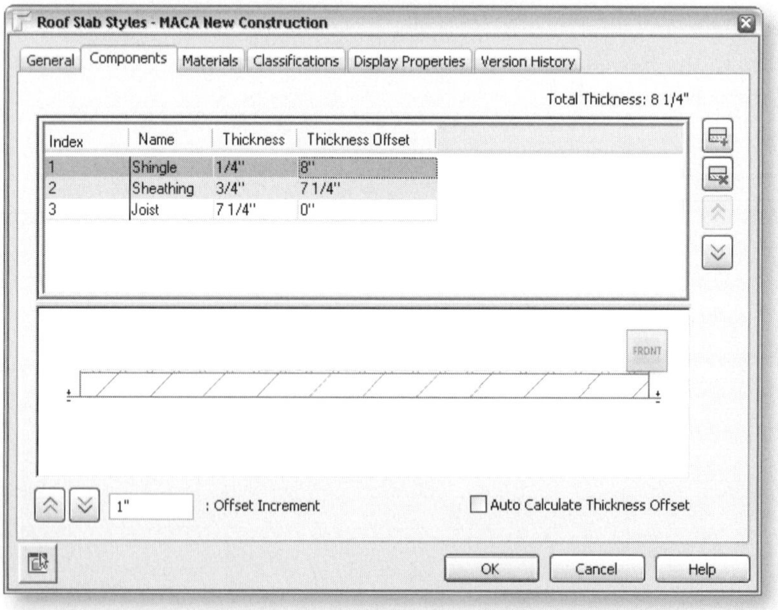

FIGURE 12.28 *Edit the style to increase the size of the Joist*

46. Click OK to complete the style edit and see the results.

    Notice that the Roof Slabs have shifted vertically relative to the other Roof Slabs and that the thickness has increased as well.

47. Select the remaining two Roof Slabs (the ones for the existing house) and on the Properties palette, change their Style to MACA New Construction. Do not use the tool this time.

Notice that the Roof Slabs have also shifted into place vertically but that the edges did *not* receive Roof Edge styles. This is because we applied the style of the Roof Slab only on the Properties palette, rather than applying both the Roof Slab and Roof Slab Edge styles as the tool did. Remember, the command on the tool's right-click menu reads "apply tool properties to," meaning that it applies *all* of the tool's properties, not just the style as we did manually. We have done it this way so that we can decide which edge styles to apply to each Roof Slab edge manually. Let's fine-tune the edge assignments.

Apply Edge Conditions

48. Zoom in on the valley between the two small Roofs (the new construction roof).

    Notice that an Edge style has been applied in a position that is concealed.

49. Select the Roof Slab that this edge belongs to, and, on the Roof Slab contextual ribbon tab on the Edge panel, choose ***Edit*** tool (see the top of Figure 12.29).

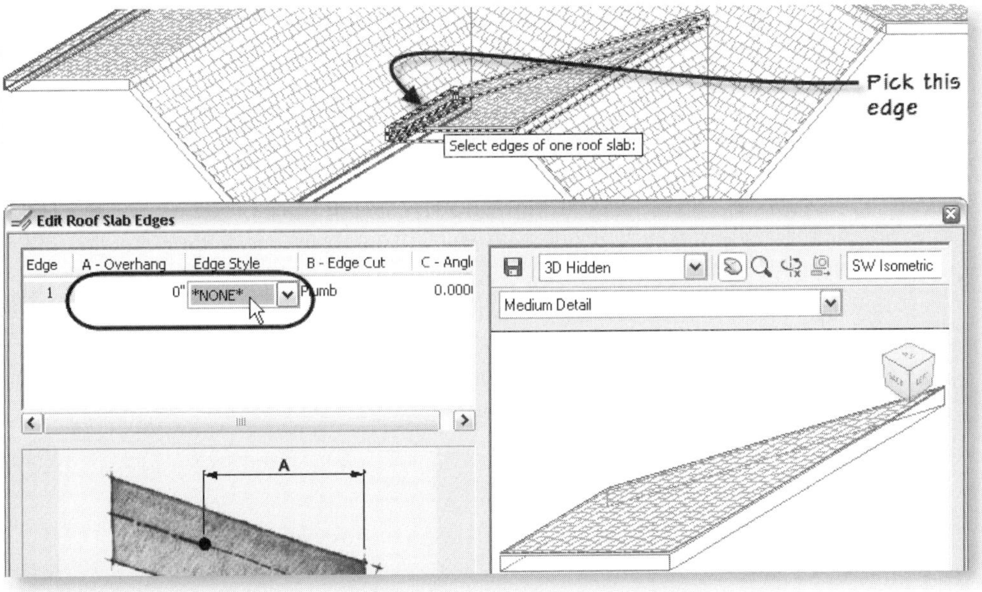

FIGURE 12.29 *Select a Roof Slab to edit edges*

50. At the "Select edges of one roof slab" prompt, click the edge with the fascia and press ENTER.

51. In the Edit Roof Slab Edges dialog box, change the A – Overhang value to **0"** [**0**], click the Edge Style list, choose ***None*** and then click OK (see the bottom of Figure 12.29).

We can use this same technique (without changing the overhang) to apply Edge styles to the fascia boards of the gable ends as well. However, we will need a different Edge style for this.

52. On the MACA Residential palette, right-click the 04 - 1×8 Fascia [100 - 25×200 Fascia] tool and choose **Import '04 - 1×8 Fascia' Roof Slab Edge Style [Import '100 - 25×200 Fascia' Roof Slab Edge Style]** (see Figure 12.30).

NOTE

If your display says "Re-import," this likely indicates that you dragged the tool into the drawing before dragging it to the palette. You can choose Re-import or just press the ESC key to cancel. Re-import means that the style is already present in your drawing; and if you choose Re-import, it will retrieve the original Style definition from the remote file and overwrite the version currently resident in your drawing. In this case, there is no harm in doing so. However, consider the ramifications of this action carefully when doing this on "real" projects.

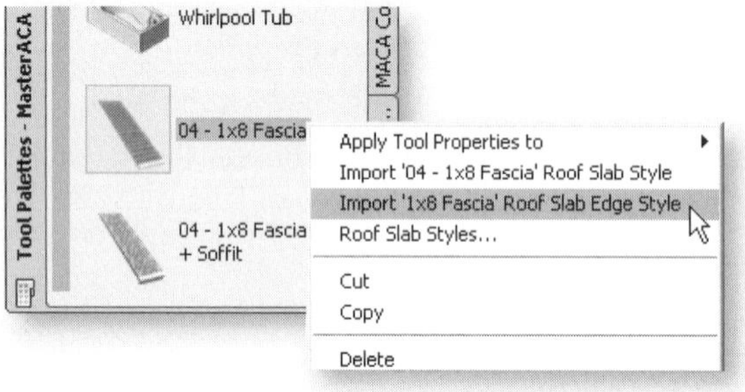

FIGURE 12.30 *Import a Roof Slab Edge style for use in the current drawing*

53. Select the same Roof Slab, and, on the Roof Slab contextual ribbon tab on the Edge panel, choose the ***Edit*** tool.
54. At the "Select edges of one roof slab" prompt, click the leading gable edge facing you and press ENTER.
55. In the Edit Roof Slab Edges dialog box, click the Edge Style list, choose 1x8 Fascia [25x200 Fascia], and click OK.
56. Repeat these steps, moving around the model and applying edges as appropriate (see Figure 12.31).

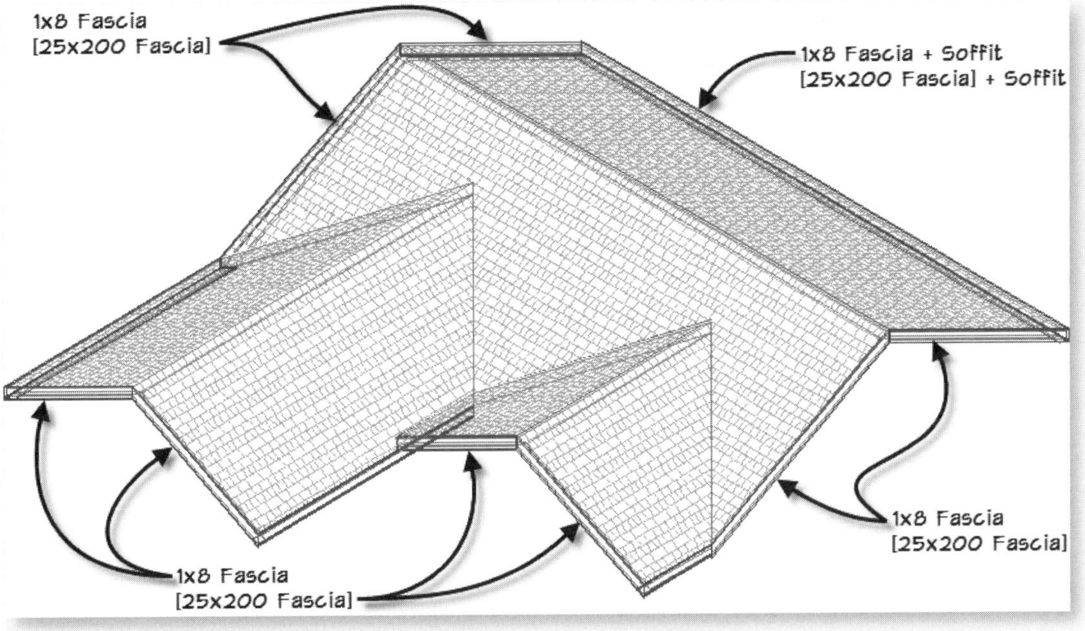

FIGURE 12.31 *Apply Edge styles as indicated*

Add Holes and Finishing Touches

The file that we inserted from the *Elements* folder (*Roof Outlines*) contained a hidden layer with a few additional polylines. We will use these now to fine-tune the Roofs.

57. Turn on the Layer named A-Temp.

    Two magenta polylines appear.

58. Orbit the model in 3D to tilt the model down slightly. You can hold down the SHIFT key and then drag with the wheel on your mouse.

    If you prefer, use the 3D Orbit tool on the floating View panel on the View split button—click the 3D Orbit tool, then place the cursor near the middle top of the drawing area, and drag down slightly. Press ESC to exit.

59. Select the leftmost Roof Slab, and, on the Roof Slab contextual ribbon tab on the Modify panel, select the Hole button and choose the ***Add*** tool.
60. When prompted, select the magenta rectangle (you may need to zoom in with your mouse wheel a bit), press ENTER and answer **Yes** to erase the layout geometry.

    A hole should appear in the Roof Slab projected from the polyline.

61. Select the long gabled Roof Slab (opposite the one we just added the hole to), and, on the Roof Slab contextual ribbon tab on the Modify panel, choose the ***Trim*** tool.
62. At the "Select trimming object" prompt, click the "L" shaped magenta polyline.
63. At the "Specify side to be trimmed" prompt, click up and to the right of the Roof Slab (see Figure 12.32).

TIP

For the "side to be trimmed" prompt, it is best to click far from the polyline to be certain that ACA trims the correct part of the slab.

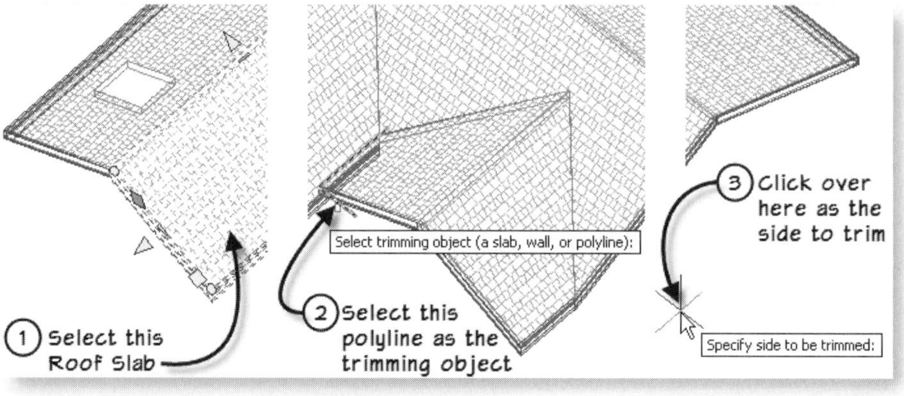

FIGURE 12.32 *Trim a slab using the provided polyline*

64. Erase the magenta polyline.

Let's add a skylight to the hole we just cut in the roof over the new addition.

65. On the Project Navigator, in the *Elements* folder, right-click the file named *Roof Window* and choose **Insert as Block**.
66. In the Insert dialog box, clear the check mark in the "Specify on Screen" checkbox for Insertion Point (accept the default 0,0,0 insertion point), place a check mark in the "Explode" checkbox and then click OK.
67. Use the Object Viewer or 3D Orbit to examine the completed roof, and then save and close the file.

Project the Walls to the Roof

Now that we have modeled the Roof, we can project the top edges of the walls in the second floor plan to follow the underside of the Roofs.

68. On the Project Navigator, Open the *Second Floor Existing* file.
69. On the Project Navigator, drag and drop the *Roof New* file into the current drawing.

    The hatching in the Roof Slab Materials may delay the regeneration a bit. To speed this up, click the small Surface Hatch Toggle icon on the Drawing status bar (shown in Figure 1.3 in Chapter 1).
70. From the floating View panel, click the ***View, SW Isometric*** tool.
71. From the floating View panel, click the ***Visual Styles, Hidden*** tool (or, on the View ribbon tab on the Appearance panel, select the Visual Styles button and choose the ***3D Hidden*** tool).

    Notice that the Walls do not follow the roof line. Notice also that there is another magenta polyline in this file (see Figure 12.33).

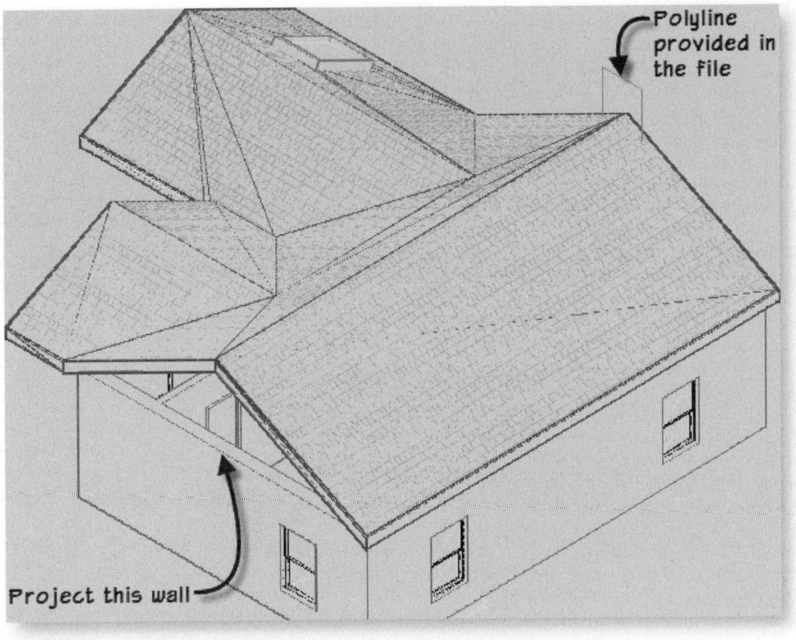

FIGURE 12.33 *The Walls do not project to the roof line*

72. Select the Wall under the gable end (as indicated in Figure 12.33), and, on the Wall contextual ribbon tab on the Modify panel, select the Roof/Floor Line button and choose the ***Modify Roof Line*** tool.
73. Select **Auto project** from the Dynamic Input menu (if on) or right-click and choose the **Auto project** option.

NOTE

Auto project is used to project to any AEC object; recall Chapter 7 when we projected a Wall to the underside of the Stairs.

74. At the "Select Objects" prompt, select the *Roof New* XREF and then press ENTER.
75. Press ENTER again to complete the command.

    If necessary, select the Wall again, on the Wall contextual ribbon tab on the Modify panel, select the Roof/Floor Line button, choose the ***Edit in Place*** tool and manipulate the vertices to fine-tune the shape.

TIP

If you have trouble projecting the Wall to the *Roof New* file, try dragging in the *Roof Exist* file and projecting to it instead. Detach the *Roof Exist* file when finished.

76. Change to SE Isometric view.
77. Select the Wall with the chimney and use the ***Modify Roof Line*** tool again.

    Use the **Project to polyline** option this time and project the Wall with the chimney to the magenta polyline. You can erase the polyline when you're done (see Figure 12.34).

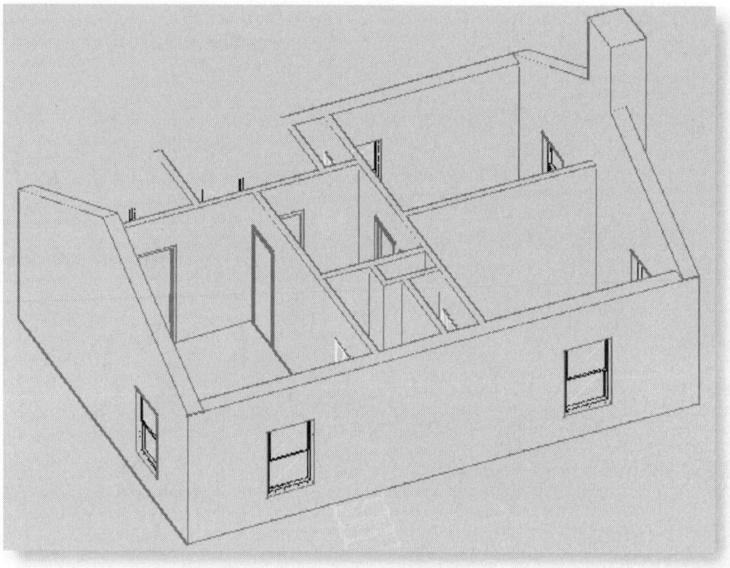

FIGURE 12.34 *The Walls now project to roof line*

78. Detach the XREF, return to Top view and then save and close the *Second Floor Existing* file.
79. On the Project Navigator, open the *Second Floor New* file.
80. Repeat the process above by dragging in the *Roof New* Construct and then projecting the Walls at the back of the house to form gable ends.
81. Detach the *Roof New* Construct and close the *Second Floor New* file when finished.

You can perform this procedure from a 3D view as we did above, or it might be easier to do it using the ***Edit in Elevation*** tool. Simply select the walls and the roof XREF, and, on the Multiple Objects contextual ribbon tab on the General panel, select the down arrow icon on the Edit in split button and choose this command. Follow the prompts to enter the Edit in Elevation mode. This will isolate just the selected objects, making it easier to see what is changing in the model. Also, in some cases, the "Auto Project" option of the Edit Roof Line command does not work. If this happens, you can use the Edit in Place option and edit the shape with the grips. Don't forget to right-click for options such as "Add Gable." You can also draw a polyline and project to it using the "Auto Project" option.

If you like, you can return to the *Roof New* file and trim the Roof Slabs of the existing house around the chimney. If you have trouble with the Roof Slab ***Trim*** tool that we used above, try the ***Cut*** tool on the same contextual ribbon tab.

Add a Dormer

Let's assume that in addition to the other improvements taking place on this house, the owner wants to add a dormer to the front of the house. To add a dormer to a roof slab, you must create all of the dormer components separately and then position them in the right place on the roof slab in a way that all of the components fully penetrate the roof slab. AutoCAD Architecture provides a dormer creation routine that, upon execution, will cut a hole in the roof slab and trim all of the dormer's components to follow the slope of the roof. The following procedure will add a dormer to the front portion of the roof in our residential project. To expedite the process, a file with the dormer's geometry has been provided.

1. In the *Elements* folder, double-click the *Dormer* drawing to open it.
2. Select all geometry and copy to Clipboard.
3. In the *Constructs* folder, double-click the *Roof New* drawing to open it.
4. On the Home ribbon tab, expand the Modify panel and select the down arrow icon at the right side of the Paste split button (second row in the expansion area, third button from left), and choose the ***Paste to Original Coordinates*** tool.

   This will insert the geometry from the *Dormer* drawing to the correct location relative to the roof.

Take a few moments to explore the dormer. Use the 3DORBIT command (hold down the SHIFT key and drag with the wheel on your mouse) to better visualize all components. Notice that the geometry of the dormer includes four walls, a roof and a window. It is important to note the presence of the back wall. Even though this wall is not necessary as a dormer component, its presence is essential so that a complete hole for the dormer can be cut in the existing roof slab. If you examine the dormer component more closely, you will see that it has been built following the same procedures already discussed in the chapter, including building a roof, converting it to a roof slab and projecting all walls to the roof line. Therefore, building a dormer is much like building the components of a small house. The objects are then simply moved in 3D space to the desired location.

5. Select the Roof Slab (the one that will be cut by the dormer), and, on the Roof Slab contextual ribbon tab on the Dormer panel, choose the ***Add*** tool.
6. Select all of the objects that form the dormer and then press ENTER.
7. When prompted to slice the walls with the roof slab, press ENTER to slice the walls.

   Manually erase the back wall of the dormer.
8. Save and close the *Roof New* file.
9. Close the *Dormer* file—it is not necessary to save it.

You can see the resulting dormer in Figure 12.36.

Updating the Residential Project Model

In Chapter 5, we built several files for each of the projects. In both projects, we created a Composite Model View file that gathered together all of the other files. Since we added a new Construct in this lesson, we should return to the Composite Model View and make some updates.

Update the Composite Model View

1. On the Project Navigator, click the Views tab.
2. Right-click on the *A-CM00* View file and choose **Properties**.
3. On the left side of the Modify View dialog box, click the Content item.
4. Clear the check mark in the *Roof Existing* checkbox, place a check mark in the *Roof New* checkbox and then click OK (see Figure 12.35).

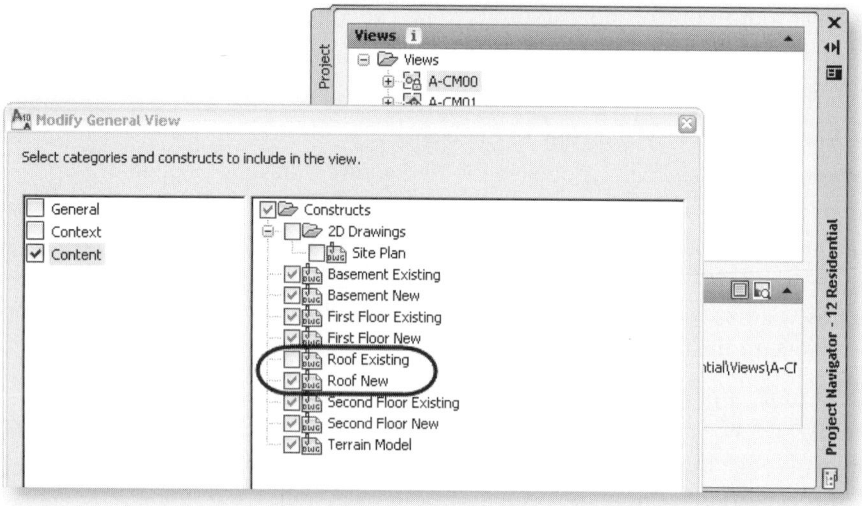

FIGURE 12.35 *Edit the Content of the Composite Model View*

5. Double-click *A-CM00* to open it.
6. From the floating View panel, click the View, NW Isometric tool (see Figure 12.36).

As you can see, there is still some work to be done. There are no floors in the house, and the patio has no Roof. Feel free to add a Roof to the patio. An additional exercise for this is provided in Appendix A. In the next sequence, we will shift our attention to Slab objects. While you can use a Slab to model any horizontal surface, in the examples that follow, we will use them primarily to model the structural components of our model.

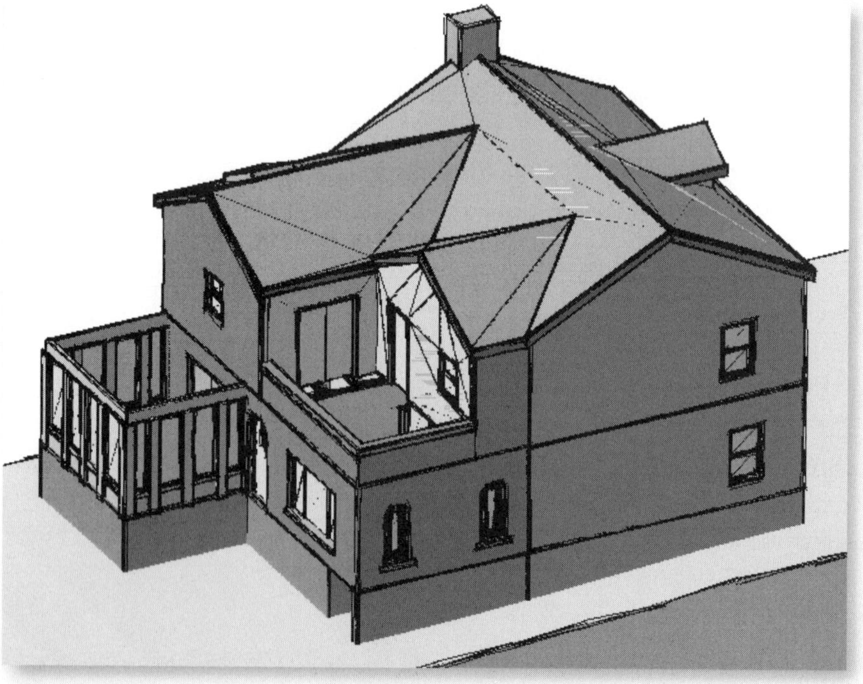

FIGURE 12.36 *The Residential Model is nearly complete*

7. Repeat these steps to update the *A-CM01* model and the *A-FP03* Roof Plan View.
8. Save and close the composite model files.

CREATING SLABS

Slabs can be used to represent any horizontal surface in your building model, whether that surface is flat or sloped. Slabs typically do not provide much benefit in plan views; they are most useful for deck-type structures such as parking structures, for quick studies of stacking flat roofs, or for use in building sections. Therefore, it is beneficial to create our Slabs in separate Constructs and XREF them back to our composite model. In this way, you can easily eliminate the Slab objects from the plan files, yet use them in the Views where they provide the most benefit: the 3D views and sections. Let's have a look at Slabs, starting in the Residential Project.

Working with Multi-Component Slabs

Slab objects can contain multiple components within their styles. For example, if you want your model to include more than one component (for, say, a concrete topping and metal deck or wood studs), you can build a style for this purpose. In many ways, a multi-component Slab style is like a Wall style that has "fallen over." Like Walls (see Chapter 10), each component can be a fixed or a variable thickness. The thickness is measured from a common point in the Slab style (see Figure 12.37).

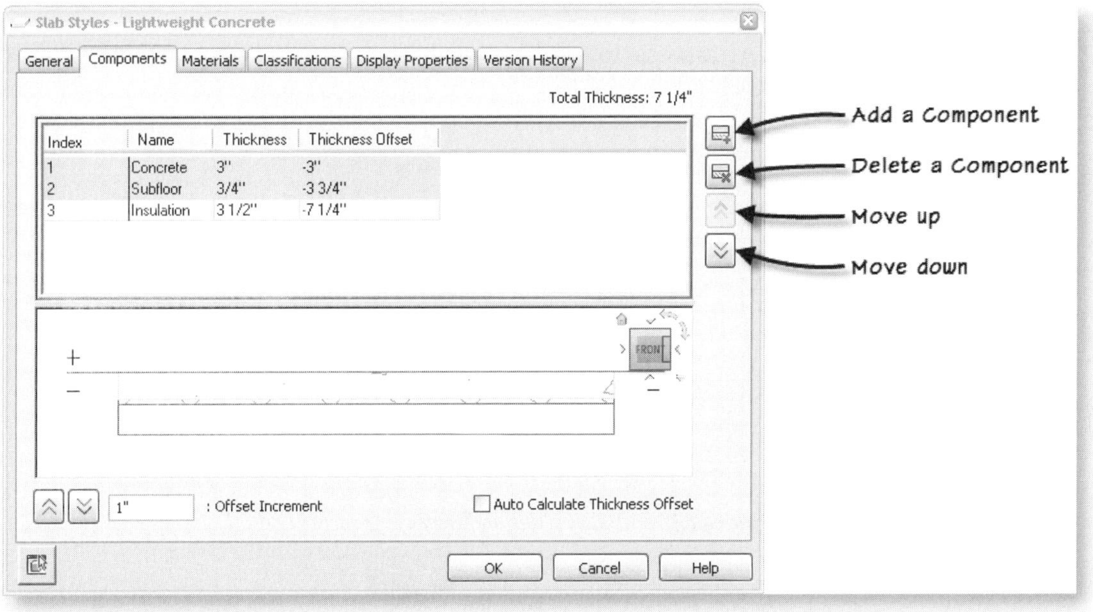

FIGURE 12.37 *The Components tab of the Slab Style dialog*

Like Walls, each component has an Index, a Name, a Thickness and a Thickness Offset (which corresponds to the Edge Offset in Walls). Unlike Walls, Slabs do not have Dimension settings, Functions and Top and Bottom Offsets (which would not apply to Slabs). The dialog pictured in Figure 12.37 shows that components can be added, deleted and moved up and down. While many similarities do exist between Slab styles and Wall styles, Slab styles are not as sophisticated as Wall styles.

(Refer to Chapter 10 for more on Wall styles.) There are also other items to consider given the difference in usage between Slabs and Walls. With Walls, it is common to see the Baseline of the style at the line that divides the structural components from the non-structural components—such as between CMU and brick veneer. With a Slab, in many cases, you will want to use the edge of the Slab that corresponds to the level height or some other meaningful baseline. Let's take a closer look at the behavior of multi-component Slabs in a prepared file before we use them in our project.

Explore Slab Styles

Several Slab styles have been included with AutoCAD Architecture. We can understand the use of multi-component Slabs by studying a few of them.

1. On the Project Navigator palette, double-click to open the file named *Understanding Slabs* in the *Elements* folder.

This is a simple file that contains a few Walls and a Slab and has some Slab styles already saved in the file. The file is saved with a Live Section active that cuts through the Walls and Slab so we can clearly see their respective components. Furthermore, the Walls have an interference condition applied to them so that the Slab cuts away from the Wall mass (see the left side of Figure 12.38).

2. Select the Slab object on the Properties palette and choose Lightweight Concrete from the Style list (see the middle of Figure 12.38).

Notice that this Style has three components: batt insulation, metal deck and concrete. Note also that the Slab maintained the same baseline when we made the switch to this style.

3. Repeat the process to choose Wood Floor System (see the right side of Figure 12.38).

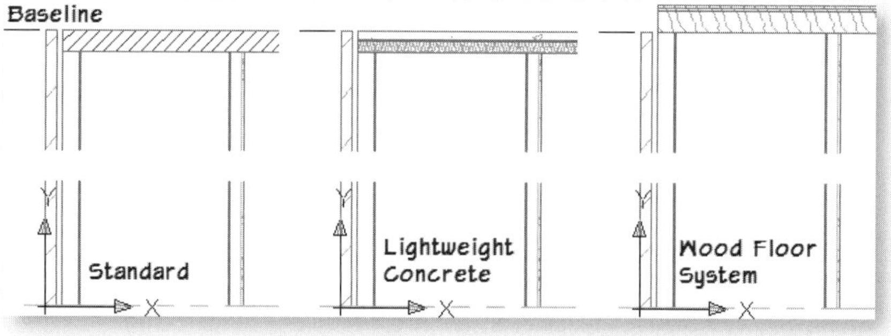

FIGURE 12.38 *Comparing different Slab styles and their components and offsets*

Notice that this style also has three components, including wood joists, subfloor and finished floor. Notice also, however, that the Slab shifted up when we made the switch to this style. The Thickness Offsets used in this style vary from those used in the other styles, which accounts for this change and gives it a different baseline. Furthermore, with most of the provided Slab styles, you can adjust the Thickness setting on the Properties palette and the Slab components will adjust in different ways according to how they are configured in the style. In some cases, the Thickness will be applied to the size of one of the components and in some cases, it will also adjust the Thickness Offset of other components—each style is a little different.

4. Select the Slab again and change the Thickness on the Properties palette to **12"** [**300**].

Notice that the subfloor and the finished floor remained the same thickness as before, but they moved up with the increasing thickness of the framing component.

5. Close the *Understanding Slabs* file. It is not necessary to save it.

Create a Slab Construct

As you can see, Slabs added some nice detail to our building sections; however, the plan Display Representation of the Slab object often proves difficult to use to control the level of precision required for most plans. For primarily this reason, it is recommended that you add Slabs to separate Constructs in the project. In this way, you can easily control when they display by not including them in plan View files created in Project Navigator. (Refer to Chapter 5 for more on the basics of Project Navigator and Chapter 14 for a more detailed look at View files.)

6. From the *Constructs* folder of Project Navigator, double-click to open the *First Floor New* file.

For the following procedures, we need to add one more tool to our MACA Residential tool palette.

7. From the Content Browser, in the Design Tool Catalog and under the "Roof Slabs and Slabs" category, choose **Slabs**.
8. Find the Wood Floor System tool and add it to the MACA Residential tool palette, as you did for Roof Slabs above.
9. From the MACA Residential tool palette, click the Wood Floor System tool.
10. Carefully trace the line of the Wall stud component within the cavity of the exterior Walls (see Figure 12.39).

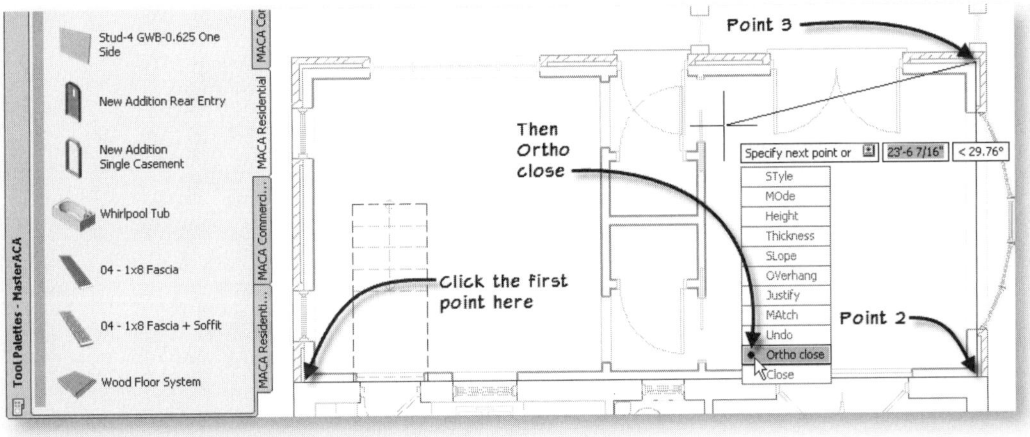

FIGURE 12.39 *Trace the exterior Walls of the new portion of the house*

As indicated in the figure, draw two segments and then use Ortho close to finish the Slab.

11. Select the new Slab; using the process outlined in the "Begin the First Floor Construct" heading of Chapter 5 (and shown in Figure 5.18), drag the Slab object from the drawing to the *Constructs* folder of Project Navigator.

This will prompt you to create a new Construct from this geometry.

12. In the "Add Construct" worksheet, type **Second Floor Slab** for the name, input **Slab for Second Floor New Construction** for the Description, and place a check mark in the Second Floor/New checkbox.
13. Click OK to complete the file, double-click the file to open it and then choose Zoom Extents.

You will see that the Slab has been removed from the *First Floor New* file and moved to this file. We want to make sure that the Slab is inserted at Z = 0. This is not always the case when you first create it.

14. Select the Slab and on the Properties palette, verify that the Elevation parameter is set to **0**. If it is not, change it now.

Create a New Slab Style

The Slab style that we have chosen here is not quite what we are looking for, but it is a decent starting point. You will recall in our explorations above that this style uses positive Thickness Offsets. This places its components above the floor plane. What we will actually do here is create a new style from this one that includes only the rough components without the finished floor or ceiling materials.

15. Select the Slab, and, on the Slab contextual ribbon tab on the General panel, choose the ***Save As*** tool.
16. On the General tab, rename the style to **MACA Wood Floor System**.
17. Click the Components tab.

Here we need to make adjustments to the existing components. We will shift all of the components below the baseline and then remove the wood flooring component and replace it with an insulation component.

18. Select component 2 – Subfloor. In the Thickness Offset field, type **-1 1/2"** [**-37**] (see Figure 12.40).

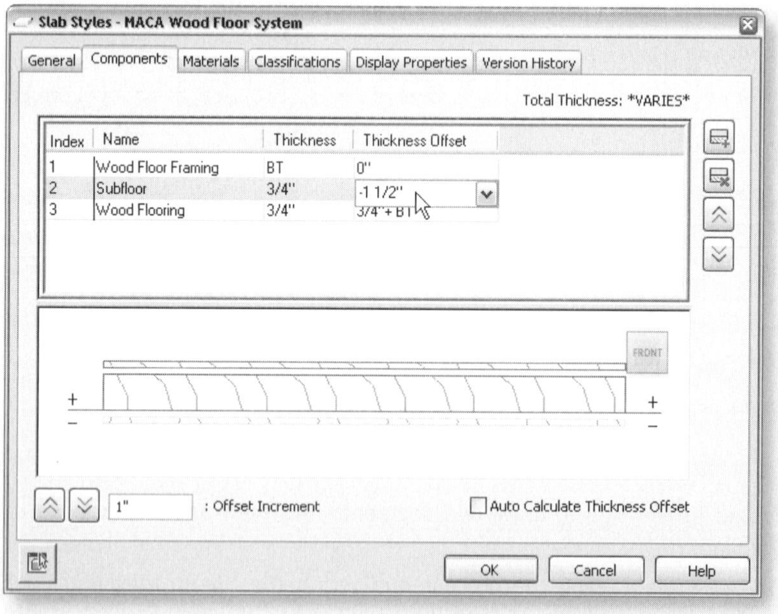

FIGURE 12.40 *Move the Subfloor component below the baseline–allow for the thickness of the finish floor*

This will move the component down in the viewer. The Joist needs to move underneath the subfloor. The chosen value allows for a gap with the finish floor material that will be part of the Space objects that will be added later. Just like Wall styles, you have two options: you can use fixed values for both the Thickness and Thickness Offset locking in that size as a parameter of the style, or you can use the "BT" (Base Thickness) variable in a formula that allows each instance of the Slab to vary. We could easily make the case for a fixed thickness in this example since the size of the joists we are using in our residential project is easily determined. However, let's take the opportunity to construct a simple formula to see how this can be done.

19. Select component 1 – Wood Floor Framing. Click in the Thickness Offset field. A pop-up menu icon will appear on the right side of the field.
20. Click the pop-up menu icon (down pointing arrow) to reveal a formula creator.
21. In the first field at the left, type **-1 1/2"** [**-37**].
22. From the pop-up in the next field, choose **Base Thickness**.
23. From the pop-up in the next field, choose * (multiply).
24. In the last field, type **-1** and then press ENTER (see Figure 12.41).

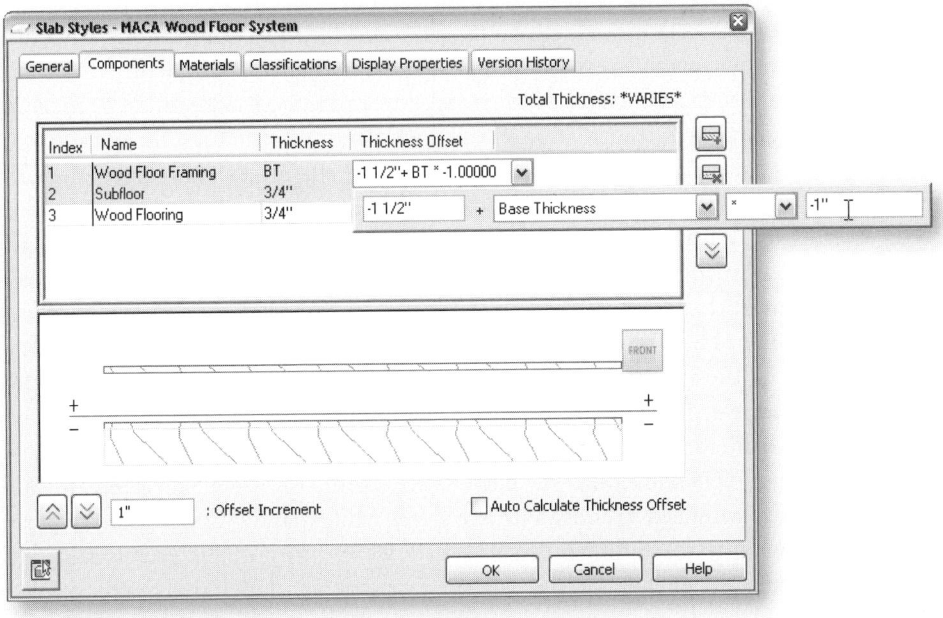

FIGURE 12.41 *Move the framing component beneath the subfloor*

The formula starts with -1 1/2" [-37] because this is where the bottom edge of the component directly above this one falls. From this point, we are adding an additional offset equal to the thickness of the component itself (Base Thickness) and multiplying it by -1 so that it offsets down rather than up. We will leave the Thickness of the Wood Floor Framing component set to BT. In this way, whatever value you type for the Thickness of the Slab on the Properties palette will be used as the size of the framing.

25. Select the Wood Flooring component and on the right side, click the Remove Component icon.

Let's change the order of these components to match the order they show in the preview.

26. Click on component 1, and then on the right side, click the Move Component Down In List icon (see Figure 12.42).

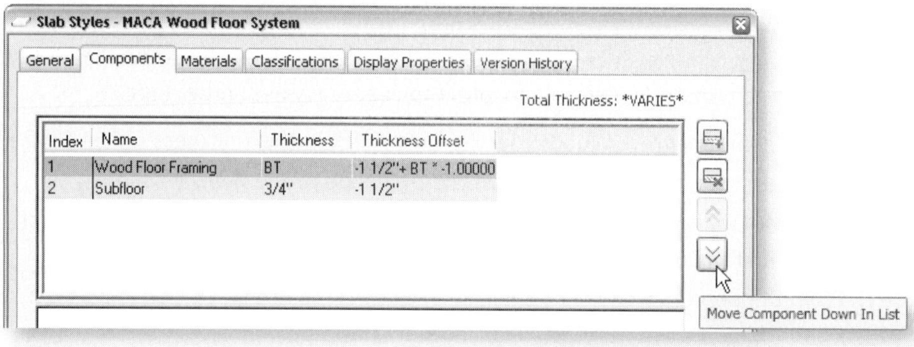

FIGURE 12.42 *Change the order of the components in the list*

At this point you could stop working on the Slab and for most applications, it would be suitable. In other words, there is always a question when working with BIM software of what to model and what not to model. For example, if we wanted to include some sound deadening batt insulation in the floor assembly structure, the question is, do we add this as a component or do we simply add this in a detail View later? In many cases, it would not only be acceptable to leave it out of the model and add it to the detail later, but it would often be preferable to do so. This is because we want to try and avoid getting carried away with modeling too much detail. Modeling too much detail can impede performance, and if there is nothing being gained except a little geometry in a single View, then the project can be better served by adding this as embellishment to the specific View in which it is needed, thereby keeping the model more clean. On the other hand, in some cases, the additional geometry serves to assist us in design coordination and decision making, thereby making it more valuable than simply providing a few additional geometric components to a detail cut later. In your own projects, you will need to consider these issues while making the decision of what to model and what to leave to details and schedules. In most of the exercises in this book, we have tended to take the "less is more" approach and included fewer components in the model with the intention of adding more embellishment directly in the detail Views cut later. (You can see more on this approach later in Chapter 17.) In this exercise, we will try the other approach and continue adding the insulation component to our Slab style and later even some framing components. We will do this for the educational value of the exercise simply to show another alternative. Once you have seen both approaches, you will be better prepared to see the impact and make decisions in your own projects.

Add a New Component

27. With the Wood Floor Framing component still selected, click the Add Component icon (on the right at the top).

    You will now have a second copy of the Wood Floor Framing component.

28. Select component 2 and rename it **Insulation**.

29. Change the Thickness to **3 1/2"** [**87**], the Thickness Offset to **-5** [**-125**] and then click OK (see Figure 12.43).

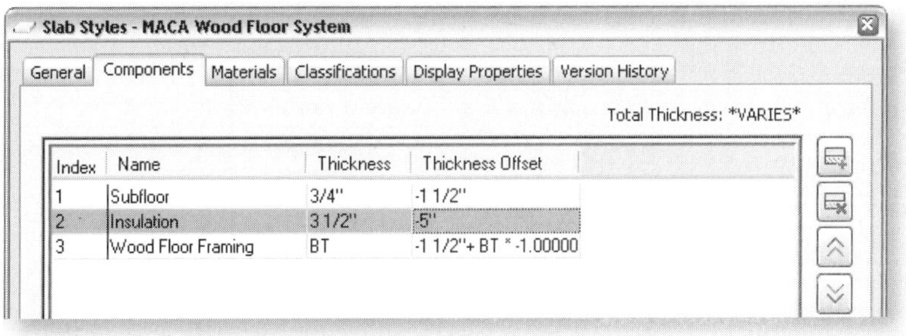

FIGURE 12.43 *Add and configure a new Insulation component*

We need to apply a Material to the new component. We will do this by creating a Material tool, starting with the one on the Design tool palette.

30. On the Tool Palettes, click the Design tab.
31. Right-click on the Material tool and choose **Copy**.
32. Change to the MasterACA tool palette group and, on the MACA Residential tool palette, right-click on the palette away from any existing tool and choose **Paste**.
33. Right-click on the copied Material tool and choose **Properties**. Verify that the Style location property points to Material Definitions (Imperial).dwg [Material Definitions (Metric).dwg].

Like other tool types, Material tools do not store the definition within the tool itself, but reference a source file from which the definition is imported, when necessary. The default location for the source files included with the program is C:\ProgramData\Autodesk\ACA 2010\enu\Styles\Imperial [C:\ProgramData\Autodesk\ACA 2010\enu\Styles\Metric], but this location can be customized. If the copied Material tool is not pointing to the appropriate source file and there is no such file in the folder noted above, check with your CAD Manager to determine where the source files have been installed.

34. Select the Definition name property. Click the pop-up menu icon (down pointing arrow) at the right side of the field and choose: Thermal & Moisture.Insulation.Batt.3.5.Horizontal [Thermal & Moisture.Insulation.Batt.064.Horizontal].
35. Change the Name of the material to: **Thermal & Moisture.Insulation.Batt.3.5.Horizontal** [**Thermal & Moisture.Insulation.Batt.064.Horizontal**] and then click OK (see Figure 12.44).

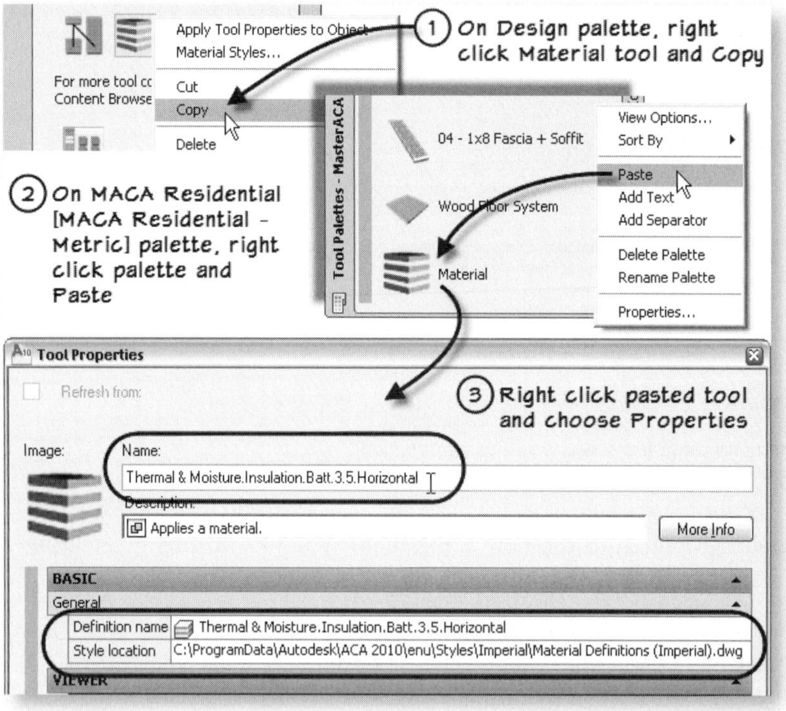

FIGURE 12.44 *Create a Material tool for an insulation Material*

To apply the insulation Material tool, we need to be able to select the component onscreen. To do so, we will enable a live section with the Edit in Section command.

36. Select the Slab, and, on the Slab contextual ribbon tab on the General panel, select down arrow icon at the right of the Edit in split button and choose the ***Edit in Section*** tool.

    Follow the prompts to cut a temporary section, zoom in to the Slab and apply the insulation Material tool (see Figure 12.45).

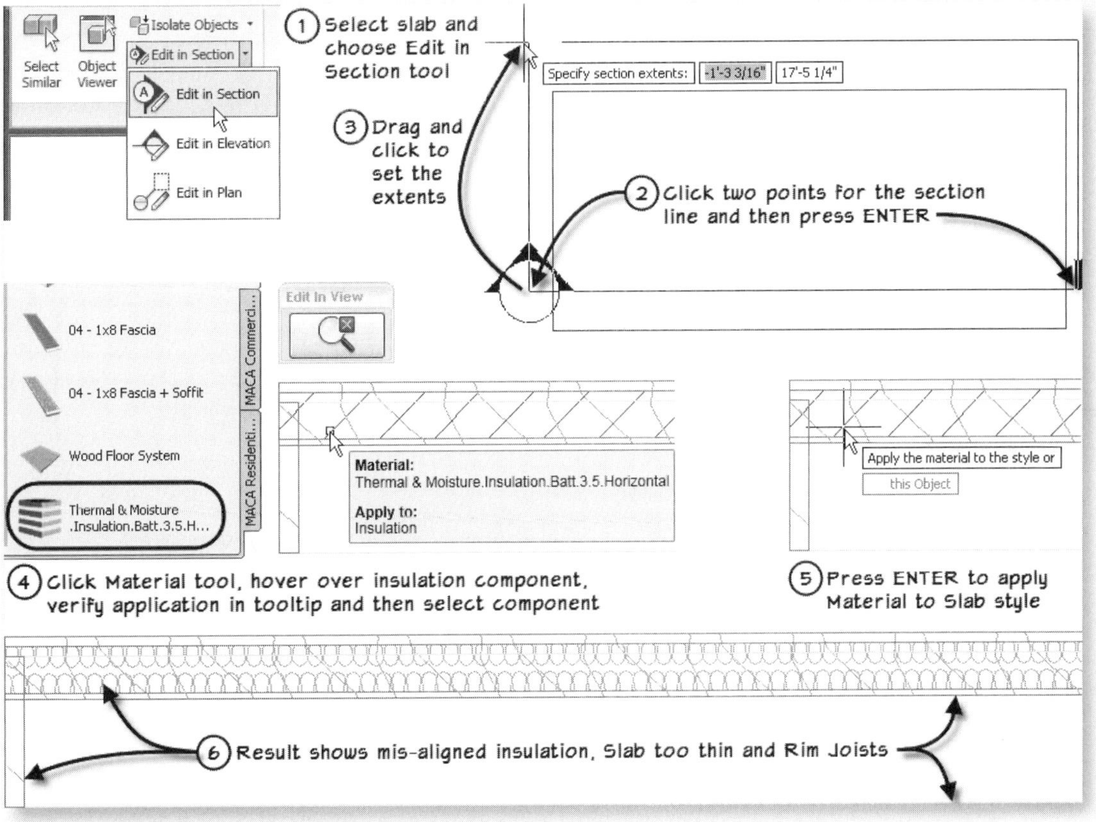

FIGURE 12.45 *Use the Edit In Section command to view and edit the model in a temporary live section*

A few things will become apparent once you view the Slab in section (see the bottom of Figure 12.45). The batt insulation hatch pattern is not aligned properly with the insulation component geometry; the Slab is too thin, and there is an edge style applied around the perimeter of the Slab. Let's address these issues.

37. Select the Slab and then on the Properties palette, change the Thickness to **9 1/4"** [**300**].
38. With the Slab still selected, edit the Style, click the Materials tab, select Insulation and then click the Edit Material icon.
39. With General Medium Detail selected on the Display Properties tab, click the Edit Display Properties icon.
40. Click the Hatching tab and change the Y Offset for Section Hatch. Try a value such as **2 1/2"** [**62**] (see Figure 12.46).

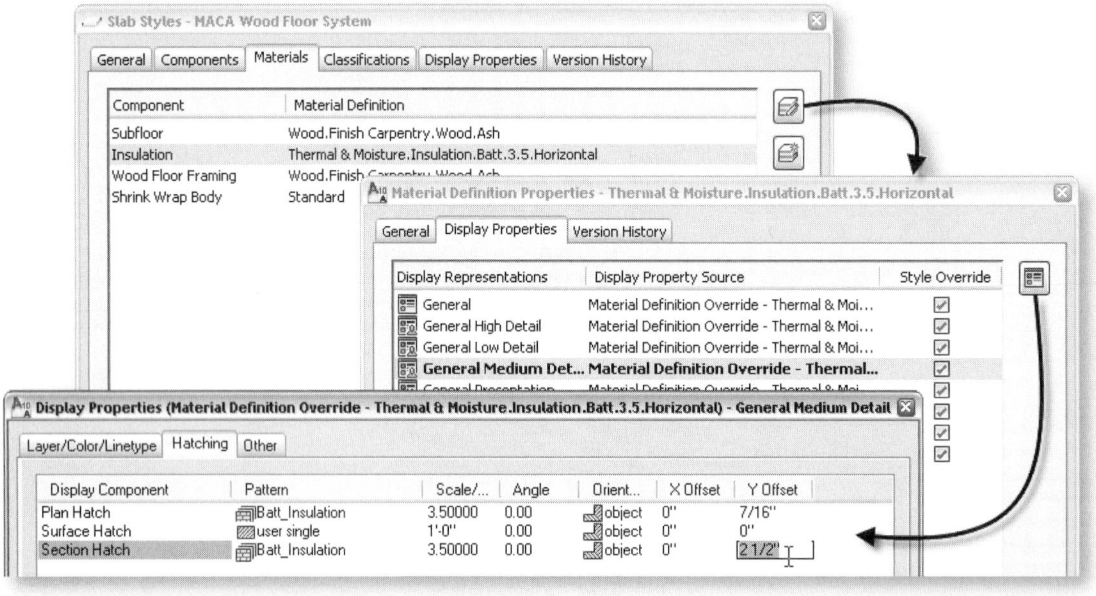

FIGURE 12.46 *Edit the Material to shift the hatching*

41. Click OK three times to return to the drawing.

The final step is to deal with the rim joist around the perimeter of the Slab. This is applied with a Slab Edge style (the same concept as the Roof Slab Edge styles used previously). When we used the Wood Floor System tool above, this edge was applied automatically. We can either edit it to the correct size and location relative to our new style, or remove it. In the steps that follow, we will remove it. If you prefer to keep it, feel free to use the in-place edit functionality to modify it instead if you choose.

42. With the Slab still selected, on the Properties palette, click the Edges worksheet icon located in the Dimensions grouping.
43. Choose ***None*** under Edge Style for all four and then click OK.
44. Click the Exit Edit In View icon and then save the file.

Add Floor Joists

As noted above, this next sequence is optional. In some cases, you may wish to see the individual framing members used in the floor construction. This can help you figure out a design problem or allow for a quick takeoff. However, remember that modeling the actual joist is not the only way to get an accurate count of them from your model. You can use Property Sets and Schedules (Chapter 15) and calculate the quantities from both schematic and highly detailed models. So again, be sure to consider all factors before making your decision about what to model.

1. From the floating View panel, choose the **View, SE Isometric** tool or on the View ribbon tab on the Appearance panel, chose **SE Isometric** from the View list box.
2. Using the Structural Member Wizard covered in Chapter 6, create a style for 2x10 [50x300] floor joists.

You can refer to the "Use the Structural Member Style Wizard" heading in Chapter 6 for a review of using the Structural Member Wizard for this task. Choose Wood, then Cut Lumber and then input the sizes indicated in the last step. Name the new

Style **2 × 10 Floor Joist [50 × 300 Floor Joist]**. Please be careful to use the proper size for the dimensions. In the case of Imperial Units, use 1 1/2'' × 9 1/4'' or 50 × 300 for Metric.

3. On the Design palette, click the Beam tool.
4. On the Properties palette, choose the style you just created.
5. In the Dimensions grouping, choose **Fill** for the "Layout Type" and verify that the "Justify" is set to **Top Center**.
6. In the Layout grouping, choose **Yes** for "Array," set the "Layout method" to **Repeat** and type **1'-4''** [**400**] for the "Bay size" (see Figure 12.47).

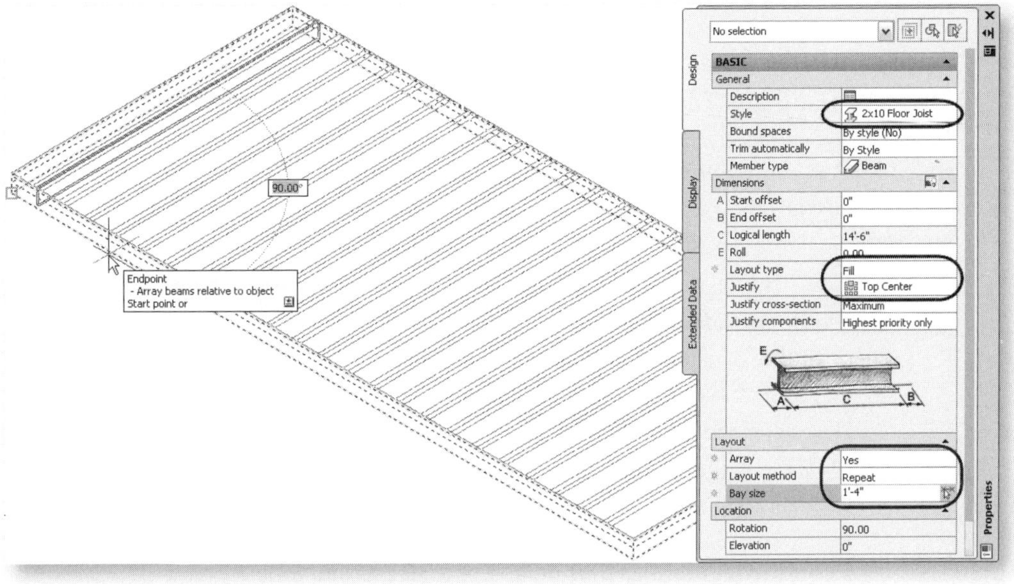

FIGURE 12.47 *Add joist using the Array option*

7. Move the mouse over the Slab.

   Move it around a bit and notice the way it previews the layout of joists. Depending on where you click, you can make the joists run horizontally or vertically.
8. Make sure that the joists run vertically (perpendicular to the long edge as shown in the figure) and then click.
9. Using the process above, cut another temporary section using the Edit In Section command. Be sure to select all joists and the Slab.

   Notice that the joists are inserted too high.
10. Select any joist, right-click and choose **Select Similar**. On the Properties palette, type **-1 1/2''** [**-37**] in the Elevation field (see Figure 12.48).

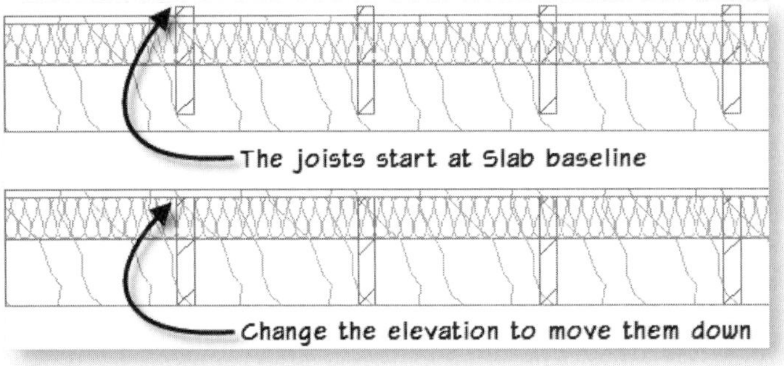
The joists start at Slab baseline
Change the elevation to move them down

FIGURE 12.48 *Move the joists down to line up properly with the Slab*

Apply Interference

To make the joists "cut" the insulation, we can apply an Interference Condition. Interference allows the 3D body of the Structural Members to interrupt the body of the Slab. Also, since we have chosen to model the individual Joists in this case, we can turn off the framing component of the Slab style so that they do not interfere with one another.

11. Select the Slab and, on the Slab contextual ribbon tab on the General panel, choose the ***Edit Style*** tool.
12. Click the Display Properties tab and place a check mark in the Style Override box next to the Model Display Representation.

    This will make the Display Properties dialog appear.
13. Click the lightbulb next to Boundary 3 (Wood Floor Framing) to turn it off and then click OK twice.
14. Select the Slab and, on the Slab contextual ribbon tab on the Modify panel, select the Interference button and choose the ***Add*** tool.
15. When prompted, select all of the joists and then press ENTER.
16. From the "Enter Shrinkwrap Effect" prompt, choose **Subtractive** (see Figure 12.49).

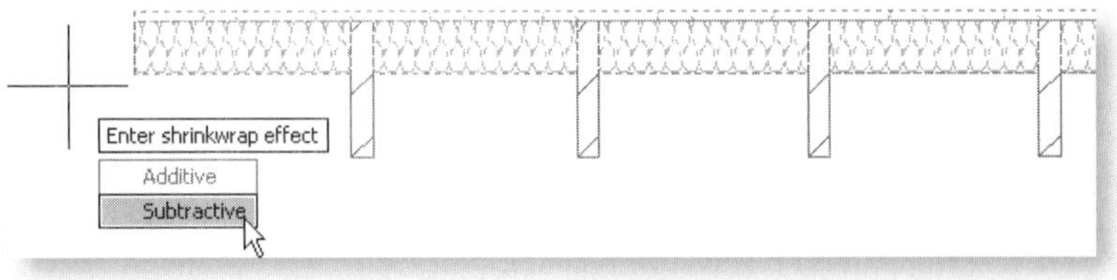
Enter shrinkwrap effect
Additive
Subtractive

FIGURE 12.49 *Apply Interference to make the joists "cut" the insulation*

17. Click the Exit Edit In View icon and then save the file.

If you wish, add a few more Beams using the joist style. You can use the Edge option instead of the Fill option on the Properties palette to create the joists going around the edges of the Slab. You can either vary the justifications or move them after placement to make them flush with the Slab edges. Apply interference on these as well. As you will see, this method allows interference, whereas had we left the Rim Joist Edge Style applied above, it would not. Edge Styles do have other advantages; however, it is worth experimenting with both approaches. Finally, we are not likely to move the Slab, so there is not much worry that it will move and leave its joists behind. You can use an Object Anchor to attach the joist to the Slab so that they move together when the Slab is moved. There is a tool for this in the Content Browser in the Stock Tool Catalog. Or in this case, it might be just as easy to type the command.

18. Press ESC to be sure no commands are active.
19. With onscreen prompts or directly in the Command Line, type **anchor**.
20. When prompted, choose **Object**.
21. When prompted, select all of the joists and then press ENTER.
22. Select the Slab at the prompt and then press ENTER to finish.

To test it out, move the Slab. Be sure to undo afterwards to return it to its proper location. You now have an assembly of components that behave as one. The final task remaining is to apply interference between the Slab and the Walls in the *First Floor New* Construct.

23. Save and Close the *Second Floor Slab* file.
24. On the Project Navigator, double-click to open the *First Floor New* Construct.
25. From the Project Navigator, drag and drop the *Second Floor Slab* Construct to the current drawing.

As we have seen in other chapters, this XREFs the *Second Floor Slab* Construct to the current *First Floor New* Construct.

Set the drawing to a convenient viewpoint such as 3D, or, using the process above, cut another temporary section using the Edit In Section command (be sure to select the Walls of the first floor and the XREF of the Slab).

26. Select one of the Walls and, from the Wall contextual ribbon tab on the Modify panel, select the Interference button and choose the ***Add*** tool.
27. Follow the prompts to select the Slab from within the XREF and make it Subtractive.

You will have to repeat this process on the other Walls as well. Also note that you may need to select the joists to interfere as well. You can make multiple selections of Walls and objects to interfere, so the process should be fairly quick.

BUILDING THE COMMERCIAL ROOF PLAN FILE

For simplicity at this stage, we will use a single flat Slab to represent the roof of the Commercial Project. In reality, there certainly would be sloped surfaces for drainage. At issue is whether the slight slope of a flat roof warrants the use of Roofs and Roof Slabs. As a rule, a Roof plan is a simple drawing. Your needs might be better served to use a single flat Slab for the 3D model and overall building section, and simply draft the slope of the Roof plan manually in the Roof Plan View file. This might sound like an odd recommendation in a book that has stressed the virtues of parametric design and building information modeling. However, the Roof and Slab objects really are a means to an end. Roof objects make good sense when working out a complex roof structure with many intersecting planes, hips, ridges and valleys. We also gain the benefit of creating linked sections and elevations directly from this geometry. (Refer to Chapter 16 for complete information on linked 2D Section/Elevation objects.) However, with a flat roof, the slope is so slight that a flat slab can do the job required by 1/8" = 1'-0" [1:100] and 1/4" = 1'-0" [1:50] drawings just as well. The true slope will then be expressed in Details. At small scales, 1/4" in 12 [1 in 50] slopes will not be perceived and the effort expended to generate correct mitering and sloping would be largely wasted.

By adding embellishments later directly in the Roof Plan View file, we achieve the requirements of a Roof Plan without adding unnecessary complexity to the model. Furthermore, by adding these embellishments only to the Roof Plan View file, we do not need to worry about freezing or thawing layers in any other files. This is because the extra linework will occur *only* in the Roof Plan file. As we noted above, let the needs of each project dictate the approach you take. In the task above, we modeled the residential floor structure in great detail. Here we are allowing the pendulum to swing in the other direction and are taking a more schematic approach. In projects where the roof covers a large surface, even a "flat" roof with 1/4" in 12 slope might be significant across the entire expanse of the roof. If you have that situation in one of your projects, you will likely find benefit in modeling the roof structure accurately instead. In this small project we have here, we do not have such a situation, and the approach mentioned above is appropriate instead.

Load the Commercial Project

Be sure that all files from the Residential Project have been closed and saved.

1. From the Quick Access Toolbar, choose the ***Project Browser*** tool.
2. Click to open the folder list and choose your *C:* drive.
3. Double-click on the *MasterACA 2010* folder, then the *Chapter12* folder.

   One or two commercial Projects are listed: *12 Commercial* and *12 Commercial Metric.*
4. Double-click *12 Commercial* if you wish to work in Imperial units. Double-click *12 Commercial Metric* if you wish to work in Metric units. (You can also right-click on it and choose **Set Current Project**.) Then click Close in the Project Browser.

NOTE

Important: If a message appears asking you to repath the project, click the "Repath the project now" option. Refer to the "Repathing Projects" topic in the Preface for more information.

Add a Wall Sweep Profile to a Parapet Wall

To save time, Slab Constructs have already been added to this project. A *Roof* Construct has also been included, complete with some Slab objects and a parapet Wall around the perimeter of the Roof to get us started. First, we will add a cap to the top of the parapet Wall; then we will update the appropriate project files.

5. On the Project Navigator palette, double-click to open the *Roof* Construct in the *Architectural* folder.
6. From the floating View panel, click the ***View, SE Isometric*** tool.

   Notice that the Parapet Wall is composed of three components, one of which is a cap component at the top (see Figure 12.50).

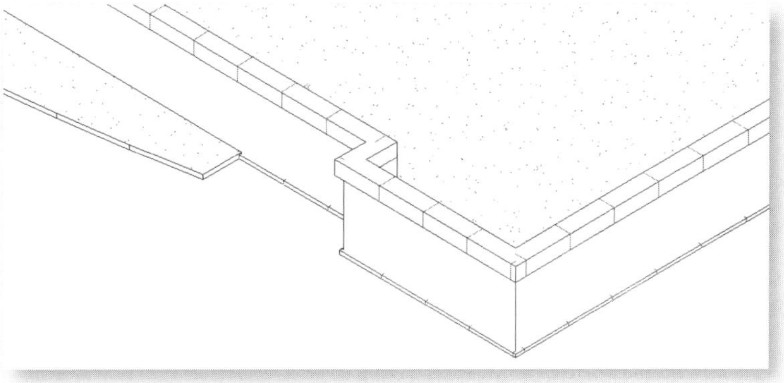

FIGURE 12.50 *The Parapet Wall Style includes three stacked components*

7. Turn on the Layer named A-Temp and then zoom in on the center Wall at the front of the building.

   There is a small magenta polyline at the position of the Parapet cap.

Wall components can have a sweep applied to them. A sweep is a custom cross-section shape that is applied to the full length of the Wall component. Sweeps are applied to individual Wall segments, not to styles. Let's take a quick look at sweeps. In the following sequence, we will add the magenta polyline shape as a sweep for the cap of all of the Parapet Walls. If you wish, you can customize the shape to your own preferences rather than use the one provided.

8. Select the Parapet Wall visible onscreen and, on the Wall contextual ribbon tab on the General tab, choose the ***Select Similar*** tool.

   All of the Parapet Walls should highlight.
9. On the Wall contextual ribbon tab on the Modify panel, select the Sweep button and choose the ***Add*** tool.
10. In the Add Wall Sweep dialog box, choose Cornice from the Wall Component list.

CAUTION

Choosing the Cornice component is important; if you forget to do this, you will be sweeping the wrong component.

11. Be sure that **Start from scratch** is chosen for Profile Definition and type **Parapet Cap** for the New Profile Name.
12. Verify that both Apply Roof/Floor Lines to Sweeps and Miter Selected Walls are chosen (see Figure 12.51).

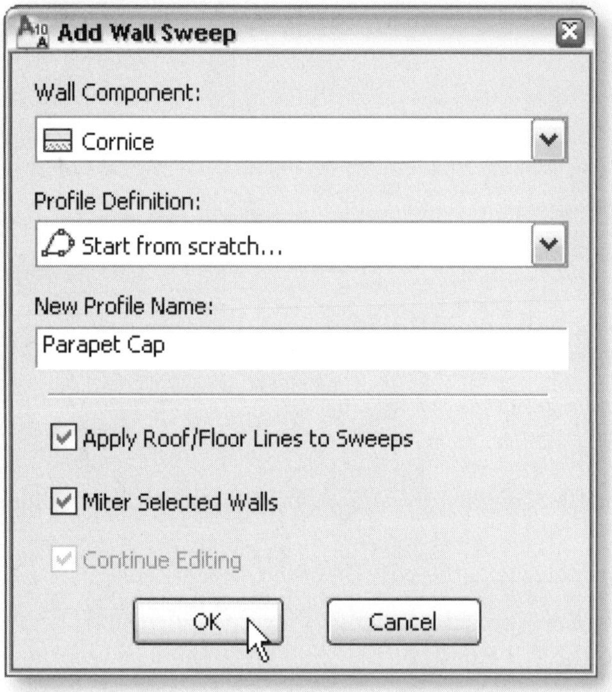

FIGURE 12.51 *Add a Wall sweep to the Cornice component of all selected Walls*

- **Apply Roof/Floor Lines to Sweeps**—Allows you to modify swept components with the Roof/Floor Line edit commands.
- **Miter Selected Walls**—Form clean intersections between all swept Wall segments. Without this setting, all sweeps produce simple straight extrusions.

13. At the "Select a location on wall for editing" prompt, click a point on the Parapet Wall near the magenta polyline (see Figure 12.52).

    It does not have to be exactly on the magenta polyline.

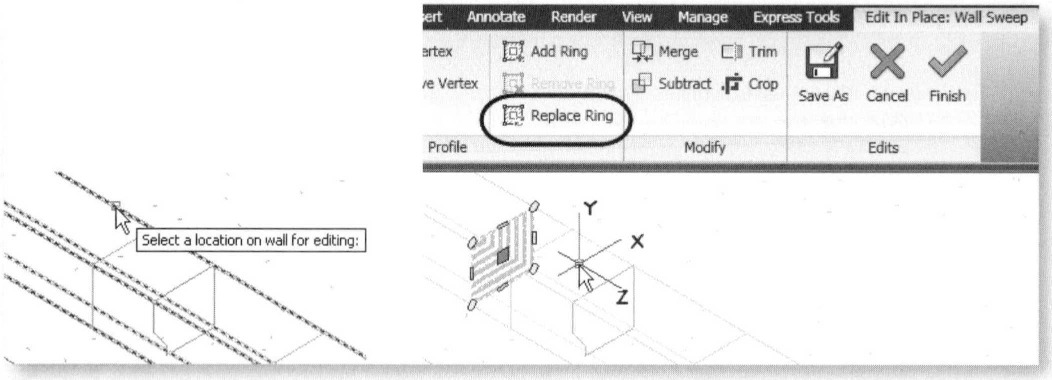

FIGURE 12.52 *Click a point to begin the Edit in Place mode for Wall Sweeps*

Feel free to experiment with the grips on the In-place Edit profile. Watch the grayed-out Walls beyond respond in real time. You can also add or remove vertices with the CTRL key options as usual. If you are happy with the profile shape that you have devised in your experimentation, skip the next Step; otherwise, proceed when you are ready.

14. Select the In-place edit profile (blue cross hatch).
15. On the Edit In Place: Wall Sweep contextual ribbon tab, on the Profile panel, choose the ***Replace Ring*** tool.
16. When prompted, select the magenta polyline and then answer **Yes** to "Erase the layout geometry."
17. On the Edit In Place contextual ribbon tab on the Edits panel, click the ***Finish*** tool to complete the operation.

    Zoom out and take note of the nicely mitered corners.
18. Save and close the file.

Update the Composite Building Section Model View

As we did above for the Residential Project, it is time to update the composite model Views for the Commercial Project. In addition to the roof files that we have worked on here, some updates have been made (and provided) in the *Ground* file. A Slab has been added and some Materials applied. Feel free to explore the objects in this file to better understand their properties and usage.

You may recall that in the Commercial Project, we have three composite model files. One is the generic 3D Model, while the other two are designed specifically to the needs of Elevations and Sections, respectively. In this exercise, we will update the *A-SC01 – Architectural Building Sections Model.* Viewing a full building section is the best way to see the impact of our new Slab objects.

19. On the Project Navigator, click the Views tab.
20. Right-click on the *A-SC01* View file and choose **Properties**.
21. On the left side of the Modify View dialog box, click the Content item (see Figure 12.53).

    Be sure that all Constructs are selected. If not, place a check mark in the *Constructs* folder at the top of the list and click OK.

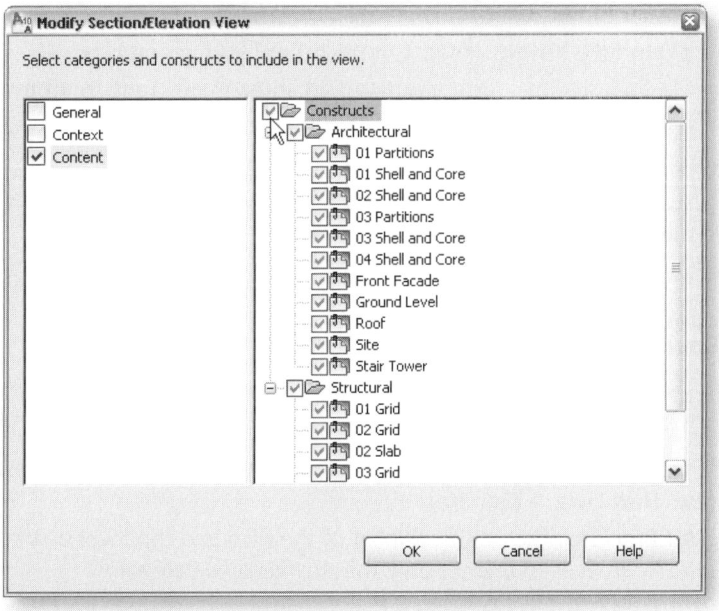

FIGURE 12.53 *Edit the Content of the Composite Model View*

22. Double-click *A-SC01* to open it.
23. From the floating View panel, click the View, SE Isometric tool (see Figure 12.54).

    It may take some time for this Model to regenerate. Material Surface Hatching can slow things down a bit.

NOTE

You can dramatically speed up the regen times of a Model like this by toggling off the Surface Hatch. The Surface Hatch toggle quick-pick icon is located on the Drawing status bar at the bottom right corner of the screen. This is shown in Figure 1.3 in Chapter 1.

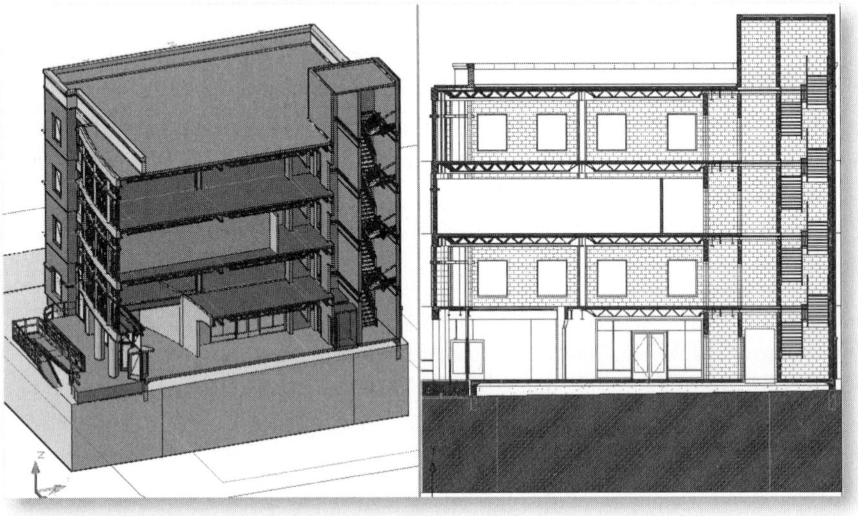

FIGURE 12.54 *Our Live Section through the Model has come a long way*

As you can see, we have come a long way on our Commercial Project. Feel free to zoom in to the various intersections between materials to see how the details are shaping up. Feel free to open any files, make adjustments and then reload the XREFs to see the results. For instance, you may want to open the *01 Partitions* file and increase the height of the Walls around the atrium space. On the other hand, you might prefer a balcony overlook, in which case you might want to add some guard rails to a new Construct named *02 Partitions*. The decision is left to you.

24. Repeat the steps to update the *A-CM00 – Composite Building* Model. For the *A-EL01 – Architectural Building Elevations* Model, add only the *Roof* Construct; it does not need the Slabs.
25. Save and close the composite model files.

Add a Roof Plan View to the Project

Once you have completed the additions to the Constructs, you are ready to create a new View in the project.

26. On the Project Navigator palette, click the View tab, right-click the *Views* folder and choose **New View Dwg > General**.
27. Name the file **A-FP05** (architectural floor plan of the fifth and top level or the roof). Choose the Roof level and select only the *Architectural* category.

28. Open another plan View, copy the elevation and section callouts and paste them to the original coordinates in the roof plan View.
29. Add a Titlemark callout and draw drainage lines directly on top of the XREFs in the file.
30. Save and close the roof plan.

You can see an example of the final result in the complete version of the project with the files from the CD.

ADDITIONAL EXERCISES

Additional exercises have been provided in Appendix A. In Appendix A, you will find exercises to add Slabs to the *Basement New* file and a Roof to the porch of the Residential Project. It is not necessary that you complete these exercises to begin the next chapter. They are provided to enhance your learning experience. Completed projects for each of the exercises have been provided in the *Chapter12/Complete* folder.

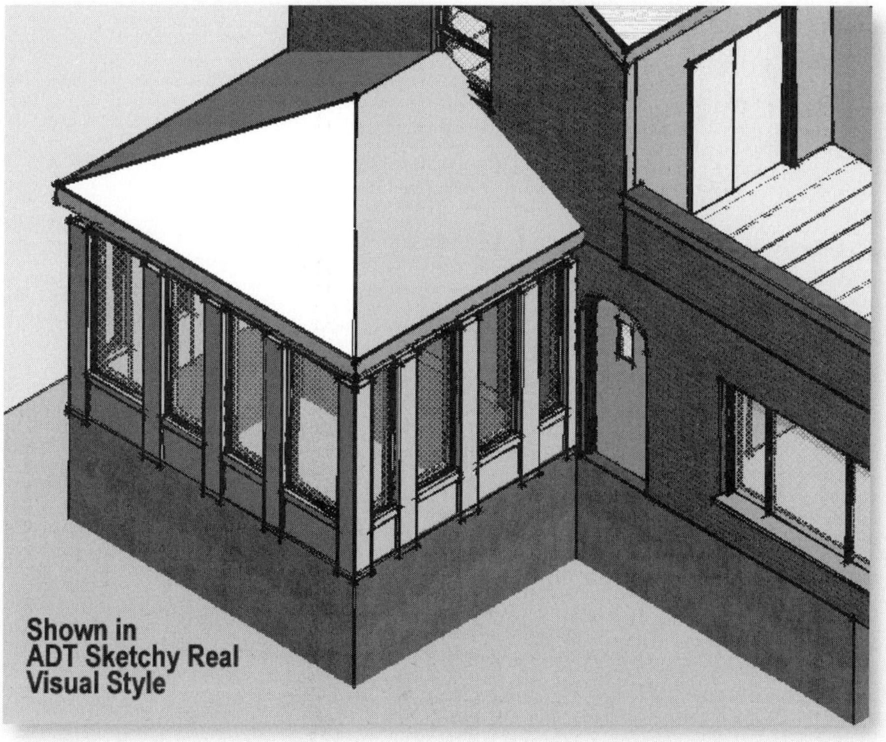

FIGURE 12.55 *Update projects in Additional Exercises—Appendix A*

SUMMARY

- The first thing you should do is rough out a roof using the one-piece Roof. When design needs warrant, you can convert it to Roof Slabs.
- Eaves can be made square by choosing the plumb option in Properties.
- Roof Slabs offer greater control and flexibility than the one-piece Roof, but they must be mitered manually.
- Roof Slab edges can be customized with Roof Slab Edge styles.
- You should use Slab objects for virtually any horizontal surface.
- Both Roof Slabs and Slabs can use styles with multiple components, much like a Wall as if it were lying flat.
- Slab edges can be customized with Slab Edge styles.
- You should keep Slabs in separate XREFs so they don't clutter your plan files.
- You should use a flat Slab with 0 slope for simple flat roofs. You should articulate the plan view with lines for drainage in a roof plan drawing.
- For more complex roof design needs, you can model the actual slope surfaces.

SECTION

III

Construction Documents

In this section, we take our building model into construction documentation. The next several chapters explore the topics of creating reflected ceiling plans, generating schedules, adding dimensions and annotation, extracting sections and elevations from the building model, creating Details and working with the Detail Component Manager. All of this data is organized onto Sheets, ready to be printed or Exported to electronic formats such as PDF and DWF.

Section III is organized as follows:

Chapter 13	Creating Reflected Ceiling Plans
Chapter 14	Generating Annotation
Chapter 15	Generating Schedules
Chapter 16	Generating Sections and Elevations
Chapter 17	Generating Details and Keynotes
Chapter 18	Plotting and Publishing

CHAPTER

13

Creating Reflected Ceiling Plans

INTRODUCTION

In this chapter, we will explore generation of a reflected ceiling plan (RCP) in AutoCAD Architecture. To facilitate the creation process, ACA includes a special Display Configuration specifically designed for reflected ceiling plans, called "Reflected." In addition to this Display Configuration, the Ceiling Grid object is also available. Use this object to create suspended ceiling layouts. Many drag-and-drop content items, such as lighting symbols and ceiling fixtures, are also at our disposal.

OBJECTIVES

A Display Configuration specially designed to display all objects with their "Reflected" Display Representation active is included in the standard ACA template files. Before work on the reflected ceiling plan can begin, this Display Configuration must be made active. (Review Chapter 2 for a detailed discussion of Display Configurations.) Working in the commercial project, we will add Ceiling Grid objects and consider ways to crop and center them within the shapes of the spaces in which they occur. The collection of content available for lighting fixtures will also be explored. The following topics will be explored in detail:

- Add Spaces object to existing files.
- Learn to switch to reflected ceiling plan Display Configuration.
- Create and modify Ceiling Grid objects.
- Clip Ceiling Grids to the shape of the room.
- Center Ceiling Grids in rooms.
- Add anchored light fixtures.
- Mask a Ceiling Grid with lights.

CREATING FLOORS AND CEILINGS USING SPACES

While Slabs (covered in the previous chapter) are useful for modeling horizontal planes in a building model, they do not necessarily lend themselves to representing the individual floor and ceiling planes or the actual rooms of an interior model. They certainly can be used, but Space objects are better suited to this task. In addition, Space objects are very useful in tracking square footage and other "room-specific" schedule data as you design a floor plan. Chapter 15 is devoted to Schedules and Schedule Data, and we will explore the data-tracking aspects of Spaces therein. In this chapter, we will focus on the physical aspects of Spaces and their ability to determine the boundaries of our ceiling grids.

INSTALL THE CD FILES AND LOAD THE CURRENT PROJECT

If you have already installed all of the files from the CD, simply skip down to step 3 below to make the project active. If you need to install the CD files, start at step 1.

1. If you have not already done so, install the dataset files located on the Mastering AutoCAD Architecture 2010 CD-ROM.

   Refer to "Files Included on the CD-ROM" in the Preface for information on installing the sample files included on the CD.
2. Launch AutoCAD Architecture 2010 from the desktop icon created in Chapter 3.

If you did not create a custom icon, you might want to review "Create a New Profile" and "Create a Desktop Shortcut" in Chapter 3. Creating the custom desktop icon is not essential; however, it makes loading the custom profile easier.

3. From the File menu, choose **Project Browser**.
4. Click to open the folder list and choose your *C:* drive.
5. Double-click on the *MasterACA 2010* folder, then the *Chapter 13* folder.

   One or two commercial Projects will be listed: *13 Commercial* or *13 Commercial Metric*.
6. Double-click *13 Commercial* if you wish to work in Imperial units. Double-click *13 Commercial Metric* if you wish to work in Metric units. (You can also right-click on it and choose **Set Current Project**.) Then click Close in the Project Browser.

NOTE

Important: If a message appears asking you to repath the project, click the "Repath the project now" option. Refer to the "Repathing Projects" topic in the Preface for more information.

GENERATE SPACES FROM EXISTING WALLS

It is often desirable to add Spaces to layouts that already include Walls and other objects. The Space auto Generate option is designed specifically for this purpose. A Space object is typically used to represent a single room (or a contiguous area in an open plan assigned to a particular function). If the room is enclosed by Walls on all sides, it is easy to make the Space. In an open plan, we sometimes need to draw the Space manually or add linework (usually non-plotting) to assist in the auto-generation process.

7. On the Project Navigator, click the Constructs tab and in the *Constructs\Architectural* folder, double-click *03 Partitions* to open it.

A selection of commercial Space style tools has been included on the Spaces tab of the tool palettes.

8. Click on the Spaces tab of the tool palettes.

   If you do not see this palette or tool, right-click the tool palettes title bar and choose **Design** (to load the Design tool palette group) and then click the Spaces tab.

9. Click on the Office (Medium) tool.
10. On the Properties palette, choose **Generate** for the Create type.
11. Move your mouse into one of the offices around the perimeter of the plan. Do *not* click yet.

    Notice how the rooms highlight when the cursor is within them (see Figure 13.1).

Verify that Associative is set to Yes and accept the default shown in the figure for the Generate Space options.

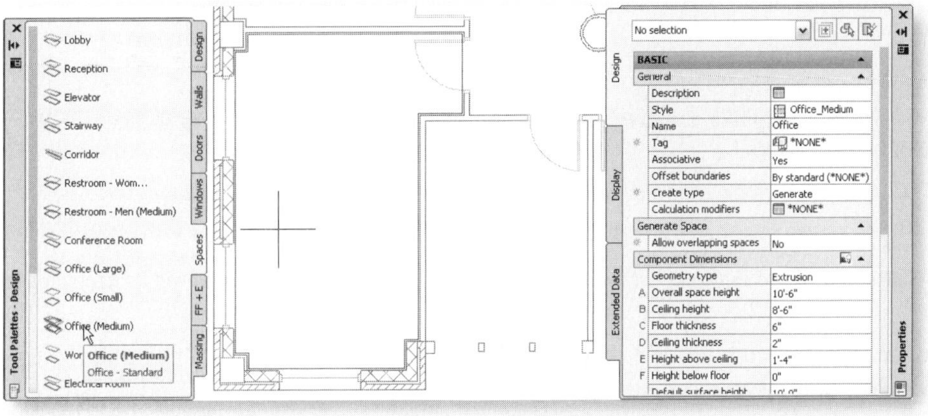

FIGURE 13.1 *With the Generate option enabled, the boundary of surrounding AEC objects is used to determine the shape of the Space*

Before you click the mouse, you can move from room to room and the outline will highlight in red.

12. Click inside the corner office at the bottom left side of the plan.
13. Repeat for the remaining offices on the left side and the two offices at the bottom (seven in all including the corner office).

TIP

If you have to pan or zoom to see all of one or more offices, you may see "Space not found" in the ToolTip at the cursor and get a "Valid boundary not found" warning message on the Command Line. Type v and press `ENTER` **(or, press the** `DOWN ARROW` **and choose reset Visible boundaries) to have previously off-screen objects included in the boundary set.**

14. On the Spaces tool palette, click on the Corridor tool.
15. Move your mouse over the corridor in the center of the plan. Do *not* click yet.

    The corridor as well as the neighboring open plan spaces such as the reception and conference room spaces should highlight (see Figure 13.2).

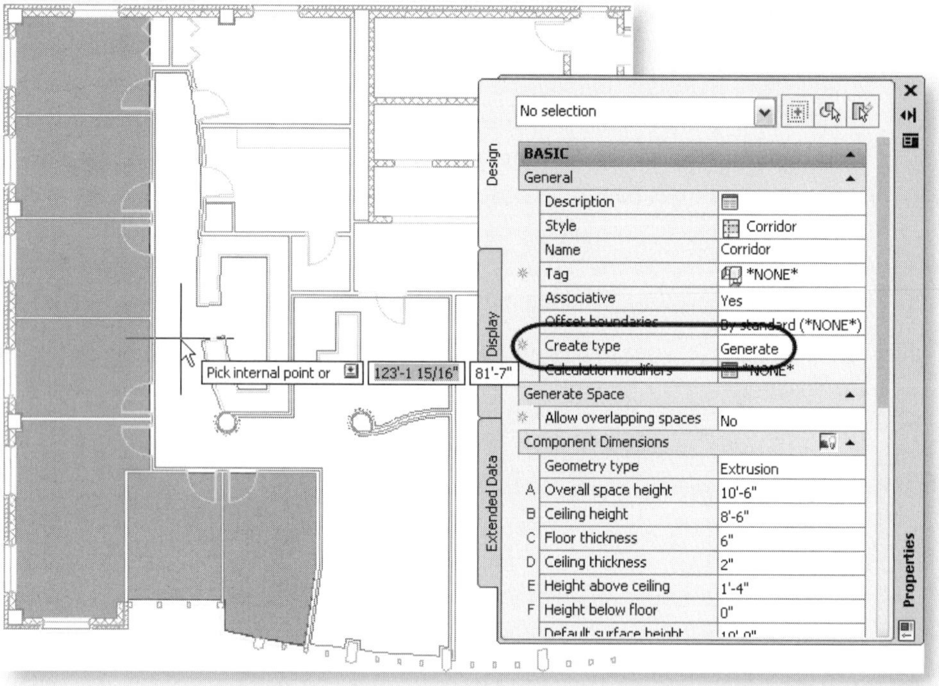

FIGURE 13.2 *When Walls do not separate the rooms, a single continuous Space will be generated*

Notice that the red boundary is highlighting not only the corridor but also the reception and conference room areas. This is because there is no clear boundary between these areas. We can draw other Walls or simple geometry-like lines or polylines. A file with such lines has been provided in the *Elements* folder.

16. Press the ESC key to cancel the command without creating any Spaces.
17. On the Project Navigator, in the *Elements* folder, right-click the *Space Outlines* file and choose **Insert as Block**.

    Use 0,0,0 for the Insertion Point and check the "Explode" box before clicking OK (see Figure 13.3).

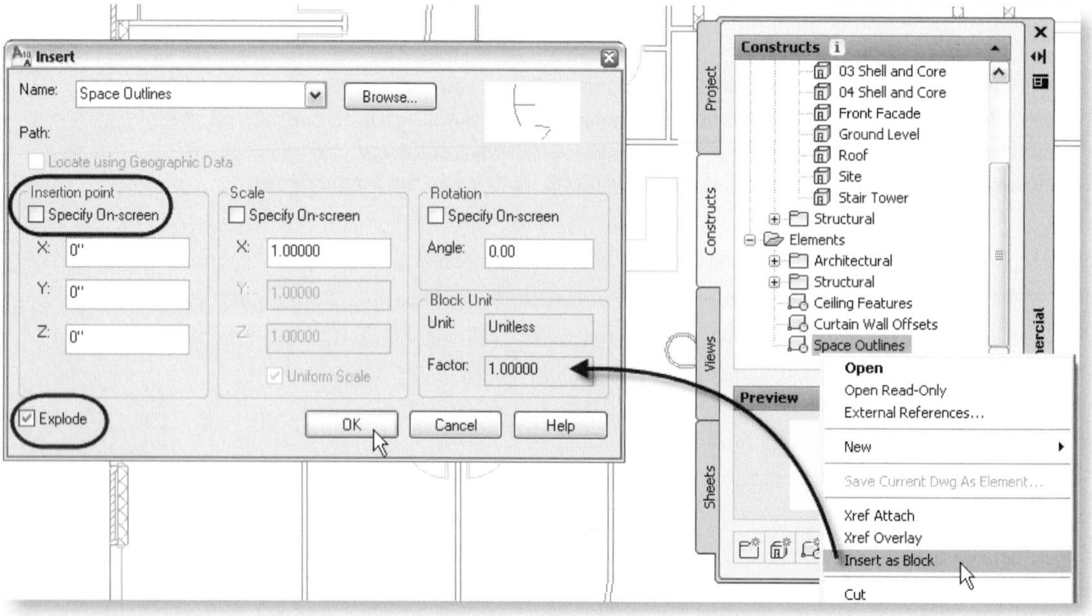

FIGURE 13.3 *Insert and explode the Space Outlines Element file*

This will add some magenta lines and arcs to the file. These will be useful in helping the Generate routine find all the desired Spaces.

18. Try the Corridor tool again.

    Notice that the magenta lines seem to be having no effect on the boundary. Press the ESC key without creating any Spaces.

19. Select the magenta polylines. On the Properties palette, beneath the Advanced grouping, set the Bound spaces property to **Yes** (see Figure 13.4).

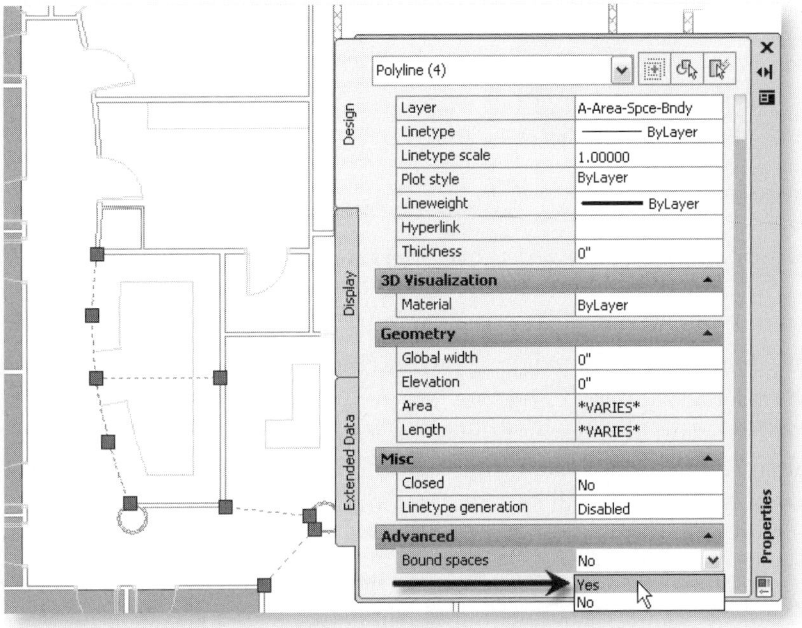

FIGURE 13.4 *Change the Bound spaces property of the polylines to "Yes"*

20. Try the Corridor tool once more.

    This time it should highlight just the corridor space using the magenta polylines as boundaries as well as the Walls.

21. Click in the area of the corridor to create the Space.

TIP

Use the Space Separator tool on the Spaces tool palette (near the bottom) to draw polylines that will have the Bound spaces property preset to Yes. This tool has the Wall layer key set in its properties; you could make a copy and change the layer key to a non-plotting layer if you do not want the polylines to plot.

22. On the Spaces tool palette, click on the Workstation (Small) tool.

23. Click in each of the workstation spaces adjacent to the corridor (see Figure 13.5).

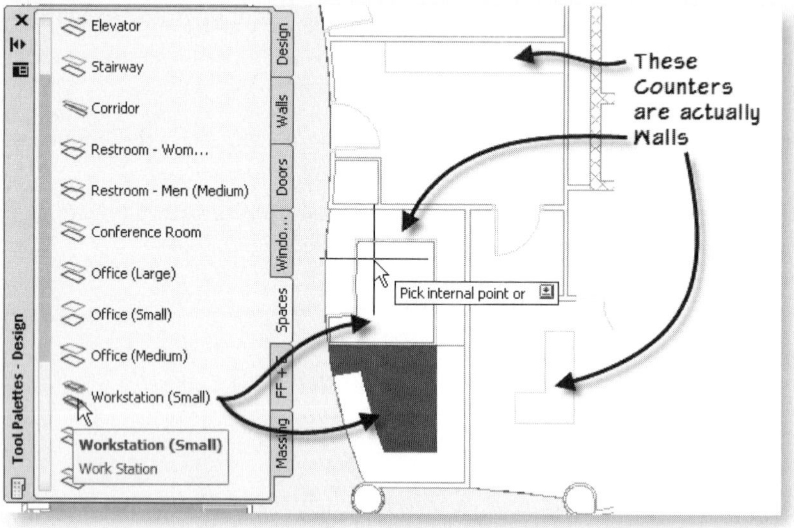

FIGURE 13.5 *Workstations treat the surrounding countertops as boundaries*

Notice that the countertops surrounding the workstations have not been included in the shape of the resultant Spaces. This is not a correct way to represent these Spaces. The reason this has occurred is because the countertops here are created from Wall styles. (Several such Wall styles are included in the out-of-the-box content files.) A simple edit to this Wall style will exclude them from the Space boundary generation process.

24. Select one of the countertop Walls, and on the Wall ribbon tab, on the General panel, click the ***Edit Style*** button (top of split button).

    It will be easier to select one in the reception or workroom space as indicated in the figure.

25. Click the General tab, remove the check mark from the "Objects of this style may act as a boundary for associative spaces" checkbox, and then click OK.

Three defect markers appear, one on the corridor Space, and one each on the two workstation Spaces. If you hover the cursor over one of the defect markers, a ToolTip providing detail on the problem and suggested solutions will appear (see left side of Figure 13.6). While it is obvious that the two workstation Spaces have had a boundary removed, ACA had used the counter Walls for part of the corridor Space also.

26. Select the two workstation Spaces, and on the Space ribbon tab on the Modify panel, select the Update drop-down button and choose the ***Selected Space*** tool (see middle of Figure 13.6).

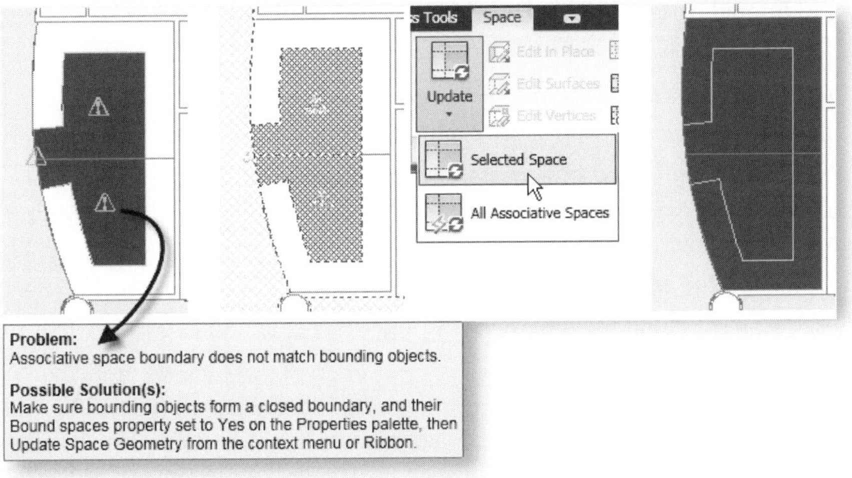

FIGURE 13.6 *After removing the countertop Wall style from boundary creation, update the Spaces*

Since the countertops in all rooms use the same style, this change will allow us to add the reception and workroom Spaces easily.

27. Using the appropriate tools on the Spaces palette, add the Spaces indicated in Figure 13.7.

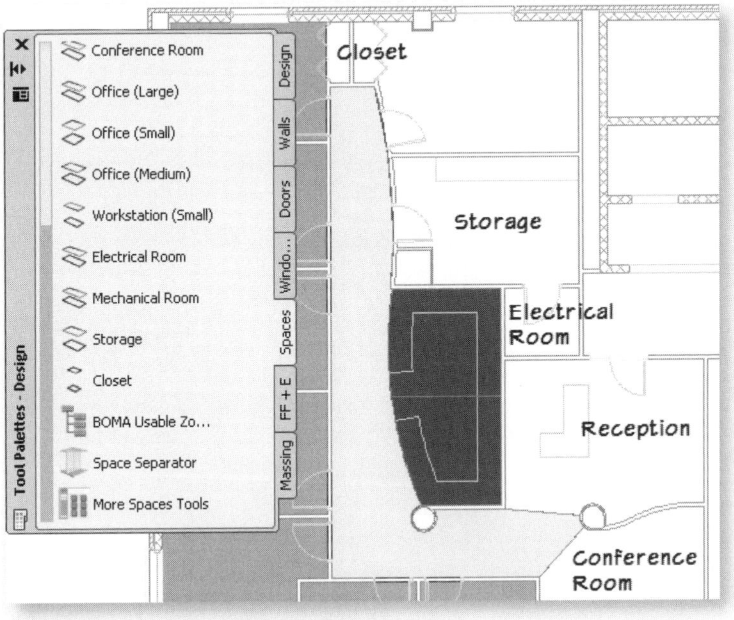

FIGURE 13.7 *Add several more Spaces from the tool palette*

The last Space that we need to add, the room in the top corner of the suite, does not have a suitable tool on the palette. Consider the tool palettes provided as samples of the total collection of content items provided. Several additional styles are provided in the library. We have discussed ways to access this library in previous chapters. The easiest method is to use the Content Browser, and an icon has been provided on the Spaces tool palette that links directly to the appropriate catalog and category containing additional Space tools. Using this icon, we can locate a suitable style for our remaining Space.

28. On the Spaces palette, click the More Spaces Tools icon.

    This tool is shown in the previous figure.
29. When the Content Browser appears, click the *Commercial* category.
30. Locate the Lounge tool and using the eyedropper icon, drag and drop it into the drawing window.

    This will run the add Space command as before.
31. Add the Space to the room in the upper right corner and then press ENTER to end the command.

You should now have Spaces for all of the unique rooms in the tenant space. We will not add Spaces to the core, lobby or unoccupied areas of the plan at this time. There remains only one bit of fine-tuning to complete. The default floor thickness for Spaces is a bit too thick. Let's adjust that now.

32. Make a crossing window selection of the entire plan.

    The Properties palette will read something like "All (91)."

"All" indicates that the selection includes a mix of object types, and the number is the quantity of objects selected. If you open this list, each type of object will be listed with its own quantity next to it.

33. Click this drop-down at the top and choose **Space (17)**.
34. Change the Floor thickness and the Ceiling thickness to **1/2"** [**12**] (see Figure 13.8).

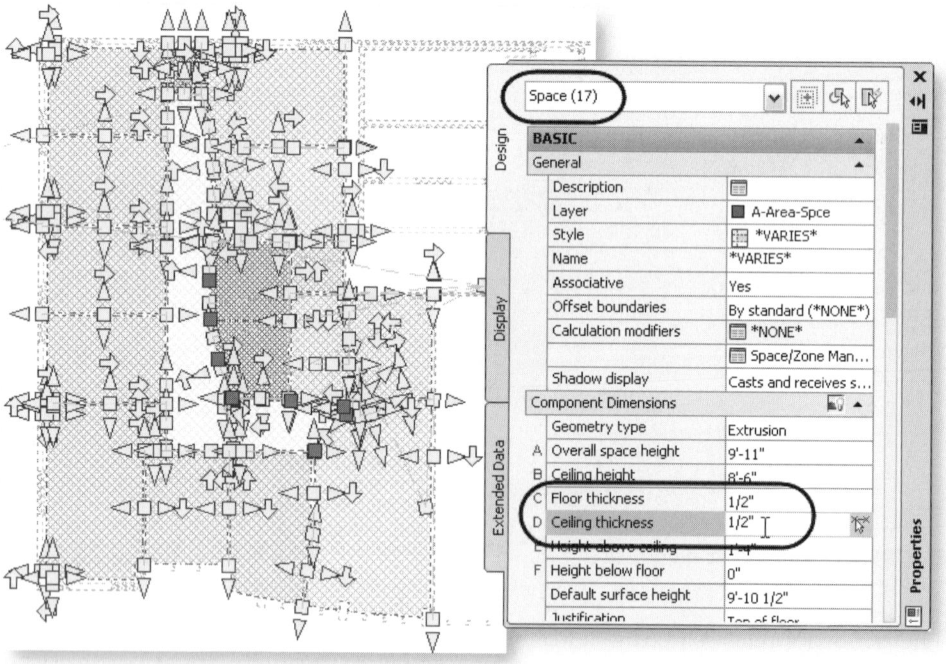

FIGURE 13.8 *Change the ceiling and floor thicknesses of all Spaces*

35. Save the file.

MANAGER NOTE CAD

In this project, we have placed the Spaces directly to the *03 Partitions* Construct. In larger projects, it may be desirable to move the Spaces to their own Construct with a name such as *03 Spaces* or *03 Spaces and Grids*. This will allow for greater flexibility in staffing issues and work flow. If both the Spaces and the Walls are in the same Construct, only one individual can be editing that particular floor plate at any given time, including both floor and ceiling plans. However, if you separate the Spaces out to their own Constructs, you can have two individuals working simultaneously on the same floor plate in separate Construct files. One person would be responsible for Walls and Doors, while the other person would maintain Spaces and Ceiling Grids. You should note that the Generate feature of the Space tools works through XREF files. So if you decide to separate them into different files, you will create a new Construct, drag the *03 Partitions* file into it and then create the Spaces. The decision is usually made on a per-project basis, and project size is the major determining factor.

WORKING IN THE REFLECTED DISPLAY CONFIGURATION

Now that we have defined the Spaces for each room, we can begin adding ceiling grids to them. Consistent with the other features of AutoCAD Architecture, Ceiling Grids have built-in intelligence and are displayed only when a Reflected Display Configuration is active. This makes it possible for the floor plan data and the reflected ceiling plan data to coexist in the same model file. In this small project, ceiling plan information will be added directly to the *03 Partitions* Construct along with the Spaces we just added.

Change the Display Configuration

As already noted, the first step in working on a reflected ceiling is to enable the proper Display Configuration.

Continue in the *03 Partitions* file.

1. On the Drawing status bar, open the Display Configuration pop-up menu and choose **Reflected**.

Notice that the graphical display of several of the objects in the drawing has changed (see Figure 13.9). (It may take a few seconds for the Display Configuration to switch.)

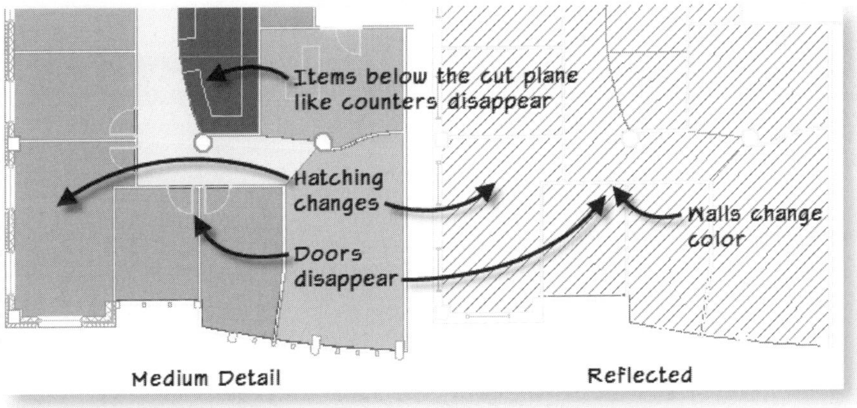

FIGURE 13.9 *Most objects change display properties with the switch to Reflected*

NOTE

See Chapter 2 for more information on the Display System.

Add Column Grid Reference and Configure Bubbles to Display in RCP

It might be helpful while working on the ceiling to have the Column Grid displayed for reference. As you recall, the Column Grid is contained in another Construct, which, in turn, references a typical *Column Grid* Element file. The *03 Grid* Construct will be added as an Overlaid XREF.

2. On the Project Navigator palette, expand the *Constructs\Structural* folder.
3. Drag the *03 Grid* Construct and drop it into the drawing window.

NOTE

Important: Resist the urge to simply overlay the *Column Grid* Element file. In the current situation, this would yield the same result; however, if at some point in the project the third floor Grid were to become unique, the third floor ceiling would no longer be coordinated.

NOTE

When you drag a Construct into another Construct as we have done here, ACA automatically uses XREF Overlay, which is exactly what we need in this case. In this way, the *03 Grid* file will be visible only here in *03 Partitions*; if it is needed in other files, it must be XREFed separately by those files.

As you can see, there is an issue with the Column Grid display. The Column Grid lines are displayed, but the Column Bubbles are not. You may find it useful to have your Column Bubbles displayed in your ceiling plans. To achieve this, we need to make a simple modification to the Column Grid Bubble Multi-View Block located in the *Column Grid* file.

4. On the Project Navigator, in the *Elements\Structural* folder, double-click the *Column Grid* Element file to open it.

   This is the typical *Column Grid* Element file (created in Chapter 6) that is nested within the *03 Grid Construct.*

5. Select any one of the Column Grid Bubbles, and, on the Multi-View Block ribbon tab, on the General panel, click the ***Edit Style*** button (top of split button, see Figure 13.10).

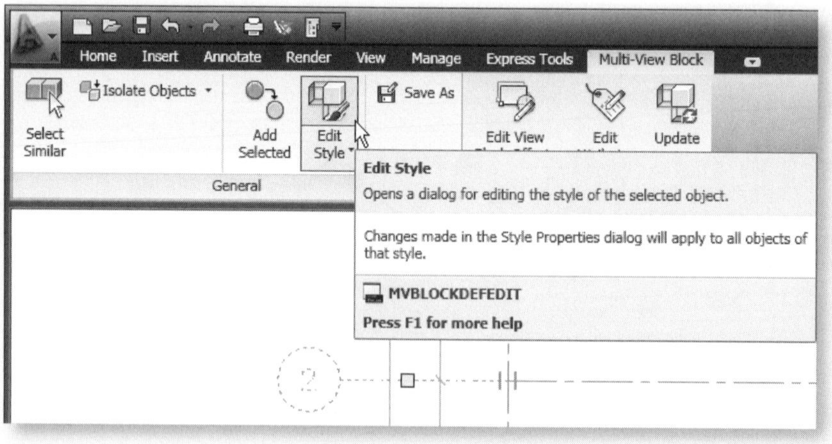

FIGURE 13.10 *Edit the Column Bubble Multi-View Block Definition*

6. In the Multi-View Block Definition Properties dialog box, click the View Blocks tab.

Notice that several Display Representations are listed on the left. (Review "Create a Custom Multi-View Block" in Chapter 11 for more information.) The Reflected representation is for reflected ceiling plans.

7. Select Reflected from the list of Display Representations.

   Notice that no View Blocks are loaded on the right.

8. Click the Add button.
9. In the "Select a Block" dialog box, choose BubbleDef and then click OK (see Figure 13.11).

   This is the same block that is loaded in the General Display Representation used for plans.

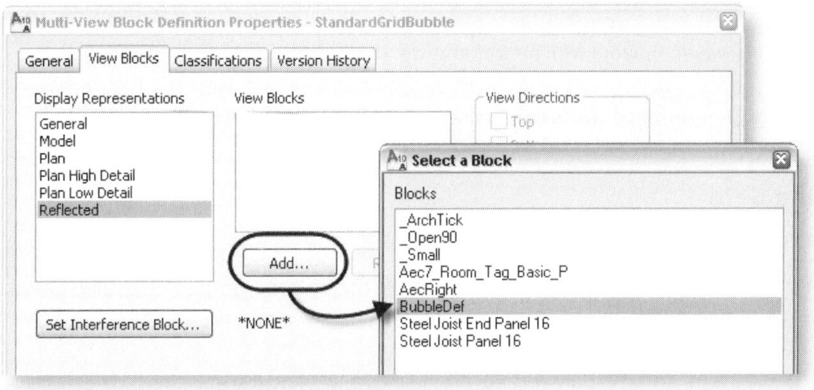

FIGURE 13.11 *Add the same View Block used for Plans to the Reflected Display Rep*

10. Click OK to return to the drawing.
11. Save and close the *Column Grid* file.

    An XREF update alert will appear at the lower left corner of the screen (see Figure 13.12).

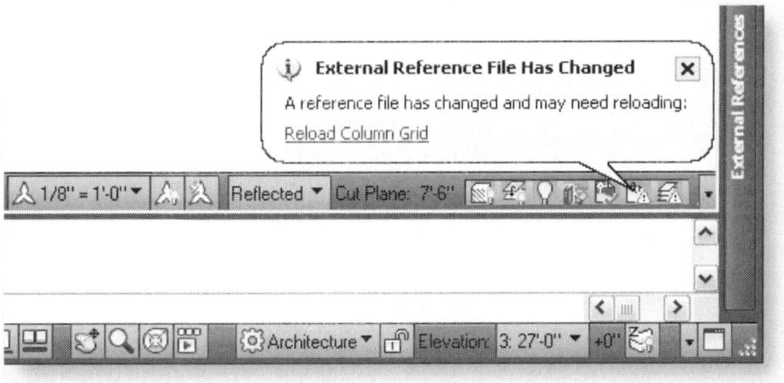

FIGURE 13.12 *Reload the XREF to see the update to the Column Bubbles*

12. Click the Reload Column Grid link (see Figure 13.12).

The Column Bubbles should now appear in the Reflected Display Configuration.

> **To make this change permanent for all drawings, edit your office standard template file(s). The Column Grid Bubble is named StandardGridBubble. ACA creates this Multi-View Block automatically when a Column Grid is labeled. If you wish to customize it, you must create your own version, name it StandardGridBubble and save it in your office standard template file.**

MANAGER NOTE CAD

WORKING WITH CEILING GRID OBJECTS

Ceiling Grid objects can be used for any type of grid pattern occurring on a reflected ceiling plan. Most typically, they are used for 2×2 [600×600] or 2×4 [600×1200] suspended ceilings. Ceiling Grid objects are added and modified in the same way as other AEC objects. Ceiling Grids are rectangular in shape; however, they can be clipped to the shape of the room in which they are placed. Both polylines and Space objects can be used as clipping boundaries. Most other parameters of Ceiling Grids are similar to Column Grids, which was covered in Chapter 6.

CAD MANAGER NOTE

Ceiling Grids are 2D objects designed for use in construction documents. Although they can be moved to the correct Z height and can be viewed from a 3D vantage point, being comprised of a grid of lines, they will not show a surface in renderings. If you plan to create hidden line renderings and walkthroughs, the Ceiling Grid placed at the correct Z height will prove sufficient. However, if you will be generating shaded or rendered output, use the Space objects (as added above) and apply a Material to the ceiling surface. The focus of this chapter and of Section III of this book is the creation of Construction Documents.

Add a Ceiling Grid

We are ready to begin adding Ceiling Grid objects to our *03 Partitions* Construct.

1. Zoom in on the room in the top right corner of the tenant space (labeled Break Room in Figure 13.13).

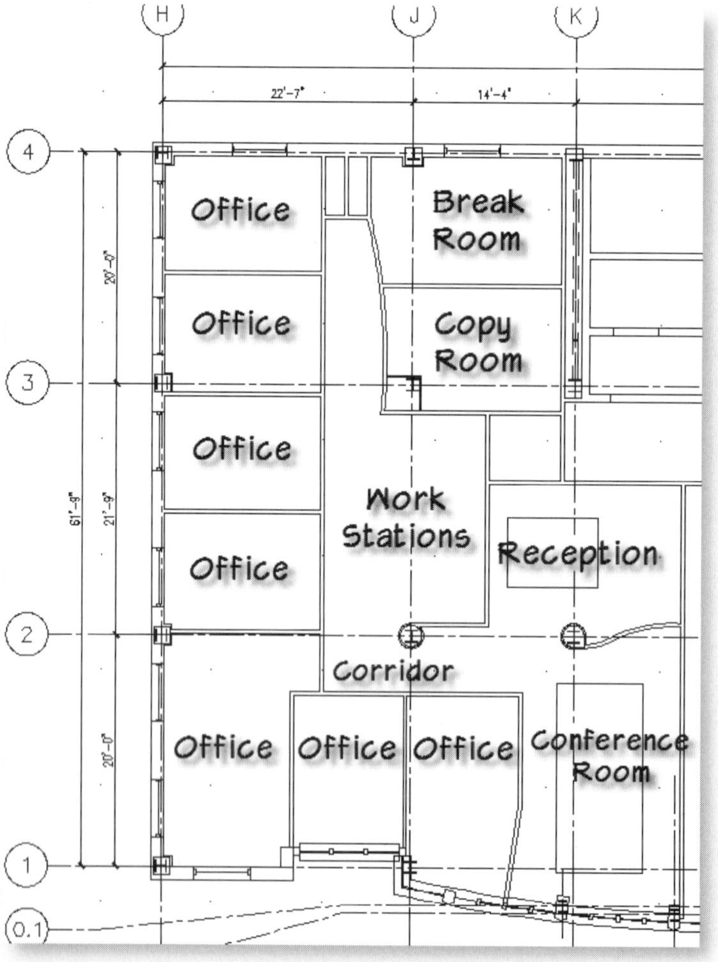

FIGURE 13.13 *Use these designations to locate individual rooms in the suite*

NOTE

The labels shown in Figure 13.13 do not appear in the drawing file. They will be referenced throughout the remainder of this tutorial for convenience. Refer to this figure throughout the exercise. We will discuss adding Room Tags to our project in Chapters 14 and 15.

2. On the Design palette, click the Ceiling Grid tool.
3. On the Properties palette, within the Dimensions grouping, set both the X - Width and Y - Depth settings (which control the overall size of the Grid) to **20'-0"** [**6000**].
4. Verify that within the X Axis and Y Axis groupings, both Bay size settings (which control the size of each tile) are set to **2'-0"** [**600**] (see Figure 13.14).

NOTE

If the Bay size fields are not available, choose Repeat from the Layout type list. Like Column Grids, Ceiling Grids can use Space evenly to establish the modulation of bays. However, because most Ceiling Grids use a fixed pre-manufactured tile size, it would be rare to use this feature.

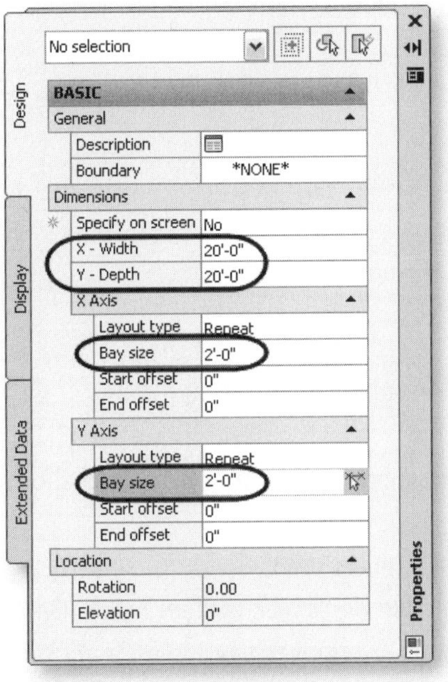

FIGURE 13.14 *Configure the parameters of the Ceiling Grid on the Properties palette*

5. Using an Endpoint Object Snap, set the Insertion point of the grid at the lower left corner of the Break Room and then press ENTER to accept the default rotation of **0°** (see Figure 13.15).

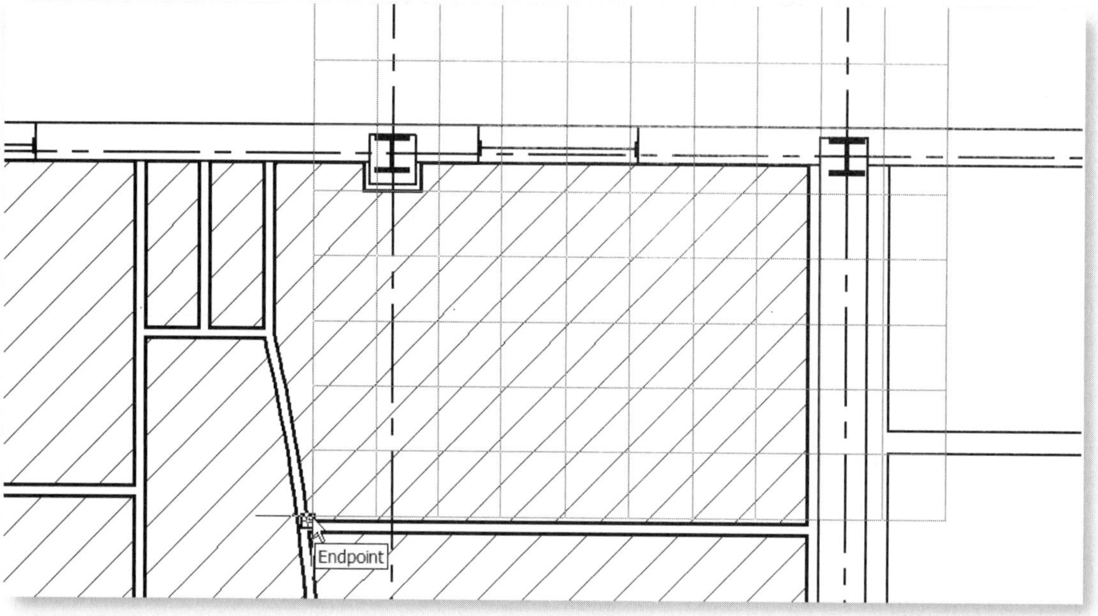

FIGURE 13.15 *Place the insertion point at the lower left corner of the room*

6. Press ENTER to complete the command.

There are several things to note about the Ceiling Grid just placed:

- It does not follow the shape of the room.
- It is bigger than the room.
- It is not centered.

7. Click on the Ceiling Grid to activate its grips.

   Notice the grips at the four corners.

We can adjust the overall size of the grid with these grips. (You might have to zoom out to accommodate the entire grid onscreen.)

8. Click the grip at the lower left corner of the Ceiling Grid.
9. Begin dragging the grip down and to the left, but don't click yet (see Figure 13.16).

   Notice that the Ceiling Grid dynamically adds or removes bays on the right side and along the top as you drag. The bottom left corner moves.

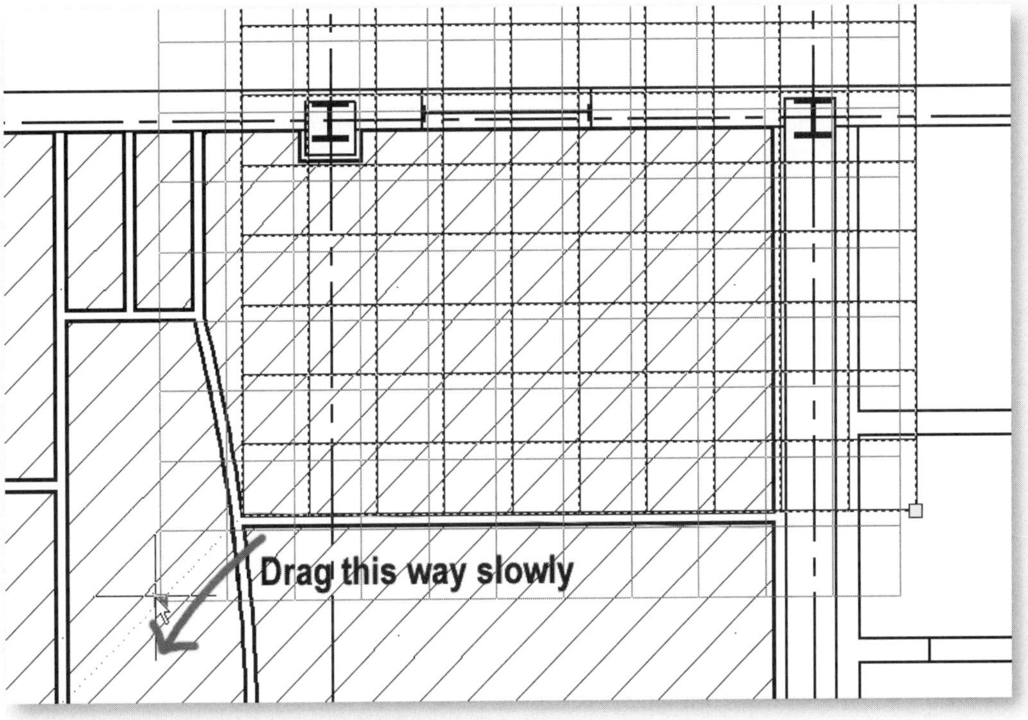

FIGURE 13.16 *Grip-edit the size of the grid*

10. Drag down and to the left far enough to add a bay or two in each direction and then click to set the corner. (Do this without Object Snaps.)

The Ceiling Grid should completely cover the space, including the small curved section at the bottom left corner of the room. Repeat the process on the upper right corner and notice the slightly different behavior. The lower left corner is the insertion point. When you dragged it, the entire Grid shifted and bays were added or removed from the opposite sides of the Grid. When you drag the upper right corner, it only adds or removes bays; the grid will stay anchored to the insertion point at the lower left. Furthermore, the bays are added or removed from the same side this time. In the next sequence, we will clip the Ceiling Grid to the shape of the room; so be sure to finish your grip editing with the grid extending past the outside of the room in all directions. Having the grid overlap on all sides gives us "extra play" when clipping and centering.

Clip the Grid to the Room Shape

Now that the Ceiling Grid covers the entire room, we still have the larger issue of the Ceiling Grid's not following the shape of the room. We will use the Clip Ceiling Grid command to resolve this issue.

11. Select the Ceiling Grid. On the Ceiling Grid tab, on the Clipping panel, click the ***Set Boundary*** tool.

"Select a closed polyline or space object for boundary" will appear onscreen as a dynamic prompt or at the Command Line. ***Set Boundary*** clips the grid to the shape of the room or to any other closed boundary (polyline) you wish. The ***Add Hole*** tool in the Clipping panel does the opposite: it creates a hole by cropping a section of the grid within. The ***Remove Hole*** deletes a clipping boundary or hole.

NOTE

You must keep the clipping boundaries. Erasing the boundary eliminates the Clip. If you do not wish to have the clipping boundaries displayed, put them on a separate layer that you freeze or designate as No Plot or use Masking Blocks. If you are clipping to Spaces, you can use Display Control to turn the Spaces off or make them non-plotting.

12. At the "Select a closed polyline or space entity for boundary" prompt, click on the Space object beneath the Grid. (Click the 45° hatching to select it.)

    Notice that the Ceiling Grid is now clipped to the shape of the room (see Figure 13.17).

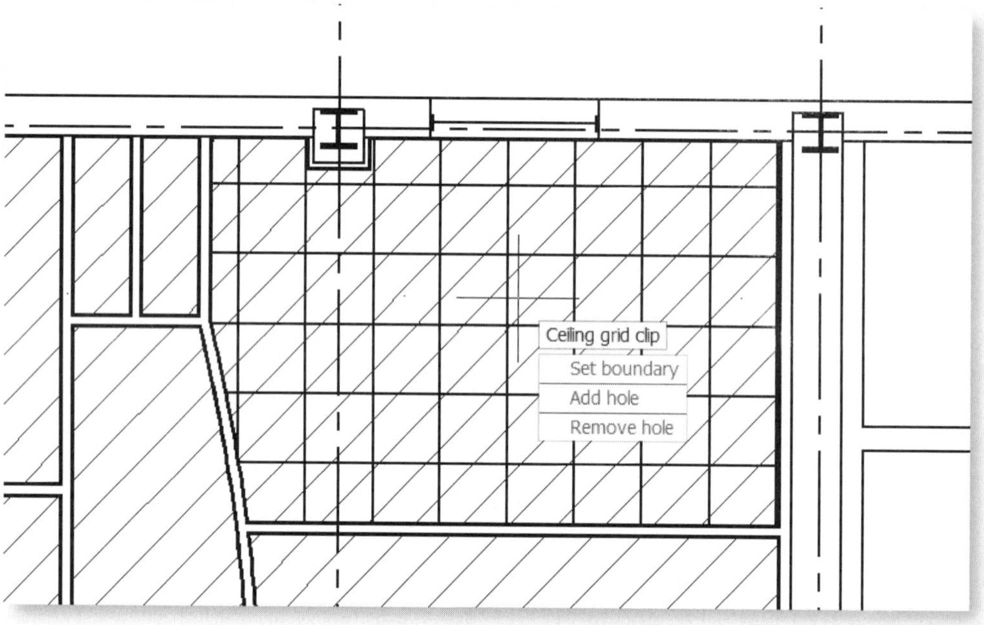

FIGURE 13.17 *The Ceiling Grid now conforms to the shape of the room*

13. Press ENTER to end the Ceiling Grid Clip command.

Add Ceiling Grid with Grid Clipping

The previous sequence illustrates the concept of clipped Ceiling Grids. In this sequence, we will clip a Ceiling Grid while it is being added to the drawing. This saves the step of our having to manually clip the grid later as previously demonstrated.

14. On the Design palette, click the Ceiling Grid tool.

    Use all of the same settings as before, but don't place the grid yet.

15. On the Properties palette, within the General grouping, choose **Select object** from the Boundary option list (see Figure 13.18).

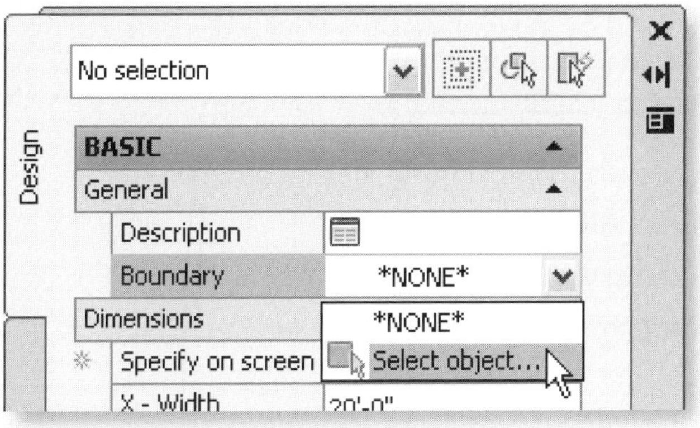

FIGURE 13.18 *Designate the clipping boundary as you add the Ceiling Grid with the Select object option*

16. At the "Select a space or closed polyline for boundary" prompt, click on the hatching in the Office in top left corner (to the left of the Break Room).
17. Move the mouse around and notice how the Ceiling Grid is dynamically cropped behind the shape of the Office space (see Figure 13.19).

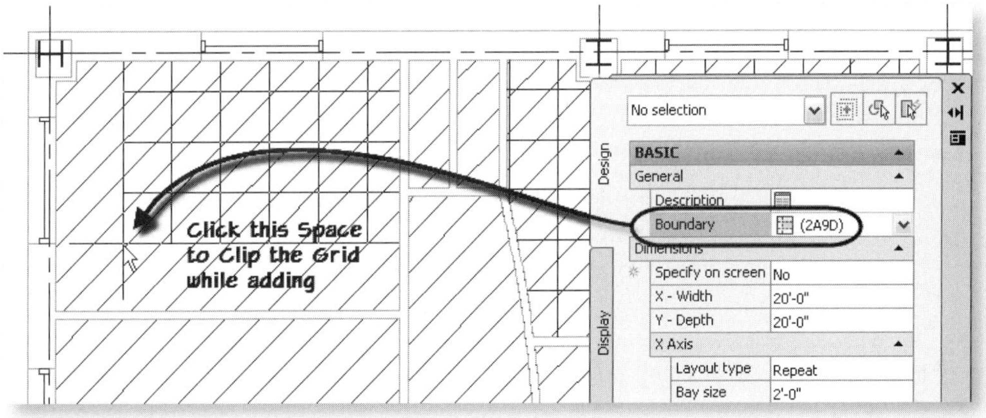

FIGURE 13.19 *The Grid is clipped "behind" the edge of the Space*

18. Move the mouse down and to the left past the lower left corner of the space.
19. Click outside the space to set the insertion point.

    Clicking outside the Space, down and to the left achieves the same goal as above in ensuring that the clipped Grid covers the entire Space.
20. Press ENTER to accept the default rotation of **0**°.

    The new Ceiling Grid is now clipped to the Office Space, and the Add Ceiling Grid command is still active and ready to place another Grid. However, notice that it is still clipped in the same Space.
21. Pan the drawing down to the room beneath this one.

    You can return to the Properties palette and change the Boundary setting to **Select object** again. However, you can also access this option on the right-click menu.
22. Right-click in the drawing and choose **Set Boundary** (or press the down arrow key to access the dynamic prompt options).
23. Click on the hatch in the next Office Space (see Figure 13.20).

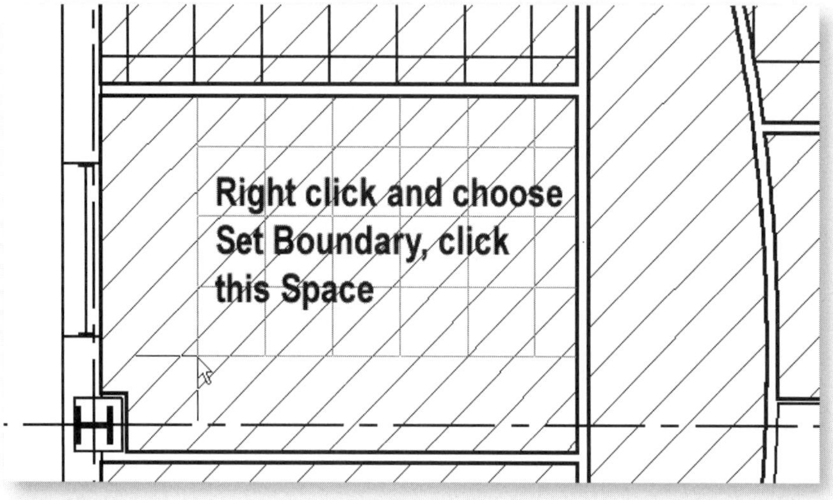

FIGURE 13.20 *Two clipped grids in the Office spaces*

The two Ceiling Grids placed so far were not centered within their rooms. A Ceiling Grid can be centered within its clipping boundary during placement in the drawing. This option will center the grid to the Space or Polyline bounding box. The bounding box is the smallest rectangle that would completely contain the entire object at its widest and tallest dimensions. For this reason, this trick works best with rectangular or nearly rectangular clipping boundaries. This applies to all of our office Spaces here. Remember that you can always move a grid after it has been placed to re-center it as necessary. Moved grids will remain clipped.

24. Right-click in the drawing again and choose **SNap to center** (or press the DOWN ARROW key for the same option).
25. Accept the default rotation by pressing ENTER.

NOTE

When you use the SNap to center option, the rotation default will be entered from the clipping boundary as well. Simply press ENTER to accept this default. If you choose a different rotation, you will lose the centering.

26. Press ENTER to end the command.

Edit the Hatch Pattern of Spaces

At this point in the process, the drawing is a bit cluttered. When you use Space objects as clipping boundaries, as we are doing here, the hatching of the space can be distracting. It would not be a good idea to turn off the hatching. If we did, it would be difficult to select the Spaces. (With only the boundaries of the Spaces showing, we would have to click at the edge of the room, which might interfere with the XREF Walls.) We would have the same difficulty if we were using polylines as boundaries; however, we can edit the display of the hatching to make it less prominent.

1. Select any Space object, right-click and choose **Properties**.
2. Click the Display tab.

Notice that the active Display representation is **Reflected** and that its Display is controlled by the Drawing default setting. This confirms what was already obvious when we switched from Medium Detail to Reflected: while the Spaces use style overrides to make them different colors in Medium Detail, here in Reflected, they all use the same simple cross-hatch pattern and color. For the Spaces in a reflected ceiling plan, this will make our current task easy. (See Chapter 2 for more information on the Display System.)

3. From the Display component list, choose the **Base Hatch** component.

   This will show the properties of this component.

4. For the Color, choose **Select color** and then in the Color dialog, choose a gray color, such as Color 9 or 254.
5. Click OK to dismiss the Select Color dialog and if a warning appears, click OK.
6. Beneath the Hatching grouping, change the Spacing to **3'-0"** [**900**] and the Angle to **60°** (see Figure 13.21).

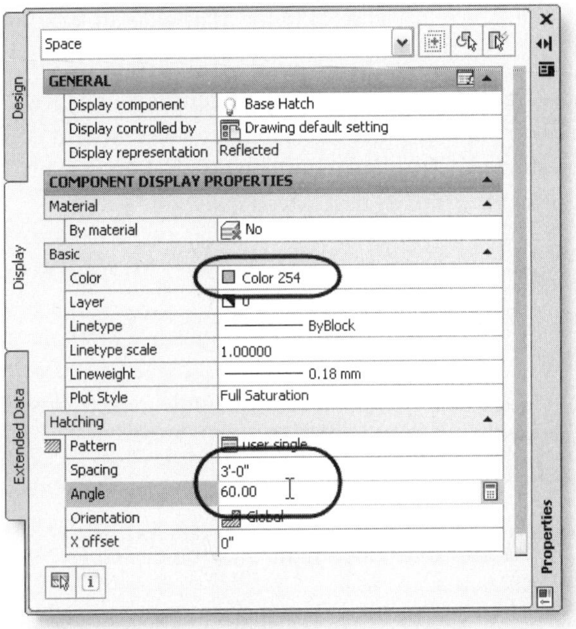

FIGURE 13.21 *Make the hatching display a gray color and change the spacing and angle*

7. Press the ESC key or right-click and choose **Deselect All** (see Figure 13.22).

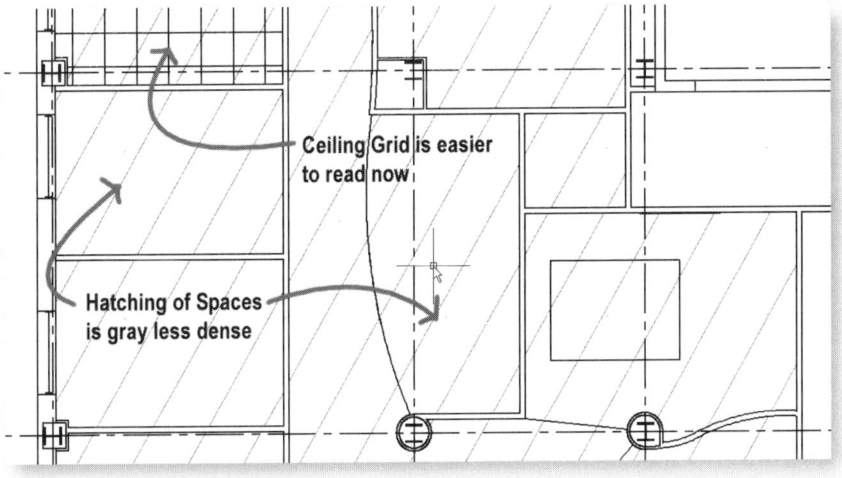

FIGURE 13.22 *The Space objects now display less obtrusive hatching as a result of the display settings*

TIP

Changes should occur immediately. If the drawing does not appear to change, choose **Regen Model** from the View menu.

Notice that this change affected all Spaces regardless of their Space Styles. This is because Reflected is the active Representation and as we saw, Reflected uses Drawing Default. This is just another example of the power and pervasiveness of the ACA Display System—in plan views, which typically use Medium Detail, each Space style displays its own unique color; but here in Reflected, all Spaces, regardless of style, display the same.

Let's now add several more Ceiling Grids.

8. On the Design palette, click the Ceiling Grid tool.
9. Repeat the steps above to add Ceiling Grids to the Reception, all Offices, and the Copy Room. (Refer to the labels in Figure 13.13 for assistance in locating each of these rooms.)

Remember to right-click and choose **Set boundary** and **SNap to center** for all Grids. Notice that despite the use of the Snap feature, the nonrectangular spaces might still need some adjustment. We will perform these adjustments below. Remember progressive refinement; for now, just place the grids as best as you can.

10. Press ENTER when finished.
11. Save the file.

Clip a Ceiling Grid to a Polyline

In addition to Space objects, Ceiling Grids can be clipped to closed polylines. A closed polyline is provided in a separate file for the Conference Room area.

12. Zoom in on the Conference Room (in the bottom right corner of the tenant space).
13. On the Project Navigator, in the *Elements* folder, right-click the *Ceiling Features* file and choose **Insert as Block**.

    Use 0,0,0 for the Insertion Point and check the "Explode" box before clicking OK (see the process outlined above in the "Generate Spaces from Existing Walls" topic).

Two polylines should appear in the file: one in the reception area and the other in the conference room.

14. On the Design palette, click the Ceiling Grid tool.
15. Change the X - Width to **10'-0"** [**3000**], leave the Y - Depth at **20'-0"** [**6000**], and set both the X Axis > Bay size and the Y Axis > Bay size to **1'-0"** [**300**].
16. Choose **Select object** from the Boundary drop-down list.
17. At the "Select a space or closed polyline for boundary" prompt, click the edge of the rectangle in the middle of the Conference Room.
18. Right-click, choose **SNap to center**, and then press ENTER to accept the default rotation (see Figure 13.23).

Content. As was already mentioned, most of the lighting symbols use an Anchor to attach themselves to the Ceiling Grids. Dragging these fixtures from the Content Browser does not properly execute the Anchor functionality. Therefore, to take full advantage of this Content, we will use the DesignCenter to access them.

1. From the Insert menu, choose **DesignCenter** (or press CTRL + 2).

The DesignCenter will appear. DesignCenter behaves similarly to the other palettes: it can float, can be docked and has the Auto-hide feature. Across the top, it has a toolbar and a string of tabs. The DesignCenter is part of the core AutoCAD functionality and, as such, has many more functions than will be covered here. To access the ACA Content library (the same library that we have been accessing with Content Browser up until now), you must click on the AEC Content tab.

2. Click on the AEC Content tab.

On the left side is a tree view, which can be toggled on and off with an icon on the toolbar at the top of the DesignCenter. Preview and Description panes appear in the DesignCenter window as well. Both of these also can be toggled on and off with icons on the toolbar (see Figure 13.30).

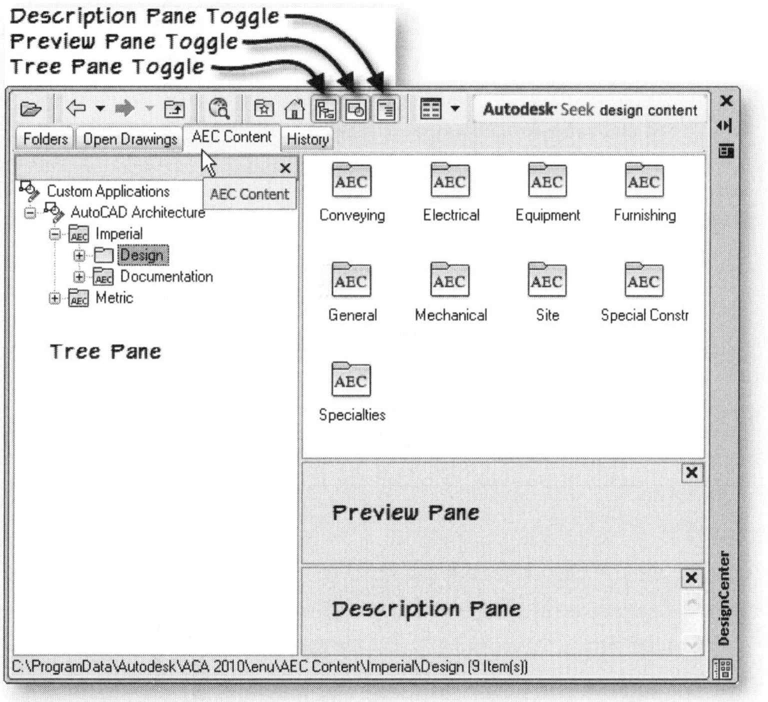

FIGURE 13.30 *Understanding the DesignCenter palette*

TIP

If you want to keep the DesignCenter open as you work, try setting it to "Allow Docking" and then anchor it to the left or right side of the screen. See Chapter 1 for more information on anchored palettes.

3. Using the tree pane, expand the *AutoCAD Architecture* root item to reveal the *Imperial* and *Metric* folders.
4. Continue to navigate to the Imperial\Design\Electrical\Lighting\Fluorescent [Metric\Design\Electrical Services\Fluorescent\600x1200] folder.

Note the various subfolders within the *Electric* folder. Each contains a different category of Electrical symbols and content.

5. Highlight the first symbol by clicking *once* on its icon on the right (do not double-click).

   Notice the larger Preview in the window pane below. This interactive Viewer is like the many other ACA viewers (see Figure 13.31).

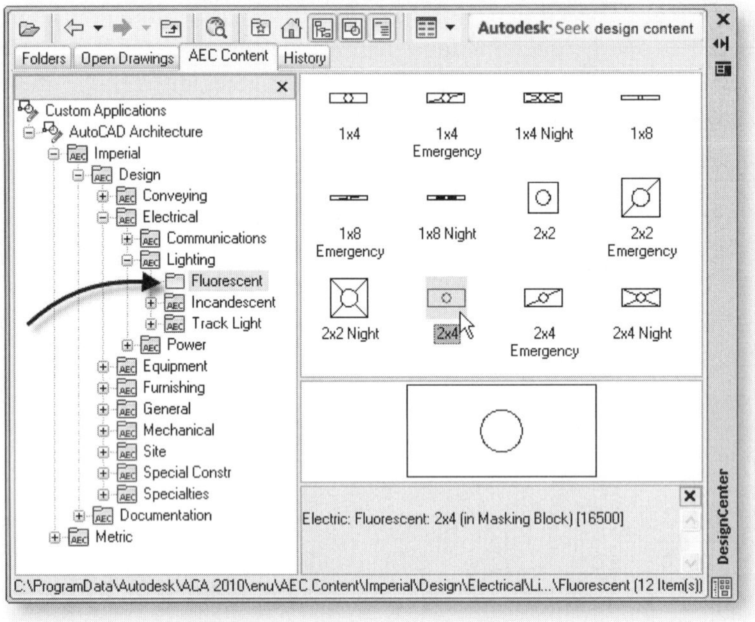

FIGURE 13.31 *Select an item to see its preview and description*

Right-click in the preview pane for the standard Viewer functions. The description field below includes the statement "in Masking Block." This statement helps you identify the symbol as a Mask Block before inserting it into the drawing.

6. Highlight other symbols and study their previews and descriptions.

Drag and Drop Content

7. Turn off OSNAP (make the Object Snap button at the bottom of the screen gray).

OSNAPs are off when the Object Snap button at the bottom of the screen is gray. The lighting symbol we are about to use automatically executes an Anchor as it is dropped into the drawing. Therefore, the OSNAPs are not necessary because the Anchor will afford us the requisite level of precision.

8. Click and hold down the mouse on the 2x4 [600x1200 Enclosed] Fixture.
9. Drag the icon into the drawing window (see Figure 13.32).

   Be sure to drag it from the icon and not the Preview pane (Viewer).

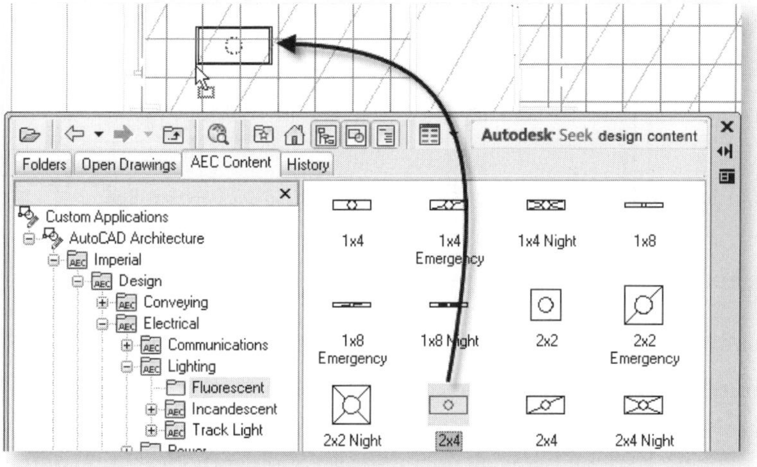

FIGURE 13.32 *Drag and drop the 2x4 light into the drawing*

10. At the "Select Layout Node" prompt, click on any grid intersection (see Figure 13.33).

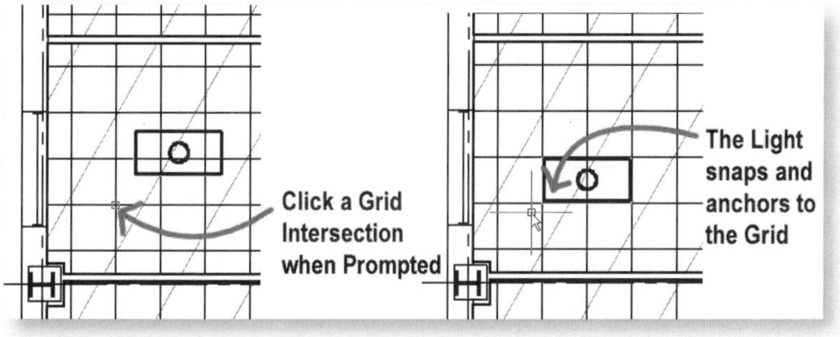

FIGURE 13.33 *Select the intersection as the Anchor parent object*

Notice that the lower left corner of the light fixture jumped to the grid intersection; this is the effect of the Anchor—in this case, a Node Anchor.

NOTE

If the light instead of a Grid intersection jumps to the center of the room, undo and try again. This indicates that you anchored to the Space and not the Grid.

A Node Anchor establishes a point-to-point relationship between the parent object (in this case, the Ceiling Grid) and the child object (in this case, the light fixture). Specifically, the nature of the relationship means that the Ceiling Grid will affect the position of the light but the light has no effect on the position of the Ceiling Grid. Recall that columns also use a Node Anchor to anchor to Column Grids. (Refer to Chapter 6.)

11. Try moving the light using the standard Move command (see Figure 13.34).

    Notice that regardless of where you move it or whether you use Object Snaps, the light jumps to the nearest grid intersection. Try moving the light a couple of times. Move it back to a good location when you are done.

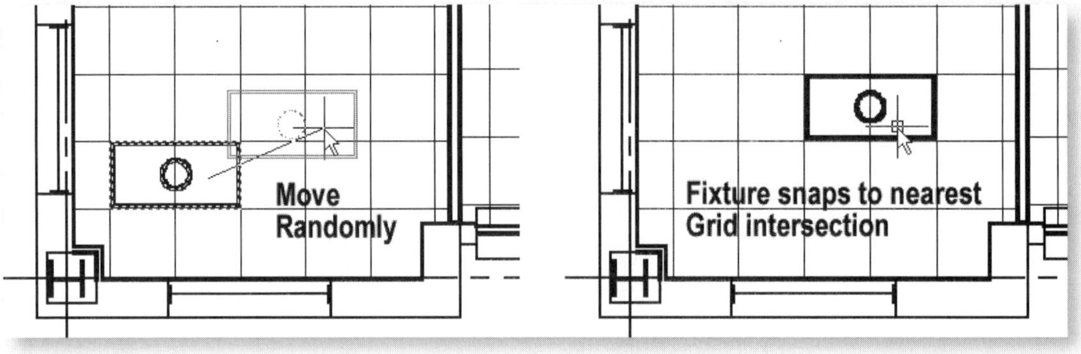

FIGURE 13.34 *Moving an anchored object shifts its Anchor to a different node*

Once the Anchor has been attached, it will control the position and orientation of the light regardless of which node it is anchored to.

CAUTION

Lights can be anchored to the nodes on the portion of your Ceiling Grid that is concealed by the clipping boundary. In the drawing, this would appear as though the light had moved off the Grid. Move a light outside the drawing area to see this.

12. From the DesignCenter, drag one light fixture into each room that has a Ceiling Grid and following the prompts, anchor the lights to the Grids.

Copy Light Fixtures

Although an Anchor can be copied from node to node on the same parent grid, it cannot be copied directly from one grid to the next. It is possible to achieve this by copying it on the same grid: right-clicking the copy and choosing **Node Anchor > Set Node** to move the copy to a different grid. However, this is neither the easiest nor the recommended procedure. Therefore, you should drag a light fixture from the DesignCenter for each room to create the first light and establish the anchored relationship. Once anchored to the Ceiling Grid, additional lights within the same Grid can be copied or arrayed.

13. Zoom in to a single room.
14. Using the AutoCAD `COPY` or `ARRAY` command, copy the existing light fixture several times to create an appropriate lighting pattern (see Figure 13.35).

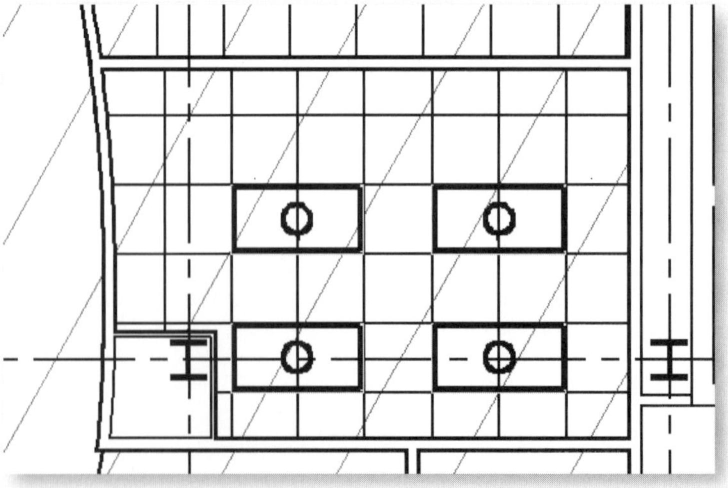

FIGURE 13.35 *Copy lights as required*

In the Copy Room, a counter runs along the north Wall; so the off-center lighting layout shown in Figure 13.35 is appropriate. However, you will undoubtedly have some rooms where the Ceiling Grid layout does not suit the light pattern required. In this case, you can move the Grid one-half tile in either direction. This will shift the grid and all of the lights while maintaining the centering. Give it a try.

Rotate Anchored Light Fixtures

Anchored objects cannot be rotated in the normal way. There are two approaches to rotating lights: the parameters of the Anchor must be adjusted to affect the rotation, or the grid itself must be rotated. However, if you perform the latter, all lights attached to the grid will be rotated. If you are interested in rotating only some of the lights, use the Anchor properties method rather than rotating the Ceiling Grid.

15. Zoom in on any room with a light fixture. Select the light, right-click and choose **Node Anchor > Set Rotation** (see Figure 13.36).

    You can select several lights at once if you wish.

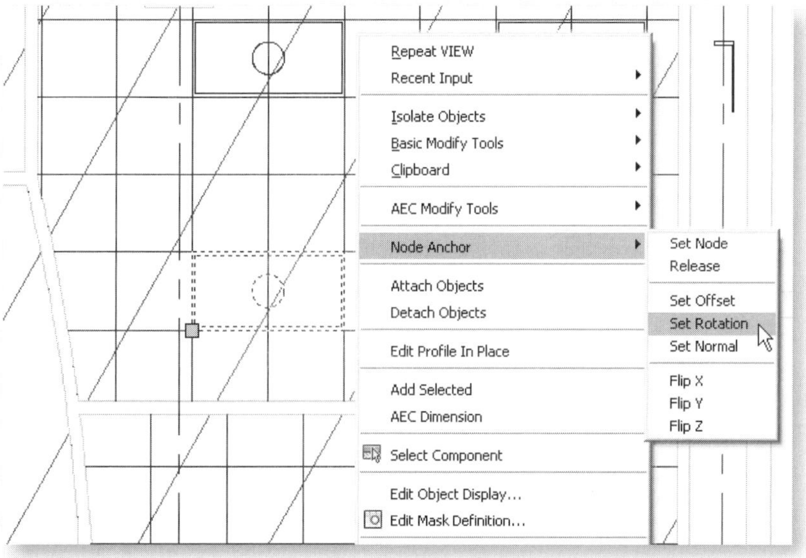

FIGURE 13.36 *Select a light (or several) and choose Set Rotation to rotate them*

    Rotating the object along the Z axis will cause a plan rotation of the object relative to its node.

16. At the “Rotation angle about X axis” and the “Rotation angle about Y axis” prompts, press ENTER to accept the default of **0**°.
17. At the “Rotation angle about Z axis” prompt, type either **90**° or **–90**° depending on the direction you need to rotate (see Figure 13.37).

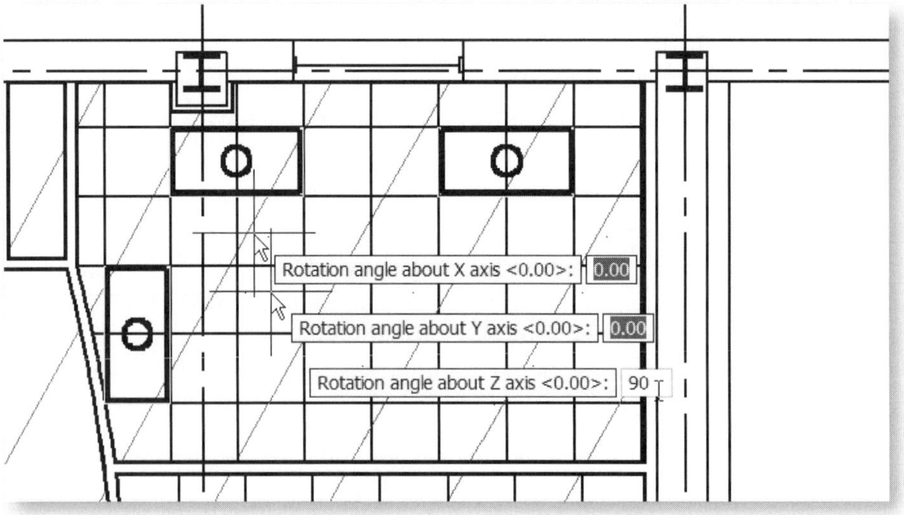

FIGURE 13.37 *The light has been rotated 90°*

18. Repeat any of the above steps as required to complete the remaining spaces.

TIP If you need to rotate lights, it is easier to rotate them before you copy and array.

Rotate a Grid

If you would rather rotate all of the lights in a room, you can rotate the entire grid. This will take all of the anchored lights with it. However, be certain to pick your base point carefully; otherwise, when you are done, you will have to re-center your grid in the Space.

TIP Try using the Center of the Boundary Space, or one of the Grid Intersections as the Base Point of the Rotation.

19. Select any Ceiling Grid with anchored lights, on the Home ribbon tab, on the Modify panel, click the Rotate tool.
20. Follow the command prompts and rotate the Grid from its center **90°**.

    Notice that the lights have also rotated.
21. Repeat any of the steps outlined here to complete a lighting layout in each room.
22. Save the file when done.

Attaching Mask Blocks to AEC Objects

As stated above, the light fixture we inserted here is a Mask Block. The Mask Block we created attached itself to the Grid automatically. Here we need to attach it as a second step. This particular Mask Block consists of a 24" × 48" [600 × 1200] rectangular mask with a light fixture Multi-View Block symbol for its "additional graphics." A Multi-View Block is used for the additional graphics to take advantage of display control. In this way, the lights appear only when the Reflected Display Configuration is active. Let's complete our lighting layout by attaching the masks to the grid.

Masking the Ceiling Grid

1. Zoom in on a room with a completed lighting layout.
2. Select all of the light fixtures in the room.

CAUTION

Be careful to select only lights, not the Ceiling Grid or any other objects.

3. On the Mask Block Reference ribbon tab on the Modify panel, choose the ***Attach Objects tool*** (see Figure 13.38).

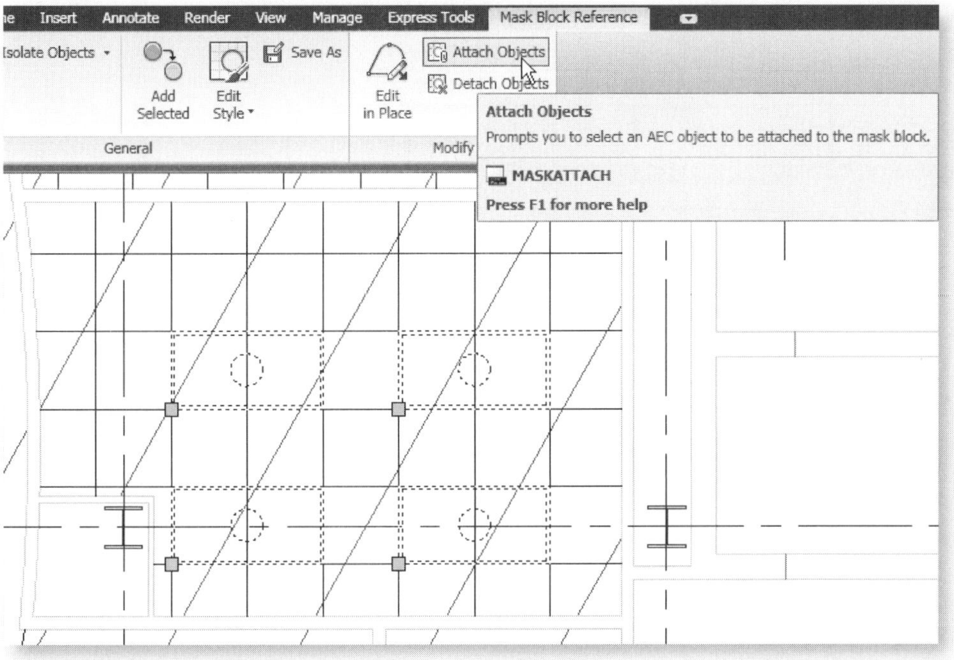

FIGURE 13.38 *Select the lights to attach*

4. At the "Select AEC entity to be masked" prompt, click on the Ceiling Grid within the room.
5. In the Select Display Representation dialog box that appears, confirm that you wish to mask the Reflected Display Representation (the only choice) by clicking OK.

If multiple Display Representations were active, the Select Display Representation dialog box would list them. In this case, the only Display Representation for the Ceiling Grid that is active is Reflected; therefore, only one Display Representation is listed in the Select Display Representation dialog box.

Notice how the lights now conceal the grid lines (see Figure 13.39).

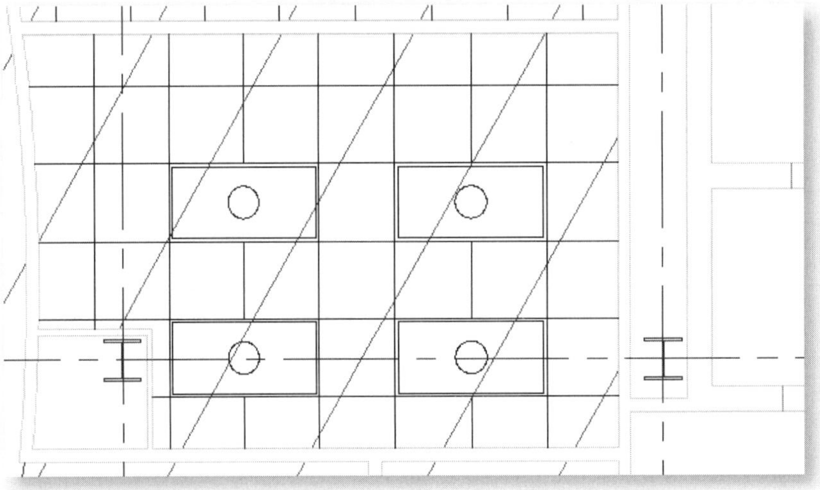

FIGURE 13.39 *The lights now conceal the Ceiling Grid*

Once you have attached the mask, you can move the object and it will stay masked.

6. Move one of the lights.

   Notice how the grid stays masked.

CAUTION

Be careful not to move an object to a different Z coordinate. Masks must be coplanar to the object they are masking.

Although copying an anchored object also copies the Anchor (as shown above), copying a masked object does not attach the copied mask. Therefore, you must copy all of the lights first, then attach the mask to the grid all at once.

7. Go room by room around the plan and repeat the steps just covered to attach the masks to all of the Grids.

TIP

Once you have attached the lights in the first room, you can repeat the `MASKATTACH` **command by pressing the space bar or Enter key to quickly attach the mask blocks in each of the remaining rooms.**

Once you have completed the steps covered here, you will have an assembly of ceiling components that behave as one. Moving and rotating the grid will also move and rotate the anchored lights, and any masked lights will remain attached. Test this out if you wish.

8. Move one of the Ceiling Grids with lights attached.

   Note that all lights move with the Grid and remain masked.

9. Undo the change.

If you ever need to detach a mask or an Anchor, select the object, and on the Mask Block Reference ribbon tab on the Modify panel, choose the ***Detach Objects*** tool to detach the mask or right-click, and select **Node Anchor > Release** to release the Anchor. Note that objects can be anchored without being masked and masked without being anchored.

10. Save the file.

OTHER CEILING FIXTURES

There are many additional lighting and electrical fixtures that we could include on a reflected ceiling plan, such as incandescent lighting, track lighting and surface mounted fixtures, to name a few. In this sequence, we will explore some of these items.

Add Surface-Mounted Lights

The same fluorescent fixtures used above and anchored to the Grid can be inserted as surface-mounted fixtures. To do so, simply skip the Anchor prompt when dragging in the fixture.

1. Zoom in to the workstations in the center of the plan.

   We have not placed a Ceiling Grid in this Space. It will have a drywall ceiling.
2. If you closed the DesignCenter, reopen it (CTRL + 2) now.
3. Navigate to the Imperial\Design\Electrical\Lighting\Fluorescent [Metric\Design\Electrical Services\Fluorescent\450x1350] folder.
4. Drag the 1x4 [450x1350 Enclosed] light fixture icon into the drawing window.
5. Drop it into the lower workstation area (see Figure 13.40).

NOTE

This time drop it in roughly where you want it to go. Because there will be no Anchor, the light fixture can be moved freely to the correct location.

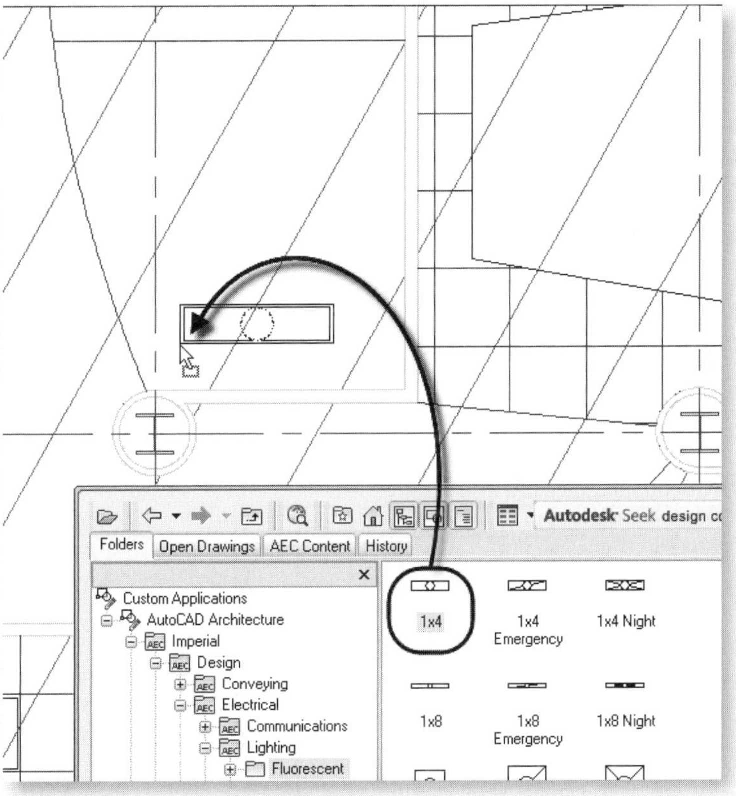

FIGURE 13.40 *Drag in a fixture for a surface-mounted light*

6. When prompted to Select Layout Node, press ENTER.

Pressing ENTER will insert the light fixture without anchoring it at the location you dropped it. Be certain to choose a layout node when adding lights to a Ceiling Grid. Press ENTER to skip the Anchor only when there is no Ceiling Grid and you wish to represent a surface-mounted light fixture. You will often need to perform an additional move to get the fixture positioned just right when it is not anchored.

Copy Surface-Mounted Lights

Because the light just added is not anchored, it can be freely moved, rotated and copied. Here is a nice place for Array. We can use the standard AutoCAD Array command on the Home ribbon tab on the extended Modify panel on first row of the extension, ***Array*** tool on the rightmost drop-down button; but for a simple linear array such as this, the ***AEC Array*** tool (on the Home ribbon tab on the extended Modify panel on first row of the extension on the rightmost drop-down button, as explored in Chapter 11) will be easier to use and will provide more visual feedback. Feel free to use the AutoCAD Array instead.

7. On the Home ribbon tab on the extended Modify panel on first row of the extension on the rightmost drop-down button choose the ***AEC Array*** tool and then select the light and press ENTER.
8. At the "Select an edge to array from or ENTER to pick two points" prompt, highlight one of the horizontal edges of the light fixture.

   In this case, it does not matter if you pick the top or bottom edge, only that you pick a horizontal edge—AEC Modify Array copies perpendicular to the edge you select.
9. At the "Drag out array elements" prompt, type **5'-0"** [**1500**] into the dynamic dimension and then press ENTER.

NOTE

Remember that distances in Array are measured from center to center. The dimension we are using here includes the size of the light fixture.

10. Drag the mouse up until four items are indicated onscreen and then click (see Figure 13.41).

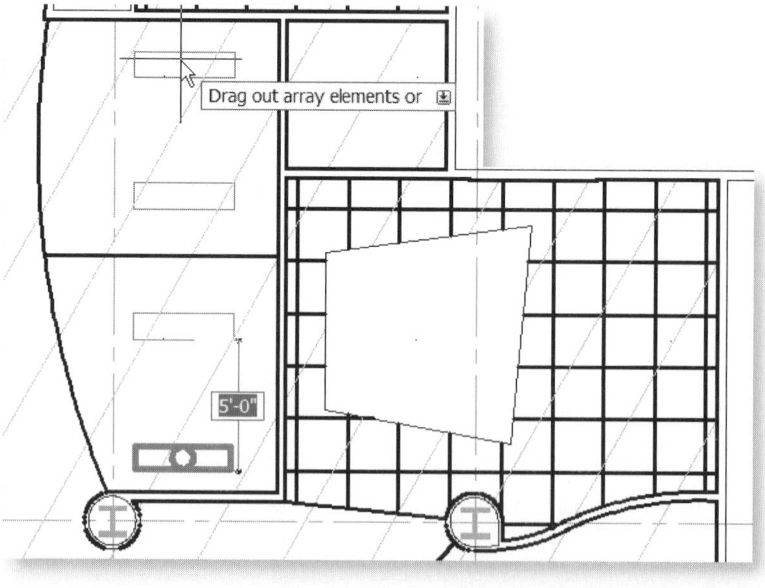

FIGURE 13.41 *Use the Array AEC Modify Tool to copy four equally spaced lights*

Add Track Lighting

Many types of lighting fixtures are included in the Content library. Let's add some track lighting to the Conference Room.

11. Zoom in on the Conference Room (the Space in the lower right corner of the tenant space).
12. If you closed the DesignCenter, reopen it (CTRL + 2) now.
13. Navigate to the *Imperial\Design\Electrical\Lighting\Track Light* folder.

> **NOTE** The Metric Content does not include track lighting. Please use the Imperial content for this exercise. The symbols, which were created in inches, will scale dynamically to an equivalent size in millimeters.

14. Drag the 4 Head – 10ft track light symbol into the drawing.
15. Drop it into the conference room.
16. Press ENTER to accept the default rotation (see Figure 13.42).

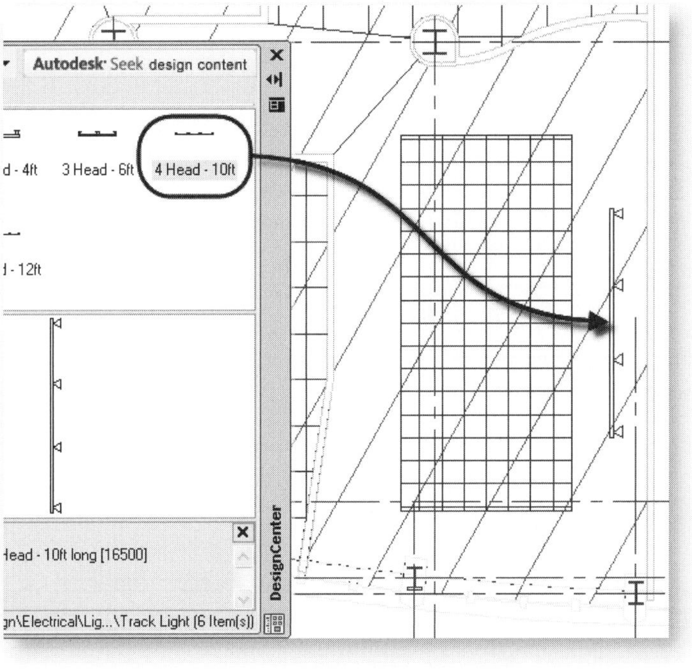

FIGURE 13.42 *Drop the Track Light in the center of the Conference Room*

17. Mirror it to the opposite side.

Add a Layout Curve

A layout curve is similar to the Ceiling Grid except that it is one-dimensional (linear) rather than two-dimensional (grid). Any linear object such as line, arc, polyline or even Wall can be turned into a layout curve. First, you draw the base object; next, you convert it to a Layout Curve and establish the spacing rules for the nodes; finally, you Anchor items to the Layout. If the shape of the Layout changes, the anchored objects will follow.

TIP

If you have been using the Divide and Measure commands in AutoCAD, you will want to begin using layout curves now. The layout curve functions like a "parametric Divide and/or Measure" tool.

18. Zoom in on the top end of the Corridor near the top left office.
19. Set the current layer to G-Anno-Nplt.

NOTE

One last reminder: We are about to draw an AutoCAD entity; therefore, unlike AEC objects, which auto-layer, we must designate the layer for the polyline manually.

20. On the Home ribbon tab on the Draw panel, select the bottom half of the Line split button drop-down and choose the ***Polyline*** tool (or type **PL** and press `ENTER`).
21. Using an Endpoint OSNAP and Figure 13.43 as a guide, click the start point at the top left Endpoint of the Corridor.

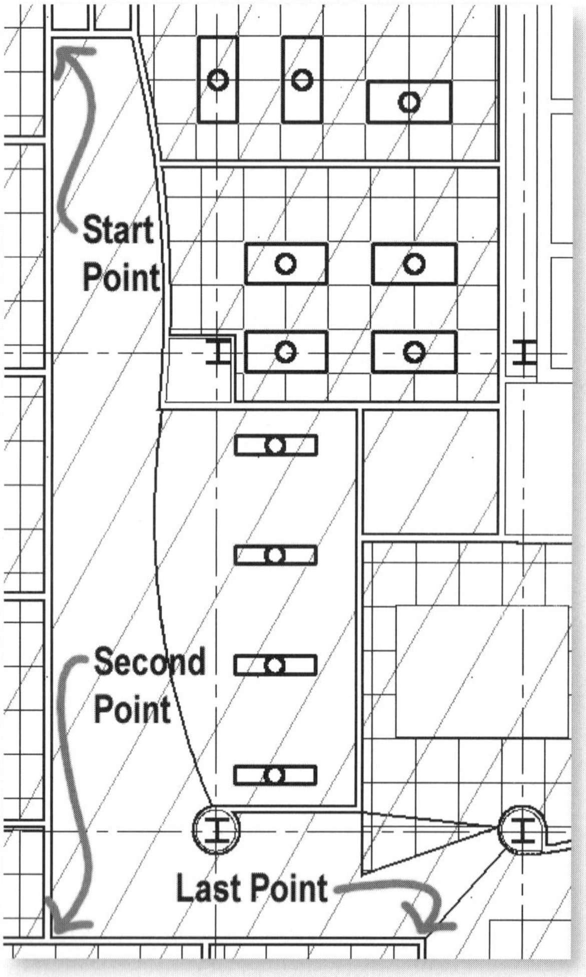

FIGURE 13.43 *Trace the Corridor with a polyline*

22. Pan down to the bottom end of the Corridor.
23. Click the second point at the bottom left corner Endpoint of the Corridor, as indicated in Figure 13.43.

24. Click the last point just outside the Conference Room, as indicated by "Last Point" in Figure 13.43, and then press ENTER to end the command.
25. On the Home ribbon tab on the Modify panel select the ***Offset*** tool, second from the left in the third row (or type **O** and press ENTER).
26. At the "Specify offset distance" prompt, type **2'-0"** [**600**] and then press ENTER.
27. Click the polyline drawn in the last step and offset it to the middle of the Corridor.
28. Erase the original polyline and set the current layer back to Layer 0.

This polyline will now be used to create a layout curve, which will in turn control the spacing of lighting fixtures running down the Corridor.

29. Open the Content Browser (the default one, not the project-based one—on the Insert ribbon tab on the Content panel, click on the top half of the Content Browser split button or press CTRL + 4).
30. Click on *Stock Tool Catalog.*
31. Navigate to the *Parametric Layout & Anchoring Tools* category.
32. Using the eyedropper icon, drag the Layout Curve tool into the drawing window.
33. At the "Select a curve" prompt, click on the polyline in the center of the Corridor (the one you just offset) (see item 1 in Figure 13.44).

    Nodes will be placed equally along the polyline, at a fixed spacing or manually based on your input.
34. At the "Select node layout mode" prompt, choose **Space evenly** (see item 2 in Figure 13.44).

The spacing can begin directly at the start and end points of the polyline, or it can be set back from them by a specified increment.

35. Type **3'-0"** [**900**] for the "Start offset" and press ENTER (see item 3 in Figure 13.44).
36. Type **3'-0"** [**900**] again for the "End offset" and press ENTER (see item 4 in Figure 13.44).

Space evenly will divide equally the linear distance from the start offset to the end offset and place as many nodes in between as you specify.

37. For the Number of nodes, type **10** and then press ENTER (see item 5 in Figure 13.44).

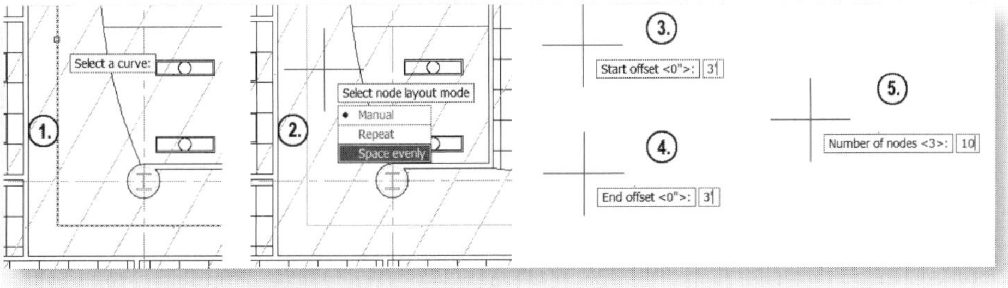

FIGURE 13.44 *Indicate the offsets and the number of nodes*

View the completed layout tool (see Figure 13.45).

Once created, a layout curve is very similar to a layout grid like the Ceiling Grid covered here or the Column Grid covered in Chapter 6.

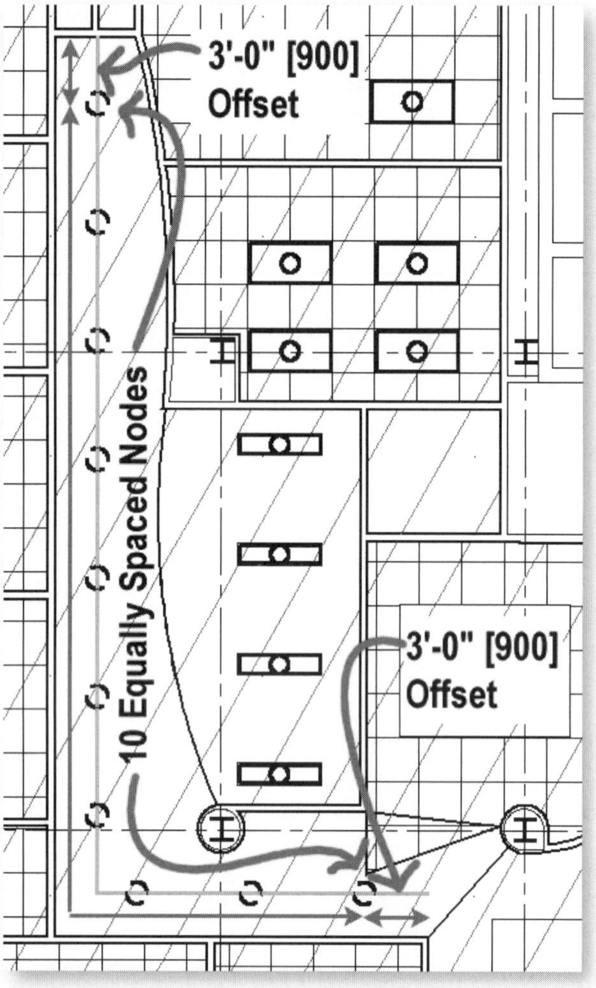

FIGURE 13.45 *The completed Layout Curve tool*

Insert an Incandescent Light Fixture

For this exercise, we will use the Imperial content for the Imperial and Metric projects. We will be assigning in appropriate units a unique scale factor to the symbol.

38. If you closed the DesignCenter, reopen it (CTRL + 2) now.
39. Navigate to the *Imperial\Design\Electrical\Lighting\Incandescent* folder.

NOTE

The Metric Content does not include incandescent lighting. Please use the Imperial content for this exercise. The symbols, which were created in inches, will scale dynamically to an equivalent size in millimeters.

40. Drag the Ceiling light fixture icon into the drawing window.
41. Drop it anywhere and press ENTER to accept the default rotation.

    Its insertion scale default is a bit large. This can be easily adjusted.
42. Select the light fixture just inserted.
43. On the Properties palette, within the Scale grouping, set the X, Y and Z scale fields at **6"** [**150**] (see Figure 13.46).

The value that we input for the scales of this Content translates into the diameter of the lighting symbol.

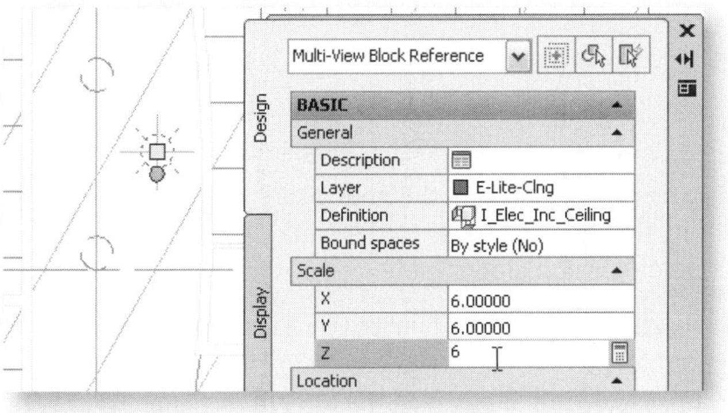

FIGURE 13.46 *Change the size of the light*

Anchor Lights to the Layout Curve

We can now copy and anchor this light fixture to the layout curve created above to give us a series of light fixtures down the length of the corridor.

44. Switch back to the Content Browser (press CTRL + 4).
45. Your Content Browser should still be showing the *Parametric Layout & Anchoring* category of the Stock Tool Catalog. If it is not, navigate there now.
46. Using the eyedropper icon, drag the Node Anchor tool into the drawing window.

The Node Anchor has three options. The "Attach Object" option establishes a Node Anchor between a single object and a single node. The "Set Node" option is essentially a move command for Anchors. It allows you to move an existing anchored object to another node on the same layout. The "Copy to Each Node" option copies the object to every node on the layout. We will use this option here.

47. From the dynamic prompt, choose **Copy to Each Node**.
48. At the "Select object to be copied and anchored" prompt, select the Incandescent Light fixture inserted in the last sequence.
49. At the "Select layout tool" prompt, click on any one of the magenta circles on the layout curve (see Figure 13.47).

    Do not click the polyline; you must click directly on one of the magenta circles.

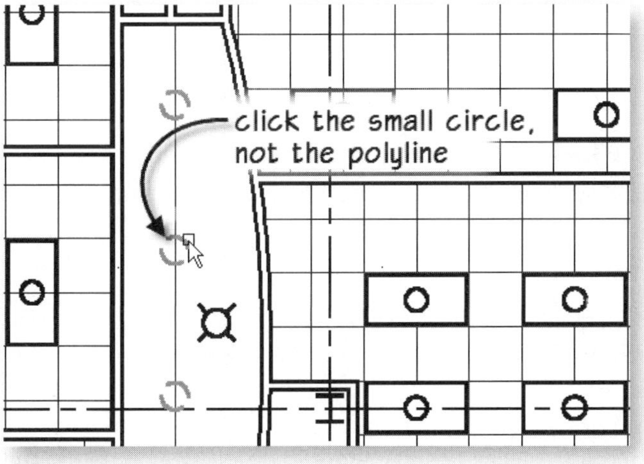

FIGURE 13.47 *Select the small magenta circle to finish the Anchor*

A light fixture is now anchored to each of the nodes along the polyline.

50. Press ENTER to end the command.

    Erase the original fixture.

51. Grip-stretch the polyline to see the benefit of this technique.

    Notice that as you grip-stretch the polyline, the nodes and their anchored lights move and respace with it. This is very similar to the behavior of the Ceiling and Column Grids, but in one dimension along the length of the Layout Curve.

You can manipulate it further by selecting the layout curve (the magenta circle), right-clicking and choosing Properties. On the Properties palette, you can change the spacing mode to **Repeat** or **Manual** or leave it to **Space evenly** and change the quantity of nodes. The trick is making sure you select the little magenta circles, which represent the actual layout curve objects. The polyline is the shape to which the layout is linked and whose shape it follows. Please note that increasing the number of Nodes will *not* automatically copy new light fixtures to those Nodes; however, removing Nodes *will* remove the anchored lights attached to them. Recall the similar "Modify Column Grids" exercise in Chapter 6.

GO FURTHER

You can change the display properties of the Doors or any other object in the Reflected Display Configuration. Zoom in on one of the offices and notice that the Doors do not display. Some firms like to see their Doors in RCP. To make this change, open the ***Display Manager*** *on the Manage ribbon tab on the Style & Display panel by clicking on the* **Display Manager** *tool. Highlight the current Display Configuration and edit the Cut Height on the Cut Plane tab. By default, it is above the height of most Doors. This is why the Doors don't show. You can also explore the Drawing Default display settings for Walls and Doors in the Representations by Object folder of the Display Manager. For example, you can select Wall on the left beneath the Representations by Object folder, double-click Reflected on the right side and edit the parameters on any of the tabs for Reflected. You can do the same for Doors (or any object). Just make sure that you are editing the Reflected Display Representation. For example, if you would rather not change the Cut Plane Height for Walls in Reflected, you could edit Doors in their Reflected Display Representation. To do this, edit the Reflected Display Representation of Doors beneath the Representations by Object folder in the Display Manager. On the right side, click the Other tab. Deselect the "Respect Cut Plane of Container Object when Anchored" checkbox. This will display Doors regardless of the cut height of Walls. Furthermore, on the Layer/Color/Linetype tab, you can edit the way the Doors look; for example make them gray in color with dashed linetype. Try it out—there is an exercise for this in* Appendix A.

RESTORE THE FLOOR PLAN

When you are finished working on the reflected ceiling plan, return to plan display.

52. On the Drawing status bar, open the Display Configuration pop-up menu and choose **Medium Detail**.

Notice that the ceiling grids disappear, but that the light fixtures do not. Starting with the 2009 release, the out-of-the-box light fixture Multi-View Blocks have had a view block added to the General Display Representation, resulting in the fixtures being visible in the Medium Detail Display Configuration. If you would prefer to have the fixtures not visible in the Medium Detail Display Configuration, you can edit the Multi-View Block Definitions for the light fixtures and remove the view block from the General Display Representation (or deselect all of the view directions for that view block). This will be the reverse of the column bubble exercise done earlier in this chapter, where a view block was added to a Display Representation. Because there are multiple Multi-View Block Definitions to be revised and because some are nested within Mask Blocks, it will be easier to use the Style Manager to make this change. On the Manage ribbon tab, on the Style & Display panel, click the ***Style Manager*** tool. In the left pane of the Style Manager under the 03 Partitions.dwg file, expand the Multi-Purpose Objects node and then the Multi-View Block Definition node. On the left pane, select each light fixture Multi-View Block Definition in turn. (All should start with I_Elec [M_Elec or M_Elect]). On the right pane on the View Blocks tab, select the General Display Representation if necessary on the left and click on the Remove button to remove the view block completely, or uncheck all View Directions on the right, to prevent the view block from displaying. After making the change to each of the lighting fixture Multi-View Block Definitions, click on OK to return to the drawing file. The light fixtures should no longer be visible with the Medium Detail Display Configuration set current. However, when returning to Reflected, they will still appear.

MANAGER NOTE CAD

As noted for the column bubbles, these edits will only affect the current drawing file. To make the change permanent for all future drawings, you will need to edit the source AEC Content files and change the Multi-View Block Definition in each. Project standards can also be helpful in applying to change to several project files.

53. Save and close the file.

The polylines in the conference room and corridor are not AEC objects and therefore remain visible. If you want them invisible onscreen, they must be turned off using layers. Or you must convert them to appropriate AEC objects. You could also assign the layer to No Plot, like the one in the corridor. So even though these polylines are showing onscreen, they will be invisible when you print the drawing. If you find them distracting as you work or you think they will be edited or deleted inadvertently, turn the layer off.

ADD AN RCP VIEW AND SHEET TO THE PROJECT

Now that we have added reflected ceiling plan geometry to the Third Floor Partitions Construct, we need to create a View file so that the construct will be able to receive annotation unique to the reflected ceiling plan and then place it on its own Sheet. We will explore the philosophy behind this approach in greater detail in the next chapter. For now, we'll simply create the required View and Sheet files so that the Project structure is up to date and ready to begin receiving annotations in the next chapter.

Create the RCP View File

Remember the rule of thumb when working in Project Navigator: you should create a new View file whenever you change discipline, scale and/or drawing type. If any of these situations occurs, create a new View file—do not try to have a single View file meet the needs of two different discipline/type/scale drawings. So in this case, we are still working in Architectural (no change in discipline), we are still working in eighth scale (1/8"=1'-0" [1:100]), *but* we are creating a different type of drawing (an RCP vs. a Plan). Therefore, creating a new View is appropriate.

1. On the Project Navigator, click the Views tab.
2. Right-click the Views folder and choose **New View Dwg > General**.

3. In the Add General View dialog, input **A-CP03** for the Name and **Architectural Third Floor Reflected Ceiling Plan** for the Description and then click Next.
4. On the Context page, place a check mark in the Third Floor checkbox and then click Next.
5. On the Content page, be sure that all *Architectural* Constructs are selected, deselect the *Structural* category, select only the *03 Grid* Construct from the Structural category and then click Finish (see Figure 13.48).

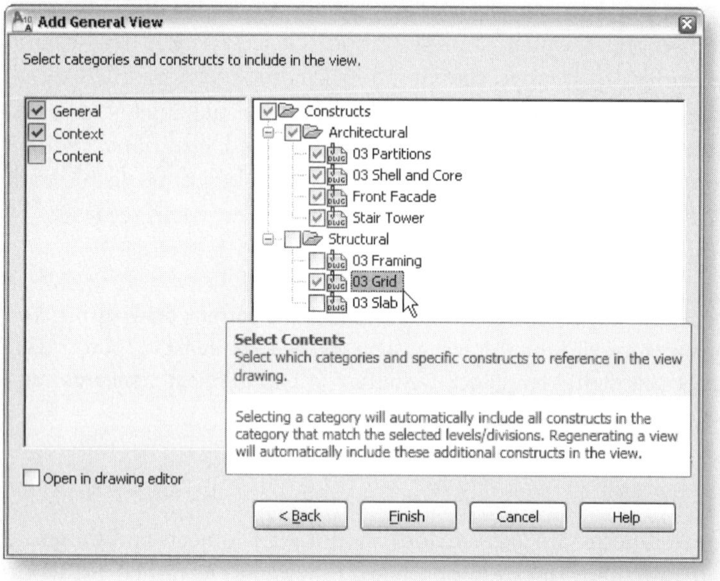

FIGURE 13.48 *Complete the Third Floor Reflected Ceiling Plan View by choosing its Content*

A new View file will appear on the Project Navigator. Click the Refresh icon at the bottom to re-sort the list and have the new *A-CP03* View appear in its correct alphabetical location. If you recall the exercises in Chapter 5 in which we configured the Floor Plan Views, we still need to add a Model Space View and a Titlemark to this file and configure it as an RCP. Let's first open the Third Floor Plan View file and borrow the Live Area Grid from it.

6. On the Project Navigator, double-click the *A-FP03* file to open it.

TIP

As an alternative, you can use the "Open in drawing editor" checkbox to have ACA open the file as you click Finish.

7. Select the Layout Grid (purple dashed rectangle) surrounding the Plan, and, on the Home ribbon tab, expand the Modify panel and click the Copy to Clipboard tool.
8. Close the *A-FP03* View file.

   It is not necessary to save the file.
9. On the Project Navigator, double-click the *A-CP03* file to open it.
10. On the Home ribbon tab, expand the Modify panel and choose the Paste to Original Coordinates tool.

As we did in the "First Floor Plan Model Space View" section of Chapter 5, we will create a Model Space View in this file based on the extents of the Layout Grid that we just pasted. We can assign properties to this Model Space View that will be used by the viewports when we drag this View to Sheet files.

11. On the Project Navigator, right-click the *A-CP03* View file and choose **New Model Space View**.

12. In the Add Model Space View dialog, type **Third Floor Reflected Ceiling Plan** for the Name and then click the Define View Window icon (see Figure 13.49).

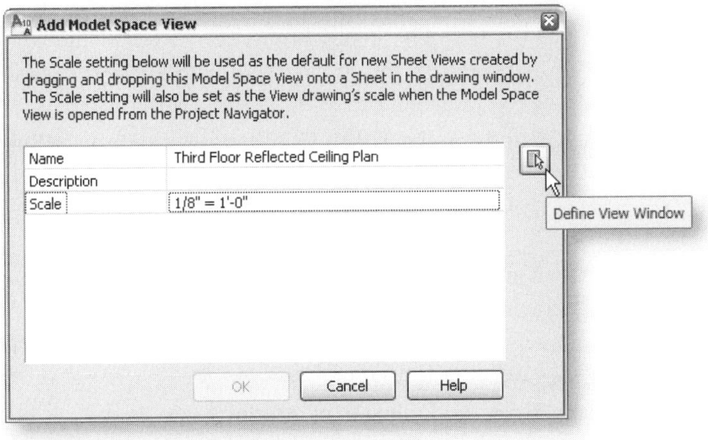

FIGURE 13.49 *Create a New Model Space View in the A-CP03 file*

13. Following the prompts in the drawing, snap to two opposite corners of the Layout Grid (the one just pasted) to define the View Window and then click OK to dismiss the Add Model Space View dialog box.
14. On the Annotate ribbon tab on the Callouts panel, select the drop-down arrow to the right of the Title button and choose the ***Title (Number)*** tool.
15. At the "Specify location of symbol" prompt, click a point within the Layout Grid beneath the model and follow the remaining prompts to complete the routine.

    The title that we assigned to the Model Space View should automatically appear in the Title Mark field.
16. On the Drawing status bar, choose **Reflected** from the Display Configuration pop-up list.

MANAGER NOTE

If you made modifications to the Reflected Display Configuration as noted in "Going Further," they will not automatically appear when you choose Reflected. This is because those changes were applied to the *03 Partitions* Construct file and not the *A-CP03* View file. Two options are available to make those modifications available here. First, we can push our changes (using the "Update Standards from Drawing" command in the Display Manager) from the *03 Partitions* file to our *Commercial Displays* [*Commercial Displays – Metric*] Standards File (created in Chapter 11) and then synchronize the project. This will apply those changes to the Reflected Display Configuration (and its nested Sets and Representations) to all drawings in the project. Please note that if you choose this approach, "Cut Plane" settings do not participate in Standards. Therefore, you will need to edit the Cut Plane manually in the *A-CP03* View file if required. This is ultimately a better approach that makes your changes available to all files in your project, but it does require a bit more effort to achieve.

The other approach would be to simply select the *03 Partitions* XREF onscreen, right-click and choose **Edit Object Display**. On the XREF Display tab, apply an override using the "Reflected" Configuration from the *03 Partitions* file. This approach may seem simpler in the short term, but it would need to be done on every file that required it. If you make the change permanently via the Display Manager and make it part of your office standard template files, you will only need to make the change once and it will become available from then on.

The Reflected Ceiling Plan View file is complete and ready to be dragged to a Sheet.

17. Save and close the *A-CP03* file.

Create the RCP Sheet File

Now that we have a reflected ceiling plan View, let's add a reflected ceiling plan Sheet file to our Project.

18. On the Project Navigator palette, click the Sheets tab.
19. Right-click on the *Plans* Sub Set beneath the *Architectural* Sub Set and choose **New > Sheet**.
20. For the Number, type **A-102** and for the Sheet Title, type **Reflected Ceiling Plans**. Click OK to accept the values and dismiss the New Sheet dialog box.
21. Double-click *A-102 Reflected Ceiling Plans* to open it.

TIP

As an alternative, you can use the "Open in drawing editor" checkbox to have ACA open the file as you click Finish.

22. On the Project Navigator palette, click the Views tab.

    Be sure that the "Third Floor Reflected Ceiling Plan" Model Space View is visible beneath the *A-CP03* View file. If it isn't, expand the plus (+) sign next to *A-CP03*.
23. Drag and drop the Third Floor Reflected Ceiling Plan Model Space View from the Project Navigator palette directly onto the Sheet Layout (see Figure 13.50).

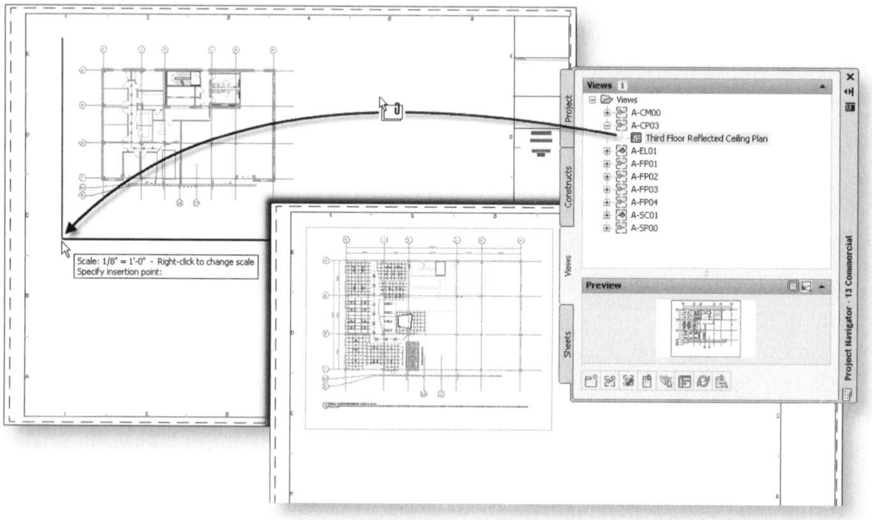

FIGURE 13.50 *Drag the Third Floor Reflected Ceiling Plan Model Space View onto the Sheet*

24. Click an insertion point on the Sheet to place the plan.

For now, we have only this single reflected ceiling plan. However, if we were to add additional RCP files later, we could easily rearrange and renumber the viewports on this Sheet. Notice that while you are still positioning the viewport, it shows the Medium Detail Configuration in the preview image. However, once you have placed the viewport, it automatically switches to Reflected. The Sheet file is now complete.

25. Save and close all project files.

NOTE

A more detailed explanation of the use of separate View files in the Project Navigator structure follows in Chapter 14. Please read on for more details on the benefits of this approach.

ADDITIONAL EXERCISES

Additional exercises have been provided in Appendix A. In Appendix A, you will find an exercise to continue refining the Commercial Project Reflected Ceiling Plans, to change the way in which Doors display on the Reflected Ceiling Plans and to add other ceiling items (see Figure 13.51). It is not necessary that you complete this exercise to begin the next chapter. It is provided to enhance your learning experience. Completed projects for each of the exercises have been provided in the *Chapter13/ Complete* folder.

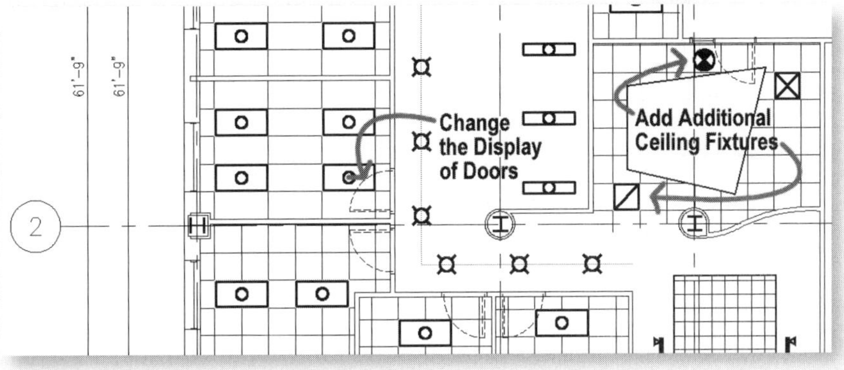

FIGURE 13.51 *Update project files in Additional Exercises—Appendix A*

SUMMARY

- Generate Spaces allows Space objects to be created from existing Walls, even those contained in XREFs.
- As the design changes, you can use Update Space Geometry to keep the Space objects up to date.
- Ceiling Grids are rectangular Grid objects; to shape them to a room, you use the clipping feature.
- You can use the Boundary option when placing a Ceiling Grid to add the grid and clip it in the same operation.
- You add Grids using rough positioning and move them later to center them or use the SNap to Center feature.
- Holes can be added to Grids to represent various design features.
- Ceiling Grids can be easily transformed from 2x2 [600x600] to 2x4 [600x1200] and vice versa.
- Ceiling Grids can be easily rotated.
- Most Fluorescent fixtures in the Content Library are Mask Blocks capable of covering up part of the grid.
- You can create your own custom Mask Blocks by drawing a closed polyline and then right-clicking it to convert.
- Content Library light fixtures use Node Anchors to attach to the Ceiling Grids.
- Anchored lights cannot be moved, copied or rotated off their parent grid. Instead, you should use Anchor properties to rotate lights.
- You can add a new light from the DesignCenter for each unique grid.
- Surface-mounted lighting can be achieved by skipping the anchor prompt (press ENTER) when inserting the lights.
- Layout curves are one-dimensional layout grids with regularly spaced nodes.
- Even if Floor Plan and Ceiling Data are contained in the same Construct, they should be annotated in separate View files.

CHAPTER 14

Generating Annotation

INTRODUCTION

In this chapter, we will add annotation required for construction documents to our files. Information such as dimensions, targets, tags, labels, leaders and notes are among the items we will explore here. In our continuing effort to work with and understand the AutoCAD Architecture Drawing Management system, we will be adding all annotation to the View files that we created in Project Navigator. The major benefit of this approach is a clean separation between modeling and annotation activities. Some firms prefer to add annotation directly to the Sheets. While this is technically possible in Project Navigator, it is recommended (with the infrastructure already available in the Project Navigator) that you use the View files for placing annotation and abandon the practice of annotating in Sheets. The entire Project Navigator infrastructure is designed around this philosophy, and the benefits of doing so are many.

OBJECTIVES

In this chapter, we will add annotation to project View files—we will add room tags to our commercial project and add dimensions to our residential plans using a variety of techniques. Our focus will be primarily AEC Tags and AEC Dimensions. We will also look at the Annotation tool palette for a sampling of the documentation content provided with ACA. This chapter will explore the following topics:

- Add Room Tags.
- Understand and create Tags.
- Use AEC Dimensions.
- Edit AEC Dimension styles.
- Access Documentation Content.
- Add text leaders and notes.

ANNOTATION AND VIEW FILES

In Chapter 5, several View files were established in each project and the concept of Views was discussed briefly. View files represent a particular type of drawing in a document set such as a "plan" or "section" and contains those project annotations like notes, dimensions and tags appropriate to the drawing type in question. Now that we are about to begin adding annotations to our project files, it is time to elaborate further on this concept.

Let's consider some of the rationale behind the organizational philosophy of the Drawing Management system. It is intended that you make a separate View file for each unique type of drawing or document required in your construction document sets (or other project deliverables). In this way, you can include completely unique annotation, dimensions and notes in each View and associated Sheets while maintaining a coordinated link back to a single source for the building graphics. In doing so, you eliminate the traditional morass of layer configurations and other issues inherent in housing data required by several drawing types and disciplines within the same file. This approach solves many common problems inherent in the process that has evolved and been employed in most AutoCAD drawing files in production today. Consider the following common problems with construction document annotation in AutoCAD drawing files:

- Various drawing types often have similar but not identical annotation needs.
- Different professional disciplines have different presentation, documentation and annotation requirements.
- Staffing needs often require multiple-user access to project files.
- Annotation is often required at multiple plotting scales.

As a point of discussion, consider the simple matter of adding room tags to your drawings. While it is true that this type of annotation would be required in nearly every type of plan (floor plan, reflected ceiling plan, MEP plans, etc.), each of these plans has its own unique and often incompatible characteristics, making it difficult to create and position a single set of room tags.

For instance, in the floor plan, the best position for a Room Tag might be in the center of the room. However, when we switch to the reflected ceiling, we may notice that this position, while optimal for the floor plan, places the symbol directly on top of a light fixture or other notes, making the drawing difficult to read. If you move the tag for the reflected ceiling, its new position often ends up obscuring information previously not obscured in the floor plan. It is very difficult to find an optimal location for such "common" annotations that satisfy all drawing types, disciplines and scales.

Furthermore, you may wish to have one type of symbol for the floor plan (including both the Room Name and Room Number, for instance), while in the reflected ceiling or the MEP plans, you may wish to see the Room Number only. Traditionally, this would require a symbol with multiple embedded layers in order to accommodate the various display needs. While reliance on layer configurations is a workable solution, it often leads to improper settings in the Sheet files or a great deal of extra coordination effort, which ultimately lead to wasted plots, wasted time and wasted money!

Another common annotation problem arises when a model file must be used at two different plotted scales, such as an overall plan and an enlarged detail plan. In this case, annotation must be scaled differently for each plotted scale. Traditionally, this would again require several scale-dependent layers, symbols and dimension styles—not to mention the amount of time wasted coordinating all variations of the items in question—particularly when changes occur.

With respect to the scaling issue, the annotation scaling feature offers a potential solution to common issues. Drawing annotation has the ability to resize automatically based on the Annotation Scale setting of a drawing file. To take advantage of this feature, text styles, dimensions styles, blocks and AEC objects must be configured as "annotative." This allows you to define some items as annotative that will automatically scale with the drawing and other items that do not as project needs dictate. (While most text and dimensions benefit from the feature, you certainly would not want all blocks to be annotative.) Most out-of-the-box annotation is already properly configured to take advantage of this powerful feature.

Annotation scaling is a powerful and exciting feature that can potentially solve the issue of multiple scales without the need for separate View files. However, with separate View files, the solution to *all* the above-sited issues is achieved, including annotation scaling. There is no conflict between drawing types because each drawing has its *own* unique annotation. Each discipline need not worry about what annotation the other disciplines have added because in their discipline-specific View files, they will see only their own. And each View has its own scale setting, so regardless of the specific annotation symbols used, all elements will be properly sized—annotative and non-annotative alike.

With separate View files, annotation symbols appear *only* in that View drawing. However (and most importantly), before assuming that this approach creates twice the work in adding and coordinating the two sets of tags, in Project Navigator, both sets of annotation reference the *same* Property Set Data! The data source lives within the Construct, *not* the separate View files. In other words, ACA tags merely reference the data that is attached directly to the object. Object data, whether graphical or non-graphical, *always* live in the Construct. (For more information on Property Sets—non-graphical data—see Chapter 15.) The tag simply reads this data and displays it. In this way, the Room Names and Numbers (or any other referenced data) remain synchronized throughout the set even though each drawing contains its own unique tag object (annotation) to display it. This setup frees us from all of the problems discussed above. Each View drawing's tags can be in a different physical location relative to the associated AEC object (Space, Door, etc). Each of those tags can use a different graphical symbol (without layers), which displays the same or different properties, and each of those tags can be inserted at its own unique scale. Therefore, when the View is dragged to the Sheet, all annotations will appear as the correct size for plotting without any further effort or layer changes required.

Finally, if Views are maintained for each type of drawing, many personnel issues are resolved as well. It becomes very easy to have two individuals working simultaneously on different annotation tasks. One person can work in a floor plan View, while another person works in the reflected ceiling. Both are able to annotate their respective files independent of each other. However, since both of their respective View files reference the same Constructs, if one of them should open one of those Constructs and move a partition, delete a Door or change the underlying annotation property data (such as room name or number), the change would be reflected in *all* Views when the XREFs were updated.

For all of those reasons and many more, the Drawing Management system in ACA is designed around the philosophy that each drawing type requiring unique annotations should be configured within its own separate View file. One or more of these Views can be dragged to the same Sheet, so there will not necessarily be a one-to-one correspondence between the Views and Sheets. (Although there certainly could be a direct correspondence if project needs warranted it.) We have already seen this throughout the Project Setup exercises in Chapter 5—for example, there are four separate floor plan View files for the Commercial Project, yet they all have been placed on the same Sheet. The opposite situation can also occur. In a very large project, a single View file can be dragged to more than one Sheet if it will not fit in a single title border and requires a matchline.

When you are contemplating whether a new View file is required, the three most important criteria are as follows:

- **Discipline**—(Architectural, Mechanical, Structural, etc.)
- **Drawing Type**—(Plan, Section, Elevation, etc.)
- **Plotting Scale**—(1/8" = 1'0" [1:100], 1/4" = 1'0" [1:50], etc.)

Variation in any one of those standards warrants the creation of a new View file. Some may argue that the annotation scaling feature eliminates the need for the third criteria. In some cases, this may be true. Theoretically, it is possible to have a single View file appear in different viewports and/or Sheets at two or more scales. However, unless the annotation for each drawing is identical at both scales, the better approach remains the creation of separate View files. Remember, there are many benefits of creating separate View files, and managing the scale of annotation was only one of them. The biggest benefit for the annotation scaling feature comes into play when you realize that project needs or drawing needs have changed and you must change the scale of an existing drawing. In this instance, annotation scaling makes the change nearly effortless, as we will see below. A fourth consideration is personnel. If you require more than one individual to work simultaneously on the same kind of drawing, you can split it into multiple View files.

Think of the entire project structure like a tree. A tree has one trunk and many branches and leaves. Constructs are close to the trunk (they are unique), while the Views and Sheets branch out from the Constructs and are more numerous. Each leaf is fed by a branch which in turn is fed by the trunk (see Figure 14.1).

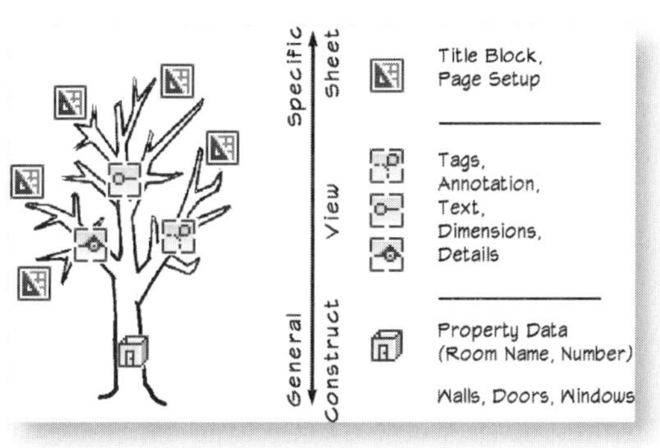

FIGURE 14.1 *The relationship of Constructs, Views and Sheets resembles a tree*

Another way to think of it is this: The more people who need a piece of data (the Walls, the Column Grid, the Room Names), the closer that data should be to the trunk. The more specialized the item (Architectural First Floor Plan at 1/8" = 1'-0" scale, stylized room tags for the mechanical equipment plan or a sheet file), the further out on the branches it should be placed. Following this logic, you can begin to make decisions about where certain project items ought to be placed. We have already discussed Walls, Doors, Windows and other "real" pieces of the model. They belong to Constructs and are required by everyone. Room designations are two separate components: the *label* (or tag) and the *data* to which the tag refers. The fact that a particular room is named "Conference Room East" is "real"; and while we cannot physically "touch" the concept of the room's being named "Conference Room East," no one can dispute that its designation as such is as "real" as the Walls which define the space. Furthermore, it would be uncommon to refer to this room by more than one name. On the other hand, the label that shows it as being "Conference Room East" is a component of a particular drawing and is not "real" in the sense that tags are not constructed and installed with the building or painted on the conference room floor. Therefore, the tag is placed in a View file and positioned in a manner convenient to the other elements of the drawing. The tag references the data contained in the Construct file, which informs it that the Space in question is named "Conference Room East."

Views used in this way provide the means for us to capture a certain slice of the building model, annotate, embellish and configure it a certain way to document and clarify our intentions. Further out on the tree's branches lie the Sheets, which have the unique purpose of gathering our documentation intent in some deliverable format, such as printed drawings or a digital Drawing Web Format (DWF) file.

ADDING ROOM TAGS

Let's explore firsthand some of the scenarios discussed in the previous section. In this exercise, we will add Room Tags to the third floor plan and reflected ceiling plan View files of the Commercial Project. We will then make a few adjustments to them and explore the flexibility inherent in having two separate View files.

Install the CD Files and Load the Current Project

If you have already installed all of the files from the CD, simply skip down to step 3 below to make the project active. If you need to install the CD files, start at step 1.

1. If you have not already done so, install the dataset files located on the Mastering AutoCAD Architecture 2010 CD-ROM.

   Refer to "Files Included on the CD-ROM" in the Preface for information on installing the sample files included on the CD.
2. Launch AutoCAD Architecture 2010 from the desktop icon created in Chapter 3.

If you did not create a custom icon, you might want to review "Create a New Profile" and "Create a Desktop Shortcut" in Chapter 3. Creating the custom desktop icon is not essential; however, it makes loading the custom profile easier.

3. On the Quick Access Toolbar (QAT), Click the **Project Browser** icon.
4. Click to open the folder list and choose your *C:* drive.
5. Double-click on the *MasterACA 2010* folder, then the *Chapter14* folder.

   One or two commercial Projects will be listed: *14 Commercial* or *14 Commercial Metric.*
6. Double-click *14 Commercial* if you wish to work in Imperial units. Double-click *14 Commercial Metric* if you wish to work in Metric units. (You can also right-click on it and choose **Set Current Project**.) Then click Close in the Project Browser.

NOTE

Important: If a message appears asking you to repath the project, click the "Repath the project now" option. Refer to the "Repathing Projects" section in the Preface for more information.

Understand Annotation Scaling

All dimensions, text and annotation routines in AutoCAD Architecture can take advantage of annotation scaling. Annotation scaling allows blocks and other annotation objects to change size automatically in order to conform to the scale setting of the drawing. Therefore, when you assign the scale setting to the View file, all annotation you add will be properly scaled based on that setting. Furthermore, if you later change the scale of the drawing, all annotation will re-scale accordingly. You can easily tell if a dimension, symbol or piece of text is annotative by hovering your mouse over it. A small symbol that looks like an architectural scale will appear next to the cursor.

7. On the Project Navigator palette, click the Views tab.
8. Double-click the *A-FP03* file to open it.
9. Move your cursor over one of the section markers (or other callouts in the file) and wait for the small annotative icon to appear (see the left side of Figure 14.2).

In Chapter 5, we designated that this file would be plotted at 1/8" = 1'-0" [1:100]. You can verify this setting by looking at the Annotation Scale setting on the Drawing status bar (also shown in the figure).

10. On the Drawing status bar, change the Annotation Scale to **1/4" = 1'-0" [1:50]** (see the right side of Figure 14.2).

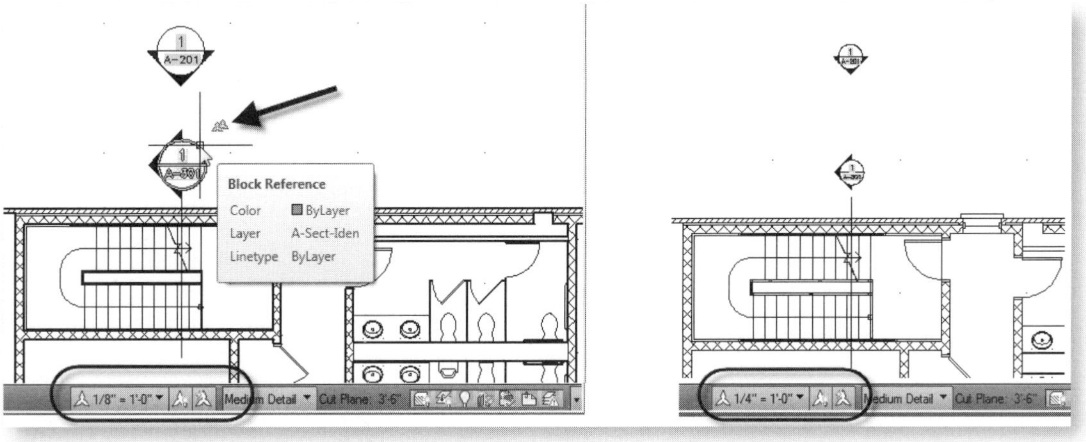

FIGURE 14.2 *Change the Annotation Scale and note the behavior of the symbols*

Notice the change in size of the section and elevation markers.

11. On the Drawing status bar, return the Annotation Scale to **1/8" = 1'-0" [1:100]**. The symbols will return to their previous size.

If you click on an annotative symbol, both versions of the symbol will appear ghosted with the selection. If necessary, you can relocate one or both of these representations relative to the overall symbol. You can also add and remove scales from any symbol using the right-click menu.

Add Room Tags

Adding tags is simple. Let's begin with the *Third Floor Plan* View file.

NOTE

Important: Be sure that the *03 Partitions* file is *not* open before continuing. The tagging routines that we will use here must have the ability to edit the referenced Construct files (in this case, *03 Partitions*). If you or anyone else has opened this or any other required Construct file in AutoCAD, the tagging routine will fail.

12. On the Annotate tab, on the Scheduling panel, click the Room Tag drop-down button and then choose the ***Room Tag – Project Based*** tool.
13. At the "Select object to tag" prompt, click on the hatch pattern of the Reception Space (on the right of the tenant space just below the elevator lobby).
14. At the "Specify location of tag" prompt, click in the center of the Reception Space (see Figure 14.3).

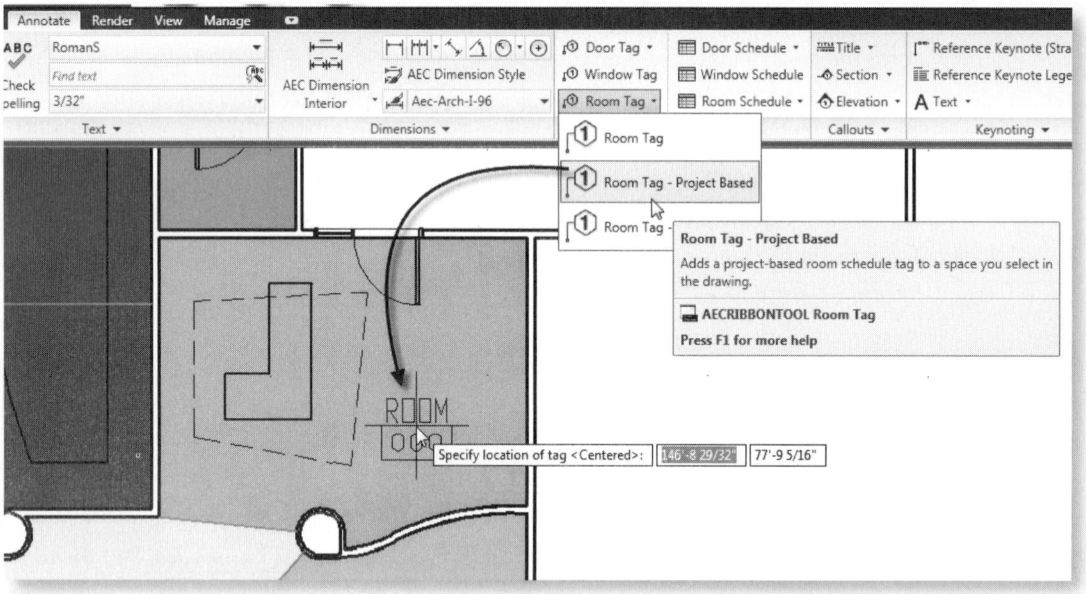

FIGURE 14.3 *Click the Reception Space to add the first Room Tag*

TIP

You can also press ENTER to automatically place the tag at the geometric center of the Space.

15. In the Edit Property Set Data worksheet that appears, collapse the Room FinishObjects grouping.
16. In the SpaceObjects grouping, examine the values automatically input for Name and NumberProjectBased (see Figure 14.4).

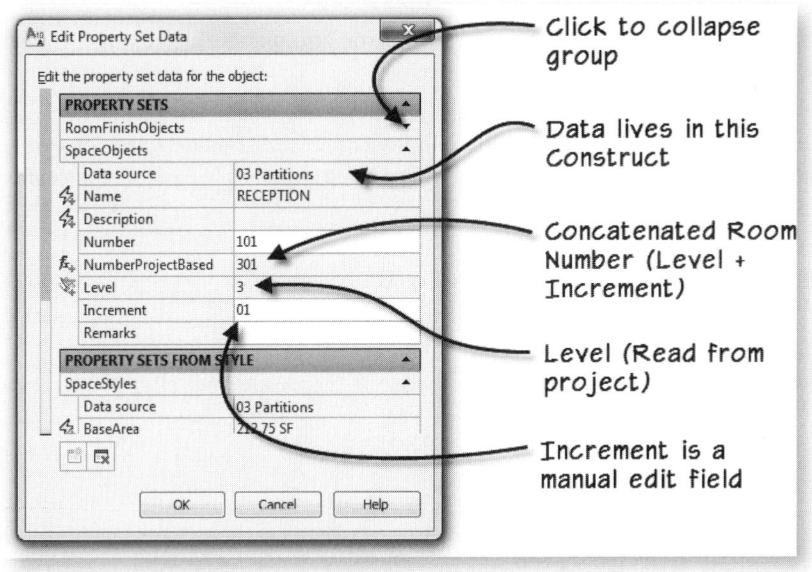

FIGURE 14.4 *The Property Set Data worksheet shows the data attached to the Space object*

When you add the tag to the drawing, it attaches one or more Property Sets to the selected object (the Reception Space object in this case). A Property Set is a collection of data that is attached to an object for tagging or scheduling purposes (see Chapter 15). In this case, we are concerned only with the SpaceObjects Property Set—specifically with the "Name" and "NumberProjectBased" fields for the tag that we have chosen. Notice that the Data Source for this Property Set is *03 Partitions*. As was mentioned in the previous paragraphs, the actual data associated with a tag will be written to the Construct even though the tag object is inserted within the View file. This is what makes tagging in Project Navigator so powerful.

Take note of the Increment and Level fields. These two fields are concatenated together to form the value in the "NumberProjectBased" field (currently 301). This number will also appear in the tag when we click OK in this worksheet. The Increment field is editable, but it will automatically increment to the next number with each Space we tag. Do not be concerned that the "Number" field (also editable) does not match the NumberProjectBased field. The Number field is used by the non-project-based tags. The Room Tag tool on the ribbon (that is not project-based) uses this field instead. We will not be using it here; therefore, you can ignore the Number field. (See Chapter 15 for more information on Schedules and Property Set data.)

MANAGER NOTE

We can hide any Property in a Property Set Definition. To do this, edit a Property Set Definition using the Style Manager on the Format menu and deselect the "Visible" checkbox. In this case, since we are using Project Navigator, it might be helpful to edit the SpaceObjects Property Set Definition and hide (deselect the "Visible" check mark next to) the Number Property. This can be done in this drawing or in our *Commercial Styles* Standards file and then synchronized to all project files. Refer to Chapter 15 for more information on Property Set Definitions. Refer to Chapter 8 for more information on Project Standards.

17. Click OK in the Edit Property Set Data worksheet.

    Notice the Room Tag as well as the room name and number values that appear (see Figure 14.5).

NOTE

If the Name reads "Room" instead of "Reception" in the tag, this will update when you complete the tagging routine. As soon as we finish tagging and press ENTER, all of the room names will update to the proper values.

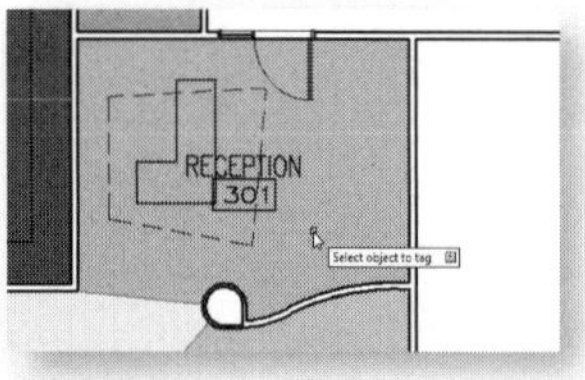

FIGURE 14.5 *The Room Tag appears showing the proper values*

18. When the "Select object to tag" prompt repeats, click the Conference Room Space, place the tag and then click OK.

    Notice that the auto-increment Number for this room is 302 and the name is "Conference Room."

19. When the "Select object to tag" prompt repeats, right-click in the drawing and choose **Multiple** (or press the down arrow to access this option from the dynamic prompt).

20. At the "Select objects to tag" prompt, click the office to the left of the Conference Room.

    The "Select objects to tag" prompt will repeat.

21. Continue clicking the offices around the perimeter of the plan. Click each office one at a time in a clockwise order. After clicking the last office, press ENTER.

You can use any selection method when you choose the Multiple option of the tagging routine, including windows and crossing windows. However, since this Property Set uses the auto-increment feature, clicking the Spaces one at a time will ensure that they are numbered in the order in which we clicked them. If you use a crossing, numbering might appear random.

TIP

You can use the Renumber Property Sets tool on the Scheduling panel to fix this and renumber all Spaces later. You must click the title of the Scheduling panel to expand it first to access this tool.

In the Edit Property Set Data dialog, the Increment field now reads "Varies." This is because several rooms have been selected and they all have a unique Number. The Name field reads "Office." When we added the Spaces to the project in Chapter 13, we used out-of-the-box Space Styles. These Space styles are associated to a list of Space Names. This makes the Name property one of the inherent properties of the Space object and makes editing the name as simple as picking from a predefined list. (The Name list is a style like other ACA styles and we can modify it to add and delete items on the list.) We will look at editing the names of the Spaces themselves later.

22. In the "Edit Property Set Data" dialog, click OK.

    Continue tagging until all rooms are tagged. Also add tags to the two closets at the top and the closet above reception. Remember to pick in the order you want them numbered.

23. When you are finished tagging, press ENTER to complete the routine (see Figure 14.6).

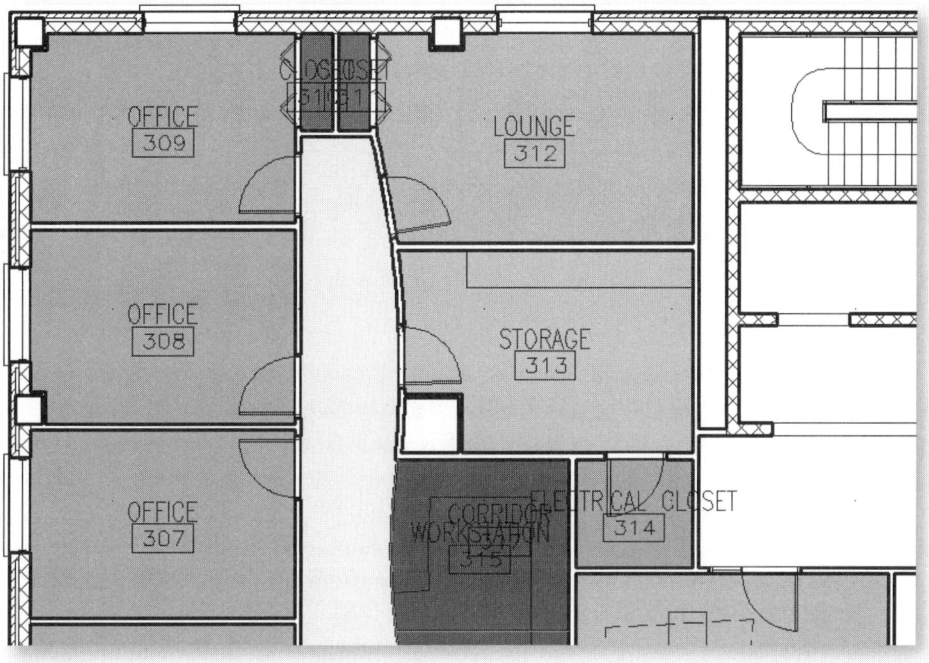

FIGURE 14.6 *All Property Set values appear when the tagging routine is complete*

If an alert balloon appears indicating that the *03 Partitions* XREF has changed, click on it to reload the XREF.

Adjust Room Tag Position

Now that all of the Room Tags have been placed, you may not be happy with the precise position of some of them. You can easily move them around onscreen to suit the needs of this Floor Plan View. Tags are anchored; but unlike other anchored objects we have seen, the location of a tag can be modified using the standard AutoCAD MOVE command or using the grips.

1. Zoom in on the top of the plan.
2. Using the standard AutoCAD MOVE command (Home tab, Modify panel), move the two Room Tags for the two small closets outside the plan and place them above their respective closet Spaces (see Figure 14.7).

TIP
If you prefer, you can also use the grips on the tags to move them.

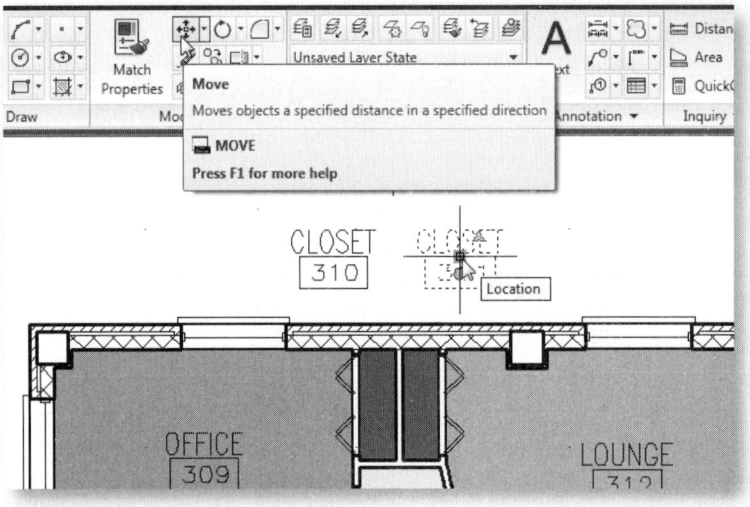

FIGURE 14.7 *Move the two Closet Room Tags outside of the Plan*

3. On the tool Annotate tab, on the Keynoting panel click the drop-down button the ***Text*** tool and choose the ***Text (Straight Leader)*** tool.

   With Leaders, the first point you click is ***the*** location of the arrowhead. Therefore, we must click our first point within the Closet Space and end at the tag. Object Snap Tracking will be helpful in keeping the points aligned.

4. At the "Specify first point of leader line" prompt, use Object Snap Tracking, acquire the corner of the Room Tag, track down from it into the Closet Space and then click (see the top right panel of Figure 14.8).
5. At the "Specify next point of leader line" prompt, snap to the same endpoint acquired in the last step (see the bottom left panel of Figure 14.8).
6. At the "Select text width" prompt, press ENTER again to accept the default.
7. At the "Enter first line of text" prompt, press ENTER again to accept the default (see the right panel of Figure 14.8).
8. In the Mtext edit window, click the OK button to dismiss the editor.

The multi-leader automatically includes a horizontal extension. You can use the grips to adjust this.

9. Use the grips to adjust the final multi-leader as shown at the bottom right of Figure 14.8.

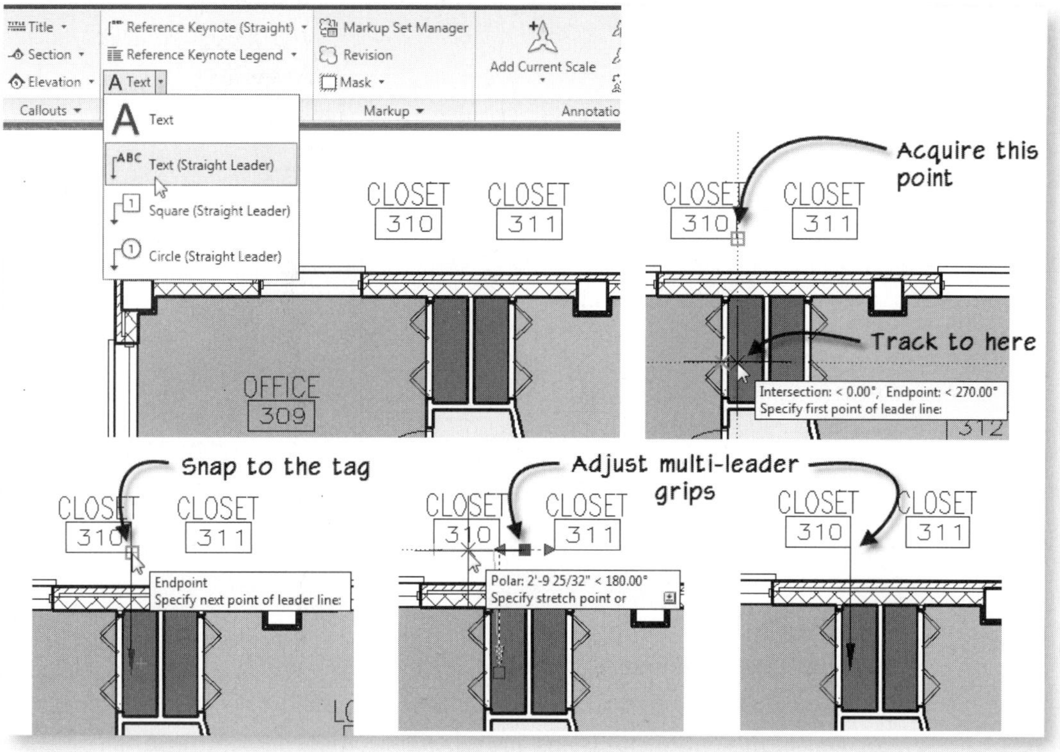

FIGURE 14.8 *Add a Leader to the tag pointing back to the Space*

This is a text leader tool. Normally you would specify with your mouse how wide you wanted the note to appear onscreen. Then you would type your text into the Mtext editor window that appears. You can also add leaders to this object on the right-click menu for cases where you want the same note to point to multiple items. However, in this case, we want only one Leader and no text. To get just the Leader, we must press ENTER at all of the default prompts and click OK in the Mtext editor. Do not press ESC. This will terminate the entire command, including the Leader.

10. On the Home tab, on the Modify panel, click the Match Properties tool.
11. At the "Select source object" prompt, click one of the Room Tags.
12. At the "Select destination object(s)" prompt, click the Leader and then press ENTER.

This matches the layer of the room tag to the leader.

13. Select the Leader. On the Properties palette, beneath the Lines & Arrows grouping, choose **Dot** from the Arrow list (see Figure 14.9).

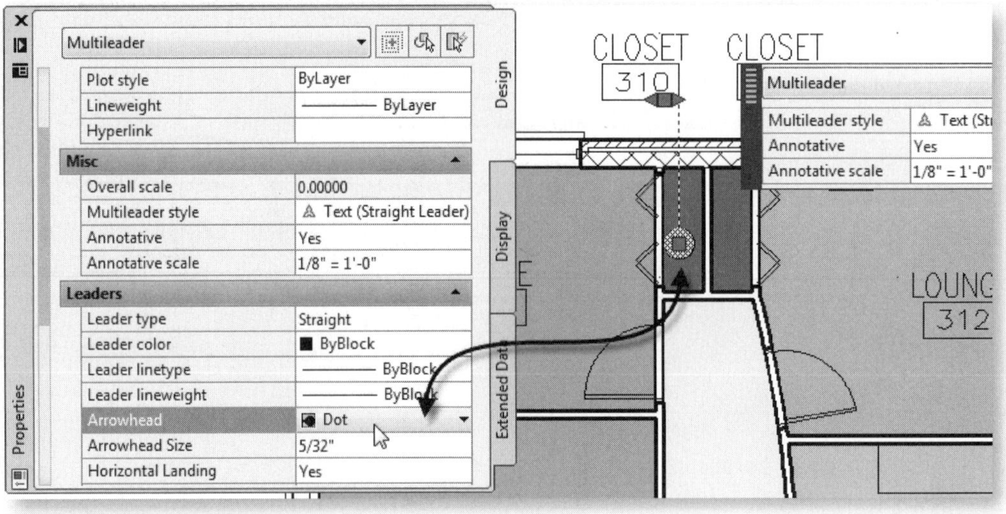

FIGURE 14.9 *Change the Leader to a Dot Arrowhead*

If you prefer a different arrowhead, feel free to choose it.

14. Copy the Leader to the other Closet Room Tag.
15. Repeat this entire process on any other ill-positioned Room Tags.

    For example, you might consider the electrical room.
16. Save the file when finished.

Edit Room Tag Property Data

As you are moving tags around, perhaps you notice a room name that is not correct. It is easy to edit the Property Data of an object. The trick is in understanding that it is not the tag that requires editing. Remember, the tag merely *refers* to the Property Data within the object (a Space object in the XREF file in this case). Therefore, to make the edit, you must edit the Space. Depending on the property you wish to edit, you can do this by opening the XREF; or in some cases, you can edit from the host file.

1. Locate a Space that you wish to edit. It is not important which one.
2. Click on any Space (click on the hatching).

   Notice that the entire XREF highlights. This is expected since the Spaces are contained in the *03 Partitions* XREF file.
3. On the External Reference tab, on the Edit panel, click the ***Open Reference*** button.
4. Select the Space object directly above the workstations, right-click and choose **Properties**.

   This will open (or shift focus to) the Properties palette. The Name is currently Storage.
5. On the Design tab, from the Name list, choose **Copy Room** (or simply type in a name if you wish to use a name that is different from what is shown on the list) (see the left side of Figure 14.10).

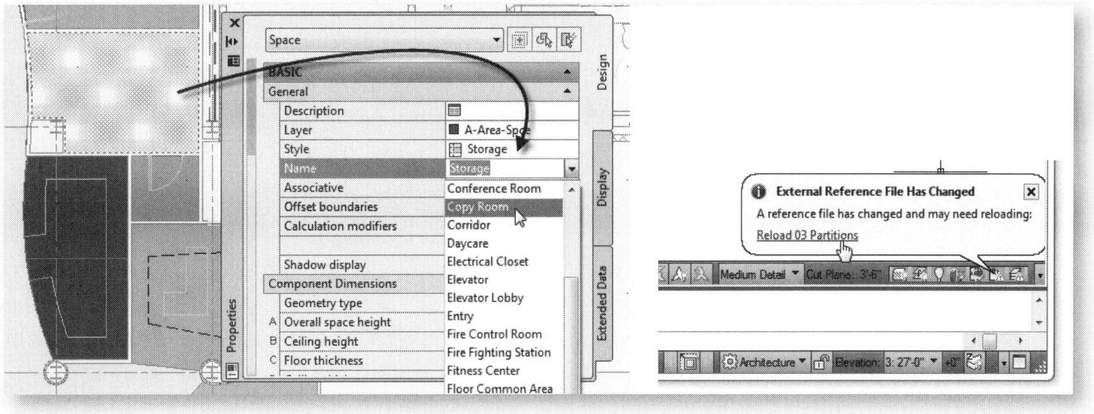

FIGURE 14.10 *Open the XREF to edit a Space Name*

6. Make any additional changes you choose to other Spaces and then Save and Close the file.
7. Return to *A-FP03* (which should still be open).

   If an alert balloon appears indicating that the *03 Partitions* XREF has changed, click on it to reload the XREF (see the right side of Figure 14.10).
8. Save and close the *A-FP03* View file.

Notice that as soon as you reload the XREF, the tags of any modified Spaces automatically update. In some cases, you can make the required edits directly from the View file and it will edit the required Construct for you. Examples of such editing will be shown below and will be further explained in the next chapter.

Add Room Tags to the Reflected Ceiling Plan

Adding tags to the Floor Plan was a fairly simple process. Adding them to any subsequent View file is even easier. The only time you need to perform the process of adding tags and inputting Property Set values (room names and numbers in this case) is the first time you add tags. Since the data to which the tag refers lives in the Construct and is passed to the tag, you can add tags in the other View files in a matter of seconds; the data values already assigned to objects in the Construct will then display in the new tags.

1. On the Project Navigator, on the Views tab, double-click the *A-CP03* file to open it.

   As before, verify that the Annotation Scale is set to **1/8" = 1-0"** [**1:100**].

NOTE

Please make sure that you closed *03 Partitions* after the previous exercise.

2. On the Annotate tab, on the Scheduling panel, click the Room Tag – Project Based tool.
3. At the "Select object to tag" prompt, click the Conference Room Space.

   This will be easiest to do by clicking on the gray hatching.
4. At the "Specify location of tag" prompt, press ENTER to accept the default of Centered.

In the Edit Property Set Data dialog, scroll down and note that all of the fields are already filled in with the same values input while you are working in the Floor Plan. For example, this is room number 302 (NumberProjectBased).

5. Click OK to return to the drawing.
6. At the return of the "Select object to tag" prompt, right-click and choose **Multiple**.
7. Using a Crossing Window, select all of the Spaces and then press `ENTER`.

A message reading "1 object was already tagged with the same tag. Do you want to tag it again?" will appear. This is referring to the tag that you just added to the Conference Room. Since we do not want two tags in the Conference Room, we will click No.

8. In the dialog that appears, click No.
9. In the Edit Property Data dialog, click OK and then press `ENTER` to complete the tagging routine (see Figure 14.11).

Notice that all of the tags appear with the same values that they had in the Third Floor Plan. Again, this is because the data to which these tags are attached lives in a common Construct file: *03 Partitions*.

NOTE

To use the "Multiple" Tag option, you must place the first tag manually. That is why we tagged one Space (the Conference Room) first.

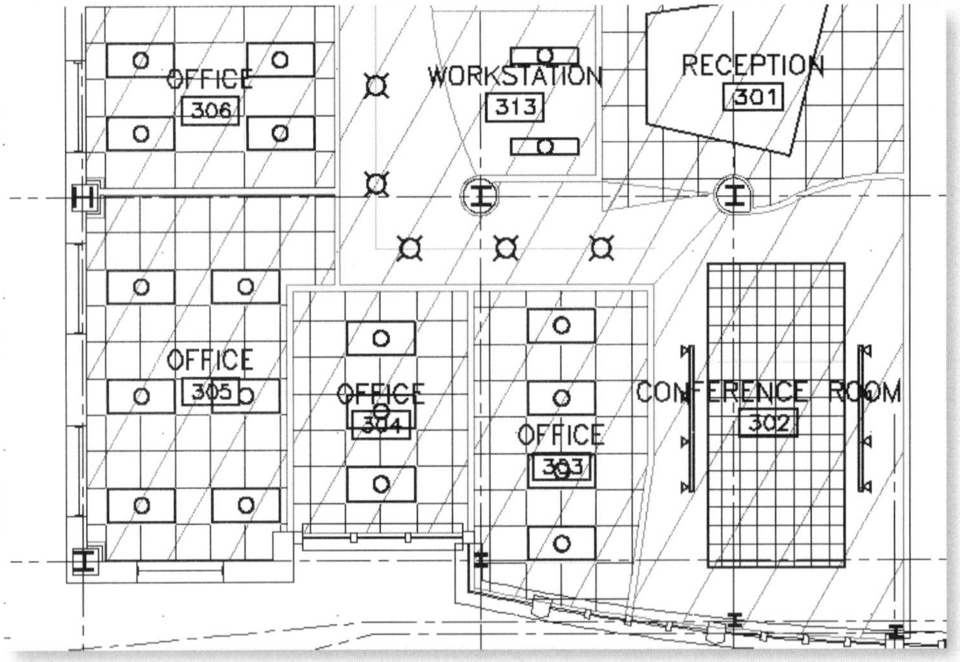

FIGURE 14.11 *All tags in the Reflected Ceiling Plan View match those of the Floor Plan*

10. Using the process above, edit the Name of Lounge Space in the upper right corner and change it to **Break Room**. (Make sure to change the Name property and not the Style.)
11. Close and save the Construct file after the edit and reload the XREF in *A-CP03*.

12. On the Project Navigator palette, double-click the *A-FP03* View file.

    If you left it open, this action will switch to it; otherwise, it will open. An XREF alert should appear.

13. Zoom in on the Lounge Space (that you just renamed) and then click the Reload link on the alert.

Note that the Lounge is now Break Room. Remember, *03 Partitions* is the common base file for each of these Views and it contains the room name data, not the tags. This is why the change occurs in both (and any other) third floor files.

NOTE **If you had any trouble getting the values to update properly, double-check that you closed the Construct and reload the XREFs.**

14. Close and save the *A-FP03* and return to the *A-CP03* View file.

Adjust the Annotation Scale

In "Understand Annotation Scaling," we were introduced to the concept of annotation scaling. Nearly all out-of-the-box annotation takes advantage of this feature. This includes the annotation that was already in the file, such as the callouts showcased above, the column bubbles and dimensions, and all of the room tags we just added. To see this, let's pretend that we wish to prepare this View for plotting at a different scale.

15. On the drawing status bar, change the Scale to **1/4" = 1'-0"** [**1:50**] (shown in Figure 14.2).

All of the room tags that you added should now be half their original size. Recall that if you pass your mouse over an annotation symbol, a small annotative icon will appear at your cursor. This was shown in Figure 14.2. Try it here on the room tags and notice the icon that appears.

16. Zoom and pan around the drawing as necessary to view other annotation.

In particular, note that the column bubble and dimensions nested within an XREF file have adjusted in size. Unfortunately, you will not be able to hover over these symbols and see the annotative icon when they are inside an XREF; but they *do* change scale, which is what is most important. We will continue with the drawing at 1/4" = 1'-0" [1:50] for the time being.

17. Save the file.

Create an Alternative Tag for the RCP

The "Annotation and View Files" section mentioned the possibility of using a different symbol in one View file than is used in another, yet keeping them linked to the same data. This is a powerful benefit of working in Project Navigator and separate View files. Let's explore that now.

1. From the Application Menu, choose **Open**. Browse to *Chapter14\MACA Commercial\Standards\Content* and open the file *Commercial Styles* [*Commercial Styles – Metric*].

We have visited this file on a number of occasions in previous chapters. Technically, you could perform the following steps in any project file; however, it is recommended that we keep all of our project-based content in a consistent location. In this case, the project standards file is the best choice.

In steps 2 through 6, we will create a piece of text and a shape to be used for the new tag's geometry. This geometry has been provided in a separate file in the *Elements* folder of Project Navigator. If you prefer, you may use this file instead. To do so, click the Constructs tab on the Project Navigator palette; in the *Elements* folder, right-click the file named *Room Tag* and choose **Insert as Block**. Choose Specify onscreen for the Insertion point and check the "Explode" checkbox. When prompted, click a point onscreen to place the objects, Zoom in on them and skip down to step 7.

2. On the Annotate tab, on the Text panel, click the Text tool.
3. At the "Specify first corner" prompt, click a point onscreen.
4. At the "Specify opposite corner" prompt, right-click and choose **Width**. At the "Specify width" prompt, type: **0** (zero) and then press ENTER.
5. In the MText editor, type **Number** and then click OK.
6. Select the piece of text and on the Properties palette, choose **Middle center** for the Justify. Set the Height to **1"** [**1**].
7. Zoom in on the text; using lines, circles, arcs or polylines (Home tab, Draw panel), draw whatever shape (rectangle, oval or pillbox) you wish to surround the text.

   Keep the size of the shape a little larger than the text. (An example appears in the preview image shown in Figure 14.12, which is also available in the *Room Tag* file noted above.)

Using the Define Schedule Tag Wizard

Be sure you are zoomed in on your text and graphics. Make sure the geometry is scaled properly: text is 1" [1] tall and the surrounding geometry is just a bit larger.

8. On the Home tab, click on the Annotation panel title bar to expand the panel.
9. Click the ***Create Tag*** tool.
10. At the "Select object(s) to create tag from" prompt, select the text and surrounding geometry and then press ENTER.
11. In the Define Schedule Tag worksheet, input **Room Tag Number Only** for the Name.

Each piece of text in the selection will be listed in the table at the bottom of the worksheet. In this case, we have a single entry labeled Number. Each piece of text in the tag can be left as is and remain text, or you can choose **Property** from the Type column. If you make it a Property, you must choose the Property Set and Property that you wish to reference.

12. From the Type column, choose **Property**. Set the Property Set to **SpaceObjects** and choose **NumberProjectBased** from the Property list (see Figure 14.12).

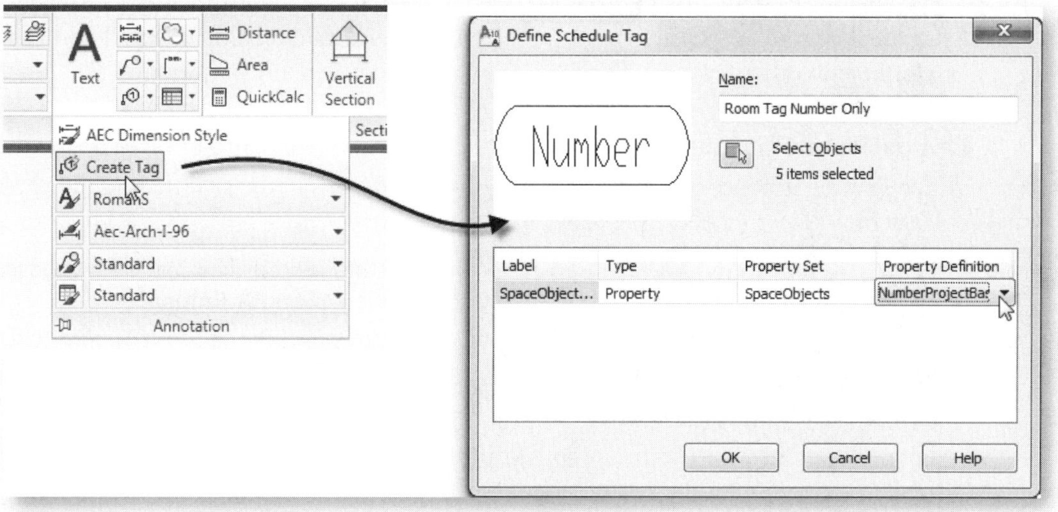

FIGURE 14.12 *Assign the piece of text as a Property that references the project-based room number*

13. Click OK to complete the worksheet. At the "Specify insertion point" prompt, click a useful insertion point relative to the geometry (such as the top midpoint or the center of the tag).

    The new tag will immediately shift in size.

14. Zoom out if necessary and hover your cursor over the new tag.

Notice that the annotation icon appears at your cursor. ACA's schedule tag wizard automatically makes the tag annotative. If you click on the geometry, you will see that it is no longer separate objects, but rather a new Multi-View Block named "Room Tag Number Only." The only problem with the way the wizard creates the tag is that it does not include any graphics in the Reflected Display Representation. Let's address that before we add it to our Project Tools palette.

15. Select the new tag, right-click and choose **Edit Multi-View Block Definition**.

> **TIP** You can also choose the Edit Style tool from Tag tab of the ribbon.

16. On the View Blocks tab, select Reflected on the left, click the Add button, choose Room Tag Number Only from the list and then click OK.
17. Save the file.

Now let's add the new tag to a tool palette.

18. Right-click on the tool palettes title bar, load the **MasterACA** tool palette group and then click the MACA Commercial palette to make it active.
19. Drag the new Room Tag Number Only object and drop it onto the Project Tools palette.
20. Right-click the new tool, choose **Properties**, change the Layer key to SPACENO and then click OK.
21. Save and close the *Commercial Styles* [*Commercial Styles – Metric*] file.

To summarize the process, you can draw any geometry using simple lines, arcs and text to make a custom tag. Make sure the text is one unit 1" [1] tall so the automated scaling routines built into AutoCAD Architecture scale it properly. Build the rest of the geometry relative to the height of the text. Be sure to create it in a library file such as your project standards file to make it accessible to other team members. Run the Create Tag tool and create the tag. Place it on a tool palette. Edit the tool and add layer keys or other settings. The tag is now ready to use in any project file.

Substitute Existing Tags

The new tag is now ready to use. Let's apply it to the tags in the reflected ceiling plan View file.

22. Return to the *A-CP03* View file, right-click the new tag tool and then **choose Import "Room Tag Number Only" Multi-View Block Definition**.
23. Select any Room Tag, on the Tag tab of the ribbon, click the ***Select Similar*** tool.

Notice the yellow grips and ghosted version of the symbols from the 1/8" = 1'-0" [1:100] scale above. If you wish, you can move each scale representation to its own unique location. You use the yellow grip to do this. In this way, you can have the small-scale version of the symbol in one spot while the large-scale version is in a different location. Try it out.

24. On the Properties palette, choose **Room Tag Number Only** from the Definition drop-down list.

Notice that all of the tags have been replaced with the new "Number Only" symbol. However, they all retained the correct reference to their individual Space object's Room Number. This is because the new tag points to the same NumberProjectBased property that the original did.

CAD MANAGER NOTE

If you wish to make a change like this to your office standard, you can create any custom tag and include it on the tool palettes deployed to all users.

25. Repeat any of the fine-tuning steps above to move Tags and/or add Leaders as required to complete the drawing and make it legible (see Figure 14.13).
26. On the Drawing status bar, change the Annotation Scale back to **1/8" = 1'-0" [1:100]**.

Remember, when working in the *A-CP03* View file, you are editing only the tag positions in that file. *A-FP03* and its tags are unaffected. However, as we saw above, if you edit the data referenced by the tag from any file, it will update in *all* files!

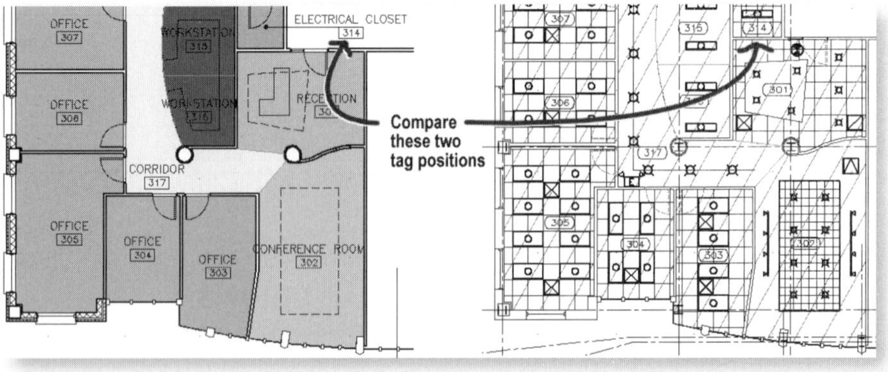

FIGURE 14.13 *All of the tags have been substituted with the new Number Only Tag*

As you can see, tagging objects in View files gives us the flexibility to use unique styles and positioning of annotation while maintaining 100 percent confidence that all data in multiple Views is coordinated back to its original source. Annotation scaling gives us additional flexibility to change plotting scale as project needs dictate.

DIMENSIONING AEC OBJECTS

AutoCAD Architecture offers several tools for dimensioning. Since ACA is built on and around an AutoCAD foundation, you have all of the AutoCAD dimensioning functionality at your disposal. However, the ACA AEC Dimension object is also worthy of serious consideration for regular Construction Document dimensioning use. We will explore this tool in the tutorials that follow. However, for the sake of completeness, here is a brief overview of the various dimensioning tools available in ACA 2010:

- **AutoCAD Dimensions**—Dimensioning tools have been a part of AutoCAD since its earliest releases. You can use this powerful and robust tool set to dimension any geometry, including AEC objects. However, you must add dimension lines point by point. If the **DIMASSOC** system variable is set to a value of **2**, AutoCAD dimensions that are added to AutoCAD drafted entities (such as lines, arcs, circles and polylines) will remain associative to those entities. AutoCAD dimensions can be used to dimension AEC objects, but they will not remain associative. To get dimensions that remain associative to AEC objects (such as Walls, Doors and Windows), use AEC Dimensions (see below). AutoCAD dimensions are drawn on the current layer.
- **AEC Content Dimension Tools**—These are accessible via the Content Browser. These dimension tools are essentially AutoCAD dimensions that auto-layer. IDrop them directly into a drawing or onto a tool palette.
- **Wall Dimensions**—These are available only at the Command Line (type **WALLDIM**), this tool applies a set of AutoCAD dimensions to a selection of Walls in the drawing. This tool provides a quick way to add a string of dimensions to a Wall or Walls. These dimensions come in on the correct layer. Since they are AutoCAD Dimensions, once placed, they can be edited using all standard AutoCAD Dimension techniques.
- **AEC Dimensions**—These are live Dimension objects that are updated automatically as the dimensioned geometry changes. AEC Dimensions sport many useful features, including the ability to edit the text and lines of AEC Dimension objects, the ability to dimension basic geometry as well as AEC objects, and the ability to attach AEC Dimensions across XREFs. In addition, AEC Dimensions are scale-dependent and use display control. This means that the same string of AEC Dimensions can be displayed differently in each Display Configuration. For all of your linear dimensioning needs, it is quite practical to consider AEC Dimensions over all of the other options. AEC Dimensions do not currently support Radial, Diameter or Angular dimensions. Use AutoCAD dimensions for those tasks. Preferably the auto-layering tools in Content Browser.
- **Content Items**—In addition to the various dimensions noted here, content items, including tags and elevation labels, read and report back on the dimensional characteristics of the drawings. Tags can read any property of an AEC object, such as width and length; and elevation labels can report heights in elevations and sections, for example. Examples of both of these items are covered below.

Room Tags with Dimensions

Above we used a basic room tag to label the Spaces in the Commercial project. In this topic, we will use a different tag in our Residential project which reports the overall dimensions of the Space object onscreen.

Change the Current Project

To explore the features of dimensioning, we will return to the Residential Project.

1. From the QAT, click the **Project Browser** icon.

Project Browser should already be in the *Chapter14* folder from above. If it is not, perform steps 2 and 3.

2. Click to open the folder list and choose your *C:* drive.
3. Double-click on the *MasterACA 2010* folder, then on the *Chapter14* folder.

   One or two residential Projects will be listed: *14 Residential* or *14 Residential Metric.*
4. Double-click *14 Residential* if you wish to work in Imperial units. Double-click *14 Residential Metric* if you wish to work in Metric units. (You can also right-click on it and choose **Set Current Project**.) Then click Close in the Project Browser.
5. If you left the commercial project loaded and files open above, you will see the "Project Browser – Close Project Files" dialog. Choose the Close all project files option.

   Save any files as prompted.

NOTE

Important: If a message appears asking you to repath the project, click Yes. Refer to the "Repathing Projects" section in the Preface for more information.

Add Room Tags with Dimensions to a View

Following the procedure used above, let's add tags to the First Floor Plan of the Residential Project. This time we will use a different tag. In the Content Browser is a tag that shows the Space style name and the dimensions of the room.

6. On the Project Navigator, click the Views tab and then double-click *A-FP01* to open it.

   We have not opened this file since the end of Chapter 5. As you can see, it has progressed nicely.
7. Zoom in on the plan a bit.

   Verify that the scale of the drawing is **1/4" = 1'-0"** [**1:50**].

Instead of the Room Tag that we used above, we will go to Content Browser and retrieve the Space Tag. This tag will show the name of the Space Style and its dimensions.

8. On the Home tab, on the Build panel, click the drop-down button on the ***Tools*** tool and then choose ***Content Browser***.
9. Click the *Documentation Tool Catalog – Imperial* [*Documentation Tool Catalog – Metric*]. Browse to the *Schedule Tags* category and then the *Room & Finish Tags* category.
10. Using the eyedropper icon, drag the ***Room Tag (w/ Dimensions)*** tool into the drawing window.
11. Follow the prompts to tag one Space and then right-click and choose **Multiple**.

12. Select and tag the remaining Spaces using the Multiple option and then press ENTER to complete the routine.
13. Make any moves or other necessary adjustments.

This tag is tied directly to the Space style name, not the room name. It also shows the dimensions of the Space. If you edit the size of the Space, the tag will adjust to show the new values. Give it a try if you like. Remember, though, that the Spaces are in the Construct; so you will have to open it to make a change and then reload the XREFs to see it. Also remember that the Spaces are associated with the Walls. So to edit them, move a Wall or Walls. If the Space does not immediately update, select the affected Space(s) and then click the **Update** tool on the Space tab of the ribbon. Be sure to undo or restore everything to their original sizes and reload the XREFs before continuing.

Match Sheet View Layer to View

Until now, we have seen that the Spaces from the tool palette use solid fill hatching and a range of colors. This makes for a nice onscreen experience and for pleasing presentation drawings. As we begin to prepare our drawings for construction documents, however, the solid hatch patterns will become less desirable. A number of ways to deal with this situation exist. We can use the display control properties of the Space objects to change the display of or to turn off the hatching. We saw general examples of Display Control in Chapter 2 and then worked specifically with the Space object hatching in the Reflected display in Chapter 13. While this method works just fine, it requires us to decide on a display for CDs, such as Low Detail. We then need to modify the display configurations and/or sets to make this change. It is a decent amount of effort at first; but with the ability to use project standards to apply the change quickly across the entire project (as we saw in Chapter 8), it becomes more manageable.

A simpler and more straightforward alternative does exist. The hatching of Spaces is assigned to its own unique layer in the style of each Space. You can see this on the Display tab of the Properties palette. To save you the effort of opening the Construct, the layer is A-Area-Spce-Patt.

Without modifying any display properties on the Spaces, we can freeze the A-Area-Spce-Patt layer in the current View file; then using the new "Match Sheet View Layer to View" Project Navigator setting (which is on by default), we can have this change automatically apply to the Sheet file that already exists in our project.

14. On the Project Navigator, click the Sheets tab.
15. Expand the *Architectural* subset and the *Plans* subset. Double-click the *A-101 Floor Plans* Sheet to open it.

Notice that in the viewport on the right, all of the Spaces appear as solid black. This is clearly not an acceptable way to plot this Sheet (see the left panel of Figure 14.14).

16. Close the Sheet without saving it.

Ultimately, we want to freeze the layer so that the Space hatching does not show at all. But before we do, let's learn how to change the solid black effect that we witnessed in the Sheet to show the actual colors used by the Space styles. The reason it is black is because the A-Area-Spce-Patt layer uses the Full Saturation plot style. This plot style substitutes all colors with black ink during printing. The sheet file is configured to preview this effect. You can refer to Chapter 18 for more on plot styles and printing.

17. Click the Project tab on Project Navigator.
18. Click the Edit Project icon at the top right corner. (This is shown in Figure 5.6 in Chapter 5.)

Beneath the "Drawing Settings" grouping, notice that the "Match Sheet View Layer to View" setting is set to Yes. (This is shown in Figure 5.4 in Chapter 5.)

19. Close the worksheet.
20. In *A-FP01*, on the Home tab, on the Layers panel, click the Layer Properties tool.
21. Locate the First Floor New|A-Area-Spce-Patt layer.

TIP

The first part of the layer name is the XREF file in which the layer is located—the *First Floor New* Construct in this case. On the left side of the Layer Properties Manager, expand the Xref item. Select First Floor New. This will make it easier to locate the correct layer on the right side.

22. Change its plot style to Standard and then click OK.

The Layer Properties Manager is a palette like Properties, Project Navigator and the Tool Palettes. You can leave it open onscreen, set it to auto-hide, dock it or leave it floating. You can also close it and reopen it with the tool the ribbon anytime.

23. Save the *A-FP01* View file.
24. On the Sheets tab, open the *A-101 Floor Plans* Sheet again.

Notice that the hatching is still displayed as solid, but it should now show its colors instead of being all black (see the middle panel of Figure 14.14).

25. Close the Sheet.
26. Back in the *A-FP01* View file, return to the Layer Manager and freeze the First Floor New|A-Area-Spce-Patt layer.
27. Click the No Plot icon next to the First Floor New|A-Area-Spce layer.

This will leave the boundaries of Spaces visible onscreen so that we can select them in View files if necessary, but will make sure that those edges do not print later in the Sheet.

28. Click OK, save the drawing and then reopen the Sheet one last time (see the right panel of Figure 14.14).

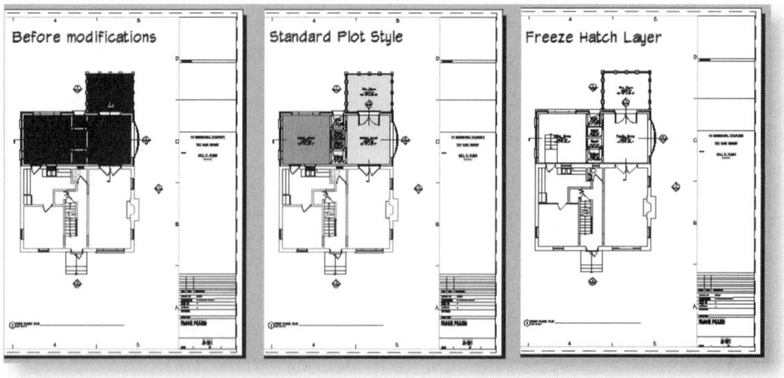

FIGURE 14.14 *Changes made to the View's layers automatically update in the Sheet*

If you forget to save the View file before opening the sheet, you can CTRL + TAB to switch back to the A-FP01 View file, save it and then toggle back to the Sheet and reload. Notice that the Space hatching is no longer displayed in either the View or the Sheet. With this feature, it is very simple to fine-tune the settings of a View file as you work without needing to repeat all of the edits later in the Sheet. With these preparations complete, we are ready to begin adding dimensions.

29. Close and save the Sheet file.

Live Dimensioning with AEC Dimensions

AEC Dimensions are live Dimension objects that are updated automatically as the dimensioned geometry changes. No manual grip editing or stretching is required. In addition, AEC Dimensions use display control. Therefore, they can be toggled on and off by loading an appropriate Display Configuration and they use annotation scaling. They automatically layer like all other AEC objects and they work across XREFs, making them the perfect complement to our Project Management system.

Add AEC Dimensions

When deciding which file to add a particular item, use the same litmus test that was applied above for room tags; dimensions are annotations that often have unique needs per drawing. Therefore, View files are the ideal location for dimensions. Part of what makes the View file an attractive location for annotation and dimensions is that tools such as AEC Dimensions and Schedule Tags (as we saw above) work across XREFs.

Remember from Chapter 5 that the magenta dashed line surrounding our plan represents the edge of the viewport on the Sheet. Therefore, when we begin adding Dimensions, we want to be certain that they do not encroach past this line. Please note that this boundary was added for convenience in Chapter 5 with this usage in mind and is not automatically added by ACA.

1. On the Annotate tab, on the Dimensions panel, click the AEC Dimension - Exterior R. O tool. (It is on the AEC Dimension split-button.)
2. At the “Select objects” prompt, click the horizontal masonry Wall at the top of the plan (between the addition and the Sun Porch) and then press ENTER.

   Notice that you are able to select a single Wall even though the Wall is part of an XREF file (see Figure 14.15).
3. At the “Specify insert point” prompt, click a point just above the Porch.

NOTE

When you are prompted to “Specify insert point,” the point you pick is the point where the first chain of dimensions will be placed (the one closest to the object being dimensioned).

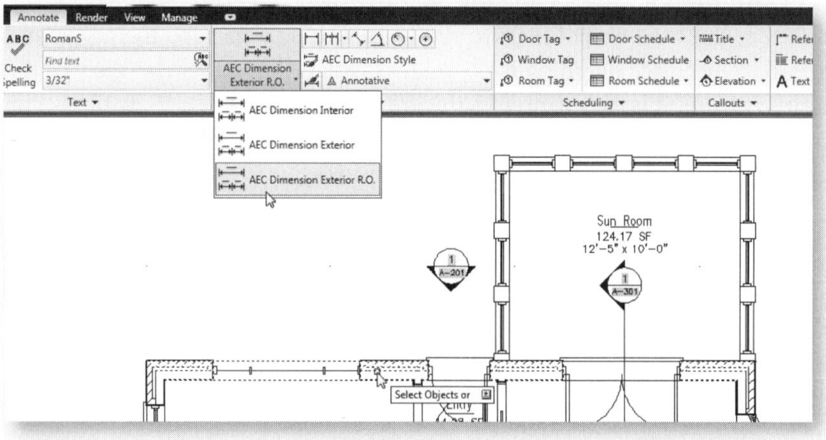

FIGURE 14.15 *Generate a string of AEC Dimensions*

4. Click anywhere on the dimensions just created.

Notice that this is a single continuous object, unlike AutoCAD dimensions, which would be several separate dimension objects.

5. Repeat these steps to add a string of AEC Dimensions on the left and right sides of the plan.

   On the left, select just the vertical masonry Wall; and on the right, try selecting the vertical masonry Wall and the vertical curtain Wall of the porch (see Figure 14.16).

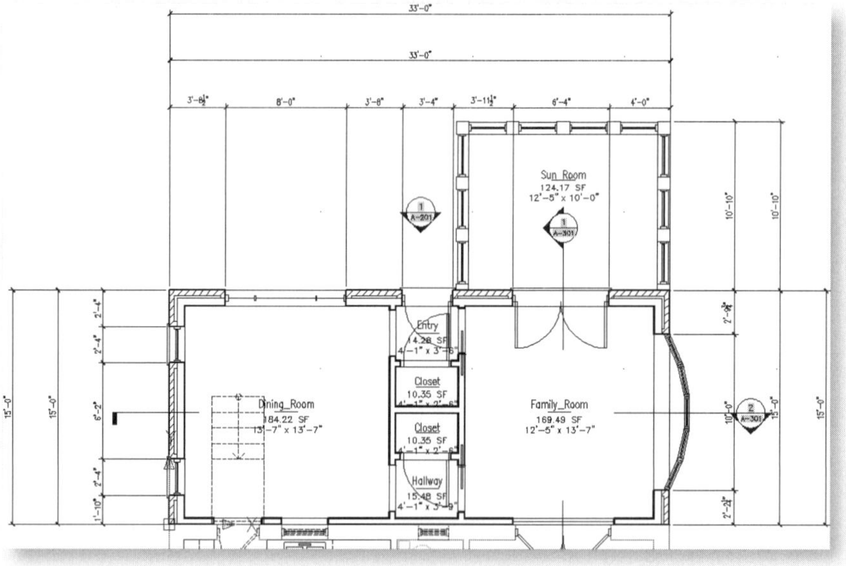

FIGURE 14.16 *Add AEC Dimensions to the right and left sides of the plan*

TIP

When selecting the Curtain Wall, be careful to select just the Curtain Wall and not the nested infill Windows.

Edit the AEC Dimension Style

Like most AEC objects, AEC Dimensions are style-based. The AEC Dimensions we have added so far were automatically assigned the Exterior - Rough Opening style by the tool on the ribbon. The AEC Dimension style establishes the quantity of strings (Chains) that AEC Dimension objects have. AEC Dimension styles also control the specific points that will be dimensioned for each type of AEC and AutoCAD object and assign an AutoCAD Dimension style that controls the display of all of the dimension components such as the lines, arrowheads and text.

6. Select any AEC Dimension, and on the AEC Dimension tab of the ribbon, choose **Select Similar**.
7. On the ribbon, click the Save As button.

TIP

You can also right-click and choose **Copy AEC Dimension Style and Assign.**

8. In the "AEC Dimension Style Properties" dialog, on the General tab, name the new Style **MACA Residential**.
9. Click the Chains tab.

   The number of chains can be between 1 and 10.
10. Change the number of Chains to **2** and then click OK.

Notice that the third chain has been removed from all dimension strings. If you were going to keep this chain, you probably would want to configure it or the second one a little differently from the way it defaulted. In this case, however, two chains will be sufficient for our needs.

11. Select any AEC dimension string and then click the Display tab of the Properties palette.

By now, this palette should look familiar. As you can see, a Style-based override has been applied to this AEC Dimension.

12. Open the Display component list.

There are four components to an AEC Dimension string:

- **AEC Dimension Group**—Contains the actual Dimension objects. This is what we see in the drawing and recognize as the Dimension objects.
- **AEC Dimension Group Marker**—An icon used to help identify each separate group of AEC Dimensions when a drawing contains several. It sits to the right of the AEC Dimension group. This component is off and is assigned to a non-plotting layer by default.
- **Removed Points Marker**—Shows dimension points that have been manually removed. This component is off and is assigned to a non-plotting layer by default, making it appear as though the points have been removed. Turn it on to restore removed points.
- **Override Text & Lines Marker**—When you override the text and/or lines of an AEC Dimension object, a small marker appears on a non-plotting layer to indicate that the dimension string has been manually modified. You should *not* turn this component off (see below for more information).

Since we saved our style from the "Rough Opening" style, all of the Windows and Doors are currently dimensioned to the opening. This is a masonry Wall, so this style is appropriate. The software comes with other styles that behave differently. For example, you can dimension to the center of openings if you wish.

13. In the Advanced grouping, click the Contents worksheet icon.
14. Select Chain 1 at the bottom and then select "Opening in Wall" in the "Apply to" list at the top.

TIP

Chain 1 is the one closest to the dimensioned geometry.

Notice that there are three options for this situation. Opening in Wall is used for any type of opening—Door, Window, Opening or Assembly. The current setting of "Opening Max. Width" gives us the rough opening of the object (see Figure 14.17).

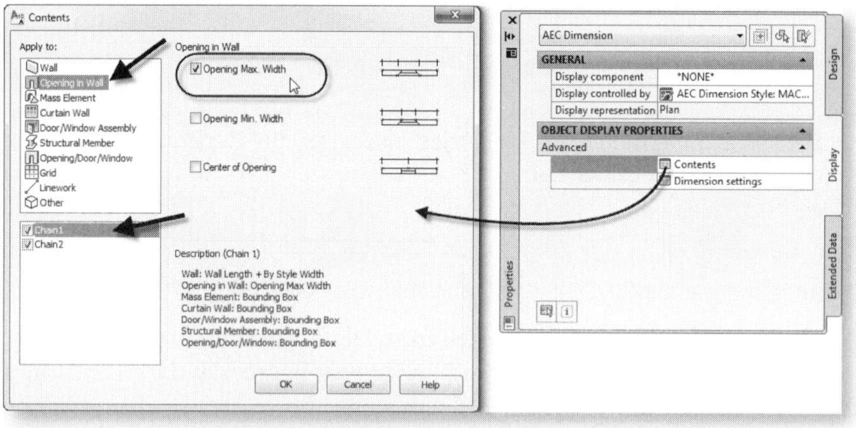

FIGURE 14.17 *Study the AEC Dimension Contents parameters for Opening in Wall*

15. Explore several of the Object types and their respective settings to get a better sense of how the AEC Dimensions operate.
16. When you are finished exploring, click Cancel to dismiss the dialog without making changes.
17. Save the file.

Edit Individual AEC Dimensions

AEC Dimensions remain linked to the objects they are dimensioning. Therefore, editing AEC Dimensions simply requires editing the model. AEC Dimensions will adjust automatically.

18. Click on one of the exterior Walls (this selects the XREF).
19. On the External Reference tab, click the Edit Reference In-Place button.
20. In the "Reference Edit" dialog box, confirm that *First Floor New* is highlighted and then click OK.
21. Select one of the Windows on the left and move it using the square location grip.

    Notice that no change to the AEC Dimensions has occurred yet. They will update as soon as we save the changes back to the XREF.
22. On the Edit Reference panel, click the Save Changes button and then click OK in the confirmation dialog box.

    Note how the drawing and the AEC Dimensions update (see Figure 14.18).

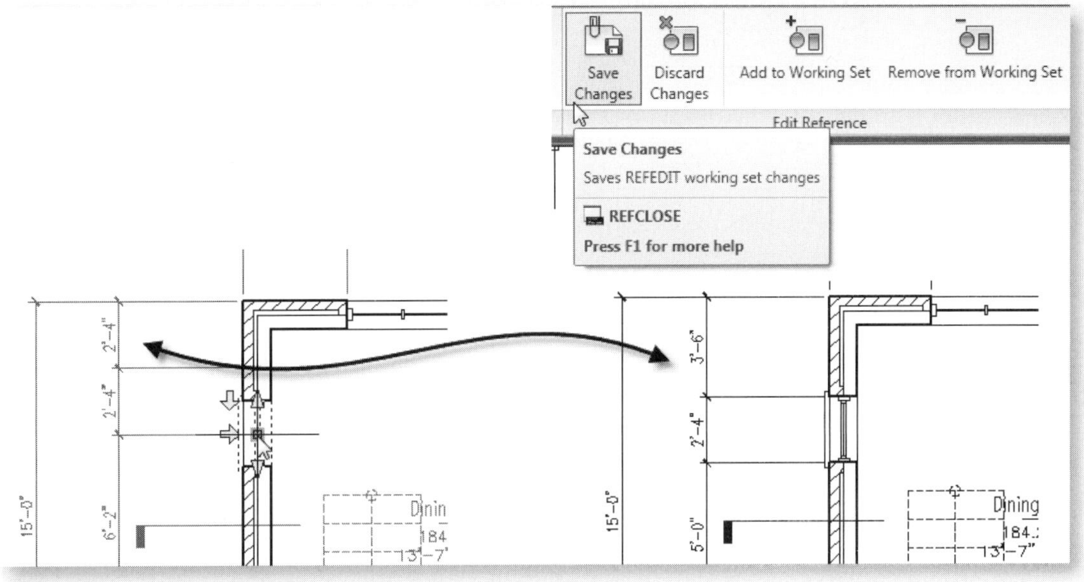

FIGURE 14.18 *Edit an object, and the AEC Dimension is automatically updated when the XREF is saved*

23. You may keep the changes or repeat the process and reverse the change.

CAUTION

You can also use Undo, but be sure to undo only the change to the geometry (not the entire Refedit session) and then click the Save Changes button on the ribbon to execute the change. If you don't, the AEC Dimensions will not update properly.

You can also grip-edit AEC Dimensions to fine-tune placement.

24. Click the AEC Dimension string at the top of the drawing.

    Several grips will appear:

- The triangular-shaped one allows you to move all Chains of the dimension string closer or farther away from the dimensioned geometry.
- The round gray grip activates the In-Place Edit mode, which we will see below.
- The small minus (−) and plus (+) sign grips allow you to add and remove points from the dimension object.
- The Arrow grip flips the text to the opposite side of the dimension line.

25. Click the triangular-shaped grip and drag all Chains up enough to allow room to dimension the porch (see Figure 14.19).

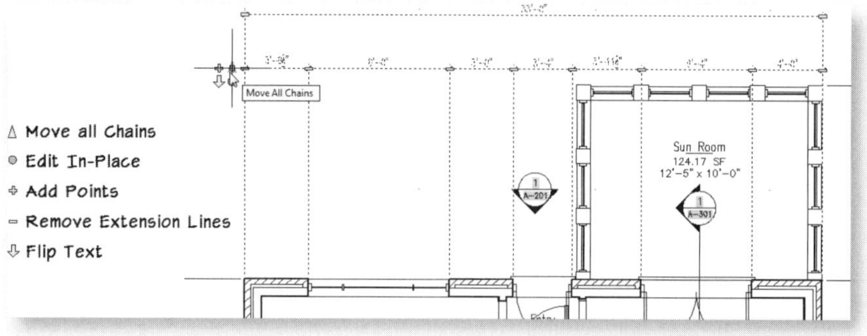

FIGURE 14.19 *Move all Chains up to allow room to dimension the porch*

AEC Dimensions are very flexible. You can attach new objects to the string at any time. You can also remove objects.

26. With the same dimension still selected, click the plus (+) sign grip.
27. At the "Select Objects" prompt, click the horizontal Curtain Wall of the porch (be certain to select the Curtain Wall and not the nested Window infills) and then press ENTER (see Figure 14.20).

    The AEC Dimension object now includes points to dimension both the exterior masonry Wall and the porch. But it does not read well.

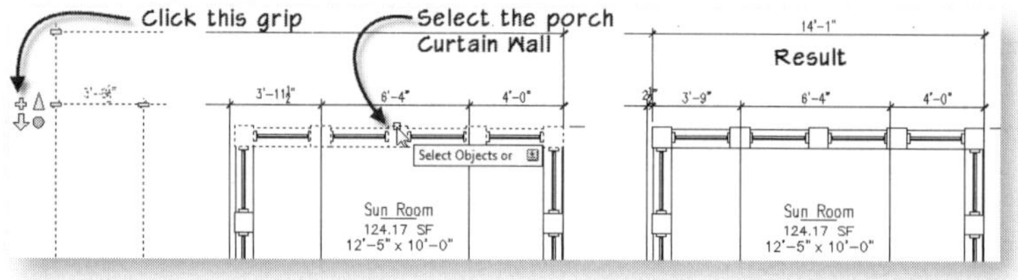

FIGURE 14.20 *Add the porch's curtain wall to the dimension string*

28. Select the same AEC Dimension object. On the AEC Dimension tab, click the **Remove Objects** tool and then click the Curtain Wall when prompted (or simply undo).

NOTE

The minus (−) sign grips are not the same as this command. The minus sign grips remove individual points; they do not remove entire objects from the dimension as the command here does.

29. Using the same grip edit method from above, move all Chains down closer to the masonry Wall.
30. Select one of the AEC Dimension objects onscreen, on the ribbon, click the Add Selected button.
31. At the "Select Objects" prompt, click only the horizontal Curtain Wall of the porch (be certain to select the Curtain Wall and not the nested Window infills) and then press ENTER.
32. At the "Specify insert point" prompt, click a point above the porch (see Figure 14.21).

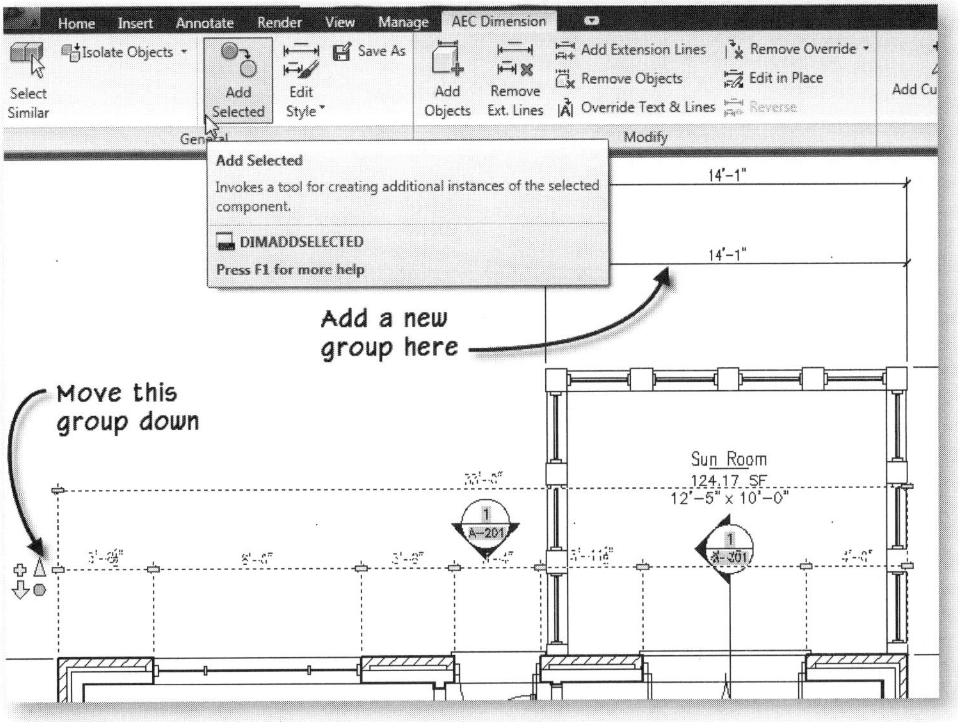

FIGURE 14.21 *Detach the Curtain Wall from the main string and add a new AEC Dimension object*

33. Save the file.

Override Text and Lines and Other Fine-Tuning

The new AEC Dimension group added to the Curtain Wall has two identical chains. It would be nice to see the overall dimension of the porch as well as the dimensions of the post spacing. We can make some other tweaks to this group as well.

34. Select the new AEC Dimension string, right-click and choose **Properties**.
35. On the Display tab, click the Contents worksheet icon.
36. Select the "Curtain Wall" entry in the "Apply to" list and then click on Chain 1.

    Remember, Chain 1 is closest to the geometry being dimensioned.

Notice that the "Bounding Box" item is selected. This is why it looks like there are two overall strings. If there were more than one segment of Curtain Wall, then each segment would have a dimension on this chain.

37. Clear the "Bounding Box" checkbox and place a check mark in the "Center" checkbox (see Figure 14.22).

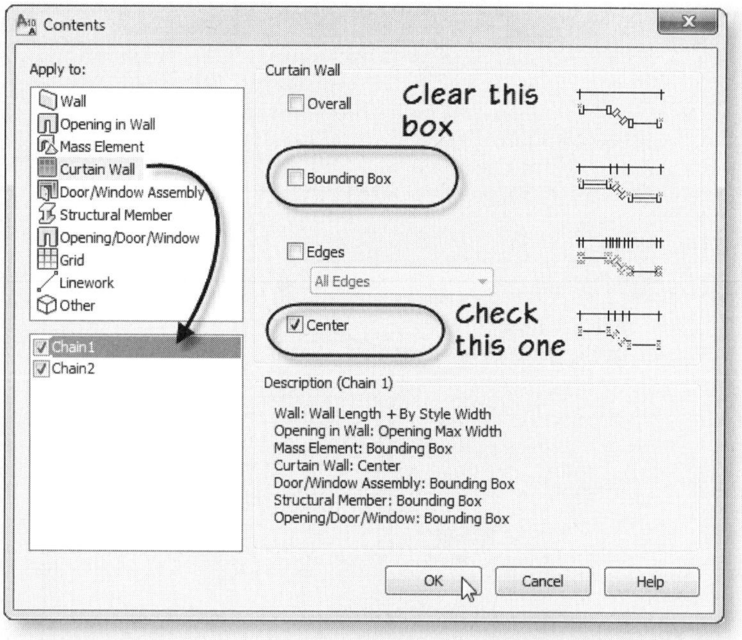

FIGURE 14.22 *Configure AEC Dimensions to dimension the mullions of Curtain Walls in Chain 1*

38. Click OK to return to the drawing and see the result (see Figure 14.23).

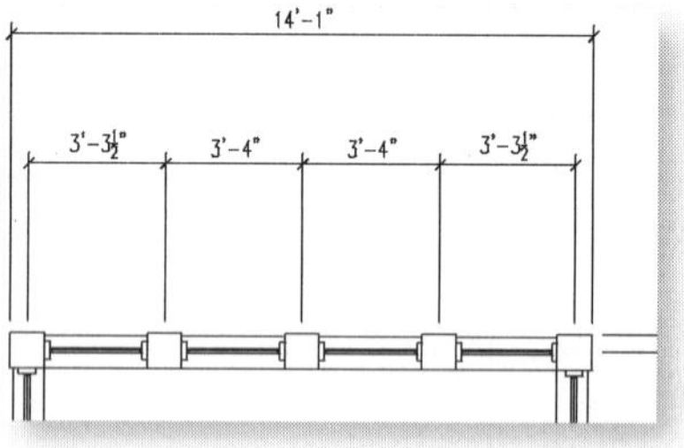

FIGURE 14.23 *The inner chain now dimensions the centers of the Curtain Wall posts*

This is better, but it still needs work.

39. Select the same dimension. On the Modify panel, click the Add Extension Lines button.
40. At the "Pick points" prompt, snap to the endpoint of the outside corner on each side of the Curtain Wall and then press ENTER (see the left side of Figure 14.24).
41. At the "Select Dimension chain" prompt, click the lower (running) Chain.

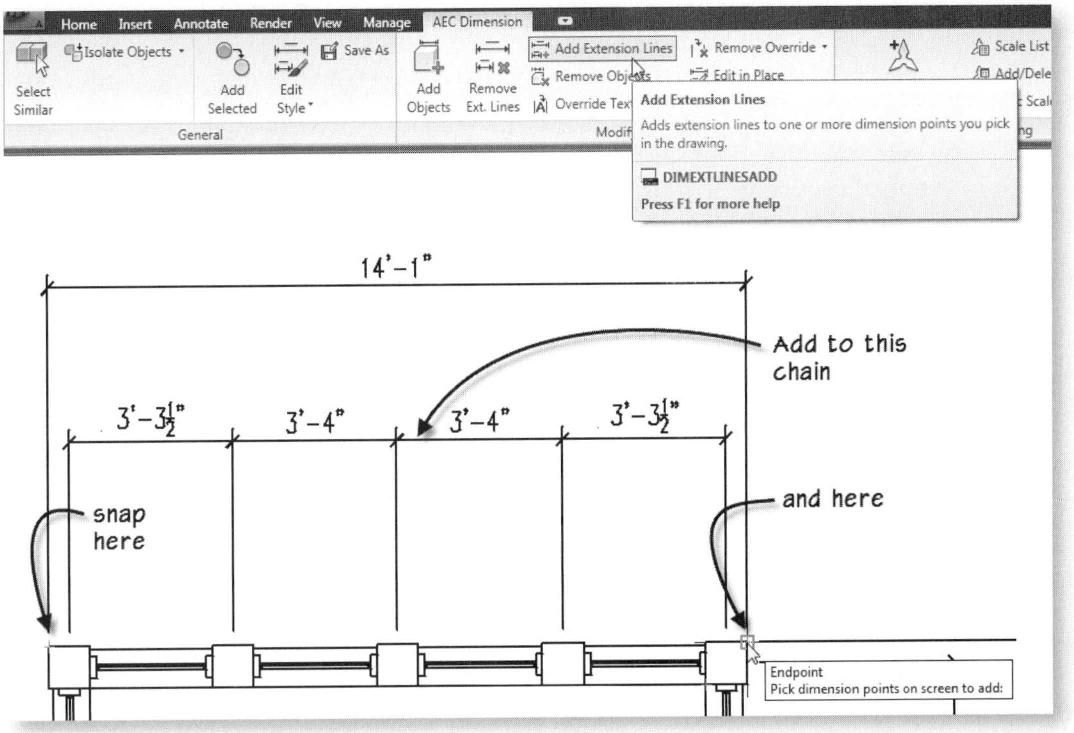

FIGURE 14.24 *Add dimension points to the two outside corners*

If you select this dimension, these two new points will appear as square grips. You can edit these manual points using these grips.

That is better still, but one more edit is in order.

42. Select the same dimension, and on the Modify panel again, click the Override Text & Lines button.
43. At the "Select dimension text to change" prompt, click on one of the middle dimensions of Chain 1 (see Figure 14.25).

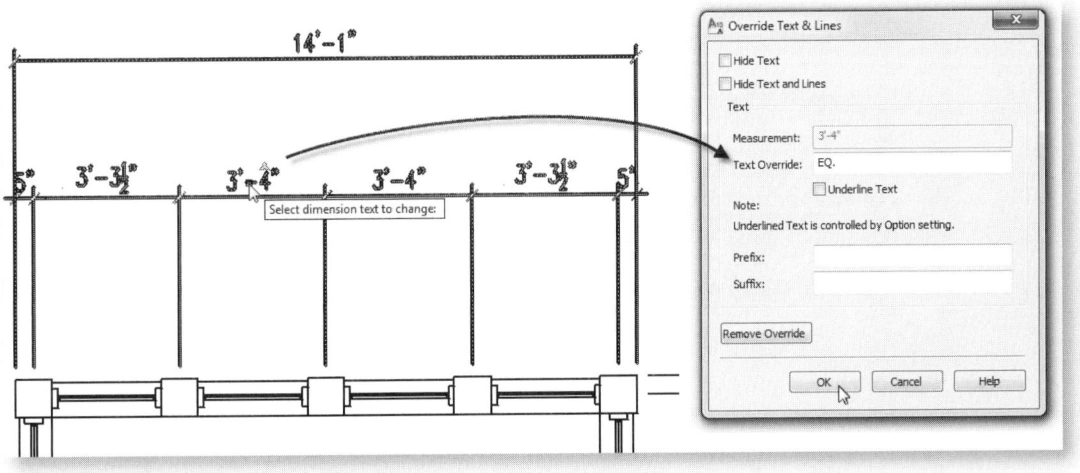

FIGURE 14.25 *Override the text to read "EQ"*

44. In the Override Text & Lines dialog box, type **EQ.** in the Text Override field and then click OK.
45. Press enter to repeat the command and override the other dimensions as well (see Figure 14.26).

Notice the small horizontal bar that appears above the text in the drawing when you apply the override. This is the Override Text & Lines Marker defined above. This marker is on a non-plotting layer and is very useful to flag dimension text that has been manually edited onscreen. Do *not* turn this component off.

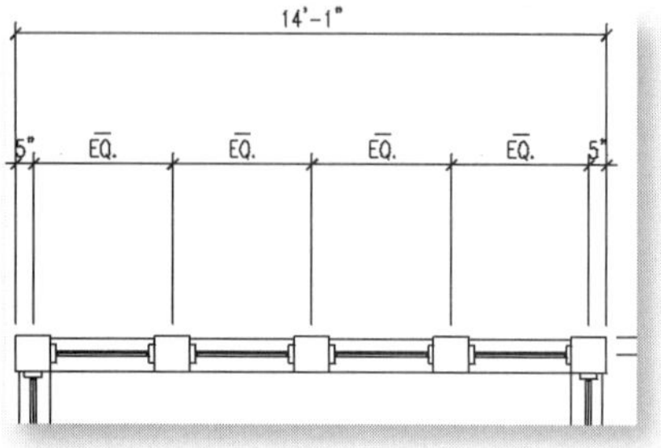

FIGURE 14.26 *The completed AEC Dimension group for the porch, including text overrides*

46. Perform similar edits on the Curtain Wall dimension string on the porch's right side.

    Return to the Override Text & Lines dialog box if you wish and experiment with other settings.
47. Save the file.

AEC Dimensions In-Place Edit

Sometimes you need to fine-tune the location of the individual dimension Chains, the text or the extension lines. This can all be done easily with in-place grip editing.

48. Select the main horizontal dimension string (the one dimensioning the horizontal Wall).
49. Click the small round gray Edit in Place grip (see Figure 14.27).

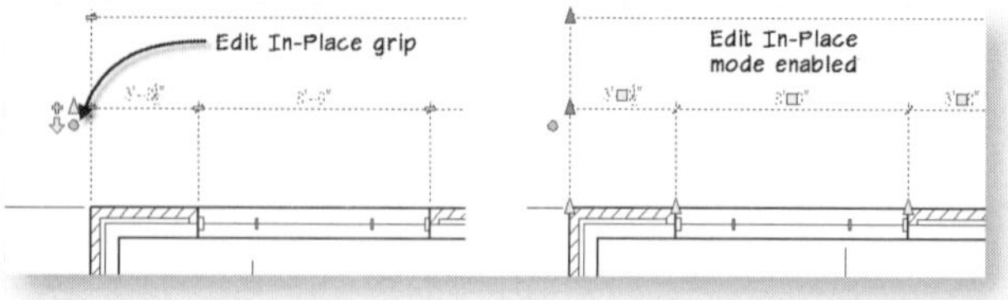

FIGURE 14.27 *Click the Edit in Place grip to reveal grips for all dimension components*

Notice the array of grip points that appears. A triangular-shaped grip appears at each extension line and dimension Chain. A square grip appears at each piece of text. Some of the triangular grips are cyan and others are magenta. The magenta ones edit a style parameter, while the cyan ones affect only the element. Therefore, if you move a chain using the magenta grip, you will be moving that chain for all AEC

Dimension objects in the drawing using that style. In this case, we want to move only one. To do this, we apply an Object Override.

With the dimension still selected:

50. On the Display tab of the Properties palette, choose **This object** from the "Display controlled by" list.

    If a warning dialog appears, click OK.

Notice that the dimension remains selected and in edit in place mode and that the magenta grips turn cyan. This means that we can now edit the dimensions on this dimension string only.

51. Click on the Move Chain grip (now cyan) of the top chain and move it above and past the AEC Dimension on the sun porch.
52. Click the Extension Line Offset grip (cyan triangular-shaped) on the right-most extension line and snap it to the corner post of the porch (see Figure 14.28).

Experiment further with the various grip points. Unfortunately, if you move text with the grips to make the dimension more legible, ACA will not create a leader pointing the text back to its dimension. You will need to draft the leader manually using the AutoCAD leader command if you choose to make such an edit.

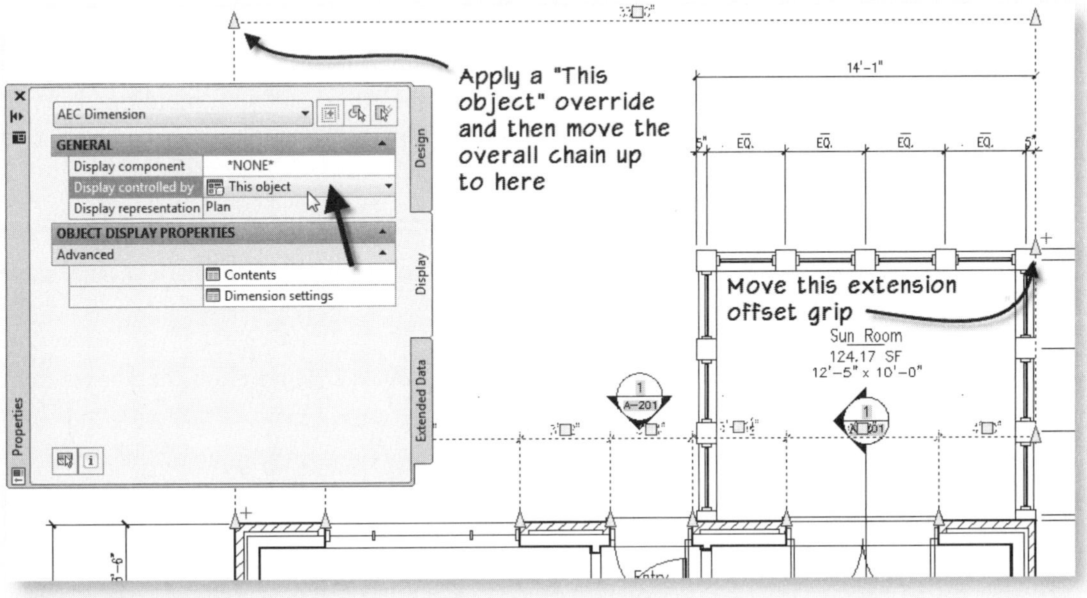

FIGURE 14.28 *Move the overall dimension away from the plan*

53. Click the small round gray Edit in Place grip again to exit the mode.
54. Save the file.

Exploring Display Settings

In addition to remaining linked to the objects they are dimensioning, AEC Dimensions interact with the display system. For example, if you want to show only overall dimensions at Low Detail and more chains at higher levels of detail, the display properties can help you achieve this with a single object. To understand this functionality, let's explore the display settings of AEC Dimensions.

Work with AEC Dimension Display

1. On the drawing status bar, open the Display Configuration pop-up menu and choose **High Detail**.
2. Zoom and pan around the drawing and study the results.
3. On the drawing status bar, open the Display Configuration pop-up menu and choose **Low Detail**.
4. Zoom and pan around the drawing again and study the results.

As you zoom and pan around the drawing, the first thing you are likely to notice is that none of the in-place edits (including text overrides) that we just performed is visible. This is because these types of edits are applied to the Display Representation (which was Plan for Medium Detail on the edits above). Therefore, you will have to repeat any edit that you wish to see at the other levels of detail. However on the positive side, since you will probably require more detailed dimensions at high detail and very schematic overall dimensions at low detail, this is probably not as big an issue as it might seem at first.

CAD MANAGER NOTE

The settings in AEC Dimension styles can be set to match the most-used cases for dimensioning in your office. For example, using the techniques that follow, you can make Low Detail show only the overall dimensions, Medium Detail show overall and one running chain and High Detail show two detailed chains and an overall.

Configure the Low Detail Display Rep of the AEC Dimension Style

For Low Detail display to be truly "low," the dimensions should be simplified. Low Detail might be used at small scales like 1/16" = 1'-0" [1:200]. As mentioned above, it is likely that we would wish to see only some overall dimension strings in this scenario.

Continue with the Low Detail display configuration active.

5. Select the AEC Dimension on the left side of the plan, right-click, choose **Properties** and then click the Display tab.
6. Click the Contents worksheet icon.
7. In the "Apply to" list, choose "Wall" and Chain 1. Remove the checkboxes from all options on the right (see Figure 14.29).

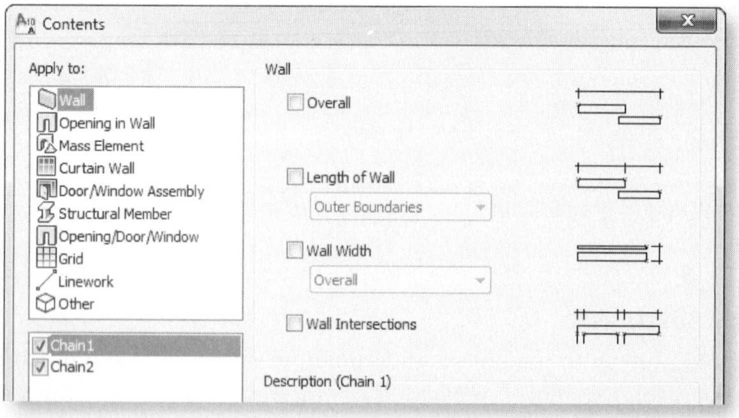

FIGURE 14.29 *Remove all dimensions from Wall in Chain1 at Low Detail*

8. Select Chain 2, deselect Length of Wall and Wall Width and check Overall instead (see Figure 14.30).

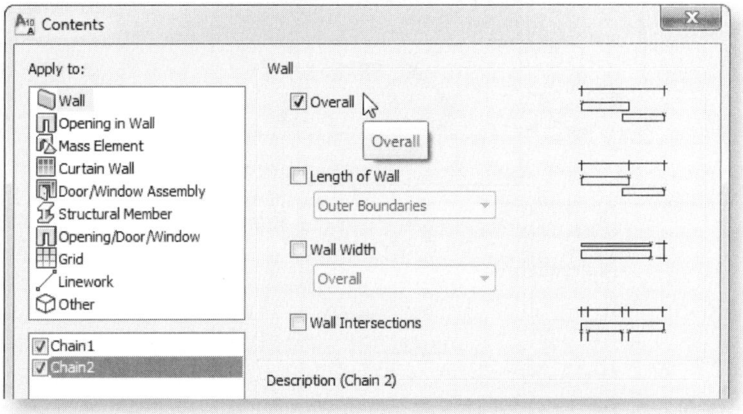

FIGURE 14.30 *Configure Plan Low Detail to display overall dimensions only*

9. Repeat the same process for the Curtain Wall, choosing the same boxes.
10. For the Opening in Wall entry, clear all boxes for both Chains.
11. Click OK.

The overall Chains (Chain 2) are a bit far away from the Walls in the default configuration, particularly since we are now essentially turning off Chain 1.

12. On the Properties palette, click the Dimension settings worksheet icon.
13. Change the Distance between Chains in the AEC Dimension Settings area to **0**.

This will place the single overall string that we configured here in the same spot as Chain 1 in the Medium Detail configuration.

14. Click OK when finished to view the results.
15. Repeat the process above to move the overall chain above the porch.

CAUTION

Don't use the Move All Chains grip; if you do, it will move the dimensions in all Display Reps. Use the process shown above to add an override to "This object" and move just the one chain.

Remember to select only the horizontal dimension and to apply a "This Object" override before moving the chain with the grip.

While these changes make for a lower detailed display, you may wish to print this drawing at a different scale. With annotation scaling, this is easy to achieve. The Residential project is configured to use 1/4" = 1'0" [1:50] for plans like this one. However, if you went to Low Detail, you might be planning to print the drawing at 1/8" = 1'0" [1:100] or even 1/16" = 1'0" [1:200]. Hover your mouse over the dimensions and notice the presence of the annotation scale icon on the cursor. You can make this change easily with the Annotation Scale pop-up menu on the drawing status bar.

16. On the drawing status bar, choose **1/8" = 1'0"** [**1:100**] from the Annotation Scale pop-up (see Figure 14.31).

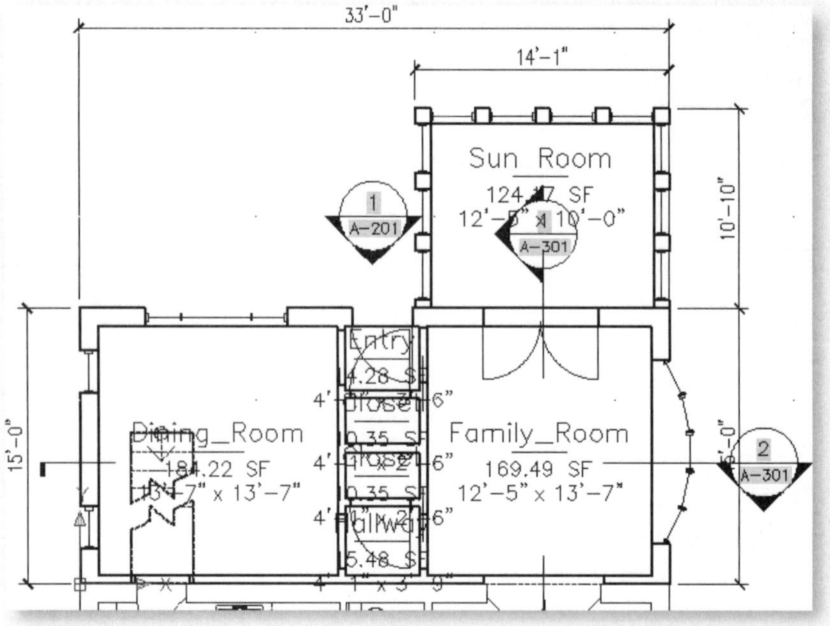

FIGURE 14.31 *Fine-tune the placement of Chains and change the Annotation scale to complete the Low Detail Display*

Notice that the AEC Dimensions have all scaled up with larger text and arrowheads. The other annotation in this View has also scaled. If you decided to stay with this scale, you would need to make some adjustments to the room tags to make them more legible. We will forgo this exercise for now. If you need an 1/8" = 1'0" [1:100] plan for the project, you could use the yellow grip on the room tags to move them around in this scale only or you could generate a new 1/8" = 1'0" [1:100] plan View file on Project Navigator. Feel free to experiment with these options before continuing or do so later as an additional exercise. Right now we will take a quick look at the AutoCAD dimension style and see the setting that makes these dimensions annotative.

17. On the Annotate tab, on the Dimensions panel, click the **Dimension style** button.
18. In the "Dimension Style Manager" select Annotative on the left side and then click the Modify button on the right.
19. Click the Fit tab (see Figure 14.32).

Notice the check mark in the Annotative box in the "Scale for dimension features" area. If you want to learn more about annotative dimensions, click the icon next to the checkbox to launch the help.

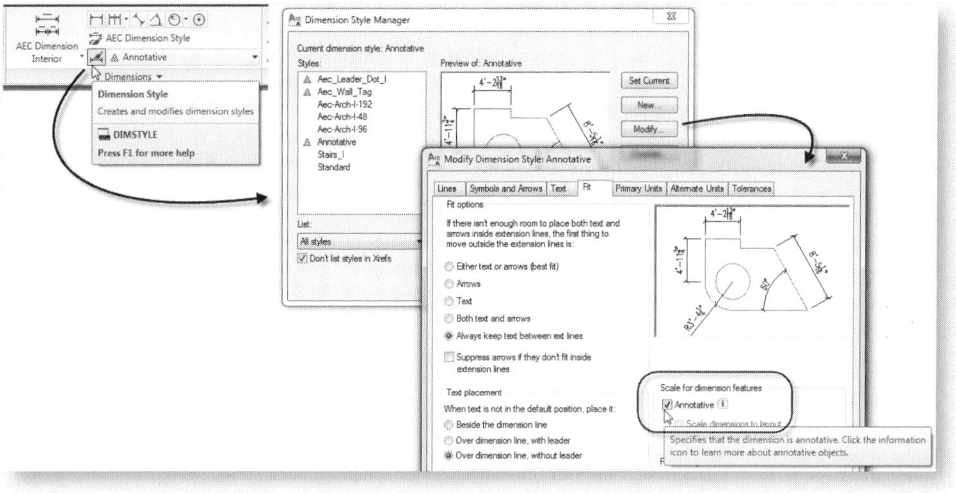

FIGURE 14.32 *The Annotative checkbox make a dimension style annotative*

20. Click Cancel and then close to return to the drawing without making any changes.
21. Change the current Display Configuration back to **Medium Detail**.

    Notice that all of the overrides made in this display are still applied.
22. On the drawing status bar, choose **1/4" = 1'0"** [**1:50**] from the Annotation Scale pop-up.

We will not bother to apply similar overrides to the High Detail configuration since we have only two chains. But in larger projects where you have more complex dimensions, you can use the process covered here to configure Low Detail to show only one chain, Medium to show two and High Detail to show three.

23. Save the file.

Linking Display Configuration to Annotation Scale

As an optional enhancement, you can link the Display Configuration to the Annotation Scale. For example, if you always want Medium Detail to display when you change the scale to 1/4" = 1'0" [1:50] and Low Detail to display at 1/8" = 1'0" [1:100], you can set the file to make this change automatically. To do this, from the Application Menu, choose **Utilities > Drawing Setup**. On the Scale tab, select a scale and then at the bottom choose the Display Configuration that you wish to associate. The effect of such a change will be that ACA will automatically change the Display Configuration when you choose a different scale in the drawing. Unfortunately, this only works one way. In other words, choosing a different scale will automatically change the current Display Configuration; choosing a different Display Configuration will not however change the scale.

Dimensioning to Wall Components

Specific dimension points can be added directly within a Wall style. AEC Dimensions can then be configured to automatically dimension to these specified points when dimensioning Walls of a particular style. Using this method, you can limit AEC Dimensions to dimension only to the face of a stud in an interior partition or only to the CMU in a block and brick Wall.

Adding Interior AEC Dimensions

Let's add a string of dimensions on the interior of the new addition and use it to explore some of the style-based capabilities of AEC Dimensions. We will create a horizontal dimension string across the middle of the plan.

1. On the Annotate tab, on the Dimensions panel, click the AEC Dimension - Interior tool.
2. Following the prompt, select each of the vertical Walls in the addition (two exterior and two interior) and then press ENTER (see Figure 14.33).

> **TIP**
>
> **If you have trouble selecting the closet walls, use a crossing window selection to select the Walls and Spaces and then hold down the SHIFT key and click the Spaces again to remove them from the selection set.**

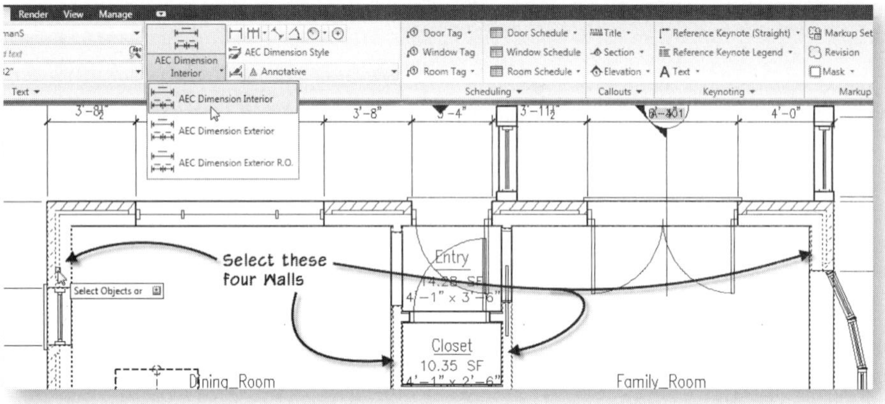

FIGURE 14.33 *Select Walls to add a Dimension on the interior*

3. At the "Specify insertion point" prompt, click a point *above* the plan.

   When you are prompted to place the dimension, if you click inside the plan at the desired location, ACA will attempt to create a vertical string. Therefore, you need to move the mouse up and outside the plan and then use the grip to move the string back into the plan after creating it.
4. Select the new AEC Dimension object, click the Move All Chains grip and drag it down into the plan (see Figure 14.34).

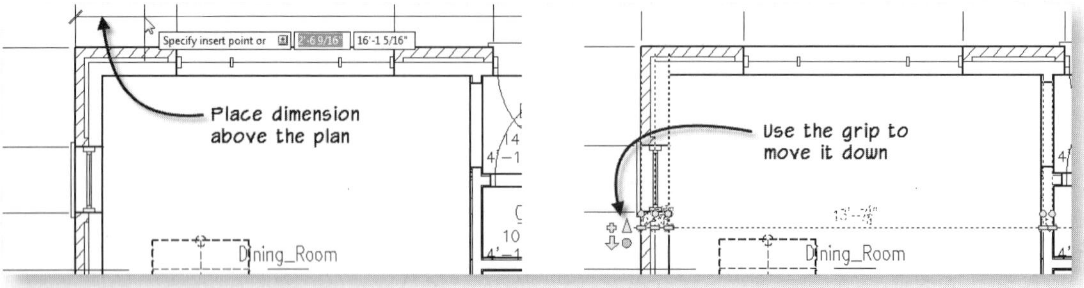

FIGURE 14.34 *Use the Move All Chains grip to move all chains down into the plan*

5. With the AEC Dimension still selected, on the ribbon, click the Save As button.
6. On the General tab, name the style **MACA Residential Interior** and then click OK.

Grip Editing Component Dimensions

7. Zoom in on the closet area (see Figure 14.35).

Notice that there is a round grip above each extension line. If you hover your mouse over one of these grips, you will receive a tool tip as with other grips. These grips control the position of style-based component dimensions. To enable such grips in an AEC Dimension style, two separate settings are required: you must choose the appropriate "By Style" option in the AEC Dimension object style, and you must indicate in the Wall style which components should be dimensioned. We discussed the editing and creation of Wall styles in detail in Chapter 10. However, we saved this bit of functionality for this chapter since it is used exclusively by the AEC Dimension objects.

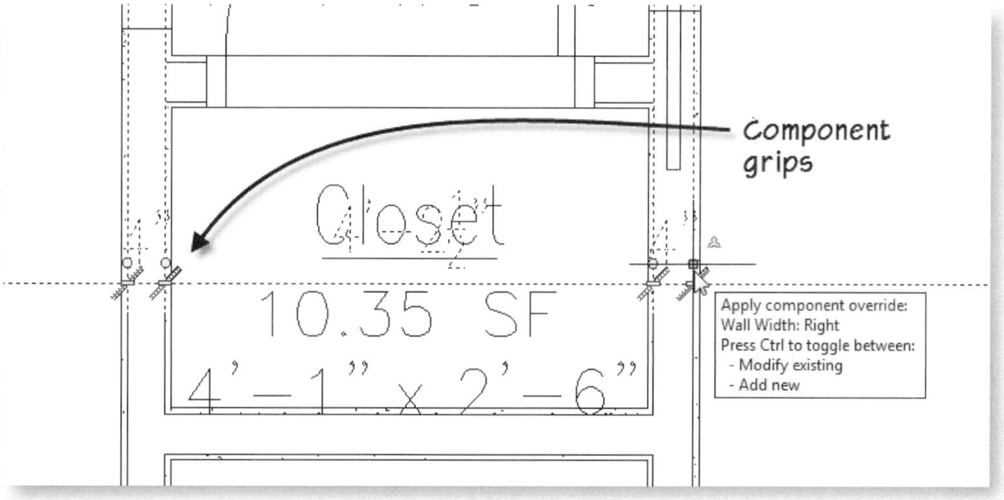

FIGURE 14.35 *Grips appear at each Wall component when configured appropriately*

8. Click one of the round grips above one of the extension lines and slowly drag it left to right.

Notice that the grip editing process will highlight available edges beneath your cursor as you drag. For example, you can snap this point to the outside of the drywall or the center of the stud.

9. Drag the grip to the outside edge of the Wall (outside the GWB component) and then click.

Notice that the a new dimension value appears with a yellow grip. The yellow color is a flag used to indicate a manually overridden dimension. This makes it very easy to identify such edits later in the project.

10. To remove a dimension point, click the minus (–) grip beneath it. Remove the yellow grip.

11. Pan over to the left side of the plan and study the same dimension string at the masonry Wall (see Figure 14.36).

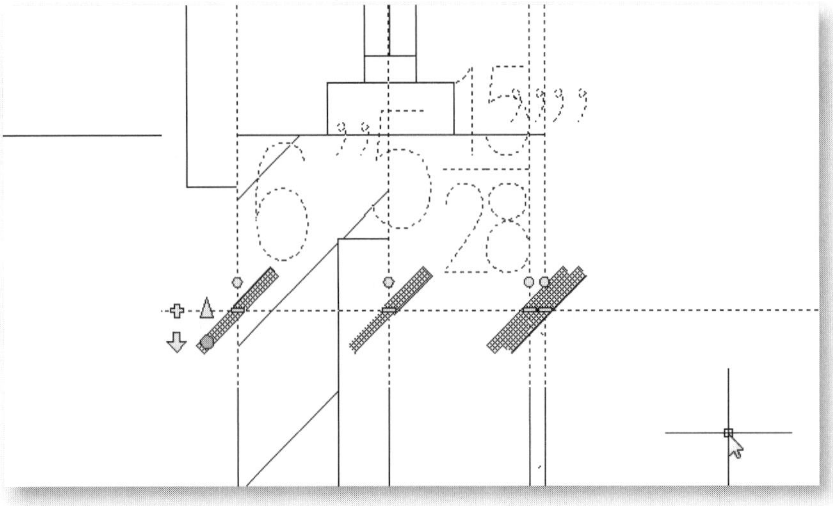

FIGURE 14.36 *The Masonry Wall indicates different dimension points than the interior stud Wall style*

12. Click the minus (–) grip on one of the middle points.

Notice the red "deleted points marker" (an 'X' in a circle). This component is turned on for AEC Dimensions and set to a non-plotting layer by default. If you prefer, you can turn it off by editing the display properties. This shows you a style-based point that has been deleted.

13. Click a round grip and drag a point back to the spot of the deleted one.

It will reappear. You can also undo.

14. Right-click and choose **Deselect All**.

Exploring Wall Style Settings

Many methods of dimensioning are used by architectural professionals. Some like to dimension to the finished face of the Walls, while others prefer to use face of stud. Either method is acceptable; it is a matter of professional preference. Rather than advocate a specific methodology here, we will focus on the procedures needed to edit the defaults.

15. Select the masonry Wall.

    The entire XREF will highlight.
16. On the ribbon, click the **Open Reference** button.

    You are now in the *First Floor New* Construct file.
17. Select the same Wall again in the Construct, on the Wall tab of the ribbon, click the **Edit Style** button.
18. Click the Components tab (see Figure 14.37).

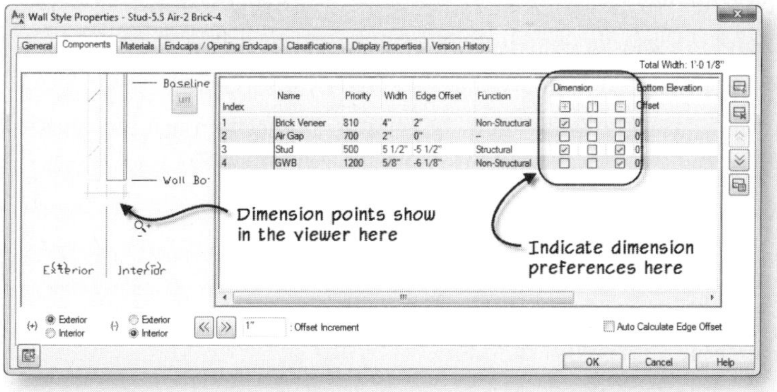

FIGURE 14.37 *Edit the Wall style in the Construct to see which components are configured for dimensioning*

Click in the viewer at the left and carefully roll and drag with the wheel to zoom in on the bottom of the image you can also right-click for Zoom and Pan. (Be careful not to drag the left button or you will change the viewing direction. If you do, you can use the ViewCube to reset to Left.) This will display some short gray lines at the bottom of the preview image. Also, there will be labels on the left and right indicating which side is exterior and which is interior. This can be controlled with the radio buttons beneath the viewer.

In the list of components at the right, scroll over to the columns indicated in Figure 14.37. Here we can indicate the function of each component. Click on an item to reveal a pop-up list. The choices are "Structural," "Non-Structural" and none (--). These three choices are fixed in the software. Next to the Function column are a series of checkboxes under the "Dimension" heading. Using these boxes, you can indicate that AEC Dimensions should dimension to either the left, right or center point of the component. You can choose multiple boxes on each component as you can see in the figure. All of the out-of-the-box Wall styles provided with AutoCAD Architecture have settings pre-configured for both the Function and Dimension columns. If you recall Chapter 10, this particular Wall style was created directly from an out-of-the-box style and we simply modified the Width and Edge offsets parameters and the Endcap conditions. Therefore the Dimension points should already be configured.

In this particular Wall style, the default settings indicate Dimension points at both side of the Stud component which is the Structural component of the Wall Style and at the outer edges of the Wall itself (outside of brick and inside of the GWB). Let's assume that we did not want to dimension the GWB.

19. Remove the check mark from the dimension point next to GWB and then click OK (see Figure 14.38).

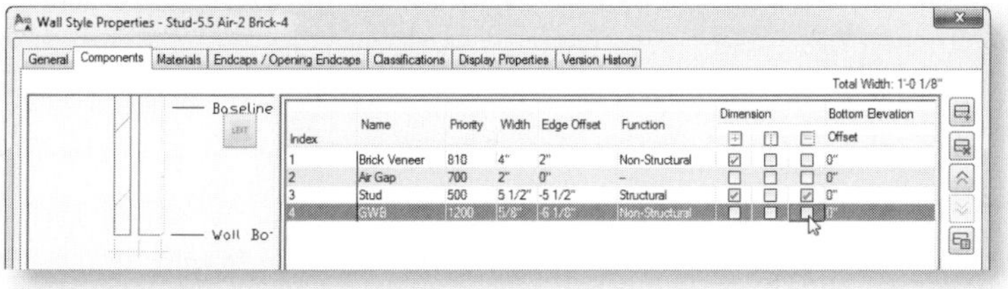

FIGURE 14.38 *Clear the Dimension points for GWB*

20. Save and close the file.
21. Back in the *A-FP01* View file (which should still be open), reload the XREFs. Note that the dimension on the drywall immediately disappears.
22. Click the Edit in Place grip (see Figure 14.27) above) and then use the grips to move the text around to make it more legible (see Figure 14.39).

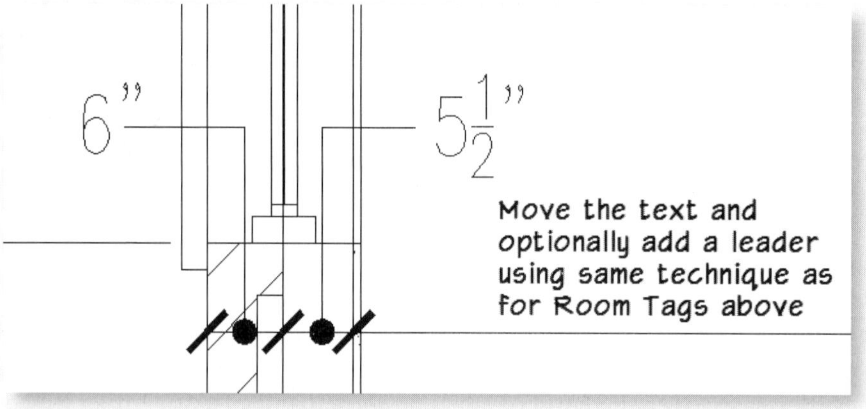

FIGURE 14.39 *Reload the XREFs, adjust and the Dimension text*

Note that this change has occurred on both sides of the plan. This is not the only way to exclude the drywall. Suppose you were interested in dimensioning the studs only—without the drywall or the brick. To do this, you could return to the *First Floor New* Construct and clear more checkboxes from the exterior Wall style. You could also make a simple adjustment directly on the AEC Dimension object itself. Recall the Function column in the Figures 14.37 and 14.38 above. There is a setting in the AEC Dimension style that will read only the Structural components of the Wall styles. Let's take a look at that setting now.

23. Select the interior AEC Dimension.
24. On the Display tab of the Properties palette, click the Contents worksheet icon.
25. Select Wall, and for Wall Width, choose **Structural By Style** (see Figure 14.40).

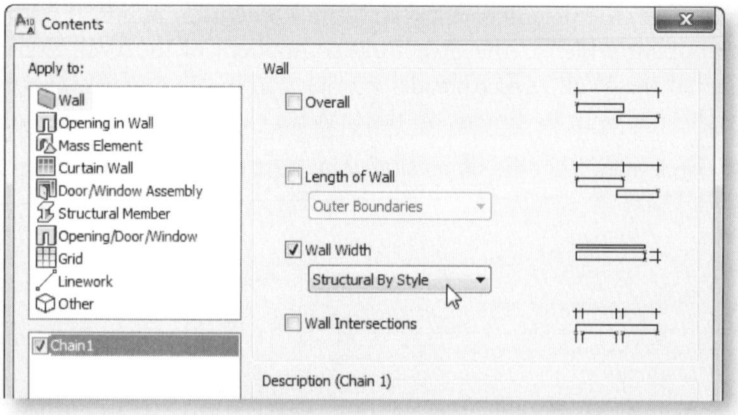

FIGURE 14.40 *Configure the Interior Dimensions to apply only to the Wall's Structural Components*

26. Click OK to see the results.

    Notice that the exterior Walls now dimension only the Stud component.

Dimension to One Face of the Stud

Sometimes people like to see a dimension on only one side of the stud. For this, we return to the Wall style.

27. Repeat the steps above to reopen the *First Floor New* Construct.
28. Select one of the interior partitions, and on the ribbon click the **Edit Style** button.
29. On the Components tab, clear the check mark from only one of the Dimension checkboxes.
30. Click OK. Save and close the file.
31. Reload the XREF (see Figure 14.41).

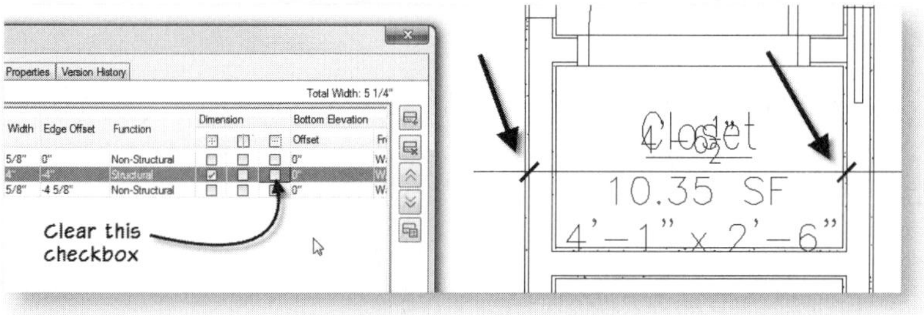

FIGURE 14.41 *Dimension to just one side of the Stud*

If you want opposite sides of the studs dimensioned, use the grip techniques shown above to override the component dimension point on one side. If you wish to experiment further, you can add other interior dimensions, such as a vertical interior string to the plan. Make any adjustments using the techniques covered here.

32. Save the file.

Using AEC Content Dimensions

For all linear dimensioning needs, you are encouraged to use the AEC Dimensions covered in the previous topic. Unfortunately, they do not allow the dimensioning of non-linear items. Therefore, for non-linear dimensions such as angular, radial and diameter, you can use the tools in the Content Library. Tools appear on the Dimensions panel of the Annotate tab, but these are the standard AutoCAD variety and do not auto-layer. If you use the versions on the Dimensions tool palette instead, they work identically and they also auto-layer. This is reason enough to use the tool palette tools instead of the AutoCAD counterparts on the ribbon.

Adjust the layer setting used by all of the ACA Dimension tools by editing the DIMLINE layer key. All of the ACA Dimension tools use the current Dimension style active in the drawing. Therefore, make sure that the current DimStyle in the template is the company standard.

MANAGER NOTE CAD

Access AEC Content Dimensions (Layer-Keyed AutoCAD Dimensions)

1. On the tool palettes, right-click the title bar spine and choose Document to load the documentation group.

   If the tool palettes are not displayed, you can click the Tools button on the Annotate tab of the ribbon.
2. On the Dimension tool palette, click the Angular tool (see Figure 14.42).
3. Follow the Command Line prompts and dimension something in the drawing; for example, the angle of the Windows in the Bow Window.

Since this is a standard AutoCAD dimension routine, you will not be able to use the select objects options; AutoCAD dimensions do not work through XREFs as AEC Dimensions do. Therefore, you must press ENTER to get the Select vertex option.

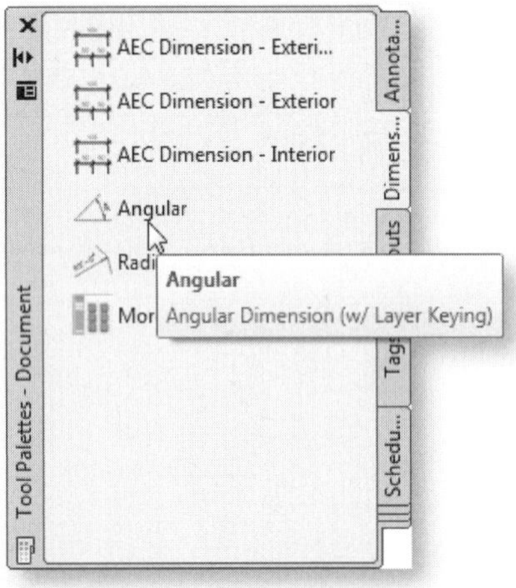

FIGURE 14.42 *The AEC Content Dimension tools*

4. The layer will not change until the command is complete, usually after you have pressed ENTER.
5. Add some Angular and Radius dimensions using the appropriate tools and following the prompts.
6. Save the file when finished.

Repeat any of the above techniques on the second floor *A-FP02* View file. You can also switch to the Commercial Project and try them out in A-FP03 as well.

DOCUMENTATION CONTENT

Within the ACA Content library are scores of symbols, routines and macros designed to add the myriad annotation symbology required by architectural construction documents. Many of these routines are simple macros that add an AutoCAD block or polyline boundary, layered and scaled properly for the drawing. The Content Browser and the DesignCenter can be used to interface with this documentation content. Because most of this content is composed of AutoCAD entities that do not use display control, it is beneficial to add these items in the View files. This will keep display management simple and layer management to a minimum. In the following sequence, we will continue to articulate the First Floor Plan View file *A-FP01*. See the introduction at the start of this chapter for more information on the topic of annotating in View files.

Add Text and Leaders

A sampling of frequently used annotation content is provided on the Annotation tool palette. To see the complete collection of what is available, open the Content Browser and browse the various categories of the *Design Tool Catalog – Imperial* [*Design Tool Catalog – Metric*].

Make sure the tool palettes are open (press CTRL + 3).

1. On the Annotation tool palette, click the Text tool.
2. Click two points within the existing house to set the width of the text block.
3. Press ENTER to open the Mtext editor. On the Text Formatting toolbar that appears, choose **Annotative** from the Style list.
4. From the Font list, choose Arial Black and set the Text Height to **1/4"** [**6**].
5. Type **Existing House** in the text edit worksheet and then click OK (see Figure 14.43).

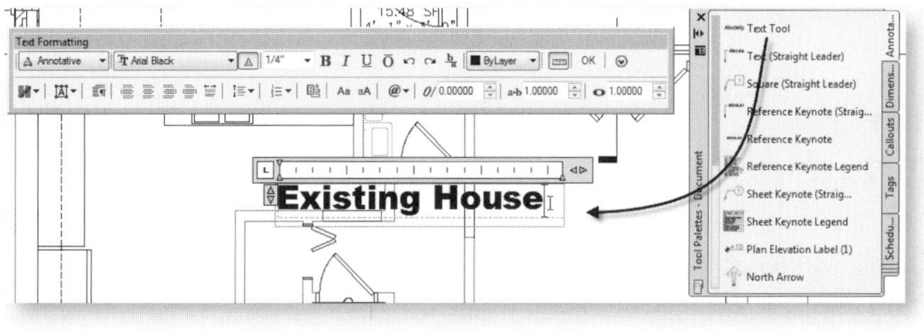

FIGURE 14.43 *Editing text in the text edit worksheet*

Using the Annotative text style means that the text will resize automatically if the scale of the drawing changes—just like the dimensions and other symbols above. If you like, you can try changing scales to see this. Text styles are annotative when the Annotative checkbox is selected in their style.

6. On the Annotation tool palette, click the Text (Straight Leader) tool.
7. At the "Specify first point of leader line" prompt, click a point near the existing kitchen window.
8. Drag out the leader, click again, click a point to indicate the width of the text block and then type the following note: **Existing Window to be removed. Install New Hardwood Pass-through**. Press ENTER to complete.
9. Adjust the position of the note to a suitable location (see Figure 14.44).

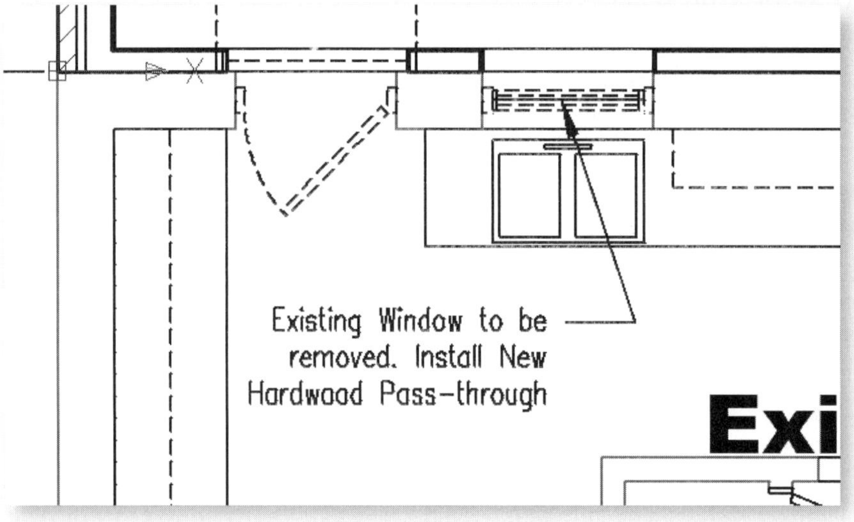

FIGURE 14.44 *Add a text note with leader*

Add Window Tags

We have already added some Room and Space tags above. Let's add some Window tags here.

10. On the Tags tool palette, click the Window Tag tool.
11. At the "Select Object to Tag" prompt, click on the lower Window to the left in the new addition.

    In the Edit Property Set Data dialog, edit any values you wish and then click OK.
12. At the "Specify location of tag" prompt, click a point just outside the Window.
13. Repeat the steps for the remaining Windows. (It is not necessary to tag the Windows of the Porch.)

    The tags may not have the exact numbering that you desire. We can renumber them sequentially with the Renumber Data Tool on the Documentation palette.
14. On the Documentation palette, click the Renumber Data Tool.
15. In the Renumber Data dialog box, choose **WindowObjects** from the Property Set list and **Number** from the Property list, leave both Start Number and Increment set to **1**, and then click OK (see Figure 14.45).

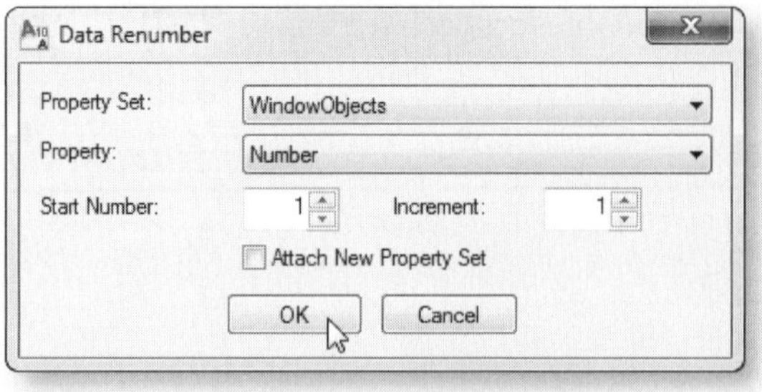

FIGURE 14.45 *Using the Data Renumber tool*

16. Following the command prompts, click the objects in the order that you would like them numbered and then press ENTER.

NOTE

This tool can be used to renumber any auto-increment Property, such as the Room Tags used in the Commercial Project at the start of the chapter.

In the next chapter, we will explore Schedules and Tags in further detail.

17. Save and close the file.

There are other tools on the Annotation tool palette and dozens more in the Content Browser library. Feel free to try other tools in this file and in the other View files in this project. We will explore the Keynote functions in Chapter 17. If you wish, you can load the Commercial Project and annotate it as well. See Appendix A for suggested exercises. In addition to dimensions, targets and tags, we can annotate our drawing sets with schedules. This topic is covered in detail in the next chapter.

Elevation Labels

1. On the Project Navigator, double-click the *A-CM01* file to open it.

This is the Section and Elevation Composite Model built in Chapter 5. Since that time, we have swapped out the *Existing Roof* file for the *New Roof* file in Chapter 12. Otherwise, there have been no changes to this file.

2. Zoom in on East Elevation.
3. On the Annotation tool palette, click on the Plan Elevation Label (1) tool.

NOTE

This symbol is meant to be used on plans, but it works equally well on elevations and sections. There are other Elevation Label symbols in the Content library. Feel free to choose a different one if you wish. They all work the same way.

4. At the "Specify insertion point" prompt, use Object Snap Tracking and line it up with the first floor line as shown in Figure 14.46.

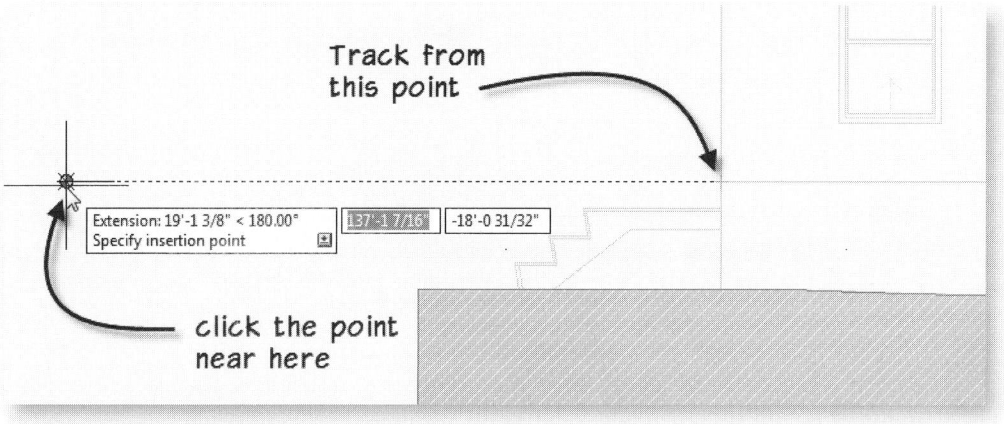

FIGURE 14.46 *Line up the Elevation Label with the First Floor Level*

5. Click a point to place the symbol.

6. In the Add Elevation Label dialog box, type **First Floor** in the Prefix field and **AFF** in the Suffix field.
7. In the bottom left corner of the Add Elevation Label dialog box, click the Define UCS icon.
8. When prompted, click the endpoint of the ground line in the Elevation as the Base point of the UCS.
9. Pull the cursor straight up and click to set the Z direction (see Figure 14.47).

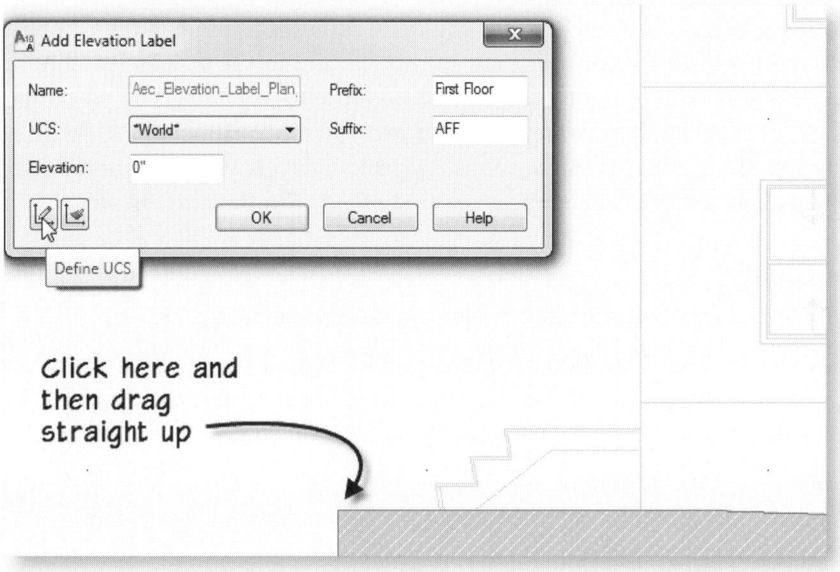

FIGURE 14.47 *Define a UCS for Elevations*

10. At the "Enter name for UCS" prompt, type **East Elevation** as the name of the UCS and then press ENTER.
11. Click OK in the Add Elevation Label dialog box to complete the routine (see Figure 14.48).

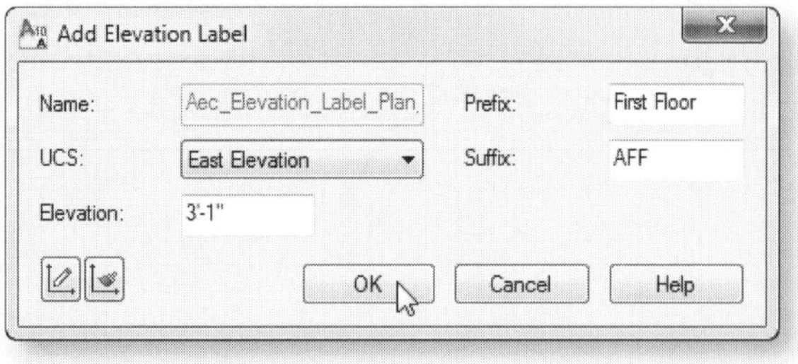

FIGURE 14.48 *Verify all values and then click OK to add the Label*

Repeat the steps to add additional labels. This time the UCS already reads "East Elevation," so you do not need to define an additional UCS. Simply type in prefixes such as "Second Floor" and "Eave" and place the labels (see Figure 14.49). The nice thing about these routines is that although they reference a UCS, they do not actually make it active. Therefore, your current UCS in the drawing remains the World Coordinate System for all other drawing operations. Try moving one of the labels.

You will notice that the elevation changes. This is because it is linked to that UCS. Add an Elevation Label to the basement level; notice that it automatically registers as a negative number.

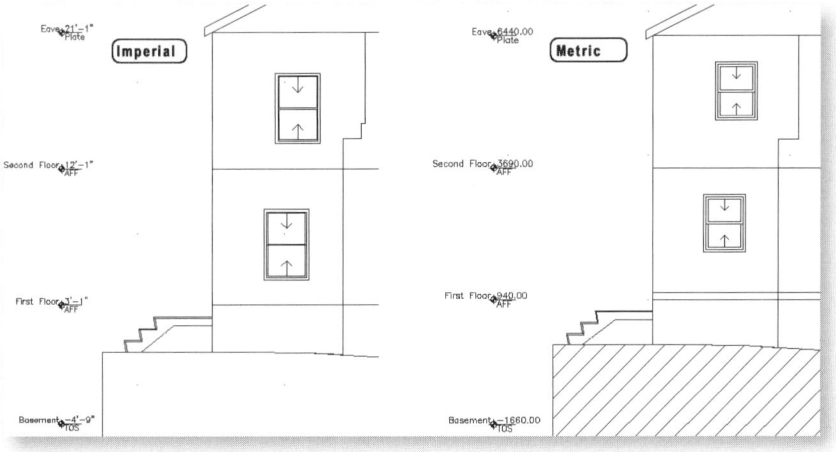

FIGURE 14.49 *Labels added to all key points on the Elevation*

If you later decide to reference another benchmark rather than the ground line we picked here, simply redefine the UCS; all of the labels that reference it will update automatically.

12. Save and close all project files.

ADDITIONAL EXERCISES

Additional exercises have been provided in Appendix A. In Appendix A, you will find exercises to add dimensions and annotation to each of the remaining View files in both the Residential and Commercial Projects. It is not necessary that you complete these exercises to begin the next chapter. They are provided to enhance your learning experience. Completed projects for each of the exercises have been provided in the *Chapter14/Complete* folder.

SUMMARY

- You want to add all annotation content to View files to take full advantage of the ACA Drawing Management features.
- You should create a new View file for each different type of drawing in each discipline at each unique scale.
- Room Tags are added with a simple Content routine.
- Multiple Tags can be added at the same time after the first one is placed.
- The Same Tag added to different View files will always remain synchronized to the Property Set Data stored in the Construct file.
- The Tags in each View can be placed in different locations and at different scales and can even use different symbols.
- Creating new tags is easy with the Define Schedule Tag wizard.
- AEC Dimensions are updated automatically with objects as they change.
- AEC Dimensions work with ACA and AutoCAD objects.

- AutoCAD associative dimensions work only on AutoCAD entities and not on AEC objects.
- AutoCAD dimensions do not use display control; AEC Dimensions do.
- AEC Dimensions can be displayed at different scales dynamically.
- AEC Dimensions can dimension objects through XREFs.
- AEC Dimensions can key into specific points within complex Wall styles.
- Break marks, north arrows, bar scales, revision clouds and scores of additional content are available as drag-and-drop content from the Content Browser, tool palettes or DesignCenter.

CHAPTER 15

Generating Schedules

INTRODUCTION

Schedules are an important part of any architectural document set. Creating a Schedule presents many unique challenges, among them deciding what to schedule, how to format it and (most importantly) how to keep the information up to date and accurate. ACA Schedule objects are ideally suited for creating any type of architectural schedule, such as Door Schedules, Equipment Schedules, Wall Schedules and Room Finish Schedules. Schedules can also play an important role in tracking key quantity information within the project at any phase regardless of whether the Schedule is intended for publication or internal use. When using AutoCAD Architecture as a Building Information Modeling (BIM) solution, schedules provide the "Information". In this chapter, we will explore the many facets of the Schedule Table tool set that AutoCAD Architecture provides.

OBJECTIVES

In this chapter, we will be working on our Commercial Project. We will begin by adding a simple Space Inventory Schedule using the default styles. With this Schedule style as our lab, we will explore the many tools and functions available in the complete Schedule Table tool set. At the completion of the exercise, we will have fully customized the Schedule in format and in the data it tracks. At the end of the chapter is an advanced tutorial on creating a Project-Based Door Schedule and associated tags for the complete building. We will also revisit the Display Theme objects. The following topics will be explored in this chapter:

- Learn to use the built-in Schedule Tables and Styles.
- Understand Property Sets.
- Work with Schedule Table Styles.
- Learn to adjust formatting and presentation of Schedule Data.
- Explore the pros and cons of automatically updating Schedules.
- Work with Display Themes.
- Explore Project-Based Schedule tools.

OVERVIEW AND KEY FEATURES

The Schedule Table objects offer many features and benefits:

- **Schedules can be linked to ALL objects**—When you decide what to schedule, both standard AutoCAD objects (such as lines, polylines and circles) and AEC objects (such as Walls, Doors and Windows) can be included in a Schedule. This allows for greater flexibility than that of AEC objects alone.
- **Fully customizable**—The formatting of the Schedule Table object and the object properties that it tracks can be customized to suit specialized needs, from simple to complex.
- **Dynamic live link**—Reporting Property Set Data to a Schedule Table object is maintained with a "direct link" to the drawing data being scheduled. This guarantees that Schedules are kept up to date. Automatic update can even be enabled to make the process seamless.

THE SCHEDULE TABLE TOOL SET

The Schedule Table tool set in AutoCAD Architecture consists of a collection of interconnected components. Before you begin to work with Schedules, it is important to understand the function of each of these components:

- **Object**—Any object in the drawing whose properties you wish to track in a Schedule. (AutoCAD and AEC objects are eligible.)
- **Property Set Definition**—Establishes a set of object data specific to a particular type of object or objects. This data determines the available columns of an associated Schedule Table. Property Set Definitions are flexible and can be applied at the style or object level.
- **Property Data**—The data from one or more Property Set Definitions attached to a specific object. This data can feed one or more Schedules.
- **Property Data Format**—Transforms raw Property Set Data from the objects into the desired presentation format prior to its appearing in the Schedule Table or other Schedule components. For example, expressed as raw data, the width of a typical door is 36 units in Imperial measure. Using the appropriate Property Data Format, the expression on the Schedule would read 3'-0."
- **Schedule Table Style**—Like other ACA Styles, the Schedule Table style controls the configuration and overall appearance of the Schedule Table object. The style also determines the types of objects to which the Schedule Table is linked.
- **Schedule Table**—The actual Table object. This includes the borders, titles, headers, row and column cell divisions and cell data (text). Each row item within the Schedule Table is linked to an object within the drawing.
- **Object Tag**—As required by construction documentation needs, Tags *can* be included in drawings and function as an additional report of the attached Property Data. When used, Property Data from the object is fed to the Tag. Multi-View Blocks defined specifically to receive data from a Property Set Definition can be used as Tags. For more information on the process of Tagging, refer to Chapter 14.

Putting It All Together

Objects (AutoCAD or AEC) populate the drawing. One or more Property Set Definitions establish data for each column we wish to see in the Schedule. Property Data is attached to each of the individual drawing objects or Object styles (AEC objects only). These objects are selected to appear in the Schedule Table. As appropriate, each piece of data is formatted by a Property Data Format. Finally, a report on object Property Data is generated in the form of a Schedule Table or an Object Tag (or even exported to Excel). A Schedule Table Style governs the Schedule Table's overall format and appearance (see Figure 15.1).

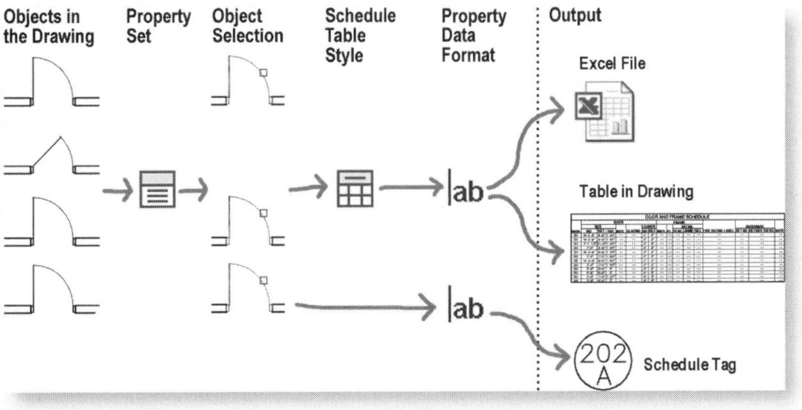

FIGURE 15.1 *The interrelationship of components in the Schedule Table tool set*

GETTING READY TO USE SCHEDULE TABLES

From a thousand-foot level, getting started with Schedules involves a few basic steps:

- **Choose**—First you must decide what information you want to schedule.
- **Format/Link**—The styles and components from which the Schedule will be generated must be imported or built next.
- **Report**—Generate the Schedule and/or insert the Tags, which will remain linked and up to date.

MANAGER NOTE CAD

Many Schedule Table Styles have been included with ACA. Start with these styles to become acquainted with the tool. Custom solutions can be created from scratch, or they can be created by modifying the existing offerings. For this reason, it is beneficial to become familiar with the configuration and intent of the samples provided with the software. You can build tool palettes containing the Schedule Table Styles that your firm uses frequently. For more information on creating custom Schedule Table Styles, Property Set Definitions and other schedule tools, consult Chapter 7 in *Autodesk Architectural Desktop: An Advanced Implementation Guide* by Paul F. Aubin and Matt Dillon.

ADDING SCHEDULE COMPONENTS

In the following tutorial, we will begin with a Schedule Table of Spaces showing department, geographical information, areas and quantities in the third floor of the Commercial Project. We will use this project to explore the many features of the Schedule Table tool set. Following the precedent established in the previous chapter, we will add Schedule Tables and Tags in View files.

Install the CD Files and Load the Current Project

If you have already installed all of the files from the CD, simply skip down to step 3 below to make the project active. If you need to install the CD files, start at step 1.

1. If you have not already done so, install the dataset files located on the Mastering AutoCAD Architecture 2010 CD-ROM.

   Refer to "Files Included on the CD-ROM" in the Preface for information on installing the sample files included on the CD.
2. Launch AutoCAD Architecture 2010 from the desktop icon created in Chapter 3.

If you did not create a custom icon, you might want to review "Create a New Profile" and "Create a Desktop Shortcut" in Chapter 3. Creating the custom desktop icon is not essential; however, it makes loading the custom profile easier.

3. From the Quick Access Toolbar (QAT), choose **Project Browser**.
4. Click to open the folder list and choose your *C:* drive.
5. Double-click on the *MasterACA 2010* folder, then the *Chapter15* folder.

   One or two commercial Projects will be listed: *15 Commercial* and/or *15 Commercial Metric.*
6. Double-click *15 Commercial* if you wish to work in Imperial units. Double-click *15 Commercial Metric* if you wish to work in Metric units. (You can also right-click on it and choose **Set Current Project**.) Then click Close in the Project Browser.

NOTE

Important: If a message appears asking you to repath the project, click the "Repath the project now" option. Refer to the "Repathing Projects" topic in the Preface for more information.

Create a Schedule View File

Let's begin by creating a View file in which to generate our first Schedule Table. We are going to create a View file of the third floor that will be very similar to the other third floor Views we have created. The major difference will be the way it is used in our project and the type of data it contains.

7. On the Project Navigator, click the Views tab.
8. Right-click the *Views* folder and choose **New View Dwg > General**.
9. Name the View **A-SH03**, give it a Description of **Architectural Third Floor Schedules** and then click Next.
10. Choose the third floor and then click Next.
11. Clear the checkboxes for all Constructs except *03 Partitions* and then click Finish.

This gives us a new View file of the third floor that contains only the *03 Partitions* Construct. We have deliberately omitted the others for the time being. We will load them in later.

Add a Schedule Table

12. On the Views tab, double-click the new *A-SH03* file to open it.

    If you left the "Open in drawing editor" checkbox selected, the file will open automatically.
13. Zoom the drawing out a bit to allow room to place the Schedule Table to the left.

14. On the Scheduling tool palette, click the Space Inventory Schedule tool (see Figure 15.2).

    If you do not see this palette or tool, right-click the Tool Palettes title bar and choose **Document** (to load the Documentation Tool Palette Group) and then click the Scheduling tab.

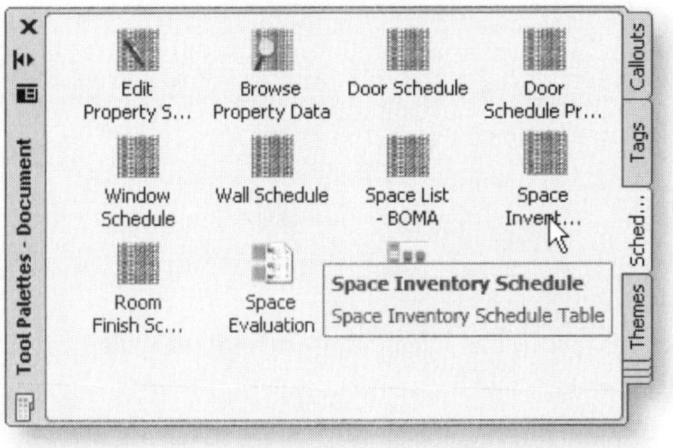

FIGURE 15.2 *Add Schedule Table from the Scheduling tool palette*

As with any AEC object, when we are adding a Schedule Table, the Properties palette includes several settings. Many are preset by the tool that we picked. For instance, since we clicked a Space Inventory Schedule tool, the Style will naturally be preset to Space Inventory. The Scale is also preset to the current annotation scale factor of the drawing. Some additional settings that are available when you are adding Schedule Tables warrant discussion here:

- **Update automatically**—When **Yes** is chosen, the Schedule Table dynamically updates as changes to the drawing take place. Use this feature sparingly because it can have a negative impact on the performance of your system, particularly with large projects.
- **Add new objects automatically**—Automatically adds newly created drawing objects directly to the table if they meet the original table selection criteria. For example, in a Door Schedule, if a new Door were added to the drawing, it would appear on the Schedule immediately.
- **Scan xrefs and Scan block references**—Allow objects nested within blocks or XREFs to be included in the Schedule.
- **Layer wildcard**—Allows the selection of objects for the Schedule to include only those on specified layers. Any standard Windows wildcard can be used, such as (*) for any character string and question mark (?) for a single character.

You can change any of these settings after placing the Schedule. When scheduling objects in XREFs (as we are here), make sure the Scan xrefs is set to **Yes**. If you wish to select only certain objects within the XREF, you can use the pipe (|) character in your Layer wildcard. For example, **01 Partitions|*** would find objects on any layer within the first floor partitions XREF only.

15. Change "Update automatically" and "Add new objects automatically" to **Yes** (see item 1 in Figure 15.3).

    Verify that Scan xrefs is also set to **Yes**. Leave the remaining presets as they are.

16. At the "Select objects or Enter to schedule external drawing" prompt, click on the *03 Partitions* XREF in the drawing and then press `ENTER` to end the selection (see item 2 in Figure 15.3).

17. At the "Upper left corner of table" prompt, click a point off to the left in the drawing to place the corner of the Schedule (see item 3 in Figure 15.3).

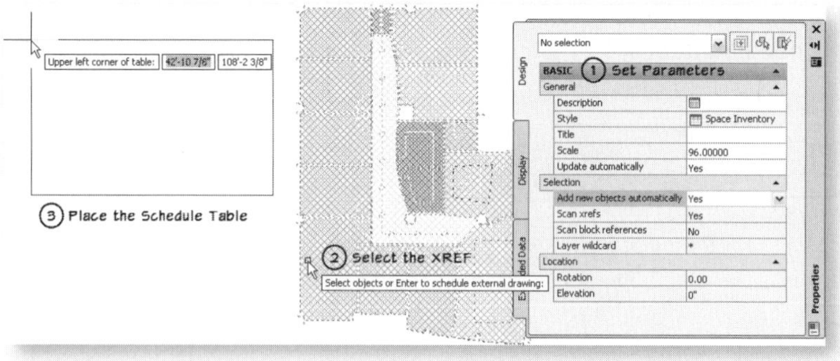

FIGURE 15.3 *Set the Parameters, select the XREF and place the Schedule at the default scale*

18. Press ENTER at the "Lower right corner (or Enter)" prompt.

    This makes the Schedule Table the default size without scaling it. Schedule Tables will be scaled automatically to the Drawing Scale (on the Drawing status bar).

A Schedule Table object will appear in the drawing. However, most of the fields in the Schedule show a question mark (?) (see Figure 15.4). The reason is that the required Property Set Data has not yet been attached to the individual Space objects (see the following sequence). Since no data is attached to the Spaces for the missing fields, the Schedule shows a question mark. Property Set Data can be attached to objects within the drawing in a few different ways.

SPACE INVENTORY							
LOCATION						AREA	QTY
SITE	BUILDING	FLOOR	ZONE	DEPARTMENT	OWNER		
?	?	?	?	?	?	242.26 SF	1
?	?	?	?	?	?	141.62 SF	1
?	?	?	?	?	?	139.45 SF	1
?	?	?	?	?	?	143.19 SF	1
?	?	?	?	?	?	140.16 SF	1
?	?	?	?	?	?	132.12 SF	1
?	?	?	?	?	?	165.92 SF	1
?	?	?	?	?	?	8.66 SF	2
?	?	?	?	?	?	181.16 SF	1
?	?	?	?	?	?	35.43 SF	1
?	?	?	?	?	?	155.44 SF	1
?	?	?	?	?	?	293.26 SF	1
?	?	?	?	?	?	330.18 SF	1
?	?	?	?	?	?	212.75 SF	1
?	?	?	?	?	?	84.97 SF	1
?	?	?	?	?	?	74.44 SF	1
?	?	?	?	?	?	? SF	1
							18

FIGURE 15.4 *Several fields in the Schedule Table are missing data*

19. Save the file.

PROPERTY SET DATA

Property Set Definitions (as defined in "The Schedule Table Tool Set" section above) determine which Property Set Data will be available to the objects and Schedules in the drawing file. Property Set Definitions can be referenced by styles or referenced directly by individual objects. In the current example, question marks occur in our Schedule where object-based Property Sets are referenced. The question marks indicate that the required data has not yet been attached. Attaching object-based Property Sets can be accomplished using a few techniques:

- Attach Schedule Tags to objects (which will also attach the Property Sets)
- Attach all Property Sets at once via the Schedule Table contextual ribbon tab
- Attach Property Sets manually to a selection of objects

Generally, the last option requires the most effort and should be avoided. The Tagging option was used in the last chapter (in the "Adding Room Tags" heading) while we were Tagging rooms. We will see additional examples below. The second option will be explored here.

Attach Property Set Data via the Schedule Table

The fastest way to attach all of the required Property Sets is via the Schedule Table.

1. Click on the Schedule Table, and on the Schedule Table contextual ribbon tab on the Modify panel, choose the ***Add All Property Sets*** tool (see Figure 15.5).

   The change to the Schedule Table will be subtle. In place of the questions marks in each field will be a double dash (–).

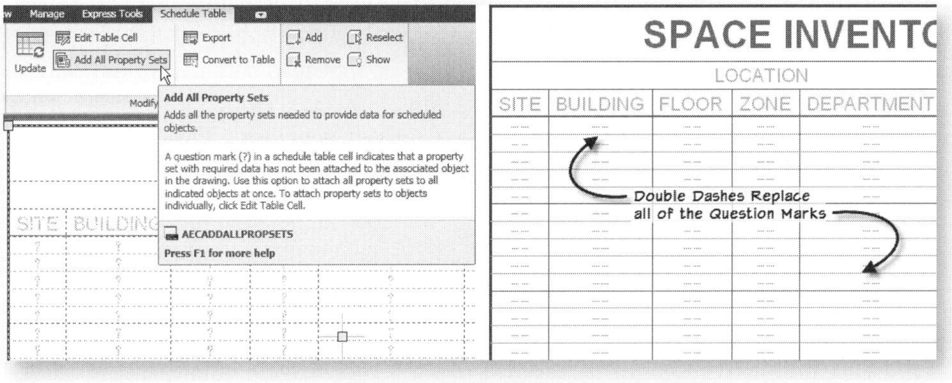

FIGURE 15.5 *Attach All Property Sets via the Schedule—All Question Marks are replaced by a placeholder value (–)*

A double dash is simply a null value (see the right side of Figure 15.5). The Property Set is attached; but because a value for the field has not been input yet (or is not applicable), the default value (–) is displayed in the field. All of these fields are now ready to receive typed in values. Unlike the columns on the right (which are automatic fields—see below), these fields are all manual type-ins.

We can edit the values assigned to each field in a few ways. Let's take a look.

2. Select the *03 Partitions* XREF, right-click and choose **Edit Referenced Property Set Data** (see the left side of Figure 15.6).
3. At the Select Objects Prompt, click on one of the Office Space objects and then press ENTER (see the right side of Figure 15.6).

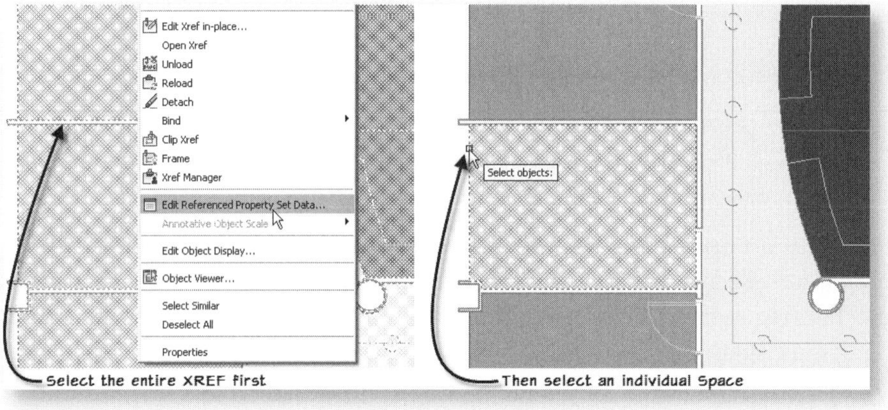

FIGURE 15.6 *Edit Referenced Property Set Data to edit the values of one or more Spaces*

The Edit Referenced Property Data worksheet will appear.

Each Property Set attached to the selected Space is indicated with a gray title bar bearing the name of the Property Set Definition. All of the Properties contained within each Property Set are grouped beneath this gray bar. You can use the small arrow icon at the right side of each of these groupings to collapse and expand the group (see Figure 15.7). You will recognize several of the names of the Properties within the GeoObjects grouping as several of them appear as columns in our Schedule Table. These are the fields that we will edit. However, notice that some of the fields available in GeoObjects do not appear on the Schedule. This illustrates the point that defining a property within a Property Set does not require that it be used by the Schedule Table.

4. In the Edit Referenced Property Data worksheet, fill in any of the fields within the GeoObjects grouping that you wish and then click OK (see Figure 15.7).

TIP

If the Schedule Table does not update on its own, select it, and on the Schedule Table contextual ribbon tab on the Modify panel, choose the *Update* tool.

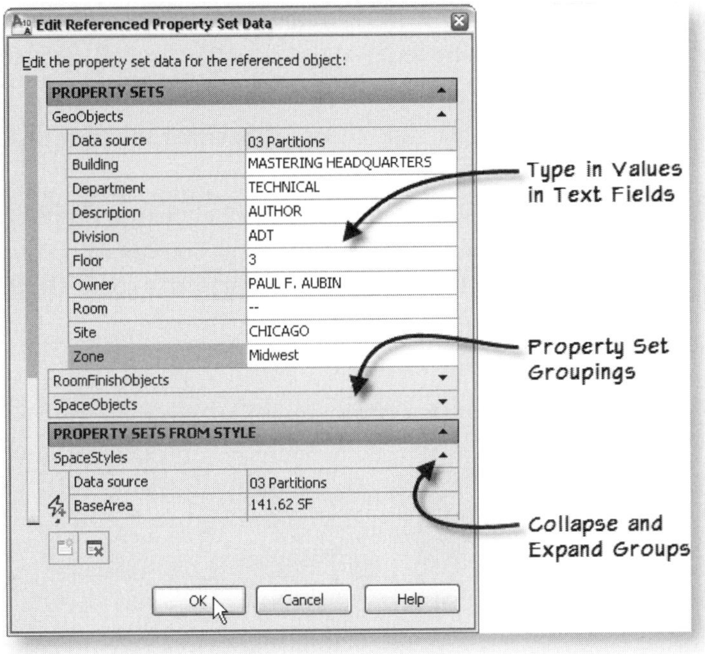

FIGURE 15.7 *Edit Referenced Property Set Data worksheet editing GeoObjects fields*

The Edit Referenced Property Set Data command can be used on one object at a time or on a selection of several. However, if you choose more than one object, remember that any field you edit will apply to *all* objects in the selection. This can be very handy and also potentially problematic. Pay close attention to your object selections for the best results.

5. Repeat the process, selecting more than one Space to edit this time (see Figure 15.8).

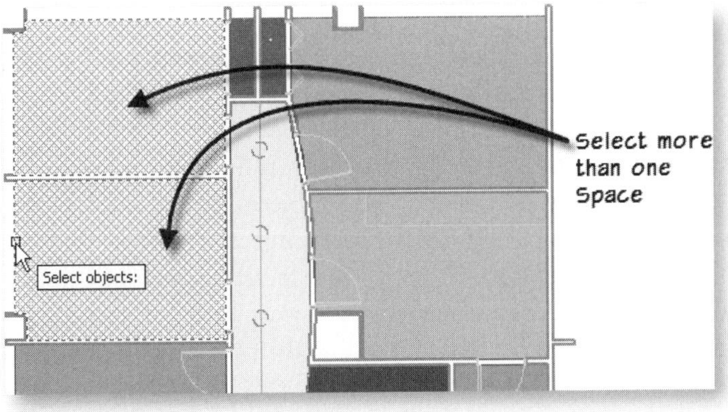

FIGURE 15.8 *Repeat Edit Referenced Property Set Data and select more than one Space*

6. Edit the GeoObjects field for the group selection and then click OK.

Notice that any change you made has been applied to all objects in the selection. Remember, the Property Sets are attached directly to the objects within the Construct. Therefore, in addition to this technique, you can also open the XREF and edit the Properties by selecting the objects directly.

7. Select the XREF, and on the External Reference contextual ribbon tab on the Edit panel, choose the ***Open Reference*** tool.

   The *03 Partitions* Construct file will open onscreen.

8. Select one of the Office Spaces, right-click, choose **Properties** and then click the Extended Data tab (see Figure 15.9).

Notice that the same information that was included in the Edit Referenced Property Set Data worksheet is contained here, because it *is* the same data. You can edit it the same way. This is simply another method to edit it. Go ahead and edit some of the values if you like; you will see any changes reflected in the steps to follow.

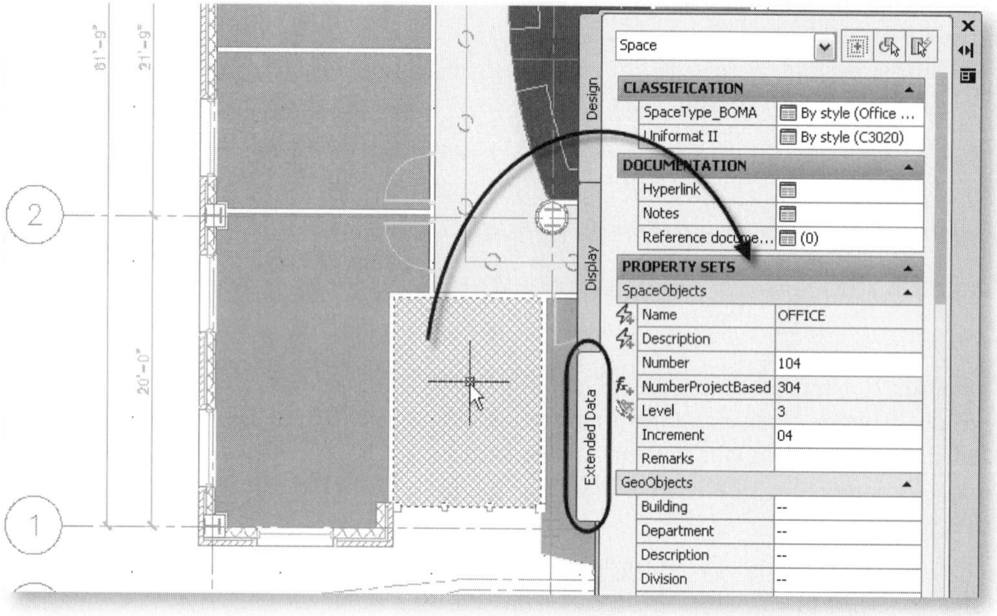

FIGURE 15.9 *Edit Property Data on the Properties Palette for selected objects*

As before, you can collapse any Property Sets that you are not currently editing to make the palette easier to manage. As noted above, all of the fields of the GeoObjects Property Set are editable text fields and are the ones shown in the Schedule in *A-SH03*. Other Property Sets are attached to the Spaces in the *03 Partitions* Construct, however; namely, RoomFinishObjects and SpaceObjects. If you scroll down to and view some of them, you will notice that RoomFinishObjects and SpaceObjects have editable text fields. In the SpaceStyles Property Set, however, you will notice that all of the properties have a small lightning bolt icon next to them and *cannot* be edited. These are Automatic Properties that come directly from the drawing (see Figure 15.10). Style-based property sets also appear on the Properties palette for easy access. You can see this on the right side of the figure. Automatic and Style-based properties will be discussed below.

Copying Tags Manually (Should be Avoided)

At this point, it might be nice to add Tags to the rest of the Spaces. Copying Tags from existing Tags in the drawing is *not* recommended. Simply copying a Tag from an existing object to another does *not* associate the data within the Tag with the new object. Proximity to an object does not determine its relationship to the Property Set Data within the object. A Tag Anchor is used to create this link. Let's try an experiment.

26. Copy the Tag just added to another room (particularly one of a different size) using the standard AutoCAD Copy command.

    Use the **Copy** in Basic Modify Tools; do *not* use Copy and Paste.

27. Change the current Display Configuration to **Diagnostic**.

    Use the pop-up menu on the Drawing status bar (see Chapter 2 for more information).

Notice the change in the drawing. As its name implies, the Diagnostic Display Configuration is used to help you troubleshoot problems in the drawing. The Diagnostic Display has the Space object's Decomposed Display Representation active, which makes it very difficult to see anything else. Let's turn this off.

28. On the Manage ribbon tab on the Style & Display panel, choose the **Display Manager** tool, expand Sets, select Plan Diagnostic and then, on the Display Representation Control tab, clear the Decomposed checkbox (next to Space objects) on the right side.
29. Click OK to dismiss the Display Manager (see Figure 15.15).

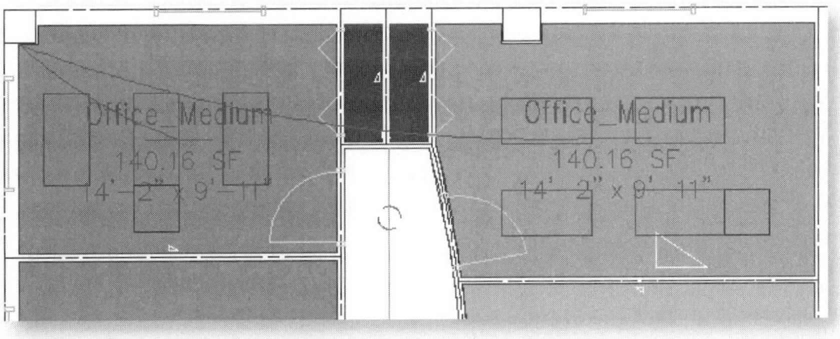

FIGURE 15.15 *Turn off Decomposed and turn on Diagnostic to see the Tag Anchors*

One of the most useful features of the Diagnostic Display (once you have removed the Decomposed Display Rep) is the display of the Anchor Tag to Entity (or Tag Anchors), seen here with the curved lines that connect the Tags to a corner of Space to which they are anchored. Notice that both the original Tag and the copied Tag are anchored to the same Space object. The copy operation copied only the Tag; it did *not* attach the Anchor to the new Space.

30. Delete the copied Tag and then restore the **Medium Detail** Display Configuration before continuing.

When you add a Tag from the tool palette or Content Browser, it does not merely insert a symbol; it actually runs a Schedule Tag command—AecScheduleTag. This command imports and attaches the required Property Sets and correctly anchors the Tag to the object it is Tagging. This process also allows the correct values to be input within the attributes of the Tags. Therefore, the quickest way to add multiple Tags is not to copy them, but to use the "Multiple" option and the process covered in the previous chapter.

A Tag is a Multi-View Block object, as we saw in the previous chapter. In previous versions of ACA, MVBs used as Tags did not "know" they were Tags. To use them as Tags required detailed and complex configuration of DesignCenter AEC Content items and tool palette tools. As we saw in Chapter 14, it is now very easy to create a custom Tag using the wizard on the Format menu. Once a Tag is created, it will "know" it is a Tag in the drawing. Select any Tag, right-click and note the appearance of the "Tag Anchor" right-click menu. If the Tag is already attached to an object, this menu will show options for attaching and releasing the Anchor. If the Tag is not attached to any object, this menu will give only one option—**Set Object**. You can experiment with the Tags onscreen. Try releasing the Anchor on one and then right-clicking the Tag to see this menu. When you drag a Tag to a tool palette, the resultant tool automatically contains Tag insertion properties. This, too, was explored in Chapter 14.

CAD MANAGER NOTE

In the "Using the Define Schedule Tag Wizard" heading in Chapter 14, we created a Tag Tool on our MACA Commercial palette. Tools can also be made that only attach the Property Set and don't insert a Tag. This can be valuable in instances where you want an easy way to apply Property Set Data to objects without needing to add a Schedule or Tags.

Add the Rest of the Space Tags

Adding Tags is a very effective and simple way to add Property Set Data to objects that require it. However, the process can be slow and tedious if you place them one at a time, even more so if the Edit Property Set Data dialog box pops up between each insertion. In most cases, you will want to add all of your Tags to the drawing quickly and then refine the Property Set Data progressively as more design detail becomes available. We have two tricks to facilitate speedy Tag insertion. First, we can turn off the setting that makes the Edit Property Set Data dialog box appear (if it is not already off on your system), and we can use the Multiple feature of the Tag add routine (as we did in the last chapter) to add a collection of Tags all at once.

31. From the Application Menu, choose **Options** (or right-click in the Command Line and choose **Options** from the shortcut menu).
32. On the AEC Content tab, clear the Display Edit Property Data Dialog During Tag Insertion checkbox and then click OK (see Figure 15.16).

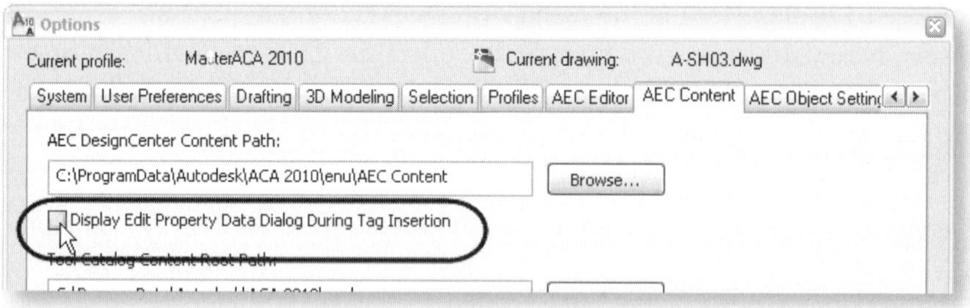

FIGURE 15.16 *The AEC Content tab of Options*

33. Bring the Content Browser to the front again (CTRL + 4) and drag the Room Tag (w/ Dimensions) tool into the drawing, or click on the tool on the MACA Commercial palette.
34. Following the prompts as above, click a Space without a Tag and place the Tag in that room. Press ENTER to automatically place the Tag at the center of the Space object.

    Notice that the Edit Property Set Data dialog box did not appear this time.

As we saw in the last chapter, after you have placed the first Tag with the Schedule Tag Add command, you will be able to use the Multiple option. This option is not available on the first click, so you have to place the first one manually. After the first Tag, you can choose the Multiple option and then select several objects to Tag all at once. Let's use this option for the remaining Tags.

35. Right-click in the drawing (or, if you have Dynamic Input on, press the down arrow key) and choose **Multiple**.
36. At the "Select objects to Tag" prompt, use a crossing window, surround the entire plan and then press ENTER.

    A dialog box like the one shown in Figure 15.17 will appear, alerting you that some Spaces already have Tags.

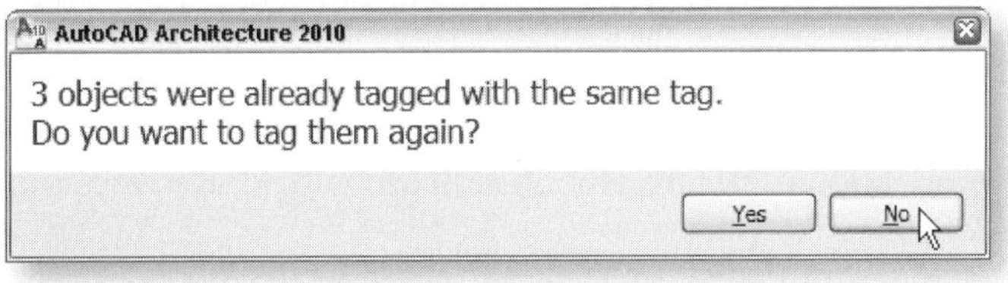

FIGURE 15.17 *Multi-Tag recognizes that some Spaces are already Tagged*

37. In the AutoCAD alert dialog box, click the No button.
38. Press ENTER to end the Schedule Tag command.

Notice that all of the Tags appear in the center. The Multiple option matches the insertion point of the first Tag placed. Inevitably, some of the Tags will need to have their placement fine-tuned. Use any of the techniques covered in the previous chapter to relocate a Tag.

39. Move any Tags as required for legibility.

NOTE

If you get a tag in the Conference Room for the Ceiling Feature, delete it.

40. The Schedule Table should update automatically. If it does not, select the Schedule Table and choose the ***Update*** tool.

Fine-Tune the Schedule's Selection

Sometimes you will want to exclude objects from the Schedule even though they are of the same type as those you are scheduling. For instance, you might want to exclude existing doors from a door Schedule and show only new ones; or as in this case, you might want only Spaces in the tenant space, not including the core.

NOTE

This chapter will not cover basic BOMA or IBC requirements for definitions on Tagging or auditing space. Terminology used to identify space in this tutorial is used for instructional purposes only. If you need to provide your clients with industry or regulatory space information, please check with those guidelines for proper space tracking requirements.

41. Select the Schedule Table, and, on the Schedule Table contextual ribbon tab on the Scheduled Objects panel, choose the ***Remove*** tool.
42. At the "Select objects" prompt, click any Space within the building *Core*.

Notice how the entire *03 Shell and Core* XREF highlights. This command is not able to select the individual Spaces within the XREF. However, depending on what goal you have for the Schedule in this View file, this may be fine. In other words, if you only intend to report the Spaces for the tenant that occupies the suite on the third floor, then removing the entire *Core* from the Schedule Table's selection is appropriate. However, if you wish instead to remove only certain Spaces from the *Core*, then you will need to use a different technique. Layer filters or Classifications can be used in that case. In the "Building a Project-Based Door Schedule (Advanced)" heading below, we will see an example of layer filters. We will look at an example of Classifications next.

43. Press ENTER to complete the sequence.

Notice that the Spaces have been removed from the Schedule. However, these Space objects remain in the drawing. This process allows you to fine-tune the selection of objects used to generate the Schedule. It does *not* change the actual objects in any way.

Within the Scheduled Objects ribbon panel are other useful tools: Add, Reselect and Show.

- ***Add***—Allows you to add objects to the Schedule Table selection and is the opposite of the Remove option shown here.
- ***Reselect***—Allows you to replace the Schedule selection with a completely new set of objects.
- ***Show***—Allows you to click a line item in the Schedule and have the corresponding item in the drawing highlighted.

If you were to Add the Core back to the selection, you would notice that the original data was restored. As was already stated, these commands affect only the selection of objects that appear in the Schedule, *not* the objects or their associated Property Set Data.

44. Practice each of these tools to get a sense of their function.

    Be sure to restore the original selection (only *03 Partitions*) when you are finished exploring.

Using Classifications to Fine-Tune Schedule Selection

The total number of Spaces now in the Schedule is 18. However, there are only 17 rooms in the tenant space. The eighteenth room is actually the Space object used to represent the ceiling feature in the Conference Room. Therefore, this particular Space should be excluded from the Schedule so that it does not distort the totals. To remove this Space from the selection used by the Schedule Table, we cannot use the options noted above. This is because as already noted, we can only select or deselect the entire XREF, not the individual Spaces within. However, two filtration methods are available: Layer Filters and Classifications. We will look at Layer Filters below. First, let's take a quick look at Classifications.

A Classification Definition is a category that can be assigned to object styles or directly to objects. AutoCAD Architecture ships with a predefined Classification Definition based on Uniformat II designations. This has been imported into the *03 Partitions* dataset and is ready to use. You can also create your own Classifications. For this exercise, we will assign one of the predefined designations to the Space style used for the ceiling feature and then instruct the Schedule not to include it.

NOTE

If you want to import the Uniformat II Classification Definition into other drawings, you can import it via the Style Manager from the *Uniformat II Classifications (1997 ed).dwg* in the Imperial folder. You can find similar Classifications in the Metric folder in the *Classifications (Metric - UK).dwg* library file.

NOTE

For simplicity in this exercise, both the Imperial and Metric versions of the project use the Uniformat II Classification Definition.

45. On Project Navigator, double-click to open the *03 Partitions* Construct.
46. Select any Space, and on the Space contextual ribbon tab on the General panel, choose the ***Edit Style*** tool.
47. Click on the Classifications tab.

Notice that two Classifications exist in this file: Space Type_BOMA and Uniformat II. For now, we will focus on Uniformat II. Notice that the office Space is already assigned to C3020 (Floor Finishes). Space objects actually have a floor and a ceiling component. All of the Spaces in this file have already been assigned to this designation.

48. Click OK to dismiss the dialog.
49. Select only the dashed rectangular Space in the conference room, and choose the ***Edit Style*** tool again (see Figure 15.18).

Notice that this Space also has been assigned to C3020 (Floor Finishes).

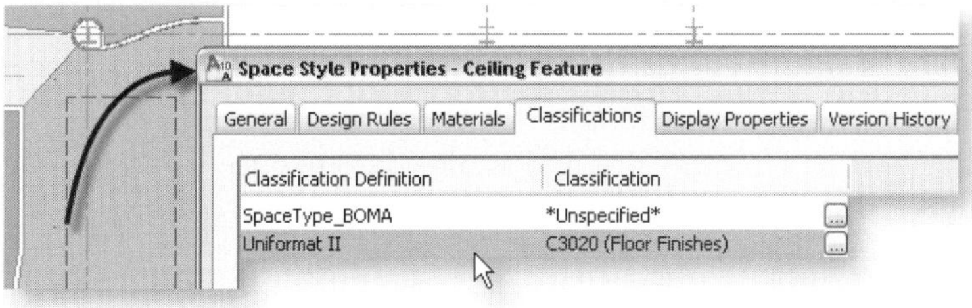

FIGURE 15.18 *All of the Spaces currently in this file have been assigned to C3020 (Floor Finishes)*

We can change the Classification at either the style or object level. If we edit in the current dialog, it applies to all Spaces of the same style. In this case, let's apply the new Classification directly to the Space object.

50. Click OK to dismiss this dialog.
51. Select the dashed rectangular Space in the conference room, right-click and choose **Properties**.

This will open the Properties palette if it is not already open.

52. On the Extended Data tab, beneath Classification, click on By style (C3020) next to the Uniformat II designation.
53. In the "Select Classification" dialog, choose C3030 – Ceiling Finishes and then click OK (see Figure 15.19).

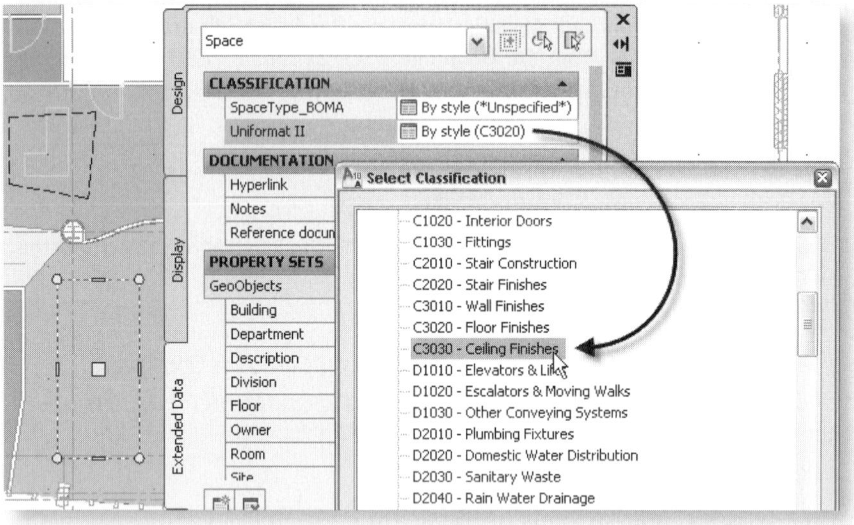

FIGURE 15.19 *Assign the C3030 – Ceiling Finishes Classification to the Ceiling Feature Space style*

This procedure has allowed us to override the style-based assignment with an object-based override. We have thereby classified only this particular Space with the Ceiling Finishes category.

54. Save the *03 Partitions* Construct.
55. Return to *A-SH03* and then reload the XREFs.

Before we can filter the Schedule using Classifications, we must import the Uniformat II Classification Definition into the *A-SH03* View file. A copy of the default *Uniformat II Classifications (1997 ed).dwg* file has been included in the *MasterACA 2010\Template* folder, which you can use for this purpose. However, in this case, since *03 Partitions* already contains Uniformat II and is already open, we will import it directly from there.

56. Select the Schedule Table.
57. On the Schedule Table contextual ribbon tab on the General panel, select the Edit Style drop-down button (bottom half) and choose the ***Classification Definitions*** tool.

    This will open the Style Manager filtered to just the Classification Definitions node. Both *03 Partitions* and *A-SH03* will be listed on the left.
58. Expand *03 Partitions* and *Multi-Purpose Objects* on the left and select the Classifications Node beneath it.
59. Drag and drop Uniformat II from *03 Partitions* and drop it on *A-SH03* (see Figure 15.20).

    If you prefer, you can right-click and use Copy and Paste instead.

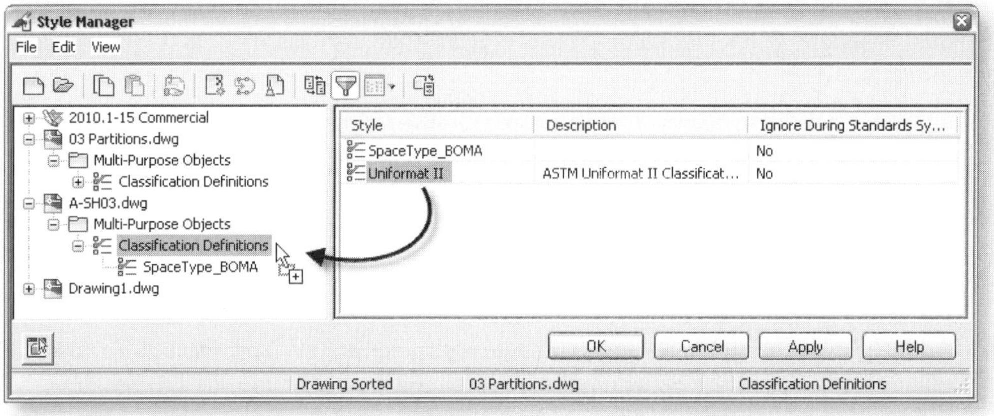

FIGURE 15.20 *Copy the Uniformat II Classification Definition to A-SH03*

60. Click OK to dismiss the Style Manager.
61. With the Schedule Table still selected, on the Schedule Table contextual ribbon tab on the General tab, choose the ***Edit Style*** tool (top half of split button).
62. Select the Applies To tab; on the right side, expand Uniformat II.
63. Place a check mark in the C3020 checkbox (see Figure 15.21).

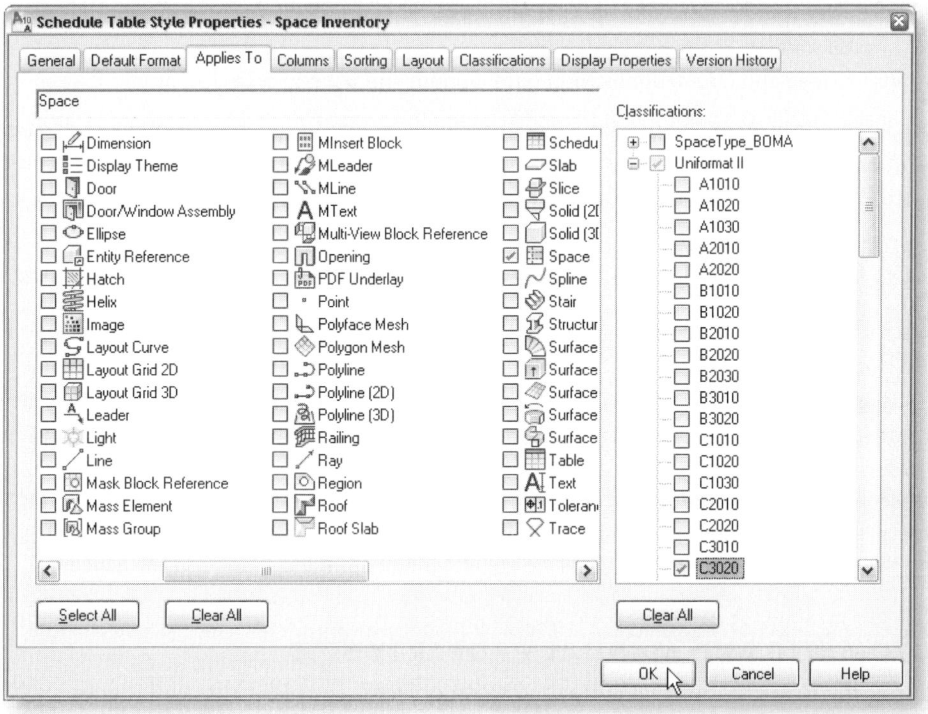

FIGURE 15.21 *Assign a Classification filter to the Schedule Table Style*

As we will see, the left side of this tab is where you choose one or more objects to which this Schedule will apply. These are the types of objects that will be included in the Schedule, in this case, Spaces. With the Classification designation(s) also being selected, you are further limiting the potential selection to objects of the type(s) chosen on the left and classified as indicated on the right. In this case, we are telling this Schedule to include only Space objects that are classified as C3020 (Floor Finishes).

64. Click OK to dismiss the dialog and see the results.

    The Schedule Table should now list only 17 items. Update the Schedule Table, if necessary.
65. Save the file.

Add and Delete Schedule Items

Adding newly created items to a Schedule is simple. If Add New Objects Automatically is set to **Yes** in the Schedule object's settings, new objects added to the drawing will be added automatically to the Schedule if they meet the original selection criteria of the Schedule Table. Otherwise, the new objects need to be added to the Schedule selection manually by using the tools covered above.

66. On the View ribbon tab on the Windows panel, select the Switch Windows drop-down and choose *03 Partitions*.
67. Select one of the existing offices, and on the Space contextual ribbon tab on the General panel, choose the ***Add Selected*** tool.

    If you add a new Space with the tool palettes, you also need to be sure to classify it.
68. Add a new Space next to the drawing using any parameters.
69. Save the *03 Partitions* file and then double-click *A-SH03* on the Project Navigator palette to switch to this file.
70. Reload the *03 Partitions* XREF and Update the Schedule Table.

Notice the addition of the new item in the Schedule. (It should appear on the last line of the Schedule.) In the same fashion, items deleted from the drawing will be automatically removed from the Schedule.

71. Return to *03 Partitions* and delete the new Space.
72. Save and close *03 Partitions*. In *A-SH03*, reload the XREF and Update the Schedule.

Notice the removal of the new line from the Schedule. The object has been removed from both the drawing and the Schedule. Adding and deleting Spaces from the drawing, as we have done in this sequence, and the impact this has on the Schedule are very different from manipulating the Schedule's selection, as we did in the last topic.

NOTE

Please do not confuse the two operations; they are quite different. When manipulating the Schedule Table selection, we are affecting the content only of the Schedule; when adding and deleting objects from the drawing, we are affecting both the drawing *and* the Schedule.

AUTOMATIC AND MANUAL PROPERTY SETS

Editing the Property Set Data attached to an object is simple. Edits will dynamically apply to all pieces in the data chain (object, Schedule and Tag). Editing Property Set Data can be done in a few ways; we have already seen some. However, you will not be able to use the methods covered so far on all Properties. The method used to edit depends on what types of Property Sets are attached to the object in question.

Property Sets can be Automatic or Manual and can be attached to Objects or Styles. Every AutoCAD or AEC object has a collection of unique defining properties inherent to its specific object type. This is true of basic drafted entities such as lines and circles and architectural objects such as Walls and Doors. These *automatic* properties include characteristics such as length, width, style, color and layer. A Property Set Definition is capable of tracking any of the object's inherent properties in an *automatic* property definition. For example, if an object is resized in the drawing, an automatic property defined to track the object's length, width or height will immediately report this change. This is very powerful indeed.

However, as useful as automatic properties are, it is often desirable to include data in the Schedule that cannot be acquired automatically. This type of data can be included in the Property Set using a nonautomatic *manual* property. Examples include cost, fire rating and material finish.

Automatic and Manual properties are articulated in the dialog boxes and worksheets with the following icons:

- **Manual property**—These properties are available for edit on the Extended Data tab of the Properties palette or on the Schedule Table itself. Editing in either place affects the entire data chain. Since they are not tied to any inherit or geometric properties, edits to the object, such as grip editing and object properties, have no impact on Manual Properties.
- **Automatic property**—Automatic properties may not be edited on the Properties palette or the Schedule. This data is available only on the object itself in the main drawing window through normal AutoCAD or AutoCAD Architecture editing such as grip editing or object properties (on the Design tab of the Properties palette).

There are several additional types of Automatic Property. Many of these offer powerful advanced functionality that fall outside the scope of this book. We will see some of these in the "Building a Project-Based Door Schedule (Advanced)" topic below. For more detail on some of the advanced automatic property types, pick up a copy of the *Autodesk Architectural Desktop: An Advanced Implementation Guide.*

- **Formula property**—An automatic property that processes the data in some way before reporting it. Examples include concatenating two or more other properties and running complex programmatic calculations.

Formula properties have a visual interface designed to make it easier to add complex formulas containing VB Script code. The dialog even allows you to input sample values and test the validity of a formula directly in the Property Set. This will save time and reduce error trapping. For more information on this feature, consult the online help.

- **Location property**—An automatic property that reads Property Set Data from a particular (often adjacent) Space or AEC Polygon.
- **Classification property**—An automatic property that reads the Classification or a particular piece of Classification Property Set Data of an object. Classifications are user-defined categories that can be assigned to AEC object styles.
- **Material property**—An automatic property that reads the Material Definition or a particular piece of Material Definition Property Set Data of an object.
- **Project property**—An automatic property that reads data from the current project database (such as floor number and project name).
- **Anchor property**—An automatic property that reads data from the parent object to which it is anchored.

- **Graphic property**—An automatic property that shows a block or raster image directly in the table cell of the schedule. It is useful for legends.

NOTE

Although extensive coverage of all automatic Property Set types is not included in this book, we will create a Graphic property and see examples of Formula, Location and Project Properties in the "Building a Project-Based Door Schedule (Advanced)" topic below. You are encouraged to experiment with these Properties on your own.

Both automatic and manual properties can be defined within "style-based" or "object-based" Property Set Definitions. A style-based Property Set is attached to an AEC object style and therefore applies automatically to all objects belonging to that style. For instance, if you assign a "Wall Type" property to a Wall Style Property Set, you can change the Wall Type of all Walls that belong to that style by editing the Wall Type Property at the style level. AutoCAD objects cannot use style-based Property Sets. Object-based properties, on the other hand, are attached individually to each object and must be edited individually by selecting each associated object. The GeoObjects Property Set used above is an example of an object-based Property Set.

Identify and Edit Object-Based Manual Properties

All of the properties under the Location heading in the Schedule we have onscreen (which belong to the GeoObjects Property Set) are manual (nonautomatic) properties.

Continue in the *A-SH03* View file. If you closed the file, double-click it on Project Navigator to reopen it. Make sure that *03 Partitions* is closed.

1. Click on the *03 Partitions* XREF onscreen, right-click and choose **Edit Referenced Property Set Data**.
2. At the "Select Objects" prompt, click on any Office Space and then press ENTER.

This is the technique that we used above. All of the manual Properties will appear as editable text fields. All Properties in the GeoObjects Property Set are manual.

3. Type **Jane Doe** in the Owner field and then click OK.

   If the Schedule does not update automatically, select it and on the Schedule Table contextual ribbon tab on the Modify panel, choose the ***Update*** tool.

Multiple spaces also can be selected before editing. This will allow you to edit the same property for several spaces at once. This technique was covered above.

NOTE

If the fields in your Edit Property Set Data dialog box are unavailable for edit, you have at least one object in your selection that does not have Property Set Data attached. Use any of the methods covered above to attach the Property Sets to the objects.

Edit a Table Cell

Manual properties can also be edited directly within the Schedule Table object's cells.

4. Click the Schedule Table object, and on the Schedule Table contextual ribbon tab on the Modify panel, choose the ***Edit Table Cell*** tool.
5. Click the double dash (–) in the Site column (directly on the Schedule in the same row as Jane Doe).

6. In the Edit Referenced Property Set Data dialog box, change the value to **Chicago** and then click OK.

   Notice the change to the Schedule. Also notice that regardless of how the data is entered, it appears in the Schedule as uppercase because of the Property Data Format applied to these fields. (Refer to "The Schedule Table Tool Set" section above for a definition of Property Data Format.)

With the Edit Table Cell command still active, take note of the Command Line, which reads "Select schedule table item (or the border for all items), hover for information, or Ctrl-select to zoom." If you click on any borderline of the Table, it will call the Edit Property Set Data dialog box and allow the global edit of all objects in the Schedule (similar to the process completed in the last sequence). Exercise caution here because in some cases, you will not want to perform a global edit.

7. Click on any Table border.
8. In the Building field, type **Mastering Headquarters** and then click OK (see Figure 15.22).

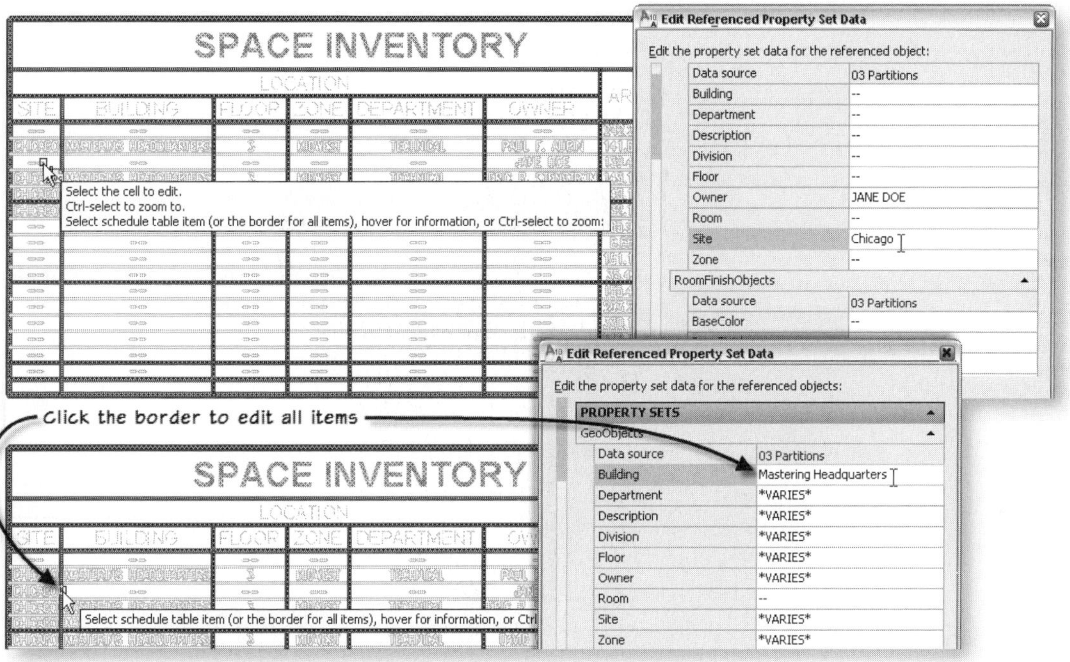

FIGURE 15.22 *Select any border of the Schedule Table using Edit Table Cell to edit all items*

   Notice that the change occurs to all items in the Schedule.

With the Edit Table Cell command still active, if you hover over an item, you will get information pertinent to that item.

9. Hover your cursor over the Zone column for any space.

   Notice the small tooltip that appears.

10. Hover your cursor over the Area column for any space.

    Notice that the message is different this time. Here you are being told that you cannot edit this cell directly because it has an automatic source.

11. Press ENTER to end the command.
12. Using either method, change more values before proceeding to the next step.

Edit Automatic Properties

Automatic properties can be edited only by directly editing the object. This is because an automatic property is a direct link to some inherent property of the object. To see this, open the *03 Partitions* Construct.

Take note of the Areas of the two office Spaces between Column Lines 2 and 3.

13. Select the *03 Partitions* XREF onscreen, and on the External Reference contextual ribbon tab on the Edit panel, choose the ***Open Reference*** tool.

NOTE

If you prefer, you can use Edit XREF in-place functionality to complete this sequence.

14. Zoom in on the Spaces between Column Lines 2 and 3.
15. Move the Wall between the two Spaces up **2'-0"** [**600**] (see the left side of Figure 15.23).
16. Select both Spaces impacted by the change, and on the Space contextual ribbon tab on the Modify panel, select the Update drop-down button and choose the ***Selected Space*** tool (see the right side of Figure 15.23).

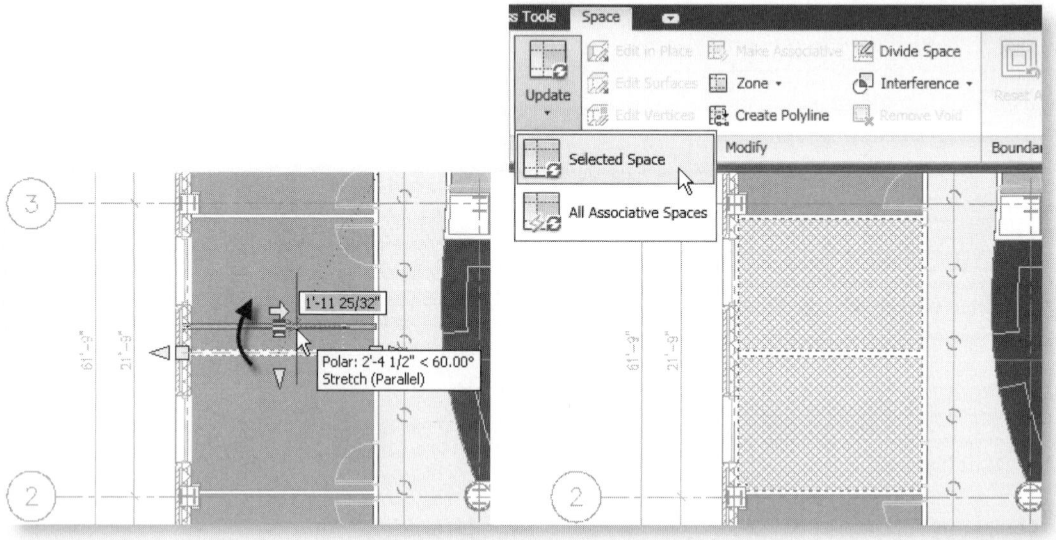

FIGURE 15.23 *Move a Wall in the Construct and then update the Space Geometry*

17. Save *03 Partitions* (don't close it), switch to *A-SH03*, reload the XREF and then update the Schedule Table.

The Area column of the Schedule noted the change and updated accordingly. The Tags also reflect the new dimensions.

18. Return to the *03 Partitions* file and undo the change to return the Space to normal.
19. Save and close *03 Partitions*, then reload the XREF and update the Schedule Table.

The areas should return to the original values. The same basic process is required for any geometric change to the Space objects. It is not possible to use Edit Table Cell to make changes to the automatic (inherit) properties of an object.

Edit Style-Based Property Data

As was noted previously, Property Sets can also be assigned to an object style. (This is true only of AEC objects as AutoCAD objects do not use styles.) This allows properties to be assigned globally to all objects referencing a particular style. The likelihood of accidentally missing an object is greatly diminished with style-based properties. The real power of style-based properties comes from the ease of editing them. Should the design change, the edit needs to be made only once at the style level to update the entire drawing and Schedule at once. Like object-based Property Sets, style-based Property Sets can be both automatic and manual.

20. Open the *03 Partitions* XREF, select one of the office Spaces (in the upper left corner) and on the Space contextual ribbon tab on the General panel choose the ***Edit Style*** tool.
21. Click the General tab and then click the Property Sets button.

A single Property Set named "SpaceStyles" is attached to this Style. Notice that all of its Properties come from an automatic source. (They all have the small lightning bolt icon, and none can be edited in this dialog box.) They must be edited on the drawing objects as we did in the sequence above.

22. Click Cancel twice to return to the drawing.

We also mentioned that you could now access Style-based properties on the Extended Data tab of the Properties palette.

23. Select the same Space.
24. On the Properties palette, click the Extended Data tab and scroll to the bottom of the Property Set list.
25. Click the small Edit Property Set Data worksheet icon.

A worksheet containing the same automatic properties will appear. Click Cancel to dismiss it when finished.

Before closing *03 Partitions*, let's take a look at another style-based Property Set that contains manual properties.

26. Within the tenant space, click one of the interior Walls.

    On the Properties palette, on the Extended Data tab, notice the "Property Sets From Style" heading and worksheet icon.
27. Click the Edit Property Set Data worksheet icon (see Figure 15.24).

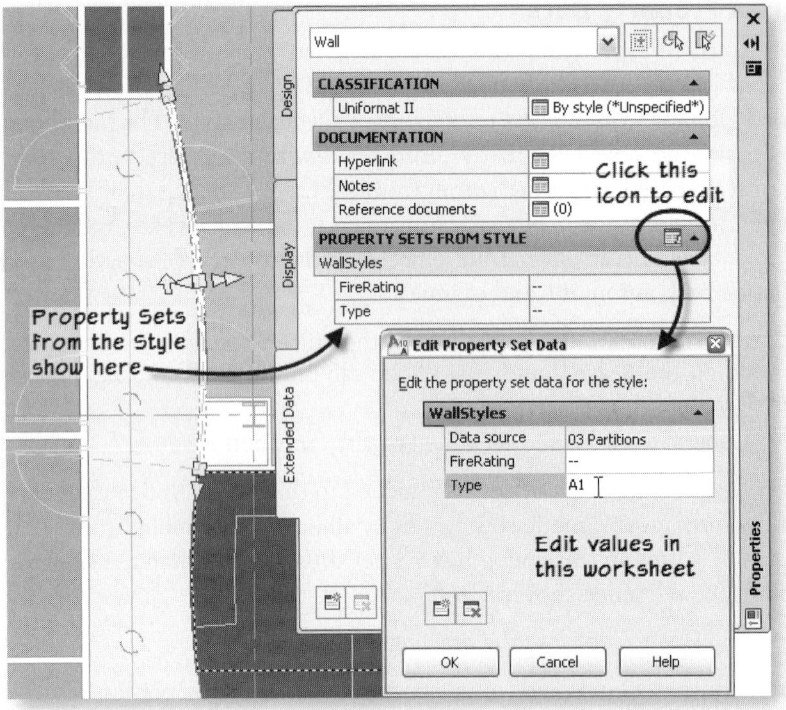

FIGURE 15.24 *Editing style-based manual properties on the Properties palette*

A single Property Set is also attached here. However, both of its Properties are manual. (They have editable type in text fields.) For instance, if we were to edit the Type field, that change would apply across the Style to all Walls belonging to Wall Style Stud-X.

28. Edit the Type and then click OK to return to the drawing.
29. Select a different Wall and repeat the process.

Note that the value you edited for the first Wall appears here as well. This is a Style-based Manual property. This means that you can input any manual value you wish, but it will apply to all objects belonging to that same Style.

30. Save the *03 Partitions* Construct file (do not close it yet).

NOTE

A Display Theme that applies to the FireRating property is seen here. We first used this Display Theme in Chapter 2. Display Themes were discussed in Chapter 12 and will be explored further below.

PROPERTY SET DEFINITIONS

Property Set Data attached to objects is comprised of one or more object properties defined by one or more Property Set Definitions. Property Sets establish the link between objects and the Schedules that report them. A Property Set Definition determines how a Property Set will be applied (object-based or style-based), what properties it contains and how the properties are configured. Analyzing the Property Set Definitions of the sample Content provided in ACA is a good way to begin to understand how they work.

Explore a Property Set Definition

1. Return to the *A-SH03* drawing (choose it on the View ribbon tab on the Windows panel from the Switch Windows drop-down list, press CTRL + TAB or double-click it on Project Navigator).
2. Select the Schedule Table. On the Schedule Table contextual ribbon tab on the General panel, click the Edit Style drop-down button (bottom half) and choose the ***Property Set Definitions*** tool.
3. In the Style Manager, right-click GeoObjects from the list on the right and choose **Edit**.

TIP

You can also double-click on the Style name in Style Manager or select the name in the left pane to edit it.

4. Click the General tab.

The text in the Description field reads: "Object-based geographic schedule properties for all objects." This Property Set is defined for use in tracking the geographic location of objects within the project. This is a good example of how Property Sets and Schedules can be used as an aid in facilities management.

5. Click the Applies To tab.
6. A Property Set can apply to individual objects or to object styles and definitions, but not to both at the same time. At the top of the Applies To tab, note that this particular Property Set applies to objects (see Figure 15.25).

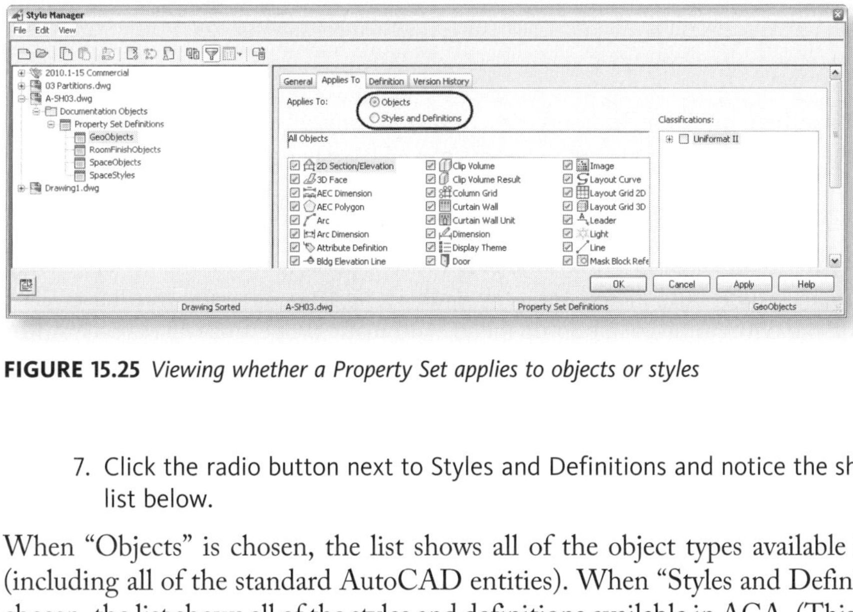

FIGURE 15.25 *Viewing whether a Property Set applies to objects or styles*

7. Click the radio button next to Styles and Definitions and notice the shift in the list below.

When "Objects" is chosen, the list shows all of the object types available in ACA (including all of the standard AutoCAD entities). When "Styles and Definitions" is chosen, the list shows all of the styles and definitions available in ACA. (This list does *not* include AutoCAD styles.) The buttons below each list, Select All and Clear All, allow easier selection within the lists. Because geographic location is not a property unique to any particular object or style, the GeoObjects Property Set is object-based and applies to all objects.

8. Click the Objects radio button to select it.
9. Click the Select All button to be sure all entities are checked.

10. Click the Definition tab (see Figure 15.26).

    Each individual property of the Property Set is configured on this tab.

A Property Set can have one or many properties. The only limit is practicality. All properties in this list are user-defined. You can tell this by the manual property icon next to each name. When a property is manual, you will be able to set its "name," "description," "type," "default" and "format." When a property is automatic, you will be able to set the "name," "description" and "format," as well as establish to which object property it should link. Refer to Figure 15.26 and review the following terms:

- **Name**—Should be descriptive and short and must *not* include spaces.

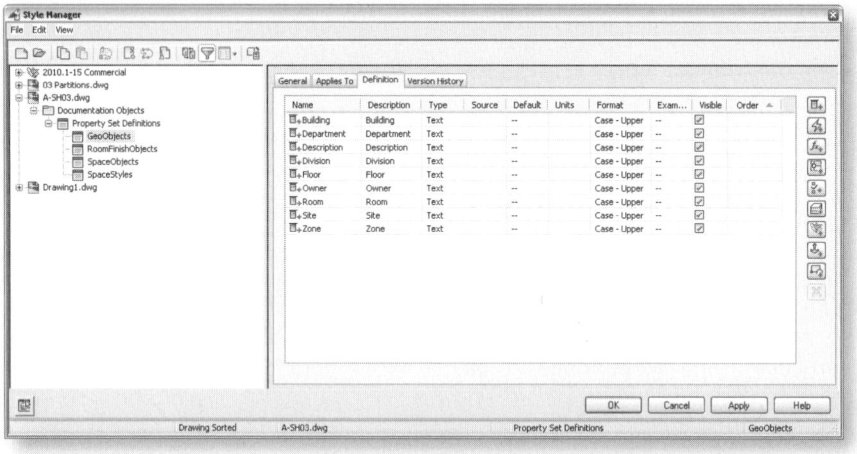

FIGURE 15.26 *The Definition tab of the Property Set Definition Properties dialog box*

- **Description**—A longer, more descriptive version of the name used to convey the intention of the property. Spaces can be used in descriptions. When a property is added as a column in a Schedule Table Style, the property description becomes the default text for the column header.
- **Type**—(Manual properties only) Sets the kind of data the property represents. Types include auto increment, real numbers, integers, text and true/false. Click on the entry to reveal a pop-up menu. Automatic properties will read as "Automatic," or as the type of automatic property ("Formula," "Location," etc.).
- **Source**—(Automatic properties only) Sets the automatic property to which the property is linked.
- **Default**—(Manual properties only) An initial value input automatically in the Property Data. Default is typically two dashes (–), which is recommended to facilitate Table Cell editing. This field can be left blank; but if no value is assigned, the user will be unable to use Edit Table Cell because there will be no way to select the "existing" value to edit.
- **Units**—Allows you to override the input and display units for a real number manual property, when the assigned Property Data Format has a Unit Type set and you wish to use a different unit from that set in the Property Data Format. This is useful for formula properties where you wish to calculate the value in units other than the default of the drawing or where the value is something other than a linear distance. A wide range of Unit Types is supported.

For example, use this to calculate formulas in inches when Feet and Inches is the default of the drawing.

- **Format**—References the list of available Property Data Formats to convert raw data to the desired presentation format (such as Feet and Inches, Case - Upper).
- **Example**—This field shows a sample value for manual properties, based on the Default value entered and the Format selected.
- **Visible**—Some properties are used only in formulas or nongraphical reports. If you do not wish to see these items on the Properties palette, you can change their Visible status. For example, if you are using Project Navigator, as we are in this book, you do not need to see the SpaceObjects-Number property. An example of this feature being used appears in the out-of-the-box DoorObjects Property Set (see below).
- **Order**—With this field, you can establish a custom sort order for the properties in the Property Set. This is the order that the properties will display in the Properties palette and in worksheets. An example of this feature being used appears in the out-of-the-box DoorObjects Property Set (see below).

For Manual properties, there are several types, as mentioned above. Auto Increment begins at whatever value you designate and steps sequentially—there are both numeric and character options. Real Numbers can be any numeric value with any quantity of decimal places. Integers allow whole numbers only (no decimals). Text is used for any character or numeric values that do not fit into one of the other categories. Any value can be input in a text field. True/False is a binary "on/off" type value. Use this for any property that has only two possibilities. A Property Data Format can be designed that includes any two values desired, such as Yes/No or In/Out.

MANAGER NOTE CAD

Property names should never include spaces if you want to create a custom Tag to accompany your Schedule. This is because AutoCAD attributes are used to define the text fields within the Tags and AutoCAD attribute names do not support spaces. The property name is used for internal configuration purposes, so not using spaces shouldn't be a problem. However, the description can contain spaces and should be written in language that makes each property's intention clear to the everyday user.

The GeoObjects Property Set does not offer much variety. All of the properties are manual (nonautomatic) text values.

11. On the left side, in the tree, expand the *03 Partitions* file, then the *Documentation Object* category and then the *Property Set Definitions* category. Finally, click on FrameStyles.

NOTE

If you closed *03 Partitions* above, click OK to close Style Manager, reopen *03 Partitions* on the Project Navigator, and then return to Style Manager to continue.

12. Click the Applies To tab.

This Property Set applies to Styles and Definitions, and it is more focused than the previous one. It applies only to Door, Door/Window Assembly and Window Styles.

13. Click the Definition tab.

Study the list of properties. Notice that there are some automatic and some manual properties.

14. Select the FrameWidth property in the list.
15. This is an automatic property, as you can see from the lightning bolt icon and the word *Automatic* in the Type column.
16. Click in the Source column and then click the small browse icon that appears (see Figure 15.27).

    In the "Automatic Property Source" dialog box, notice the check mark in the box next to Frame Width for Door (and Window). Door/Window Assembly has nothing checked. Take a moment to review the complete list of properties available.

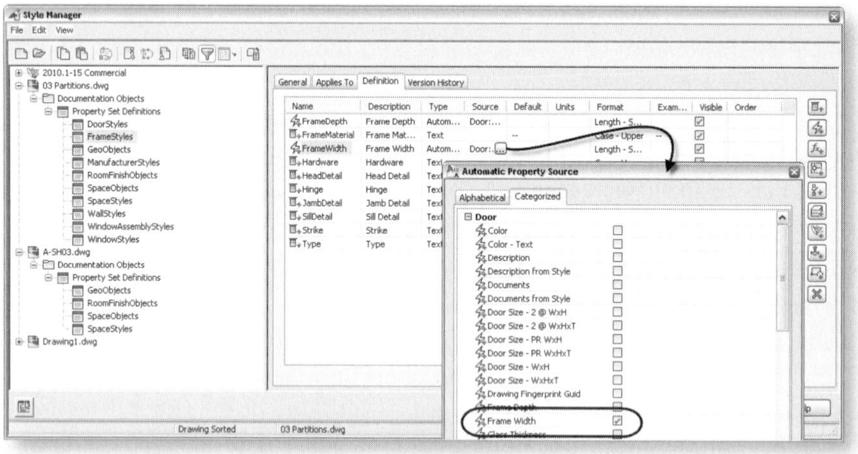

FIGURE 15.27 *The Automatic Property Source dialog box*

17. Click OK to dismiss the Automatic Property Source dialog box.
18. Continue to explore the various properties and their settings. When you are satisfied, click Cancel to return to the drawing.

SCHEDULE TABLE STYLES

Like all style-based AEC objects, the format and configuration of the Schedule object is controlled by a Schedule Table Style. The function of Schedule Table Styles can be broken down into two major functions: configuring the data content of the Schedule and graphically formatting the look of the Schedule Table. Let's begin our exploration of the Schedule Table Style with its graphic formatting.

Schedule Table Style Graphic Formatting

Of the many tabs in the Schedule Table Style Properties dialog box, Default Format, Layout and Display Properties control the format and visual characteristics of the Schedule. The Default Format tab is used to establish the text defaults for the entire Schedule Table style. On the Layout tab, you can assign text override formatting for the title and headers of the Schedule. On the Columns tab, you can assign an override to the header and/or the cells of just that column. Finally, Display Properties for Schedules is the same as it is for other AEC objects—here you control the Layer, Color, Linetype, Lineweight and Plot Style parameters of all Schedule components.

Examine Schedule Table Text Formatting

The Schedule Table style allows for a different Text style for each major Schedule component, including the main title, headings and the data entries. Typical AutoCAD Text Styles are used within the Schedule Table Style to determine text formatting (font, width factor, etc.) of a Schedule's components. Because they have not included a means to edit Text Style settings from within the Schedule Table Style dialog box itself, it is useful to remember to set up any Text Styles needed prior to editing the Schedule Table Style.

1. On the Project Navigator palette, on the Views tab, double-click *A-SH03* to open it.

NOTE **If you left this file open above, this action will simply make that file active.**

2. On the Annotate ribbon tab on the Text panel, select the Text Style drop-down button (upper right corner of the panel, displaying the name of the current text style) and choose the ***Manage Text Styles*** tool.

Notice that three styles for Schedules are included in the list: Schedule-Data, Schedule-Headers and Schedule-Title. These Text styles have been set up for use in the sample Schedule Table Styles provided with the software.

3. Choose the **Schedule-Data** Text Style from the list.

   Study the settings and look at the preview.

4. Repeat for the other two styles as well.

As you can see, these styles are well suited to their tasks. For instance the Schedule-Title Style uses a bold font, while the Schedule-Data Style does not. If you wish, you can change the settings; otherwise, click Cancel to return to the drawing.

Explore the Schedule Table Style Default Format

5. Select the Schedule object in the drawing, and, on the Schedule Table contextual ribbon tab on the General panel, choose the ***Save As*** tool.
6. On the General tab, name the new style **MACA Space Allocation Schedule** and give it a Description of **Mastering AutoCAD Architecture Space Allocation Schedule**.
7. Click the Default Format tab (see Figure 15.28).

This tab establishes the basic text parameters and other formatting considerations of the Schedule. Use this tab to set the way you wish the rows of data to be displayed. Titles and headers are formatted on the Layout tab (see below).

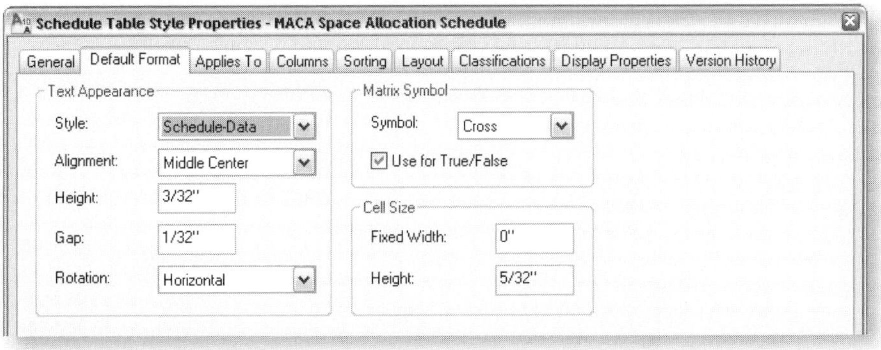

FIGURE 15.28 *The Default Format tab of the Schedule Table Style Properties dialog box*

- **Style**—Allows the choice of any previously defined Text style. This Text style is used for the entire Schedule unless overrides are attached on the Layout tab.
- **Alignment**—Choose from all the standard text alignments, such as left or center.
- **Height**—Sets the height of the text throughout the Schedule.

NOTE

Do not use scale factors; the Schedule Table object is already scaled using the value from Drawing Setup dialog box (also on the Drawing status bar). However, it is important to note that the Annotation Plot Size value (from Drawing Setup dialog box) does not have any effect on Schedules.

- **Gap**—Sets the space around the text within each cell. This is applied to all sides. For example, if the text Height is 1/8" [3] and the Gap is 1/16" [1.5], then the total height of the cell will be 1/4" [6].
- **Rotation**—Choose from either horizontal or vertical. Vertical is sometimes used for column headers, but rarely on the Default Format tab.
- **Matrix Symbol**—When using Matrix columns (such as in a residential finish Schedule), a choice of symbols is available (see below).
- **Use for True/False**—Some Property Set Data return a true/false value. If this box is checked, a symbol from the matrix symbol list will be used for true values; the cell will be blank when the value is false.
- **Fixed Width**—This value forces the width of cells to a set number of units. Text will wrap to this width if the value is too long to fit. This will enlarge the height of the cell. If the width value remains 0, then cells will widen as the value within them grows. The final width of a cell will be determined by the widest entry in a particular column.

TIP

Be careful when assigning a fixed width (other than 0). Although the data within the cell will wrap, long words might run over the cell borders and bleed into the next cell. This is because the word wrapping does not have the ability to hyphenate words. There is no way to prevent this other than to use a variable width (width = 0).

Override Formatting

After establishing the basic text formatting of the Schedule on the Default Format tab, you can assign overrides to various pieces on the Layout tab.

8. Click the Layout tab.

   The default title that appears at the top of the Schedule is entered here.

9. Change the table Title to **SPACE ALLOCATION SCHEDULE** (see Figure 15.29).

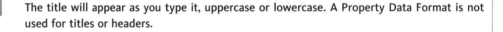

NOTE

The title will appear as you type it, uppercase or lowercase. A Property Data Format is not used for titles or headers.

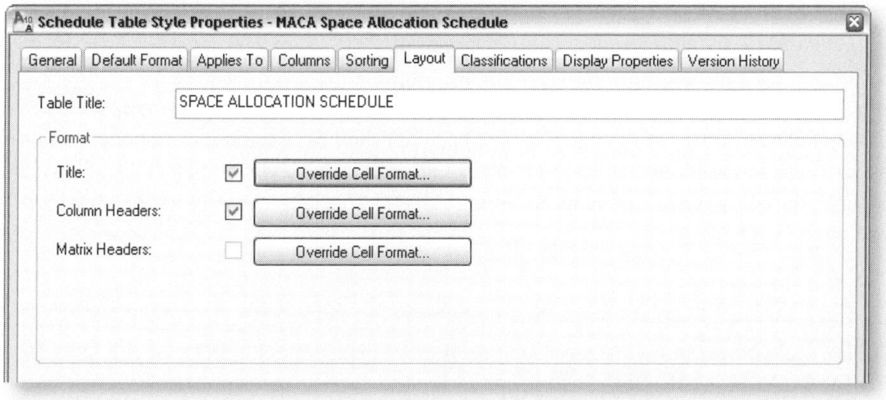

FIGURE 15.29 *A specific title can be assigned to the Schedule Table Style on the Layout tab*

The three buttons below the title field on the Layout tab can be used to assign text overrides to the title and the headers of the Schedule.

10. Click the Override Cell Format button next to Title.

    The fields in this dialog box match the ones on the Default Format tab. Override values will appear in red to help distinguish them from defaults.

    Notice that the Style, Height and Gap already have overrides applied. The effect is to make the title larger and bolder (see Figure 15.30).

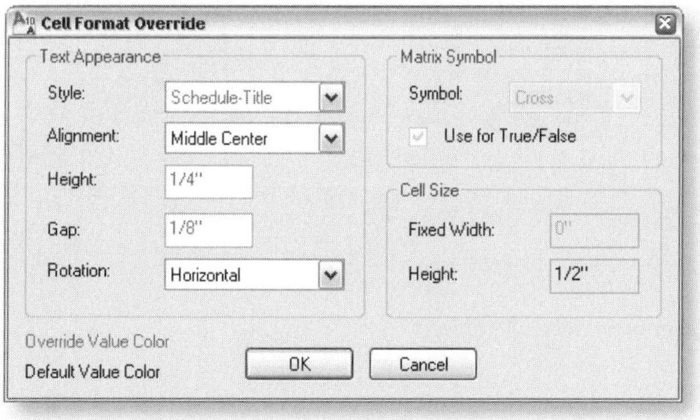

FIGURE 15.30 *Overriding Schedule title cell format properties*

11. Click OK to return to the Layout tab.

Configure Borders, Colors and Lineweights

Every component of the Schedule Table can be modified to achieve the exact graphic display and printed output desired. The Display Properties tab gives access to settings such as Layer, Color and Lineweight for each component. The settings established with the default out-of-the-box content are well-conceived. Regardless, let's have a look to see if there is something you wish to change.

12. Click the Display Properties tab.

    This reveals the standard ACA Display Properties tab. Notice that Schedule Tables have just one Display Representation: General. This is appropriate considering that Schedules are typically drawn the same regardless of the drawing on which they are displayed.

CAD MANAGER NOTE

Typically, you will wish to enforce a single officewide standard regarding the graphical display of Schedules. In this case, the goal is best accomplished by assigning all Schedule Table Display settings at the Drawing Default level. Editing at the style or object level works against uniform consistency but may be appropriate in specialized scenarios or on a per-project basis.

13. Click the Edit Display Properties icon.
14. Several components are shown here. As you can see, each piece of the Schedule Table can be configured individually.
15. Select the Header Bottom Row Line component.
16. Change its Color, Lineweight and Plot Style to match the Outer Frame component and change the Out of Date Marker color to Magenta (see Figure 15.31).

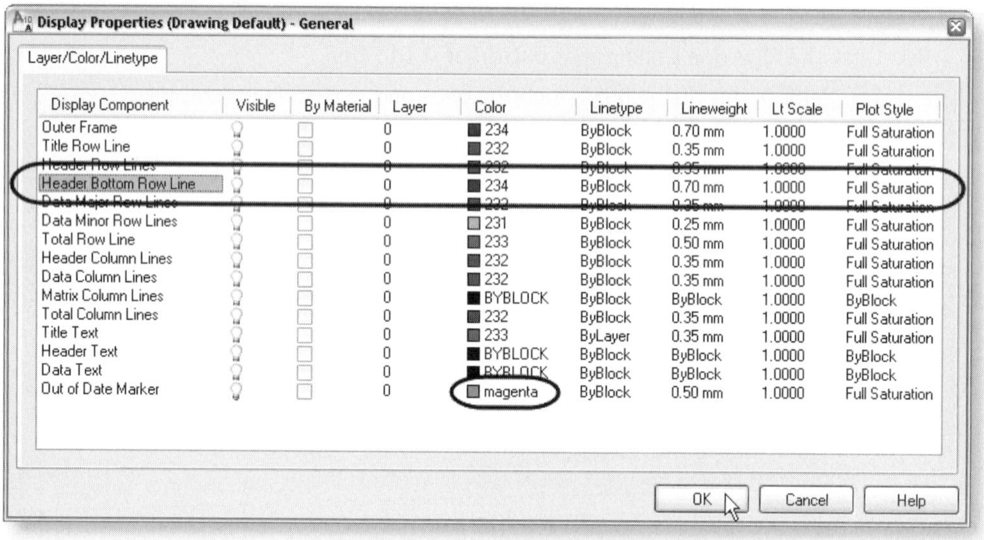

FIGURE 15.31 *Manipulating the Display Props of Schedule objects*

17. Review the remaining settings and make any desired changes.
18. Click OK twice to return to the drawing. If the drawing is not updated on its own, on the View ribbon tab on the Appearance panel, select the down arrow on the Regenerate split button (right side) and choose the ***Regenerate Model*** tool and then press ENTER.

Note the changes to the title and the row line under the headers. Also, a diagonal line will likely appear across the Schedule. This is the "Out of Date Marker." This line is a visual cue that your Schedule is out of date and needs to be updated. To update it, select the Schedule Table and, on the Schedule Table contextual ribbon tab on the Modify panel, choose the ***Update*** tool.

19. To see the lineweights displayed, click the Lineweight (LWT) toggle button at the bottom of the screen on the Application status bar (see Figure 15.32).

Lineweight display in model space is relative to screen size and not truly indicative of final plotted appearance. Paper space layouts are better suited to accurate onscreen display of lineweights. (Refer to Chapter 18 for information on using layouts.)

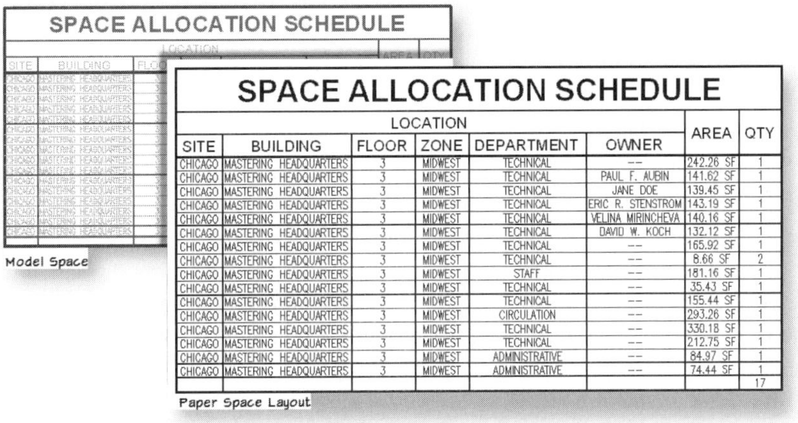

SPACE ALLOCATION SCHEDULE

LOCATION						AREA	QTY
SITE	BUILDING	FLOOR	ZONE	DEPARTMENT	OWNER		
CHICAGO	MASTERING HEADQUARTERS	3	MIDWEST	TECHNICAL	--	242.26 SF	1
CHICAGO	MASTERING HEADQUARTERS	3	MIDWEST	TECHNICAL	PAUL F. AUBIN	141.62 SF	1
CHICAGO	MASTERING HEADQUARTERS	3	MIDWEST	TECHNICAL	JANE DOE	139.45 SF	1
CHICAGO	MASTERING HEADQUARTERS	3	MIDWEST	TECHNICAL	ERIC R. STENSTROM	143.19 SF	1
CHICAGO	MASTERING HEADQUARTERS	3	MIDWEST	TECHNICAL	VELINA MIRINCHEVA	140.16 SF	1
CHICAGO	MASTERING HEADQUARTERS	3	MIDWEST	TECHNICAL	DAVID W. KOCH	132.12 SF	1
CHICAGO	MASTERING HEADQUARTERS	3	MIDWEST	TECHNICAL	--	165.92 SF	1
CHICAGO	MASTERING HEADQUARTERS	3	MIDWEST	TECHNICAL	--	8.66 SF	2
CHICAGO	MASTERING HEADQUARTERS	3	MIDWEST	STAFF	--	181.16 SF	1
CHICAGO	MASTERING HEADQUARTERS	3	MIDWEST	TECHNICAL	--	35.43 SF	1
CHICAGO	MASTERING HEADQUARTERS	3	MIDWEST	TECHNICAL	--	155.44 SF	1
CHICAGO	MASTERING HEADQUARTERS	3	MIDWEST	CIRCULATION	--	293.26 SF	1
CHICAGO	MASTERING HEADQUARTERS	3	MIDWEST	TECHNICAL	--	330.18 SF	1
CHICAGO	MASTERING HEADQUARTERS	3	MIDWEST	TECHNICAL	--	212.75 SF	1
CHICAGO	MASTERING HEADQUARTERS	3	MIDWEST	ADMINISTRATIVE	--	84.97 SF	1
CHICAGO	MASTERING HEADQUARTERS	3	MIDWEST	ADMINISTRATIVE	--	74.44 SF	1
							17

FIGURE 15.32 *Comparing lineweight display in model space and paper space*

MANAGER NOTE **CAD**

The Color, Lineweight and Plot Style were all assigned in the preceding exercise. Some firms use color, others use the Lineweight property and still others use Plot Style to assign Lineweights for plotting. Use whichever setting is appropriate for your firm's standards in real practice.

Schedule Table Style Data Content

The tabs covered so far in the Schedule Table Style relate to a Schedule's graphical display. The remaining tabs—Applies To, Columns and Sorting—establish what data the Schedule contains and how it is presented. Let's begin with the Applies To tab.

Determine which Object Types Appear in the Schedule Table

1. Select the Schedule object, and on the Schedule Table contextual ribbon tab on the General panel, choose the ***Edit Style*** tool.
2. Click on the Applies To tab.

The Applies To tab establishes the link to a particular type of object or objects. This works in the same way that it does in the Property Set Definition. By clicking the same object type(s) in both the Property Set Definition and the Schedule Table style, you bind the two together. You can check more than one item in Applies To. In order for a Property Set to be available to the Schedule Table style, the Property Set Definition must apply to at least all of the items that the Schedule style applies to. The Property Set Definition can apply to more than the Schedule, but not vice versa.

Notice that this Schedule has a check mark in the Space entry only. Therefore, any Property Set Definition that applies to at least Spaces will be available on the

Columns tab. Again, Property Sets can apply to more object types than the Schedule style, the way GeoObjects does for instance, but they must *at least* apply to Spaces to be included in this particular Schedule style.

Determine which Properties will Appear in the Schedule Table

The Columns tab establishes the columnar structure of the Schedule Table, and any headers. Each column contains the data of a single Property from a single Property Set. Each column can reference Properties from a different Property Set or all columns can reference Properties from the same Property Set. Any combination is also possible.

3. Click the Columns tab.
4. Scroll horizontally and make note of the various columns.
5. If you can, position this dialog box so that the Schedule Table in the drawing is visible beyond. Then compare the columns listed in the Columns tab with those actually in the drawing. You can also resize the Schedule Table Style Properties dialog box. Modifying any of these columns will have a direct effect on the structure of the Schedule in the drawing (see Figure 15.33).

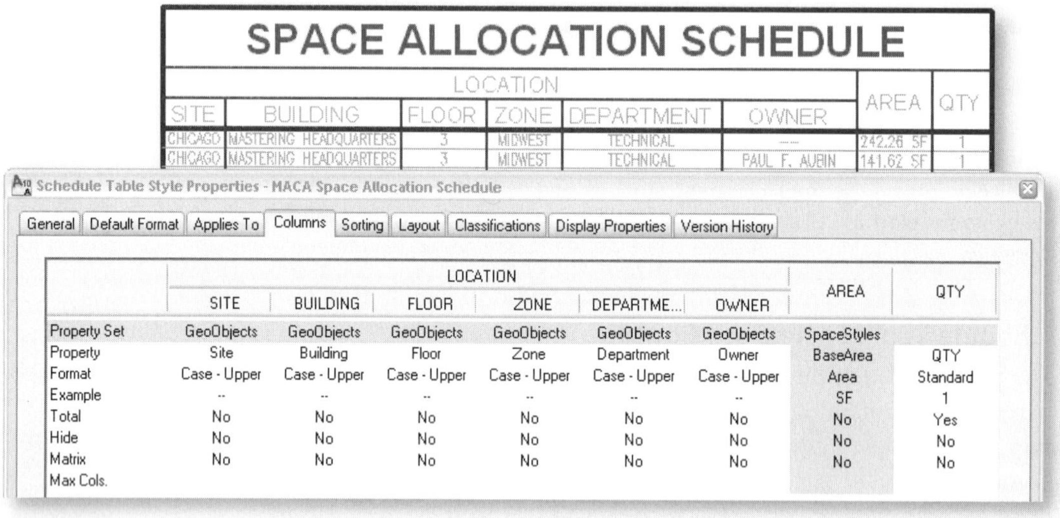

FIGURE 15.33 *Position the Schedule Table Style Properties dialog box so that the Schedule in the drawing is also visible*

6. Click the ZONE column (it will be highlighted), and then click the Modify button at the bottom of the dialog box (see Figure 15.34).

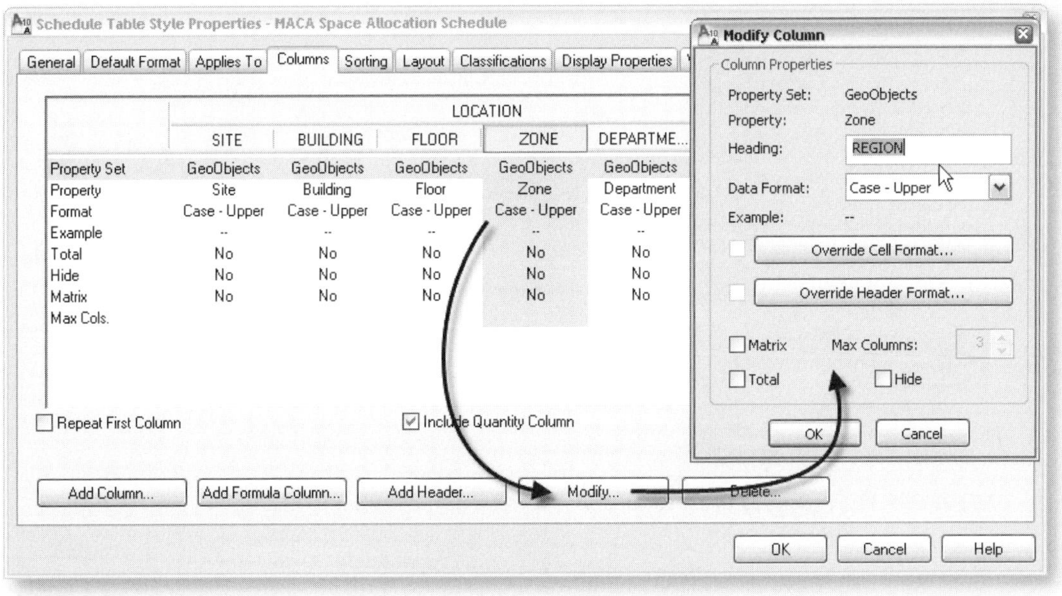

FIGURE 15.34 *Selecting columns to modify in the Schedule Table Style Properties dialog box*

Each column of the Schedule refers to a single property of a single Property Set. The first two items in the Modify Column dialog box show exactly which Property Set and specific Property this column accesses. The Schedule Table style can change the way a Property is formatted in the Schedule. The Heading box allows you to enter any column heading desired. This is the actual text that will appear at the top of the column on the Schedule itself. This does not change the Property Set Definition in any way.

7. Change the heading from ZONE to **REGION** and then click OK.

The Data Format drop-down list shows all of the Property Data Formats currently available in the drawing. Its value defaults to whatever was set in the Property Set Definition. Notice that this column is assigned to Case – Upper. This means that regardless of how the data is input by the user, it will be formatted in upper case in the Schedule Table. Please note, however, that this formatting does not apply to the titles and headers. These must be typed in uppercase if you wish them displayed as such.

Override Cell Formatting

8. Select the Area column and then click the Modify button.
9. Click the Override Cell Format button.

This button provides access to the same settings outlined above in the Default Format tab. Any of the values discussed previously can be edited here. However, the overrides apply to this column only.

10. Change the Alignment to **Bottom Right**.
11. In the Fixed Width field, type **1 1/2"** [**30**] and then click OK.
12. Back in the Modify Column dialog box, place a check mark in the Total checkbox (see Figure 15.35).

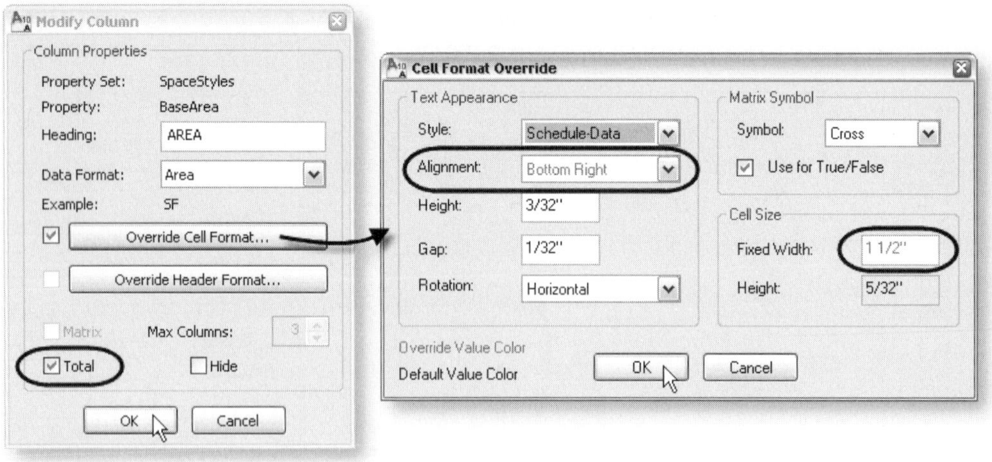

FIGURE 15.35 *Configuring the Area column for a total at the bottom*

13. Click OK twice more to return to the drawing.

Notice the change to the Zone and Area columns of the Schedule; Zone is now REGION and all of the values in the AREA column now line up properly at the right side. There is a total area at the bottom of the AREA column and there is more room to the left of the column. If your Schedule now overlaps the plan, move it over to the left.

Modify a Property Data Format Style

Some firms like to round off the Area value to the nearest whole unit. To do this, modify the Area Property Data Format style.

14. Select the Schedule Table. On the Schedule Table contextual ribbon tab on the General panel, click the Edit Style split button (bottom half) and choose the Property Data Formats tool.
15. On the left side, select the Area Format and then click the Formatting tab.
16. From the "Precision" list, choose **0** and then click OK to see the results (see Figure 15.36).

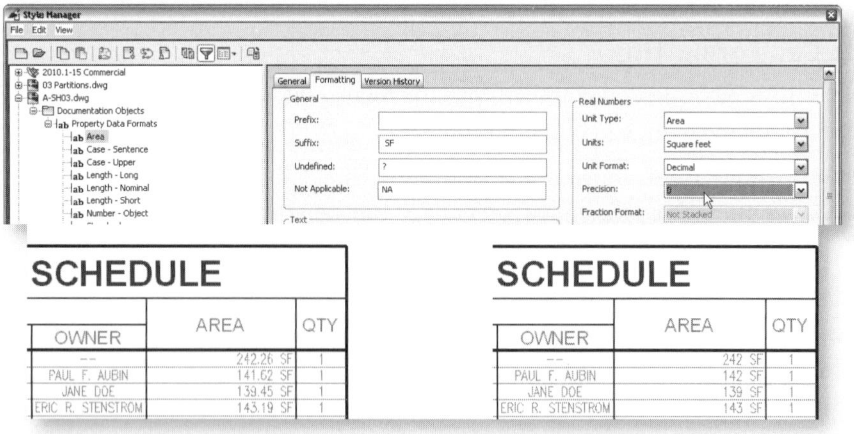

FIGURE 15.36 *Edit the Area Property Data Format to change the number of decimal places*

Note that the values round off using standard conventions in the before and after illustrations shown at the bottom half of the figure.

Move, Delete and Add Columns

17. Select the Schedule object, choose the ***Edit Style*** tool again and then return to the Columns tab.
18. Click the REGION heading and drag it on top of the FLOOR heading (see Figure 15.37).

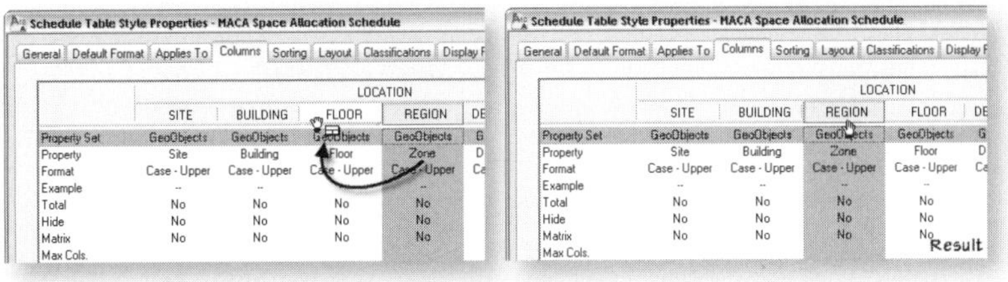

FIGURE 15.37 *Drag columns to change their order*

19. Click OK to view the change.

    Notice the new order of the REGION and FLOOR columns.
20. Select the Schedule object, choose the ***Edit Style*** tool again and then return to the Columns tab.
21. Select the BUILDING column and then click the Delete button at the bottom of the window.
22. Click OK when asked to confirm and click OK again to return to the drawing.

    Notice the removal of the BUILDING column.
23. Select the Schedule object, choose the ***Edit Style*** tool again and then return to the Columns tab.
24. Click the Add Column button at the bottom of the dialog box.

In the Add Columns dialog box, available Properties are listed on the left. Unavailable items (grayed out) have already been added to the Schedule. Column properties for the selected item can be edited on the right before clicking OK (this is the same as clicking the Modify button later). Use the area at the bottom to decide where in the existing column order to place the new column (or if you prefer, you can drag it after you place it).

25. Select the Categorized tab and scroll through the list of properties.
26. Locate the SpaceObjects Property Set and select "Name" (Room Name) (see Number 1 in Figure 15.38).
27. In the Heading box type **ROOM NAME** (remember uppercase) (see Number 2 in Figure 15.38).
28. At the bottom of the dialog box, choose **Insert Before** and then choose **GeoObjects:Site** from the Column list (see Number 3 in Figure 15.38).

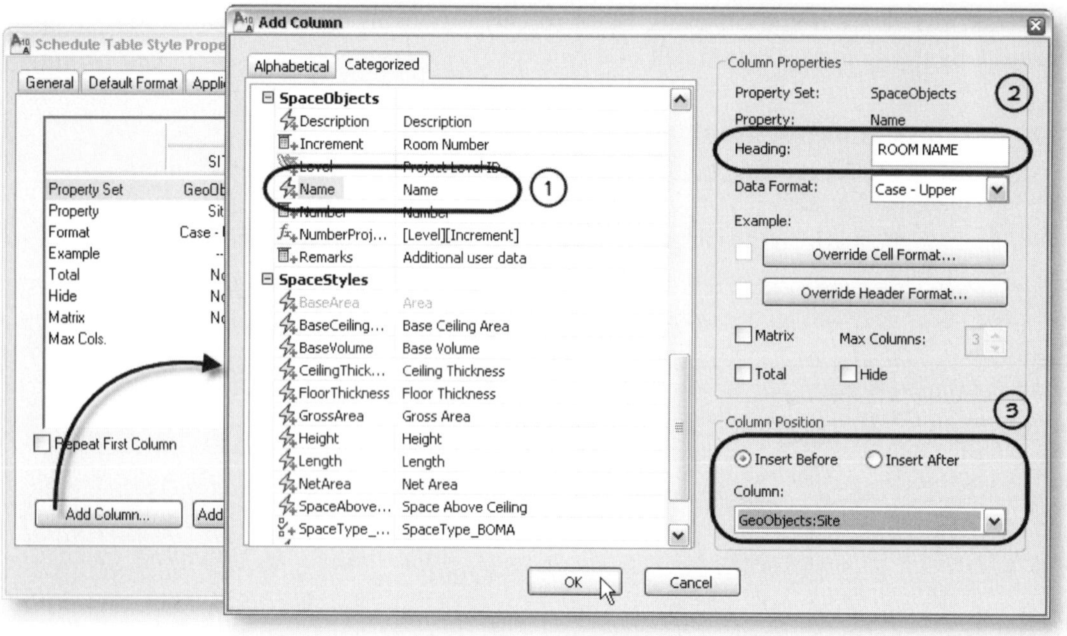

FIGURE 15.38 *Adding a column to the Schedule style*

29. Click OK and note the new column at the left.
30. Click OK again to view the change in the drawing.

There is now a Room Name column at the beginning of the Schedule. The Room Names have already been filled in based on the Property Sets we added in Chapter 14. (See the "Adding Room Tags" heading in Chapter 14 for more information.)

31. Modify the alignment of some of the text columns (such as Room Name) to make them left-justified. (Review the "Override Cell Formatting" topic above for assistance if necessary.)

Work with a Matrix Column

In this sequence, we will change the format of the DEPARTMENT column to a "Matrix" column, which offers a more graphical display of the information in that column. Before we can gain much value from this change, we need to finish editing the values in this column.

32. Using the procedures outlined above, fill in the values in the DEPARTMENT column.

You can edit the Spaces directly in *03 Partitions* on the Properties palette, or close *03 Partitions* and use Edit Referenced Property Set Data command or Edit Table Cell from the *A-SH03* file. Remember, you cannot use these two methods if *03 Partitions* is open—editing Property data requires that the Construct can be edited and saved. For the offices along the bottom and left side, and the two Workstation Spaces, use a mix of Department names like: **Marketing**, **Sales** and **Technical**. Make the Reception, Conference Room and Corridor use the name: **Public**. Make the Department name for the Break Room, Copy Room and Electrical Closet: **Common**. Make the Closets the same as the Spaces to which they are attached (see Figure 15.39).

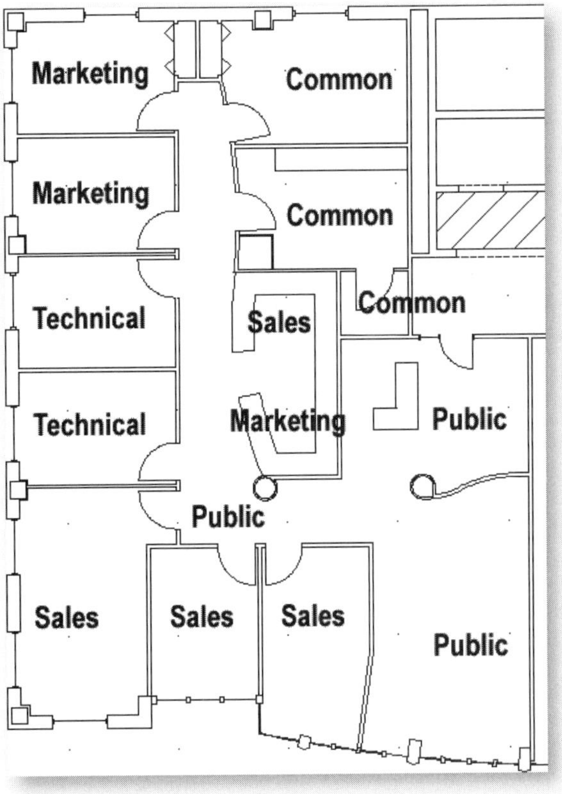

FIGURE 15.39 *Edit the Department names of all Spaces*

33. Select the Schedule object, choose the ***Edit Style*** tool again, and then return to the Columns tab.
34. Select the DEPARTMENT column and then click the Modify button.
35. Put a check mark in the Matrix checkbox and change the "Max Columns" to **6** and then click OK.
36. Click the Default Format tab and in the Matrix Symbol area, open the list of symbols and choose **Dot** (see Figure 15.40).

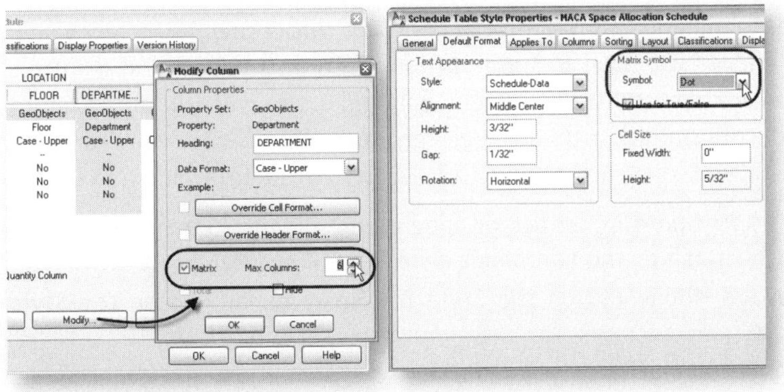

FIGURE 15.40 *Changing the Department column to a Matrix column and the default Matrix symbol to a Dot*

37. Click the Layout tab.
38. Next to Matrix Headers, click the button labeled Override Cell Format (don't click the checkbox).
39. From the Style list, choose Schedule-Header.
40. From the Rotation list, choose **Vertical** and then click OK (see Figure 15.41).

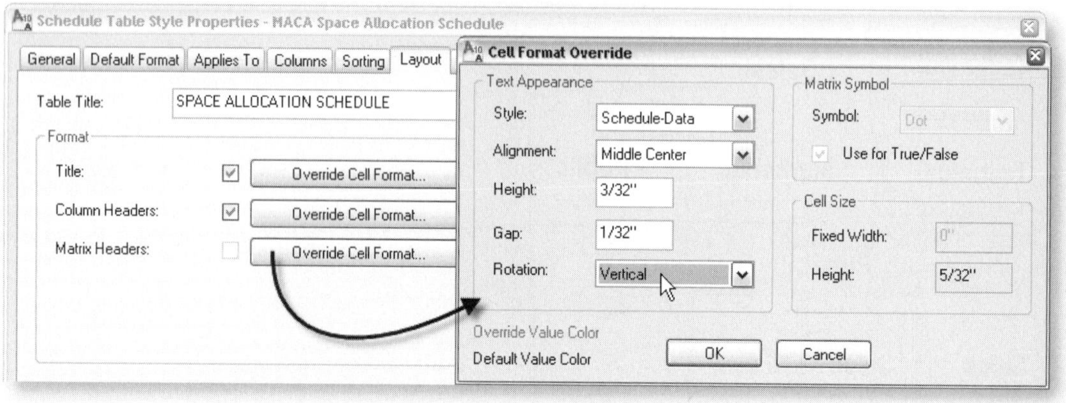

FIGURE 15.41 *Changing the orientation of Matrix Headers to vertical*

41. Click OK again to view the results.

Several changes have occurred in the Schedule Table. The individual department names are running vertically as subheadings beneath the DEPARTMENT column heading. A dot appears in the Schedule as each department occurs. Matrix Headers occur only for Properties actually in use. To test this out, select the XREF, right-click and choose **Open XREF**, which opens *03 Partitions*. Then select any Space object in the drawing and change the value of the GeoObjects:Department property to **Standard** on the Extended Data tab of Properties palette. Save and Close the *03 Partitions* file. Reload the *03 Partitions* XREF and update the Schedule Table if necessary. Notice the addition of a new Matrix column named "Standard." Repeat the steps to reverse the change.

Add a Graphic Property

Sometimes you want to include an image in the Schedule rather than just a text value. To do this, we can add a Graphical Property Set Definition. Let's look at a simple example of a Graphical Property in the current Schedule. We will add an image to represent the Region column rather than the current text value. To do this, we must return to the *03 Partitions* Construct and edit a Property Set Definition.

42. Select the *03 Partitions* Construct onscreen, and, on the External Reference contextual ribbon tab on the Edit panel, choose the ***Open Reference*** tool.
43. On the Manage ribbon tab on the Style & Display panel, choose the ***Style Manager*** tool.
44. Expand *Documentation Objects*, select Property Set Definitions and then edit the GeoObjects Property Set Definition.
45. On the Definition tab, select Zone and then click the Remove icon.

46. On the right side, just above the Remove icon, click the Add Graphic Property Definition (see Figure 15.42).
47. In the "Graphic Property Definition" dialog, name the Property **Zone** and then choose Image for the Source.

To create a Graphic Property, you need to point to an image file (BMP, TIF, PNG, etc.) or a Block. Some image files have been provided in the project folders for expediency's sake.

48. Click the Browse button and navigate to the *C:\MasterACA 2010\Chapter15\MACA Commercial\Standards\Graphics* [*C:\MasterACA 2010\Chapter15\MACA Commercial Metric\Standards\Graphics*] folder.
49. Select the *US_regional_map-Central.png* image file and then click Open.
50. For the Path type, choose **Full Path**.
51. Clear the "Use image name for property description" checkbox.
52. Leave the remaining settings at their defaults and then click OK (see Figure 15.42).

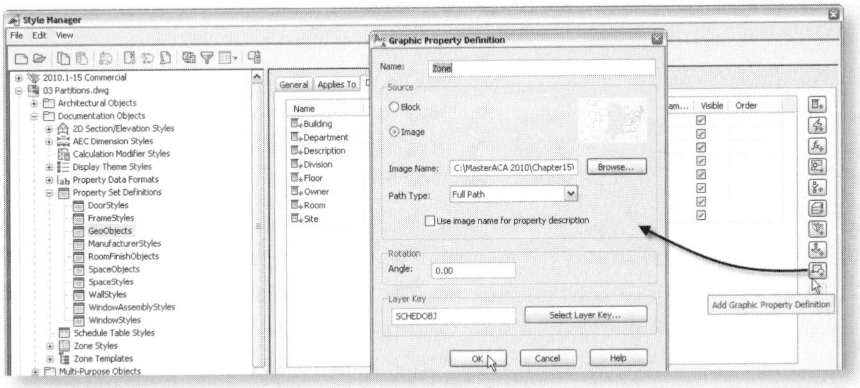

FIGURE 15.42 *Add a Graphic Property for the Division*

The Description is typically used as the default column header in the Schedule Table. This is why we cleared the checkbox above. You can now click in that field and edit it to a more useful Description for the Schedule column header.

53. Click in the Description field (currently empty), click the small browse icon that appears and type **REGION** (remember uppercase).
54. While still in Style Manager, drag and drop or copy and paste GeoObjects from *03 Partitions* to *A-SH03*.
55. When prompted, choose Overwrite Existing and then click OK (see Figure 15.43).
56. Click OK to close the Style Manager.
57. Select the two office Spaces at the bottom between the corner office and the conference room.
58. On the Extended Data tab of the Properties palette, beneath the GeoObjects Property Set, click on the Zone field.
59. In the "Graphic Property" dialog that appears, click the Browse button, navigate to the same folder as above and choose the *US_regional_map-East.png* image file (see Figure 15.43). Click OK to accept the change.

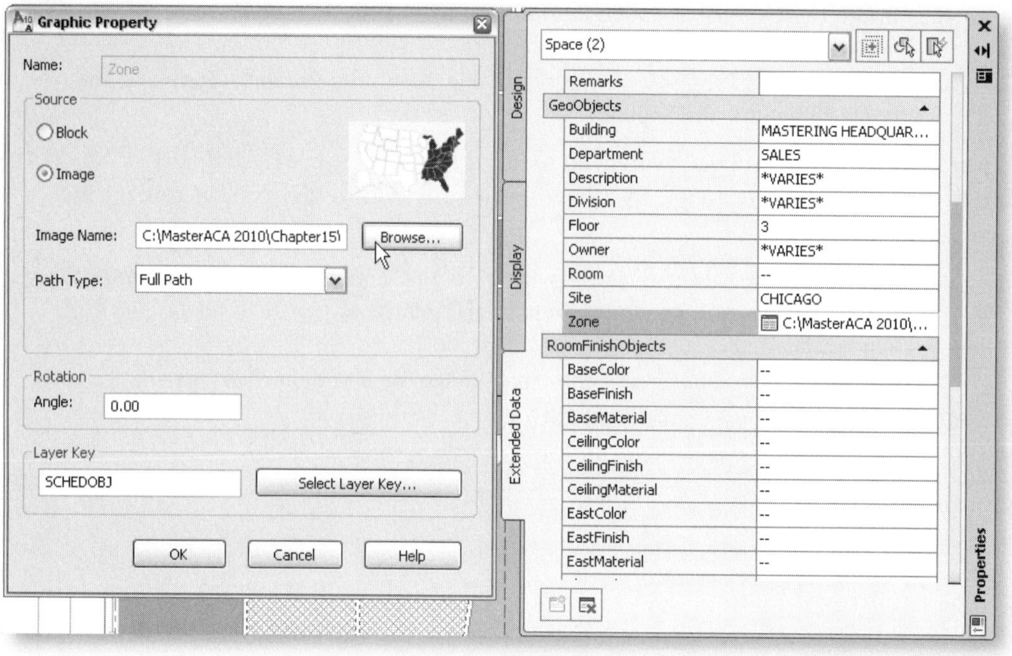

FIGURE 15.43 *Assign a different image to some of the Spaces*

60. Select a few other offices, repeat the process and choose *US_regional_map-West.png* instead.

An additional image named simply *None.png* has also been provided. You can use this one to override the Conference, Reception, Corridor, Break Room, Electrical Room and Copy Room Spaces. Since these are all common Spaces, they would not belong to a specific Division. You can skip this step if you wish. You will still get the sense of the Graphic Property even without this change.

61. Save and close *03 Partitions*.
62. Back in the *A-SH03* View file, reload the XREFs and then Update the Schedule table.

The REGION column has been removed from the Schedule Table. Let's add it back.

63. Select the Schedule and, on the Schedule Table contextual ribbon tab on the General panel, select the ***Edit Style*** tool. Click on the Columns tab if it is not current.
64. Select the Site Column, click on the Add Column button and choose the GeoObjects:Zone property.
65. Verify the Heading is set to REGION, the Column Position is set to Insert After GeoObjects:Site and press OK twice to return to the drawing.

The images should appear automatically in the REGION column. However, they will likely be tiny. We need to make an edit to the height of the column to fix this.

66. Select the Schedule, and choose the ***Edit Style*** tool, again.
67. Select the Region column, click the Modify button and then in the "Modify Column" dialog, click the Override Cell Format button.
68. For the Height, type **3/8"** [**10**] and then click OK three times to return to the drawing (see Figure 15.44).

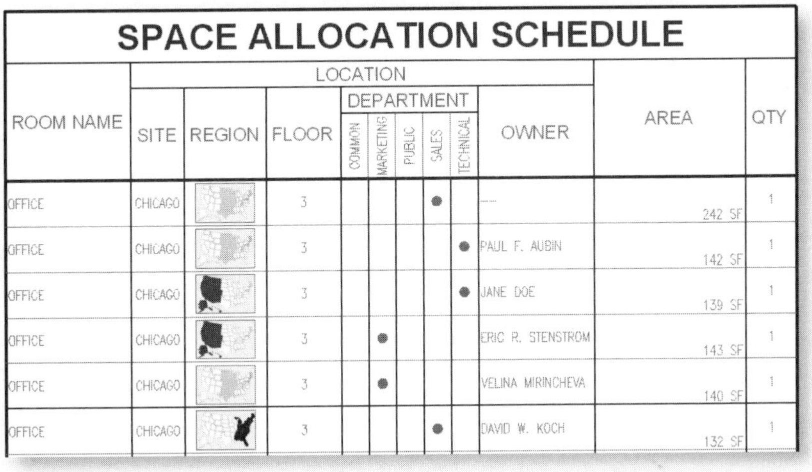

SPACE ALLOCATION SCHEDULE											
ROOM NAME	LOCATION								OWNER	AREA	QTY
	SITE	REGION	FLOOR	DEPARTMENT							
				COMMON	MARKETING	PUBLIC	SALES	TECHNICAL			
OFFICE	CHICAGO		3				●		---	242 SF	1
OFFICE	CHICAGO		3					●	PAUL F. AUBIN	142 SF	1
OFFICE	CHICAGO		3					●	JANE DOE	139 SF	1
OFFICE	CHICAGO		3		●				ERIC R. STENSTROM	143 SF	1
OFFICE	CHICAGO		3		●				VELINA MIRINCHEVA	140 SF	1
OFFICE	CHICAGO		3				●		DAVID W. KOCH	132 SF	1

FIGURE 15.44 *The Graphic Properties appear in the Schedule in the Region column*

69. Save the file.

Sort a Schedule Table

There is one more tab left to consider in the Schedule Style. This is the Sorting tab. Here we can designate the column(s) from which to sort the data in the Schedule Table. You can choose ascending or descending, and you can sort by more than one column if you wish.

70. In the *A-SH03* View file, select the Schedule and, on the Schedule Table contextual ribbon tab on the General panel, choose the ***Edit Style*** tool.
71. Click the Sorting tab.
72. Click the Add button.
73. Choose SpaceObjects: Name and then click OK twice to return to the drawing and view the change.

    The Schedule now sorts alphabetically (ascending) by Room Name.

The Schedule customization is now complete. Edit the Property Set Data of the remaining Spaces to complete the Schedule. Tweak any other settings you wish to fine-tune the Schedule style to meet your own standards.

74. Save the file.

Special Column Types and Features

There are some additional items on the Columns tab of the Schedule Table Style Properties dialog box worthy of mention.

- **Quantity**—Identical objects can have their line items in the Schedule grouped together and expressed as a quantity rather than being listed separately. The Schedule used in this tutorial uses a quantity column. In order to be quantified, duplicate line items must be *identical* in all columns. Include a quantity column by putting a check mark in the Include Quantity Column checkbox.
- **Formula**—With a Formula Column you can include any valid VBScript expression and have the values calculated and included in a Schedule Table. This is a very powerful way to add robust calculations to your Schedule Tables.

CAD MANAGER NOTE

If you wish to use this Schedule Table style in other drawings, copy and paste the style to a library file and save it. Create a new tool palette or use an existing one and make it active. Drag this Schedule Table from the library drawing onto a tool palette. A new tool will be created from the Schedule Table.

Add a Model Space View

In the next topic, we will do an advanced tutorial adding a complete project-based Door Schedule. In that exercise, we will create a new Sheet file for our Project in which to insert the Door Schedule. We will then add the Schedule created here to that Sheet. In preparation for that, let's make a Model Space View that defines only the area occupied by our Space Allocation Schedule to be included on the Sheet.

1. On the Project Navigator, right-click on *A-SH03* and choose **New Model Space View**.
2. In the Add Model Space View dialog, type: **Third Floor Space Allocation Schedule** for the Name and accept the remaining defaults.
3. Click the Define View Window icon on the right and in the drawing, click two points defining a rectangular region just a bit larger than the Schedule Table.
4. Click OK to complete the Model Space View.

We will drag this View onto the *A-601 Schedules* Sheet below.

Change the Title of the Schedule Table Object

Each Schedule Table can have its own unique Title.

5. Select the Schedule, right-click and choose **Properties**.
6. On the Properties palette, change the Title property to: **THIRD FLOOR SPACE ALLOCATION** (upper case) (see Figure 15.45).

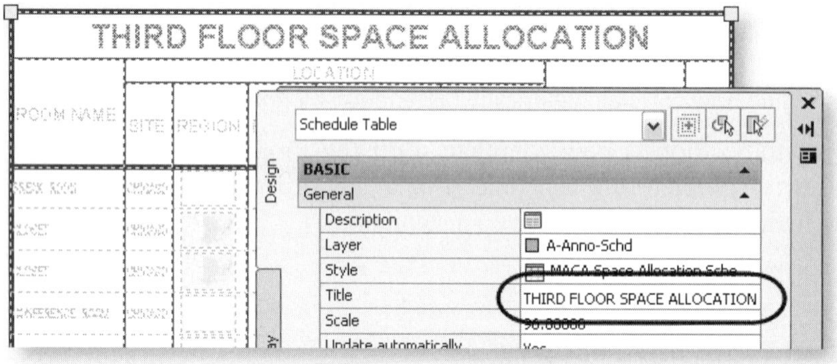

FIGURE 15.45 *Assign a unique Title to this Schedule object*

7. Save and close the file.

BUILDING A PROJECT-BASED DOOR SCHEDULE (ADVANCED)

The remainder of this chapter is more advanced. If you are not interested in linking Door numbers to Room numbers, you can skip this topic. In this topic, we will explore a project-based Door Schedule of the entire building. There are many exciting features of the Schedule Table tool set that we will explore. For example, in the exercise that follows, we will add Door Tags to the first floor plan and the third floor plan View files, build a new Sheet file for Schedule Tables and add a complete Door Schedule of the entire Commercial Project. This process is involved but very beneficial.

Following the logic used above, we could create our new Door Schedule within its own View file. In order to schedule the entire project, this would need to be a View much like our Composite Model and include all of the Constructs that contained Doors. There is nothing wrong with that approach, and you are free to follow it if you wish. However, there is an even better approach that takes advantage of an exciting feature of Schedule Tables: the ability to schedule a remote drawing. Let's explore this feature next.

Create a New Sheet and Schedule a Remote File

A Schedule Table can be set to schedule a remote drawing file. In this case, the Schedule becomes a one-way report with a live link to the data contained in the drawing that it schedules. When you use this feature, it is unnecessary to create a View file for Schedules and then reference that View file to a Sheet. Instead, you simply add the Schedule Table directly to a Sheet file in paper space, and link it to your composite building model (or any other file that you wish to schedule).

While this approach might seem contradictory to the definition of Sheets presented in Chapter 5, actually it is not. The fact that this Schedule, once added and linked to a remote file, is a one-way report, means that it will require no further intervention from a user. Therefore, it is fine (and preferable) to have it directly on the Sheet. Every time that Sheet is opened, it will automatically gather the latest Schedule Data, and be "ready to print" – exactly what we would expect from a Sheet file.

1. On the Project Navigator, click the Sheets tab.
2. Right-click on *Architectural – Schedules and Diagrams* Subset and choose **New > Sheet**.
3. Type: **A-601** for the Number and type: **Schedules** for the Sheet title, and then click OK (see Figure 15.46).

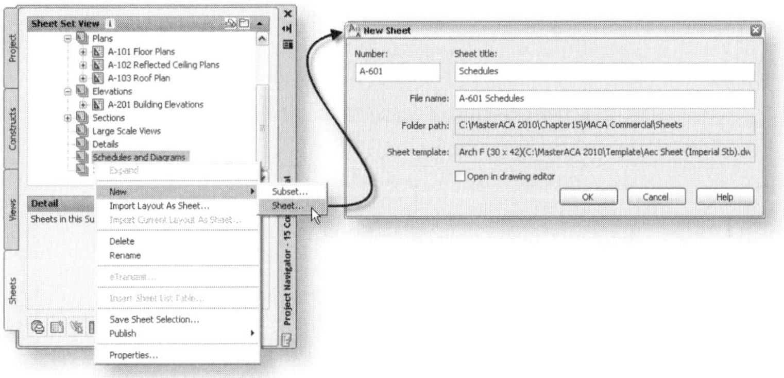

FIGURE 15.46 *Create a new Sheet file for Project Schedules in the Schedules and Diagrams Subset*

4. Double-click the new *A-601 Schedules* to open it.

   New Sheet files open into a single paper space layout named the same as the file, which contains a title block.

5. On the Scheduling tool palette, click the Door Schedule Project Based tool.

   If you do not see this palette or tool, right-click the Tool Palettes title bar and choose **Document** (to load the Documentation Tool Palette Group) and then click the Scheduling tab.

6. At the "Select objects or Enter to schedule external drawing" prompt, press ENTER.

   A rectangle will appear at your cursor and the command prompt will request the "Upper-left corner of table."

7. Click a point near the top-left corner of the sheet and then press ENTER to accept the default size.

   An empty Door Schedule will appear showing only the title and headers.

8. Select this Schedule and on the Properties palette, click the Design tab and scroll down to the Advanced grouping.

9. In the External Source grouping, change Schedule external drawing to **Yes**.

   An additional field labeled "External drawing" will appear.

10. Open the menu in External drawing (click on *__None__*).

    A list of all of the View files in the *Views* folder will appear. If the file that you wish to schedule does not appear on the list, you can also choose **Browse** at the bottom of the list and locate any drawing.

We are going to choose the Composite Building Model to schedule. This is because it contains all of the Constructs for the entire project. Therefore, if we schedule it, we will be sure to include all of the Doors.

11. From the list, choose the Composite Model file: *.\Views\A-CM00.dwg* (see Figure 15.47).

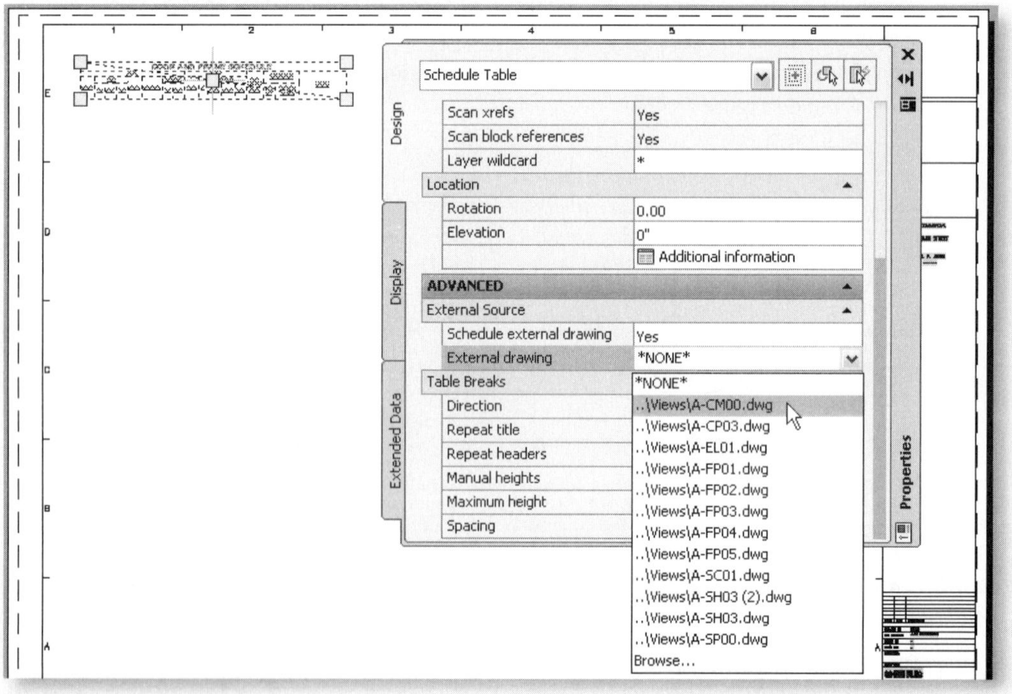

FIGURE 15.47 *Choose the Composite Model (A-CM00)*

12. With the Schedule still selected, on the Schedule Table contextual ribbon tab on the Modify panel, choose the ***Update*** tool.

When the Table completes the update, there will now be several rows of data. The Schedule Table has extracted information about every Door in the project! If you select this Schedule Table again and check its properties, you will notice that many are grayed out. This means that we will not need to do anything more to this Schedule Table. Whenever the Doors in the project change, those changes will be read directly by this Schedule Table each time the *A-601 Schedules* Sheet file is opened—usually for printing.

Manipulate Schedule Table Size and Scale

13. Select the Schedule to reveal its grips.
14. Hover over any of the four grips at the corners.

Notice the dynamic dimensions that appear. The overall size of the Schedule Table is revealed as well as the scale. As you can see, since we added this Schedule Table in paper space, the scale is set to 1.

15. Click the small triangular grip at the bottom edge of the Schedule.
16. Drag it up and click again.

Notice that this grip changes the Maximum page height. This particular Schedule is not very tall, but on very large projects where there are hundreds of Doors, the Schedule can get quite long. Use this grip to "wrap" the Schedule on the Sheet. Additional parameters for this feature appear on the Properties palette.

That is all that we need to do to this Schedule Table for now. However, if you zoom in on it and look at the data, you will see that we still have quite a bit of work in the project files. Our Doors do not have any object-based data yet.

17. Save and close the file.

Add Tags to XREFed Doors

We are now ready to add Door Tags. As we saw above in the Space Allocation Schedule tutorial, adding Tags does more than just insert a Multi-View Block. This is how we will also import all of the object-based Property Set Data that is required for our Door Schedule, attach it to the Doors and anchor the Tags to those Doors. For this sequence, we will use the Tags on the Tags tool palette.

18. On the Project Navigator, click the Views tab.
19. In the *Views* folder, double-click the *A-FP01* file to open it.

You will note that Space objects have been added to the Constructs referenced by this file. They will be important to the process of Tagging Doors. You will also note that the *Core* file XREF has been unloaded. We will reload it later in the tutorial.

There are two Door Tags on the Tags tool palette. The Door Tag is a simple auto-incrementing Door Tag much like the Window Tag that we used in the last chapter. The Door Tag – Project Based is a more robust Tag that references the Room number of a neighboring Space object. In this way, we are able to link the Door numbers to the Room numbers.

20. Zoom in on the central lobby space (just below the elevators and above the curved Wall).
21. On the Tags tool palette, click the Door Tag – Project Based tool.

22. At the "Select object to Tag" prompt, click one of the two Doors facing into this Space.
23. At the "Specify location of Tag" prompt, click a point near the Door.

TIP It will be easier to place the Tag if you turn off Object Snap.

Don't exit the command yet.

Notice that the number appears as "?A." As you recall, the question mark indicates that the Property Set Data has not yet been added, yet we have just Tagged the Door, which is supposed to attach the required Property Set Data. The problem is that this particular Tag uses a more advanced Property Set. The Door Number property is a Formula property (see the definition above in the "Automatic and Manual Property Sets" topic). The formula in use here is a simple concatenation of the adjacent room number and a letter suffix. The question mark in this case is indicating that the Property Set is missing from the Space, not the Door.

The command prompt again reads "Select object to Tag."

24. Tag the Door on the opposite side of the lobby, the three revolving Doors at the building entrance and the exit door near the Stair and then press ENTER to complete the command (see Figure 15.48).

    Right-click and use the Multiple option if you wish.

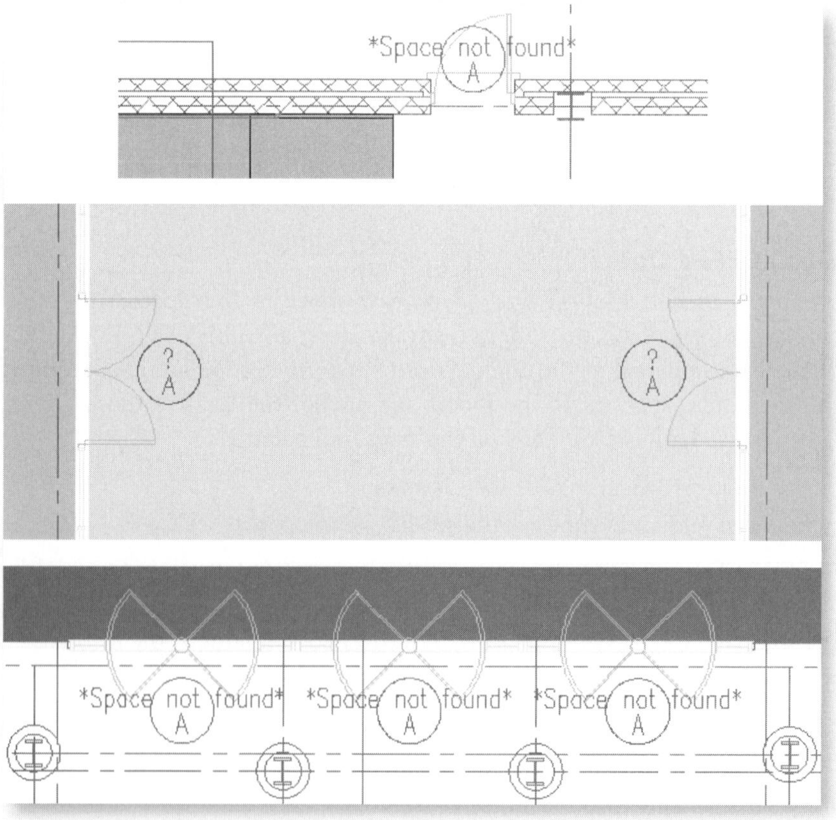

FIGURE 15.48 *Various errors appear in the Door Tags*

NOTE

If an XREF alert appears stating that your reference files have changed, it is OK to ignore these. When you Tag View files, it is actually adding the Property Set Data to the Construct files, meaning that the XREFs (Constructs in this case) have actually changed. However, graphically there will be no change to the drawing, so an update at this time is not necessary.

The problem seems a bit worse on the three revolving Doors and the rear exit Door. Let's deal with each issue separately starting with the retail lobby Doors. We need to make two adjustments in order to correct the Door Tag numbers. The Door Tags use a Location Property (see the definition in the "Automatic and Manual Property Sets" heading above) to query the Room Number of the Space in which they swing. So first, we must attach the required Property Sets to the Spaces. The easiest way to accomplish this is to Tag the Spaces.

25. On the Tags tool palette, click the Room Tag – Project Based tool.
26. Follow the prompts as before and Tag each of the Spaces and then press ENTER to exit the command.

    Start with the main entrance lobby at the bottom of the plan (the one with the three revolving Doors), Tag the retail lobby next and then the two retail tenant spaces. Tagging them in this order will ensure that they are numbered as such.
27. Open *01 Partitions* and edit the Room Names of each of the four Spaces.

    The room Tags should update with the new names.

Edit the Number Suffix

When you finish with the room Tags, the door Tags in the center of the plan (in the retail lobby Space) should update immediately. If they do not, on the View ribbon tab on the Appearance panel, click the down arrow on the Regenerate split button (right side), select the ***Regenerate Model*** tool and then press ENTER. The three revolving Doors will remain incorrect.

Even though the two retail lobby Doors did update, they will both have the same number (or specifically the same "Number Suffix").

28. Click on the retail lobby Space to select the *01 Partitions* XREF, right-click and choose **Edit Referenced Property Set Data**.
29. At the "Select Objects" prompt, click the retail lobby Door on the right side of the plan and then press ENTER.
30. In the Edit Referenced Property Set Data dialog, change the Number Suffix to: **B** and then click OK (see Figure 15.49).

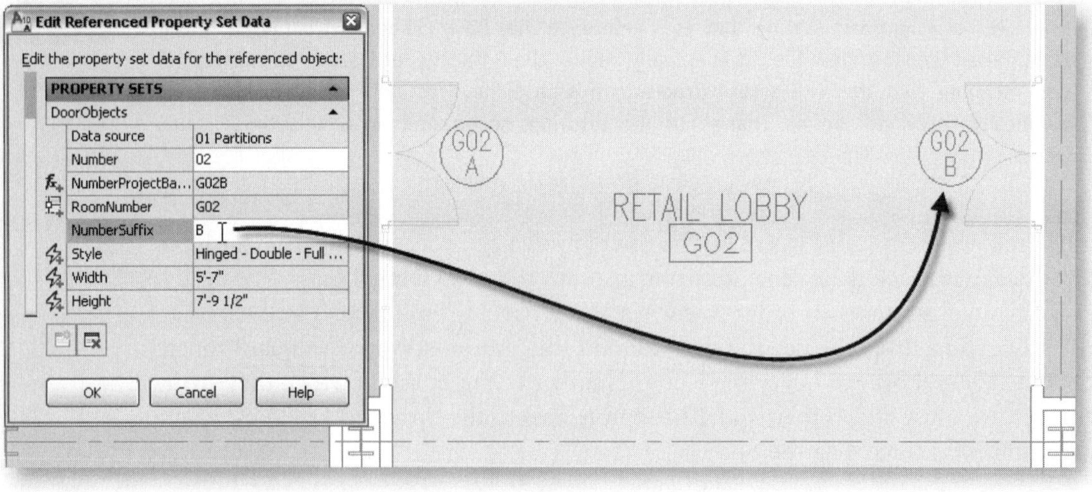

FIGURE 15.49 *Edit the Number Suffix of the second Door in the retail lobby*

Adjust the Location Grip

The three revolving Doors in the main entrance lobby still do not show a Room Number. They are also all assigned to Number Suffix "A" like the Doors above.

31. Click on any of the three revolving Doors, and, on the External Reference contextual ribbon tab on the Edit panel, choose the ***Open Reference*** tool.

    The *01 Shell and Core* Construct will open.

32. Click any one of the Revolving Doors.

In addition to the normal grips, note the star-shaped grip with the curved tail attached to it. This is a Location Grip. It indicates into which space the Door belongs. ACA will search your model for a Space or AEC Polygon beneath this grip. The first one that it finds will be reported as this Door's location. In this case there is no Space outside of the building. This is why we received the error message in the *A-FP01* file.

33. Click the location grip and drag it into the building (see Figure 15.50).

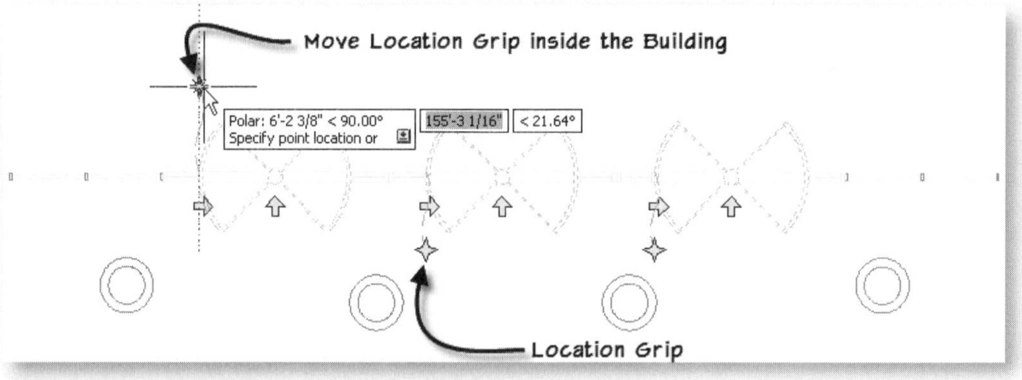

FIGURE 15.50 *Move the Location grip into the building*

Perform the same action on the exit door by the Stair. It will not update right away, but later when we reload the *Core* it will.

34. Repeat for all three revolving Doors and then save and close the *01 Shell and Core* file.
35. Back in the *A-FP01* file, reload the *01 Shell and Core* XREF by clicking the link in the balloon that appears.

The three revolving Door Tags should update to the correct room number, but they still all contain the "A" suffix.

36. Repeat the process outlined in the "Edit the Number Suffix" heading above to change the Number Suffix of two of the revolving Doors to "**B**" and "**C**," respectively (see Figure 15.51).

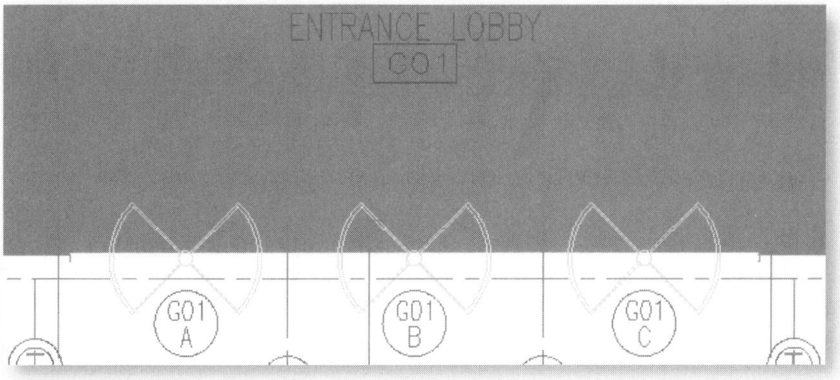

FIGURE 15.51 *Edit the Number Suffix of each of the revolving Doors*

Property Sets and Element Files

The way that we have structured our Commercial Project, the *Core* file is a typical configuration that repeats on four floors. There are five Doors in the *Core* Element file. However, in the project, this is really 20 Doors since the Element repeats four times. If you returned to the *A-601 Schedules* Sheet file and made a count of the total number of Doors, you would see that the actual quantity of 20 Doors is being properly represented within the Schedule. However, in order to correctly label each of these Doors, we really need each of the five Doors in the Element to realize that they really represent four Doors each. To accomplish this, we must first add the Property Sets to the objects within the Element file, and then perform the normal steps to attach the actual project-based Properties in the various Constructs and Views. The first values in the Element file itself will become overridden by the ones we apply to the Constructs via the View file.

If you recall our discussion in the last chapter regarding View files, it was noted even though we Tag in the View file, and the data to which the Schedule Tags refers actually lived within the Construct. The same is true in the case of the Elements. Even though Property Sets can and must be attached to the Doors within the Element file itself, ultimately it is not this data that is read into the Tags and Schedules, but rather the data that lives within the Construct. Therefore, even though there are really only five Door objects, they are able to correctly represent a total of 20 actual project Doors. This occurs because Property Set Data overrides are attached to each of the

Doors from the *Core* Element file within each floor's respective Construct files. These overrides are the data that is then passed to the schedule.

In order to make this work properly, when typical Element files are involved in objects you wish to schedule, you must follow a fairly strict process. First open the Element and attach the Property Sets to the object within. It is not important what values you assign to these Properties as each Construct will ultimately carry its own values; it only matters that the Property Sets be attached. Once this is done, the normal procedures covered throughout this chapter can then be employed.

37. On the Project Navigator palette, click the Constructs tab.
38. In the *Elements\Architectural* folder, double-click *Core* to open it.

All we need to do here is attach the required Property Sets. We have covered a few techniques to do this in this chapter so far. However, unless you know exactly which Property Sets are needed, and are certain that they are already resident in the file, or you know from where to import them, the easiest way to add the Property Sets is by using the Tag tools. Naturally we don't want to actually add the Tags in this file, but we can use the Tag tools to apply the Property Sets only.

39. On the Tags tool palette, right-click the Room Tag – Project Based tool and choose **Apply Tool Property Set Data to Objects**.
40. At the "Select objects to apply property set data to" prompt, select the Elevator Lobby Space. Press ENTER to end the selection. If the Edit Property Set Data dialog opens, scroll down to the Space Objects Property Set and change the Increment property to **101**.
41. Click OK to end the command.

    If that dialog did not open, select the Elevator Lobby Space, right-click and choose **Properties** and, on the Extended Data tab, set the SpaceObjects:Increment property to **101**. Press ESC to deselect the Space.

The Increment property contributes the incrementing portion of the room number. Setting the first value to 101 establishes the base number from which subsequent Spaces will be auto-incremented.

42. Right-click the Room Tag – Project Based tool and choose **Apply Tool Property Set Data to Objects** again.
43. At the "Select objects to apply property set data to" prompt, click each of the remaining Spaces and then press ENTER to exit the command. If the Edit Property Set Data dialog opens, click OK to exit the dialog and end the command.

    Be sure to click the Spaces in the order you wish them to be numbered (refer to Figure 15.52).

Notice that the first part of the Room Number, beneath the SpaceObjects Property Set on the Extended Data tab of the Properties Palette currently reads "NA." This first part of the Room Number is a Project Property (see the definition in the "Automatic and Manual Property Sets" heading above). It is configured to read the level from the Project Database. Since we are currently working directly in the Element file, this value is not applicable (NA). Elements do not have a level designation. This value will be replaced with the correct level indication within each Construct.

Even though we stated above that the actual values of the Properties assigned to the Element file were not important, the values assigned here will be used as a default within each Construct. If you do not want to retype an incorrect Increment value in each of the four floor plan Constructs, verify that the desired value is set here and it will be used as the default in each Construct when the Construct's Property Set Data override is applied. The SpaceObjects:Name is an exception to this; because it is an automatic property, reading the Name property on the Design tab of the Properties palette, it can not be overriden in the Construct. Verify that the desired room name is set for each Space in an Element file.

44. On the Tags tool palette, right-click the Door Tag – Project Based tool.
45. Follow the prompts as before and click each of the Doors and then press ENTER to exit the command.
46. Edit the Number Suffix of the three Doors of the left Corridor Wall making them **NA102A**, **NA102B** and **NA102C**.

    Since we are working directly in the file with the Doors, simply select the Door and edit the Property Sets on the Extended Data tab of the Properties palette.
47. Move the Location Grip for the Stair Door into the Corridor Space.

We now have all of the Property Sets needed attached to the various objects within the *Core* Element file.

48. Save and close the *Core* Element file.

Tag the First Floor Core

The First Floor Plan file (*A-FP01*) should still be open onscreen. If it is not, open it now from the Views tab of the Project Navigator palette. Now that Property Sets have been attached to the Core Element file, let's attach the required overrides to those Properties for the First Floor Plan.

49. On the Tags tool palette, click the Room Tag – Project Based tool.
50. Follow the prompts as before and Tag each of the Spaces in the Core ending with the Space in the Stair Tower and then press ENTER to exit the command.

    Use the Multiple option if you wish.

Notice that the Names and Numbers assigned within the Element file have been assigned here as well; however, all of the Numbers correctly begin with the prefix *G* (for Ground Level) rather than *NA*, as was the case in the Element file. If you are not sure where the *G* comes from, review the "Establish the Project Framework" topic in Chapter 5. It is the Level ID, and it can be viewed or edited on the Project tab of the Project Navigator palette (click the Edit Levels icon).

51. On the Tags tool palette, click the ***Door Tag – Project Based*** tool.
52. Follow the prompts as before and Tag each of the Doors and then press ENTER to exit the command.
53. Fine-tune the position of any Tags as desired and edit the suffix of the exit door to **D** (see Figure 15.52).

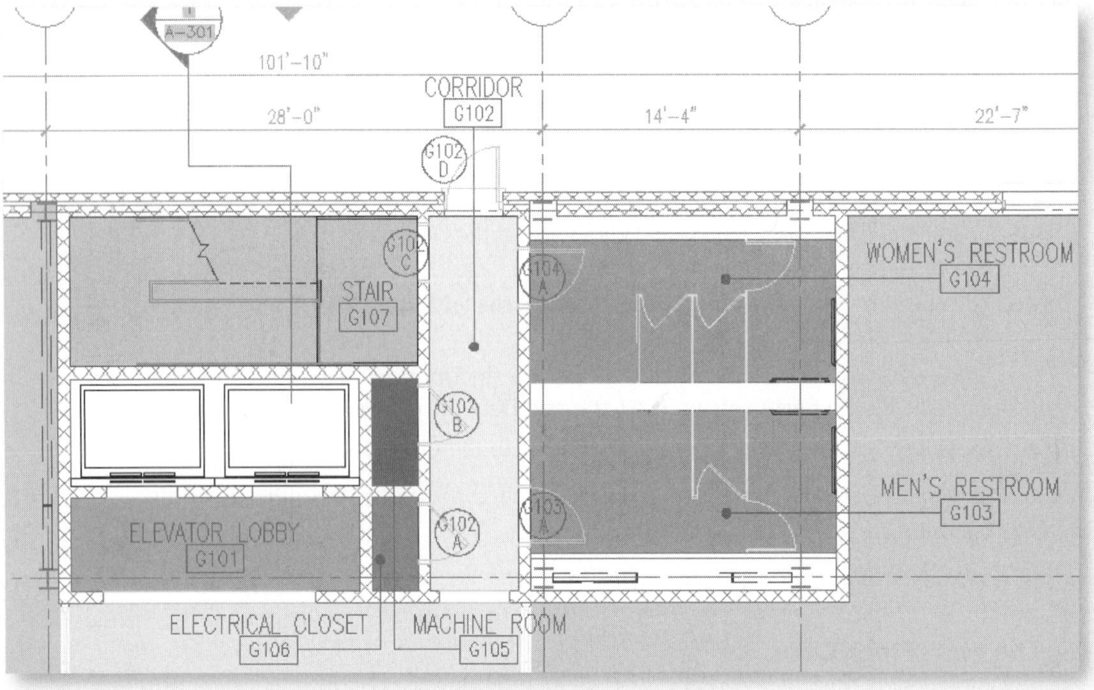

FIGURE 15.52 *Add Tags to the First Floor Core – Virtually no editing is required*

Notice how it was not necessary to edit the door Tags this time. This is because they read their default values from those in the Element file. If we needed to edit them further on a particular floor, we could do so, but the advantage of adding good default values to the Element file first is that we often will not need to change them later.

54. Save and Close the *A-FP01* file.

Tag the Upper Floors

Compared to this floor, the upper floors will be easy.

55. On the Project Navigator, on the Views tab, double-click *A-FP02* to open it.
56. Repeat the process just followed in the "Tag the First Floor Core" topic.
57. Save and Close the *A-FP02* file.

NOTE

While the Stair Tower is a Spanning Construct, there is a Space for the Stair in the *Core* Element file. That results in a Space at each level for the Stair, when the *Core* is attached to the *Shell and Core* Construct for each level. This allows the Stair to have a unique room number for each level. There is a style-level override set on the Model Display Representation for the Stairway Space Style so that these Spaces will not be seen in any sections cut through the Stair.

58. On the Project Navigator, on the Views tab, double-click *A-FP03* to open it.

For the *Core*, use exactly the same process. For the Tenant Space, the room Tags were added already in Chapter 14. Simply add the door Tags.

59. Repeat the above process for the *Core*.
60. Tag the Doors starting with the entry Door to the suite.

    The one in the Reception Space with the sidelight is the entry to the suite.
61. Right-click and choose **Multiple**, and Tag the rest of the Doors in the tenant suite.

Notice how all of these Doors automatically read the room number of the adjacent Spaces. Also notice that the room numbers reference the Level from the Project database—all of the numbers on this floor begin with a "3." If you are unhappy with the default Space referenced by a particular Tag, open the *03 Partitions* file on the Project Navigator, and edit the Location grip.

62. Save and Close the file.
63. Repeat once more for *A-FP04* and *A-FP05* (the Roof Plan). After tagging the Stair Space in *A-FP05*, set the SpaceObjects:Increment property to **107**.
64. Save and Close all files.

Open the Schedule Sheet and View the Results

We have finished numbering and editing all of the Doors in the Project. Let's check our progress in the Schedule Table and reopen *A-601* and see how things are shaping up.

65. On the Project Navigator, click the Sheets tab and then double-click *A-601 Schedules* to open it.

Notice that all you have to do is open the file and the Schedule automatically updates. Much of the data has filled in nicely. There are still several rows of question marks, however. It turns out that the original criteria that we used to make the Schedule Table selection were too broad. This Schedule is reporting *all* Doors in our entire model. This currently includes all of the toilet stalls in the rest rooms as well as the actual Doors. This situation is easily resolved.

66. Select the Schedule and on the Properties palette (on the Design tab), within the Selection grouping, type ***Door** [***Door-G**] for the Layer wildcard and press ENTER (see Figure 15.53).

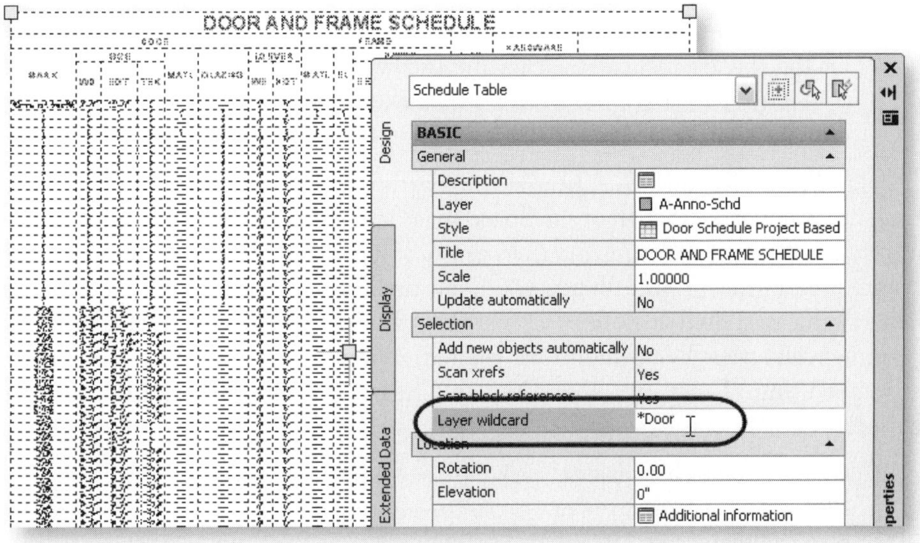

FIGURE 15.53 *Add a more restrictive Layer Wildcard*

The Schedule Table should update and remove all extraneous toilet stall Doors. All that remains to do is add our Space Allocation Schedule from earlier in the chapter to this Sheet.

67. On the Project Navigator palette, click the Views tab.
68. Click the small plus sign next to *A-SH03* to expand its Model Space Views.
69. Drag the Third Floor Space Allocation Schedule Model Space View onto the Sheet.
70. Save and Close all project files.

If you prefer, you can copy this single Door Schedule four times (five total) and assign each one to one of the floor plan View files (*A-FP01*, *A-FP02*, etc.). Then, using the new ability to title each one separately (see above), you can name each copy according to its respective level, such as "First Floor Door and Frame Schedule." This task is left to the reader as an additional exercise.

UNDERSTANDING DISPLAY THEMES

In Chapter 2, we took a brief look at Display Themes. A Display Theme is an object that applies a display override to some or all objects in a drawing and presents the Theme in a legend inserted in the drawing. The change is temporary and applies only as long as the Display Theme remains active.

Using Display Themes

Like most objects in AutoCAD Architecture, Display Themes are style-based objects. They key into Property Set Data attached to the objects and use rules based upon those properties to modify the display. Display Themes do not apply to AutoCAD entities like lines, arcs and polylines. A few styles have been provided as out-of-the-box samples. Let's take a brief look at them now before building our own style below.

1. On the Project Navigator palette, click the Views tab and then double-click the *A-FP03* View file to open it.

   The third floor plan opens and all of the Spaces added to the *03 Partitions* file appear via XREF in this drawing.
2. On the tool palettes, right-click the title bar and choose **Document** to load the Document tool palette group and then click the Themes tool palette to make it active.
3. On the Themes tool palette, click the Theme by Space Type - Commercial tool.
4. At the "Upper-left corner of display theme" prompt, click a point off to the side of the plan and then press ENTER.

A Display Theme legend will appear at the location where you clicked. If you study the legend, you will see that all of the Space styles included in the *Spaces - Commercial (Imperial).dwg* [*Spaces - Commercial (Metric).dwg*] are included even though not all of them are used in this project. When you build the Display Theme Style, you decide which criteria it should include. In this case, this particular Style includes all of the commercial styles. We could, if we wanted, modify it to eliminate the ones that we are not using. There are other Display Themes on this palette. Let's look at one more.

5. On the Themes tool palette, click the Theme by Space Size tool.
6. At the "Upper-left corner of display theme" prompt, click a point to side of the plan and then press ENTER.

This Theme uses different colors and codes by size rather than type. Notice that only one Theme can be active at a time. When you added the second one, the first was automatically disabled. You can right-click either one and chose to apply or disable them.

7. On the Sheets tab of Project Navigator, in the *Schedules and Diagrams* subset, create a new Sheet named A-602 Display Themes.
8. Open the new Sheet, drag the *A-FP03* Third Floor Plan View file and place it on this new Sheet.
9. Copy the Viewport twice (for a total of three) and position them on the Sheet.

   If necessary, choose **Regenall** from the View menu to refresh the display.
10. On the Themes tool palette, click the Theme by Space Size tool and when prompted, select the first Viewport.
11. At the "Upper-left corner of display theme" prompt, place the legend in proximity to the Viewport and then press ENTER to accept the default size and scale.
12. Repeat this process using the Theme by Fire Rating and Theme by Space Type – Commercial Display Theme tools on the Themes tool palette and apply them to the other two viewports.

NOTE

If the Display Theme legend or the themed objects appear solid black, open the Layer Manager and change the Plot Style of the A-Anno-Legn layer to Standard and then click OK. On the View ribbon tab on the Appearance panel, click on the down arrow at the right side of the Regenerate split button and choose the *Regenerate Model* tool and then press ENTER to update the drawing display.

13. Save the file.

The first thing that you will notice is that different Display Themes can be applied to different Viewports yielding a completely different graphical look, even when the contents of the Viewports are the same. Now let's edit one of the Display Theme styles to get an understanding of how it works. The Theme by Fire Rating Display Theme is perhaps the simplest one onscreen. Let's start with that one.

14. Select the Theme by Fire Rating legend, and, on the Display Theme contextual ribbon tab on the General tab, choose the ***Edit Style*** tool.
15. Click the Design Rules tab (see Figure 15.54).

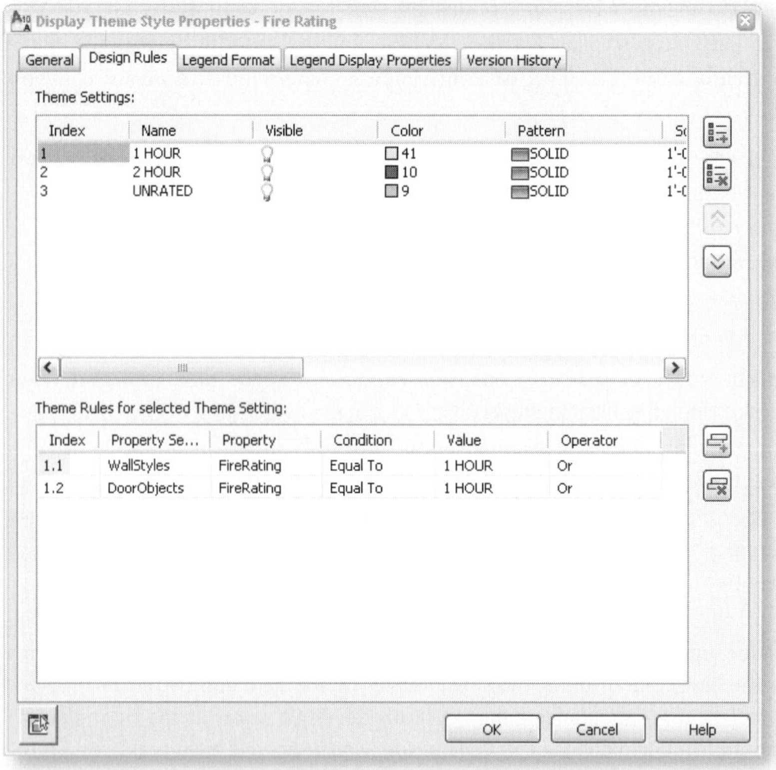

FIGURE 15.54 *The Display Theme Design Rules theme objects based on Property Set values*

A Display Theme contains one or more components at the top, that each have one or more Rules at the bottom. In this case, there are three components: "1 Hour," "2 Hour" and "Unrated." Selecting any one of these components at the top reveals two rules (4 for unrated) for each at the bottom; one for Wall objects, and another for Door objects. Each Rule contains a criterion composed of a Property from a Property Set and a Condition against which it is tested. If the object type and property in question meets the condition, then the object is themed. If it does not meet the criterion, then it is not affected. In this case, the first component at the top looks at Wall and Door objects. If either object type has their FireRating Property set to "1 Hour" then the objects are colored color number 41. Color 10 is used if the FireRating equals "2 Hour" and if it is blank, or set to a double dash (--) they are colored gray (color 9). Currently there are no one or two hours Walls in our project.

The Display Theme looks at the style-based WallStyles Property Set and the object-based DoorObjects Property Set.

16. Using the techniques covered above, open the *Core* Element file and edit the WallStyles Property Set of core Walls to be "1 Hour" and/or "2 Hour" rated.

    For the complete effect, edit the Doors Property Sets as well and then close and save the file.

17. When the XREF balloon appears, reload the *Core* file.

The Theme will update immediately.

Let's look at the Theme by Space Type – Commercial Style next. In Chapter 13, we used several out-of-the-box Space Styles and applied them to the Spaces in this project. The legend, however, shows all Space Types, not just those we are using. We can edit the Legend and remove the Styles that we aren't using.

18. Select the Space Style – Commercial legend, and, on the Display Theme contextual ribbon tab on the General tab, choose the ***Save As*** tool.
19. On the General tab, rename the Style to **MACA Space Style**.
20. On the Design Rules tab, in the top pane, highlight Index 1 – Atrium Ground and then click the Remove Component icon on the right.
21. Repeat for each Style that is not in use in our project and then click OK.

Create a Custom Display Theme

Like most Styles, it is easy enough to create your own Display Theme Style—simply begin with an existing one and modify it. Choose an existing one that is either close in terms of the Design Rules so that you will have minimal editing, or pick one that already has a color scheme that you like. Ideally you can find one that has a little of both. There are some additional Display Theme tools in the *Documentation Tool Catalog - Imperial* [*Documentation Tool Catalog – Metric*] in the Content Browser.

22. Copy one of the Viewports to create a fourth Viewport and then add a Display Theme to it.

    For example, try Theme by Space Type – Medical on the Themes palette.

We are going to build our Theme based on the GeoObjects Property Set. However, it is not currently part of this drawing. The easiest way to add it is to use the Space Inventory Schedule tool that we used above.

23. On the Scheduling tool palette, click the Space Inventory Schedule tool and then press ESC without adding it to the drawing.
24. Select the Theme and, on the Display Theme contextual ribbon tab on the General tab, choose the ***Save As*** tool.
25. Name it **MACA Theme by Department** and then click the Design Rules tab.
26. Rename the first component to **Marketing**; at the bottom, next to Index 1.1, choose GeoObjects from the Property Set list, **Department** from the Property list and type **Marketing** in the Value field.
27. Repeat this for each of the Departments that we used above.
28. Delete all unused components (see Figure 15.55).

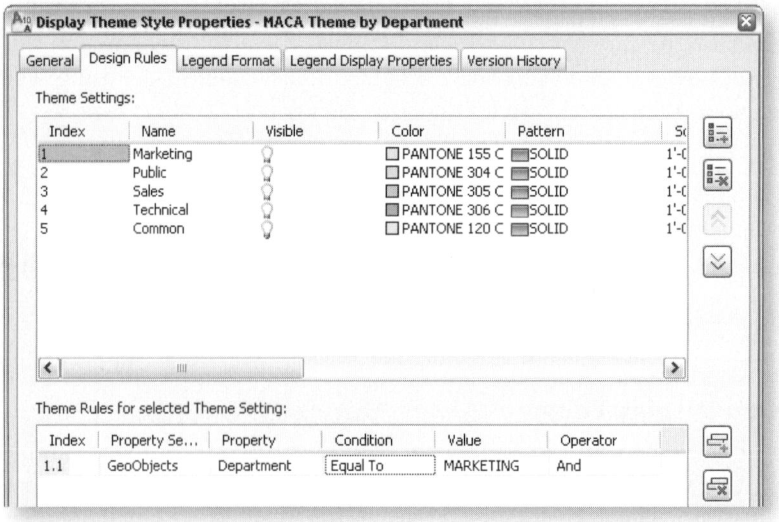

FIGURE 15.55 *Build a custom Display Theme to show Departments*

29. Click OK to see the results.

    If the Theme does not update immediately, select its legend, right-click and choose **Apply Display Theme** and then select the Viewport when prompted.

Display Themes offer a vast array of possibilities of which we have only scratched the surface of here. Please feel free to experiment further. All of the out-of-the-box themes utilize solid fill hatching and pantone colors; however, if you scroll to the right you will note that other properties are also available like hatch patterns, linetype, lineweight and plot style.

30. Close and Save all commercial project files.

ADDITIONAL SCHEDULE TOOLS

Several other tools are available to manipulate Schedules once they have been added to the drawing.

Renumber Data

This command allows you to renumber any Property Set that uses automatic increment (such as Room Number). Simply click the Renumber Data tool on the Tags tool palette and choose the property to renumber, the number to start at, and the amount to increment by. Follow the command prompts to select the objects in the order in which you want them to be renumbered. This command was used in the previous chapter.

Exporting Schedules

Schedule Tables can be exported to popular file formats like Microsoft Excel. To do so, select a Schedule Table in the drawing, right-click and choose **Export**. In the dialog box that appears, choose a file format such as Microsoft Excel 97 (*.xls) from the Save As Type list. Type a name for the export file or click Browse to set a new location and name in separate dialog box. Click OK to complete the export. If you are working in Imperial units, a Format dialog box will often appear, indicating that Excel does not support the Architectural Units format. Choose Convert to Formatted Text, put a check mark in Apply to All Columns, and then click OK. Excel cannot understand Feet and Inch values, so this will convert it to plain text, which Excel can understand. If you choose not to convert the values to text, they will be in raw numeric format instead. In other words, 6'-0" will become 72.

CAUTION

This is an "export" command. The Excel spreadsheet is *NOT* linked back to the drawing objects in any way.

Out of Date Marker

Automatic update is a valuable feature of Schedules. The advantage of automatic update is clear; however, it can cause a significant drain on drawing performance. Manual update imposes no such performance detriment, but it does require user intervention to keep the data in the Schedule current. When you choose manual update, it is imperative that the Display Configuration settings of the Schedule Table objects be configured properly to alert the user when the Schedule needs updating. Schedule Tables contain a Display Component called Out of Date Marker. Edit the Display Properties of Schedule Tables to turn this on or off. When this is turned on, and Automatic Update is turned off, a line will appear through the Schedule when the data in it no longer matches the drawing. To update, you then select the Schedule and, on the Schedule Table contextual ribbon tab on the Modify panel, choose the ***Update*** tool.

MANAGER NOTE CAD

There is no harm in having the Out of Date Marker turned on even when Schedules are set to Automatic Update. However, in contrast, it could be very damaging to productivity to have the component turned off in situations where it is needed. Making this modification to your template files will serve as a valuable preventive measure. Regardless, get people in the habit of performing a manual update before critical submissions.

ADDITIONAL EXERCISES

Additional exercises have been provided in Appendix A. In Appendix A you will find exercises to add additional Schedule Tables in both the Residential and Commercial Projects. It is not necessary that you complete this exercise to begin the next chapter, it is provided to enhance your learning experience. Completed projects for each of the exercises have been provided in the *Chapter15/Complete* folder.

SUMMARY

- Schedule Tables link directly to drawing objects.
- In order for the correct data to appear in the cells of the Schedule, an associated Property Set must be attached to the objects (or their styles) listed in the Schedule.
- Objects can be added and deleted from Schedules by adding or removing them from the Schedule selection.
- Adding or deleting the objects in the drawing changes both the drawing and the Schedule.
- Use Classification Definitions to selectively filter out elements from the Schedule.
- Style-based properties are edited at the object-style level and affect all objects of the same type in the Schedule and the drawing.

- Property Set Definitions can apply to objects or styles.
- Individual properties within the Property Set Definition can be Automatic or Manual.
- Automatic properties can use formulas and track physical location relative to Spaces and Areas.
- The text formatting of Schedule objects can be customized with AutoCAD Text styles and Format settings in the Schedule Table style.
- Layers, Colors, Linetypes and Lineweights are all fully accessible for Schedule Table styles with the Display Properties settings.
- Schedule columns and headers can be moved and edited to suit specific needs.
- Add a Graphic Property to insert images or blocks directly into the Schedule Table cells.
- Doors Tags can reference the Room numbers of adjacent Spaces.
- Room numbers can automatically reference the level from the Project database.
- When you add a Schedule Table to a Sheet, you can reference a remote drawing that will update automatically each time the file is opened.
- Display Themes key into Property Sets attached to objects. Edit the Display Theme Style to modify this behavior.
- Schedule Tables can be exported to Microsoft Excel; however, the data is not linked back to ACA.
- When using manual update, make sure that the Out of Date component is active in the Display Properties.

CHAPTER

16

Generating Sections and Elevations

INTRODUCTION

There are two basic approaches to generating sections and elevations in AutoCAD Architecture 2010: sections and elevations can be generated from the ACA model as a linked graphical "report" of the data contained within it, or the ACA model can be viewed "live" in an appropriate Display Configuration. When generating sections (the "linked report" approach), ACA offers a three-dimensional Section/Elevation object that is suitable for presentation drawings and "cut away" perspectives and a two-dimensional Section/Elevation object that is useful for inclusion in design development and construction documents. Live sections are also very useful for design and presentation purposes. The 2D Section/Elevation object is style-based and robust. It will be the main focus of this chapter.

OBJECTIVES

In this chapter, we will look at the 2D Section/Elevation object in detail. We will cover ways to make this tool produce top-quality sections and elevations from your ACA model. We will work in the Residential Project, as we work through the process of creating Sections and Elevations. At the end of the chapter, we will also look briefly at Interior Elevations and Live Sections. In this chapter, we will explore the following topics:

- Learn to Add Section/Elevation lines.
- Working with Callouts.
- Generate a 2D Section/Elevation object.
- Work with 2D Section/Elevation Styles.
- Update 2D Section/Elevation objects.
- Understand Edit Linework and Merge Linework commands.

WORKING WITH 2D SECTION/ELEVATION OBJECTS

2D Section/Elevation objects are useful for generating section and elevation drawings from an ACA model suitable for design development and construction documents. 2D Section/Elevation objects have a broad scope; use them for full building sections and elevations, interior elevations, as an underlay for wall sections and even to get started with details. To create a 2D Section/Elevation, you must first add a Section/Elevation Line object to indicate where you wish the section cut to occur and in which direction it ought to look. Section/Elevation lines are added when you run the tools on the Design tool palette and through the various Callout tools on the Callouts tool palette. Callouts are robust routines that add required annotation and cross-link it throughout the project. The tools on the Design palette add only the Section/Elevation Line object with no cross-referenced annotation. You configure and fine-tune the appearance of the 2D Section/Elevation object in much the same way as other AEC objects. You can edit its style, change its Display Properties and/or edit the actual component linework within the object.

The Bldg Section Line and the Bldg Elevation Line

The Bldg Section Line and Bldg Elevation Line objects are actually three-dimensional "boxes." The purpose of this three-dimensional box is to determine what portion of the Building Model will be included in the Section or Elevation (see Figure 16.1).

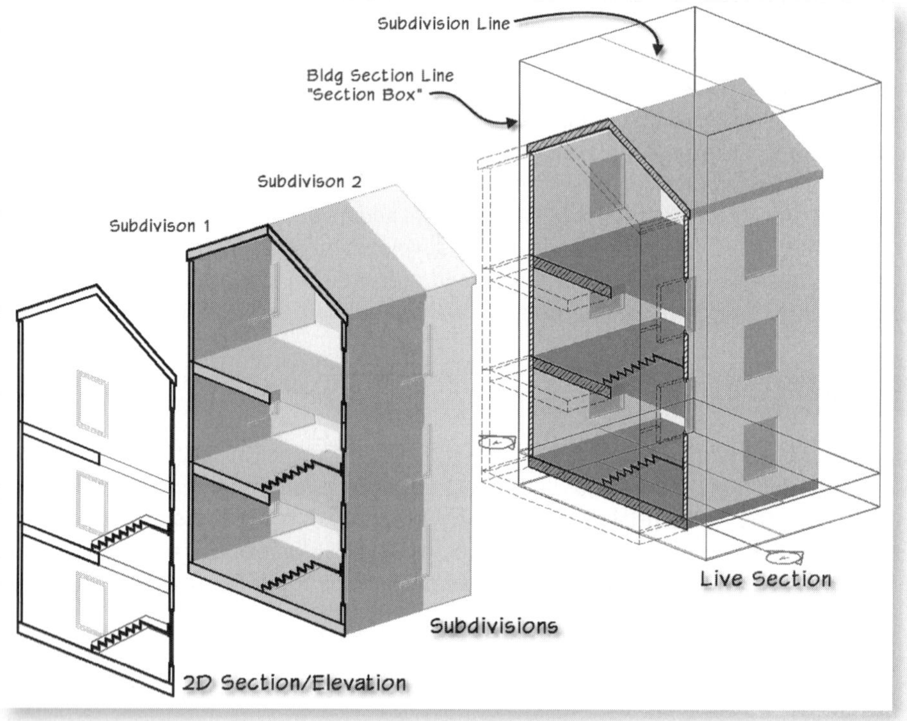

FIGURE 16.1 *Bldg Section Line at right with a Live Section, middle showing subdivisions and left showing 2D Section/Elevation*

In the illustration shown in Figure 16.1, the Bldg Section Line is sized to give a full building cross-section. If the size of the box is adjusted, in both plan and Z heights, we can effectively create an entirely different type of drawing like the interior elevation shown in Figure 16.2.

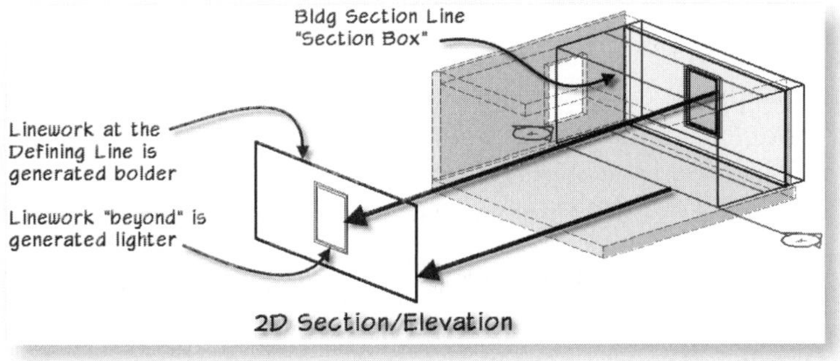

FIGURE 16.2 *Resize the Bldg Section Line to give an Interior Elevation*

The Display Representations of the Bldg Section Line and Bldg Elevation Line objects contain three sub-components (see Figure 16.3). Two of the three subcomponents: the Boundary and the Subdivisions are used merely for purposes of configuring the 2D Section/Elevation object (as shown in the above two figures). The third component, the defining line, is the only component that would potentially have value when printed; at least for Sections (you will likely not want it printed for Elevations). The Defining Line can be used in conjunction with a Section Bubble in your drawings, or you can simply use the bubbles by themselves. By default, all of these components are on a non-plotting layer. The Defining line is the "cut line," drawn through the building in plan view. It forms a plane three-dimensionally that determines where the bold cut line in the Section will be. The Boundary *is* the "box" (illustrated above). Nothing outside the boundary is included in the Section or Elevation. The subdivisions are drawn as lines parallel to the back edge of the Section box and determine where the Lineweight zones occur. Subdivisions must be enabled for each section or elevation individually. We will look more carefully at subdivisions on the later in the chapter.

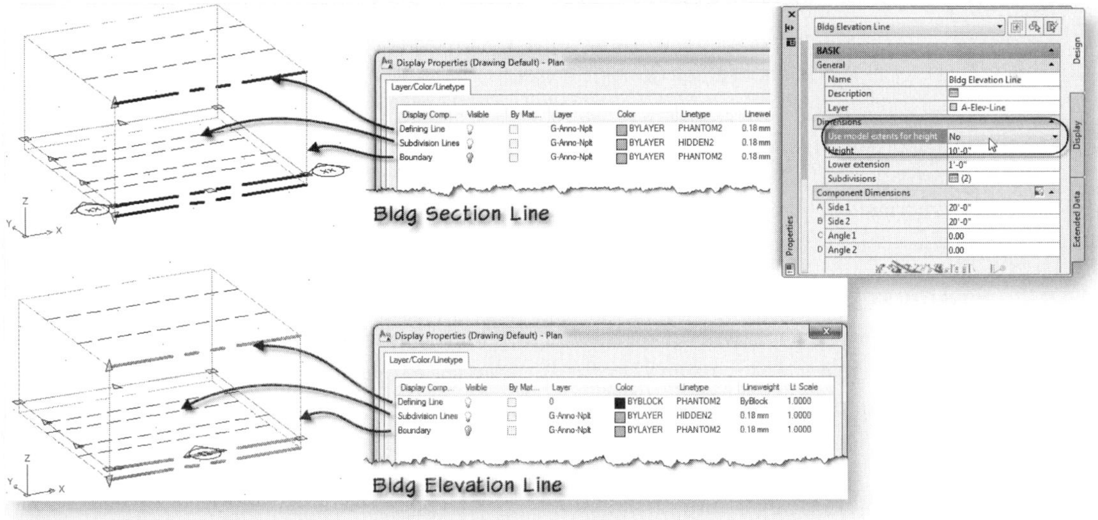

FIGURE 16.3 *The components of the Bldg Section Line and Bldg Elevation Line objects*

Another way to think of the Bldg Section Line and Bldg Elevation Line objects is like the field of view for a camera. When you look through your camera lens, you can only see so much of the scene both side to side and moving back. If you imagined mapping the field of view of your camera on the ground, you would have a pretty good approximation of the Section/Elevation Line object. Even though this boundary is actually three-dimensional, by default ACA will automatically include the entire height of the model in the 2D Section/Elevation object. This default can be changed if required. Ironically, when this option is active ("Use model extents for height" is set to **Yes** on the Properties palette), no height will be shown graphically in 3D views since it includes *all* of the height. When it is set to "No" you see a 3D box when you view the model (see the right side of Figure 16.3).

Install the CD Files and Load the Current Project

If you have already installed all of the files from the CD, simply skip down to step 3 below to make the project active. If you need to install the CD files, start at step 1.

1. If you have not already done so, install the dataset files located on the Mastering AutoCAD Architecture 2010 CD-ROM.

   Refer to "Files Included on the CD-ROM" in the Preface for information on installing the sample files included on the CD.
2. Launch AutoCAD Architecture 2010 from the desktop icon created in Chapter 3.

If you did not create a custom icon, you might want to review "Create a New Profile" and "Create a Desktop Shortcut" in Chapter 3. Creating the custom desktop icon is not essential; however, it makes loading the custom profile easier.

3. From the File menu, choose **Project Browser**.
4. Click to open the folder list and choose your *C:* drive.
5. Double-click on the *MasterACA 2010* folder, then the *Chapter16* folder.

   One or two residential Projects will be listed: *16 Residential* and/or *16 Residential Metric*.
6. Double-click *16 Residential* if you wish to work in Imperial units. Double-click *16 Residential Metric* if you wish to work in Metric units. (You can also right-click on it and choose Set Current Project.) Then click Close in the Project Browser.

NOTE

Important: If a message appears asking you to repath the project, click the "Repath the project now" option. Refer to the "Repathing Projects" heading in the Preface for more information.

Adjust the Bldg Elevation Line

In this exercise, we will revisit the Section and Elevation Composite Model View file that we created in Chapter 5 for the Residential Project. At that time, we built a composite model of the entire project and cut four elevations and two sections using the Callout routines. One of those elevations, the East Elevation, has been removed from the file for this chapter. We will begin our exploration of 2D Section/Elevation by re-creating this elevation.

7. On the Project Navigator, click the Views tab, and then double-click *A-CM01* to open it.

This is the Section and Elevation Composite Model View file that was created in Chapter 5 (available as a PDF on the book CD-ROM). As was mentioned above, the East Elevation has been removed from this file and we will re-create it below.

For the time being, let's focus our attention on the Bldg Elevation and Bldg Section Lines that already appear in this file.

8. Click to select any one of the three elevations or the two sections.

   Notice a dashed red line will also highlight in the plan. This is the Bldg Section or Bldg Elevation Line associated with the selected section or elevation.

9. Right-click and choose **Deselect All**.

   Repeat the process to see which section or elevation belongs to each Bldg Section or Bldg Elevation Line.

10. Select the Elevation immediately to the left of the model (North Elevation).

    This will highlight the Bldg Elevation Line running horizontally across the north side of the model.

11. Zoom in on the model.
12. Click to select the Bldg Elevation Line running horizontally along the top of the plan.

Several grips of varying shape will appear. Hover your mouse over each grip to see its function (see Figure 16.4).

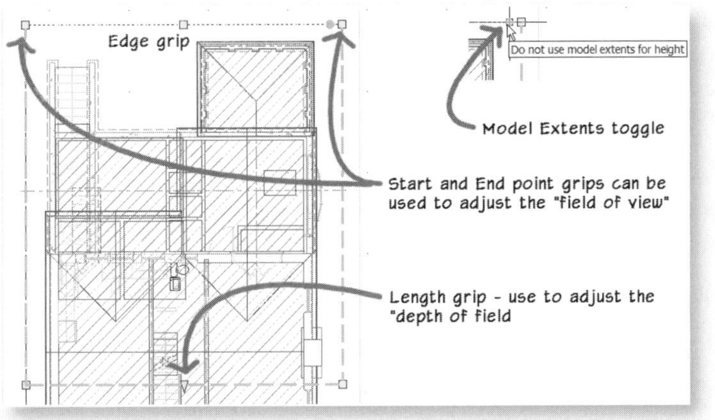

FIGURE 16.4 *Examine the Bldg Elevation Line Object Grips*

Let's take our camera analogy from above a bit further. You are able to adjust what the camera sees by adjusting the focal length of your lens and your f-stop for the depth. With grips, you can make the similar adjustments to what the Bldg Section/Elevation Line boundary "sees." The three grips on the back edge (left side in this case) change the "depth of field." However, to keep the back edge parallel to the defining line, you should always use the middle triangular-shaped grip. The two ends of the defining line (right side in this case) can be used to widen or narrow the field of view. A small gray grip appears on the defining line with which to toggle the "Use Model Extents for Height" feature on and off.

13. Experiment with the Grip points if you wish.

    When you are finished experimenting, undo any grip edits you made.

Make the Section/Elevation Line Easier to Read

The display properties of the Section/Elevation line are assigned to a non-plotting layer by default. If you wish, you can edit this in the same way as other AEC objects.

Bldg Section Line and Bldg Elevation Line objects are not style-based. Therefore, you can either edit the Drawing Default display properties of these objects or apply object level overrides.

14. Select the same Bldg Elevation Line object in the drawing again, right-click and choose **Properties**.
15. Click the Display tab.

Like most AEC objects, there are several Display Representations. However, unlike more complex objects like Doors and Walls, the Bldg Section Line and Bldg Elevation Line objects show the same three components in all Display Reps. Currently the Plan Display Rep is active. In the Display Component list, there are three components:

- Defining Line—This is the cut line akin to the cut plane for plans. Geometry cut by this line will typically be automatically rendered in a heavy lineweight.
- Subdivision Lines—As you recede back from the defining line, you can define "zones" or subdivisions that have different (often receding in thickness) lineweights as they move further from the defining line (see below).
- Boundary—This is the outer edge of the Section/Elevation Line object.

NOTE

Another way to see the components is to right-click the object and choose Edit Object Display. On the Display Properties tab, double-click a Display Representation to view or edit its properties. An example of these dialogs is shown above in Figure 16.3.

The Boundary Line is off by default. This is fine for our purposes here. However, later in the chapter when we add subdivisions to some of our elevations, it might be easier to read if the Subdivision Lines are a different color.

16. Select the Subdivision Lines component and assign a different color such as magenta to them. If the confirmation dialog appears, click OK (see Figure 16.5).

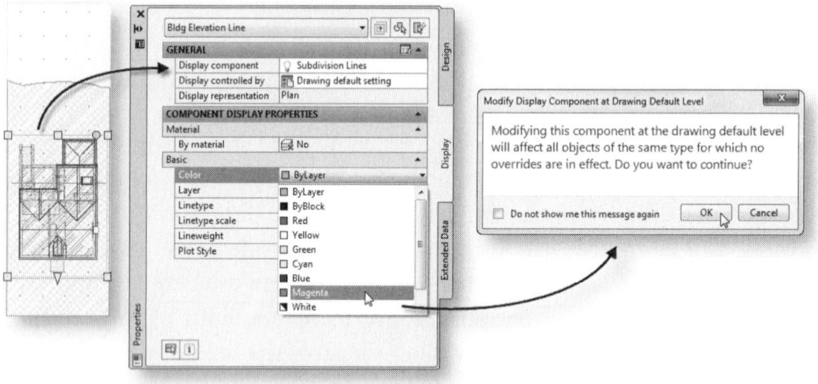

FIGURE 16.5 *Assigning colors to the Display Components of the Section/Elevation Line object*

We don't have any subdivisions yet, so this change will not become evident until later.

You could change the settings of the other components if you wish. The process would be the same.

17. Save the file.

Generating a 2D Section/Elevation Object Using a Callout

Now that we have an understanding of how the Bldg Section Line and Bldg Elevation Line objects are used to generate sections and elevations, let's re-create the East Elevation in the Section and Elevation Composite Model file. Although this can be done manually, it is much easier to use a Callout routine as we did in Chapter 5. We will review that process next.

Section and Elevation objects in ACA can be thought of as graphical "reports" of the data in the drawing model. The zone defined by the Bldg Section Line object and an object selection made while generating the 2D Section/Elevation determines the specific objects that will be included in this report. Using our camera analogy, it is the "snapshot."

We will begin in the First Floor Plan where we will add an elevation Callout. The Callout routines are powerful tools that are capable of performing several steps in one operation. The typical Callout routine will add one or more Callouts to the current drawing, create a Bldg Elevation Line (in the same or another View file), add a Model Space View with association to the 2D Section/Elevation, add a Title Mark and then Generate a 2D Section/Elevation object. Later when you add an elevation created this way to a Sheet, the callout's annotation will be linked.

Add a Callout

You typically execute the Callout routine within the drawing where you wish to have the Callout appear. Since indicators for elevations and section are typically placed in plans, in this case we will begin in the First Floor Plan View file. However, we want the 2D Section/Elevation object to be created in the *A-CM01* View file (where all of the other elevations and sections are placed). The Callout routine will prompt us for our preferred location at the appropriate time and then generate the 2D Section/Elevation object within the file we designate automatically.

1. On the Project Navigator, click the Views tab, and then double-click *A-FP01* to open it.
2. On the Callouts palette, click the Elevation Mark A2 tool (see item 1 in Figure 16.6).

   If you do not see this palette or tool, right-click the Tool Palettes title bar and choose **Document** (to load the Documentation Tool Palette Group) and then click the Callouts tab.

   Several notes have been added to this file to aid you in this task. These labels are on the G-Anno-Nplt layer so they won't print, but you should erase them when you are finished.
3. At the "Specify location of elevation tag" prompt, click the Midpoint of the cyan rectangle, as indicated by the "SNAP to MIDPOINT HERE" leader (see item 2 in Figure 16.6).

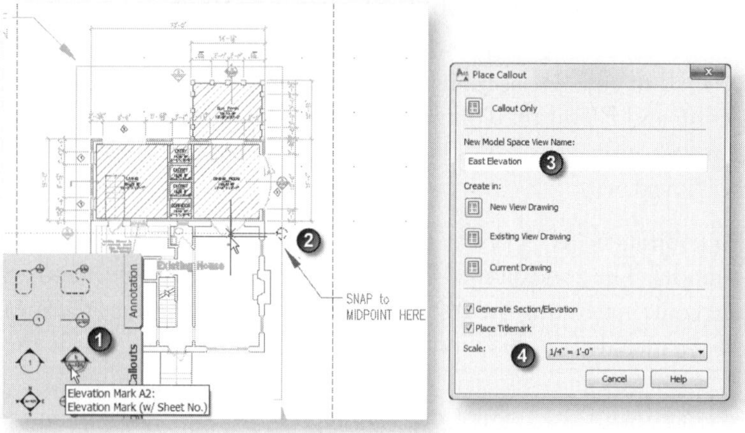

FIGURE 16.6 *Add a Callout and then fill in the required items in the Place Callout Worksheet*

4. At the "Specify direction of elevation" prompt, move the mouse directly to the left (using POLAR or ORTHO) and then click.

   This determines the direction from which you want to "look" at the elevation.

5. In the Place Callout worksheet, type: **East Elevation** for the New Model Space View Name (see item 3 in Figure 16.6).

NOTE

This Model Space View Name must be unique in your project. Project Navigator will not allow you to create a New Model Space View using a name that already exists in the Project, even if it is within a different drawing.

6. From the Scale list at the bottom, choose **1/4" = 1'-0"** [**1:50**] (see item 4 in Figure 16.6).

   Be sure that both "Generate Section/Elevation" and "Place Titlemark" are checked.

When you instruct the Callout routine to "Generate Section/Elevation" it will create the 2D Section/Elevation object for you. Place Titlemark will add a Title Mark Callout to the drawing you specify in the Create in area above and that Title Mark will be scaled to whatever you indicate in the Scale list. This scale will also be assigned to the New Model Space View named at the top of the worksheet. For more information and other examples of Callouts, see the "Create the Building Elevation View" heading in Chapter 5.

7. Click the Existing View Drawing icon in the center of the worksheet (see Figure 16.7).

   An Add Model Space View worksheet will appear listing all of the View files within the current project.

8. Select *A-CM01* and then click OK (see Figure 16.7).

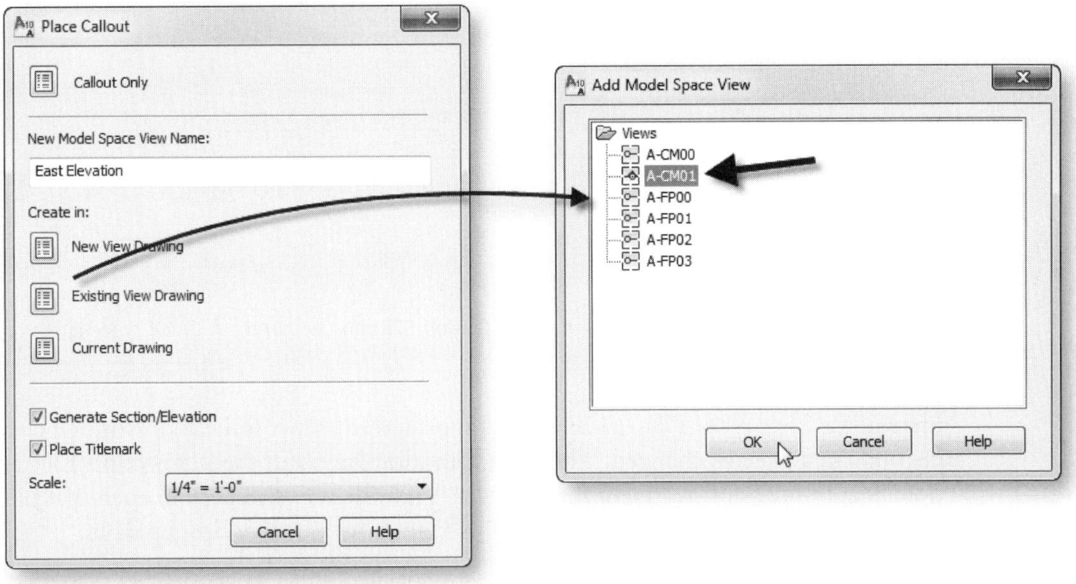

FIGURE 16.7 *Choose the Section and Elevation Composite Model—A-CM01*

9. At the "Specify first corner of elevation region" prompt, snap to the upper left corner of the cyan rectangle as indicated by the "FIRST CORNER OF ELEVATION REGION" text leader.
10. At the "Specify opposite corner of elevation region" prompt, snap to the lower right corner of the cyan rectangle as indicated by the "OPPOSITE CORNER OF ELEVATION REGION" text leader.

CAUTION

Do not press `ENTER` **or hit the** `ESC` **key. You are not done with the Callout routine yet!**

Look at the Command Line and notice the message that has appeared. It will read:

```
** You are being prompted for a point in a different view
drawing **
```

When you create elevations using the Callout routine to an existing or new View file, you still must indicate within the current drawing where you would like the elevations to be created in that file. This prompt serves to inform you of that. It is usually best to pick a point off to the side of the plan. Since we already have several elevations and sections in the *A-CM01* View file, ACA will highlight these temporarily until you click the insertion point. Each elevation and section will show the name of its associated Model Space View. In this case, we want to click a point between the North and South Elevations that already exist in that file. The text leader at the right side of the plan will help you to do this.

11. At the "Specify insertion point for the 2D elevation result" prompt, click a point in the drawing to the right of the floor plan where indicated by the "PLACE INSERTION POINT OF ELEVATION NEAR HERE" text leader (see Figure 16.8).

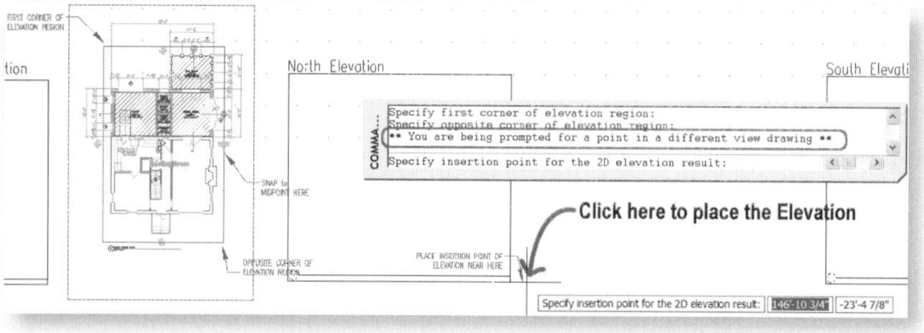

FIGURE 16.8 *Pick an insertion point for the 2D Section/Elevation within the A-CM01 drawing*

Here in the First Floor Plan, a Callout has appeared where we indicated. Nothing else has appeared to have changed. The Bldg Elevation Line and the 2D Section/Elevation object were both created in the *A-CM01* View file. We will need to open that file to see them. Before we leave the First Floor Plan, however, let's cleanup a bit.

12. Erase the four text leaders and their associated notes. Erase also the cyan rectangular Layout Grid that we used to set the boundaries of the elevation.

    Erase only the inner (and smaller cyan colored) Layout Grid. Do not erase the outer purple dashed one.

If you wish to reference the East Elevation from the other Floor Plans, copy the Callout that we just added to the clipboard and then on Project Navigator, open each Floor Plan View: *A-FP00*, *A-FP02* and *A-FP03*, on the Home tab, expand the Modify panel and choose Paste to Original Coordinates from the Paste drop-down button in each of those files.

13. Save and close all Floor Plan View files.
14. On the Project Navigator palette, open the *A-CM01* file if it is not already open.
15. Zoom in on the newly created East Elevation (third elevation from the right).

TIP

If the file is already open and the elevation does not appear immediately, Regen the drawing.

As you can see, we have come a long way since Chapter 5! This Elevation is nearly OK as is, but we can certainly find a few things to enhance the drawing.

Reposition the Elevation for the Sheet

Notice that there is a horizontal line with a note pointing to it. This line matches up with the first floor of the other Elevations in this file. In Chapter 14 we added Elevation Labels to this file. In order for those heights to be correct relative to this new elevation, we must move it to line up precisely with the others in this file. The line has been provided to simplify the process. We will now move the Elevation to line up with this line.

16. Click on the East Elevation 2D Section/Elevation object.

Notice the dashed gray box that surrounds the elevation. This is the Model Space View that is associated with this elevation. It has a grip on each edge that can be used to edit the extents of this Model Space View.

17. Click the square Location grip at the left side of the elevation.

    Use this grip to move the elevation within its Model Space View.

18. Move the mouse down and snap using Intersection or Perpendicular to the provided guide line (see Figure 16.9).

    Zoom as required.

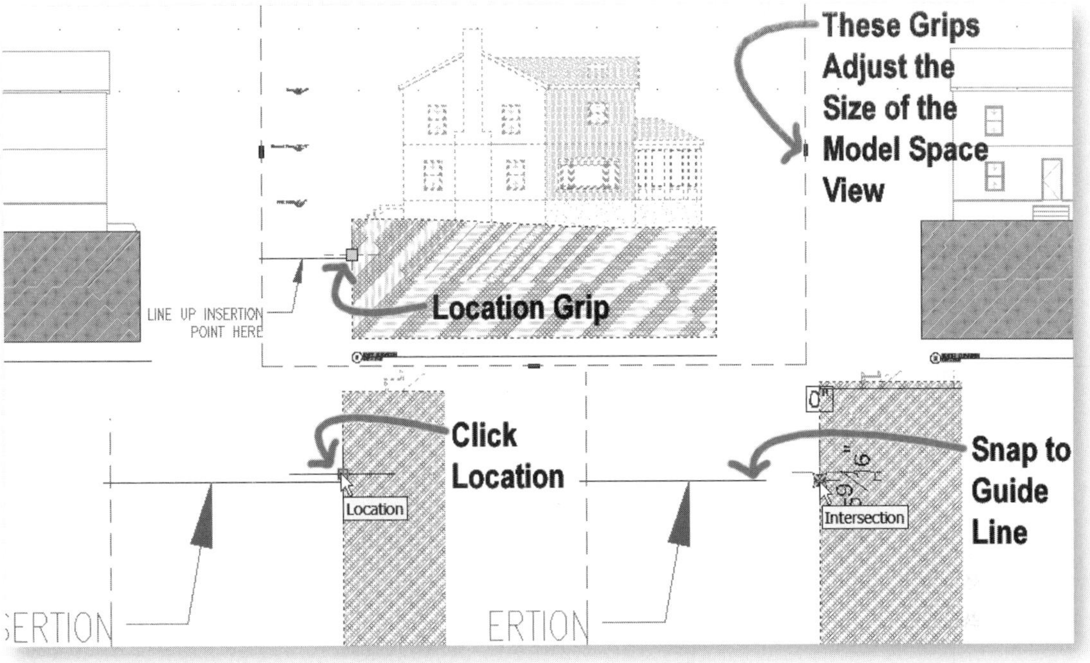

FIGURE 16.9 *Use the Location Grip to align the new elevation to the others*

If you prefer, the AutoCAD MOVE command can be used. If you use Move, set the Base Point at the Insertion point of the elevation and then snap perpendicular to the guide line.

NOTE

The Location Grip is useful for moving the elevation object within its Model Space View boundaries. If you wish to move the elevation and its associated Model Space View together, then use the AutoCAD MOVE command instead.

19. Erase the line and the note.
20. Save the file.

Updating and Modifying Section/Elevation Objects

2D Section/Elevation objects remain linked to the building model. When changes occur in the building model, you can perform an update on the 2D Section/Elevation objects. This greatly reduces the amount of rework required to keep Sections and Elevations up to date.

NOTE

2D Section/Elevation objects are not live data; they can be edited for their own purposes as we will see below, but manual update is required to keep them current with the state of the model. There is also a batch process routine available that will update all elevations and sections within an entire project. On the Home tab, expand the Section & Elevation panel and then click the Batch Refresh tool.

Modify the Model

Suppose a design change caused the position of one of the windows to move. Let's open the Second Floor New file, make this change and then return to the Elevation and update it to see the change.

Be sure to keep the *A-CM01* file open.

1. On the Project Navigator, click the Constructs tab and then double-click the *Second Floor New* file to open it.
2. Zoom in to the Bedroom in the top right corner.
3. Select the Window in the right vertical Wall of the Bedroom.
4. Using the Location grip (the square one in the middle), move the Window up **2' 0"** [**600**] (see Figure 16.10).

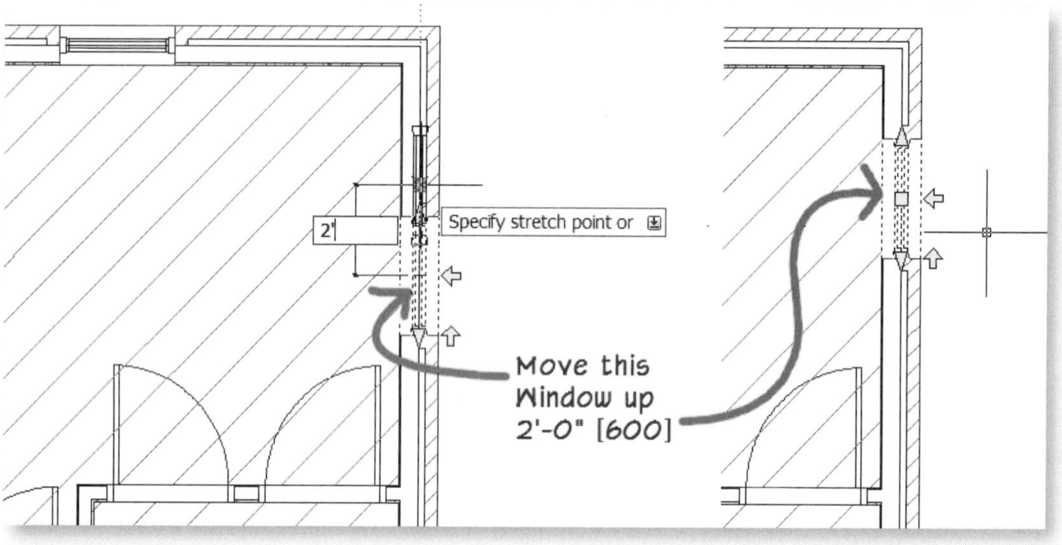

FIGURE 16.10 *Move a Window on the Second Floor*

5. Save and close the file.

Refresh the Elevation

Back in the *A-CM01* file, you should receive an alert that the *Second Floor New* XREF has changed at the lower right corner of your screen (see Figure 16.11).

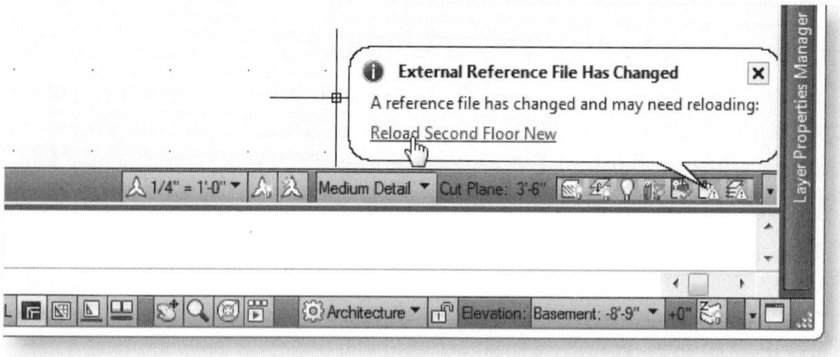

FIGURE 16.11 *An XREF Alert will appear*

6. Click the link on the balloon to reload the XREF.

TIP

You can also right-click the XREF quick-pick icon for a menu to open the XREF Manager. Use this technique if the balloon does not appear.

7. Select the East Elevation (the one we added above), on the 2D Section/Elevation ribbon tab, click the Refresh button.

Keep your eye on the second floor Window as the elevation refreshes.

Notice the update to the Elevation. The Window on the second floor has moved 2'-0" [600] to the right (see Figure 16.12).

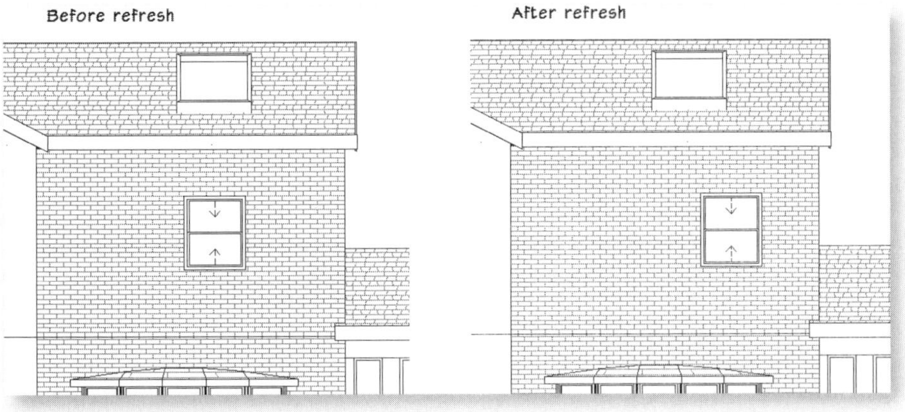

FIGURE 16.12 *Reload the XREFs and then refresh the Elevation to see the change*

NOTE

Important: It is very important that you first update the XREFs, and then refresh the Elevations. If you refresh first, you will see no change in the Elevation since the change took place in a remote file. We have to load those remote changes before the Elevation can "see" them.

Modify the Chimney

One of the advantages of studying Elevations is that you can discover flaws in the design or the drawing components used to portray the design that are not always evident in the plan views. For this reason it is good practice to set up the Elevations and Section early in the project and refresh them often throughout the design process. (This was certainly the rationale behind the setting up of the current file back in Chapter 5.) Here we have such an example. The Chimney was created with Plan Modifiers which are effective for the plan representation and when there are no sloped surfaces in elevation. However, if we want to have the chimney taper properly as it goes up, we will need to model it differently. Let's add a simple Body Modifier to what we already have thus far.

8. On the Project Navigator, click the Constructs tab and then double-click the *Second Floor Existing* file to open it.
9. Click the Wall on the right (the one with the chimney) on the Wall tab, click the drop-down button on the Edit in Section button and choose **Edit in Elevation**.
10. At the "Select linework or face under the cursor or specify reference point for view direction" prompt, click the mouse to the right of the chimney (see the left side of Figure 16.13).

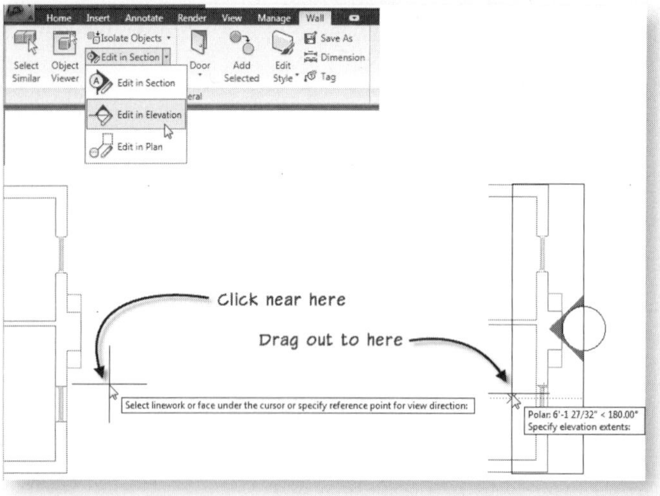

FIGURE 16.13 *Select the outside edge of the chimney for the reference view location*

11. At the "Specify elevation extents" prompt, drag to the left just beyond the inside edge of the Wall and then click again. (You just need to include the full thickness of the selected Wall.) (See the right side of Figure 16.13.)

    All objects except the selected Wall will be hidden and the drawing will switch to an elevation view looking at the chimney.
12. On the Home tab, click the drop-down button on the Line tool and choose the Polyline tool (or type **PL** and then press `ENTER`).
13. Using the illustration in Figure 16.14 as a guide, draw a polyline describing the shape of the desired taper of the chimney.

    Use Object Snaps and Object Snap Tracking to draw with precision.

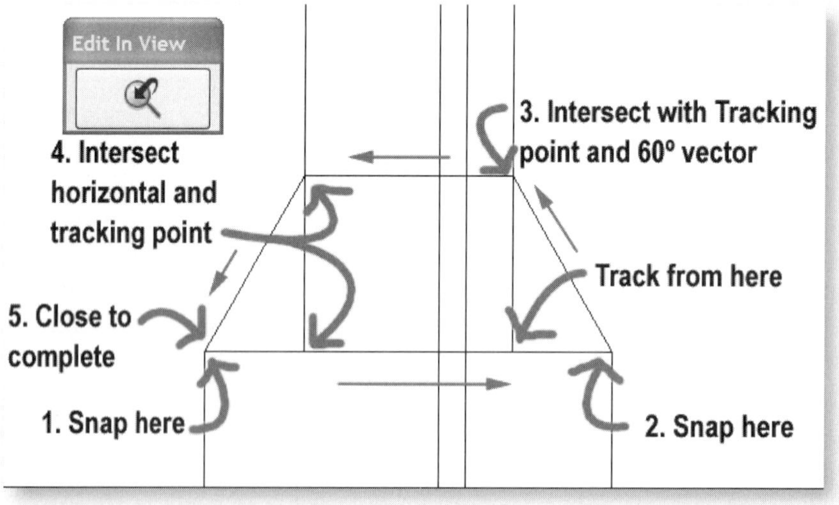

FIGURE 16.14 *Draw a polyline to describe the shape of the desired chimney taper*

14. When the polyline is complete, select it, right-click and choose **Convert To > Mass Element.**
15. At the "Erase selected linework" prompt, choose **Yes**.
16. At the "Specify extrusion height" prompt, type **1'-3"** [**380**] and then press ENTER.

    You should now have an extruded Mass Element in place of the polyline.
17. Select the Wall, on the Wall tab, on the Modify panel, click the Body Modifier drop-down button and then choose Add.

A Body Modifier is a piece of 3D geometry that modifies the shape of a Wall. You can apply it to the mass of the Wall using a choice of operations such as "Additive," "Subtractive" and "Replace." If you anticipate needing to place a Door, a Window or another opening in the space occupied by the Body Modifier, choose **Additive Cut Openings**. This will allow a Door or Window to later cut a hole in the shape formed by the Body Modifier.

18. At the "Select objects to apply as body modifiers" prompt, click the Mass Element and then press ENTER (see the left side of Figure 16.15).

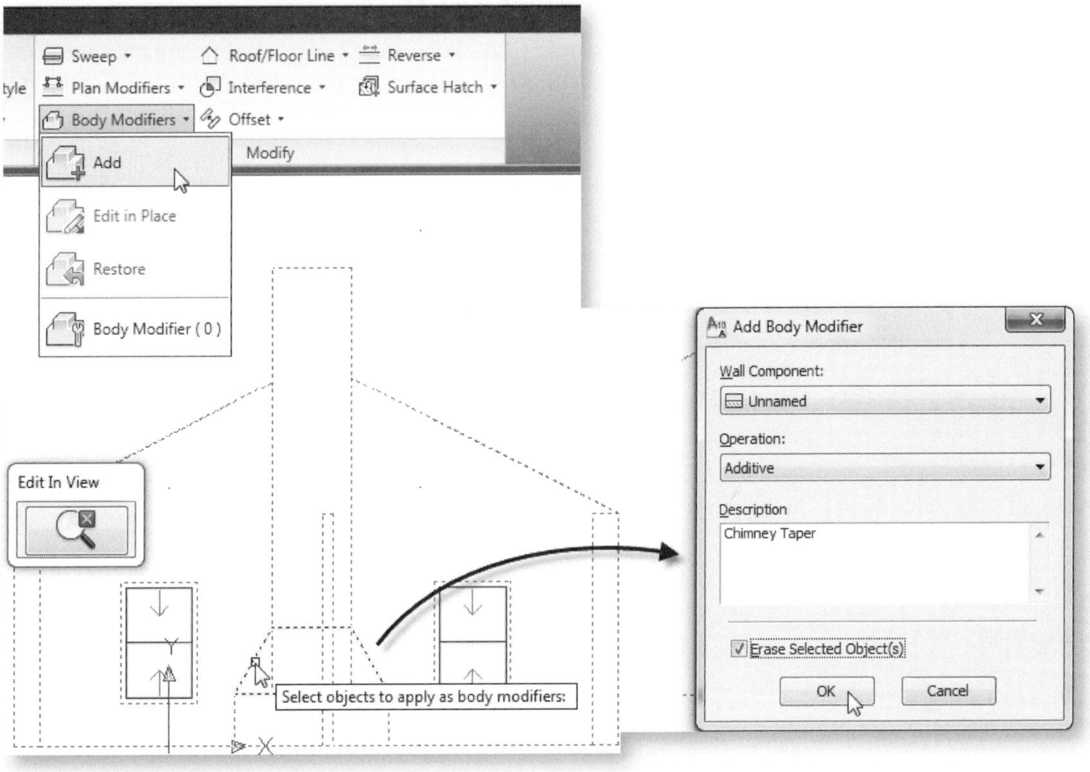

FIGURE 16.15 *Apply the Mass Element to the Wall as a Body Modifier*

19. In the Add Body Modifier worksheet, choose **Additive** from the Operation list and type **Chimney Taper** in the Description field.
20. Place a check mark in the Erase Selected Object(s) checkbox and then click OK (see the right side of Figure 16.15).

> **NOTE**
>
> **You may want to view the wall in a 3D view at this point to verify that everything is correct. For instance, if the profile snapped to the wrong face of the chimney, select the Wall, on the Wall tab, click the Body Modifier drop-down button and then choose Edit in Place to correct. Move the Mass to the correct location and then click Finish.**

21. Click the Exit Edit in View icon on the floating Edit in View toolbar to exit the Edit in Elevation mode and return to the previous plan view.
22. Save and close the file.
23. Back in the *A-CM01* file, repeat the steps above in the "Refresh the Elevation" topic to reload the XREF and then refresh the elevation.

Apply a Material Boundary

The hatching on the Elevation was generated automatically based on the Material Definitions applied to the various pieces of the model (see below for more information on Material Definitions). Sometimes showing hatching all the way across the surface of the Elevation can be a bit too busy. We can limit the extent of the hatching on each 2D Section/Elevation object very simply.

24. Draw a closed polyline like the one shown in Figure 16.16.

    Make sure that you draw only three sides and then right-click and choose **Close** for the last side. The exact size or shape is not important.

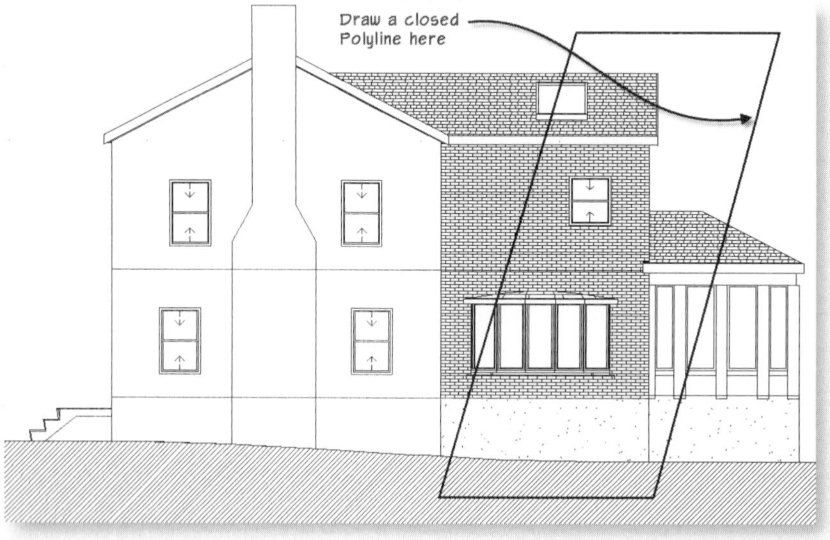

FIGURE 16.16 *Draw a polyline to use for the Material Boundary edge*

25. Select the Elevation, on the 2D Section/Elevation tab, on the Material Boundary panel, click the Add button.
26. At the "Select a closed polyline for boundary" prompt, click the polyline that you just drew.
27. At the "Erase selected linework" Prompt, choose **Yes**.

    The 2D Section/Elevation Material Boundary dialog box will appear.
28. Accept all defaults for now and click OK (see Figure 16.17).

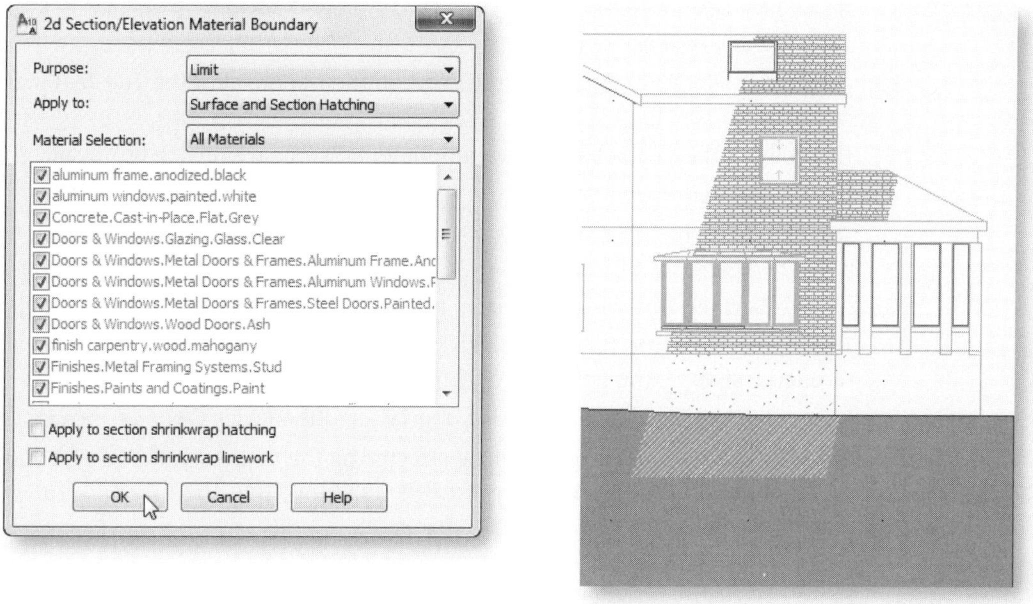

FIGURE 16.17 *Applying a Material Boundary with the default settings*

Material Boundaries are quite exciting, but the default settings do not give us such a good affect in this case. All of the hatching outside of the selected polyline has been erased. We can edit the Material Boundary any time.

29. Select the Elevation, on the 2D Section/Elevation tab, on the Material Boundary panel, click the Edit in Place button.

    You can grip edit the shape of the Material Boundary in real time. Give it a try (see Figure 16.18).

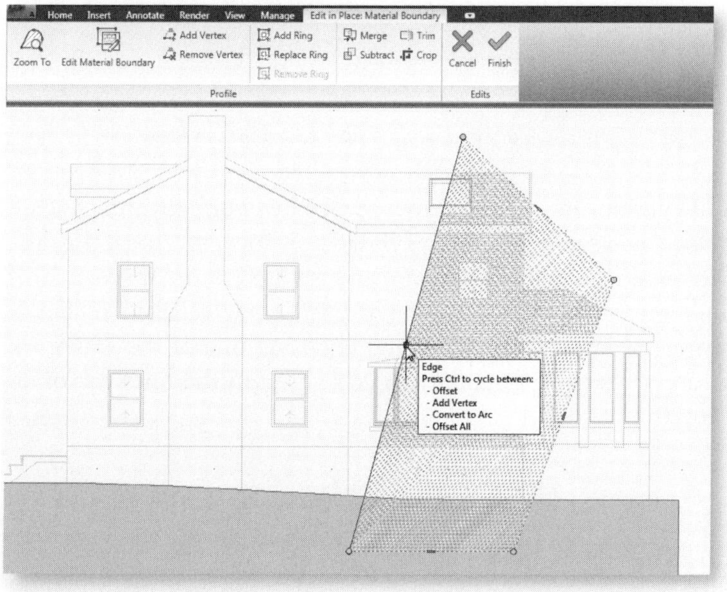

FIGURE 16.18 *Grip edit the shape of the Material Boundary and see the results in real time*

Hover over each grip to see its CTRL key options. Try some of them out. You can undo any of these edits.

30. With the In-Place Edit boundary selected, on the ribbon, click the Edit Material Boundary button.

    This will call the "2D Section/Elevation Material Boundary" dialog box again.

31. Change the Purpose to **Erase**.

    This will show the hatching everywhere except the region within the polyline. It is like reversing the polyline.

32. Choose **Surface Hatching Only** from the Apply to list.

    This will exclude the hatching on the terrain that we are actually sectioning through and apply the boundary only to hatches seen in elevation.

33. Leave Material Selection set to **All Materials** and then click OK.

    With this chosen, all materials will be affected by the boundary. If you wish you can choose **Selected Materials** instead and choose from the list of materials only those that you wish to change.

34. On the ribbon, click the Finish button to complete the operation (see Figure 16.19).

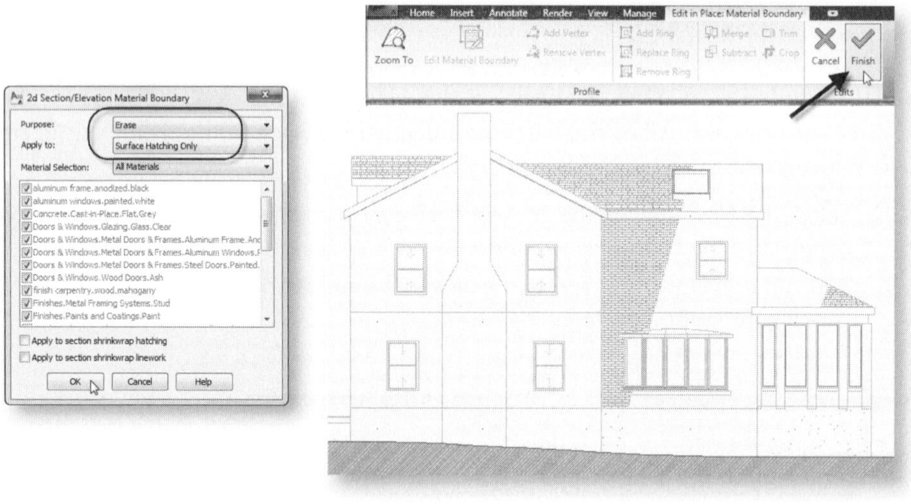

FIGURE 16.19 *Reverse the effect of the boundary and apply it only to hatches in Elevation*

Continue to perform In-place Edits and experiment with the boundary until you are fully satisfied. For instance, you can draw another closed polyline, and repeat the process to add a second Material Boundary. Each one can be edited in the In-place Edit mode. Try also changing the Material Selection to just a few selected materials as well. Also, by applying a Material Boundary and choosing one of the Linework options, you can even use a Material Boundary to erase or crop the linework of an elevation (see Figure 16.20).

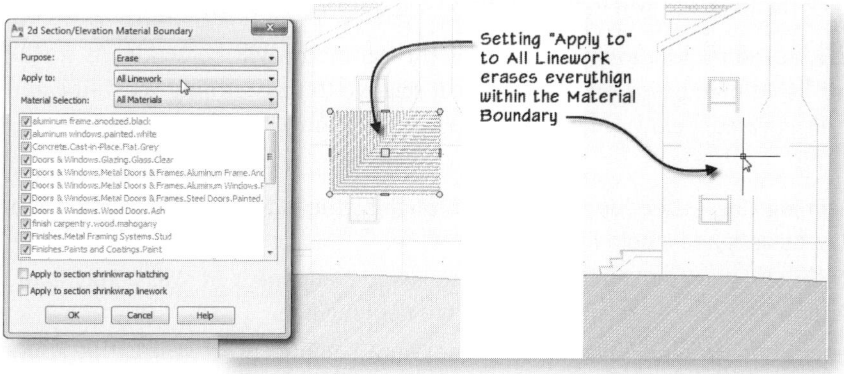

FIGURE 16.20 *You can have more than one Material Boundary on an elevation and it can even erase all hatching and linework*

35. When you are satisfied with the Material Boundary, Save the file.

2D SECTION/ELEVATION STYLES

2D Section/Elevation objects are controlled by styles in much the same way as other AEC objects. By means of the style, we will be able to adjust the graphical display of virtually all of the linework in the 2D Section/Elevation object. By adding layers and lineweights to the linework of the section, we will help the key features to "punch" and achieve an overall better read from the Section/Elevation object.

Explore the 2D Section/Elevation Style

A large part of the configuration of the 2D Section/Elevation Style is the display control. As we have seen in previous chapters, display control allows us (within specific Display Representations) to assign Layer, Color, Linetypes, Lineweights and Plot Styles to the various components of an AEC object. Many objects offer additional display parameters as well, such as Cut Plane, Custom Block Display and Hatching. 2D Section/Elevation objects have only a single Display Representation called "General." Currently all of the Sections and Elevations in this drawing use the 2D Section/Elevation style named "2D Section Style 96 [2D Section Style 100]." This is the default used by all Callout routines. Let's take a quick look at the Display settings of this style.

1. Select the East Elevation, on the 2D Section/Elevation tab, click the Edit Style button.
2. Click the Display Properties tab.

   Notice that General is the only Display Representation, and that a Style Override has been applied.
3. Click the Edit Display Properties icon (see Figure 16.21).

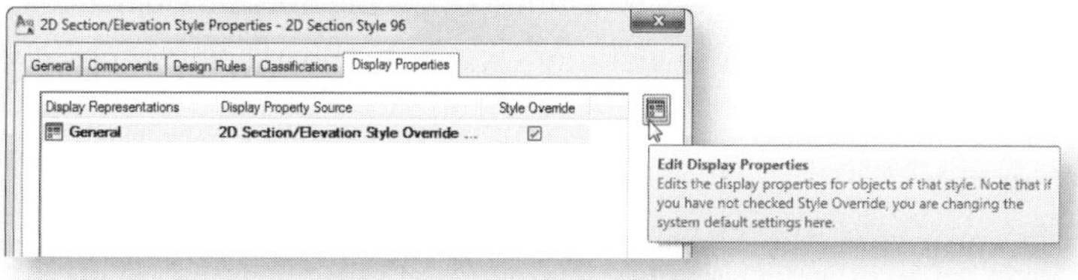

FIGURE 16.21 *Edit Display Properties of the 2D Section Style*

4. Click the Layer/Color/Linetype tab and scroll through the list of components.

When a 2D Section/Elevation is cut, all of the geometry will be rendered to the components listed here based on how they fall relative to the defining (cut) line and other criteria covered below. Here is a brief description of each component (see Figure 16.22):

- Defining Line—Used for objects cut through by the Bldg Section/Elevation line. Usually assigned a bold lineweight.
- Outer Shrinkwrap—Similar to the shrinkwrap component of Walls. This is the outermost edge of the all objects on the defining line.
- Inner Shrinkwrap—Similar to the shrinkwrap component of Walls. This is the innermost edge of the all objects on the defining line. It can be thought of as "holes" in the defining line.
- Shrinkwrap Hatch—A hatch pattern that fills in the space between the outer and inner shrinkwrap.
- Surface Hatch Linework—All of the hatching on surfaces shown in elevation.
- Section Hatch Linework—All of the hatching of materials cut through at the defining line. Section Hatch Linework differs from the Shrinkwrap Hatch in that it applies individually to each model component, rather than the entire space between the shrinkwrap components.

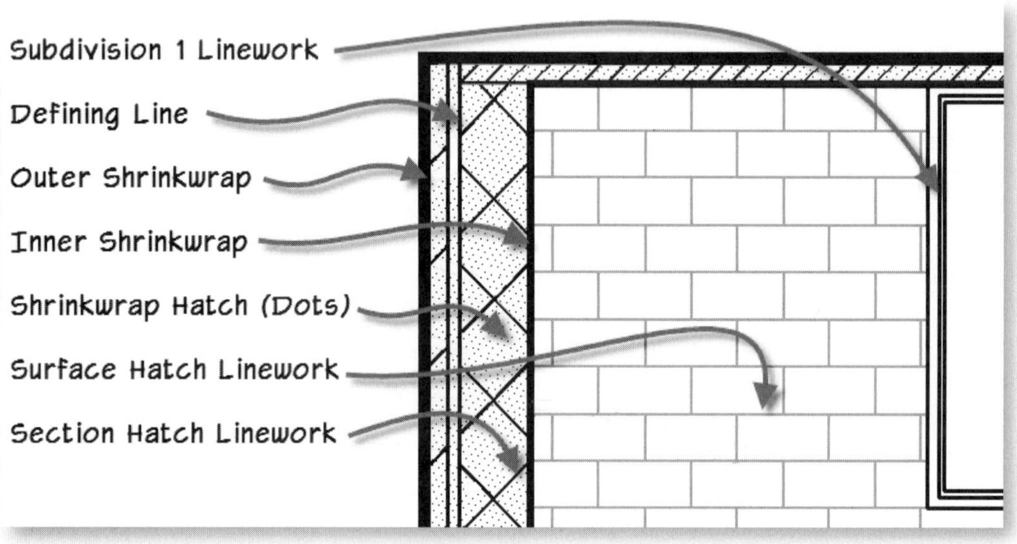

FIGURE 16.22 *The 2D Section/Elevation Style Components in context*

- Hidden—Used for objects concealed from view.
- Erased—Used to store linework that is manually edited and erased.
- Unknown Component—Used for errors encountered by the Section objects.
- Subdivision 1–10—Zones beyond the defining line used to display receding lineweights.

5. Click the Hatching tab.

   There is a single entry here, the Shrinkwrap Hatch. If you turn on the Shrinkwrap Hatch, configure its pattern and dimensions here. It is currently set to Solid Fill. We'll skip the Other tab for now.

Edit a 2D Section/Elevation Style

Now that we have seen some of the settings available for 2D Section/Elevation styles, let's make a few minor changes.

6. Click back on the Layer/Color/Linetype tab and turn off the Shrinkwrap Hatch component (dim the lightbulb icon).

Notice that the Defining Line, Outer Shrinkwrap and Inner Shrinkwrap components have their layers set to 0 and most of the other properties set to ByBlock. ByBlock is an old AutoCAD term. This setting means that the particular property in question will be inherited from the parent object. (It is called ByBlock simply because Blocks were the first objects to be able to do this.) In other words, the Defining Line does not have its own explicit Color, Linetype, Lineweight or Plot Style designation; rather it inherits these properties from the 2D Section/Elevation object itself. The Shrinkwrap components do likewise (with the exception of Color which is set explicitly to Red). Therefore, the properties of the 2D Section/Elevation object will be inherited by these components. If the linetype, lineweight or Plot Style of the 2D Section/Elevation object itself changes, then the linetype, lineweight and/or Plot Style of all Defining Line and Shrinkwrap components will also change. (This is also true for Color in the case of the Defining Line.)

MANAGER NOTE CAD

Before you panic and begin changing all of the hundreds of display components from ByBlock to ByLayer, remember that the object itself is almost always set to ByLayer, so that the net result of any ByBlock component is typically ByLayer. It is unnecessary, therefore, to change all of the Display Properties of the AEC objects to ByLayer internally. Use this setting only if you explicitly assign a layer in the Display Properties. You will see examples of this below.

It is rare that properties like Color, Linetype, Lineweight and Plot Style are assigned directly to objects in the drawing. Typically, individual objects use the setting: ByLayer. ByLayer means that the object will inherit the properties of the layer upon which it resides. This is standard industry practice. Therefore, when the internal components of an object are set to ByBlock, and the object itself is set to ByLayer, the net result is that the components also behave as if they were set to ByLayer. Typically you will find the Color, Linetype, Lineweight and Plot Style settings assigned either directly in the Display Properties dialog box or via the Layer. You should never apply these properties directly to the objects themselves. This is generally considered bad practice and will not be looked on favorably by most CAD Managers and co-workers. In other words, there is little good reason to select the 2D Section/Elevation object and make its color Green. Rather, you would move the 2D Section/Elevation object to a Green-colored layer.

It is, however, fairly common for colors, linetypes, lineweights and plot styles to be assigned to object components within a particular Display Representation. For instance, as you can see here, the two Shrinkwrap components have been assigned to Color Red, while the Shrinkwrap hatch is assigned Color 9. For instance, to better understand which components are being rendered to Inner and Outer Shrinkwrap, it might be helpful to assign them different properties.

7. Select Outer Shrinkwrap, and set its Color to **154**, its Lineweight to **0.70 mm** and its Plot Style to **Full Saturation**.
8. Select Inner Shrinkwrap, and set its Color to **45**, its Lineweight to **0.50 mm** and its Plot Style to **Full Saturation** (see Figure 16.23).

NOTE

If you do not have Full Saturation available, please refer to the "Named Plot Style Tables included in-the-box" topic in the Preface for information on the shipping plot style tables.

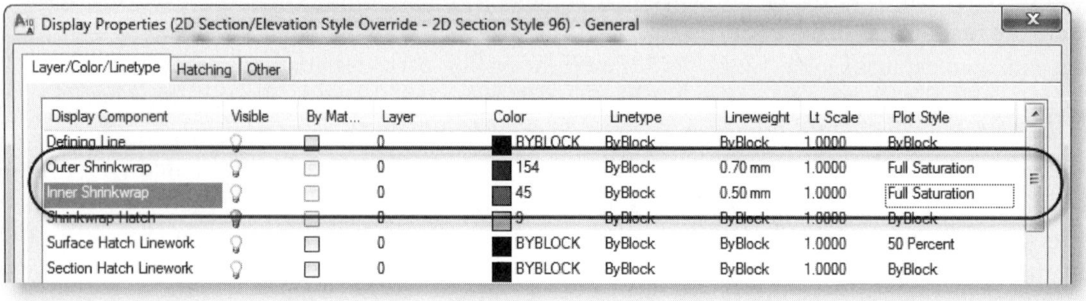

FIGURE 16.23 *Change the Lineweight and Color for the Shrinkwrap components*

9. Click OK twice when finished to return to the drawing.

The most obvious change was the elimination of the solid fill hatch from the terrain object beneath the elevation.

CAD MANAGER NOTE

There are various approaches to the process of manipulating the graphical display of a 2D Section/Elevation object. Conventional AutoCAD wisdom uses a series of layers; each assigned a unique color, which in turn is assigned a Lineweight while plotting. We can also have the layer assign the Lineweight or Plot Style properties or assign all three. Finally, all of these properties could be assigned directly within the 2D Section/Elevation dialog box without need for further layers. It is a matter of CAD management philosophy. Regardless of the CAD management philosophy implemented at your firm, ensure that your standards and templates are documented so the staff is clear on the method. In this exercise, we will explore the process by using a little of each technique. If you decide to use layers, make sure that all of the layers that you need are created in the file before you begin editing the 2D Section/Elevation style. You will not be able to create a new layer or edit the properties of an existing layer while in the Display Properties dialog box.

10. Save the file.

Update the Sections

To better see the effects of the edits we made to the Shrinkwrap components, let's shift our attention to the Sections for a while.

11. Pan over to the left side of the drawing.
12. Select both of the Section objects (to the left of the model), on the 2D Section/Elevation tab, click the Refresh button (see Figure 16.24).

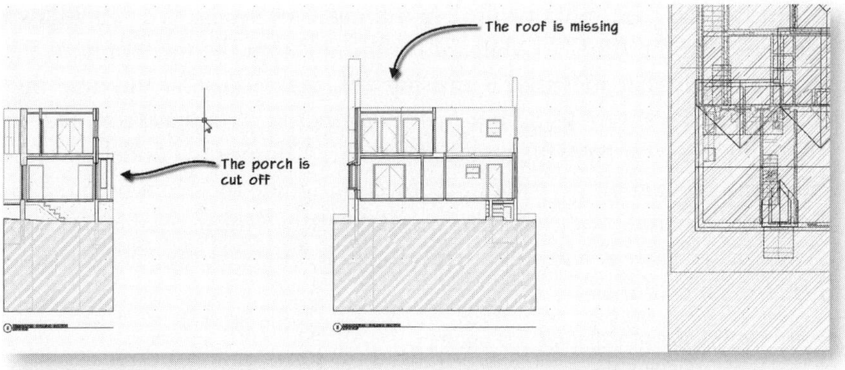

FIGURE 16.24 *Refresh the two Sections*

You will see an immediate change in the color that outlines the cut objects. The sections will also update to reflect the latest changes in the model.

13. Zoom in on each Section and study them.
14. On the Application Status Bar, click the Show/Hide Lineweight toggle.

With the Inner and Outer Shrinkwrap components now being assigned to different colors and different lineweights, you should be able to see them clearly in the sections. You should also notice some problems that we will need to resolve, like the cavity in the exterior Wall (see Figure 16.25).

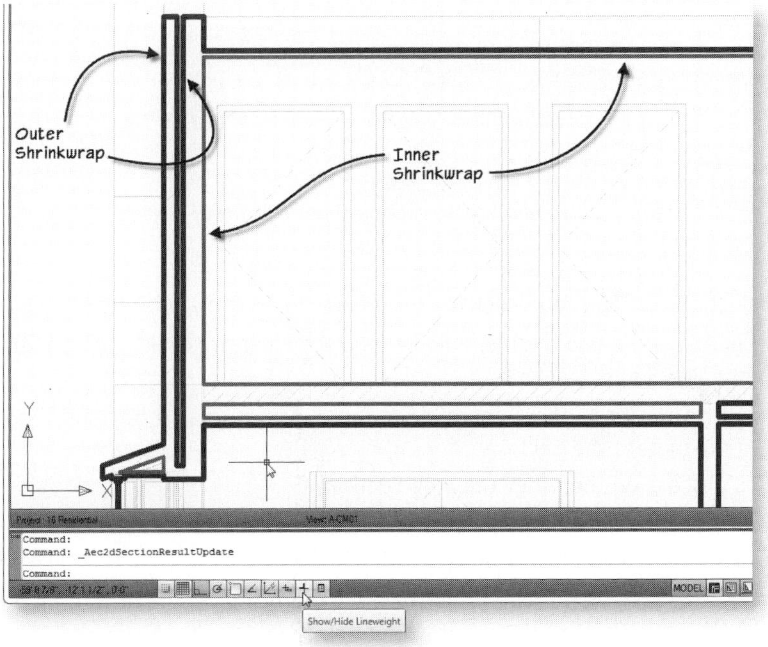

FIGURE 16.25 *After changing the colors and lineweights of the two Shrinkwrap components, it is easier to understand the section*

The sections clearly need a bit more work than did our Elevations. We will address air gap issue in the "Edit the Air Gap Material Definition" topic below. For now, the most obvious problem is that the Roof is missing. This is because at the time that these Sections were cut, we were using the *Roof Existing* file. You may recall that in Chapter 12 we built the *Roof New* file and updated this Composite Model to reference it instead of the original file. We did not, however, update the Sections and Elevations at that time. Therefore, rather than use Refresh, we must regenerate these Sections and the other three Elevations. Unfortunately, regenerating 2D Section/Elevation objects must be done one at a time.

15. Toggle the Lineweight display off again.
16. Select the Longitudinal Building Section, on the ribbon, click the Regenerate tool.

    All of the XREFs we need are included in the selection for this Section except the Roof New file. Rather than replace the entire selection, we will simply add to it.
17. Click the Select Additional Objects icon (see Figure 16.26).

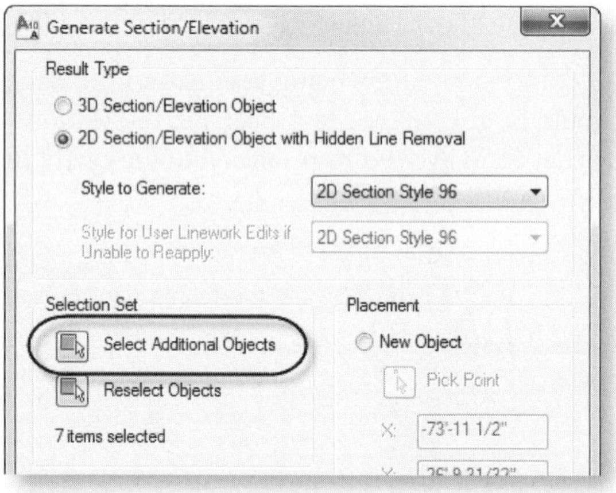

FIGURE 16.26 *You can add to the existing selection by clicking Select Additional Objects*

18. At the "Select objects" prompt, click the Roof New file in the model at the right.

    You may need to zoom in a bit. It should be easy to select, try clicking on one of the ridge or valley lines to select it.
19. Press ENTER to return to the Generate Section/Elevation dialog box and then click OK to regenerate the Section.
20. Repeat this process on the other Building Section.

Adjust the Bldg Section Line Position

When we added the Bldg Section Line in Chapter 5, we did not have the porch yet. If you zoom in on the Transverse Building Section, you will notice that the porch has been cropped out of the section. Zoom in on this area in the model and you will discover the reason. The Section line passes directly through the middle of a Wall (and even though we cannot see it here, the Door as well). This problem is very easy to correct.

Simply widen the Bldg Section Line with the grips and then Refresh the Section.

21. Select the Bldg Section Line for the Transverse Building Section.

If you have trouble locating it, remember you can click on the 2D Section/Elevation object first and the Bldg Section Line will highlight in red. Furthermore, you can click the Cut Plane item on the Drawing Status Bar and raise the Cut Plane up past the terrain model. This will remove some of the hatching on the model and make it a little less busy. Try a value of about 10'-0" [3000]. However, the Spaces will still show hatching, so this will help some, but you will still want to zoom in to make a good selection.

22. Click the square End grip at the top of the Section Line and drag it up using POLAR or ORTHO.
23. Click just outside the porch.
24. You might also want to adjust the Length grip (triangle shape) so it is outside the building as well (see Figure 16.27).

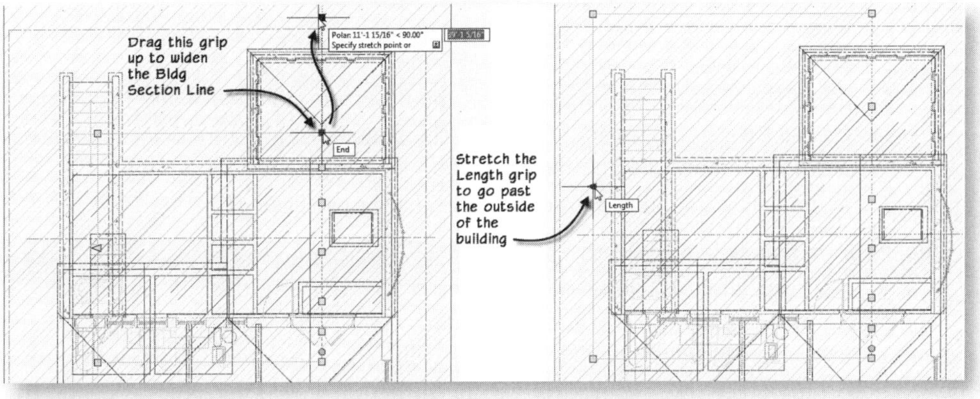

FIGURE 16.27 *The Bldg Section Line needs to be widened to include the porch*

25. Deselect the Bldg Section Line, select the Section and on the ribbon, click the Refresh button.

    If the section line now cuts through one of the porch piers, you can simply move the entire Bldg Section Line slightly and then refresh again.

26. Click the Section object and use the small magenta edge grips (attached to the gray dashed lines) to widen the extents of the Model Space View.

Fine-Tune the Model

There is one other very obvious issue with the model illuminated by these Sections: The Terrain Model has not been cut (excavated) to receive the house. You may recall that we used the Drape command in Chapter 5 to build the *Terrain Model* file. The Drape command simply creates free-form Mass Elements. Therefore, it is a simple matter to subtract geometry equivalent to the shape of our model to form the cut in the Terrain. To do this, we will use the actual Basement files and some of the techniques we learned earlier. To properly cut away what we don't want from the *Terrain Model* file, we need a "solid" version of our Basement. (Imagine filling the Basement with concrete, and then using this to subtract away the terrain.) To get that from the files we have, we will enable the Volume Display Rep of Space objects as we did in Chapter 2.

Leave the *A-CM01* file open while you perform these steps.

27. On the Project Navigator, double-click the *Terrain Model* Construct to open it.
28. From Project Navigator, in the *Constructs* folder, drag the *Basement Existing* file and drop it into the drawing window of the *Terrain Model* file. Repeat for *Basement New*.

    They should insert in exactly the correct location.

In Chapter 2, in the "Add a Set" heading, we learned how to make Space objects display a 3D solid representing their volume. By repeating that process now, and enabling something similar for the Stair leading up from the Basement, we will have a solid object to subtract from our terrain model.

29. On the Manage tab, on the Style & Display panel, click the Display Manager button.
30. Expand Sets, select Model (it will be bold) and then on the right side, on the Display Representation Control tab, select Space.
31. Place a check mark in the Volume checkbox and then click OK.
32. Select the *Basement New* file, on the External Reference tab, click the Open Reference button.
33. Select the Stair object leading out of the Basement, right-click and **Properties**.
34. On the Display tab, open the Display component list and turn on the Clearance component (click the lightbulb icon).
35. In the dialog that appears, confirm the change by clicking OK.

The Stair treads will appear to "grow" up as the Stair clearance is represented three-dimensionally with a volume. In this case, we are using the volume to help us cut away from the terrain, but you can use this to assist you when planning Stairs to make sure you have enough head clearance as well. You can control the height of this clearance volume on the Properties palette with the Stair selected. Look for the Headroom height parameter in the Advanced grouping.

36. Save and close the file and then back in the *Terrain Model* file, reload the XREF to Basement New.

We are now ready to subtract the volume of these two XREFs from the mass of the *Terrain Model.*

37. Select the large terrain Mass Element.

    A blizzard of grips will appear. Time and space do not permit us to discuss them here, but feel free to explore on your own.

38. On the Mass Element ribbon tab, click the Boolean drop-down button and choose Subtract.
39. At the "Select objects to subtract" prompt, click on both the *Basement Existing* and *Basement New* files and then press ENTER.
40. At the "Erase layout geometry" prompt, choose **No**.

We don't want to erase the XREFs. Erasing them is not the same as detaching and unloading. If you no longer want a particular XREF, Detach it. If you just want it to be invisible for a while, you can maintain the XREF by choosing Unload instead.

You should now have a hole in the terrain for the excavation. If you find it difficult to see the results, select just the Terrain Mass Element, right-click and choose **Object Viewer** (see Figure 16.28).

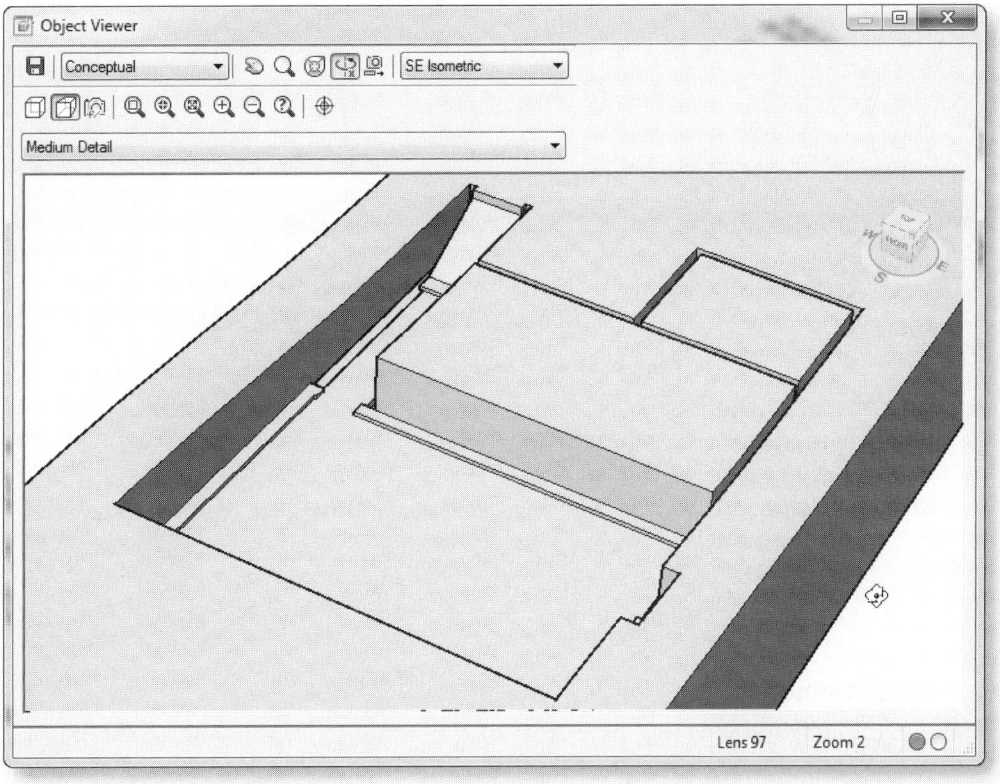

FIGURE 16.28 *Producing the excavation in the Terrain Model with a Boolean Subtraction*

41. Re-open Basement New and turn off the Clearance Component of the Stair object, Save and close the file.

    You can also restore the display of Spaces in the *Terrain Model* back to Model instead of Volume as well.

The Boolean functions use the active display graphics. This is why we changed both Spaces and Stairs in their respective files to a volumetric display. Had we not done this, the basement would have appeared to be filled with dirt, since the Walls and slabs would be the only objects to subtract.

42. On the Project Navigator, right-click the *Terrain Model* Construct and choose **External References**.
43. In the "External References" dialog that appears, right-click the *Basement New* XREF and then choose **Detach**. Repeat for Basement Existing.
44. Close the "External References" dialog.
45. Save and close the file.
46. Back in the *A-CM01* file, repeat the process from above to first reload the XREFs and then refresh the two Sections (see Figure 16.29).

TIP

Unlike Regenerate, with Refresh, you can select several elevations or sections at the same time and Refresh together.

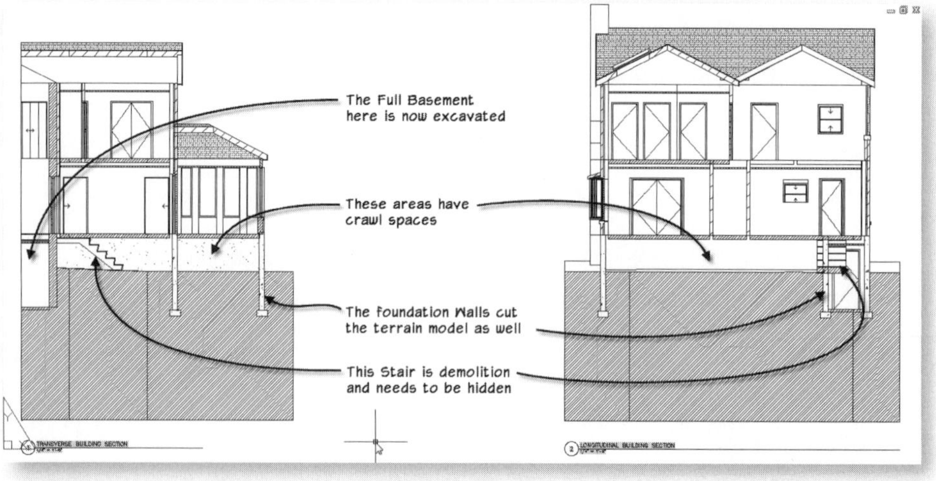

FIGURE 16.29 *After Reloading the XREFs and Refreshing the Sections, the Terrain now displays with the proper excavation*

47. Save the *A-CM01* file.

Freeze Demolition

Look carefully in the crawl space areas of the sections and you will see the existing exterior Stair seeming to float in the Basement. We assigned this to a Demolition layer back in Chapter 10. It is, however, not showing as dashed here, and it is hiding a portion of the Section beyond it. Let's remove these items from the section.

48. In the "Layer Properties Manager," locate all "demolition" layers and freeze them.

    The layer names will have XREF names as a prefix, like First Floor Existing|A-Wall-D [First Floor Existing|A-Wall-GR] for example. Demo layers might end in "-Demo" or simply "-D" ["-Demo" or "-GR"].

You can use Search for Layer box at the top right corner of the palette to make this task easier. In the search field, type: ***D** [***R**]. This will show all layers ending in D [R] (see Figure 16.30). Repeat for ***Demo**. Notice that this filter will also capture the threshold layers like A-Door-Thld. This is because this layer also ends in "*d*." This is fine as our goal here is to shorten the list of layers so that we can easily locate the demolition layers.

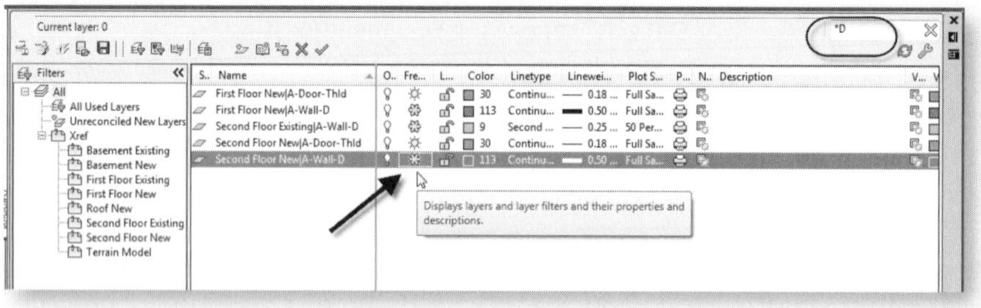

FIGURE 16.30 *Search for layers with a Filter*

49. After you have frozen all "demo" layers, clear the search field in the "Layer Properties Manager" to return to an unfiltered list and then click OK to apply the changes and dismiss the Layer Properties Manager.

NOTE **Be sure to use Freeze, turning them Off will not work.**

50. Refresh the two Sections.

The Basement Stairs should no longer appear in the Sections. If you look carefully in the Longitudinal Section, the demolished Window and Door also disappear during this refresh.

SUBDIVISIONS

Subdivisions are physical zones within the Bldg Section/Elevation Line boundary that designate different Display properties when the Section/Elevation is generated. Typically, each zone is assigned a lighter lineweight as it moves farther from the defining line. In this way, you can begin to introduce depth to your Sections and Elevations.

Regenerate the Remaining Elevations

The North and West Elevations are good places to explore subdivisions because the plan steps back in a few places. Before we begin, let's add the *Roof New* file to these Elevations as we did with the Sections above.

1. Select the North Elevation, on the 2D Section/Elevation tab, click the Regenerate button.
2. From the Style to Generate list, be sure that 2D Section Style 96 [2D Section Style 100] is selected.
3. As we did above, click the Select Additional Objects icon, pick the *Roof New* file in the drawing (remember, click the eaves or valleys for easy selection) and then click OK to finish and regenerate the elevation.
4. Repeat this on each of the other two elevations.

Add Subdivisions

5. Zoom the drawing so that you can see both the North Elevation and the house model comfortably onscreen.
6. Click to select the North Elevation.

   Notice how one of the Bldg Elevation Lines in the model has highlighted in red. This is the Bldg Elevation Line used to generate this elevation.
7. Select the highlighted Bldg Elevation Line, right-click and choose **Properties**.

   At the top of the Properties palette, "All (2)" will appear in the selection list.
8. From the selection list at the top of the Properties palette, choose **Bldg Elevation Line (1)**.
9. In the Dimensions grouping, click the Subdivisions worksheet icon (see Figure 16.31).

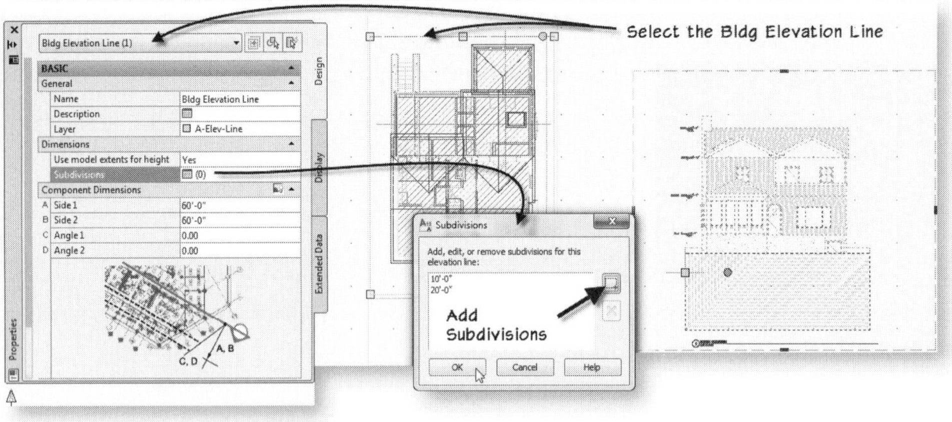

FIGURE 16.31 *Add Subdivisions*

10. In the Subdivisions worksheet, click the Add icon.

    A Subdivision will appear automatically set to 10'-0" [3000]. It may be edited here, but it is usually easier to grip edit it in the drawing instead.

11. Click Add again.

    This one will come in at 20'-0" [6000].

12. Click OK to dismiss the worksheet and add the subdivisions to the drawing.

Since we changed the Display Properties of the Bldg Section /Elevation Line object earlier in this chapter, the two Subdivision lines come in magenta. This makes them easier to see and edit. Notice that each subdivision has a triangular-shaped grip. If you hover over this grip, the dimension of the subdivision will appear. The Subdivision lines are located pretty well where the default dimensions placed them. The one further away at 20'-0" [6000] sits in the space between the back Wall of the addition and the Wall of the patio on the second floor. This will make the linework of Wall behind the patio Wall lighter than the back Wall of the addition. The closer subdivision may need some adjustment. The transition between one subdivision and another is abrupt. If the subdivision cuts across the hip portion of the porch Roof you will get a sharp line on that Roof surface indicating the break between subdivisions. In this case, you would want to move the subdivision using the grip back a bit to cut through the ridge of the porch roof.

13. Using the grips on the subdivisions, make any necessary adjustments to their position.
14. Refresh the North Elevation.

You should see a shift in color with the porch reading in one color, and the rest of the elevation using a different color as it recedes from us.

15. Repeat the process on the West Elevation. Be mindful of where the Roof ridges and valleys occur as you are placing the subdivision lines.

The difference in color is very subtle in the default 2D Section/Elevation Style. Furthermore, the color used for Subdivision 3 is the same as Subdivision 2, so it is not as obvious where this break occurs.

Let's edit those colors so that the transition from one subdivision to the next becomes more recognizable.

16. Open the Layer Properties Manager again.
17. Change the color of A-Sect-Thin to **20** and the color of A-Sect-Fine to **31** and then click OK.

These colors will have no impact on plotting. The Lineweight and Plot Style settings will determine how these layers plot. We are choosing brighter colors for the items that are closer to use and softer colors for those that recede back. This is being done simply to make the drawing easier to read onscreen.

NOTE

The default out-of-the-box for ACA is Named Plot Styles, if you use Color-Dependent Plot Styles in normal production, then a change like this might affect plotting.

18. Select either elevation, on the ribbon, click the Edit Style button.
19. Click the Display Properties tab and then the Edit Display Properties icon.
20. Select Subdivision 1, and set its Layer to **A-Sect-Medm**, select Subdivision 2, and set its Layer to **A-Sect-Thin**. Subdivision 3 can remain **A-Sect-Fine** (see Figure 16.32).

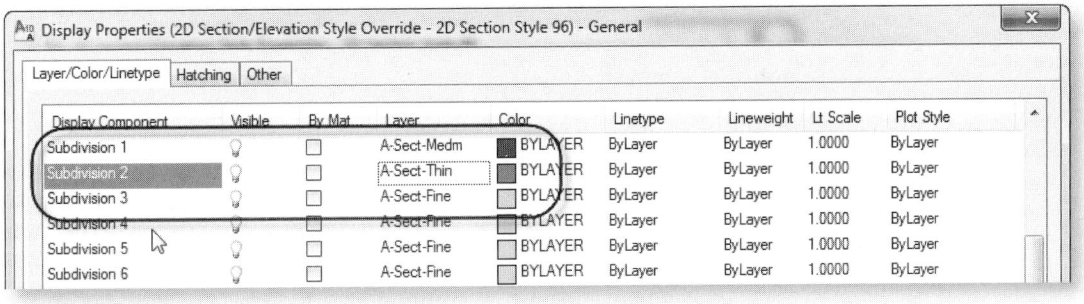

FIGURE 16.32 *Change the layer assignments of the Subdivision components*

21. Click OK twice to return to the drawing.

    Refresh the elevation if necessary. You can also toggle the Lineweight display to help see the effect of the change.
22. Save the file.

You will see some of the linework change to the new color. Notice how all of the Hatching remains unchanged. If you wish, you can make the Surface Hatching use the same properties as its Subdivision. To do this, edit the Style again, choose Edit Display Properties, click the Other tab and then place a check mark in the "Use Subdivision properties for surface hatching" checkbox. Although this might at first seem a logical option to enable, if you try it you will see that there will no longer be any contrast between the Surface Hatching and the Subdivision linework. Also, the hatching in the foreground (Subdivision 1) will display much too bold. It is not recommended that you use this setting.

2D SECTION/ELEVATION STYLES DESIGN RULES

Subdivisions allow us to address the overall needs of the Section/Elevation object, but they don't offer enough flexibility. If a piece of geometry falls within a particular subdivision, it will use those display properties assigned to that subdivision regardless of any other display settings the object itself may have. Design rules can be used to give more control over precise graphical display.

Door and Window Swing Design Rules

Design rules are linked to object colors in the model. A design rule will search the drawing model for a particular color and render the objects of that color to a particular component when generating the 2D Section/Elevation. To take fullest advantage of this functionality, you need to be familiar with which colors have been assigned to objects in the template files.

If you look at the Doors shown in the North Elevation, you will notice that their swings display in dashed lines despite the particular subdivision in which they occur. As we mentioned above, the Section_Elev Display Set is used to generate Elevations and Sections. If you were to edit this Display Set in the Display Manager (Chapter 2), you would learn that it uses the Door object's Elevation Display Representation. If you were to then open any Construct, and edit any Door's Elevation Display Rep and examine its Display Properties, you would further find that the Doors use color number 54 for their Swings by default. Therefore, to build a Design Rule for Door Swings, it must make reference to Color Number 54. This has been done already in the default 2D Section Style 96 [2D Section Style 100] Style that we are using here. This is why Door swings are dashed.

1. Select any Section or Elevation onscreen, on the ribbon, click the Edit Style tool.
2. Click the Design Rules tab.

   Take notice of Rule 1.

This rule states that if an item is found on color 54, and it is visible, then it should be rendered by the 2D Section/Elevation Style to the "Swing Lines" component (see Figure 16.33). Remember, the 2D Section/Elevation object performs a hidden line removal when it generates the section or elevation. Therefore, this rule (because the objects must be visible) ignores all items that are not visible regardless of color. The "Swing Lines" component is a custom component added to this style specifically for Door and Window Swings. You can see this on the Components and Display Properties tabs.

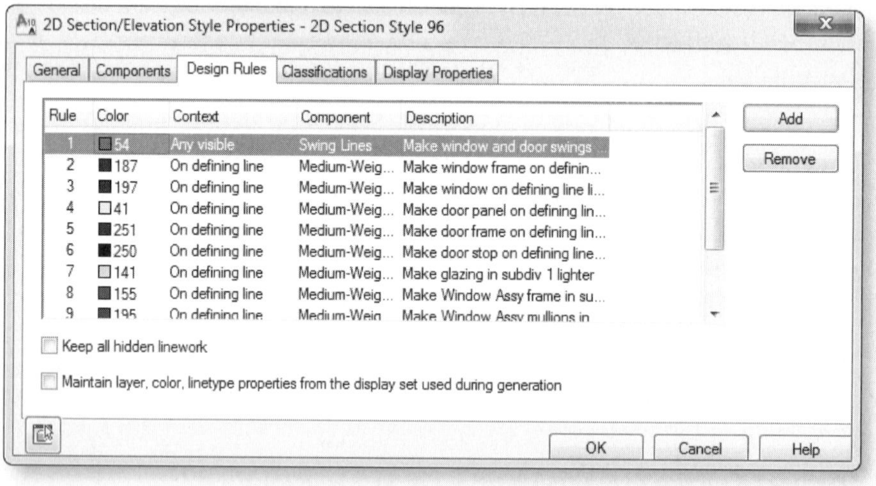

FIGURE 16.33 *Many Design Rules have been included in the default 2D Section/Elevation Style*

Feel free to further examine the other rules on this screen. The descriptions are helpful in explaining the purpose of the rule. In order to understand and ultimately to build your own rules, the most critical requirement is a color that you can assign to a unique purpose. In this case, color 54 has been reserved in the default templates to Door and Window Swings only. If you were to assign some other object to color 54, and then generate an elevation from it using this style, those objects would render dashed in the elevation object. Using this logic, let's make a simple Design Rule.

For Doors and Windows that actually swing, having the Swing indications dashed is useful. However, perhaps the small arrow swing indicator on the double hung Windows is not desirable. We can create a Design Rule to erase all of these automatically provided that we can assign a unique color to this component in the model. We will use color 56 for this purpose. However, since we are already editing the 2D Section/Elevation Style, let's add the rule first.

3. Click the Add button.

   Rule 14 will appear.
4. Next to Rule 14, in the Color column, click color Red.
5. In the Select Color dialog box, choose color **56** (you can just type the number), and then click OK.
6. In the Context column, choose **Any visible** from the drop-down list.
7. In the Component column, choose **Erased** from the drop-down list.
8. In the Description field, type **Erase Double Hung Window Swings** (see Figure 16.34).

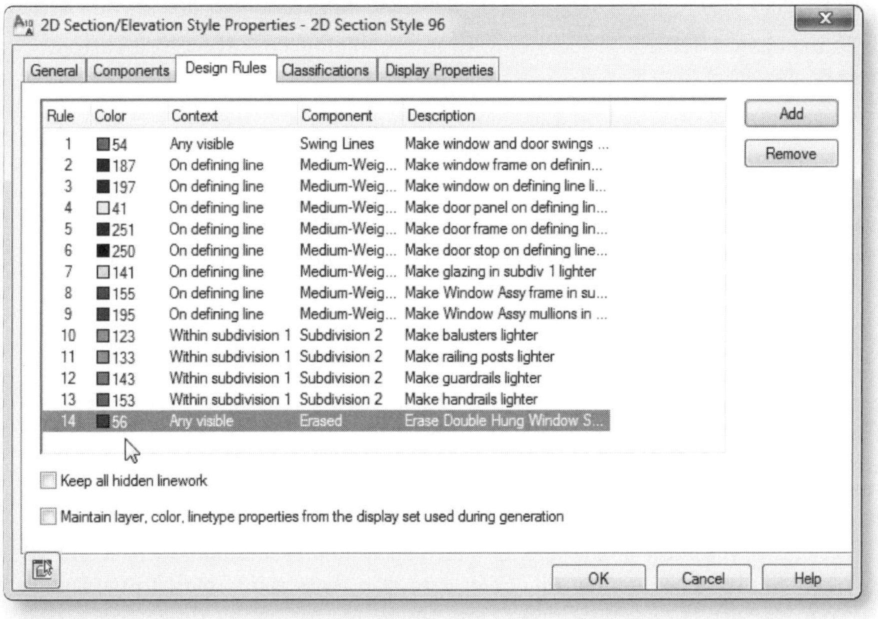

FIGURE 16.34 *Create a rule to delete the swings for Windows*

9. Click OK to return to the drawing.

   At the moment, there will be no change evident.
10. On the Project Navigator palette, click the Constructs tab, and then double-click *First Floor Existing* to open it.

11. Select any Double Hung Window in the drawing, on the ribbon, click the Edit Style button.
12. On the Display Properties tab, place a check mark in the Style Override checkbox next to Elevation (it will not be bold).

    In the Display Properties dialog, on the Layer/Color/Linetype tab, notice that the Swing color is currently 54, as we noted above.
13. Change the color of the Swing component to **56** and then click OK twice to return to the drawing.
14. Save and close the file and then repeat the process in the *Second Floor Existing* Construct.
15. Back in the *A-CM01* View file, reload the XREFs.
16. On the Home tab, expand the Section & Elevation panel, click the Batch Refresh button.
17. In the "Batch Refresh 2D Section/Elevations" dialog, be sure that Current Project is chosen and then click the Begin button.

    In the background behind the dialog, you will see each elevation and section highlight as it is being refreshed.

This is a very powerful command that can be used to refresh every 2D Section/Elevation object in the entire project. It will scan every Project drawing and then refresh the sections and elevations. In this case, the current file is the only one that contains 2D Section/Elevation objects. Therefore, we could also have simply selected them all and manually chosen Refresh from the ribbon. Use caution with this command as it will refresh every section and elevation. If for some reason there are elevations or sections that you do not wish to refresh, do not use this command, or use the Folder option instead.

18. In the "Batch Refresh 2D Section/Elevations" dialog, click the Close button.
19. Zoom and Pan the drawing and examine the results.

    Notice that Door and Window Swings are still dashed except the Double Hung Windows in the existing house which have disappeared.

NOTE

Other Double Hung Windows are unaffected. If you wish, however, you can edit those Styles and change the Swing color to 56 and then refresh the elevations to apply the rule to them as well.

CAD MANAGER NOTE

You will want to reserve a pool of colors for this type of editing. By setting some colors aside, you will ensure that someone in the office will not inadvertently choose a color already being used by other objects. This will help you avoid future hassles in trying to track down the reason that the section design rules do not work correctly. You can also pre-assign as many colors as you wish in the appropriate Display Representations to facilitate 2D Section/Elevation object generation. Don't forget to map those same colors to the Design Rules in your 2D Section/Elevation styles. Materials make configuring Design Rules a bit more challenging. When a particular component is set to By Material, it will look to the Material Definition for its color, rather than the component color. It may not always be possible to reserve a color for a Design Rule and for its purposes in a Material Definition. In this case, you may need to build a Custom Display Set for generating 2D Section/Elevations.

Maintaining Layer, Color and Linetype Properties

Despite the power of Subdivisions and Design Rules, sometimes it is desirable to simply generate the elevations using the same properties as the original model. A simple checkbox in the 2D Section/Elevation style toggles this behavior on and off.

20. Select the East Elevation object, on the 2D Section/Elevation tab, click the Save As button.
21. On the General tab, name the new Style: **MACA 2D Section Style**.
22. Click the Design Rules tab.
23. Place a check mark in the "Maintain Layer, Color, Linetype properties from the display set during generation" checkbox (see Figure 16.35).

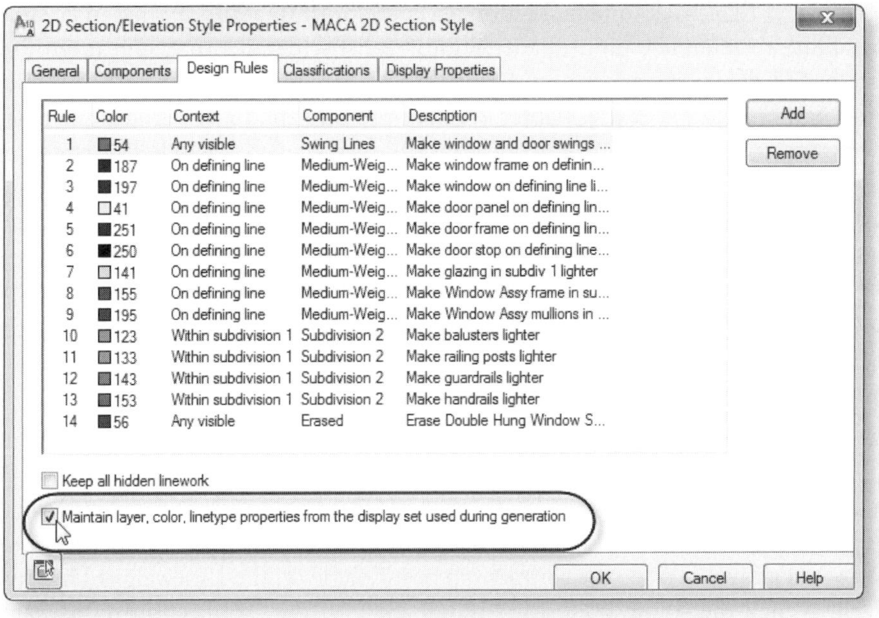

FIGURE 16.35 *You can instruct the section/elevation style to use the layer settings for model geometry*

24. Click OK to return to the drawing.

Notice that a line appears through the elevation. This indicates that the elevation is now out of date.

25. On the ribbon, click Refresh.

If you like this result better, you can assign this style to the other sections and elevations as well. The choice is left to the reader. It should be noted that if you edit the Display Properties of this style, that Subdivision 1 will no longer be available. The "Maintain Layer" setting overrides the geometry in Subdivision 1 only. As such, you cannot apply any settings to Subdivision 1 in such a style. However, if you have a Bldg Section Line and corresponding section that use Subdivisions, Subdivision 2 and higher will not use the model layer colors, but will continue to behave as they have before the change. This allows you to use model layer settings in the foreground, and receding lineweights for the other Subdivisions.

EDITING MATERIALS

We have already seen quite a bit of materials throughout the chapters of this book. Perhaps it is time we took a slightly more formal look at them. This topic is brief, but should prove sufficient to give you some idea of what the materials functionality in AutoCAD Architecture is all about. A Material Definition is a complete collection of display settings (plan, section, elevation and 3D rendering), designed to portray a single real-life material. Several dozen pre-made materials have been defined and included with ACA out-of-the-box. We have seen brick, concrete, roof shingles, drywall, paint, wood and more so far in the exercises in this book. Materials are assigned to objects via their object style. For example, each component of a Wall style is assigned to a particular Material Definition. When you assign a brick or concrete material to a component in a Wall style, the material controls the hatching and linework used to represent that brick in plan, section and elevation. In addition, materials also have the ability to reference high-quality photo-realistic textures that appear within ACA in shaded viewports and in renderings. It is used to generate photo-realistic renderings and animation. (See Chapter 20 for more information.) Perhaps the best feature of materials is that they allow you to think of your ACA Models in real-life terms. If your project will use three types of brick and two types of CMU, you define these five materials in ACA and use them in your project wherever they occur. One set of settings will govern your brick in all plans, sections, elevations and 3D renderings. If brick number two changes mid design from red to blond brick, you simply need to edit the Material Definition, and all of the objects using it will update.

Edit the Air Gap Material Definition

If you zoom in on the Sections again, and take a close look at the exterior Walls, you will notice that the Air Gap for the Wall Style is rendering "hollow" and that in some cases you can see linework for other Walls beyond. In addition, since the Air Gap is being represented as a void, this space is also being shrink-wrapped by the Section (this was noted above). To see the shrinkwrap best, toggle on the Lineweight Display temporarily—click the Show/Hide Lineweight icon on the Application status bar. Let's modify the Material Definition used for Air Gap to make this void less prominent in the Sections.

Leave the *A-CM01* file open while you perform these steps.

1. On the Project Navigator, open the *First Floor New* Construct.
2. Select one of the exterior masonry Walls, on the ribbon, click the Edit Style button.
3. Click the Materials tab.

   Each material of the Wall style is listed here with its material assignment.
4. Click on the Air Gap component and, at the top-right corner of the dialog box, click the Edit Material icon (see Figure 16.36).

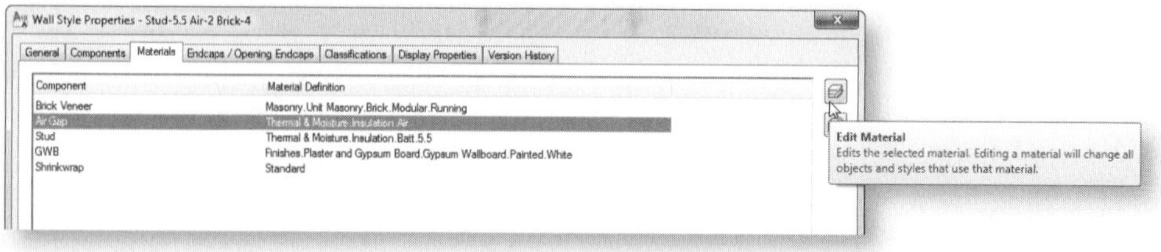

FIGURE 16.36 *You can edit Material Definitions directly from the Materials tab*

5. Click the Display Properties tab.

Even though there are eight Display Representations for Material Definitions, the one we want to edit is the one used by the Section_Elev Display Set. This is General Medium Detail (which also happens to be the currently active Display Rep). To see this for yourself, choose **Display Manager** from the Manage tab, expand Sets and select the Section_Elev Set. On the Display Representation Control tab, notice that General Medium Detail is checked for Material Definition.

6. On the Display Properties tab, with General Medium Detail selected, click the Edit Display Properties icon.
7. Click the Layer/Color/Linetype tab.

Material Definitions contain eight Display Components:

- Plan Linework—This is the linework used to draw the shape of the component in plan. For instance, for Walls it would be the two parallel lines and the Endcap shape of the component.
- 2D Section/Elevation Linework—This is the linework of components that you are looking at "beyond" in Sections and Elevations, in other words, any linework contained in the subdivisions.
- 3D Body—This is used to determine the linework for objects cut by the defining line in 2D Section/Elevation objects. It is also used to hide the object behind the material. In Live Sections and Models, this is the actual 3D object displayed for each material.
- Plan Hatch—Any plan hatching within the Plan Linework components, such as the hatching for brick in plan.
- Surface Hatch—Used for all surfaces that you are looking at "beyond" in Sections and Elevations, in other words, any hatching contained in the subdivisions.
- Section Hatch—This is the hatching for objects cut by the defining line.
- Sectioned Boundary—In Live Sections, this is the outline of the defining line.
- Sectioned Body—In Live Sections, this is the portion of the 3D object that is sectioned away. Render materials can be applied to this to make it display.

As you can see, in this case nearly every component is turned off. In order for other objects to not appear beyond the Air Gap void and to prevent it from shrinkwrapping, we must turn on the 3D Body component. As was mentioned above, one of the functions of the 3D Body is to hide other components behind it.

8. Click the lightbulb icon next to "3D Body" to turn it on.

   By turning on only the 3D Body and not the hatching, the Air Gap linework will still display as a gap, but it will no longer show objects behind nor will it shrinkwrap.
9. Click OK three times to return to the drawing.

Edit the Glazing Material

While we are in the *First Floor New* file, it might also be a good idea to make a slight modification to the glazing material used by the Windows. When we section a Window, you probably don't want the shrinkwrap to outline the glass. This makes the glass too bold. Let's edit the glass material to fix this.

10. Select one of the Windows, on the ribbon, click the Edit Style button.
11. Click the Materials tab.

12. Click on the Glass component and at the top-right corner of the dialog box, click the Edit Material icon.
13. On the Display Properties tab, with General Medium Detail selected, click the Edit Display Properties icon.
14. Click the Other tab.
15. Below the 2D Section Rules item, place a check mark in the "Exclude from 2D Section Shrinkwrap" checkbox (see Figure 16.37).

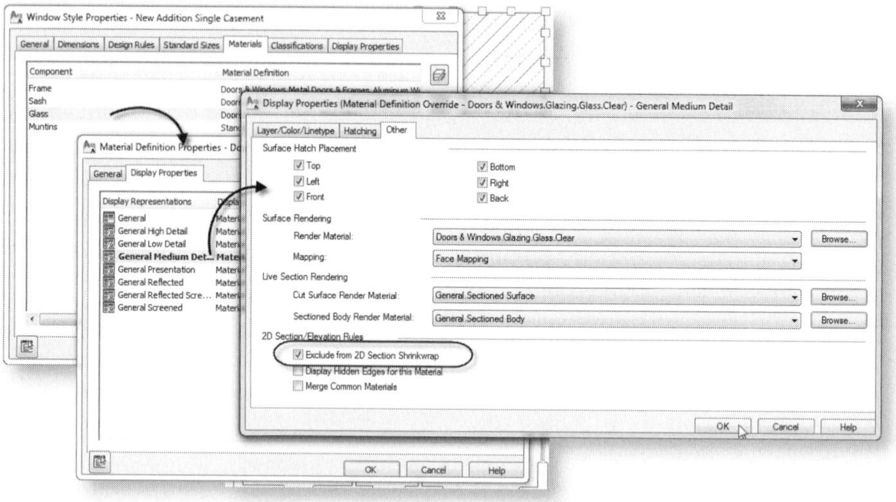

FIGURE 16.37 *Excluding the glass material from the 2D Section/Elevation Shrinkwrap*

As you can see, this is also the tab where you choose Render Materials and set up Live Sectioning Rules.

16. Click OK three times to return to the drawing.
17. Save the file.

Export Changes to the Second Floor

Both of these changes are needed on the *Second Floor New* file as well.

18. On the Project Navigator, open the Second Floor New Construct.
19. On the Manage tab, on the Styles & Display panel, click the Style Manager button.

We can use Style Manager to copy the modified definitions from the *First Floor New* file and update those contained in the *Second Floor New* file.

20. On the tree at left, below the *First Floor New.dwg* entry, expand the *Multi-Purpose Objects* folder and then highlight *Material Definitions* (see the item 1 in Figure 16.38).
21. Hold down the CTRL key and select Doors & Windows.Glazing.Glass.Clear and Thermal & Moisture.Insulation.Air.

    They should both be highlighted.
22. Right-click and choose **Copy** (see item 2 in Figure 16.38).

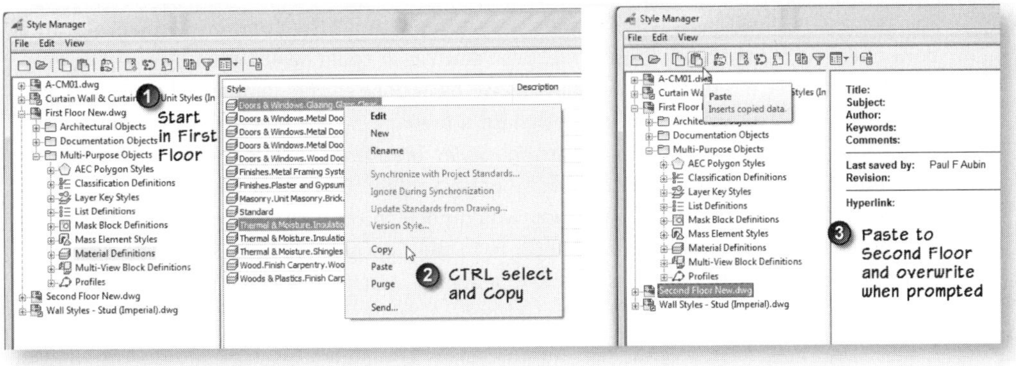

FIGURE 16.38 *Copy the two modified Material Definitions from the First Floor New file*

23. On the left side in the tree view, right-click on the *Second Floor New.dwg* entry and choose **Paste** (see item 3 in Figure 16.38).

An alert dialog box will appear warning you that the two Definitions already exist in the destination drawing. By choosing the Overwrite Existing option, we will be updating them to match the new versions that edited in the First Floor.

24. In the Import/Export – Duplicate Names Found dialog box, choose **Overwrite Existing** and then click OK (see Figure 16.39).

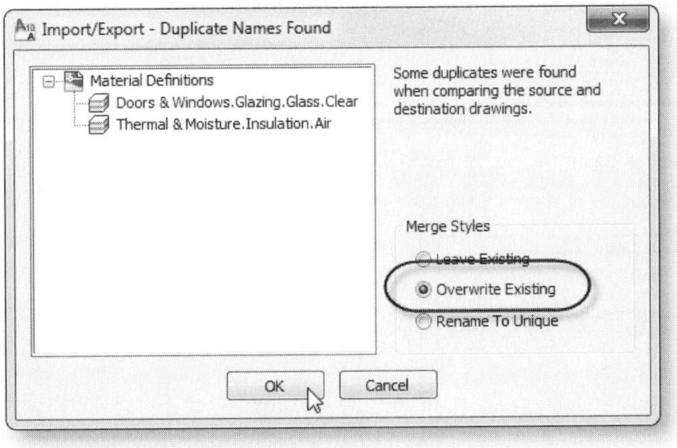

FIGURE 16.39 *Choose the Overwrite existing option to update the Second Floor with the Definitions from the First*

25. Click OK to close the Style Manager and accept the changes.

If you would like to verify that the changes have been copied to the *Second Floor New* file, feel free to repeat the steps used above to edit the Materials in the *First Floor New* file.

CAD MANAGER NOTE

The process outlined here is the manual way to update a Style from one project file to a newer version from another project file. The same result could be achieved by enabling Project Standards for the residential project as we have done in the commercial project. If you were to do so, you would need to designate a drawing as the Standards Drawing for the residential project such as the *Residential Styles* [*Residential Styles – Metric*] file in the *Standards\Content* folder at the root of the project folder. Open that file and add the modified Material Definitions to it. Next, you would need to configure Project Standards as we did for the commercial project in Chapter 8. In the Configure Project Standards dialog we could assign the *Residential Styles* [*Residential Styles – Metric*] file as our Standards Drawing. Be sure to check "Material Definitions" as one of the Style Types to synchronize. Finally, perform synchronization.

26. Save and close both the *First Floor New* and the *Second Floor New* files.

The *A-CM01* file should still be open, if you closed it, use the Project Browser to re-open it.

27. Back in the *A-CM01* file, reload the XREFs when prompted.

Update the Sections

Back in the *A-CM01* file, you should receive an alert that the *First Floor New* and the *Second Floor New* XREFs have changed at the lower-right corner of your screen (similar to Figure 16.11).

28. Select both Sections, on the ribbon, click Refresh (see Figure 16.40).

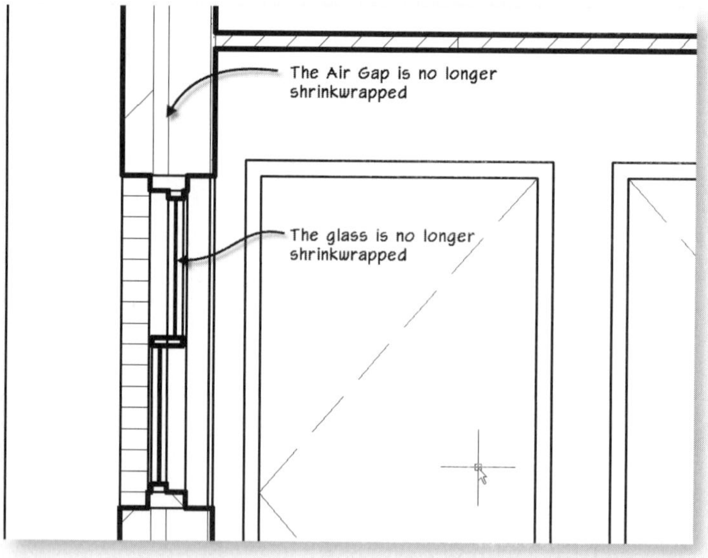

FIGURE 16.40 *Windows and Air Gaps no longer have shrinkwrap applied (toggle the Lineweight display to see clearly)*

If necessary, you may need to move the Bldg Section Line objects slightly to get them to cut through a Window to see the results.

Edit Brick Coursing

Zoom in on the East Elevation at the point where the First and Second Floors meet. Notice that the brick coursing does not match. This is because the height of the Walls on the First Floor is 9'-0" [2750] which does not fall on an even brick dimension.

29. On the Project Navigator, open the *Second Floor New* Construct.
30. Select the right vertical exterior Wall, on the Wall tab of the ribbon, click the Edit in Section drop-down button and choose Edit In Elevation.
31. Follow the prompts like we did for the chimney above to isolate just the Wall.

Material Definitions are "sub objects" meaning that you cannot select a Material and then click the Edit Style button or go to Properties. You must first select an object to which the Material is assigned and then follow the editing procedure of choice. Above in the "Editing Materials" topic, we saw a few examples of editing the Materials via the Wall Style dialog box. You can continue to use that method if you prefer, but presented here will be an alternative using the Display tab of the Properties palette.

Walls use "Drawing default" display settings and have all components assigned to "By Material." This means that the Display component list on the Properties palette will have names like: Boundary 1, Boundary 2, etc. Therefore, you will have to either be familiar with the Wall style in question in order select the correct component or perform some trial and error to "discover" the right one. In this case, we have worked with our brick Wall style enough to remember that the brick is Boundary 1.

32. On the Display tab, from the Display component list, choose **Boundary 1**.

In the Component Display Properties grouping, notice that the By material setting is set to Yes and the name is Masonry.Unit Masonry.Brick.Modular.Running. If you use this technique with other Walls, and the Material you expected is not listed here, simply choose a different boundary from the list to find the right one.

33. Beneath the Material name, from the Component list, choose **Surface Hatch**.
34. In the Hatching grouping, in the Y Offset field, type: **-1.33"** [**-34**] and then press enter.
35. In the confirmation dialog, click OK (see Figure 16.41).

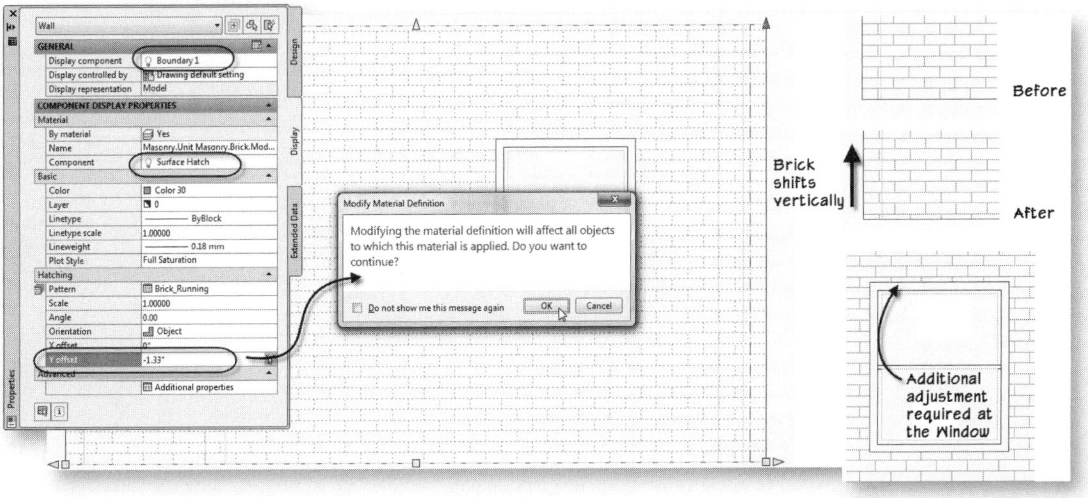

FIGURE 16.41 *Edit the Y Offset of the Material Definition Surface Hatching to shift the Brick Coursing*

You will see the results of the Brick Hatch Offset right away in the model file (see right side of Figure 16.41). However, this edit now makes the coursing around the Window incorrect. The easiest way to fix this is to adjust the Window Head height. Do this on the Properties palette on the Design tab. This adjustment will be left to the reader. Let's return to the Section and Elevation Composite Model file and refresh the elevation to see the overall effect.

36. Click the Exit Edit in View icon to return to the previous view and restore the hidden objects.
37. Save and close the *Second Floor New* file.

    Back in the *A-CM01* file, you should receive an alert that the *Second Floor New* XREF has changed.

38. Reload the XREFs.
39. Zoom in on the East Elevation at the joint between the brick on first and second floor.
40. Refresh the elevation.

Eliminate the Lines Between Floors

The brick coursing looks a lot better, but you may have noticed that there is a line between floors in the elevations. This line is the top and bottom edge of the individual Walls for the First and Second Floors. We can, however, configure that Material to remove this line for us. We do this by instructing the Material to merge with similar Materials. We can make this change directly in the Section and Elevation Composite Model file.

41. On the Manage tab, on the Styles & Display panel, click the Style Manager button.

All Materials used in the sections and elevations of this file are automatically imported into this file. To make the common Materials from different XREFs merge together, we edit the imported Material Definition here.

42. Expand Multi-Purpose Objects, then select Material Definitions.
43. Double-click on the Material Definition named: Masonry.Unit Masonry.Brick.Modular.Running to edit it.
44. On the Display Properties tab, with General Medium Detail selected, click the Edit Display Properties icon.
45. Click the Other tab and place a check mark in the "Merge Common Materials" checkbox (see Figure 16.42).

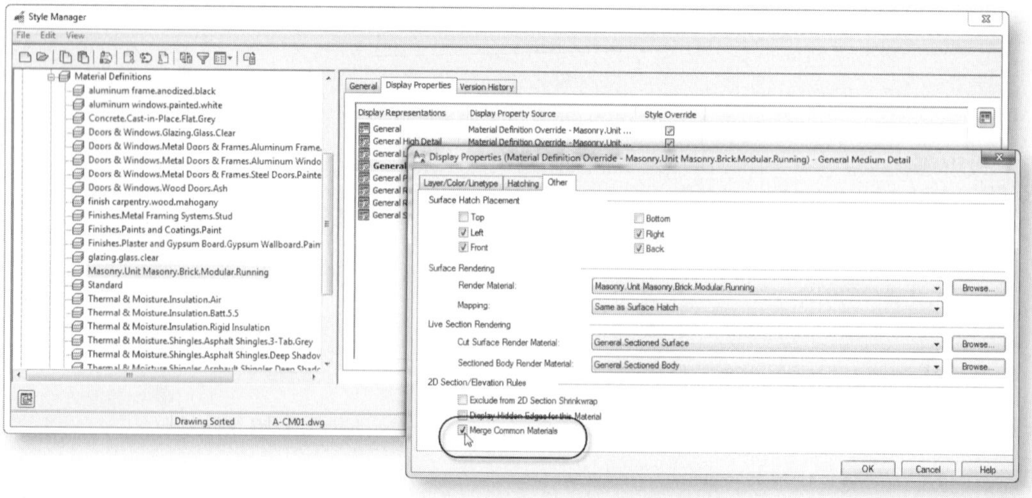

FIGURE 16.42 *Merge Common Materials to eliminate the "Lines between floors"*

46. Click OK twice to return to the drawing.
47. Select the East Elevation and choose **Refresh**.

Notice that the line between the brick of the First Floor and the brick of the Second Floor has disappeared (see Figure 16.43).

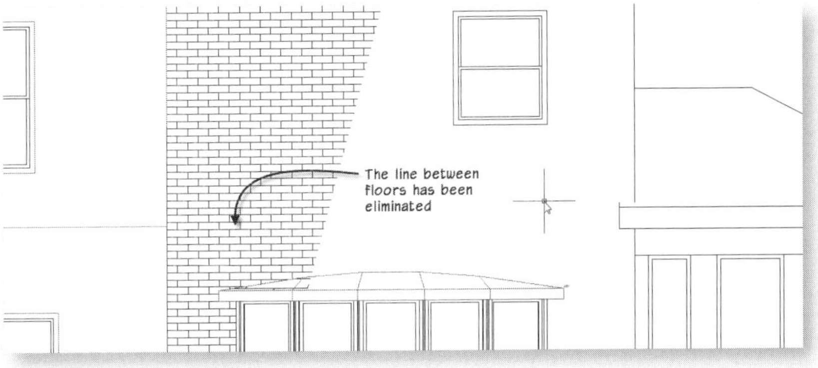
The line between
floors has been
eliminated

FIGURE 16.43 *The Brick now appears continuous with the Materials merged and the line between floors removed*

NOTE

While this technique produces the desired merged brick effect, we have now created a slightly different version of the Material in the elevation file than occurs in the Constructs. It should, however, not cause any problems.

Showing Hidden Materials Beyond

In some cases, you wish to have a particular Material show even though it is hidden from view. For instance, it is often desirable on elevations to have foundation Walls and footings appear dashed below grade. There is a setting in the Material Definition to control this.

48. On the Manage tab, on the Styles & Display panel, click the Style Manager button.
49. Expand Multi-Purpose Objects, then select Material Definitions.
50. Double-click on the Material Definition named: Concrete.Cast-in-Place.Flat.Grey to edit it.
51. On the Display Properties tab, with General Medium Detail selected, click the Edit Display Properties icon.
52. Click the Other tab and place a check mark in the "Display Hidden Edges for this Material" checkbox.
53. Also place a check mark in the "Merge Common Materials" checkbox as we did with Brick.

This Material will now show dashed whenever it is hidden rather than being removed as other hidden linework is. Also, this material will merge as the Brick did above.

54. Click OK twice to return to the drawing.
55. Select the North Elevation and choose **Refresh**.

Notice that the foundation Walls and Footings now display as dashed lines (see Figure 16.44).

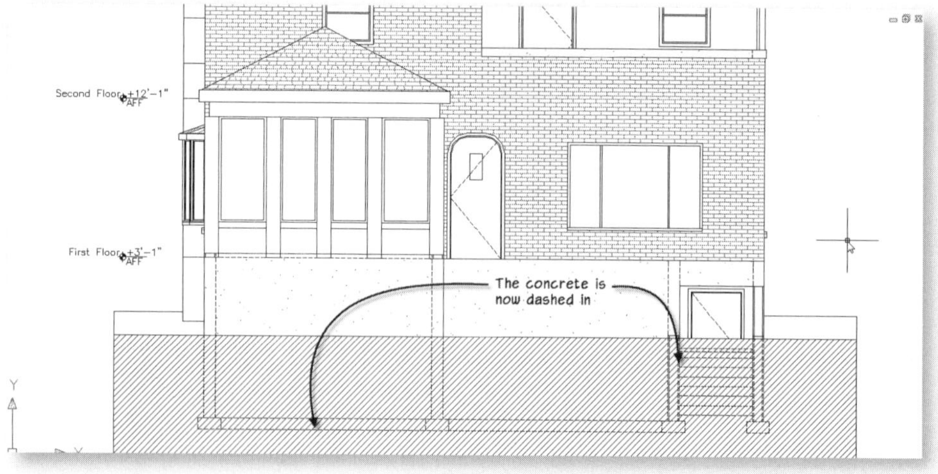

FIGURE 16.44 *The Concrete Material now shows dashed automatically when hidden*

56. Refresh the remaining elevations and save the file.

CAD MANAGER NOTE

If you wish, you can include your most commonly used Material Definitions with the merge and/or display hidden edges options enabled in your Section/Elevation View Template file. On the Project Navigator palette, on the Project tab, click the Edit Project Details icon to access the settings for the project. There, you can assign a different template file to General, Section/Elevation and Detail View files. You may include certain Materials in this file that have the settings you wish enabled already configured. This will not guarantee that users will not need to edit these settings for some Materials. Rather this approach would simply eliminate a few steps for the most commonly used Materials.

Create a New Material Definition and Tool

It might be nice to have a more appropriate hatch pattern for the Terrain Model in our Sections. To do this, let's create a new Material Definition.

57. On the QAT, click the Open icon. Browse to the *C:\MasterACA 2010\Catalog* folder.
58. Open the *Residential Styles* [*Residential Styles – Metric*] file.

We last added to this file in Chapter 10.

59. Right-click the tool palettes title bar and choose **MasterACA** and then click the MACA Residential tab.
60. On the Manage tab, on the Styles & Display panel, click the Style Manager button.
61. Expand Multi-Purpose Objects, then select Material Definitions.
62. Right-click on the Standard Material and choose **Copy**, right-click again and choose **Paste**.
63. Double-click on Standard(2) to edit it.
64. On the General tab rename it to: **MACA.Site.Earth**.
65. On the Display Properties tab, make sure General Medium Detail is selected and then click the Edit Display Properties icon.
66. On the Layer/Color/Linetype tab, set the Color of the Section Hatch to **44**, its Lineweight to **0.18 mm** and the Plot Style to **Full Saturation** (see Figure 16.45).

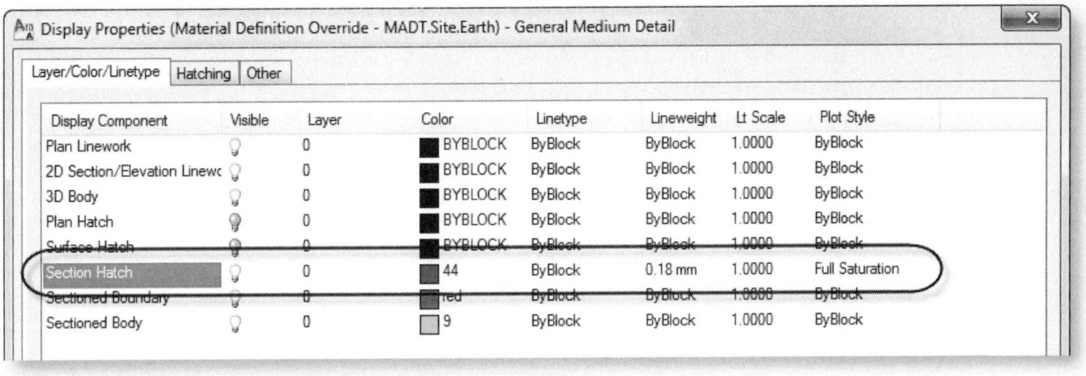

FIGURE 16.45 *Set the properties of the Section Hatch*

67. Click the Hatching tab.
68. Click on the entry in the Pattern column next to Section Hatch (currently User Single).

    This will call a Hatch Pattern dialog box.
69. In the Hatch Pattern dialog box, choose **Predefined** from the Type list and **Earth** from the Pattern list, and then click OK.
70. In the Scale/Spacing column next to Earth, type **40** [**40**] (see Figure 16.46).

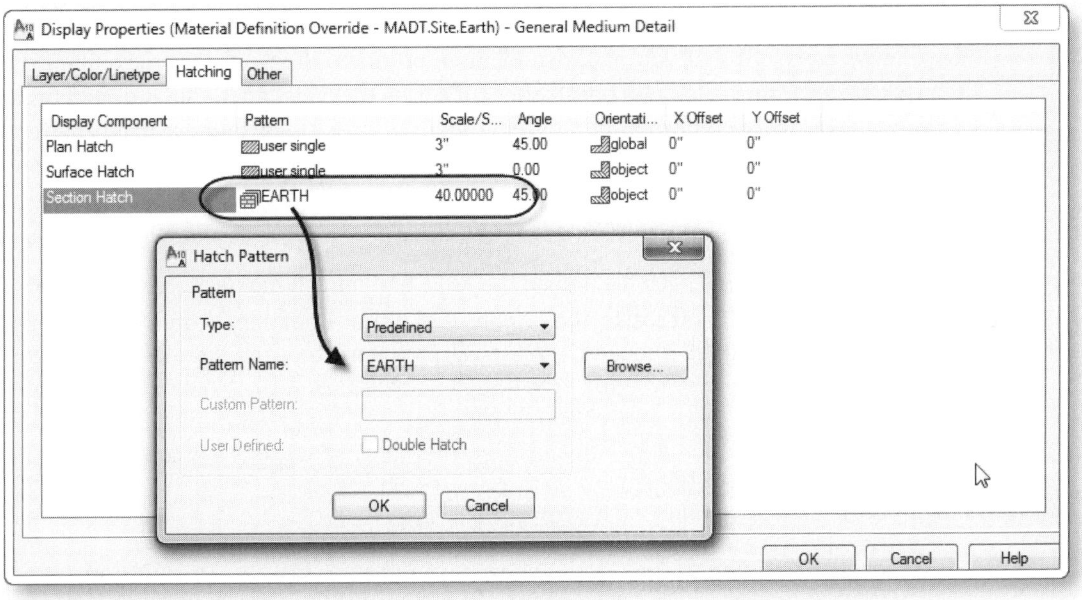

FIGURE 16.46 *Assign the Earth hatch pattern and a scale*

71. Click OK to return to the Style Manager.
72. Drag the **MACA.Site.Earth** Material from Style Manager to the Project Tools palette.
73. In the warning that appears, click OK. Click OK to dismiss the Style Manager and then Save the file.

You have created a new Material Definition and a tool referencing it. We can now use this tool to quickly apply this new material to other objects like the Mass Element in our *Terrain Model* Construct.

74. Close the *Residential Styles* [*Residential Styles – Metric*] file.

Apply a Material Tool to an Object

75. On the Project Navigator, open the *Terrain Model* Construct.

As we have already seen, the Terrain object is a Mass Element. Mass Elements have materials assigned to them via their styles like all other AEC objects. Our primary concern in this topic is the Section Hatch for the Mass Element. We will apply our new Material Definition to this Mass Element.

76. Select the Terrain Mass Element, on the Mass Element tab, click the Save As button.
77. On the General tab, name the Style: **Terrain** and then click OK to return to the drawing.
78. On the MACA Residential palette, click the new **MACA.Site.Earth** Material tool, then at the "Select a component or an object:" prompt, select the Terrain Mass Element.
79. At the "apply the material to the style or" prompt, press ENTER.

    Do not choose "this object."

If you want to see the result right away, select the Mass Element and then on the Mass Element tab, click the Edit in Section tool. The process is very similar to Edit in Elevation except that you pick two or more points to define the section line. Following the prompts, click two points that cut across the Mass Element and then press ENTER. You will be zoomed to the section cut and will see the new hatch pattern applied on the cut surface. Click the Exit Edit in View icon to restore the previous view and exit the Edit in View mode.

80. Save and close the file.
81. Back in the *A-CM01* file, reload the XREF and refresh the Sections.
82. Following the steps in the "Apply a Material Boundary" topic above, draw some polylines and add a Material Boundary to each side of the Section (see Figure 16.47).

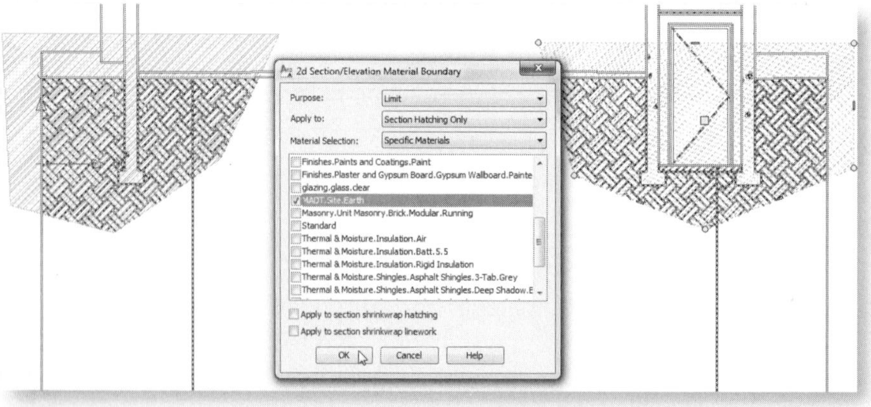

FIGURE 16.47 *You can add Material Boundaries to crop out part of the Earth hatching.*

To make a Material Boundary like the one shown here, draw the polyline boundary, select the section and on the ribbon, on the Material Boundary panel, click the Add button. Select the polyline and answer Yes to erase it. Leave the Purpose set to: **Limit**. Apply it to: **Section Hatching only**, and then from Material Selection, choose: **Selected Materials**. Finally check only the MACA.Site.Earth material and then click OK. Repeat on the other side with a new polyline. You can add as many Material Boundaries as you want to a single Section or Elevation. Add some more for the surface hatching on the Roof. For instance, you would not want to see shingles on the inside of the house.

83. Save the file.

EDITING AND MERGING LINEWORK

Subdivisions give a broad-brush level of control over 2D Section/Elevation Display Properties. Design rules and materials allow for more focused refinement of the 2D Section/Elevation. The final level of control over the display of Sections and Elevations comes from the Edit Linework and Merge Linework commands. With these commands, you can "reach into" the 2D Section/Elevation object and edit the actual linework from which the Elevation is comprised. The editing capabilities are limited to changing selected linework from one component index to another, deleting unwanted linework while editing, and adding new linework while using Merge. In most cases, these will prove sufficient to fine-tune the Section/Elevation in acceptable fashion.

Erase 2D Section/Elevation Linework

It is nice to have a bold line at the ground line, but we probably don't want it to continue all the way around the terrain Mass Element, particularly if you have added Material Boundaries to crop the Earth hatching. Let's use Edit Linework to remove it.

1. Select the Section and then click the small round gray Edit Linework grip.

   When you enter the Edit Linework mode, the hatching will temporarily disappear. Don't worry—it will return when you are finished.

2. Use a crossing selection to select the bottom horizontal line, and the two vertical lines that make up the bottom of the terrain object, as well as two stray vertical lines within the terrain boundary in the section (see Figure 16.48).

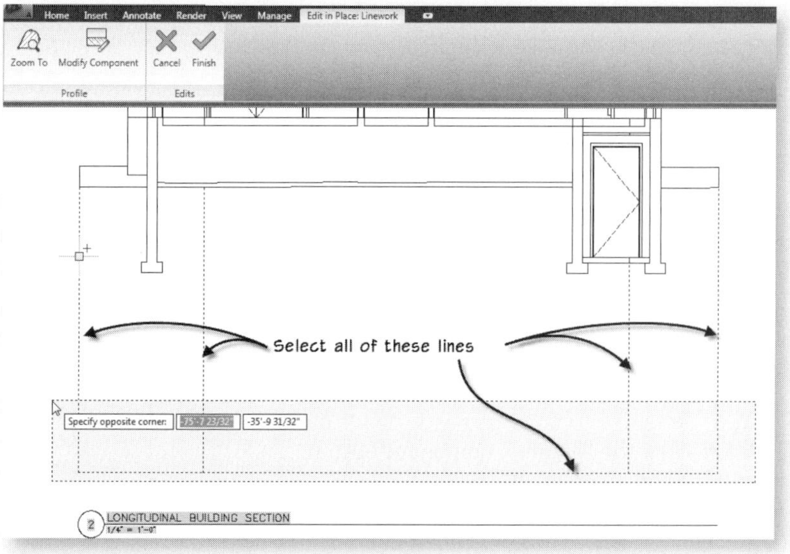

FIGURE 16.48 *Select bottom, sides and stray lines of the Terrain to erase*

3. Press the DELETE key to erase the three lines.
4. On the on the ribbon, click the Finish button (see Figure 16.49).

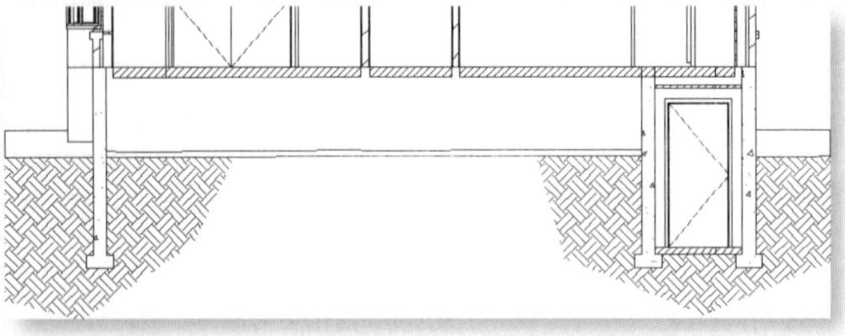

FIGURE 16.49 *The Section with terrain edges removed*

5. Repeat these steps on the other section and all elevations.

Zoom around the drawing and look for other lines to erase. Add any other Material Boundaries you may need to crop hatching as well.

Modify 2D Section/Elevation Linework

Sometimes you will want to edit the way a particular line appears. The lines of the gables facing us on the North Elevation could be a little bolder.

6. Zoom over to the North Elevation, select it and then on the Linework panel, click the Edit button.
7. Select the lines of the top edges of the left-hand gable as shown in Figure 16.50.

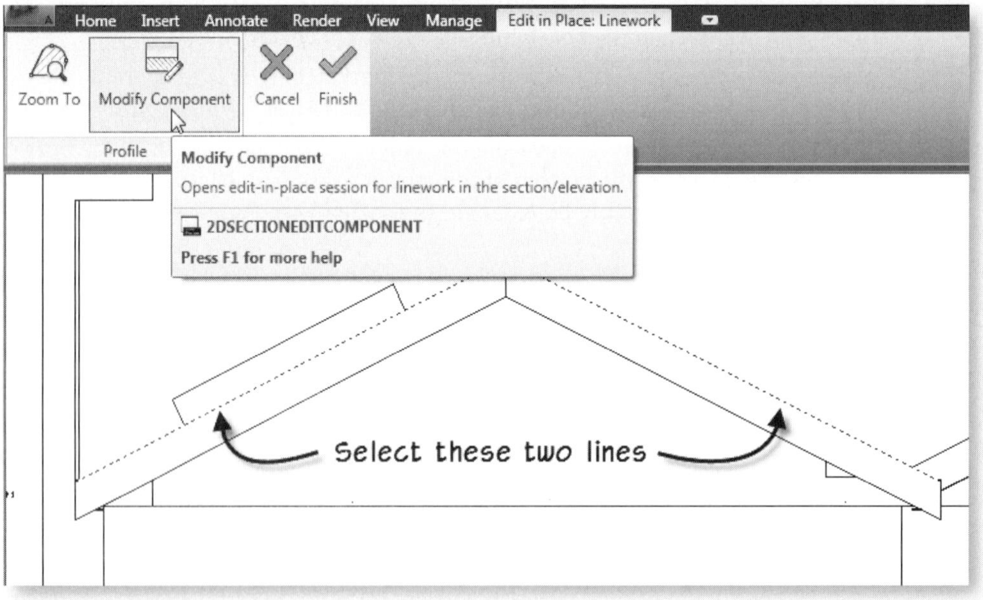

FIGURE 16.50 *Select the lines of the gable and Modify the Component*

8. On the ribbon, click the Modify Component button.

In the “Select Linework Component” dialog box, the Linework Component of the selected lines is currently set to Subdivision 2. This makes sense considering how we configured the subdivisions above. To make these lines display a bit bolder, we can move them up one subdivision. In the Linework Component list are all of the display components of the 2D Section/Elevation object. Simply choose Subdivision 1 to make these lines that physically fall within Subdivision 2 display as though they were in Subdivision 1.

9. Choose **Subdivision 1** from the Linework Component list and then click OK (see Figure 16.51).

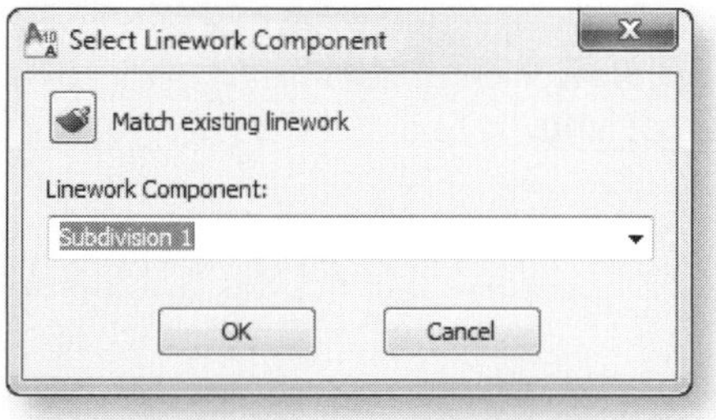

FIGURE 16.51 *Choose the new component for display*

10. Repeat the process on the gable at the right, choosing **Subdivision 2** this time.
11. On the Edit in Place Linework tab, click the Finish button.

Merge Linework

Sometimes to edit linework, it is easier to re-draw it. You can draw any linework with the standard tools on the Home tab, and then merge them into the Section. When you do, you will be prompted to choose a component, just like the Modify Component commands above. This will replace any existing linework under the drawn elements with the ones being merged in.

12. Zoom in on the bottom of the porch on the East Elevation.

The boards of the screen porch pilasters overlap the concrete foundation, but in this elevation they do not appear correctly. We could certainly open the model and try to fix the actual geometry, but sometimes a quick linework edit will be all you need to get a plot out quickly. You may be tempted to use the technique above and simply erase the stray lines. The problem is that the line of the foundation Wall is one continuous line. Feel free to try. Instead try this:

13. On the Home tab, click the Line button and draw some small line segments with the Intersection Osnap as shown in Figure 16.52.

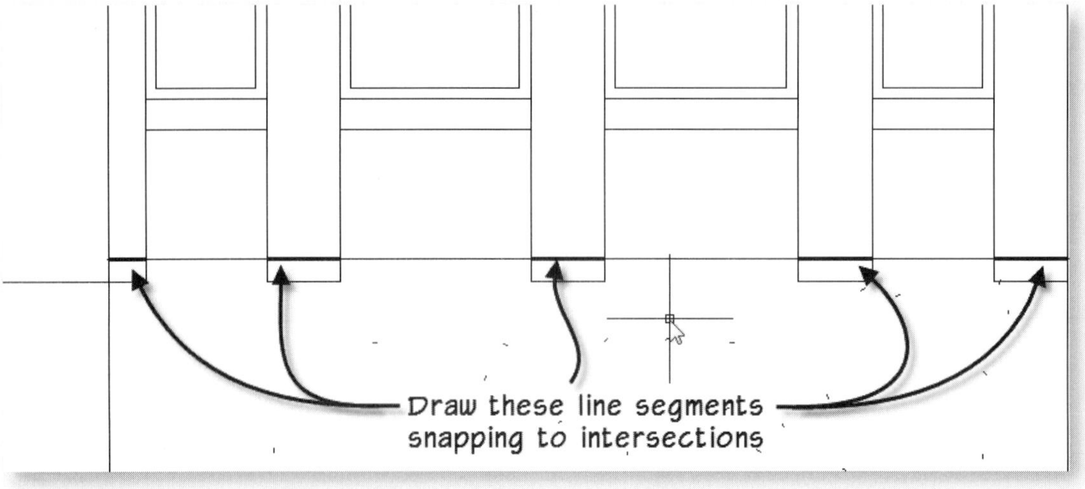

FIGURE 16.52 *Draw several small segments at the points that you want erased (Lines in the figure shown bold for clarity)*

14. Select the Elevation and on the 2D Section/Elevation tab, on the Linework panel, click the Merge tool.
15. At the "Select objects to merge" prompt, select all of the lines drawn in the previous step and then press ENTER.
16. In the "Select Linework Component" dialog box, choose **Erased Vectors** from the Linework Component list and then click OK (see Figure 16.53).

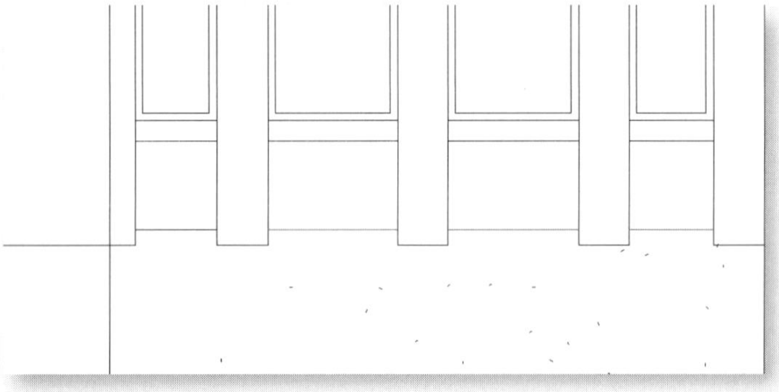

FIGURE 16.53 *By merging lines to the Erased Vectors Component, you can erase the underlying linework*

This technique is a little counterintuitive, but as you can see, by drawing the linework that you need, you can use Merge to modify the underlying linework in the elevation or section. The same technique works regardless of the Linework Component you select. So while we used Erased Vectors in this example, we could have used Hidden to make the lines appear dashed, or one of the Subdivisions to change how bold they were and so on.

Update 2D Section/Elevation Objects with User Edits

Inevitably the design will change and the section will need to be updated. When the update occurs, the 2D Section/Elevation object will automatically re-apply all user edits. However, sometimes the nature of the change is such that some of the edits will no longer be in the same physical location as the newly regenerated model geometry. When this occurs, user edits can be saved to a second 2D Section/Elevation object and merged back into the section after the update. To do this effectively, you need to build another 2D Section/Elevation style. The basic process is as follows:

1. Create a New 2D Section/Elevation style (Manage tab, Styles and Display panel, Style Manager button) named: User Edits.
2. In this new style, On the Display Properties tab, turn on *all* components, especially Erased. Set the Erased component to an alert color such as Magenta.

This is very important. Most user edits are erasures. However, erased in elevation and section user edits really means that the linework is simply invisible. This is the desired effect in the actual elevation, but if it is invisible, during the refresh process, you will not be able to reapply your user edits because you will not be able to see them.

3. Regenerate (not Refresh) the Section and choose the User Edits style from the "Style for User Linework Edits if Unable to Reapply" list (see Figure 16.54).

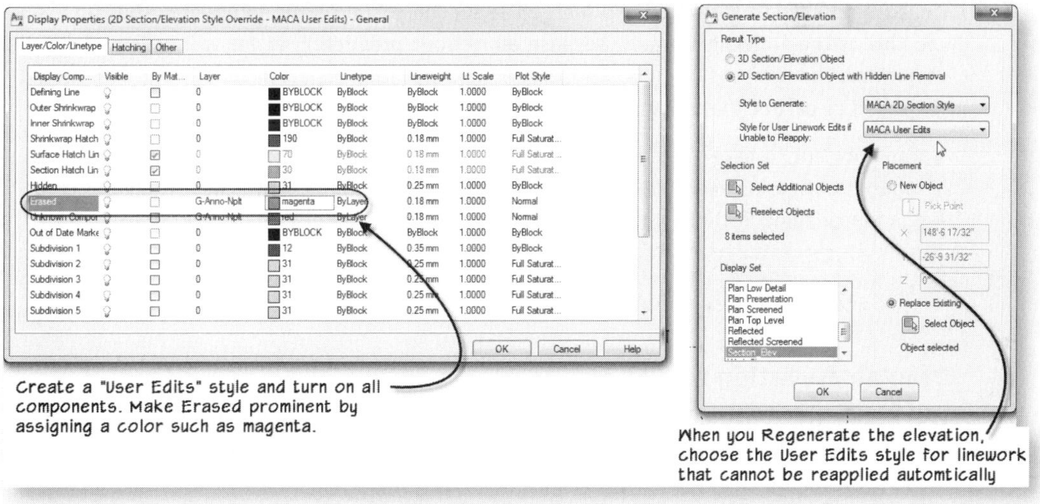
Display Properties (2D Section/Elevation Style Override - MACA User Edits) - General
Generate Section/Elevation
Create a "User Edits" style and turn on all components. Make Erased prominent by assigning a color such as magenta.
When you Regenerate the elevation, choose the User Edits style for linework that cannot be reapplied automtically

FIGURE 16.54 *User Edits can be saved to another style if ACA is unable to re-apply them automatically*

4. After the update, explode the User Edits Section, move the linework into place on the Section, and then reapply it with the Merge command (see Figure 16.55).

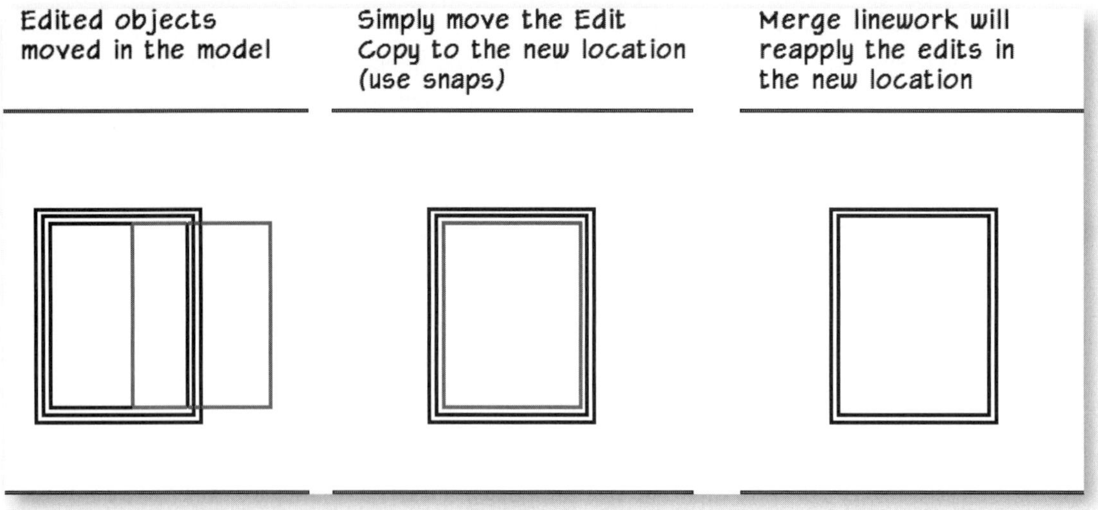
Edited objects moved in the model
Simply move the Edit Copy to the new location (use snaps)
Merge linework will reapply the edits in the new location

FIGURE 16.55 *Move saved copy of user edits into position and then Merge Linework*

CAD MANAGER NOTE

Although "off" is the proper setting for Erased Vectors in styles used in production, it is recommended that one style be maintained for saving user edits that has the Erased component turned on and set to color 6-Magenta. You can name the style "User Edits." This will make it possible to easily see and merge the second section after an update. You can even do this as the Drawing Default, because all of your production styles will have style-level overrides. The choice is up to you. All 2D Section/Elevation styles, including this one, should be saved as part of the office standard template files.

It is important to have the colors used for Design Rules established and well documented. Properly configuring and documenting this powerful tool will enhance the leverage of creating and managing Sections and Elevations from the ACA model.

5. Save and close the *A-CM01* Section and Elevation Composite Model file.

Drag an Elevation to a Sheet

We began this chapter by re-creating the East Elevation. As a result, it must be placed on its Sheet over again. This will also complete the cross-referencing of the field codes within the Elevation Callouts on the plans.

6. On the Project Navigator palette, click the Sheets tab and then double-click *A-202 Elevations* to open it.
7. On the Project Navigator palette, click the Views tab and then expand the plus (+) sign beneath *A-CM01* to reveal the Model Space Views contained within.
8. Drag the East Elevation Model Space View and drop it on the Sheet.
9. At the "Insertion point" prompt, click a point to place the Elevation on the Sheet.
10. Save and close the file.

    If you wish, open any of the Floor Plan View files to see the updated Callouts referencing the East Elevation as drawing 1 on Sheet *A-202*.

CREATING INTERIOR ELEVATIONS USING CALLOUTS

Interior Elevations are achieved simply by manipulating the size and shape of the Bldg Section and Bldg Elevation lines. By default ACA uses the full extents of the model for the height of the Elevation or Section. By changing this setting to a fixed height that matches your ceiling height and cropping the sides of the Section/Elevation Line to the size of the room, your result will be an interior Elevation. You can do this manually, or this can be achieved automatically using the Callouts designed for this purpose.

Use an Interior Elevation Callout

1. On the Project Navigator, open the *A-FP01* View file.

As you recall, this is our First Floor Plan View file. We will create the Callouts here and through the routine create a new View file scaled for Interior Elevations.

2. On the Callouts palette, click the Interior Elevation Mark B1 tool.

   If you do not see this palette or tool, right-click the Tool Palettes title bar and choose **Document** (to load the Documentation Tool Palette Group) and then click the Callouts tab.
3. At the "Specify location of elevation tag" prompt, click a point within the Dining Room Space.
4. At the "Specify direction for first elevation number" prompt, move the mouse straight up with POLAR or ORTHO and then click.

This will be the direction of Elevation 1. There will be four total going clockwise from the first. The Place Callout worksheet will appear. We have seen this worksheet on several previous occasions. In the New Model Space View Name field there is only one name suggested this time. You can still enter the name for all four Model Space Views. Simply separate the names with a semicolon. It is recommended that you input four unique names, otherwise you will get names that simply have a numeric suffix appended to the end, such as Elevation, Elevation (2), etc.

5. In the New Model Space View Name field, type: **North Dining Room Elevation;East Dining Room Elevation;South Dining Room Elevation;West Dining Room Elevation**.

CAUTION

Be certain to include the semicolon separators between each name and do not put a space after the semicolons.

6. Accept the remaining defaults and then click the New View Drawing icon (see Figure 16.56).

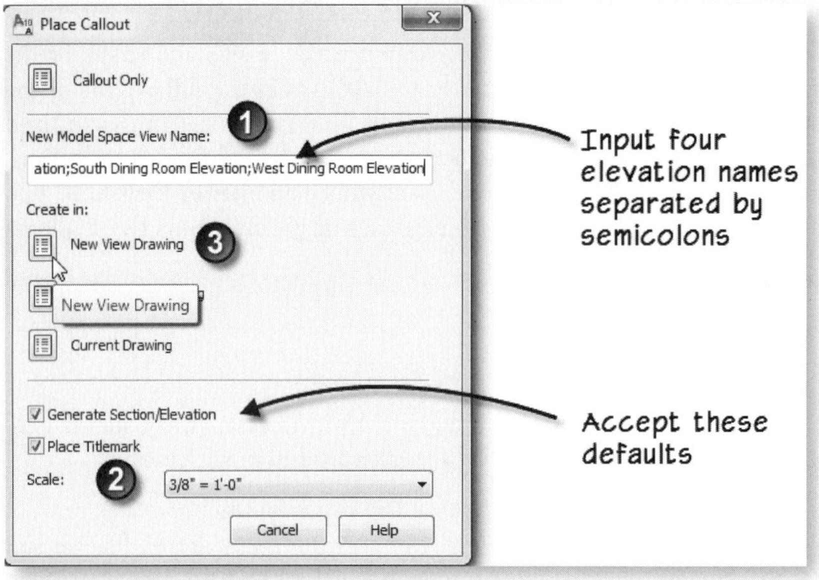

FIGURE 16.56 *Setting up interior Elevations in the Callout Worksheet*

Again, by now in this text, we have created several View files, so this process should be review. We are creating a new View file because the interior elevations are a different scale than any of the other Views we have created so far.

7. Name the new View: **A-EL01** with a Description: **Architectural Interior Elevations**.
8. Click Next, verify that only the First Floor (both Existing and New Divisions) is selected, click Next again.
9. Verify that *First Floor New* and *First Floor Existing* Constructs are selected and then click Finish.
10. At the "Select space(s) and area(s)" prompt, select the Dining Room Space (click the hatching) and then press ENTER.

The full prompt here includes an option to "ENTER to pick region to specify elevation line width." If you have Space objects as we do here, then simply select the Space or Spaces. The Bldg Elevation Lines will be created to match the width and height of the Space object. If you press ENTER instead, you will be prompted to select a rectangular region, which will be used to determine the widths of the elevations and later you will be prompted for the height. Regardless of the option you select, you will be prompted next for the Depth of the elevations.

11. At the "Specify elevation line depth" prompt, drag into the room slightly and then click.

If you wait a second or two, you will see some temporary graphics being drawn onscreen to represent the extent of the elevations. Just get them approximately correct with your mouse click. You can always adjust each Bldg Elevation Line later as required.

At this point the now familiar "** You are being prompted for a point in a different view drawing **" prompt will appear.

12. At the "Specify insertion point for the 2D elevation result" prompt, click a point to the right side of the plan, drag slightly to the right (using POLAR or ORTHO) and then click again.

As with other Callout routines, you will see a progress bar as the elevations are generated.

13. On the Project Navigator palette, double-click the new *A-EL01* View file to open it (see Figure 16.57).

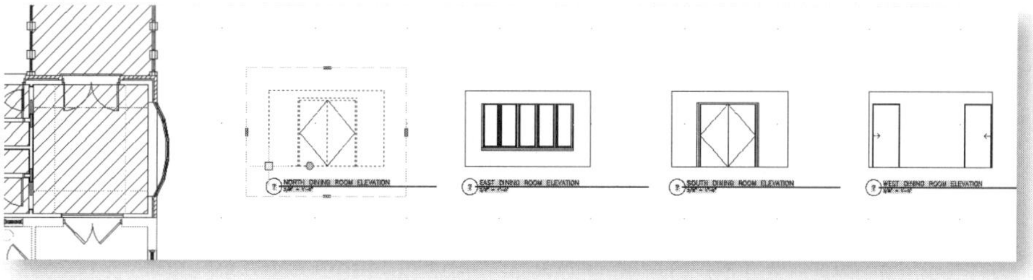

FIGURE 16.57 *Interior Elevations generated automatically in their own View file*

Using the same Callout Routine, create additional interior elevations of the other major Spaces in the First Floor Plan. Generate any additional elevations in the same *A-EL01* View file (choose the Existing View Drawing icon this time). Create interior elevations of the Second Floor Plan in a new View file named *A-EL02*. You can drag them to the same Sheet.

14. Refer to the process in the "Create the Elevation Sheet File" heading in Chapter 5 and create a new Sheet in the Enlarged Views Subset. Name it *A-401 Interior Elevations* and drag the *A-EL02* View file onto it. Follow the prompts to place each Model Space View in sequence.

    Note the update of all Callout numbers and references throughout the Project files.

15. Save and close all open Project files.

LIVE SECTIONS

The *A-SC00* View file in the Commercial Project was set up to use a Live Section. A Live Section operates on the actual building model data and can be edited directly, unlike the 2D Section/Elevation object. A Live Section *is* the model. Live Sections make great design tools. Adding one is simple—just add a Bldg Section Line where you would like the Section to be cut, right-click it and choose **Enable Live Section**. (There is a generic Bldg Section Line tool on the Design tool palette that adds a Bldg Section Line without a Callout.) Switch to 3D View and have a look. It is that simple! Even though the Live Section that we added was of the entire Commercial Building model and has proved very useful for viewing our progress as we have updated our model, to fully see the benefit of a Live Section you should add one to one of your Construct files. They only display when you are in 3D (refer to the "View Direction Dependent Configurations" topic in Chapter 2 for an example). In plan (Top View) the entire model will show.

Live Sections are applied to the active Display Configuration. So if you wish to have it applied to a Configuration other than the currently active one, be sure to choose the appropriate Display Configuration prior to enabling the Live Section. Load the Commercial Project and view the Live Section in *A-SC00*. Create one in a Construct in either project if you wish and then play around.

SHEET FILES

The Sheet files for plotting Elevations and Sections were created and configured in Chapter 5. Open them now to view the fruits of your labors in this chapter. *A-201*, *A-202* and *A-203* display the Elevations, while *A-301* is the Sections. All files were saved with the paper space layout active and Plot Styles displayed. Toggle on the Lineweight display to get a good preview of how these drawings will plot.

ADDITIONAL EXERCISES

There is plenty more work to be done on all of the Sections and Elevations that have been worked on here. Additional exercises have been provided in Appendix A. In Appendix A you will find exercises to add additional Sections and Elevations in the Commercial Project (see Figure 16.58), as well as further refine those created here in the Residential Project. It is not necessary that you complete these exercises to begin the next chapter, they are provided to enhance your learning experience. Completed projects for each of the exercises have been provided in the *Chapter16/Complete* folder.

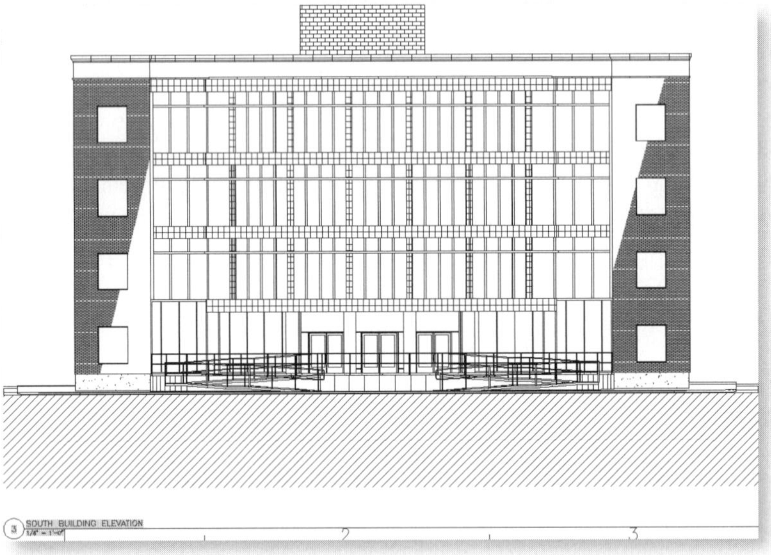

FIGURE 16.58 *Additional Exercises in Appendix A—Complete the Commercial Elevations*

SUMMARY

- The Section Line boundary determines how much of the model will be considered by the Section.
- The Section must be updated to reflect changes to the floor plan.
- Callouts completely automate the process of adding a Bldg Section Line and then generating the Section or Elevation including placement of a linked Callout.
- 2D Section/Elevation styles can be assigned to the Section and Elevation to give them more graphical definition.
- Subdivisions are used to assign lineweight and other properties to objects as they recede from the defining line.
- Hatching generates automatically from the Material Definitions in the Model.

- When cutting a Section or Elevation from XREF models, remember to first reload the XREFs and then update the Section/Elevation.
- 2D Section/Elevation styles offer a great way to manage Layer, Color and Linetype settings on 2D Section/Elevation objects.
- Layers used in the 2D Section/Elevation style must exist in the drawing prior to being assigned in the Style Display Props.
- Design rules offer a way to assign custom display settings to objects within a 2D Section/Elevation regardless of the subdivision in which they occur.
- Edit Linework allows the 2D Section/Elevation object to be directly edited.
- Merge Linework allows custom drawn linework and previously edited linework to be incorporated into the 2D Section/Elevation object after it has been updated.
- Interior Elevations use the same tools with different parameters assigned to the Bldg Elevation Line. Callout with automated routines are provided.

CHAPTER

17

Generating Details and Keynotes

INTRODUCTION

We could not complete our discussion of Construction Documents in AutoCAD Architecture without a look at Details and Keynotes. All of the AEC objects covered so far serve overall drawing and modeling needs. Even a very complex and detailed Wall style can really only accommodate the needs of general plans, sections and elevations at low and medium levels of detail. When you are ready to begin drawing construction details, ACA offers a robust detailing module and a complete keynoting system. In this chapter we will explore both of these tools to help round out the CDs for our two projects.

OBJECTIVES

In this chapter, we will look at the Detail Component Manager and its associated tools and tool palettes. The Keynoting system, which is tied to a central Microsoft Access database, will allow us to quickly annotate our details and View files. We will also complete our exploration of the Callout tools begun in the earlier chapters of this book with a look at the Callout routines designed to assist in detailing. In this chapter, we will explore the following topics:

- Learn to use Detail Callouts.
- Use the Detail Component Manager.
- Explore the Detailing Tool System.
- Explore Keynote Assignments.
- Add Reference Keynotes.
- Add Sheet Keynotes.

DETAILS

The concept behind detailing in ACA is simple. Standard AutoCAD-drafted entities are created from exact specifications contained in a central database. These components are not connected to the model in any way, but models built with AEC objects such as Walls, Doors and Windows provide an excellent framework for creating such details. Using the tools on the Callouts tool palette, we can crop out areas of the model that we wish to detail. A 2D Section/Elevation object of the designated area is generated using a special non-plotting 2D Section/Elevation style (see the previous chapter for more information). We then use the robust and fully extensible Detail Component Manager to draft our details directly on top of this sketch 2D Section/Elevation framework. The basis of the Detail Component Manager is a collection of industry standard building components (bricks, steel shapes, bolts, fasteners, insulation, etc.) in a variety of standard sizes. Each is drawn as a two-dimensional graphic from a certain view direction such as plan or section view.

Create a Detail View File

We will work in the Residential Project where we will create a typical wall section. The first step in the process is to decide from what point in the model you wish to reference the detail. Then use a Callout routine to create a new View file for details from this region at an appropriate scale for detailing. Once we have this rough linework as a guide, we add Detail Components directly in the View file on top of the generated linework.

Install the CD Files and Load the Current Project

If you have already installed all of the files from the CD, simply skip down to step 3 below to make the project active. If you need to install the CD files, start at step 1.

1. If you have not already done so, install the dataset files located on the Mastering AutoCAD Architecture 2010 CD-ROM.

   Refer to "Files Included on the CD-ROM" in the Preface for information on installing the sample files included on the CD.
2. Launch AutoCAD Architecture 2010 from the desktop icon created in Chapter 3.

If you did not create a custom icon, you might want to review "Create a New Profile" and "Create a Desktop Shortcut" in Chapter 3. Creating the custom desktop icon is not essential; however, it makes loading the custom profile easier.

3. From the File menu, choose **Project Browser**.
4. Click to open the folder list and choose your *C:* drive.
5. Double-click on the *MasterACA 2010* folder, then on the *Chapter17* folder.

   One or two residential Projects will be listed: *17 Residential* and/or *17 Residential Metric*.
6. Double-click *17 Residential* if you wish to work in Imperial units. Double-click *17 Residential Metric* if you wish to work in Metric units. (You can also right-click on it and choose **Set Current Project**.) Then click Close in the Project Browser.

NOTE

Important: If a message appears asking you to repath the project, click the "Repath the project now" option. Refer to the "Repathing Projects" heading in the Preface for more information.

NOTE

The Metric Complete version of the project (provided with the dataset files from the Mastering AutoCAD Architecture 2010 CD ROM) varies slightly from the results indicated here and those included in the Imperial Complete version.

Using Detail Callouts

There are several Callout tools specifically designed for details. We can use any of these as a starting point. Please note that you can start a detail without first using a Callout. However, the Callout approach gives you a nice framework upon which to construct your detail. If you already have an ACA model (as we do in the projects we have been building throughout the book), then this is the recommended way to begin a new detail.

7. On the Project Navigator, click the Views tab, and then double-click *A-CM01* to open it.

This is the Section and Elevation Composite Model View file that was created in Chapter 5, which was extensively modified in the previous chapter. You can generate callouts from the model directly as plan cuts (using a process similar to overall building sections), or from an existing elevation or section. We will do the latter here.

8. Zoom in on the Longitudinal Building Section.
9. On the Callouts tool palette, click the Detail Boundary B tool.

   If you do not see this palette or tool, right-click the Tool Palettes title bar and choose **Document** (to load the Documentation Tool Palette Group) and then click the Callouts tab.
10. At the "Specify one corner of detail box" click just above the eave to the left (see Figure 17.1).

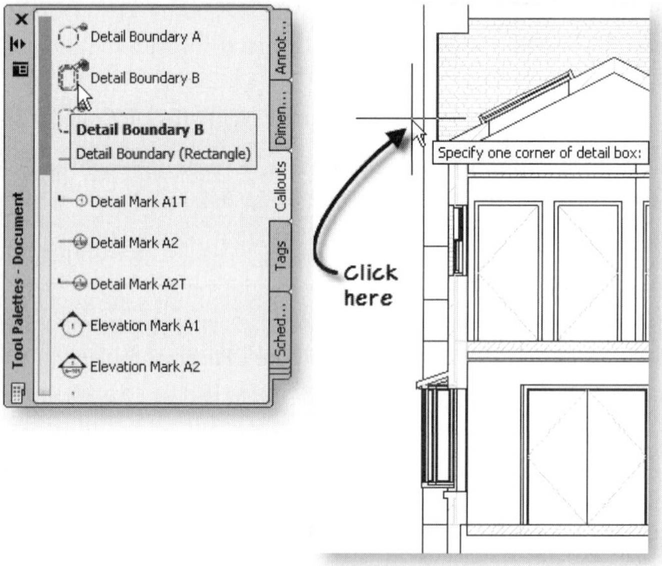

FIGURE 17.1 *Click a point at the Roof Eave*

11. At the "Specify opposite corner of detail box" prompt, click a point below and to the right of the footing (see Figure 17.2).

    Try not to include the Roof Window in the region.

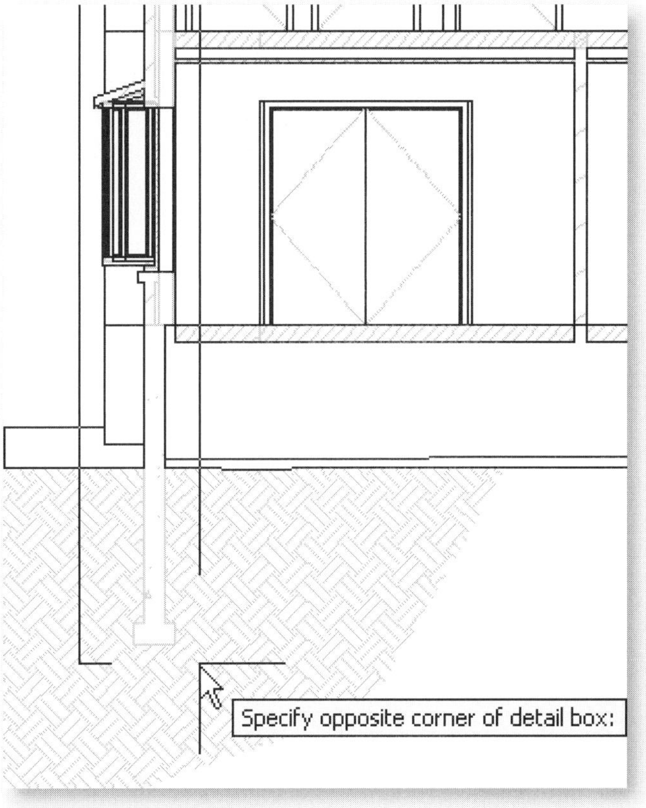

FIGURE 17.2 *Click the other point below the footing*

12. At the “Specify first point of leader line on boundary” prompt, click a point to the left of the boundary and then press ENTER (see Figure 17.3).

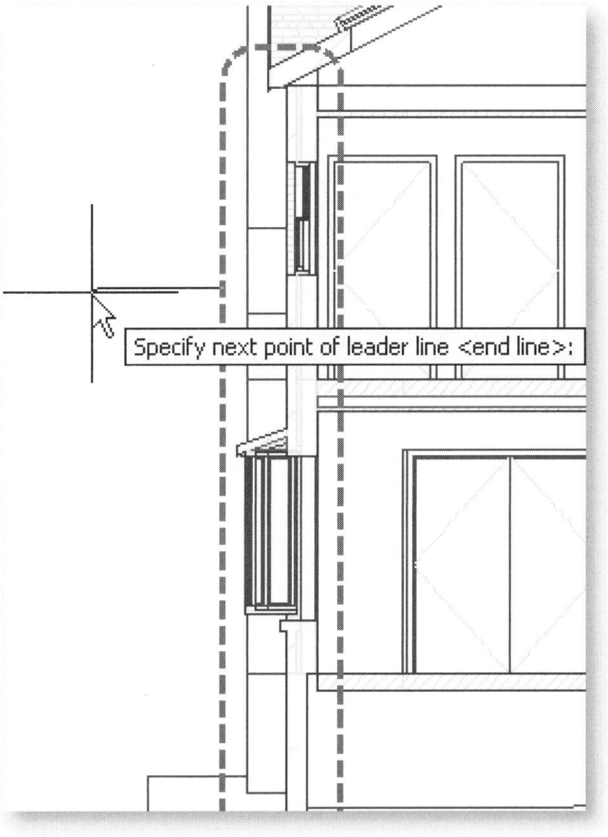

FIGURE 17.3 *Indicate the location of the Callout*

13. In the Place Callout worksheet, type **Typical Wall Section** for the New Model Space View Name.
14. At the bottom of the worksheet, change the Scale to: **1" =1'-0"** [**1:10**].
15. In the Create in area, click the New View Drawing icon (see Figure 17.4).

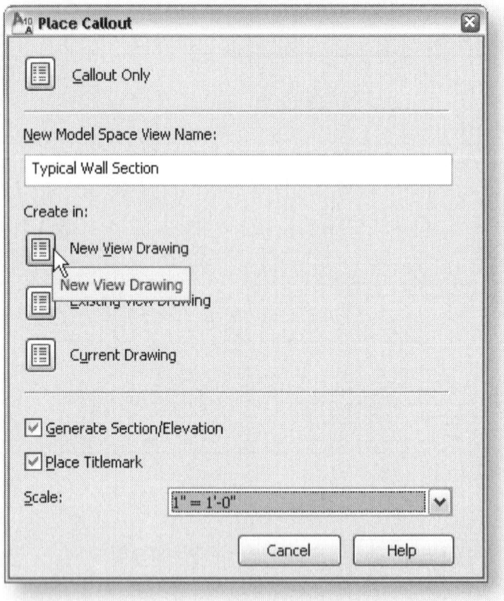

FIGURE 17.4 *Configure settings for a New View Drawing in the Place Callout worksheet*

The Add Detail View Wizard will appear. This is identical to the other View Wizards that we have seen; however, it uses different default settings. (You can also optionally assign a different template to Detail Views in the Project's Properties.)

16. In the Add Detail View wizard, type **A-DT01** for the Name and **Architectural Details** for the Description, and then click Next.

On the Context page, the Detail View wizard has selected all Levels and Divisions. However, in our case, this is a new construction detail and it is therefore not necessary to include the Existing Division. It would not actually cause any detriment to our detail if we were to leave the Existing Division selected; it will just help to simplify the View file we are generating a bit by excluding unnecessary XREFs.

17. On the Context page, right-click on the Existing Division column and choose **Clear Model Division** (see Figure 17.5). Click Next.

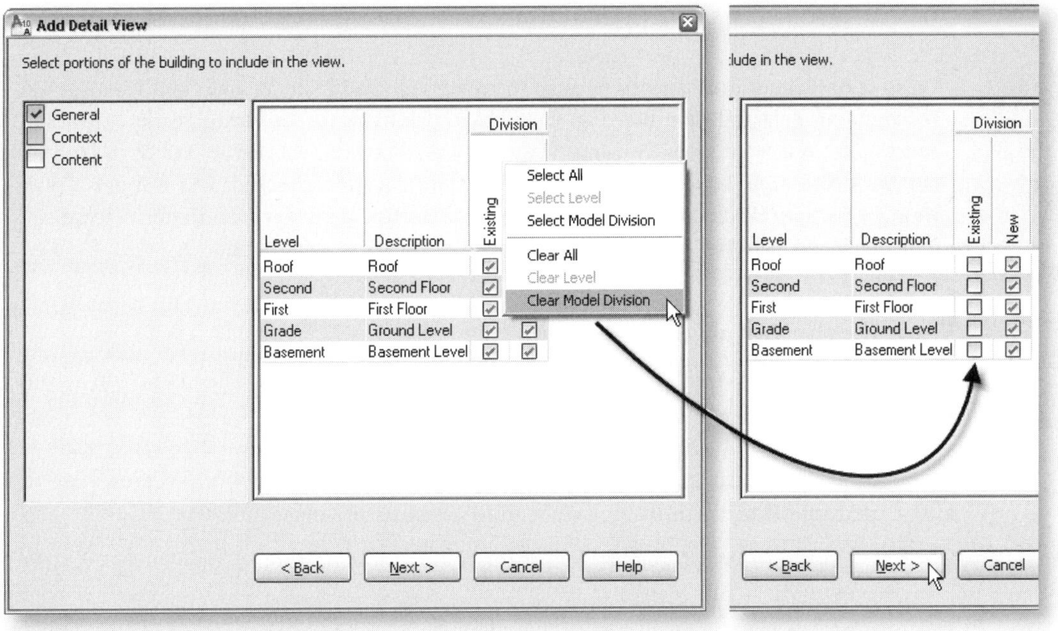

FIGURE 17.5 *Clear the Existing Division to exclude all of its Constructs from the Detail View file*

18. On the Content page, clear the checkbox next to the 2D Drawings folder and then click Finish.

The routine is almost complete and a polyline boundary surrounding the designated area has appeared on the section. A detail callout has also appeared. As with other Callout routines used in previous chapters, this one shows temporary placeholder values. At the Command Line will be the now familiar notice:

```
**You are being prompted for a point in a different view
drawing**
```

19. At the "Specify insertion point for the 2D section result" prompt, click a point to the right of the Longitudinal Section (see Figure 17.6).

    The Detail Callout will now appear with a "?" in both the Sheet and Detail Numbers. This is correct for now. Later, when you add this detail to a Sheet, those question marks will update to the correct values.

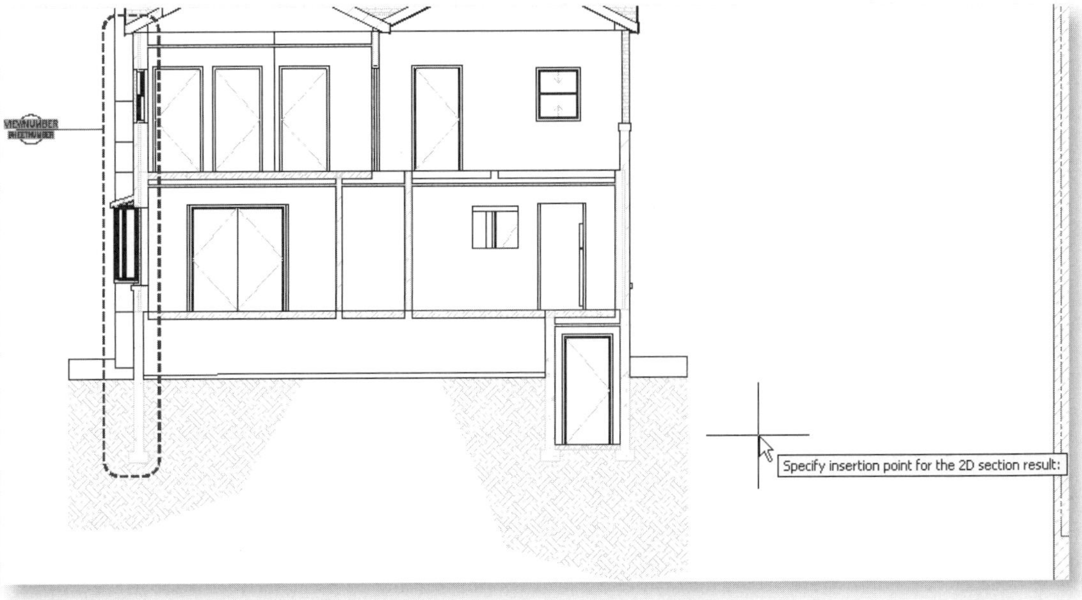

FIGURE 17.6 *Insert the new 2D Section/Elevation result to the left of the drawing*

20. Save and close the A-CM01 file.

NOTE

These same Callout routines can be used to create Enlarged Plan drawings and Plan Details. To create an Enlarged Plan drawing, clear the check mark for Generate Section/Elevation and Create in a New View Drawing. The new View drawing will use an XCLIP to crop all but the detail area. If you leave Generate Section/Elevation checked, you will get a plan view 2D Section/Elevation object. This is a useful starting point for Plan Details. Please see the "Challenge Exercise" at the end of this chapter for more information.

Simplify the Detail Background

Let's now open the *A-DT01* View file and see the results. We want to create a complete Wall Section detail from the footing to the roof. However, since the full height of the Wall is too tall to be inserted on the Sheet at the 1"=1'-0" [1:10] scale we designated, we will need break lines along the height of the section. We can use the Cut Line tool on the Annotation palette to assist us in this.

21. On the Project Navigator, click the Views tab, and then double-click *A-DT01* to open it.

    Locate the new wall section (it will be drawn in blue linework) and zoom in on it.

Notice that all of the linework in these 2D Section/Elevation objects is a cyan color. This indicates that all of the linework of the section is on a non-plotting layer. This is done deliberately since the section is intended to be an underlay upon which you can build a detail using ACA Detail Components. If you wish to see how this is accomplished, select the 2D Section/Elevation object, and, on the 2D Section/Elevation contextual ribbon tab, on the General panel, choose the ***Edit Style*** tool. Click the Display Properties tab and click the Edit the Display Properties icon. On the Layer/Color/Linetype tab, notice that all components are assigned to a non-plotting layer, except for the Out of Date Marker. Cancel to return to the drawing without making changes. Now let's locate the Bldg Section Line from which this 2D Section/Elevation object is generated.

22. Toggle off Surface Hatch Display with the toggle icon on the Drawing status bar (see Figure 17.7).

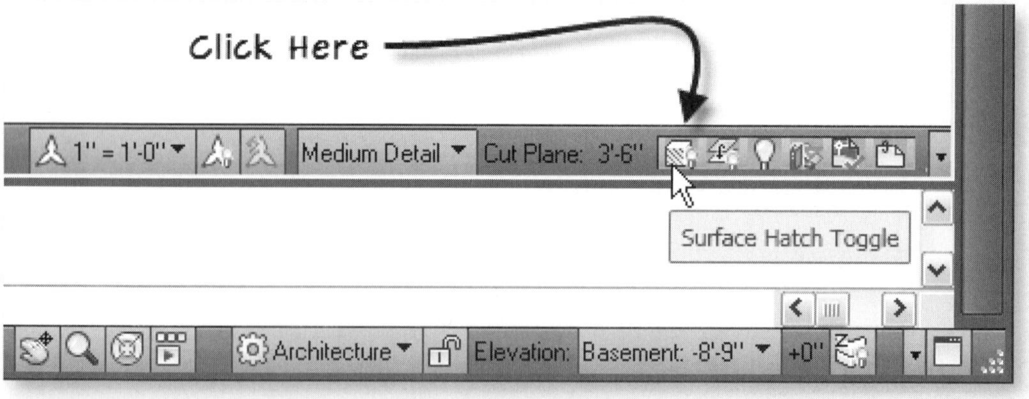

FIGURE 17.7 *Toggle off the surface hatching*

23. Click on the 2D Section/Elevation object.

NOTE

The 2D Section/Elevation object was covered in detail in the previous chapter.

Look carefully at model to the right and locate the Bldg Section Line object. It will be highlighted in red while the associated section object is selected. Notice that the location of this Bldg Section Line matches the location of the Longitudinal Building Section from which it was generated in *A-CM01*.

24. Click on the Bldg Section Line object on the right (it should still be highlighted in red).

Notice how deep the Bldg Elevation Line is. This does not pose a major problem, but the sketch linework of our section will appear cleaner if we reduce the depth of the Bldg Elevation line. We can do this interactively onscreen with the Length grip (see the left side of Figure 17.8) or on the Properties palette (see the right side of Figure 17.8). If you still have both the 2D Section/Elevation object and the Bldg Elevation Line object selected, the Properties palette will read "All (2)" at the top.

25. On the Properties palette, choose **Bldg Elevation Line (1)** from the object list at the top.

When you have more than one type of object selected at the same time, the Properties palette reveals only generic parameters. Use this technique to edit the object-specific parameters of a particular class of object in a group selection.

26. In the Component Dimensions grouping, change both Side 1 and Side 2 to: **1'-0"** [**300**], or use the grip (see Figure 17.8).

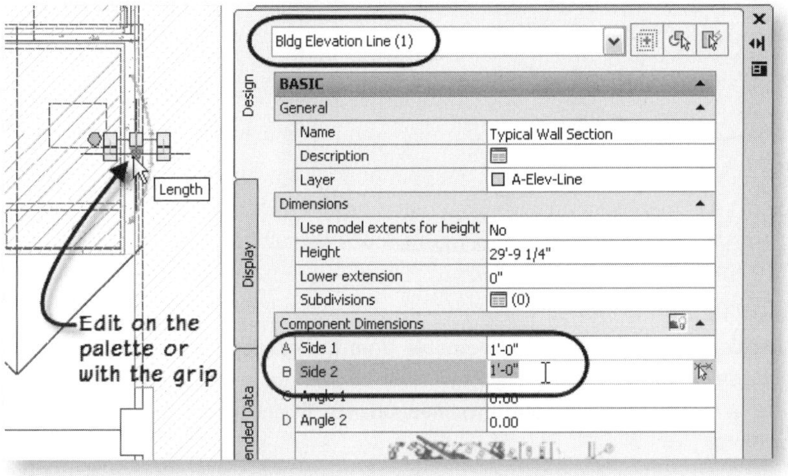

FIGURE 17.8 *Reduce the depth of the Bldg Elevation Line Object*

When we Refresh the section, some of the extraneous lines beyond will be removed, making the section easier to read.

27. Right-click in the drawing and choose **Deselect All**.
28. Select the 2D Section/Elevation object, and, on the 2D Section/Elevation contextual ribbon tab on the Modify panel, choose the ***Refresh*** tool.

Adding Break Marks

Now that we have simplified our sketch section background, we can add some break lines to crop unnecessary portions of the detail. This will allow us to exclude items like Windows so that our section is more generic in nature, as is appropriate for a "typical" detail. In this View file, the overall floor-to-floor height will remain unaltered. We will use the Cut Line tool to crop out the portions that we don't wish to include on the final printed detail. We will then rely on Model Space Views and Paper Space Viewports to crop out typical portions of the Wall so that the detail will fit vertically on the Sheet. However, before we can begin, we need to create a custom Cut Line tool. The tool provided on the Annotation tool palette includes a break line on only one side. We need one that draws a break on both sides.

1. On the Annotation tool palette, right-click the Cut Line (1) tool and choose **Copy**.

   If you do not see this palette or tool, right-click the Tool Palettes title bar and choose **Document** (to load the Documentation Tool Palette Group) and then click the Annotation tab.
2. Right-click the tool palettes title bar and choose **MasterACA** and then click the MACA Residential palette.
3. Right-click and choose **Paste** (see Figure 17.9).

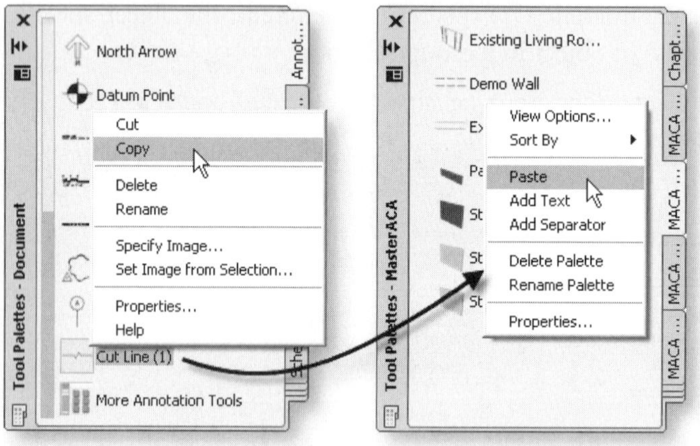

FIGURE 17.9 *Using OSNAPS to move the sections together*

NOTE

If your MACA Residential tool palette is refreshable from the catalog (look for the refresh icon in the lower corner on the tab side), you will not be able to paste. Right-click on the tool palettes title bar, create a new palette named Chapter17 and paste the copy of the Cut Line (1) tool there.

4. Right-click the new tool and choose **Properties**.
5. At the top of the worksheet, rename the tool to **Cut Line (2)**. Change the Description to **Straight Cut Line (Double "Z")**.
6. At the bottom of the worksheet, choose **Dual Break** from the Type list and then click OK (see Figure 17.10).

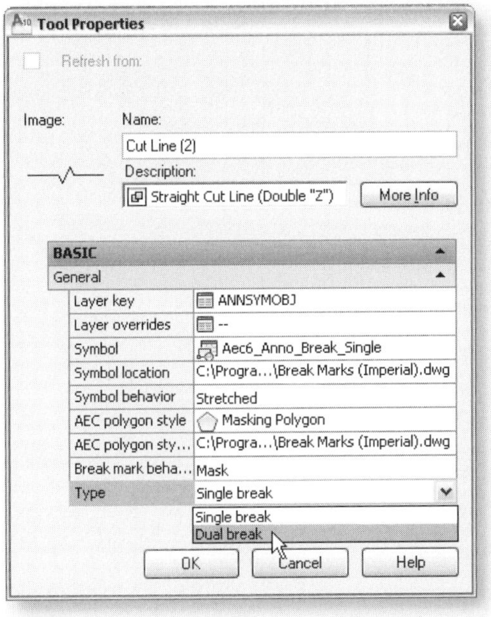

FIGURE 17.10 *Change the new Cut Line (2) tool to a Dual Break*

7. Click the new Cut Line (2) tool.
8. At the "Specify first point of break line" prompt, click a point below and to the left of the eave.
9. At the "Specify second point of break line" prompt, using Polar Tracking or Ortho Mode, drag straight across the detail to the right and then click again.
10. At the "Specify break line extents" prompt, drag down past the bottom of the window and above the second floor and then click (see Figure 17.11).

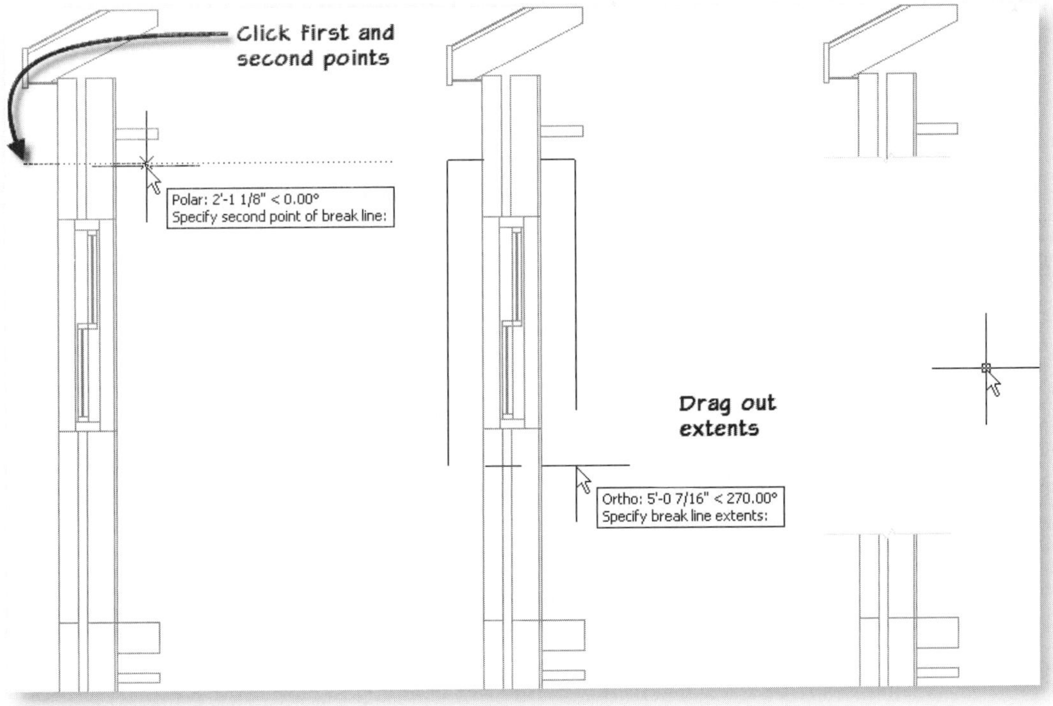

FIGURE 17.11 *Click points to designate the extents of the break*

11. Repeat twice more to create two more breaks as indicated in Figure 17.12.

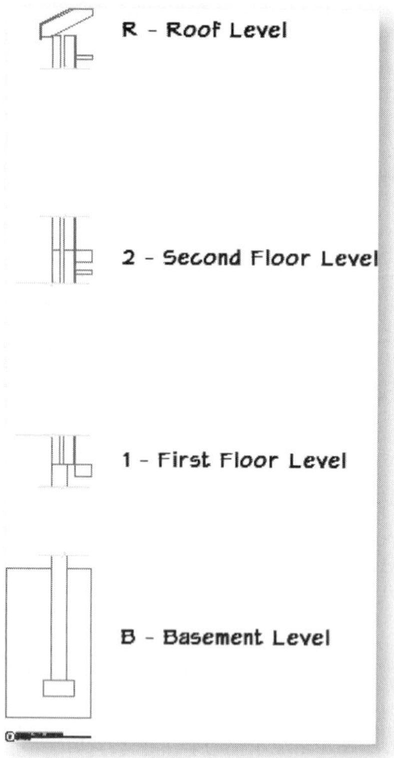

FIGURE 17.12 *Add additional break marks to create four zones—these designations will be referenced throughout the remainder of the tutorial*

NOTE

For the remainder of this tutorial, the labels on the right of Figure 17.12 will be used for reference. Therefore, if the tutorial calls for work to be done in the area of the second floor, it will simply direct you to work in region 2.

12. Click near any of the breaks.

Notice that a highlighted shape masks the underlying geometry. This is an AEC Polygon object. AEC Polygons are AEC objects that are very similar to polylines except they also have opaque surfaces. This surface can be colored, hatched or made into a mask as we have here. Once the Cut Lines are drawn, you can use the grips on the masking polygon to adjust its shape as required. On the AEC Polygon contextual ribbon tab on the General panel, choose the ***Edit Style*** tool to explore its settings if you wish.

13. Save the file.

Create a Detail

We are now ready to begin adding Detail Components to our drawing. We will use the 2D Section object as a guideline to help us place our Detail components. This will make the creation of the detail go quickly, and ensure greater accuracy and fidelity to the model.

Detailing Tool Palettes

You will create Detail Components from tools on tool palettes (in the same way as other ACA tools) or with the Detail Component Manager. Since many common components used in details are already available on tool palettes, we will begin our detail using them.

1. Right-click the Tool Palettes title bar and choose **Detailing** and then click the Exterior tab.

   This will load the Detailing Tool Palette Group and the Exterior tool palette.
2. Zoom in on region 1 of the detail (as shown in Figure 17.12).
3. On the Exterior tool palette, click the Standard Brick - 3/8" Jt [Standard 65mm Brick - 10mm Jt] tool.

A single brick in section view will be attached to your cursor. You can start placing the brick right away, or you can make adjustments to it on the Properties palette first.

NOTE

Please note, however, that unlike other ACA tools, if you begin placing a Detail Component, and then change parameters on the Properties palette before completion of their placement, the routine will start again and cancel the placement of the Detail Components in progress.

4. In the Specifications grouping, verify that Show mortar reads: **Yes**.
5. In the Mortar grouping, from the Right joint type list, choose **Flush [Struck Flush]** (see bottom right side of Figure 17.13).

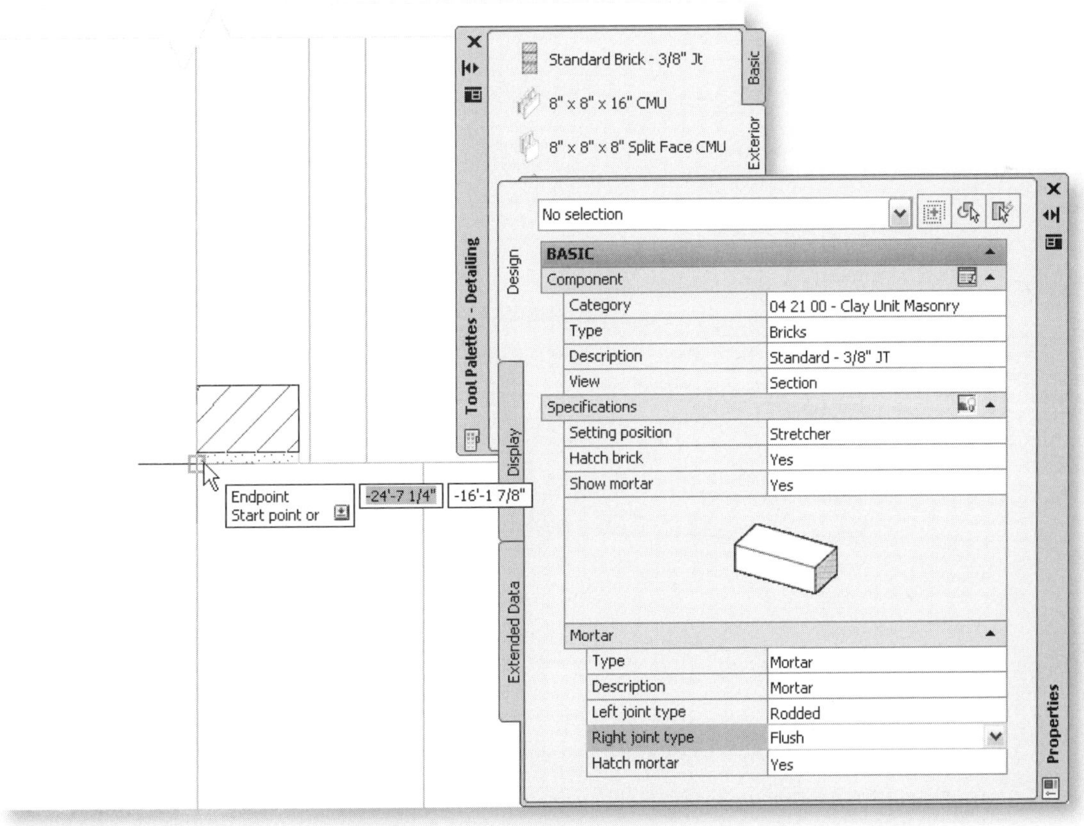

FIGURE 17.13 *Change the mortar joint type and begin placing the brick*

6. At the "Start point" prompt, click the bottom outside edge of the brick in region 1 of the section (see left side of Figure 17.13).
7. Drag the mouse straight up to the top of the detail and click at the Endpoint of the brick just beneath the roof eave (in region R) and then press ENTER to complete the routine (see Figure 17.14).

   Zoom and Pan as necessary.

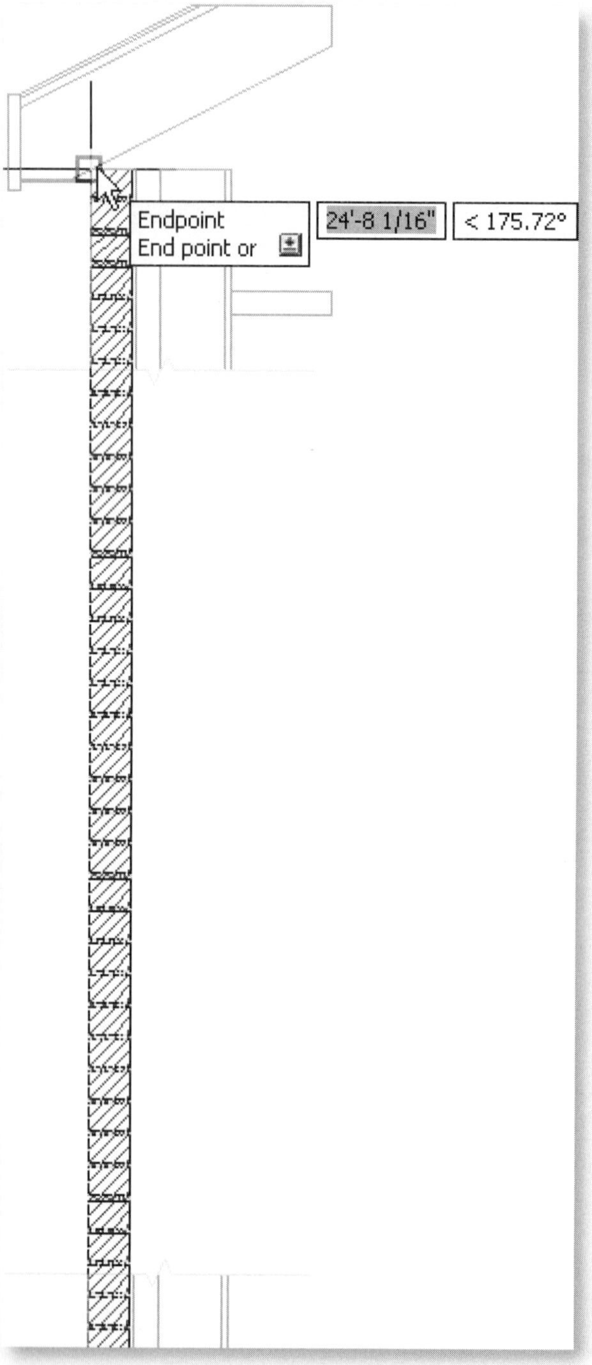

FIGURE 17.14 *Drag up to draw continuous courses of brick; click a point near the eave*

Notice that as you move the mouse, bricks will be drawn filling in from the point where you started to wherever you click the "End point." When you are finished, your bricks might be showing on top of the breaks that we built above. This is easy to address.

8. Click near the edge of each of the masking polygons.

   The edge lines up with the endpoints of the Cut Lines.

9. Right-click and choose **Basic Modify Tools > Display Order > Bring to Front** (see Figure 17.15).

   Alternatively, on the Home ribbon tab, on the Modify panel, you can click the Draw Order split button and choose the ***Bring to Front*** tool, as shown in the bottom left corner of the figure.

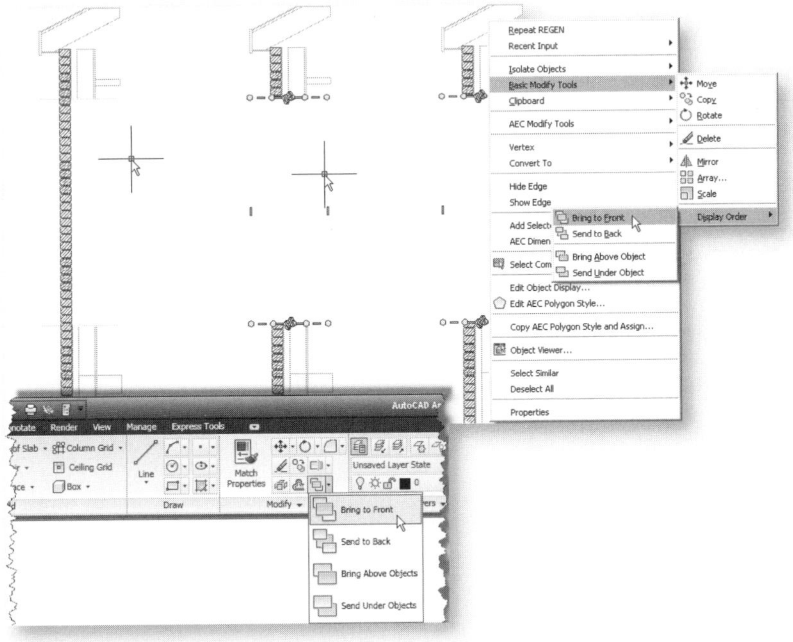

FIGURE 17.15 *Bring the masking polygon to the front*

If you wish, you can wait till the end to perform this step since we are likely to need to repeat it when we add more components. Also, feel free to delete the hidden bricks if you wish.

Adding Wood Framing

Sometimes the component you need is not configured on the palette exactly as you need it. This is no problem as you can easily modify the parameters of any tool directly on the Properties palette before you place the component. For instance, the framing of the exterior Wall uses 2×6 [50×150] framing. The tool on the tool palette is for 2×4 [50×100] framing. We can simply use this tool and then change the size.

10. On the Interiors tool palette, click the 2×4 [50 × 100mm Nominal] tool.

11. On the Properties palette, choose **2X6 [50 X 150mm Nominal]** from the Description list.

12. From the View list, choose **Elevation**.

13. Right-click in the drawing and choose **X Flip**. (You can also press the DOWN ARROW and choose **X Flip** from the dynamic prompt.)
14. At the "Start point" prompt, click the bottom of the stud within the air gap in region 1 (see Figure 17.16).

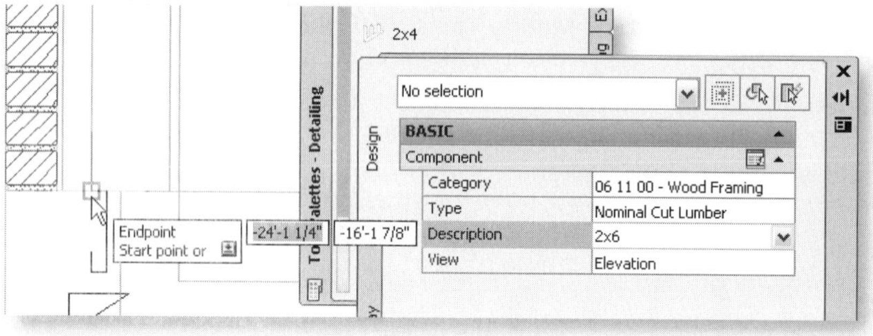

FIGURE 17.16 *Draw the Stud component from the air gap side*

15. At the "End point" prompt, drag straight up using Polar Tracking or Ortho Mode and click within the sloped rafter at the roof (see Figure 17.17).

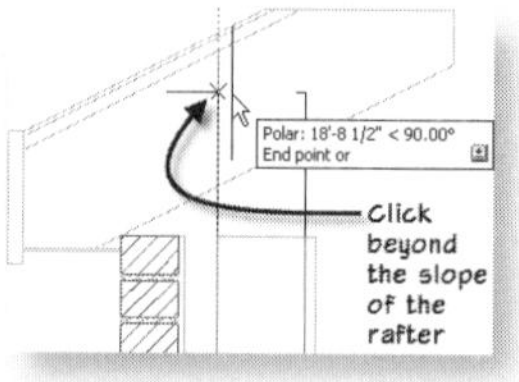

FIGURE 17.17 *Draw the stud all the way to the roof rafter*

16. On the Properties palette, change the View to **Section**.
17. Right-click in the drawing and choose **Rotate** (or use the DOWN ARROW and the dynamic prompt).
18. At the "Rotation" prompt, type **90** and then press ENTER.
19. In region 1, snap the lumber to bottom of the stud drawn above to make a bottom plate for the Wall.
20. Using the underlying section object guidelines, snap another bottom plate at the base of the second floor Wall (see Figure 17.18).

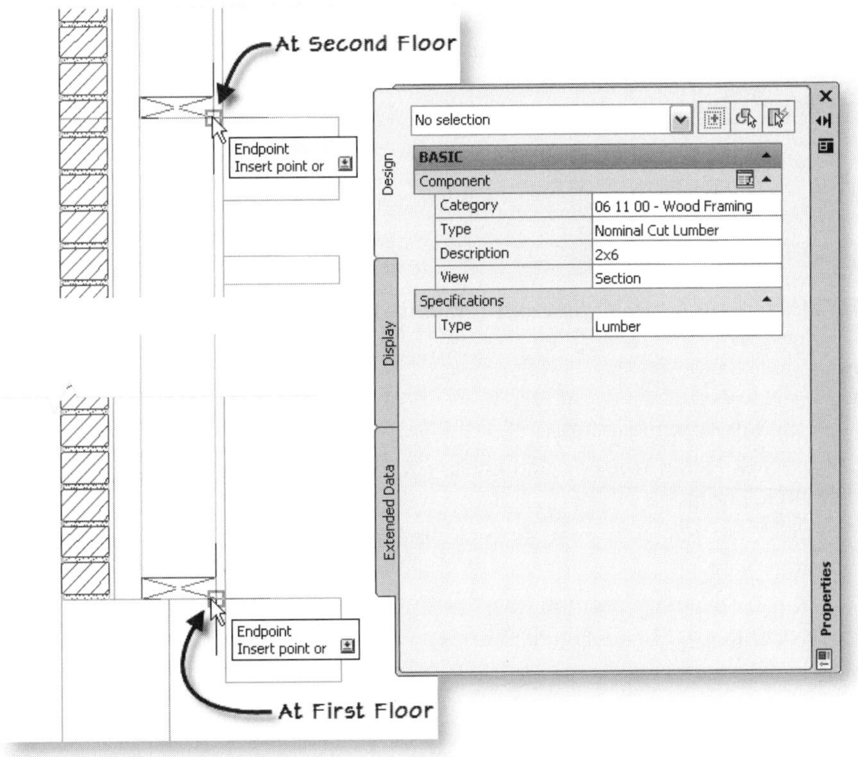

FIGURE 17.18 *Add bottom plates at the first and second floors*

21. Right-click in the drawing and choose **X Flip**.
22. Using the Intersection OSNAP, add a double top plate at the point where the roof rafter intersects the vertical stud (drawn above) and then press ENTER (see Figure 17.19).

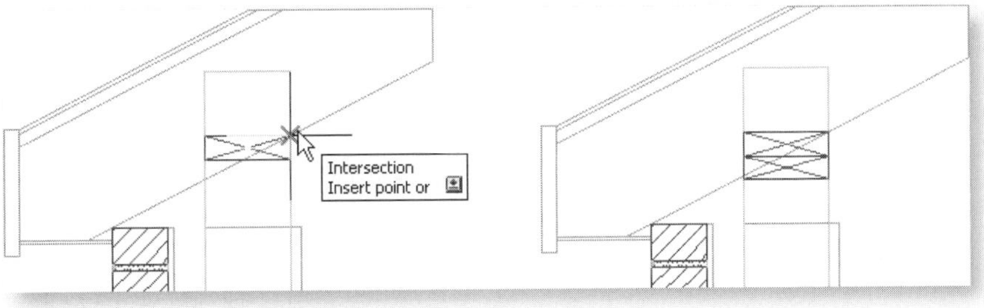

FIGURE 17.19 *Add a double top plate at the roof rafter*

23. Select the vertical stud drawn above, and, on the Home ribbon tab, on the Modify panel, click the Trim/Extend split button and choose the ***AEC Trim*** tool.
24. At the "Select the first point of the trim line" prompt, click the same intersection used to place the top plate.
25. At the "Select the second point of the trim line" prompt, use Polar Tracking or Ortho Mode to create a horizontal trim line.
26. At the "Select the side to trim" prompt, click anywhere above the trim line (see Figure 17.20).

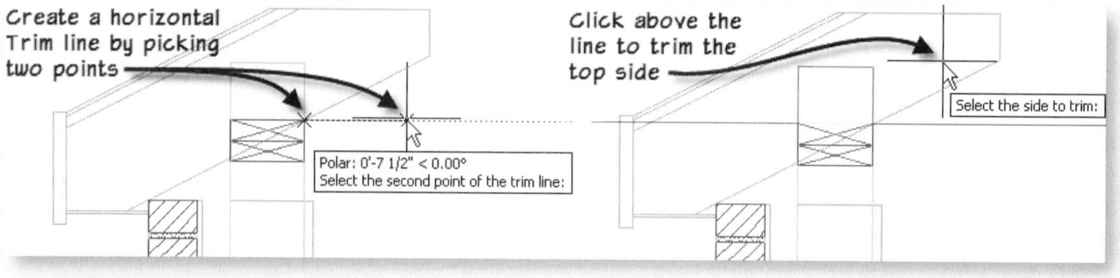

FIGURE 17.20 *Use the AEC Modify Tools to trim off the excess stud at the roof*

27. On the Interiors tool palette, click the 5/8" Plywood [15mm Plywood] tool.
28. Right-click in the drawing and choose **X Flip** (or use the arrow keys and the dynamic prompts).
29. At the "Start point" prompt, snap to the bottom left Endpoint of the first floor bottom plate.
30. At the "End point" prompt, snap to the Endpoint of the underlying section object to the right (see Figure 17.21).

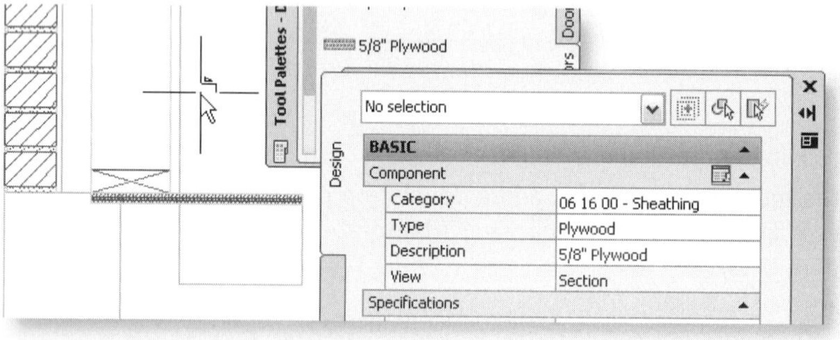

FIGURE 17.21 *Add a plywood subfloor*

31. Repeat this process on the second floor.
32. Select the vertical stud component, right-click and choose **Add Selected**.
33. On the Properties palette, choose **2×10** [**50 × 250mm Nominal**] from the Description list.
34. Draw a floor joist beneath each of the two plywood subfloors just drawn.

TIP **Don't forget to right-click and change the reference point to Left.**

35. Change the Description back to **2×6** [**50 × 150mm Nominal**] and draw a ceiling joist starting as the double top plate in region R, and then press ENTER to complete the routine (see Figure 17.22).

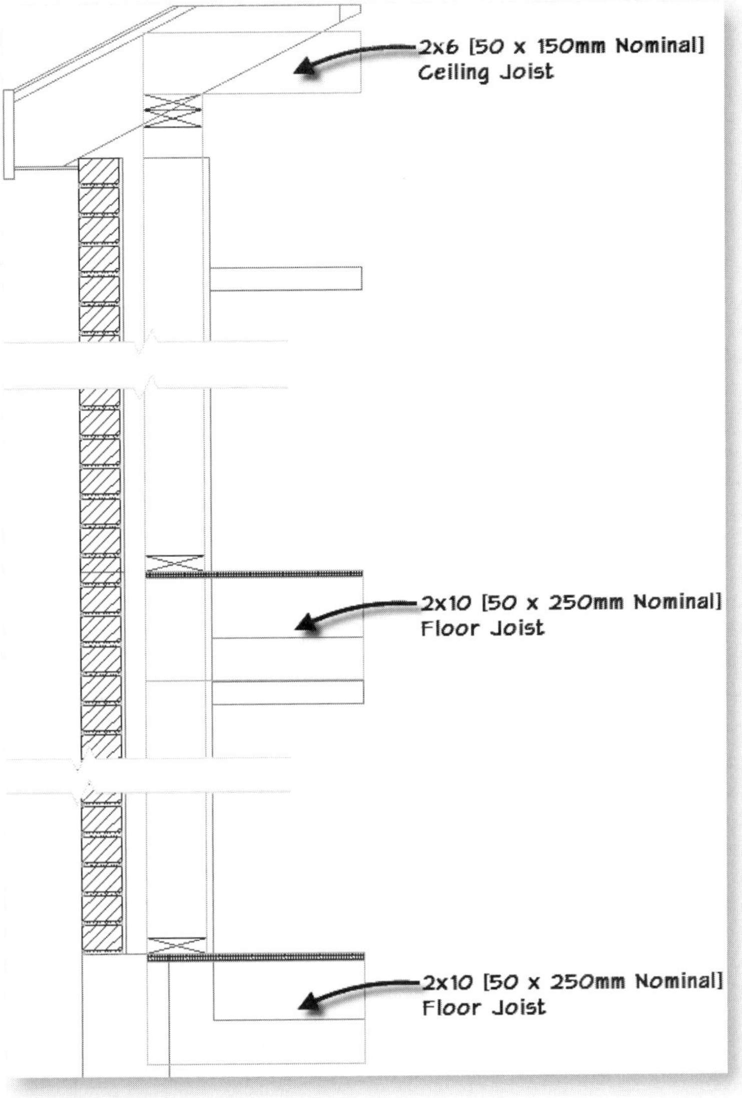

FIGURE 17.22 *Add Floor and Ceiling Joists*

36. Save the file.

Add Roof Rafters

The Roof Rafters present a bit of a challenge since we don't have all of the reference points that we need. This is easily solved by adding some construction lines.

37. On the Home ribbon tab, on the Draw panel, click the Line split button (bottom half) and then choose the ***Construction Line*** tool.
38. At the "Select linework under cursor" prompt, mouse over one of the sloped rafter lines and click.
39. At the "Specify offset" prompt, click the point where the top plate intersects the rafter and then press the ESC key (see Figure 17.23).

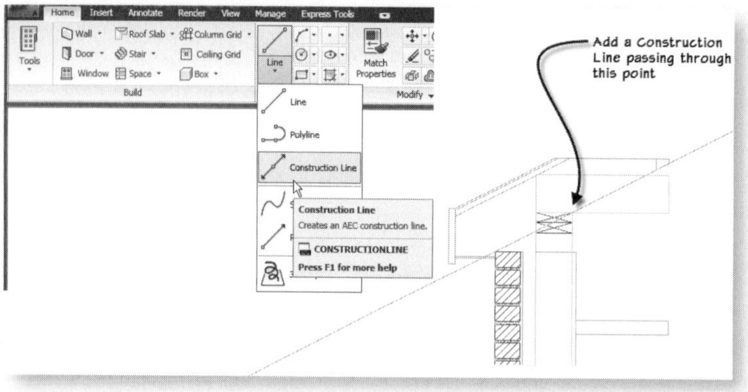

FIGURE 17.23 *Add a Construction Line following the slope of the Roof Rafter*

40. Select the Ceiling joist, right-click and choose **Add Selected**.
41. On the Properties palette, change the Description to **2×8** [**50 × 200mm Nominal**].
42. At the "Start point" prompt, using the Nearest OSNAP, click a point on the construction line to the left of the roof eave.
43. At the "End point" prompt, using the Nearest OSNAP, click a point on the construction line to the right side of the detail and then press ENTER.

    Make sure the rafter is too long in both directions (see Figure 17.24).

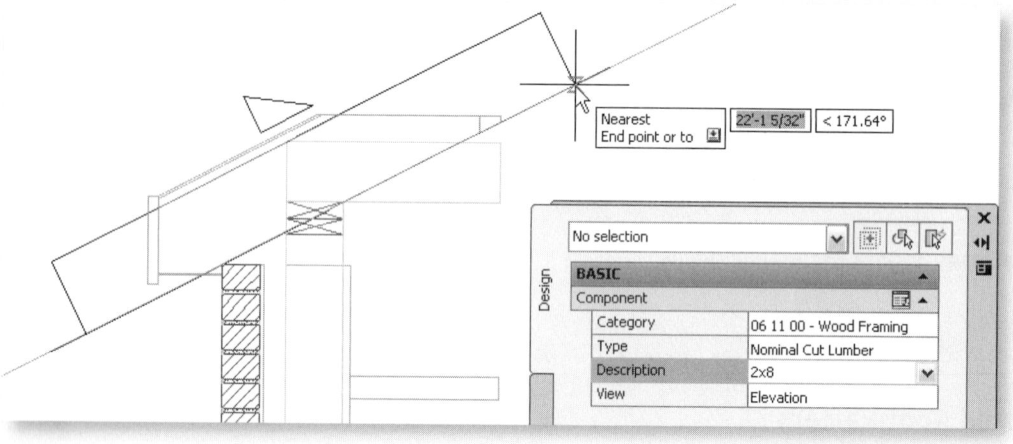

FIGURE 17.24 *Draw the Roof Rafter "too long"*

44. Follow the process in the "Adding Wood Framing" section above, and use the **AEC Modify Tools > Trim** command to trim off the unwanted parts of the roof rafter (see Figure 17.25).

NOTE

Important: Do not use the normal AutoCAD TRIM command for this operation. AEC Modify Tools preserve the integrity of the Detail Component object, but this is not necessarily the case with normal AutoCAD commands.

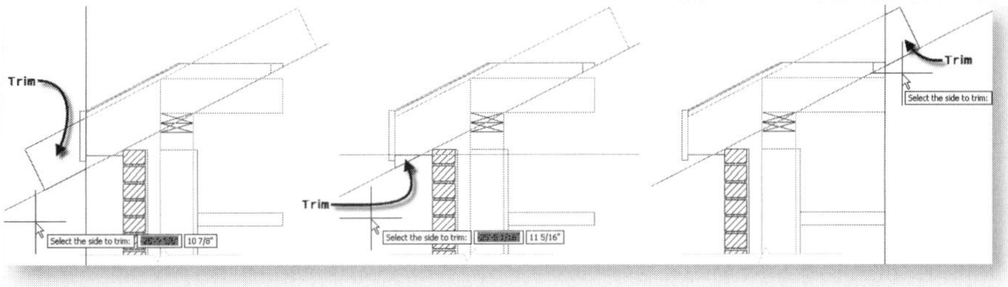

FIGURE 17.25 *Use AEC Modify Tools to trim the roof rafter to the correct shape*

45. Offset the construction line up **5"** [**125**] and using it and **AEC Modify Tools** > **Trim**, chamfer the corner of the ceiling joist.

TIP

You can use the AEC Modify Tools, such as Trim on standard AutoCAD entities as well as AEC Objects.

46. Delete the construction lines.
47. Click on the newly trimmed roof rafter and on the Properties palette, click the Extended Data tab.

Notice that all of the Detail Component information has been retained on this object even though we have given it a custom shape. This is true for all Detail Components. You can always see the Detail Component Extended Data by selecting the component and viewing its properties on the Extended Data tab of the Properties palette this way. Try this on some other Detail Components. Let's make a few finishing touches to the roof framing members.

48. Return to the Design tab of the Properties palette.
49. Select the sloping roof rafter.
50. On the Home ribbon tab, expand the Modify panel, click the Merge/Subtract split button and choose the ***Subtract*** tool.
51. When prompted, select both of the top plate members and press ENTER. Answer **No** to erasing them.

We can show the ceiling joist as if it were behind the roof rafter.

52. Select the horizontal ceiling joist.
53. On the Home ribbon tab, expand the Modify panel, click the Obscure/Crop split button and choose the ***Obscure*** tool.
54. At the "Select obscuring object(s)" prompt, click the sloping roof rafter and then press ENTER (see Figure 17.26).

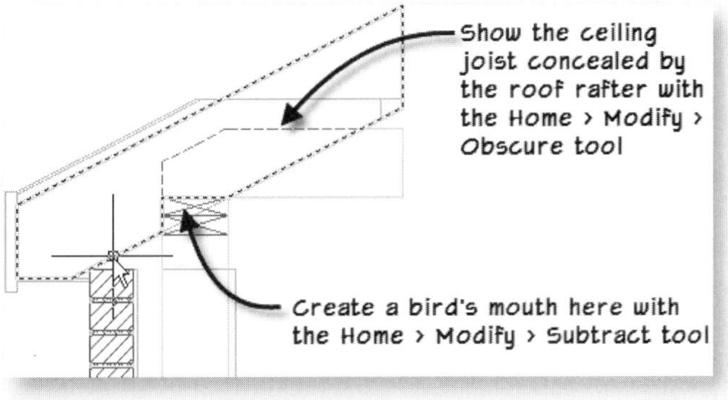

FIGURE 17.26 *Use AEC Modify Tools to fine tune the roof rafter and ceiling joist*

The end of the rafter that overlaps the sloping rafter will now be dashed and on a different layer.

55. Save the file.

Add Remaining Framing Components

There are still some framing components required. We can use the Add Selected functionality to add these.

56. Using Add Selected, add a double top plate for the first floor snapping to the bottom of the second floor joist.
57. Using Add Selected, add a sill plate beneath the first floor joist.
58. Using Add Selected, add a joist in section at each floor.
59. Using Add Selected, add plywood sheathing from the sill plate to the double top plate at the ceiling joists and along the top edge of the roof rafter (see Figure 17.27).

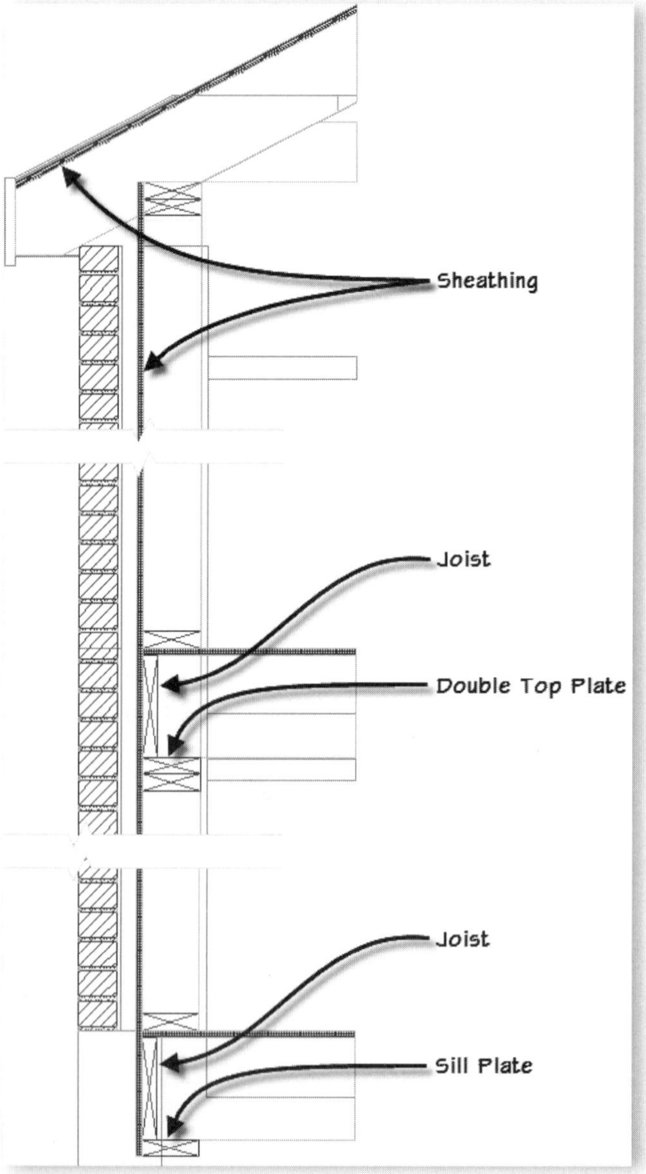

FIGURE 17.27 *Add remaining framing components*

60. Select the vertical stud.
61. On the Home ribbon tab, expand the Modify panel, click the Align/Reposition From/Space Evenly/Center/Divide split button and choose the ***Divide*** tool.
62. Follow the prompts and use Figure 17.28 as a guide to divide the vertical stud into two pieces at the double top plate.
63. Using the ***Trim*** tool on the Modify panel, remove the piece of the upper vertical stud that overlaps the floor joist and floor sheathing (see Figure 17.28).

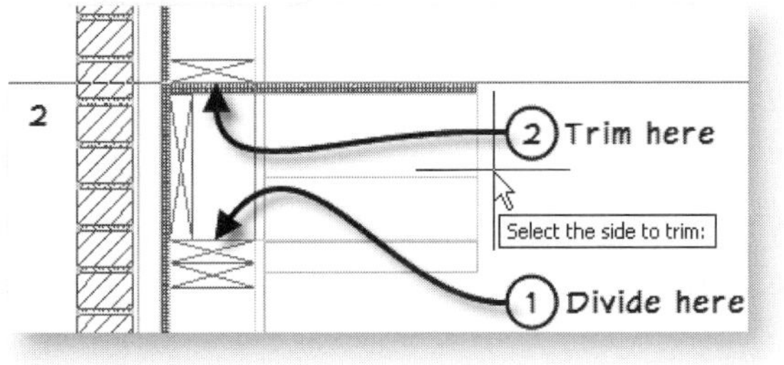

FIGURE 17.28 *Divide the vertical stud and then trim the portion at the floor joist*

64. Select any lumber component, right-click and choose **Add Selected**.
65. On the Properties palette, change the Description to **1×8** [**25 × 200mm Nominal**], change the View to **Section** and then beneath the Specifications Grouping, change the Type to **Plank**.
66. Add this component to the fascia of the roof.
67. Save the file.

Detail Component Manager

Although all of the Detail Components that we have added so far have come from tools, the Detail Component Manager (see Figure 17.29) is the primary interface to the ACA Detailing System. Tools are simply "shortcuts" to specific items in the Detail Component Manager. If an item that you wish to add cannot be found on an existing tool palette, use the Detail Component Manager. You may also add new sizes to existing components in the database with Detail Component Manager, and you can drag items from it to tool palettes for quick future access.

The detail component database is organized in the MasterSpec 2004 format.

1. On the Home ribbon tab, on the Details panel, choose the ***Detail Components*** tool.

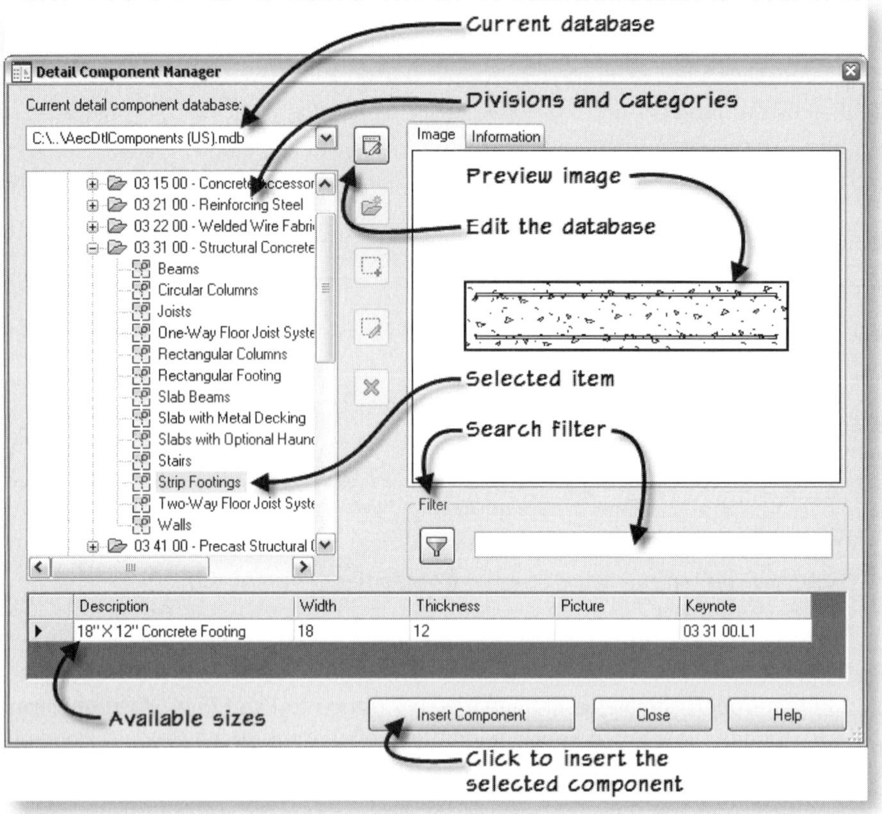

FIGURE 17.29 *The Detail Component Manager*

2. Browse to the correct category and item:

   In Imperial: *Division 3 – Concrete,* then *03 31 00 - Structural Concrete,* and finally *Strip Footings.*

   In Metric: [*E - In Situ Concrete/Large Precast Concrete,* then *E10 - Mixing/ Casting/ Curing In Situ Concrete, then Strip Footings*]

In imperial, there is only one size listed for Strip Footings and it is not the size that we need. However, it turns out that we can easily add sizes to the database. Once we add an item, it will be available from that point on.

CAD MANAGER NOTE

All Detail Components are saved in a Microsoft Access database file. New sizes that are added become new fields in the database. You will likely want to locate the standard database for the office on your server. You can do this in the Options dialog. You may also want to consider access rights to this central database. However, if you limit user write access to the database, you must provide a process by which users can add the additional components that their designs require. Assuming that you allow write access, the database can be edited directly from the Detail Component Manager dialog. Use this functionality to add sizes to existing components (see below) and to add custom groups and components. You can also edit components directly in the database using the edit icon. This will call a Component Properties wizard which will give access to all of the component's custom parameters.

While not covered in this book, you can also add custom detail components. To do this, select an existing group (or add a custom group using the Add Group icon), and then click the Add Component icon. This will call the New Component worksheet. Several types of detail component templates called "recipes" are available. Visit the online help for more information on the options available. In addition, for recommendations on detail and keynote customization, you can consult Chapter 8 in *Autodesk Architectural Desktop: An Advanced Implementation Guide* by Paul F. Aubin and Matt Dillon.

3. At the top of the dialog, click the Edit Database icon.

   A blank line—with a star (*) next to it—will appear at the bottom of the list of sizes.
4. Click in the last line of the size list (the blank one that just appeared) in the Description column.
5. Type **20" x 10" Concrete Footing** [**500mm x 250mm CONCRETE FOOTING**] and then press the TAB key.
6. Type **20** [**500**] in the Width column, and press TAB again, type **10** [**250**] in the Thickness column and press TAB twice.
7. Right-click in the Keynote column and choose **Edit**. Pick the same keynote listed for the other sizes and then click OK.
8. Click the Edit Database icon again, to exit edit mode. When prompted to save changes, click Yes.
9. With this new item selected, click the Insert Component button.
10. On the Properties palette, in the Rebar - Longitudinal grouping, change the Bars value to **2**. In the Rebar - Lateral grouping, change the Edges to **Center**.
11. Place the Footing component relative to the upper-left corner of the section underlay and then press ENTER.

> **NOTE**
> **The Footing that you are placing will be larger to the right and project lower than the outline provided by our underlain 2D Section/Elevation object. This is OK, the detailing process has revealed a flaw in the design of the foundation. There is a suggested exercise to edit this in the model in Appendix A.**

Add the Foundation Wall

Let's return to the tool palette for the Concrete Foundation Wall. There is not a specific tool for this, however, on the Basic tool palette; there is a general tool for each major category of Detail Component. (You can also find the same component we will use in the Detail Component Manager instead if you wish.)

12. On the tool palettes, click the Basic tab and then click the 03 Concrete [E - In Situ Concrete/Large Precast Concrete] tool.
13. On the Properties palette, choose **Walls** from the Type list.
14. From the Description list, choose **12" Concrete Wall [300mm CONCRETE WALL]**.
15. Verify that View is set to Section, and from the Show Reinforcing list, choose **No**.
16. At the "Start point" prompt, click the Midpoint of the top of the footing.
17. At the "End point" prompt, snap Perpendicular to the bottom edge of the sill plate.

Brick Haunch

Let's cover the floor construction at the first floor with some bricks.

18. Copy seven bricks down to fill in the space between the foundation Wall and the brick veneer.

> **NOTE**
> **Even though the bricks are covered by the masking polygon, you can still select and copy them.**

Approximately three bricks will overlap the foundation wall. Let's create a haunch for them.

19. Draw a rectangle starting at the point where the sheathing intersects the foundation wall and with its opposite corner aligned with the point where the overlapping brick intersects the foundation wall (see Figure 17.30).

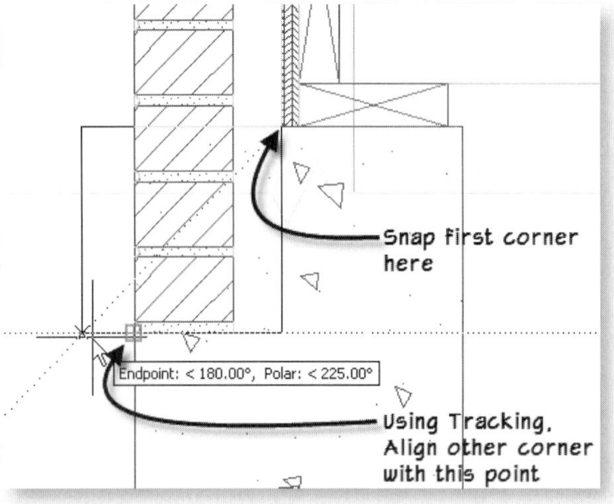

FIGURE 17.30 *Draw a rectangle relative to the bricks and the sheathing*

20. Select the foundation wall.
21. On the Home ribbon tab, expand the Modify panel, click the Merge/Subtract split button and choose the ***Subtract*** tool.
22. At the "Select object(s) to subtract" prompt, click the rectangle and then press ENTER.
23. At the "Erase selected linework" prompt, choose **Yes**.

Footing Key

24. Draw another rectangle **4"** [**100**] square and then move it so that its geometric center is snapped to the Midpoint of the top edge of the footing (see the left side of Figure 17.31).

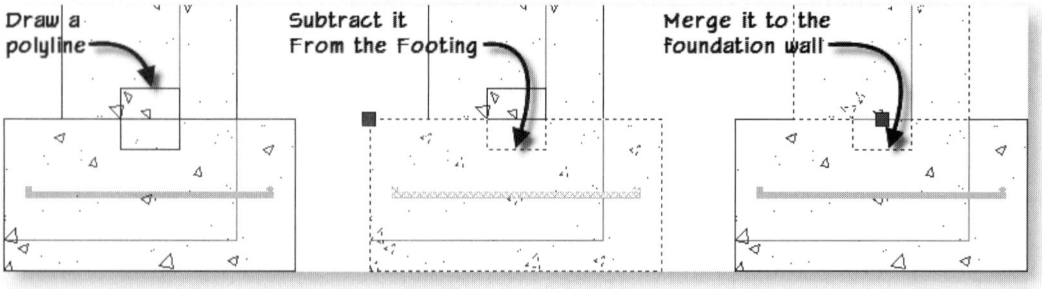

FIGURE 17.31 *Add a key to the footing using AEC Modify Tools*

25. Select the footing. On the Home ribbon tab, expand the Modify panel, click the Merge/Subtract split button and choose the ***Subtract*** tool.
26. Select the square to subtract, but do not erase it this time (see the middle of Figure 17.29).
27. Select the foundation wall. On the Home ribbon tab, expand the Modify panel, click the Merge/Subtract split button and choose the ***Merge*** tool.
28. Select the square to merge and do erase it this time (see the right side of Figure 17.29).

NOTE

Be careful not to mistake the underlying 2D Section/Elevation linework as part of the detail at this point. The 2D Section/Elevation linework is on a non-plotting layer.

29. Save the file.

Add Insulation

30. On the Interiors tool palette, click the 3-1/2" Acoustical Batt Insulation [89mm Acoustical Batt Insulation] tool.
31. On the Properties palette, choose **5-1/2" Acoustical Batt Insulation** [**140mm Acoustical Batt Insulation**] from the Description list.
32. At the "Start point" prompt, snap to the top Midpoint of the sole plate.
33. At the "Next point" prompt, snap to the bottom Midpoint of the top plate. Press ENTER twice to complete the routine.
34. Repeat the steps on the next floor.

TIP

Use Add Selected to avoid having to reset parameters on the Properties palette.

Zoom in on the floor structure of the first floor in region 1.

35. Using Add Selected, select and add batt insulation. Right-click and choose **Right**.
36. At the "Start point" prompt, snap to the bottom Endpoint of the first floor plywood sub-floor on the right side of the detail.
37. At the "Next point" prompt, snap to the top right Endpoint of the sectioned joist.
38. At the "Next point" prompt, move the mouse down and snap to the bottom right corner of the same joist. Press ENTER twice to complete the routine (see Figure 17.32).

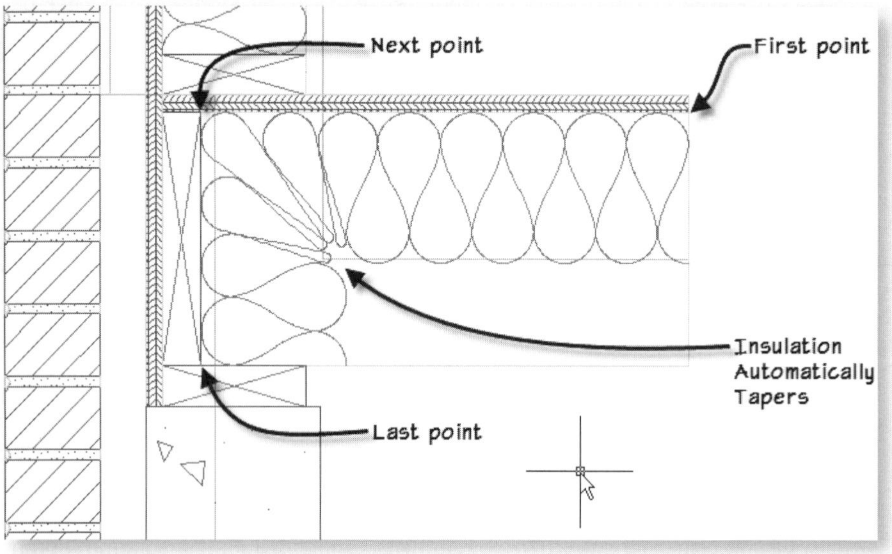

FIGURE 17.32 *Add batt insulation around a corner – the shape automatically conforms to the turn*

We will use the Add Selected command and create and taper the Batt Insulation along the ceiling joist.

39. Zoom into the roof line in Region R. Select the batt insulation, right-click and choose **Add Selected**.
40. Right-click and choose **Right**.
41. Pick the first Endpoint in the lower left hand corner of the ceiling joist and the second point in the lower right hand corner of the ceiling joist and then press ENTER.
42. At the "Select first point of first taper boundary" prompt, snap to one lower left Endpoint of the ceiling joist chamfer.
43. At the "Select second point of first taper boundary" prompt, snap to the other Endpoint of the ceiling joist chamfer and then press ENTER (see Figure 17.33).

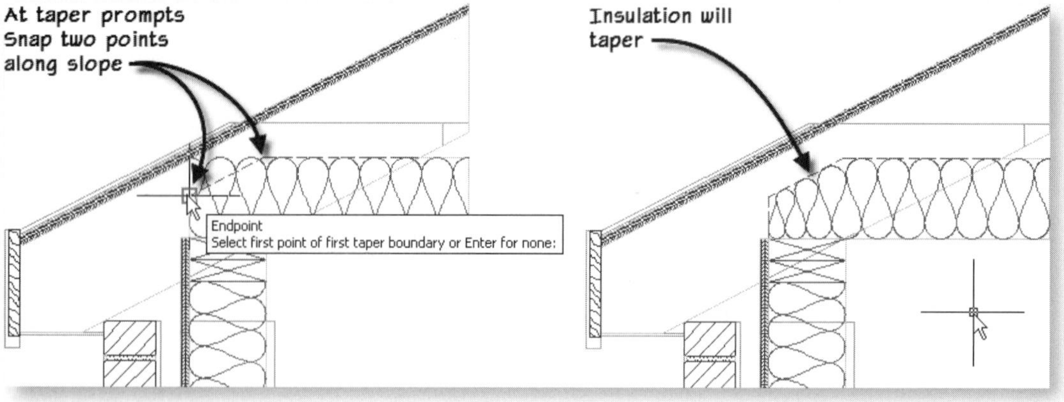

FIGURE 17.33 *Taper Batt Insulation with two points*

44. Save the file.

Flashing

To draw items like flashing, or any type of membrane, draw a polyline of the desired shape first. Then insert the Detail Component as normal. You will be prompted to select objects, at which point you can select the polyline to convert it. This will automatically change the polyline to the predefined layer and add the proper keynote detail component associations.

1. At the base of the brick cavity, draw a polyline to represent flashing.
2. On the Home ribbon tab, on the Details panel, choose the ***Detail Components*** tool.
3. In the Filter field, type **flashing** and then press ENTER.

   The tree list on the left side will shorten to show only flashing items.
4. Select the Sheet Metal Flashing [Flexible Flashing] component, select the Copper Flashing component and click the Insert Component button.
5. At the "Select Objects" prompt, click the polyline you just drew and then press ENTER twice to complete the command.

   To see the changes applied, select the new flashing component and check the properties of this converted polyline. Choose the Extended Data tab and observe the Component information and keynote information.

Complete the Detail

The detail still needs drywall on the inside, building felt on the outside of the sheathing, compacted gravel at the footing, soil, rigid insulation on the inside of the foundation wall, furring strips and drywall at the ceiling and building paper and shingles on the roof. At this point, you should be familiar enough with the Detailing tool palettes and the Detail Component Manager to locate and add all of these remaining components. The Detail Component Manager also contains Masonry Anchors, Control Joints, Sealant and Backer Rods, Caulking, Metal Soffit Vents and much more. Add any of these items as well. Do this now before moving on.

If you would like to have a bold outline around the entire detail, you can use the Shrinkwrap tool on the Basic tool palette of the Detailing tool palette group. This tool will create a polyline outline around any object(s) that you select. To add a bold shrinkwrap around the outer edge of the entire detail, simply select all detail components, being careful not to select the Cut Lines, the underlain 2D Section or the masking polygons. You can then edit the resultant polyline to suit your needs and desired graphical appearance of the detail.

6. On the Annotation tool palette (in the Document tool palette group) click the Cut Line (1) tool.
7. Following the prompts, add three cut lines to the right of the detail at the first floor, the second floor and the roof.
8. Repeating the steps covered above, use **Basic Modify Tools > Display Order > Bring to Front** to move all of the masking polygons back on top as required (see Figure 17.34).

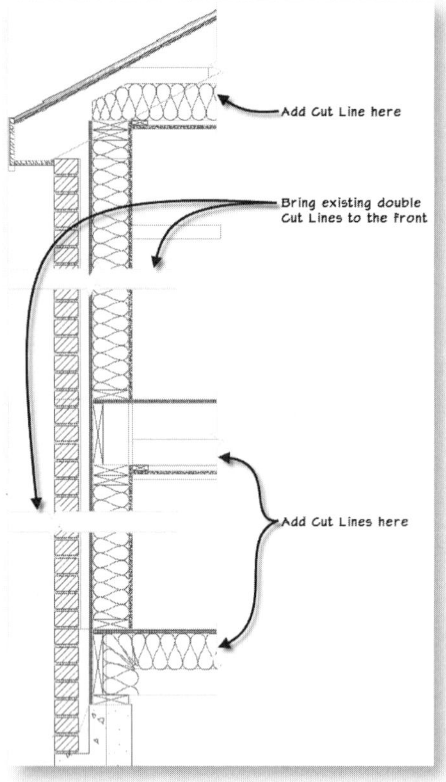

FIGURE 17.34 *Add single Cut Lines and bring the existing double Cut Lines to the front*

9. Save the file.

Modify a Detail

You can modify an existing detail using the same tools that were used to create it. One additional tool that is very handy when modifying Detail Components is "Replace Selected." Since Detail Components are not "true" objects, but rather very smart drafted entities, they cannot take advantage of many of the normal progressive refinement techniques promoted throughout this book. However, with Replace Selected, they come very close. We saw above that any Detail Component will remember its parameters (visible on the Extended Data tab of the Properties palette). After selecting one, right-click and choose Add Selected; a new Component routine is started using matching parameters. Replace Selected is the same basic concept except that instead of adding a new Component and keeping the original, this command will erase the original selected Detail Component, and populate the Properties palette with all of its original settings so that you can add a new Component in its place. You use this when you need to make a change to a Component size, or some other parameter. Replace Selected is often the quickest way to progressively refine details and Detail Components.

Be sure to also rely heavily on the AEC Modify Tools as we have above. While some components can be edited with grips in the normal fashion, others cannot. The AEC Modify Tools, however, work on *all* detail components. You can use the Trim function to cut a detail component, and crop and subtract can be used (as we saw) to apply the shape of another object to the selected detail component as a means of editing its shape. Obscure (also shown) is also a very handy tool that will make a selected detail component appear to be behind another one. Also included are Merge and Divide which can be very handy as well.

KEYNOTES

Once you have generated elevations, sections (in Chapter 16) and details (this chapter), your next task will be to add notes and annotation to them. Some techniques for this have already been covered in Chapter 14. There we added Elevation labels to the elevations and sections to indicate their floor heights and we added some basic text leaders. You can also use the dimensioning techniques covered in that chapter on your elevations, sections and details as well. In this topic, we will explore the ACA Keynoting feature. Keynotes can be added to any ACA drawing: plan, section, elevation or detail.

Keynotes Assigned to Styles

Keynotes are standard notes that are pre-assigned to both ACA object styles and Detail Components. Keynotes are stored in a Microsoft Access database that can be modified and added to as the needs of your firm dictate. They can be added with or without text leaders as reference keynotes, or in keynote symbols tied to individual Sheets called Sheet keynotes. Let's begin by taking a look at the Keynote references within ACA styles.

1. On the Project Navigator, open the *First Floor New* Construct.
2. Select one of the exterior masonry Walls, and, on the Wall contextual ribbon tab, on the General panel, choose the ***Edit Style*** tool.
3. Click the General tab.
4. On the right side of the tab is a field that lists the currently assigned Keynote. There is also a Select Keynote button that you can click to change the Keynote designation (see Figure 17.35).

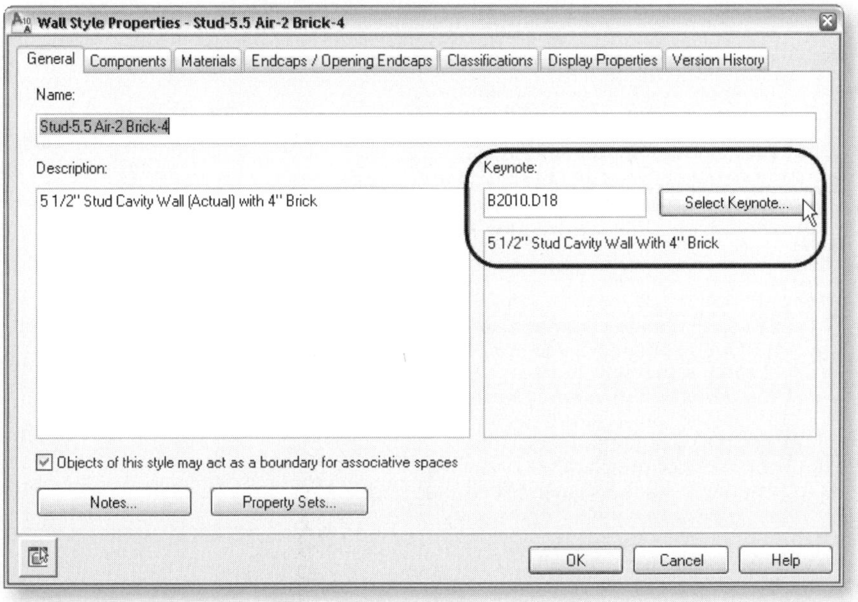

FIGURE 17.35 *You can assign a Keynote to an ACA object style on the General tab*

CAD MANAGER NOTE

Keynotes reference a Microsoft Access database file (*.mdb*). ACA ships with a few databases and you can also create your own. Database files can be saved and accessed from a network file server so that all members of your firm access the same keynotes. The path to the Keynote databases is configured in the Options dialog on the AEC Content tab. There you can add multiple Keynote Database paths. You can also assign custom Keynote databases to the current Project. This can be done on the Project Navigator palette on the Project tab. Click the Edit Project icon and then the Add/Remove button next to the "Project Details Component Databases" and "Project Keynote Databases" entries. If you wish to create your own custom Keynote database, template files have been provided in the ACA *Template* folder. By default this is located in the following path: *C:\ProgramData\Autodesk\ACA 2010\enu\Template\Details and Keynotes.*

Use caution when creating Databases based on these templates. You should attempt this only if you are familiar with Microsoft Access.

If you already have a custom Keynote database that was in use in a previous version of Architectural Desktop, use the utility provided in the Autodesk group of the Windows Start menu to migrate it to 2010. Choose **Start** > **All Programs** > **Autodesk** > **AutoCAD Architecture 2010** > **Detail Component – Keynote Database Migration Utility**. Use this tool to merge your existing database(s) into the 2010 one. Also in the same location on the Start menu, is the **Keynote Editor**. Use this tool to open existing keynote databases and add or edit keynote entries. You can also create a custom database using this tool.

5. Click the Select Keynote button.

You can choose any Keynote from the list that appears. Notice that at the top of this dialog, you have the option to choose a database, and then all of the Keynotes within that database will be listed. At the bottom, you can type in a key word and then click the filter icon to shorten the list as we did above in the Detail Component Manager. On the right side are icons to edit the database directly in this dialog (see Figure 17.36).

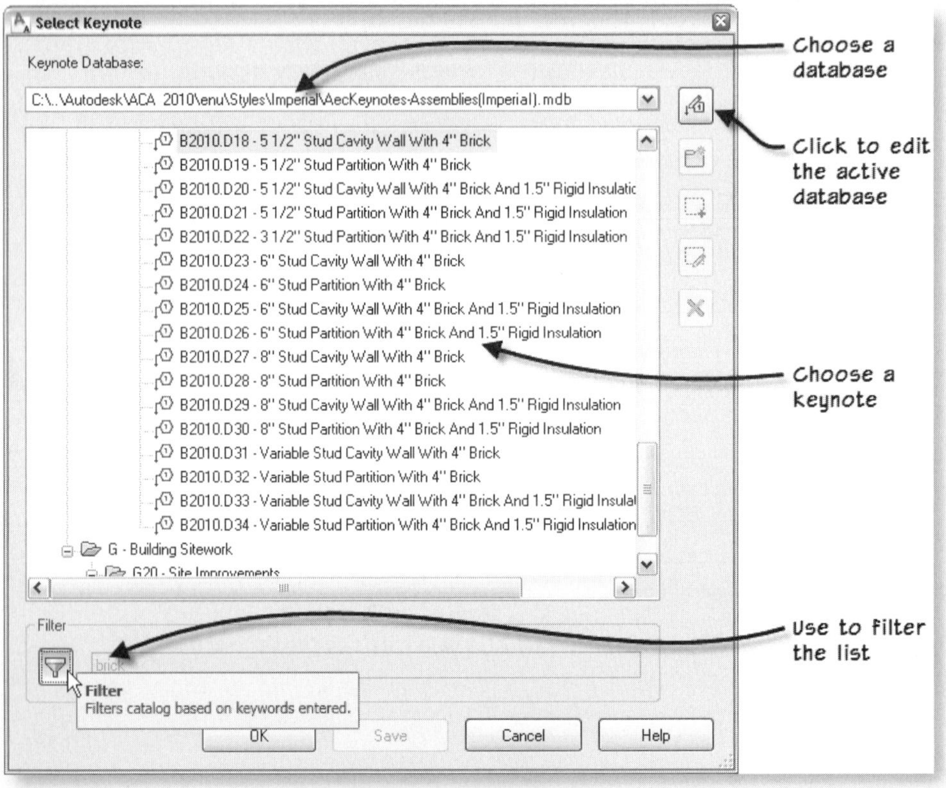

FIGURE 17.36 *Filter the Keynote list by typing in a key word*

6. Click Cancel to return to the Wall Style Properties dialog.
7. In the Wall Style Properties dialog, click the Materials tab.
8. Select the Brick Veneer component and then click the Edit Material icon.
9. In the Material Definition Properties dialog, click the General tab.
10. Notice that the Material Definition also has a Keynote designation.
11. Click Cancel three times to return to the drawing.
12. Close the *First Floor New* file. It is not necessary to save it.

Add Keynotes to Sections and Elevations

The Keynotes referenced by the Wall styles and Material Definitions that we just explored can be accessed by the tools on the Annotation tool palette.

1. On the Project Navigator palette, on the Views tab, double-click the *A-CM01* file to open it.
2. Zoom in on the East Elevation.
3. On the Annotation tool palette, click the Reference Keynote (Straight Leader) [Keynote (Straight Leader)] tool.

   If you do not see this palette or tool, right-click the tool palettes title bar and choose **Document** (to load the Documentation tool palette group) and then click the Annotation tab.
4. At the "Select object to keynote" prompt, click on the Brick Hatching on the elevation.
5. The Select Keynote dialog will appear (see Figure 17.37).

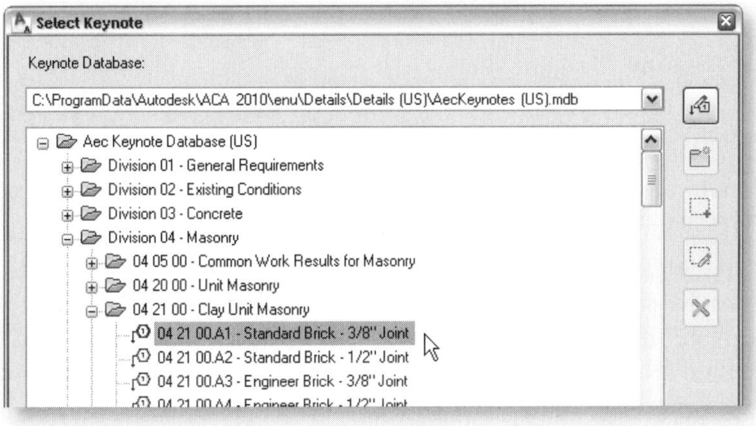

FIGURE 17.37 *The Select Keynote dialog jumps directly to the item referenced by the Material Definition*

The Keynote choice will jump directly to the Keynote category indicated by the Material Definition, in this case "04 21 00 – Clay Unit Masonry [F10 - Brick/Block Walling]."

6. Select **Standard Brick – 3/8" Joint** [**F10/110 - Clay Facing Brickwork**] and then click OK.
7. At the "Select first point of leader" prompt, click a point for the leader and then follow the remaining prompts to place the note.
8. Continue this process to add Keynotes to all the sections and elevations (see Figure 17.38).

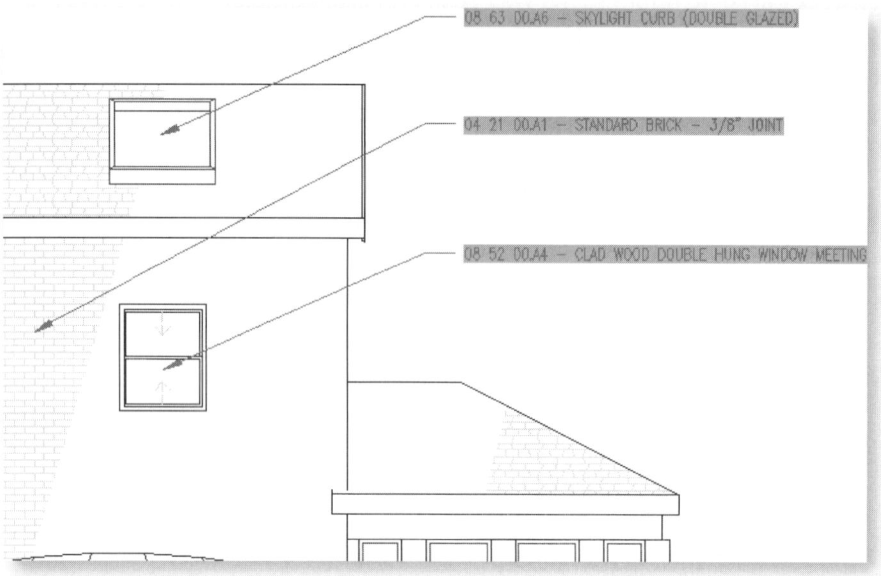

FIGURE 17.38 *Add Keynotes to the elevations and sections*

If the item you select does not have an explicit keynote assigned to its style, it will either jump to the general category of the material or simply open the keynote dialog to the top of the list. If this happens, navigate to the desired keynote and choose it manually. To prevent this from occurring, edit the style of the selected component and choose an appropriate keynote for that style.

Change Keynote Display

You can change the way that Keynotes display in your drawings. They can show the Keynote number, the Keynote text or both.

9. On the Annotate ribbon tab, click on the Keynoting title bar to expand the panel, and choose the ***Reference Keynote Display*** tool.

The three choices are: "Reference Keynote - Key only," "Reference Keynote - Note only" and "Reference Keynote - Key and Note." Figure 17.38 shows "Reference Keynote - Key and Note" display. In Figure 17.39, "Reference Keynote - Key only" is shown on the left and "Reference Keynote - Note only" is shown on the right. In addition, you may also choose your desired format in lower or upper case.

10. Choose your desired Keynote Display option and then click OK.

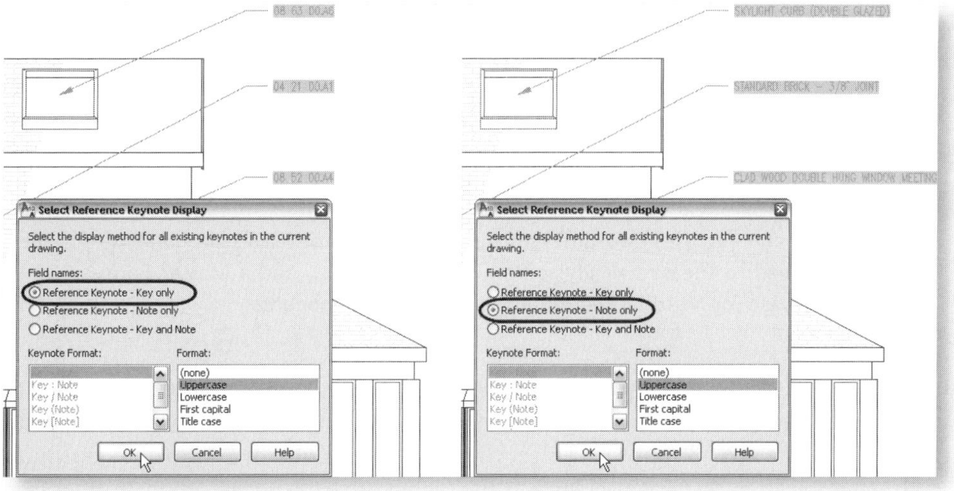

FIGURE 17.39 *Changing the method of Display for Keynotes*

11. Save and Close the file.

Keynoting Plans

In addition to keynoting elevations and sections, you can also keynote plans.

12. On the Project Navigator palette, on the Views tab, double-click the *A-FP01* file to open it.

This is the First Floor Plan View file. We added some simple notes and dimensions to it in Chapter 14. Let's add a few keynotes to it now. You may have noticed that when we added keynotes to the elevations, they automatically used the keynote assigned to the Material Definition. When you keynote in plan, you get the choice to use either the keynote assigned to the Wall style or the ones assigned to the individual components (via Materials).

13. On the left side of the plan, add a Reference Keynote pointing to the exterior Wall.
14. In the Select Element to Keynote dialog, place a check mark in the style checkbox (see Figure 17.40).

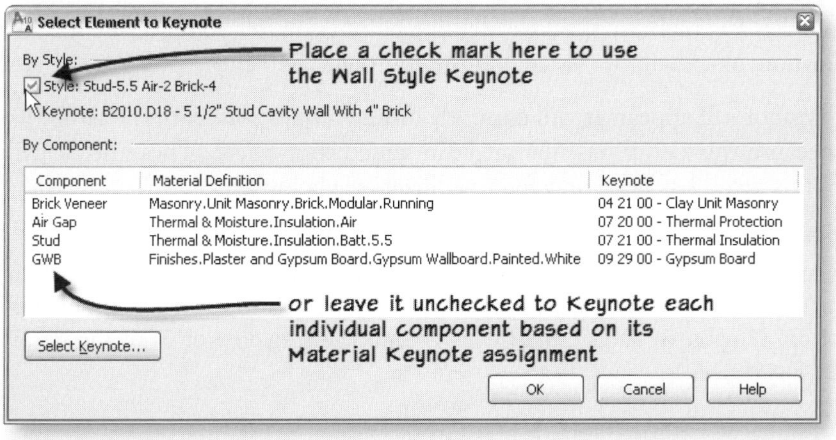

FIGURE 17.40 *Keynoting in Plan gives the option of the Wall style or Component Material Keynotes*

TIP

Before placing any keynotes, check the Drawing Scale of the file (on the Drawing Status Bar). Keynotes, like other ACA annotation, use the drawing scale to automatically scale the text and the leader.

CAUTION

A single Keynote Legend (see below) can only reference one database. If you want all of your keynotes in one legend, you will need to use only keynotes from one database. The out-of-the-box content uses two different databases, a Uniformat-based database for the keynotes assigned to the overall Styles (Imperial and Metric), and a Master Format 2004 [UK NBS] database for Material Definitions and Details Components.

If you want to wrap the keynote to more than one line, you can select the text, and then change the width in the Properties palette. Make the width some value other than zero. When the width of text is set to zero, it does not word wrap and continues on in one long line. After you change it to a value other than zero you can then fine tune the width with the grips.

15. Save and close the file.

Keynoting Details

Keynoting Details uses the same tools and procedures. Since we used Reference Keynotes in the previous examples, we will use Sheet Keynotes here. Either type of Keynote, Reference or Sheet can be used in either situation; we are switching here merely to show both types in practice. A Sheet Keynote will be assigned a numeric designation that will be used for each instance of a particular note. Therefore if you note the same brick five times on a Sheet, they will all use the same numeric designation that refers back to a Keynote Legend (see below). These designations will be applied when the drawings are added to a Sheet.

Return to *A-DT01*. If you closed it, re-open it from Project Navigator now.

1. On the Annotation tool palette, click the ***Sheet Keynote (Straight Leader)*** tool.
2. At the "Select object to keynote" prompt, click on a Detail Component to select and Keynote it.
3. At the "Select first point of leader" prompt, click the point where you wish the arrowhead to be located.
4. At the "Specify next point of leader line" prompt, click your next leader point.

The Block (Straight Leader) Multileader Style used by the Sheet Keynote (Straight Leader) tool takes a maximum of two leader line points, so after you pick the second point, the keynote block will be placed and the command will end.

A Keynote symbol will appear. It will currently display a question mark (?) within its field code because this detail has not yet been added to a Sheet. These fields will update once this detail has been dragged to a Sheet (see below).

5. Continue to add as many Sheet Keynotes as you wish.

   Be sure to keynote the same type of Component in more than one location on the detail. For instance, keynote the brick at the top (region R) and the bottom (Region B) and perhaps even the middle (region 1 or 2) of the detail (see Figure 17.41).

NOTE

Create a Construction Line on each side of the detail using the ***Construction Line*** tool. (Home ribbon tab, on the Draw panel, Line split button). Snap to this construction line when placing Keynotes or edit the second segment length after placement to keep them all lined up neatly.

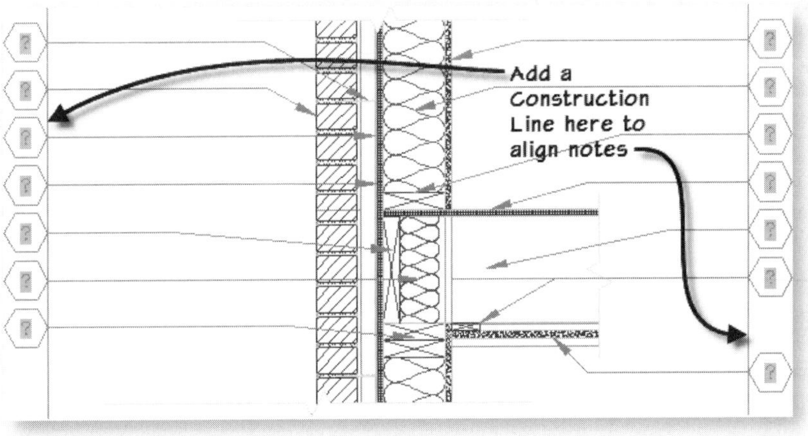

FIGURE 17.41 *Add several Sheet Keynotes to the Detail*

6. Locate the underlying 2D Section and click on it. Verify that all of the notes fit within the dashed gray boundary that appears. If they don't use the grips to adjust the width of the boundary.

   These grips adjust the size of the Model Space View that we will drag to the Sheet next.

7. When you have finished Keynoting, save and close the file.

Add Details to Sheets

Let's add our detail to a Sheet and then create some Keynote Legends.

8. On the Project Navigator palette, click the Sheets tab.
9. In the *Architectural* > *Details* Subset, double-click the *A-501 Details* Sheet to open it.

   The Sheet was provided for convenience and it is currently empty.

10. On the Project Navigator palette, click the Views tab.
11. Click the plus (+) sign beneath the *A-DT01* View file to reveal the Model Space Views contained in the file.
12. Drag Typical Wall Section Model Space View onto the Sheet and snap its lower-left corner to the lower left corner of the Sheet to place it.

    The Viewport created will be too tall for the Sheet.

13. Copy (on the Home ribbon tab, on the Modify panel, select the ***Copy*** tool) the Viewport three times next to itself (you will have four total).
14. Use the grips on the Viewports to reduce the height only and crop each Viewport to one portion of the detail (B, 1, 2 and R) (see Figure 17.42).

    Be careful not to change the width of any of the Viewports, maintaining the width will allow us to stack them up and keep everything properly aligned.

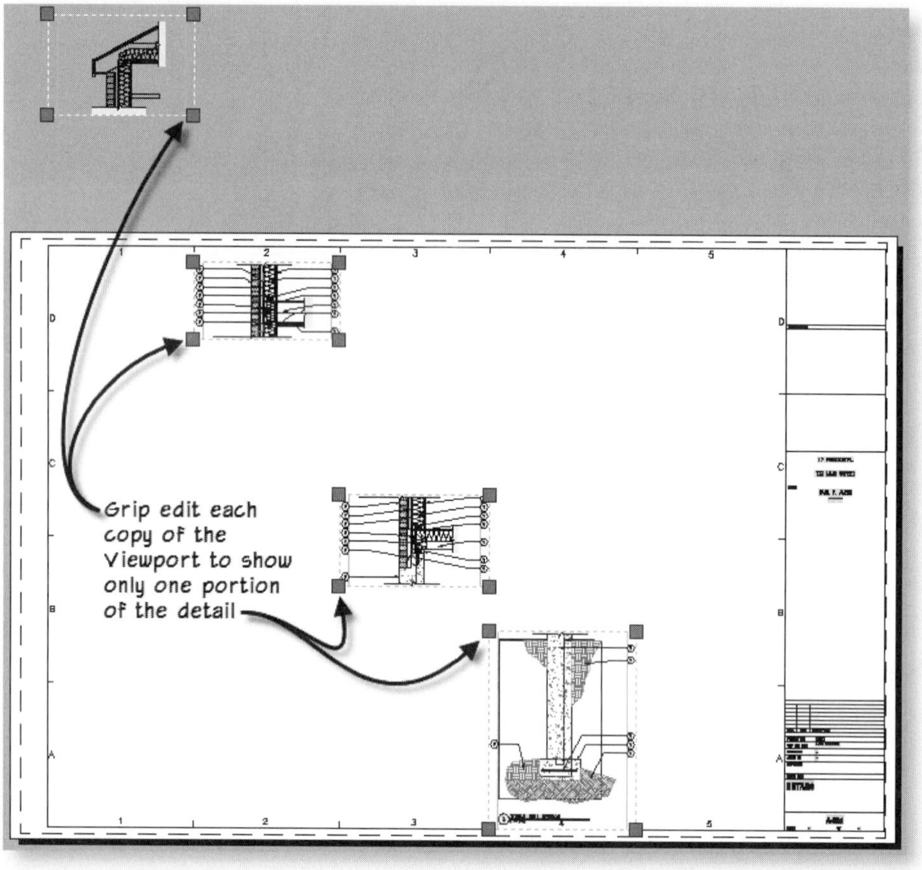
Grip edit each copy of the Viewport to show only one portion of the detail

FIGURE 17.42 *Copy the Viewport and adjust each copy to view only one section of the detail each*

15. Move all of the Viewports to the left edge of the Sheet and use object snaps to stack them up on top of each other (see Figure 17.43).

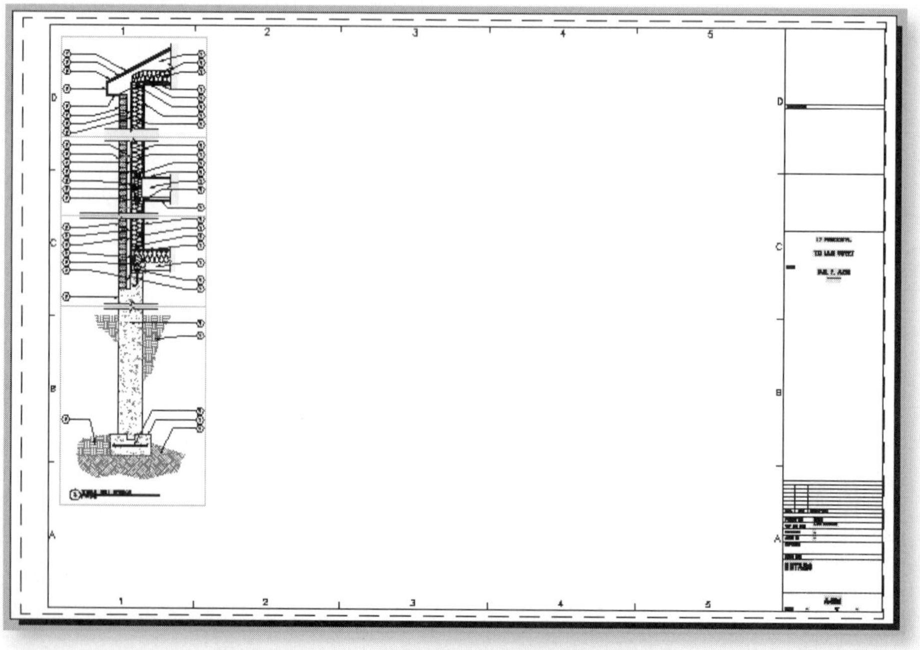

FIGURE 17.43 *Move all of the Viewports together and snap them to one another*

16. Save the file.

NOTE

The Metric Complete version of the project (provided with the dataset files from the Mastering AutoCAD Architecture 2010 CD-ROM) varies slightly from the results indicated here and those included in the Imperial Complete version.

Keynote Legends

When you use Keynotes, you can place a legend on your Sheet files that references all of the Keynotes showing on a particular Sheet. If they are Reference Keynotes, the legend is organized logically by category. If they are Sheet Keynotes, then the Legend will enumerate the Keys and update all of the field codes throughout the set.

Sheet Keynote Legend

1. On the Annotation tool palette, click the Sheet Keynote Legend tool.
2. At the "Select keynotes to include in the keynote legend" prompt, make a window around all Sheet Keynotes (across all four Viewports) and then press ENTER.

   This can be done from Paper Space *without* making the Viewport active.
3. At the "Insertion point of table" prompt, click a point on the Sheet to place the Table (see Figure 17.44).

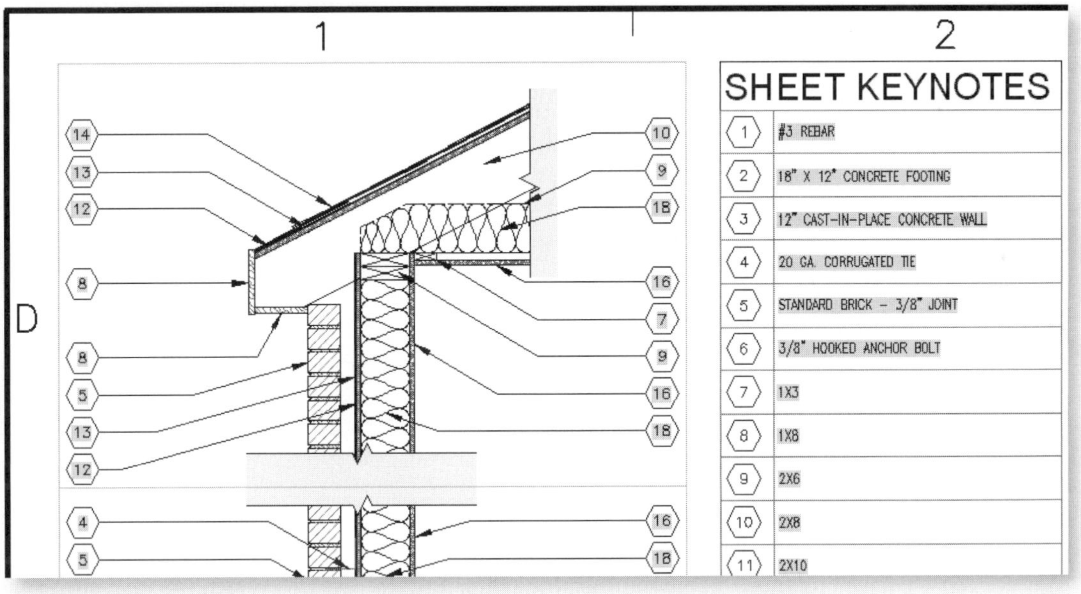

FIGURE 17.44 *Place a Sheet Keynote Legend to enumerate and describe the Sheet Keynotes*

4. Save and close the file.

If you wish, you can create additional details for this project following the same techniques covered previously. When finished, add Sheet Keynotes, drag them to this Sheet and then update the Sheet Keynote Legend. The Sheet Keynotes will renumber appropriately to create a single legend that incorporates all of the details with Sheet Keynotes displayed across the entire Sheet. Each Sheet will be unique; however, the Keynote List is compiled on a sheet-by-sheet basis.

Reference Keynote Legend

5. On the Project Navigator palette, click the Sheets tab.
6. In the *Architectural > Elevations* Sub Set, double-click the *A-202 Elevations* Sheet to open it.
7. On the Annotation tool palette, click the Reference Keynote Legend tool.
8. At the "Select keynotes to include in the keynote legend" prompt, make a window around all Reference Keynotes and then press ENTER.

   This can be done from Paper Space *without* making the Viewport active.
9. At the "Insertion point of table" prompt, click a point on the Sheet to place the Table (see Figure 17.45).

TIP

After selecting the Keynotes to include in the legend, right-click and choose Sheets. A Worksheet will appear in which you can select several or all of your Sheets to include in the Legend.

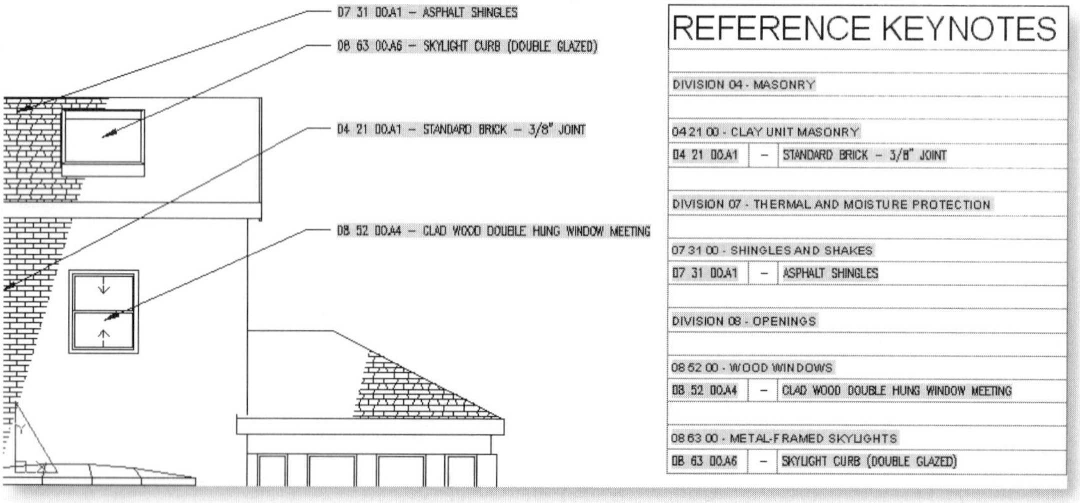

FIGURE 17.45 *Place a Reference Keynotes Legend*

10. Repeat for any of the other Sheets that have Keynotes.
11. Save and close all files.

Insert a Sheet List

We have one more Table to insert (or rather update). At this point, we are nearing the end of the book and have added many Views and Sheets since starting our two projects back in Chapter 5. From the Sheet Set, we can insert a Sheet List. In Chapter 5, we did this. However, it is time to update that list to reflect the new Sheets that have been added to the project.

12. On the Project Navigator palette, click the Sheets tab.
13. In the General Sub Set, double-click the *G-100 Cover Sheet* to open it.
14. Right-click on the Sheet List in the lower right corner of the Sheet and choose **Update Sheet List Table**.

    The Table will update to reflect the added Sheets.

The object that is placed here is an AutoCAD Table object. It is a style-based object similar to the type of table that you might add in Microsoft Word. The style used here is generated automatically for the Sheet Index and Keynote Legends. While this object at first appears similar to an ACA Schedule Table as covered in Chapter 15, it is not the same type of object, nor does it share the same features. Tables do not interface with Property Sets, nor do they use ACA Display Control. They can have Field codes inserted within their cells. ACA Schedule Tables cannot. So while these two objects are similar in use and function, each has unique uses.

15. If you wish, follow the steps in Chapter 5 and plot the set.
16. Save and close all residential project files.

CHALLENGE EXERCISE

Section III has introduced us to Tags and Dimensions in Chapter 14; Schedules, Property Sets, Tags and Display Themes in Chapter 15; Callouts, Sections and Elevations in Chapter 16; and finally Details, Keynotes and Legends here in Chapter 17. While presented individually across four chapters, all of these tools work together to give us a complete Construction Documents package. In this exercise, we will use several of the tools from each of these chapters to create an enlarged plan detail of the commercial project.

Load the Commercial Project

1. From the File menu, choose **Project Browser**.
2. Click to open the folder list and choose your *C:* drive.
3. Double-click on the *MasterACA 2010* folder, then on the *Chapter17* folder.

   One or two commercial Projects will be listed: *17 Commercial* and/or *17 Commercial Metric.*
4. Double-click *17 Commercial* if you wish to work in Imperial units. Double-click *17 Commercial Metric* if you wish to work in Metric units. (You can also right-click on it and choose **Set Current Project**.) Then click Close in the Project Browser.

NOTE

Important: If a message appears asking you to repath the project, click the "Repath the project now" option. Refer to the "Repathing Projects" topic in the Preface for more information.

Create a Plan Detail Using a Callout

The first step in our process is to create a plan view detail. We can use the same Callout routine that we used at the start of this chapter for this purpose.

5. On the Project Navigator, click the Views tab, and then double-click *A-FP01* to open it.

This is the First Floor Plan View file. We will create a Callout around the Core area in this file.

6. Zoom in on the building core.
7. On the Callouts tool palette, click the Detail Boundary B tool.

   If you do not see this palette or tool, right-click the Tool Palettes title bar and choose **Document** (to load the Documentation Tool Palette Group) and then click the Callouts tab.
8. At the "Specify one corner of detail box" click just above and to the left of the Stair tower.

9. At the "Specify opposite corner of detail box" prompt, click a point below and to the right of the Men's Restroom.

   Click both points close to but outside of the masonry Walls.
10. At the "Specify first point of leader line on boundary" prompt, click a point to the left of the boundary and then press ENTER (see Figure 17.46).

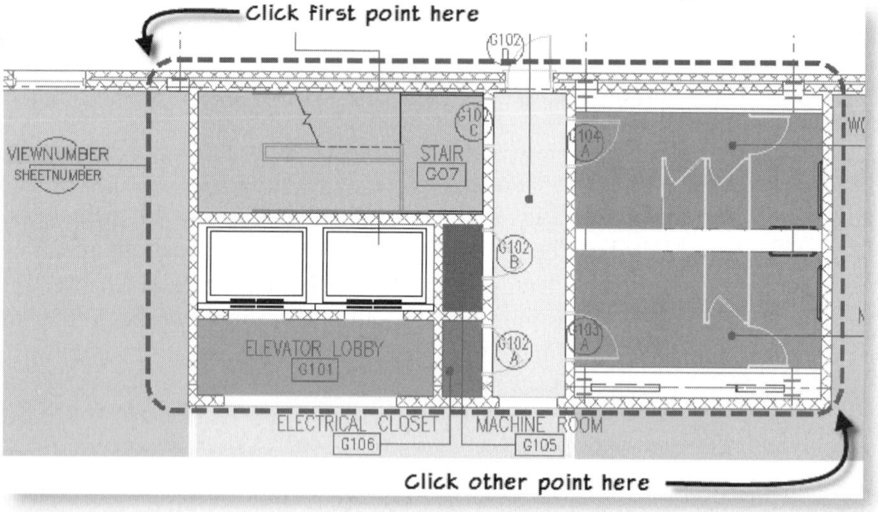

FIGURE 17.46 *Create a Detail Boundary around the Core area*

11. In the Place Callout worksheet, type **Enlarged Core Plan** for the New Model Space View Name.
12. At the bottom of the worksheet, remove the check mark from the Generate Section/Elevation checkbox.
13. Change the Scale to **1/4"=1'-0"** [**1:50**].
14. In the Create in area, click the New View Drawing icon (see Figure 17.47).

FIGURE 17.47 *Deselect "Generate Section/Elevation" to create an Xclipped Plan View file*

The Add Detail View Wizard will appear. This is identical to the other View Wizards that we have seen; however, it uses different default settings. (You can also optionally assign a different template to Detail Views in the Project's Properties.)

15. In the Add Detail View wizard, type **A-EP01** for the Name and **Architectural Enlarged Floor Plans** for the Description, and then click Next.
16. On the Context page, the Detail View wizard has selected the First Floor to match the current file. Click Next.
17. On the Content page, be sure that all Constructs are selected and then click Finish.

The routine is almost complete and a polyline boundary surrounding the designated area has appeared on the plan. The last prompt requests the corners of the Model Space View. When you clear the "Generate Section/Elevation" checkbox, you get a plan detail view in which all XREFs are clipped to the shape of the Callout boundary. However, you will likely want an area larger than this as a Model Space View so that the Viewport of this enlarged plan has enough room for notes, dimensions and a title mark.

18. At the "Specify first corner for model space view" prompt, click a point above and to the left of the Callout Boundary allowing plenty of room on both sides.
19. At the "Specify opposite corner for model space view" prompt, click a point down and to the right of the Callout Boundary again allowing plenty of room on both sides (see Figure 17.48).

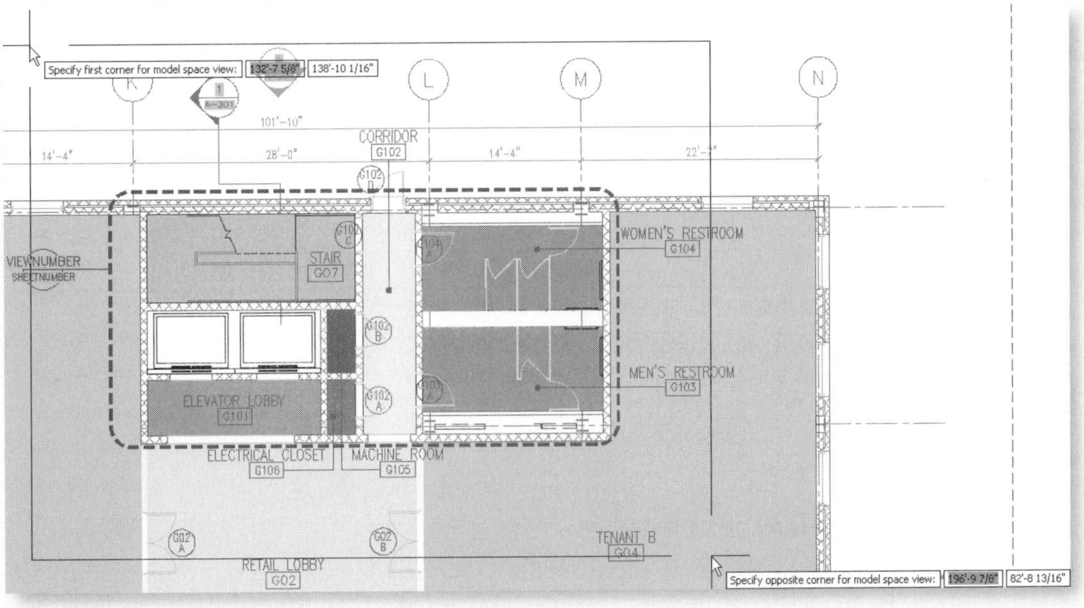

FIGURE 17.48 *Create a Detail Boundary around the Core area*

20. On the Views tab of Project Navigator, double-click to open *A-EP01*.
21. Manually drag in the *Elevators* file from the *Elements* folder on the Constructs tab.

Notice that the XREFs here have been clipped to the shape indicated by the Callout Boundary. Also note that like the other Callouts, this one created a title mark beneath the plan area. The drawing is ready to receive embellishment. Use the techniques covered in this and the previous three chapters to add Tags, Dimensions, Elevation and Section Callouts and Keynotes. You can also add Schedules or Display Themes if you wish. You might want to select the Grid XREF and, on the External Reference contextual ribbon tab, on the Clipping panel, choose the ***Create Clipping Boundary*** tool and adjust the Clip so that some of the column bubbles show. When you are finished, drag the View to a new Sheet. You can find additional Tags and Annotation routines in the Content Browser in the *Documentation Tool Catalog – Imperial* [*Documentation Tool Catalog – Metric*] catalog (see Figure 17.49).

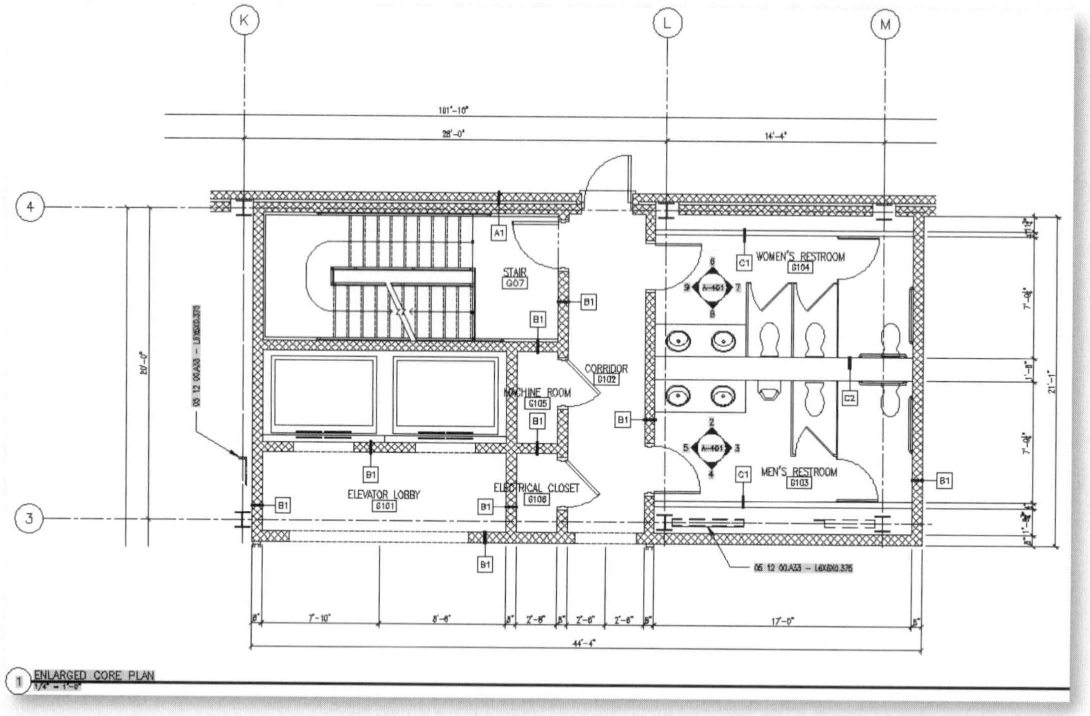

FIGURE 17.49 *Add annotation to the enlarged Core Plan*

22. Save and close all commercial project files. Plot the set if you wish.

ADDITIONAL EXERCISES

There are certainly plenty more details to be drawn in both of our projects. Feel free to create additional details, keynotes and legends. Additional exercises have been provided in Appendix A. In Appendix A, you will find exercises to add additional Sections and Elevations in the Commercial Project, as well as further refine those created here in the Residential Project (see Figure 17.50). It is not necessary that you complete these exercises to begin the next chapter, they are provided to enhance your learning experience. Completed projects for each of the exercises have been provided in the *Chapter17/Complete* folder.

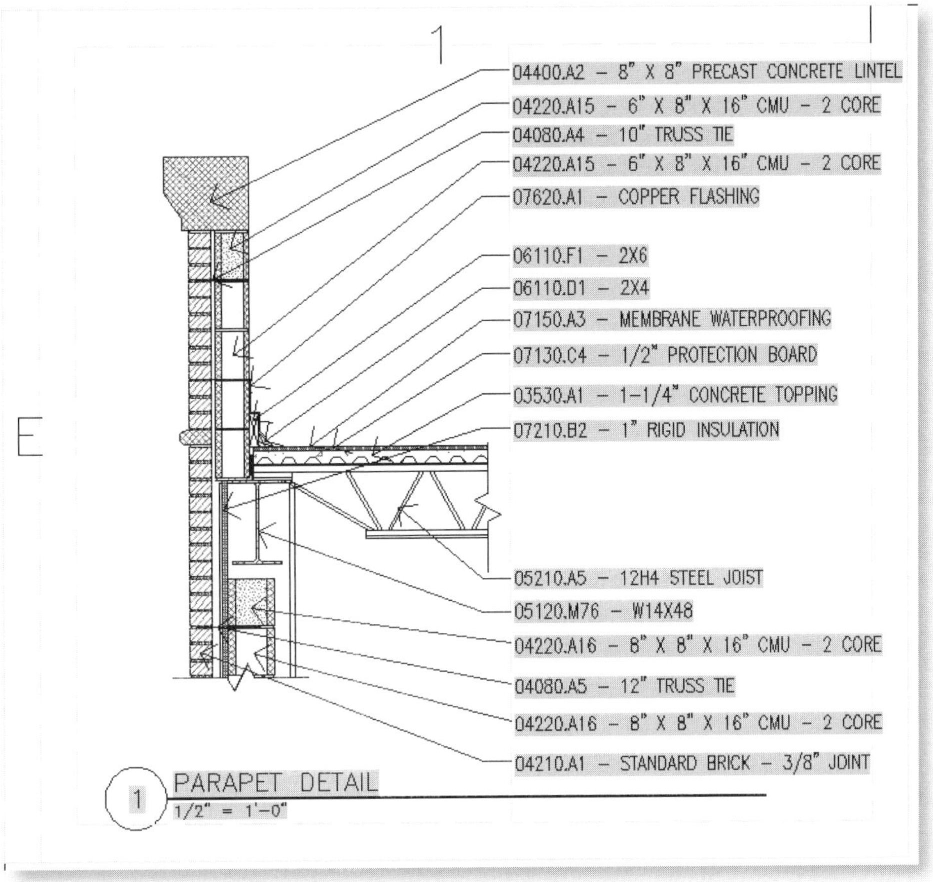

FIGURE 17.50 *Additional Exercises in Appendix A—Add Details*

SUMMARY

- Details in ACA are created from a series of predefined components saved in a central database file.
- Use Callouts to designate a region of the Model that you wish to Detail.
- The Callout tools will create a guideline "sketch" 2D Section/Elevation object on top of which you can draft your detail.
- Details with break lines can be created from several smaller 2D Section/Elevation objects lined up one on top of the other.
- The Detailing tool palettes contain a wide variety of preconfigured Detail Components.
- Use the Detail Component Manager to access the complete database of Detail Components.
- New sizes can easily be added to the database directly within the Detail Component Manager.
- Use Add Selected and Replace Selected to progressively refine details.
- AEC Modify Tools offer the ability to customize the shape of any standard Detail Component.
- Keynotes can be assigned to object styles and Material Definitions.

- The Keynote Assignments made within the model carry through to the linework and hatching on the 2D Section/Elevation objects.
- Reference Keynotes can include a Key, a Note or both.
- Sheet Keynotes are enumerated at the time that they are added to a Sheet and a Sheet Keynote Legend is added.
- Keynote Legends and Drawing List Tables can be added to automatically display an inventory of Keynotes and/or Sheets in the Sheet Set.

CHAPTER

18

Plotting and Publishing

INTRODUCTION

Conceptually, plotting in AutoCAD Architecture is no more difficult than printing a document from any other computer program. The major difference lies in the complexity of the data being sent to the printer. The major contrast between AutoCAD plotting and printing in other software applications is the use of "Plot Style Tables." The data flow for plotting AutoCAD objects is as follows: Objects are drawn and assigned properties (Layer, Color, Linetype, Lineweight and Plot Style). This object data interacts with the Plot Style Table and is then sent to the plotter. When AutoCAD entities interact with a Plot Style Table, the result of the interaction often modifies the look of the objects in the final plot. This is because the Plot Style Table can optionally change an object's properties at the time of printing. For example, colored lines onscreen become pure black when printing. There is typically no need to do this in other Windows applications.

You can preview the result of this interaction of parts with great accuracy before committing to final plot in a "paper space layout." This gives you much better control over the entire process. If you don't take advantage of this, what you see onscreen may not be what you see in print.

With AutoCAD Architecture objects, there are a few more interactions happening before the data hits the plotter. As we have seen throughout this text, all AEC objects have one or more Display Representations. It is the Display Representation that actually determines what graphical entities are drawn to the screen and sent to the plotter. Display Representations also are responsible for the assignment of all AutoCAD properties like Color, Layer and Plot Style. If you want to print a plan, the Display Representation sends 2D plan graphics; if you want a model, it sends 3D. Therefore, with AEC objects, the flow is as follows: the Display Representation determines the Object components that will be drawn; it then assigns properties to each of these components; the assigned properties interact with the Plot Style Table; and the result is sent to the plotter.

Understanding how this data flow works can help achieve more successful plots. It will certainly aid you in troubleshooting plotting problems. Plotting troubles with AutoCAD entities can therefore be addressed most often in layers or plot style tables. For AEC objects, look to the Display Representation first, then the Layers and/or Plot Style Tables.

OBJECTIVES

This chapter gives an overview of the plotting process. We will look at Paper Space Layouts, Page Setup, Plot Style Tables, Sheet Sets, eTransmit, Transmittal Setups, Plotting, Publishing and 3D DWF Export. The following topics will be explored:

- Understand data flow in Plotting.
- Understand Layouts.
- Work with Page Setup Manager.
- Transmit Sheet Sets.
- Publish construction documents.
- Sheet Sets.
- 3D DWF Output.

SHEET FILES

A "Sheet File" is an ACA drawing configured specifically for plotting purposes. The goal is to create a "ready-to-plot" drawing file that can be opened and printed without need for detailed configuration or checking. We have created several Sheets throughout this book. XREFs and Paper Space Layouts are used to create sheet files. Several sheet files can be gathered together and organized into "Sheet Sets." Sheet Sets are fully incorporated into the ACA Project Navigator on the Sheets tab. Several sheet files were built to generate our cartoon set at the beginning of this book. (Review Chapter 5 for complete information on Sheet files.) We have continued to add additional sheets to both projects with each successive chapter.

Install the CD Files and Load the Current Project

If you have already installed all of the files from the CD, simply skip down to step 3 below to make the project active. If you need to install the CD files, start at step 1.

1. If you have not already done so, install the dataset files located on the Mastering AutoCAD Architecture 2010 CD-ROM.

   Refer to "Files Included on the CD-ROM" in the Preface for information on installing the sample files included on the CD.
2. Launch AutoCAD Architecture 2010 from the desktop icon created in Chapter 3.

If you did not create a custom icon, you might want to review "Create a New Profile" and "Create a Desktop Shortcut" in Chapter 3. Creating the custom desktop icon is not essential; however, it makes loading the custom profile easier.

3. From the Quick Access Toolbar (QAT), choose the ***Project Browser*** tool.
4. Click to open the folder list and choose your *C:* drive.
5. Double-click on the *MasterACA 2010* folder, then on the *Chapter18* folder.

   One or two commercial Projects will be listed: *18 Commercial* and/or *18 Commercial Metric*.
6. Double-click *18 Commercial* if you wish to work in Imperial units. Double-click *18 Commercial Metric* if you wish to work in Metric units. (You can also right-click on it and choose **Set Current Project**.) Then click Close in the Project Browser.

IMPORTANT

If a message appears asking you to repath the project, click the "Repath the project now option. Refer to the "Repathing Projects" heading in the Preface for more information.

LAYOUTS

Layouts provide the means to emulate a sheet of paper and the composition of all its components organized to scale. The sheet is typically set up to facilitate plotting. The ACA drawing environment consists of model space and paper space. Model space emulates "real space." It is a full-scale, full-size environment without physical limit. The model space environment is 3D, but the actual model needn't be. Any drawing created in this environment is referred to as a "model," regardless of whether it is two-dimensional or three-dimensional. In contrast, paper space is an environment made up of one or more "paper space layouts," or simply layouts. A layout is a "2D only" drawing environment. Typically, a layout is used to organize the various components that comprise the printed sheet. These often include a title block, general notes and one or more Viewport objects. The viewports are used to show the model from various vantage points and at specific architectural scales. In this capacity, a layout is a page layout/plotting tool. The main goal is to provide very accurate preview capabilities, which eliminate the need to generate endless "test" plots. This helps save paper, time and money.

- Access layouts by clicking the icon on the status bar (or if you displayed them, the tabs at the bottom of the screen).
- Create a new layout from Quick View Layouts or, from the right-click menu on one of the existing layout tabs, choose **New layout** or **From template**. To display the layout tabs, right-click the layout icon on the Application status bar (see Figure 18.1).

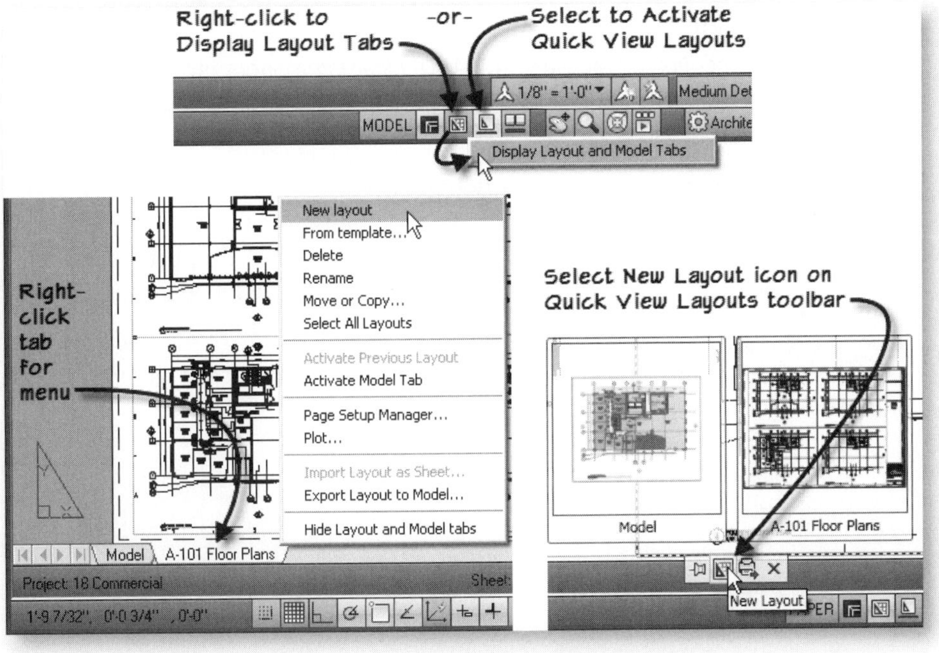

FIGURE 18.1 *New Layout: Display Layout Tabs and right-click for menu or activate Quick View Layouts*

WORKING LAYOUTS

It is also possible to set up "working" layouts, where the model is viewed in a particular Display/Layer Configuration conducive to the task at hand. One of the advantages of this approach is that you can work in the drawing in a format that is very similar to the way it will appear when plotted (see the "Manipulating Door and Window Display" topic in Chapter 11 for an example). The template files used to generate Elements, Constructs and Views in ACA 2010 all contain a Work layout tab. To be most effective, you should set a scale to the viewports in this layout and lock them while you work. You can even edit the Page Setup to "Display Plot Styles" in the layout (which usually makes the drawing appear in black and white). This is most effective when your AutoCAD background color is set to White, so that lines appear black. There is also the "Maximize Viewport" icon that allows you to temporarily fill the screen with the contents of a particular viewport. The focus of this chapter is plotting, so we will not look further at this technique, but you are encouraged to experiment with it on your own.

PAGE SETUP MANAGER

Like all Windows applications, ACA uses Page Setup to configure the printer, page size, scale and other output settings. Page Setup in ACA has some unique features that other Windows programs do not share. For instance, a Page Setup configuration in ACA can be saved and recalled later. Page Setup configurations are created, edited and deleted from the Page Setup Manager dialog. Let's look at some of the key features of Page Setup.

Explore Page Setup

1. On the Project Navigator, open the *A-101 Floor Plans* Sheet file.

   This is the Sheet file generated in Chapter 5 containing all of the floor plans for the Commercial Project.

As you may recall, this Sheet file XREFs floor plan View files in model space and has four viewports in the Plot Layout. Each viewport is configured to "look" at just one of the plans. This occurred automatically when we dragged and dropped the various floor plan View files into the Sheet. (Unique layers for each XREF were added automatically by ACA to accommodate the process.)

2. From the Application Menu, choose **Print > Page Setup** (see Figure 18.2).

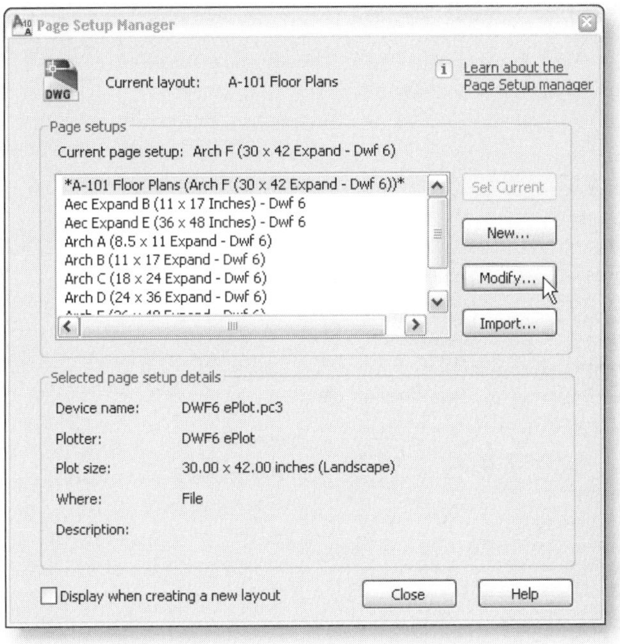

FIGURE 18.2 *The Page Setup Manager dialog*

In this dialog are listed all of the Page Setups saved in the current drawing. The template file used to create this Sheet is responsible for adding all of the Page Setups we see here.

You might want to consider creating your own Named Page Setup configurations. You can add them to your office standard Sheet template file. They will then appear in addition to or in place of the Page Setups shown in Figure 18.2. Making a Page Setup active will set all of the plotting settings automatically. This can be a great way to standardize plotting settings.

The current Page Setup: Arch F (30 × 42 Expand – Dwf 6) [ISO A0 (841 × 1189 Expand – Dwf 6)] is listed at the top and selected in the list.

3. Be sure that Arch F (30 × 42 Expand - Dwf 6) [ISO A0 (841 × 1189 Expand - Dwf 6)] is selected and then click the Modify button (see Figure 18.2).

Outlined here is a brief explanation of each setting in the Page Setup dialog box. You can change any of the settings you wish to meet your specific needs. As a general rule of thumb, move through the dialog on the left first, moving top to bottom, then make any adjustments on the right. Refer to Figure 18.3 as you work through each description.

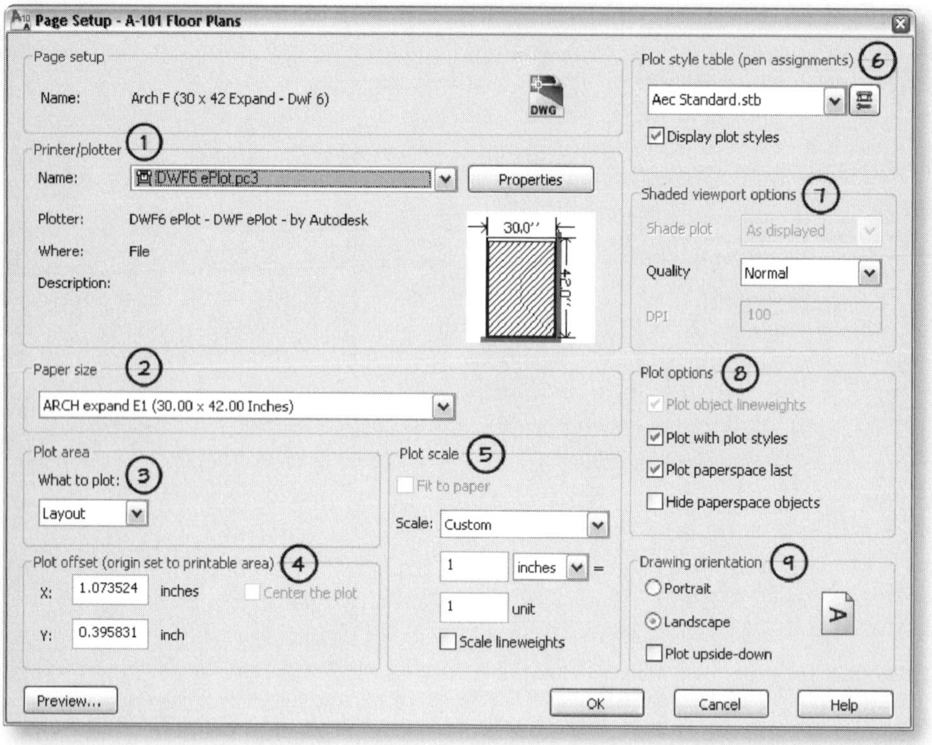

FIGURE 18.3 *The Page Setup dialog*

1. Printer/Plotter

- **Name**—All plotters available on your system will be listed here. This list often includes all of the printers in the *Windows Printers* folder as well. Windows Printers have a small printer icon next to them, while AutoCAD plotters have a small plotter icon.
- **Properties**—This button gives access to hardware settings in the printer/plotter driver. You can optionally save your changes to a new plotter configuration file (*.pc3*).

2. Paper size

- Choose from a list of standard sheet sizes. This list is unique to each plot device. Therefore, it is critical that you choose your plotter/printer first.

3. Plot area (What to plot list)

- **Layout**—Most of the time you should choose Layout as the Plot area. This setting prints the entire Layout area as defined by the paper size. This guarantees an exact fit to the paper. This setting is recommended.
- **Extents**—Sets the print area to the outer edge of the actual Drawing objects.
- **Display**—Sets the print area to the view currently onscreen.
- **View**—Available if Named Views have been created in the drawing. Drawing Management creates a Named View of each drawing dragged to the Sheet.
- **Window**—Use the mouse and pick a rectangular print area in the drawing.

4. Plot offset (origin set to printable area)

- **X and Y**—Shift the plot relative to the lower left corner of the paper.

5. Plot scale

- **Scale**—Long list of predefined plotting scales.

NOTE

Most often, you will choose 1:1 (shown as 1'-0" = 1'-0" in Imperial) as the plot scale when working from a layout. This is because drawings have already been scaled in the viewports. If you are plotting from the Model tab, choose the appropriate scale here.

- **Custom**—Type a scale factor ratio if the scale you wish to use is not in the list.
- **Scale lineweights**—Adjust the thickness of the lineweights relative to the scale chosen. This is very useful for half-size plots.

6. Plot style table (pen assignments)

- Drop-down list includes all of the Plot Style Tables available on your system. There are two types of Plot Style Tables: Named and Color Dependent. Drawings can use only one type at a time. Check with your CAD support personnel for the type your firm uses. Check the online help for complete information on the differences between the types. ACA 2010 ships with Named Plot Styles set as the default. The precise table used was changed in ACA 2008; see the "Plot Style Tables" topic below for more information.
- **Edit icon**—This icon loads the Plot Style Table Editor with the current Plot Style loaded for editing. When you save your changes in the Plot Style Editor, you will be returned to Page Setup.
- **Display plot styles**—With this function turned on (check mark in the box), the layout becomes a live preview of the drawing as it will actually appear when plotted. This setting used in conjunction with Lineweight display and properly scaled viewports is highly recommended.

7. Shaded viewport options

- **Shade plot**—With this option, you can plot the image shaded as it appears in the drawing, using Hidden, Shaded or Gouraud Shaded.
- **Quality**—Several preset qualities from Draft to High quality are available for shaded plotting. The higher the quality, the longer it will take to plot.
- **DPI**—If you choose "Custom" quality, you can set any DPI (Dots Per Inch) that you wish for plotting shaded viewports.

8. Plot options

- **Plot with lineweights**—Use this option to toggle on and off lineweights where available.
- **Plot with plot styles**—Check this to use the settings in the Plot Style Table. Recommended.
- **Plot paperspace last**—Check this to make sure paper space objects are not concealed by model space objects. Recommended.
- **Hide objects**—Use if the drawing is 3D to create a hidden line rendering. (If you are plotting 3D from a layout, use the Hideplot feature of the viewport instead.)

9. Drawing orientation

- **Portrait**—Sheet-oriented short side horizontal.
- **Landscape**—Sheet oriented long side horizontal.
- **Plot upside-down**—Image rotated 180° on the sheet.

10. Click the Preview button to get an onscreen plot preview of the current drawing.

11. Right-click and choose Exit to leave the Plot Preview and return to the Page Setup dialog.
12. Click OK to accept any changes and return to the Page Setup Manager.

    If you are finished in the Page Setup Manager, click the Close button, otherwise, select a different Page Setup to Modify, click New to create a New Page Setup, or click Import to browse to another drawing and import its Page Setups.

VIEWPORTS

Viewports are used to crop out sections of the building model and present them on the layout sheet. On the View ribbon tab, use the tools on the Viewports panel to manually create viewports of varying sizes and shapes. Entities such as closed polylines and circles can be converted to viewports. Use the Properties palette to assign a scale to the viewport. Each viewport can have its own Scale, Layer and Display Configuration settings. If you are using the Project Management features of AutoCAD Architecture as we have throughout this book, Viewports are created for you and automatically scaled properly when you drag a View file or a Model Space View saved within a View file (on the Views tab of the Project Navigator) onto a Sheet file. This is the recommended way to set up Sheet files and Viewports (see Chapter 5 for more information).

PLOT STYLE TABLES

Plot Style Tables can assign a variety of plotting attributes, such as color, half tone, lineweight and join and end styles to the final plotted linework in your drawings. Join and end style, and in some cases halftone, must be set in the Plot Style Table. Settings such as Lineweight and Linetype can (and often should) be set in the drawing instead of the Plot Style. The specific approach varies from office to office. There are two types of Plot Style Table: Named Plot Style Tables (*.stb*) and Color Dependent Plot Style Tables (*.ctb*). Named Plot Style Tables are user defined and can be assigned ByLayer, within Display Representations, or directly to individual objects. Named Plot Styles are the ACA 2010 default and have been used throughout this book. This varies from traditional AutoCAD usage where Color Dependent Plot Style Tables are more commonly used. A Color Dependent Plot Style Table assigns plotting attributes to objects based on their color as they are printing. In other words, a permanent mapping exists between each of the 255 AutoCAD colors and a Plot Style within the Color Dependent Plot Style Table.

NOTE

The Plot Style Table used by default in AutoCAD Architecture 2010 and the dataset in this book is the *AEC Standard.stb* plot style table. While every attempt has been made to incorporate this superior plot style table into the datasets used in this book and its accompanying CD-ROM, in some cases you might find the inclusion of legacy plot styles used by the 2004–2006 versions of the software. Please see the "Out-of-the-Box Named Plot Style Tables" topic in the Preface for further explanation and a remedy for this situation.

Edit a Plot Style Table

1. Return to Page Setup Manager (Application Menu, **Print > Page Setup**), modify the current Page Setup and then click the Edit icon next to the Plot style table list.

- Click the Form View tab (see Figure 18.4).

Plot styles are listed on the left. They are named for the function they serve. For instance, Full Saturation uses Black ink and the Lineweight assigned in the drawing. In the Properties area, you can configure the properties listed below for the selected Plot Style on the left. (Select and configure multiple entries with the SHIFT and CTRL keys.)

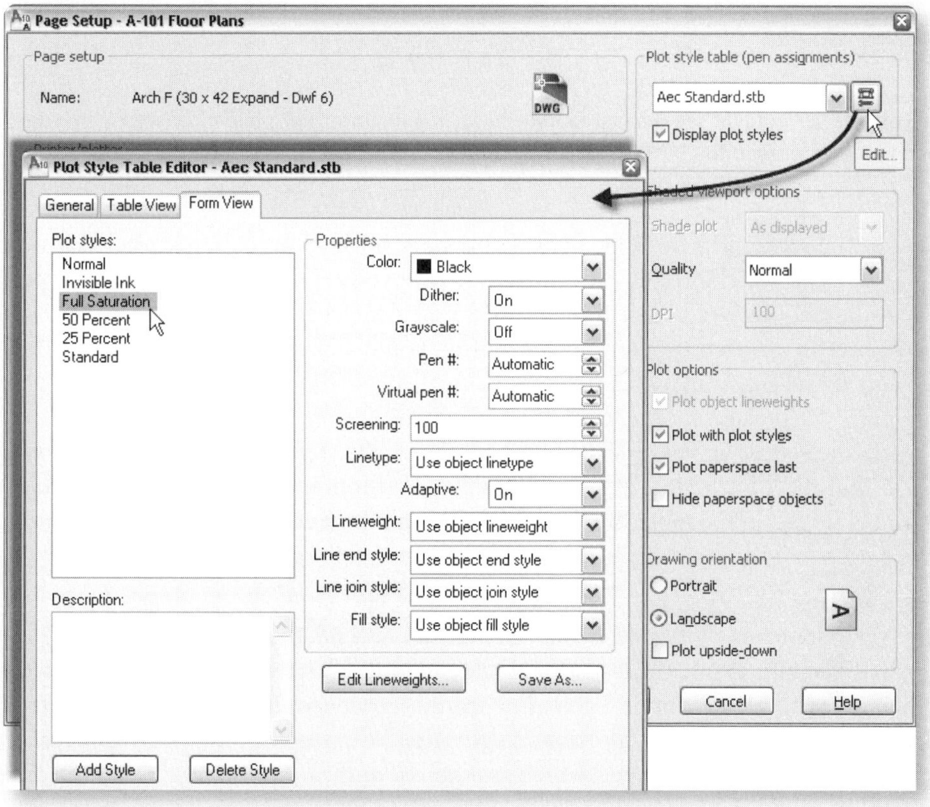

FIGURE 18.4 *The Plot Style Table Editor*

The Plot Style Table can be used to affect the following printing attributes:

- **Color**—Color of the ink used to plot items of this style.
- **Dither**—Enables the process of simulating colors unavailable on your plot device by mixing colors that are available.
- **Grayscale**—Translates the value of the color to an equivalent shade of gray.
- **Pen #**—For pen plotters, assigns the pen to use.
- **Virtual pen #**—For plotters with pen plotter emulation, assigns the pen to use.
- **Screening**—Uses a lower intensity of ink expressed in a percentage from 0 to 100. 100 is full ink, 0 is no ink.
- **Linetype**—Assign hardware linetypes if your plotter supports them.
- **Adaptive**—Works with the hardware linetypes to make the linetype wrap around corners.
- **Lineweight**—Overrides the Lineweight property in the drawing.
- **Line end style**—Choose from a list of end shapes.
- **Line join style**—Choose from a list of corner conditions.
- **Fill style**—Choose from a list of patterns.

If you use Color-based plotting instead, you will have all of the same settings, but instead, there will be 255 colors listed on the left. You cannot add to, delete from or rename the list. It is fixed.

TIP

If you want to convert a Named Plot Style drawing to Color Dependent or vice versa, use the `CONVERTPSTYLES` command at the Command Line.

CAD MANAGER NOTE

If you use an outside service bureau to manage your plotting, please consult with your vendor to determine the best setup parameters for plotting.

Most of the settings in the Plot Style Table have the option to "Use object" setting. For instance, if you wanted to use **AutoCAD linetypes** instead of hardware linetypes, you would choose Use object linetype and not turn on Adaptive. For construction documents on a typical modern ink jet plotter, you will use Plot Style Tables to force all colors to use Black ink when plotting. Some firms set lineweights in the drawing as a property of the layers; others use the lineweight option in the Plot Style Table to override the setting in the drawing. Whichever method your firm uses, be sure you realize that the Plot Style Table gets final "say." If a lineweight is assigned both in the drawing and in the table, the Plot Style Table's lineweight will win.

AEC Standard Plot Style Table (ACA 2010 Default)

The AEC Standard Plot Style Table—*AEC Standard.stb* is the AutoCAD Architecture 2010 default. While the last several releases of ACA have used named plot styles as their default, this Plot Style Table, first introduced in the 2008 release, represents a departure from the previous strategy. In the AEC Standard Plot Style Table, there are only six plot styles: Normal, which is required and cannot be modified, and five others that are described here:

- **Full Saturation**—This plot style changes the color of objects to black ink and plots at 100% screening or full intensity. This is the most common plot style used for all of the out-of-the-box content.
- **50 Percent**—This plot style changes the color of objects to black ink and plots at 50% screening.
- **25 Percent**—This plot style changes the color of objects to black ink and plots at 25% screening.
- **Invisible Ink**—This is another way to achieve a "No-Plot" setting. Objects assigned to Invisible Ink will plot at 0% screening, which will make them invisible.
- **Standard** - This plot style is a copy of the Normal plot style, and can be used for full intensity color plotting. In the 2004 and 2005 releases, this plot style was set to a color of Cyan and a fixed lineweight of 0.18 mm. It was assigned to non-plotting layers and served as a warning in plot previews that a layer that was not meant to be plotted had been changed to plotting.

The "Out-of-the-Box Named Plot Style Tables" topic in the preface notes that while this Plot Style Table is the ACA 2010 default, some of the datasets provided with the book have been authored with previous releases. Therefore, some of the objects or drawings might reference another Plot Style Table named "AIA Standard." This Plot Style Table is also included out-of-the-box with AutoCAD Architecture.

It follows a slightly different strategy than the AEC Standard Table. The next topic discusses this "legacy" Plot Style Table.

The AEC Standard Plot Style Table represents a simpler strategy than was used in the previous releases. Basically, all that the Plot Style Table is responsible for is ensuring that plots use black ink and determining whether the effect should be screened. This means that in ACA 2010, *all* lineweights are assigned directly in the drawing by either Display Control settings or Layers. The author agrees that this is a superior approach to previous releases, and it is recommended for all new projects created in AutoCAD Architecture 2010. However, if you are upgrading from a release that used the AIA Standard Plot Style Table (2004, 2005, 2006 or 2007), you may experience difficulties in migrating to this new Plot Style Table. There are two solutions: edit all of your drawings and custom content to utilize the new plot styles outlined above or edit your default Plot Style Table to include both the old and new plot styles. Please note that all AEC Content and Styles included with AutoCAD Architecture 2010 already utilize the new plot styles of Full Saturation, 50 Percent and 25 Percent. You do *not* have to edit any out-of-the-box content to use the AEC Standard Plot Style Table. The issue is in any existing drawings created in a pre-2008 release that you open in ACA 2010. These will continue to utilize and look for the plot styles included in the AIA Standard Plot Style Table (see next page). Rest assured that endeavoring to perform such modifications is no small undertaking. Therefore, while theoretically possible, the simpler approach is to edit the AEC Standard Plot Style Table and add the needed plot styles from AIA Standard (or vice versa). An example of this has been provided in the *MasterACA 2010\Plot Styles* folder of the files installed from the Mastering AutoCAD Architecture 2010 CD-ROM (see Figure 18.5).

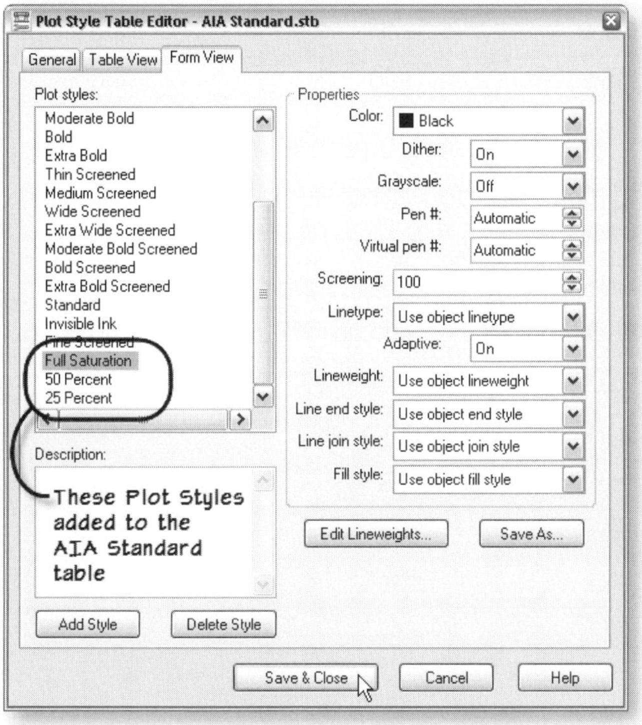

FIGURE 18.5 *A modified version of AIA Standard.stb Plot Style Table including all the plot styles from the AEC Standard.stb Plot Style Table*

AIA Standard Plot Style Table (ACA 2004, 2005, 2006 and 2007 Default)

The releases of AutoCAD Architecture prior to 2008 (under the name Autodesk Architectural Desktop) used the *AIA Standard.stb* Plot Style Table as the default. This Plot Style Table is still included in the *Plot Styles* folder with ACA and is discussed here because it may be in use in your firm if you are upgrading from one of those releases. There are two basic groups of styles in this table: The Black ink styles and the Screened styles. Each group contains a collection of Lineweights configured according to the recommendations of the U.S. National CAD Standard (see Table 18.1). This is the fundamental difference between the two tables showcased here: AIA uses embedded lineweights and AEC does not.

TABLE 18.1 *Plot Style Settings for AIA Standard.stb*

Plot Style	Color	Lineweight	Screening
Normal	Use object color	Use object lineweight	100
Fine	Black	0.18	100
Thin	Black	0.25	100
Medium	Black	0.35	100
Wide	Black	0.50	100
Extra Wide	Black	0.70	100
Moderate Bold	Black	1.00	100
Bold	Black	1.40	100
Extra Bold	Black	2.00	100
Thin Screened	Black	0.25	50
Medium Screened	Black	0.35	50
Wide Screened	Black	0.50	50
Extra Wide Screened	Black	0.70	50
Moderate Bold Screened	Black	1.00	50
Bold Screened	Black	1.40	50
Extra Bold Screened	Black	2.00	50
Standard	Use object color	0.18	100
Invisible Ink	Cyan	Use object lineweight	0
Fine Screened	Black	0.18	50

- Click Cancel to close the Plot Style Table Editor without saving.
- Click OK to close the Page Setup dialog and then click Close to dismiss the Page Setup Manager.

If you wish to use the modified version of AIA Standard included with this book and noted above, please copy it to your *Plot Styles* folder on your computer or network. If you work in a multiperson firm, talk to your network administrator or CAD manager before you proceed to be sure that you are adhering to established company standards.

PLOTTING

If you wish to plot a single drawing file, you can use the Plot command by selecting **Print** on the Application Menu. The dialog that appears is nearly identical to the Page Setup dialog pictured in Figure 18.3. The only difference is that the right side is hidden from view. You can expand the right side with the small icon at the bottom right corner of the plot dialog. To see this, choose **Print** from the Application Menu (see Figure 18.6).

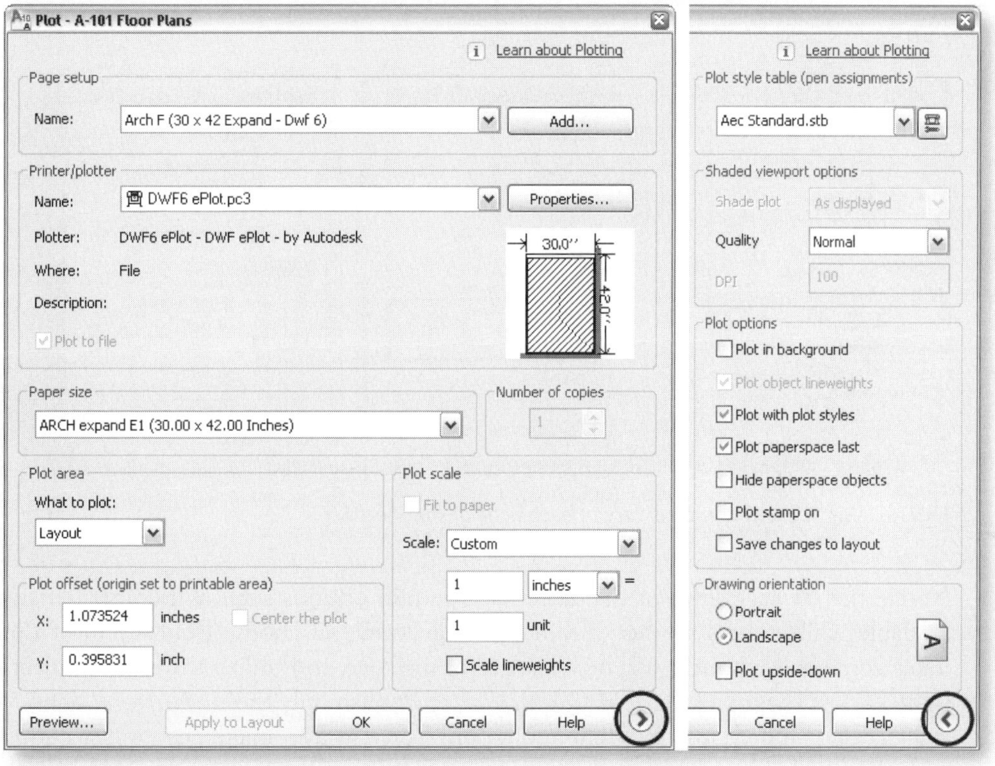

FIGURE 18.6 *The Plot dialog is nearly identical to the Page Setup dialog*

Simply choose a Page Setup from the list at the top, verify and modify any settings as required and then click OK to plot. Although drawings can be printed one at a time this way, it is much more effective to "Publish" drawings from your Sheet Set contained in Project Navigator. You will get much more control and reliability.

PUBLISH A SHEET SET

Our drawing set has come a long way since we first plotted it in Chapter 5. Let's review that process now and explore some of the many features available on the Sheet tab for publishing drawing sets.

- On the Project Navigator, click the Sheets tab.

As we have seen already, the Sheets tab incorporates the AutoCAD Sheet Set functionality. A Sheet Set gathers a collection of drawing Layouts for plotting. The Sheet Set can be organized into Subsets. The order of the drawings as they appear in the Sheet Set will be the order in which they will list when adding a Sheet List (see Chapter 5) and the order in which they will plot. Using the functions inherent to the Sheet Set, you can print the entire set of project drawings, or any subset you wish without the need to open and plot each one individually. Let's take a look at what functions are available at each level of the Sheet Set.

- On the Project Navigator, on the Sheets tab, right-click the *MACA Commercial* Sheet Set node at the top of the list (see the left side of Figure 18.7).
- On the Project Navigator, on the Sheets tab, right-click any Subset, such as Architectural (see the middle of Figure 18.7).
- On the Project Navigator, on the Sheets tab, right-click any Sheet, such as *A-100 Site Plan* (see the right side of Figure 18.7).

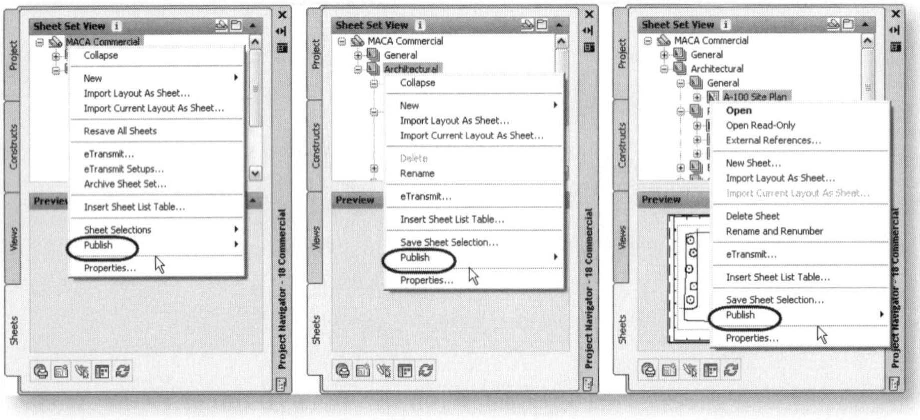

FIGURE 18.7 *Right-click menus vary at each node of the Sheet Set*

Notice that at each level of the Sheet Set, certain options such as Publish remain available while others are not. From whatever level you choose Publish, all of the items contained within it will be chosen. For instance, to Publish the entire project, right-click at the top on *MACA Commercial*; to Publish only the *Architectural* Subset, right-click it and choose **Publish** and so on. You can also make custom selections with the SHIFT and CTRL keys. For instance, let's say that for a Design Development submission, you only need the Plans and Elevations, not the Site, nor any Details.

Publish a Sheet Set to DWF

1. Select the *Architectural – Plans* subset, hold down the CTRL key and then click the *Architectural – Elevations* subset.

Once you have a custom Selection, you can right-click to access the Publish and other options, or you can save the selection for future retrieval. Right-click the *MACA Commercial* Sheet Set node to restore saved selections later.

- With both items selected, right-click and choose **Save Sheet Selection**. In the dialog, name it **Design Development**.

Since plotters vary widely, in this exercise, we will plot to a DWF file. If you prefer, feel free to create a hard copy plot of the set. When we explored the settings in the Page Setup we saw that the *A101 Floor Plans* file is set up to print to the DWF6 ePlot.pc3 plotter. (This is the default of all the files in our project.) *DWF6 ePlot.pc3* is a digital plotter designed to create a DWF file. A DWF (Design Web Format) is a highly compressed, vector-based file format designed for viewing and distributing drawing files over the Internet and by e-mail. What makes the DWF file so powerful is that it is a vector-based, high-quality drawing file that is read only. This means it can be distributed to consultants and clients without fear of unauthorized editing. DWF preserves access to Layers and can even include the Property Set Data attached to the objects within the drawing. DWF files can also be embedded in Web pages for viewing in a browser with the plug-in provided free from Autodesk. Anyone with a copy of the Autodesk Design Review software, available as a free download on the Autodesk Web site (*http://www.autodesk.com/*), can view, zoom, pan, turn on and off layers and print the DWF file. If the recipient has a copy of Autodesk DWF Composer, they can add redline comments to the DWF file, which can then be loaded back into ACA. Creating a DWF is simple, because it is the same as printing to a hard copy device. Before creating our DWF, let's make a modification to the Publish Options.

DWF files can be attached to drawings as references. The attached DWF file will behave as an underlay in the drawing file in which it is attached. You can even use object snaps on it! Use the Reference Manager palette (the same one that is used for XREFs) to attach and detach DWF files.

- Right-click the *MACA Commercial* Sheet Set node at the top and choose **Publish > Sheet Set Publish Options** (see Figure 18.8).

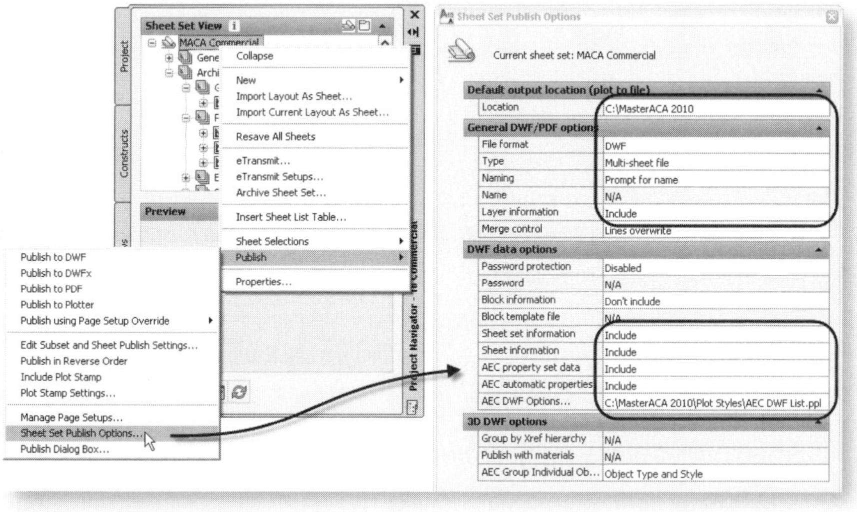

FIGURE 18.8 *Sheet Set Publish Options*

- In the Default output location, accept the initial *C:\MasterACA 2010* location or click the browse icon (...), and then choose your desired location.
- Choose a file format of DWF, a type of Multi-sheet file and **Include** as the Layer information value in the General DWF/PDF options area.

- In the DWF data options area, choose **Include** from the "Sheet set information," "Sheet information," "AEC property set data" and "AEC automatic properties" options.
- Click in the AEC DWF Options field, click the small Browse icon (...) and then place a check mark in the "Publish Property Set Data" and "Publish All Automatic Properties" checkboxes. Click OK twice.

Configuring those options will make a more robust DWF. (Note, the more recent format is actually DWFx. The DWFx format can be viewed by recipients on Windows Vista and Windows 7 without need for Design Review. Feel free to use this newer format instead). All of the Property Set Data and Sheet information will now be included with the DWF file. When this DWF is opened in Autodesk Design Review, the recipient will be able to select any object that has Property Set Data and view it directly.

- Right-click the *MACA Commercial* Sheet Set node at the top and choose **Publish > Publish to DWF** (or Publish > Publish to DWFx).

NOTE

You can also choose Publish > Publish to PDF if you prefer to make a PDF file instead of a DWF or DWFx.

As we saw in Chapter 5, this is all we need to do to publish the entire set. Use the same process to publish a subset or custom selection. When the Publish is complete, you can view a report or the DWF file itself by right-clicking on the Plot and Publish icon on the Application status bar (see Figure 18.9).

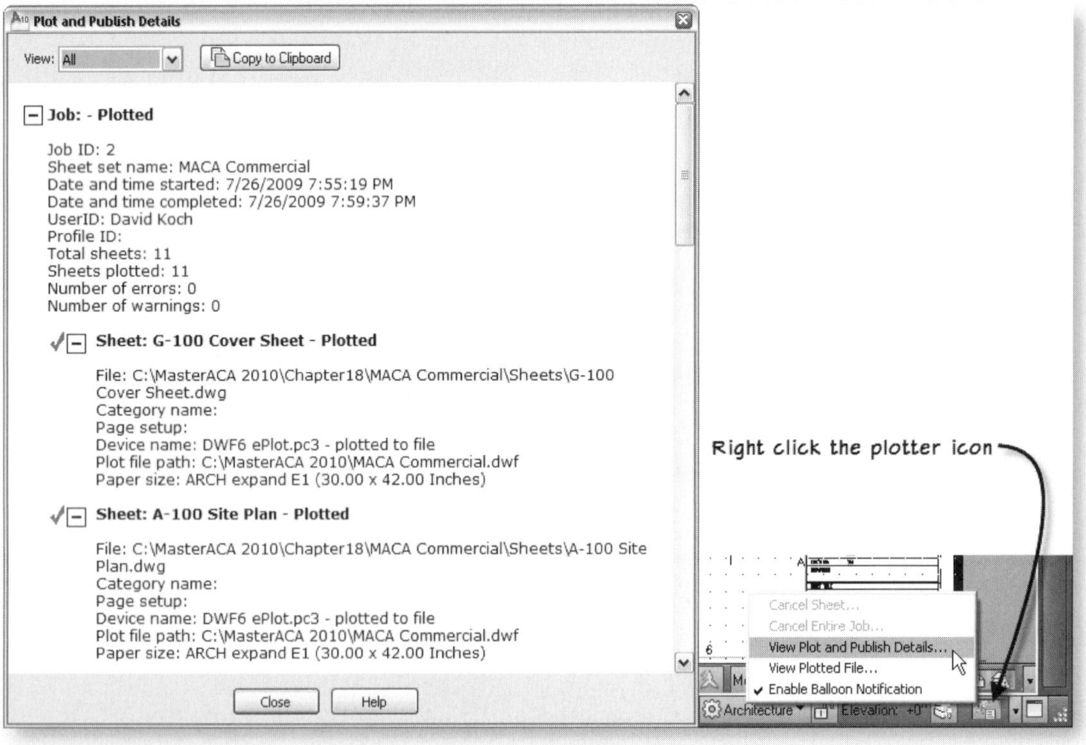

FIGURE 18.9 *View Plot and Publish Details*

If you wish to view the DWF, right-click the Publish icon and choose **View Plotted File** (you can also double-click it from wherever you saved it). In Autodesk Design Review, select a Sheet that you wish to view on the left. Click the Selector icon on the toolbar and then click on an object in the drawing. They will highlight blue under your cursor as you mouse over. When an object is selected, you can view its Property Set Data on the left. In Autodesk Design Review, you can add redline markups (see Figure 18.10).

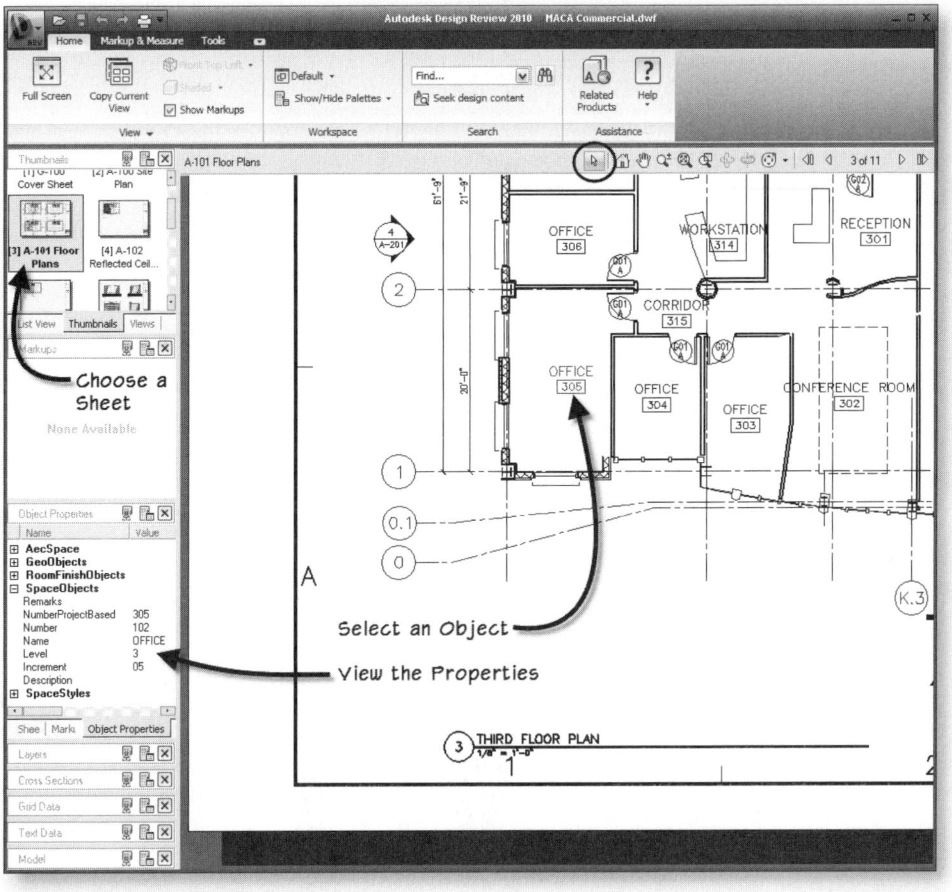

FIGURE 18.10 *Open the DWF and view the embedded Property Set Data*

3D DWF

AutoCAD Architecture 2010 also allows you to publish 3D Models to DWF files. Use this feature to output a 3D Model containing Property Set data in a compact DWF file. Just like the 2D DWF set published above, all your recipients need is a copy of the free Autodesk Design Review application to view, orbit, query and print the 3D model.

- On the Project Navigator, on the Views tab, double-click the *A-CM00* file to open it.
- From the Application menu, choose **Export > 3D DWF** (see Figure 18.11).

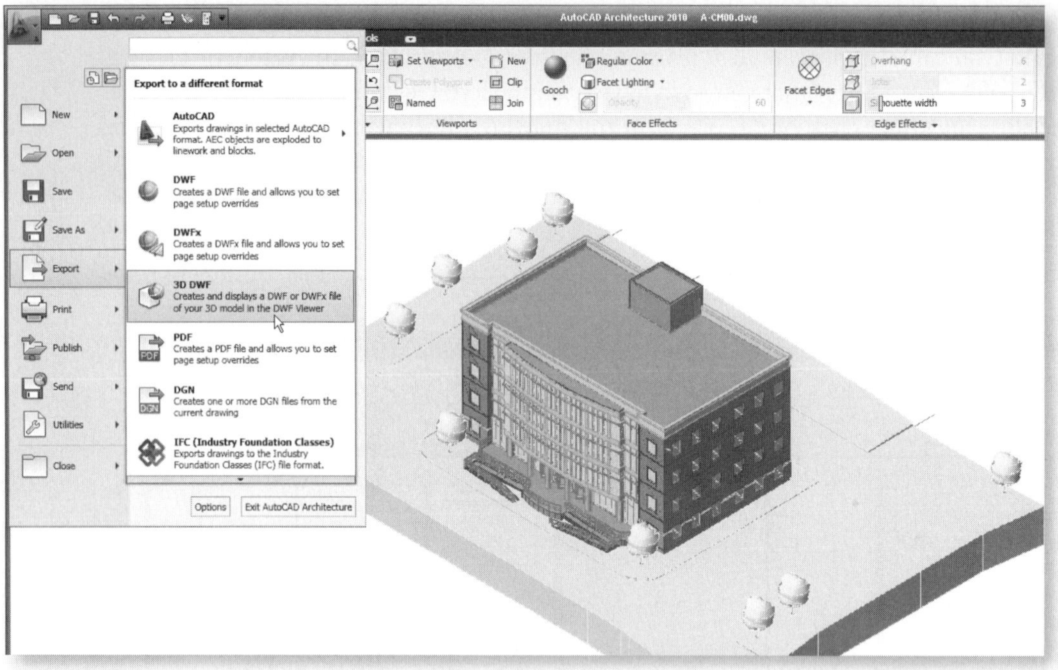

FIGURE 18.11 *Publish a 3D DWF*

- In the "Export 3D DWF" dialog, type in a name for the file and then click Save.

NOTE

Depending on your hardware specifications, it may take a little while for the 3D DWF to generate. Please be patient.

- Open the new DWF file as before.

You will have slightly different icons this time. You can select objects in the DWF and view their properties, you can also orbit the model, zoom, pan and isolate objects. A tree hierarchy of all objects appears on the left. Use it to select objects, and right-click to access isolate options (see Figure 18.12).

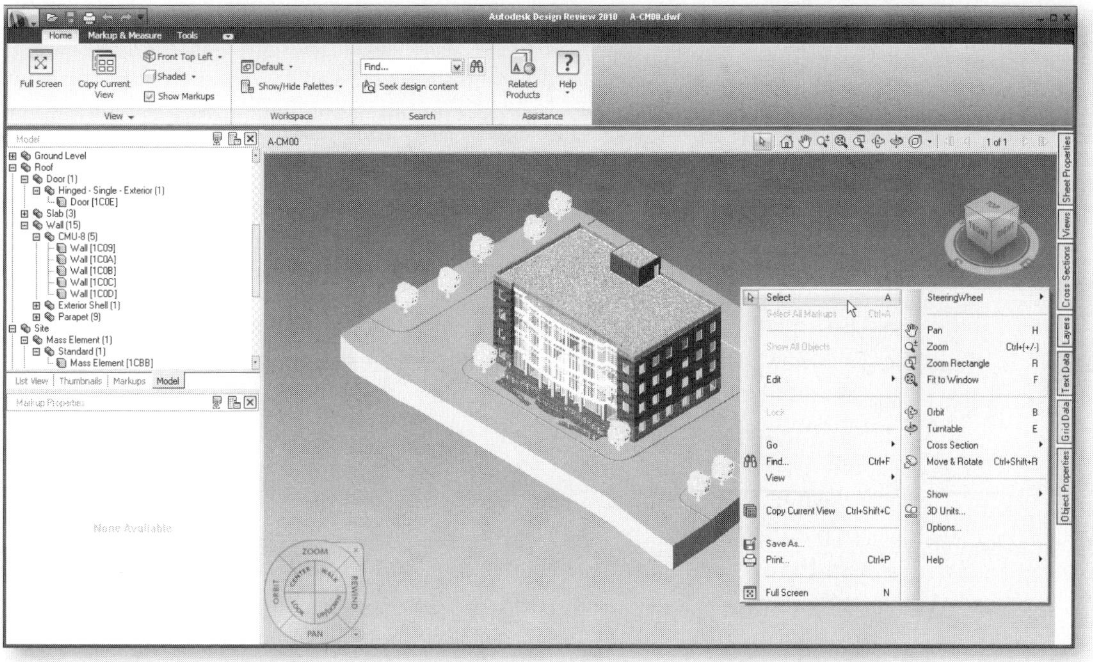

FIGURE 18.12 *View the model and select objects in the 3D DWF*

ETRANSMIT AND ARCHIVE

If you wish to send the actual drawing files to a recipient, you can use the eTransmit from the Project Navigator. With this tool, you can gather all of the drawings, their XREFs, fonts and other dependent files and package them all up into a single ZIP file and even automatically send the ZIP file as an e-mail attachment. Use the eTransmit Setups option on the right-click menu to determine which settings you want. The Archive command is nearly identical to eTransmit except that it does not include the e-mail option.

PUBLISH TO WEB

If you generate lots of DWF files and wish to include them in a project Web site for online viewing on the Internet, use the Publish to Web Wizard by typing **PUBLISH-TOWEB** at the Command prompt to generate the DWFs, rather than plotting them manually. This wizard will create the DWFs and accompanying HTML Web pages ready to post to the Web. This wizard has many options. Be sure to check it out.

PUBLISH TO PDF

AutoCAD Architecture includes a PDF printer driver. If you wish, you can use this driver to create a plotter and publish your Sheets and Sheet Sets to PDF files instead of DWF. PDF files have the advantage of being well known and universal. There are pros and cons to PDF and DWF. In general DWF is purpose-built for digital delivery of design files, while PDF is a more general-purpose format suitable for any kind of digital document. Ultimately the decision will have to be made within each project team as to which format is most suitable.

ADDITIONAL EXERCISES

Additional exercises have been provided in Appendix A. In Appendix A you will find exercises to plot the Residential Project.

SUMMARY

- The properties of objects are assigned through a variety of hierarchical settings, starting with the object Display Representation and ending with the Plot Style Table.
- Sheet files are valuable tools to enhance plotting productivity.
- Use Layouts and Page Setup to set up the "sheet of paper" exactly as you want it plotted.
- Page Setups can be saved and named for easy retrieval.
- Use viewports to crop out individual views of your building model.
- Each viewport can be any shape, and it can have its own layer and unique Display Configuration.
- The Plot Style Table gets the "final word" in plotting attributes like color and lineweight.
- Assign Plot Style Tables to your layouts to make the drawing "black and white" for plotting.
- Use the Publish utility to create groups of files that can be printed together unattended.
- Create a multi-sheet DWF file that includes embedded Property Set Data.
- Publish any ACA file to a 3D DWF and view it in Autodesk Design Review.
- eTransmit and Archive options are available for the Sheet Set.

SECTION

IV

Appendices

Appendix A includes the additional exercises referenced throughout the text. Appendix B summarizes the rules of Wall Cleanup detailed in Chapter 9. You can find many Web sites and other online resources listed in Appendix C. (Shortcut files of each URL are also included with the files installed from the CD.) Appendix D covers the process of using Spaces to generate BOMA area calculations. Appendix E provides some guidelines for sharing files with external consultants who may or may not be using AutoCAD Architecture. Finally, Appendix F gives the solution to the additional Wall Cleanup exercise from Chapter 9 (included in Appendix A).

Section IV is organized as follows:

Appendix A Additional Exercises
Appendix B Wall Cleanup Checklist
Appendix C Online Resources
Appendix D Space Area Calculations
Appendix E Sharing Files with Consultants
Appendix F Wall Cleanup Solution

APPENDIX a

Additional Exercises

INTRODUCTION

This Appendix includes several practice exercises furthering the topics covered in many of the chapters. It is intended that you will visit this appendix at the completion of each chapter. Once you have finished the lessons in a particular chapter, perform the exercises herein for that chapter. Each of the projects has been provided in completed form in a folder named *Complete* within each respective chapter's folder. You are encouraged to experiment in each of these exercises. The notes given here are merely guidelines for your further explorations. Feel free to perform other tasks not listed and experiment with other tools. You can use Saveas to explore alternatives. If you wish to create a complete variation of a project, create a new project in the Project Browser using the existing one as a Template Project.

NOTE

In all of these exercises, work in the non-complete versions of the files for the chapter in question. In some cases, these exercises have already been completed in the "Complete" version from the CD. Not all exercises have been completed in the Complete CD versions.

INSTALL THE CD FILES AND LOAD THE CURRENT PROJECT

If you have already installed all of the files from the CD, simply skip down to step 3 below to make the project active as appropriate per the exercises that follow. If you need to install the CD files, start at step 1.

1. If you have not already done so, install the dataset files located on the Mastering AutoCAD Architecture 2010 CD-ROM.

   Refer to "Files Included on the CD-ROM" in the Preface for information on installing the sample files included on the CD.

2. Launch AutoCAD Architecture 2010 from the desktop icon created in Chapter 3.

If you did not create a custom icon, you might want to review "Create a New Profile" and "Create a Desktop Shortcut" in Chapter 3. Creating the custom desktop icon is not essential; however, it makes loading the custom profile easier. In some of the exercises that follow, you will work in stand-alone files provided in the *C:\MasterACA 2010\Appendix-A* folder. In other cases, you will work in the project files for the corresponding chapter. To work in a project for a particular chapter, you must first load the project files for that chapter.

3. On the Quick Access Toolbar (QAT), choose the **Project Browser** icon.
4. Click to open the folder list and choose your *C:* drive.
5. Double-click on the *MasterACA 2010* folder, then the appropriate chapter folder (depending on the particular exercise).

   You will find either the Metric or Imperial version of *Commercial* and *Residential*.

6. Double-click *XX Commercial* or *XX Residential* (where XX equals the chapter number) if you wish to work in Imperial units. Double-click *XX Commercial Metric* or *XX Residential Metric* if you wish to work in Metric units. (You can also right-click on it and choose **Set Current Project.**) Then click Close in the Project Browser.

NOTE

Important: If a message appears asking you to repath the project, click the "Repath the project now" option. Refer to the "Repathing Projects" topic in the Preface for more information.

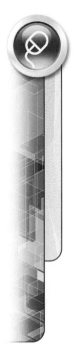

CHAPTER 4
Residential Project

Here are some additional exercises to practice topics covered in the Chapter 4 Residential Project.

Please note that for Chapter 4, there is not yet a project to load. Therefore, simply open the files noted here using the open icon on the Quick Access Toolbar.

EXERCISE A4.1: BASEMENT EXISTING CONDITIONS

The basement Existing is a simple file to create.

1. Start with the *First Floor Existing* file that you created in the chapter's lessons. Select all four exterior Walls, and copy them to the clipboard. Create a new file using the same template that you used in Chapter 4 for the First Floor file. On the Home tab of the ribbon, on the Modify panel, choose the Paste to Original Coordinates tool. Select the right vertical Wall, on the Wall tab, on the Modify panel, choose **Plan Modifiers > Remove**. Remove the firebox and the hearth (see Figure A.1).
2. Save the file as *Basement Existing.dwg*. Close the file.

FIGURE A.1 *Basement Existing Conditions Plan—Residential Project*

EXERCISE A4.2: SECOND FLOOR EXISTING CONDITIONS

The Second Floor Existing Conditions can be built in much the same way as the First Floor.

1. Start with the *First Floor Existing* file. Select all four exterior Walls. On the home tab, on the Modify panel, choose Copy to Clipboard. Create a new file using the same template that you used in Chapter 4 for the First Floor file. On the Home tab of the ribbon, on the Modify panel, choose the Paste to Original Coordinates tool. Select the right vertical Wall, on the Wall tab, on the Modify panel, choose **Plan Modifiers > Remove**. Remove the firebox and the hearth.
2. Save the file as *Second Existing.dwg.*
3. Using the process followed in the text of Chapter 4 for the First Floor, offset, trim, extend and fillet Walls as required to lay out the Second Floor following the dimensions in Figure A.2.
4. Use the Existing Conditions Wall style from the *First Floor Existing* file. Set the Width of Exterior Walls to **12"** [**300**] and the interior Walls to **5"** [**125**]. Set the height of all Walls to **9'-0"** [**2750**].
5. Use the Automatic Offset/Center option for Doors and Windows and an offset of **4"** [**100**] unless noted otherwise. For the hinged Doors, use the Single – Hinged tool and choose the **2'-6"** × **6'-8"** [**750×2200**] Standard Size. For the Bi-fold Doors, pick sizes appropriate to the various closets. The Windows are all Double Hung, **3'-0"** × **4'-8"** [**900** × **1200**] with a Head Height of **6'-8"** [**2200**]. The two bathroom Windows are **3'-0"** × **3'-0"** [**900** × **900**].
6. Save and close the file.

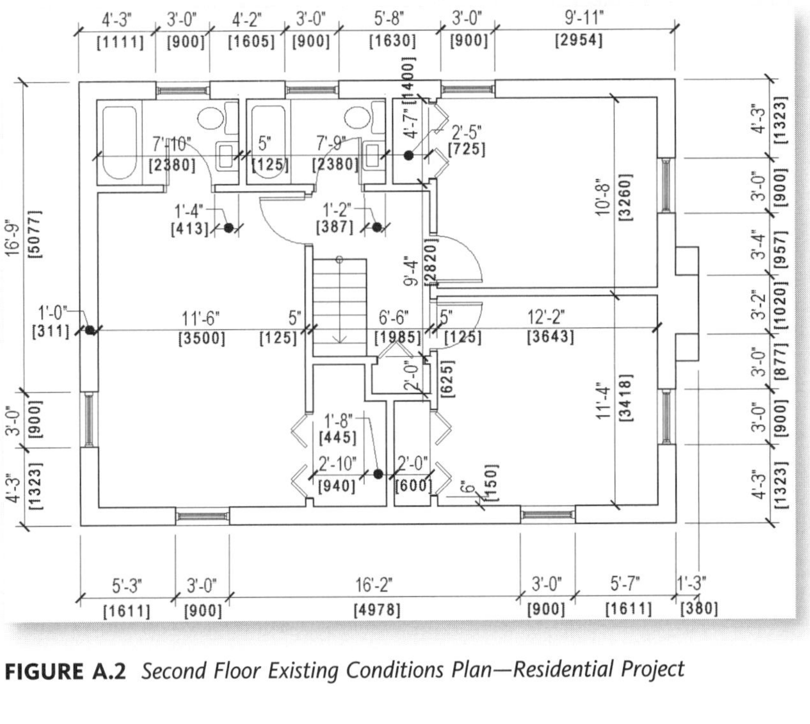

FIGURE A.2 *Second Floor Existing Conditions Plan—Residential Project*

Commercial Project

EXERCISE A4.3: THIRD FLOOR BUILD OUT

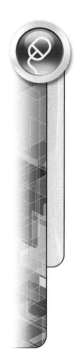

1. In the *C:\MasterACA 2010\Appendix-A* folder (from the CD), open the file named *Chapter04 Commercial.dwg* [*Chapter04 Commercial - Metric.dwg*] and add the Walls shown in Figure A.3. Use the same techniques as above. For the curved Walls, simply draw them with the Wall tool, using a curved Wall segment, and use grips to edit the curves to the approximate shapes and dimensions shown.
2. Add Doors as appropriate using the standard tools and sizes.
3. Save the file as *Third Floor Build Out* and then close the file.

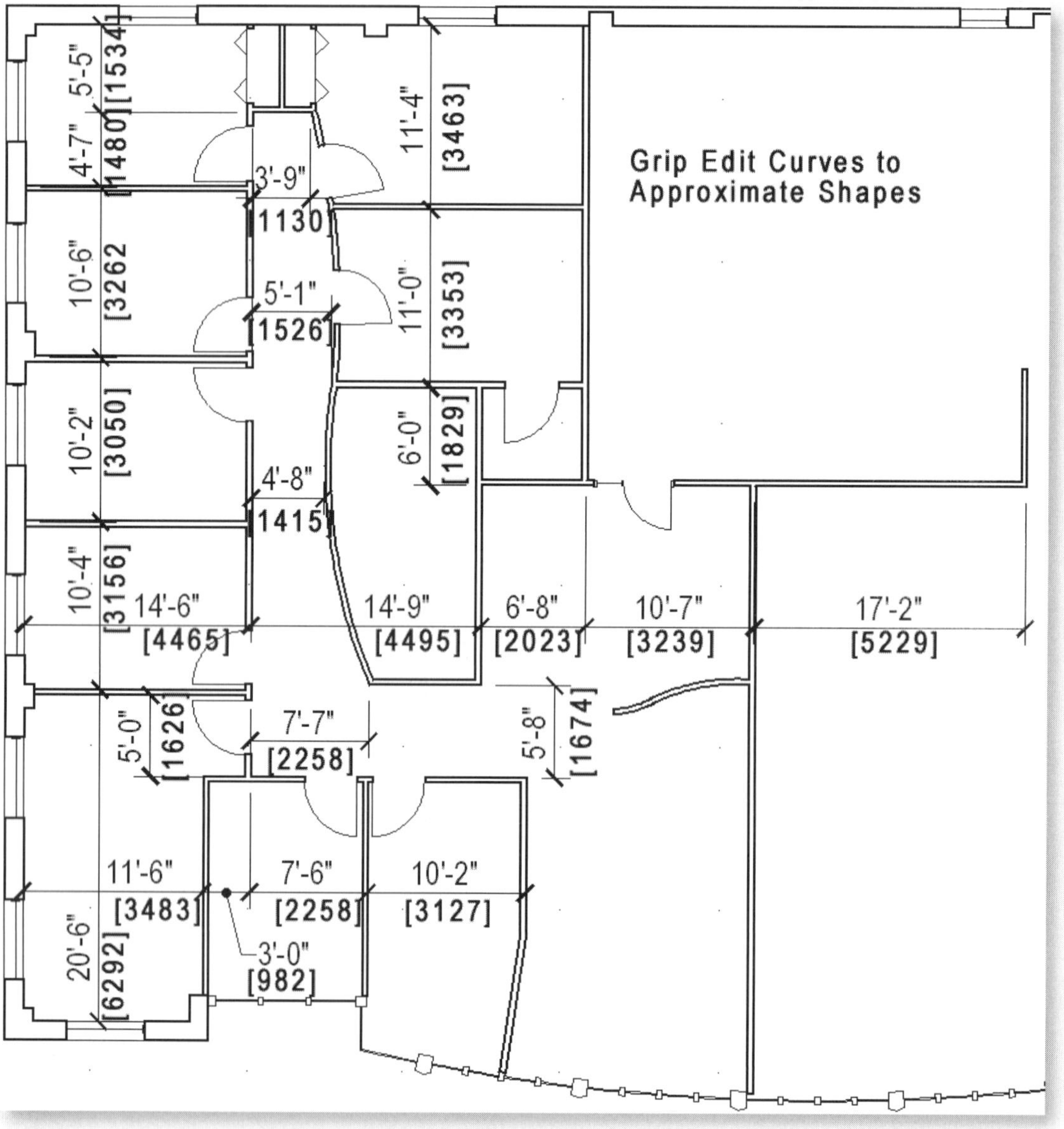

FIGURE A.3 *Third Floor Build Out—Commercial Project*

CHAPTER 5

Residential Project

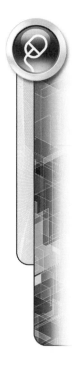

Included on the CD-ROM is a PDF mini-chapter with detailed instructions for creating all of the required residential project files. Using the same process outlined in Chapter 5, you will create a new project in Project Navigator, set up the levels and division, import files created in Chapter 4 and create several new Constructs, Views and Sheets. Please open and/or print the provided PDF mini-chapter and keep Chapter 5 handy as you work through this tutorial. This mini-chapter is provided for additional practice in using Project Navigator to set up new projects. You do not need to complete the mini-chapter in order to advance to Chapter 6 and beyond. Each subsequent chapter includes the required files for the residential project with the files installed from the CD. It is provided merely for your information and practice.

Commercial Project

The two projects that we are building in this book do not take full advantage of the use of Elements in a Project Structure. With an Element, you can create a portion of the building model that is reused in more than one location in the complete building model. For instance, a typical Stair Tower or Typical Restroom layout are excellent examples. You can also use an Element to assist with Furniture Layout. The *C:\MasterACA 2010\Appendix-A* folder (from the CD) contains two files, *Office Furniture.dwg* [*Office Furniture – Metric.dwg*]. The files contain some sample furniture and a rectangle representing the typical office size of the Commercial Project.

EXERCISE A5.1: CREATE A FURNITURE LAYOUT ELEMENT FILE

1. From the *C:\MasterACA 2010\Appendix-A* folder, open *Office Furniture.dwg* [*Office Furniture – Metric.dwg*]. Using the Rectangle as a guide, create a *typical furniture* layout using the symbols provided in the file. (If you wish to add others, there are others in the library. The Content Library is covered in detail in later chapters.)

NOTE The lower-left corner of the rectangle is 0,0. Name the file Typical Furniture.

2. On the Project Navigator, right-click the Elements folder and choose **Save current drawing as Element**.
3. Open the *Third Floor Build Out* file created in the previous exercise and on the Project Navigator, right-click the Constructs folder and choose **Save current file as Construct**. Check Third Floor for the assignments.
4. Drag the *Typical Furniture* Element from the Project Navigator and drop it into the *Third Floor Build Out* file. Move it into position in one of the offices. The single grip at the insertion point of the file is helpful for this. Copy and mirror it into several offices. Save the *Third Floor Build Out* file.
5. Return to the *Typical Furniture* layout Element file, and make a change to the layout. Move a piece of furniture, add something, delete something. The exact change is unimportant. Save the *Typical Furniture* Element.
6. Return to the *Third Floor Build Out* file, open the External References palette (use the quick pick on the lower-left corner of the Drawing Status Bar) and reload the *Typical Furniture* XREF. Note the change. Continue to experiment.
7. Save and close all files.

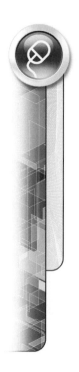

EXERCISE A5.2: USING THE COMMERCIAL TEMPLATE PROJECT

1. Following the procedures outlined in Chapter 5, create a new project but use the *Commercial Template Project (Imperial)* [*Commercial Template Project (Metric)*].

When the project Navigator loads this time, you will already have several premade files in the *Constructs*, *Views* and *Sheets* folders ready to receive project geometry. Naturally, you can edit the number of levels and add or delete files as required by your project. For now, simply add some simple geometry to each Construct and then load the Views and Sheets to understand the value of the template.

2. On the Constructs tab, expand the *Architectural\Shell* folder and then open the *00 Shell* file. Add four Walls within the guide onscreen. (Use the Wall tools on the Project Tools palette if you wish.)
3. Repeat in the other two *Core* files. (Draw the Walls in each file, or Copy and Paste.)
4. In the *Architectural\Roof* folder, add a simple Roof object.
5. In the *Elements* folder, expand the *Architectural* folder and then open the *Typical Toilet Room* file. Use the toilet room layout provided in the DesignCenter and drag it into the file. Close and save the *Typical Toilet Room* file.
6. In the *Constructs\Architectural\Core* folder, open each *Core* file and add some interior Walls, Doors and other objects. Do the same in the files within the *Architectural\Interior* folder.
7. The *Constructs\Architectural\Site* folder contains a file named *Terrain*. You can use the procedures covered in Chapter 5 to make a simple Mass Element terrain model upon which your building can sit.
8. The *Constructs\Architectural\Slab* folder contains three *Slab* files. Open and add floor Slabs to these if you like.
9. Finally, structural column grids can be added to the files in the *Constructs\Structural\Grid* folder.
10. Save and close all Construct and Element files before continuing.
11. On the Project Navigator Views tab, in the *Architectural* folder, you will find several prebuilt plan, elevation, section and detail View files. Open each one and study the results.

    Notice that all of the Constructs are already present in each file. In the Section and Elevation files, select the 2D Section/Elevation files within these files (provided as placeholders), right-click and then choose **Refresh**.
12. Close and save any files you opened and then go to the Sheets tab and open the Sheets.

    The plan Sheets are already set up. The elevation and section Sheets require you to drag the appropriate View files to the Sheets within. Do this now to complete the cartoon set.

Feel free to continue your exploration in this project based upon the *Commercial Template Project (Imperial)* [*Commercial Template Project (Metric)*] project. Make whatever changes and adjustments you wish. Be sure to read the topic in the help file that explains each file in detail. You can find the name of this topic in the bulletin board for the project. The help also explains how to add and remove levels to the project. You can make modifications to this project and use the modified version as your office standard template project or build your own from scratch.

CHAPTER 6

Residential Project

Using the Structural Member Catalog, we can import some shapes for the beams and columns needed in the Basement of the Residential Project.

EXERCISE A6.1: ADD COLUMNS AND BEAMS TO THE BASEMENT

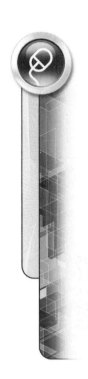

1. Open the Structural Member Catalog as done for the Column Grid in Chapter 6. Import (double-click to make styles) Shapes appropriate for a column and beam in the Residential Basement. Add two Beams and two Columns in the center of the *Basement Existing* file as shown in Figure A.4.
2. Use the Elevation setting on the Properties palette to get the height correct.

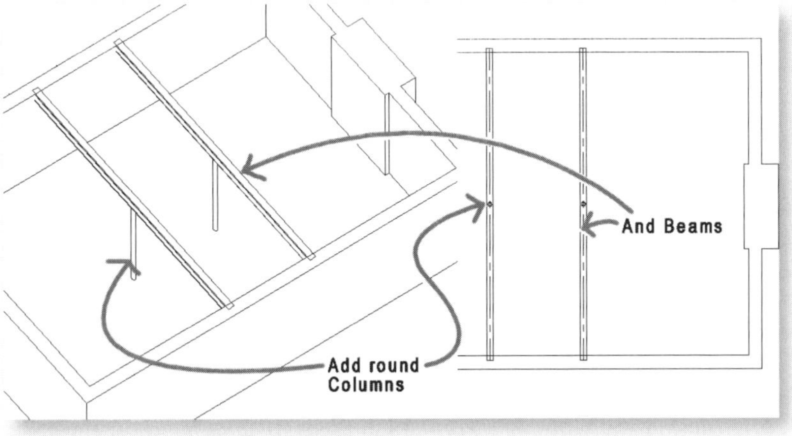

FIGURE A.4 *Third Floor Build Out—Commercial Project*

EXERCISE A6.2: ADD A BEAM HAUNCH

1. Draw a Mass Element (Design tool palette group > Massing tab) big enough for the overlap of the Beam on the Wall. Position it at the top of the Wall.
2. Select the Wall. On the Wall tab, on the Modify panel, choose Body Modifiers > Add. When prompted, select the Mass Element. In the Add Body Modifier dialog box, choose Subtractive for the Operation. Put a check mark in the "Erase Selected Objects" checkbox to delete the Mass Element after the operation (see Figure A.5). The result will be that the Mass Element carves away a haunch for the Beam.

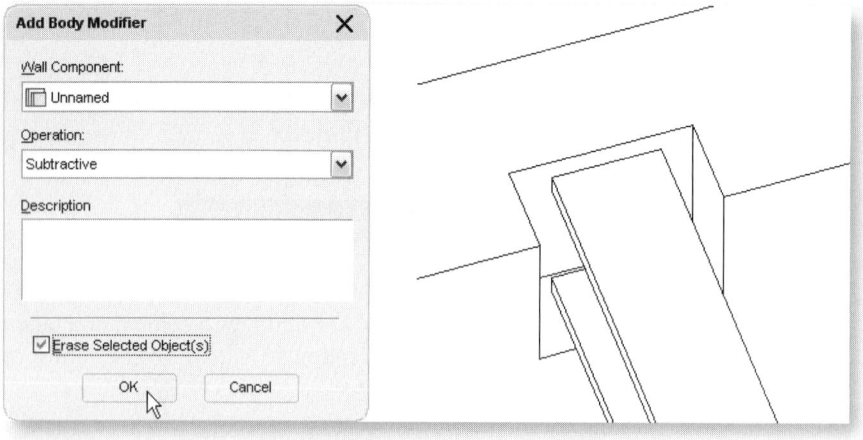

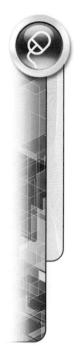

FIGURE A.5 *Add a Subtractive Mass Element as a Beam Haunch*

CHAPTER 7

Residential Project

Add some Stairs to the new Residential Addition.

EXERCISE A7.1: ADD BASEMENT STAIRS

1. The small space between the two vertical Walls on the left of the *Basement New* file for the Residential Project needs some Stairs to the Basement. Use the Content Browser, *Design Tool Catalog – Imperial* [*Design Tool Catalog – Metric*], Stairs and Railings category to import the Concrete Stair Style. Set the Width to **4'-4"** [**1300**] and the Height to **4'-4"** [**1254**]. Use Right justification and trace the edge of the Wall. Move the Stair down about **12"** [**300**] from the top edge of the Walls. Make sure that the Elevation of the Stairs is set to **0**. Set the Tread size to **12"** [**300**] (see Figure A.6).
2. When you are finished, save the file, open the Composite Model file *A-CM00* and view the model from the NW Isometric view to see the results. The Stair should come up to the level of the terrain. In a later chapter, we will carve out the terrain where the Stairs occur. For now, simply verify the heights in wireframe.
3. Save and close all files.

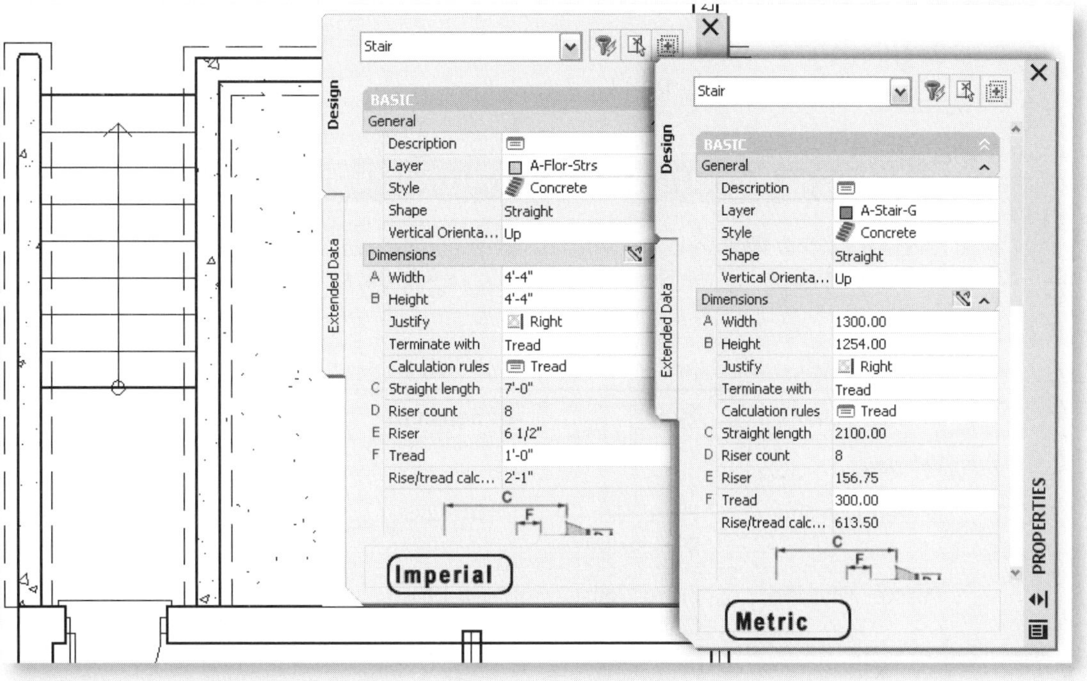

FIGURE A.6 *Setting the parameters for Basement Stairs in the New Construction*

Commercial Project

Add some Railings to the *Ground* Construct file.

EXERCISE A7.2: CONVERT LINEWORK TO RAILINGS

Choose a Railing Style from the library and import it into the *Ground Level* Construct file. Right-click the Railing tool on the Design tool palette and choose **Apply Tool Properties to > Linework**. Choose the Blue lines in this file. Erase the layout geometry. Select the resultant Railings and change their style to the style that you imported.

4. Verify that the heights are correct and, if necessary, adjust the Elevation of the Railing objects.
5. Save and close all files.

CHAPTER 8

Residential Project

Add a Porch to the new Residential Addition.

EXERCISE A8.1: CREATE A CURTAIN WALL FOR A SCREEN PORCH

Create a Curtain Wall style to use for a Screen Porch on the Residential Project. Work in the First Floor New file of the Residential Project. Define the following elements:

TABLE A.1 *Residential Project Porch Curtain Wall Style Elements*

Element Name	Type	Dimensions	Other
Divisions			
Screen Division	Fixed Cell Dimension	9'-0" [2750]	Shrink Top
Pilaster Division	Fixed Cell Dimension	3'-0" [900]	Shrink Left & Right Maintain half Cell Offset Start & End 8" [180]
Infills			
Screen Infill	Style	N/A	Porch Window Style Create a Window Style using 2"×4" [50×100] Frame and a zero Sash
Frames			
Corner Pier Frame	Basic (No profile)	10" [250] wide × 10" [250] deep	X Offset = 5" [125] End Offset = 12" [300]
Half Pilaster Frame	Basic (No profile)	5" [125] wide × 10" [250] deep	End Offset = 12" [300]
Cornice Frame	Basic (No profile)	4" [100] wide × 12" [300] deep	
Knee Wall Frame	Use Profile	8" [200] wide × 24" [600] deep	Y Offset = 1" [25]
Mullions			
Pilaster Mullion	Basic (No profile)	10" [250] wide × 10" [250] deep	

1. Define all Element Definitions. Be sure to make the Window style and the Profile Definition required first. The easiest way to create the Profile Definition is to create the Curtain Wall with a basic rectangular Frame definition and then select it in the drawing and, on the Curtain Wall contextual ribbon tab on the Modify panel, choose the ***Frame/Mullion > Add Profile*** tool. Create a new Profile from scratch and then add a few vertices to shape it as shown in Figure A.7.

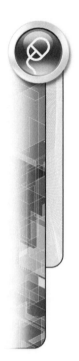

FIGURE A.7 *Draw a Profile to use for the Knee Wall Frame*

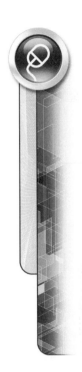

2. Create a new style and name it **Screen Porch**. For the Primary Grid, assign the **Pilaster Division**. Assign **Cornice Frame** to the Default Frame Assignment for Top, Left and Right (not **Bottom**). Set Mullion Assignment to **Pilaster Mullion**. For the Secondary Grid, use the **Screen Division**; the Cell Assignment should be the **Screen Infill**, and the Frame Assignment is **Knee Wall Frame**. The Mullion Assignment does not matter since there are no Mullions in this Grid (see Figure A.8).

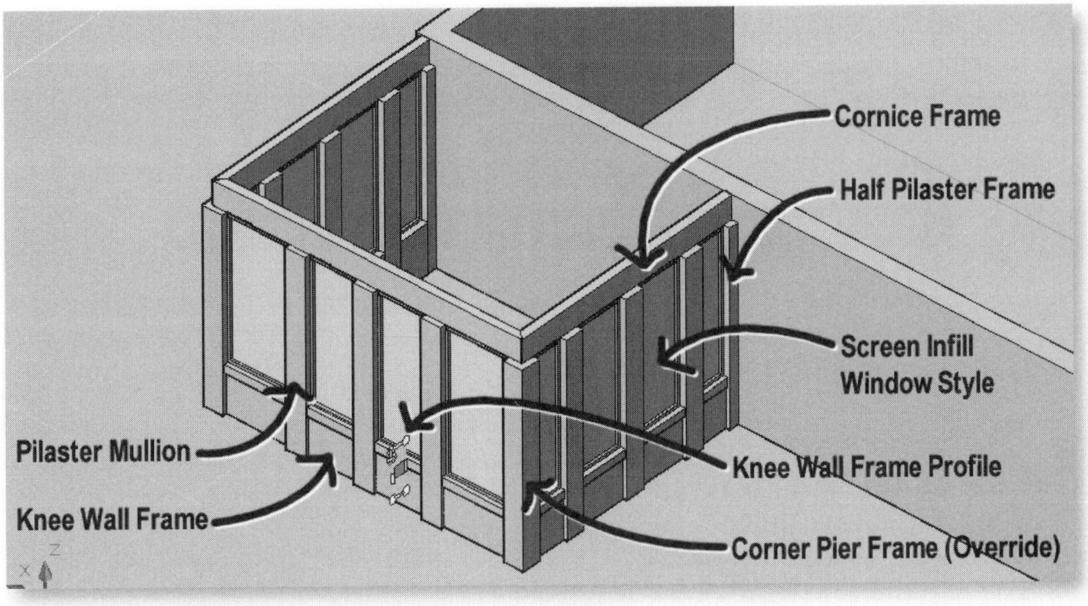

FIGURE A.8 *Assemble the kit of parts to build a Screen Porch Curtain Wall*

3. Use the Curtain Wall contextual ribbon tab, Modify panel ***Frame/Mullion > Override Assignment*** tool to change the Corner Frames to the Corner Pier Frame and the Frames against the Wall of the house to the Half Pilaster Frame.
4. Draw a three-sided porch using the new style on the top-right side of the plan of the *First Floor New* file.
5. Save and close the file.

CHAPTER 9

Commercial Project

Practice additional Wall Cleanup.

EXERCISE A9.1: PRACTICE EDIT IN PLACE

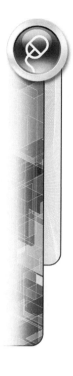

1. From the *Chapter09* folder, open the file named *Wall Cleanup7.dwg*.
2. Zoom in on the intersection of three walls to the left of the closet and select one of the Walls. On the ribbon, click Cleanup Edit in Place. Select one of the Walls in the intersection, click the Hide Edge tool and then click the edge to hide.
3. Repeat for the other Walls. You will have to complete the Edit in Place and then go back in with a different Wall selected to do all three Walls. When you are finished, the result should look like the right side of Figure A.9.

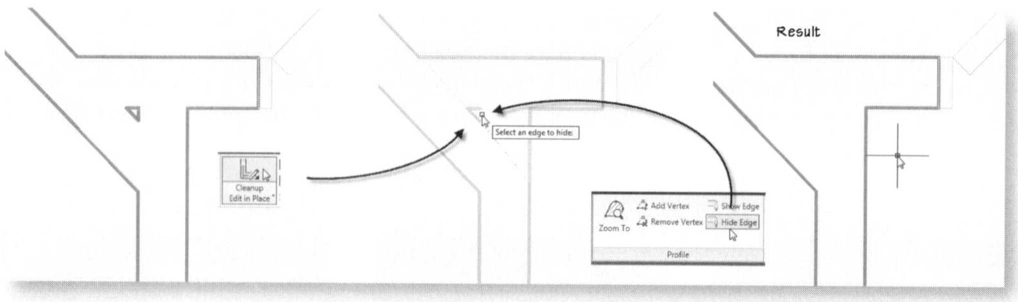

FIGURE A.9 *Add a Bow Window*

EXERCISE A9.2: FIX CLEANUP PROBLEMS ON THE THIRD FLOOR

4. Load the Commercial Project for Chapter 9. Open the *03 Partitions* Construct in the Project Navigator. Follow the "Rules" in Chapter 9 and see if you can solve all of the Cleanup Problems.
5. If you get stuck, see Appendix F for the solution.

CHAPTER 10

Residential and Commercial Projects

Add additional components.

EXERCISE A10.1: ADD CASEWORK

Work in the First Floor Existing file for the Residential project; the upper-left space is the kitchen. Work in the 03 Partitions file for Commercial. The Workstations and Copy Room in the middle of the plan need counters.

1. Open the Style Manager or Content Browser and load the *Wall Styles - Casework (Imperial).dwg* [*Wall Styles - Casework (Metric).dwg*] content file.

   All of the styles in this content file have their Baseline assigned to the back edge of the counter.

2. Add them the way you would any other Wall, using the Baseline justification. However, before you begin to add countertops, choose **Options** from the Application Menu and on the AEC Object Defaults tab, turn off the Autosnap New Wall Baselines option. (If you don't, the ends of your countertops will snap to the centerline of your Walls.) Explore the Styles, the Endcaps and the Components. Look at the Display Properties and the Cut Plane height. Make changes as you see fit. (For instance, remove the bullnosed Endcap Style and use Standard instead.) Get a complete sense of how these styles work.

Also try the Casework in the Content Browser's Design catalogs. There are dozens of "drag-and-drop" content items within. Try them out in your drawings.

EXERCISE A10.2: ADD EQUIPMENT AND FURNITURE

Equipment and Furniture can be found in Content Browser as well.

1. Drag in some appliances in the Residential Project and some office equipment in the Commercial Project.

CHAPTER 11

Residential Project

Add additional components.

EXERCISE A11.1: ADD BOW WINDOW

Load the Residential Project and open the First Floor New Construct. Add a Bow Window to the vertical Wall on the right side of the Dining Room. You will find a premade Bow Window style in the Content library.

1. Open the Content Browser and navigate to *Design Tool Catalog – Imperial.*

> **NOTE**
> **Please note that there is no Bow or Bay Window style in the Metric catalog, but you can use the one in the Imperial catalog and simply change the dimensions to suit.**

2. Open the *Doors and Windows* category and then the *Windows* category.
3. Locate the Bow Window style (it is on page 2). Drag it into the drawing (or to a palette first if you like) to add it to the drawing.
4. Add it to the vertical Wall on the right side of the Dining Room as noted above. On the Properties palette, set the Width to **10'-0"** [**3000**], the Height to **5'-0"** [**1800**], and the Head Height to **6'-8"** [**2200**] (see Figure A.10).

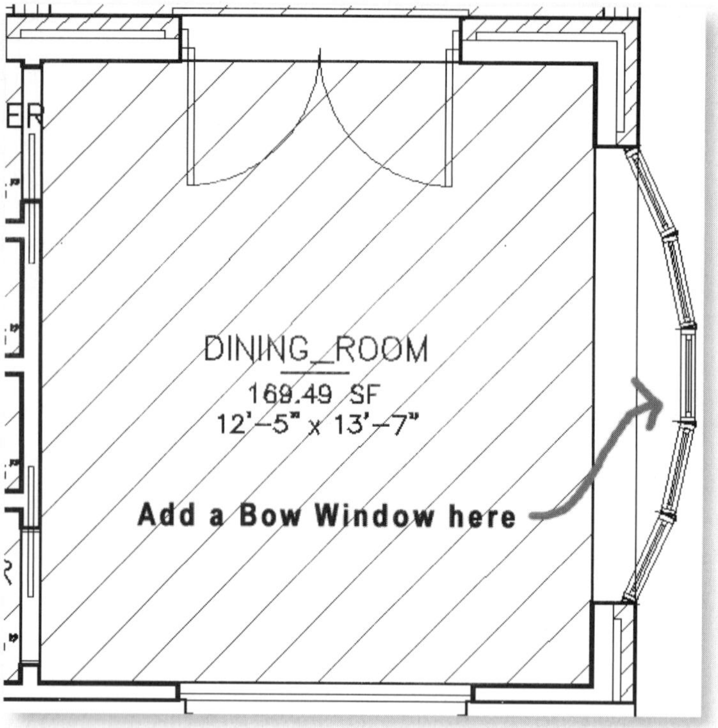

FIGURE A.10 *Add a Bow Window*

The Bow Window style makes use of a Custom Display Block named Aec_Window_Bow. This block contains several Window objects of the style Bow – Unit organized in a Bow configuration. You can insert this block and refedit it to change the configuration (quantity of Windows, type of Window, etc.). You can also open the Style Manager and edit the Bow – Unit Window style if you wish. For instance, you could follow the steps in Chapter 11 *to add Muntins to the Window units. Experiment with both the Display Block and the Window style to see what you can achieve. For more information on Custom Display Blocks, refer to the "Adding Custom Display Blocks in Plan" topic in* Chapter 11.

5. Save and close the file when finished.

Commercial Project

Add Column Enclosures and use Wall Interference.

EXERCISE A11.2: BUILD A MULTI-VIEW BLOCK FOR COLUMN CUTOUTS—INTERFERENCE WITH WALLS ON SHELL FILE

This exercise covers two concepts: Multi-View Block Interference blocks and Wall interference. An Interference condition enables one object to interact with the mass of another object. In the case of Wall objects, interference is used to make a separate object interact with the shrinkwrap of the Wall(s) to which it is attached. There are three possible shrinkwrap effects: Additive, Subtractive and Ignore. Use Additive to make the shrinkwrap include (wrap around) the object, use Subtractive to make the object appear to carve away from the object and use Ignore to have the shrinkwrap unaffected by the interfering object. In this example, we will carve out a pocket for each of the Columns in the shell Wall. Interference will be used to achieve this. You can create interference between a Wall and any other AEC object. Mass Elements are often used for this. In this case, we will take advantage of the ability that multi-view blocks have to contain an Interference block.

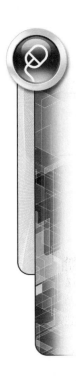

1. Load the Commercial Project and open the *01 Shell and Core Element* file.
2. Create a Mass Element Box (from the Massing palette in the Design tool palette group) with the dimensions **1'-6" × 1'-6" × 12'-0"** [**450 × 450 × 3650**]. Using the Midpoint of one of the sides as a base point, create a block from this Mass Element named Column Enclosure_M.
3. Open the Style Manager and in the Multi-Purpose Objects folder, create a new Multi-View Block named Column Enclosure. Edit the Multi-View Block and add Column Enclosure_M to the General Display Rep in **Top** and **Bottom** views only. Also click the Set Interference Block and add the same block there. Drag the Multi-View Block to your MACA Commercial tool palette. Close the Style Manager, save the drawing and then use the new tool to add the Multi-View Block to the drawing.
4. In the Project Navigator, right-click on the *Column Grid* Element file in the Structural subfolder and choose **XREF Overlay**. Move the Multi-View Block that you added in the last step into position relative to one of the columns. Copy it to the other columns as well.
5. Select one of the Walls, right-click and choose **Interference Condition > Add**. Select all of the Multi-View Block Column Enclosures that overlap the selected Wall. For the Shrinkwrap effect, choose **Subtractive**.
6. At the corners, you need to perform the Interference for each of the Walls. However, choose **Subtractive** for the first Wall and **Ignore** for the second (see Figure A.11).

The reason for this is that if you use Subtractive for both, the Subtractive on the second one will override the Subtractive of the first one. When you choose Ignore, it prevents this from happening.

7. Select the Multi-View Block, right-click and choose **Edit Multi-View Block Definition**. On the General Display Rep, deselect the Top box. This will make the multi-view invisible in this view. If you ever need to edit the definition, use the Style Manager or switch to Bottom view to show them and then select.
8. Save and close the file. Repeat on the other floors.

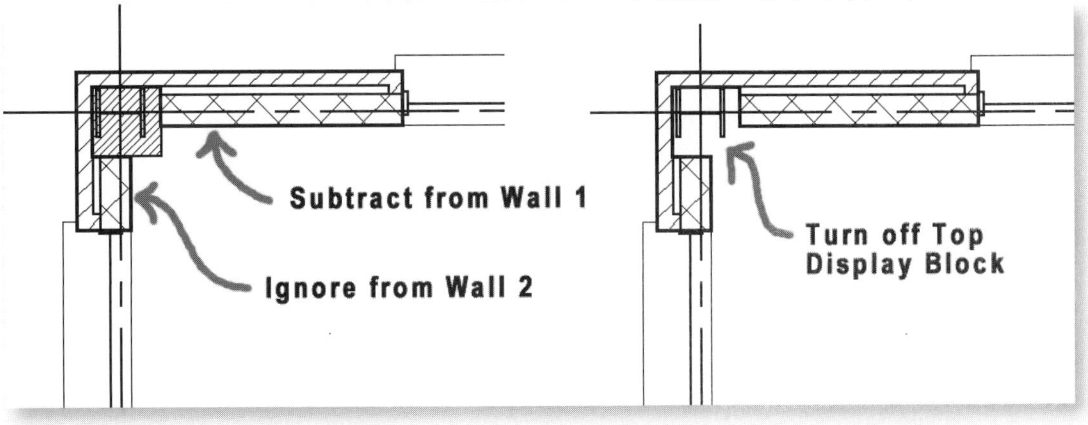

FIGURE A.11 *Adding Interference to Walls*

CHAPTER 12

Residential Project

Add Floor Slabs and a Roof.

EXERCISE A12.1: ADD BASEMENT FLOOR SLABS

1. Load the Residential Project and open the *Basement New* file. Add Floor Slabs to the Stair galley and the main Basement space of the new addition. Use the techniques covered in Chapter 12 to import an appropriate Slab style. You can simply trace the spaces with the Slab command or draw polylines first and convert them.
2. Save and close the file.

EXERCISE A12.2: ADD A ROOF TO THE PORCH

1. Open the *Roof New* file and add a Roof for the Porch.
2. On the Project Navigator, right-click the *First Floor New* file and choose **XREF Overlay**. This will add it at the correct height relative to the Roof. Using the techniques covered in Chapter 12, draw a Roof over the screen porch as shown in Figure A.12.
3. Detach the XREF and save and close the file.

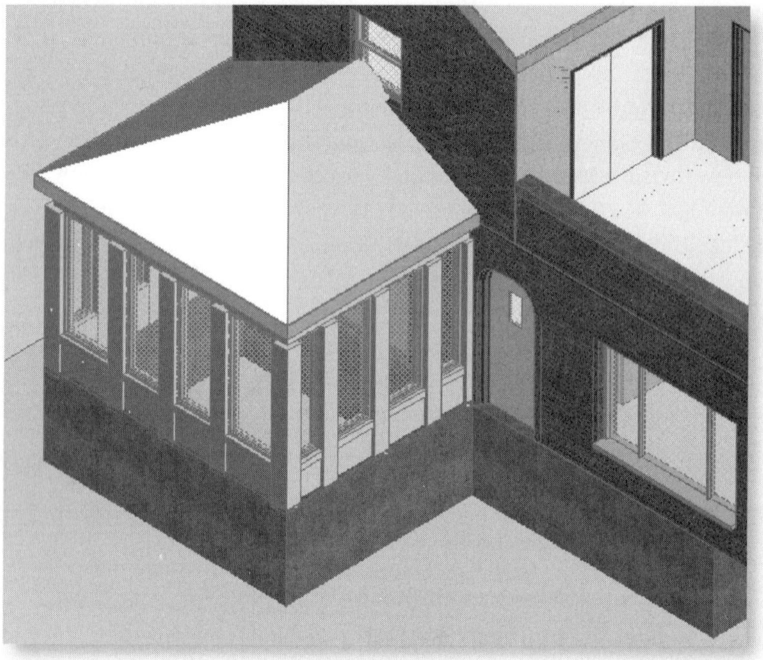

FIGURE A.12 *Adding a roof to the screen porch*

CHAPTER 13

Commercial Project

Continue to refine the Third Floor Reflected Ceiling Plan. Add additional elements and configure Door Display in Reflected.

EXERCISE A13.1: EDIT DOOR DISPLAY IN REFLECTED

There are a few ways that you can configure Doors to display in Reflected Ceiling Plans. Each firm has its own standards. Here are a few techniques to try.

1. Load the Commercial Project and open the *03 Partitions* file. On the Drawing Status Bar, load the **Reflected** Display Configuration.
2. Select one of the interior Walls, right-click and choose **Edit Object Display**. On the Display Properties tab, highlight Reflected and then click the Edit Display Properties icon. On the Layer/Color/Linetype tab, turn on the Below Cut Plane component. Configure the Above Cut Plane component to your desired Layer, Color, Linetype and Plot Style settings. (This is the "header" component.) Click the Cut Plane tab, place a check mark in the "Override Display Configuration Cut Plane" checkbox, change the value to **6'-6"** [**1800**] and then click OK back to the drawing.

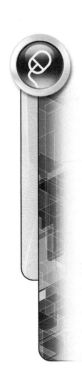

   The location of the openings within the Walls should now appear. Doors will also appear and be fully closed. You can change the way they display based on your preferences.
3. Select one of the Doors, right-click and choose Edit Object Display. On the Layer/Color/Linetype tab, turn off components that you don't wish to see. If you do not want Doors to display at all in the Ceiling Plan, turn off all components and then click OK back to the drawing. If you wish some components to display, you can leave them on and change their settings. For instance, you may wish to leave the Frame, Swing and Panel on, but change them to a gray color and a dashed linetype and a lighter lineweight. Check the Other tab and review the "Override Open Percent." If this is selected and set to 0, then the Door swing will appear closed. Experiment with this feature and see that the Door swing can be configured differently between Display Configurations. Set to your office standard or desired effect. OK back to the drawing when finished (see Figure A.13).
4. Save and close all files.

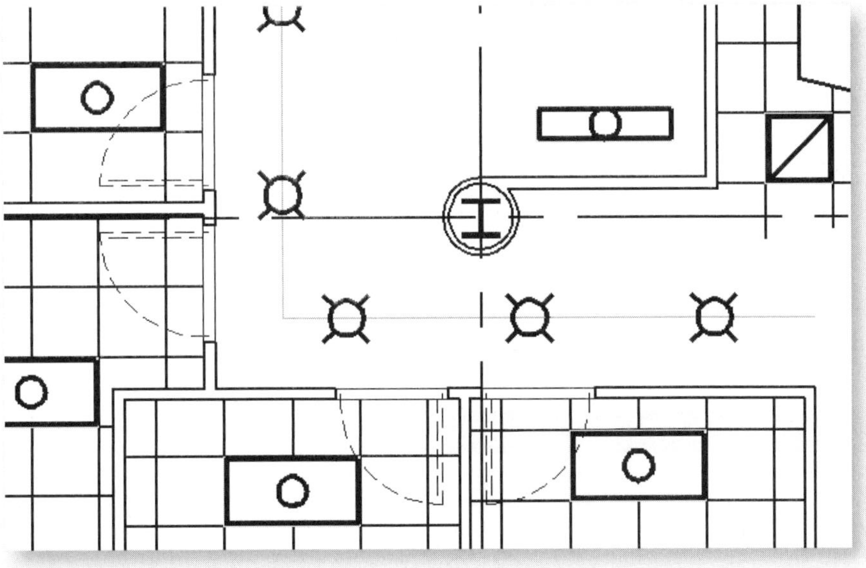

FIGURE A.13 *Change the Display settings of objects in the Reflected Display Configuration*

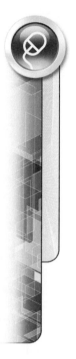

EXERCISE A13.2: COMPLETE THE CEILING PLAN

1. Finish adding all of your Ceiling Grids and lights.
2. Add some other ceiling fixtures (using the Content Browser or the DesignCenter). There are exit signs, diffusers and other types of lights. The process for everything in the Content Browser and DesignCenter is "drag and drop" and then read the Command Line for options.
3. Try the other electrical items, such as switches, outlets, bells and fire alarms.
4. Save and close all files.

You may also repeat any of the techniques covered in Chapter 13 on the Residential Project if you like. Files have been provided in the *Chapter13\Residential* folder for practice.

CHAPTER 14

Residential and Commercial Projects

Annotate the remaining View files.

EXERCISE A14.1: ADD AEC DIMENSIONS AND ANNOTATION

1. Load either the Residential or the Commercial Project.

   Open any of the View files for either the Commercial or Residential project. Use the techniques covered in Chapter 14 and perform the following:
2. Add AEC dimensions to each *Floor Plan* View file.
3. Add detail clouds, notes and revision clouds using the tools on the palettes and the Content Browser.
4. Open the *Elevation and Section Compo*site Model View files and add Elevation Labels to each Elevation and Section. Remember to define a new UCS for each Elevation and Section as required.

   There are also elevation tags, north arrows, bar scales and many other symbols on tool palettes, Content Browser and in the DesignCenter. Try several of them to get comfortable with what is available. Be sure to work in the View files of each project.
5. Add Room Tags to other View files to practice techniques covered in the chapter.
6. Repeat on the other Levels.
7. Save and close all files when done.

CHAPTER 15

Residential and Commercial Projects

Add additional Schedules.

EXERCISE A15.1: ADD OTHER SCHEDULES

Included on the tool palettes are two other Schedule Table styles: Window Schedule and Room Finish Schedule. In addition, there are several more examples in the Content Library.

1. Load either project. Create additional Schedule Table View and Sheet files. If you want to use the Edit Table Cell functionality, create a View file for the

Schedule that you wish to create; otherwise, simply make a new Sheet file in the "600" series (A-601, A-602, etc.), and add a Schedule there using the procedure for adding the Door Schedule covered in Chapter 15.

2. Open the Content Browser (CTRL + 4) and Click on the *Documentation Tool Catalog – Imperial* [*Documentation Tool Catalog – Metric*].
3. Navigate to the *Schedule Tables* category (see Figure A.14).

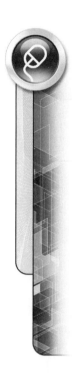

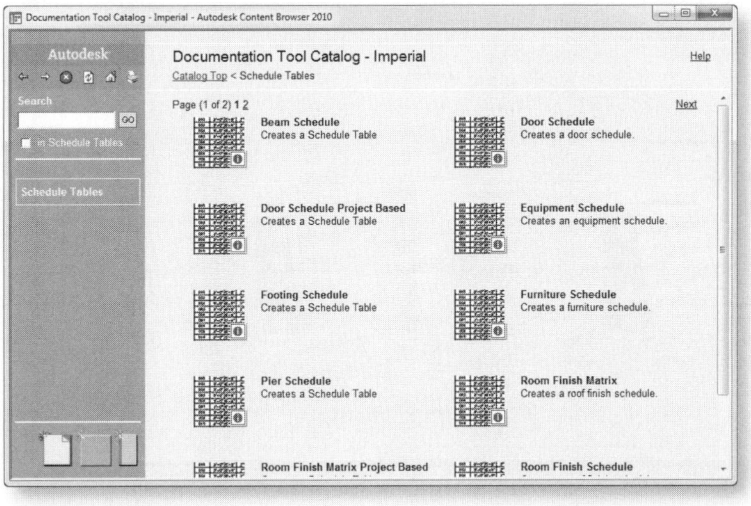

FIGURE A.14 *Many Schedule Table tools are available in the Content Browser*

4. Add some more Schedules. Follow the same basic procedures we followed in this chapter. If you are unhappy with the format of any Schedule, see if you can edit the style to change it.
5. Save and close all files.

CHAPTER 16

Residential Project

Refine Sections and Elevations.

EXERCISE A16.1: MATERIAL BOUNDARIES

Add more Material Boundaries to all Sections and Elevations as appropriate.

EXERCISE A16.2: OTHER REFINEMENTS

Add notes and dimensions to the elevations and sections. Do general cleanup of any extraneous linework.

Commercial Project

Update and add Elevations and Sections. You can open the complete version from Chapter 15 for this exercise.

1. Update all of the Elevations in the *A-EL01*. Repeat all of the techniques discussed in Chapter 16 to create pleasing Building Elevations (see Figure A.15).

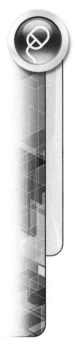

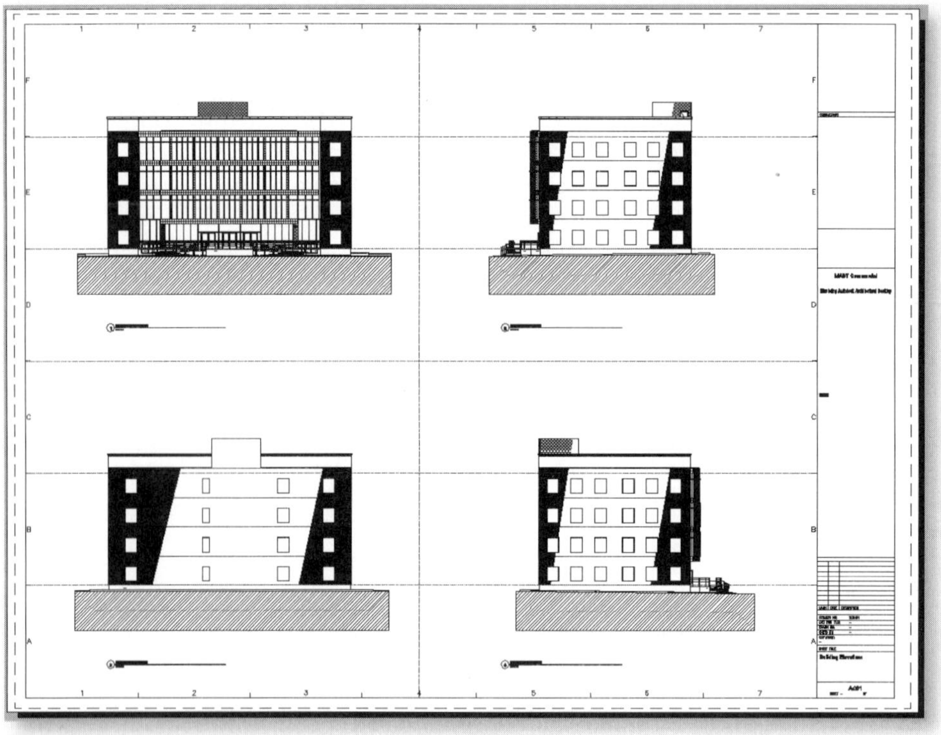

FIGURE A.15 *Set up an Elevation Sheet for the Commercial project*

2. Add Material Boundaries.
3. Add labels, notes and dimensions as appropriate.
4. Open *A-201* Sheet file to see the results. To make the *A-201 Sheet* file load more quickly, unload all XREFs except the *A-EL00* XREF.

A Live Section was built in the *A-SCoo* View file in the early stages of this project. You can continue to keep this section live and up to date as the project progresses and even print it as part of the final set. However, it will probably be more useful in the later stages of Design Development and Construction Documents to cut some 2D Section/Elevation objects for the Building Sections instead.

5. Open the View file named *A-SC01*.
6. Switch to the **Medium Detail** Display Configuration.
7. In Top view, follow steps similar to those covered in Chapter 16 and update the Section.
8. If you wish to add some more Sections, create them from the Plan View files using the appropriate Callout tools on the tool palette. Be sure to choose the "Existing View Drawing" option to create the new sections in the *A-SC01* View file.
9. Add Subdivisions, Material Boundaries, Notes, Labels, Dimensions and Edit Linework as appropriate on the existing and any new sections you create.
10. Save and close all files.

CHAPTER 17

Residential Project

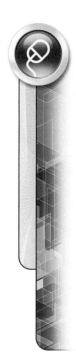

The Typical Wall Section Detail created in the Residential project exposes an issue with the dimensions of the foundation Wall used. It is too narrow for the construction above it. This is exactly the kind of thing that early creation and blocking out of details is meant to reveal. Try correcting these problems in the *Basement New* Construct and then updating the underlying section beneath our detail to verify.

1. Open the *Basement New* Construct.
2. Select all Foundation Walls and using the Save As tool on the ribbon to create a new style for these Walls. Edit the components to match the sizes used for the detail components (**12"** [**300**] Wall width, **20"** × **10"** [**500 × 250**]). Be sure to keep the reference points relative to the Baseline intact; in other words, change the Width of the Wall component to **12"** [**300**] and the Edge offset to **-12"** [**-300**]. (Refer to Chapter 10 for assistance with Wall Style editing.)
3. Open the *A-DT01* View file and refresh the background 2D Section/Elevation object to coordinate it with the detail.

EXERCISE A17.1: COMMERCIAL PROJECT DETAILS

Using the techniques covered in the chapter; create details in the Commercial project.

CHAPTER 18

Residential Project

Plot the Residential Project.

EXERCISE A18.1: PLOT THE RESIDENTIAL PROJECT

1. Repeat the steps covered in Chapter 18 to plot the Residential Project.

   Save different Sheet Selection lists for different purposes; for example, one list might be for plans only, while another is the complete set. To do this, use the `SHIFT` and `CTRL` keys to select one or more Sheets on the Sheets tab, right-click and choose **Save Sheet Selection**. Give it a name.
2. Create a 3D DWF of the Residential project.

APPENDIX b

Wall Cleanup Checklist

AUTOMATIC WALL CLEANUP

Automatic Wall cleanup will occur when:

- The justification line of one Wall intersects the justification line of another Wall.
- The justification line of one Wall intersects the cleanup radius of another Wall.
- The cleanup radius of one Wall intersects the justification line of another Wall.

Rule 1—Use Wall Justification Display

- Select a Wall. On the Wall ribbon tab, on the Cleanup panel, click the Justification Display button.

Rule 2—Set the Default Cleanup Radius to 0

- Properties palette and Wall tool defaults (already set to 0 in out-of-the-box templates).

Rule 3—Practice Good Clean Drafting

This is the "Golden Rule" of Wall cleanup:

- Avoid doubles.
- Use Offset, Fillet, Trim and Extend.
- Use L and T cleanup tools (on the Wall ribbon tab).
- Use Object Snaps (F3).
- Autosnap (**Application Menu** > **Options**: AEC Object Settings tab).

Rule 4—Adjust the Cleanup Radius

- Use the Cleanup Radius grip (visible when justification display is on).
- Or edit on the Properties palette.

  For Center and Baseline justification—set between ½ and ¾ × Wall Width.

  For Left and Right justification—set between ½ and 1 × Wall Width.

OTHER CONSIDERATIONS

- Justification can impact cleanup. Experiment with Left, Right, Center and Baseline to yield variations in cleanup behavior. Try Baseline for exterior Walls, Center for interior Walls and Left or Right as needed.
- A Cleanup Group limits cleanup to Walls that are part of the same group.
- To Make XREFs clean up with the host drawing, edit the Cleanup Group definition.

- Complex Wall styles use component priorities to determine how their individual subcomponents clean up.
- If all attempts at Automatic Cleanup fail, use "manual cleanup" (Wall Merge and Edit in Place).

MANUAL WALL CLEANUP

When Automatic Cleanup fails to give the desired result and the items listed in Other Considerations have been ruled out, try manual cleanup:

- Try to trigger automatic cleanup before resorting to manual cleanup.
  Option 1: Apply a Wall Merge (expand the Cleanup ribbon panel, choose Add Wall Merge Condition).
  Option 2: Use Cleanup Edit in Place (Wall tab, Cleanup panel).

WALL COMPONENT PRIORITIES

Wall Component priorities impact the way components clean up relative to one another:

- Components with the same priority number will clean up.
- Lower-numbered components will interrupt (pass through) higher-numbered components.
- Wall priorities will take precedence over drawing order. (The order in which Walls were drawn has no bearing.)
- It is highly recommended that you adopt the out-of-the-box priority list shown in Table 9.1 in Chapter 9.

APPENDIX C

Online Resources

INTRODUCTION

This appendix provides several Web sites and other resources that you can visit for information on AutoCAD Architecture and related topics. Internet shortcuts for each of these sites can be found in the *Appendix C* folder created when you extracted the datasets from the CD.

WEB SITES RELATED TO THE CONTENT OF THIS BOOK

Books, Training
Implementation Services
Project Coaching
PAUL F. AUBIN
CONSULTING SERVICES
www.paulaubin.com

http://www.paulaubin.com

Web site of the author. Includes information on this book and Aubin's other books, such as *Autodesk Architectural Desktop: An Advanced Implementation Guide* (co-authored with Matt Dillon), as well as Aubin's books on previous versions of ACA. Check the site for ordering information and addenda. Paul also offers training and consulting services nationwide. Please visit the site for details and contact information.

http://paulfaubin.blogspot.com/

Paul F. Aubin's Blog. Thoughts on publishing CAD books.

http://www.autodeskpress.com

Web site for Autodesk Press. Visit for information on other CAD titles, online resources, student software and more.

http://www.autodesk.com

Autodesk main Web site. Visit often for the latest information on Autodesk products.

WEB SITES OF RELATED INTEREST

http://discussion.autodesk.com

Autodesk Discussion Groups main page. Online community of Autodesk users sharing comments, questions and solutions about all Autodesk products.

http://architects-desktop.blogspot.com

David Koch, based in Upper Darby, Pennsylvania, an architect employed by Ewing-Cole in its Philadelphia office. His blog, titled "The Architect's Desktop" is about harnessing the Power of Autodesk AEC products and includes many useful ACA resources, tutorials and musings.

http://modocrmadt.blogspot.com

Matt Dillon, based in San Antonio, Texas, specializes in consulting with architectural and engineering firms to make the most of their ACA and other BIM software. His blog, titled "Breaking down the walls" includes many useful Revit and ACA resources, tutorials and musings.

http://adt_blog.typepad.com

Started by Chris Yanchar, a product designer on the AutoCAD Architecture team, and now continued by Shaan Hurley (see *Between the Lines*, below), this blog shares and aggregates information on AutoCAD Architecture and architecture. At the blog site, you will find links to how-to's and articles about ACA features.

http://autodesk.blogs.com/between_the_lines

Shaan Hurley, a technical marketing manager for the AutoCAD group and manager of most of the beta programs for Autodesk, shares his views on AutoCAD, technology and life. Not everything is official Autodesk opinion, endorsement or recommendation; it is a blog from Shaan. This approach provides direct contact between customers and Autodesk personnel most familiar with the products.

***Cadalyst* Magazine Web Forum**

http://forums.cadalyst.com

Online user forum hosted by *Cadalyst* magazine and moderated by Paul F. Aubin.

http://www.cadalyst.com/

Main home page for *Cadalyst* magazine. View magazines online or subscribe to print edition.

http://www.nibs.org

Web site of the National Institute of Building Sciences.

buildingSMARTalliance Sites

http://www.buildingsmartalliance.org/index.php

Main home page of the buildingSMARTalliance.

http://www.buildingsmartalliance.org/ncs

Web page for information about and purchase of the United States National CAD Standard.

http://www.aia.org

Web site of the American Institute of Architects.

ONLINE RESOURCES FOR ACA PLUG-INS AND TRAINING

PAUL F. AUBIN
CONSULTING SERVICES
www.paulaubin.com

http://www.paulaubin.com

Web site of this book's author. Paul F. Aubin Consulting Services provides AutoCAD Architecture training and implementation services. Visit the site for details on services available. Contact Paul F. Aubin to discuss your ACA training and implementation needs:

http://www.paulaubin.com/contact.php

http://www.studiovim.com

Design and CAD Consulting/3d Modeling

Web site of Velina Mirincheva, editorial and dataset contributor to the 2008 edition of *Mastering AutoCAD Architecture*. Studio VIM provides architects and engineers with design and CAD consulting, online and live support for AutoCAD Architecture, single-user and network setup and complex 3D modeling for use in construction documentation. For contacts, send an e-mail to mail@studiovim.com.

http://au.autodesk.com/

The annual conference and premiere learning event for users of Autodesk software. With more than 9,000 people in attendance last year and more than 600 classes being offered by industry experts from around the globe, this is the training and networking event of the year. The AU Online Web site extends the learning year-round.

http://www.GreenBuildingStudio.com

Green Building Studio is a free Web service that provides architects and engineers using Autodesk Revit, AutoCAD Architecture or Autodesk Building Systems with early design stage whole-building energy analysis and product information appropriate for their building design.

http://www.e-specs.com

Built around its e-SPECS technology, which links the project drawings to the specification documents, InterSpec has a variety of products and services to help manage construction specifications in the most accurate, efficient and cost-effective manner possible.

http://www.archidigm.com

The world's largest independent online source of architectural desktop information featuring tips, tricks, news, downloads and a complete subscriber-only area with several eGuides on ACA and AutoCAD.

http://www.augi.com

The Autodesk User Group International (AUGI). Home of resources, training, content and membership information for AUGI, the largest international Autodesk user's group.

Several additional sites are provided with the files from the CD in the *Appendix-C* folder. All URLs were tested and active at the time of publication.

APPENDIX d

Space Area Calculations

INTRODUCTION

Throughout the course of this book, we have used Space objects as a means to represent the rooms in our projects and as a place to store such room-specific schedule data. In addition to these uses, Space objects provide an easy and sophisticated means of tracking room area.

Many building projects require calculation of critical areas in some form. The extent of such need will vary depending on whether you seek to calculate the building Floor Area Ratio (FAR), determine leasing rates based on Building Owners and Managers Association (BOMA) standards or generate a Proof of Areas report for building department officials. Regardless of the specific requirement, Spaces provide many powerful features to assist in making these required calculations.

OBJECTIVES

- Understand Space boundaries.
- Use Offset boundaries.
- Use Automatic and manual boundaries.
- Understand Calculation Standards.
- Generate BOMA Space Schedule.

SPACE GEOMETRY

Space objects serve a variety of functions in an AutoCAD Architecture project. In the chapters of this book, we have used Spaces as general representations of the rooms in our projects. Spaces can serve other functions in a project as well. They can also be represented in a variety of ways. On the Properties palette, three geometry types are available: 2D, Extrusion and Freeform (see Figure D.1).

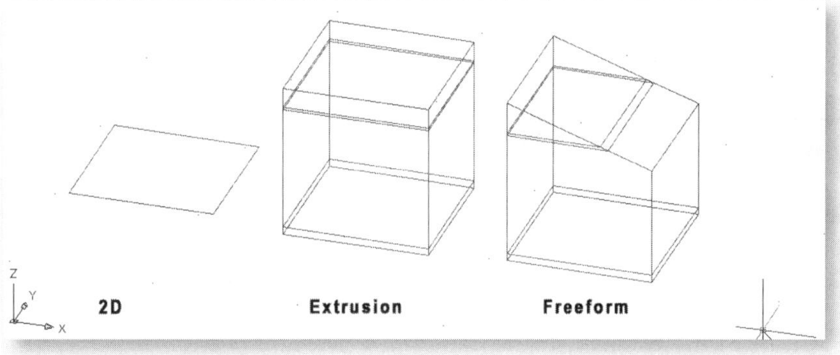

FIGURE D.1 *Spaces can be drawn in three geometry types*

Choose the 2D option if area calculations and space tagging are your only concerns. The extrusion option adds a simple third-dimensional characteristic to a Space and exposes the floor, ceiling and volume components of the Model display representation. When you choose a free-form Space, you gain the ability to modify the three-dimensional form of the volume component. In each case, the underlying Space object is the same; the three choices simply control how the Space is represented graphically in 3D.

When a Space is drawn, its actual area, perimeter and volume can be seen on the Properties palette. These are referred to as the "base" dimensions (Base Area, Base Volume, etc) and are representative of the actual Space geometry (see Figure D.2).

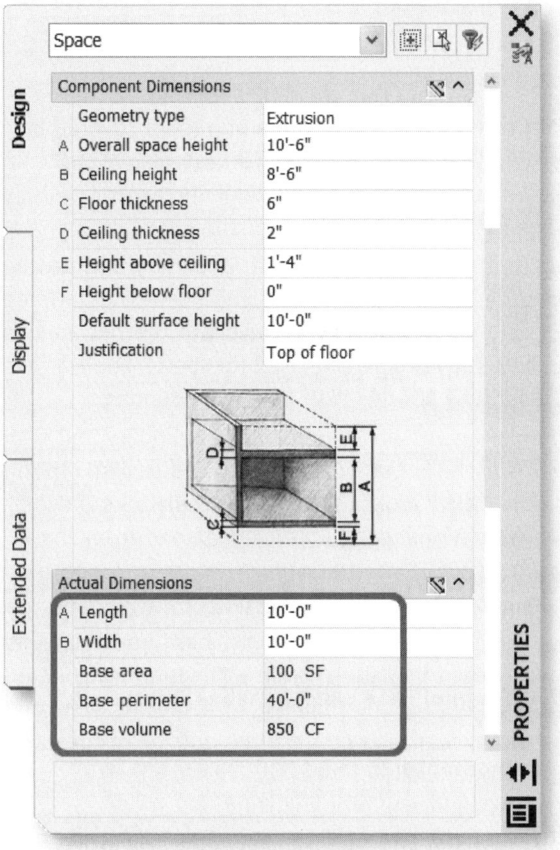

FIGURE D.2 *Base dimensions are the actual dimensions not based on calculations or interpretations*

While useful, these base dimensions are often not suitable to the kinds of calculations (particularly for area) that are often required by building officials, codes and leasing agents. For more control and detail in such calculations, we have several alternative boundaries available on each Space object. To see these, click on a Space and on the Properties palette and change the Offset boundaries to Manual. Click the Space again to see additional grips at the center of the Space. If you hover over each of these, you will see that you can enable and disable one of four different boundary types. Look at Figure D.3 for a brief explanation of the process. For a definition of each boundary, see the next topic.

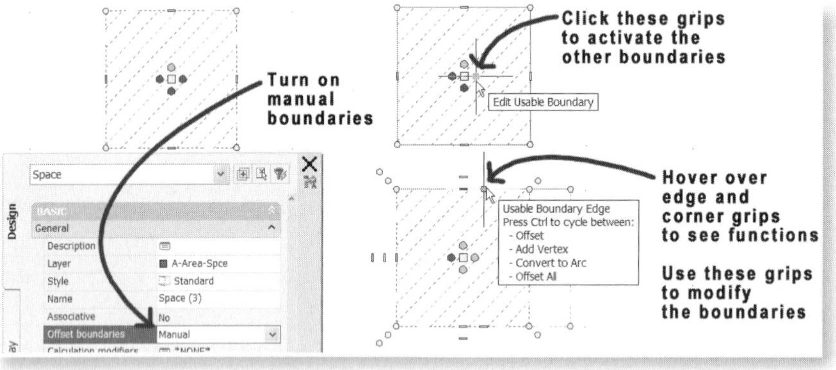

FIGURE D.3 *Manual boundaries can be used to modify the Base, Net, Usable and Gross areas*

SPACE BOUNDARIES

Spaces have four different boundaries, each of which displays a different aspect of the Space and can be scheduled and edited individually:

- **Base boundary**—Normally representing the inner area of a room covered by a space. This is the area generated by bounding objects in an associative space. In most cases, the base boundary is identical to the net boundary, except in some area calculation standards such as the Swedish SIS standard.
- **Net boundary**—This boundary is offset from the base boundary and can be used for planning and detailed design. For example, if you need to determine the hiring of cleaning personnel for an office, you would use the net area as the calculation basis. The net boundary can also be used for special applications when the calculated area of a space is smaller than the base boundary.
- **Usable boundary**—This boundary is offset from the base boundary and is in many area calculation standards used for planning and detailed design, renting calculations, tax and other duty calculations, statistical calculations, maintenance, pricing and more. The usable boundaries typically extend from the inside of the exterior walls to the middle of the interior walls (or a specified distance into the interior walls).
- **Gross boundary**—The gross boundary is offset from the base boundary and can be used in connection with cost calculation, price estimation, calculation of tax and other duties, key numbers for the building or a specific floor and more. Normally, the gross boundary is measured from the outside of the exterior walls to the middle of the interior walls.

NOTE The preceding definitions were excerpted from the AutoCAD Architecture online help.

AutoCAD Architecture 2010 provides a collection of tools that when enabled, give us a quick and effective way to create area takeoffs for planning, leasing and other common scenarios. In the remainder of this appendix, we will use the Imperial Commercial project and the out-of-the-box BOMA calculations standard. BOMA stands for Building Owners and Managers Association, an organization that publishes the standard for determining leasable area in the United States and Canada. If you do not use BOMA in your own calculations, ACA does include a few alternative standards. At this time, it is not possible to build your own standard. However, you can turn on manual boundaries if none of the out-of-the-box standards meet your needs.

Install the CD Files and Load the Current Project

If you have already installed all of the files from the CD, simply skip down to step 3 below to make the project active. If you need to install the CD files, start at step 1.

1. If you have not already done so, install the dataset files located on the Mastering AutoCAD Architecture 2010 CD-ROM.

   Refer to "Files Included on the CD-ROM" in the Preface for information on installing the sample files included on the CD.
2. Launch AutoCAD Architecture 2010 from the desktop icon created in Chapter 3.

If you did not create a custom icon, you might want to review "Create a New Profile" and "Create a Desktop Shortcut" in Chapter 3. Creating the custom desktop icon is not essential; however, it makes loading the custom profile easier.

3. From the File menu, choose **Project Browser**.
4. Click to open the folder list and choose your *C:* drive.
5. Double-click on the *MasterACA 2010* folder, then the *Appendix-D* folder.

   Only one project will be listed: *D Commercial*.
6. Double-click *D Commercial* and then click Close in the Project Browser.

NOTE

Important: If a message appears asking you to repath the project, click the "Repath the project now" option Refer to the "Repathing Projects" topic in the Preface for more information.

Working with the By Style Boundary Offset

There are three types offset boundaries: By Style, By Standard and Manual. By Style and By Standard are both automated ways of determining offsets of the Net, Gross and Usable areas relative to the Base area. We looked briefly at the manual option above. You would enable the manual option if you could not make either of the automated options suit your needs. Then you would simply use the grips to manipulate the boundaries as necessary. Let's take a brief look at the By style option. This option simply applies a uniform offset all the way around the Space for each of the other boundaries. To see and modify the By style settings, edit the Space style.

7. Double-click to open *03 Partitions* on the Constructs tab of Project Navigator.
8. Select any office Space onscreen, right-click and choose **Properties**.

Notice that the Offset boundaries option is set to **By Style** (see the left side of Figure D.4).

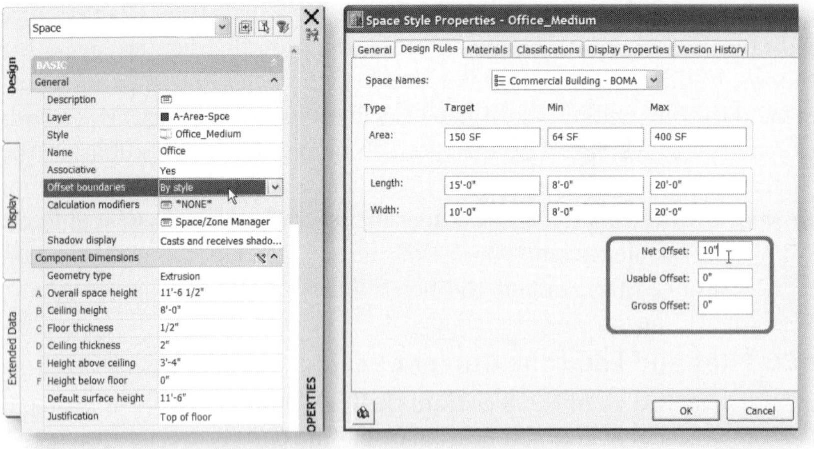

FIGURE D.4 *Space style offset boundaries*

9. With the Space still selected, on the Space tab of the ribbon, click the **Edit Style** button.
10. Click the Design Rules tab.

Notice the Net, Usable and Gross Offset fields. Here we could input values to offset these boundaries relative to the Base Area. All Spaces of this style would be affected.

11. Type **10** in the Net Offset field and then click OK to dismiss the dialog.

Notice that all office Spaces now have an additional dark green dashed boundary all the way around. While potentially useful in some circumstances, it is unlikely that a uniform offset like this would provide much value in generating meaningful area takeoffs. Let's try the BOMA Standard instead.

Working with the BOMA Standard Boundary Offset

Four standards come with AutoCAD Architecture: Basic, BOMA, DIN and SIS. Basic is fairly generic, but it is more useful than the By style options shown above. DIN is used in German-speaking countries; SIS is used in Scandinavian countries; and as noted above, BOMA is prevalent in the United States and Canada. To work with a Calculation Standard, you must make two changes: the Spaces in your file must have the Offset boundaries changed to By standard and you have to enable the Calculation Standard in the "Options" dialog.

12. On the Properties palette, click the Quick Select icon (upper right corner).
13. In the "Quick Select" dialog, choose **Entire drawing** from Apply to, **Space** from Object type and **Layer** from the Properties list and type **A-Area-Spce** in the Value field (see Figure D.5).

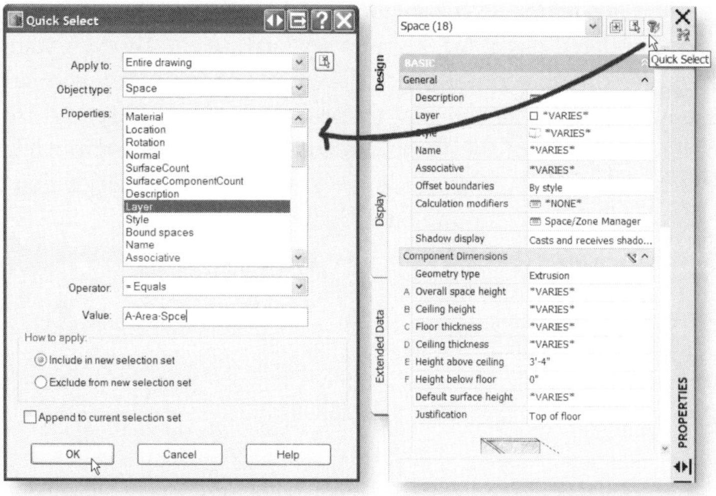

FIGURE D.5 *Use Quick Select to select all Spaces*

This selects all Space in the drawing on the default Space layer. Recall from Chapter 13 that there is one additional Space in this file used to represent a ceiling feature. We do not want this selected; and since it is on the ceiling layer, this approach to selection easily excludes it.

14. Click OK to select all Spaces.
15. On the Properties palette, choose **By standard** from the Offset boundaries list.

Notice that the green dashed boundaries disappear. This is because they were displayed based upon the setting of By Style. The new setting of By Standard uses different rules for the offsets as we will see.

16. From the Application Menu, choose **Options**.
17. On the AEC Object Settings tab, choose **BOMA Standard** from the Calculation Standard list (see Figure D.6) and then click OK.

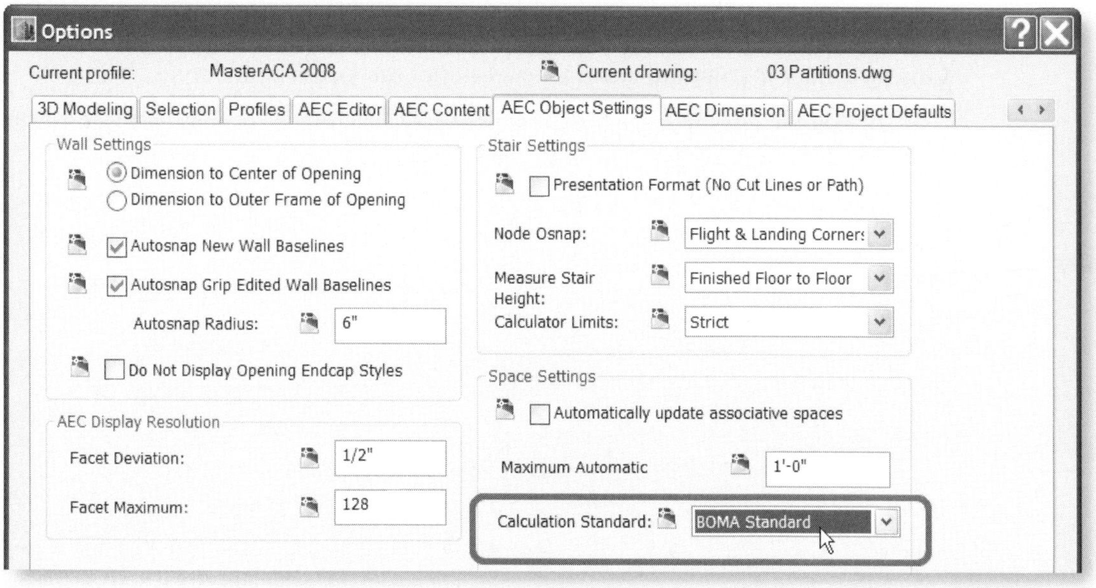

FIGURE D.6 *Turn on the BOMA Standard in the Options dialog*

The drawing should update immediately. If you zoom and pan around, you will see that all of the Spaces have updated based on the rules set forth in the BOMA standard. For example, if you look at the corner office (lower left of the plan), you will notice that the Gross boundary goes all the way to the exterior Wall edge and the Net boundary goes to the inside face of the Windows and Walls on the bottom and left sides and to the center of the Walls on the interior. The Usable boundary follows the inside edge of the Walls all the way around (see Figure D.7).

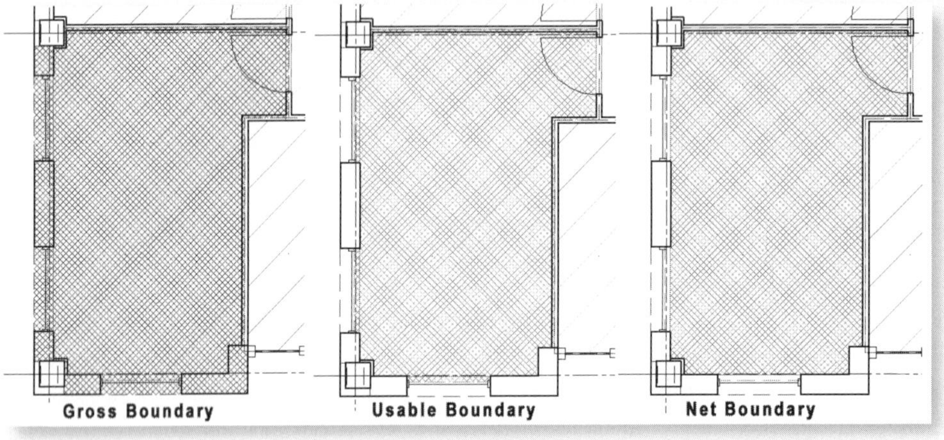

FIGURE D.7 *Compare the automatically created Gross, Usable and Net Boundaries*

You may find that you are not satisfied with the results at the corners or around columns. In this case, it has to do with the way in which the columns, the Walls and the interference between the two have been built in this dataset. We could modify the columns and their enclosures to try to achieve a better automated solution, or we could simply modify the affected Spaces manually. Let's try the manual modification approach on the corner office.

18. Select the corner office.
19. On the Properties palette, change the Offset boundaries setting to **Manual**.
20. Click the gray "Edit Gross Boundary" grip (Use the tooltips to find it).

Grips will appear around the entire perimeter of the Gross boundary.

21. Edit the grips to make the Gross boundary include the columns (see Figure D.8).

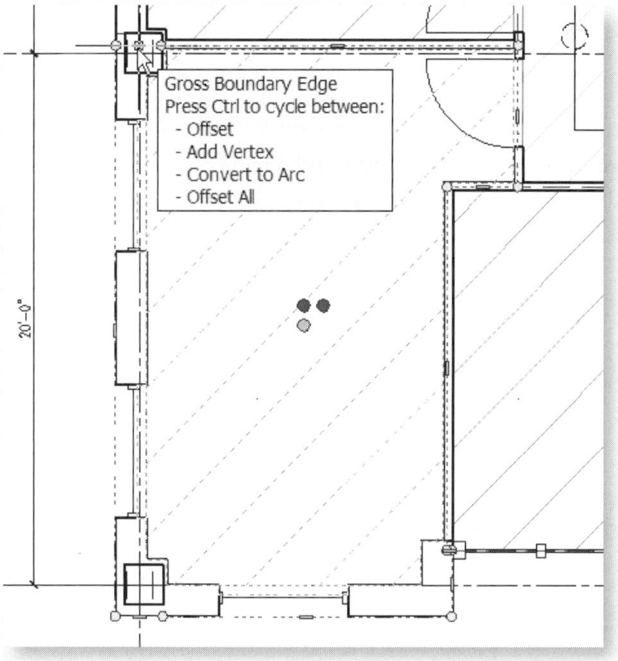

FIGURE D.8 *Change a Space to manual and edit the Gross boundary with grips*

BOMA CLASSIFICATIONS AND SCHEDULES

In the previous topics, we focused on the geometry of the Spaces and their respective boundaries. Once you have the geometry correct, you will want to generate a report of the totals and analyze the results. This can be done with Schedules as we learned in Chapter 15. ACA ships with a premade Schedule style for use in generating a BOMA Space list. As we saw in Chapter 15, to create a Schedule, you need both a Schedule Table style and a Property Set definition. In addition, the BOMA Schedule also makes use of a special BOMA Classification definition. Classifications were also explored in Chapter 15.

Understanding the BOMA Space Type Classification

All of the Spaces used in our projects throughout this book have come directly from the out-of-the-box styles or have been created as copies of an out-of-the-box style. This was done back in Chapter 13 primarily. One aspect of those out-of-the-box styles not previously explored was their Classification. Nearly all AEC objects can have a Classification applied to them. In Chapter 15 we discussed how this was useful to filter Schedules. In this sequence, we will see that all of the Spaces in our project have a preassigned Classification that is used by the BOMA Schedule to determine which type of Space and therefore which BOMA rules should be applied to it. Let's have a look.

1. Select one of the office Spaces, right-click and choose **Properties**.
2. Click the Extended Data tab (see Figure D.9).

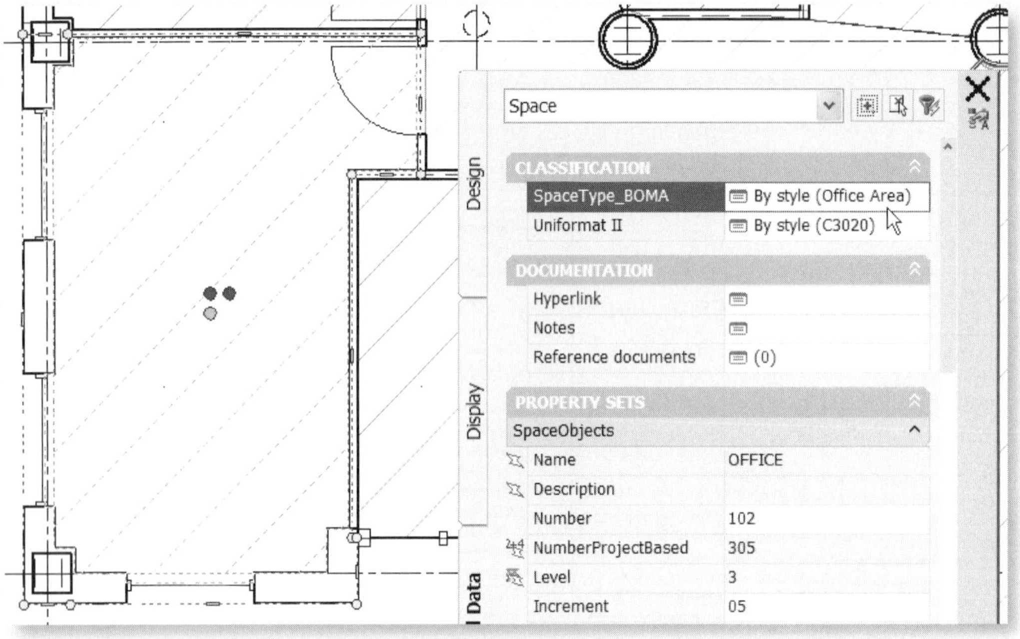

FIGURE D.9 *Check the Classification on the Properties palette*

At the top of the palette is the Classification grouping. In the case of the Spaces we have here, there are two Classification definitions listed: SpaceType_BOMA and Uniformat II. We assigned this Uniformat II Classification to these Spaces in Chapter 15. Now let's take notice of the SpaceType_BOMA Classification. Notice that for this (and any office) it reads "By style (Office Area)." This means that the Classification is Office Area and it is applied at the style level. Like most things in ACA, it is better to apply such settings at the style level where possible.

3. With the Space still selected, on the Space tab of the ribbon, click the **Edit Style** button.
4. Click the Classifications tab.

Here you will simply receive confirmation of what we already learned on the Properties palette. However, if you wish to experiment, you can click on the browse icon next to Office Area and choose something else for the Office_Medium style. Remember this change will affect all Spaces using this style. When you click OK, and select another office, you will receive confirmation on the Properties palette. Be sure to undo any such experimentation that you do. If while you have a Space (or any object) selected, you click on the designated Classification and change it, this change will, by contrast, apply only to the selected item; not to the style. So if you wish to reclassify all objects of a particular style, edit the style again. If you wish to apply the Classification to just a single object, you change it on the Properties palette instead.

5. On the Project Navigator palette, double-click to open *01 Partitions*.
6. Repeat the process above to select all Spaces and change the Offset boundaries to **By standard** and then turn on the BOMA Standard in the Options dialog.

NOTE

Notice the "Current drawing" icon next to this setting in the Options dialog; recall that this means that Calculation Standard setting affects only the drawing we are in.

Study the results.

7. If necessary, change any of the Spaces to Manual and adjust the boundaries accordingly.
8. Click either of the two large Spaces on the left or right.

   On the Extended Data tab of the Properties palette, check the Classification.

Notice that the Classification for each of these Spaces is Store Area and it is assigned By style. These two Spaces are on the street level, however, and should more appropriately be classified as Street Frontage.

9. On the Properties palette, change the SpaceType_BOMA to Street Frontage.

If you open additional files in the project such as the *Core* Element file and look at how the Spaces are classified, you will begin to anticipate the way that final totals in the Schedule will break down. For example, in the *Core* file, the toilet rooms are classified as Floor Common Areas while the elevator lobby is classified as Building Common Area. If you open the *Stair Tower* Construct, you will see that its Space is classified as Major Vertical Penetration.

Understanding the Space List—BOMA Schedule Table

The Classifications shown here impact the way the BOMA Schedule performs its calculations. Let's add the BOMA Schedule next and see how it functions. This is the last piece of BOMA content that we will explore. To add this Schedule, we will open the Content Browser.

10. Close and save any open Constructs or Elements.
11. On the Project Navigator palette, on the Views tab, double-click to open the *A-SH03* View file.

    This file was last visited in Chapter 15 when the Schedule was added to the left.
12. On the Home tab, from the Tools drop-down button, choose Content Browser or press CTRL + 4.
13. In the Documentation Tool Catalog - Imperial, navigate to the *Schedule Tables* category.
14. On the second page, locate and then iDrop the Space List - BOMA tool into the drawing.

    If you prefer, you can iDrop it to the Project Tools palette first so that you can access it more readily.
15. Follow the prompts to complete placement of the Schedule beneath the plan.

    Make sure that the Scan XREFs option is selected on the Properties palette and select the XREF containing all the Spaces (*03 Partitions*).
16. Zoom in on the Schedule.

Notice all of the question mark symbols. As we learned in Chapter 15, we must have a Property Set applied to the object being scheduled or no values will show.

17. Select the Schedule, on the Schedule Table tab, on the Modify panel, click the **Add All Property Sets** button (see Figure D.10).

    Remember, you will not be able to edit (add Property Sets) to the Construct if it is still open, so be sure all Constructs are closed.

BOMA SUMMARY OF AREAS

				Usable Areas						Basic Rentable Areas							
Gross Building Area	Gross Measured Area	Major Vertical Penetration	Floor Rentable Area	Office Area	Store Area	Building Common Area	Floor Usable Area	Floor Common Area	Floor R/U Ratio	Office Area	Store Area	Building Common Area	Building Rentable Area	Building R/U Ratio	Office Area	Store Area	Total Rentable
290.56 SF	252.16 SF	0 SF	252.17 SF	252.17 SF	0 SF	0 SF	252.17 SF	0 SF	1	252.17 SF	0 SF	0 SF	252.17 SF	1	252.17 SF	0 SF	252.17 SF
159.70 SF	147.88 SF	0 SF	147.88 SF	147.88 SF	0 SF	0 SF	147.88 SF	0 SF	1	147.88 SF	0 SF	0 SF	147.88 SF	1	147.88 SF	0 SF	147.88 SF
158.04 SF	145.71 SF	0 SF	145.71 SF	145.71 SF	0 SF	0 SF	145.71 SF	0 SF	1	145.71 SF	0 SF	0 SF	145.71 SF	1	145.71 SF	0 SF	145.71 SF
160.29 SF	149.45 SF	0 SF	149.45 SF	149.45 SF	0 SF	0 SF	149.45 SF	0 SF	1	149.45 SF	0 SF	0 SF	149.45 SF	1	149.45 SF	0 SF	149.45 SF
171.42 SF	147.33 SF	0 SF	147.33 SF	147.33 SF	0 SF	0 SF	147.33 SF	0 SF	1	147.33 SF	0 SF	0 SF	147.33 SF	1	147.33 SF	0 SF	147.33 SF
139.11 SF	137.83 SF	0 SF	137.83 SF	137.83 SF	0 SF	0 SF	137.83 SF	0 SF	1	137.83 SF	0 SF	0 SF	137.83 SF	1	137.83 SF	0 SF	137.83 SF
174.02 SF	172.34 SF	0 SF	172.34 SF	172.34 SF	0 SF	0 SF	172.34 SF	0 SF	1	172.34 SF	0 SF	0 SF	172.34 SF	1	172.34 SF	0 SF	172.34 SF
13.07 SF	10.36 SF	0 SF	10.38 SF	10.36 SF	0 SF	0 SF	10.38 SF	0 SF	1	10.36 SF	0 SF	0 SF	10.38 SF	1	10.38 SF	0 SF	10.38 SF
0.06 SF	0.06 SF	0 SF	0.06 SF	0.06 SF	0 SF	0 SF	0.06 SF	0 SF	1	0.06 SF	0 SF	0 SF	0.06 SF	1	0.06 SF	0 SF	0.06 SF
208.51 SF	186.90 SF	0 SF	186.90 SF	0 SF	0 SF	186.90 SF	186.90 SF	0 SF	1	0 SF	0 SF	186.90 SF	186.90 SF	1	0 SF	0 SF	0 SF
40.51 SF	41.71 SF	0 SF	41.71 SF	0 SF	0 SF	0 SF	0 SF	41.71 SF	1	0 SF	0 SF	0 SF	0 SF	1	0 SF	0 SF	0 SF
166.13 SF	159.02 SF	0 SF	159.02 SF	0 SF	0 SF	159.02 SF	159.02 SF	0 SF	1	0 SF	0 SF	159.02 SF	159.02 SF	1	0 SF	0 SF	0 SF
311.84 SF	325.94 SF	0 SF	325.94 SF	0 SF	0 SF	0 SF	0 SF	325.94 SF	1	0 SF	0 SF	0 SF	0 SF	1	0 SF	0 SF	0 SF
347.41 SF	338.49 SF	0 SF	338.49 SF	0 SF	0 SF	338.49 SF	338.49 SF	0 SF	1	0 SF	0 SF	338.49 SF	338.49 SF	1	0 SF	0 SF	0 SF
225.83 SF	216.20 SF	0 SF	216.20 SF	0 SF	0 SF	216.20 SF	216.20 SF	0 SF	1	0 SF	0 SF	216.20 SF	216.20 SF	1	0 SF	0 SF	0 SF
86.56 SF	86.43 SF	0 SF	86.43 SF	86.43 SF	0 SF	0 SF	86.43 SF	0 SF	1	86.43 SF	0 SF	0 SF	86.43 SF	1	86.43 SF	0 SF	86.43 SF
77.21 SF	75.94 SF	0 SF	75.94 SF	75.94 SF	0 SF	0 SF	75.94 SF	0 SF	1	75.94 SF	0 SF	0 SF	75.94 SF	1	75.94 SF	0 SF	75.94 SF
122.67 SF	122.67 SF	0 SF	122.67 SF	0 SF	0 SF	0 SF	0 SF	0 SF	1	0 SF	0 SF	0 SF	0 SF	1	0 SF	0 SF	0 SF
2854.75 SF	2716.42 SF	0 SF	2716.42 SF	1325.49 SF	0 SF	900.81 SF	2226.10 SF	387.65 SF	1.22	1325.49 SF	0 SF	900.81 SF	2226.10 SF	1.679	1325.49 SF	0 SF	1325.49 SF

FIGURE D.10 *The BOMA Summary of Areas appears in the Schedule*

There is much more that can be done with this project to finalize our BOMA calculations. For example, the way the third floor schedule file (*A-SH03*) is configured, it references only the *03 Partitions* and *Core*. If you like, you can add the *Stair Tower* to show the major vertical penetrations in the totals. You can also add the *Front Façade* and use it to assist you in adding Spaces for the empty tenant space on the right side of the plan.

To Add Additional Constructs to this View

18. On the Project Navigator, right-click the *A-SH03* file and choose **Properties**.
19. On the Content tab, check the boxes next to *Front Façade* and *Stair Tower* and then click OK.

This will automatically add XREFs for these files to the current View file. You do *not* need to add XREFs manually.

To Adjust the Selection of the Schedule Table

Schedules list only those items that you actually select when adding the Schedule. Since you are adding new XREFs, they must be added to the Schedule selection.

20. Select the Schedule table. On the ribbon, on the Scheduled Objects panel, click the **Add** button.
21. Click to select the *Core* and the *Stair Tower* file and then press `ENTER`.
22. On the ribbon, click the **Add All Property Sets** button again.

To Add Ancillary Spaces to the Plan

In some cases, you will want to report on areas that are not occupied in a plan or areas that will be completed in a future phase of the project. For example, the large open area on the right side of the third floor is currently not occupied by a tenant. If you wanted to know the square footage of this tenant space, you could certainly open the appropriate Construct and add new Spaces to that area. An alternative would be to simply add the Space object here directly in this View file. In this case, since you are concerned only with the area of the empty space, this would be an acceptable alternative. To do this, add the Space using the 2D geometry option (noted at the beginning of this appendix). By adding the Space directly to this View, it will not appear in any other project Views or Sheets. Adding such a Space to the Constructs is technically the "correct" approach, but since we are not doing any work in this vacant space, and all we really want to do is record the square footage of the empty space on the report for the third floor, the alternative suggested here can be an effective way to manage such data. Naturally you should discuss such strategies with your project team to arrive at the most suitable approach for your specific needs.

23. Use the basic Space tool (on the Design tab) with the 2D geometry and Generate options to add a Space to the unoccupied areas.
24. Select the new Space in the large unoccupied tenant area and on the ribbon click the **Save As** button.
25. Name the new Space style **Unoccupied – Not in Contract** (see Figure D.11).
26. Select the Schedule table. On the ribbon, on the Scheduled Objects panel, click the **Add** button, and then select the new Spaces.
27. Click the **Add All Property Sets** button again.

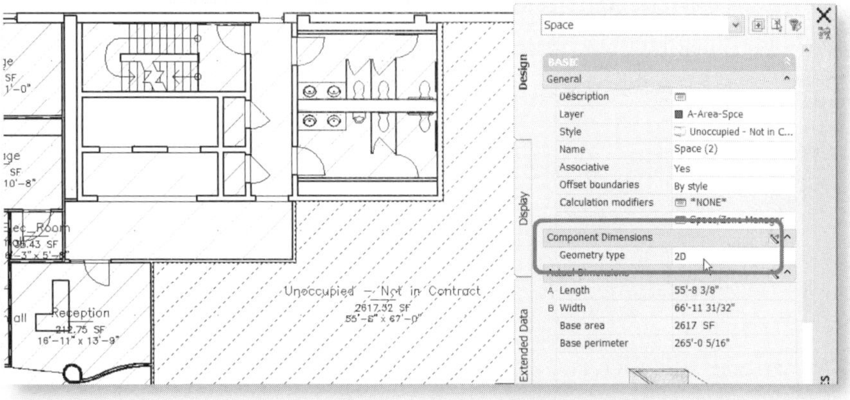

FIGURE D.11 *Add a 2D Space to represent the unoccupied area of the plan*

There is more you can do. If you would like to generate a complete report of the entire building, open each of the Constructs and enable the appropriate Space Standards features as outlined in this appendix. Open the Constructs and make any required manual modifications to the Spaces. Next, add additional View files to the project—one for each of the first, second and fourth floors. Name them *A-SH01*, *A-SH02* and *A-SH04*, respectively. Review the process for creating General View files outlined in Chapter 5, 14 or 15 if necessary. In each of these files, you can add any 2D Spaces as we have done here to flesh out the floor plate and then add the Space List – BOMA Schedule using the process outlined above. Create a Sheet, and then drag each of these Schedules to that Sheet to present the final BOMA calculations for the entire building.

SUMMARY

- Spaces can be 2D, Extrusion or Freeform. Each type exposes successively more of the three-dimensional characteristics.
- You can manually modify each of the Base, Net, Gross and Usable boundaries of Space objects using the grips.
- Space styles can have a uniform offset from the Base boundary for each of the other three boundaries. This is on by default with zero offsets.
- Enabling the By standard option for Spaces allows the Net, Gross and Usable boundaries to react to the bounding geometry and automatically adjust to rules built into the Standard.
- There are four out-of-the-box Standards: Basic, BOMA, DIN and SIS. Each uses rules appropriate to the jurisdiction for which it is designed.
- If the automatically generated boundaries are not correct, you can change an individual Space to manual and use the grips to modify it. Other Spaces remain automatic.
- Classification definitions applied to Space styles assist the BOMA Schedule in determining the proper designation and calculated areas.
- You can modify Classification assignments at the style or object level.
- In general, style-level assignments are preferred over object overrides.
- Use the provided Space List – BOMA tool to generate a complete list of all Spaces and their respective BOMA calculated areas.
- You can choose to add 2D Spaces directly to View files in cases where the actual model geometry is not required elsewhere in the project and you simply need to calculate the square footage of a space.

APPENDIX e

Sharing Files with Consultants

INTRODUCTION

In nearly every project, you will need to share digital design data with other individuals and potentially other software packages. For instance, preparing drawings for distribution to mechanical, electrical and plumbing (MEP) engineers and other consultants offers some challenges in ACA. The objects that make ACA so powerful do not exist in the base version of AutoCAD or in other CAD software. Complicating matters is the fact that you may be dealing with a consultant who is not using AutoCAD, but some other application altogether. This appendix is focused on the various issues related to distributing ACA drawings to consultants who may be using a variety of alternative ACA and AutoCAD versions or other software applications not based on AutoCAD at all.

OBJECTIVES

In this appendix, we will discover what is required to translate drawings into formats readable by consultants not using ACA. Due to the potentially destructive nature of the commands being covered, be sure to practice on files unrelated to any "real" projects until you are familiar with all of the issues covered in this appendix. The following summarizes topics covered in this appendix:

- Understand file formats.
- Understand Object Enablers.
- Understand Proxy Graphics.
- Use Export to AutoCAD.
- Export to non-AutoCAD applications.

DO THEY NEED A DWG?

In some cases, your recipient does not need a DWG at all—he or she only needs to review or print a drawing, for example. In this case, consider sending the recipient a DWF file instead. The DWF format is more compact than DWG, making it easier to e-mail. You can plot the entire set of drawings to a single multi-sheet DWF file (see Chapter 18). Also, you can include Property Sets, layers and Sheet Set data in your DWF files. Recipients need only install the free Autodesk Design Review software to view and print the files. Autodesk Design Review is available free of charge from the Autodesk Web site. Redmarks created in Design Review can be loaded back into ACA for review. All Autodesk products support the creation and importation of DWF files. You can even XREF DWF files and snap to their geometry! Therefore, depending on the specific type of collaboration required, this can be a viable alternative to DWG sharing.

EXPORT TO AUTOCAD

If the recipient needs a DWG, sometimes the best approach in sharing data with consultants is simply sending along a standard AutoCAD drawing file. The DWG file format is widely used and readable by most CAD packages. To save as a standard AutoCAD file, you must *remove* all AEC objects from the drawing. You could try to do this manually with Explode, but you would not achieve much success. The proper way to explode and remove all AEC objects from a drawing is to use the Export to AutoCAD commands on the File menu. This routine eliminates the AEC objects from a drawing file and replaces them with lines, arcs and circles. Additionally, it can bind any external reference files that may be attached or overlaid. It saves the resultant file in one of several versions of DWG or DXF. Use this only if the file will not be returned to you for editing.

CAUTION There is NO way to retrieve the AEC objects once this export has been performed.

Using Export to AutoCAD

1. Open the file you wish to convert. (You can open within the Project Navigator or from the standard Application Menu > Open command.)
2. Be sure that the view direction and Display Configuration are set to the view that you wish your recipient to see.

   For example, if you want them to receive a floor plan, open a floor plan View file and be sure that you set the drawing to Top view and Medium Detail.
3. Depending upon the recipient's version, choose one of the following options:

- *If the recipient has AutoCAD 2010 or an AutoCAD 2010-based vertical product:*

  From the Application Menu, choose **Export** > **AutoCAD** > **AutoCAD** 2010.
- *If the recipient has AutoCAD 2009, 2008 or 2007 or an AutoCAD 2009-based, 2008-based or 2007-based vertical product:*

  From the Application Menu, choose **Export** > **AutoCAD** > **AutoCAD** 2007.
- *If the recipient has an older version, you can choose one of the older formats.*

4. Confirm the file name and location and then click Save.

If the recipient is using a non-AutoCAD–based product that does not read DWG, use one of the DXF options. If the recipient is using Microstation, from the Application Menu choose **Export > DGN** or type Export at the Command Line and then choose the V7 or V8 DGN format.

Using eTransmit and Archive Project

If you wish to send an entire project (or any portion of it) in AutoCAD format, you can use the eTransmit or the Archive function on the Project Navigator. Simply load the project, decide which files you wish to send and then use the right-click functions to eTransmit or Archive the project. Both functions are very similar in process; so once you learn the use of one, the other will be very simple. eTransmit has a few more options. You can eTransmit from any tab of the Project Navigator. It also has the option to send the files directly as an e-mail attachment. Let's look at an example from the Sheets tab, using eTransmit to send the entire project set.

1. On the Project Navigator palette, click the Sheets tab.
2. Right-click the Sheet Set node at the top (it has the same name as the currently active project) and choose **eTransmit Setups**.

3. Click the New button and name the New Transmittal Setup **CD Submission** and then click Continue (see Figure E.1).

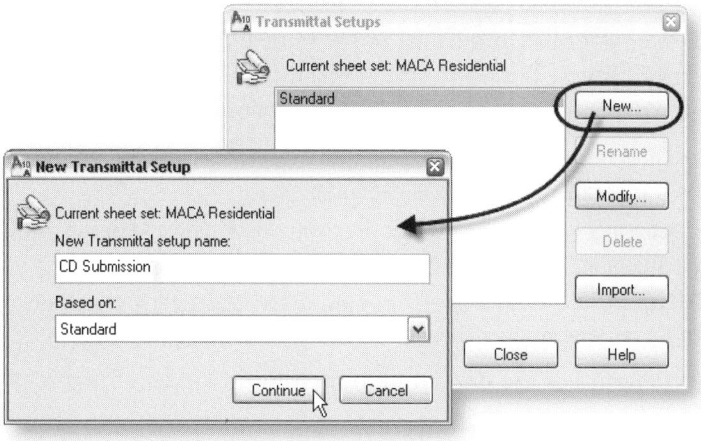

FIGURE E.1 *Creating a New Transmittal Setup*

Several options will appear in the Modify Transmittal Setup dialog. At the top left, in the Transmittal package type list are three options (see Figure E.2).

- **Folder (set of files)**—This option will copy all of the required files to a new folder.
- **Self-extracting executable (*.*exe*)**—This option will create a single compressed self-extracting archive file containing all of the selected files. Recipients simply double-click the *.exe* file to extract all of the files.
- **Zip (*.*zip*)**—This option will create a single compressed archive file containing all of the selected files. To open the ZIP file, the recipient must have compatible extraction software such as WinZip or the native Windows XP Zip file capabilities.

In the File Format list are nine options, including four that match the Export to AutoCAD functions discussed above:

- **Keep existing drawing file formats**—This option maintains the file format of each drawing transmitted.
- **AutoCAD 2010 Drawing Format**—This option will simply save all drawing files in 2010 format without translation.
- **AutoCAD 2007 Drawing Format**—This option will perform a Saveas to AutoCAD 2007 file format. However, the results with AEC objects could be unexpected. This option is not recommended when files contain AEC objects.
- **AutoCAD 2010 Drawing Format with Exploded AEC Objects**—This option is the same as Export to AutoCAD discussed above. The result will be AutoCAD drawing files containing only AutoCAD entities with no AEC objects in AutoCAD 2010 format.
- **AutoCAD 2007 Drawing Format with Exploded AEC Objects**—This option is the same as Export to AutoCAD discussed above. The result will be AutoCAD drawing files containing only AutoCAD entities with no AEC objects in AutoCAD 2007 format.

The Maintain visual fidelity for annotative objects checkbox offers the opportunity to maintain the appearance of annotative content when viewed in Autodesk

Architectural Desktop/AutoCAD 2007 or earlier. An anonymous block with graphics for each scale representation on a separate layer is generated for each annotative object when this box is checked. Refer to the AutoCAD Help topic "Save a Drawing (Concept)" for more details on this setting.

Next is the Transmittal file folder list. It defaults to the same location as the current project, or you can click the Browse button to save it to a different location. Beneath this is the Transmittal file name list, which contains three options:

- **Prompt for a filename**—This option prompts you with a dialog to input the file name as the eTransmit routine is executed.
- **Overwrite if necessary**—This option overwrites any existing files with the same name(s) as those being created by the transmittal.
- **Increment file name if necessary**—This option creates a new transmittal file or files with an incremental suffix added to the file name(s).

The next set of options determines the organization used in the folder structure of the eTransmitted files or archive.

- **Use organized folder structure**—This option matches the eTransmitted folder structure to the folder structure chosen from the list. Use Browse to choose a different root folder.
- **Place all files in one folder**—This option is useful when the recipient has different server names than you and will be viewing the files in vanilla AutoCAD. Using this option, you are able to keep all XREFs attached (not Bound) and not worry that their paths will be broken. This is because AutoCAD always searches the current folder for XREFs.
- **Keep files and folders as is**—This option uses the same folder structure as the original project without modification. This option is best for recipients who are using ACA 2010, 2009, 2008, 2007, 2006, 2005 or 2004.

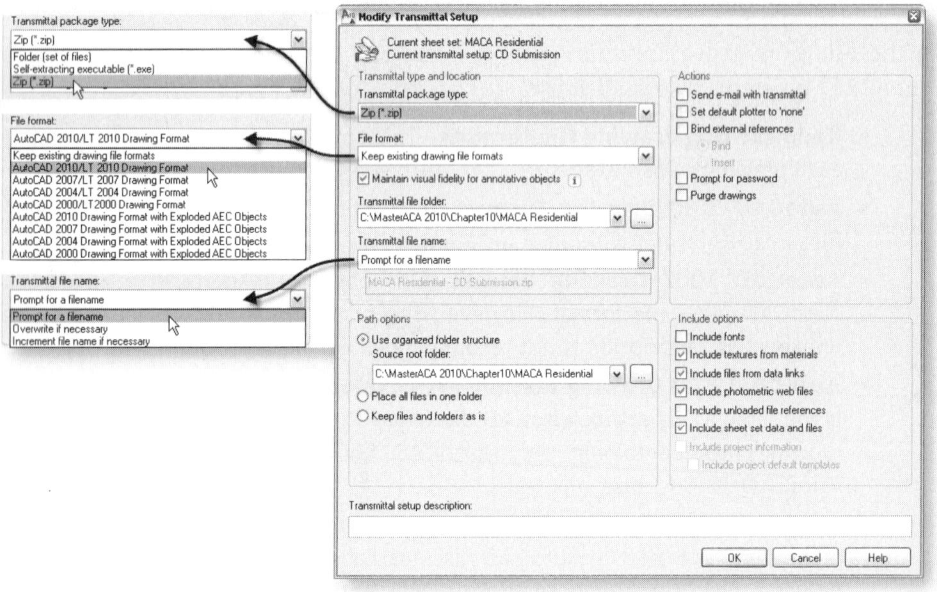

FIGURE E.2 *Configuring The New Transmittal Setup*

At the top right of the dialog, the following Actions may be specified:

- **Send e-mail with transmittal**—This option launches your default e-mail application and sends the file(s) created by the transmittal as e-mail attachments.
- **Set default plotter to 'none'**—This option is useful if your recipient does not have the same default plotter as you. Before printing, the recipient will need to choose a plotter in the files you send.
- **Bind external references**—Use this option if you do not want external references included in the drawing files. All XREFs will be bound to their hosts and those files saved using whatever settings you designated above. This setting is useful with the four "Exploded AEC Objects" options above for recipients that need only a simple background file. Select either the Bind or Insert option when using this option.
- **Prompt for password**—Use this option with the *.zip* and *.exe* options to require a password to open the archive. Don't forget to share the password with the recipient.
- **Purge**—Use this option to do a complete, silent mode purge of all drawings transmitted.

Options for controlling what is to be included with the transmitted files are found at the lower right:

- **Include fonts**—This option includes the required font files. If you have used only standard AutoCAD fonts in your drawings, this option is not necessary.
- **Include textures from materials**—Use this option to add the materials that are used by the objects in the drawing.
- **Include files from data links**—This option will include any external file that is referenced by a data link in the transmittal package.
- **Include photometric web files**—Photometric web files assigned to web lights in transmitted drawings will be included when this option is selected.
- **Include unloaded file references**—Select this option to have any unloaded external reference files included.
- **Include sheet set data and files**—This option includes the Sheet Set, all Subsets and all Sheet Set settings. This option includes the DST file with the transmittal.
- **Include project information**—Use this option to include the Project APJ and XML files with the eTransmittal. This is useful if your recipient is an ACA 2009, ACA 2008, ADT 2007, ADT 2006, ADT 2005 or ADT 2004 user.
- **Include project default templates**—This option includes all of the Drawing Template (DWT) files with the transmittal. This option is only active when the Include project information option is used.

The Transmittal setup description edit box at the bottom of the dialog allows you to add a detailed description of the setup.

4. Make your desired changes (use Figure E.2 as a guide) and then click OK to create the Transmittal Setup.

   Create alternative ones if you wish and then click Close to finish.

5. Right-click the Sheet Set node at the top again and choose **eTransmit**.

   A progress bar will appear as the list for required files is compiled.

6. Choose CD Submission on the right side (see Figure E.3).

Click the various tabs on the left to see all of the files that will be included in the transmittal. The Preview area will display a thumbnail image when selecting a drawing file on either the Files Tree or Files Table tab. Before clicking OK, you can uncheck any files that you do not wish to include. You can also click the View Report button to see a detailed report of what will be included. There is also a notes field where you can type in any message you wish. This will be included as a text file with the transmittal and in the e-mail message as well.

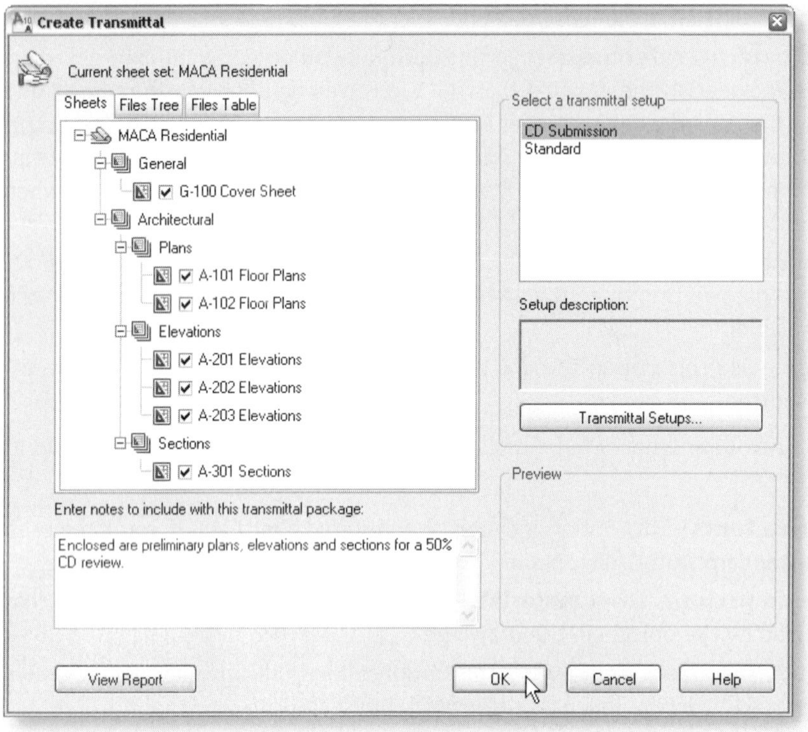

FIGURE E.3 *Creating the eTransmittal for the entire project*

7. Click OK to generate the transmittal and then click Save in the dialog that appears.

When the ZIP file creation is complete, you will be prompted to send the e-mail. You can continue with the e-mail and send a test e-mail to yourself or simply cancel. The Archive command works nearly the same way except that it will not offer the e-mail option. You can also eTransmit from any node on the Project Navigator, Constructs, Views, Sheets and Sheet Subsets. Feel free to experiment.

DETERMINING THE REQUIRED TRANSLATION

A recipient using AutoCAD Architecture 2010 can open, edit and resave any file that you send to them with complete "round-trip" ability. If you save down to a previous version of a DWG file, AEC objects will either appear as "proxies" in the resulting file or be exploded to AutoCAD primitives.

AutoCAD 2010 has built-in awareness of AEC objects—all required Object Enablers (see below) are included in the software. Therefore, if your recipients are using AutoCAD 2010, there is no translation required. However, it is important to note that even though the recipients can open ACA files, they still do not have all of the ACA tools and can perform only limited edits. It is also important that your AutoCAD recipients be made aware of the fact that exploding AEC objects will destroy their files irrevocably.

AutoCAD Architecture 2010 uses the 2010 DWG file format. Versions of AutoCAD (and associated vertical application like AutoCAD Architecture or AutoCAD MEP) older than 2010 are *not* capable of properly displaying AutoCAD Architecture 2010 objects natively. There are three ways to share ACA 2010 drawings with these non-ACA users: the consultant can install an Object Enabler, you can save proxy graphics into the ACA 2010 format file, or you can use the **Export to AutoCAD** command prior to sending the consultant the file.

Use the following chart to determine the relevant issues.

TABLE E.1 *Determining Translation Requirements per Software Version (currently retired versions not included)*

Consultant Software and Version	Translation Required	AEC Objects Preserved
AutoCAD Architecture		
ACA 2010	No Translation Required	Yes
ACA 2009, 2008 or Architectural Desktop 2007	Save As 2007 or	Proxies
	Export > AutoCAD 2007	No
AutoCAD MEP		
AutoCAD MEP 2010	No Translation Required	Yes
AutoCAD MEP 2009, 2008 or Building Systems 2007	SaveAs 2007 or	Proxies
	Export > AutoCAD 2007	No
AutoCAD		
AutoCAD 2010	No Translation Required	Yes
AutoCAD 2009	Object Enabler 2009 or	Proxies
	Export > AutoCAD 2007	No
AutoCAD 2008	Object Enabler 2008 or	Proxies
	Export > AutoCAD 2007	No
AutoCAD 2007	Object Enabler 2007 or	Proxies
	Export > AutoCAD 2007	No
Revit		
Revit 2010 releases	Export > AutoCAD 2010 or	No
	IFC Export	Limited
Revit prior releases	Export > AutoCAD 2007 or	No
	IFC Export	Limited
Other CAD Packages		
Non-AutoCAD CAD software that reads DWG format	Export > AutoCAD (DWG format)	No
Non-AutoCAD CAD software that does not read DWG format	Export > AutoCAD (DXF format)	No
Microstation V7 or Higher	Export > DGN, then choose the V8 DGN or V7 DGN format	No

NOTE

Depending on the release, some objects might appear as proxies or with limited functionality. For example, Annotation objects with multiple scale representations appear either as proxies or separate objects on multiple layers in releases older than 2008. Field codes appear as normal text with no background shading in release 2007 or prior.

SHARING ACA FILES WITH OTHER ACA USERS

If you wish to share an ACA 2010 file with users of a previous version of ACA or Architectural Desktop, you will need to translate the files to plain AutoCAD files. The process of doing so—**Application Menu > Export > AutoCAD > AutoCAD 2007**—will destroy all AEC objects and their underlying intelligence and replace them with representative AutoCAD geometry. Saving directly as 2007 or 2004 DWG (using the SAVEAS command) will create proxy objects and render your AEC objects unusable in the resulting file. Therefore, despite the fact that proxies might, at first, seem preferable, exporting to AutoCAD is actually the recommended course of action for most situations.

NOTE

Important: Take care to draw the distinction between the two methods of saving an ACA file down to an earlier version of AutoCAD. Saving your file as an earlier version by using the SAVEAS command or configuring ACA to save to an earlier version of AutoCAD by default results in proxy graphics and renders your AEC objects unusable. Export to AutoCAD is located on the Application Menu and is recommended instead. Do *not* under any circumstances configure the default of ACA 2010 to save as an earlier version of AutoCAD.

UNDERSTANDING OBJECT ENABLERS

To share drawings with consultants who are using AutoCAD or an AutoCAD-based vertical product, Autodesk provides a free software plug-in called an *Object Enabler*. An Object Enabler, as its name implies, "enables" the otherwise unknown AEC objects directly within the vanilla version of AutoCAD (or other AutoCAD-based vertical products) without the need for a copy of ACA. As mentioned above, an Object Enabler is not required for AutoCAD 2007 or later—it is already built into the software for those versions. Users of Object Enablers will be able to correctly view and print AEC objects and will be able to perform limited grip editing and Properties palette functions upon the AEC objects contained within a file that they receive. They will not be able to add new AEC objects to the drawing or perform most AutoCAD Architecture specific commands. Without an Object Enabler, sharing drawings with consultants using other versions of AutoCAD will require the use of proxy graphics (simplified geometric approximations of the actual AEC object) or the need to use Export to AutoCAD.

At the time of this writing, you can find the latest AutoCAD Architecture Object Enabler online on the Autodesk Web site at:

http://www.autodesk.com/autocadarchitecture-support.

Click on **Data & Downloads > Utilities & Drivers** to get to the ACA page with enablers and other downloads. If this URL is not functioning (or if you simply do not want to type the above URL into your browser address bar manually), visit www.autodesk.com, click the search link, type *object enabler* and then click Search. This process should locate the latest download location of the Object Enabler.

UNDERSTANDING PROXY GRAPHICS

AEC objects automatically generate the graphics used to represent themselves in different views based on the parameters of the specific object. We have seen examples of this behavior throughout this book. The generic AutoCAD package is incapable of generating these representational graphics and simply ignores the "unknown" objects under typical circumstances. However, within ACA, a feature called Proxy Graphics can be turned on. When enabled, ACA creates two sets of graphics for the AEC object when the file is saved: the parametric one used by ACA and the one saved with the file for generic AutoCAD. As the name *proxy* implies, proxy graphics are "stand-in" objects that appear onscreen only when the host application that created them is not present on the machine. In this case, that host application is AutoCAD Architecture. A proxy graphic is not editable in any way. Therefore, if the recipient of the file with proxies needs to edit the data, this would not be a good choice of formats.

Despite the noted limitations, if you choose to share your AutoCAD Architecture drawings using proxy graphics, it is important to understand how to do so successfully. As we have seen, AEC objects have multiple Display Representations. However, each object can store only a single proxy representation; so it is important to configure your work session to be sure the file you are saving displays correctly for your recipients.

For people needing to view the data in the file only for review purposes, proxies can provide a workable solution. This is because no special requirements are placed on recipients. They simply open files as they normally would. One small caveat: a message will typically appear alerting the recipients of the presence of proxy graphics and requesting their input on how to deal with them. The choices are to display the proxies, show the bounding box only or ignore them. Please instruct your recipients to choose to **display proxy graphics**. If they choose not to display them, they will see nothing and will most likely call you to ask why you sent an empty file. If they choose bounding box, each object in the file will appear as a box that matches the overall size of the total object. This option will not reveal very detailed information and is not very useful.

Avoid using proxy graphics if you can. Again, these are stand-in graphics, not the real thing. They cannot be edited, and they provide only limited visual information from whatever view was active when the file was saved. Finally, proxies nearly double the size of ACA files. Depending on the file size without proxies, this size can be significant.

Turning Proxy Graphics On

To keep file sizes small, Proxy Graphics is turned off by default in ACA. For your recipients to see proxy graphics, you must turn it on and set the drawing viewport to the configuration (Medium Detail, Low Detail, etc.) and view the direction you wish them to see (Plan, Model, etc.) prior to saving and sending the file.

1. Type **PROXYGRAPHICS** at the Command Line and then press ENTER.
2. Type **1** and press ENTER again.
3. Save the file (usually Saveas and choose a new name) and then send this file to your recipient.

After saving, you can return to the original, turn off proxy graphics and resave to reduce file size again.

SHARING ACA FILES WITH REVIT USERS

With the building information modeling products on the Revit platform from Autodesk gaining in popularity, it is conceivable that at some point you will find yourself working with a consultant or collaborator who is using Revit Architecture for architectural design and documentation, Revit Structure for structural engineering or Revit MEP for HVAC and electrical design. While the Revit file format (RVT) is not directly compatible with ACA's DWG format, you can still share your geometry with users of these products.

All of the Revit products can import and export AutoCAD DWG formats. While Revit does not utilize a layering system like AutoCAD, its objects are organized into "object categories" and subcategories. These categories can be mapped to AutoCAD layers by the Revit users prior to export, allowing for compliance with any given layer standard (see Figure E.4). In addition, once the layer mappings have been established, they can be saved to a file for easy retrieval in the future. Therefore, if you are sharing data with a Revit user, you should provide them with documentation on your layer standard to assist them in exporting data to you. You can easily document a good part of your layer standard by simply exporting your Layer Key style to an Excel spreadsheet.

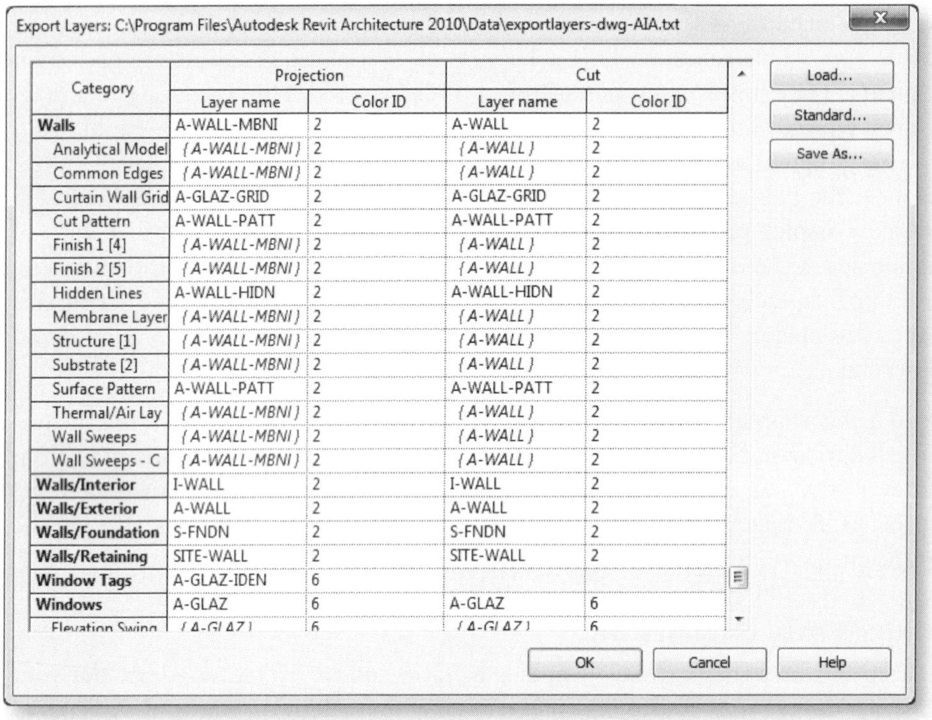

Category	Projection		Cut	
	Layer name	Color ID	Layer name	Color ID
Walls	A-WALL-MBNI	2	A-WALL	2
Analytical Model	{A-WALL-MBNI}	2	{A-WALL}	2
Common Edges	{A-WALL-MBNI}	2	{A-WALL}	2
Curtain Wall Grid	A-GLAZ-GRID	2	A-GLAZ-GRID	2
Cut Pattern	A-WALL-PATT	2	A-WALL-PATT	2
Finish 1 [4]	{A-WALL-MBNI}	2	{A-WALL}	2
Finish 2 [5]	{A-WALL-MBNI}	2	{A-WALL}	2
Hidden Lines	A-WALL-HIDN	2	A-WALL-HIDN	2
Membrane Layer	{A-WALL-MBNI}	2	{A-WALL}	2
Structure [1]	{A-WALL-MBNI}	2	{A-WALL}	2
Substrate [2]	{A-WALL-MBNI}	2	{A-WALL}	2
Surface Pattern	A-WALL-PATT	2	A-WALL-PATT	2
Thermal/Air Lay	{A-WALL-MBNI}	2	{A-WALL}	2
Wall Sweeps	{A-WALL-MBNI}	2	{A-WALL}	2
Wall Sweeps - C	{A-WALL-MBNI}	2	{A-WALL}	2
Walls/Interior	I-WALL	2	I-WALL	2
Walls/Exterior	A-WALL	2	A-WALL	2
Walls/Foundation	S-FNDN	2	S-FNDN	2
Walls/Retaining	SITE-WALL	2	SITE-WALL	2
Window Tags	A-GLAZ-IDEN	6		
Windows	A-GLAZ	6	A-GLAZ	6
Elevation Swing	{A-GLAZ}	6	{A-GLAZ}	6

FIGURE E.4 *Layer mapping from Revit Architecture*

Sharing Geometry with Revit Users

While Revit Architecture and Revit MEP do not directly open DWG files, they can import directly from an AutoCAD DWG file. Like AutoCAD, however, Revit Architecture and Revit MEP are not able to read AEC object data and geometry. Worse, there is no object enabler for products based on the Revit platform. To work with users of either of these two products, the best solution at this time is to use the Export to AutoCAD feature in ACA to generate a 2D drawing of geometric primitives or a 3D model made up of generic ACIS solids. Set your ACA drawing to the desired display configuration and view before export (plan view to generate 2D graphics and any 3D isometric view to create solids).

When you need to import data from a user of Revit Architecture or Revit MEP, the data must first be exported to AutoCAD DWG file format as either 2D drawings made up of generic AutoCAD geometry or a 3D model consisting of either polyface meshes or ACIS solids.

It should also be noted that at the time of this writing, users of Revit MEP also own AutoCAD MEP, as Revit MEP is typically sold as part of a bundle that includes AutoCAD MEP. Ideally, in these cases, your MEP engineer can provide you with native AutoCAD MEP files, which are compatible with ACA. Likewise, your ACA geometry can be opened directly into AutoCAD MEP. It is up to the engineer, then, to process the geometry further to make it compatible with Revit MEP. Work with your consultants in such scenarios to establish the workflow that is most desirable and productive for all parties.

Sharing Geometry with Revit Structure Users

Revit Structure, although built on the same platform as Revit Architecture and Revit MEP, has some unique capabilities when it comes to reading and writing ACA data. When an ACA model is imported into Revit Structure, the geometry is imported as graphically correct "anonymous blocks" that are devoid of any data. What this means is that the structural engineer can bring your ACA model directly into Revit Structure as geometry only; it will not have any "intelligent" data or properties. In fact, it must remain a single "import instance." Exploding the imported model will cause any graphics generated by ACA to be deleted.

The graphical information can be used by the structural engineer in the initial layout of the structural model. Column Grid lines can be used to generate Revit Structure grid lines, and Walls can be used to aid in the creation of Revit structural walls.

When exporting a Revit Structure model, there is an additional option that is not present in Revit Architecture or Revit MEP to export the model as ACA geometry. When this option is chosen, Revit Structure columns, beams and braces are exported as ACA Structural Members. Slabs, walls and other types of 3D objects become ACA Mass Elements.

NOTE

When exporting as AEC objects from Revit Structure, the file format must be set to AutoCAD 2010 DWG. Additional options that have an impact on graphical accuracy and quality must be considered when exporting geometry from Revit Structure. Refer to the Revit Structure Users Guide for more information.

Understanding IFC

IFC, or Industry Foundation Classes, is a developing standard for the interoperability of objects between different modeling platforms. You can import from and export to IFC directly within the application. Currently, IFC translation between ACA and Revit is in its infancy; not all objects are translated directly between the two products. For example, while Walls, Doors and Windows from ACA 2010 will translate into Walls, Doors and Windows in Revit using the IFC utility, Curtain Walls become generic masses in Revit.

You can find the IFC options on the File menu in ACA. The IFC utility will attempt to translate the levels in your projects and various AEC objects. For more information on the IFC capabilities of AutoCAD Architecture or Revit, see the online help within each product.

APPENDIX f

Wall Cleanup Solutions

This illustration gives the solution to the commercial project Wall cleanup exercise in Appendix A.

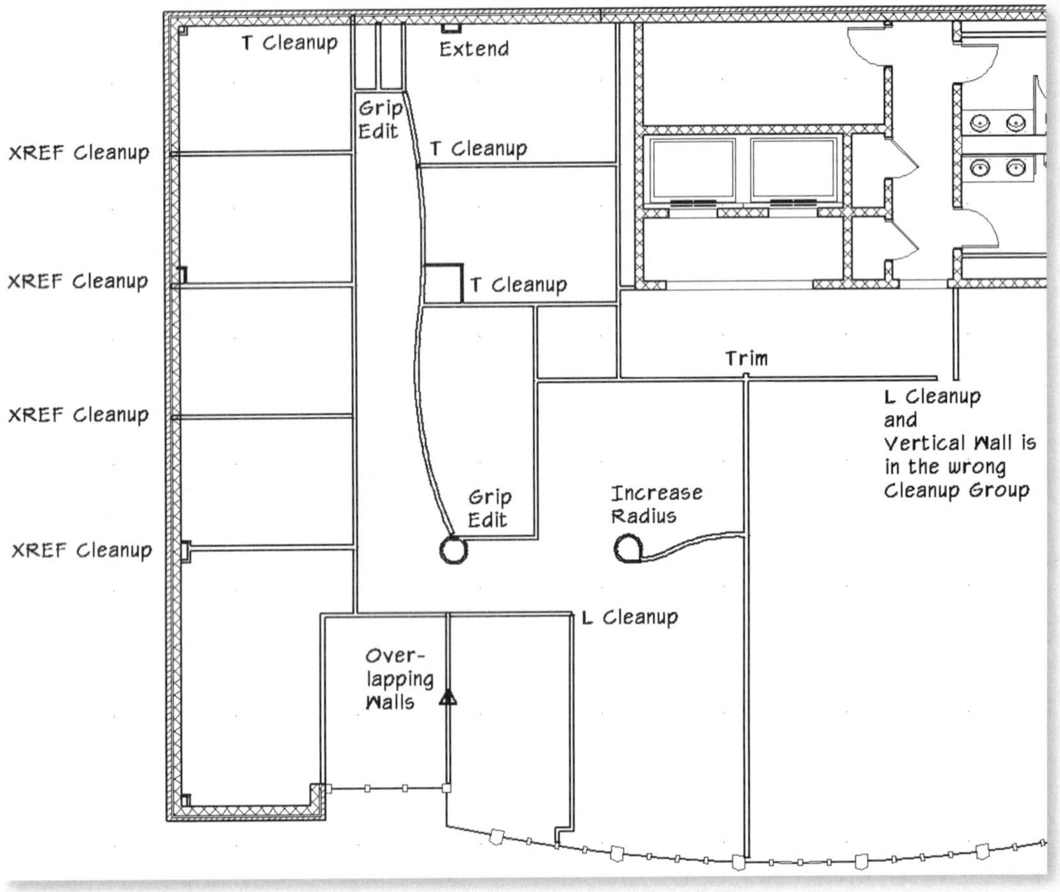

FIGURE F.1

INDEX

A

Acoustical Batt Insulation, 841–842
Adding floor slab and roof, 10–11
AEC Model, 127
AEC Model, 294–295
AEC Standard Plot Style Table, 870–871
AIA Standard Plot Style Table, 872–873
Air Gap width changes, 452–454
Anchor property, 715
Anchors
  exploring objects with, 115–118, 120–122
  layout tools and, 114–115, 120–122
  Object Anchor, 118–120
  overview of, 113
  types of, 113–114
Annotation
  accessing AEC Content Dimensions (layer-keyed), 686
  adding AEC Dimensions, 665–666
  adding AEC Dimensions/Annotations, 900
  adding interior AEC Dimensions, 680–681
  adding Room Tags, 648–651
  adding Room Tags to RCP, 655–657
  adding Room Tags with Dimensioning Tools, 662–663
  adding text/leaders, 687–688
  adding Window Tags, 688–689
  adjusting position of Room Tags, 651–654
  and AEC Dimensions In-Place edit, 674–675
  changing Current Project with Dimensioning Tools, 662
  configuring Low Detail display Rep of AEC Dimension Style, 676–679
  creating alternative tag for RCP, 657–658
  dimensioning to Wall components, 679
  editing AEC Dimension Style, 667–668
  editing individual AEC Dimension Style, 668–671
  editing Room Tags Property Data, 654–655
  Elevation Labels and, 689–691
  exploring Display Settings with Dimension Tools, 675
  exploring Wall Style settings with Dimension Tools, 682–685
  grip editing component dimensions with Dimension Tools, 681–682
  installing CD files/loading Current Project for Room Tags, 646–647
  linking Display Configuration to Annotation Scale with Dimension Tools, 679
  live dimensioning and, 665
  matching Sheet View Layer to View with Dimensioning Tools, 663–665
  One Face of the Stud with Dimension Tools, 685
  overriding Text/fine-tuning with Dimension Tools, 671–674
  overview of dimensioning tools, 661, 667
  and Room Tags with Dimensions, 662
  scaling and, 647, 657
  substituting existing Tags, 660–661
  using AEC Content Dimensions, 685
  using Define Schedule Tag wizard, 658–660
  View Files and, 643–646
  working with AEC Dimension Display, 676
Application Menu, user interface and, 38–39
AutoCAD Architecture 2010 (ACA) overview
  adding callouts and elevations, 25–26
  adding first floor plan view, 22–24
  adding floor slab and roof, 10–11
  adding second floor plan view, 24
  changing drawing scale, 24
  creating sheets, 26–28
  difference from AutoCAD, 75
  editing elevation, 12–14
  inner workings (underpinnings) of. *See* Parametric design of ACA
  laying out simple building, 1–10
  setting up project with floor levels, 14–22
  workspace, 33–37
Autodesk Architectural Desktop: An Advanced Implementation Guide, 715
Automatic/Manual Property Sets of Schedules, 714–720
Automatic Wall Cleanup, 904–905
Auto Snap options, as ACA prerequisite, 71
Autosnap, 420–421

B

Base boundary, 912
Baseline and Wall cleanup, 412
Beam Haunch, 889–890
Blocks, as ACA prerequisite, 71
Body modifier
  adding to stairs, 330–331
  customization of, 311–313
BOMA
  Classification, 917–919
  Schedule Table, 919–920
  Standard Boundary Offset, 914–917
Boolean operations, 308–311
Bow Window, 895–896

Brick Haunch, 839–840
Building model. *See also* Commercial Core Plan; Residential Building Model
  adding Elevation/Section Callouts to upper floor plans, 255–256
  adding First Floor Plan View for, 239–241
  adding Titlemark to, 241–243
  beginning First Floor Construct, 228–230
  building composite model View for, 235–237
  building digital cartoon set, 210–211
  building terrain model for, 226–228
  creating building Elevation View for, 246–251
  creating Constructs for, 224
  creating Cover Sheet for, 263–265
  creating Elevation Sheet file for, 261–263
  creating First Floor Plan View for, 239
  creating Floor Plan Views for, 238
  creating remaining Floor Plan sheet files for, 259–261
  creating Second Floor Plan View for, 243
  creating Section View for, 252–254
  creating Site Plan Sheet File for, 257–259
  creating Site Plan Views for, 238–239
  creating Spanning Construct for, 233–234
  creating Third/Fourth Floor Plan Views for, 245
  creating upper floor Constructs for, 231–233
  elevations/sections and, 245–246
  enabling Live Section for, 254–255
  enabling View layer Synchronization for, 234–235
  and naming files, 237–238
  opening existing Site Conditions/creating Construct for, 224–226
  posting linking field codes for, 244
  preparing for Project Standards, 230–231
  and project navigator terminology (ACA Model files), 219–220
  and project navigator terminology (ACA Sheet files), 220–221
  and project navigator terminology (Levels/Divisions), 217–218
  and project navigator terminology (Model/Sheet files), 218
  publishing Cartoon Set for, 265–267
  Residential Building Model, 1–12 (Chapter 5a)
  setting up commercial project, 211–217
  setting up Project Levels for, 221–224
  setting up residential, 267
  Sheet files/Cartoon Sets and, 256–257
Building shell
  adding Curtain Walls, 363–365
  adding Door/Window Assembly to 01 Partitions Construct, 408–409
  adding Front Entry Infill override, 367–368
  applying Miter to corners, 402–403
  assigning Materials, 390–392
  building Grid structure, 386–390
  checking Dimensions, 392–395
  converting linework to Door/Window Assembly, 406–408
  converting Walls to Curtain Walls, 382–383
  and copying Walls between files, 357–359
  creating custom Curtain Wall style, 381
  creating custom Door/Window Assembly tool, 408
  creating Divisions, 383–385
  creating Infills/Frames/Mullions, 385–386
  creating masonry shell for, 356
  creating New Style of, 383
  Curtain Wall terminology and, 369–370
  and Curtain Wall Units and Door/Window Assemblies, 381
  customizing Mullion profile via direct manipulation, 403–405
  end bays and, 398–399
  exploring element definitions of Curtain Walls, 372–374
  exploring grid structure of Curtain Walls, 374–376
  exploring interface of Curtain Walls, 370–372
  installing CD files/loading Current Project for, 357
  merging cells in Curtain Walls, 365–366
  and out-of-the-box Curtain Wall styles, 376–378
  overriding corner conditions of Curtain Walls, 400–402
  process for designing custom Curtain Wall style, 378–381
  refining Maca Front Façade design, 398
  and setting up Project Standards, 361–363, 361–363
  synchronizing single drawing, 397–398
  trimming Curtain Walls, 365
  updating Project Standards, 395–396, 405–406
  and working with Project Standards, 359–361

C

Callouts and elevations, 765–768, 811–813
  adding (overview), 25–26
  challenging exercise for, 855–859
  Details and, 818–822
Ceilings. *See* Reflected Ceiling Plan (RCP)
Cell and anchor, 114
Chimneys, 771–774
Classification property, 715
Cleanup. *See* Wall cleanup
Cleanup circle and Wall cleanup, 412

Column Grid Labels/Dimensions
adding, 289–291
adding AEC Dimensions, 294–295
adding labels/extensions to second Grid, 293–294
creating extensions/loading commercial Palette, 291–292
Set Drawing Scale and, 289
Column Grids
adding Columns to new Grid, 287–288
adding/deleting Grid Lines, 288
anchored column addition to, 277–279
converting linework to, 286–287
and identifying anchors, 279–280
manipulating spacing of, 283–285
modifying, 282–283
moving, 277
and moving Grid to correct coordinates, 280–282
removing unnecessary Columns, 285
and rotating anchored Columns, 285
working with Structural Members, 276–277
Columns
adding to Basement, 889
building Multi-View Block for Column Cutouts, 896–897
Matrix, 734–736
Schedules and, 739
Command Line
right-clicking in, 55–56
user interface and, 64–65
Commercial Core Plan. *See also* Building shell; Progressive refinement
adding AEC Dimensions/Annotations, 900
adding Casework, 894–895
adding Equipment/Furniture, 895
adding other Schedules, 900–901
adding Railing to, 335–336
adding ramps/elevators, 349–353
adding Roof Plan View, 588–589
adding stairs to, 332–333
adding toilet rooms, 353–354
adding Wall Sweep Profile to Parapet Wall, 584–587
building Multi-View Block for Column Cutouts, 896–897
completing Ceiling Plan, 900
and copying/assigning Stair Style, 334–335
editing Door display in Reflected Ceiling Plans, 899
and editing in place, 894
extending landings, 333–334
fixing Cleanup problems on Third Floor, 894
loading, 331–332
Third Floor Build Out, 886
updating/adding Elevations/Sections, 901–902
updating Composite Building Section Model, 587–588
using Commercial Template Project, 888
Consultants. *See* Sharing files with consultants
Content Library, and parametric design of ACA, 126
Core plan. *See* Commercial Core Plan
Curtain Walls
adding, 363–365
adding Door/Window Assembly to 01 Partitions Construct, 408–409
adding Front Entry Infill override to, 367–368
applying Miter to corners, 402–403
assigning Materials, 390–392
building Grid structure, 386–390
checking Dimensions, 392–395
converting linework to Door/Window Assembly, 406–408
converting Walls to, 382–383
creating custom Door/Window Assembly tool, 408
creating custom style of, 381
creating Divisions, 383–385
creating Infills/Frames/Mullions, 385–386
creating New Curtain Wall Style, 383
and Curtain Wall Units and Door/Window Assemblies, 381
customizing Mullion profile via direct manipulation, 403–405
end bays and, 398–399
exploring element definitions of, 372–374
exploring grid structure of, 374–376
exploring interface of, 370–372
merging cells in, 365–366
and out-of-the-box styles of, 376–378
overriding corner conditions of, 400–402
process for designing custom style of, 378–381
refining Maca Front Façade design, 398
synchronizing single drawing, 397–398
terminology, 369–370
trimming, 365
updating Project Standards, 395–396, 405–406
Curve and anchor, 114
Custom Doors/Windows. *See also* Doors/windows
creating, 523–528
creating Custom Multi-View Block, 533–538
Custom Display Blocks and, 517–523

D

Demolition
and creation of new layer based on Layer Standard, 478–479
Demolition Wall tool testing, 479
of existing items, 475–476
of existing Wall, 480–481
Wall style, 476–477
DesignCenter, RCP and, 620–624
Design Web Format (DWF), publishing Sheet Set for, 874–879
Detail Component Manager, 837–839
Details. *See also* Keynotes
adding Break Marks, 824–825
adding Brick Haunch, 839–840

Details (*continued*)
adding Foundation Wall, 839
adding Insulation, 841–842
adding remaining Framing components, 833–834
adding Roof Rafters, 833–836
adding to Sheets, 851–852
adding wood framing, 829–833
challenging exercise for, 855–859
creating (overview), 826
and Detail Component Manager, 837–839
final completion of, 843–844
flashing and, 843
Footing key and, 840–841
installing CD files/loading Current Project for, 817
Keynoting Details, 850–851
modifying, 844–845
overview of, 816–817
simplifying background of, 822–823
Tool Palettes and, 827–829
using Callouts, 818–822
Dimensioning Tools
accessing AEC Content Dimensions (layer-keyed), 686
adding AEC Dimensions, 665–666
adding interior AEC Dimensions, 680–681
and AEC Dimensions In-Place edit, 674–675
challenging exercise for, 855–859
changing Current Project with, 662
configuring Low Detail display Rep of AEC Dimension Style, 676–679
dimensioning to Wall components, 679
editing AEC Dimension Style, 667–668
editing individual AEC Dimension Style, 668–671
exploring Display Settings, 675
exploring Wall Style settings with, 682–685
grip editing component dimensions, 681–682
linking Display Configuration to Annotation Scale with, 679
live dimensioning and, 665
matching Sheet View Layer to View with, 663–665
One Face of the Stud with, 685
overriding Text/fine-tuning with, 671–674
overview of, 667
Room Tags and, 662–663
using AEC Content Dimensions, 685
working with AEC Dimension Display, 676
Display system
CD file installation/load sample files and, 81–82
component relationship of, 80–81
Configuration tab and, 92–94
Display Representations and, 98–104
Fixed View Direction Dependent Configuration and, 89–90
key features/benefits of, 79
loading Display Configuration and, 82–86
and plan/section/elevation/schedule views from single model, 77–78
relationship to layers of, 78–79
Sets and, 94–98
tool set of, 79–80
using Display Manager and, 90–91
View Direction Dependent Configuration and, 86–89
Display Themes
challenging exercise for, 855–859
and parametric design of ACA, 122–125
Schedules and, 752–756
Divisions, 383–385
Doors/windows
adding a Door/Window assembly, 186–187
adding Bow Window, 895–896
adding Doors, 171–176
adding new Windows to Upper Floors, 509–511
adding Openings, 183–184
adding remaining Doors, 180
adding Sill extensions, 498–500
adding Tags to XREFed Doors (advanced), 743–745
adding Window Muntins, 530–532
adding Windows, 180–182
adding Window Tags, 688–689
adjusting Cut Plane, 182–183
adjusting Door Swing angles, 188–189
adjusting Door threshold display, 189–191
adjusting Location Grip (advanced), 746–747
Assembly tool for, 406–409
changing display properties in Reflected Display Configuration, 636
changing Door size with direct manipulation, 177–178
changing swing, 176–177
completing Custom Window Style, 500–502
converting Window to Door, 511–512
copying/assigning New Window Style, 494–495
copying existing Windows, 507
creating Custom Multi-View Block, 533–538
creating Custom-Shaped Doors/Windows, 523–528
creating New Sheet/Remote File (advanced), 741–743
Custom Display Blocks (Door/Window display) and, 517–523
Door display properties and, 515–517
editing New Window Style, 495–498
editing Number Suffix (advanced), 745–746
enabling Plot Preview (Door/Window display), 513–515
Idropping a Tool Palette, 186
loading custom Tool Palette, 184–185
manipulating Table size/scale (advanced), 743
modifying Doors/Windows, 187–188
moving Door with Object Snap Tracking, 178–179
opening Schedule Sheet/View results (advanced), 751–752
Property Sets/Element Files (advanced), 747–749

re-importing Door/Window Styles, 532–533
revolving Doors, 517–518
synchronizing Project Standards, 502–503
Tags for First Floor (advanced), 749–750
Tags for Upper Floor (advanced), 750–751
using AEC Modify array, 507–508
Window Anchors and, 503–506
Dormers, 568–569
Draw Once, as principle of ACA, 76
Drawing Editor, right-clicking in, 54–55
Drawing scale, changing (overview), 24
DWG, 933
Dynamic Input, user interface and, 57–63

E

Edge grips, user interface and, 63–64
Elevation. *See also* Sections/Elevations
adding callouts and, 26–28
challenging exercise for, 855–859
editing overview, 12–14
Elevation Labels and, 689–691
updating/adding Sections and, 901–902
Elevators, adding, 352–353
End bays, 398–399
Endcaps
adding Brick Sill to, 466
assigning different, 456–457
conditions for, 455–456
creating custom, 463–464
Customizing Wall style and, 461–463
editing in place of, 458–460
invisible segments and, 460–461
opening styles of, 464–465
overriding (2nd floor) of, 486–487
eTransmit/Archive
Plotting/Publishing and, 879
and sharing files with consultants, 924–928
External References, as ACA prerequisite, 71

F

First Floor Plan. *See also* Building model
adding, 22–24, 239–241
AutoCAD Architecture 2010 (ACA) overview, 22–24
beginning First Floor Construct, 228–230
creating, 239
Flashing, 843
Floor joists, 580–583
Floor levels. *See also* Building model
adding first floor plan view, 22–24
adding second floor plan view, 24
setting up project overview, 14–22
Floor plan layout. *See also* Building model
adding a Door/Window assembly, 186–187
adding curved Wall segments, 160
adding Doors, 171–176
adding Openings, 183–184
adding plumbing content, 192–194
adding remaining Doors, 180
adding Windows, 180–182
adjusting Cut Plane, 182–183, 182–183
adjusting Door Swing angles, 188–189
adjusting Door threshold display, 189–191
adjusting lavatory [basin] height, 199–200
CD file installation and, 156
changing Door size with direct manipulation, 177–178
changing Door swing, 176–177
configuring Osnap settings (wall plan modifiers), 200–202
converting Polylines to Wall Modifiers, 203–204
creating/assigning Wall styles, 169
creating existing conditions plan (Walls), 160–161
creating layers (Walls), 170
creating with Spaces, 594
Edit in Place for Plan Modifiers, 204–206
getting started with Walls, 156–157
Idropping a Tool Palette, 186
importing Objects with clipboard (wall plan modifiers), 202–203
layout remaining, 164–169
loading custom Tool Palette, 184–185
major fields/controls with Walls, 157–159
modifying Doors/Windows, 187–188
modifying Walls and, 164
moving Door with Object Snap Tracking, 178–179
offset Walls and, 162–163
stairs and, 206–207
using Object Viewer, 194–198
using Ortho Wall, 161–162
Footing key, 840–841
Foundation plan, residential project and, 305–307
Foundation Wall, 839
Frames/Mullions, 367–368, 385–386
Furniture Layout Element File, 887, 895

G

Graph line and Wall cleanup, 412
Graphic property, 716, 736–739
Gross boundary, 912

H

Haunch
Beam, 889–890
Brick, 839–840

I

Infills/Frames/Mullions, 367–368, 385–386
Insulation, 841–842
IntelliMouse, user interface and, 66

J

Joists
Justification line and Wall cleanup, 412–415, 424–426

K

Keynotes. *See also* Details
  adding Details to Sheets, 851–852
  adding to Sections/Elevations, 847–848
  assigned to Styles, 845–847
  challenging exercise for, 855–859
  changing Display of, 848–849
  and inserting Sheet List, 854–855
  Keynoting Details, 850–851
  Keynoting Plans, 849–850
  Reference Keynote Legend, 854
  Sheet Keynote Legend, 853

L

Land T Cleanups, 418–419
Landing Slabs, Stair Tower Generation, 337–340
Layers, as ACA prerequisite, 70
Laying out simple building (overview), 1–10
Layout Curve, as one-dimensional tool, 114
Layout Grid 2D, 115
Layout Grid 3D, 115
Layouts (Paper Space), as ACA prerequisite, 71
Leader and anchor, 114
Light fixtures
  and accessing electrical content, 620–624
  adding surface-mounted, 629–630
  adding track lighting, 631–634
  anchoring to layout curve, 635–636
  attaching Mask Blocs to AEC objects, 626–628
  copying, 624–625
  copying surface-mounted, 630
  inserting incandescent, 634–635
  rotating, 625–626
Live data, as principle of ACA, 77
Location property, 715

M

Maca Front Façade design, 398
Manual Property Sets of Schedules, 714–720
Manual Wall Cleanup, 905
Masking Block, RCP and, 614–615
Masonry shell
  and copying Walls between files, 357–359
  installing CD files/loading Current Project for, 357
  and setting up Project Standards, 361–363
  and working with Project Standards, 359–361
Material property, 715
Matrix columns, Schedules and, 734–736
Miters, 402–403
Model. *See* Building model
Mullions, 367–368, 385–386, 403–405
Multi-View Block, 533–538
Muntins, 530–532

N

Net boundary, 912
Node and anchor, 114

O

Object and anchor, 114
Object Snap Tracking, as ACA prerequisite, 72
Object Snaps, as ACA prerequisite, 70
Object styles
  accessing Tool Catalog, 107–109
  adding Palettes, 109–110
  applying tool properties to drawing objects, 110–113
  content browser and, 104–107
  and styles in Current Drawing, 105–106
One-dimensional tool, Layout Curve, 114
Online resources, 906–909
Overview of AutoCAD Architecture 2010 (ACA)
  adding callouts and elevations, 25–26
  adding first floor plan view, 22–24
  adding floor slab and roof, 10–11
  adding second floor plan view, 24
  changing drawing scale, 24
  creating sheets, 26–28
  editing elevation, 12–14
  laying out simple building, 1–10
  setting up project with floor levels, 14–22
  workspace of, 33–37

P

Palettes
  adding in object styles, 109–110
  Column Grid Labels/ Dimensions and, 291–292
  Details, 827–829
  group creation (work space) of, 134–136
  loading/verifying (work space) of, 133
  user interface and, 48–53
Panels, user interface and, 42–46
Parametric design of ACA
  accessing Tool Catalog (object styles), 107–109
  adding Palettes (object styles), 109–110
  applying tool properties to drawing objects (object styles), 110–113
  CD file installation/load sample files (display system) and, 81–82
  component relationship of display system, 80–81
  Configuration tab (display system) and, 92–94
  content browser (object styles) and, 104–107
  Content Library and, 126
  Display Representations (display system) and, 98–104
  and display system's relationship to layers, 78–79
  Display Themes and, 122–125
  exploring objects with anchors, 115–118, 120–122
  Fixed View Direction Dependent Configuration (display system) and, 89–90

key features/benefits of display system, 79
layout tools (anchors) and, 114–115, 120–122
loading Display Configuration (display system) and, 82–86
Object Anchor and, 118–120
overview of anchors, 113
and plan/section/elevation/ schedule views from single model display, 77–78
principles of, 76–77
Sets (display system) and, 94–98
and styles in Current Drawing, 105–106
tool set of display system, 79–80
types of anchors, 113–114
using Display Manager (display system) and, 90–91
View Direction Dependent Configuration (display system) and, 86–89
PDF, publishing to, 879
Plans. *See* Floor plan layout; Wall plan modifiers
Plotting/Publishing
AEC Standard Plot Style Table, 870–871
AIA Standard Plot Style Table, 872–873
editing Plot Style Tables, 868–870
eTransmit/Archive and, 879
installing CD files/loading Current Project for, 862
Layouts and, 863–864
overview of, 861
Page Setup Manager and, 864–868
Publishing Sheet Set, 873–879
for Residential Project, 903
Sheet Files and, 862
single drawing file, 873
Viewports, 868
to Web/PDFs, 879
Plumbing
adding content, 192–194
adjusting lavatory [basin] height, 199–200
using Object Viewer, 194–198
Polar tracking, as ACA prerequisite, 72
Polylines
as ACA prerequisite, 71
RCP and, 612–614
Porch, 892–893, 898
Progressive refinement
adding new Windows to Upper Floors, 509–511
adding Sill extensions, 498–500
adding Window Muntins, 530–532
applying new Wall style to model (2nd floor), 490–491
applying Tool Properties to other file (2nd floor), 486
building custom Wall style from scratch (2nd floor), 487
building/editing Wall styles and, 448–451
building new Wall style (2nd floor), 487
changing Air Gap width, 452–454
completing Custom Window Style, 500–502
converting Window to Door, 511–512
copying/assigning New Window Style, 494–495
copying existing Windows, 507
creating Custom Multi-View Block, 533–538
creating Custom-Shaped Doors/Windows, 523–528
creating custom tools (2nd floor), 482–484
creation of new layer based on Layer Standard, 478–479
Custom Display Blocks (Door/ Window display) and, 517–523
customizing Wall style, 461–463
Demolition of existing items, 475–476
Demolition of existing Wall, 480–481
Demolition Wall style, 476–477
Demolition Wall tool testing, 479
Door display properties and, 515–517
editing New Window Style, 495–498
enabling Plot Preview (Door/ Window display), 513–515
endcap overriding (2nd floor), 486–487
endcaps (adding Brick Sill), 466
endcaps (assigning different), 456–457
endcaps (conditions for), 455–456
endcaps (creating custom), 463–464
endcaps (editing in place), 458–460
endcaps (invisible segments), 460–461
endcaps (opening styles), 464–465
endcaps (view opening in 3D), 473–474
installing CD files/loading Current Project for, 494
as principle of ACA, 76
re-importing Door/Window Styles, 532–533
setting up components of Wall style, 454–455
setting up shared Tool Palette (2nd floor), 485
swap styles and, 444–448
synchronizing Project Standards, 502–503
using AEC Modify array, 507–508
using Wall style Components browser (2nd floor), 487–490
Wall style Display object-level override, 471–473
Wall style Display properties, 467–471
Wall styles and, 439–444
Window Anchors and, 503–506
Project property, 715
Project Standards
preparing for, 230–231
setting up, 361–363
updating, 395–396, 405–406
working with, 359–361
Property Sets/Element Files (advanced), challenging exercise for, 855–859
Proxy Graphics, 931

Q

Quick Access Toolbar (QAT), user interface and, 39

R

Radius Cleanup, 415–416, 421–424
Railings. *See also* Stairs
- adding, 329–330
- anchoring to Slab, 339–340
- CD file installation and, 316
- overview of, 315–316

Ramps, adding, 349–352
Reflected Ceiling Plan (RCP)
- accessing electrical content via DesignCenter, 620–624
- adding Ceiling Grid, 604–607
- adding Ceiling Grid with Grid clipping, 608–610
- adding RCP View/Sheet to Project, 637–639
- adding Room Tags to, 655–657
- adding surface-mounted lights, 629–630
- adding track lighting, 631–634
- anchoring lights to layout curve, 635–636
- attaching Mask Blocs to AEC objects, 626–628
- centering Ceiling Grid in Space, 616–617
- changing Ceiling Grid Bay sizes, 619–620
- clipping Ceiling Grid to polyline, 612–614
- clipping Ceiling Grid to room shape, 607–608
- copying light fixtures, 624–625
- copying surface-mounted lights, 630
- creating alternative tag for, 657–658
- creating Masking Block, 614–615
- creating RCP Sheet file, 640
- creating with Spaces, 594
- editing boundaries of Ceiling Grid, 617–619
- editing hatch pattern of Spaces, 610–612
- fine-tuning Ceiling Grid, 616
- generating Spaces from existing Walls, 594–601
- inserting incandescent light fixture, 634–635
- installing CD files/loading Current Project for, 594
- restoring floor plan, 636–637
- rotating anchored light fixtures/ Grid, 625–626
- working in Reflected Display Configuration, 601–603

Residential Building Model. *See also* Building model; Dimensioning tools; Railings; Stairs
- adding AEC Dimensions/ Annotations, 900
- adding Basement Floor Slabs, 898
- adding Basement Stairs, 890–891
- adding Beam Haunch, 889–890
- adding Bow Window, 895–896
- adding Casework, 894–895
- adding Columns/Beams to Basement, 889
- adding Equipment/Furniture, 895
- adding other Schedules, 900–901
- adding Roof to Porch, 898
- Basement Existing Conditions, 884
- body modifier customization and, 311–313
- building, 3–7 (Chapter 5a)
- changing Sheet template for Set, 11–12 (Chapter 5a)
- converting Linework to Railings, 891
- Create Furniture Layout Element File, 887
- creating, 2–3 (Chapter 5a)
- creating Curtain Wall for Screen Porch, 892–893
- and creating foundation plan, 305–307
- creating Sections in existing View, 10–11 (Chapter 5a)
- framework for, 2 (Chapter 5a)
- Model Space Views/Titlemarks for, 8–9 (Chapter 5a)
- plotting Project, 903
- and problems with Foundation Walls, 903
- publishing Cartoon Set for, 13 (Chapter 5a)
- Second Floor Existing Conditions, 885
- setting up, 1 (Chapter 5a)
- setting up Elevation/Section View for, 9–10 (Chapter 5a)
- setting up General Views for, 7–8 (Chapter 5a)
- setting up Project Sheets for, 12–13 (Chapter 5a)

Resources, online, 906–909
Revit, 932–933
Revolving Doors, 517–518
Ribbon panel tools, user interface and, 44–46
Ribbon view state, user interface and, 43–44
Ribbons, user interface and, 40–42
Right-clicking
- in application status bar, 56–57
- in Command LIne, 55–56
- in Drawing Editor, 54–55
- while command is active, 56

Roof Rafters, 833–836
Roofs/slabs
- adding, 542–545
- adding Basement Floor Slabs, 898
- adding Dormers, 568–569
- adding floor joists, 580–582
- adding holes/finishing touches, 565–566
- adding new Component, 576–580
- adding Roof Plan View (Commercial Plan), 588–589
- adding Roof to Porch, 898
- adding Wall Sweep Profile to Parapet Wall (Commercial Plan), 584–587
- applying Edge conditions, 563–566
- applying interference (joists), 582–583
- and Commercial Plan loading, 584
- converting to Roof, 545–549
- converting to Roof Slabs, 550–553
- creating, 540–541
- creating New Construct, 541–542
- creating new Slab style, 574–576
- creating Slab Construct, 573–574
- creating Slabs, 571–572
- exploring Slab styles, 572–573

installing CD files/loading Current Project for, 541
mitering Roof Slabs, 558–559
modifying Roof edges, 549–550
projecting Walls to Roof, 566–568
trimming Roof Slabs, 553–558
updating Composite Building Section Model (Commercial Plan), 587–588
updating Composite Model View, 569–571
working with Roof Slabs styles, 559–563
Room tags. *See* Annotation; Dimensioning tools

S

Schedules
adding components, 695
adding/deleting items, 714
adding Graphic Property, 736–739
adding Model Space View, 740
adding other, 900–901
adding Space Tags, 708–709
adding Table, 696–698
adding Tags, 704–706
adding Tags to objects with Existing Property Data, 706
adding Tags to XREFed Doors (advanced project-based Door), 743–745
adjusting Location Grip (advanced project-based Door), 746–747
Automatic/Manual Property Sets, 714–720
challenging exercise for, 855–859
configuring Borders/Colors/Lineweights, 727–729
content/properties of Table, 729–731
creating New Sheet/Remote File (advanced project-based Door), 741–743
creating View File, 696
Display Themes and, 752–756
editing Automatic Properties, 718
editing Number Suffix (advanced project-based Door), 745–746
editing style-based Property Data, 719–720
editing Table Cells, 716–717
exploring Property Set Definition, 721–724
Exporting, 756–757
fine-tuning selection of, 709–714
installing CD files/loading Current Project for, 696
manipulating Table size/scale (advanced project-based Door), 743
manually copying Tags, 707–708
Matrix columns and, 734–736
modifying Property Data Format Style, 732–733
moving/deleting/adding Columns, 733–734
opening Schedule Sheet/View results (advanced project-based Door), 751–752
and Out of Date Marker, 757
override formatting, 726–727
overriding Cell formatting, 731–732
overview of, 694–695
Property Set Data and, 699–704
Property Sets/Element Files (advanced project-based Door), 747–749
Renumber Data tool and, 756
sorting Table, 739
special Column types/features, 739
Table Style default format, 725–726
Table Style Graphic formatting, 724, 724–725
Tags for First Floor (advanced project-based Door), 749–750
Tags for Upper Floor (advanced project-based Door), 750–751
Screen Porch, 892–893
Second floor refinement. *See also* Building model
adding new Windows, 509–511
applying new Wall style to model, 490–491
applying Tool Properties to other file, 486
AutoCAD Architecture 2010 (ACA) overview, 24
building custom Wall style from scratch, 487
building new Wall style, 487
creating custom tools, 482–484
creating Floor Plan View for, 243
endcap overriding, 486–487
Second Floor Existing Conditions, 885
setting up shared Tool Palette, 485
using Wall style Components browser, 487–490
Walls and, 481–491
Sections/Elevations
2D Style settings for, 777–778
adding Keynotes, 847–848
adjusting Bldg Elevation Line, 762–763
adjusting Bldg Section Line Position (2D Style), 782–783
applying Material Boundary, 774–777
applying Material Tool to Object, 804–805
Bldg Section Line/Bldg Elevation Line and, 760–762
challenging exercise for, 855–859
creating Interior Elevations using Callouts, 811–813
creating New Material Definition/Tool, 802–804
Door/Window Swing 2D design rule, 790–792
dragging Elevation to Sheet, 810
ease of reading, 763–764
editing 2D Air Gap Material, 794–795
editing 2D Glazing Material, 795–796
editing 2D Style, 779–780
editing Brick Coursing, 799–800
eliminating Lines between floors, 800–801
erasing 2D Linework, 805–806
exporting changes to Second Floor (2D), 796–798
fine-tuning Model (2D Style), 783–786

Sections/Elevations (*continued*)
Freeze Demolition (2D Style) and, 786–787
installing CD files/loading Current Project for, 762
Layer/Color/Linetype Property maintenance (2D), 792
Live Sections, 813
merging 2D Linework, 807–808
modifying 2D Linework, 806–807
modifying Chimney, 771–774
modifying Model, 770
refreshing Elevation, 770–771
repositioning Elevation for Sheet, 768–769
Sheet Files and, 814
showing hidden Materials beyond, 801–802
subdivisions, 787–789
updating (2D), 798
updating 2D Objects with User Edits, 809–810
updating 2D Style, 780–782
updating/adding, 901–902
use of Callout for generation of, 765–768
Sharing files with consultants
determining required translation, 928–930
and exporting to AutoCAD, 924
Industry Foundation Classes (IFC), 933
and need for DWG, 923
Object Enablers and, 930
Proxy Graphics and, 931
Revit users and, 932–933
and sharing geometry with Revit Structure users, 933
and using eTransmit/Archive Project, 924–928
Sheet Set publishing, 873–879
Sheets, creating (overview), 26–28
Shrinkwrap, 779–780
Sill extensions, 498–500
Slabs. *See* Roofs/slabs
Sloped Walls, Cleanup Groups and, 426
Solution Tip ison and Wall cleanup, 413
Space
adding Ancillary Spaces, 920–921
adding Constructs, 920
BOMA Classification, 917–919
BOMA Schedule Table and, 919–920
BOMA Standard Boundary Offset and, 914–917
boundaries, 912–913
geometry, 910–912
installing CD files/loading Current Project for, 913
By Style boundary offset and, 913–914
Stair Tower Generation
adding Landing Slab, 337–338
anchoring Railing to Slab, 339–340
and attaching Core to Constructs, 343–344
editing Landing Slab, 338–339
editing Slab Display, 340
generation, 341–342
moving Stair/Railings to Spanning Tower Construct, 340–341
and overriding Xref Display, 344–345
overview of, 336–337
using Isolate Objects, 337
Stairs. *See also* Railings
adding, 316–319
adding Basement Stairs, 890–891
adding Body Modifier to, 330–331
adding Railing to, 329–330, 335–336
adding to Commercial Plan Core, 332–333
and adjusting Wall Roof Line, 327–328
CD file installation and, 316
copying/assigning Stair Style, 334–335
creating, 324–326
custom creation of, 345–348
display components for, 322–323
extending landing of, 333–334
modifying, 321–324
overview of, 315–316
stair edge, 326–327
styles of, 319–321
wall plan modifiers and, 206–207
Standards. *See* Project Standards
Steering Wheels, user interface and, 67–68
Structural Framing
adding beams, 295–299
adding braces, 299–300
adding joists, 301–302
adding Structural Category, 302–303
and creating Structural Grid Construct files, 303–304
and updating project Views, 304–305
Structural Members. *See also* Column Grids
and accessing Structural Member Catalog, 271–273
body modifier customization and, 311–313
and creating foundation plan, 305–307
and creating new Element File, 270–271
custom block customization and, 308–311
overview of, 269–270
and Structural Styles in Content Browser, 307–308
using Style Wizard with, 273–274
viewing Structural Member Shapes in Style Manager, 274–276
working with, 276–277
Style, as principle of ACA, 76–77
Subdivisions, 787–789

T

Tables (AEC/AIA Standard Plot Style), 870–873
Template files, as ACA prerequisite, 71
Terrain Model, 783–786, 802–804
Three-dimensional tool
Layout Grid 3D, 115
publishing to DWF files, 874–879
Toilet rooms, 353–354
Tool Palettes. *See also* Palettes
Details and, 827–829
user interface and, 48–53
ToolTip assistance/ALT-KEY command access, 46–48

Two-dimensional tool
2D Style settings for, 777–778
adjusting Bldg Section Line Position (2D Style), 782–783
Door/Window Swing design rule, 790–792
editing 2D Style, 779–780
editing Air Gap Material, 794–795
editing Glazing Material, 795–796
erasing Linework, 805–806
exporting changes to Second Floor, 796–798
fine-tuning Model (2D Style), 783–786
Freeze Demolition (2D Style) and, 786–787
Layer/Color/Linetype Property maintenance, 792
Layout Grid 2D, 115
merging Linework, 807–808
modifying Linework, 806–807
updating, 798
updating 2D Style, 780–782
updating Objects with User Edits, 809–810

U

Usable boundary, 912
User interface
Application Menu of, 38–39
Command Line and, 64–65
Dimension Input and, 60–61
direct manipulation, 61–63
Dynamic Command Prompting and, 61
Dynamic Input and, 57–60
edge grips and, 63–64
IntelliMouse and, 66
panels and, 42–43
prerequisite skills - "The Rules", 70, 73
prerequisite skills - tools/entities, 70–72
Quick Access Toolbar (QAT) of, 39
ribbon panel tools and, 44–46
ribbon view state and, 43–44
ribbons and, 40–42
right-clicking and, 53–57
Steering Wheels and, 67–68
Tool Palettes and, 48–53
ToolTip assistance/ALT-KEY command access and, 46–48
View Cube and, 69
View Navigation and, 67
View Panel and, 67
workspace and, 33–37

V

View Cube, user interface and, 69
View Navigation, user interface and, 67
View Panel, user interface and, 67
Volume and anchor, 114

W

Wall cleanup
Autosnap and, 420–421
avoiding doubles, 416–417
changing component priorities of, 434–435
checklist, 904–905
Cleanup Groups and, 426
Cleanup radius and, 415–416, 421–424
exploring component priorities of, 433–434
fixing problems on Third Floor, 894
installing CD files/opening Sample File, 413
Land T Cleanups, 418–419
manual, 427–432
solutions, 934
terminology, 412–413
understanding component priorities of, 435–437
using clean drafting, 416
using Extend/Trim, 417–418
using Wall Justification Display, 413–415, 424–426
Wall plan modifiers
configuring Osnap settings, 200–202
converting Polylines to, 203–204
Edit in Place for, 204–206
importing Objects with clipboard, 202–203
stairs and, 206–207
Walls. *See also* Building shell; Curtain Walls; Progressive refinement; Wall cleanup
adding curved segments, 160
adjusting Wall Roof Line, 327–328
CD file installation and, 156
Cleanup Checklist, 904–905
cleanup solutions, 934
creating/assigning Wall styles, 169
creating existing conditions plan, 160–161
creating layers, 170
getting started with, 156–157
layout remaining, 164–169
major fields/controls with, 157–159
modifying, 164
offset, 162–163
and problems with Foundation, 903
second floor refinement of, 481–491
using Ortho Wall, 161–162
Websites
publishing to, 879
resources, 906–909
Windows. *See* Doors/windows
Wood framing, 829–833
Work space
desktop shortcut creation and, 138–139
inclusion (template files), 146–151
layer standards (drawing setup) and, 141–145
out-of-the-box (template files), 145–146
palette group creation, 134–136
palette loading/verifying, 133, 139–141
profile completion/saving, 137
profile configuration, 130–133
profile creation, 128–129